D0857278

The Encyclopedia *of* Herbs

The Encyclopedia
of
HERBS

A Comprehensive Reference to
Herbs of Flavor and Fragrance

Arthur O. Tucker
and
Thomas DeBaggio

Edited by Francesco DeBaggio

JERICHO PUBLIC LIBRARY

Timber Press
Portland • London

Copyright © 2009 by Arthur O. Tucker and
Thomas DeBaggio. All rights reserved.

Illustrations copyright © 2000 by Marjorie C. Leggitt.
Frontispiece: *Wasabia japonica*. Opposite: *Geranium macrorrhizum*.

An earlier edition of this volume was published as
The Big Book of Herbs (Interweave Press, 2000).

Published in 2009 by Timber Press, Inc.

The Haseltine Building
133 S.W. Second Avenue, Suite 450
Portland, Oregon 97204-3527
www.timberpress.com

2 The Quadrant
135 Salusbury Road
London NW6 6RJ
www.timberpress.co.uk

ISBN-13: 978-0-88192-994-2

Printed in China

Library of Congress Cataloging-in-Publication Data

Tucker, Arthur O.
    The encyclopedia of herbs : a comprehensive reference to herbs of flavor and fragrance /
Arthur O. Tucker and Thomas DeBaggio ; edited by Francesco DeBaggio. — [2nd ed.]
        p. cm.
    Earlier edition published as: The big book of herbs, Interweave Press, 2000.
    Includes bibliographical references and index.
    ISBN 978-0-88192-994-2 (alk. paper)
  1. Herbs. 2. Herb gardening. 3. Herbs—Utilization. I. DeBaggio, Thomas, 1942–
II. DeBaggio, Francesco. III. Tucker, Arthur O. Big book of herbs. IV. Title.
    SB351.H5T777 2009
    635'.7—dc22
                                                                2009016700

A catalog record for this book is also available from the British Library.

Contents

Introduction

THIS BOOK PROVIDES accurate information to help identify, grow, and use hundreds of herbs. Although it draws heavily on scientific research from around the world, it is tempered by personal gardening experience and written in a simple understandable style.

No single book is big enough to describe all the plants called herbs, so we have focused on herbs that are most common in home gardens, catalogs, restaurants, and markets (or should be). For the purpose of this book, we define an herb as any temperate climate herbaceous or woody plant used for flavor or fragrance. This excludes a wide range of herbs for medicine, dyes, fibers, insecticides, soap, and rubber.

We believe our range, while limited, remains wide. Old favorites, such as basil, dill, parsley, coriander, lavender, mint, sage, rosemary, tarragon, and thyme are included in detail and many species that have not reached a wide audience are included. Among the unusual or hard to find herbs are *rau răm* or Vietnamese cilantro (*Persicaria odorata*), which immigrated to the United States along with the airlift of 140,000 Vietnamese in 1975. Another cilantro-flavored ethnic herb, *papaloquelite* (*Porophyllum ruderale* subsp. *macrocephalum*), comes from south of the border. This nine-foot marigold relative has been used in Mexican cooking for centuries but only entered Texan cuisine around 1990.

The Encyclopedia of Herbs grew from our frustration with the superficial treatment of our favorite herbs and the gross errors about them in many popular herb books (a recent one erroneously claimed that dill "resembles fennel in appearance and aroma"). We have spent years searching for thorough, unbiased research to dispel many cultivation myths perpetuated by four centuries of misinformation.

The most interesting data we uncovered was not in the popular press but in small circulation technical books and journals where scientists use shorthand and jargon to communicate with each other. This is one of the first times that most of these research findings have been available in a non-scientific venue.

We rely on botanists and agricultural scientists for an understanding of herbs and their cultivation, and we believe that their research provides useful guidelines, but it is not infallible and should not be read as the last word on the subject. Every spring brings new revelations to the observant gardener, as well as to the careful scientists.

The first edition of this book, entitled *The Big Book of Herbs* and published by Interweave Press, was extremely well received, earning awards from both the International Herb Association (2001 Book Awards) and The Herb Society of America (Gertrude B. Foster Award, 2004). However, in the intervening years, amounting to almost a decade of newly published literature, new information has emerged (e.g., absinthism was probably due to adulterants, not the content of thujones) and scientific names have changed (e.g., vetiver is now *Chrysopogon zizanioides*). In addition, we found a number of typographical errors or species that we had inadvertently excluded (e.g., *Agastache scrophulariifolia*). Other sections (e.g., *Pelargonium*) have been completely revamped. We thank all those conscientious readers who wrote to us with these enlightenments and hope that this book will be your ultimate reference on culinary and fragrant herbs for years to come.

Many readers, from gardeners to academics, also wrote to thank us for including the references. Actually, this is not just academic show-and-tell or some sort of weird academic compulsive disorder; it protects us legally. Pay particular attention to our wording in the following chapters. In accordance with the First Amendment of the U.S. Constitution, we may freely (1) quote scientific literature, (2) quote ethnic or historic literature, or (3) cite how we personally use herbs. However, as soon as we use terms like "recommend," "prescribe," or show advocacy for consumption for herbs that are not GRAS (Generally Recognized As Safe) by the U.S. Food and Drug Administration, then we (and the publisher) are legally liable. Readers should pay particular attention to this when advocating herbs like sassafras, which is not GRAS and has been shown to be a pre-hepatocarcinogen; while you may not accept the scientific literature, you are legally liable if you advocate its consumption and somebody does develop liver cancer (which may not even be related to the consumption of sassafras). In our litigious society today, this warning is not just scientific arrogance, and even if you win a legal suit, you still have to pay lawyers in most states and go through the hassle and time. When we make a statement, such as garlic being antifungal, we have cited scientific papers to support that statement. Herbs also fight a long uphill battle to prove their efficacy. Popular medical journals will publish poorly conducted research that shows negative effects, and the popular press will subsequently seize upon this, disregarding the many other well-conducted positive studies. We also hope that these references will prompt readers to locate the original scientific literature from their libraries and investigate a topic further to make their own well-informed decisions, and if we have inspired at least one student to research a topic further, then we have succeeded.

How to Use the Book

In this book we have attempted to update the lore of the past with current horticultural practices from around the world to prepare you for the garden of your life. The book is arranged in two large sections. The first section provides a detailed overview of herb growing, harvesting, and preserving techniques.

The second section is an alphabetized listing intended to equip you with the details to identify, understand, cultivate, care for, and use herbs of flavor and fragrance. Each entry is filled with detailed descriptions and histories of individual herbs. A typical entry provides the plant's botanical name and family, whether it is an annual or perennial, and its height, hardiness, light requirements, water consumption, required soil type and pH. The plant's name in various languages is included, as is a history of the plant, its chemistry, how to propagate the plant, and its culinary and landscape uses. A botanical key is given to identify the plant, and its description includes its country of origin and various data on the leaves, flowers, fruits, and seeds.

Who We Are

We have known the thrill of discovery in the garden and share a longstanding passion for cultivating the earth, and between us we have over eighty years of dirty knees. Art is Dr. Tucker to his students and many others. He spends much of his time in the highly technical milieu of a botanist who has specialized in the identification and chemistry of herbs. He has published and lectured widely and has a list of degrees that ends in a Ph.D. from Rutgers.

Tom had a more checkered career. He was a reformed journalist who since 1976 has been a commercial grower and seller of herb plants and has written for numerous publications about herbs. While Art has familiarity with Latin, French, German, and "Botanese," Tom needed translations of all four. Tom's expertise was passed onto his son, Francesco, upon Tom's diagnosis of Alzheimer's, and Francesco has continued the tradition.

We both marvel at the intense interest that Americans have shown recently in herbs. Pollsters estimate that over 6 million U.S. households grow herbs and they found that over half of the nation's population recognized garlic, parsley, dill, chives, and basil. Commercial growers responded to this increasing hunger with record fresh herb harvests. All this interest helped to fuel new research and made this book possible and more worthwhile.

Our aim has been to fill a gap between the highly technical scientific research of herbs and the homey, anecdotal approach bathed in generalities. We set out to compile diverse information and offer it in a single volume that will appeal to a wide range of gardeners and specialists, from home gardeners to commercial growers as well as professional horticulturists and academics. We think of this book, in a modest way, as a modern, updated version of the great herbals of the past. We hope that it will encourage more Americans, and others around the globe, to successfully grow and enjoy these beautiful and useful plants.

CHAPTER 1.
Plant Identification

IDENTIFYING A PLANT usually requires some knowledge of its origin. Taxonomic literature is organized along the lines of floras for specific geographical regions. If the plant is from cultivation, its geographical provenance may be unknown and its identification more difficult.

Two manuals for the identification of cultivated plants published in 1949 have become standard texts: L. H. Bailey's *Manual of Cultivated Plants* and A. Rehder's *Manual of Cultivated Trees and Shrubs Hardy in North America*. These two books provide information about plant families and genera. While these classic texts are now out of print, the more recent six volume *The European Garden Flora* (1984–2000) is exemplary in its approach, including identification, descriptions, and nomenclature.

Revisions of genera occur from time to time and are published in scientific journals or other publications. These provide identification tools for species within the genus. We have tried to cite important revisions for the genera within this book. We have tried to supplement this with the most up-to-date nomenclature available on reputable Internet sources, such as USDA's GRIN database (http://www.ars-grin.gov/cgi-bin/npgs/html/taxgenform.pl).

Species are identified by dichotomous keys. These keys are artificial analytical arrangements of two contradictory propositions. A choice is provided whereby one proposition, called a couplet, agrees with the specimen at hand, while the other couplet must be rejected. Within each couplet, another set of contradictory propositions are included and must be read for the specimen at hand. For example, the following key might be constructed for three species of *Origanum*:

1. Calyces (green tube of united sepals) with five equal to subequal teeth .... *O. vulgare.*
(If the specimen does not match, proceed to the next description.)

1a. Calyces two- or one-lipped (i.e., with three upper teeth fused to form a single upper lip, two lower teeth often well developed) 2
(If the specimen matches this description, go to the next paragraph, 2, which presents further refinement.)

2. Calyces 4 to 9 mm long; bracts (green leaves accompanying flowers) 3 to 24 mm long, membranous, usually purple, sometimes yellowish green, more or less glabrous (hairless) . . . . *O. rotundifolium.*

(If your specimen doesn't match here, go to 2a.)

2a. Calyces 1.5 to 3.5 mm long; bracts 2 to 5.5 mm long, leaf-like, in texture and color, somewhat hairy . . . . *O. onites*

If the specimen does not match any of these, it may not be an origanum or the key may not include a description of it.

Obviously, identifying a plant with a key will require a ruler, many times a 10× hand lens or other method of magnification, and a concentration on the terms in the key. In this book we have tried to give English equivalents to scientific terms whenever possible except in the scientific descriptions and keys. For further reading in this area three books may be helpful—*How to Identify Plants* by H. D. Harrington and L. W. Durrell, *A Glossary of Botanic Terms and Their Derivation and Accent* by B. D. Jackson, and *Plant Identification Terminology* by J. G. Harris and M. W. Harris.

How to Use the Plant Profiles

Vital statistics

Because authorities differ on how to pronounce scientific names, we tried to reproduce the most common pronunciation used in North America; most books on pronunciation are published in Great Britain and thus use a British pronunciation. These pronunciations are uniformly simplified to long and short syllables as shown in Table 1:

English pronunciation of common names is also indicated when we have experienced mispronunciations or when the English name is adopted from a foreign language. Accented syllables are indicated by underlining. Features of hardiness and pH range are modified from J. A. Duke's *Ecosystematic Data on Medicinal Plants*. Hardiness is also based upon limited scientific data and our personal experience. Where climatic zones are noted, they refer to the 1990 revision of the USDA Plant Hardiness map and noted as, say, Zone 4. Seeds per ounce and normal germination are

TABLE 1. Pronunciation guide.	
ă as in fat	ĭ as in pin
ā as in fate	ī as in pine
ä as in far	ŏ as in not
â as in fall	ō as in note
ā as in fare	ö as in move
å as in Persia	ô as in nor
ĕ as in met	ŭ as in tub
ē as in meet	ū as in mute
ē as in her	

garnered from many sources, including commercial catalogs. In some instances, this information is not available.

Species and common names

We begin with the complete scientific name, followed by the authority who named it, an accepted abbreviation of the book or journal according to *Taxonomic Literature*, second edition, by F. A. Stafleu and R. S. Cowan, and the year of publication. The etymology of the scientific names is derived primarily from *Plant Names Simplified* by A. T. Johnson and H. A. Smith. Common names are from various sources, such as L. L. Balashev's *Dictionary of Useful Plants in Twenty European Languages*.

Description

The attempt here is to provide a description which would not necessitate a glossary. Thus, the meanings are presented first, followed by the technical terms in parentheses. We hope the beginning gardener will gradually start to read the technical terms. In time, with repeated reading, it will be realized that their precision is to be preferred for exact, proper descriptions.

Culture

The attempt here is to quote, as far as possible, original research which may not have been assimilated by former writers. However, we have tempered it with our own practical experience.

Fungi are identified according to *Fungi on Plants and Plant Products in the United States* by D. F. Farr, G. F. Bills, G. P. Chamuris, and A. Y. Rossman, published in 1989.

Important chemistry

We have listed those chemicals which are the major components, usually greater than 10 percent, of extracts or essential oils.

Uses

Those herbs which are GRAS (Generally Recognized As Safe) by the U.S. Food and Drug Administration have been quoted from A. Y. Leung and S. Foster's 1996 *Encyclopedia of Common Natural Ingredients Used in Food, Drugs and Cosmetics*, and the third edition (1975) of T. E. Furia and N. Ballanca's *Fenaroli's Handbook of Flavor Ingredients*. These GRAS listings have been modified by Dr. James A. Duke (pers. comm., 1989). Lack of GRAS status is noted as well. Additional studies of the potential toxicity of fragrance substances applied to the skin is covered by the International Fragrance Association's *Code of Practice* (1989) and Tisserand and Balacs's *Essential Oil Safety* (1995). For information about the dose of a substance that kills 50 percent of test animals (the LD_{50}) of principal chemicals, we relied upon T. C. Zebovitz's *Compendium of Safety Data Sheets for Research and Industrial Chemicals*. Medical terms are defined according to the 1990 revised edition of *Mosby's Medical, Nursing, and Allied Health Dictionary* by W. D. Glanze, K. N. Anderson, and L. E. Anderson.

Botanical key and description

We have sought to describe plants in a way that does not require a glossary, but we have included metric measurements for precision.

Selected references

For those readers who desire additional reading, we list the major reviews and research papers used to compose the plant profiles. More importantly, these reviews and research papers supply the substantiation for our statements. These references are compiled by chapter and follow the plant profiles.

CHAPTER 2.
What's in a Name?

IF YOU'VE EVER heard a group of botanists talk about plants, you probably gained a new appreciation for the phrase "speaking in tongues." Plant scientists' conversation is so sprinkled with words and phrases in Latin that an outsider might find it meaningless. While some gardeners may view scientific names as arcane, irrelevant jargon, or as a secret code of botanists, the names are meant to bring order and understanding to the chaos of nature.

Knowing official plant names provides essential access to information. The two or three Latin words that make up a botanical name may sketch information on the plant's geographic and ecological distribution, cultivation, propagation, pests, diseases, chemistry, or uses. A further advantage of scientific names is that they are precise in meaning and indicate the relationships of plants with similar attributes and uses. For instance, from the popular name "scented geranium," you might assume that these are closely related to the hardy geraniums of our temperate woods and meadows. Both are in the family Geraniaceae, but scented geraniums are semitropical *Pelargonium* species. They differ in appearance, hardiness, and use from wild geraniums that comprise the *Geranium* species.

Latin names are assigned according to simple, logical rules that are periodically revised by an international congress of experts and recorded as the International Code of Botanical Nomenclature. The intent of using them is to standardize the names of plants the world over and help communication, so a plant known in Boston as *Alchemilla mollis* is known in Amsterdam by the same name. In print, the scientific name is always italicized or underlined. The generic name is always capitalized, but the specific epithet is not.

Latin is not the only ancient language a gardener may encounter when dealing with plants; Greek also shows up from time to time. For example, the science of the classification of plants is called taxonomy, a word that comes from the Greek word *taxis*, meaning "arrangement" or "division." Any unit of taxonomic classification is a taxon (plural, taxa).

The basic unit of scientific names is the species (singular and plural), a two-part name consisting of the genus and specific epithet, or name. Bear in mind that a species does not actually exist in nature; instead, individuals are organized into populations. The human concept of "species" is an attempt to impose order upon a bewildering array of natural variation. A species is relatively easy to define when variations are clearly abrupt. More often than not, however, variation is continuous.

Not surprisingly, scientists define species differently. Morphologists—those who study the shape and form of plants—place great weight upon the characteristics of a plant's flowers and vegetative parts to define a species. Geneticists, on the other hand, see a species as a potentially interbreeding group of individual plants. To molecular biologists, a species is defined by its bands of DNA fragments or proteins.

Botanists have not yet achieved a synthesis of these differing viewpoints, but from a practical standpoint we can use the definition of Arthur Cronquist: "Species are the smallest groups that are consistently and persistently distinct, and distinguishable by ordinary means." Not all taxonomists will agree with this definition, but for horticulturists, it is practical above all else. For example, true lavender, *Lavandula angustifolia*, and spike lavender, *L. latifolia*, are readily distinguishable by using a 10× hand lens, noting flowering time, and/or observing plant height.

Genus and Species

Groups of one or more similar species are combined into a genus (plural, genera). For example, all species in the genus *Rosa*—the roses—have woody stems, compound leaves, five or more petals, and many pistils enclosed within a hypanthium, a structure formed by the fusion of sepals, petals, and stamens. All species of *Mentha*—the mints—have four perfect stamens of equal length, and the calyx and corolla are almost radially symmetric.

The scientific name of European field mint, *Mentha arvensis*, for instance, is composed of two portions: the genus (*Mentha*) and a descriptive word called the specific epithet (*arvensis*). The genus is rather like a surname, while the specific epithet reflects a given name; it's like writing John Smith's name as Smith John.

Both genus and specific epithet are necessary when naming a plant. The citation of only *arvensis* means only "of the cultivated fields," and *arvensis* is not the species, only the specific epithet; you must cite both to correctly name the species. A species can have only one name, and a name can be used for only one species.

To distinguish the scientific name of European field mint, the authority who first coined *Mentha arvensis*, Carl von Linné (Latinized to Linnaeus and abbreviated L.), may follow the scientific name; it is not italicized. *Mentha arvensis* L. refers to the field mint of Linnaeus. In 1753, he published *Species Plantarum*, the book that is the starting point of botanical nomenclature. For most common species, the authority may be omitted, but it is cited in formal literature.

Sometimes, if the meaning is clear, writers abbreviate the name of a genus with an initial. For example, in an article about mints, when first naming the species the author writes "*Mentha arvensis*." In following text, "*M. arvensis*" may be used, although starting a sentence with the initial of the genus is considered confusing by international authorities.

Plant Families

Just as similar species are grouped into a genus, similar genera are grouped into a family. Many writers or lecturers misuse the term "plant family." They might refer to the "sage family," when they mean the genus *Salvia*.

A "sage family" does not exist; *Salvia* belongs to the Lamiaceae or mint family, along with true mints (genus *Mentha*), marjorams (genus *Origanum*), rosemarys (genus *Rosmarinus*), and many other herbs. All members of the Lamiaceae have four-sided (square) stems, opposite or whorled leaves, two-lipped flowers, and usually glands that produce fragrant oils. This family was once called Labiatae, but the general trend has been to spell all families with the suffix "-aceae." This is another benefit of using Latin names: You might confuse the terms "mint genus" and "mint family," but you'd never confuse *Mentha* with the Lamiaceae.

Climbing up the taxonomic ladder, families are organized into orders, orders into classes, classes into phyla (botanists used to call this rank a division), and phyla into the kingdom Planta, kingdom Planta into the domain Eucarya. Except for distinguishing between the two subclasses that differ in pattern of seed growth, the monocots and the eudicots, horticulturists are rarely concerned with taxa above the family level.

In fact, horticulturists are mostly concerned with individual variation. They prize plants which are special in one way or another, and differ from what is typical for the species. Subtle differences arise because a species includes many individuals, not all identical; thus, the taxonomy must be flexible. Sometimes the differences within a species are significant enough to warrant a separate name. Botanists assign variation within a species into three categories: subspecies (abbreviated subsp. or ssp.), varieties (var., for *varietas*), and forms (f., for *forma*).

For example, the pine-needled rosemarys are quite distinct, and naturally occurring specimens would be *Rosmarinus officinalis* var. *angustifolius*. On the other hand, forms designate very minor variations, such as floral color. Naturally occurring white-flowering rosemary, typical in all other respects, would be *R. officinalis* var. *officinalis* f. *albiflora*.

The designation of subspecies was originally proposed for taxa not quite worthy of specific rank, with or without included varieties, and has often been used to designate variation correlated with geography. The distinction of variety versus subspecies is best left to esoteric discussions by botanists; one botanist's variety is another botanist's subspecies!

Horticulturists use the term "cultivar," a portmanteau word created from "cultivated variety." However, not all cultivars correspond to botanical varieties. Like botanical varieties, some cultivars describe variation within a species. But other cultivars describe hybrids between species or even between genera. Cultivars do not occur in nature; they are maintained by gardeners. Some, like 'Munstead' lavender, must be vegetatively propagated to maintain the correct selection. Others, such as 'Long Standing' coriander, come true from seed.

In the past, cultivar names were designated in Latin; an example is *alba*, meaning "white." Since 1 January 1959, cultivar names must be given in a modern language instead of Latin. In print, they are not italicized but instead capitalized and placed in single quotes, thus now 'Alba'. The abbreviation "cv" is no longer correct to use.

The term "hybrid" has been used to represent progeny from the mating of two recognized species, but the term also refers to the progeny of any recognized taxa, from highly inbred lines (F_1 hybrids) to genera (intergeneric hybrids). Hybridization at all taxonomic levels occurs naturally and is a leading force in evolution. In nature, however, hybrids may or may not be common depending on the taxa and isolating mechanisms between taxa.

Cultivation brings previously isolated species into close contact. Seed saved from collections of closely related species often results in mixed hybrids. An oft-quoted story is that one herb nursery gathered a large basil collection and planted them all side by side. Basils are notoriously promiscuous, and in a few years the basil grown from seeds collected from these plants were all of the same hybrid progeny—regardless of the label on the seed packet in which they were sold. The only way to keep basils from interbreeding is to plant them far apart, enclose each selection separately in netting ("bag" them), or take cuttings.

Mentha species in Europe have become closely associated with agriculture. Normally isolated populations of perfectly good species have been thrown together for centuries. Today, interspecific hybrids of *Mentha* are very common. For example, peppermint is a naturally occurring hybrid of two species, water mint (*M. aquatica*) and spearmint (*M. spicata*). This hybrid nature is indicated by the use of a multiplication sign (or the small letter "x") and sometimes pronounced "notho."

Peppermint is generally sterile, but this is not the case with all interspecific hybrids. Numerous cases of fertility being restored to sterile hybrids exist both in the laboratory and nature.

Other hybrids are entirely the result of human manipulation. All our modern cultivars of roses are the result of direct manipulation by humans, bringing together roses from the Mediterranean and Orient that would never have mated under natural conditions. It is doubtful a 'Peace' rose has enough vigor to survive in nature, except perhaps in a moderate climate like Bermuda's. Gardeners supply the extra care, fertilization, winter protection, insecticides, and fungicides that make 'Peace' one of the best-known and best-loved roses worldwide. Nature ruthlessly eliminates poorly adapted genetic combinations, but humans can intervene to some extent.

Because hybrids are a mixture of genes, they will not breed true. Today's corn and petunias are the result of crossing two highly inbred lines, and seed saved from these F_1 (first filial or first generation) hybrids results in different plants; in successive generations, the desirable characteristics gradually diminish. Many named cultivars, because they are the result of hybridization, do not breed true and must be propagated by cuttings.

Conventional hybrids result from the transfer of pollen to stigma. Insects (and wind) have done this job for eons, but humans have initiated artificial pollination within the last century. New advances in biotechnology, such as somatic fusion in tissue culture, add new dimensions to hybridization, but we still depend upon the transfer of genetic material regardless of the technique.

A rose and a mint present two examples of the way scientists have dealt with subtleties in classifying plants. The autumn damask rose is sometimes classified as *Rosa damascena* Mill. var. *semperflorens* (Loisel. & Michel) Rowley, a botanical variety of the true damask rose. Other botanists classify it as a full species, *R. bifera* Pers., asserting that it differs sufficiently in particular characteristics. In this case, the different names represent different viewpoints of what defines a species.

As another example, 'Todd's Mitcham' peppermint is a cultivar derived from 'Mitcham' peppermint by gamma-irradiation. 'Todd's Mitcham' has oil that is slightly different from that of 'Mitcham' and is resistant to verticillium wilt, a soil-borne disease that weakens and kills susceptible plants by attacking their roots. If 'Todd's Mitcham' had occurred naturally, it would not have been given botanical recognition because it lacks major differences from black peppermint, *M.* ×*piperita* nothovar. *piperita*. In other words, disease resistance is important horticulturally but not botanically (although it is important in evolution).

Changing Scientific Names

While the scientific names of plants are more stable than common names, they do change. When it is discovered that prior names were published, plant names change; they also change when concepts of genera and species alter. Taxa are not static entities, especially with human disruptions of genetic barriers, and plant names change as plants evolve. The International Code of Botanical Nomenclature (ICBN) is, in itself, being constantly revised to meet the needs of the scientific society, and plant names also change as rules change. Someday a concise list of correct plant names will be formulated for the Planet Earth, but until that utopian day arrives, we will have to be content with using the most up-to-date name as the correct name.

Interpreting Scientific Names

Scientific plant names have several levels of meaning because they may be commemorative, descriptive, or derived from a vernacular name. The specific epithet *officinalis*, often attached to the names of herbs, means "medicinal"; *vulgare* means "common." The genus *Wasabia* was derived from the Japanese name for Japanese horseradish, *wasabi*.

Herbs have a rich history, and knowing the meaning of scientific names aids in interpreting their history and uses. *The Dictionary of Plant Names* by Coombes (Timber Press, 1987), *Stearn's Dictionary of Plant Names for Gardeners* (Cassell, 1992), *Plants and Their Names* by R. Hyam and R. Pankhurst (Oxford, 1995), and *The Names of Plants* by Gledhill (Cambridge University Press, 1990) are recent texts often recommended for further study of the meaning of names.

Pronouncing Plant Names

The pronunciation of the vowels and consonants of Latin now taught in American and European classrooms is the "reformed" or "restored" academic pronunciation. It was adopted by classical scholars as an approximation of the words spoken by educated Romans in the time of Cicero (first century B.C.E.). Since Cicero's time, however, this classical Latin has been corrupted by the sounds and rhythms of native languages. Erasmus, the sixteenth-century humanist theologian, remarked that a French ambassador at the court of Emperor Maximilian made a speech in Latin with so Gallic an accent that the Italians present thought he was speaking French; a German, called upon to reply, sounded as if he was speaking German. A Dane who spoke third might have been a Scotsman, "so marvellously did he reproduce the pronunciation of Scotland."

That tradition is alive today. In North America and Great Britain, most botanists and horticulturists use an English pronunciation of Latin. Botanists of continental Europe, English-speaking botanists with international contacts, and botanists whose native tongue is written in non-Latin script all attempt to use the reformed academic pronunciation of Latin. Add to this the many scientific names that are of non-Latin origin, and you have a polyglot stew that burns many a tongue. Just imagine pronouncing a Latinized Polish name!

In Latin, every vowel is pronounced (e.g., o-i-des, not -oides). In words of several syllables, the stress usually falls on the next to the last one. Diphthongs (ae, oe, au, eu) are treated as long vowels. Table 2 (see next page), as modified from W. T. Stearn's *Botanical Latin*, indicates the difference between the English and the classical Latin pronunciation.

In the end, the purpose of proper pronunciation is to facilitate the understanding of the spoken word. If you can communicate to your listeners, don't worry whether you are "proper" in your pronunciation. At least one taxonomy professor of the "old school" used classical Latin for all his pronunciations and regularly caused an uproar in class when he talked about *Pinus rigida*. Sometimes it's best to use the most melodious pronunciation, not the most correct.

TABLE 2.
Pronunciation of scientific names by Latin and English pronunciations (after Stearn).

REFORMED ACADEMIC	ENGLISH	HERBAL EXAMPLE
ā as in father	fate	*Galium mollugo*
ă as in apart	fat	*Dictamnus albus*
ae as in aisle	as ea in meat	*Tropaeolum majus*
au as in house	as aw in bawl	*Laurus nobilis*
c always as in cat	before e, i, y as in center	*Cichorium intybus*
c always as in cat	before a, o, u as in cat	*Catha edulis*
ch as k or k-has	k or ch	*Chenopodium album*
ē as in they	me	*Anthemis nobilis*
ĕ as in pet	pet	*Sesamum orientale*
ei (or ej) as in rein	height	*Satureja montana*
g always as in go	before a, o, u as in go	*Galium odoratum*
g always as in go	before e, i, y as in gem	*Genista tinctoria*
ī as in machine	ice	*Linum usitatissimum*
ĭ as in pit	pit	*Mentha citrata*
j as y in yellow	j as j in jam	*Jasminum officinale*
ng as in finger	finger	*Eryngium maritimum*
ō as in note	note	*Viola odorata*
ŏ as in not	not	*Viola tricolor*
oe as in toil	as ee in been	*Oenothera biennis*
ph as p or p-h	like f	*Daphne mezereum*
r always trilled		*Teucrium chamaedrys*
s as in sit, gas	sit, gas	*Sesamum orientale*
t as in table, native	t as in table	*Baptisia tinctoria*
t as in table, native	ti in word as nation	*Baptisia tinctoria*
ū as in brute	brute	*Calendula officinalis*
ŭ as in full	tub	*Hyssopus officinalis*
ui as oui (French)	ruin	*Sanguisorba minor*
v (consonant) as w	van	*Valeriana officinalis*
y as pur (French)	cipher	*Cuminum cuminum*
y as du (French)	cynical	*Cynoglossum officinalis*

Herbs and Etymology

IS AN HERBARIAN the offspring of an herbalist and a barbarian? What is the difference between an herbarian and herbarium? Do you have an herbary or herbour? What is an herblet? Are you herbiferous or herbless? Is this book herbose? Is an herbal accolade an herbelade?

The word "herb" is derived from the Latin *herba*, meaning "green crops" or, more literally, herbage. It is this meaning of herb that is used in Genesis 1:11, "the herb yielding seed."

Talk to a botanist, however, and you will hear "herb" used to describe any plant that is not woody, but herbaceous. In turn, a horticulturist uses the most familiar definition: a plant that may be used for fragrance, flavor, medicine, or dye.

The following are some herb-enlightenments or a little herbarized dictionary:

herbaceously with a flavoring of herbs.

herbage (1) herbaceous growth; (2) herbs for garnishing a dish; or (3) the green, succulent part of herbaceous plants.

herbal (1) a book containing the names and descriptions of plants with their properties and virtues; (2) a collection of botanical specimens (= herbarium); (3) belonging to or consisting of herbs; or (4) or the nature of an herb.

herbalism the science of herbs or plants.

herbalist (1) one versed in the knowledge of herbs; (2) a collector or writer on plants; or (3) a dealer in medicinal herbs.

herbalize to collect medicinal herbs.

herbarian one skilled in the knowledge of herbs (= herbalist).

herbarism the knowledge of herbs (= herbalism).

herbarist one skilled in herbs (= herbalist).

herbarium (1) a collection of dried plants systematically arranged; (2) a book or case contrived for keeping such a collection; or (3) the room or building in which the collection is kept.

herbarize = herbalize = herborize.

herbary (1) one skilled in herbs (= herbalist); (2) a collection of dried plants (= herbarium); (3) a place where herbs are grown; (4) a treatise on herbs (= herbal); or (5) the science of herbs.

herbelade a kind of pork sausage mixed with herbs and baked in a crust.

herbar, herber (-e, -eior, -our) Middle English forms of arbor; especially in its earlier senses as a green plot, such as an herb- or flower-garden, orchard.

herberie, erberie (1) collection of herbs, (2) an herb-market, (3) provision or store of herbs.

herbescent growing like an herb (= herbaceous).

herbid grassy.

herbiferous bearing or producing herbs.

herbish resembling an herb; greenish.

herbist, herbister herbalist.

herbless destitute of herbs.

herblet, herbling a little herb.

herb-man one who deals in herbs.

herborist = herbarist = herbalist.

herborization (1) one who herborizes; (2) a botanical excursion.

herborize (1) to tend herbs or plants; or (2) to gather herbs (botanize).

herbose abounding in herbs or herbage.

herbous belong to or of the nature of an herb.

pot-herb (1) an herb grown for boiling in the pot; (2) any of the herbs cultivated in a kitchen-garden.

And how could we forget the most hotly debated linguistic conundrum in herb-dom: How do you pronounce "herb"? In Old French and Middle English, it was only occasionally spelled with an "h," but is found written that way regularly after 1475. However, the "h" was silent until the nineteenth century, and has remained so among most Americans until its relatively recent revival.

CHAPTER 3.
The Flavors and Fragrances of Herbs

PLANTS ARE FACTORIES that produce thousands of complex chemicals, many of which have never been synthesized by humans or are too expensive to manufacture in commercial quantities. In fact, the word "chemical" is derived from the Greek *chemia*, meaning "plant juice." In turn, the Greeks supposedly derived their word from the Persian *kimiya*, a reference to a group of tonic herbs from China.

These chemicals are manufactured, or biosynthesized, throughout the plant, usually in association with specialized tissues or organs. The essential oils, for example, may be synthesized in secretory canals in anise fruits or epidermal glands on peppermint—thus anise fruits must be broken and mint leaves rubbed to release the fragrance. Although the peppermint oil is secreted outside the gland, it lies beneath a layer of plant wax, or cuticle, that is easily broken.

We can only guess why herbs produce such a large array of chemicals. Many chemicals, such as those involved in photosynthesis, are clearly an integral part of the plant's metabolism and thus absolutely necessary for survival. Most plants depend on chlorophyll to capture light energy for the synthesis of sugars. Plants that lack chlorophyll must be saprophytic (living off dead organic matter, as Indian pipes, *Monotropa uniflora*, does) or parasitic (obtaining sustenance from other living organisms, such as the *Cuscuta* spp., dodders, do).

On the other hand, why do plants secrete scents or alkaloids? Plants, unlike animals, lack an immune system and cannot move away from predators (or, in another interpretation, move but at a much slower tempo). Not all plants secrete the same array of plant compounds, so how does a plant benefit from secreting, say, menthol instead of carvone?

We have good evidence that floral fragrances attract very specific pollinators. In a review of orchid floral fragrances, researchers noted that alpha-pinene attracts male euglossine bees to *Stanhopea* orchids to accomplish pollination.

Do these same chemicals in leaves protect against animals that might find them tasty menu items? A researcher at the Pacific Southwest Forest and Experiment Station found that pine oil, which is chiefly composed of alpha- and beta-pinene, protects lodgepole pines from attack by mountain pine beetles. The pyrethrenoids of *Tanacetum ptarmici-*

florum (*Chrysanthemum ptarmiciflorum*) are effective insecticides and the source of a major industry in Kenya.

Do some plants produce chemicals to kill other plants around them—and relieve the competition for resources? At the University of California, Santa Barbara, researchers discovered that the essential oil of *Salvia leucophylla* inhibits germination of nearby seedlings; the oil is thus said to be allelopathic.

Stress in the form of extreme parameters of light, temperature, disease, or insect infestation also changes the chemical profile of plants as raw materials become less available or must be used for essential metabolic reactions. French researchers reported a peppermint that had been severely infested with a mite (*Eriophyes* sp.); the oil smelled like that of basil because of its high menthofuran content.

Regardless of the biological reasons for their existence, chemicals in herbs are also responsible for the unique flavors, fragrances, and even poisons within the plants. The chemicals also serve as markers for identifying the herbs.

Flavors and Fragrances

Flavor seems so simple and immediate when you chew a basil leaf freshly plucked from a plant in your garden, but flavor is a complex phenomenon consisting of fragrance (aroma), taste, and consistency. Fragrance is detected by the sensory cells at the upper part of the nasal cavity. The tongue senses taste. Consistency includes physical texture, including "mouth feel," a physical sensation that influences one's perception of the total flavor.

Fragrance is the most complex of the components of flavor. While the human nose can distinguish among very similar compounds—such as (*S*)(-)-carvone (d-carvone), which smells of caraway and (*R*)(-)-carvone (l-carvone), which smells of spearmint—it senses no difference between the chemically dissimilar nitro musks and steroid musks. Many theories have been put forth to explain this situation by correlating molecular structure with perceived aroma; the texts cited below contain further information.

Important fragrance chemicals occur in the essential oil. Why are oils essential? The term derives from the sixteenth-century Swiss physician and alchemist Paracelsus, who used the term *quinta essentia*, or quintessence of the plants. His term refers to the fifth essence of Aristotle, which the philosopher believed permeates all living as well as inanimate objects.

An essential oil is different from a fixed oil, one that is liquid at room temperature, or fat, which is solid at room temperature. Essential oil is highly volatile—it evaporates easily—and contains the principal components of the herb's fragrance. Fixed oils can be easily extracted from plants by pressing—as corn oil is produced, for instance—but an essential oil is usually extracted by distillation or organic solvents.

Fixed oils also differ chemically from essential oils. Fixed oils are formed by the union of glycerol and fatty acids, while essential oils include a wide variety of chemicals, all more or less volatile.

The way essential oils are derived from plants makes all the difference to the oil's odor. Dry distillation, without water, is notoriously destructive and not usually used. Water distillation introduces problems of pH and metal ions; the process is reserved for herbal material such as rose petals, which cannot be distilled easily otherwise.

Steam distillation remains the least destructive method of obtaining essential oil. Live steam is passed over herb materials and then condensed, resulting in water and essential oil that are then separated. Some companies sell distillation equipment, both for the amateur and professional, but in general the cheaper the distillation equipment, the cruder the product.

The heat of steam distillation, however, introduces its own effects. For example, lemon verbena oil obtained from distillation has a notable isocitral content, which may cause the skin to become extremely sensitive to the sun. Thus, a gentler solvent extraction method is preferred for this and some other for floral fragrances. Petroleum ether, the solvent of choice today, yields a product that is high in fats and plant waxes; it's usually yellow. This product, a "concrète," requires further treatment with ethyl alcohol to eliminate the non-fragrant materials. The resulting product is an "absolute," or if extracted from a concrète, an "absolute from concrète."

Another method of solvent extraction for flowers that continue to release their fragrance after being picked—jasmine and tuberose, for instance—is enfleurage. Flowers are spread on a layer of cold fat (usually 1 part tallow to 2 parts lard) coated on glass. After twenty-four hours (forty-eight in the case of tuberose), the flowers are removed, and the process repeated up to thirty-six times with fresh floral material.

Later the fragrance-saturated fat is washed with ethyl alcohol in a mixer; the fat is discarded or used to make soap. The saturated alcohol is frozen to remove the last bit of fat, and it may be concentrated by vacuum distillation to yield an "absolute of enfleurage." The "exhausted" flowers may be further extracted in a solvent to yield an "absolute of chassis," referring to the sheet of glass which carries the fat.

This hand labor drives up the price of the product, but the full, fine fragrance extracted by enfleurage is unequalled. The scent obtained by merely dumping the flowers in petroleum ether pales in comparison.

Amateurs may easily enjoy the process of cold-fat extraction. First, find a spanking clean, large pickling jar; pizza parlors normally discard empty pickled-pepper jars that can be thoroughly cleaned. Next, coat with vegetable shortening several layers of cheese cloth big enough to cover the inside walls of the jar. Pat the fatted cheese cloth inside the jar.

In the morning, load the jar with fragrant flowers of your choice; store in a cool, dry basement overnight. Next morning, remove the flowers and reload the jar with a fresh batch of flowers. Repeat daily for about a month.

Pour about a cup of 190 proof (95 percent) grain alcohol into the jar, gently shake, and let set overnight, shaking periodically. Decant the fragrant alcohol the next morning—it's your own absolute from enfleurage.

Cold solvents, such as butane or carbon dioxide, may also be used to extract fragrances. Carbon dioxide (supercritial fluid extraction or SFE) is especially interesting because the carbon dioxide is easily removed later, and the resulting material is food-grade. The capital investment, however, is high for the pressurized equipment.

Other fragrant materials, such as gums and resinoids, are also available on the fragrance market. They are normally extracted further by distillation or solvent extraction.

Essential oil is composed of at least three groups of chemicals: the straight-chain compounds, the monoterpenoids, and the benzene derivatives. Another way of grouping the components of an essential oil is by their reactive group, such as presented in Table 3.

Each species offers unique attributes of fragrance, so an analysis of essential oil may be used for identification. While dwarf white lavender, *Lavandula angustifolia* 'Nana Alba', may be easily distinguished by its dwarf stature and floral color; it also has an extremely

---

TABLE 3.
Principal compounds in essential oils.

REACTIVE GROUP	SUFFIX AND DESCRIPTION	HERBAL EXAMPLE
acid	-ic; contains a terminal carboxyl (COOH)	isovaleric acid in valerian oil
alcohol	-ol; contains a hydroxy group, (-OH)	menthol in peppermint oil
aldehyde	-al; contains an aldehyde group (-CHO)	neral in lemon oil
ester	-ate; alcohol + acid = two oxygens attached to carbon	menthyl acetate in peppermint oil
hydrocarbon	-ane or -ene; contains only carbon (C) and hydrogen (H)	pinene in pine oil
ketone	-one; contains a carbonyl group (-CO-)	menthone in peppermint oil
lactones	-ide; an "inner ester"	ambrettolide in ambrette seed oil
oxide	-ole; has an oxygen bridging two or more carbons	1,8-cineole in eucalyptus oil
phenol	-ol; has a hydroxyl (-OH) attached to benzene ring	thymol in thyme oil
phenolic ether	-ole; has an oxygen (-O-) between carbon and benzene ring	anethole in anise oil
sulfur compounds	-ide = sulfides; -mercaptan = thio-alcohols; -in = sulfoxides	diallyl disulfide in garlic oil

high content of terpinen-4-ol in its essential oil. Identification of 'Abrialii' and 'Super' lavandins (*L.* ×*intermedia*) is difficult because they are similar in height and floral color. The two can be readily distinguished, however, by their essential oils.

The nose is often able to detect some of these differences in fragrance, but not always. While most of the odoriferous components in a plant are released so the nose can detect them, others must break down before they can be smelled. This is why drying, which aids in the breakdown of coumarin, deepens the fragrance of sweet woodruff. Some of the principal components of essential oils of herbs are presented in Table 4. Perfumers uses the term "note," which was borrowed from music, to refer to fragrance moods or qualities.

TABLE 4.
Principal components of essential oils of herbs.

NOTE	CHEMICAL COMPONENT	HERBAL EXAMPLE
woody	patchouli alcohol	patchouli
	khusimol	vetiver
musk	ambrettolide	ambrette
amber	sclareol	clary sage
spicy	cinnamaldehyde	cinnamon basil
	eugenol	clove basil
hay-fern	coumarin	sweet woodruff
anise-basil	trans-anethole	anise
	estragole (methyl chavicol)	French tarragon, most sweet basil
	safrole	sassafras
mint	menthol	peppermint
	(R)(-)-carvone	spearmint
citrus	citral (geranial + neral)	lemon verbena
	limonene	lemon verbena
aldehydic	7-dodecanal	cilantro
floral; rose	geraniol	rose geranium
	phenylethyl alcohol	damask rose
herbaceous	linalool/linalyl acetate	lavender
	1,8-cineole	Dalmatian sage
camphoraceous-pine	borneol/bornyl acetate	rosemary
phenolic	thymol	French thyme
	carvacrol	oregano
sulfurous	diallyl disulfide	garlic oil

The Taste of Herbs

Taste consists of four basic qualities: sweet, sour, salty, and bitter; alkaline and metallic tastes are sometimes included, along with flavor intensifers such as monosodium glutamate. To this traditional classification, pungency, astringency, and coolness, all of which affect the mucous membranes, might be added.

Sweet tastes may be carbohydrates but this taste more often arises from other compounds, such as terpenoids or proteins. Organic acids produce sour tastes. Inorganic salts, such as sodium chloride, or common table salt, produce salty tastes. Bitter tastes are sometimes due to alkaloids in herbs and are usually poisonous; seco-irodoids and terpenoids may also be bitter. A number of compounds, typically cyanates, create pungency. Astringency is produced by phenolics and quinones, the chemical complexes sometimes called tannins. Coolness is a sensation elicited by compounds such as the menthols. Like herbal aromas, some of these compounds are not in a free state where they can be tasted directly. They need the action of enzymes to burst forth.

Like smell, taste is highly variable by sex, age, race, and individual; it can also be learned or acquired. Cilantro, for example, was once ignored by many Americans because it reeks of stink bugs, but now it has become a popular item in classy restaurants. Table 5 includes some of the principal components of taste in culinary herbs.

TABLE 5. Examples of principal components of taste in culinary herbs.		
TASTE	CHEMICAL COMPONENT	HERBAL EXAMPLE
sweet	stevioside	Paraguayan sweet herb
	glycyrrhizin	licorice
	estragole	sweet cicely
sour	oxalic acid	French sorrel
bitter	gentiopicroside, amarogentin	bitter gentian
	absinthin	wormwood
	humulon	hops
pungent	capsaicin	chili pepper
	allyl isothiocyanate	black mustard
cool	menthol	peppermint

Caution: Some Natural Flavors and Fragrances May Be Toxic

Just because something is "natural" does not mean it is intrinsically "good." AIDS is natural, poison ivy is natural, and comfrey leaves containing chemicals that cause liver cancer are natural. In the United States, flavor ingredients are regulated by the Food and Drug Administration (FDA) under the Food Additives Amendment, section 409 of the 1958 Food and Drugs Act. The Flavor and Extract Manufacturers Association (FEMA) provides an expert panel to determine those flavors and levels that are granted exemptions from the coverage of section 409 and whose use in food is "Generally Recognized As Safe" (GRAS). This is summarized in chapter 21, parts 182 and 184, of the Code of Federal Regulations.

In 1972, the National Academy of Sciences' Food Protection Committee reviewed GRAS chemicals, and since then the FEMA expert panel has reviewed flavor ingredients and published periodic updates in *Food Technology*. In Europe, a classification of "Nature-identical" is similar to GRAS, and the European Community (EC) is preparing inventories of flavoring materials. We have listed the GRAS status and FEMA levels allowed in foods under each herb (see, for example, pennyroyal, *Mentha pulegium*).

What does this mean for you, the consumer? Consider safrole (see herb profiles for *Sassafras albidum* and *Piper auritum*). An extract or oil of the root of sassafras, *S. albidum* (Nutt.) Nees, contains 74 to 85 percent safrole; it also causes liver cancer in mice, rats, and dogs. Safrole is viewed as a precarcinogen which is metabolized to the carcinogenic 1'-sulfoöxysafrole via 1'-hydroxysafrole (in mouse liver).

Aside from safrole's ability to cause cancer, ingestion of 5 ml of sassafras oil by an adult or a few drops by a toddler causes death or at least induces vomiting, rapid heart beat, and muscle tremors. Consumption of 10 cups or more per day of sassafras tea will induce profuse sweating in an adult. Sassafras root has been banned by the FDA since 1960 and the Council of Europe since 1974; the FDA ruling was comprehensively reviewed in 1976 and upheld.

Should you recommend the consumption of sassafras root bark? Whether or not you believe that safrole causes cancer is irrelevant under federal law. Anyone who gets liver cancer and then asserts in court that it is your fault for recommending the consumption of this or any other high-safrole plant has the backing of the U.S. Food and Drug Administration—and at taxpayers' expense.

Likewise, the International Fragrance Association (IFRA), formed in 1973, has created industry guidelines to restrict ingredient usage in fragrances as a result of oral toxicity and skin problems, including potential irritation, contact sensitization, and/or phototoxicity and skin photosensitization potential.

New fragrance ingredients for which no adequate experience exists should be used only after satisfactory evaluation by competent toxicologists. Table 6 includes the 1989 (to present) IFRA list for natural materials. These recommendations make use of the detailed findings of the Research Institute for Fragrance Materials (RIFM), which was created in 1966 by the fragrance industry for the sole purpose of establishing fragrance safety.

TABLE 6.
IFRA recommendations on fragrance ingredients.

HERB PRODUCT	STATUS
allantroot oil (elecampane oil)	prohibited
angelica root oil	restricted; limit to 3.9%
bergamot oil	restricted; limit to 2%
bitter orange oil, expressed	restricted; limit to 7%
cassia oil	restricted; limit to 1%
chenopodium oil	prohibited
cinnamon-bark oil, Ceylon	restricted; limit to 1%
costus root oil, absolute and concrète	prohibited
cumin oil	restricted; limit to 2%
fig-leaf absolute	prohibited
lemon oil, cold pressed	restricted; limit to 10%
lemon verbena absolute	limit to 1%
(lemon) verbena oil	prohibited
lime oil, cold pressed	restricted; limit to 3.5%
marigold oil and absolute (*Tagetes* oil and absolute)	restricted; limit to 0.25%
oak moss absolute and resinoid (concrète)	restricted; limit to 3%
opopanax	restricted; use only from *Commiphora erythraea* var. *glabrescens*
Peru balsam	restricted; use only from *Myroxylon pereirae*
Pinaceae family oils	specification; use only oils with peroxides level less than 10 millimoles peroxide/liter
rue oil	restricted; limit to 3.9%
sassafras oil	restricted; safrole content should not exceed 0.05%
savin oil	specification; use only from *Juniperus phoenicea*, not *J. sabina*
styrax, American and Asian	restricted; should not be used

CHAPTER 4.

How to Maximize Flavor and Fragrance

WHILE MANY HERBS may enhance the landscape, we grow them most often for their flavor and fragrance. These two essential qualities, however, are not found in all plants called herbs. To get the most flavor and fragrance from your herb garden, it is important to choose varieties from species with strong aromatic character. Unfortunately, variety selection is one of the least understood aspects of herb gardening, a state of affairs that is probably due to the way herbs have been marketed to cooks under single, vague names such as oregano, tarragon, and thyme. This may account for some of the misconceptions that sprout in the herb garden.

One of the most common misunderstandings about herbs was voiced not long ago by a gardener who asked why her oregano turned into a mint with no flavor in its second year. She was certain it had changed because she planted it too close to her spearmint. Instead, the oregano she purchased was the purple-flowered *Origanum vulgare* subsp. *vulgare*, or wild marjoram, an herb with the vigorously spreading habit of a mint but without the flavor of the culinary herb she desired. In short, her oregano was behaving the way its genes told it to and was not under the influence of bad companions.

The beginner and experienced herb gardener alike sometimes face a difficult task in choosing the right herb. Is it possible to pick just one thyme, for instance, from the more than 350 *Thymus* species, plus untold cultivated varieties? When the recipe calls for three tablespoons of fresh mint, what type should be used? There are at least nineteen very variable *Mentha* species that have been named, but thousands of hybrids have been generated in nature and in gardens. Is it too much to expect to find the right sage from more than 900 *Salvia* species? Is it any easier to pick an oregano from the thirty-six species of *Origanum*? Or a rosemary from the more than four dozen cultivars of *Rosmarinus officinalis*? Which is the best parsley—if there is one—among the more than 100 varieties grown around the world? Can you name the lavender with the best fragrance from the hundreds of choices of *Lavandula*? Well, it may be much easier, and a lot more fun than you think.

While most herb gardeners eventually settle on favorites, sometimes more from familiarity than any other reason, it is fairly simple to choose a likeable herb variety that will grow well in your area. Your anticipated use of the herb and knowledge of local growing conditions will help narrow the field. Your subjective evaluation of a plant's aromatic appeal is, of course, necessary. Part of the excitement of herb gardening is that you may experiment with one variety after another; there is no reason to believe the first choice is the best.

It's not a big deal to make a mistake in the garden, but it does help to have an idea of the how wide the herb world is and how humans have organized it. Herbs are generally classified as herbaceous or woody. A plant is herbaceous if its stems die in the winter and new spring stems appear from the roots. Lemon balm, beebalm, catnip, mints, and tarragon are typically herbaceous and tend to spread underground. Woody-stemmed herbs may be small and somewhat shrubby (suffrutescent), such as thyme, winter savory, lavender, and rosemary; or, like bay, they may resemble trees.

Herbs also may be annuals, biennials, or perennials. Some gardeners are confused about these terms, often because of climatic influences—the difference between an annual and a perennial is a little more complicated than whether a plant survives the winter. An annual germinates, grows, produces flowers and seeds, and dies in a single year. Dill, coriander, borage, summer savory, and basil are typical annual herbs.

A biennial is a two-year plant that usually flowers and makes seed during the second year, as do parsley and caraway.

Here's the confusing part: A perennial lives more than two years, but some cannot withstand severe winter temperatures or even heavy frosts. Thus a particular herb, such as rosemary, may be a perennial in a warm, sunny climate such as California's, returning year after year. In Montana, it must be grown as an annual, for it will not survive the winter.

Common herbs that are winter hardy in most parts of the United States include catnip, horehound, many mints and oreganos, some lavender varieties, and others. Cold-sensitive or tender perennials include bay, rosemary, sweet marjoram and several lavender species. Scientific research can't determine the precise fatal low temperature for individual herbs, in part because some winter conditions, such as snow cover, protect plants. Others, such as dampness, contribute to plant mortality. Local variations would skew the results.

Genetic Influences

Herb cultivars, sometimes incorrectly called strains, differ in the characteristics most desired by the gardener, the farmer, or the market place. Some of the most important characteristics to consider when choosing herbs for maximum flavor and fragrance are growth habit, productivity, and essential oil content. Cold hardiness and disease resistance are important factors in perennial herb yields because they influence the vitality and longevity of the plant. All of these qualities are established by the plant's genetic composition.

Once an herb leaves its hometown hillside or meadow and is cultivated under intense scrutiny, differences between it and other representatives of the same "typical" species may be noticed. The hometown herb may grow taller, produce larger leaves, or differ in aroma.

Such differences occur in both wild populations and the garden because of the natural variability among seeds that leads to differing characteristics among the offspring.

This variability has been underscored by one of America's top vegetable breeders, Burpee's Ted C. Torrey: "Herbs are so diverse and to my observation, so variable in seed-propagated types as to offer great opportunity for breeding programs," he told the 1990 conference of the International Herb Growers and Marketers Association.

Torrey took advantage of this variability in 1976 when he began a large herb-breeding program, including sharp observation of plants grown from herb seed available in the marketplace. 'Green Bouquet' basil is a selection from seeds purchased at Nichols Garden Nursery in Oregon, and 'Green Ruffles' is a selection from basil seeds provided by Helen H. Darrah, author of *The Cultivated Basils*. 'Fernleaf' dill, a 1992 All-America Selection winner, is a selection from Turkish seeds.

Gardeners seeking clues in their search for the best herb varieties may ask the grower whether the plants were grown from seeds. This growing method is convenient and inexpensive compared to rooting cuttings—no plants from which to take cuttings need to be maintained—and it is virtually the only way herbs such as chives, parsley, chervil, caraway, and others reproduce.

Yet, for some species, the genetic variability of seeds leads to uncertain results. After many years, most major seed merchants no longer offer seed of French tarragon (*Artemisia dracunculus* 'Sativa'), a sterile plant unable to reproduce from seed. The seed they sold produced a rank-growing, poorly flavored plant called Russian tarragon.

Despite this experience, catalogs of major companies continue to list a number of herbs that should not be produced from seed. Lavender is one; its seed is too genetically variable to produce named varieties. Much of the oregano seed now sold produces vigorously spreading, tasteless plants, an exceedingly poor choice for cooking. Seed of peppermint, an intensely sterile plant, is also on many lists. With these varieties and many other perennials, asexual reproduction is the most reliable way to produce plants with the desirable parental characteristics.

Natural genetic mutations within plants are another source of unintended diversity. These genetic changes, called sports, might cause the green leaves on a single branch of the plant to become variegated or to differ in some other noticeable way. Such a mutation occurred to create the variegated rosemary 'Joyce DeBaggio', and a similar genetic fluke produced the variegated thyme 'Wedgewood'.

To capture and preserve the unique genetic material of these sports, horticulturists root cuttings from stem tips, a method of vegetative propagation (also called asexual propagation) that maintains the purity of the new cultivar without the risks of seed variability.

Varieties also differ in invisible characteristics such as winter hardiness or resistance to disease. One of our most winter hardy rosemarys (*Rosmarinus officinalis* 'Arp') would have gone unnoticed but for the sharp eye of herb grower Madalene Hill. She discovered it in 1972 behind a house in Arp, Texas, where it had grown for several decades; no one is quite sure of the plant's origins. The new rosemary, however, allowed many northern gardens to welcome the aroma of a rosemary bush.

An equally salutary discovery occurred when nurseryman Pierre Grosso found a single lavender plant that had survived an attack by a deadly mycoplasm that threatened a segment of the French lavender-oil industry in the early 1970s. The survivor, which created a new future for French agriculture, was the mycoplasm-resistant *Lavandula ×intermedia* 'Grosso'. It is comforting to know that in a world guided by technology and test tubes, chance and human observation still play important roles in the development of new herbs.

What's the "Best" Variety?

There are several approaches to choosing the most flavorful variety of herb. The simplest is to sniff through a selection and pick the one that most appeals to you. In doing this, don't try to match the aroma of the fresh herb to that of the dried product available on store shelves. A jar of imported dried oregano, for instance, may contain four or five different species or cultivars of oregano, along with dissimilar herbs such as lemon balm.

Using another method of comparison, a gardener may seek a variety to match an herb-industry standard. For sage, that standard is often said to be Dalmatian sage (*Salvia officinalis*), but over a dozen varieties of sage grow along the Dalmatian coast, an area of the former Yugoslavia and Albania. The varieties, or chemotypes, vary in essential oil content, but three make up about 70 percent of the sages found in the area.

Our research at Delaware State University analyzed the essential oils of eight sage varieties found in the American herb trade ('Albiflora', 'Compacta', 'Icterina', 'Purpurascens', 'Rubriflora', 'Tricolor', 'Berggarten' and 'Woodcote Farm') to ascertain if any match the Dalmation coast's sage varieties.

We found that while sage oils from the Dalmatian coast vary widely and imports are mixtures of several oils, 'Rubriflora' came closest to mimicking the standard, but 'Berggarten' and 'Purpurascens' produce better foliage yields and are runners-up in aroma.

Israeli researchers examined the idea of "the best herb" from a different perspective. Knowing that much commercial dried sage combines *Salvia officinalis* and *S. fruticosa*, they carefully crossed the two species, harvested seeds, and then selected from the hybrid plants to create a new variety. This new sage contained the essential oil characteristics found most desirable in the marketplace and gave Israel's fledgling herb industry a chance to challenge the dominance of the Dalmatian sage product. It wasn't long, however, before European growers began to produce this new sage, and it probably won't be long before U.S. gardeners find it in garden centers, properly labeled as 'Newe Ya'ar', but often incorrectly sold as "silver sage."

It's fine to follow your own aromatic instincts and choose an herb variety without the help of test tubes. Commercial herbs may not be "the best" for your purpose. The herb could be the most plentiful when the industry began, or one that is easy to cultivate and harvest.

Nonetheless, home gardeners face a formidable task in sniffing and munching through the thyme and parsley varieties alone. Fortunately, Harriet Flannery Phillips offers some guidelines on thyme selection. Phillips did what many herb enthusiasts only dream of when she bought all the thyme she could find—some 400 plants that represented all the thyme in the United States—and began her landmark study of the genus.

One of her major discoveries was that French thyme, which she characterized as *Thymus vulgaris* 'Narrow-leaf French', is virtually the only seed-grown culinary thyme generally available in the United States (English thyme has only female flowers and cannot come true from seed, she reported). More than fourteen plants, all offered under separate names, turned out to be *T. vulgaris* 'Narrow-leaf French'. The plants varied in leaf color, size, and growth habit, but they were linked by their revolute leaves—the leaf-margins rolled downward.

In addition, the essential oil of all contained thymol as a chief component. Although this chemical provides important flavoring, it varied as much as 42 percent within the species she defined. Phillips's research, besides clarifying much of the complex thyme nomenclature, underscored once again that selecting the best herbs for flavor and fragrance is best done by the nose, not by the plant name.

The yield of an herb, or how much can be harvested from a plant, is something no nose can smell and close observation of a seedling cannot reveal. James E. Simon, a vegetable and herb specialist at Rutgers University, has spent many years studying parsley; an examination of his 1987 and 1988 field tests of fresh yields of parsley reveals a difference of nearly 1,300 percent between the lowest and the highest yields. While Simon compared only seventeen strains, 'Gigante d'Italia' ('Giant Italian'), a flat-leaved parsley grown from seed imported directly from Italy, had the largest leaf production; second place went to 'Extra Curled Dwarf', a curly variety sold by Burpee.

Simon's tests have shown repeatedly that both seed source and variety play important roles in productivity. While his research has yet to end the age-old debate whether curly-leaved parsley or flat-leaved parsley has the most flavor, Simon has found that curly-leaved varieties can produce just as much essential oil, although the essential oils have not been compared or analyzed for flavor. Besides flavor and yield, parsley's genetics also controls stem length, leaf color, size and tightness of the curl and resistance to heat tip-burn.

How Environmental Factors Influence Flavor

Light, temperature, soil, water, and nutrients are indispensable in growing herbs. While a plant's genes determine many essential characteristics, the environment in which the plant is cultivated plays an indirect part in altering and enhancing these traits.

Most gardeners are familiar with some common factors that influence plants. Plants with insufficient light become spindly. Temperatures too cold may kill sensitive plants, just as surely as too much heat may fry them. Stiff soil permits water to run off, and low fertility produces runts. Water applied to a wilted plant will quickly revive it. These are all profound and palpable effects of the environment on a plant, but there are subtle changes wrought by cultivation that influence the accumulation of volatile oils, the chemicals that give herbs their aromatic character and commercial value.

The idea that the environment has the power to change how a plant tastes or smells is hardly a revolutionary idea. Gardeners, cooks, and scientists have known for decades that certain vegetables benefit from cool temperatures and even a light frost. With the cold comes a change in plant metabolism that turns starches into sugars in parsnips, carrots, cauliflower, kale, mustard greens, collards, brussels sprouts, beets, leeks, kohlrabi, and turnips.

The science of herb cultivation, unlike that of many other crops, is still in its infancy. But enough research has been done to satisfy many scientists that the most common environmental agents in altering essential oil production of herbs are the length and intensity of light, the mean temperature of the climate, and the nutrient levels and water availability of the soil.

Cold is perhaps the most common influence an herb grower recognizes. It does not take severe cold to kill plants like basil. Cold winter temperatures can kill a number of herbs that would otherwise be perennials and knock down the tops of hardy herbaceous varieties. But cold can also trigger other responses. Although parsley is regarded as a biennial that normally flowers the second year, temperatures below 45°F (7°C) for a month or two in spring will cause it to produce seed the first year.

Minor daily changes occur in the composition of an herb's essential oils. These are called diurnal fluctuations and are believed to be caused by changes in the intensity and length of daylight, air temperature and pressure, and other climatic factors.

Other changes within the plant, however, occur gradually over a long period; these may be influenced by cultivation and the environment. Light is often a key factor; in 1976 researchers found that long days enhance growth and increase the content of aromatic oils in peppermint. They also found another environmental factor, temperature, contributed to change: cool nights coupled with long days improved the quality of the plant's aromatic oils. Long days and high temperatures create high oil yields in basil. High light intensity alone increases oil production in chamomile plants.

When we placed a 1-inch layer of white sand beneath hybrid lavandin plants (*Lavandula* ×*intermedia* 'Dutch') in our research field at Delaware State University, growth and flower production increased and essential oil yields soared up to 771 percent compared to plants of the same cultivar without the mulch. We believe that increased light reflected from the sand into the plant was largely responsible for increased growth and oil yields.

Day-length is important to a number of herbs for growth and maturity. Under short days, French tarragon forms a rosette and remains dormant, even with otherwise ideal growing conditions. This dormancy ceases as days lengthen toward spring and may be eliminated artificially through the use of supplemental light. At Cornell University, a researcher established that two 75-watt incandescent bulbs hung 1 foot above tarragon plants for sixteen hours a day provide enough light to maintain vegetative conditions indoors.

Commercial growers near the equator who benefit from naturally long days use this factor to produce tarragon year-round without a dormant period. The same long-day conditions provide the energy for bay laurel (*Laurus nobilis*) to continue vigorous growth through winter. Given long days—artificially or naturally—coriander and dill begin to flower as few as six weeks after germination; oregano plants will also flower.

Water is the life blood of plants, but vary in their response to it. When stressed by lack of water, some react by producing more aromatic oils; others decrease production. The quantity and quality of the aromatic oils in tarragon (*Artemisia dracunculus* 'Sativa'), for instance, improve when plants are watered only at shoot formation early in the year, again when secondary shoots form, and after harvest.

Low to moderate water stress on peppermint increases essential oil yields per leaf (probably because the leaf area became smaller but contained the same number of oil glands), but the entire plant actually produced less oil after two weeks of water deprivation. Overhead irrigation of mint with sprinklers decreases aromatic oil yields by 20 to 30 percent because the soaking and drying of the oil glands causes cracks that increase oil evaporation.

Much of the reaction of herbs to water can be traced back to their native adaptability, says Brian M. Lawrence, a scientist in private industry noted for his work with herbs. "The adaptability of an essential oil-bearing plant to a dry habitat (xerophyte) or an environment that is neither too wet nor too dry (mesophyte) has a profound effect upon the influence of water stress and intake on oil yield," he told an American Chemical Society symposium in 1985. Coriander (*Coriandrum sativum*), clary sage (*Salvia sclarea*), lavender (*Lavandula angustifolia*), and chamomile (*Matricaria chamomilla*), among other herbs, "produce an increased oil yield under moisture stress," he said. "In contrast, mesophytic plants such as *Carum carvi* [caraway], *Levisticum officinale* [lovage], *Anethum graveolens* [dill], *Ocimum basilicum* [basil], and so on produce a decreased oil yield under moisture stress. They require a regulated water supply throughout their growth cycle to maximize oil yield. If such a regimen were applied to xerophytic plants, their oil yield would be lower than if they were under moisture stress."

Scientists have discovered that aromatic chemicals are formed by plants primarily during vigorous growth, and for some when they flower or fruit. While a good supply of nutrients encourages growth, it is important to make some distinctions. Nitrogen increases plant mass by growing more and larger leaves. For plants that produce oil on the leaves, nitrogen increases yields.

Contrary to a common belief held by herb gardeners, nitrogen does not significantly alter the relationship of the chemical constituents of aroma-producing oils for herbaceous plants in the Lamiacae and Compositae families, according to Lawrence. No matter what size the plant reaches, its genes control the relationship of the chemicals that make the aromatic oils.

Yet the type of nitrogen alters the quantity of aromatic oil in sweet basil, according to researchers at Purdue University. While leaf size was not affected, ammonium fertilizer reduced sweet basil's essential oil content by 28 percent and altered the oil's composition by reducing two key components—but not the composition of the oil. Nitrate forms of nitrogen did not have this effect. Ammonium, the cheapest and most readily available fertilizer source, breaks down slowly when soils are cold or acidic.

Ammonium nitrate is found in both organic and inorganic fertilizers. Most organic fertilizer materials break down first into ammonium nitrogen. While ammonium nitrogen usually breaks down quickly, we think the frequent side-dressings of nutrients required by herbs like sweet basil should be made with liquid fertilizers that use calcium nitrate as their source of nitrogen.

Two other nutrients, phosphorus and potassium, are essential for good plant growth. High amounts of phosphorus are important for herbs raised for their seeds, such as fennel, dill, and coriander; too much nitrogen on such herbs is likely to produce foliage at the expense of seed production.

Potassium has the capacity to make minor alterations in the quality of aromatic oils in at least one herb. Italian researchers found the concentration of the leading component in Dalmatian sage oil, beta-thujone, was proportional to the concentration of potassium in the soil.

While fertilizer may affect the aromatic properties of some herbs, it is also important to maximize yields. How much fertilizer does it take to get the most from an herb garden, and when should it be applied for best results? An Israeli scientist studied basil, sweet marjoram, lemon balm, oregano, and thyme and concluded that proper fertilization depends upon plant age and soil condition; further, herbs grow best when nourished at about the same rate as vegetable crops. This conclusion is at odds with the common wisdom that herbs produce best on poor soils of low fertility.

The Israeli study employed a regimen that included liquid nitrogen applied to fertile soil after each herb harvest at a rate of approximately 20 grams of nitrogen per square meter during the first year of herb growth. This amount of added nitrogen—equal to the nitrogen in 1 pound of 10-10-10 granular fertilizer spread on 100 square feet—improved harvests of marjoram by 32 percent and oregano by 23 percent compared to plants that did not receive the extra nutrient.

In the second year of growth, fertilizer rates were doubled and produced the greatest improvement for marjoram (26 percent), oregano (73 percent), and lemon balm (36 percent). There was little difference between the two application levels in sage, producing about 20 percent more at both application rates.

Basil reacted to increases in nitrogen when larger yields of foliage nutrient levels reached three times the lowest level; then yields took a dive. "The fact that no artificial fertilizer was given to the field [prior to planting] may cause a shortage of various elements," stated the report, "so the shortage of elements other than nitrogen may have caused the reduction in yield."

In research performed on rosemary, however, too much nitrogen clearly reduced yields. Potted rosemary fertilized at moderate rates once a week produced the highest foliage yields, while overfertilized plants produced 33 percent less foliage.

Thus it appears that moderate amounts of fertilizer increase the growth of herbs and their yields without a detrimental influence on aroma, but the environmental manipulation of cultivation does little more than enhance what nature provided genetically to herbs. Varietal selection and its purity remain keys to producing herbs with good aroma that adapt well to specific climates.

All this research can help you to understand the many variables that affect herbs and the questions to ask before purchasing a particular plant. In the end, however, maximum flavor or fragrance of the herbs in your garden depends upon choosing a variety that appeals to you through a sniff test and then produces vigorous, healthy plants on well-drained, fertile soil.

CHAPTER 5.

How to Create the Best Growing Conditions

THE RETURN TO a plant's origins may be the most important journey a gardener takes, for that original environment often reveals the limits of a plant's ability to live on its own. The native habitat also provides important clues to methods of cultivation and to a plant's cold hardiness—environmental information on which the gardener may base many decisions.

What characteristics in the plant's hometown environment provide the most important cultivation clues? The essentials for plant growth are annual rainfall, the amount of sun, minimum and maximum annual temperatures, and soil conditions.

An understanding of insects and diseases a plant may encounter in its hometown is helpful, too, even when soil and climate seem perfect. As an herb grower in the Pacific Northwest once commented about rosemary plants: "If the verticillium doesn't get it, the phytophthora does." These two wilt diseases are common enemies of Mediterranean herbs.

Changing one element in the environmental equation may disable the best intentioned efforts and leave a withered, stunted plant. For example, knowing that native rosemary plants are found in stony soil is not enough—perhaps rosemary roots thrive under Spartan conditions, or they need good drainage, little water, loose soil, soil of low fertility, or warm soil in winter. Further, rosemary can be cultivated in circumstances that differ significantly from those of its native habitat—but differ in what ways?

In short, rosemary's hometown conditions represent the minimum and maximum environmental tolerances of the species, but not necessarily its ideal cultural conditions. Only experimentation—something gardeners, horticulturists, and scientists do all the time—will provide a deep understanding about the needs and responses of the plants.

When uprooted from their native lands, any herbs are ill-prepared to cope with new diseases and pests, as plant diseases common to one part of the world may be sometimes unknown in others. Some oregano varieties that survive hometown temperatures as high as 86°F (30°C) in summer and winter lows of −22°F (−30°C) apparently can't survive winters in some areas of United States. Moisture may be an overriding factor in this climatic equation. These oregano varieties, native to high, dry mountainous habitats in the eastern Mediterranean, adapt poorly to the diseases that accompany high humidity and poor air circulation. Where winters are cloudy and damp, disease-weakened plants die.

Such adaptation problems are not immediately apparent. Nearly 125 years after black peppermint (*Mentha* ×*piperita* 'Mitcham') was introduced to the United States, it became infested with verticillium wilt, a soil-borne disease that causes stunted plant growth and eventual death. Peppermint had no natural resistance to the disease, and its propagation through root divisions spread the infection. Eventually the disease forced the abandonment of thousands of acres that formerly nourished the herb. Fortunately, M. J. Murray rescued the declining peppermint industry in less than two decades by creating new resistant varieties, the irradiation-induced mutations named 'Todd Mitcham' and 'Murray Mitcham'.

Does one hometown environmental factor outweigh others? James A. Duke of the U.S. Department of Agriculture compiled information about native and cultivated plants to be used to advise farmers of alternative crops. Duke found it difficult to form a consensus among agricultural scientists on just what single environmental factor is the most important to plant growth. "There is a tendency of soil scientists to assert that soil is the determinant in the distribution and yield of economic plants," he wrote, "of some climatologists to believe the climate is the determinant, and of some plant ecologists to believe the vegetation type is the determinant. I suspect that all plant distributions are determined by interaction of all three and other factors as well."

How these elements—soil, climate and plant type—are linked is often what the observant gardener discovers in the struggle to produce vigorous, healthy herbs in the conditions that exist in the microclimate of a backyard or farm. Our own experience, the research of knowledgeable scientists, and interviews with growers all over the nation remind us that there are many ways to grow herbs successfully.

Looking for a "cookbook" on commercial herb growing? We recommend five texts that may help. The most readily available is a spiral-bound booklet, *Manual for Northern Herb Growers* by Seija Hälvä and Lyle E. Craker; *Breaking Ground* by Kara M. Dinda and Lyle E. Craker may also be useful. N. Kumar and his associates in India have written *Introduction to Spices, Plantation Crops, Medicinal and Aromatic Plants*, which may be purchased from Rajalakshmi Publications, 28/5–693, Veppa Moodu (JN), Nagercoil, 629 001 India. More technical information is provided in Robert K. M. Hay and Peter G. Waterman's *Volatile Oil Crops* and E. A. Weiss's *Spice Crops*.

How to Get Started Growing Herbs

Some of us wake up one fine spring morning and decide it is a good day to start an herb garden and without further planning proceed to a garden center to select some plants. A minority of us spend the winter studying, planning, and then creating a detailed plan of what plant goes where.

There is nothing wrong with either method, but it is a good idea to give some thought to desirable species and the conditions under which they will grow well. Gardens, however, are constantly in flux and no gardener should be so foolish as to let nature take care of it or to think that the plan cannot be altered in the future as the plants begin to communicate their delight or unhappiness at the chosen placement.

In general, a location that receives unshaded sun between 10 a.m. and 4 p.m. suits herbs. A site with moderately fertile soil that is loose, well-drained, and full of decayed vegetable matter will produce steady, even growth of healthy, vigorous, aromatic herbs. In addition, access to irrigation is helpful. Good air circulation around and through the plants decreases many diseases. A method to control temperature is helpful to meet various needs and extend the season.

The minimum amount of sunlight required to produce adequate growth of most herbs is four hours when counted after 10 a.m. More sun is recommended because herbs, for the most part, are plants of sunny fields and withstand and, in fact, require a great deal more sunlight and heat than many gardeners realize; rosemary suffers not at all under temperatures exceeding 110°F (43°C). Commercial fields of tarragon thrive in Arizona, where temperatures reach well over 100°F (37.7°C) in the shade during the day (but where the nighttime temperatures are chilly).

Although herbs are often said to prefer poor soil, in fact, these plants tolerate low soil fertility but do not flourish under those conditions. Why is soil so important? It physically supports the crop by housing the growing roots and supplies nutrients to feed the plants. Gardeners often look at the color or texture of the soil, but what isn't visible is just as important: Good soil must supply air to plant roots. Scientists consider soils to be adequate for sustaining vigorous plant life when they contain at least 5 percent organic matter and 50 percent pore space that is open for air and water. At least 20 percent of the pore space should be available for air.

While most herbs need attention to special cultivation details, some generalities can be made about soil conditions to provide optimum growth. Clay soils are heavy, tough, and often poor in nutrients. They lack pore space and when wet get sticky and drain poorly. Sandy soils have an abundance of pore space but are so light that water runs through it, taking nutrients with it. Replacing such soils is expensive, hard work, and, because of the low quality of much topsoil, probably not worth it unless the garden-to-be is a rock pile.

It's much easier to improve the soil's texture and capacity for holding water and air by adding large quantities of humus, decayed vegetation that has reached a crumbly texture. This lovely, dark stuff can come from your own compost pile or from the garden center; a variety of sphagnum peat moss products that are bagged and readily available make excellent soil amendments. Compost and sphagnum peat may be mixed with equal amounts of aged, composted animal manure for soil enrichment.

Preparing garden soil

Faced with converting lawn or a weed patch into a garden, the first inclination of the American gardener is to grab a gas-powered tiller. While this may be the quickest way to loosen soil, it may also be the worst method. Where do you find the maximum number of weed seeds? In the top 2 to 3 inches (5.1 to 7.6 cm) of soil. What happens when you expose all those weed seeds to optimum light, water, and soil? They germinate!

Here's a method to counteract this problem. Some may say it is backbreaking labor, but think of all the good money people spend for health-club memberships because they've heard that daily vigorous exercise counteracts heart disease, cancer, and diabetes. This type of soil preparation has many advantages besides lowering weeds and aerating the soil. It's cheap exercise, the hours are flexible, you can work at your own pace, and you have something besides an empty wallet to show for your labor.

Our method is a variation of double digging, an annual practice applied to the borders at the Royal Horticultural Society's gardens at Wisley.

1. Dig out any bulbous weeds, such as wild garlic, by hand. Crush the bulbs on a rock or pavement or discard them to a landfill. Wild garlic has resisted our eradication efforts, including using the recommended concentrations of 2,4-D or glyphosate weed killers. Physical removal is the easiest and cleanest method.
2. Mark out a 3 × 6 foot (0.9 × 1.8 m) section with stakes. As you become accomplished at this, you can do without the stakes and estimate.
3. Six feet away from the narrow side of your plot, spread two sheets of 3 × 6 foot (0.9 × 1.8 m) landscape plastic, burlap, old plastic tablecloths, or canvas tarps.
4. Remove the surface soil in sections 2 to 3 inches (5.1 to 7.6 cm) deep and pile it on one of the sheets of landscape plastic. If the area is sodded, after you remove the first section, the rest should peel up as if you were lifting a carpet. A weedy plot, however, is slower going.
5. Dig down another 12 to 18 inches (30.5 to 45.7 cm) and pile this soil on the other piece of landscape plastic.
6. Next to this plot, stake off another 3 × 6 foot (0.9 × 1.8 m) section.
7. On the new section, prepare the surface as indicated above, but place the surface soil or sod face-down into the pit that you've just dug. Step on it firmly.
8. Dig the new section 12 to 18 inches (30.5 to 45.7 cm) deep, and place the soil in the previous pit.
9. Continue the process until the plot is the desired size. For the last section, use the sod and soil that you have reserved on the landscape plastic. Level the soil of the entire plot with a rake.
10. Spread an even layer of compost, leafmold, or sphagnum moss 4 to 6 inches deep atop the newly dug area, moistening dry material before spreading it. Use the fork to

work this into the soil. Where soil is heavy, spread 2 to 3 inches of builder's sand, granite sand, perlite, turface, or chicken grit over the raised bed area and work it into the soil. This will provide additional aeration to keep the soil loose.

This method creates a raised bed 6 to 8 inches above the ground level, the most desirable way to grow herbs, and it puts the weed seeds on the bottom of a pit, where they can gradually rot. Do not disturb this bottom for at least another five to ten years, for not all seeds lose their powers of germination; pokeweed over thirty years old can germinate. When the plant roots reach 12 to 18 inches (30.5 to 45.7 cm) deep, you'll be repaid with the resulting luxuriant growth.

The height of a raised bed will improve air circulation around your plants and encourage drainage; the soil will become warm earlier in the spring, and plants will be easier to reach for harvest. An edging of treated lumber, stones, old concrete, or similar materials will help to keep the soil from washing away and will also keep the water from running off. If each side of the bed slants gently toward the middle, water will remain in the beds even during heavy rains.

If you use lumber to support the sides of your raised beds, select it carefully. Fred Lamb, an extension specialist in Wood Products, Virginia Tech and Virginia State University, lists cypress (old growth), cedars, black cherry, junipers, black locust, white oak, redwood, and black walnut as being the most enduring lumbers. However, unless you harvest from your own wood lot, all are very expensive and last about fifteen years—at the most—in contact with soil.

Home gardeners thus turn to pressure-treated ("salt-treated") lumber. Although the manufacturers and engineers assure us that pressure-treated lumber is perfectly fine for gardens, pawing through the biological literature has turned up a number of papers that are alarming.

If you buy pressure-treated lumber, buy lumber rated for ground contact use (usually labeled "L22"). Properly inspected lumber will be marked with a "cloverleaf" stamp, the symbol of the American Wood Preservatives Bureau. The most common preservative used to be CCA (chromated copper arsenate). That sounds rather poisonous, and it certainly was. CCA-treated lumber had been available for decades but it didn't become the outdoor product of choice until the 1970s, being wisely used for decks and playground equipment. As of 30 December 2003, U.S. chemical companies no longer had EPA approval to sell CCA to treat lumber, and retailers had until 16 May 2004 to sell CCA-infused lumber. Fortunately, alternatives are now available on the market, but much CCA-treated lumber is still recycled by homeowners.

The contamination problem will arise twenty-five to thirty years in the future, when this lumber starts to decay. How do you dispose of it, besides sending it to a landfill? Burning, according to the Koppers Company in Pittsburgh, "has been shown in laboratory testing not to produce any more toxic off-gases than burning untreated wood," but we know of one wood-burning enthusiast who was treated for arsenic poisoning after burning CCA-treated wood. The resulting ash (and fly ash) is high in toxic metals and should not be inhaled, touched, or spread on the garden, and any sawdust should be treated as a toxic material, too.

Cheryl Long and Mike McGrath of *Organic Gardening* produced a popular review of the literature on treated lumber, backed by a bibliography available upon written request. They summarized some of the scientific reports on the topic.

- Heavy metals (chromium, copper, and arsenic) are leached from both new and weathered pressure-treated wood in acidic environments. Remember acid rain?
- Vegetable composts produce greater leaching of heavy metals than distilled water, weathering, or exterior soil burial.
- Even after two years of weathering, chromium, copper, and arsenic are still leached in high enough levels to warn against drinking the water that runs off the lumber.
- The arsenic leached in one week from a 2 × 2 inch (5 × 5 cm) piece of pressure-treated lumber is enough to kill a mouse.
- In some spots on weathered pressure-treated lumber, neither copper nor arsenic could be detected, indicating complete removal of these metals.

Discarded railroad ties, preserved with creosote, are sometimes available. While the major creosote components biodegrade, newly creosoted timbers can cause skin irritations and possible migration of chemicals into the soil. Pentachlorophenol once readily available, is now restricted, like creosote, by the EPA (Environmental Protection Agency). Copper naphthanate remains available and is thought to be less toxic than creosote or "penta" to plants, but it has not been studied much.

Research continues to find an environmentally safe wood preservative. For a while, wood on the market was preserved with CDDC (copper dimethyldithiocarbamate) and marketed as Kodiak Lumber. The EPA did not classify this as a hazardous waste material, unlike CCA-treated wood. New products continually appear on the market; do your homework first before purchase and use. Ask questions like the following: How far do the contaminants migrate from the source? Can they bind to the soil, thereby preventing or slowing their migration? Does pH or soil type affect the migration? Are they absorbed by plant roots and other organs?

So what is the best material now available for raised beds? We recommend stones, bricks, or concrete blocks. Many ornamental blocks are now available in today's markets, and some molds are even sold to create your own blocks.

Why go to all this trouble for a few plants? Plant roots extend far into the soil in search of moisture and nutrients. Parsley, considered a rather shallow-rooted plant, reaches 18 to

24 inches into the soil. Moreover, many herbs are perennials, plants that will stay put for years, a lot longer than short-lived herbs such as parsley, basil, dill, and coriander.

Soil fertility is basic

While creating a loamy garden bed may be the kind of hard labor that disciplines prisoners in a penal colony, it's only the first step to a successful herb garden. Fertility is equally important and it needs attention every year and sometimes more often, because many crops are improved with side-dressings of fertilizer after each harvest.

As with other plants, herbs require three basic chemicals for growth: nitrogen, phosphorous and potassium. The formulas on fertilizer packages, such as 5-10-5, designate the percentages of each chemical—in this case, 5 percent nitrogen, 10 percent phosphorus pentoxide, 5 percent potassium oxide—contained in the fertilizer. This nutrient triumvirate is supplemented by other chemicals, referred to as micronutrients, that are needed in small amounts. Examples include boron, copper, iron, manganese, molybdenum, and zinc. A soil test from a private company or from the U.S. Department of Agriculture Extension Service is usually the first step to soil improvement. The test results report the levels of key nutrients in your soil so that proper amounts of nutrients and amendments may be added.

Nitrogen. Soils can attain some fertility just by hanging onto the globe. "Some nitrogen accumulates in the soil from rainfall," says Allen V. Barker, a soil scientist at the University of Massachusetts, "and from nitrogen fixation (the conversion of gaseous nitrogen in the atmosphere to organic nitrogen) by free-living microorganisms. This accumulation rarely exceeds 10 pounds per acre per year, however, and cannot support much crop production."

A more purposeful use of these ingenious natural occurrences is called green manuring, the cultivation of leguminous plants to produce nitrogen, a key nutrient that is rapidly depleted. Such plants as garden beans and alfalfa produce, respectively, from 50 to 200 pounds of nitrogen per acre. "For soil to be nitrogen enriched by leguminous plants," Barker said in an article in *The Herb, Spice and Medicinal Plant Digest*, "the growing crop . . . must be turned into the ground while at a green, succulent stage. If the top growth of the legume is harvested, no enhancement of nitrogen levels in the soil occurs. Thus, production of a green manure crop for nitrogen fertilization requires that land be set aside from the production of a cash crop for at least one year."

Little residual nitrogen remains after the first year a crop is grown, Barker added. This makes green manure of minimal value for the production of perennial herbs that remain in the soil for years. As herb researcher Eli Putievsky of Israel's Agricultural Research Organization put it in 1990 to a group of herb growers, "Under intensive agricultural conditions, when plants are harvested for their foliage several times each year, heavy fertilization is required." Rain and green manure aren't enough to supply adequate nitrogen to growing plants.

Natural fertilizers or synthetic equivalents are used to replenish nutrients for herbs. Synthetic fertilizers are usually available in granular form or as a powder to be mixed with water and used as a liquid; they contain specific amounts of nutrients that are readily available to herbs. Natural fertilizers (manures and composted vegetative material are the most common) do not release nutrients as rapidly and are often quite bulky. "The actual nitrogen content of manures varies with the type of animal and feed given to the animal," Barker noted. "Poultry manure is considerably higher in nitrogen than the manures from larger farm animals, and the better livestock is fed, the richer the nutrient content of the manure." Manures improve soil friability by adding organic matter and often contain important micronutrients; synthetic fertilizers often do not. However, organic herb growers should be acutely aware of possible lethal strains of *E. coli* that have surfaced recently, so do not apply any animal manures less than 60 days before harvest (and clean as discussed under harvesting). Fall application is best, allowing breakdown of the pathogens over the winter, just to be sure.

The amount of fertilizer to add to soil depends on a number of factors. One of the most important is the soil's past history of cultivation. The type of soil also determines how quickly nutrients are leached from it. Fertilizers work best when applied to newly prepared beds three to four weeks before planting. The amount of fertilizer depends on the type of material to be applied and on existing soil nutrients, as well as the herb varieties.

For the average garden, James E. Simon of Rutgers University recommends fertilizer applications consistent with those commonly given American vegetable growers—a per acre rate of 100 pounds of nitrogen, 200 pounds of phosphate, and 200 pounds of potassium. On a smaller scale, this translates to about 4 ounces of nitrogen for each 100 square feet of garden or about 4.5 to 5 pounds of 5-10-10 granular fertilizer per 100 square feet prior to planting.

To bring a home garden up to these recommended nitrogen levels with natural manures may require a surprisingly large quantity of material. To achieve the 4-ounce rate per 100 square feet (100 pounds of nitrogen per acre) would take any one of the following: 2 pounds of blood meal (12 percent N), 14 pounds of poultry manure (3 percent N), 23 pounds of dried cow manure (2 percent N), or 92 pounds of moist compost (0.5 percent N). These figures are adapted from Barker's research.

Part of the reason so much manure is needed is that it is low in nitrogen and all the nutrient is not available to the plant immediately. While 100 percent of the nitrogen in dried blood is available the first year, according to Barker, only half the nitrogen in manure and compost is ready to use in the same time.

When fresh manure is used, it's important to incorporate it into the soil immediately (but not around plant roots, where it might burn them). Otherwise, Barker said, half of its nitrogen content is lost to the atmosphere within two to four days. Fresh manure applications are best made in the fall before planting the following spring, so tender new roots are not damaged.

Fertilizer applications during the growing season, sometimes referred to as side-dressing, are useful to supplement nutrients lost through leaching or used by the plants. One-third to one-half the rate of the fertilizer applied initially should be scratched in carefully around the base of the plants after each harvest, according to Simon. These side-dressings are placed where the plant's roots can get to them quickly, but not so close to the plant that foliage or roots are burned. Compost and manures can be applied with little fear of plant damage, but they act slowly. Liquid fertilizers (20-20-20 is a good formula) are easy to place around plant roots with a watering can and have nearly immediate acceptance by the plants.

Phosphorus and Potassium. Two other nutrients, phosphorus and potassium, are essential for good plant growth. High amounts of phosphorus are important for herbs raised for their seeds, such as fennel, dill and coriander. Both phosphorus and potassium take longer to build up and become available for plant growth with organic methods. Complete granular and liquid fertilizers contain various amounts of nitrogen, phosphorus, and potassium more quickly used by plants. Composts and manures also contain phosphorus and potassium in small amounts. Bone meal is high in phosphorus, with much of it readily available to the plant. Wood ashes provide a good source of available potassium.

Acid or alkaline?

Plenty of sun, fertility, and drainage won't help an herb planted in a soil that is mismatched in pH, a measure of the soil's acidity. A plant's ability to use soil nutrients is hampered or choked off when the pH is too high or too low for the crop. Moreover, acid soils can cause toxic levels of aluminum and manganese. Fortunately, most herbs respond to soils with a wide range of pH. Basil, bay, chives, coriander, dill, fennel, lemon balm, marjoram, mints, oregano, parsley, rosemary, sage, tarragon, and thyme are all found growing naturally in soils that range from an acid 5 all the way up to an alkaline 8 on the pH meter. Somewhere in the middle of these ranges—perhaps 6 to 6.5—is where most herbs will prove their worth in flavor and growth.

Lime is the most common material used to bring acid soils up to a pH that will release nutrients to herbs. "Measuring the soil pH is the principal and most practical means for determining and estimating lime requirements," according to Barker. "This pH measurement, however, is only an expression of the active acidity, the hydrogen ions in the soil solution. Most of the acidity of soils, referred to as reserve acidity, resides on the soil colloids, primarily clays and organic matter. While only a small amount of limestone, possibly only a few pounds, is needed to neutralize the active acidity within an acre of land, many tons will be required to neutralize the reserve fraction." For instance, to raise the pH of a sandy soil from 4.5 to 6.5 takes 2,200 pounds of limestone per acre (5 pounds per 100 square feet), but on a clay loam soil with a similar pH, it requires nearly four times as much, 8,400 pounds per acre (20 pounds per 100 square feet).

Carbonates, hydroxides, or oxides of calcium and magnesium are different materials that horticulturists refer to as lime. Each of these materials differs in the speed with which it reacts to neutralize soil acidity. Quicklime, sometimes called burnt lime or caustic lime, and hydrated lime, or slaked lime, work more rapidly than limestone or other materials because they are more water soluble, Barker explained in the winter 1989 issue of *The Herb Spice and Medicinal Plant Digest*. "Dolomitic limestone (limestone containing more than 5 percent $MgCO_3$) generally reacts more slowly with acid soils than calcitic limestone ($CaCO_3$). . . . In practice, most agricultural limestones are a mixture of dolomitic and calcitic limestones." This material moves through the soil at the rate of about an inch per year.

As a rule, the more quickly the lime acts, the less residual effect it has and the more often it must be applied to maintain the desired pH. "Once the acidity of a field is neutralized to about pH 6.5," Barker says, "the pH should remain constant with only moderate applications of lime (2 tons per acre, 90 pounds per 1,000 square feet) about every five years. More frequent applications of lime will maintain a more constant pH from year to year. The need for reapplying lime is governed by soil texture, leaching, cropping, cultivation practices, fertilization and fineness of the original liming material."

To keep pH above 6, Barker recommended a soil test every two to three years. The Agriculture Extension Service in your area can have your soil tested and tell you the amounts of lime to add to adjust the pH.

Soil tests are a sure way to discover the pH and fertility levels, but if you already have a crop in the ground and something doesn't seem quite right with it, there may be a quick way to find out what's wrong—ask the plant. It's not as absurd as it sounds. Herbs and other plants communicate their condition visually. If you can translate this visual language, you can have an educational chat. For instance, some of your herbs appear stunted and the stems are hard, thin and upright; the leaves are a bit yellow and smaller than they should be. Translation: nitrogen deficiency. Perhaps the underside of the leaves of another plant is flushed with purple—and it shouldn't be—and the stems are stunted and thin, and growth is slow. Translation: the plant needs phosphorus. Yet another plant develops a gray or tan coloring near the leaf margins. This scorched appearance spreads around the leaf margins. Translation: possible potassium deficiency.

Talking to your plants this way might make the difference between a successful garden and a season of failure. Close observation is the first rule of a good gardener.

TABLE 7.
pH range of common herbs.

COMMON NAME	BOTANICAL NAME	SOIL pH MINIMUM	SOIL pH MEAN*	SOIL pH MAXIMUM
basil	*Ocimum basilicum*	4.3	6.6	9.1
bay laurel	*Laurus nobilis*	4.5	6.2	8.2
borage	*Borago officinalis*	4.5	6.6	8.2
calendula, pot marigold	*Calendula officinalis*	4.5	6.6	8.2
caraway	*Carum carvi*	4.8	6.4	7.8
catnip	*Nepeta cataria*	4.9	6.6	7.6
chives	*Allium schoenoprasum*	5.0	6.5	8.2
chives, garlic	*Allium tuberosum*	4.5	6.0	7.0
comfrey	*Symphytum officinale*	5.5	7.1	8.7
coriander	*Coriandrum sativum*	4.9	6.6	8.2
dill	*Anethum graveolens*	5.0	6.5	8.2
fennel	*Foeniculum vulgare*	4.8	8.2	6.6
horehound	*Marrubium vulgare*	4.5	6.9	8.4
lavender	*Lavandula angustifolia*	6.4	7.1	8.2
lemon balm	*Melissa officinalis*	4.5	6.6	7.6
marjoram, sweet	*Origanum majorana*	4.9	6.9	8.7
mint, pennyroyal	*Mentha pulegium*	4.8	6.9	8.2
mint, spearmint	*Mentha spicata*	4.5	6.3	7.5
nasturtium	*Nasturtium officinale*	4.3	6.3	8.0
oregano	*Origanum vulgare* subsp. *hirtum*	4.5	6.7	8.7
oregano (rigani)	*Origanum onites*	6.5	6.8	7.2
parsley	*Petroselinum crispum*	4.9	6.2	8.2
rosemary	*Rosmarinus officinalis*	4.5	6.8	8.7
sage	*Salvia officinalis*	5.3	5.8	6.8
savory, summer	*Satureja hortensis*	5.6	7.0	8.2
savory, winter	*Satureja montana*	6.5	6.7	7.0
tansy	*Tanacetum vulgare*	4.8	6.3	7.5
tarragon	*Artemisia dracunculus* 'Sativa'	4.9	6.9	7.5
thyme	*Thymus vulgaris*	4.5	6.3	8.0

* Mean pH approximates optimum.
Source: Duke, J. A., *Quart. J. Crude Drug Res.*, 15 (1977), 189–233.

Irrigation

Natural rainfall is one gauge of how much water herbs will tolerate. Many of the most common herbs will tolerate low water levels, even if they won't thrive on them. A respectable herb garden can be put together of plants that require an average of an inch of water a month or less—it might contain bay laurel, borage, calendula, chives, coriander, fennel, horehound, lavender, pennyroyal, rosemary, sage, and tarragon.

Virtually all the major culinary herbs could get by in areas receiving an average of 2 inches or less of precipitation a month, but only if they were already well-established. However, this may not be enough to maximize production. Israeli researcher Eli Putievsky studied the reaction to water of essential oil and foliage yields of scented geraniums, sweet marjoram, lemon balm, and sage. He found that yields of foliage and essential oils increased with the amount of water given to the plants. We think herbs in the home garden need about 1 inch of water a week for vigorous growth and health.

Many herbs have adapted to dry conditions, but the extent to which they can tolerate dryness has remained little known outside the small circle of horticulturists and scientists who study the special requirements of plants. James A. Duke has spent years collecting what he calls "ecosystematic data" on a variety of plants, including most of the common herbs. The information was collected from hundreds of sites around the world in an effort to find the range of climatic conditions under which a plant might grow.

Duke's study showed that basil grows in areas that receive only 21 inches of rain a year and in climates that receive nearly 170 inches of rain annually. French tarragon, on the other hand, had a more limited range—from 8.3 to 54 inches annually. Spearmint, often thought to be a thirsty herb, ranged from a minimum of 20.5 to 109 inches annually.

Of course, all plants on the list are not at each site. And conditions (such as soil type) may also influence the plant's ability to sustain itself. "Means reported are usually closer to the optima than the extremes," according to Duke. "Hence the means are useful criteria in determining the suitability of a habitat for the species."

The information in the chart below is adapted from Duke's article, "Ecosystematic Data on Economic Plants," published in the *Quarterly Journal of Crude Drug Research* (1979, No. 3–4, pp. 91–110). It should be understood as a guide, not as an absolute, and should be tempered with average temperatures during the growing season. For orientation, consider the total annual precipitation in inches for some cities in 1984: Albany, NY (37); Albuquerque, NM (12); Atlanta, GA (55); Boston, MA (50); Dallas, TX (34); Indianapolis, IN (42); Little Rock, AR (64); New Orleans, LA (52); Los Angeles, CA (8); Portland, OR (38); San Francisco, CA (14); and Tampa, FL (32).

TABLE 8.
Water tolerances of herbs.

COMMON NAME	BOTANICAL NAME	ANNUAL PRECIPITATION (INCHES)		
		MIN.	MEAN	MAX.
basil	*Ocimum basilicum*	20.9	63.8	168.9
bay laurel	*Laurus nobilis*	12.2	36.2	89.8
borage	*Borago officinalis*	12.2	33.5	53.9
calendula, pot marigold	*Calendula officinalis*	12.2	30.7	53.9
caraway	*Carum carvi*	13.8	29.5	53.9
catnip	*Nepeta cataria*	13.8	29.5	53.9
chives	*Allium schoenoprasum*	12.2	39.8	158.7
chives, garlic	*Allium tuberosum*	24	47.6	109.5
comfrey	*Symphytum officinale*	18.9	55.5	146.5
coriander	*Coriandrum sativum*	12.2	32.7	51.6
dill	*Anethum graveolens*	16.5	33.5	69.3
fennel	*Foeniculum vulgare*	12.2	38.6	103.2
horehound	*Marrubium vulgare*	11.4	27.6	53.9
lavender	*Lavandula angustifolia*	12.2	28	53.9
lemon balm	*Melissa officinalis*	19.7	33.9	60.2
marjoram, sweet	*Origanum majorana*	18.9	53.1	107.1
mint, pennyroyal	*Mentha pulegium*	12.2	27.6	7.2
mint, spearmint	*Mentha spicata*	20.5	36.2	109.4
nasturtium	*Nasturtium officinale*	15.8	40.6	168.9
oregano	*Origanum vulgare* subsp. *hirtum*	17.3	1.6	107.1
parsley	*Petroselinum crispum*	12.2	35.4	111
rosemary	*Rosmarinus officinalis*	12.2	51.6	107.1
sage	*Salvia officinalis*	12.2	36.2	60.2
savory, summer	*Satureja hortensis*	13.8	33.1	53.9
savory, winter	*Satureja montana*	26	42.5	68.1
tansy	*Tanacetum vulgare*	13.8	31.1	53.9
tarragon	*Artemisia dracunculus* 'Sativa'	8.3	27.6	53.9
thyme	*Thymus vulgaris*	15	37	111

Watering garden-grown herbs is one of the most important, yet often most instinctual and little understood, factors in producing plants with vigor and flavor. The vapid axiom, "Apply the right amount of water at the right times," is repeated even by otherwise well-informed specialists. The obvious question is, "The right times for what?"

Unlike many other crops, herbs are watered for two reasons—for health and vigor and to produce the highest quality and quantity of aromatic oils. The right times for health are fairly obvious and normal. Young seedlings need special care, including adequate water to establish them in the garden. In addition, soil plays an important role in the access of water to the plant; some soils can hold more water than others. In most areas of the United States, some irrigation may be necessary during the summer for most herb crops. The normal rule-of-thumb: Water in a way that the plant can maintain steady, vigorous growth from transplant to harvest.

Overhead watering by sprinklers is wasteful and can foster a multitude of diseases in many herbs. Underground systems using pipes from which water oozes have found acceptance in many home gardens where regular irrigation of an inch or more per week is necessary. These supply water at the root level without loss to evaporation. Such a system is best installed prior to planting.

Mulches also conserve water. Where humidity is high in summer and fungus problems are manifold, mulches of organic materials should be avoided; peat moss, wood chips, and rotted sawdust all promote sudden wilt by *Phytophthora* and other root fungi on dense Mediterranean subshrubs such as rosemary, lavender, hyssop, and sage. For these herbs, mulches of sand or small pea gravel, 1 to 2 inches deep, retain moisture quite well. Our studies at Delaware State University revealed that 1 inch of sand under lavender plants vastly increased flower production, aided growth (mulched plants were twice the size of their unmulched counterparts) and significantly improved winter survivability.

Researchers at the University of Illinois found that black polyethylene mulch increases the fresh and dry weight of basil and rosemary, but parsley does not respond to this type of mulching. Colored plastic mulches and woven plastic mulches may be advantageous for herb cultivation, but scientific results have not yet been published.

Cool-Weather Crops

While most herbs grow well within a wide range of temperatures, a few, when grown for their foliage, perform best in cool weather. These herbs' optimum growing temperatures fall between 55°F (12.6°C) and 70°F (21°C). Included in this category are annuals such as dill, chervil, and coriander.

There are two approaches to the cultivation of these plants. One method is to start them in early spring and harvest them before long, hot days bring on their flower stalks. Cutting the flower stalk helps to prolong foliage production from these plants, but it will not keep them vegetative through summer as it does an annual such as basil. Flowering has been found to change the flavor as well as the shape of the foliage in coriander. A second approach is to sow seed toward summer's end and finish the crop in cool fall weather. All of these herbs will withstand some light frost.

We have noticed that many gardeners delay initial foliage harvest on coriander and dill and thus lose significant benefit from the herbs. As an experiment, we planted seven-week-old coriander transplants in early June in an East Coast garden to see how many times the plants' foliage could be harvested. We used a site that received five hours of direct sun. Soil temperatures were in the 70s and daytime highs had begun to reach the mid 90s regularly. The soil was heavily amended with sphagnum peat and perlite and fertilized heavily with slow-release 14-14-14 Osmocote; plants were watered every few days to assure adequate water.

The first harvest was made one week after transplanting and continued at approximately ten- to fourteen-day intervals through the first week in August. The plants were harvested an average of five times each, indicating that harvesting early and continuing on a regular basis increases overall yields of coriander. In fall trials of four dill varieties, findings were similar.

Some success can be had with dill, chervil, and coriander as a warm-weather crop where it is sown thickly and harvested by pulling all the seedlings when they reach 5 or 6 inches high—about sixty days from planting. Many gardeners and commercial growers use this method coupled with periodic seed sowing to produce continuous crops. Bolt-resistant varieties are best for foliage production of chervil, dill, and coriander.

While seed sown directly in the garden or field is common for chervil, dill, coriander, and Florence fennel, transplants are sometimes used in small-scale operations or in the home garden. Transplants of dill and coriander, preferred by some home gardeners, are sometimes of harvestable size when purchased and may not last long after transplanting because of their age. Direct-sown plants seem to be able to withstand more heat stress before bolting than those transplanted from pots. It is not true that dill and coriander do not transplant well from pots; however, bare-root transplanting outdoors should be avoided.

Florence fennel is often grown in spring as a transplant, especially where cool weather does not last long. It should be heavily fertilized and provided with adequate water so that vigorous growth is continuous. Bulbs should be harvested before seed stalks form; these stalks form a hard, inedible core in the bulb. Summer transplants can be held longer in the cool weather of fall before flower stalks form. A minimum of about 100 days is need for crop maturity.

Sorrel, a perennial grown for its large, tart, green leaves, also performs best under cool temperature conditions. It sends green shoots from dormant roots in late winter. As temperatures reach the 80s, foliage production slows and long, tough stems ascend in profusion, producing a mass of small, unattractive flowers. These stems should be removed as they form. Regular water and liquid fertilizer during summer heat will encourage only moderate growth. As cool weather returns in fall, the plant returns to foliage production.

These cool-weather crops are excellent for winter production in the southern and southwestern United States where temperatures remain above 40°F (4.4°C). They can also be grown in cold frames and other devices that extend the season by protecting plants from frigid weather.

Extending the Season

Because climates often are unpredictable, horticulturists seek methods to prolong the proper growing temperatures for their plants without the clutter and inefficiency of plants on a windowsill. Fall, winter, and early spring present major challenges to herb growers anxious to lengthen the season or overwinter tender herbs outdoors. Extension of the season allows seeds and transplants to be planted sooner and produce earlier harvests. At the other end of the growing cycle, season extenders offer protection to later crops and permit delayed harvests.

Some of the best herbs to grow under extended-season conditions are often miserly producers during warmer weather. Chervil, dill, coriander, and parsley can become monsters under long, cool growing conditions. Other herbs particularly suited to extended growing conditions are crops such as sorrel, rosemary, oregano, thyme, and sweet marjoram.

Greenhouses control environmental conditions, but they are expensive and permanent. Cold frames are less cumbersome and more portable than a greenhouse and can provide significant protection. While it's no relation to an ice box, this miniature greenhouse requires only modest skill and investment to build and can become the most valuable tool in the herb garden.

Good cold frames keep temperatures at 15 to 20 degrees Fahrenheit (8.3 to 11.1 degrees Celsius) higher than outside without heating apparatus. This, along with their size and portability, has made them essential for early seed starting and to prepare seedlings for spring transplanting. In many areas of the United States, cold frame protection can mean the difference between life and death for many herb varieties.

There are many styles and sizes of cold frames. The most common is made from old window sashes and 2 × 8 inch (5 × 20.3 cm) treated lumber. The wooden frame is sized to the sash widths. The back faces north and is about twice as high as the front. The window sashes are slanted to slough off rain and snow and to capture the maximum winter sun. Where plants are grown directly in the earth inside the frame, the soil should be improved. If potted plants are to have a winter home in the cold frame, 6 inches (15.2 cm) of earth inside the frame is removed and replaced with 3 inches (7.6 cm) of crushed stone overlaid with bricks to hold heat. For added heat-retention, water bottles painted black may be stationed around the perimeter of the cold frame.

A more ambitious and portable cold frame can be erected to cover a raised garden bed. This design takes the cold frame to the plants rather than the plants to the cold frame. It can be rolled up at the end of winter and stored. To make one, insert 2-foot-long pieces of electrical conduit, about 1 inch (2.5 cm) in diameter, into the ground beside the herb bed opposite each other and spaced every 4 feet (1.2 m). To pound the pipe into the ground without damaging the lip, place an oversized bolt in the top of the pipe.

Into opposite pipes, shove a 10- or 20-foot (3 or 6 m) flexible, ½-inch (1.3 cm), white plastic water pipe or gray plastic electrical conduit. These arch over the bed to make a hooped support for a layer of clear 6-mil polyethylene sheeting. Sometimes two beds can be covered at one time.

A walk-in cold frame made this way is easy to tend. If the structure is too low to stand in, one side can be folded and stapled to the wooden bed support with heavy-duty, ½-inch (1.3 cm) staples. The ends and the remaining side, held down by heavy cement blocks, permit easy access and can be opened when the sun warms the interior too much.

Variations on this scheme can provide hot-water heat under the plant bed. A double layer of polyethylene inflated with a special fan insulates by adding an air space between layers of plastic and keeps the covering from flapping in the wind. A cold frame with a double layer of plastic keeps temperatures inside as much as 20 degrees Fahrenheit (11.1 degrees Celsius) warmer than outside.

Rigid steel components for making cold frames are available commercially; the hoops connect with pieces of straight steel. This steel is hinged on one side with an ingenious "T" made of two pieces of welded pipe. The side rail runs through the horizontal piece of the T, while the vertical piece slips over a ground stake to form a hinge. The entire top can be lifted for access and ventilation.

To cultivate plants in a cold frame successfully, the inside temperature must be controlled; it can heat up fast and cook the plants. Automatic sash lifters, which operate when inside temperature reach a preset maximum or minimum, will provide convenient ventilation. Where there is height and access to electricity, thermostatically controlled fans can ventilate automatically by drawing fresh air into the cold frame.

To limit fungus diseases spawned by high humidity inside a cold frame, regular ventilation is important to increase air movement. If necessary, an application of liquid garden sulfur may be needed to kill mildew; unfortunately, some herbs show an intolerance for sulfur on their foliage, and the material should be tested on a few plants before it is sprayed or dusted on an entire crop.

Horticulturists have for decades sought ways to take the cold frame to the field. An early answer came with the nineteenth-century cloche, an invention of French market gardeners. The word *cloche* means "bell" or "dish-cover." The French gardeners' cloche was a blown-glass bell 12 to 18 inches (30.5 to 45.7 cm) in diameter that was placed over young vegetable plants. This method had two drawbacks. First, the glass cloche was easily broken; secondly, it covered such a small area that heat dissipated quickly at night. Modern versions of the cloche include upturned plastic milk bottles and milkshake cups with their bottoms removed.

The gardeners of Britain went beyond the cloche and perfected a row cover made of glass panes clipped together, an A-frame tent that covered more space, but it, too, could be easily broken.

With the advent of specialized plastics, the transformed glass row cover has become a popular season-extender in the United States. These latest developments are soft, billowy, lightweight row covers that are held up by the plants themselves. The materials from which they are made vary among four plastics: polyethylene, polyester, polypropylene, and polyvinyl alcohol.

The modern row covers are lightweight and allow sunlight and air to pass through their woven, breathable surfaces. They actually do double duty by protecting the plants from cold as well as insects. As a blanket against cold, the best of them, Tufbell Livecover made from polyvinyl alcohol, adds 5 to 10 degrees Fahrenheit (2.7 to 5.7 degrees Celsius) of protection. It has a useful life of four to eight years and admits 93 percent of the light.

The popular polyester material called Remay lasts for up to three years, admits 83 percent of light and offers up to 5 degrees Fahrenheit (2.7 degree Celsius) of protection. Other materials fall into somewhat similar protective and light-admission categories, according to test results published in *Harrowsmith Country Life Magazine*

Research with vegetables has shown that these protective coverings work. Nine types of lettuce survived a New Hampshire winter under a double cover of Argyle polypropylene row covers, while uncovered lettuce perished. Strawberries covered with similar row covers have matured two weeks earlier with a 50 percent increase in yields.

Heat buildup can be a problem even with these self-ventilating materials. Temperatures at plant level under row covers can reach 10 to 15 degrees Fahrenheit (5.7 to 8.3 degrees Celsius) above ambient air. Care must be taken to remove the row cover at the appropriate time for a specific crop—much sooner for a cool-weather crop like dill than for a heat lover like basil.

With ingenuity and the proper materials, many herbs too tender for some climates can be brought through frigid periods outdoors without damage. But the gardener still plays an important role in the choice of materials and the way they are handled. It is this balance between an herb gardener's skill at cultivation and knowledge of plant species that elevates growing herbs to a near-art and makes the herb garden a place of constant experimentation and excitement as well as a place from which to draw pleasure and sustenance.

CHAPTER 6.

Container Cultivation

MOST HERBS ADAPT readily to containers, as many herb growers have known for years. Potted plants are easily relocated for optimum sun or maximum impact in the landscape. The same plants can be brought indoors for winter and enjoyed for their fragrance and welcome harvests of fresh foliage for cooking. The seductive allure and a hard-won practicality of gardening in a movable few square inches may have inspired the Egyptians to take up container gardening some four thousand years ago.

Growing herbs in containers provides the gardener the ultimate in control and pleasure but brings new responsibilities, too. Container gardening requires more cultivation skills than growing plants in the garden or field, because a potted plant relies totally on the gardener's knowledge and ability to create the necessary growing environment. A plant above ground in a container is exposed to the elements in ways a plant in the ground is not. Wind and sun will dry container plants rapidly; without the protection of the ground around them, roots reach colder, even detrimental, temperatures in winter. If the container plant is brought inside, the gardener must place the plant carefully for maximum sunlight, and perhaps provide supplemental light to encourage growth during the short days of winter.

Direct care of the container herb's roots also becomes the gardener's concern. The roots of an herb in a container cannot roam underground in search of water and nutrients as they do in the garden, and the gardener must attentively supply these essentials. Roots may circle the pot's interior, creating a rootbound condition and slowing or preventing plant growth and foliage production; eventually, the plant will die. Thus the gardener must inspect the rootball frequently and periodically transplant the herb to a larger pot.

Growing Media

The composition of the potting mix is the most important ingredient of growing herbs in containers successfully. A good potting soil is free of weed seeds, pests, and disease organisms; and it should also have lots of air space and hold a moderate amount of water. An initial low level of fertility is also desirable to allow the grower more control of nutrient levels. Soil dug from the garden is inappropriate for use in containers because it lacks the porosity necessary for a good container growing medium and may contain disease organisms, pests, and weed seeds.

The phrase "growing medium" has a scientific twang to it and doesn't sound very down to earth; it is meant to be a bit vague, too, because there are many concoctions put in containers to grow herbs that contain no soil at all. Organic purists sometimes call these soilless mixes "artificial," but there is nothing unnatural about them, nor are they necessarily new. Soilless media contain natural and processed materials such as (1) shredded sphagnum peat moss, which comes from partially decomposed perennial mosses (*Sphagnum* spp.) that grow in freshwater acid bogs; (2) sand; (3) composted bark, peanut hulls, or sawdust; (4) perlite, a volcanic rock that is expanded by heating it to 1800°F; and (5) vermiculite, a layered mica that is heated to 1400°F to expand it.

Soilless growing media have several advantages over those that contain soil: they are lighter, drain better, easier to store, pest free and generally disease free. There is no need to go through the smell and mess to pasteurize these mixtures as you would if you dug garden soil from the garden (soil is pasteurized to remove the harmful organisms; sterilization would destroy it). Traditional pasteurizing methods for home gardeners use 3 to 4 inches of damp soil in a baking or roasting pan covered with aluminum foil and placed in a 250°F (121°C) oven; when the soil reaches 180°F (83°C), the oven temperature is reduced slightly so that the soil temperature can be maintained for 30 minutes; higher temperatures destroy soil structure. Expect a rancid odor when pasteurizing soil. The smell does not remind you of something mother used to make! All this may sound as far away from a sunny Mediterranean hillside covered with herbs as you can get, and you may wonder whether herbs can grow in this stuff. There is persuasive evidence that growing media without soil produce healthier herbs with an increased foliage yield. A study of lemon balm, peppermint, and sage by Susan M. Bell and Gerald D. Coorts at Southern Illinois University revealed that a medium with equal parts soil, peat, and perlite produced the smallest plants while the plants grown in soilless mixes were all larger (the largest and fullest plants were produced in a medium of 30 percent vermiculite and 70 percent composted and milled pine bark). Similar results were produced at the University of Massachusetts in a test of rosemary's response to growing media. "Reduced water-holding capacity and increased porosity may have been responsible for the slight enhancement of growth obtained in the soilless mix," the team of scientists led by Thomas H. Boyle concluded of their rosemary test plants. The rosemary in the soilless medium produced 12 percent more foliage than plants grown in soil-peat-perlite.

While the idea of a potting soil without soil may be new to you, French horticulturists experimented with peat, leafmold, and pine needles to grow azaleas before 1892, and peat-sand combinations were used experimentally in the 1930s by the renowned American horticultural scientist Alex Laurie of Ohio State University. Commercial growers the world over now use growing media without soil, and most are based on peat and sand or some other aggregate.

In the United States, soilless media frequently follow formulations established in the 1950s at the University of California and at Cornell University in New York. Scientists at both universities were aware that topsoil was a dwindling resource for the nursery industry and they arrived at similar goals: the reduction of soil-borne diseases and pests, and a lightweight, uniform, less expensive growing medium that was suitable to grow many plant varieties; they both developed growing media based on sphagnum peat moss.

In California, fine sand was the favored aggregate to combine with the peat, while the Cornell scientists used perlite and vermiculite. Kenneth F. Baker at the University of California favored fine sand with the peat because the mixture, he said, "approaches loam in water and nutrient retention." He also advocated the use of some organic sources of nitrogen or a mixture of organic and inorganic nutrients. "Organic forms are desirable from the standpoint of providing slowly available nitrogen over an extended period of time," he said. At Cornell University, J. W. Boodley and R. Sheldrake put emphasis on inorganic nutrient sources because they could be mixed with the medium and stored for long periods when kept dry, an advantage that California's Baker also acknowledged. Scientists at both universities saw the advantage of adding composted tree bark, or sawdust (waste products of the lumber industry) to their mixes.

Soilless growing media are available under many trade names today and purchasing a bag at a garden center is the easiest way to start a container herb garden, but you can also make your own. Beyond their historical interest, we think it useful to list the ingredients in several mixes so that home gardeners may prepare their own. Liquid fertilizer may be added after transplanting to the mix instead of potassium nitrate, potassium sulfate, and single superphosphate. All ingredients should be added dry and it is best to mix them well. They are easiest to dampen with warm water and may need to be mixed or sit for a while before the water is evenly absorbed. The University of California mixes contain manure as a source of reserve nitrogen and should not be stored longer than one week before use.

University of California Soil Mix

To one cubic yard of equal parts sphagnum peat and fine sand, add:

5 pounds hoof and horn, or blood meal	2.5 pounds single superphosphate
4 ounces potassium nitrate	7.5 pounds dolomite lime
4 ounces potassium sulfate	2.5 pounds calcium carbonate lime

One cubic yard of mix has 27 cubic feet; a cubic foot of mix will fill 16 round, plastic 6-inch pots.

The Cornell Peat-lite Mix

To one cubic yard containing equal parts of sphagnum peat moss and perlite, add:

1.5 pounds potassium nitrate	5 pounds ground limestone
2 pounds superphosphate	2 oz. fritted trace elements

Osmocote 14-14-14, a slow-release fertilizer, may be substituted for the potassium nitrate and superphosphate if desired. Otherwise begin liquid fertilization two weeks after transplanting. This mix may be stored indefinitely when kept dry.

The Cornell scientists also developed a growing medium for plants that tolerate dry conditions, which should work well for herbs grown indoors during winter, where its quick-drying characteristics combat root-rot.

The Cornell Epiphyte Mix

To a cubic yard containing equal parts of sphagnum peat (screened through a $1/2$-inch mesh), Douglas red or white fir bark ($1/8$ inch to $1/4$ inch), and 1 part medium perlite, add:

1 pound potassium nitrate	7 pounds dolomite limestone
4.5 pounds superphosphate	8 oz. iron sulfate
2.75 pounds 10-10-10 fertilizer	2 oz. fritted trace elements

If Osmocote 14-14-14 is added at a rate of five pounds a cubic yard, omit first three ingredients.

The Cornell Foliage Plant Mix

Garden centers often offer this mix, or a variation of it, bagged and ready to use. It suits most herbs.

To 1 cubic yard, containing 2 parts sphagnum peat, 1 part number 2 grade vermiculite, and 1 part medium perlite, add:

1 pound potassium nitrate	8 1/4 pounds dolomite limestone
2 pounds superphosphate	3/4 ounces iron sulfate
2 3/4 pounds 10-10-10 fertilizer	2 ounces fritted trace elements.

For those who feel it's a sacrilege to grow plants without some soil in the growing medium, we include the recipe for the famous John Innes Compost that was developed in Britain.

> **The John Innes Growing Mix**
>
> To 1 cubic yard containing 7 parts composted medium loam, 3 parts sphagnum peat, and 2 parts coarse sand, add:
>   1.5 pounds ground limestone
>   12 pounds 5-10-10 fertilizer or 8.5 pounds of the base fertilizer which consists of 2 parts hoof and horn, 2 parts superphosphate, and 1 part sulfate of potash.

Growing media that contain sand, according to recent research by C. A. Martin and D. L. Ingram, become warmer when exposed to sun than those with a higher content of organic matter; this may be an important factor to determine which growing medium to use in summer when heat is an enemy, and in winter when heat is desirable.

The problem with most growing media is that attempts to pasteurize them often leave unwanted diseases that attack the roots and crowns of herbs. Soilless media have this problem to a lesser extent, but as the 1990s got under way a new generation of potting materials became available that promised to suppress the microorganisms (*Phytophthora, Pythium, Rhizoctonia,* and *Fusarium*) that cause root and stem rot and sudden wilt disease. The key to the new growing media was composting.

The major researcher of this new media was Harry Hoitink of Ohio State University who found that composted bark contained a diversity of organisms that successfully competed with the deadly microorganisms to suppress diseases. Another researcher, Frank Regulski in North Carolina, discovered what he believed to be even more powerful disease suppressive properties in composted peanut hulls. The formulas for the media developed by these two researchers (even their composting methods, which are said to inactivate disease-causing pathogens) are closely held or have been patented. "A specific method of composting developed by the company actually encourages the growth of certain beneficial saprophytic bacteria and fungi, such as the fungus *Trichoderma,*" Regulski told David L. Kuack in a report in *Greenhouse Grower Magazine.* The beneficial organisms compete with disease pathogens for food and in some cases become parasites that inhibit the growth of some pathogens, he said. Some control of diseases such as fusarium, phytophthora, and rhizoctonia have been seen. "The control of *Phytophthora* and *Rhizoctonia* is not nearly as good as for *Pythium,*" Regulski told Kuack. "In an experiment done with *Fusarium* on cyclamen we had only a two- to three-percent loss of plants grown in the suppressive . . . mix compared to a 80 to 100 percent loss of plants produced in peat-vermiculite mixes." Such disease-suppressive mixes promise more carefree container growing of herbs, but are not as widely available as the more easily obtainable peat-based media.

Because of the high organic content of soilless media, a pH lower than normally recommended for herbs is sometimes advisable. A pH somewhere between 5.0 and 6.0 will create conditions for the best uptake of nutrients and micronutrients by plants.

Types of Containers

Containers come in a variety of sizes and shapes. They can be utilitarian or artistic and are made from cement, wood, metal, plastic, and clay. The material from which it is made is not as important as the container's ability to drain water. Containers that do not drain well may cause waterlogged roots and encourage serious diseases for herbs.

There is considerable confusion among gardeners about how water percolates through growing media and leaves a container. Scientists have discovered that the position of the drainage holes is important for the pot to drain well. "The most effective position of the drainage hole was found to be in the base of the pot," A. C. Bunt said in summarizing the research. "When the same number of drainage holes were positioned around the side of the pot so that the lower edge of each hole was directly at the base, drainage was less effective." The common wisdom that stones or broken pieces of pottery should be placed at the bottom of a pot to "improve drainage" is worthless and can actually cause more water to be retained in the container.

Clay and plastic are the most common materials used for pots and window boxes. Aside from their appearance, they differ in several ways. Clay breaks easily, is heavier than plastic and is usually more costly; many plastics become brittle after lengthy exposure to intense sun. However, the most important difference between the two materials is porosity, a characteristic that keeps the growing medium in an unglazed clay pot cooler. This can be an advantage in summer when high media temperatures can stunt growth. In winter, however, research indicates that plastic pots maintain media temperatures and plants produce 15 percent more growth in plastic than in clay containers.

Clay containers have an increased water loss due to their porous nature and this also means there is some minor nutrient loss from the growing medium. Research at the Glasshouse Crops Research Institute in England showed that water evaporation from a clay pot is 50 percent greater than plastic in summer and 85 percent greater at other times. The reason for this seasonal difference is that more water is lost through evaporation from plastic pots during summer, while the clay pot wicks water through its side wall in winter. But evaporation from the pot is not the sole criterion to govern watering of containers, the researchers discovered. "In the case of mature pot plants with large leaf areas, there will be very little difference in the frequency with which the different containers require watering," according to A. C. Bunt.

Because most herbs' roots are easily suffocated by overwatering, clay containers have an advantage over plastic for winter growing conditions. However, a loose, well-drained growing medium that dries quickly will narrow the gap between clay and plastic. During summer when heat causes rapid water evaporation, plastic may be a better choice for hot spots like decks and sunny balconies.

Specialty containers

Used half whisky barrels and strawberry jars (tall clay containers with many holes for planting in their sides) are two types of specialty containers often pictured with herbs growing in them. Large tubs and multi-port pots tempt the gardener to crowd plants too closely and to grow too many plants for the growing medium available. At best these containers, while creating decorative visual effects, are useful for short-term use only and often fail to produce the healthy, vigorous growth that herbs require for maximum foliage production.

When using a large tub or barrel, weight is an important factor to consider; not only are these containers difficult to move after being filled with growing medium and planted, but they may cause architectural damage if placed where support is inadequate, or where water drainage will cause damage. Except in frost-free areas or where mild winters are experienced and plants may grow year-round, the amount of growing medium in a large tub is often greater than needed by the plants for one season of growth. Eight to ten inches of area for the growing medium is usually sufficient to sustain a season's growth. Some gardeners fill the excess space with lightweight broken pots or gravel to improve drainage. However, the filler may actually inhibit drainage somewhat and significantly increase the weight of the container. Spacing plants in a barrel is also a critical consideration and it is important not to crowd the herbs or plant fast-growing, tall plants where they will shade shorter varieties. When plants grow too large, they can be transplanted to individual pots.

The low volume of soil and the difficulty of watering it are drawbacks of strawberry jars. Getting water to the bottom of the pot is difficult, but it is made easier by placing a hollow watering tube down the center before the container is filled with growing medium. Such a tube, made from rolled screen wire or an old hose with holes drilled through its sides, allows easy irrigation from top to bottom. Planting is made easier when transplants are placed in the holes before the pot is filled with growing medium; start at the bottom and fill the pot after each level of transplants has been put in place. It is almost impossible to remove plants from these containers without severe root damage which makes them useful for annuals; perennials are unlikely to reach their full potential because the small amount of growing medium in a strawberry jar is insufficient to sustain growth for more than one season.

Plastic bags filled with loose (instead of compressed) soilless growing media combine the best aspects of both container culture and outdoor gardens and are ideal for those who lack space for a garden but want to grow in containers on the cheap. These bags hold 2 cubic feet (56.6 l) of mix and are 48 inches (3 m) long, 16 inches (40.6 cm) wide, and 4 inches (10.2 cm) deep. They are used by commercial tomato growers in the United States and have become a hot item in England for home gardeners; they work splendidly for herbs, especially annuals. These grow bags provide all the convenience of being able to have several plants in a single container without the permanence of wood, clay, or plastic; transplanting perennials to other containers at the close of the growing season is easy.

To use the bag, place it where the plants will be grown (one of the disadvantages is that the bag is difficult to move once it is wetted and planted), punch random holes in one side of the bag for drainage and then turn it over and cut an "X" several inches long in the middle of the bag and additional Xs half way toward each end. Put a flowerpot in each hole made by the Xs and then pour several gallons of hot water through the flowerpots to wet the growing medium; remove the pots. A 3-foot (0.9 m) length of hose in which holes have been drilled randomly is inserted in the hole on one end of the bag and worked toward the opposite end; future watering of the bag will be easily accomplished through this hose. Wait several hours to allow the mix to become thoroughly wet and begin transplanting your herbs by cutting small Xs in the plastic to insert transplants, and space them as you would in the garden. Begin fertilizing with liquid nutrients after two weeks.

We think potted herbs will grow best over an extended period when there is one plant per container. This allows you to tailor growing conditions to a single herb's requirements. If you want a grouped effect, place the individual pots in a larger, decorative container but be sure to space them so that the leaves of the different plants do not touch.

Sizing Pots

Matching the size of the container to the plant calls for personal judgment based on expected plant growth and climatic conditions. The pot should be large enough to provide adequate root growth for at least several months. Pots chosen for growing during summer may be larger in relation to the transplant's root structure than at other times of the year because plants grow more rapidly when days are long and warm. A transplant with a small root system is easily overwatered, often with fatal results, when it is placed in a container that is far too large for it. Even in summer, water may not evaporate rapidly enough to provide sufficient air to the young roots. As a rule of thumb, transplants from 2.5-inch (6.4 cm) pots can easily handle a 6- to 8-inch (20.3 cm) pot when planted in late spring and grown outdoors. Indoors, where light levels are lower and temperatures more moderate, a 4-inch (10.2 cm) pot may prove quite adequate. As plants grow larger, the pot sizes grow proportionally. A rosemary in a 6-inch pot will easily fill a 13 or 14 inch (33 to 36 cm) pot over a summer of growth. The best time to pot up new seedlings or to repot older plants is spring; fall is the worst time because plant growth slows and days become shorter, which increases the chances that roots will sit in water-logged growing media and die. Plants should be placed in pots only large enough to accommodate one year's growth.

Root Pruning

Eventually, larger-growing herbs will outsize the largest pot available, but they need not become rootbound and die slowly. By pruning the roots, the plant may be returned to the same pot filled with fresh growing medium. Root pruning may sound like major surgery, but most plants take it in stride without noticeable stress.

To root prune a plant, knock it out of the pot as you would for any transplanting: hold the pot upside down and jiggle it with one hand so that the rootball falls into your free hand (you may have to put a large pot between your knees and let the rootball fall into both hands). Put the rootball on some paper or clean plastic and with a sharp knife remove the bottom third of the rootball; then trim an inch or so from around the sides if the rootball is at least 6 inches wide. The plant is then ready to be repotted into fresh growing mix. Place the plant in a sheltered spot for several days to recuperate; it is often wise to prune and shape the plant's branches at the same time to put the new root system in better proportion with the top of the plant.

Watering and Feeding Container Herbs

Next to the growing medium, water and nutrients are of greatest concern to container herb gardeners; no plant can live without them and the proper amounts of both need to be applied at the right time. Water is the first thing a plant needs to live and thrive; it is its life-blood and without it the tiny cells that form the plant cannot multiply and grow. Water also carries a host of chemical nutrients to the plant cells that are converted into food.

Water comes to most of us through pipes from municipal water supplies or from wells, and we turn on the faucet when we want some. The ease with which most of us obtain water can lead us to take its quality for granted. But plants are a bit more particular about what's in the water than we are and can be damaged by excessive amounts of sodium bicarbonates, boron, and to a lesser extent fluoride found naturally in water or introduced into it for public health reasons. Little research on the effect of water quality on herbs has been done, but much is available for bedding and foliage plants and there is no reason to believe that herbs will react much differently. However, it should be noted that even where research has shown damage from these chemicals, not all plants react to the same levels of these substances in the water. With naturally occurring chemicals, it is usually the ability of the water to change the soil pH that creates problems for the plant by hindering its ability to absorb necessary nutrients. These problems are usually associated with continued use of mineral-rich "hard" water (where "hard" water is softened for household use with sodium, it should not be used on plants). Although boron is a necessary nutrient, it can be found in some water supplies in amounts than can prove toxic to plants. Fluoride can cause leaf damage to some foliage plants, but we know of no research that links harm to herbs from it.

The application of water, to some extent, determines the growth rate of herbs. Stress from too little water slows a plant's growth. Many commercial producers of potted plants create stress intentionally by limiting the frequency (not the amount) they water plants to keep them more compact, a technique of little value to most home gardeners who strive to get maximum growth from their herbs. Even if you want to use water to control growth, it is important to irrigate the plant thoroughly so that the growing medium is wetted from top to bottom.

When to water is often the most crucial decision a grower of container herbs must make because there are so many variables that influence the timing. Most herbs should be allowed to become dry, but not to the wilting stage, between irrigations. So, how do you tell when it's dry? The color of peat-based growing medium changes from dark to light as the amount of water diminishes. If you know the weight, or feel, of the pot when wet, its light weight can be another clue that it is time to water. Some gardeners stick a finger in the pot to determine how dry the growing medium is, but this method can cause your pot to look like a cratered moonscape and can damage roots. The finger method really only gives half the story. It can tell you how wet the growing medium is near the top and whether you shouldn't water. Even if the pot appears to be dry at the top, there may be plenty of moisture where the majority of the roots are, at the bottom.

A good question to ask before you water is, "Will the plant wilt if I don't water it today?" That consideration brings in these additional factors:

- the size of the plant and its relation to the container
- the material from which the pot is made
- the season of the year
- the day and night temperatures
- the amount of sun the day before and the expected weather
- the type of growing medium.

It's a complicated decision because watering is more art than science, but the job becomes easier with experience.

Plant Nutrients

Herbs and other plants need sixteen essential elements to maintain health and vigor. Water (H_2O), delivered to the plant roots by rain or the gardener, is a liquid that contains hydrogen (H) and oxygen (O), two of the elements necessary for plant growth. Additional oxygen and carbon (C), a third major element essential for growth, are taken into the plant through its leaves as carbon dioxide (CO_2), an atmospheric gas. The other major elements enter the plant through the roots from the soil or growing media. Nitrogen (N) is an element with which most gardeners are familiar because it makes up nearly 50 percent of living plant cells which is why plants need so much of it. Plant roots absorb nitrogen in several forms: nitrates (NO_3), ammonium (NH_4+), nitrite (NO_2-), or organic forms (NH_2+). Nitrates are the form most readily available to the roots. Plants need only small amounts of phosphorus (P), but it is important because it becomes part of a plant's cells and is needed for seed germination, seedling growth, and root growth. It is usually delivered to the plant in the form of phosphate, which helps to stabilize plant cells. Potassium (K) acts as a catalyst and regulator inside the plant and helps combine carbohydrates and proteins, regulates water, and plays a part in photosynthesis which is the method by which the plant converts light into energy. Calcium (Ca) is part of a plant's cell wall and is important for root growth; it also helps the plant absorb nitrogen and regulates potassium. Limestone is the usual way calcium is added to soil or growing media and is used to help raise soil pH. Magnesium (Mg) is the chief constituent of chlorophyll and is often added to deficient soil in the form of Epsom salt. Sulfur (S), along with nitrogen and phosphorus, is combined in amino acids, which make up plant proteins and is useful in lowering the pH of soil.

Minor or trace elements are essential for plant growth and health, too, but they are needed in minute amounts. Among them are iron (Fe), molybdenum (Mo), boron (B), copper (Cu), manganese (Mn), zinc (Zn), and chlorine (Cl). Most of these trace elements are to be found in soil, but they are not in soilless media and must be added as part of the regular fertilizer. Liquid fertilizers formulated for use with soilless media often have these trace elements added and will say so on the bag or box; otherwise the trace elements will have to be added separately. Trace elements to add to fertilizers are available at many garden centers.

In one way or another, container gardeners have to make sure their herbs get the proper nutrients. Fertilizer, either organic or inorganic, is the usual answer to supply these nutrients. When scientists talk about fertilizers in general, they call them salts. This may sound odd to an ear that has always heard that salt (sodium chloride) was something to put on food, but scientists are describing a class of elements that are needed for plant growth when they call them salts. To the gardener who is not a chemist this may be techno-babble, but the scientists are just being precise: a salt is a chemical created by mixing acids and bases; bases remove hydrogen to create a salt.

There are many types of fertilizer available to container gardeners today and it is not unusual to find ten or more pages in a grower's catalog devoted to container fertilizers. The job to select one is no more complicated than picking the right breakfast cereal: the easiest way is to read the label.

Reading a fertilizer label

Among the fertilizer choices are dozens of different formulations. The formulas are generally specified with three connected numbers as in 12-10-17 or 19-7-10. These numbers tell you, in order, the balance of the most important elements in the fertilizer: nitrogen, phosphorus, and potassium. The 12-10-17 formulation, for instance, has 12 percent nitrate, 10 percent phosphate, and 17 percent potassium oxide by weight. For herbs, a 20-10-20 or 20-20-20 formula will work well; if such a formula is not available, one with the same balance (a 10-5-10 or 5-2-5, for instance) will do just as well. (It's obvious that the numbers don't equal 100, so what's the rest of it? Inert material makes up the remainder of container; in fertilizer-lingo, it's called a carrier.)

Don't stop reading once you've gotten as far as the formula; be sure to read the fine print on the label. The small type on the label will also tell you the rest of the information you need to find the right fertilizer. The first thing to look for is the source of nitrogen. Plants have difficulty digesting nitrogen from ammonia during winter or when the growing medium is cold. Ammonia also tends to slowly lower pH, a characteristic that can cause most herbs difficulty digesting nutrients. Nitrogen from nitrates are the most readily useful to herbs and most of the nitrogen should come from that group.

A second important piece of information on the label is something called "potential acidity," a phrase that indicates the fertilizer's potential to lower the pH of growing media. Most often this potential for acidity is expressed in the number of pounds of calcium carbonate it would take to maintain the current pH for each ton of fertilizer applied. Because few herbs do well in acidic growing media, look for the lowest "potential acidity." The label will also tell you if micro-nutrients have been added, and they are an important feature for soilless media.

Choosing a Fertilizer Form

The type of fertilizer used for containers differs to some extent from that used in the garden. In the garden, large bags of granular fertilizer, rotted manure, or a combination of granular organic ingredients are used. These types of fertilizers, for the most part, are inappropriate for use in containers because it is difficult to determine how much of the essential nutrients are applied to the smaller area of the pot. Granular fertilizers do not break down or liquify quickly and may cause fertilizer burn and kill plants with excess nutrients (liquid fertilizers used in containers, however, can be used in the garden). Water-soluble and slow-release fertilizers are the most common types used for container growing and should be mixed and applied according to directions on the box or bag. Water-soluble fertilizers are sold as a powder or as a liquid concentrate. Both types are dissolved in water (usually hot water is best if a powdered fertilizer is to be mixed as a concentrate to be further diluted) and applied when plants need irrigation. Powdered, water-soluble fertilizers are most often manufactured from inorganic sources. The most common liquid concentrates are from organic sources and are usually fish emulsions or fish hydrolysates in which waste from the fish processing industry are used. Hydrolysates are new on the market (Squanto's Secret is the name of one) and are often made with fresh fish byproducts that have a less "fishy" odor. Phosphoric acid is used in the process, which turns a slurry of water and fish waste into a stable liquid that is milled and screened; sulfate of potash and citrus extract are sometimes added. While little research with any fertilizers has been done with potted herbs, we know of none using fish hydrolysate (FH), but comparisons with other horticultural crops have shown impressive growth with the fish product. In two tests at the University of Massachusetts, fish hydrolysate produced 86 percent more flower buds on chrysanthemums, and a 76 percent larger yield of jalapeño peppers when compared with a traditional 20-20-20 inorganic, water-soluble fertilizer. Researchers Amul Purohit and Ronald Athanas expressed surprise at the results of the chrysanthemum study because "from pure N-P-K analysis point of view, it seems that Peters fertilizer [20-20-20] should out perform FH." They added: "We do not know the precise mode of action of FH, but it seems that due to the abundant source of amino acids [in fish hydrolysates], the building block of proteins, plants are reacting quite differently."

Another fish byproduct fertilizer, fish soluble nutrients, which is commonly called fish emulsion, has been widely tested on container-grown plants (everything from tomatoes to bedding plants) with results that compare favorably with inorganic liquid fertilizer. Significantly larger yields or sizes were not noted by researcher Everett R. Emino at Texas A&M University, who tested a variety of flowering plants and houseplants, or in tests of tomato plant growth and yield by L. H. Aung and G. J. Flick Jr. at Virginia Polytechnic Institute and State University. Emino noted that the odor of the fish emulsion increased and "became undesirable" if it was left to stand more than several hours after being mixed from the concentrate.

Applying Fertilizers

If you have only a few pots, fertilizer is easily mixed and applied with a watering can. As your collection of container-herbs increases, an inexpensive siphon device that sucks liquid fertilizer concentrate from a bucket and mixes it into the flow of water through a hose makes the job easier and quicker. Such a device is available at many garden centers as a Hyponex siphon mixer; depending on water pressure, one gallon of concentrate can make 12 gallons of liquid fertilizer. Commercial growers often use a more sophisticated siphon device called an injector, a more sophisticated siphon, to precisely mix fertilizer in the water supply. Either siphon device can be used in the garden or greenhouse with herbs in ground beds, as well as with container plants. Inorganic water-soluble fertilizers usually contain a marking dye so that the gardener can see when fertilizer is coming through the hose.

Slow-release fertilizers made their way into the market as the result of polymer technology, which allows small granules of water-soluble nutrients to be coated with a thin plastic resin film. These small plastic-coated beads are mixed with the growing medium or placed on top of it and through osmosis the encapsulated nutrients are slowly drawn out to feed the plant's roots over a period of time. These fertilizers come in a wide array of formulations and last from several months to over a year. Their advantage is simplicity of use.

How much fertilizer is necessary to maintain adequate growth for herbs grown in containers? It is important to remember that each herb variety has its own requirements; all herbs don't react identically. Two research projects illustrate this point. S. M. Bell and G. D. Coorts reported in *Florists' Review* in 1979 that sage (*Salvia officinalis*), lemon balm (*Melissa officinalis*), and peppermint (*Mentha ×piperita*), had an unquenchable thirst for nutrients—the more nitrogen the two researchers fed their plants weekly, the larger their herbs became. But a study of rosemary (*Rosmarinus officinalis*), and its reaction to fertilizer came to a different conclusion. Researchers Thomas Boyle, Lyle Craker, and James Simon reported: "In our study, rosemary plants were shortest and lowest in fresh weight at the highest fertilization rate . . . suggesting that this rate of fertilization suppressed growth of potted rosemary." Rosemary plants grown with a liquid fertilizer applied weekly were largest and had the highest essential oil content and those with a single application of a controlled-release fertilizer were similar.

A weekly feeding of a 20-10-20 fertilizer will probably produce optimum growth for rosemary grown outdoors in summer, and most other herbs will flourish under such feeding. However, weekly feeding is not necessary when herbs are not in active growth. During the short days of winter or under cool conditions, plants lose three to four times less water through their leaves than in summer, according to British researcher A. C. Bunt. So, it's important to cut back on water and fertilizer in winter and carefully monitor your herbs' irrigation needs; too much fertilizer will accentuate thin, wispy growth, and liquid fertilizer should be applied about every fourteenth irrigation. Another factor to keep in mind is that the walls of clay pots wick nutrients along with moisture into their porous walls; the water will evaporate but the fertilizer salts remain there and can be seen as a white coating on the outside of the pot. When British scientists tested nutrient levels in clay pots, they found high concentrations of nutrients in the center of the growing medium and low levels near the clay walls.

Growing Herbs Indoors

Light is the most critical factor for the indoor gardener, and unlike all the other variables of plant growth, it is the most difficult to control. You'll have less trouble growing container herbs indoors, and your plants will be healthier and more vigorous, when they are positioned to receive five to six hours of direct sunlight during the day. This is often quite difficult in the typical home or apartment due to windows that don't face south or because of obstructions that prevent the entry of sunlight. There are some rules of thumb to determine whether your plants have enough light. If stems are so thin they tend to bend under their own weight and if leaves are sparsely arranged along the stems, it is likely due to a lack of sunlight. While many herbs will often adjust to less than optimum light, the good health and growth of the plants often dictates the use of supplemental light from artificial sources.

A fluorescent light garden is one way to give your herbs and other plants near-perfect light conditions. Expensive plant lights aren't any better than a combination of one warm white fluorescent and one cool white tube in a two-light fixture. Fluorescent tubes are usually placed horizontally above the plants and should be no more than 6 to 8 inches (15 to 20 cm) above the top leaves with light 16 to 18 hours daily. Where tall plants are being grown the lower leaves often will be too far from the lights for good growth. For larger plants, place the fluorescent fixtures vertically on at least two sides of the plant and 6 to 8 inches (15 to 20 cm) from it; rotate the container one-half turn daily.

A Greenhouse for Herbs

If herbs are a passion on the way to becoming an obsession, a greenhouse is either already in the garden or you are thinking of putting one there. It's a wise solution to the problem of how to keep the family together when the last windowsill is filled with overwintering herbs.

Greenhouses are surrounded by a beautiful, romantic aura that pictures them as horticultural cathedrals where rituals bring forth magical, mystical events. However, the cynic, blessed with perfect, year-round weather, sees a greenhouse as the quickest place to kill herbs with disease and insects. Both views have a kernel of truth. But like it or not, greenhouses are sometimes essential, and almost always a gardener's fondest dream.

Before selecting a greenhouse, you want to consider carefully what herb plants to grow in it and why you want to grow them there. For some gardeners, overwintering tender plants is the only reason they'd use a greenhouse. A cold frame with a sand and gravel floor heated by hot water may be a much less expensive alternative for them. Others might want to use a greenhouse for growing a variety of annual and perennial crops during the winter, as well as overwintering tender perennials and propagating plants. If that's your desire, you'll want to consider how your herbs will perform during the long nights of winter. While most herbs grow in the winter greenhouse just as they do in the summer garden, some herbs rest during the winter whether temperatures are warm or cold. Others flower and do not produce useful foliage during this time.

Another important element is the temperature to be maintained in the greenhouse during winter. Will the plants you want to grow do well at the temperature you can afford? Heating even the most efficient greenhouse is expensive. Generally, most herbs can be classified as heat-savers which perform well in a cool greenhouse.

Gardeners often have a frugal streak; it's a characteristic that gives them a creative bent and sometimes lends them an idiosyncratic air. In purchasing a greenhouse and maintaining it, frugality is best submerged temporarily. While you can build greenhouses from urban flotsam, or a variety of kits, it is less trouble in the long run to go first class right from the start. From experience, we know how quickly a greenhouse will fill, so pick a model that is as large as the budget will allow, but which is probably twice as big as you think you'll need; it's also helpful if the model chosen can be easily enlarged later. Unless you want to be tied to your greenhouse in a connubial knot, automate as much of the tedium (like watering and ventilating) as you can.

There are several styles of greenhouses and different types of materials for covering them. The lean-to fits against the house or a shed. It's usually less expensive to heat, but it doesn't come in as wide a range of sizes. Free-standing greenhouses sit by themselves. The glass and aluminum, peaked-roof style is typical of greenhouse architecture and is the type that most people see when they dream of a greenhouse in the backyard. Glass is least efficient at keeping heat inside during the winter. Greenhouse grade fiberglass and structured polycarbonate sheets are heat-efficient alternatives to glass; they offer as much as a 50 percent savings in fuel costs over glass and provide an even, diffused light. The least expensive greenhouse is probably the pipe-frame quonset style covered by a double layer of air-inflated, 6 mil thick polyethylene. Air pumped between the two layers of poly keeps it from flapping in the wind and provides dead-air insulating space. The initial cost is low and operating costs are also reduced. Because even special greenhouse grade poly deteriorates under the sun's punishing gaze, these structures need to be re-covered every two or three years.

All of these types of greenhouses have their proponents. Herbs can be well grown in all of them. The key to herb cultivation probably isn't the greenhouse, it's the knowledge behind the grower, just as it is in the outside garden. Greenhouse growing, however, requires considerably more skill and attention to detail because the gardener has to control almost every aspect of the environment.

For growing herbs, site the greenhouse where it will receive the most sun possible. Usually greenhouses are sited so their ends face east and west, so that the sun hits the length of the greenhouse all day as it moves across the sky.

After you've decided on a style of greenhouse and where it will be sited, you should think about equipping it. The equipment you'll need is likely to cost at least as much as the greenhouse structure, sometimes considerably more; benches, heat, electricity, and water are essential in the greenhouse.

Here is where you'll have to make another important decision. Will you grow your greenhouse herb garden in ground beds or in containers? A combination of both is probably desirable. This decision is important to the selection of a method of heating the greenhouse. Recent research shows that heating the plants rather than the air around them is the most cost efficient. It also produces healthier plants. Radiant heat is one way this can be done, but this heat source usually requires a height in the greenhouse that the structures favored by home gardeners lack. Heating at the root zone of the plants is a second method and is usually achieved by circulating heated water under the plants, whether on benches or in beds. In some cases, a supplemental source to heat the air in the greenhouse may also be necessary.

One thing many greenhouse gardeners don't think about at the start is monitoring the interior temperature of the greenhouse, especially when it is some distance from the house. Greenhouse heaters have an uncanny knack for failing on the coldest night of the year and if undetected, such emergencies can prove fatal to your plants. There are temperature warning devices that will actually make phone calls and play pre-recorded messages to warn of emergencies; they are state-of-the-art and costly. A Thermalarm is a much less expensive device that will ring a bell in the house when the greenhouse temperature goes above or below preset points. A temporary heat source, such as a kerosene heater with a blower (probably in the 30,000 BTU range) is a good idea for substitute heat while the plumber is on the way.

Next to heating, ventilation and air movement are most important to greenhouse cultivation of herbs. Stale, damp air fosters an array of diseases that trouble herbs. Greenhouses, particularly the air-tight, double poly-types, need ventilating fans to cool them and change the air. During winter, condensation forms on the greenhouse covering material when the interior is warmer than the exterior air. These droplets of condensate cause humidity to rise and increases the likelihood of fungus diseases like botrytis, sometimes called gray mold. Constantly moving air helps dry the foliage and retards disease growth but it is sometimes necessary to dry the interior of the greenhouse and the plants in it by using the ventilating fans while the heater runs.

Two different types of fan systems are used in greenhouses. The ventilating fan is used to pull overheated air out of the structure. This is especially valuable during spring, summer and fall. The principle is simple: a fan at one end of the greenhouse pulls cooler, outside air through an opening at the opposite end of the structure. The fan may also be placed in the middle of the side wall of the greenhouse and draw air through openings in both ends. It is beneficial to have the fans and the shuttered openings work automatically so you don't have to constantly monitor the greenhouse; let a thermostat and electric motors do that job for you.

The second type of fan system moves air inside the greenhouse when the ventilating fans are not needed. Heavy-duty fans are necessary. When properly positioned, these fans will push rising hot air from the "attic" of the greenhouse back down around the plants, making for heating efficiency, and they keep air moving around plants to reduce disease. Two methods are used to achieve this. One uses a special device known as a fan-jet. It is mounted near the roof at one end of the greenhouse and has its own shuttered opening a foot or so behind it. In front of the fan is a long poly tube with holes punched in it. The fan inflates the tube and air is forced through the holes and down into the greenhouse. Fresh air can be mixed with the air in the greenhouse by opening the shutter behind the fan-jet. This type of fan is also used to carry warm, heated air from furnaces. Fan-jets vary in size with the greenhouse. A second method of moving interior greenhouse air uses a less costly type of fan. This method works on a slightly different principle called horizontal air flow. A series of fans moves air up one side of the greenhouse and down the other, mixing air and drying foliage. These fans, constructed to withstand the caustic greenhouse atmosphere, are not cheap but they are worth every penny.

Supplemental lighting of the greenhouse may be necessary during the short days and low light levels of winter, especially if high-quality, optimum yields of crops like tarragon and basil are your goal. More than fluorescent lights may be necessary to do an adequate job. High pressure sodium or metal halide lamps are the type most commonly used in greenhouses. To light a 100 square-foot area with 800 footcandles, a measure of light intensity, it would be necessary to have four fixtures. These lights are not inexpensive. The lights do help heat the greenhouse, so all the energy used does not go for light alone.

If your greenhouse will be used for overwintering and growing potted plants, benches are a good idea. They put the plants where you can reach them easily. It's important that air circulate through the benches. This allows air to move around the plants more effectively. There are a number of materials used for benches and they vary in expense and longevity. Snow fence is a popular inexpensive material often used for greenhouse benches. It is usually mounted on two-by-fours and placed on cinderblock pillars. Under greenhouse conditions, the snow fence does not have an extended life and often has to be replaced every four or five years when it rots. Metal wire, expanded metal, and poly benches are more durable but cost considerably more.

One of the great joys of owning a greenhouse is having a proper propagation area in which to root cuttings. A small area should be set aside to contain a mist system and heat mats. It needn't be large and can be used for growing potted plants when not used for propagation. The most economical, small-scale misting system is a Mist-A-Matic; with it a gardener can obtain professional results. It uses a small-mesh screen to capture mist produced by misting nozzles. This screen is part of an apparatus that controls an electrically operated valve, which turns mist off and on.

The medium in which the plants grow inside the greenhouse is as important as the atmosphere. Ground beds should be carefully constructed so that they drain well and contain copious amounts of humus. This humus may be in the form of compost, manure or sphagnum peat moss. A combination of these materials should make up at least half the composition of the ground bed growing medium. Ground beds are best for plants that will be permanent residents in the greenhouse and for short-term annual crops that can be planted and harvested, as they would be in the garden outside.

An automatic watering system for the beds is a time-saver. An underground irrigation pipe that oozes water should be installed before the beds are planted. A system with overground pipes and spaghetti tubes with tiny nozzles to water plants can be installed after planting. Overhead watering systems should be avoided because they increase humidity and wet foliage.

Greenhouse, patio, living room window—no matter where you grow your potted herbs it will require more knowledge and skill than an outside garden plot because you become responsible for a greater part of the plants' growing environment. But because you have greater control over the plants, your container herbs may well outperform those in a backyard garden. In any event, your versatile potted herbs will provide summer glory to refresh the kitchen and your spirit year-round.

CHAPTER 7.

Propagation and Planting

PROPAGATION IS AS OLD as the world, and in the garden its ancient ways are still at work with only minor variations. It is the magic of the garden that earth and sun meet to create new plants from parts of old ones. At its most basic, the plants take care of reproducing and creating new varieties themselves by casting pollen and seeds to the wind, insects, birds, or bats or by sending creeping stems across the soil to root. Playful *Homo sapiens* developed methods to, if not improve, at least to complicate the original simplicity.

Scientists refer to seed propagation as sexual reproduction and to methods that use roots, stems, or other plant parts as asexual reproduction. Both procedures require the propagator's knowledge of special techniques, some easily acquired skills, and a certain amount of special equipment to make the job easier and the outcome reliable.

Sexual Reproduction

Seeds often appear to be dried husks, but they are actually tiny embryos, the offspring of sexual unions that take place in a plant's flower where sperm in the stamen's pollen fertilizes an egg in the ovule found in the ovary. The ovule matures to form the seed, while the ovary matures to form the fruit. Some seed coats are closely attached to the fruit wall, making seed and fruit essentially synonymous for the home gardener; examples include cumin, dill, coriander, and other members of the carrot family.

Most herb species pollinate themselves with the help of wind currents and insects to reproduce plants of similar size and aroma, but sometimes species within a genus, or cultivated varieties of a species, cross-pollinate to create a hybrid. This may happen as an accident of nature or through the intentional intervention of a plant breeder. These hybrids are often genetically unstable or sterile and cannot reproduce sexually. In rare cases, herbs such as English thyme have only one sex and cannot reproduce from seed.

Because seed is produced through a sexual process, care must be taken to prevent unwanted cross-pollination that will create plants that vary from the parent. This means that space—sometimes as much as a mile or more—must be maintained to isolate species or cultivated varieties and prevent cross-pollination. Alternatively, cages can keep pollinators from reaching the plants or trap pollinators, such as bees, inside the cages to perform their pollination chores. Pollination can also be performed by hand, using soft brushes.

The knowledge needed to propagate herbs successfully includes knowing which herb varieties do not produce viable seed or vary widely when grown from seed. Seed to be avoided includes that of herbs such as French tarragon, English and several other thyme varieties, all named lavenders, rosemary, mints, and many oregano cultivars (see individual listings for varietal characteristics). Of course, a certification that plants are grown from vegetative cuttings is no guarantee of varietal purity, but a plant in hand provides the gardener or the farmer a way of assessing the plant's quality and pedigree—foliage to sniff and flowers to see, at the very least.

Whether you have a small backyard plot or several acres, the seed quality is important. As a living embryo, the seed needs special care to maintain viability while awaiting the proper conditions for growth. Viability is partly genetic, but proper temperature and humidity control help to maintain the natural vigor of most seeds. Packets of seeds enclosed in a sealed container and put in a refrigerator provide the home gardener with the best chance of maintaining seed viability. However, many seeds—parsley, chives, and coriander to name only a few—have a naturally short lifespan of about one year.

Your seed merchant's reputation and the germination rate of the seed you choose indicate its quality. Although government regulations require germination tests on large seed lots, small packets are not required to show test results. Most American seed firms do not routinely offer germination data on the herb seed intended for home gardeners. This policy of nondisclosure has been criticized by experts in the field. "Stricter quality control on seed purity and trueness to type as well as seed vigor for basil varieties and other culinary herbs is needed," according to leading U.S. herb researcher James E. Simon. "Basic information such as germination percentage should be included on every herb seed packet, as this alone would aid in ensuring minimum seed viability and improve the performance that commercial growers and home gardeners expect."

Simon did not reach this conclusion from his ivory tower; he found out the hard way through experience. He is known for his extensive studies of basil and parsley, but he has also studied many other annual and perennial herbs grown from seed. His disquieting conclusion on herb seed quality: "We . . . found that many seeds were of poor quality: low viability and vigor; others were composed of many seed types and were not uniform in growth and visual appearance. Several herbs were incorrectly labeled in commercial seed catalogs."

Basil-seed germination was so variable from the different firms supplying the seed that in the first year of Simon's trials it was almost too difficult to make research comparisons. Future studies used transplants instead of direct seeding in order to make comparisons less complex. Simon found the names on the basil-seed packets were often incorrect and recommended efforts to correct the misidentification of cultivated basil varieties.

Other researchers have expressed concerns about seed viability. Robin Cowen, Charles

Voigt, and Joe Vandemark looked at germination rates of thyme, oregano, and marjoram and agreed with Simon that "the source of seed is important in percentage germination," but they noted that the growing media used to germinate seeds is another factor that is often overlooked. In their study, University of Illinois researchers discovered that oregano seed from the same supplier varied from 60 to 100 percent germination, depending on the germination medium used; marjoram and thyme showed similar reactions. Nine major brands of soilless and other growing media were tested. "Overall" the researchers concluded, "Fafard no. 2 and Metro mix had the highest percent germination for all seed sources. Both seed source and media are important in obtaining high germination percentages. If the lowest percent germination sources were dropped out, any of the soilless mixes except Grendell [Farms Growing Mix] would give quality results. All seedlings in the other soilless mixes grew on very well."

If germination rate is one standard of seed quality, government regulation of these standards has been minimal under the U.S. Federal Seed Act. The law establishes minimum germination for only three herbs: chives (50 percent), parsley (60 percent), and sorrel (65 percent). In Europe, more herb seed is regulated and minimum germination standards are more stringent. Under Common Market regulations, at least 75 percent of chive seed must germinate. Minimum germination is regulated as well: dill (75 percent), chervil (80 percent), sorrel (75 percent), summer savory (75 percent), thyme (70 percent), fennel (75 percent), basil (70 percent), marjoram (70 percent) and parsley (75 percent). These higher standards may spring from a more intense European interest in herbs and in gardening, as demonstrated by French national newspapers that publish independent germination tests comparing vegetable and herb seeds from different firms to help seed buyers determine quality.

Seeding Methods

While the majority of vegetable seeds are directly sown in the garden or field, only a few herbs are usually handled this way. The minute seed size of many herbs and their slow germination and growth often necessitate growing them to transplanting size in pots. Slow-growing herbs with tiny seeds are best started indoors so that established plants can be set out to receive extra garden time to provide a shorter interval to the first harvest. Perennials with large seeds and rapid germination, such as sorrel (about 34,000 seeds per ounce), sage (3,400) and chives (26,000), may be sown directly in the garden, but harvests may be delayed more than a year while the plants mature to cutting size. But small-seeded perennials such as thyme (about 100,000 seeds per ounce), sweet marjoram (120,000 seeds per ounce), oregano (300,000 seeds per ounce), catnip (48,000 seeds per ounce), and lemon balm (56,000 seeds per ounce) benefit from a controlled indoor environment. Large-seeded annual herbs like basil (18,000 per ounce), dill (21,800 seeds per ounce), borage (1,600 seeds per ounce), coriander (2,000 seeds per ounce), chervil (12,000 seeds per ounce), and parsley (18,000 seeds per ounce) can be direct seeded.

Earlier yields from these seed-grown plants may be obtained with transplants where cost is not a consideration. Parsley transplants, for instance, can be ready for the garden and near harvestable size in the time it takes for the seed to germinate outdoors.

Most annual herb seeds are direct-sown outdoors like vegetable seeds: Once the soil warms in spring, seed is covered in rows to a depth twice its thickness and kept moist until germination. After germination, the seedlings are thinned to prevent overcrowding.

Not all seed lends itself to direct-sowing, however. Parsley seed can be troublesome because, like many of its umbelliferous relatives, parsley seeds ripen unevenly, resulting in low germination rates; even viable parsley seeds germinate slowly and unevenly in cold, wet ground. The cause of this poor germination is the presence in the seed of a germination inhibitor, a water-soluble chemical called heraclenol, a furanocoumarin. The common advice to soak parsley seed is on target, but it takes more than a quick soak to get rid of heraclenol—several days is required, according to researchers. Simon recommends the use of aerated water, such as might be found in an aquarium. The seed is soaked in the bubbling water in a mesh bag or panty hose for several days and then dried before planting. Jack Rabin, a researcher with Rutgers Cooperative Extension in New Jersey, recommends a similar method but allows water to run through the mesh bag to carry the germination inhibitor away to prevent any from remaining on the seed coat. Such a procedure improved germination of seed sown in late February and early March in New Jersey by 78 percent, according to Rabin. As ground warms, however, there is almost no difference in germination, according to Rabin. Parsley sown indoors under optimum conditions takes about eight days to germinate; outdoors, it can take four times as long.

Parsley is not the only herb whose seeds need special treatment to germinate; some, like sweet cicely (*Myrrhis odorata*), for instance, won't sprout at all without special treatment. Sweet cicely's splinter-like seeds should be harvested as soon as they are dark and ripe, then placed in a plastic bag and mixed with damp sphagnum peat moss. The bag is sealed and placed in a refrigerator where the seeds will begin to germinate in five months; then they can be planted and grown as other seedlings described below. Seed of sweet bay (*Laurus nobilis*) needs a similar hot/cold treatment to help it break dormancy.

Starting herb seedlings indoors takes little special equipment other than fluorescent lights. This supplemental light is necessary because the days of late winter and early spring are not long enough or intense enough to promote sufficient growth. A shop light with two 4-foot (1.2 m) long fluorescent tubes produces enough light for sixty-four plants in 2.5-inch (6.4 cm) pots. Special plant lights aren't necessary; instead, install one warm-white tube and one cool-white tube in the fixture. Keep the light no more than 6 to 8 inches (15.2 to 20.3 cm) from the tops of the seedlings. The lights should illuminate the seedlings for sixteen hours per day.

A growing medium made of equal parts of sphagnum peat moss and perlite along with some lime works well to grow seeds from germination to transplant size because it is sterile, holds moisture, and drains well. Such soilless mixes are available from a number of companies. Dampen such growing medium with warm water prior to filling flats or pots. Seeding mix should not be so wet that you can squeeze water from it.

New, sterile plastic pots should do fine for a few seedlings, but don't use any much deeper than 2 inches, or the volume of growing medium will not dry quickly and may lead to disease problems. In a plastic nursery tray, or flat, measuring 10 inches wide by 20 inches (25.4 × 50.8 cm) long and filled with soilless medium, sow seed in twelve 10-inch (25.4 cm) rows to produce 200 to 500 finished plants. Two of these germination trays can be accommodated under one 4-foot fluorescent fixture.

Seeds of chive and similar herbs without traditional stems can be successfully sown directly in a pot, but herbs with stems or those that grow from a rosette are better transplanted from the pot or flat into individual pots, in which they will grow to transplant size. This additional transplanting helps prevent new seedlings from falling over because their young stems are rather soft.

Because some seed requires light to germinate, it should be left uncovered when sown outdoors; other types of seed germinate best when covered with soil. When grown indoors, the high humidity of the germination chamber minimizes such seed differences. Two methods of seed sowing are generally used: broadcasting the seeds on the surface of the growing medium, and sowing seeds in evenly spaced rows. If you choose to use small pots, the broadcasting method is best; for more seedlings, flats are better. If different seed varieties must be sown in the same flat or pot, choose varieties that germinate within a day or two of each other and grow at the same rate; this allows simultaneous transplanting of the varieties and little risk of one or two varieties becoming too large and shading smaller seedlings near them. Air circulation is improved for seedlings grown in rows, an important factor to eliminate potential disease problems. A small piece of metal that is shaped like a V is handy to press rows into the dampened growing medium. Seeds are sown into these depressions, and some care should be taken to space the seed correctly. Seed-germination rates enter into spacing decisions; for instance, if the rate is 50 percent, you'll know that only half the seed sown will germinate. Seed sown too thickly will lessen air circulation among the seedlings and encourage diseases.

After the seed is sown, water it with a gentle spray and immediately wrap the top of the flat with plastic wrap or place it in a clear plastic bag to prevent the growing medium from drying before the seeds germinate. Garden centers often sell special seed-starting kits that contain a flat equipped with a plastic dome. Place the covered germination containers in a bright, warm room with temperatures ranging between 70 and 80°F (21 to 26.8°C) but away from direct sunlight.

Once the seed germinates, remove the plastic covering and place the pot or tray under the fluorescent lights, maintaining similar temperatures. Temperature when the lights are off may drop to the 60 to 65°F (15.6 to 18.2°C) range; however, plant researchers have discovered that nighttime temperatures that are 5 to 10 degrees Fahrenheit (2.7 to 5.7 degrees Celsius) warmer make seedlings and plants stockier.

Depending on the temperature under the lights and the moisture level in the seedling flat, it is usually not necessary to water the seedlings until the second or third day under the lights. When it becomes necessary to water, the peat moss will lighten in color. A gentle flow of water that does not knock the seedlings down is best to moisten the growing medium; this can be achieved by watering between the rows or watering from the bottom if the pots sit in a saucer.

Fertilization of seedling herbs is an important but often overlooked aspect of growing healthy, vigorous plants. Israeli scientist Eli Putievsky performed experiments on seed-grown marjoram, lemon balm, and thyme that dramatically illustrated the importance of fertilizer application even at the earliest stages of growth. He began fertilizing seedlings after germination with one gram of 7-3-7 (N-P-K) in a liter of water (a 20-20-20 water-soluble fertilizer at 1/20 ounces per gallon would be the closest commercial American equivalent) every two days. Within thirty days, the marjoram was 1,033 percent larger than unfertilized seedlings. Lemon balm and thyme seedlings did not show such dramatic increases but were 600 percent or more larger than their unfertilized counterparts. After sixty days, or at transplant size, all fertilized seedlings were at least 100 percent larger (marjoram, 138 percent; lemon balm, 103 percent; and thyme, 176 percent) than their unfertilized counterparts.

Transplanting to pots can occur when the plants' first true leaves are well developed and the second begins to emerge. If left in their first homes, the crowded seedlings will become stringy, and disease may become established.

Two to 2.5-inch plastic pots with the same sterile growing medium used to start the seedlings are ideal for transplants. If you must reuse pots, plastic pots are easy to sterilize in a mixture of bleach, soap, and water.

Traditionally, each pot receives a single transplant, but healthier, fuller transplants develop quicker with clump transplanting, a method that groups three to six seedlings into a single pot. This method decreases the seedlings' stress because removing a small clump of seedlings reduces root damage, and the greater number of roots in the pot use water and nutrients that might otherwise build up to create disease problems.

To use the clump method, gently remove a small clump of up to five seedlings from the flat or germination pot. It's not necessary to count the seedlings in the clump; instead take what comes apart easily with the least root damage. The clump size also depends on the physical stature of the seedlings: the larger the leaves on the seedling, the fewer seedlings go in the clump.

TABLE 9.
Sow-to-plant data for seventeen culinary herbs grown from seed.

HERB[1]	SEEDS PER OUNCE	VIABILITY[2]	SOW SEED	GERMINATION @ 70°	FROM GERMINATION TO TRANSPLANT	TRANSPLANT TO GARDEN[3]	TEMP.[4]
basil	17,750	60%	uncovered	4 days	18 days	11 days	65°F
borage	1,600	70%	covered	5 days	15 days	11 days	55°F
catnip	41,000	40%	uncovered	5 days	25 days	14 days	50°F
chamomile	275,000	40%	uncovered	4 days	20 days	14 days	45°F
chervil	10,000	65%	covered	7 days	10 days	12 days	45°F
chives	22,000	50%	covered	6 days	direct seeded	25 days	45°F
coriander	1,700	70%	covered	6 days	13 days	10 days	50°F
dill	21,800	60%	covered	5 days	11 days	16 days	50°F
lemon balm	50,000	60%	uncovered	7 days	21 days	15 days	50°F
lovage	8,000	50%	covered	8 days	21 days	12 days	45°F
marjoram	165,000	50%	uncovered	5 days	12 days	14 days	55°F
oregano	354,400	50%	uncovered	4 days	30 days	14 days	50°F
parsley	15,000	60%	covered	8 days	12 days	14 days	50°F
sage	3,400	60%	covered	9 days	17 days	14 days	55°F
savory, winter	49,700	55%	uncovered	5 days	20 days	24 days	55°F
sorrel	33,00	65%	uncovered	2 days	14 days	14 days	45°F
thyme	98,200	50%	uncovered	4 days	40 days	19 days	50°F

[1]See text for botanical names and cultural data.
[2]Average viability based on data from Park Seed Company and Johnny's Selected Seeds.
[3]Plants should be conditioned to the outdoors before planting in the garden. This should be done in a cold-frame and should take about a week.
[4]Transplanting temperatures are estimates based on average nighttime lows and are related to transplanting common vegetables: broccoli or cabbage, 45°F; tomato or pepper, 55°F; eggplant, 60°F.

Hold this clump by the leaves to avoid damage to the soft stems, and shove the index finger of your free hand into the center of the transplant pot. Then gently settle the clump into its new home, planting it deeper than it was growing in the seedling flat. Set the clump upright so the seedlings' true leaves lie on or close to the surface of the growing medium. This method often buries the plants' cotyledons, often called first leaves or nurse leaves, which look different from the plants' true leaves. This deep transplanting of the seedlings helps them stand up much better after watering and develop stockier stems. Indoors, the transplants are grown under lights just as the seedlings were and with similar fertilization.

Asexual Propagation

When home gardeners need only a few perennial herb plants to give to a friend or to enlarge their own herb patch, their own gardens may be able to produce the additional plants. Two no-hassle methods of ancient vintage are up to the task of propagation.

One method called layering takes advantage of woody herbs' low growing branches. In a technique copied from nature, the gardener selects pliable branches near the ground and, without breaking them, strips them of leaves except for about 2 to 3 inches at the tip. Next, a narrow strip of bark is scraped from the outer layer of the branch with a sharp knife to enhance rooting. The branch, still connected to the plant, is then covered with soil except for the leafy tip. A stone or a brick will be necessary to hold the stem in place. This is not a method to use when quick results are required, and it may take six or more months for the roots to grow substantially. After the roots form, the stems are cut from the plant, and the rooted cutting is potted and grown to transplanting size.

A second technique, division, involves dividing clump-forming herbaceous species as spring growth commences. The plants to be divided are carefully dug from the ground where the gardener can look at the root structure to determine where the most advantageous areas to cut occur. For some plants, the previous year's growth was abundant, and there are many areas where many roots will remain after several divisions are taken; in other, slower growing species, growth is slower and fewer divisions can be cut. After the divisions are made, the plants may be planted in the garden immediately, or, alternatively, the divisions may be potted and kept in the shaded garden for several weeks to recover from the trauma of surgery before they are placed in a sunny spot. After growth is observed, the divisions may be planted in the garden.

Both propagation methods are easy, but they have limited usefulness because only small numbers of plants can be reproduced and the gardener must already possess the plants to be multiplied. The traditional way perennial herbs are reproduced is by stem cuttings. Two types of cuttings are used. Softwood cuttings originate in green, immature growth; hardwood cuttings are taken from mature growth that is wounded by scraping away the bark to expose its cambium layer.

The typical tip cutting is 3 to 4 inches long and is removed from the growing end of the stem with a sharp knife or scissors. The cutting instrument should be disinfected frequently in bleach or other sterilizing solution to decrease the chance of transmitting disease. One-third to one-half of the lower portion of the cutting is stripped of leaves before it is stuck in the rooting medium. The traditional rooting medium of sterile sand has been largely replaced by the use of soilless growing media, often amended with an equal volume of perlite or calcined clay (sterilized, pelleted clay also known as cat litter).

Rooting cuttings relies on many plants' almost magical ability to reproduce by thrusting life-sustaining roots out through their stem walls. Scientists reduce this magic to a single word, mitosis, which describes a plant's ability to duplicate cells with chromosomes that are identical to its parent. H. T. Hartmann and D. E. Kester, in their book *Plant Propagation*, describe mitosis as "the basic process of normal vegetative growth, regeneration, and wound healing." This is the process with which gardeners are so familiar: the elongation of stems and the production of new leaves, the growth of large root systems, and the ability of plants to heal wounds with new growth. Under the proper conditions, stems form a swollen cluster of new cells called a callus, from which roots will spring.

Most named varieties of perennial herbs are reproduced with this method, assuring that the plant's offspring retain the parent's characteristics. Because it is necessary to have plants, or access to them, before this type of propagation can occur, commercial growers and advanced experienced gardeners most typically root cuttings to increase their plant stock. But this should not dissuade even the beginning home gardener from trying the process when given the opportunity.

Stem-tip cuttings 3 to 4 inches long from many herbs can be rooted in a glass of water on a windowsill, but two things should be remembered: change the water daily to prevent disease, and give the stems about twice as long to root as needed for other methods.

The key to successfully rooting large numbers of stem-tip cuttings is an environment that encourages roots to form quickly: high humidity, strong to moderate sunlight, a day length of at least ten hours, and temperatures at the root zone of 10 to 15 degrees Fahrenheit (5.7 to 8.3 degrees Celsius) above a cool-to-moderately warm ambient air. This environment keeps the cuttings from wilting and dying and allows root formation.

Over the years, plant propagators have developed several methods of achieving conditions needed to root cuttings. The simplest method requires a large, sterilized plastic pot, sometimes cut in half to shorten it and reduce the amount of rooting medium, and covered with a clear polyethlene bag to provide a humid atmosphere. Usually some type of support, such as a clean, stainless steel fork, keeps the bag from touching the cuttings. The bag-covered pot is placed in bright but indirect sunlight; direct sun creates lethal temperatures inside the plastic bag. An alternative is a 10-inch by 20-inch (2.5 by 50.8 cm) flat with a humidity dome similar to that used for starting seeds.

The bag or humidity dome should be removed several times a day to allow fresh air to circulate through the cuttings. If the cuttings appear to wilt, they may be misted with fresh water from a hand-held pump sprayer.

As the gardener becomes more ambitious, a larger rooting area may become necessary, but always humidity is required to maintain cutting turgidity. Cold frames and hot beds are low structures with sides made of treated wood, have glass-sash tops, and are traditional garden accoutrements that are used for both seed-starting and rooting cuttings in both spring and fall. Today's commercial cold-frame kits are lighter and more portable than traditional ones. Hot beds differ from cold frames only in that they have packed, fresh manure or heating cables buried under them to provide heat; keeping such structures from overheating and cooking the plants takes skill and constant attention.

In the early stages of rooting cuttings, the sashes of the cold frame are often left closed to hold humidity when temperature permits. During warm periods, automatic mist systems or hand watering with a hose and fine-spray water breaker can maintain humidity until roots form. Lathhouses are structures usually made of narrow pieces of wood nailed to a frame to limit the amount of sun; the shade they create cools summer temperatures around cuttings. Because these structures are so open to air currents, hand watering or automatic misting is often necessary to maintain humidity.

Inside a greenhouse, benches or ground areas are sometimes set aside to root cuttings and sometimes have overhead frames covered with clear poly and 50-percent shade cloth to retain humidity and protect tender cuttings. These poly tents may cause trouble, and frequent hand misting may be necessary until roots form. The most common method of propagating cuttings in greenhouses uses a bench—or an entire greenhouse—equipped with an overhead, automatic mist system that emits regular bursts of fine spray to maintain leaf moisture. Fog systems produce very fine spray particles that cool the greenhouse by raising humidity. The most effective system for rooting cuttings automates as much of the process as possible so that constant manual adjustments are unnecessary.

In a small greenhouse, a typical propagation area consists of a bench with heating mats that are thermostatically controlled to maintain a preset root-zone temperature. Over the bench hangs a mist line, a long water pipe with numerous mist nozzles. Water to the mist line is controlled by a computer or other device that turns the water line on as moisture evaporates from the cuttings. Although some greenhouses have special beds of sand for the cuttings, most commercial growers now use flats or small containers filled with soilless growing media into which the cuttings are inserted.

Whether you plan to grow just a few cuttings or thousands, begin with strong, healthy cuttings taken from plants that are in vigorous growth. Stems from such plants are thicker than those suffering from lack of sun or nutrients. Tip cuttings should be free of diseases and insects; this is especially important because cuttings are placed close together—often the leaves barely touch each other—and their rooting environment is ideal for the spread of disease.

Because the interaction of the cutting with the environment is important, the condition of the cutting is also a crucial factor. The age of the wood that makes up the cutting definitely affects its ability to root. Despite the oft-repeated advice to take a bit of old wood with lavender and lavandin (*Lavandula angustifolia*, *L.* ×*intermedia*) cuttings and to take them in the fall, our research shows that at this age lavender stems root slowly and unreliably. The best lavender cuttings for rooting are taken from the tips of stems in the active growth that typically coincides with the onset of flower-bud formation. Nearly 100 percent of cuttings taken at this time will strike roots in twenty-one days under intermittent mist, if the weather is not extremely hot. Most *Lavandula angustifolia* and *L. ×intermedia* varieties in outdoor environments are not in full growth in fall, but cuttings may be obtained from four- or five-month-old potted plants.

Rooting aids in the form of liquids or powders are often used on the bare stems, and some horticulturists consider these products essential to producing roots. These rooting aids, called rooting hormones, usually contain varying concentrations of indole-3-butyric acid (IBA) and naphthaleneacetic acid (NAA). There is some controversy over whether these rooting compounds actually induce rooting, but there is evidence that they improve the number and vigor of roots on some herbs.

Tests we made on rosemary and bay cuttings illustrate the old grower's axiom that rooting compounds are sometimes a more effective psychological aid to the uncertain propagator than they are to the initiation of roots on cuttings. We took a group of cuttings from *Rosmarinus officinalis* 'Mrs. Reed's Dark Blue' and treated half with a rooting powder containing 0.8 percent indole-3-butyric acid, one of the strongest formulas available. Both sets of cuttings were grown side by side on a heat mat under intermittent mist. The results showed no difference in the time it took to root the cuttings, but the treated cuttings had larger, more vigorous root clusters.

A second test using the same rooting aid on cuttings of *Laurus nobilis* produced results that conflicted with the rosemary. Bay is one of the toughest herbs to root; the condition of the cutting and even the timing of the cutting are critical to achieve fast, reliable rooting. While fresh new growth of most herbs roots well, it fails with bay and rots instead of rooting. Over the years, we have discovered that first-year growth of bay stems that are half-ripe root best. A half-ripe cutting is somewhat stiff but still green; soft bay cuttings that bend without much resistance usually rot before they root. Because bay grows in spurts several times a year, it is best to take tip cuttings 4 or 5 inches long from stems that have ceased active growth for several weeks.

Bay's sensitivity to the rooting environment hints of important factors in the propagation environment. Our experience has shown that wounding bay cuttings by scraping the butt half of the stem produces better roots quicker. To judge the effect of wounding, rooting aids, and root-zone heat on these hard-to-root bay cuttings, we set up a test that compared cuttings treated in different ways. Cuttings were stuck in 3-inch-deep tapered pots filled with a soilless growing medium enhanced by an equal amount of perlite.

All the cuttings were grown under intermittent mist but divided into two broad groups: One had root-zone heating that was 15 to 20 degrees Fahrenheit (8.3 to 11.1 degrees Celsius) above ambient air temperatures; the other had no heat. Within the two large groups were subgroups of cuttings that were wounded and unwounded, and treated with a rooting aid and untreated. Cuttings were prepared and stuck 1 December; nine weeks later they were checked. Here are the results:

- Without root-zone heat, there were no rooted cuttings; 42 percent of the heated cuttings had produced roots.
- Of the heated cuttings, twice as many of those that were wounded and had no rooting powder were as well rooted as were those that received the rooting aid.
- It took another four weeks for the unheated cuttings to send out any roots, and again the wounded cuttings without rooting powder were the best rooted, double in number of those that received no rooting aid.
- However, the cuttings that were not wounded and received rooting powder produced 36 percent more rooted cuttings than the unaided and unwounded counterparts.

The results show the importance of root-zone heating to speed the rooting process under intermittent mist and indicate that the treatment of the cutting plays an important part in how it roots and the effectiveness of rooting aids.

Fortunately, not all herbs are as temperamental as bay, but our comparison of different methods may provide some clues to the most important factors that apply to rooting any cutting. Little information from the scientific literature about herbs is available on this subject, but some observations from experience and our comparison tests are worth considering. Extreme heat, especially accompanied by hot sun, as sometimes occurs in late spring or during summer, can make rooting cuttings difficult, no matter what method is used. When temperatures exceed 85° or 90°F, it is difficult to keep cuttings from wilting or becoming stressed to the point that it is difficult to achieve quick rooting. The longer it takes a cutting to root, the lower the success rate is likely to be.

Our experience in the laboratory and in the greenhouse has also shown that providing high humidity, especially with intermittent mist or fog, is probably the most important environmental factor when it comes to rooting cuttings. The second factor is probably root-zone heating accomplished with heat mats embedded with electric cables.

Another important factor in producing heavily rooted cuttings was discovered by Israeli researchers. They found that fertilizer, an often-overlooked aspect of the rooting process, may also play a key role in root formation. Eli Putievsky of the Israeli Agricultural Research Organization reported increased rooting and root development of sage cuttings with the addition of 1 gram of 7-3-7 fertilizer in 1 liter of water (a 20-20-20 water-soluble fertilizer at 1/20 ounce per gallon would be the closest commercial American equivalent) applied every two days. With fertilization, 90 percent of the sage cuttings rooted, while only 79 percent of the unfertilized cuttings did so, and the fertilized cuttings had a 128 percent increase in the number of roots.

After cuttings have rooted, they are removed from the propagating environment and introduced to bright sunlight for a few days before being transplanted. Each rooted cutting is placed in a 2- to 3-inch pot filled with soilless growing media. The tip is pinched out of the cutting when it is transplanted so that the stem will begin to branch as the roots

TABLE 10.
Cutting to plant for selected perennial herbs.

NAME	TIME TO ROOT	TRANSPLANT TO GARDEN READY
mints	13 days	14 days
oregano	14 days	14 days
sage	13 days	14 days
rosemary	21 days	28 days
tarragon	18 days	15 days
thyme	20 days	20 days

begin to grow in the pot. If the weather is warm, the potted cutting can be grown in a cold frame; when the weather is inhospitable, an indoor garden with fluorescent lights, a sunny window, or a greenhouse are suitable sites for growing the cutting. When the roots begin to reach the sides of the pots, it is time to transplant the herbs to the garden.

A Healthy Propagation Environment

To be successful at propagation, rigorous control must be exercised over the environment to prevent the invasion of diseases at a time of a plant's greatest vulnerability. Where seeds or cuttings are to be started in a controlled indoor environment, the use of new or sterilized pots and trays is important from the start. Plastic containers are a good choice because they are sterile when new and if reused they can be sterilized easily with chlorine bleach, hot water, and soap.

The medium used for seeding and rooting cuttings may vary slightly, but it should consist of material that has not been contaminated with disease by standing in water or sitting in an open bag where diseases could infect it. It is a smart precaution to use a newly opened bag of material wetted especially for the day of use. If you feel unsure about the seed starting material, it can be sterilized with heat: a temperature of 180°F (83°C) for 30 minutes will kill nematodes and other soil insects, damping-off organisms, bacteria and fungi, and most viruses. The tools used to take stem tip cuttings should be cleaned and disinfested frequently so that they do not spread viruses and diseases; cuttings should not be taken from plants on which disease or insects are visible. The area in and around which the rooting or seedling growth is to take place should be scrubbed with a solution of hot water, detergent, and bleach (one cup of bleach per gallon of hot water) to kill any diseases that might be present; be sure to wear rubber gloves and other protective clothing.

Water, the essential ingredient for seed germination and for rooting cuttings, is also one of the most important factors in the transmission and spread of diseases. The management of moisture, along with sanitation, is the key to seedling and cutting root growth, as well as the control of the typical root rot and damping-off diseases that may romp through the propagation area. *Pythium*, *Rhizoctonia*, *Phytophthora*, and *Botrytis* are fancy names for organisms that are commonly called water molds and root rots and may attack seedlings or cuttings. Water molds like *Pythium* and *Phytophthora* go through a spore stage that swims in water; the disease can be splashed easily from one container to another. These fungi are unlikely to live in a well-drained growing or seeding medium.

Pythium can cause trouble to a seed before it emerges by preventing germination; avoid overwetting of the growing medium when sowing seeds to help control this problem. *Rhizoctonia*, *Pythium*, and *Phytophthora* may all be responsible for post-emergent damping-off, a condition in which disease organisms attack the stem at the soil and cause it to collapse. In addition *Pythium* and *Phytophthora* may attack seedling and cutting roots causing poor growth and leaf-yellowing. Overwatering encourages these organisms and their spread, but excessive dryness can also weaken young plants and damage them so that when water is applied the diseases they cause have an easy time of destroying the crop. "Frequent light waterings keep the upper part of the medium moist, which promotes the growth of disease organisms," according to researcher Charles C. Powell of Ohio State University. "When the medium is irrigated thoroughly and less often, leaving the area at or near the surface slightly drier, it is less likely to see the growth of damping-off pathogens." In our experience, the ideal combination of good drainage, light, and temperature should allow the seeding medium to dry each day to permit daily irrigation at the beginning of the lights-on cycle.

Foliar diseases can also present obstacles to propagation success. Mildews, rusts, botrytis, and fungal blights caused by *Septoria* and *Alternaria* may be encountered in the propagation area, especially in the humid atmosphere where cuttings are rooted. The use of disease-free cuttings, environmental sanitation, and moisture management lessen chances that these organisms will attack seedlings and cuttings. Air circulation through the rooting or seedling area aids in the drying of the medium and helps to dry vegetation; this will also lessen the spread of water-borne diseases. When seedlings or cuttings are too close together they cut down on this beneficial air circulation and hold water on their foliage longer, which aids the spread of disease organisms. Chapter 8 contains detailed descriptions of all these diseases and a further discussion. Whether with seeds or rooted cuttings, starting herbs from scratch provides the gardener with a sense of self-reliance and participation in the magic of the birth of nature. It is something that can be looked back upon later in the gardening process with pride and a sense of personal accomplishment.

Transplanting

Spring is the best time to transplant herbs. It's the season of new growth with a ready availability of plants from specialists and garden centers. It also reveals the need to replace plants killed by winter, as well as the necessity of rejuvenating older plants by dividing thick clumps of roots. Most of these tasks can also be tackled in fall, but the wise gardener gets started early to allow 45 to 60 days before the first frost hits new transplants.

More than physical labor is needed to transplant herbs. Timing is often critical, as with so much else in the garden. The ideal air and soil temperatures to transplant encourages steady plant growth; these are not the same for all herbs. Some herbs—chervil, coriander, dill, sorrel, tarragon, and parsley—respond to cool weather to produce their best foliage growth. Herbs such as basil don't take off until the nights get hot. Sage, mint, thyme, rosemary, winter savory, oregano, and a host of others put forth steady growth over a longer period of the year and are usually transplanted between the cool-weather-lovers and basil.

When the job at hand requires moving a plant from its current site in the ground, air temperature, maturity, and the condition of the plant are first considerations. They are important to minimize water loss by the plant, often manifested by wilted foliage after transplanting. The best time to move established plants is when they are still dormant—usually late winter or early spring. This is true for woody-stemmed perennials such as rosemary, hyssop, lavender, sage, and thyme, as well as herbaceous ones that die to their roots each year. Woody plants show their eagerness to grow with small, swollen, green growth nodes along their stems.

Soil prepared before transplanting speeds the process and makes it easier to prevent root exposure to drying air. When digging the plant, as many roots should be held in the ball of soil as possible. Stress that hinders growth or may be fatal is lessened by disturbing the roots as little as possible.

A second reason for transplanting established herbs is to divide herbaceous roots to increase their numbers in the garden or to thin out plants whose roots have become crowded and need thinning. When the tiny, green-capped nodes of French tarragon push their heads through the soil, dormancy is broken and the plant will begin vigorous growth soon. French sorrel also begins to grow at this time by pushing thin spears from its crown. At this stage of spring development, it is easiest to make divisions. Weather can be changeable and observation is the best guide to determine when the time is right, but both tarragon and sorrel begin observable growth when temperatures start to top 40°F (4.4°C) regularly and produce foliage rapidly until night temperatures push 65 to 70°F (18.2 to 21°C). As these two plants begin growth, divisions may be made from other herbaceous herbs.

Finding the roots of herbaceous herbs is simplified when the gardener is a bit lazy and hasn't cut away all the dead plant tops. Pushing a shovel through the crown of a large plant is the easiest approach to root division; digging the whole clump and using a knife to cut new plants is a more exact method. Use the new buds showing on the roots to guide your work and choose new crowns with several growth buds for each new plant.

New plants that have come from a windowsill or a greenhouse need different treatment because they are not accustomed to the fractious atmosphere outside. Because vegetable transplanting schedules are readily available for every area of the United States through local agricultural extension offices and are well known to experienced gardeners, herb transplanting dates are easily related to them. The earliest date for transplanting cool-weather annual herbs and many perennials parallels the time recommended to transplant lettuce and broccoli. Most other potted herbs go in about the same time as tomato plants or around the time minimum night temperatures hover around 50°F (9.9°C). Basil should wait until the ground is warm and nights are above 55°F (12.6°C) and daytime highs reach the upper 70s, about the time eggplants and watermelons are planted.

Before transplanting potted herbs, their tender foliage and soft stems need to be protected from sudden temperature swings, extreme cold and hot sun. A cold frame or a protected place next to a building will help moderate air currents and shelter the potted plants from blistering sun. (Although the air is rarely as hot in April as it is in August, the sun can be as scalding.) If the plants are not protected from temperatures below 40°F (4.4°C) in a cold frame, they should be brought inside for a few nights until their leaf and stem tissues stiffen or, as gardeners say, harden off. The process takes four to five days. Once the plants are acclimated, knock them gently from their pots—pulling them out by grabbing them by their tops may rip roots from the stem and kill them. Hold the rootball in one hand and gently spread the roots with your other hand, if necessary, before placing the plant in the hole.

Before soft soil is pushed around the roots, puddle the roots in the hole with a solution of liquid fertilizer. After the hole is filled, leave a slight dimple in the soil around the stem so that water will run toward the roots. A second drench with liquid fertilizer finishes the transplanting.

Getting your herb plants off to a good start in their new home is one of the most important things you can do to create a successful garden. Timing is important, but it's a lot more flexible than serving a tennis ball or casting a fly rod. The plant will present signals when the time is right, but it's a good idea to be aware of local weather patterns and seasonal changes as they also govern what you do and when.

Spacing Herbs

The distance between an herb plant and its nearest neighbor—be it another plant or an object like a fence or a wall—can be crucial to its survival. It's also an important consideration for those who husband large acreages and expect top yields.

Proper spacing can boost yields and help to control pests and diseases. Foliage production of dill in commercial fields can increase spectacularly when proper spacing is used, Nancy Garrabrants and Lyle Craker discovered in research conducted at the University of Massachusetts. When spacing went from 1 plant per square foot (10/square m) to 6 plants per square foot (68/square m), yields soared from 8 tons per acre to 27 tons per acre (9.9

t/ha). This high yield was achieved with plants 4 inches (10.2 cm) apart in rows 10 inches (25.4 cm) from each other, a spacing that would be inadvisable with many herbs that require more time to develop, or have a longer growing season.

In commercial fields where several acres of dill might be grown, spacing is easier than it is in a home garden where many different herbs share a small common area. At home, yields are important but they are not the governing principle—separation is important for visual effect and to foster air circulation, availability to sunlight, and access to the plants for harvest. An herb's growth rate and ultimate height and width are important pieces of the spacing puzzle in the home garden. Tall plants improperly sited can cut off essential sunlight to shorter plants. Likewise faster growing plants can crowd slower ones and smother them. The intended effect of the planting should be considered, also. Obviously, if a hedge or a groundcover is desired, spacing will be closer.

There are some general rules to aid gardeners through the spacing maze. Rapid-maturing annuals produced for their foliage can be planted close together because they are harvested often, while those annuals grown for their seeds should be separated a bit more. This is one reason annuals and perennials are often relegated to their own portions of a garden.

Non-invasive perennials should be spaced according to their mature height and width. Taller herbs are placed where they will not shade the shorties. The important number to know to separate plants from each other, or from stationary objects, is one and one-quarter the plant's expected diameter. This is known as the spacing factor. A perennial that will mature at 12 inches (30.5 cm) wide, for instance, has a spacing factor of 15 inches (38.1 cm).

A good rule of thumb is to separate plants of the same species a distance equal to the spacing factor, or one and a quarter times their mature width. If you had two upright thyme plants that would be expected to become 18 inches in diameter, space them about 22.5 inches (57.2 cm) apart (18 + 4.5= 22.5) on centers. Herbs of different species use a different equation. To arrive at the distance between them, take the spacing factor of each, add them together and divide by two. The result is the distance to separate them. If you have a plant that will become 12 inches (30.5 cm) wide at maturity and one that will become 6 inches (15.2 cm) wide at maturity to be sited next to each other, add one-quarter the expected diameter of each, add the results together, and divide by two to achieve the spacing (15 + 7.5 = 22.5 ÷ 2 = 11.25).

Even the best gardeners' efforts to correctly space herbs sometimes fall short because a number of factors influence growth. If plants become too close, they can be pruned to improve air circulation, or moved. Where a species may take a number of years to achieve its mature width, annuals or short-lived perennials are sometimes planted around it to achieve a more pleasing balance in the garden and make use of the empty space.

CHAPTER 8.

Keeping Herbs Healthy

HEALTHY HERBS IN the garden or field begin with high-quality, disease-free plants and careful garden planning to suit specific cultivar requirements. These cultural needs include awareness of whether the plant grows best in full sun or in shade, dotes on dry or moist soil, or needs a high, low, or medium pH for optimum growth. Although large, healthy roots may be the most important part of the young transplant, the final stature of the plant is also important. Herbs may be small when you buy them at a nursery, but it is their *ultimate* height and width that determines the best site and spacing to grow them. Careful attention to all these factors early in the growing process is the key to healthy herbs.

Fertile soil is equally important for healthy, vigorous plant life, as is the variety's ability to adapt to local climatic conditions. The identification tag that comes with the plant is the first place to look for cultural help. Many thoughtful herb specialists supply most of the basic information to grow healthy herbs on their plant tags or through free information available at their nurseries.

Successful gardeners have not only learned about plants' unique requirements; they have also developed understanding of the visual language of plants. Plants communicate their internal condition visually, and the careful gardener learns to interpret the language accurately.

We have tried to outline much of the data specific to individual herbs later in the book. In this section, we want to concentrate on some simple, all-purpose gardening strategies to foster healthy herbs. Be mindful that no approach to plant health will succeed without frequent, even daily inspection of the herb garden to assess the plants' condition. These visits to the garden will be more valuable when the gardener is familiar with the telltale signs that signal future problems.

Weeds

It is difficult to define a weed, although every gardener recognizes what one is. It is, first of all, an unwanted plant that becomes undesirable vegetation in the garden. Herb gardeners are often sensitive to the word "weed" because so many cultivated herbs that are useful for food, flavoring, and medicine, are considered weeds somewhere in the world, sometimes in American backyards. The list of plants that reflect this duality is long; it includes such familiar flora as yarrow (*Achillea millefolium*), couch grass (*Agropyron repens*), lamb's quarters (*Chenopodium album*), chicory (*Cichorium intybus*), chamomile (*Matricaria recutita*), sheep sorrel (*Rumex acetosella*), chickweed (*Stellaria media*), and dandelion (*Taraxacum officinale*). The problem with weeds is not that they present a universal evil, or an uncontrollable menace; they are just plants that sprout at the wrong time and place.

Small, slow-maturing herbs are no match for fast-growing weeds, harbingers of potential garden disasters. Such weeds cut off air and light as they crowd small plants. Weedy growth robs herbs of necessary moisture and nutrients and creates breeding areas for insects and fungal diseases. To the farmer, weeds cut profits because they lower yields and increase expenses for pest and disease control. To the home gardener, they present a never-ending chore that diminishes the pleasure of gardening.

While elimination of weeds appears to be a desirable goal, Stephen C. Weller, a weed scientist at Purdue University, notes that "eradication is seldom achieved." Few herbicides that might do the job effectively are registered for use with herbs. "Even when herbicides are available," Weller concedes, "their usefulness is limited due to the nature of the crop and the overall effectiveness of the herbicide available." For the herb grower, he concludes, cultivation techniques that include "extensive hand hoeing" may be the most common way to control weeds.

Gardeners are greatly vexed by weed seeds that can stay dormant deep in the ground for many years. When they rise to the soil's surface during soil preparation, they germinate and become problems. Anyone who has seen weeds growing in the cracks of city sidewalks must admire, even grudgingly, their tenacity and omnipresence.

Like other plants, weeds fall into three classifications: perennials, biennials, and annuals. Perennial weeds live for two or more years on winter-hardy roots. Many of these weeds are produced from seeds, but creeping varieties may also reproduce from spreading roots or root-like structures called rhizomes. Buckthorn plantain, pokeweed, and dandelion are examples of seed-grown perennials that overwinter on hardy roots. Ground ivy, bindweed, quackgrass, Johnson grass, and Canada thistle are common creeping weeds encountered by American growers. A few biennial weeds also trouble perennial herb growers. These plants produce seed after exposure to cold, usually in the second year of life, and then die. Wild carrot, common mullein, and bull thistle may take up residence in the field and garden.

Annual weeds germinate, grow, flower, produce seed, and die in a single year. They are divided by the time of year they grow. Some annuals come to life under cool fall conditions and overwinter; they flower and set seed in the spring or early summer before dying. Examples of these are chickweed, henbit, Virginia pepperweed, speedwell, and shepherd's purse. Summer annuals begin growth in the spring and die with fall's hard frosts. Purslane, ragweed, ivy-leaf morning glory, crabgrass, and yellow foxtail are examples of these.

Perennial weeds are the most difficult to control; those with long taproots seem to defy banishment. Even careful soil preparation to eliminate these weeds in the home garden—the best way to conquer them—is often marked by failure. A small morsel of root overlooked in the garden will spring to life and eventually stiffen the back of even a careful and forgiving gardener. Where many acres are cultivated, a program of plowing unplanted land to control annual weeds and applying herbicides on perennial species is often effective, according to Weller.

Herbicides are traditional remedies for weeds in agricultural crops. Two types of weed killers are used. A pre-emergent herbicide is applied before the weed seeds germinate; a post-emergent herbicide is applied to weeds in full growth. But Weller points out restrictions on using these herbicides: "Outside of spearmint and peppermint, few herbicides are presently registered for use in other herbs." Little research has been performed to determine the effect of herbicides on herbs because of the high cost of registration. This high cost, coupled with the limited acreage in herbs, has deterred large agrichemical firms from registration testing.

In recent years, a federal government program called IR-4 has permitted researchers to perform much of the preregistration herbicide and pesticide analysis for minor crops such as herbs. Their work has led to the use of some herbicides and pesticides on a state-by-state emergency basis.

Hand weeding is not an unpleasant task in a small herb garden, but even there it is a chore that is easily postponed. A variety of mulches, inert materials that smother weeds as they germinate, may prove to be an alternative and lessen the need for hand cultivation. Straw, leaves, sand, small stones, wood and bark chips, and even newspaper have traditions of use as mulch. Plastic mulches met immediate acceptance with American farmers and many home gardeners; the material now covers hundreds of thousands of acres.

Plastic mulches are favored by many commercial growers because they are easy to apply. Two basic types of plastic sheet mulches are available. One is made from woven strands or from a solid plastic sheet with tiny holes punched in it. This type permits water to flow through to plant roots while suffocating weeds. A more traditional type is a solid black sheet of poly that does not permit water penetration; some system of drip irrigation to supply moisture is needed under this type of plastic mulch.

The weight of the plastic material and method of manufacture provide a guide to its lifespan in the garden or field. Two polyethylene mulches provide up to three years' protection—VisPore Black Mulch, a 4-mil fabric, and Weathashade Weed Stop, weighing in at 7 mil. Weed-X Landscape Fabric, a 7-mil polyolsin material that is black on one side and white on the other, has a life of about five years.

Some vegetables respond to specific wavelengths of light reflected from plastic mulch, USDA researchers Michael J. Kasperbauer and Patrick G. Hunt found. A red mulch increased tomato yields by about 20 percent and improved the quality of the fruit. Tests on peppers showed yields increased about 20 percent with a white plastic mulch. Although they have not been tested thoroughly, herbs may also respond to reflected color. White sand has been shown in at least one case (with 'Dutch' lavandin) to provide increased yields, and white plastic may prove efficacious for herb growers. Mulching with light-colored sand, small stones, marble chips, and/or ground oyster shells also smothers weed growth, cools the soil, and radiates drying light and heat through plant interiors, lessening the spread of diseases; marble and oyster shells also supply extra calcium for the herbs from the Mediterranean. Dark organic matter used as a soil mulch around herbs has been associated with some soil and foliage diseases, partly because of its ability to retain moisture.

Allen Barker of the University of Massachusetts considers sand, gravel, and stones beneficial only in the short term. "Over time," he says, "the weed growth in the sand or gravel and around stones destroys the effectiveness of these materials, making the planting unattractive and requiring control by hand or herbicides." Barker favors 3 or 4 inches of straw or sawdust for weed control. "Composts are excellent for weed control and usually contain few weed seeds," he says, but hay and manures often contain weed seeds. Aggressive weeds such as nutsedge, dock, perennial grasses, or Jerusalem artichoke can be controlled with plastic sheets or heavy paper. "A layer of newspaper about five to eight sheets thick placed underneath 1 or 2 inches of straw, compost, or manure will control most weeds," he believes.

An innovative mulch, suggested by Barker, consists of vegetable garbage ground in a garden shredder and poured around plants. The concoction dries into an impervious mat.

Mulches of clear plastic can be used to warm soil 6 to 10 degrees Fahrenheit to a depth of 6 inches for an early spring start. "At a depth of 4 inches," says Barker, "soils under leaves can be as much as 20 degrees Fahrenheit cooler."

Along with the benefits of mulches, there are disadvantages. "Several cultural problems can counter any beneficial effects of mulching," according to Barker. "Packed mulches will reduce plant stands, especially with perennial herbs where each year's new growth must emerge through the mulch." Another problem pointed out by Barker is that mulched crops have shallower root systems; as mulches decay, the root systems come closer to the surface, where they require more water and become vulnerable to physical damage.

Living mulches composed of alfalfa and red clover in northern climates and subterranean clover in southern areas also provide weed control, prevent erosion and pests, and may add nitrogen to the soil. It is important to grow herbs in an 18-inch strip with the living mulch growing on either side. The mulch should be kept cut low.

Pruning to Ensure Healthy Plants

It is easy to see why stem pruning becomes almost instinctual around herb plants. The foliage begs to be touched and release its aroma; it insists on being cut away and savored. This constant pruning is good for herbs because it shortens their stems, reducing their natural tendency to become leggy, tangled whips that provide ideal conditions for the spread of disease.

Where climates have high summer humidity, pruning is often necessary to keep plants disease-free or to restore fungus-plagued plants. Humid conditions and rapid new growth often coincide with many herbs' most handsome period; it is also a time when summer turns on its furnace and trifling rain showers provide the perfect conditions for rapid fungus growth.

Fungus grows in a moist, shaded atmosphere and spreads on droplets of water. It thrives on dead leaves and other interior plant debris and goes unnoticed by the garden stroller. One day, often after a summer shower, the darkened, fungus-killed leaves suddenly show through their green canopy. Unfortunately, it is necessary, when faced by these conditions, to make gorgeous herbs look ugly.

A midsummer "buzz" haircut with sharp pruners helps fungus-susceptible herbs such as culinary sages, whether variegated, small or large-leaved; semi-upright thymes that make thick mounds; French tarragon that bends under its own weight; thickly branched santolina; tangled oregano; heavy stands of thick mints; floppy lavender; unruly rosemary; wildly spreading lambs' ears; and others herbs that embrace the earth too closely. If the disease has not progressed too far, a quick cleanup and pruning—the horticultural equivalent of a shave and a haircut—does the trick. Once the dead foliage is removed and the plant is opened to drying air and sunlight, the need for other preventive treatment decreases.

This polite surgery, often undertaken in late spring or early summer, is definitely not a whack-whack affair, though. One third to one half of each stem, especially those nearest the ground, should be carefully removed. The remaining stems, usually covered with soggy dead foliage, are thoroughly cleaned, and debris on the ground removed. At the plant's base, extremely low branches may need to be removed to permit air circulation under the plant. The purpose of this gentle beheading of herbs is not only to root out sources of evil; it also encourages new, vigorous growth that produces a bountiful late summer harvest.

Part of the need for this midsummer snipping session is the speedy growth of some established herbs. In addition, if spring pruning was skipped, summer disease problems are more likely. Spring is when careful herb gardeners create stick gardens to rejuvenate many woody-stemmed perennial herbs and to control their growth according to the space available in the garden. When one plant grows faster and larger, its neighbor may suffer from disease fostered by lack of air and light.

The spring pruning ritual begins when small nodules begin to swell along herb stems. These infantile branches will burst into growth after pruning. Thyme, sage, lavender, rosemary, and other woody perennials welcome these spring rites. It is useful to look among the sprouting wood carefully for winter damage and remove dead branches and stems. As with summer pruning, shorten the branches of these budding herbs by one third to one half their length. If plants have been wintered indoors, more of the stem length may need to be removed. Inside or outside, leave some greenery on the branches or make sure there are plenty of growth nodules remaining on bare stems.

The goal of this spring amputation is to energize the lower reaches of the plant with new growth. Branching often comes at the end of unpruned stems, and if they are not cut as spring growth commences, the lower part of the plant becomes woody and barren of foliage. Pruning herbs is not a simple indulgence that begins the process of adding flair to food; it also provides a practical means to grow healthy plants.

Is It Alive?

After a tough winter—almost every winter to those who garden where temperatures drop below 25°F (−4°C)—gardeners are flushed with both enthusiasm and anxiety. The anxiety is created by concern over the continued existence of their perennial herbs: Did they survive the winter?

The wait for the first signs of spring growth is sometimes agonizing, partly because replacement plants may not be available if the wait is too long. How long should you wait to write the death certificate? Spring comes at different times of the year throughout the United States, despite what the calendar may say. There are guidelines for some common culinary herbs, based on observable growth of other plants.

French tarragon, French sorrel, and chives are among the first herbaceous herbs to show new growth, which springs from energy stored in the roots. Look for this growth as the daffodils and forsythia bloom. Cut last year's top growth from these plants shortly after the plants die back in the fall, or during the winter to decrease chances of disease after the new growth appears.

Thyme, lavender, and sage begin to show swelling growth nodes along their woody stems about the time the lilacs bloom. Mints and oregano begin to push fresh shoots through the spring soil around the same time. The evergreen rosemary will begin to show new growth at this time also.

These benchmarks are general, for some variations occur among cultivated herb varieties. Severe cold or a late hard freeze sometimes stuns unprepared plants and cautions them to be slow starters. Sadly, new growth on a winter-damaged plant is often feeble and weak, and while it is alive, it may not be worth saving; most severely damaged plants should be replaced.

What's Wrong? Ask the Plant

Nearly everybody recognizes that a droopy plant needs water; wilting is a plant's visual messages about its health. If you're an attentive gardener, it's as if your plants talk to you.

Misinterpreting a plant's subtle visual messages is common because people and plants don't speak the same language. For instance, when rosemary leaves turn black or brown and drop, it is commonly believed to signal an insufficient humidity in the air. This prompts the often-heard advice to mist the plants.

What usually makes rosemary leaves turn color and drop has to do with moisture, but not around the leaves. Too much water around the roots makes them rot and discolors the leaves at the other end of the plant.

As even a wallflower at a high school dance knows, one glance does not a conversation make. It takes more than a wink and a hello to create meaningful dialog with your herbs. Just as our own language is tangled with ambiguity, an herb's messages may have several translations. A thorough assay of all the possibilities is useful when testing possible ways to rescue sick plants, but it is essential to have some basic information about the cultivar under study. What are the herb's optimum cultural requirements: light, temperature, fertility, water needs, and soil pH? What insects and diseases typically attack this cultivar?

It is not easy to find a good grammar explaining plant language, either. Many herb books give pests and diseases a quick brush-off, as if problems didn't exist or didn't matter much. Unfortunately, herbs have as many of these problems as other plants.

Here's an example of how a concerned gardener might develop a good bedside manner. Let's have a conversation with four basils, beginning with a general examination that leads to questions that probe the vital signs. From ten yards away, it appears that the basils have been pitifully neglected. The plants are stunted. The leaves are limp and yellowish. Days of hot sun have caked and split the soil. It is easy to see that the plants are too dry and need water. But what caused the lack of growth and the anemic leaf color?

To quiz plants, a basic vocabulary of plant sign language is necessary. The yellowed leaves are saying something. Now, basil is a big nitrogen gobbler, and yellowed leaves and failure to grow might be a way of showing a lack of water-soluble nutrients. To test this hypothesis, mix and apply 20-10-20 liquid fertilizer (expressed as 20 percent nitrogen, 10 percent phosphorous pentoxide, and 20 percent potassium oxide) in the amount of water recommended by the manufacturer (fish emulsion may be substituted). This remedy combines prompt irrigation and essential nutrients for growth. If the plants are no longer wilted in a matter of hours, part of the cure is clearly working. If the color has returned to the basils' leaves in a week and the plants begin to grow again, we know the procedure has succeeded; the interpretation was correct.

When plants yellow, even with optimum nitrogen levels, pH may be the culprit. When the pH is too high or too low for the specific herb, the plant cannot take up nutrients and break them down into a useable form. This single problem can be devilishly difficult to diagnose. A pH test of both irrigation water and soil should be taken. Home soil test kits are available or soil samples may be sent through a U.S. Department of Agriculture extension agent for analysis.

Later in the season, the same basils that perked up quickly with a dose of fertilizer may appear wilted again, and even lose some leaves, although the soil does not appear dry and most leaves look quite normal. On careful inspection, however, brown lesions can been seen on the stems just below the wilted area. This is a telltale sign of a moisture-loving basil killer called *Erwinia* that performs its dirty work by interrupting the flow of water and nutrients up the stem. Some research has indicated bark mulch around the base of basils may effectively combat *Erwinia's* debilitating actions, but certainly the plant's diseased stems should be removed, and a general cleanup of dead foliage is in order.

Even something as simple as an overabundance of nitrogen may become a problem. While there is little evidence that an herb's flavor is affected by such a condition, herbs grown for their flowers respond to a nitrogen glut with few blooms, although they appear super healthy and have large, dark-green leaves. Too much shade may produce similar symptoms, but plants grown in poor light tend to appear thin and lack the bushiness of those grown in full sun.

Problems occur with more obscure nutrients from time to time, in even the best-kept garden. Accordingly, here are the symptoms of a variety of nutrient deficiencies.

Too little phosphorus in the soil may bring about unusually small plants with thin stems and smaller-than-typical leaves. Foliage and stems may take on a purplish tint followed by early defoliation. On the other hand, too much phosphorus, although rare, may cause conditions resembling nitrogen, potassium, or zinc deficiency.

Uncommonly weak growth and green leaves with abnormal browning along their margins and sometimes leaves that are unnaturally curled may herald a potassium deficiency. An excess of potassium mimics magnesium deficiency.

Leaf yellowing followed by browning of leaf tissue is symptomatic of deficient magnesium, iron, or boron.

Yellow, young terminal growth with the older, lower leaves remaining green is a sign of a lack of calcium. As the process continues, growth becomes stunted and stem-tips die; new shoots exhibit abnormal growth and then die. An examination underground will reveal stubby roots with dark spots. Ammonium-based fertilizers used on container plants often cause calcium problems. Using fertilizers from calcium nitrate are recommended to keep calcium levels stable. Ground limestone may also be added. Too much calcium may cause leaves to yellow, a condition termed chlorosis.

Diseases and insects also leave telltale signs that speak to the educated gardener. In some cases, the disease attack may be caused by environmental conditions over which the gardener has little control, such as an extremely wet summer or winter. Diseases also take advantage of plants' weaknesses created by lack of nutrients; the disease may enter through dying foliage or soft growth created by an overabundance of nitrogen in the soil.

The following conversations with plants offers some solutions, as well as a methodology of communicating with herbs and other garden plants. As with any conversation with a plant, a translation of the original message is necessary before a response can be formulated.

Message: Brown leaf tips.
Translation: Over- or underwatering may be the culprit, but too much fluoride, copper, or boron in the water can produce the same appearance; so can excessive fertilizer.
Response: If changed watering and fertilizing techniques fail to alleviate conditions on new leaves, check water quality with a comprehensive test.

Message: Foliage is covered with a white powdery substance.
Translation: Suspect powdery mildew.
Response: Plants are most susceptible to powdery mildew when humidity is high, temperatures are below 80°F, and there's poor air flow. Leaf dampness and low light conditions also favor mildew growth, which is why plants such as rosemary become infected when they are brought into the house for winter. Powdery mildew is usually not a problem where plants are out in the open, especially when afternoon temperatures are above 86°F (30°C) and air is continually circulating through the foliage.

Combat this infection with sprays of a solution of 2 tablespoons of baking soda in one quart of water. If this fails, try sprays of garden sulfur. Use caution, however: high temperatures combined with sulfur sprays are sometimes toxic to plants.

Message: Leaves have an oily, greasy appearance or have water-soaked spots; plant stems wilt and blacken.
Translation: Probably a bacterial disease.
Response: Destroy infected plants; do not reuse their potting soil. Space healthy plants so that air can circulate around and through plants. Water so that foliage receives little moisture. Keep plants in as much sunshine as they can stand to create strong leaf tissue.

Message: Plant roots are brown to black instead of their usual firm consistency and light or white color.
Translation: Could be root rot.
Response: Roots need air. When they are irrigated, water fills the small holes in the growing media that contain air. If plants are watered too often, or given too much water, air cannot reach the roots, and they begin to die. It is sometimes helpful to test

how long a plant can go without water before it shows signs of stress and then adjust the quantity and frequency of irrigation.

Message: Leaves and stems of new and old tissue are covered with a gray or brown mold.
Translation: Likely culprit: Botrytis.
Response: Botrytis is encouraged by cool, damp weather and conditions that cause stress to plants. Provide plants with plenty of sun or longer hours of plant lights. Be careful not to overwater; instead, toughen plant tissue by withholding water. Keep plant leaves from touching so that air can circulate through and around them. Indoors, use a fan to gently push air through the plants.

Message: Dead leaves hanging on branches low to the soil, while upper leaves are healthy.
Translation: Suspect fungus disease.
Response: The disease is spread by moisture and reduced air flow. Remove infected, dead, yellowing, and damaged foliage. Increase air circulation within and around the plant by judicious pruning and increased spacing. Add a pea-gravel mulch or white sand to reflect heat into the plant and help keep leaves dry.

Message: Lower leaves wilt, yellow, and die. Process proceeds up the plant. Plants may suddenly wilt and die.
Translation: A good chance that the soil is infected with *Pseudomonas*, *Verticillium*, or *Fusarium*.
Response: Plant resistant varieties or set new, disease-free plants in uncontaminated soil.

Message: Sudden collapse or wilting of the plant when adequate irrigation is available.
Translation: Suspect *Phytophthora*, *Fusarium*, *Verticillium*, and/or *Pythium*, soil diseases that attack many herbs native to the Mediterranean basin. These diseases clog the plants' vascular tissue and reduce the transmission of water.
Response: *Phytophthora*, *Fusarium*, *Verticillium*, and/or *Pythium* are molds and cause damage to a wide variety of cultivars. These diseases are often accelerated by over-watering, poor drainage, and inadequate air circulation. Copper foliar sprays are sometimes effective on infected plants. Changing the plant's location may be helpful, but a fresh start with new plants is desirable. Incorporate abundant sand and gravel into the soil, enough to raise the planting bed's level above the rest of the garden. Consider a light-colored mulch of sand, gravel, marble chips, or ground oyster shells. Mycorrhizal (beneficial) fungal dips may be helpful in some instances.

Message: Your chive shoots in early spring are covered with black insects.

Translation: Aphid infestation.

Response: Aphids are among the most common garden pests, with more than 4,400 species. They feed by sucking plant sap, and a heavy infestation can stunt and deform their hosts. In addition, about 60 percent of plant viruses are transplanted by these little critters. Aphids are often seasonal in the garden, especially during periods of cool nights.

Light aphid infestations in the garden can be handled with a strong spray of water that knocks the insects from the plants. If the garden or greenhouse is overrun, spray a combination of insecticidal soap and rotenone. Biological controls include ladybugs, lacewings, parasitic wasps, and insect-pathogenic fungi.

Message: Bay tree leaves feel sticky and are covered with a soot-like substance.

Translation: Most likely a scale infestation, especially if the bay tree was summered outdoors and brought in for winter.

Response: Scale, a tiny sucking insect, is commonly found on bay plants. Coating the plant with a fine horticultural oil mixed with water and applied either by spraying or dipping (if the plants are small) suffocates the insects and gives the plant a pleasant, healthy shine.

Message: Tiny flies float around potted plants.

Translation: Fungus gnats, probably.

Response: In greenhouses, stores, and homes where light levels are low and soil moisture is high, fungus gnats are likely inhabitants. The adults are merely unsightly, but their offspring burrow into roots and stems and often transmit diseases such as pythium, fusarium, phoma, and verticillium. *Bacillus thuringiensis* (BT) is a spore-forming bacterium that destroy the larvae of fungus gnats; use it to drench the soil.

Message: Green or yellowing leaves show pinhead discolorations

Translation: Thrips or spider mites. Thrips leave an irregular, discolored pattern that looks like the pigment has been sucked from small areas of the leaves. Spider mites leave many tiny, round marks on leaves from their feeding; the color has been drawn from these areas. Minute webbing with tiny insects scooting over it may be visible during major infestations of spider mites.

Response: Sprays of insecticidal soap and rotenone every three days for two weeks can break the insect life cycle and control the pests, if not totally eradicate them.

Message: Wiggly discoloration through leaf surfaces, especially sorrel.

Translation: Probably leaf miners, the larva of the flying adult. Little clusters of eggs are often clearly visible on the undersides of leaves.

Response: Create a barrier to prevent the adults from laying eggs by covering foliage with spun-bonded poly, especially in spring and fall.

Message: Ragged holes in leaves or leaf-margins, particularly basil and sorrel.

Translation: Probably night-foraging slugs who spend their days under layers of mulch, large stones, and sidewalks, wherever there is darkness and moisture. Also look for caterpillars; they normally feed during daylight hours.

Response: Seek out and destroy these pests' resting places. Trap the pests by placing flat pieces of wood or inverted, scooped-out melon shells on the soil—a veritable slug hotel—on the soil. During the day, destroy the guests. Four-inch-high copper flashing pushed into the soil on its edge makes an impervious slug fence. Some mail-order garden-supply firms sell copper material to block slug attacks, and copper flashing is available at roofing supply firms. Recent tests of beer as a bait and trap for slugs showed the brew was not effective at significantly reducing slug predation of strawberries, and the beer-baited traps are effective for only a few feet.

Message: Poor growth, yellowing leaves, dying growing tips.

Translation: After ruling out pH imbalance, poor drainage, and lack of nutrients, consider microscopic soil insects called nematodes. These pests burrow into roots, causing raised nodes, interfering with nutrient uptake, and slowly killing the crop. Nematode-infested roots can spread the critters to previously uncontaminated areas, particularly when field-grown plants are dug and sold or new plants are created from divisions. Nematodes also promote the spread of soil-borne fungi.

Response: Soil enriched with grass clippings destroys most nematodes. If infestation is severe, turn to container gardening using a growing medium containing equal parts of peat moss and perlite.

In rare occasions, the coveted plant is simply the wrong one for the site or the climate. This was the case with lavenders planted on the edge of nineteenth-century London in the famous fields of Mitcham. The lavenders grown in Mitcham were gorgeous and profitable, but they were ravaged by shab (*Phoma lavandulae*), a disease prevalent in Great Britain. The disease causes young spring growth, which carries lavender's expressive flowers, to yellow and wilt. After the shoots die, the disease spreads into the plant and eventually kills it. Selection of lavender varieties resistant to shab, a disease unknown in the United States, eventually overcame the problem.

To grow healthy, vigorous herb plants, gardeners are wise to practice the art of observation. Reading herb leaves may at first seem as tricky as reading a crystal ball, but this plant language can be learned by observation, knowledge, and repeated close encounters with failure. For most gardeners, failure is the second-best teacher; the first is having a wise, old gardener for a neighbor. When your own talent as a reader of herb leaves is unequal to the task, the local agricultural extension agent may be able to help or can refer you to a specialist at the state university, whose experience is probably wide enough to interpret your plant's vital signs.

Companion Planting

Many herbs, as well as other plants, have gained reputations as nurses who help restore vigor to ailing flora, ward off insect infestations, and by their mere presence make nearby plants grow better. Such ideas have existed for centuries in folklore and were widely spread in the United States beginning in the 1940s, when interest in French intensive gardening methods grew. The idea that was eventually called companion planting was popularized by Rudolf Steiner's bio-dynamic movement and takes its common name from a 1943 pamphlet called *Companion Plants*, written by Richard B. Gregg.

The movement got a large boost by the publication in 1966 of *Companion Plants and How to Use Them* by Gregg and one of the method's leading champions, Helen Philbrick. Rodale Press' *Organic Gardening Magazine*, the largest home-gardening publication in the United States at the time, also promoted the method by publishing numerous articles. Increasing environmental awareness and the desire to produce vegetables and herbs without using pesticides buoyed the movement's popularity. Companion planting has taken on a life of its own, separate from its narrow beginning in a small cultish group, and now has a ready acceptance.

From the beginning, the idea of placing differing plants close to each other to provide improved growth or keep insects at bay was more than a simple gardening technique. "Among the plants, symbiotic relationships usually depend upon immediate touch or some other close connection," Philbrick wrote in the 1969 *Herbarist*, a publication of The Herb Society of America. "They may be caused by root secretions between two species of plants. They may be caused by leaf secretions. Finally, they may even be caused by scent between two plants—or as the books elegantly term it, 'exhaled aromatic substances.'"

Philbrick identified seven ways that plants influenced each other:

- Some plants directly aid other plants
- Some enrich the soil, indirectly providing assistance to others
- Some oppose or harm each other

- Some provide positive influence for some of their brethren, helping them grow, and at the same time hinder or harm other plants
- Some repel harmful insects
- Some attract useful insects
- Some even repel animals

Philbrick believed in symbiosis among numerous plants. Late cabbage and early potatoes are good together, she said. Carrots go well in the garden with peas, lettuce, and chives. Asparagus was aided in growth by tomatoes and parsley. Garlic benefits nearby roses.

Herbs play a large part in the companion-planting scheme. While basil is "generally compatible and good for the whole garden," she says, it does not "get along" with rue. In "small quantities," chamomile increases the essential oil of peppermint and aids cabbage. She recommends chamomile blossoms soaked in cold water for two days to control seedling damping-off diseases. Coriander aids germination, growth, and seed formation of anise, but hinders seed formation of fennel. Watch out for wandering dill; it greatly reduces carrot yield, according to Philbrick. Hyssop increases grape yields, but is "not good close to radishes," she warned. Pennyroyal repels ants and mosquitoes, while peppermint reduces flea beetles and white cabbage butterflies. Spearmint comes in handy to repel rodents, ants, and aphids.

Rosemary and sage are said to stimulate each other. Summer savory, when used as a border, "helps" onions and beans. Southernwood repels moths on fruit trees and cabbages, while tansy keeps flies and ants away. Thyme is another barrier to the ever-present cabbage moth. Yarrow, said Philbrick, increases the "aromatic quality of all herbs and their general health."

"What we see in the garden is real," Philbrick wrote of companion planting. "It is now provable by scientific methods in a biochemical research laboratory where everyone can see and measure it." Chromatography, a scientific method that breaks a plant's essential oils into color bands, was the tool she believed proved her point. "Having once discovered that one plant extract always produces the same picture," Philbrick wrote, "laboratory technicians have now experimented with combinations of plant extracts. Plants known to be mutually helpful produced harmonious pictures when extracts were combined. Plants having a harmful effect on each other produced pictures showing confusion or disharmony, or a canceling out of the finer forms of the individual pictures." For Philbrick, these pictures drawn by chemical mixes became a truthful pseudo-scientific validation of her garden observations, when they could just as easily have been viewed as fanciful interpretations without scientific validity.

Companion planting was a palatable doctrine, delivered with evangelistic fervor, that went unchallenged for many years. Its appeal was almost mystical: Plants work together to enhance their lives for the benefit of humans. Scientists and experienced gardeners who might have been expected to question some of the claims made for companion planting may have had their doubts, but they also saw the possibilities of using companion planting to reduce the use of expensive and often harmful pesticides in gardens and farms.

In their usual quiet way, plant scientists began testing the claims made for companion planting. After more than half a century of independent investigation of companion planting, what can be said for certain about the symbiotic relationships among plants? In his 1986 book *Designing and Maintaining Your Edible Landscape Naturally*, Robert Kourik sought to summarize research on the subject. "For eight years, I have looked for 'hard data' to double-check and substantiate the traditional companion planting guidelines," he wrote. "I found a mixed bag of results: less than half of the studies confirmed the recommendations; the majority seemed to indicate that faith, not fact, may have been an important aspect of specific recommendations."

Following are some of the positive study results that concern companion planting, according to Kourik's review of the scientific literature.

While you can forget about marigolds to keep insects away, some herbs have shown promise as companion plants. For instance, catnip and tansy both reduced Colorado potato-beetle infestations on potatoes by more than 70 percent. Catnip reduced by 91 percent green aphid populations on peppers. Squash had fewer squash bugs when interplanted with tansy and catnip. Most studies found some reduced yields due to interplanting with herbs, which could have been due to overcrowding.

Another part of the garden environment has been elevated due to the scientific interest in companion planting. For some plants, particularly the brassicas, simple weeds are excellent protectors. The weeds fill in the space between the plants, thus confusing flying predators, while those that stand out provide a bare, earth-highlighted target. Unfortunately, weeds may also compete with crop plants for nutrients, and the end result may be a reduction in pests as well as lower yields. Weedy groundcovers also reduced common pests on apples, beans, cabbage, cauliflower, collards, corn, grapes, mung beans, peaches, and walnuts.

While companion planting may be unreliable, herbs can be used in different forms to solve garden problems. Sprays of essential oils or aqueous suspensions of ground herbs may repel insects. J. Hough-Goldstein at the University of Delaware found that aqueous sprays of tansy were an effective antifeedant of cabbageworm, while sprays of tansy, sage, basil, catnip, dill, or rue deterred feeding of adult and larval Colorado potato beetle. Catherine Regnault-Roer and associates in France found that the essential oil of marjoram and mother-of-thyme were toxic against a bruchid insect that attacks kidney-bean plants. A review of the use of essential oils as potential repellents and insecticides was published by Dan Palevitch and Lyle E. Craker in 1993; they noted some effective uses of the oils of anise, basil, catnip, chamomile, coriander, dill, eucalyptus, fennel, feverfew, garlic, hyssop, pennyroyal, ponderosa pine, rosemary, rue, sage, sour orange, tansy, and wormwood. In the greenhouse, I. Tunç and S. Sahinkaya of Turkey found that the essential oils of cumin, anise, oregano, and eucalyptus were effective against the carmine spider mite and the cotton aphid.

Nematodes are particularly noxious in the soil despite their near-invisibility. Jerry T. Walker at the University of Georgia found that many herbs may resist or tolerate nematode infections. Yet, such nematode infestations are often followed by soil-borne, sudden-wilt fungi, such as *Phytophthora*, that ultimately kill the herb. Synthetic nematicides may be effective, but they are one of the chief, persistent pollutants of ground water. One of the best natural nematicides is released by the roots of marigolds (*Tagetes* spp.), but in the field it shows rather weak nematicidal activity; fresh grass clippings are often just as effective. Since nematodes are composed of chitin, mulches of ground crab shells, also composed primarily of chitin, have been thought to foster fungi that degrade chitin, but the field results are very mixed.

Good news for weed lovers also comes from Mexico. It was there that farmers discovered a common weed that enhanced corn yields if it was managed in a way that kept it from becoming tall and competing with the corn for nutrients. Francisco J. Rosado-May, a scientist at the University of California, Santa Cruz, wanted to find out why. In 1990, he and his university colleagues discovered the roots of the weed (*Bidens pilosa*) secreted compounds that killed corn-destroying fungi and nematodes. The farmer's practice of keeping the weed mowed until harvest let the weed control soil pests without stealing nutrients from the corn, the scientists concluded.

The difficulty of making sweeping generalizations about the benefits of companion planting, or about gardening in general, is that everybody's garden is not the same; soils differ, as do climates. The environment is such an important determinant of growing conditions (and pest populations), and local fluctuations so numerous, that it is often difficult to reach precise and universal advice for growing a single plant.

As most experienced horticulturists know, there are few universal truths to be found in the cultivation arts except that farming and gardening are hard, often satisfying work. The subtleties in local environments and microclimates make it almost impossible to universalize personal experience. A method of companion planting that is successful in an East Coast location may not work in the mountains of West Virginia or in Berkeley, California. When it comes to having healthy herbs, nothing can replace the continual care and attention of a knowledgeable gardener.

CHAPTER 9.

The Harvest

THE LEVEL OF mystery and misunderstanding about harvesting herbs grows almost daily. A typical example of the way misinformation gains credibility occurred in a major American paper when a garden writer offered this tip of the week to her readers: "Many herbs are reaching full maturity just now. For best flavor, pick basil, parsley, thyme, and others in early morning or evening. Their aromatic oils dissipate in the heat of the sun and, after the sundown, fade completely to the human palate."

We have been growing herbs for decades and collecting data on their aromatic properties for as long, and the information was news to us. Because the newspaper has a circulation that tops 800,000, which puts its readership well over 1 million, we decided to look into the claim in hopes of discovering the basis for it. The garden writer quickly conceded that the tip was based solely on her own experience and was limited almost entirely to her perception of basil. Although her words implied that an herb's aromatic properties disappeared after dark, she actually meant that she thought there was an "astonishing" loss of aroma. That night, we went out to sniff the basil in our respective gardens—and found no noticeable loss of aroma.

This is not to say the garden writer was totally wrong, but her generalization was not universally true or based on wide experience. Unfortunately, this sort of statement often occurs in the world of gardening, where folklore sometimes plays a more prominent role than does scientific inquiry.

The flavor and aroma of fresh herbs is so appealing, and the desire to preserve these qualities so strong, that for centuries, herbs have been surrounded by an aura of mysticism and secrecy. The aromatic character of herbs is elusive and difficult to capture and preserve, and scientists have begun to use new, sensitive equipment to test plant chemistry and thus reach a better understanding of this aspect of herb plants.

The chemicals that give an herb its characteristic aroma are called essential oils and are usually contained in microscopic pouches or modified hairs on the surface of the leaves, stems, roots, and flowers; sometimes the essential oils reside in internal canals. The content of these oils consists of a variety of chemicals whose proportions may shift constantly during the plant's growth cycle. As scientists probe the mysteries of herbs' essential oils, their findings have challenged many assumptions held by gardeners.

An herb's heredity plays a critical role in both the amount and content of its essential oil. Dramatic alterations in chemical composition have been reported in chamomile, dill, and coriander in the short time it takes for the plant to flower and form seed or fruit. In coriander, for instance, trans-2-decenal and decenal are slightly over 50 percent of the essential oil as flowers open, but drop to 5.5 percent as fruits ripen. At the same time, linalool increases from 0.34 percent to 60.37 percent of the oil.

Even something as apparently insignificant as the mulch around a lavender plant may influence essential oil yield dramatically. Scientists at Delaware State College found in 1981 that essential oil yields of *Lavandula* ×*intermedia* 'Dutch' increased as much as 771 percent when a 1-inch topdressing of white sand was used as a mulch under the plants. In a footnote to a scientific paper, two Finnish scientists reported that greenhouse-grown basil and marjoram contained greater quantities of essential oils than similar field-grown plants. The quality and quantity of an herb's essential oil often determines the optimum time to harvest. The intended use of the herb—fresh, dried foliage, or distilled aromatic oil—also plays a role in harvest timing.

The high commercial value of herbs and of their essential oils adds to the importance of maximizing harvest yield and quality, especially for commercial growers. For many years, the time of plant flowering was believed to be the best time to harvest foliage. Research indicates, however, that as some herb plants grow, the chemicals that make up essential oils actually rearrange themselves. Italian scientists found that the essential oil of sage (*Salvia officinalis*), for example, was high in camphor, an undesirable component, during the spring. As the plant continued to grow, however, the camphor content peaked and then declined. Thus, harvests of sage in July and October will produce finer flavor and aroma. Similar seasonal, or periodic, variations have also been reported in sweet marjoram (*Origanum majorana*), lemon balm (*Melissa officinalis*), basil (*Ocimum basilicum*), oregano (*Origanum vulgare* subsp. *hirtum*), thyme (*Thymus vulgaris*), and other herbs.

The Italians built their findings on research done in 1978 in Israel. The Israeli report was one of the first to challenge the contention that herbs attain their highest quantity and quality of aroma and fragrance at the time of flowering. The Israeli scientists, D. Basker and E. Putievsky, concluded that "the simple criterion of flowering onset is not adequate" to signal harvest.

The Israelis studied lemon balm, oregano, sage, sweet marjoram, thyme, and basil. While they found the highest yield of oil occurred around the time of flowering, the largest quantity of dried leaves and the highest quality of oil occurred at other times (one reason for the highest quantity of oil occurring at flowering is that the oil in the flowers adds to the total). The most leaves could be gathered from lemon balm, oregano, and sage, the scientists discovered, between 18 July and 13 August. The highest quality essential oil occurred in lemon balm about 3 September, in oregano 29 September, and in sage 19 July. The harvest dates are specific to the unique Israeli climate.

The scientists concluded, "Three processes appear to be involved in yield development: firstly, new leaves form, particularly on the upper portions of the plants; secondly, the volatile oil content of the leaves increases with time, with the presumably older leaves on the lower portions of the plants attaining the highest content; and finally, leaves are shed, particularly those on the lower portions of the plant. The balance among these three processes thus determines the various components of the yield, and also results in the seasonal periodicity noted in the volatile oil content of the dried leaves."

The harvest of foliage for the extraction of essential oils is not the primary reason the home gardener cuts herbs, so the detailed information from scientific essential oil analysis, while useful to commercial growers, does not reflect the needs and uses of the home gardener. Nonetheless, this information suggests that multiple harvests can be important. Four or more harvests are possible in commercial fields, as well as in the home garden, depending on climate. Whether in the home garden or in the commercial field, multiple harvests maximize the annual yield of herbs to be consumed and preserved. We consider a harvest different from an occasional picking of leaves to use for the evening meal; instead, harvest is undertaken for the purpose of storing herbs for later use. Here are some guidelines for the home gardener about to embark on an herb harvest:

- Remove as much as half the foliage of perennial and annual herbs during early and mid-season; never more than 20 percent of perennials late in the season where cold winters may cause damage. Annuals such as dill and coriander have a short period of leaf production and are harvestable three to six times before the initiation of flowering signals the end of leaf production. Once these plants begin to flower, foliage production ends and seed creation begins.
- Harvesting in the cooler parts of the day decreases the need for cooling the foliage to reduce loss of aromatic oils and leaf deterioration.
- Use sharp tools—pruners, knives, sickles, shears—for cutting. Rubber bands to bunch stems are useful, too.
- To prevent foliage from wilting, immerse cut stems immediately in a bucket of water.
- Cut only what can be handled quickly with the freezing or drying equipment available.

Disinfection of Herbs

Periodically, an especially virulent bacterium, known as *E. coli* 0157:H7, has appeared in hamburger, unpasteurized apple juice, sprouts, and mesclun mixes in the United States and Japan. Not only does this bacterium cause severe diarrhea and abdominal cramping, but it has been reported to kill children and elderly because of hemolytic uremic syndrome (HUS), wherein kidney function is impaired. Organically grown herbs are especially prone to infection because this strain of *E. coli* is often found in cow manure; it has also been reported in deer excrement. Most organic standards prohibit the use of raw manure on a crop within 60 days of harvest, but *E. coli* can live for 70 days or longer in manure. It takes more than tap water to dislodge *E. coli* and other microbes. Though cooking can kill these microbes, basil for pesto, sprouts, or any other herbs that may be eaten without cooking should be first treated.

Susan Sumner, a food scientist at Virginia Polytechnic Institute and State University, has found that two sanitizing sprays are very effective in dislodging and killing infectious microbes. Firstly, a 3 percent hydrogen peroxide solution (the same strength available at drug stores for disinfecting wounds or gargling) is squirted on the vegetables or herbs. Then, this is followed with a mist of mild acetic acid (household vinegar). Actually, the sequence of hydrogen peroxide or acetic acid solutions is not critical, and a common household sprayer for dampening clothing before ironing may be used.

Postharvest Care

As soon as a stem is removed from an herb plant, it begins to deteriorate. Time from cutting thus becomes a determinant of quality, but not the only one. Both temperature and light are factors that can be used to buffer the effect of time on foliage deterioration. Low temperatures and darkness are important factors to preserve the visual quality of harvested culinary herbs.

The key to retain high quality in herb foliage after harvest is storage at temperatures between 32°F (0°C) and 41°F (5°C), according to research at the University of California, Davis. Of the major culinary herbs, only basil reacted negatively to such treatment; temperatures below 50°F (10°C) were detrimental. Chervil, chives, dill, marjoram, mint, rosemary, sage, tarragon, and thyme remained at or near optimum condition visually for ten days when stored at 32°F (0°C).

Storage at 50°F (10°C) for ten days yielded quite different results. Thyme, sage, rosemary, and marjoram remained in similar condition, but the other herbs studied lost up to 50 percent of their visual quality. Only rosemary and thyme had any quality left after the full ten days of storage.

Preserving the Harvest

Drying was the first and remains a standard way for home gardeners to preserve herb foliage for later use, but modern technology has added special freezing techniques, sonic drying, microwave drying, and irradiation as ways to improve traditional methods. Alas, each method results in some loss of flavor and aroma. Microwave drying alters essential oils of many herbs, and at 140°F (60°C) most of the volatile aromatic oils are lost. A study in

TABLE 11.
Recommended shelf pull dates for culinary herbs.

ITEM	CARDBOARD AND TIN (YRS.)	GLASS (YRS.)
anise seed	3	4
anise, star	3	3
arrowroot	4	4
basil, whole leaves	3	3
basil, ground leaves	3	3
bay leaves, whole	4	4
caraway seed, whole	4	4
cardamom seed, whole	3	4
cardamom seed, ground	3	4
chervil leaves, whole	2	2
chives	2	–
coriander, whole	3	4
coriander, ground	3	3
cumin seed, whole	4	4
cumin seed, ground	3	3
dill seed, whole	4	4
dill weed, whole	2	2
fennel seed, whole	3	4
fenugreek	3	–
garlic products	3	3

Finland discovered that freeze-drying dill caused a 75 percent loss of aroma, but when parsley and bay laurel were dried in the same fashion, there were no significant changes in essential oil content. A second Finnish report found almost no loss of essential oils in marjoram and oregano. This seemed to suggest that not all herbs have essential oil constituents that resist attempts to preserve them.

Some of the most popular herbs, however, do not make ideal subjects for preserving. In the case of dill, the key aromatic ingredient, benzofuranoid, is extremely volatile and is lost in drying. The main aromatic components of chives, disulfides, are severely reduced by freezing, freeze-drying, or air drying. Basil is notorious for the speed at which its aroma deteriorates after drying. Within three months of drying, 19 percent of basil's preserved essential oil is gone, and within six months, 62 percent of basil's aroma has disappeared. For this reason, Italians pack their fresh basil leaves in olive oil and keep them in the dark.

How long you can expect dried herbs to retain their aromatic character in storage

TABLE 11. (continued) Recommended shelf pull dates for culinary herbs.		
ITEM	CARDBOARD AND TIN (YRS.)	GLASS (YRS.)
marjoram, whole	3	3
marjoram, ground	3	3
mustard, whole	4	–
mustard, ground	3	4
oregano, whole	3	3
oregano, ground	3	3
parsley	–	2
peppermint leaves	2	3
poppy seed	3	3
rosemary, whole	3	3
saffron, whole	4	4
sage, whole	3	3
sage, ground	3	3
savory, whole	3	3
savory, ground	2	3
sesame seed	2	3
spearmint, whole	2	3
tarragon, whole	3	3
thyme, whole	3	4
thyme, ground	3	4

Source: The American Spice Trade Association

depends on several factors. Herbs that have been ground, for instance, deteriorate in storage more rapidly than the whole product. The type of container used for storage is also important. While dark-colored glass has been a standard for years, aluminum foil bags and waxed paper proved superior to traditional glass in a 1989 Russian study. A Finnish researcher showed that 44 percent of dill's aromatic compounds were preserved in an aluminum foil laminate after nine months; high-density poly bags preserved only 20 percent of the dill aroma.

Once the herbal bounty has been preserved, how long can it be expected to remain useful? The American Spice Trade Association has established recommendations for discarding dried herbs. While these dates are useful, they were established more to aid grocery chains than to inform purchasers. Most purchased containers of dried herbs reveal no packing date, so purchasers have no idea how long the product has sat in a warehouse or on the shelf. Storage at less than optimum conditions lowers shelf-life. Once the container is opened at home, further loss of flavor will occur.

Drying Herbs the Traditional Way

The goal of herb drying is to remove 85 to 90 percent of the moisture while preserving the aromatic oils of the herbs, as well as the color of the material. To achieve this, drying should be done in the dark with temperatures about a maximum of 100°F (37.7°C). Drying should be slow but take no more than 30 to 100 hours, depending on the herb and the thickness of the material to be dried. The plant material to be dried must be disease free because the drying temperatures are ideal for fungal growth.

Drying herbs and their flowers can be done simply on an old window screen placed in a well-ventilated location where darkness and low humidity can be maintained. Lay the herbs on the screens and gather them up again when dry. Most herbs can also be dried in bunches of six to ten stems. The tied bunches are often hung from hooks fastened to the ceiling; low humidity and darkness help to preserve color. When plants are properly dried, the material is easily powdered with the hands. A commercial moisture meter comes in handy during the process.

As the volume of foliage and flowers increases, more sophisticated equipment may be desired, and it too can be built at home. In 1988 at the Third National Herb Growing and Marketing Conference, Art Tucker and Michael Maciarello of Delaware State University described two prototype dryers, one heated by electricity and the other by the sun. The homemade electric "coffin" dryer, with 55 square feet of shelf space, cost about $1,000 in 1988; the solar-heated dryer, with about half as much square feet of shelf space, was about $200. The electric dryer is particularly useful for rapidly drying roots. For drying leafy herbs in areas of high temperature and humidity, a dehumidifier, instead of the heating elements, would lower the humidity while maintaining the temperature below the maximum of 100°F (37.7°C).

Cooking with Fresh and Dried Herbs

When herbs dry, they shrink and become lighter in weight as moisture exits the leaves. Along with the moisture, some essential oils may also be lost. The fact that all herbs do not dehydrate at the same rate makes the situation even more complex. Trying to compensate for the difference between dried and fresh herbs is difficult, and skillful tasting becomes a necessary art.

A study of herb drying done by students at Delaware State University in 1990 provides some helpful guidelines to help cooks compensate for the shrinkage of herbs that occurs between garden and jar, but it could not incorporate the differing flavor intensities of fresh and dry material. The study showed that, on average, 4.8 grams of fresh herb produced 1 gram when dried; parsley, for instance, hugged the average. Oregano averaged 3.6 grams fresh to produce 1 gram dried, but that average was derived from three fresh samples, ranging in weight from 2.8 to 5 grams, that yielded 1 gram dried herb. For 1 gram of sweet marjoram, another species of *Origanum*, 3 grams of fresh material were required. Bowles's mint (*Mentha ×villosa* nothovar. *alopecuroides*) took 3.5 grams of fresh leaves to produce 1 gram dried.

Here is a list of the herbs and the number of grams of fresh material, on average, it takes to make 1 gram of dried: basil, 6.7 grams; dill ('Mammoth'), 4.5 grams; rosemary, 3.2 grams; French tarragon, 4.9 grams; and winter savory, 6.1 grams. For cooks, the most useful data from the study was the finding that, on average, 3 teaspoons of fresh herb is equal to 1 teaspoon of dried.

Harvesting Seed

There are times in the life of an herb gardener when it is desirable to harvest seed from favorite plants. This is a chore that befalls herb growers more than other gardeners because of the whims of the seed market. One year, gardeners may find abundant herb seed for special basils, such as 'Purple Ruffles' or 'Green Ruffles', for instance, but the next, no catalog company lists them. Such are the vagaries that make saving seed, or even growing your own, necessary.

Storing seed from year to year is as easy as placing the extra seed packets in plastic zipper bags and then storing them in the refrigerator until next spring. When it comes to saving seed from plants grown in the garden, usually annuals that come true from seed, advanced planning is advisable.

Make sure that only one variety of a species is present in the garden; this will eliminate cross pollination that might create a hybrid rather than the desired variety. Single out the plants that are for seed and the ones that are to be used for cooking or other purposes; cutting herb foliage for cooking during the summer may prevent flowering and seed formation. Flowering and seed maturation can take several months, especially when stems flower at different times during the summer.

Once the seeds have formed, remove the stems just below the seed pods. Place the stems loosely in open paper bags (grocery bags are good for this purpose). Each herb variety should have a clearly labeled bag of its own; be sure to mark the year and date of the seed harvest on the bag. Place the bags with the seeds and their stems in a warm, dry place inside the house for at least several weeks so they can dry further.

When the seeds are dry, loosen them by rubbing the seed pods against screen wire with small-diameter openings. Ideally, the screen openings will be large enough for the seed to slip through, but small enough to keep the leftover plant material atop the screen. Sometimes it is necessary to use several seed screens of different sizes, depending on the diameter of the seeds. Rather than investing in professional-grade sifters, the home gardener can substitute a variety of strainers and sifters from a kitchenware shop and supplement these with different meshes of screens from the hardware store.

Carefully blow away any chaff that remains with the seeds so they are as clean as possible. This can be easily accomplished by placing the seeds in a small bowl or canning jar and, while tapping the bowl or jar, *gently and slowly* lower the nozzle of a vacuum cleaner into the jar so that only the chaff is removed, leaving the heavier seeds behind. This is easier if your vacuum cleaner allows adjustment of intensity of the air flow. Another way to remove the chaff is to place the seeds on an old sweater of coarse, heavy wool; the chaff, but not the seed, sticks to the wool. Clean seeds are ready to use for next year's garden, or they may be stored until sowing time. Sealing them in a jar in the refrigerator will lengthen their life, and this is more successful if the jar also contains a small packet of silica gel or other desiccant—even a small envelope of brown sugar could be substituted in a pinch—to absorb any residual moisture.

Herb Teas

Infusions of herbs in hot water have been drunk for centuries for pleasure as well as their perceived medicinal effects. Supermarket shelves are now stocked with many brands and combinations of herbs to be used as a tisane or tea. The public perceives herbs as generally safe to consume, and little has appeared in the popular press about the possible danger of drinking herb teas.

Several scientists have raised questions about the regular consumption of some herbal beverages. In addition, some herbs have the potential of carcinogenocity and should be avoided: bayberry (*Myrica cerifera*), calamus (*Acorus calamus*), coltsfoot (*Tussilago farfara*), comfrey (*Symphytum officinale*), golden ragwort (*Senecio aureus*), and sassafras (*Sassafras albidum*).

HERB
PROFILES

Acorus

āk-ō-rŭs
sweet flag

Family: Acoraceae
Growth form: herbaceous perennial to about 3 feet (1 m) high
Hardiness: hardy to Nova Scotia and Quebec (at least Zone 4)
Light: full sun
Water: constantly moist to edge of standing water
Soil: rich in organic matter, pH range 5.0 to 7.5, average 6.2
Propagation: divisions in spring
Culinary use: none (potentially carcinogenic)
Craft use: potpourri
Landscape use: edges of ponds, swampy wildflower garden

French: *calamus, acore vrai, acore odorant, calamus aromatique, ruseau aromatique*
German: *Kalmus*
Dutch: *kalmoes*
Italian: *calamo aromatico, acoro aromatico*
Spanish: *calamo aromático, acoro verdadero*
Swedish: *kalmus*
Chinese: *ch'ang-p'u*
Japanese: *ch'ang*
Arabic: *akaron, vaj*

Sweet flag or calamus resembles a yellow-green cattail and is scented in all its parts with a delicate combination of green leaves, roses, and orris with nuances of a clean, fatty odor. Its fragrance has been appreciated since ancient times; along with myrrh, cinnamon, cassia, and olive oil, the rhizomes of sweet flag were used in the Oil of Holy Ointment (Exodus 30:23). Calamus is rarely, if ever, used to season food, but in Joel Chandler Harris's Uncle Remus tales, Br'er

Rabbit touts the combination of chicken and calamus as so good that once he tasted it he never wanted the bird another way. It's just as well that the poultry dish never met wide public acceptance; calamus is now known to cause duodenal and liver cancer.

The dried rhizomes of sweet flag were once widely used in the preparation of bitters and vermouths, and the essential oil was used for the preparation of liqueurs and sweets; sometimes the rhizomes were candied. None of these uses are permitted today by the U.S. Food and Drug Administration. The leading component of the essential oil, beta-asarone, is carcinogenic (but sedative and reputedly hallucinogenic). High doses of rhizomes that are beta-asarone-free have been reported to relieve spasms or

Acorus calamus

cramps, but it is difficult to certify the rhizomes as free of beta-asarone, and so sweet flag should not be ingested. The essential oil prevents the growth of fungi and bacteria and also has potential use as an insecticide and mosquito repellent. The rhizomes, either whole or sectioned, are easily dried over screens and may be substituted for the traditional orris root in potpourri.

The genus *Acorus* consists of three species (*A. calamus*, *A. americanus*, and *A. gramineus* Ait.) of European, Asian, and North American wetlands, and the genus is in its own family, the Acoraceae. These are hardy, perennial herbs with tufted and iris-like or grass-like leaves arising from pencil- to cigar-shaped horizontal underground rhizomes (modified stems). Calamus produces tiny, inconspicuous, greenish flowers on a green, thick, fleshy spike (spadix) attached to the upper half of a leaf-like blade (spathe); this type of inflorescence is typical of the genus. Recent work on DNA has confirmed that *A. calamus* is the primal extant monocotyledon, i.e., sweet flag represents the oldest living lineage of the monocots. The treatment of *Acorus* in *Flora of North America* recognizes only two species, *A. calamus* and *A. americanus*. However, this treatment is based on research that did not examine the worldwide distribution of these species. In addition, herbarium specimens that we have seen, even those cited in this treatment, are not easily identified with this key. More research needs to be done. In the interim, we have combined the treatment in *Flora of North America* with research that examined the worldwide distribution and recognize two species, *A. calamus*, with two varieties, and *A. americanus*. *Acorus calamus* var. *calamus* is found in Europe and Asia and was introduced into North America by early European settlers; it is a sterile triploid that is vegetatively propagated. *Acorus calamus* var. *angustatus* has both temperate and subtropical forms distributed from East Asia and Japan to South Asia; it is a fertile tetraploid. *Acorus americanus* is distributed in northern North America; it is a fertile diploid. Humans have spread all three forms in their conquests and travels. The Mongolians (Tartars), invading Russia and Poland, brought sweet flag along with them in the belief that it purified water. Today, an attractive variegated cultivar, 'Variegata' (a tetraploid), is sometimes sold by those who also deal in waterlilies and lotus.

Sweet flag was once used for treating eye diseases, and thus its generic name, *Acorus*, is derived from the Greek word *akore*, meaning "without pupil." The specific name *calamus* comes from the Arabic *kalon*, and means "reed," referring to the iris or flag-like foliage.

While the scent is concentrated in the rhizomes, the blades, or rushes, are also scented and were once scattered on the floors of Medieval and Renaissance castles along with other "strewing herbs" such as lavender and pennyroyal, to ward off fleas, lice, and other vermin. Even the serfs and peasants gathered it for their humble homes, but sweet flag was especially appreciated in churches for religious holidays. During the era of King Henry VIII in England, one of the charges brought against Cardinal Wolsey was the extravagance shown by his liberal use of sweet flag rushes; the herb did not grow near London, and the rushes had to be brought from Norfolk and Suffolk at considerable expense.

Sweet flag is found in the wild growing along wet places and borders of quiet water in full sun and is easily cultivated in similar circumstances. In pots, this robust plant quickly outgrows its bounds and forms spreading clumps. Propagation is by division in early spring of the rhizomes; lift, then split them apart with a sharp shovel, and set the rhizomes at ground level.

Important chemistry: The essential oil of sweet flag rhizome (taxa usually not designated in the literature) consists primarily of trace to 96 percent beta-asarone, depending upon the geographical source; the content of beta-asarone is highest in some forms from Asia but lowest in those from Canada. In contrast, the alcoholic extract of sweet flag rhizome (which was once used in liqueurs) contains only 1,723 ppm beta-asarone and the major component is 5,246 ppm acorone. The chemical that gives the characteristic odor of green-fatty-rose-orris has been identified as (*Z,Z*)-4,7-decadienal. Other chemicals contributing to the odor of this very variable essential oil include 0 to 34 percent furanoeudesma-1,3-diene, 0 to 30 percent α-asarone, trace to 30 percent camphene, trace to 19

percent (*Z*)-beta-ocimene, 0 to 18 percent acorenone, 0 to 18 percent preisocalamenediol, 0 to 15 percent (*Z*)-sesquilavandul, 0 to 15 percent curzerene, 0 to 13 percent lindestrene, 0 to 13 percent isoshyobunone, 0 to 11 percent isocalamenediol, and 0 to 11 percent acorone.

Botanical Key and Description

Until a comprehensive worldwide analysis of this genus is conducted with modern techniques, we have merged the keys of Röst and Thompson. We do not consider this a satisfactory solution but only a momentary exigency.

Key:

1. Less than 19 air canals per 0.62 mm2 of the transverse section of leaf blades, midvein plus 1 to 5 additional veins equally raised above leaf surface . . . . *A. americanus*

1a. More than 25 air canals per 0.62 mm2 of the transverse section of the leaf blades; midvein prominently raised above leaf surface, other veins barely or not raised 2

2. 26 to 51 air canals per 0.62 mm2 of the transverse section of the leaf blades . . . . *A. calamus* var. *calamus*

2a. More than 71 air canals per 0.62 mm2 of the transverse section of the leaf blades . . . . *A. calamus* var. *angustatus* Bess., *Flora* 17 (Beibl. 1): 30. 1834 (*A. triqueter* Turcz. Ex Schott).

A. americanus (Raf.) Raf., New Fl. 1:57. 1836 (*A. calamus* L. var. *americanus* Raf.) and
A. calamus L., Sp. pl. 324. 1753.
Native country: Sweet flag occurs around the globe throughout northern regions of Asia, Europe, and North America.
General habit: Sweet flag is an herbaceous perennial to 1 m high.

Leaves: Leaves are 0.5 to 1 m long, 0.7 to 2 cm broad, borne on a rhizome.
Flowers: The leaf-like bract (spathe) subtends the inflorescence (spadix) and is prolonged 30 to 80 cm beyond the spadix.
Fruits/seeds: The inflorescence is a thick and fleshy spike, first appearing in late spring, 4 to 9 cm long, in fruit becoming 1.2 to 2 cm thick.

Agastache

ăg-ă-stā-kē
agastache

Family: Lamiaceae (Labiatae)
Growth form: short-lived herbaceous perennial to about 3 feet (1 m) high
Hardiness: many hardy to Wisconsin and Vermont (at least Zone 4)
Light: part shade to full sun
Water: does best in dry, well-drained soil
Soil: rich in organic matter, near pH 7.0
Propagation: seeds in spring
Culinary use: tea, substitute for French tarragon, flowers in salads; not GRAS
Craft use: dried flowers, potpourri
Landscape use: edges of shaded areas, mid-section of borders, bee plant

Agastache is derived from the Greek roots *agan*, "very much," and *stachys*, "spike," referring to the numerous flower spikes tightly packed with whorls of brightly colored pink, violet, blue, greenish yellow, or white flowers, reminiscent of hyssop (*Hyssopus officinalis*). All *Agastache* species are excellent ornamentals in the July garden and provide good bee forage. The flowering plants go very well with the silver-leaved species

Agastache

of mountain mint (*Pycnanthemum*), which flower about the same time.

Most of the thirty species of *Agastache* attract bees and produce abundant honey, but four species are most often found in herb gardens: *A. foeniculum*, *A. mexicana*, *A. rugosa*, and *A. scrophulariifolia*. Many of the offerings of "*A. foeniculum*" in the U.S. herb trade are actually *A. scrophulariifolia*, and one commercial seed listing, 'Fragrant Delight', is marketed as a mixture of species but is primarily *A. scrophulariifolia*. Adding further confusion, experts have found hybrids of *A. foeniculum* × *A. scrophulariifolia* in the cultivated material.

Agastache foeniculum, *A. rugosa*, and *A. scrophulariifolia* are generally stated to be anise-scented, but the principal component of anise, anethole, is not found in high amounts in *Agastache*. These plants might be more correctly described as basil or French tarragon-scented. Other scents revolve around peppermint and pennyroyal. Harvest leaves early in the day during a sunny, rain-free spell near flowering, then dry the leaves. While the leaves of all three species have been used as a substitute for French tarragon or brewed into tea and the flowers mixed in mesclun salads, no *Agastache* species has GRAS status. However, the flowers dry rather well, and both the leaves and flowers make good additions to potpourri.

Agastache species need little more than partly shaded to sunny, well-drained, acid to near-neutral soil. The seeds (actually tiny nuts, or nutlets) are most easily started by broadcasting; established clumps readily reseed themselves, often in tiny nooks and crannies. Alternatively, seeds may be sown in the greenhouse with transplants in six to eight weeks. Clumps generally last two to three years, becoming very woody at the base and eventually dying out.

The two-spotted cucumber beetle is an occasional pest in the garden, while green aphids may be attracted to these plants in the greenhouse.

Agastache foeniculum
ăg-ă-stā-kē fē-nĭk-ĕw-lŭm
anise hyssop

Agastache foeniculum derived its scientific name from its hay-like scent and its common name from its anise-like scent, although today the scent is more closely associated with basil or French tarragon. Alternate common names are blue giant hyssop, fennel giant hyssop, or fragrant giant hyssop. Attempts at commercial cultivation in Finland found 22 to 55 pounds (10 to 25 kg) dry, marketable drug per 1076 square feet (100 m2). Anise hyssop does not perform well as far south as Zone 9 because of the summer heat. The young, broad, dark green leaves are often tinted purple, especially in cool weather; the newly emerged leaves in spring are usually a medium shade of purple that goes well with spring bulbs. Flowers are commonly lavender-blue and borne above the purple-tinged

leaves, but a white-flowered form, 'Alabaster' (a.k.a. 'Alba'), has pale green leaves.

Important chemistry: The principal constituent of the essential oil of anise hyssop is usually 21 to 97 percent estragole (methyl chavicol), modified by trace to 20 percent germacrene D, 0 to 43 percent limonene, and 0 to 9 percent (*E*)-ocimene, providing a scent reminiscent of French tarragon or basil. One form has been reported with 29 percent gamma-cadinene, 16 percent alpha-cadinol, 12 percent beta-caryophyllene, and 11 percent spathulenol, providing a woody-floral odor. Another form has been reported with 50 percent spathulenol and 18 percent bornyl acetate, providing a balsamic odor. Still other forms have been reported with 27 to 37 percent isomenthone, 23 to 31 percent pulegone, and 2 to 16 percent estragole, which would be scented of peppermint-pennyroyal-French tarragon and are probably hybrids with *A. scrophulariifolia*.

Agastache mexicana
ăg-ă-stā-kē mĕk-sē-kâ-nå
Mexican giant hyssop

Mexican giant hyssop is often identified as "mosquito plant," but we find no evidence, anecdotal or otherwise, that this plant repels mosquitoes. To further add to the confusion, many commercial sources of *A. mexicana* germinate, instead, to the French tarragon-scented *A. foeniculum*. The true Mexican giant hyssop is usually scented of mint (although much unre-

ported chemical diversity undoubtedly exists in this species) and hardy only in Zones 9 and 10, although it can be grown as an annual elsewhere. The flowers are usually a pale rosy pink to near crimson; a rare white form has also been reported. Flowering spikes can reach up to one foot in favorable sites.

Important chemistry: The principal constituents of the foliar essential oil are 14 to 73 percent menthone and 14 to 75 percent pulegone, providing a peppermint-pennyroyal odor.

Agastache rugosa
ăg-ă-stā-kē rū-gō-så
Korean mint

Korean mint or wrinkled giant hyssop acquired its Latin name from the rugose, or wrinkled, leaves. The leaves of Korean mint are slightly larger than those of anise hyssop. Korean mint has rose to violet flowers and is otherwise similar to anise hyssop but slightly more tender. The essential oil is anti-fungal against *Trichophyton* species that cause tinea infections and has been found to selectively inhibit the proliferation of human cancer cells in vitro.

Important chemistry: As in anise hyssop, the principal constituent of the essential oil from the foliage is commonly 20 to 96 percent estragole with 0 to 45 percent isomenthone and 4 to 12 percent limonene, but a variant has been reported to contain 84 to 92 percent methyl eugenol and only 2 to 6 percent estragole. This latter variant is somewhat clove-scented in contrast to the French tarragon odor of the normal plant. A plant from China has been reported with 37 percent patchouliol and 12 percent alpha-guaiene, providing a woody, patchouli-like fragrance.

Agastache scrophulariifolia
ăg-ă-stā-kē skrōf-ū-lā-rē-ĭ-fō-lē-å
purple giant hyssop

Purple giant hyssop derives its specific name from the resemblance to the leaves of the genus *Scrophularia*. It is frequently cultivated in the U.S. herb trade as *A. foeniculum* but can be distinguished by its minty scent vs. the French tarragon scent of anise hyssop. Furthermore, the leaves of purple giant hyssop are green, rather than white, felty below as in anise hyssop.

Important chemistry: The essential oil of purple giant hyssop contains 26 to 50 percent isomenthone, 20 to 45 percent pulegone, and 11 to 16 percent limonene, providing a peppermint-pennyroyal odor.

Botanical Key and Description

Key:
1. Stamens two pairs, lower pair ascending under the upper lip, the upper pair thrust down and exserted between the lower pair. 2
    2. Corolla tube 7 to 10 mm long; calyx teeth 1.5 to 2.5 mm long; floral bracts lance-shaped, inconspicuous . . . . *A. rugosa*
    2a. Corolla tube mostly less than 7.5 mm long; calyx teeth 1 to 2 mm long; floral bracts egg-shaped, tapering to the apex or pinched at the tip, more or less conspicuous but shorter than the calyces . . . 3
        3. Leaves white beneath, feltlike; calyx hairy, blue at least distally. . . . . *A. foeniculum*
        3a. Leaves green beneath, not feltlike, calyx hairless, green, pale green or pink-tinged . . . .
        . . . . *A. scrophulariifolia*
1a. Stamens two pairs, parallel, both pairs exserted from the tube . . . . *A. mexicana*

A. foeniculum (Pursh) Kuntze, Rev. gen. pl. 511. 1891 [*A. anethiodora* Nutt. ex Britt., *Lophanthus anisatus* (Nutt.) Benth.].

Native country: Anise hyssop is native to the United States through Wisconsin, Minnesota, Iowa, North and South Dakota, to Wyoming and Colorado, and in Canada from western Ontario to Alberta.

General habit: This short-lived perennial is an erect herb coated with fine hairs, less than 1 m high.

Leaves: Leaves are opposite, egg-shaped or triangular-egg-shaped, the median mostly 5 to 8 cm long, 3 to 5 cm broad, tapering to the apex or somewhat pinched, rounded or tending to squared at the base, with sharp teeth; white, feltlike below.

Flowers: Spikes are 4 to 8 cm broad at maturity. Bracts are egg-shaped, pinched at the tip, mostly shorter than the calyces, uniformly coated with fine, spreading hairs, often violet-tinged. Calyces are coated with fine spreading hairs throughout, the tubes 5 to 7 mm long, the teeth narrowly triangular and tapering to the apex, 1 to 2 mm long, always violet-tipped except in albino forms. Corollas blue, the tubes 6.5 to 7.5 mm long.

Fruits/seeds: Nutlets are about 0.8 to 1.2 mm long.

A. mexicana (Humb., Bonpl. & Kunth) Lint & Epling, *Amer. Midl. Nat.* 33:227. 1945 [*Brittonastrum mexicanum* (Humb., Bonpl. & Kunth) Briq., *Cedronella mexicana* (Humb., Bonpl. & Kunth.) Benth., *Gardoquia betonicoides* Lindl.].

Native country: Mexican giant hyssop is a short-lived perennial native to Mexico.

General habit: This short-lived perennial is an erect, nearly smooth herb, 50 to 60 cm tall.

Leaves: Leaves opposite, lance-shaped or lance-egg-shaped, the median mostly 4 to 6 cm long, 1.5 to 2 cm broad, tapering to the apex, rounded or somewhat squared at the base, with sharp teeth.

Flowers: Spikes are 30 cm long and usually about 3 cm broad. The calyces are mostly green but more or less tinged with rose, the tubes 6.5 to 11.5 mm long, coated with fine, spreading hairs, the teeth narrowly triangular or triangular-lance-shaped (deltoid-lanceolate), tapering to the apex, 2.4 to 4 mm long. The corollas are rose or crimson, the tubes 19 to 27 mm long.

Fruits/seeds: Nutlets are 1.5 to 2 mm long.

A. rugosa (Fisch. & C. A. Mey.) Kuntze, Rev. gen. pl. 2:511. 1891 (*Lophanthus rugosus* Fisch. & C. A. Mey.).

Native country: Korean mint is native to China, Japan, and Korea.

General habit: This short-lived perennial is an erect, smooth or finely hairy herb, commonly 1 m tall.

Leaves: Leaves are opposite, egg-shaped, the median mostly 6 to 8 cm broad, generally pinched at the tip above the middle, mostly heart-shaped at the base, but sometimes rounded, with coarse, sharp teeth.

Flowers: Spikes are 5 to 10 cm long, mostly 1.5 to 2 cm broad. Bracts are lanceolate, thin, and inconspicuous. Calyces have fine hairs throughout, or smooth, tending to membranous, and often colored rose or violet, or white at the tips, the tubes 4 to 5 mm long at flower expansion, increasing somewhat at maturity, the mature teeth narrowly triangular, tapering to the apex, 1.5 to 2.5 mm long, rarely 3 mm. The corollas are violet, pallid, or rose, the tubes mostly 7 to 8 mm long, infrequently 10 mm.

Fruits/seeds: Nutlets are 2 mm long.

A. scrophulariifolia (Willd.) Kuntze, Rev. gen. pl. 2:511. 1891 (*Hyssopus scrophulariifolia* Willd.).

Native country: Purple giant hyssop is native to North America, from Ontario to South Dakota and South Carolina.

General habit: This short-lived perennial is an erect, smooth or finely hairy herb, commonly 1 m tall.

Leaves: Leaves are opposite, egg-shaped, the median mostly 8 to 15 cm long, 3.5 to 7 cm broad, generally pinched at the tip above the middle, mostly heart-shaped at the base, but sometimes rounded, with coarse, sharp teeth.

Flowers: Spikes are 5 to 50 cm long, mostly 1.5 to 2 cm broad. Bracts are egg-shaped, sharply pointed, hairless, tending to membranous and often colored at the margins, about as long as the calyces. Calyces are smooth, whitish or rose, the tubes 3 to 5 mm long at flower expansion, the mature teeth narrowly triangular, 2 mm long. The corollas are rose or purple, the tubes mostly 6 to 7 mm long.

Fruits/seeds: Nutlets are 1.5 mm long.

Allium

ål-ē-ŭm
allium

Family: Liliaceae

Growth form: herbaceous perennials

Hardiness: many hardy to Nova Scotia (at least Zone 5)

Light: full sun

Water: moist and well drained

Soil: soil rich in organic matter, pH 4.5 to 7.5, average 6.3 (*A. ampeloprasum*)

Propagation: seeds or bulbils in spring, 11,000 seeds per ounce (395/g) (*A. ampeloprasum*)

Culinary use: almost all foods except desserts

Craft use: dried bulbs or flower heads in wreaths

Landscape use: front of perennial border or vegetable garden

The Celtic *all*, which translates as "pungent" or "stinky," supplied the original basis for the Latin name of this genus, and it describes an aromatic characteristic that certainly epitomizes it. But who can imagine life without onions, garlics, and scallions? Certainly not the breath-mint industry!

These vegetables and herbs have the power to turn plain cooking into the spectacular, and the glorious things alliums do when combined with other foods are revered around the world; in addition, some alliums have reputed medical benefits as well. Most of the 700 species of *Allium* are also good garden ornamentals, while some, such as chives, function as both herb and ornamental.

The genus *Allium* consists of rhizomatous or bulbous plants, mostly perennial, that have subbasal hollow leaves and flowers in a terminal umbel that emerges from a membranous, leafy cap.

Allium ampeloprasum

ǎl-ē-ŭm ǎm-pěl-ō-prā-sǔm

elephant garlic

French: *ail d'orient*

German: *Pferdknobloch*

Elephant garlic is sometimes purchased as a larger version of regular garlic (*A. sativum*), but more than size differentiates the two. The simpler chemical composition of elephant garlic makes it milder than its smaller relative; it's so mild that it can be cooked and eaten as a vegetable. It is also known as giant garlic, jumbo garlic, great-headed garlic, or Mama La Salle's French garlic; the term elephant garlic may have been first used by Luther Burbank in 1919. The species also includes the pearl onion (*A. ampeloprasum* var. *sectivum* Lueder), ancestors of the leek (*A. porrum* L.), and the kurrat (*A. kurrat* Schweinf. ex K. Krause).

Few studies have been done on the medicinal value of elephant garlic, but researchers in Thailand found that it had beneficial effects on cutaneous immunological function, protecting against toxins.

Since elephant garlic is essentially sterile, it is propagated from the cloves (bulbils) covered with 1 to 4 inches (2.5 to 10 cm) of soil, 8 to 12 inches (20 to 30.5 cm) apart on raised rows. Choose soil in full sun that is well drained with a pH range between 6.5 to 7.0. The largest cloves will produce the largest bulbs; cull out the smallest cloves. Plant in the fall, fifteen to seventy-five days before the first frost. Since elephant garlic is shallow-rooted, irrigate to maintain even moisture; mulching may promote rotting but will allow winter protection in northern areas, and bulbs will be much larger following mild winters.

Elephant garlic is a heavy feeder and benefits from sidedressings of poultry or other manure. The new bulb will divide into distinct cloves around the time of flowering; flower stalks should be removed at this time because they divert energy from clove formation. About five percent of the cloves may never form new bulbs, but save them and replant. Bulbs are ready for harvest two to three weeks after leaves start to yellow. After bulbs are lifted, peel off one or two of the outer leaves to expose clean bulbs, trim off roots, then dry on a chicken-wire rack in the shade for three to seven days. The tops may also be left to braid bulbs together garlic-style. Finish curing at 80 to 100°F for four to six weeks or until the papery skin changes from pure-white to off-white and becomes crisp.

Where the weather does not expose the cloves to cold, they will sprout but fail to form new bulbs. To remedy this situation, vernalize the cloves by storing at 40 to 50°F between summer harvest and fall planting, but storage at less than 40°F (4.4°C) will produce misshapen bulbs.

Nematodes and other pathogens peculiar to alliums may multiply on the soil, so rotate to another crop after the elephant garlic is harvested. While few insects attack elephant garlic, it is vulnerable to some diseases, such as white rot.

Important chemistry: By low-temperature analysis (Si-HPLC), the oil of elephant garlic contains 28 to 29 percent S-2-propenyl methanesulfinothioate and 9 to 11 percent (*Z,Z*)-2,3-dimethyl-1,4-butanedithial S,S'-dioxide. By conventional high-temperature analysis (GC/MS), the oil of elephant garlic contains 55 percent diallyl disulfide and 31 percent allyl methyl disulfide.

Allium fistulosum

ål-ē-ŭm fĭs-tēw-lō-sŭm

Welsh onion, Japanese bunching onion

French: *ciboule*
German: *Winterzwiebel, Schnittzwiebel*
Italian: *cipoletta*
Spanish: *ceboletta*
Russian: *pjesotshnyi luk, kitaiski luk, tatarka, louka riezanets*
Chinese: *ts'ung, hiai, kiai, kiai-pe, chang fa*
Japanese: *negi*

The Latin name *fistulosum* describes the hollow green leaves. This is a versatile species with a broad geographical cultivation across Europe and Asia and hence many intergrading varieties, all derived from the wild *A. altaicum* Pall. The smaller forms may be used for seasoning in a manner similar to chives in salads, stews, soups, or vegetable medleys; alternatively, the larger forms may be consumed as vegetables (sometimes called "scallions," which also refers to the green tops of onions). In its native Southeast Asia, the cultivars of *A. fistulosum* can be subjectively divided into two groups: (1) *taai ts'ung* refers to the larger forms and (2) *koo ts'ung* (stable, or lasting, onion) includes the smaller plants. Listed commercial seed lines of Japanese bunching onion include 'Evergreen', 'Evergreen Long White', 'Ishikuro', 'Iwatsuki', 'Kujuhoso', 'Nebuka' ('He-shi-ko' or 'Japanese Bunching'), 'Prolific', and 'White Lisbon'. This species also includes forms known as multiplier onion (which proliferates bulbils in the inflorescence), cibol, and stone leek.

Few studies have been done on Welsh onion, but it has been found to be antioxidant due to both the enzymes and α-tocopherol content.

The Japanese bunching onion or Welsh onion is easily grown from seeds planted 6.5 mm (¼ inch) deep in circum-neutral garden loam high in nitrogen in early spring. Sow seeds in rows 14 to 18 inches (36 to 46 cm) apart and thin to 4 inches (10 cm) apart in each row. Allow the plants to grow to mature size the first year. You may harvest by cutting or uprooting as early as sixty days after planting, or, alternatively, up to the second year after planting. In the spring of the second year, transplant to trenches 6 inches (15 cm) deep and fill with garden soil to bleach the bases.

Japanese bunching onions are subject to attack by downy mildew (*Peronospora destructor*), purple blotch (*Alternaria porri*), and white rot (*Sclerotium cepivorum*).

Important chemistry: By low-temperature analysis (Si-HPLC), the oil of Japanese bunching onions consists of 33 percent S-1-propyl 1-propanesulfinothioate, 22 percent S-(*Z*)-1-propenyl methanesulfinthioate plus S-(*E*)-1-propenyl methanesulfinothioate, and 11 percent S-methyl 1-propanesulfinothioate. By conventional high-temperature analysis (GC/

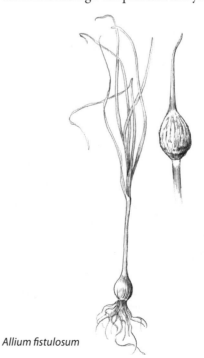

Allium fistulosum

MS), the volatile component of Japanese bunching onion consists primarily of 4 to 65 percent di-n-propyl disulfide, 7 to 53 percent 2-tridecanone, trace to 16 percent 2,3-dihydro-2-octyl-5-methylfuran-3-one, trace to 15 percent methyl-n-propyl disulfide, and up to 13 percent methyl propyl trisulfide.

Allium sativum
ăl-ē-ŭm să-tē-vŭm
garlic

- **French:** *ail commun*
- **German:** *Knoblauch*
- **Dutch:** *knoflook*
- **Italian:** *ai, aglio*
- **Spanish:** *ajo commún*
- **Portuguese:** *alho*
- **Swedish:** *vitlök*
- **Russian:** *tschesnok*
- **Chinese:** *suan*
- **Japanese:** *ninniku*
- **Arabic:** *toum*

The Latin name means "cultivated onion," while the common name is derived from the Anglo-Saxon *garleac*, or "spear-leek." Three botanical varieties are known, but many cultivars show combinations of characteristics from two or more varieties, and botanical classification seems to offer little advantage.

The var. *sativum* (garlic), alias the "stinking rose," needs no introduction. Juvenal and Pliny tell us mockingly that in Egypt garlic and onion were esteemed as gods; the Egyptians took their oaths upon them. Egyptian clay models of garlic bulbs date to 3000 B.C.E., and actual bulbs, dating to 1500 B.C.E., were found in the tomb of Tutankhamun. When the Israelites wandered in the desert, they recalled "the fish which we did eat in Egypt for nought; the cucumbers and melons, and the onions and the garlic" (Numbers 11:5, compiled c. 900–750 B.C.E.).

Since garlic is not native to the eastern Mediterranean (the ancestral species, *A. longicuspis* Regel, is native to south-central Asia, and a population of *A. sativum* with fertile pollen has been located in central Asia), it must have been one of the first cultivated plants. In addition, because garlic is usually vegetatively propagated, we may be consuming the exact ancient germplasm that our ancestors presented upon their tables with crusty bread and wine—an edible antiquity!

The var. *ophioscorodon* is the serpent garlic or rocambole, also known in French as *rocambole*, in German as *Rocambol*, in Italian as *aglio d'India*, in Chinese as *ta suan*, *hu suan*, or *hu*, and in Russian as *ispansky tschesnok*. Serpent garlic is similar to wild garlic in character and flavor. The semi-wild taste, combined with easily removed skins, makes serpent garlics popular gourmet items. However, serpent garlics require more management and skill in production. All of the serpent garlics produce woody flower stalks that produce not fertile flowers, but bulbils. Underground, around the central woody stalk, a circle of four to fourteen cloves is produced. The var. *pekinense*, or Peking garlic, called *ta suan* in China, is apparently similar to the serpent garlic and may be correctly classified with it.

The presence of many clones that show combined characteristics of all three varieties of *A. sativum* indicates that these taxa may not be correct; they are maintained here because of their frequent use.

Three cultivars of garlic grown extensively in California are 'California Early', 'California Late', and 'Creole' ('American'). 'California Early' produces the most abundant crop and is less fussy about day length. 'California Late' is the most popular variety around Gilroy, California. 'Creole' ('Mexican Pink') is also not daylength sensitive and is a major crop in Louisiana. 'Chileno' ('Chilleno'), 'Egyptian', 'Formosan', and 'Italian' seem to do well in southern and desert regions. 'Silverskin' is a name applied to many strains of garlic with white sheathing. 'German Red' and 'Valencia' do well in the eastern United States, while 'Susanville' thrives on the western coast. An Italian study found that 'Paceco' and 'Campobello di Licata Bianco' had the highest levels of allicin. Further discussions of garlic varieties are covered in the excellent catalog of Filaree Farm (182 Conconcully Hwy, Okanogan, WA 98840).

Intact garlic is odorless, but cellular disruption results in enzymatic breakdown and the release of odorous compounds. The essential oil is GRAS at 0.01 to 40 ppm.

Garlic is a mandatory ingredient of many southern European and central Asian dishes. Garlic is also effective against bacteria, stopping their action or killing them, depending upon the organism; fungus, especially yeast; internal parasites such as worms and protozoa; insects; and to some degree, nematodes. Garlic extracts do not repel mosquitoes, but garlic oil is an effective repellent for sandflies and birds. Does garlic have antithrombotic effects? Well, we know that processed garlic (oil, dried, cooked, etc.) has very little effect other than producing bad breath. Looking at fresh garlic, the overwhelming number of research papers show benefits to the heart. One clinical trial conducted at Stanford University, however, found no effect of fresh garlic on low density lipoproteins (LDL). Although this has received the most press, it must be put in perspective of the other potential cardiovascular benefits; more controlled studies are needed. Allicin is a potent blood thinner, dissolving blood clots. Garlic also retards lipoprotein oxidation, reduces hepatoxicity from toxins, lowers blood sugar, reverses tumor development, lowers blood pressure, relieves asthmatic symptoms, and relieves flatulence and abdominal distension. Garlic promotes healing of warts and corns. The diallyl sulfide in garlic offers protection against gastrointestinal cancer, but the mechanism may or may not be by inhibiting *Helicobacter pylori*. Refer to the selected references for the original scientific reports, pro and con, on these claims.

Fresh garlic has the highest content of active ingredients. Properly freeze-dried garlic is second to fresh garlic in activity, but further processing (encapsulating with soybean oil and so on) further lowers the active ingredients, and tests of commercial products show considerable variation from pill to pill and from batch to batch. The active principles are completely eliminated in deodorized products. Studies in the references that show garlic to be ineffective usually used commercially processed material, not fresh garlic.

Few negative effects, other than occupational asthma, contact dermatitis with prolonged handling, some gastrointestinal reactions in sensitive individuals, and bad breath have been confirmed for garlic. Bad breath from garlic primarily results from tiny pieces remaining on the teeth and gums; vigorous brushing, mouthwash, fresh lemon juice, and chewing parsley have been recommended but never fully tested. Milk or milk components will reduce the odor of garlic. Confirmed garlic lovers will also find their body odor altered by garlic consumption; little is recommended for this problem other than (1) don't sweat, (2) keep your mouth shut, and (3) choose your friends wisely.

Selections of *Allium sativum* are generally sterile and are propagated from the cloves (the cloves, or bulbils, are often called "seed," while the entire bulbs are called "sets") covered (pointed ends up) with 1 to 2 inches (2.5 to 5 cm) of soil and planted 3 to 6 inches (8 to 15 cm) apart and 12 to 32 inches (30.5 to 80 cm) between rows in fall three to four weeks before the ground freezes in well-drained, highly organic loam with a slightly acid pH (6.5 to 6.7); a position in full sun is necessary.

Planting recommendations for the eastern United States, on a per-acre basis, include 1,375 pounds (624 kg), or 10,400 bulbs, planted 4 inches (10 cm) apart and 18 inches (45.7 cm) between rows, assuming each bulb weighs 2 ounces and only the six to eight largest cloves of each bulb are used. To best avoid disease build-up, plant in soil where onions have not been grown in the past five years.

Garlic yields in California are highest when 100 to 200 pounds nitrogen per acre is applied at planting (112 to 114 kg/ha). In the east, adequate yields may be achieved with the application of 35 to 60 pounds per acre (39 to 67 kg/ha) in the fall, and another 20 pounds per acre (22 kg/ha) applied once or twice in the spring. Rotation of land with legumes may help to reduce these inputs of nitrogen. Soils low in sulfur will also benefit from 2.2 pounds sulfur per acre (5 kg/ha), while soils low in phosphorus will benefit from the application of 235 pounds per acre (263 kg/ha.).

Home gardeners should add 2 to 3 pounds (0.9 to 1.4 kg) of a common 5-10-5 fertilizer or its equivalent to every 100 square feet (9 square meters) of garden area. Distribute 1 pound (0.5 kg) of the same fertilizer along a 50-foot (15 m) row as a sidedressing. Since the largest cloves will produce the largest bulbs, cull out the small-est cloves. Mulch lightly with straw for winter protection, increased yields, and suppression of weeds. Studies done in Illinois showed that black plastic mulch produced greater marketable weights and bulb diameters than bare soil or a wheat straw mulch treatment. Garlic cloves may also be planted in spring six weeks before the last frost, but the resulting bulbs will not be as large as those sown in autumn.

Temperature and day length are extremely important in garlic production. Garlic requires temperatures below 40°F (4.4°C) for six to eight weeks to vernalize the plant. Once vernalized, the plant initiates bulbing when the day length reaches approximately thirteen hours and soil temperatures are above 60°F (15.6°C). Prolonged temperatures below 32°F (0°C) cause rough-shaped bulbs and small axillary cloves. Temperatures above 80°F (26.8°C) speed up bulb formation under favorable day length. Warm temperatures continuously above 60°F (15.6°C) and/or days with fewer than twelve hours daylight prevent bulbs from forming.

Maintain even moisture during the growing season, using a mulch if possible. Irrigation should be adequate to moisten the soil to a depth of 12 to 18 inches (30.5 to 45.7 cm) for proper bulb development. While moisture is critical as the bulb develops from late May until July, withhold additional water two to three weeks before harvest. Vegetative growth is greatest around 61°F (16°C) in short days, while bulbs are formed and enlarged in long days with temperatures above 68°F (20°C).

The flowering stalks of garlic should be removed to assure energy focus on the bulb; flowering stalks may be finely chopped and used for salads and garlic butter. The bulbs are ready to harvest when the leaves turn yellow, weaken, and fall over. As a second test of harvest readiness, inspect the leaves at the soil level near the bulb; they turn from a succulent, fleshy texture to a dry, papery sheath at harvest time.

Once the bulbs are lifted, peel off one or two of the outer leaves to expose the clean bulb and trim off roots. If you wish to braid the tops, leave them on and do so while they are somewhat dry but remain pliable. Dry in a shady place with a relative humidity of 60 to 70 percent and temperatures of 60 to 70°F (15.6 to 21.0°C); allow a week or two for drying. Chicken-wire racks work well for drying. Finish curing at 80 to 100°F for four to six weeks or until the papery skin changes from pure-white to off-white and becomes crisp.

Prolonged storage of garlic at 39°F (4°C) and above and at humidities greater than 70 percent will lead to high losses due to sprouting and mold, respectively. Optimum storage conditions for garlic are eight to ten days at 68 to 86°F (20 to 30°C), followed by temperature reduction to 32°F (0°C) and maintenance at 32±0.9°F (0±0.5°C) and relative humidity of 65 to 70 percent with permanent air circulation. Under these conditions, storage life is 130 to 220 days, depending on cultivar type and cultivation practices. Garlic may also be dehydrated at a maximum temperature of 140°F (60°C).

In general, 2.2 pounds (1 kg) of planted garlic yields 11 to 15 pounds (5 to 7 kg) harvested. Yields reflect the garlic variety used, soil quality, moisture, nutrition, weed competition, and planting density. Good garlic yields in California (with denser populations of plants) are 10 tons per acre (22,417 kg/ha) for dehydrator garlic and 7 tons per acre (19,054 kg/ha) for fresh-market garlic.

Grade standards for garlic include "USDA No. 1" and "unclassified." USDA No. 1 consists of garlic of similar varietal characteristics with mature, compact, plump cloves free from mold, dirt, sunburn stains, cuts, sprouts, roots, in-

sects, or other mechanical damage. An unclassified grade does not meet USDA No. 1.

Reductions in yields may indicate the presence of viruses, particularly onion yellow dwarf virus, and virus-free stock should be sought. The most damaging pest in commercially grown garlic in America is the stem and bulb nematode (*Ditylenchus dipsaci*), followed by onion thrips (*Thrips tabaci*). Army worms, wireworms, and the onion maggot (*Hylemya antiqua*) are minor pests. Garlic is subject to attacks of downy mildew (*Peronospora destructor*), basal or bottom rot (*Fusarium oxysporum*), clove rot (*Penicillium corymbiferum*), white rot (*Sclerotium cepivorum*), onion smut (*Urocystis magica*), neck rot (*Botrytis allii*), and pink root (*Pyrenochaeta terrestris*). The crop of garlic in California has been particularly beset with garlic rust (*Puccinia allii*), and the most environmentally friendly solution has been selection of resistant cultivars. Stored bulbs may be attacked by the eriophyid mite (*Aceria tulipae*). Gophers are also reputed to like garlic.

The information just supplied for garlic also generally applies to rocambole.

California, especially the area centered around Gilroy, leads in the domestic production of fresh and dehydrated garlic. Dehydrated garlic is also imported, mainly from Taiwan and mainland China.

Important chemistry: By low-temperature analysis (Si-HPLC), the oil of garlic contains 59 to 89 percent S-2-propenyl 2-propene-1-sulfinothioate and 3 to 27 percent S-propenyl methane-sulfinothioate. By conventional high-temperature analysis (GC/MS), garlic oil contains of 30 to 74 percent diallyl disulfide, 2 to 61 percent allyl methyl trisulfide, 6 to 42 percent diallyl trisulfide, trace to 33 percent allyl methyl disulfide, trace to 32 percent diallyl sulfide, and trace to 10 percent dimethyl trisulfide. Diallyl disulfide is formed from allicin (2-propenyl 2-

propenethiosulfinate, up to 0.4 percent of fresh bulbs), which, in turn, is formed from odorless, sulfur-containing amino acid alliin (S-(2-propenyl)-L-cysteine S-oxide, 0.9 percent of fresh bulbs) by the enzyme alliinase upon crushing or bruising the bulb. (E) and (Z)-ajoene [(E)- and (Z)-4,5,9-trithiadodeca-1,6,11-triene-9-oxide]

are also formed by self-condensation of allicin. The major components in human breath after ingestion of garlic are 2-propene-1-thiol and diallyl disulfide. The principal lacrimatory (tear-causing) factor of onion, (Z)-propanethiol S-oxide, is absent from garlic.

Allium schoenoprasum

ăl-ē-ŭm skĕ-nō-pră-sŭm

chives

> **French:** *ciboulette*
> **German:** *Schnittlauch*
> **Dutch:** *bieslook*
> **Italian:** *erba cipollina, aglio di serpe*
> **Spanish:** *cebolleta, cebollino*
> **Portuguese:** *ceboletas de França, cebolinha*
> **Swedish:** *gräslök*
> **Russian:** *luk-rezanyets*
> **Chinese:** *hsia-ye-ts'ung*
> **Japanese:** *asatsuki*
> **Arabic:** *basal*

The marriage of chives from the Old World and potatoes from the New World was truly inspired. Baked potatoes with sour cream and chives is a standard offering in American restaurants, although cut onion or Japanese bunching onion tops are sometimes substituted for chives. Pennsylvania German potato salad is incomplete without chives. The leaves of chives are used for soups, salads, and vegetable dishes. The edible colored blossoms may be pickled in vinegar. Chives are considered GRAS (Generally Recognized As Safe) by the U.S. Food and Drug Administration.

The Latin name *schoenoprasum* was derived from the Greek name for leek, while chive is an English corruption of the Latin *cepa*, or onion.

"Large" chives, called *Alpenschnittlauch* in Germany, have been separated as var. *alpinum* Gaudin, but these garden forms cannot be reliably associated with wild material. Both the wild and garden plants have hybridized; large chives have double the normal number of chromosomes of the normal or "fine" chives. One botanical form (*f. albiflorum* Döll.) is listed with white flowers, and a selected form (by Mark McDonough) is 'Corsican White'. Other chives cultivars include 'Grosser Riesen', 'Mittelgrosser Schnittlauch', 'Feiner Schnittlauch',

Allium schoenoprasum

and 'Forescate', which has pink flowers. A cultivar of large chives is 'Fruhlau'.

Chives grow easily in full sun in a moist, near-neutral garden loam. Chives may be grown from seeds, and clumps should be divided every three or four years. Chives' native habitat is stream banks and damp meadows; the herb will not withstand prolonged drought. Topdressings of nitrogen at 45 pounds per acre (50 kg/ha) should be given during the season according to the vigor of the crop and level of production required. One study in sandy soil in Florida found that topdressings of 14 to 28 pounds per acre (16 to 31 kg/ha) per week of each nitrogen and potassium oxide in liquid fertilizer is a desirable range of fertilization; much higher rates, above 56 pounds, result in yield reduction and excess fertilizer accumulation. Organic mulch improves the yields, and grass straw is particularly recommended.

At home, harvest chives as needed, taking the outside leaves first rather than shearing the entire plant. One study in Germany found that the base and center were "juicier and crisper," while the tips were "strawy/fibrous and drier."

In commercial production, where this is not feasible, the entire clump of plants is cut 2 inches (5 cm) above the ground, but the clump regenerates only after several weeks, and then with very tender new growth. Cutting also encourages new bulbets and discourages flowering. Chives may also be forced for winter consumption.

For storage, chives may be freeze-dried; those that are fast-frozen under low pressure (0.1 mm Hg) are superior to those slow-frozen and dehydrated under higher pressure (1.5 mm Hg). Chives are subject to attack by downy mildew (*Peronospora destructor*) and onion smut (*Urocystis magica*).

Important chemistry: By low-temperature analysis (Si-HPLC), the oil of chives contains 58 percent S-1-propyl 1-propanesulfinothioate, 16 percent S-n-propyl (*E*)-propenesulfinothioate, and 15 percent S-propyl methanesulfinothioate. By conventional high-temperature analysis (GC/MS), the oil of chives contains primarily of 8 to 65 percent di-n-propyl disulfide and up to 23 percent methyl-n-propyl disulfide.

Allium tricoccum

ăl-ē-ŭm trī-cŏ-kŭm

ramps

If you are unfamiliar with ramps, the name *pikwute sikakushia* ("the skunk") of the midwestern Menominee Indians says it all. According to legend, Shikako was once a favorite ramps-gathering place in rich woodlands near the southern end of Lake Michigan; ergo, Chicago. Ramps are a potent substitute for garlic, and as one of the first wild edibles to appear in spring, they are truly a spring tonic. Ramps festivals, where they are fried and served with ham,

beans, cornbread, and greens, are a popular rite of spring in the Appalachians. Ramps omelettes and ramps with morels are also delicious.

The name "ramps" can be traced to early English dialects that survived in the semi-isolated communities of the Appalachians; the word was derived from the European "ramsoms" (properly *A. ursinum* L.). Ramps are distinctive in that they bear a broad, flat leaf that disappears by flowering time in midsummer. While usually harvested from the wild, ramps may be cultivated in partial shade in a well-drained but moist soil rich in leafmold. Seed germination can take up 18 months, so bulbs,

Allium tricoccum

transplanted September to March, are recommended for the beginner. Plant bulbs 3 inches deep and 4 to 6 inches apart, keeping just the tip of the bulb above the surface of the soil. Mulch the bed with 2 to 3 inches of leaf litter. When harvesting, take 5 to 10 percent but no

more than 15 percent of the ramps. Harvesting should be carefully done with a handheld ramp "digger" tool, similar to a mattock. Ramps have no GRAS (Generally Recognized As Safe) status from the U.S. Food and Drug Administration.

Important chemistry: Analysis of supercritical fluid extracts (SFE) of frozen ramps analyzed by LC-APCI-MS (liquid chromatography-atmospheric pressure chemical ionization-mass spectrometry) revealed 26.7 percent allicin, 2 to 25 percent methanesulfinothioic acid S-(*E*)-1-propenyl ester/methanesulfinothioic acid/methanesulfinothioic acid S-(*Z*)-1-propenyl ester/(*E*)-1-propenesulfinothioic acid S-methyl ester, 7 to 34 percent methanesulfinothioic acid S-2-propenyl ester/2-propene-1-sulfinothioic acid S-methyl ester, trace to 17 percent methanesulfinothioic acid S-methyl ester, 8 to 29 percent 2-propene-1-sulfinothioic acid S-(*E*)-1-propenyl ester/2-propene-1-sulfinothioic acid S-(*Z*)- 1-propenyl ester/(*E*)-1-propenesulfinothioic acid S-2-propenyl ester, and related compounds.

Allium tuberosum

ăl-ē-ŭm tū-bĕ-rō-sŭm

garlic chives, Chinese chives, Oriental chives

Russian: *kitaiski tschesnok*
Chinese: *jiu*
Japanese: *nira-negi*
Javanese: *puchai, pootjaj*

Just as Europeans are devoted to European chives (*A. schoenoprasum*), the Chinese prefer their own *A. tuberosum*. The flat-leaved garlic chives is native to eastern Asia, and the Chinese have a number of names for this plant: *jiu cai*

(green garlic chives), *jiu huang* (blanched garlic chives), *gow choy, cuchay,* or *kiu-ts'ai*.

Versatile garlic chives may be used in a manner similar to chives, onions, or garlic, but the taste is most similar to a delicate garlic. Add garlic chives only during the last minutes of cooking to avoid stringiness. The buds and blossoms are also edible and may be pickled in vinegar. Garlic chives have no GRAS (Generally Recognized As Safe) status from the U.S. Food and Drug Administration.

While garlic chives may enliven a stir-fry, they are sometimes unwanted in the garden. The prolific seeds seem to sprout everywhere, and kneeling on a clump of garlic chives surprises both the senses and the laundry bill. Dead-heading, or removal of the blossoms before seed-set, can be practiced, but because individual clumps are often short-lived, some seeds may be allowed to form.

The traditional Chinese method of growing garlic chives is direct sowing of fresh seeds into beds 3 feet by 15 feet (1 × 5 m) in 4-inch (10 cm) deep drills as soon as the ground can be worked in the spring. Faster and more even germination results from pre-germinated seed: (1) soak seeds overnight in warm water, (2) strain off water, (3) wrap in clean wet cloth, (4) place them at 65 to 76°F (18 to 25°C) for four to five days, (5) sow, and (6) cover with a thin layer of straw. The following spring, transplant in clumps of twenty to thirty seedlings 4 to 6 inches (10 to 15 cm) apart in rows 20 inches (51 cm) apart.

The range of optimum temperature for growth of Korean germplasm is between 68°F (20°C) and 77°F (25°C). Leaves can be harvested the second year, with three harvests per season. After the third or fourth year, the chives plants deteriorate.

In China, the leaves are commonly blanched under clay "chimney pots" and topdressed with ½ to 2 inches (1.5 to 5 cm) sand to produce delicately flavored yellow leaves. A well-grown clump can yield over 8 pounds (4 kg) of chives per year. Garlic chives may also be forced for winter production.

Important chemistry: By low-temperature analysis (Si-HPLC), the oil of garlic chives consists of 72 percent S-methyl methanesulfinothioate and 13 percent S-2-propenyl methanesulfinothioate. By conventional high-temperature analysis (GC/MS), the volatile component of garlic chives consists primarily of 5 to 57 percent methyl allyl disulfide, 7 to 39 percent dimethyl disulfide, and 6 to 27 percent dimethyl trisulfide.

Botanical Key and Description

Key:
1. Leaves cylindrical and hollow 2
   2. Naked flowering stems inflated . . . . *A. fistulosum*
   2a. Naked flowering stems not inflated . . . . *A. schoenoprasum*
1a. Leaves flat, not hollow 3
   3. Bulb consisting of 1 to 60 bulbils enclosed within a common membrane; flowers often displaced by bulbils 4
      4. Convex inflorescence with youngest flowers in center (umbel) 2.5 to 5 cm in diameter, flowers mostly abortive, bulbils frequent . . . . *A. sativum*
      4a. Convex inflorescence with youngest flowers in center (umbel) 5 to 9 cm in diameter, some fertile seed set, bulbils infrequent . . . . *A. ampeloprasum*
   3a. Bulb consisting of 1 to 3 bulbils enclosed within a common membrane; flowers not displaced by bulbils 5
      5. Leaves 3 to 9 cm wide . . . . *A. tricoccum*
      5a. Leaves 2 to 6 mm wide . . . . *A. tuberosum*

A. ampeloprasum L., Sp. pl. 294. 1753.

Native country: *A. ampeloprasum* is native to southern and western Europe.

General habit: Elephant garlic is a perennial herb reaching to 1.5 m when flowering.

Leaves: Each bulb bears four to ten flat, keeled leaves with rough margins, 50 cm × 5 to 40 cm, sheathing one-third to one-half of the stem.

Flowers: The pink to purple-red (usually sterile) flowers are borne on a dense convex inflorescence with the youngest flowers in the center 5 to 9 cm in diameter, subtended by a deciduous scape 4 to 11.5 cm on a bract (scape).

Bulbs: Bulbs are 2 to 6 cm in diameter; outer tunics are membranous covering eight to fourteen yellowish cloves (bulbils).

A. fistulosum L., Sp. pl. 301. 1753.

This cultivated species is derived from the wild *A. altaicum* Pall. Many botanical varieties have been described but not thoroughly compared.

Native country: Welsh onion or Japanese bunching onion is unknown in a wild state but originated in eastern Asia, where it is widely cultivated. It is cultivated as a vegetable/herb in Europe and found as an occasional escape.

General habit: Japanese bunching onion is a perennial herb reaching to 12 to 70 cm when flowering.

Leaves: The two to six completely hollow, terete leaves are 6 to 30 cm × 5 to 15 mm wide, circular in cross section, smooth, upright, and shorter than or as long as the scape.

Flowers: The whitish flowers are borne in a dense convex inflorescence with the youngest flowers in the center, 1.5 to 5 cm in diameter, subtended by a 1 to 2 cm spathe on an inflated bract.

Bulbs: The bulbous base is cylindrical, 1 to 2.5 cm in diameter, attached to a short rhizome; the membranous outer tunics are at first white, later brown.

A. sativum L., Sp. pl. 296. 1753.

Native country: *A. sativum* probably originated from *A. longicuspis* Regel of south-central Asia and spread with nomadic tribes.

General habit: Garlic is a perennial herb growing 25 to 200 cm high.

Leaves: Garlic bears six to twelve leaves, circular in cross-section, which are up to 60 cm long × 12 to 30 mm wide, linear, flat, and keeled. The leaves sheath the lower one-half of the naked flower stem.

Flowers: The few pinkish flowers are often sterile and replaced by bulbils in a dense, convex inflorescence with the youngest flowers in the center and measuring 2.5 to 5 cm in diameter. The flowers are subtended by a bract up to 9¾ inches (25 cm) long on a scape 25 to 200 cm high.

Bulbs: The bulbs are 3 to 6 cm in diameter and have five to sixty bulbils, or cloves, all enclosed within a silky white or pink membranous tunic.

Allium tuberosum

Key:

1. Leaves narrowly linear, under 2 cm wide, narrowing upward... 2
    2. Leaves somewhat keeled, rough on the edges; naked flowering stem before blooming mostly
        upright; bulbils uniformly long .... var. *sativum*
    2a. Leaves flat, not rough, smooth on the edges; naked flowering stem before blooming crooked or
        coiled worm-like; bulbils uniformly round............ var. *ophioscordon* (Link) Döll, Rhein Fl. 197. 1843.
1a. Leaves broadly linear, over 2 cm wide, limp, more or less twisted together, later almost falling on the
    ground............................... var. *pekinense* (Prikh.) Maek. apud Makino, Ill. Fl. Japan. 748. 1954.

A. schoenoprasum L., Sp. pl. 301. 1753.

Native country: Chives are native to northern regions of Europe, Asia, and North America.

General habit: *A. schoenoprasum* is a perennial herb 5 to 61 cm high. The morphology is diverse and encompasses at least three subspecies.

Leaves: Chives bear one or two hollow leaves, circular in cross-section, up to 35 cm × 1 to 6 mm, sheathing the lower one-third of the stem.

Flowers: The lilac to rose flowers are borne in an convex inflorescence with the youngest in the center, 1.5 to 5 cm in diameter, subtended by a bract up to 1.5 cm long on a naked flowering stem.

Bulbs: The bulbous bases are $^3/_{16}$ to $^3/_8$ inch (0.5 to 1 cm) in diameter and form firm tufts; the outer tunics are membranous, sometimes splitting into leathery strips.

Key:

1. Umbel hemispherical, globose, or fasciculate; tepals lanceolate, acute 2
    2. Umbel globose or hemispherical; pedicels two or three times shorter than the perianth ....
        .... subsp. *schoenoprasum*
    2a. Umbel arranged in a tight bundle, 1.5 to 2 cm in diameter; pedicels equal or shorter than the
        perianth; style equal or slightly longer than the tepals..
        ....subsp. *latiorifolium* (Pau) Rivas Martinez et al., Opusc. Bot. Pharm. Complut. 2:103, 1986.
1a. Umbel globose; tepals broad-lanceolate, obtuse ....
    .... subsp. *orosiae* Montserrat, Soc. Ech. Pl. Vasc. Eur. Occid. Bassin Medit. Bull. 19:110, 1984.

A. tricoccum Solander in Aiton, Hort. kew. (ed. 1) 1:428, 1789.

Native country: Ramps are native to North America from Nova Scotia to Georgia, west to the eastern Dakotas.

General habit: *A. tricoccum* is a perennial herb 15 to 40 cm high when flowering.

Leaves: Ramps bear two or three fleshy, flat leaves, widest in the center with the two ends equal or lance-shaped with narrowed base leaves, 15 to 40 × 3 to 9 cm.

Flowers: When the leaves turn yellow, the 20 to 60 cream-colored flowers are borne in a hemispherical convex inflorescence with the youngest flowers in the center, subtended by a bract about as long as the inflorescence on a naked flowering stem; both scapes and bracts are red.

Bulbs: The bulbs are slenderly ovoid, 4 to 6 × 1.5 to 3 cm, forming a crown on a rhizomatous base; the tunic is fleshy.

A. tuberosum Rottler ex Spreng., *Syst. Veg.* 2:38, 1825 (*A. odorum* auct.).

Native country: Garlic chives are native to eastern Asia.

General habit: *A. tuberosum* is a perennial herb 30 to 45 cm high when flowering.

Leaves: Garlic chives bear 2 to 5 flat leaves, 25 cm × 2 to 6 mm.

Flowers: The many fragrant flowers are white with a brownish or greenish nerve and borne in a convex inflorescence with the youngest flowers in the center subtended by a bract, 4 to 5 × 2 mm.

Bulbs: One to three bulbs are clustered together and attached to a horizontal rhizome; tunics are brownish.

Aloysia citriodora

ă-lō-ĭs-ē-a sĭ-trĭ-ō-dôr-å
lemon verbena

Family: Verbenaceae
Growth form: shrub to 8 feet (2.4 m)
Hardiness: coastal North Carolina (Zone 8) with protection
Light: full sun
Water: moist but not constantly wet
Soil: friable and porous
Propagation: cuttings in summer
Culinary use: teas and desserts
Craft use: potpourri
Landscape use: container plant or protected next to house; may be pruned into standards

French: *verbein citronelle, verbein odorante*
German: *Zitronenkraut, Punschkraut*
Italian: *erba Luisa, limoncina, cedrina*
Spanish: *cedrón, yerba Luisa*

Lemon verbena was very popular with Victorian ladies, who tucked sprigs into hankies or floated them in finger bowls, or simply rubbed the herb on their necks for its refreshing scent. Lemon verbena is a shrub with arching stems and narrow, pointed, pale green leaves in whorls of three or four. The tiny, almost scentless, pale pink or white flowers appear from April to August.

The Latin name of the genus was published by Palau in 1784 to honor Maria Luisa, Princess of Parma, wife of King Charles IV of Spain; the specific epithet refers to the delicious lemony odor of the leaves (the original publication of Palau was *Aloysia citrodora*, but the Interna-

Aloysia citriodora

tional Code of Botanical Nomenclature allows this to be treated as a spelling error). The genus includes thirty-seven species of the Americas.

Lemon verbena, or verbena, is considered one of the best lemon-scented herbs. It is cultivated for its essential oil, concrète, and absolute in France, Algeria, and Morocco. The leaves are prized for tea or as a flavoring in food, especially desserts. Leaves or oil of lemon verbena add a superb lemon fragrance to potpourri and sachets. Oil of verbena was once widely used in fragrance compositions, but the presence of up to more than 1 percent (Z)- and (E)-isocitral (artifacts of steam distillation) produces photosensitization of skin, so concrètes and absolutes are preferred in perfumery. Extracts and tinctures of verbena are also used in the formulation of liqueurs, and the liquid extract has GRAS status. Lemon verbena oil is also somewhat antifungal. The leaves are antioxidant and may be effective as a digestive aid. Japanese researchers identified acetoside (verbascoside) as a pain-relieving principle in alcoholic extracts of the herb. Mexican researchers have documented the antidiarrhoeal activity of lemon verbena oil as due to one minor compound, nonanal.

Lemon verbena is marginally hardy in Zone 8; at this extreme of its hardiness it should be protected from excessive frost and wind; it's best to plant it along a south wall. For added winter protection, it may also be cut back and mulched with straw. Most gardeners, however, treat lemon verbena as a tender perennial and grow it as a potted plant that can be wintered in the house or in a cool greenhouse.

Lemon verbena prefers a near-neutral garden loam and full sun if grown outside, but pot culture demands a very friable, porous soil; a peat/perlite mixture with water-soluble fertilizer works well, but heavy, wet soils spell its death. In a cool greenhouse during the winter, lemon verbena often drops its leaves and appears dead, but leaves typically reappear when the temperature and day length increase. Plants grown during winter with supplemental light to extend the day to twelve hours remain evergreen, continue to grow, and produce flowers in the spring. Plants should be pruned to maintain a bushy appearance and may be successfully grown as standards.

Lemon verbena is best propagated by cuttings from new growth, although it may also be grown from layers or seeds (in cooler climates, seeds do not always fully ripen). Lemon verbena is highly susceptible to spider mites and whiteflies, particularly under hot, dry conditions.

Important chemistry: The essential oil of typical lemon verbena consists of 11 to 38 percent geranial, 6 to 30 percent neral, and 4 to 23 percent limonene, providing a rich lemony odor. The geranial + neral (citral) content is highest in November to December in Chile. Oil from plants cultivated in Argentina revealed 37 percent myrcenone, 13 percent alpha-thujone, and 9 percent lippifoli-1(6)-en-5-one with a citrusy tansy odor, while plants cultivated in Morocco had 12 percent 1,8-cineole and 10 percent geranial and a lemony eucalyptus odor. Two other forms from Argentina had either 40 percent limonene and 22 percent citronellal or 73 percent beta-thujone. The oil of the flowers from plants cultivated in Argentina is rich in 31 percent myrcenone and 17 percent alpha-thujone. The major flavonoid from the leaves is luteolin 7-diglucuronide.

Botanical Description

A. citriodora Palau, Bot. Parte Práct. Bot. 1:768. 1784 [*Lippia citriodora* Kunth in Humb. & Bonpl., *A. triphylla* (L'Hér.) Britton, *L. triphylla* (L'Hér.) Kuntze].

Native country: Lemon verbena is native to Argentina.

General habit: Lemon verbena grows as a shrub or small tree, 1 to 2.5 m high.

Leaves: Leaves are lance-shaped, 3.5 to 7.5 cm by 1 to 1.5 cm, in whorls of three or four, short-stalked, smooth, and densely covered beneath with lemon-scented oil glands.

Flowers: Appearing in very late fall, the flowers are white, pink, or pale lilac, 6 mm long in axillary or terminal compound inflorescences with the younger flowers at the apex.

Fruits/seeds: The fruit is dry, becoming two separate nutlets.

Anethum graveolens

å-nē-thŭm grå-vē-ō-lĕnz
dill

Family: Apiaceae (Umbelliferae)

Growth form: annual to 20 inches (50 cm, *A. graveolens*) or 40 inches (100 cm, *A. sowa*)

Hardiness: seedlings can withstand minor frost

Light: full sun

Water: moist but not constantly wet

Soil: light, pH 5.0 to 8.2, average 6.5 (*A. graveolens*)

Propagation: seeds in spring, 27,000 seeds per ounce (952/g)

Culinary use: vinegars, pickles, baked goods, and so on

Craft use: none

Landscape use: short-lived; use at rear of border, best in vegetable plot

French: *aneth*
German: *Dill, Indische Dille*
Dutch: *dille, iundische dil*
Italian: *aneto puzzolente*
Spanish: *éneldo, anega*
Portuguese: *endro, aneto*
Swedish: *dill*
Russian: *ukrop*
Chinese: *shih lo*
Japanese: *diru*

Arabic: *shibith*
Hindi: *sowa*
Sanskrit: *satapushpi*

Dill has been cultivated since at least 400 B. C.E. and is mentioned in the New Testament (Matthew 23:23) in Christ's sevenfold condemnation of the Pharisees: "Woe unto you, scribes and Pharisees, hypocrites! for ye pay tithe of mint and dill [incorrectly translated as anise in the King James version of 1611] and cumin, and

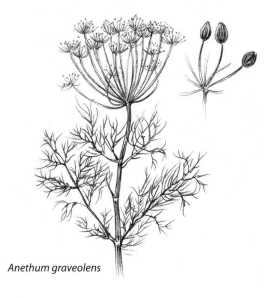

Anethum graveolens

have omitted the weightier matters of the law, judgment, mercy, and faith."

Dill's uses range from flavoring to medicine and witchcraft, yet the herb is considered rather lowly and unexciting today: "An herb without glitz," as cookbook author Carolyn Dille has described it.

Dill's cultivation humbles and mystifies many home gardeners, in large part because of the dual uses of the plant. In the youthful stage of the plant's growth, dill's blue-green, feathery foliage with its rather delicate and perishable aromatic tones is used fresh (as dillweed) to flavor chicken and fish, and in egg and potato dishes. As the herb matures, foliage production ceases as long stems shoot up, and dill's second product, pungent seeds (technically fruits), appear. These enhance vinegars, pickles, breads, crackers, cookies, cakes, and pies.

Dill's rapid growth is acknowledged in its botanical name: *Athenon* (Latinized to *Anethum*) was the ancient Greek name for dill derived from *ano* (upward) and *theo* (I run). Our common name for the plant, dill, probably derives from the Norse verb, *dilla* (to lull), a tribute to claims that dill reduces flatulence and abdominal distension (and thus serves as a carminative). Dill seed oil has some antimicrobial antigenotoxic effects.

While native to the Mediterranean, dill has been primarily, but not exclusively, employed in northern Europe. The aroma of dillweed is delicate, with tones of anise, parsley, and celery. The flavors are easily lost on drying. The seeds give off aromatic tones of caraway and anise. Dill and Indian dill are sometimes listed as separate species in the genus *Anethum*, but they are so similar that most botanists consider them as variants of only one species, *A. graveolens*. Both are characterized by small yellow flowers held on green stalks that are clustered together in a flat-topped, half-round construction about the size of a small grapefruit, which botanists call a compound umbel. The yellow-petaled flowers develop into tiny elliptical fruits with a ridged brown center surrounded by a narrow cream band.

Anethum graveolens translates as the "strong-smelling dill" and yields different commercial products depending upon the maturity and processing of the crop: dillweed, dillweed with umbel, dill seed, and dill oil. India is the major producer of dill seed imported to the United States; domestically, Oregon, Washington, and Nevada are the leading producers of dill oil. Approximately 80 to 85 percent of the dill oil is used in the pickling industry; 15 to 20 percent is used in general flavoring and seasoning. Dill seeds are considered GRAS at 1,200 to 8,200 ppm, while the oil is GRAS at 1 to 750 ppm. The seeds of Indian dill are considered GRAS at 3.3 to 400 ppm, while the oil is GRAS at 3 to 750 ppm.

Seed lines include 'Bouquet', 'Crown', 'Diwa', 'Dukat', 'Dura', 'Elefant', 'Fernleaf', 'Gewöhnlicher', 'Herkultes' ('Hercules'), 'Long Island Mammoth', 'Mammut', 'Sari', 'Tetra', and 'Vierling'. 'Bouquet' is fairly compact for the home garden; 'Fernleaf', a selection by Burpee Seed Company from Turkish seeds, is unique in that it grows only to 18 inches (46 cm) tall, a size that makes it ideal for pot culture. 'Long Island Mammoth' and 'Tetra' produce high leaf and total fresh weight, while 'Long Island Mammoth' and 'Bouquet' produce high flower fresh weight. As one might suspect, each seed line has slightly different aromatic characteristics and selections for the home gardener may take some experimentation.

The uses and culture of Indian dill are the same as dill, and, in fact, P. K. Mukherjee and L. Constance's *Umbelliferae* (*Apiaceae*) *of India* considers Indian dill as merely a variant of regular dill. Indian dill is primarily cultivated in India, Bangladesh, China, and Japan. The leading seed lines are 'Variyali' ('Dark Variyali' and 'Pale Variyali'), 'Ghoda', and 'Vizag'.

Once dill is established in the home garden, it resows. A large plant can yield up to a cup of seeds. Dill responds to cool weather and long days, so as soon as a minimum 25°F (-4°C) night temperature is reached, direct seeding is done on a smooth, well-prepared field from early spring to late summer. Separate plantings a few weeks apart will provide a continuous crop of dill weed for the fresh market. Home gardeners usually snip foliage, but marketer gardeners typically pull plants and sell them bundled.

Soil should be light and neither too sandy nor too stony; a medium to heavy, well-drained, organic soil is preferred. Germination may be enhanced by soaking seeds for four days with 50 mg/l of ascorbic acid (vitamin C). Seeding after late summer will produce mostly seeds and little dillweed.

The home gardener should plant fifteen to twenty seeds per foot of row and thin to three or four plants per foot with rows 1 to 3 feet apart; the thinned seedlings may be used in the kitchen. For seed production, plant twenty to twenty-four seeds per linear foot in early plantings and thirty-five to thirty-six seeds per linear foot in late plantings with two rows per bed row and 30 to 36 inches (76 to 91 cm) between bed rows for an average yield of 1,000 to 1,400 pounds seed per acre (1,019 to 1,427 kg/ha).

For maximum dillweed production, plant 4 inches (10 cm) apart with rows 6 inches (15 cm) apart, or 6 plants per square foot (68 plants/square meter) to produce a yield of 27 tons per acre (61 t/ha). Seed takes seven to nine days to germinate, and flowering commences forty to sixty-seven days after germination, depending upon sowing time, soil, and weather.

While it has often been said that dill transplants poorly, that advice is good only for bare-root transplants; young potted plants transplant readily. The home gardener should remember that the age of the plant determines how quickly the plant will end foliage production to begin making seeds.

Dill is sensitive to water stress, so overhead sprinkling may be used from the time of seeding to 2 feet (60 cm) in height, then switching to furrow irrigation to reduce disease and risk of seed-shattering that spills seed on the ground. Starting recommendations for fertilizer levels are 40 to 60 pounds per acre (45 to 67 kg/ha) available nitrogen, 20 to 30 pounds per acre (22 to 34 kg/ha) available P_2O_5, and 20 pounds per acre (22 kg/ha) of available K_2O.

Healthy vegetable-garden soil suits dill well in the home garden. Early-fall dill plantings will produce leaves for several weeks, even after the first light frosts; late-fall sowings will germinate the following spring. Dill may be grown in the greenhouse but requires full sun.

Dill competes poorly with weeds. Weeds may be controlled with Linuron, the only herbicide registered for dill in the United States. While this pre-emergent herbicide controls weeds at one-half pound per acre (0.55 kg/ha), it may also produce crop injury.

Dillweed may be harvested throughout the season, but seeds should be harvested as soon as they start to turn brown. Freeze drying is recommended over hot-air drying for dillweed, but even freeze drying causes the loss of 75 percent of the aroma compounds. Thus, dillweed is best used fresh. For fresh-market sales, package twelve to fifteen plants to the bunch.

Dill is subject to attack from a *Fusarium* root rot and a powdery mildew caused by *Erysiphe heraclei*, but the latter has not been reported in the United States. Aphids are the herb's worst pest and particularly colonize the dill heads.

Important chemistry: The essential oil of dill seed (fruit) contains 18 to 81 percent $(S)(+)$-carvone, 0 to 55 percent limonene, 0 to 53 percent dill apiole, and 0 to 23 percent alpha-phellandrene. An unusual cultivar has been reported with 44 percent limonene, 41 percent (*S*)(+)-carvone, and 12 percent myristicin (with no dill apiole). The leading essential oil components of Indian dill seed (fruit) include 17 to 46 percent (*S*)(+)-carvone, 15 to 45 percent limonene, and 0 to 27 percent dill apiole. The essential oil of dillweed contains 9 to 76 percent alpha-phellandrene, 2 to 53 percent limonene, trace to 35 percent (*S*)(+)-carvone, and 0 to 60 percent anethofuran (dill ether); alpha-phellandrene and anethofuran contribute primarily to the unique odor of dillweed.

Botanical Description

A. graveolens L., Sp. pl. 263. 1753 (including *A. sowa* Roxb. ex Flem.).

Native country: Dill is native to southern Europe.

General habit: Dill is a smooth annual 20 to 50 cm high.

Leaves: Leaves are feathery with threadlike lobes.

Flowers: Yellow flowers are arranged in a large umbel, 10 to 15 cm in spread, with fifteen to forty smaller umbels.

Fruits/seeds: Fruit is 3 to 6 mm × 1.5 to 3 mm, dark brown with a pale wing.

Angelica

ăn-jĕl-ĭ-kå
angelica

Family: Apiaceae (Umbelliferae)

Growth form: biennial to short-lived perennial to 6 feet (1.8 m) (*A. archangelica*) or 3 to 10 feet (1 to 3 m) (*A. atropurpurea*)

Hardiness: hardy to Minnesota (Zone 4)

Light: full sun (in areas of cool summers) to part shade (areas of hot summers)

Water: moist but not constantly wet

Soil: rich in organic matter, pH 4.5 to 7.4, average 6.3 (*A. archangelica*)

Culinary use: candied stems have limited use for cake decoration

Craft use: none

Landscape use: bold, lush backgrounds (when flowering); attracts bees

All parts of angelicas—the fruits, leaves, and roots—are scented with a sweet aromatic oil.

Watch out, though; these parts contain a number of furanocoumarins (the so-called psoralens) which may heighten one's sensitivity to light, resulting in skin reactions to sunlight. Even when not combined with light, these compounds are documented to be toxic, cause genetic damage, and possibly cancer. To make matters even worse, collectors of wild angelica often confuse the species with poison hemlock (*Conium maculatum* L.).

With a name such as *Angelica*, you might assume that this genus of about fifty species of the northern hemisphere and New Zealand would be blessed with graceful beauty, but instead the herb possesses a stalwart presence judged by many gardeners to be large and rank. The name is derived from the Latin *angelus*, meaning "angel" or "angelic," an allusion to the reputed healing properties of this herb; one legend says that angelica was revealed to humans by an angel as a cure for the Black Plague.

These tall plants are biennials or short-lived perennials ("triennials") that are adapted to soils high in organic matter, constant moisture, and relatively cool summers. Many *Angelica* species are found in the semishade near cool mountain streams. If your summers are hot, plant these in part shade in the coolest part of your garden and hope for a mild summer.

Angelica archangelica
ăn-jĕl-ĭ-kå är-kăn-jĕl-ĭ-kå
angelica

> **French:** *angélique cultivée, Saint-Esprit*
> **German:** *Engelwurz, Garten-Angelika, Echtes Engelwurzkraut, Brustwurz*
> **Dutch:** *tuin-angelica, engelkruid*
> **Italian:** *angelica*
> **Spanish:** *angelica*
> **Chinese:** *ch'ien-tu*

Angelica, according to the peasant folklore of Old Europe, was revealed to humanity by the archangel Raphael as a gift with potent, magical powers. *Angelica archangelica* is characterized by spindle-shaped, fleshy roots; an erect, hollow stem to 6 feet; large, lobed alternate leaves; and large umbels of greenish yellow flowers that are followed by oblong, off-white fruits. It is a biennial that flowers the second year after the seed is planted.

Angelica leaves have been used as a vegetable and to flavor fish, poultry, cooked fruits, soups, or stews, while the leaf and inflorescence stalks have been candied for cake decorations, especially in England. The fresh, succulent stems are sometimes prepared like asparagus, chopped and stewed with rhubarb and apples, or minced in preserves or marmalade. The dried roots find extensive use in liqueurs, vermouths, and bitters. The essential oil of the roots is used in the formulation of Benedictine and Chartreuse-type liqueurs. The dried seeds are often used in combination with the roots for distilled liquors, while the root oil is used in liqueurs. The flowers are also a source of nectar for bees.

Angelica is cultivated commercially in France, Belgium, Germany, Hungary, Poland, and several other Northern European countries. It is easily started from seeds (actually fruits) planted immediately after ripening in late summer in nursery beds. As with most umbellifers, freshness of the seed is of utmost importance. Seeds from the primary (central) inflorescence typically exhibit the highest germination rate. Light is necessary for germination, so the seeds are planted in shallow drills and only barely covered with fine sand. Fresh seeds may be stored dry at 41°F (5°C) for up to two years but must

Angelica archangelica

be subsequently stratified in vermiculite and stored at 41°F (5°C) for six weeks. Seeds may also be germinated indoors if shallowly sown in moist soil at 72°F day/64°F night (22°C/18°C) under artificial light; the plants should be 5 inches, or 12 cm, from cool white fluorescent lights at a day length of sixteen hours. Transplant young seedlings from the nursery bed to the field when 3 to 4 inches (7.6 to 10 cm) high, which is about four to six weeks after germination, spaced 12 inches (30 cm) between plants in rows 2 to 3 feet (61 to 91 cm) apart for a population of 20,000 plants per acre (49,420/ha).

The soil should be evenly moist but well drained, slightly acid, and high in organic matter. Soil analysis may indicate a need to add boron and other micronutrients to the field before planting. Investigating greenhouse-grown plants, a team of scientists at Laval University found that angelica plants grown in a sand-hydroponic system with inorganic fertilizers and supplementary light (16 hours) yielded more roots than plants grown in peat moss and an organic fertilizer system under natural light during the winter.

Leaves and flowering stalks may be harvested from the plants in the second year of growth. Viral and fungal diseases may attack the leaves in late summer, making the leaves unappealing. If roots are desired, flowering stalks must be removed to prevent loss of growth or quality. Harvest the roots in the fall of the second year of growth or the following spring. After digging, the roots should be washed to remove any attached soil. Dry the roots slowly in a clean room with good air circulation; rapid oven drying is not recommended because of the loss of oil. An average yield of fresh roots is approximately 12,000 pounds per acre (13,500 kg/ha).

Studies done at ENSI Chemie and Université Blaise Pascal de Clermont in France indicate that distillations performed with the plant ma-

terial in or out of water gave similar compositions, irrespective of how the roots had been dried or for how long. The optimum conditions for distillation were obtained in the French study when the reactor was 40 percent full of plant material in water with a plant:water ratio of 1:4. The essential oil of angelica root is recognized as GRAS at 0.03 to 60 ppm; the extract of angelica root is GRAS at 1 to 100 ppm. The essential oil of angelica seed is GRAS at 1.5 to 32 ppm; the extract of angelica seed is GRAS at 10 to 1,100 ppm. The essential oil of angelica stem is GRAS at 0.5 to 24 ppm.

The fresh, succulent stems are sometimes prepared like asparagus, chopped and stewed with rhubarb and apples, or minced in preserves or marmalade. The dried roots find extensive use in liqueurs, vermouths, and bitters.

The coumarins in angelica root exhibit calcium-antagonistic activity in rat pituitary cells. The seeds contain archangeline, a furanocoumarin that causes photosensitization, including symptoms similar to poison ivy when affected skin is exposed to sunlight. The alpha-copaene and alpha-ylangene in the seed oil are attractive to the male Mediterranean fruit fly, *Ceratitis capitata*.

Important chemistry: The seed oil of angelica is dominated by 34 to 87 percent beta-phellandrene and 4 to 16 percent alpha-pinene, providing a pepperminty-pine odor. The root oil is dominated by trace to 57 percent beta-pinene, trace to 46 percent alpha-terpinolene, 2 to 40 percent alpha-pinene, trace to 30 percent beta-phellandrene, 0 to 24 percent alpha-phellandrene, 8 to 16 percent delta-3-carene, 0 to 16 percent cedrol, trace to 14 percent p-cymen-8-ol, and 0 to 12 percent osthol, yielding also a minty-pine odor. *Angelica archangelica* var. *norvegica* has a root oil with 13 percent delta-3-carene The pentane extract differs radically from the essential oil with 53 percent osthol, 9 percent isobergapten, 9 percent bergapten, 6 percent palmitic acid, and 6 percent pentadecanolide. The roots are rich in furanocoumarins, particularly 2'-angeloyl-3'-isovaleryl vaginate, archangelicin, isoimperatorin, psoralen, and oxypeucedanin.

Angelica atropurpurea

ăn-jĕl-ĭ-kå ăt-rō-pē-pŭ-rē-å
purplestem angelica

Also called American angelica or Alexanders, purplestem angelica has similar uses and culture similar to angelica. Purplestem angelica is less robust than angelica and has stems tinged with purple at the base; the fruit also differs. Purplestem angelica has no GRAS status, and little has been published on its chemistry.

Botanical Key and Description

Key:
1. Fruit with thick corky wings, stems tinged purple at base . . . . *A. archangelica*
1a. Fruit with thin corky wings, stems prominently purple at base . . . . *A. atropurpurea*

A. archangelica L., Sp. pl. 250. 1753 (*Archangelica officinalis* Hoffm.).

Angelica includes two subspecies, but only one, *archangelica*, is cultivated.

Native country: Angelica is native to damp places in northern and central Europe, west to the Netherlands and Iceland, and south to Central Ukraine; frequently naturalized elsewhere.

General habit: Angelica is a biennial with purple-tinged smooth stems to 6 feet (1.8 m).

Leaves: Leaves are divided up to three times with smooth leaflets 5 to 7.6 cm long.

Flowers: Flowers are greenish to cream in an umbel.

Fruits/seeds: Fruit is 6 to 8 mm long, nearly oblong, with wings and prominent dorsal ribs.

A. atropurpurea L., Sp. pl. 251. 1753.

Native country: Purplestem angelica is native to swamps and wet woods from Labrador to Minnesota, south to Delaware and West Virginia.

General habit: Purplestem angelica is a short-lived perennial 3 to 10 feet (1 to 3 m) with purple-stained smooth stems.

Leaves: Leaves are divided up to three times with smooth leaflets 4 to 15 cm long.

Flowers: Flowers are white in an umbel.

Fruits/seeds: Fruits are oblong-elliptic, 4 to 7.5 mm long, rounded at base, with wings and prominent dorsal ribs.

Anthoxanthum

ăn-thō-zăn-thŭm
sweet vernal grass

Family: Poaceae (Gramineae)

Growth form: short-lived herbaceous
perennials

Hardiness: hardy to Zone 4

Light: full sun to part shade

Water: moist to constantly wet; can withstand mild drought

Soil: garden loam

Propagation: divisions in early spring or
seeds

Culinary use: none (not GRAS)

Craft use: potpourri, perfumery, baskets,
incense

Landscape use: cottage garden, wildflower
meadow, groundcover

The genus *Anthoxanthum* includes about fifteen species of the temperate region. Most are
scented on drying. The genus is derived from
the Greek *anthos* ("flower") and *xanthos* ("yellow"), a reference to the abundant yellow anthers on flowering.

Anthoxanthum nitens

ăn-thō-zăn-thŭm nī-tĕns
holy grass

French: *herbe de la Sainte Vierge*

German: *Wohlriechendes Mariengras*

Dutch: *Veenreukgras*

Chinese: *pai-mao-hsiang*

Previously known as *Hierochloë odorata*, holy
grass has also been used by North American Indians (particularly the Plains Indians) to weave
sweet grass baskets and incense-ropes, and as a
medicine and cosmetic. Women in the Black-
foot tribes underwent a purification ceremony
in water scented with holy grass thirty-four
days after giving birth. Holy grass is also used
to flavor vodka to produce zubrowka. Because
holy grass has an appreciable content of coumarin, it is prohibited by the FDA in foods and
permitted only in alcoholic beverages and tobacco (see sweet woodruff for a further discussion of coumarin).

Holy grass is usually sold as a potted plant
and used as a groundcover; in the ground it will
very quickly colonize large areas with creeping

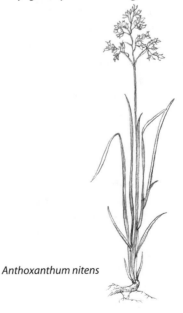

Anthoxanthum nitens

rhizomes. The specific epithet, *nitens* refers to the shiny leaves. Height is variable, but the holy grass now circulating in the herb trade in North America seldom grows higher than 12 inches (30 cm). It appreciates slightly acid, cool, moist soil rich in organic matter and can be found in moist meadows, swales, and shores around the world.

Important chemistry: The principal component of the ethanol extract from the leaves of holy grass is 62 percent coumarin, providing a vanilla-like odor. Also notable is a trace of the coconut-scented massoialactone (dec-2-en-5-olide).

Anthoxanthum odoratum
ăn-thō-zăn-thŭm ō-dŏ-rā-tŭm
sweet vernal grass

> **French:** flouve odorante, gazon de vanille
> **German:** Geruchgras, Ruchgras
> **Dutch:** reukgras
> **Italian:** paleo, paleo odoroso, antosassanto
> **Spanish:** grama de olor
> **Portuguese:** feno de cheiro

Sweet vernal grass, a short-lived herbaceous perennial, is a frequent component of hay fields in North America and is sometimes planted on purpose, although the fodder has relatively little nutritive value. When the herb is dried, it has a typical new-mown hay odor and is used to weave sweet grass baskets. Can withstand mild drought and moist but not constantly wet soil. Since sweet vernal grass is actually native to Europe, this use is adapted from the Native Americans' use of *Anthoxanthum nitens*.

Sweet vernal grass is a tight tuft of hairy grass blades, reaching to about 20 inches (50 cm) on flowering. Warning: This grass may spread aggressively, so plant it where it can reseed with abandon, such as a cottage garden or wildflower meadow.

A commercial essential oil or absolute (alcoholic extract of a petroleum ether extract) called "flouve" is composed primarily of sweet vernal grass hay and used in tobacco flavorings. Flouve has an odor that is intensely sweet, haylike, and herbaceous. In perfumery, flouve blends well with fougères, chypres, new-mown hay bases, Oriental bases, ambers, and so on, although always at very low concentrations. Neither sweet vernal grass nor flouve has GRAS status from the U.S. Food and Drug Administration, although flouve has been used in the past to modify maple and other flavors. In addition, cattle fed home-grown sweet vernal grass have exhibited internal hemorrhaging, so the

Anthoxanthum odoratum

use of sweet vernal grass for flavoring should be discouraged.

Important chemistry: The odor of dried sweet vernal grass is dominated by 47 to 96 percent coumarin with an odor similar to that of sweet woodruff (*Galium odoratum*).

Botanical Key and Description

Key:
1. Lower florets awnless. . . . . *A. nitens*
1a. Lower florets awned. . . . . *A. odoratum*

A. nitens (Weber) Schouten & Veldkamp, Blumea 30:348. 1985 [*H. odorata* (L.) Wahlenb.].

Native country: Holy grass is mainly found in moist soil, meadows, and bog-margins from northwestern Europe to North America, where it is found from Maine south to Indiana and west to Arizona.

General habit: Holy grass is a rhizomatous perennial.

Leaves: Leaves are linear or narrowly elliptic, edged with tiny teeth, 3.0 to 6.0 mm broad.

Flowers: Flowers are arranged in a compound inflorescence with the younger flowers at the apex, 25 to 60 cm high in mature condition.

Fruits/seeds: Fruit is a grain but rarely produced.

A. odoratum L., Sp. pl. 28. 1753.

Native country: Sweet vernal grass is native to Europe but now grows in North America.

General habit: Sweet vernal grass is a tufted, short-lived perennial 15 to 50 cm high.

Leaves: Leaves are mostly near the base, flat, smooth to sparsely hairy, 2 to 8 mm wide, the upper much shorter.

Flowers: Flowers are arranged in a compound inflorescence with the younger flowers at the apex, cylindrical, dense.

Anthriscus cerefolium

ăn-thrĭs-kŭs sĕr-ĕ-fō-lē-ŭm
chervil

Family: Apiaceae (Umbelliferae)

Growth form: short-lived annual to 28 inches (60 cm)

Hardiness: withstands frost

Light: part shade to full sun

Water: moist but not constantly wet

Soil: rich in organic matter, pH 5.7 to 8.2, average 6.7

Propagation: seeds in spring, 10,000 seeds/ oz (353/g)

Culinary use: fish, poultry, vegetable, and egg dishes, salads, sauces

Craft use: none

Landscape use: short-lived; use at edge of border, best in vegetable plot

French: *cerfeuil*
German: *Kerbel, Gartenkerbel*
Dutch: *kervel*
Italian: *cerfoglio, mirride, felce muschiata*
Spanish: *cerafolio, perfolio*
Portuguese: *cerefolho, cerifólio*
Swedish: *körvel*
Russian: *kervel'*
Chinese: *san-lo-po*
Japanese: *chābiru*
Arabic: *maqdunis afranji, khalai-i-khalil*

No herb, except perhaps tarragon, is quite so French as chervil, an association that is not surprising for a nation known for its celebration of fine food and the subtle use of herbs. A simple description of the plant might quickly capture a bit of the spirit of France and its people: although chervil resembles a delicate parsley with somewhat lacy, fernlike foliage, the spirit of its flavor betrays an aristocratic subtlety. Is it any wonder that a synonym for chervil is French parsley?

Chervil's unique flavor, also described by many gourmets as resembling a refined combination of French tarragon and parsley, complements fish and egg dishes and is an essential component of *fines herbes*, a French combination of freshly chopped basil, parsley, thyme, and tarragon. It also finds its way into salads, a variety of sauces, and poultry and vegetable dishes. In addition to its delightful taste, chervil has antioxidant activity. Chervil leaves are considered GRAS at 50 to 1,140 ppm.

While the French may be most closely associated with chervil today, the Romans were probably the ones who popularized its cultivation and use. Apicius, the first-century Roman gourmet, included green chervil sauce in his *De Re Coquinaria*, one of the world's earliest surviving cookbooks. In John Edwards's modern translation of the tome, coriander, chervil, lovage, and mint are listed as key herbal ingredients.

The delicate flavor of chervil is easily destroyed by drying and the heat of cooking, so it is best used fresh from the herb garden. Add it to hot dishes after cooking is nearly complete.

The generic name, *Anthriscus*, is derived from the Greek name for the plant, and the specific name, *cerefolium*, means waxy-leaved, alluding to the shiny leaves. The genus includes twelve Eurasian species. Mountainous areas of east-central and southeastern Europe are home to chervil, but it is widely dispersed elsewhere.

Chervil is a short-lived but rather cold-hardy annual that some home gardeners might characterize as finicky. Successful cultivation of the plant depends on timing because it grows best in cool, moist soil in full winter sun or part shade in late spring and fall. Chervil also prefers soils that drain well and have a nearly neutral pH; good soil drainage and fertility are important factors to achieve large, productive plants. In areas as far north as Zone 7, chervil is best grown as a fall/winter crop; in the colder reaches of this growing area, a cold frame or similar winter protection is advisable.

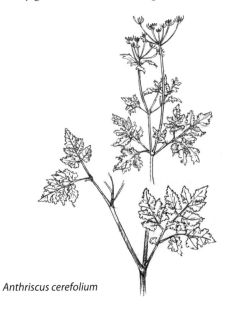

Anthriscus cerefolium

Chervil flourishes in cool spring and fall conditions, especially when mid-day temperatures hover at 40 to 50°F, when plants become lush and richly textured and may reach diameters over 12 inches. When warm weather arrives, overwintered plants cease foliage production and send up flower stems 24 to 30 inches (70 cm) high that are topped by umbels of small, white blossoms which produce seed before the plant dies. The chervil cultivar 'Brussels Winter' tolerates cold well and is a little slower to begin flowering. In areas where summers are hot, chervil does best in part or full shade, although the combination of heat and shade seems to render the plants weak and susceptible to spider mite infestation.

Chervil produces dark brown, 1-inch, splinter-like seeds (really fruits) that may be planted directly in the garden or started indoors and transplanted to pots. The latter technique is useful when an early start is needed to catch the most desirable weather. Bare-root seedlings of chervil transplanted directly to the garden often fail, but pot-grown transplants take hold quickly during cool growing conditions. When taking advantage of warm soil to start the seedlings indoors or in a greenhouse, four to five weeks should be allowed from seeding to transplanting to the garden. Chervil seed will not germinate in soil that is too warm; this characteristic keeps chervil seed that is scattered in spring from germinating during summer heat when the plants are most likely to struggle or die. Seeds sown in early spring or late fall when soil temperatures are cooler germinate in about fourteen days.

In commercial cultivation in California, chervil plants are spaced about 6 inches (15 cm) apart, with 30 inches (76 cm) between rows. In home garden, plants may be cultivated in staggered rows 6 to 8 inches apart in raised beds. Chervil grows like parsley to produce a rosette of stems with light green leaves. Plants are harvested by removing the outer stems and leaving the young tender shoots to grow from the center. The harvest begins in earnest about ninety days after the direct sowing indoors. Plants produced in the greenhouse or indoors under lights are ready to harvest lightly about forty to sixty days after the seeds are sown.

Important chemistry: The essential oil of chervil leaves is dominated by 64 to 83 percent estragole (methyl chavicol) and 15 to 34 percent 1-allyl-2,4-dimethoxybenzene, providing a tarragon and parsley-like odor.

Botanical Description

Two varieties (var. *cerefolium* and var. *trichocarpa* Neilrach) are recorded, but var. *cerefolium* is the chervil of gardens.

A. cerefolium (L.) Hoffm., Gen. pl. umbell. 41. 1814.

Native country: Chervil is native to mountainous areas of east-central and southeastern Europe but widespread elsewhere.

General habit: Chervil is a wiry annual to 70 cm.

Leaves: Leaves are fernlike, lobed three times.

Flowers: Flowers white, borne in an umbel.

Fruits/seeds: Fruits are 7 to 10 mm long, needle-like.

Armoracia rusticana

är-mör-ă-sĭ-å rŭs-tĭ-kā-nå
horseradish

Family: Brassicaceae (Cruciferae)
Growth form: herbaceous perennial to 3 feet (1 m) or more
Hardiness: hardy to Maine (Zone 5)
Light: full sun
Water: moist but not constantly wet; can withstand some drought
Soil: average garden loam, pH 5.0 to 7.5, average 6.5
Propagation: divisions in early spring
Culinary use: sauces
Craft use: none
Landscape use: edges of borders

French: *raifort, cran*
German: *Meerrettich, Kren*
Dutch: *mierikswortel*
Italian: *barbaforte, ramolaccio*
Spanish: *cochlearia, rábano rusticano*
Portuguese: *armorácio*
Swedish: *skörbjuggsört*
Russian: *khren*
Chinese: *lagen*
Japanese: *seiyō wasabi*
Arabic: *fujl har*

The Oracle at Delphi told Apollo that the radish was worth its weight in lead, the beet its weight in silver, and the horseradish its weight in gold. We don't place such values on our plants today, but it's hard to imagine Passover or hot roast beef without grated horseradish, or cold seafood without cocktail sauce. Actually, horseradish only appeared in the Passover *seder* as *maror* in the Middle Ages (c. 1215–1293) as Jews migrated north and eastward into colder climates. Horseradish provides a unique pun-

gency different from that of black and red peppers, and the tall, broad leaves provide a textural contrast in the herb garden. Horseradish is also notably high in vitamin C and has antimicrobial activities to preserve meat. The root of horseradish is considered GRAS. Excessive doses of horseradish may lead to diarrhea or night sweats. One case of a heart attack has been recorded—the patient survived.

Once you grow horseradish, you'll have this hardy perennial forever; even the smallest piece of horseradish root can grow a new plant, and whenever you are absolutely sure you've eradicated the horseradish bed *this* time, lo and behold, it comes back. Superficially, horseradish resembles dock (*Rumex* spp.) with tall, stalked, slightly rumpled leaves.

Armoracia rusticana is one of three species in the genus, and may be an ancient hybrid of the other two species. All are smooth-leaved, perennial herbs with deep roots or rhizomes. The leaves are strap-like, either simple or dis-

Armoracia rusticana

sected, and the flowers have four sepals and petals. *Armoracia* was the old Latin name for horseradish, while *rusticana* means "rustic" or "of the country." The most primitive name seems to be *chren*, still common to Slavic languages and introduced into German and French dialects in variations. The German *Meerrettich* means literally sea-radish, as it sometimes naturalizes near seasides, and this name provided the later English name horseradish; *meer* seems to have been misunderstood by the English for *mähre*, an old horse, as if for the rankness and toughness of the roots. Some have made the apocryphal claim that horseradish, an herb of northern Europe, was cultivated prior to the Exodus of the Hebrew slaves (c. 1500 B.C.E.) from Egypt. In England, it only became popular in England in the late 1600s. From there it was transferred to North America.

Commercial cultivation of horseradish in the United States is centered around Chicago; plants were brought to this area about 1856 by a German family named Sell, who gave roots to the Sass family. St. Louis is another commercial area, where horseradish has been grown since the 1890s. Today the United States produces around 6 million gallons of horseradish sauce, enough to season a line of sandwiches that would circle the globe an estimated twelve times!

In the United States, the commercial practice is to plant root cuttings ¼ to ¾ inches diameter and 8 to 14 inches long obliquely (an estimated 30° angle from horizontal is claimed to be best) to horizontal in shallow furrows with a large crown bud end resting slightly higher than the small or lateral root end. These are spaced 18 to 24 inches within the row and 30 to 36 inches between rows, and produce 8,900 to 9,700 plants per acre. The sets are covered with 2 to 4 inches of soil; rolling then firms the soil. Soil should be pH 6.0 to 6.5; liberal applications of manure prior to planting are recom-

mended. Addition of boron in boron-deficient soils will increase yields.

During growth, roots increase in diameter but little in length. Water stress produces bitter roots. To produce a high-quality marketable root, the roots are "lifted"—the crown of the plant is pulled up and small lateral roots removed; then the root is replanted in its original position. Suggested times for lifting are when the largest leaves are 8 to 10 inches long and again about six weeks later. Lifted roots are more uniform and easier to clean, but the total yield is reduced by this procedure. Roots are dug either in fall or early spring. Harvested lateral roots are stored until spring for replanting the next crop.

If you grow horseradish in the home garden, early spring is the best time to plant the pencil-thin branches trimmed from larger roots. If you cannot plant the roots immediately, store them in plastic bags in the refrigerator until ready to plant. Choose a sunny location and work in plenty of rotted manure or compost to a depth of 10 inches. Depending upon your needs, plant one or two dozen roots, spacing them 12 to 18 inches apart. Set each piece so that the top is at ground level in a trench 3 to 5 inches deep. You may dig the roots as you need them, but after fall's first heavy frost is when the flavor is at its peak. In areas where the ground does not freeze, you may harvest throughout the winter! Remove only the largest roots, leaving the small ones to survive another season; roots that are more than three years old should be discarded as too tough.

Horseradish is commercially dehydrated for export but tastes best when served fresh. The root may be shaved into curls to decorate and flavor beef. To prepare horseradish sauce, scrape the roots, grate (with good ventilation to avoid asphyxiation), and combine ½ cup white vinegar and ¼ teaspoon salt with every cup of grated root. Bottle tightly and refrigerate for up to two months; grated red beets or various mustards may also be added. For longer storage, freeze the grated horseradish. Mix the sauce with ketchup to taste for cocktail sauce. If you harvest too many roots in the fall, store them in damp sand or in the refrigerator for grating later. Serve horseradish only in porcelain or glass, never silver, which blackens on contact with horseradish.

Numerous cultivars of horseradish exist, most sterile. The most attractive for the garden is an unnamed variegated cultivar with white-splashed leaves; another unnamed cultivar has dark purple-green leaves. Both of these ornamental cultivars are difficult to locate and recommended only for the collector.

Cultivars may be grouped into one of three types: Type I has leaves with a heart-shaped base, Type III has leaves with a tapering base, while Type II is intermediate. Cultivars also vary as to whether the leaves are smooth or crinkled and on the yield per acre. Of more than thirty cultivars, some of the more common ones and their chief characteristics are listed here.

Cultivar: 'Big Top Western'
Leaf type: I, smooth
Yield per acre: 1.6 pounds per root with 4.65 tons per acre
Disease resistance: highly resistant to turnip mosaic 1, slightly resistant to white rust

Cultivar: 'Bohemian'
Leaf type: I, smooth
Disease resistance: highly resistant to turnip mosaic 1, highly resistant to white rust

Cultivar: 'Maliner Kren' ("common")
Leaf type: III, crinkled
Yield/acre: 1.1 pounds per root with 2.79 tons per acre

Disease resistance: highly susceptible to turnip mosaic 1, highly susceptible to white rust

Cultivar: 'Sass'
Leaf type: I, smooth
Yield/acre: 1.7 pounds per root with 4.81 tons/acre
Disease resistance: highly resistant to turnip mosaic 1, slightly resistant to white rust

Cultivar: 'Swiss'
Leaf type: II, smooth
Yield/acre: 1.1 pounds per root with 3.19 tons per acre
Disease resistance: highly susceptible to turnip mosaic 1, highly resistant to white rust

Cabbageworms will feed on horseradish foliage, but these are easily controlled with strains of *Bacillus thuringiensis*. A worse problem is the imported crucifer weevil, *Baris lepidii*; the white grublike larvae tunnel in the roots and reduce both quality and yield. Dipping the roots in a 0.1 to 5.0 percent permethrin solution for 30 to 120 minutes effectively kills this pest before planting. Horseradish flea beetle, *Phyllotreta armoraciae*, may also present a problem but is easily controlled with carbaryl (Sevin), an insecticide registered for horseradish. Horseradish may also be troubled by harlequin bugs and cabbage loopers.

White rust, caused by *Albugo candida*, is one of the most prevalent and destructive diseases. Bacterial leaf spot (*Xanthomonas campestris* var. *armoraciae*) is sometimes quite severe. Alternaria, a fungal disease, will cause lesions on older leaves similar to early blight of tomatoes. Some root rots also have been reported. Turnip mosaic 1 virus causes the formation of somewhat sunken black streaks in the leaf stalks and midribs that reach the crown as the season progresses, with blackening of the smaller leaf veins in some cultivars. Disease-free planting stock and wisely chosen cultivars are the best means of controlling these diseases.

Important chemistry: In an ether extract of the ground root, the dominant components are 76 to 80 percent allyl isothiocyanate and 16 to 18 percent beta-phenylethyl isothiocyanate, or mustard oils, which irritate the ending of olfactory nerves and cause tears and salivation. Normally the mustard oils are bound with sugars as either sinigrin (allyl glucosinolate) or gluconasturtin (beta-phenylethyl glucosinolate) in the vacuoles of the cells, separated from a membrane-bound enzyme, myrosinase, but rupture of the cells allows hydrolysis of the sugar bonds by myrosinase, thereby releasing free isothiocyanates.

Botanical Description

A. rusticana P. Gaertn., B. Mey. & J. Scherbius, Oekon, Fl. Wetterau 2:426. 1800 (*A. lapathifolia* Gilib., *Cochlearia armoracia* L.).

Native country: Horseradish is probably native to southern Russia and eastern Ukraine but is cultivated widely in Europe and North America, where it has frequently escaped.

General habit: Flowering stems rise to 1 m or more.

Leaves: Basal leaves are 30 to 50 cm long, egg-shaped or oblong-egg-shaped, round-toothed, with a stalk to 30 cm.

Flowers: Flowers are yellow with petals 5 to 7 mm long.

Fruits/seeds: Fruits are dry globose or egg-shaped pockets 4 to 6 mm long with 4 to 6 seeds in each pocket.

Artemisia

är-tĕ-mĭz-ĭ-å
artemisia

Family: Asteraceae (Compositae)

Growth form: shrubs or herbaceous perennials, rarely annual

Hardiness: most hardy to Maine (Zone 5)

Light: full sun

Water: many can withstand drought

Soil: most require extremely well-drained soil, pH 4.9 to 7.5, average 6.9 (*A. dracunculus*)

Propagation: cuttings or divisions; seeds also possible in some, 270,000 seeds per ounce (9,524/g) (*A. absinthium*)

Culinary use: little except for French tarragon

Craft use: wreaths, potpourri, smudge sticks, moth and mosquito repellents

Landscape use: from herbaceous border to shrub border

Artemis, the Greek goddess (Diana of the Romans), may have been the ultimate inspiration for this genus, but the immediate inspiration was probably Queen Artemisia of Caria (Helicarnassus), a Turkish female botanist who lived about 400 B.C.E. and was the wife of Mausolus. The handsome memorial she built to her husband became one of the "Seven Wonders" of the ancient world and the origin of the word "mausoleum."

The genus *Artemisia* includes about 300 species, but only a few are appropriate for the garden; most are large, rank perennials grown for their scented, fine foliage, but a few species are annuals. The foliage can be harvested anytime, and prunings should be saved and dried.

The gray, silky-haired leaves and shrub-like nature of many species add interest to the herb garden. These silky leaves also prevent evaporation of moisture in their native habitats which are sunny, hot, and dry; because of this characteristic, particular care should be taken to site these plants in bright, sunny areas of the garden, preferably with good morning sun, in order to dry the dew quickly from the leaves. Soil drainage should be sharp, and the liberal addition of sand, or even gravel, will be rewarded with shorter but harder growth that is more resistant to fungal blights.

The descriptions of many of the species sound alike, but these plants are easily distinguished by degree of the silkiness of the leaves, the divisions of the leaves, and the arrangement of the small (usually yellow) disk-like heads (capitula) of flowers. Further distinctions can be made by the number and fertility of the individual flowers and the bracts subtending the capitula, but this requires a dissecting microscope. Many species have a bitter taste and smell from the thujone content, but French tarragon is unique in the genus for its estragole content and importance in haute cuisine.

Artemisia abrotanum
är-tĕ-mĭz-ĭ-å å-brō-tā-nŭm
southernwood

> **French:** *citronelle, aurone mâle*
> **German:** *Stabwurz, Eberraure, Eberreis, Citronkraut, Stabkraut, Aberraute*
> **Dutch:** *citroenkruid*
> **Italian:** *abrotano macho, cidronella*
> **Spanish:** *abrótano macho, boja, hierba lombriguera*
> **Chinese:** *ch'ing hao*
> **Arabic:** *afsantin-e-hind*

Abrotanum is an ancient Latin name used for southernwood, also called "old man" from the graying sage-green leaves arranged in clusters of uneven lengths. Lad's love and maiden's ruin are other names. Another name, *garderobe*, from the French meaning "closet," became attached to this plant because the strongly scented leaves were placed in closets to ward off moths, but the effectiveness of doing so has never been experimentally tested.

Foliage is finely divided and greenish on a plant that can become very woody at the base. Southernwood can be easily trained into small

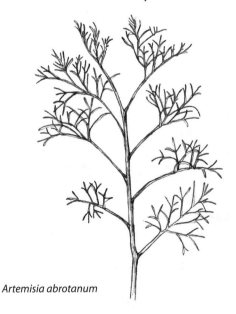

Artemisia abrotanum

hedges for the herb garden, but the growth of the untrained plant is rangy.

The botanical and chemical variation in this species has not been fully assessed, and the relationship of "camphor-scented," "lemon-scented," and "tangerine-scented" southernwood is unknown. Part of the problem is that this species rarely flowers in North America, and because this plant grows with long, rangy stems, frequent pruning is practiced, which further reduces the chances of flowering. One very hairy cultivar is known as 'Silver' in the trade.

Southernwood is easily cultivated on well-drained, garden loam with a near-neural pH where it receives full sun. Propagation is usually from stem tip cuttings, which root quickly, but layering is even easier for the home gardener. A well-established plant typically arches down to the soil and layers itself, forming a gradually increasing mound. Heavy pruning in early spring will prevent this and maintain a compact form.

Southernwood does not have GRAS status. Olaf Renderath and his associates at the University of Cologne noted a high frequency of respiratory tract infections in professional ice hockey players in Germany. Investigating the effects of "Herba-abrotani-Tee" (southernwood tea) on oral immunomodulation with *Propionibacterium avidum*, they stated it "may be considered to be a safe possibility to reduce immunosupression-induced infectious diseases in athletes."

Important chemistry: One study found that the essential oil of southernwood consists of 40 percent camphor and 11 percent limonene + 1,8-cineole; another study found 28 to 42 percent 1,8-cineole and 18 to 23 percent davanone. The very similar *A. paniculata* Lam. (sometimes considered as a cultivated variant of *A. abrotanum*) has 39 to 48 percent davanone, 5 to 10 percent 1,8-cineole, and 1 to 5 percent camphor.

Artemisia absinthium
är-tĕ-mĭz-ĭ-å ăb-sĭn-thē-ŭm
wormwood

French: *grande absinthe, herbe d'absinthe, herbe aux vers, herbe-sainte, alvire*
German: *Wermutkraut, Bitterer Beifuss*
Dutch: *absintkruid, absint-alsem*
Italian: *assenzio*
Spanish: *ajenjo mayor*
Portuguese: *vermout, losna, sintro, absint, alosna*
Swedish: *malört*
Arabic: *shagaret (shadjret) mariam, afsantin-e-hindi, kashus-rumi*

Absinthium was the Latin name for this plant. The "worm" in its common name has two meanings. Wormwood is anthelmintic, that is, it can eliminate the common roundworm, *Ascaris lumbricoides*, from the intestines. Wormwood has also been used against fungal infections of the skin ("worm" in Anglo-Saxon frequently referred to fungal infections such as ringworm). Wormwood is still used in some topical antifungal preparations, especially for athlete's foot.

This is one plant that has received unwarranted bad press. For many years, the claims were made that thujone, one of the principal components of wormwood, apparently acts similarly to tetrahydrocannabinol (THC), found in marijuana, and was the reason for the banning of the potent green liqueur, absinthe. If thujone were the culprit, then Dalmatian sage, which has a similar concentration of thujones, should also have similar properties, which it does not. Close chemical examination of pre-ban (pre-1915) absinthe found an average concentration of 25.4 mg/liter, while an examination of post-ban (1915–1988) absinthe showed similar levels. The addiction called absthinism was probably simply alcoholism, further complicated by toxic adulterants, such as copper sulfate, which was used as a colorant. Yet low doses of thujone-free wormwood are considered GRAS (plant parts are GRAS at 360 ppm, the essential oil is GRAS at 60 ppm, and the extract is GRAS at 170 ppm). Thus, while the recommendation of an upper limit of wormwood oil is approximately 5.7 drops per quart of water, any finished food must be free of thujone under current FDA rules. New companies producing absinthe are today working to moderate these rules.

One study done at the Aga Khan University Medical College in Pakistan found that the crude aqueous-methanolic extract of *A. absinthium* appears to provide protection to the liver, validating one traditional use of this plant. Nonetheless, the herb gardener is best advised

Artemisia absinthium

to limit the use of wormwood to crafts such as making wreaths or potpourris or antifungal preparations to be applied to the skin. Wormwood oil is also toxic to mites.

Wormwood is easily grown in garden loam with a near-neutral pH, and the herb has even become a naturalized weed in northern North America. The gray-velvety leaves of wormwood are conspicuous but become brown and scraggly at the base by midsummer.

The flowering branches typically reach about 39 inches tall and then flop over. Cut the flowering plants back to promote branching and force more growth from the base of the plant. Seed is readily available from the larger seed merchants, but the finest varieties for landscaping are propagated through cuttings or layerings taken annually, since wormwood is often a short-lived plant. Of the varieties available, 'Lambrook Silver' has good silvery foliage and controlled growth compared with the species. 'Powis Castle' is a hybrid of this species with *A. arborescens* L. It is hardy to Zone 7 in well-drained soil and bright sun.

Important chemistry: The bitter principles of wormwood are absinthin (a dimeric guaianolide), anabsinthin, and artabasin (the latter two compounds formed from absinthin). Additional lactones contribute to the bitterness.

The essential oils are very variable. A high (*Z*)-epoxy-ocimene chemotype occurs in alpine Italy, while a high alpha-thujone chemotype occurs at lower elevations in Italy. French plants may occur as either a chrysanthenyl acetate or a sabinyl acetate chemotype. Plants from Siberia and Romania and some from Italy belong to a mixed chemotype. The essential oil of wormwood may thus contain 0 to 85 percent sabinyl acetate, 0 to 54 percent (*Z*)-6,7-epoxy-ocimene, 0 to 60 percent beta-thujone, 0 to 42 percent *cis*-chrysanthenyl acetate, and 0 to 27.8 percent *trans*-sabinene hydrate + lavandulyl acetate.

Plants from Greece have 25.3 percent caryophyllene oxide and 16.8 percent *p*-cymene. Plants raised in Cuba have been reported with 23 percent bornyl acetate. The essential oil of 'Powis Castle' is rich with 41 percent beta-thujone and 25 percent (*Z*)-6,7-epoxy-ocimene. All these forms generally smell of wormwood but with differing nuances of daisy, pine, and tansy.

Artemisia annua
är-tĕ-mĭz-ĭ-å ăn-ū-å
annual wormwood

Chinese: *qing hao*

Annual wormwood produces many finely divided leaves on a large, bushy plant. Also known as sweet Annie or sweet wormwood, it has become popular for use in dried wreaths due to its strong aroma and copious foliage production. Be forewarned, however, that allergic reactions to sweet Annie are not uncommon, and many individuals develop headaches after being around the plant or products made from it.

Since 1971, when Chinese researchers discovered its anti-malarial activity against several microorganisms, including the rodent parasite *Plasmodium berghei*, annual wormwood, or *qing hao*, has been repeatedly researched. Malaria, a disease caused by the four major parasite species of the genus *Plasmodium*, is spread by the *Anopheles* mosquito and kills around 1.5 to 2.7 million people annually in tropical and subtropical areas.

Quinine, derived from the bark of *Cinchona* species, has long been the standard treatment for malaria, but resistant strains of malaria have been reported. Artemisinin, or *qinghaosu* (literally, "the active principle of qing hao"), and artemether, the methyl ether of dihydroartemisinin, have received the most study. Several studies have shown artemether as effective as quinine in treating severe cases of malaria, and both compounds have few side effects, offering a ray of hope against new strains of the deadly illness.

The oil of *A. annua* also displays antifungal, antibacterial, and antioxidant activity. Artemisinin shows no immunomodulatory activity.

Seeds of annual wormwood can be direct-sown in the spring garden, but plants will also readily reseed on a soil with a pH between 5.5 and 6.5 with 59.8 pounds nitrogen per acre (67 kg/ha). However, the very small size of the seeds prevents a uniform stand from developing, so transplants are recommended. Plants are ready to transplant six weeks after seeding at a rate of 44,966 plants per acre (111,111 plants per ha) or individual spacing of 12 × 12 inches (30 × 30 cm). Annual wormwood is a short-day plant with a critical photoperiod of 13 hours and 31 minutes, and non-juvenile plants flower

Artemisia annua

two weeks after induction. Artemisinin content is higher in the inflorescences than in the leaves and is highest at the time of anthesis (pollen release). In subtropical areas, planting in September is recommended for the highest concentration of artemisinin. Recommendations for subtropical cultivation also include dense stands, 8.9×10^4 plants/acre (2.22×10^5 plants/ha) for maximum yield of artemisinin.

Field trials in Brazil have shown a production of 5 lb/acre (6 kg/ha) of artemisinin. If grown for the artemisinin content, a high-artemisinin seed line should be grown, and harvest should be timed prior to flower bud-formation. Water stress during the two weeks before harvest will lead to reduced leaf artemisinin content, as will prolonged drying. For optimum artemisinin content, dry plants at ambient air temperature for the shortest period possible or at 176°F (80°C) for twelve hours.

Important chemistry: The essential oil of the leaves is composed of 6 to 76 percent artemisia ketone, 0 to 44 percent camphor, 0 to 32 percent 1,8-cineole, 0 to 33 percent germacrene D, trace to 16 percent alpha-pinene, and 0 to 15 percent alpha-guaiene. Artemisinin is found only in the aerial parts of the plant, and the inflorescence produces ten times more than the leaves and will vary from trace to 0.8 percent of dry matter.

Artemisia dracunculus

är-tĕ-mĭz-ĭ-å drā-kŭn-kū-lŭs
tarragon

French: *estragon*
German: *Estragon, Dragon*
Dutch: *dragon, slangenkruid*
Italian: *targone, dragone, targoncello, estragone*
Spanish: *estragón, dragoncillo*
Portuguese: *estragao*
Swedish: *estragon*
Arabic: *tharchoûn*

Plant names often appear to have blown in from left field, and when their derivation is examined, the mystery of the name remains; *A. dracunculus* is like that. *Dracunculus* means little dragon, and curiously both tarragon and dragon have the same derivation, the Greek *drákon*. The Arabic name translates as dragonwort. The precise derivation of the name is unknown, but it may allude to the resemblance of tarragon's brown, coiled roots to a cluster of small, arched serpents.

Tarragon is found in Europe, Asia, and North America, but only the so-called Russian and French plants have been cultivated, and France today is the chief source of imported tarragon leaves. The Russian tarragons are extremely vigorous and seed-fertile but have a balsamic leather odor. In contrast, French tarragon, designated as the cultivar 'Sativa', was

Artemisia dracunculus

selected as a seed-sterile derivative sometime during the Middle Ages. The earliest reference to French tarragon that we can locate is the *tarkhon* of Ibn Beithar, a physician and botanist who lived in Spain in the thirteenth century, although French tarragon may be the same as the *altarcon* of Gerard of Cremona of 1187. French tarragon has an anise- or basil-like flavor, and is also antibacterial. If you buy seeds of tarragon, you are planting the Russian type, not the French; French tarragon is propagated only by cuttings or divisions. After you purchase (unsprayed) French tarragon plants, take off a small leaf and bite into it; the herb gives a sweet, numbing sensation.

Tarragon is propagated from stem tip cuttings, root cuttings, and divisions, but the latter two methods carry the risk of spreading diseases and insects, such as nematodes, which burrow into the plant's rhizomes. The herb prefers a site with well-drained, fertile soil with a pH between 6 and 6.5, and full sun. Space plants 15 to 24 inches apart; commercial operations use about 1,000 plants per acre. We have found that if plants are spaced 2 feet (0.6 m) apart with 3 feet (0.9 m) between rows, yields of French tarragon were as follows: first year (September) 1,062.1 pounds dry herb/acre (1.190.0 kg/ha), second year (May) 649.8 pounds dry herb/acre (728.0 kg/ha), second year (September) 1,162.0 pounds dry herb/acre (1,301.9 kg/ha).

Many gardeners look at their thin-stemmed, narrow-leaved tarragon and believe that they see fragility, but there is nothing delicate about this herb except its flavor; it can withstand climates with as little as 12 inches of rain annually. It stands up to the excessive heat of Arizona, where it is grown commercially with irrigation. Tarragon is not so sanguine, however, in climates with high humidity or poor air circulation, as both conditions foster deadly disease problems.

Removal of diseased and discolored foliage along with methods that limit the amount of moisture on plant foliage effectively combats diseases. Providing sufficient space between plants to permit good air circulation, frequent harvest of stems to reduce foliage density, and no overhead irrigation goes a long way to minimizing disease. A sand mulch 1 inch deep on top of the soil under the plant will aid moisture evaporation from the plant's interior. The division of plants every three to five years also provides an opportunity to reduce the plant density and improve air circulation.

Tarragon can be grown for year-round harvest in the greenhouse under long-day photoperiods of sixteen hours by supplementing the natural day length with incandescent lights. While cold storage is not necessary for year round growth, plants exposed to six to eight weeks of 37°F (4°C) cold storage with eight hours of incandescent light daily will increase total production.

French tarragon is the key ingredient in Sauce Béarnaise and an important ingredient in salad dressings and poultry dishes. French tarragon is considered GRAS (leaves are GRAS at 2,731 ppm, while the essential oil is GRAS at 441 ppm). Tarragon oil with 60 percent methyl chavicol has been found to be genotoxic to *Saccharomyces cerevisiae* (yeast), an indication that it may be carcinogenic. Whether this represents a human health hazard is still open to speculation. Tarragon oil is also antifungal.

Tarragon plants can be troubled by rust (*Puccinia dracunculina*) and nematodes. Hot water treatment (113°F for 25 minutes) of the roots will kill most of the root-knot nematodes (*Meloidogyne hapla*) but also produce a 32 percent reduction in rhizome viability.

Important chemistry: The Russian tarragons have an essential oil with trace to 55 percent (*E*)-isoelemicin, trace to 60 percent elemicin (which provides a resinous odor), and 4 to 30 percent methyl eugenol (scented of cloves). French tarragon oil is high in methyl chavicol (estragole), 60 to 80 percent. Plants of "Turkish" tarragon have been reported with 81 percent (*Z*)-anethole and 7 percent (*Z*)-beta-ocimene.

Plants grown in Oregon of unknown origin had 25 percent terpinolene and 22 percent (*Z*)-beta-ocimene. The latter two chemotypes illustrate the diversity within this species that has not been explored.

Artemisia genipi

är-tĕ-mĭz-ĭ-å jē-nī-pī
genépi

> **French:** *genépi*
> **Italian:** *genipi*

Genépi is usually harvested from the wild in the Alps of Europe and primarily used in some liqueurs. While currently not cultivated in North America, genépi deserves to be introduced because of its fine odor. Genépi has no GRAS status.

Important chemistry: The essential oil of genépi consists of 26 percent alpha-thujone and 12 percent terpinen-4-ol.

Artemisia glacialis

är-tĕ-mĭz-ĭ-å glā-sē-ā-lĭs
genépi des glaciers

> **French:** *genépi des glaciers*
> **German:** *Gletscherreute*

Genépi des glaciers is used in a similar manner to *A. genipi*. It is not in current cultivation in North America but should be introduced. Genépi des glaciers has no GRAS status.

Artemisia herba-alba

är-tĕ-mĭz-ĭ-å hĕr-bā-ăl-bå
armoise

> **French:** *armoise*
> **Arabic:** *shih*

The Latin name literally means "white herb." Armoise is primarily used in perfumery but is also possesses antibacterial and antispasmodic properties. While not now cultivated in North America, the species deserves increased attention because of its fragrance and historical use.

Important chemistry: The essential oil of armoise consists of 0 to 84 percent beta-thujone, 0 to 74 percent alpha-thujone, trace to 69 percent camphor, 1 to 50 percent 1,8-cineole, trace to 39 percent davanone, trace to 18 percent *p*-cymene, 0 to 17 percent *trans*-pinocarveol, and 0 to 16 percent chrysnathenone, a very variable odor that could best be described overall as green-herbaceous, chrysanthemum-like.

Artemisia maritima

är-tĕ-mĭz-ĭ-å må-rĭt-ĭ-må
Levant wormseed

> **French:** *armoise maritime*
> **German:** *Strand-Beifuss*
> **Dutch:** *zee-alsem*
> **Italian:** *assenzio marino, santonica*
> **Arabic:** *afsantin-el-bahr*

Levant wormseed is sometimes used in Middle Eastern cooking but is not cultivated in North America. *Maritima* refers to the sea-coast habitat of this plant. Levant wormseed has no GRAS status.

Important chemistry: The primary constituents of the essential oil are 53 to 82 percent linalool and 6 to 20 percent 1,8-cineole, providing a lavender/eucalyptus-like odor.

Artemisia pallens

är-tĕ-mĭz-ĭ-å păl-ĕnz
davana

Davana, as it is almost universally known, is used in flavor compositions for beverages, candies, tobacco, and baked goods; *pallens* refers to its gray foliage. The essential oil is GRAS up to 11 ppm. Despite the wide use of davana, it is currently not cultivated in North America.

Davana is used in India for garlands and bouquets and in folk medicine as a treatment for diabetes. Research with methanol extracts of davana done at the Tropical Botanic Garden and Research Institute in Kerala, India, showed a significant blood-glucose lowering effect in diabetic rats.

This annual is easily propagated from seeds. Prior to sowing, the seed is usually mixed with sand, tied in a cloth bag, and kept moist for forty-eight hours before sowing in nursery beds. Prior to transplanting, the soil is fertilized with liberal manure, 36 pounds per acre (40 kg/ha) phosphate and 36 pounds per acre (40 kg/ha) potash. Nitrogen at 48 pounds per acre (53 kg/ha) is applied ten days, twenty-five days, and forty days after transplanting. Transplants are normally planted out five weeks after sowing, spaced 3 inches (7.5 cm) between plants and 6 inches (15 cm) between rows. Harvesting is done when a large number of flower buds open. Infestations by root-knot nematodes (*Meloidogyne* spp.) will decrease yields.

Important chemistry: The essential oil is primarily composed of 38 percent cis-davanone and 10 percent nerol, providing a fruity-rose fragrance.

Artemisia pontica

är-tĕ-mĭz-ĭ-å pŏn-tĭ-kå
Roman wormwood

> **French:** *petite absinthe*
> **German:** *Römischer Beifuss*
> **Dutch:** *roomse alsem*
> **Italian:** *assenzio pontico, assenzio gentile*
> **Spanish:** *ajenjo menor, ajenjor romano*

Roman wormwood is also known as Hungarian wormwood or small absinthe. *Pontica* refers to the south shore of the Black Sea. The delicate, thread-like gray leaves of this herb may remind the gardener of frost patterns.

In situations of full sun and well-drained garden loam, Roman wormwood spreads widely and easily into the lawn; it is not a good edging. Yet the delicate foliage is indispensable in the herb garden. Since wormwood was banned from liqueurs, Roman wormwood has been substituted in the formulation of Pernod, the replacement for absinthe. Roman wormwood has no GRAS status.

Important chemistry: The essential oil of Roman wormwood consists of 0 to 34 percent artemisia ketone, 24 to 25 percent 1,8-cineole, 21 to 23 percent alpha-thujone, and 0 to 16 percent camphor.

Artemisia vulgaris

a är-tĕ-mĭz-ĭ-å vŭl-gā-rĭs
mugwort

> **French:** *armoise commune, herbe de St. Jean*
> **German:** *Echter (gemeiner) Beifuss, Mugwurz, Gánsekraut*
> **Dutch:** *bijvoet*
> **Italian:** *erba di San Giovanni, amarella, campaccio, assenzio selvatico*
> **Spanish:** *ajenja, artemisia, hierba de San Juan*
> **Portuguese:** *artemisia verdadeira*
> **Chinese:** *ai-hao, ch'i-ai, i-ts'ao, k'i-ai, chih-ts'ao, chiu-ts'ao*
> **Arabic:** *afsantin-e-hindi*

Mugwort is also known as Indian wormwood. *Vulgaris* means "common". Mugwort is a potentially noxious weed and very difficult to eliminate because of its rhizomatous roots; it is not a plant for the controlled herb garden. Edges of fields and forests would suit this herb perfectly. Mowing does not seem to harm it where it is established.

Mugwort has been used in cooking, and it is an effective mosquito repellent when burned. Mugwort has no GRAS status.

Artemisia princeps Pamp., Japanese mugwort, is called *yomogi* or *kazuzaki-yomogi* in Japan. This herb is very similar to *A. vulgaris* and is sometimes classified as a variety of that species (*A. vulgaris* var. *maximowiczii* Nakai).

Artemisia vulgaris

Important chemistry: The essential oil of mugwort consists of trace to 27 percent 1,8-cineole, trace to 20 percent camphor, 1 to 19 percent borneol, 0 to 16 percent sabinene, 0 to 14 percent myrcene, and 0 to 13 percent terpinen-4-ol, providing an overall odor of green-herbaceous.

Botanical Key and Description

Key:

1. Most leaves on the flowering stems undivided . . . . *A. dracunculus*
1a. Most leaves on the flowering stems divided. 2
   2. Annual. 3
      3. Hairless . . . . *A. annua*
      3a. Covered with grayish white interwoven tangle of hairs. . . . . *A. pallens*
   2a. Perennial 5
      4. All florets hermaphrodite and fertile. 5
         5. Leaves rarely more than 10 mm, mostly in axillary fascicles on the flowering stems . . . .
         . . . . *A. herba-alba*
         5a. Most leaves more than 10 mm, not in axillary fascicles on the flowering stems. . . . .
         . . . . *A. maritima*
      4a. Outer florets female, with thread-like floral envelope 6
         6. Inflorescence compound with the younger flowers at the apex; stems usually at least
            30 cm . . . . *A. absinthium*
         6a. Inflorescence with stalked flowers borne along a more or less elongated axis, the
            youngest flowers near the apex or head, sometimes with a few short branches; stems
            usually less than 30 cm 7
            7. Involucral bracts hairy all over . . . . *A. glacialis*
            7a. Receptacle smooth. 8
               8. Terminal lobe of leaves on the stem at least 2 mm wide at base. . . . . *A. vulgaris*
               8a. Terminal lobe of leaves on the stem less than 2 mm wide at base. 9
                  9. Small heads (capitula) ten or fewer . . . . *A. genipi*
                  9a. Capitula more than ten. 10
                    10. Capitula in a simple or very slightly branched inflorescence along a more
                       or less elongated axis with the younger flowers at the top . . . . *A. genipi*
                    10a. Capitula in a much-branched inflorescence with the younger flowers at
                       the center; branches sometimes short but numerous. 11
                      11. Lower leaves on the stem stalkless, the lowest pair of segments usually
                       more or less stem-clasping with a dilated base . . . . *A. pontica*
                      11a. Lower leaves on the stem distinctly stalked. . . . . *A. abrotanum*

A. abrotanum L., Sp. pl. 845. 1753.
Native country: Southernwood is found in Europe but its native country is unknown.

General habit: Southernwood is a woody perennial shrub to 1 m.
Leaves: Leaves are pinnately lobed halfway to

the midrib once to three times, the thread-like lobes bearing glandular dots, smooth above and grayish-hairy beneath; leaf stalks short, not with a basal lobe.

Flowers: The inflorescence consists of small heads. The flowers are yellow.

A. absinthium L., Sp. pl. 848. 1753.

Native country: Wormwood is native to Europe.

General habit: Wormwood is covered with long, straight, soft, appressed hairs, giving it a silky texture, 30 to 100 cm tall.

Leaves: Leaves are pinnately divided two to three times, stalked, lobes 5 to 20 × 1 to 6 mm, usually blunt at the apex.

Flowers: The inflorescence consists of small heads, nodding, in a compound inflorescence with the youngest at the tip.

A. annua L., Sp. pl. 847. 1753.

Native country: Annual wormwood is native to southeast Europe but naturalized throughout Europe, Asia, and North America.

General habit: Annual wormwood is a smooth annual, 5 to 150 cm tall.

Leaves: Lower and middle leaves are pinnately lobed halfway to the midrib three times, stalkless; lobes 1 to 5 × 0.5 to 1 mm, linear-lance-shaped, tapering to the apex. Upper leaves are pinnately lobed halfway to the midrib once or twice.

Flowers: The inflorescence consists of small heads arranged in a lax compound inflorescence with the youngest at the apex.

A. dracunculus L., Sp. pl. 849. 1753.

Native country: Tarragon is native to Asia, Europe, and North America.

General habit: Tarragon is a much-branched smooth perennial, 60 to 120 cm tall.

Leaves: Basal leaves are three-lobed at the apex,

the other leaves 2 to 10 × 0.2 to 1 cm, linear to lance-shaped, with a smooth edge or weakly toothed.

Flowers: The inflorescence consists of small heads arranged in a small compound inflorescence with the youngest at the apex. Flowers are yellowish.

A. genipi Weber in Stechm., Artem. 17. 1775 [*A. spicata* Wulfen, *A. laxa* (Lam.) Fritsch., *A. mutellina* Vill., *A. glacialis* Wulfen, non L.].

Native country: Genépi is native to the Alps of Europe.

General habit: Genépi is densely grayish; long, straight, soft, appressed hairs give a silky texture to this 25 cm perennial.

Leaves: The stem-leaves are stalked, pinnately lobed, or deeply toothed.

Flowers: The inflorescence consists of small heads, dense and nodding. Flowers are densely hairy.

A. glacialis L., Sp. pl. ed. 2. 1187. 1763.

Native country: Genépi des glaciers is native to the southwestern Alps of Europe.

General habit: Genépi des glaciers is a densely tufted perennial to 18 cm; long, straight, soft, appressed hairs give a silky texture.

Leaves: Leaves are stalked, five-parted, with segments divided into threes, the lobes narrowly linear, almost blunt at the apex; the upper stem-leaves less divided.

Flowers: The inflorescence consists of small heads crowded into a terminal flat-topped or convex open inflorescence. Flowers are bright yellow, smooth.

A. herba-alba Asso, Syn. Strip. Arag. 117. 1779.

Native country: Armoise is native from Spain to southern France and from Morocco to Israel and Iran.

General habit: Armoise is a woody perennial to 60 cm, spreading.

Leaves: Leaves are 2 to 5 mm, pinnately lobed halfway to the midrib once or twice, the lower shortly stalked, the others stalkless.

Flowers: The inflorescence consists of small heads in a freely branched compound inflorescence with the youngest at the apex.

A. maritima L., Sp. pl. 846. 1753.

Native country: Levant wormseed is native to the coasts of western and northern Europe.

General habit: Levant wormseed is a perennial covered with a gray to white dense, wool-like covering of matted, tangled hairs of medium length, rarely approaching smooth with a horizontal to slightly ascending, usually rather slender stalk; flowering stems are 5 to 60 cm, often woody below.

Leaves: The lower stem-leaves wither at flowering and are pinnately divided two or three times, stalked, often with small, earlike lobes at the base. The lobes are 3 to 15 × 0.4 to 0.9 mm, rounded at the apex to linear, almost tapering to the apex to blunt at the apex; upper leaves stalkless, the uppermost undivided or with a few lobes basally.

Flowers: The inflorescence consists of small nodding or erect heads.

A. pallens Wall. ex DC., Prodr. 6:120. 1838.

Native country: Davana is native to India.

General habit: Davana is an erect annual covered with a grayish white, dense covering of matted, tangled hairs of medium length, 45 to 60 cm tall.

Leaves: Leaves are stalked, lobed to halfway to the midrib, gray.

Flowers: The flowers consist of small heads arranged in a lax inflorescence with the stalked flowers formed along a more or less elongated axis with the younger flowers near the apex. Flowers are yellow.

A. pontica L., Sp. pl. 847. 1753.

Native country: Roman wormwood is native to central and eastern Europe and naturalized throughout Europe.

General habit: Roman wormwood is a rhizomatous perennial with stems 40 to 80 cm tall, grayish with a dense covering of matted, tangled hairs of medium length, almost smooth below.

Leaves: Leaves are 3 to 4 cm, pinnately compound halfway to the midrib once or twice, stalkless, with small earlike lobes at the base, densely hairy on both surfaces; lobes are up to 0.5 mm wide, linear-lance-shaped, tipped with a small tooth-like shape.

Flowers: The inflorescence consists of small heads in a narrow compound inflorescence with the youngest at the tip. The flowers are yellow.

A. vulgaris L., Sp. pl. 848. 1753.

Native country: Mugwort is native to most of Europe and naturalized in North America.

General habit: Mugwort grows in tufts but without an overwintering rosette. Stems are 30 to 120 cm, sparsely hairy, often almost smooth, usually reddish or purplish.

Leaves: Leaves are pinnately lobed halfway to the midrib, with ear-shaped appendages at the base, usually smooth above, covered with a tangle of hairs beneath. Lower leaves are shortly stalked, upper stalkless.

Flowers: The inflorescence consists of numerous small heads, almost stalkless, erect or slightly recurved, crowded on the branches of a large compound inflorescence with the younger flowers at the apex. Bracts are leaf-like, the upper small and simple. The flowers are usually reddish brown.

Asarum canadense

ăs-å-rŭm kăn-ă-dĕn-sē
wild ginger

Family: Aristolochiaceae

Growth form: creeping herbaceous perennial to 6 inches (15 cm)

Hardiness: hardy to New Brunswick and Quebec (Zone 4)

Light: shade

Water: constantly moist to edge of standing water

Soil: rich in organic matter, pH 5.0 to 6.0

Propagation: primarily by divisions in early spring, but fresh seeds may also be used

Culinary use: substitute for ginger

Craft use: potpourri

Landscape use: shady border, groundcover, wildflower garden

French: *serpentaire du Canada*
German: *Canadische Schlangenwurzel*
Italian: *asaro*
Spanish: *asaro, serpentaria*

The wildflower books call this wild ginger, but the name of the commercial product is Canadian snakeroot. The genus name is derived from an unknown ancient Roman and Greek word and currently includes about seventy species of the north temperate areas of the northern hemisphere.

The heart-shaped leaves of *A. canadense* are a good accent in a shady, moist garden with acidic soil. The tubular dark red flowers, borne at the base of the leaves, go almost unnoticed. In the wild, this herb is found in humusy soil near moist seeps or along streams in northeastern North America. Allowed to colonize, the plant can actually be used as a groundcover. Wild ginger is easily propagated by divisions in early spring. Fresh seeds may also be pressed into the soil where new colonies are desired.

Wild ginger is grown primarily for its ginger-scented creeping rhizomes, but don't expect a windfall of ginger for your kitchen. The plant is rather delicate and slow growing compared to true ginger (*Zingiber officinale*), so it is more of a curiosity than a useful herb. Other species of *Asarum*, such as *A. europaeum* L., are also good ornaments in the garden and often have ginger-scented rhizomes but are not recommended for human consumption (the oil of *A. europaeum* is actually poisonous). The rhizomes of wild ginger have been used as a substitute for true ginger and even candied, but only the essential oil has GRAS status at 1 to 8.3 ppm in nonalcoholic beverages, ice cream, candy, baked goods, and condiments.

Important chemistry: The essential oil of the rhizomes of wild ginger (Canadian snake-

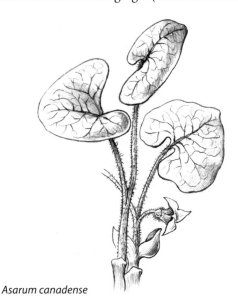

Asarum canadense

root) is dominated by 36 percent methyl eugenol and 28 percent linalyl acetate, providing a
spicy-lavender note. The rhizomes of wild ginger also contain aristolochic acid, an anti-tumor
compound.

Botanical Description

At least two varieties may be distinguished: var.
canadense with calyx lobes spreading from the
base, curved upward beyond the middle and
gradually narrowed into a rolled-backward-
margined slender tip 0.5 to 2 cm; and var. *re-
flexum* (E. P. Bicknell) B. L. Robinson, with
reflexed calyx lobes closely appressed to the
ovary and triangular, abruptly contracted into
a short, tubular 2 to 4 mm tip.

A. canadense L., Sp. pl. 442. 1753.

Native country: Wild ginger is native to rich
woods from New Brunswick and Quebec
to Ontario and Minnesota, south to North
Carolina, northern Alabama, and northern
Louisiana.

General habit: Wild ginger is a hairy, deciduous, herbaceous perennial rising to about
15 cm.

Leaves: Leaves are heart-round to heart-kidney-
shaped, 8 to 12 cm wide at the time of pollen
release, larger at maturity.

Flowers: The flowers are actually composed
of three calyx lobes and no petals. These appear in May and are basal, bell-shaped, and
deep red.

Bergera koenigii

bĕr-gĕr-å kĕ-nīg-ē-ī
Indian curry leaf

Family: Rutaceae
Growth form: shrub to small tree
Hardiness: hardy to Zone 9
Light: full sun
Water: evenly moist
Soil: garden loam
Propagation: cuttings, seeds
Culinary use: curry, but not GRAS
Craft use: none
Landscape use: interesting container plant

Hindi: *mitha neem, kurry-patha*

Bergera koenigii

Indian curry leaf is an essential ingredient of
curries throughout southeastern Asia. The
smell has been described as distinctly curry-like

with the overtones of gasoline. Nonetheless, the herb harmonizes well with curry mixtures for vegetables, fish and meat dishes, soups (rasams), pickles, buttermilk preparations, chutneys, scrambled eggs, and so on. It does not, however, have GRAS status from the FDA.

An organic solvent extract of the leaves is somewhat antibacterial. An aqueous extract of the leaves inhibits ethanol-induced lesions in the stomach.

Most publications list Indian curry leaf as *Murraya koenigii*, but the correct name is *Bergera koenigii*. The latter scientific name apparently commemorates Alexander Malacias Berger (1737–1804), a student of Linnaeus, and J. G. Koenig (1728–1785), a botanist in India.

Important chemistry: The essential oil of Indian curry leaf is very diverse and contains 0 to 45 percent sabinene, 0 to 68 percent alpha-pinene, trace to 54 percent beta-caryophyllene, trace to 70 percent beta-pinene, trace to 49 percent beta-phellandrene, 0 to 21 percent beta-gurjuenne, and 0 to 10 percent bicyclogermacrene. Both the leaves and seeds are rich in numerous carbazole alkaloids of unknown toxicity, and the seeds are considered poisonous.

Botanical Description

B. koenigii L., Mant. Pl. 2:563. 1771 [*Murraya koenigii* (L.) Spreng.].

Native country: Indian curry leaf is native to the foot of the Himalayas, eastward to Myanmar (Burma), Indochina, southern China, and Peninsular India, and is widely cultivated in various tropical countries.

General habit: Indian curry leaf is a shrub or small tree to 5 m in height.

Leaves: Leaves are spiralled-alternate, pinnate, crowded at twig-ends, mostly 15 to 30 cm long, leaflets 15 to 25, dark green above, paler beneath.

Flowers: The small, white fragrant flowers are borne in a dense, corymbose paniculate, terminal inflorescence.

Fruits/seeds: The fruit is a subglobose berry containing one or two green seeds.

Borago officinalis

bôr-ā-gō ŏ-fĭs-ĭ-nā-lĭs
borage

Family: Boraginaceae

Growth form: annual to about 28 inches (70 cm)

Hardiness: seedlings do not withstand frost well

Light: full sun

Water: constantly moist but not wet

Soil: average garden loam, pH 4.5 to 8.2, average 6.6

Propagation: seeds in spring, 2,000 seeds per ounce (70/g)

Culinary use: historically eaten but not recommended today

Craft use: none

Landscape use: allow to reseed cottage-garden style

French: *bourrache*
German: *Boretsch, Borretsch, Gurkenkraut*
Dutch: *prikneus, bernagie*
Italian: *borrana, borragine, buglossa vera, vorraccio*
Spanish: *borraja, becoquino*
Portuguese: *borragem*

The ancients found in borage the perfect pick-me-up, a quick cure for what they called melan-cholia, or, as we know it today, the blahs. Although this cure for boredom was usually created by mixing borage stems, leaves, and/or flowers with alcohol and drinking the concoction, you don't have to go that far. The plant itself is cheery, in an awkward way; a bit clumsy of stem with a sprawling footprint, but bearing beautiful blue flowers that sparkle against its large, coarse green leaves.

The derivation of the generic name, *Borago*, is unknown but it probably derives from the medieval Latin, *borra* or *burra*, meaning "rough hair" and referring to the prickly stems and leaves. Linnaeus stated that the name was a corruption of *corago* (Latin *cor*, the heart, and *ago*, to act) from its use in medicine as a heart seda-

Borago officinalis

tive. The genus *Borago* includes three species native to the Mediterranean region and Europe.

Borage has long been employed as bee-fodder, and the cucumber-flavored leaves have been eaten like spinach or used to flavor apertifs such as Pimm's No. 1 Cup. The flowers of borage are also candied and used for cake decoration or used in jams and jellies. Not only do raw, hairy borage leaves taste like cucumber-flavored caterpillars, recent research has found that both flowers and leaves contain pyrrolizidine alkaloids, which cause liver cancer, and hydrocyanic acid.

However, borage seeds (actually small nuts, or nutlets) contain gamma-linolenic acid. This unusual fatty acid is an intermediate in the biosynthesis of prostaglandins, a class of metabolic regulators in mammals. Dietary supplements of gamma-linolenic acid may be beneficial in the treatment of health problems associated with deficiencies in essential fatty acids and prostaglandins. Gamma-linolenic acid has shown therapeutic promise in the treatment of atopic eczema, premenstrual syndrome, diabetes, alcoholism, and inflammation. Gamma-linolenic acid may help prevent heart disease. We do not recommend the consumption of raw borage seeds, however, because they also contain at least one pyrrolizidine alkaloid.

Borage germinates quickly from direct-sown seed in spring and grows rapidly up to about 28 inches (70 cm) with coarse 8-inch (20 cm) leaves and blue flowers around June and July. Borage prefers well-drained, stony soil in full sun and only a moderate amount of water. In conditions to its liking, borage will reseed.

Important chemistry: The foliage of borage is rich in pyrrolizidine alkaloids in the range of 2 to 8 mg/kg. The principal alkaloids detected in the leaves include 16 to 39 percent lycopsamine, 12 to 36 percent supinine, 13 to 35 percent amabiline, 9 to 31 percent acetyllycopsamine, $\leq$ 2 percent 7-acetylintermedine, more than 1 percent intermedine, and cynaustine [(+)-supinidine viridiflorate]. In addition, borage plants contain hydrocyanic acid (15 mg HCN/kg of young nonflowering plants). The flowers contain the alkaloid thesinine. The seeds contain thesinine (300 mg/kg in mature seeds), lycopsamine, 7-acetylintermedine, and seneciphylline in addition to 13 to 33 percent oil with 34 to 39 percent linoleic acid, 20 to 26 percent gamma-linolenic acid, 15 to 19 percent oleic acid, and 9 to 12 percent palmitic acid.

Botanical Description

B. officinalis L., Sp. pl. 137. 1753.
Native country: Borage is native to southern Europe but naturalized in the warmer parts of central, eastern, and western Europe.

General habit: Borage is an annual to 15 to 70 cm high.

Leaves: Basal leaves are 5 to 20 cm long, egg- to lance-shaped, and stalked. Upper leaves are stalkless, clasping the stem.

Flowers: Flowers are five-pointed blue stars, rarely white, lobes 8 to 15 mm long, lance-shaped, tapering to the apex.

Fruits/seeds: Nutlets are 7 to 10 mm long, oblong to slightly egg-shaped.

Brassica

bră-sē-kå
brassica

Family: Brassicaceae (Cruciferae)
Growth form: annual to about 39 inches (1 m) or more
Hardiness: withstands frost
Light: full sun
Water: moist but not constantly wet
Soil: good garden loam, pH 4.3 to 8.2, average 6.2 (*B. juncea* var. *juncea*); pH 4.9 to 8.2, average 6.5 (*B. nigra*)
Propagation: seeds in spring, 15,000 seeds per ounce (535/g)
Culinary use: mustards
Craft use: none
Landscape use: wildflower garden

Brassica

The genus *Brassica* includes the cole crops (cabbage, cauliflower, broccoli, brussels sprouts, kohlrabi, and so on), and its name is derived from the Latin for cabbage. All thirty species of this genus contain allyl thiocyanates, or mustard oils, providing them with their own particular pungency, but only two members of the genus are considered to be herbs because their seeds are ground and used to make mustard.

To most Americans, mustard is the commercial yellow product slathered upon hot dogs. Mustards, either alone or with other flavors (such as dillweed or tarragon), go well beyond this simple concept, and those resourceful enough to prepare their own mustards are in for a real treat.

As a food, mustard dates back as far as the Han Dynasty in China (206 B.C.E.–221 C.E.), and the Romans also spread mustard in their conquests. The word mustard is derived from the French *moutarde*, which, in turn, is derived from the Latin *mustum ardens*, or "burning must." This etymology arose because of the medieval French practice of preparing culinary mustard by pounding the seeds with honey and either vinegar or must (partially fermented or "new" wine). The English of this time prepared their mustard differently, grinding the seeds coarsely with flour and sometimes cinnamon, moistening the paste, and forming it into balls which were then dried for later use.

Modern medical application of the mustards is limited to external poultices on top of cheesecloth ("plasters") to increase blood flow by dilating the blood vessels, but prolonged contact with skin will produce blistering. Internally, the effect is the same, and the irritants in mustard stimulate blood flow in all tissues, but damage to the digestive tract can result with overdoses. Mustard can depress thyroid function, so individuals with hypothyroidism should generally avoid mustards.

Besides the species of *Brassica* listed below, *Sinapis alba* (which see) yields yellow or white mustard, the source for many American prepared mustards.

Brassica juncea
bră-sē-kå jūn-sē-å
brown and Indian mustard

French: *moutarde brune, moutarde de Chine*
German: *Rutensenf, Sareptasenf, Indischersenf*
Dutch: *bruine mosterd*
Italian: *senape indiana, senape cinese*
Spanish: *mostaza de Indias, mostaza hindu*
Swedish: *sarepta senap*
Russian: *gorchitsa sareltskaya*
Chinese: *chieh*
Japanese: *karashi*

The brown and Indian mustard seeds are used for their pungent aroma and bite similar to horseradish. Chinese restaurant mustard, hot English mustard, Dijon mustard, and German mustard all owe their pungency to brown mustards.

This species name, *B. juncea*, means "rush-like mustard," referring to the inflorescences arising in tight clusters. Depending upon the variety, mustard may be used either as a potherb or for seasoning. Only var. *juncea* is considered here as an herb, although this species also includes var. *crispifolia*, curled mustard or Southern curled mustard; var. *integrifolia*, broad-leaved Chinese mustard; var. *japonica*, Japanese mustard or potherb mustard (*takana* in Japanese); var. *megarrhiza*, turnip-rooted mustard or tuberous-rooted Chinese mustard; and var. *tumida*, swollen-stemmed mustard.

Since World War II, brown and Indian mustards have supplanted black mustard in the condiment trade because mechanical harvesting of the latter is difficult—it shatters easily. Prepare garden loam with near-neutral pH in the fall for sowing as early as possible the following spring. Seeding is at the rate of approximately 3 pounds per acre (3⅓ kg/ha). For the home gardener, plant seeds about 9 inches apart and about ⅛ to ¼ inch deep. Succulent thinned seedlings can be consumed in salads. The yellow flowers have a sweet fragrance that permeates the garden.

The crop may be ready for harvest in August or as early as late May. When the seed pods turn brown, cut the plants down and stack them in an airy place to dry with a tarp underneath to catch fallen seeds. Home gardeners may hang plants to dry with the pods enclosed in a strong paper bag. Later roll the closed bag with a heavy rolling pin and winnow the seeds by lowering the nozzle of a vacuum cleaner until the chaff is picked up, leaving the heavier seeds behind. Yields of up to 1,000 pounds per acre (1,121 kg/ha) of cleaned seeds may be expected, or about 2 tablespoons of seeds for each foot of plants. Generally about a dozen plants will yield enough seeds to prepare at least a few batches of homemade mustard. All mustards self-sow freely and can become weedy quickly; seeds last for about two years in soil.

Brown and Indian mustards are subject to attack by the *Brassica* seed weevil (*Ceutorrhynchus assimilis*), pollen beetle (*Meligethes aeneas*), flea beetle (*Phyllotreta cruciferae*), and the mustard beetle (*Phaedon cochleariae*), but all are easily controlled by insecticides.

Brown and Indian mustards are primarily imported from Canada, but some is produced in the northern Plains States of the United States. Brown mustard seeds (23,000 to 101,503 ppm) and essential oil (201 ppm) are considered GRAS.

Important chemistry: The seeds of brown and Indian mustards contain the enzyme myrosinase and a mixture of two glucosides: sinigrin, or potassium allyl glucosinolate, and 3-butenyl glucosinolate. In the presence of water, the enzyme and the glucosides interact, liberating allyl isothiocyanate (44 to 69 percent of the volatile oil) and 3-butenyl isothiocyanate (5 to 6 percent of the volatile oil). The volatile isothiocyanates are responsible for the pungent flavor, or "heat," of brown and Indian mustards. This reaction is somewhat different in hot water; at temperatures greater than 110°F (43°C), the somewhat toxic and bitter nitriles are liberated. This may account for the bitterness of adding uncooked mustard seeds early in cooking, which can be alleviated by soaking the seeds in cold water before cooking. Heating in oil does not liberate the isothiocyanates, and mustard seeds may be popped and ground as is done in many Indian masalas.

Generally about a dozen plants will yield enough seeds to prepare at least a few batches of homemade mustard.

Brassica nigra
br̆ă-sē-k̊å n̄ī-gr̆ă
black mustard

    French: *moutarde noire, moutarde grise,*
      sénevé noir
    German: *Schwarzer Senf, Senfkohl*
    Dutch: *zwarte mosterd*
    Italian: *senape nera*
    Spanish: *mostaza negra*
    Portuguese: *mostarda, mostarda negra*
    Swedish: *svartsenap*
    Russian: *gorchitsa chernaya*
    Chinese: *chi'ing-chieh, tzu-chieh*
    Arabic: *khardal*

Black mustard is no longer a commercial commodity because it requires hand-harvesting. Since World War II, the brown mustards have replaced black mustard for use in prepared mustards. Indian cooks, however, use black mustard seeds in hot oil to impart a rich, buttery taste to curries.

Try raising your own black mustard to prepare a really unique spread! Seeds of *B. nigra* are considered GRAS at 2,300 to 5,200 ppm.

Important chemistry: Seeds of *B. nigra* contain myrosinase and sinigrin (potassium allyl glucosinolate), which liberates allyl isothiocyanate (trace to 2 percent of the volatile oil) upon mixing with water.

Botanical Key and Description

Key:

1.   Long capsules appressed to the stem; beak thread-like . . . . *B. nigra*
1a. Long capsules, spreading to erect or curved outward; beak gradually narrows to a tip to cylindrical . . . . . .
. . . . *B. juncea*

B. juncea (L.) Czern., Consp. Pl. Charc. 8. 1859 var. *juncea* (*B. besseriana* Andrz., *Sinapis ramosa* Roxb., *B. juncea* Coss., *B. juncea* Coss. var. *sareptana* Sinskaia)

Native country: *B. juncea* is probably an ancient hybrid (*B. nigra* × *B. rapa* L.) and is native to southern and eastern Asia.

General habit: *B. juncea* var. *juncea* is a smooth annual herb. The principal stem is up to 1.2 m high; branches are long and spreading to erect.

Leaves: Lower leaves are egg-shaped to broad with parallel sides to narrowed at the base, with leaf stalk, with opposite lobes with one or two pairs of lobes on each side and a larger terminal lobe sparsely beset with bristles; upper lobes almost smooth, shortly stalked.

Flowers: Flowers are bright yellow, 1 cm long, scattered in the raceme or more typically aggregated at the end and overlapping the unopened buds.

Fruits/seeds: Fruit is an elongated, two-celled capsule, 30 to 60 × 2 to 3.5 mm. Brown mustard is distinguished by its reddish brown to dark brown seeds, while Indian mustard is distinguished by its mostly light yellow seeds; both seeds are about 2 mm in diameter.

B. nigra (L.) W. Koch in Röhling, Deutschl. Fl. ed. 3. 4:713. 1833.

Native country: Black mustard's origin is uncertain, but it is probably native to the Middle East.

General habit: The principal stem of this

annual herb is up to 1 m or more, branched from the middle or from near the base.

Leaves: Lower leaves are lobed, with one to three pairs of lateral lobes and a much larger terminal lobe, with stiff bristles on both surfaces; upper leaves are narrow with parallel sides, without teeth, or strongly wavy-margined, smooth; all leaves stalked.

Flowers: Flowers are bright yellow, 7 to 9 mm long.

Fruit/Seeds: Fruit is an elongated two-celled capsule, 10 to 20 × 1.5 to 2 mm. Seeds are about 2 mm or less in size but tend to be more oblong than spherical.

Calamintha

kăl-å-mĭn-thå
calamint

Family: Lamiaceae (Labiatae)
Growth form: herbaceous perennials to about 32 inches (80 cm)
Hardiness: hardy to at least Zone 6
Light: full sun
Water: well-drained soil
Soil: average garden loam
Propagation: divisions in spring, seeds
Culinary use: limited (not GRAS)
Craft use: potpourri
Landscape use: cottage gardens, wildflower meadows, or along paths

The genus name is from the Greek for "good mint," and while that judgment deserves attention, the calamints have been generally ignored by herb growers. Calamint's late summer flowers are small, but the mint-scented foliage is abundant; they are tough but short-lived, straggly perennials rather resistant to heat, cold, excess moisture, and drought. They bloom in late summer. The seven species of calamints are easily cultivated on a near-neutral garden loam. The abundant seeds and rampantly spreading nature of the herb, however, mean that the cala-

mints are better suited to the wild or cottage garden, not tightly controlled borders.

These European plants grow almost too well sometimes, and have readily naturalized themselves in North America. None of the calamints have GRAS status, although some books recommend the following two species of calamint in teas, and Italian cookbooks occasionally rec-

Calamintha

ommend these calamints (often called *nepetella*) for sauces.

Recently, the treatment in *The European Garden Flora* by D. R. McKean and A. C. Whiteley has alerted us to the fact that the names *C. nepeta* and *C. officinalis* have been misapplied, and what was formerly known as *C. nepeta* should be *C. glandulosa*. *Calamintha menthifolia* is now the correct name for *C. sylvatica*.

Calamintha glandulosa
kăl-å-mĭn-thå glăn-dū-lō-så
lesser calamint

> **French:** *menthe de montagne, calament clinopode*
> **German:** *Meeresminze, Wald-Quendel, Wald-Melisse, Basilien-Quendel, Berg-Melisse, Kalamint, Wirbeldast*
> **Dutch:** *alpen-steenthijm, berg-melisse, berg-steenthijm*
> **Italian:** *calamento, menta cendrata, clinpodio*
> **Spanish:** *calamenta, calaminta, albahaca silvestre mayor, calaminta de montaña*
> **Arabic:** *asaba-el-fatiyat*

Some American herb companies have mislabeled *C. glandulosa* as "*Nepeta nepetella*," an entirely different plant, apparently confused by some Italian cookbook authors who call this *nepetella*. This short-lived perennial bears hairy, egg-shaped leaves on wispy stems with tiny white or lilac flowers. The oil is antimicrobial.

Important chemistry: Misapplication of the names in *Calamintha* makes the interpretation of the chemical literature a bit difficult, so the original names in the literature are reported here. The essential oil reported as *C. nepeta* subsp. *nepeta* leaves consists of trace to 65 percent menthone, 12 to 62 percent pulegone, trace to 38 percent piperitenone oxide, trace to 26 percent isomenthone, trace to 17 percent piperitone oxide, and trace to 16 percent menthol. The essential oil reported as *C. nepeta* subsp. *glandulosa* leaves consists of 0 to 89 percent (*R*)(+)-carvone, trace to 76 percent pulegone, 0 to 56 percent menthone, 1 to 52 percent *trans*-piperitone oxide, trace to 44 percent piperitenone oxide, 0 to 40 percent carvacrol, 0 to 27 percent isomenthone, 0 to 28 percent menthol + neoisomenthol, 0 to 40 percent piperitenone, 0 to 13 percent piperitone, and 0 to 13 percent limonene.

Calamintha menthifolia
kăl-å-mĭn-thå měn-thĭ-fō-lē-å
calamint

Calamint is primarily used for teas. The essential oil has sedating, antipyretic (reducing fever), and antimicrobial activity.

The wispy aspect, leaves, and flowers of *C. menthifolia* are very similar to *C. glandulosa*. An unnamed variegated form with white streaks also exists.

Important chemistry: Misapplication of the names in *Calamintha* makes the interpretation of the chemical literature a bit difficult, so the original names in the literature are reported here. The essential oil reported as *C. sylvatica* subsp. *sylvatica* leaves consists of 57 percent piperitenone epoxide and 17 percent limonene or 63 to 75 percent piperitone oxide. The essential oil reported as *C. sylvatica* subsp. *ascendens* leaves consists of 31 percent 1,8-cineole, 17 percent isomenthone, 16 percent neoisomenthol, and 15 percent menthol. The essential oil reported as *C. menthifolia* has 63 to 68 percent piperitone oxide. The essential oil reported as *C. officinalis* has 47 percent carbone, 25 percent limonene, and 22 percent pulegone.

Botanical Key and Description

Key:

1. Lower calyx-teeth 2 to 4 mm long, usually densely set with long marginal hairs; hairs in mouth of calyx more or less included. . . . . *C. glandulosa*
1a. Lower calyx-teeth 1 to 2 mm long, without or with very few long marginal hairs; hairs in mouth of calyx somewhat exserted . . . . *C. menthifolia*

C. glandulosa (Req.) Benth. [*C. nepeta* (L.) Savi subsp. *glandulosa* (Req.) P. W. Ball; *C. nepeta* misapplied].
Native country: Lesser calamint is native to southwest and south-central Europe.
General habit: Lesser calamint is a sparsely to densely hairy perennial herb 30 to 80 cm tall.
Leaves: Leaves are 8 to 20 × 8 to 16 mm, broadly egg-shaped, blunt at apex, almost without teeth or with shallowly to deeply rounded teeth, up to five teeth per side, glandular spotted.
Flowers: Five to twenty white or lilac flowers are arranged in a flower cluster that blooms from the top down.

C. menthifolia Host (*C. sylvatica* Bromf., *C. officinalis* misapplied)
Native country: Calamint is native to western, southern, and south-central Europe.
General habit: Calamint is a hairy, stoloniferous perennial 30 to 80 cm tall.
Leaves: Leaves are 20 to 70 × 10 to 45 mm, egg-shaped or rounded-egg-shaped, slightly tapering to the apex to blunt at the apex, almost without teeth to coarsely large-toothed or with rounded teeth and five to ten teeth per side.
Flowers: Three to nine pink or lilac flowers with white spots on the lower lips are arranged in a cluster that flowers from the top down.

Calendula officinalis

kå-lĕn-dū-lå ŏ-fĭs-ĭ-nā-lĭs
poet's marigold

Family: Asteraceae (Compositae)
Growth form: annual to 8 to 20 inches (20 to 50 cm)
Hardiness: seedlings can withstand minor frost

Light: full sun
Water: moist but not constantly wet
Soil: average garden loam, pH 4.5 to 8.2, average 6.6

Propagation: seeds in spring, 3,500 seeds per ounce (123/g)

Culinary use: cheese, butter, custards, vinegars, salads, soups

Craft use: dye for hair and fabrics

Landscape use: border edges

French: *souci*

German: *Ringelblume, Studentenblume, Totenblume, Goldblume*

Dutch: *goedsbloem-wratten-kruid*

Italian: *calendula gialla, fiorrancio, calenzola*

Spanish: *calendula, flamenquilla, maravilla, flor de muerto*

Portuguese: *maravilhas, marianas*

Swedish: *ringblomma*

Russian: *nogotki lekarstvennye*

Chinese: *chin-chan-hua*

Arabic: *janvah, azariyunah, azarboya*

The genus *Calendula* includes about twenty species of the Mediterranean, but only *C. officinalis* has been used in medicine or the kitchen. The generic name is derived from the Latin *calendae*, the first day of the month, probably alluding to the flowering of the plant throughout the year in mild climates. The derivation of "marigold" is the Anglo-Saxon *merso-meargealla*, the marsh marigold, although the herb later became associated with both the Virgin Mary and Queen Mary. Large yellow to deep orange daisies, sometimes tipped in red and up to 3 inches across, are borne from tufted, light green, lance-shaped foliage, making this a very attractive annual for the border.

The subject of many poems because of its beauty and nature of closing at around 3 p.m. and opening again at about 9 a.m., calendula has achieved the English name of poet's marigold, but it also goes under the names of pot marigold, Scotch marigold, golds, or ruddles (ruddes). The derivation of "pot marigold" is either a shortening of "poet's marigold" or because of its free-flowering habit when housed in pots in cool winter greenhouses.

The carotenoid-rich yellow to orange petals of this annual daisy were once used to color butter, cheeses, and custards and to thicken soups and add a pleasant, spicy taste to salads, and to substitute for expensive imported saffron. From reading the first edition of John Gerarde's *Herball* of 1597, we know that it was especially popular during the time of Queen Elizabeth I (1533–1603). Recipes that call for marigold petals generally refer to this plant, not the Mexican/African/French marigolds (*Tagetes* spp.), although the latter are indeed used today as a supplement in chicken feed to color the fat yellow. The flowers of poet's marigold are listed as GRAS at 11 to 44 ppm.

The petals of poet's marigold also yield a dye for fabric or hair. Wide-ranging medicinal claims have been made for poet's marigold petals, but little research has tested these assertions. The petals have been found to be anti-inflammatory and promote wound-healing and may aid in the treatment of acute dermatitis, due to the content of isorhamnetin and faradiol mono-

Calendula officinalis

ester. The faradiol esters also provide anti-oedmatous activity. In addition, the high concentration of carotenoids, which are antioxidant, is well documented and provides scavenging activity against free radicals. The flower extract may be both genotoxic and anti-genotoxic. Flowers also exhibit both spasmolytic and spasmogenic constituents and may be useful in abdominal cramps and constipation. The flowers of *C. officinalis* contain 0.009 percent pyrethrins, so an extract would also be effective as an insecticide.

Some single and many double forms ('Bon Bon', 'Gitana', 'Prince', and 'Touch of Red' series) are currently cultivated. One quaint form, 'Prolifera', is the hen-and-chickens poet's marigold because of the "proliferated head," which radiates smaller heads out from it in the manner of hen-and-chickens (houseleek), *Sempervivum tectorum* L. Gerarde called this form "Jacke-an-apes on horsebacke." An investigation of ten cultivars of *C. officinalis* in Italy showed that 'Calypso Orange Florensis" produced the highest amounts of bioactive monoesters, followed by 'Fiesta Gitana Gelb' and 'May Orange Florensis'. Another study done in Austria with eight cultivars in two different locations found that the diameter of the flower heads, dry weight of the inflorescences, and content of faradiol-3-monoesters proved to be stable parameters, regardless of the environment. A study by the same authors found that the inheritance of the faradiol monoesters was complex and polygenic and not correlated with flower size.

Plants are easily started indoors four to six weeks before the last expected frost. The seeds, shaped like stiff and twisted vipers, may be directly sown in friable garden loam in full sun about 9 to 12 inches apart. Flowers are generally produced from May until frost if summers are cool. Seeds ripen in August and September, and poet's marigold often reseeds itself in the gar-

den. Heat is inimical to poet's marigold, and southern gardeners will find that their plants cease flowering and suffer from spider mites and black aphids in July and August; partial shade and moist soil will sometimes counterbalance the summer's heat. Researchers in Egypt found that pre-sowing seeds at a low temperature (5°C for 7 days) caused the most pronounced increase in the essential oil.

Flower production is particularly increased by fertilizers high in phosphorus, so fertilizers with an N-P-K ratio of 1-2-1 are recommended. A study done in Egypt also found that an application of urea at the rate of 106 pounds per acre (119 kg/hectare) gave the highest flower numbers and weight. Researchers in New Zealand found that the total flower yield was not significantly different at populations over 46 plants/m2. A mechanical harvester has been described by M. Herold and others of the VEB Pharmazeutisches Werk in Halle, Germany (see selected references).

Home gardeners may harvest flowers by cutting the heads from the stems and drying them in the shade on paper; the petals will stick to screens. Overlapping of the petals results in discoloration. Store the dried petals in tight, opaque containers to prevent fading and discoloration.

Important chemistry: The essential oil of poet's marigold flowers is dominated by 2 to 64 percent alpha-cadinol, 8 to 10 percent eudesmol, and 2 to 23 percent cadinene, along with many fatty acid esters and sesquiterpenes, providing a pleasant, spicy odor. The bitter principle is (-)-loliolide (calendin). The carotenoids, which provide the distinct yellow to orange of the petals, are beta-carotene, lycopene, violaxanthin, and lutein; in addition, flavonoids, narcissin, and glycosides of quercetin and isorhamnetin provide some color. At least eight faradiol and calenduladiol monoesters are bioactive.

Botanical Description

C. officinalis L., Sp. pl. 921. 1752.
Native country: Poet's marigold is native from Europe to Iran and North Africa.
General habit: Poet's marigold is an annual to perennial, woody only at the base, with stems 20 to 50 cm high.
Leaves: Leaves are 7 to 14 × 1 to 4 cm, lance-shaped with narrowed bases, narrowly parallel-sided, or spoon-shaped, shortly tapering to the apex or blunt, glandular-hairy to sparsely spidery-cottony hairy, usually with a smooth edge to obscurely wavy-toothed.
Flowers: Flowers are 4 to 7 cm in diameter, yellow or orange.
Fruits/seeds: Outer fruits (achenes) are incurved (or rarely flat) narrowly beaked, 2 to 2.5 cm, alternating with shorter boat-shaped (rarely three-winged) achenes.

Capparis spinosa

kă-p̱ār-ĭs spĭ-nō̱-så
capers

Family: Capparaceae
Growth form: shrub to 5 feet (1.5 m)
Hardiness: hardy to western California and central Florida (Zone 9)
Light: full sun
Water: withstands drought when established
Soil: well drained, pH 6.3 to 8.3
Propagation: cuttings preferred; seeds slow and variable
Culinary use: sauces and salad dressings
Craft use: none
Landscape use: pots, desert garden, walls

French: *câprier épineux, câpre*
German: *Kapernstrauch, Kappern, Kaper*
Dutch: *kappertjesstruik*
Italian: *capperi, cappero*
Spanish: *alcaparro, alcaparna, tápana, cabriola*
Portuguese: *alcaparra*
Swedish: *kapris*
Russian: *kapertsy*
Arabic: *kiabara*

While most people have tasted capers, few have actually seen them growing or attempted to grow them. Those tiny, pale green lumps are actually unopened flower buds pickled in a vinegar and brine solution. The genus includes about 250 species native to warm regions. *Capparis* was the classical name of capers, originally from the Arabic *kabar*, while *spinosa* refers to the spines at the base of the leaves. Capers are traditionally used in sauces for fish, mutton, salads, or *hors d'oeuvres*. Classic French sauces

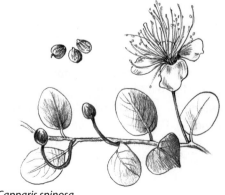

Capparis spinosa

featuring capers include *tartare*, *remoulade*, *ravigote*, and sometimes vinaigrette.

Capers are borne on a shrub that thrives in full sun. The caper bush has long, sprawling branches that can trail down walls or slopes or gently mound until about 5 feet high and 10 feet across. Leaves are roundish, dark green, and somewhat fleshy. Flower buds in each leaf joint appear from spring to fall. A three-year-old plant will yield just over 2 pounds of buds per year, and a plant older than four years may produce over 20 pounds per year. If left to open, the buds produce attractive 2- to 3-inch flowers with four crepe-like white petals. While freezing weather will cut this plant down to the ground to resprout later, prolonged weather at 32°F (0°C) will kill the plant. Caper's very deep roots help it resist drought, and very few diseases or insects attack capers.

Capers are propagated by cuttings or roots because of the variability of seed. Cuttings are rooted in the greenhouse and matured for at least one year before they are planted in the field and spaced 16 feet apart in rows 16 feet apart (5 × 5 m); in California, field planting is usually done from February to March. During the first two summers, plants may require irrigation two or three times per year but none after establishment. Spring fertilization with a 16-16-16 fertilizer at the rate of ½ pound per plant per year is advisable, followed by watering. Mature caper plants are pruned to ground level during November or December in California. The new tender shoots in spring may be consumed as a vegetable. Harvest flower buds from mid-May to mid-August.

Germination of seed is irregular and slow, but Demetrios G. Kontaxis of the University of California has outlined a procedure to enhance germination. Seeds are soaked in a jar filled with warm water (100 to 115°F, 38 to 46°C) for twelve hours while the water cools to room temperature. Then the seeds are wrapped in a moist towel, placed in a plastic bag, and refrigerated for 65 to 70 days. The seed is removed, resoaked as above, and then planted in a soilless mix in pots or flats. The seed is watered and kept at 70 to 85°F (21 to 29°C) in part to full sun. Germination may take from three weeks to three months. Seedlings should be 3 to 5 inches tall before transplanting. Another study, performed by Gabriel O. Sozzi and Angel Chiesa in Argentina, found high germination by soaking seeds in concentrated sulfuric acid for twenty minutes followed by a ninety-minute soak in a solution of 100 ppm gibberellin.

Capers are considered GRAS, but consumption of too many at once can cause stomach distress. While used primarily as a condiment, capers are also used in cosmetics to improve dry skin. Morocco, Spain, and Turkey are the chief exporters of capers to the United States. The small caper buds, called *nonpareil* or "nonesuch" capers, are usually preferred by chefs, but some prefer the larger *capot* buds. Raw capers are unpalatable and must be pickled in the same manner as cucumbers for pickles before consumption.

The home gardener may harvest buds every day early in the morning, wash them, drop them in salted vinegar, and refrigerate them for at least two weeks. Alternatively, mix caper buds with salt overnight and then drop into vinegar. The addition of French tarragon leaves to the solution improves the flavor, as does a pickling solution boiled with bay leaves and black pepper. The immature fruit, the *taperon*, is also pickled and eaten in Spain and Portugal, but the flavor is not very pleasant. Caper paste is often prepared from these immature fruits. The root bark has been shown to be antihepatotoxic.

Four primary cultivars are listed in the literature: 'Nuciddara' and 'Testa di Lucertola' from Italy and 'Comun' and 'Mallorquina' from

Spain. Additional cultivars include 'Dolce de Filicudi e Alicudi', 'Josephine', 'Nuciddara' ('Nucidda'), 'Nocella', 'Senza Spina', 'Testa di Lucertola', and 'Tondino'.

Important chemistry: The principal flavor constituents of capers include 2,290 ppm acetonitrile, 1,920 ppm octanoic acid, 1,310 ppm methyl isothiocyanate, and 1,050 ppm cytooctasulfur. The principal flavor constituents of pickled capers are octanoic acid, (*E*)-cinnamaldehyde, methyl isohiocyanate, benzaldehyde, ethyl hexadecanoate, and benzyl alcohol.

Botanical Description

The var. *inermis* Turra is a coastal variant in Europe; this differs from the typical form in having pendant branches, somewhat succulent leaves, and no stipular spines. Forms have also been selected for large flower buds.

C. spinosa L., Sp. pl. 5-03. 1753.
Native country: Capers are native to the Mediterranean region.
General habit: Capers are a small mounding shrubs to 1 to 1.5 m and 3 m across; individual branches can reach 2 to 3 m long.
Leaves: Leaves are smooth, stalked, rounded egg-shaped, and blunt at the apex. Spines at the leaf bases are recurved, sometimes weakly developed.
Flowers: Flowers are 5 to 7 cm in diameter, white, slightly bilaterally symmetrical. Sepals are purplish.
Fruits/seeds: Fruits are green, elongated, 3 to 5 × 1 to 1.5 cm with 200 to 300 seeds.

Capsicum

kăp-sĭ-kŭm
red pepper, chile

Family: Solanaceae
Growth form: shrubby perennials from 20 inches to almost 10 feet
(0.5 to 3 m) tall
Hardiness: hardy only in frost-free locations
Light: full sun
Water: moist but not constantly wet
Soil: friable and porous, pH range 4.3 to 8.7, average 6.1 (*C. frutescens*)
Propagation: seeds in spring, 4,500 seeds per ounce (160/6) (*C. annuum*)
Culinary use: myriad
Craft use: wreaths, ristras
Landscape use: annual border, vegetable garden

Cultivated red peppers originated in South America about 7500 B.C.E., and Europeans were first exposed to them with Columbus's arrival in the New World in 1492. By 1494, Dr. Diego Alvarez Chanca, physician to Columbus's fleet, wrote back to Spain of the *agí* used by the natives in Hispaniola (Dominican Republic and Haiti). When the Spanish arrived in Mexico, they picked up the native name *chilli*, from the Nahuatl language of the Aztecs; in Nahuatl, *chil* refers both to the red pepper and the color red. Today *chile* is the word used in Mexico with a descriptive adjective, as *chile poblanos*.

Chiles spread very rapidly to Europe, Africa, and the Far East and were immediately accepted, unlike the tomato, also a member of the Solana-ceae, which was imported with dire warnings of potential toxicity. In the Far East today, "chillie" or "chilly" is used for the pungent types, while the larger, milder peppers are called "capsicums." Americans seem to use all names and spellings, including "pimento," the anglicized version of the Spanish word for pepper. The American Spice Trade Association (ASTA) defines "red pepper" as any ground product of hot peppers, while "chili peppers" are any large, mild peppers that go into chili powder. Sharon Hudgins has provided further discussion of the etymology and use of the names pepper and chile.

The genus *Capsicum* includes about twenty-two species, but only five are cultivated, with *C. annuum* comprising most of the domesticated germplasm. The genus is fittingly named, from the Greek *kapto*, "to bite," a reference to the pungency of the fruits.

Chili flavor varies with the cultivar, process-ing, and climate; cultivar and processing aside, generally the hotter the climate, the hotter the pepper. Peppers ripening between 86°F and 95°F (30 to 35°C) have twice the fire as those which develop between 59°F and 72°F (15 to 22°C).

Capsaicinoids, the active components of hot peppers, transfer easily to your hands when you touch hot peppers; this can become a painful experience if you touch your eyes, mouth, geni-talia, or other mucous membranes. Capsaicin-oids have particular affinities with plastic con-tact lenses, and no amount of washing seems to remove them completely. Capsaicin, one of the capsaicinoids, is the effective burning agent used in personal protection sprays and animal repellents. Unless you really enjoy pain, the best precaution is to wear disposable plastic gloves, especially when chopping or seeding chiles. If you get hot pepper on your hands, washing with a small amount of chlorine bleach or am-monia will stop the burning sensation; the

chlorine or ammonia changes capsaicin into water-soluble salts. For burning in the mouth, cheap vodka can be used as a mouthwash; the capsaicin is alcohol-soluble. Alternatively, the casein in dairy products will break the bond of capsaicin with the pain receptors in the mouth.

The burning sensation caused by hot peppers is commonly referred to as "heat" and is mea-sured in Scoville Heat Units (SHU). This method was developed in 1912 by Wilbur L. Scoville, a pharmacologist with Parke Davis, a drug company that used capsaicin in its muscle salve, Heet™. Because of the inadequate chemi-cal tests of the time, five human heat samplers tasted and analyzed a solution made from exact weights of chiles. The pungency was recorded in multiples of 100 units. Pure capsaicin and dihydrocapsaicin are rated at sixteen million Scoville Heat Units; the analogues of capsaicin have lower ratings: 9.3 million for nordihydro-capsaicin, 8.1 million for homodihydrocapsai-cin, and 6.9 million for homocapsaicin. Recent-ly, the cultivar 'Bhut Jolokia' (primarily *C. chinense*, perhaps with some introgression from *C. frutescens*) was introduced at 855,000 SHUs, the hottest known pepper, beating out *C. chi-nense* 'Red Savina' at 577,000 SHUs. A relative heat scale rates heat from 0 to 10. The 'Habañe-ro', perhaps the hottest, commonly available pepper, rates a 10, with 200,000 to 300,000 Scoville Heat Units. At the other end of the scale, a bell pepper has 0 Scoville Heat Units and a rating of 0.

Within the past few decades, high-pressure liquid chromatography (HPLC) has been used to measure the Scoville Heat Units and relate them to actual capsaicinoid content. The ppm of capsaicinoids can be approximated by dividing SHU by 15. The American Spice Trade Associa-tion (ASTA) uses ASTA Heat Units based upon the ppm of capsaicinoids. Some peppers are ar-ranged on the relative heat scale in Table 12.

TABLE 12.
An average relative heat scale
of some pepper types,
from mildest (0) to hottest (10+).

0 = 'Bell'
1 = 'Anaheim Mild'
2 = 'Anaheim'
3 = 'New Mexico 6-4'
4 = 'Ancho'
5 = 'Floral Gem'
6 = 'Sante Fe Grande'
7 = 'Jalapeño'
8 = 'Cayenne'
9 = 'Scotch Bonnet'
10 = 'Habañero'
10+= 'Bhut Jolokia'

The distribution of the fiery principles within chiles is uneven, but they appear to be concentrated on the partitions, or placenta, of the fruit. The pure seeds themselves contain none or up to 10 percent of the total capsaicinoids; the heat on the seeds primarily arises from contamination from the placenta. Conical, thinner-walled fruits generally are more pungent than rounder, thicker fruits.

Don't feed hot peppers to dogs or cats. They can be lethal for some breeds.

Julia Child claimed that chiles produce "palate death." According to research performed by Harry Lawless, Paul Rozin, and Joel Shenker at the University of Pennsylvania, regular users of chiles rate the intensity of orally induced irritation from capsaicin as markedly lower than non-users. Despite this difference, the partial masking of the magnitude of olfactory or gustatory sensations by capsaicin is about equal in the two groups. This research also indicated that decrements in flavor identification under capsaicin are greater in chile non-eaters.

On the other hand, Beverly Cowart of the Monell Chemical Senses Center found that "even for individuals who are rarely exposed to hot species, and who find the irritant sensations they produce intense and quite unpleasant, the ability to appreciate basic tastes in the presence of such irritation seems remarkably unaffected." At the most, Julia Child may have been partially correct for non-chileheads, and certainly for hellfire cultivars like 'Bhut Jolokia'.

Capsaicin has been characterized by Young-Joon Surh and Sang Sup Lee as a "double-edged sword," and studies on the toxicity, mutagenic, and carcinogenic/co-carcinogenic/anticarcinogenic activities of capsaicin have yielded conflicting results, mostly depending upon the dose. Most studies have indicated that low consumption of chiles is beneficial but high consumption of chiles may be deleterious. Indeed, while it may be macho to consume the hottest peppers possible, clinical studies have shown that oral administration of capsaicinoids can damage the gastrointestinal tract to produce ulcers, act as a laxative, or even be fatal in massive doses. The dose of orally administered capsaicin that will kill 50 percent of the mice ranges from 97 to 294 mg/kg. Capsaicin in the amount of 0.232 to 0.706 ounces would have about the same effect on 150-pound humans. Assuming a median capsaicinoid content of 0.5 percent of dry weight and an approximate capsaicin content of 50 percent of the total capsaicinoids, that would be 93 to 282 ounces of dried chiles.

Remember, though, that other capsaicinoids accompany capsaicin, and while their toxicological effects have not been well estimated, a better guess at the fatal level of dried chiles would be 47 to 141 ounces. While only a fool would eat 2.9 to 8.8 pounds of dried hot chiles, remember that people have done more bizarre things to join fraternities or beat world records.

Chile consumption may create risk for gastric cancer, yet it also protects against aspirin-induced injury of the gastroduodenal mucosa in humans and exhibits a protective factor against peptic ulcers. Conflicting experiments have shown that capsaicin may either aggravate ethanol-induced damage of the gastric muscosa of rats or exert strong gastroprotective activity against damage induced by ethanol in rats. Orally administered capsaicin also exhibits chemoprotective activity against some chemical carcinogens and mutagens, but one study in Chile (no pun intended) found that gallbladder carcinoma was correlated with the high intake of both green and red chiles.

Capsaicin has been used to deaden nerve pain in the treatment of rheumatoid arthritis, osteoarthritis, and peripheral neuropathies. Capsaicin is a bronchoconstrictor and produces hypothermia. It displays both antiarrhythmic as well as anti-ischemic effects in isolated heart preparations similar to those of a calcium-channel antagonist. Capsaicin prevents chemically induced skin inflammation and can act as an anesthetic; it effectively treats pruritic psoriasis. Researchers at Kyoto University have reported that capsaicin enhances lipid metabolism (and thus decreases adipose tissue weight) by promoting the secretion of catecholamine from the adrenal medulla of the brain, although capsaicin may also damage acetylcholine chloride receptors on the adrenal medulla. A topical application of 0.075 percent capsaicin may be of value in diaetic neuropathy and intractable pain and particularly in postherpetic neuralgia.

Capsaicin is an antioxidant and prevents decomposition of fats in cooking, giving two reasons for including hot peppers in fatty foods. The discovery of vitamin C was made in paprika, and later studies have confirmed that red peppers are rich in vitamins. Capsanthin, the leading carotenoid, is also antioxidant. The fruits of red peppers are considered GRAS at 1 to 910 ppm, the oleoresin at 0.5 to 900 ppm, and the extract at 12 to 1,200 ppm.

Repeated application of capsaicin may relieve idiopathic rhinitis. Alkamides from the fruits of red pepper are antimicrobial as are the carbohydrates of red pepper seeds.

Peppers are self-pollinating, but insects can cause considerable crossing. Steven Tanksley at New Mexico State University found that the natural cross-pollination was 42 percent with the rates for individual plants as high as 91 percent. If you grow more than one type, be sure to clothe separate cultivars with mosquito netting or, even better, a spun polyester cloth (Reemay) to prevent cross-pollination if you plan to save seeds from year to year. Some breeders separate their plots by ⅛ mile just to make sure.

Real chileheads plan their chile plots the fall before. Choose a sunny, well-drained site, pH 5.5 to 6.5, and work in soil amendments and fertilizers as you would for a general vegetable garden soil (as determined by a soil test at least two months before planting). A medium-textured sandy loam or loam is best. To minimize problems of diseases, choose a site where no solanaceous plants (peppers, tomatoes, eggplants, or potatoes) have been grown at least for the past three years. Avoid intermixing peppers with other solanaceous vegetables, and rotate frequently to avoid the spread of diseases. Also avoid soils where the herbicides Karmex, Tenoran, Cotoran, or Lorox were previously used; these chemicals kill peppers.

The average yield of peppers is one pound per plant. One ounce of seeds, or 4,500 seeds, will provide enough for about an acre. Treated seeds are less susceptible to disease, particularly bacterial spot. Besides Thiram or Captan, which will control fungi, seeds may be treated with 1 part Clorox to 4 parts water at the rate of 1 gallon per pound of seed. Wash seed in the solution for forty minutes, stirring often. Discard Clorox solution as it becomes dirty. Spread seed to air-dry promptly.

Peppers are best grown from transplants because they require a long growing season, and gardeners usually purchase plants or grow their own indoors in a greenhouse to gain the maximum yield. Start seeds indoors in a flat or other shallow container filled with pasteurized, soilless mix as indicated in the preliminary chapters. Sow seeds ¼ to ½ inch deep. Keep evenly moist at 72 to 82°F (22 to 28°C). Temperature stress increases the time of germination, so a constant temperature of 81°F (27°C) is best. Slight scarification by placing the seeds in a plastic bag and gently rolling with a rolling pin will also reduce germination time. Oxygen will enhance germination, while light will not.

According to research conducted at the Louisiana Agricultural Experiment Station at Baton Rouge, germination may be enhanced by soaking the seed in 1,000 ppm gibberellic acid for forty-eight hours and priming in 2.75 percent potassium nitrate for 144 hours. Germination will take up to two weeks, with the hybrids germinating faster than the open-pollinated selections. Pregermination in a gel is used commercially.

After seedlings are up, place in the sun. Fluorescent lights (cool white) should be used if the seedlings become spindly, with the lights about 4 inches above the leaf tips for twelve to fourteen hours per day. Grow seedlings at 70 to 80°F (21 to 27°C) during the day and 63 to 70°F (17 to 21°C) during the night.

When the first set of true leaves appear, seedlings may be transplanted into 2.5- to 3-inch pots filled with a loose, pasteurized soil; stems may be covered to the first set of true leaves. Continue growing the potted plants under lights. At transplant time, choose stocky plants with good root systems for the garden; leggy plants must be clipped to perform as well (or better) than stocky ones. A transplant should have no flowers or fruit but six to eight true leaves and be less than 10 inches tall. Harden plants for about ten days before transplanting directly into the ground; acclimate the plants by setting them outside for longer and longer each day.

Plant one or two weeks after all danger of frost is past or when the soil temperature at the transplanting depth reads above 55°F (13°C) for three consecutive days. A properly hardened plant rarely wilts, but if in doubt, choose a cloudy day or cover the transplants with cloches to reduce wilting. Plant in full sun at 12- to 24-inch intervals (depending upon the mature size of the cultivar) in raised rows 36 inches apart; furrows next to the raised row will aid in irrigation and help to prevent root rot. Feed lightly; a 5-10-5 water-soluble fertilizer has been recommended by one grower.

Peppers are best grown from transplants because they require a long growing season, and gardeners usually purchase plants or grow their own indoors in a greenhouse to gain the maximum yield.

Staggered double rows are also recommended to use space more efficiently, with 12 to 18 inches between plants but 12 to 15 inches between individual rows and 36 inches between each set of double rows. Plants may need staking; the effort will result in more attractive fruit. Plants will generally bear fruit in 65 to 80 days, depending upon the variety. Avoid fertilizers high in nitrogen, which will produce lush foliage at the expense of the fruits. If plants have poor color or stunted growth, additional fertilizer may be needed. Soil should be evenly moist, and if rainfall does not provide about 1 inch per week (65 gallons/100 square feet), additional watering may be required. Straw and rotted sawdust mulches will help to conserve moisture and reduce weeds.

Even for the quick-maturing sweet peppers,

at least three months of warm weather are required for good yields and four or five months for most other cultivars. Peppers are very sensitive to temperature changes. Blossom drop occurs below 70°F (21°C) and above 90°F (32°C), and fruit sets poorly when day temperatures exceed 85°F (29°C). Fruits set at temperatures above 81°F (27°C) are likely to be small or poorly shaped because of heat injury, and above 95°F (35°C) few fruits will set, even if the air is very dry. Thus, uniform temperatures of 70 to 85°F (21 to 29°C) are recommended in the literature for maximum yields of sweet peppers. The smaller-fruited chiles are more tolerant of temperature extremes, but they need a longer growing season than sweet peppers.

Pepper color changes from green to red or yellow, but fire starts to peak when the peppers assume full size. Harvest peppers by cutting, not pulling. Chiles may be roasted and peeled, frozen, dried, and/or pickled; drying on the plant is probably the most primitive method. In Mexico, the peppers are gathered when completely mature and immediately spread on *paseras*, raised soil beds oriented to receive maximum sun and slanted so that the rain water will run off. The peppers are spread over a layer of straw or dry grass to allow air circulation and water drainage. Fruit is turned daily and will take twenty to thirty days to dry completely.

In a modified *pasera* recommended by Jean Andrews, inclined platforms are covered with sheets of clear plastic and weighted with stones. This method requires less turning and results in better color, according to Andrews. The fruit may also be spread on other clean, flat, dry surfaces or strung as *ristras*. Commercial drying requires gentle heat. In Mexico, 'Jalapeño' chiles are typically dried by smoking, resulting in a new product, chipotle. Smoked peppers without seeds, *capones* (the "castrated ones"), command higher prices.

Pepper seeds will germinate best after a period of dormancy. Storage conditions before planting also influence germination. After cleaning, seed should be dried to 5 percent moisture or lower and stored in refrigerated, sealed, moisture-proof containers; a small bag of dried silica gel in a sealed jar works well for the home gardener. Seeds stored for six months will germinate better than freshly gathered seeds.

Aphids spread viral diseases (curly top virus, pepper mottle virus, alfalfa mosaic virus, cucumber mosaic virus, and tomato spotted wilt) and must be controlled. Researchers at Louisiana State University have found that an aluminum-foil mulch repels aphids and aluminum-painted polyethylene mulch produces significantly greater yields as compared to that obtained from herbicide or hand-cultivated treatments, but we suppose that white sand may have similar properties.

To partially control anthracnose, which causes circular sunken brown spots on fruits, remove any plant debris and water only in the early morning. Mottled or twisted plants should be removed immediately and sent to the nearest landfill; they are infected with viruses. Do not smoke tobacco near peppers, and wash hands exposed to tobacco to avoid the spread of tobacco mosaic virus. Chile wilt, caused by *Phytophthora capsici*, results from poorly drained soils and/or heavy rainfall. Verticillium wilt also is soil-borne and best avoided by crop rotation. A host of other diseases include blossom-end rot, phytophthora pod rot, fusarium pod rot, black mold, rhizoctonia root rot, bacterial spot, and cercospora leaf spot. Cutworms, tomato hornworms, and tomato fruitworms are some of the major insect pests. Root-knot nematodes may cause serious yield losses and increase root rots. Peppers are also susceptible to sunscald, salt injury, and wind injury.

Capsicum annuum

ka̱p-sĭ-kŭm ă̱n-ū̱-ŭm

common red pepper

> **French:** *piment commun, poivron, poivre (piment) de Guinée, poivre rouge*
> **German:** *Paprika, Roter Pfeffer*
> **Dutch:** *spaanse peper*
> **Italian:** *peperone, peperoncino, pepe di caienna*
> **Spanish:** *pimiento, paprica, pimentón*
> **Portuguese:** *pimento, pimentão*
> **Swedish:** *spansk peppar*
> **Russian:** *perets ovoshchnoy, struchkovy pyerets*
> **Chinese:** *hsiung-ya-li-chiao*
> **Japanese:** *papurika*
> **Arabic:** *filfil ahmar*

The var. *annuum* of this species, meaning "annual" (a misnomer, since they can be grown in the greenhouse for the winter), includes most of the familiar peppers, and they are classified into at least five groups. The most prominent is the Longum Group, alias capsicum pepper, chili pepper, and paprika. Mexico, China, India, and Pakistan provide most of the imported capsicum peppers.

The use of ground sweet peppers as a product called paprika reputedly dates to an Ottoman invasion of Hungary in the sixteenth century. A young Hungarian girl was forced into the harem of the pasha of Buda, and she saw how the palace gardeners grew red peppers. When Hungarians stormed the palace, she was freed and fled back to her village with the peppers. These peppers, originally from the Americas via India, became "paprika" in Hungarian and gave rise to a whole series of parikashes, or dishes incorporating paprika. Today, Kalocsa, Hungary, hosts a Paprika Museum and an annual Paprika Festival in October. Paprika even has its own popular folkloric figure in Hungary called Jancsi

Paprika, often represented by a puppet embodying a Hungarian version of Sancho Panza.

In the Old World, the traditional peppers became milder, some still with a distinctive bite, others sweet. Despite Hungarian initiative in the development and spread of paprika, Spain provides most of the paprika imported into the United States, with Hungary and France second and third. Paprika today strictly refers to the ground product, not a pepper cultivar. Paprika can be made from any variety of *C. annuum* that is relatively low in heat but not devoid of it, and with brilliant red color. In the western United States, 'NuMex R. Naky' and 'NuMex Conquistador', two "mild" hot peppers, are grown for processing into paprika. Other peppers recommended for paprika are 'Hungarian', 'Kalosca' (especially recommended for home growers), 'Paprika Supreme' and 'Papri Mild II'.

With new cultivars being introduced every year, it would be impossible to list all cultivars of *C. annuum*, and some, such as 'Chilhuacle Negro', which is used to prepare the black molé sauces of Oaxaca, are quite obscure. Some of the

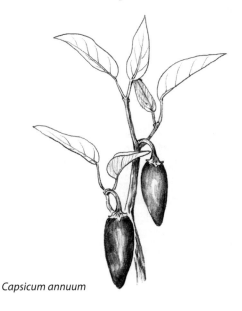

Capsicum annuum

more popular cultivars readily available in the United States are listed here. We have omitted the vegetable types with a heat rating of 0, such as 'Banana', 'Bell', 'Cubanelle', and 'Pimento'.

Cultivar: 'Anaheim' or 'New Mexican'/'New Mexico'
Synonyms: 'Chile Colorado', 'California Green Chile', 'Long Green/Red Chile'
Origin: released in 1903 by H. L. Musser; developed by Emilio Ortega in 1896
Relatives: 'Aconcagua', 'Anaheim M', 'Anaheim TMR', 'Anaheim TMR 23', 'Anaheim TMR 24', 'California Chili', 'Chimayó', 'Diablo Grande', 'Dixon', 'El Paso', 'Española Improved', 'Fresno', 'Fresno Chile Grande', 'New Mexico No. 6-4', 'New Mexico No. 9', 'NuMex Big Jim', 'NuMex Conquistador', 'NuMex Eclipse', 'NuMex Joe E. Parker', 'NuMex R. Naky', 'NuMex Sunrise', 'NuMex Sunset', 'Rio Grande', 'Sandi', 'Sweet-Cal', 'Tam Chile'
Availability: canned, fresh, or dried
Uses: stews, sauces, ristras, stuffed for rellenos
Color: green or red
Heat rating: 2 to 3

Cultivar: 'Ancho'
Synonyms: 'Poblano' (a generic name), 'Chile Poblano', 'Chile Para Rellenar', 'Chile Joto', 'Pasilla' (an incorrect designation)
Origin: ancient
Relatives: 'Ancho Esmeralde', 'Ancho Flor de Pabellon', 'Ancho Verdeno', 'Ancho 102', 'Chile de Chorro', 'Miahuateco', 'Mulato Roque', 'Mulato V-2'
Availability: fresh (*poblano*) or dried (*ancho*)
Uses: stuffed for rellénos, used in sauces including molé sauce
Color: brick red to dark mahogany
Heat rating: 3 to 5

Cultivar: 'Cayenne'
Synonyms: 'Ginnie'
Origin: pre-Columbian
Relatives: 'Cayenne Larger', 'Cayenne Pickling', 'Come d'Orient', 'Dwarf Chili', 'Du Chili', 'Hades Hot', 'Hot Portugal', 'Japanese Fuschin', 'Jaune Long', 'Large Red Chili', 'Large Thick Cayenne', 'Long Cayenne', 'Long Narrow Cayenne', 'Long Red', 'Long Thin', 'Mammoth Cayenne', 'New Giant Cayenne', 'New Quality', 'Prolific', 'Rainbow', 'Red Chili', 'Red Dawn', 'Ring of Fire', 'Rouge Long Ordinaire', 'Super Cayenne', 'Trompe d'Elephant', 'True Red Chili'
Availability: bottled sauces, dried, and powdered
Uses: sauces, soups
Color: bright red
Heat rating: 8

Cultivar: 'Cherry'
Synonyms: 'Hungarian Cherry'
Origin: pre-Columbian
Relatives: 'Bird Cherry', 'Bird's Eye', 'Bolita', 'Cascabel', 'Cerise', 'Cherry Jubilee', 'Cherry Sweet', 'Cherrytime', 'Christmas Cherry' (not Jerusalem cherry, *Solanum pseudocapsicum* L.), 'Creole', 'Holiday Cheer', 'Hot Apple', 'Japanese Miniature', 'Large Red Hot', 'Red Cherry Hot', 'Red Giant', 'Super Sweet', 'Tom Thumb'
Availability: pickled
Uses: salads
Color: deep red
Heat rating: 1 to 5

Cultivar: 'De Arbol'
Origin: Mexico, related to 'Cayenne'
Relatives: 'NuMex Sunburst', 'NuMex Sunflare', 'NuMex Sunglo'
Availability: dried
Uses: sauces, soups, stews, wreaths, ristras

Color: bright red
Heat rating: 7.5

Cultivar: 'Fips'
Synonyms: 'Fiesta'
Origin: pre-1965 House of Venay, Germany
Availability: potted plants
Uses: primarily ornamental, but also salsas, soups, stir-fries
Color: yellow to red
Heat rating: 6 to 8

Cultivar: 'Floral Gem'
Origin: 1921
Relatives: 'Floral Gem Jumbo', 'Floral Grande'
Availability: pickled (Torrido Chili Peppers or Trappey's of Louisiana)
Uses: salads, gravies, beans, meat dishes
Color: used when yellow
Heat rating: 5

Cultivar: 'Fresno'
Synonyms: 'Chile Caribe', 'Chile Cera'
Origin: 1952, Clarence Brown Seed Co.
Relatives: 'Cascabella'
Availability: fresh
Uses: salsas, ceviches, seasoning, sauces, pickling (*en escabeche*)
Color: red, but used primarily when green
Heat rating: 6.5

Cultivar: 'Jalapeño'
Origin: pre-Columbian, named for town of Jalapa in state of Veracruz, Mexico
Relatives: 'Early Jalapeño', 'Espinalteco', 'Jalapa', 'Jalapeño M. Americano', 'Jarocho', 'Meco', 'Mitla', 'Morita', 'Mucho Naco', 'Papaloapan', 'Peludo', 'Rayada', 'San Andres', '76014 Jumbo-Jal', 'Tam Jalapeño', 'Tam Mild Jalapeño-1', 'Típico'
Availability: pickled (*en escabeche*), canned (*mora*, *morita*), fresh, smoked (*chipotle*)

Uses: salsas, sauces, ristras
Color: green or red
Heat rating: 5.5

Cultivar: 'Mirasol'
Synonyms: 'Guajillo', 'Cascabel'
Origin: Mexico
Relatives: 'De Comida', 'La Blanca 74', 'Loreto 74', 'NuMex Mirasol', 'Real Mirasol'
Availability: dried
Uses: salsas, sauces, soups, stews
Color: deep orange-red with brown tones
Heat rating: 2 to 5

Cultivar: 'Pasilla' (not the 'Ancho' types offered in California)
Synonyms: 'Chile Negro', 'Chilaca'
Origin: Mexico
Relatives: 'Apasceo', 'Pabellón 1', 'Salvatierra'
Availability: dried, powdered
Uses: molé sauce, seafood
Color: dark raisin brown when dried
Heat rating: 3 to 5

Cultivar: 'Peter'
Synonyms: 'Penis'
Origin: unknown
Uses: primarily an ornamental conversation piece but can be used in salsas if Freudian significance is desired. (Caution: if you make and sell a "penis pepper jelly," as one of our friends did, make sure that you have a warning label "not for topical application.")
Color: bright red
Heat rating: 7.5

Cultivar: 'Santa Fe Grande'
Synonyms: 'Güero' (a generic term for yellow peppers)
Origin: Mexico
Relatives: 'Caloro', 'Caribe', 'Hybrid Gold Spike'

Availability: fresh
Uses: yellow molé sauces, pickled (*en escabeche*), hot vinegars
Color: pale yellow
Heat rating: 6

Cultivar: 'Serrano'
Origin: mountain ridges (serranías) north of Puebla and Hidalgo, Mexico
Relatives: 'Altamira', 'Cotaxtla Cónico', 'Cotaxtla Gordo', 'Cotaxtla Típico', 'Cuauhtemoc', 'Huasteco-74', 'Panuco', 'Super Chili', 'Tam Hidalgo', 'Tampiqueño 74', 'Veracruz S69'
Availability: fresh, dried
Uses: sauces (*salsa verde*, *pico de gallo*), pickled (*en escabeche*)
Color: orange-red
Heat rating: 6 to 7.5

Cultivar: 'Tomato'
Synonyms: 'Squash'
Origin: pre-Columbian Mexico
Relatives: 'Canada Cheese', 'Early Sweet Pimento', 'Red Cheese Pimento', 'Sunnybrook', 'Tomato Pimento', 'Yellow Cheese Pimento'
Availability: dried, fresh
Uses: dried and powdered as paprika (but rather bland), salads
Color: red
Heat rating: 0

The var. *aviculare* is the chiltecpin pepper, alias the chiltepin, chilipiquin, or tepín (Nahuatl *chilli* + *tepectl*, "flea chile"). Many other synonyms are also used, but the most common name is "bird pepper" because birds eat the tiny round fruits with impunity and spread it in their droppings. It is considered the wild form of *C. annuum* and distinguished primarily by fruit size. It may be used for salsas, soups, stews,

and flavored vinegars; its heat rating is 8. Improved cultivars are 'Hermosilla Select', 'NuMex Bailey Piquin', 'NuMex Centennial', 'NuMex Twilight', 'NuMex Piquin', 'Pequín' ('Piquin'), 'Texas', and 'Tuxtla'.

Within the last decade or so a number of peppers from Southeast Asia and Africa have revisited North American shores; these often incorporate various flavors along with varying degrees of heat. These so-called exotic or as-yet-unclassified peppers vary from the size of a chiltecpin pepper to cayenne types and include 'Barbere', 'Calistan', 'Pili-Pili', 'Thai Hot', and 'Yatsafusa'. We know that by 1542 three races of peppers were being grown in India, yet today the pepper cultivars of Africa and Asia remain relatively unknown. More remains out there for the pepper explorers.

Important chemistry: The red peppers are rich in carotenoids (3 to 66 g/kg), primarily capsanthin (23 to 69 percent of total pigment), crytocapsin (trace to 19 percent of total pigment), and beta-carotene (4 to 13 percent of total pigment). Measured as provitamin A content, the red cultivars have 928 to 5,232 IU/g (0.06 to 3.13 mg/g) fresh weight (the optimum amount of vitamin A_1 for an adult is about 5,000 IU daily).

Of the other fat-soluble vitamins, vitamin D_2 varies from 80 to 240 IU/g (0.004 to 0.012 mg/g) dried weight of paprika (400 IU of vitamin D daily is recommended for babies, children, adolescents, and pregnant and lactating women). Vitamin E varies from 160 to 880 IU/g (0.16 to 0.88 mg/g) dried weight of paprika. Of the water-soluble vitamins, vitamin C (ascorbic acid) content varies from 1.60 to 58.80 IU/g (0.08 to 2.94 mg/g) fresh weight (1,500 IU of vitamin C daily is recommended for adults).

Chile heat is due to capsaicin and its vanillylacyl amide analogues with the degree of pungency related to the length of the acid side-chain. The heat of *C. annuum* is primarily due to 33 to 95 percent capsaicin of the total capsaicinoid content accompanied by trace to 51 percent dihydrocapsaicin and 7 to 22 percent nordihydrocapsaicin. Total capsaicinoid content will vary from 0 to 1.3 percent by dry weight. The var. *aviculare*, the bird pepper, has 54 to 62 percent capsaicin and 22 to 32 percent dihydrocapsaicin.

The characteristic odor of peppers is primarily due to pyrazines. The essential oil of 'Bell' peppers, for example, has 16 percent 2-methoxy-3-isobutylpyrazine, alkylmethoxypyrazine, and nona-(*E,E*)-2,5-dien-4-one; 10 percent limonene; and 11 percent (*E*)-beta-ocimene. The six primary compounds of chile aroma are hexanal, 2-isobutyl-3-methoxypyrazine, 2,3-butanedione, 3-carene, *trans*-2-hexenal, and linalool, producing a green grassy aroma.

Capsicum baccatum
kăp-sĭ-kŭm bă-kā-tŭm
ají, Brown's pepper, piris

Baccatum means "fleshy," or having berries with a pulpy texture. This species is difficult to distinguish from *C. annuum* in the fruiting stage, as it has many of the same fruit forms. The var. *baccatum* is probably the wild progenitor of the cultivated var. *pendulum*. Two cultivars are derived from var. *pendulum*, 'Kellu-Uchu' ('Aji Amarillo', 'Cusqueño') and 'Puca-Uchu'; both of these little-known South American peppers are used locally in soups and stews and have a heat rating of 7 to 8. 'Kellu-Uchu' is widely used in Peru to accompany many dishes but particularly the potatoes of the region. Attempts to grow 'Kellu-Uchu' in Texas resulted in a 5-foot shrub that barely matured before winter; thus this pepper is best consumed as imported fresh or dried fruits.

Important chemistry: The fruits of *C. baccatum* var. *pendulum* have 32 to 67 percent capsaicin and 27 to 53 percent dihydrocapsaicin of the total capsaicinoid content, which is 0.1 to 0.2 percent of the dried fruit. The fruits of *C. baccatum* var. *baccatum* have 61 to 72 percent capsaicin and 29 to 28 percent dihydrocapsaicin.

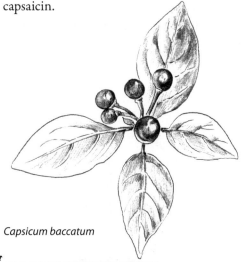

Capsicum baccatum

Capsicum chinense
kăp-sĭ-kŭm chī-nĕn-sē
Chinese pepper

Capsicum chinense was named by Baron von Nikolaus Joseph Jacquin, but why he chose the epithet *chinense* for this South American plant has never been adequately explained. The differences between this species and *C. frutescens* are slight and perhaps they should be combined into one species, *C. frutescens*. The many unnamed cultivars (in red, orange, and brown) also have extreme variations in fruit shape and size, merging one into the other; 'Scotch Bonnet' is milder and more squashed in appearance compared with 'Habañero' but otherwise differs little.

These "Chinese" peppers are the hottest known. The germination of the seeds of these cultivars, however, is longer than types from *C. annuum*, as is the length of growing season required for full fruit maturation, and so cultivation of these peppers serves to separate the dabblers from the devotées.

Capsicum chinense

Cultivar: 'Bhut Jolokia'
Origin: Assam, northeastern India
Relatives: 'Red Savina'
Availability: fresh
Uses: one pepper can supply a family of chile-heads for a week!
Color: bright red when fully ripe
Heat rating: 10+

Cultivar: 'Habañero'
Origin: probably Cuba
Availability: fresh, dried, bottled
Uses: salsas, chutneys, seafood marinades, pickled (*en escabeche*)
Color: dark green to orange, orange-red, or red when fully ripe
Heat rating: 10

Cultivar: 'Rocotillo'
Synonyms: 'Red Squash', 'Rocoto' (not the true rocoto pepper)
Availability: fresh, pickled
Uses: ceviches, pickled (*en escabeche*), tasty as a hot snack
Color: green, orange-yellow, or red
Heat rating: 7 to 8

Cultivar: 'Scotch Bonnet'
Origin: Caribbean
Relatives: 'Jamaican Hot', 'Ají Dulce' (a low heat/sweet cultivar)
Availability: fresh, sauces
Uses: Jamaican jerk sauce, Caribbean curries
Color: pale yellow-green, orange, or red
Heat rating: 9 to 10

Important chemistry: The fruits of *C. chinense* have 65 to 75 percent capsaicin and 21 to 32 percent dihydrocapsaicin of the total capsaicinoid content, which is 0.3 to 1.2 percent of the dried fruit.

Capsicum frutescens

kăp-sĭ-kŭm frū-tĕs-ĕnz
Tabasco pepper

French: *piment enragé*
German: *Beissbeere*
Dutch: *spaanse peper*
Italian: *peperone*
Spanish: *chile, malagueta*
Portuguese: *pimentão picante*
Swedish: *spansk peppar*
Russian: *struchkovy pyerets*
Chinese: *hung-fan-chiao*
Japanese: *tōgarashi*
Arabic: *filfil*

Capsicum frutescens (*frutescens* means bushy) has given us the 'Tabasco' pepper cultivar with a heat rating of 8 to 9. "Tabasco," in reference to a pepper, first appeared in print on 26 January 1850, in a letter to the editors of the *New Orleans Daily Delta*. The name Tabasco, however, was used as early as 1519 by Hernán Cortez; it was ultimately derived from the Nahuatl *tapa-cho-co*, "place of coral (or oyster) shell." During two centuries of Spanish dominion in Louisiana, goods passed from the inland port of Tabasco (currently San Juan Bautista) in Mexico to New Orleans. New Orleans also played an important role in the war with Mexico (1846–1847), and Com. Matthew Galbraith Perry, who directed the second seizure of Tabasco with 420 marines, shipped his ill men back to New Orleans.

Currently this pepper is used to make a hot sauce manufactured by the McIlhenny Company of Avery Island, Louisiana, and the name Tabasco™ is the firm's exclusive trademark for the sauce. An additional cultivar, 'Greenleaf Tabasco', is resistant to tobacco etch virus with heavy yields. Another cultivar derived from *C. frutescens* is 'Uvilla Grande', but this is primarily an ornamental.

Important chemistry: The heat of *C. frutescens* is primarily due to 50 to 79 percent capsaicin of the total capsaicinoid content accompanied by 21 to 50 percent dihydrocapsaicin. The fragrant components isolated by lyophilization include 38 percent isohexyl-isocaproate, 22 percent 4-methyl-1-pentyl-2-methyl-butyrate, and 13 percent 3-methyl-1-pentyl-3-methyl-butyrate.

Capsicum frutescens

Capsicum pubescens

kăp-sĭ-kŭm pū-bĕs-ĕnz

rocoto

Spanish: *rocoto, chile manzana*

The rocoto pepper is distinguished by its large violet flowers held erect above the foliage and its hairy leaves (*pubescens* means "downy"). The seeds are also unique, wrinkled and blackish brown. The rocoto grows at higher elevations than any other pepper and may become a shrub reaching above 6 feet. Fruits are yellow-green, orange, red, or lemon-yellow in at least fourteen different shapes; heat ratings are 8 to 9. The rocoto probably originated in Peru in pre-Columbian times but was introduced into Central America and Mexico in the twentieth century. Named landraces include 'Chiapas', 'Huatusco I', 'Huatusco II', 'Perú', 'Puebla', and 'Zongolica'.

Important chemistry: The fruits of *C. pubescens* have 44 to 54 percent dihydrocapsaicin, 25 to 39 percent capsaicin, and 4 to 15 percent nordihydrocapsaicin of the total capsaicinoid content, which is 0.1 to 0.4 percent of the dried fruits.

Botanical Key and Description

Key:

1. Seeds dark, flower purple. . . . . *C. pubescens*
1a. Seeds straw-colored, flower white or greenish white (rarely purple). 2
   2. Flower with diffuse yellow spots at bases of lobes. . . . . *C. baccatum*
   2a. Flower without diffuse yellow spots at bases of lobes 3
      3. Flower purple. 4
         4. Flower solitary. . . . . *C. annuum*
         4a. Flowers two or more at each node . . . . *C. chinense*
      3a. Flower white or greenish white. 5
         5. Calyx of mature fruit with ringed constriction at junction with flower stalk . . . . *C. chinense*
         5a. Calyx of mature fruit without ringed constriction at junction with flower stalk. 6
            6. Flowers solitary. 7
               7. Flower milky white, flower stalks often declining at pollen release. . . . . *C. annuum*
               7a. Flower greenish white, flower stalks erect at pollen release. . . . . *C. frutescens*
            6a. Flowers two or more at each node 8
               8. Flower milky white. . . . . *C. annuum*
               8a. Flower greenish white. 9
                  9. Flower stalks erect at pollen release, flower lobes usually slightly turned
                    backward. . . . . *C. frutescens*
                  9a. Flower stalks declining at pollen release, flower lobes straight . . . . . *C. chinense*

C. annuum L., Sp. pl. 188. 1753.

The two varieties of this pepper are distinguished primarily by fruit size.

var. *annuum*

Native country: The common red pepper originated in Mesoamerica but is now cultivated worldwide.

General habit: The common red pepper is a much-branched, smooth, shrubby, perennial herb or subshrub, 45 to 100 cm tall, typically grown as an annual.

Leaves: Leaves are lance-shaped, 1.5 to 13 × 0.5 to 7.5 cm, stalked. Base is pinched, base is wedge-shaped or tapered.

Flowers: Flowers are solitary at each node, flower stalks declining at pollen release. Corolla is milky white (occasionally purple) without diffuse spots at the base of the lobes. Corolla lobes are usually straight. The calyx of the mature fruit has no ringed constriction at the junction of the flower stalk (though sometimes irregularly wrinkled).

Fruits/seeds: Fruit is an indehiscent, many-seeded berry extremely variable in size, shape, and color. Seeds are straw-colored.

var. *aviculare* (Dierb.) D'Arcy & Eshbaugh, Phytologia 25:260. 1973 [*C. annuum* L. var. *glabriusculum* (Dunal in DC.) Heiser & Pickersgill].

Native country: The bird pepper or chiltecpin originated in southern Mexico or northern Colombia but is distributed today in southeastern and southwestern United States into northern Peru.

General habit: The chiltecpin is a short-lived perennial herb or small shrub to 2 m, smooth or rarely slightly hairy.

Leaves: Leaves are lance-shaped.

Flowers: Flowers are solitary, rarely two to three pairs. The flower stalk is slender, enlarging just beneath the fruit. The corolla is white, rarely greenish; anthers are violet to blue.

Fruits/seeds: The fruit is green suffused with dark purple to black when immature, red when mature, erect, small, globose or egg-shaped, 5 to 10 mm in diameter, rarely ex-

ceeding 15 mm in length. Seeds are cream to yellow.

C. baccatum L., Mant. pl. 47. 1767.
Two varieties of this pepper are known. The primary difference is in the position of the fruit, mostly erect in var. *baccatum* and mostly pendant in var. *pendulum*. Another difference between the two varieties is the length of the filaments, 1.2 to 3.1 mm in var. *baccatum* and 2.6 to 4.2 mm in var. *pendulum*.

var. *baccatum*

Native country: The var. *baccatum* has a center of distribution in Bolivia and northern Argentina.

General habit: The var. *baccatum* is a much-branched, smooth (sometimes slightly hairy), shrubby, perennial herb, 0.5 to 3.0 m tall.

Leaves: Leaves are lance-shaped.

Flowers: Flowers are white to off-white with a pair of yellowish to tan to greenish spots at the base of each lobe.

Fruits/seeds: Fruit is an erect, indehiscent, many-seeded berry. Seeds are straw-colored.

var. *pendulum* (Willd.) Eshbaugh, Taxon 17:51–52. 1968.

Native country: The var. *pendulum* is native from the lowlands to middle elevations in South America with its primary center in Peru and Bolivia.

General habit: The var. *pendulum* is a much-branched, smooth, shrubby, perennial herb, 1 to 1.5 m tall.

Leaves: Leaves are lance-shaped.

Flowers: Flowers are solitary at each node. Flower stalks are erect or declining at pollen release. Flower is white or greenish white with diffuse yellow spots at the base of the flower lobes on either side of the midvein. The flower lobes are usually slightly turned backward. The calyx of the mature fruit has no ringed constriction (though sometimes irregularly wrinkled).

Fruits/seeds: Fruit is a pendant, indehiscent, many-seeded berry. Seeds are straw-colored.

C. chinense Jacq., Hort. Bot. Vindobon. 3:38. t. 67. 1776.

Native country: The Chinese pepper is widespread in northern South America, southern Central America, and the West Indies; domestication probably occurred in South America.

General habit: The Chinese pepper is a much-branched, smooth (rarely with dense, short hairs), shrubby, perennial herb, 45 to 75 cm tall.

Leaves: Leaves are egg-shaped to egg-lance-shaped, to 10.5 cm broad, smooth or wrinkled.

Flowers: Flowers are two or more at each node (occasionally solitary). Flower stalks are erect or declining at pollen release. Flower is greenish white (occasionally milky white or purple) without diffuse spots at the base of the lobes. The flower lobes are usually straight. The calyx of the mature fruit usually has a ringed constriction at the junction with the fruit stalk.

Fruits/seeds: Fruit is an indehiscent, many-seeded berry, 1.0 to 12.0 cm long, varying from spherical to elongate, smooth or variously wrinkled. Seeds are straw-colored.

C. frutescens L., Sp. pl. 189. 1753.

Native country: The Tabasco pepper probably originated in the western Amazon River basin of lowland Colombia and Peru.

General habit: The Tabasco pepper is a much-branched, smooth (to slightly hairy), shrubby, short-lived perennial herb 0.5 to 1.5 m high, living for two or three years.

Leaves: Leaves are widest at the center with equal ends.

Flowers: Flowers are solitary at each node (occasionally two or more). Flower stalks are erect at pollen release but flowers are nodding. Flower is greenish white without diffuse spots at the base of the lobes. The corolla lobes are often slightly turned backward. Calyx of mature fruit has no ringed constriction at the junction with the fruit stalk, though often irregularly wrinkled.

Fruits/seeds: Fruit is an indehiscent, many-seeded berry typically 0.7 to 3.0 × 0.3 to 1.0 cm, but larger fruited forms occur. Seeds are straw-colored.

C. pubescens Ruiz. & Pav., Flora peruv. prodr. 2:30. 1799.

Native country: The rocoto pepper is native to relatively high elevations in Andean South America.

General habit: The rocoto pepper is a much-branched, hairy, shrubby, perennial herb.

Leaves: Leaves are lance-shaped, hairy.

Flowers: Flowers are solitary at each node. Flower stalks are erect at pollen release but flowers are nodding. Flower is purple (occasionally with white margins to lobes and/or white tube), without diffuse spots at the base of the lobes. The lobes are usually straight. Calyx of mature fruit has no ringed constriction at the junction with the fruit stalk.

Fruits/seeds: Fruit is an indehiscent, many-seeded berry. Fruit flesh is thick and firm. Seeds are wrinkled and blackish brown.

For further reading: The red or capsicum peppers or chiles deserve a whole book, and indeed several already exist. We recommend, in particular, Jean Andrews's *Peppers: The Domesticated Capsicums.* This book suits the coffee table, kitchen, bedside, library, botany laboratory, classroom, and so on—it is a perfect synthesis of science, history, art, and humor. All chile-heads must have it!

Other good chile books include Mark Miller's *The Great Chile Book*, which has excellent color photographs and a compact size. Dave DeWitt and Nancy Gerlach's *The Whole Chile Pepper Book* gives additional information on cultivation and culinary uses. J. W. Purseglove, E. G. Brown, C. L. Green, and S. R. J. Robbins have provided an excellent survey of

commercial cultivation, processing, and standards of chiles in volume one of their *Spices*; we have not expanded upon these commercial features here and advise you instead to read their comprehensive treatment. Amal Naj's *Peppers: A Story of Hot Pursuits* features interviews with people working on peppers interwoven with a very readable fabric of pepper history and uses. Finally, for the chilehead and pungent-herb connoisseur, we recommend the magazine *Chile Pepper*.

Carthamus tinctorius

kär-thăm-ŭs tĭnk-tō-rĭ-ŭs
safflower

Family: Asteraceae (Compositae)
Growth form: annual to 47 inches (1.2 m)
Hardiness: seedlings can withstand some minor frost
Light: full sun
Water: moist but not constanstly wet
Soil: light
Propagation: seeds in late winter or early spring
Culinary use: traditional saffron substitute but without GRAS status
Craft use: dried flowers, wreaths
Landscape use: rear of annual border, wildflower garden

French: *carthame des teinturiers, safran bâtard, faux safran, graine de perroquet*
German: *Färberdistel, Wilder Safran, Bastard Safran, Färber-Saflor*
Dutch: *saffloer, wilde safraan*
Italian: *cártamo, zafferano falso, croco batardo*
Spanish: *alazor, cártamo, azafrán romi*

Portuguese: *açafrão, assaflor*
Swedish: *safflor*
Russian: *saflor*
Chinese: *hong-hua*
Arabic: *kurthum, usfar*

Carthamus tinctorius

Safflower is a multifaceted plant; its seeds yield a cooking oil and its flower petals provide a cheap substitute for the more expensive saffron, accounting for the alternative name "false saffron." Safflower production probably arose in Syria in the Neolithic. The use of safflowers for their yellow dye is reflected in the generic name, which is derived from the Hebrew *qarthami* ("the painted one") and the specific name, which means "of the dyers." The genus *Carthamus* includes about thirteen species native to the Mediterranean region.

Safflower is a much-branched annual to 4 feet (1.2 m) with bristly leaves. The golden-orange flowers are thistle-like with twenty to eighty florets per head; each floret has the potential to mature into a seed (technically a fruit called an achene). The heads do not shatter, thus preserving the oil-rich seeds, but many seed lines are very spiny, presenting difficulty at harvest.

Safflower produces large seed harvest in climates with low relative humidity from the time of flower formation until maturity; a dry atmosphere is necessary for good seed-set and high oil content. Thus, safflower raised for oil does not do very well in the eastern or southern United States but rather well from the western part of the northern Great Plains to the Southwest. As an oil crop, safflower falls outside the scope of this book, but if raised as a saffron substitute, then high humidity presents fewer problems.

Commercial safflower for oil is raised in rows 10 to 40 inches (25-102 cm) apart (solid drilled) at the rate of 15 to 30 pounds per acre (17 to 34 kg/ha), planted 1.5 to 2 inches (3.8 to 5 cm) deep in late winter or early spring; similar rates would be used for flower production. Safflower is a poor weed competitor and grows slowly for the first three or four weeks after emergence; good weed control is necessary for high yields (several herbicides are registered for safflower).

Safflower requires about the same amount of nitrogen as spring barley. Under irrigation in Washington, the recommendation is for 100 pounds nitrogen and 50 pounds phosphorus pentoxide per acre (112 and 56 kg/kg, respectively) incorporated into the top 4 inches (10 cm) of soil. Safflower tolerates drought better than other oilseed crops but less than wheat. Soil moisture is particularly important at the time of seed germination. Safflower is subject to attacks by rust (particularly *Puccinia calcitrapae* var. *centaureae*) and root rot (*Phytophthora drechsleri*). Insects are of minor importance, but safflower may be attacked by lygus bugs and bean aphids.

Flower petals of safflower have been sold as a saffron substitute, but these petals apparently do not have GRAS status. The chemistry of safflower flower petals is also unknown, but stigmasterol (71 percent in the methanol extract of the dried petals) has been shown to inhibit tumor promotion in mouse skin two-stage carcinogenesis.

Important chemistry: The reddish pigment of safflower petals is quinochalcone. The petals of the white cultivar have no quinochalcone and four flavonols with 6-hydroxykaempferols. The petals of yellow safflower are rich in hydroxysafflor yellow A, safflor yellow B and safflomin C and nine flavonoils containing four 6-hydroxy-kaempferols. The petals of the orange cultivar produce six quinochalcones and eleven flavonols containing five 6-hydroxykaempferols.

Botanical Description

C. tinctorius L., Sp. pl. 830. 1753.
Native country: Safflower is native to western Asia but widely escaped wherever it has been cultivated.
General habit: Safflower is an almost smooth annual to 1.2 m.

Leaves: Leaves along the stem are undivided or rarely deeply lobed, egg- to lance-egg-shaped, toothed with spines or smooth-edged.

Flowers: Flowers are yellow, orange, or reddish and arranged in heads that are egg- to conical-egg-shaped.

Fruits/seeds: Fruits (achenes) are almost pyramid-shaped, more or less smooth, shiny, white.

Carum carvi

kā-rŭm kăr-vĭ
caraway

Family: Apiaceae (Umbelliferae)

Growth form: biennial or annual forms exist to 59 inches (150 cm)

Hardiness: seedlings can withstand frost

Light: full sun

Water: moist but not constantly wet

Soil: light, pH 4.8 to 7.8, average 6.4

Propagation: seeds in fall or spring, 11,000 seeds/oz (388/g)

Culinary use: breads, pickles, meats

Craft use: none

Landscape use: short-lived; middle of border, best in vegetable plot

French: *carvi, cumin des prés*

German: *Kümmel, Wiesen-Kümmel*

Dutch: *karwij, gewone kummel*

Italian: *carvi, cumino dei prati, cumino tedesco*

Spanish: *hinojo de prade, alcaravea, alcarahueya*

Portuguese: *cominho*

Swedish: *kummin*

Russian: *tmin*

Chinese: *yuan-sui*

Japanese: *karuwai*

Arabic: *karawya*

Urdu: *kala zira*

The aromatic seeds (really fruits) of caraway are closely associated with cuisines of northern and eastern Europe, particularly rye bread and Irish soda bread, and find their way into cheese, cole slaw, sauerkraut, potato salad, beef or lamb roast, liqueurs (e.g., Kümmel), salad dressings, soups, applesauce, and baked fruit. The foliage is sometimes added to cheeses, salads, soups, or stews, but the flavor is rather bland. Caraway is a corruption of the Latin name, *Carum carvi*.

Carum carvi

Carum was the Greek herbalist Dioscorides' name for caraway, so named from Caria, the ancient district of Hellenized southwestern Asia Minor where it was grown; *carvi* was used by the Romans to refer to caraway.

The genus *Carum* includes about thirty species native to temperate and warm Eurasia. Caraway seed is primarily imported into the United States from the Netherlands, but Hungary and Egypt also supply the American market.

Foliage is ferny, not unlike a coarse dill or a finely textured anise. Caraway is commonly a biennial, but annual forms are also available. These annual forms require a longer growing season than the biennial forms, and the annual forms have a lower essential oil content in the seeds. The biennial forms tend to be dark brown-seeded, while the annual forms tend to be light brown ("blond")-seeded. The seed line called 'Mogador' is light brown and long-seeded; 'Dutch' cultivars are darker. Other seed lines reported in the literature include 'Konigsberger' and 'Neiderdeutsch' from Germany. A study done by Bertalan Galambosi and Pekka Peura in Finland found that the highest oil contents (7.6 percent and 7.5 percent) were found in a cultivated Swiss and a wild Finnish population. 'Karzo' is recommended for highest seed yield and highest essential oil content in western Canada.

Caraway seeds are sown from mid-spring to midsummer in full sun and well-tilled, humus-rich soil with good moisture retention; a position in full sun is best. The optimum temperatures for germination are 59°F (15°C) for eight hours and 50°F (10°C) for sixteen hours. Germination may be increased to nearly 100 percent by soaking the seeds for three to six days and drying for four hours before planting.

For field production, space plants 14 to 24 inches (35 to 60 cm) apart between and within rows; this translates to a seed rate of 3.6 to 4.5 pounds per acre (4 to 5 kg/ha). In Israel, the optimum density is thirty-one plants per square yard (thirty-seven plants/square meter). In the normal biennial form, during the first year after sowing, a foot-high (31 cm) mound of finely cut leaves is produced. Flowering occurs early the next summer with 2-foot (61 cm) hollow stems topped with white flowers. Seven weeks of cold temperatures 46°F day/41°F night (8°C day/5°C night) is optimal for flowering, but root-stocks with a diameter below ⅓ inch (8 mm) require longer vernalization. Seed yield is directly correlated with the amount of sunlight between flowering and yield. Harvest plants with a sickle as soon as the oldest seeds mature and partially dry in sheds before threshing to avoid shattering. Commercial yields are 696 to 1,784 pounds per acre (780 to 2,000 kg/ha) of seed for the biennial and 696 pounds per acre (780 kg/ha) for the annual.

Translated for the home gardener, a large plant will produce about ⅓ cup of seeds. Because of the waste of space on a biennial crop like this, vegetables (such as peas) are sometimes intersown for maximum use of land. Caraway is subject to attack from a number of fungal diseases. The most injurious insect is the caterpillar of the caraway moth.

The essential oil of caraway seed is listed as GRAS at 63 to 10,000 ppm. Oddly enough, in spite of the wide use of whole caraway seeds, we find no GRAS listing for them. Caraway may be antispasmodic, a relaxant for smooth muscles. The seed oil is antibacterial and inhibits skin tumors. It also protects gastric mucosa against ethanol-induced damage.

Important chemistry: The essential oil of caraway seeds is dominated by 39 to 68 percent (*S*)(+)-carvone and 26 to 50 percent limonene. The immature inflorescences have 82 percent (*S*)(+)-carvone and 12 percent limonene; the leaves have 59 percent germacrene D, 27 percent beta-elemene, and 13 percent (S)(+)-carvone; and the stems have 62 percent germacrene D, 25 percent beta-elemene, and 10 percent (S)(+)-carvone. The whole herb has 75 to 81 percent germacrene D.

Whereas both spearmint and caraway contain carvone as a principal constituent, spearmint has laevorotary carvone [(R)(-)] while caraway has dextrorotary [(S)(+)] carvone. While the human nose normally cannot distinguish optical isomers of this nature, these two forms of carvone certainly smell different.

Botanical Description

C. carvi L., Sp. pl. 263. 1753.
Native country: Caraway is native to most of Europe.
General habit: Caraway is a biennial or annual smooth herb to 150 cm.
Leaves: Leaves are feather-like and divided two or three times; lobes are 3 to 25 mm long, linear-lance-shaped or linear.
Flowers: Flowers have white or pinkish petals and are arranged in an umbel.
Fruits/seeds: The egg-shaped fruit is 3 to 6 mm in diameter with low ridges.

Cedronella canariensis

sĕ-drō-nĕl-å kå-nār-ĭ-ĕn-sĭs
balm of Gilead

Family: Lamiaceae (Labiatae)
Growth form: somewhat succulent shrub to 59 inches (150 cm)
Hardiness: cannot withstand frost
Light: full sun
Water: moist but not constantly wet
Soil: light
Propagation: cuttings or seeds
Culinary use: none
Craft use: potpourri
Landscape use: pots

Large terracotta pots of balm of Gilead on the patio bring back memories of the warm, blustery winds of the Canary Islands, but why this fragrant herb acquired the popular English name of balm of Gilead is anyone's guess. The true balm of Gilead is *Populus balsamifera* L., a tree. One clue to their similar names may be

that both plants share a resinous odor, and *Cedronella*, a genus of only one species, is the diminutive of *Cedrus*, or cedar, so the name is not too far-fetched. The slightly hairy, lance-shaped

Cedronella canariensis

leaves are divided into threes perched on rather succulent stems of a shrub that may reach to almost 5 feet (150 cm).

Balm of Gilead is excellent in potpourri to provide a balsamic odor. While this herb has no GRAS status, the oil has been demonstrated to be active against bacteria and fungi, particularly *Bordetella bronchiseptica*, which causes whooping cough, and *Cryptococcus albidus*, a cause of meningitis and pulmonary infections. This finding vindicates the popular use of balm of Gilead in the Canary Islands as a respiratory decongestant. This herb deserves further investigation for use as an inhalant for upper respiratory infections.

Balm of Gilead is easy to grow from cuttings, and the seeds (actually tiny nuts, or nutlets) germinate fairly easily. A friable soil in full sun is recommended, but since this tender perennial is only hardy to about Zone 9, it should be carried over on a cool, sunny windowsill or in the greenhouse during the winter.

Important chemistry: The primary form of balm of Gilead cultivated in the United States has an essential oil with 47 to 63 percent pino-

carvone and 10 to 30 percent beta-pinene, providing a resinous balsamic odor. Another form from the Canary Islands has 76 to 82 percent estragole (methyl chavicol) and 6 to 11 percent beta-pinene, providing an odor of balsamic French tarragon, while still another form has 76 percent *p*-allyl anisole and 12 percent pinocarvone, providing a balsamic anise odor.

Botanical Description

C. canariensis (L.) P. Webb & Berthel., Hist. Nat. Iles Canaries 3:87. 1845.

Native country: Balm of Gilead is native to the Açores (Portugal), Arquipélago da Madeira (Portugal), and Islas Canarias (Spain).

General habit: Balm of Gilead is a perennial, smooth, shrubby herb to 150 cm.

Leaves: Leaves are three-foliate; the leaflets are 6 to 13 × 1.5 to 4.5 cm, lance-shaped, pinched at the tip, stalked, smooth above, hairy beneath, toothed.

Flowers: The flowers are pinkish to lilac, rarely white, hairy.

Chamaemelum nobile

kăm-ĕ-mē-lŭm nō-bĭl-ē
Roman chamomile

Family: Asteraceae (Compositae)

Growth form: perennnial to 12 inches (30 cm) high when flowering

Hardiness: hardy to Zone 5

Light: partial to full sun

Water: moist but not constantly wet

Soil: rich in organic matter, pH 5.0 to 8.3, average 7.0

Propagation: seeds, layerings, or cuttings

Culinary use: teas (but not for ragweed-sensitive individuals)

Craft use: potpourri, hair rinses (but not for ragweed-sensitive individuals)

Landscape use: groundcover and along walking stones

French: *chamomille romaine*
German: *Gartenkamille, Römische Kamille, Doppel-Kamille*
Dutch: *roomse kamille*
Italian: *camomilla romana (odorosa), manzanilla*
Spanish: *manzanilla romana, manzanilla officinal*
Arabic: *babunj, babunaj*

Roman chamomile may be every herb gardener's favorite plant to simply walk on; a barefoot sunrise meander through a patch of chamomile on a dewy summer morning may bring to the body a soft tranquility and to the nose a fruity aroma reminiscent of bananas and apples when crushed. The sweet scent of the plant masks the somewhat bitter taste of the soft, ferny foliage and daisy-like flowers. *Chamaemelum nobile* was first called "Roman" by the German herbalist Joachim Camerarius the Younger, who noticed it growing abundantly near Rome, in 1588 (the year he published *Hortus Medicus et Philosophicus*).

By any name, Roman chamomile makes a fast-spreading, aromatic groundcover in the herb garden and is sometimes included with grass-seed mixtures in England or used by itself to create a chamomile lawn, which provides the alternative name of English chamomile.

The genus *Chamaemelum* includes about three species of herbs from Europe. The generic name was derived from Greek *chamos*, "ground," and *melos*, "apple," alluding to the prostrate habit and apple-like fragrance. Roman chamomile used to be listed as *Anthemis nobilis* L., but a taxonomic realignment of many plants of the Asteraceae forced a change of the scientific name.

At least two different cultivars are available. 'Flore Pleno' has double white flowers rising to about 3 inches (7.6 cm). 'Treneague' generally does not flower, thus making it ideal for lawns or as a nonflowering groundcover.

The essential oil of Roman chamomile is listed as GRAS at 0.1 to 20 ppm; the extract is GRAS at 6.7 to 10 ppm. The essential oil is used commercially in ice cream, ices, candy, baked goods, alcoholic and nonalcoholic beverages, gelatins, and puddings.

Ingestion of Roman chamomile tea, bee-pollen, and even honey can induce various allergenic reactions in susceptible individuals (particularly ragweed-sensitive individuals), including skin and respiratory reactions, abdominal pain, and vomiting. Roman chamomile rinses and cosmetics may also induce localized allergic reactions in sensitive individuals, such as conjunctivitis (inflammation of mucous membranes, as around the eyelids).

Commercial cultivation centers upon the cultivar 'Flore Pleno'. Densities of 10,117 plants per acre (25,000 plants/ha) are recommended. This translates to double rows 28 inches (70 cm) apart and 63 inches (160 cm) between double rows with plants 20 inches (50 cm) apart within rows. Flowers are harvested from late July to

Chamaemelum nobile

early August in France and then either dried or distilled. Gardeners with hot summers will find that Roman chamomile will not grow as abundantly as seen in England. Under the best circumstances, the plant should be allowed to ramble cottage-garden style through the moist, humusy border along walking stones.

The Roman and German chamomiles (*Matricaria recutita*) are often confused in the literature; please see the entry for German chamomile for additional information. Argentina is a major producer of dried Roman chamomile blossoms.

Important chemistry: The essential oil is dominated by 3 to 39 percent isobutyl angelate, 0 to 23 percent 3-methylamyl angelate, 0 to 21 percent 3-methyl amyl isovalerate, 0 to 18 percent isoamyl angelate, 0 to 16 percent methylallyl angelate, 0 to 14 percent 2-methyl butyl angelate, and 0 to 13 percent 3-methyl amyl isobutyrate. While German chamomile oil is blue from the chamazulene content, we find no chemical report of an authentic Roman chamomile oil which reports azulenes.

Botanical Description

C. nobile (L.) All., Fl. pedem. 1:185. 1785 (*Anthemis nobilis* L.).

Native country: Roman chamomile is native to western Europe northward to northern Ireland on roadsides and damp grasslands.

General habit: Roman chamomile is a more or less hairy perennial, decumbent, 10 to 30 cm high.

Leaves: Leaves are oblong in outline, stalkless, deeply lobed two or three times, linear, with a tooth-like tip.

Flowers: Flowers are yellow and white daisies.

Fruits/seeds: Fruits (achenes) are about 1 mm long.

Chrysopogon zizanioides

krī-sō-pō̆-gŏn zī-ză-nĭ-ōy-dēz
vetiver

Family: Poaceae (Gramineae)
Growth form: perennials to about 8 feet (2.4 m)
Hardiness: marginally hardy to Zone 8
Light: full sun
Water: not constantly moist; can withstand drought and flooding
Soil: average garden soil; sandy preferred for harvesting
Propagation: divisions in spring with an ax or saw
Culinary use: none
Craft use: potpourri, perfumery, baskets

Landscape use: middle to rear of herb or perennial border

French: *vétyver, costus arabique, cus-cus, chiendent des Indes*
German: *Vetivergras, Arabischer Kostus, Ivarancusa, Mottenwurzel*
Dutch: *vetiver*
Hindi: *khus-khus, khas*
Sanskrit: *reshira, sugandhimula*
Javanese: *akar wangi*

Vetiver is a large, coarse grass that grows up to 8 feet (2.4 m) tall. Where it is hardy (Zone 9, marginally Zone 8), the tops are evergreen and pale green; often in Zone 8 the tops are killed back but the tops come back in spring. Vetiver, alias vetivert, Arabian kuss-kuss, cuscus grass, or khus-khus grass, is one of 29 species of the genus *Chrysopogon*. Previously, vetiver was put into its own genus, *Vetiveria*, but recent studies have found that *Vetiveria* and *Chrysopogon* are hardly distinct. The name *Chrysopogon* means "golden beard," referring to the flowers; the specific name means "wild rice-like," after the genus *Zizania*.

The massive, fibrous, fragrant roots are distilled for perfumery and also woven into mats, baskets, screens, and fans, which give off a scent when sprinkled with water. The Mogul emperors were particularly fond of the *khus khus tatti*, a screen woven of vetiver roots, soaked with water to both cool and perfume the air that passed through the arches of their pavilions. Recently, vetiver has been advocated as a plant to control erosion in tropical and subtropical areas because of the large, extensive root system.

Chrysopogon zizanioides

The odor of vetiver has been described as heavy and woody-earthy. Vetiver oil is used extensively in perfumery as a fixative and blends well with bases such as fougère, chypre, modern woody-aldehydic or amber-aldehydic bases, Oriental bases, moss and woody notes, and rose bases. Vetiver oil has also been used as a repellent to cockroaches, termites, and flies, and in Europe vetiver root used to be placed in clothes closets and was called "mothroot." Essential oil of vetiver is antioxidant. French traders first introduced vetiver to Louisiana and Haiti, and vetiver is now imported from Haiti, Réunion, China, Brazil, India, and Angola.

Growing vetiver is usually no problem; it will grow in wet or dry areas and even in almost pure sand. Harvesting the massive roots, however, is the problem. Remember, these roots can withstand even torrential monsoons and floods with no apparent damage! Robert P. Adams and Mark R. Dafforn have extensively characterized the genetic diversity of vetiver but found that the clone 'Sunshine' accounts for almost all the germplasm utilized outside South Asia. R. K. Lal and his associates in India have also identified germplasm for oil yield and soil conservation.

Rooted cuttings are normally planted in full sun in Asia at a depth of approximately 12 inches (30 cm) during the rainy season. Harvest is about 18 to 22 months later during the dry season. High-nitrogen fertilizers produce the best growth; the yield in Asia amounts to about 2,677 to 5,355 pounds per acre (3,001 to 6,002 kg/ha). This means approximately 909 tons (1,000 metric tons) of soil must be worked in order to harvest approximately 0.9 ton (1 metric ton) of roots. After being dug out, the rootballs must be completely free of soil residues before they can be processed. Sandy soils are more easily removed, and roots from sandy soils have a higher percentage of oil than roots from heavy soils anyway. Chopped roots are soaked in water up to twelve hours and then charged to the stills. Because of the high-boiling point constituents in vetiver, a single distillation can take up to 24 to 48 hours.

Important chemistry: The essential oil of vetiver is dominated by 3 to 31 percent khusimol, trace to 17 percent isovalencenol, and 2 to 11 percent alpha-vetiselinenol backed by a rich array of sesquiterpenoids, providing a rich woody fragrance.

Botanical Description

There are two types of vetiver in India. The northern type flowers freely and sets viable seed, while the southern type does not usually flower. The plant cultivated in North America seems to be thus from the southern population.

C. zizanioides (L.) Roberty, Bull. Inst. Franç. Afrique Nord 22:106. 1960 [*Vetiveria zizanioides* (L.) Nash].

Native country: Vetiver is native to tropical India.

General habit: Vetiver is a dense, clumping grass to 2.4 m.

Leaves: Leaves are smooth, stiff, 8 mm wide.

Flowers: Flowers are large, erect panicle, 14 to 40 cm long, slender, with gray-green or purplish spikelets.

Citrus hystrix

sĭt-rŭs hĭs-trĭx
Kaffir lime, makrut, Mauritius papeda

Family: Rutaceae
Growth form: small, thorny tree 6 to 25 feet (1.8 to 7.6 m)
Hardiness: hardy to Zone 9
Light: full sun
Water: moist but not constantly wet
Soil: rich in organic matter
Propagation: seeds, layerings, or cuttings
Culinary use: Thai curries, esp. with coconut milk
Craft use: insect repellent
Landscape use: generally a container plant outside of California or Florida

French: *combava*
German: *Kaffir Limette, Makrut Limette*
Dutch: *Kaffir limoen, Djerook pooroot*
Javanese: *jeruk purut*

Malay: *limau purut*
Thai: *makrut*
Japanese: *swangi*

The specific epithet *hystrix* means "porcupine," probably referring to the numerous spines. Kaffir lime has been used in the English language as far back as 1888. Kaffir means "infidel" in Arabic and was applied by Arab slavers to the inhabitants of the east coast of Africa; thus, it is now viewed by some as offensive, but in Indonesia the word *kafir* (*kaffir, kapir*) is a non-judgmental word. If kaffir lime offends you, then call this by the Thai name makrut (pronounced "ma-gruud"), which is easier to say than the alternate English name Mauritius papeda.

In Thailand, leaves of makrut are used in

curries, especially in combination with coconut milk. It provides a unique tang to tom-yam soup, a Thai delicacy. The fruit is so sour that it cannot be eaten fresh, but the juice is used in food products.

The leaves are unique with a swollen, leafy petiole and the scent of citronella candles with nuances of lime. The knobby green fruits have a lemon/lime odor, and the oil provides a stimulating effect when inhaled. Glyceroglycolipids from the leaves exhibit anti-tumor properties, while coumarins from the fruit inhibit nitric oxide generation. The fruit peel also has an anti-fertility effect, inhibiting implantation.

Important chemistry: The leaves of makrut are rich in 65 to 82 percent citronellal. The oil of the fruit peel is rich in 5 to 31 percent limonene, 19 to 31 percent beta-pinene, 2 to 23 percent sabinene, and trace to 11 percent terpinen-4-ol.

Botanical Description

C. hystrix DC., Cat. Pl. horti monsp. 97. 1813.
Native country: Makrut is native to China and Southeast Asia but widely naturalized.
General habit: Makrut is a thorny tree 1.8 to 7.6 m tall.
Leaves: Leaves are blunt-pointed, usually of medium size, 8 to 12 × 3 to 5 cm, more or less irregular at the tip. Margins are more or less scalloped. The winged petiole, usually two-thirds to three-fourths as long as the leaf blade, is broadly rounded and blunt at the base, more or less with scalloped margins.
Flowers: Flowers are small with short, entirely free stamens.
Fruits/seeds: Fruits are almost always bumpy or tuberculate, similar in size to a lime.

Coriandrum sativum

kō-rē-ăn-drŭm să-tē-vŭm
coriander

Family: Apiaceae (Umbelliferae)
Growth form: annual to 3 feet (90 cm)
Hardiness: seedlings can withstand light frost
Light: full sun
Water: moist but not constantly moist
Soil: light, pH 4.9 to 8.2, average 6.6
Propagation: seeds in spring or fall, 3,000 seeds per ounce (106/g) (var. *sativum*)
Culinary use: curries, pickling spices, sauces, cakes, beverages (fruits); salsas, soups, salads (leaves)
Craft use: none
Landscape use: short-lived; may be used in the middle of the border, but best in vegetable plot

French: *coriandre, persil arabe*
German: *Koriander, Wanzendill, Schwindelkorn*
Dutch: *koriander*
Italian: *coriandolo*
Spanish: *culantro, cilantro, cilandriom coriandro*
Portuguese: *coentro*
Swedish: *koriander*
Russian: *koriandr*
Chinese: *hu-sui, hsiang-sui, yuan-sui*
Japanese: *koendoro*
Arabic: *kuzbara, kuzbura*

Those who believe a taste for coriander is acquired with difficulty love to point out that its botanical name is derived from the Greek *koriannon*, one of the earliest words deciphered of Linear B of Crete, 1500–1200 B.C.E. ("*ko-ri-ja-do-no*"). The root of both words is *koris*, or bedbug.

Despite its smell, coriander has achieved a world-wide popularity that provides palatable synonyms, too. In English, the "seed," technically a fruit, is termed coriander, but the foliage is referred to as Chinese parsley or cilantro, a term preferred by Latin Americans. While many species of *Coriandrum* were defined in the past, the tendency today is to consider them all as variations of only two species, *C. sativum* and *C. tordylium* (Fensl) Bornm.

Along with a galloping international popularity, this annual herb has two lives. First, it resembles a flat-leaved parsley with stems that extend from a crown to hold green segmented leaves; it is in this stage that the leaves are harvested. Its second life occurs about thirty days later, as a tall stalk rises from the plant's crown;

Coriandrum sativum

this stem will bear the umbels with white to pink flowers that produce the hard coriander fruits.

Young coriander leaves are added to salads, sauces, and soups and are especially popular in Oriental and Mexican cuisines. While the odor of the leaves may be repulsive to some, the taste becomes muted when cooked and provides a deep flavor rather than a sharp accent to accompany food. The leaves do not dry well but can be preserved by freezing or storing in salted oil. The ripe fruits in their crisp, tan spheres are an essential ingredient in curries and pickling spices and are sometimes sugar-coated and called "coriander comfits." The essential oil from ripe coriander seeds is a commercial flavoring for foods, alcoholic beverages (chiefly gin and some liqueurs), and tobacco. The fruits (5,200 ppm) and essential oil (120 ppm) are considered GRAS. The seed oil is antimicrobial and antioxidant. Cilantro is effective against both *Listera* and *Salmonella*.

Morocco, Romania, and Mexico are the principal commercial sources for American imports of coriander. The Russian corianders (var. *microcarpum*) are higher in essential oils than the other commercial corianders (var. *sativum*).

Prior to planting coriander, consideration should be given to proper varietal selection because of the plant's dual harvests of leaves and fruits. There are several dozen selected strains of coriander in the trade in the United States, Europe, and Asia. Some, like 'Leaf' and 'Long Standing' in the United States are more adapted to foliage production; they are slower to make flowers and thus provide an increased harvest of foliage. The best slow-bolting varieties now available increase the time of foliage production by about two weeks. Moderating heat with 30- to 50-percent shade cloth also extends the period of foliage harvest.

Coriander is grown from seed sown in near-neutral garden loam where it will receive full sun. Seed sown directly in the field or the garden exhibits a low germination rate, usually less than 50 percent. Germination may be enhanced above 60 percent by rubbing the fruits until the seed-halves, or mericarps, separate. The seed is then soaked for three or four days and dried for eight hours before planting. Seeds are planted 1 inch (2.5 cm) deep at the rate of 10 to 25 pounds per acre (11 to 28 kg/ha). For the home gardener, the seeds may be broadcast or planted in rows or raised beds, allowing 9 to 32 inches (23 to 76 cm) between rows for cultivation. Maximum germination occurs when day temperatures are about 80°F and nights are in the upper 60s (27°C/20°C).

Seed is sown as soon as soil can be worked and after danger of heavy frost is past. Germination begins about four days after sowing when the scraping and soaking method is used or after about twenty-five days otherwise. Coriander does not successfully compete with weeds, so mulch or cultivation are important cultural factors. Plants require about 16 inches (400 mm) of rain during development, comprising about 4 inches (100 mm) for germination and 12 inches (300 mm) for stem elongation.

Leaves are harvested about one month after sowing. Foliage is usually hand-harvested by shearing the rosette's outermost leaves. New growth commences within a few days from the center of the plant. Leaf-harvesting continues until the central flower stem rises and leaf production ceases.

In climates with long, hot summers, coriander is often considered a cool-weather crop to be planted in early spring or late summer and fall; low temperatures tend to temper the plant's desire to run to seed. Seed may be sown in successive rows every few weeks during hot weather and harvested by pulling the plants when sufficient leaves appear.

Seeds mature about 90 to 105 days after sowing. The concentration of essential oils in the fruits decreases at temperatures above 70°F (21°C); the ideal temperature for maturation of the fruits is 59 to 64°F (15 to 18°C). Green seeds smell of the foliage but acquire a spicy aroma and a chestnut-like color when dry. Over-ripening results in scattering and losing the seeds during harvest.

Harvest coriander seeds when about half of the seeds have changed from green to gray or when the seeds on the central umbels are ripe, preferably in the morning, when dew acts to prevent shattering. Commercially, fruits may be harvested by taking up the entire plant for threshing or by using a wheat combine harvester. Fruit yields of 1,000 to 5,000 pounds per acre (1,123 to 5,616 kg/ha) are considered normal. For essential oil distillation, grind seeds immediately before distillation. Yield of oil is 0.4 to 1.8 percent with the small-fruited types, while the large-fruited types yield only 0.1 to 0.4 percent oil.

Coriander is susceptible to a gall-forming fungus (*Protomyces macrosporus*), a wilt disease (*Fusarium oxysporum* f. sp. *corianderii*), a leaf/flower spot (*Pseudomonas syringae*), and a powdery mildew (*Erysiphe polygoni*). Late-maturing varieties are especially prone to powdery mildew. Occasional minor insect infestations include some caterpillars and boring grubs.

Important chemistry: The principal constituent of the essential oil of the ripe seeds is 56 to 86 percent linalool. The foliage is given its distinctive aroma by a combination of chemicals, principal among them are 0 to 38 percent linalool, 2 to 59 percent (*E*)-2-decenal, 1 to 22 percent (*E*)-2-dodecenal, and 4 to 18 percent decanal, and trace to 45 percent (*E*)-2-tetradecenal.

Botanical Description

C. sativum L. Sp. pl. 256. 1753.

Native country: Coriander is native to southern Europe, Asia Minor, and the Caucasus.

General habit: Coriander is a short-lived annual that grows erect and is 20 to 90 cm high.

Leaves: The smooth leaves are borne singly on stems that rise in rosette fashion from a crown. The immature plant has basal and lower stem leaves that are egg-shaped with a wedge-shaped base and irregularly cut segments. As the plant matures, a single tall stem emerges from the crown and the leaves become more finely dissected into narrow linear segments, presenting a fern-like appearance.

Flowers: Flowers have white, rose, or lavender petals and are arranged in an umbel.

Fruits/seeds: The spicy-scented fruits are egg- or globe-shaped. Two botanical varieties of coriander are cultivated, *C. sativum* var. *sativum* and *C. sativum* var. *microcarpum* (small-fruited). The two are distinguished by the size of their hard, ribbed fruit, which varies in diameter between 1.5 to 2.5 mm for var. *microcarpum* and 3 to 6 mm for var. *sativum*.

Crocus sativus

krō-kŭs så-tē-vŭs
saffron crocus

Family: Iridaceae

Growth form: cormous perennial to 6 inches (15 cm)

Hardiness: routinely hardy to at least southern Pennsylvania (Zone 6)

Light: full sun

Water: must be well-drained soil at all times

Soil: rich in organic matter, pH 6.0 to 8.0, average 6.9

Propagation: separation of small corms (cormels)

Culinary use: soups, stews, rice dishes, breads

Craft use: limited use for dye

Landscape use: front of perennial border or along paths

French: *safran*
German: *Safran*
Dutch: *saffraan*

Italian: *zafferano*
Spanish: *azafrán*
Portuguese: *açafrão*
Swedish: *saffran*
Russian: *shafran*
Chinese: *fan-hung-hua*
Japanese: *safuran*
Arabic: *za'farān*

Saffron may be one of the oldest herbs of commerce and the most expensive, but the origin of the word saffron is a matter of conjecture; it may be derived from the Arabic. The earliest reference to the word saffron dates to 2300 B.C.E. when Sargon, one of ancient Babylonia's leaders, was born at a village on the Euphrates called Azupirano, or "Saffron Town." The Papyrus Ebers, written about 1550 B.C.E. (but probably copied from a manuscript from about 2650

B.C.E., about the time Cheops built the Great Pyramid), includes saffron as a remedy for rheumatism.

Saffron crocus is also pictured on a Bronze Age pottery jug found at Crete and in the Xeste 3 fresco in Akrotiri, Thera, dating to c. 3000–1100 B.C.E. The saffron crocus has lent its name to ancient Corycos in Cilicia (on Turkey's Mediterranean coast), Krokos in Greece, Safranbolu in Turkey, and Saffron Walden in England.

The genus *Crocus* includes about eighty species from the Mediterranean to China. As distinguished from the fall crocus, *Colchicum* of the Liliaceae, the genus *Crocus* has corms (not bulbs) and three stigmatic branches. Saffron crocus is a fall-blooming crocus with deep lilac-purple flowers; the long, linear leaves persist over winter and gradually turn brown in late spring, only to reappear again in fall.

The generic name is derived from the Greek *kroke*, or "thread," alluding to the dried, orange, thread-like stigmas, which are the source of the commercial saffron. About 70,000 flowers are needed to produce 1 pound of saffron; a harvest of this size takes an experienced picker twelve days of backbreaking labor. Ounce for ounce,

Crocus sativus

saffron is the most expensive spice or herb in the world, with natural vanilla second. Adulteration is common, sometimes with false saffron (*Carthamus tinctorius*), poet's marigold (*Calendula officinalis*), turmeric, and even dyed corn silk.

Saffron imparts a peculiar, perfumed, slightly bitter taste to a wide array of dishes. Many cultures consider it essential, for both color and flavor, in the best-loved, traditional dishes. It is added to Spanish *paella*, a seafood and rice casserole; Italian *risotto*, or rice; Provençal *bouillabaisse*, a fish stew; Russian *kulich* or Easter bread; Pennsylvania Dutch *bot boi*, or chicken noodle stew; and Swedish *lussekatter*, or St. Lucia's cakes. Saffron may also color cheeses and liqueurs such as Fernet-Branca.

More than six saffron strands per person will make a dish too bitter as well as excessively expensive; ingesting 0.05 oz (1.5 g) of saffron has resulted in death. Saffron was once used as a dye (1 part saffron/10,000 parts water, or approximately 1 g saffron/gallon water). Saffron was also used to color paints, stained glass, and foil to produce an imitation gold. In ancient times it had limited use as a perfume. Today, the dye that colors the golden-yellow robes of Buddhist monks is most typically from the heartwood of the jack-fruit tree, *Artocarpus integrifolius* L., not saffron.

Saffron crocus is primarily cultivated in Spain among a network of families whose methods of cultivation and negotiation date back to the Arab introduction of the plant around 921 C.E. Although commercial cultivation has been attempted at various times in other European countries, the Mediterranean, the Middle East, India (particularly Kashmir), China, South America, tropical island nations, and Pennsylvania, Spain continues to supply most of the world's saffron.

Traditionally in Spain, saffron planting begins during the feasts of Saint John and Saint

Peter at the end of June. Corms are planted 5 to 7 inches (12 to 18 cm) deep, 6 to 8 inches (15 to 20 cm) apart and 4 inches (10 cm) between rows, in May or June in well-drained, loose, sandy or calcareous soil that has been dressed with rotted manure well before planting; blossoms are fewer with corms planted at more shallow depths. The corm lies dormant from about May to September. Autumn moisture is required for blossom production. Weeds are controlled by hoeing.

In Spain, a crop of one million blooms per 2.5 acres (1 hectare), yielding 22 pounds (10 kg) of dried saffron, is considered satisfactory, although higher yields have been reported in Italy, India, and Spain. New Zealand has reported 24.3 kg/ha, but labor costs prohibit saffron cultivation there.

Saffron imparts a peculiar, perfumed, slightly bitter taste to a wide array of dishes.

After morning gathering, the flowers are spread on a table, and the crocus blossom is split down the stem. Nimble fingers remove the three-part stigma. The full plate of fresh saffron is turned onto a fine-meshed sieve and dried over gentle heat, developing full flavor and reducing its weight by 80 percent. The final product is dry to the touch with its significant flavor intact. Saffron should be stored at a relative humidity that does not exceed 57 percent.

During a good crocus season, a field may be picked five times as successive blooms appear. Every three years the corms must be dug up, separated (each corm produces four to ten daughter corms each season), selected for size and health, and transplanted to avoid disease and crowding. For the next twelve years, the saffron fields are planted with other crops; then saffron may be returned to the site.

Several fungal diseases, particularly *Rhizoctonia violacea* and *Fusarium oxysporum*, attack saffron; they may be controlled by selection of disease-free stock, cultivation in new soil, and by dipping corms in solutions of copper sulfate. The chief enemies of saffron crocus are mice, voles, chipmunks, and other rodents. Rabbits also relish the green tops during the winter, so rabbit-proof fencing may be required in some areas.

Saffron crocus is sterile and hybridization or selection by conventional means to improve flower yield are thus impossible, but it may be possible to use natural variation to gain improved harvests; an Iranian researcher has reported finding up to ten stigmatic divisions per flower. Other researchers have reported the formation of stigma-like structures and pigments in cultured tissues of *C. sativus*. Other species, such as *C. haussknechtii* Boiss. & Reut. ex Boiss., also yield comparable pigmented stigmas. Will saffron of the future be grown in a flask or harvested from other species? If so, it will have to meet rigid standards now in place for saffron:

1. *Very select* saffron has an average stigma length of 53 mm and only a small portion of the yellow style at the base. The color is orange-red and the odor is strong and penetrating.
2. *Select* saffron has average length of 53 mm of stigma and style together. The color is bright red and the odor is good.
3. *Superior* saffron has an average length of 50 mm of stigma and style together. The color is dark red and the odor is good.
4. *Medium* saffron has an average length of 46 to 50 mm of stigma and style together. The color, appearance, and odor are good.

The stigmas of the saffron crocus are considered GRAS at 1 to 969 ppm, while the extract is GRAS at 1 to 50 ppm. Saffron has been shown to exhibit antisecretory and antiulcer activities in rodents. Stigma and petal extracts of saffron are antinociceptive, anti-flammatory, and antidepressant in mice. Crocetin, one of the carotenoids in saffron, has been documented in animal experiments to cut serum cholesterol in half when injected into rabbits. Crocin, safranal, and picrocrocin have also been documented to inhibit the growth of human cancer cells (HeLa and HL-60) in vitro, and crocin and crocetin derivatives inhibit skin tumor promotion in mice. Safranal and crocin are anticonvulsant in mice. A glycoconjugate isolated from corms of saffron is highy cytotoxic. Crocin has also been shown to reduce the ethanol-induced impairment of learning behavior of mice.

Important chemistry: Saffron has 0.1 percent vitamin B_2 (riboflavin). The principal water-soluble pigment, providing the orange-red color, is alpha-crocin, which is composed of the carotenoid crocetin bound to glucose [crocetin-di-(-D-glucosyl) ester]. The bitter taste is due to picrocrocin. The odor in the essential oil is primarily due to 47 to 60 percent safranal, which is released from picrocrocin upon drying.

The pigments in the petals are primarily five kaempferol derivatives.

Botanical Description

C. sativus L., Sp. pl. 36. 1753 [*C. orsinii* (Parl.) Maw, *C. sativus* L. var. *casmirianus* Royle].

Native country: Saffron crocus is not known in the wild. *Crocus sativus* is considered to be a sterile triploid hybrid of *C. cartwrightianus* Herbert of open, rocky hillsides or sparse pinewoods in Greece, most probably with *C. thomasii* Ten. from the mountains of Italy and the Adriatic Coast.

General habit: Saffron crocus is a 3 to 5 cm corm covered with a fibrous tunic.

Leaves: Slightly grayish green leaves are narrow and grass-like, 1.5 to 2 mm wide, about 5 to 11 per corm.

Flowers: One to four flowers per corm, appearing in fall, are deep lilac-purple with darker veins and a darker violet stain toward the base of the segments; the throat is hairy, white or lilac. Perianth segments are 3.5 to 5 × 1 to 2 cm. Three orange-red style branches or pistils are 2.5 to 3.2 cm long.

Fruits/seeds: Saffron crocus is a sterile triploid and does not set fruits or seeds.

Cryptotaenia japonica

krĭp-tō-tē-nĭ-å jå-pŏn-ĭ-kå
mitsuba, Japanese honewort, wild parsley or chervil

Family: Apiaceae (Umbelliferae)
Growth form: short-lived perennial to about one foot (30 cm) or more
Hardiness: hardy to at least southern Pennsylvania (Zone 6)

Light: part sun
Water: moist but not constantly wet
Soil: rich in organic matter
Propagation: seeds in spring

Culinary use: substitute for parsley or chervil but not GRAS

Craft use: none

Landscape use: edge of perennial border or along paths

Japanese: *mitsuba, itomitsuba*

Mitsuba looks like a dark green, non-glossy, broad, flat Italian parsley but tastes more of chervil. In Japan, this is used as a topping for vegetables and is believed to have a stimulating effect on the appetite.

During its vegetative stage, it lies close to the ground; when flowering, it reaches up to 1 foot (30 cm) or more. The tiny white flowers sparkle along a woodland walkway. The forma *atropurpurea* (Makino) Ohwi, or *murasaki-mitsuba*, has dark purple leaves. Named cultivars include 'Yanagawa 1 goh', 'Kanto-masumori', and 'Kantomasumori (B)'.

Give mitsuba moist but well-drained humusy soil in the shady herb garden. This is a short-lived perennial which readily reseeds and may

become weedy. This is very similar to honewort, *C. canadensis* (L.) DC., which is found in Piedmont forests in eastern North America and has been similarly employed as a chervil substitute.

While this has been cultivated for centuries in Japan, Korea, and China, it has no GRAS status. Consumption of large quantities may be poisonous.

Important chemistry: The essential oil of mitsuba is rich in 26 percent germacrene D, 13 percent alpha-selinene and 11 percent *trans*-farnesene, providing a chervil-like odor.

Botanical Description

C. japonica Hassk., Retzia 1:113. 1855 [*C. canadensis* (L.) DC. var. *japonica* (Hassk.) Makino].

Native country: Japanese wild chervil is native to the woods of the hills and mountains in Korea, China, and Japan.

General habit: Japanese wild chervil is a smooth perennial with short rhizomes and rather thick roots.

Leaves: Leaves at the base are long-stalked with blades heart-triangular-shaped, 1 to 5 cm wide, with three leaflets, the leaflets stalkless, the terminal one broadly diamond-egg-shaped to broadly egg-shaped, 3 to 8 cm long, 2 to 6 cm wide, tapering to the apex, abruptly narrowed to the tapering base, incised or irregularly toothed, rarely deeply lobed, the lateral leaflets at base with a slightly dilated outer margin, the leaves of the inflorescence very short, often undivided, linear to lance-shaped.

Flowers: The white flowers, appearing in June and July, are borne in an umbel.

Fruits/seeds: Fruit, appearing in August, is 3 to 4 mm long, smooth, ribbed, the halves oblong-cylindric, narrowed at the apex.

Cryptotaenia japonica

Cuminum cyminum

kū-mĭn-ŭm sī-mĭn-ŭm
cumin

Family: Apiaceae (Umbelliferae)
Growth form: annual to 20 inches (50 cm)
Hardiness: can withstand light frost
Light: full sun
Water: moist but not constantly wet
Soil: light, pH 4.5 to 8.2, average 7.3
Propagation: seeds in spring, 11,000 seeds per oz (388/g)
Culinary use: curries, chilis, pickles, meats, soups, and stews
Craft use: none
Landscape use: short-lived; use at front of the border, but best in vegetable plot

---

French: *cumin*
German: *Römischer Kümmel, Kreuzkümmel*
Dutch: *komijn*
Italian: *comino*
Spanish: *comino*
Portuguese: *cominho*
Swedish: *spiskummin*
Russian: *kmin*
Chinese: *ma-ch'in*
Japanese: *kumin*
Arabic: *kamun, kammon*

The genus *Cuminum* includes two species; black cumin is an entirely different plant, *Nigella sativa*. Both the genus name for cumin and specific epithet are derived from the ancient Arabic name, *kamun*. Cumin has been cultivated since at least the times of the Minoans (c. 2200–1400 B.C.E.) for its aromatic "seeds" (technically fruits). Cumin is extensively used in curries and chilis and used to flavor meats, pickles, cheeses, sausages, soups, and stews. Cumin fruits (300 to 4,308 ppm) and essential oil (247

ppm) are considered GRAS. The essential oil of cumin is antibacterial and antioxidant. Cumin also inhibits arachidonic acid-induced aggregation of blood platelets and reduces thromboxane formation. The essential oil of cumin is both anti-nociceptive and anticonvulsant.

Cumin is primarily imported from Turkey, China, and India. The fruits lose their viability quickly after one year, and seed lots should be tested if germination is unknown; good seeds will have at least 70 percent germination. Cumin is commercially cultivated in India on a garden loam of fine tilth with a near-neutral pH; fruit is sown at the rate of 11 to 13½ pounds/acre (12 to 15 kg/ha), ½ to ¾ inches (1.5 to 2.0 cm) deep.

For the home garden, plant seeds about 2.5 to 3 inches apart. Germination is improved by soaking fruits in running water for twenty-four

Cuminum cyminum

to thirty-six hours before planting to remove germination inhibitors. Cumin is a cool-weather crop, so it must be planted in early spring or early fall, as it requires three to four months of growth to produce mature seeds. Cumin is picky; plants refuse to grow in spots that are too windy, too wet, too dry, too cold, too hot, and so on.

At best, cumin plants seldom exceed 6 inches high and are spindly with threadlike leaves. They may be engulfed by weeds if the gardener is not diligent. Manures (17 to 22 tons per acre or 40 metric tons/ha) along with ammonium sulfate (133 pounds per acre or 150 kg/ha) or urea (54 pounds per acre or 60 kg/ha) are recommended in India. Yields of 714 to 892 pounds per acre (800 to 1000 kg/ha) are reported under optimum conditions.

The home gardener might try a pot planted with ten seeds, which will yield about a tablespoon of seeds. Cumin is subject to powdery mildew (*Erysiphe polygoni*), blight (*Alternaria burnsii*), wilt (*Fusarium oxysporium* f. sp. *cumini*), and aphids.

Important chemistry: The essential oil of cumin is primarily composed of trace to 72 percent cuminyl alcohol, 24 to 45 percent 1,4-*p*-menthadiene-7-al, 16 to 54 percent cuminaldehyde, 7 to 30 percent gamma-terpinene, 3 to 20 percent beta-pinene, 4 to 14 percent 1,3-*p*-menthadien-7-al, 5 to 12 percent *p*-cymene, trace to 12 percent acoradiene, and 0 to 11 percent safranal.

Botanical Description

C. cyminum L., Sp. pl. 254. 1753.
Native country: Cumin is native to northern Africa and southwestern Asia.
General habit: Cumin is a slender annual 10 to 50 cm high.
Leaves: The two or three leaves are thread-like lobes 2 to 5 cm long, bluish green with sheathed bases.
Flowers: Three to five white or rose-colored flowers are borne in an umbel.
Fruit/Seeds: The fruit is 4 to 5 mm long, egg-shaped with parallel sides, beset with fine bristles or non-hairy.

Cunila origanoides

kŭ-nī-lå ō-rĭ-gå-nōy-dēz
Maryland dittany

Family: Lamiaceae (Labiatae)
Growth form: clumping herbaceous perennial to about 16 inches (40 cm) tall
Hardiness: hardy to at least southern Pennsylvania (Zone 6)
Light: part shade
Water: moist but well drained at all times
Soil: rich in leafmold

Propagation: divisions or seeds in early spring
Culinary use: limited (not GRAS)
Craft use: dried flowers, wreaths
Landscape use: front of shaded perennial border, along woodland paths

Cunila origanoides

Maryland dittany may be a minor member of the herb garden, but it is delightful for its thyme/marjoram-scented leaves and a curious physical property: in winter the hollow stems act as capillaries to form "frost-flowers" of ice crystals. This unusual trait is responsible for an alternative name for the herb, frost mint. Alternative hypotheses beyond simple capillary action have been devised to explain this phenomenon; some elaborate explanations require living roots, but dead plants also exhibit frost flowers. We have also observed frost flowers on dead stems of *Lippia micromera*, a Jamaican oregano that had been dead for more than a month.

Maryland dittany's mass of tiny, wispy rose-purple flowers seems to glow from a shaded corner of the herb garden from August to October. The herb is usually found on rocky hillsides or hummocks in Piedmont forests (another name is stone mint); thus, it must have very good drainage and acid, humusy soil.

Cunila was an ancient Latin name for a now-forgotten fragrant plant that now refers to about fifteen species of plants, primarily tropical, from eastern North America to Uruguay. The specific name, *origanoides*, means "like *Origanum*."

The scented leaves of Maryland dittany were once used to brew tea, but the herb does not have GRAS status.

Important chemistry: The essential oil of Maryland dittany collected from Virginia is dominated by 38 percent thymol and 27 percent gamma-terpinene, providing a thyme/marjoram-like fragrance.

Botanical Description

C. origanoides (L.) Britt., Mem. Torrey Bot. Club 5:278. 1894 (*C. mariana* L.).

Native country: Maryland dittany is native to dry or rocky roods from southern New York and Pennsylvania to Indiana, Illinois, and Missouri, south to South Carolina, Tennessee, Arkansas, and Oklahoma.

General habit: Maryland dittany is an herbaceous perennial, slightly woody at the base, 20 to 40 cm tall.

Leaves: Leaves are almost stalkless, egg- to triangular-egg-shaped, 2 to 4 cm long, tapering to a point, smooth, commonly with a few teeth, rarely smooth-edged.

Flowers: Rose-purple to white flowers appear in August to October in clusters of three to nine.

Cymbopogon citratus

sĭm-bŏ-pō-gŏn sĭ-trå-tŭs
lemongrass

Family: Poaceae (Gramineae)

Growth form: herbaceous perennial to 2 feet (60 cm)

Hardiness: cannot withstand frost

Light: full sun

Water: moist but not constantly wet

Soil: well drained, sandy, pH 4.3 to 8.4, average 6.0

Propagation: divisions anytime

Culinary use: Asian stir-fry, meats, teas

Craft use: potpourri, perfumes

Landscape use: container plant, or annual accent in border

French: *lemongrass de l'Amerique Centrale*

German: *Lemongras*

Spanish: *pasto limón, cedrón paja, citronel*

Portuguese: *capim-limão*

Chinese: *iang mao*

Vietnamese: *xå, så*

Cymbopogon citratus

At the base of lemongrass's many fibrous leaves is a paler, more succulent core resembling a scallion that is sliced into Southeast Asian dishes to impart a pungent lemon flavor. The leaves are also used in teas and potpourris.

While commonly called lemongrass in the herb trade, the commercial name for *Cymbopogon citratus* is West Indian lemongrass to differentiate it from East Indian lemongrass [*C. flexuosus* (Nees es Steud.) Wats. in Atkinson] and Jammu lemongrass [*C. pendulus* (Steud.) Wats. in Atkinson]. The genus *Cymbopogon*, with fifty-six species, is unique among grasses because the leaves are scented. Other economically important species include *C. martinii* (Roxb.) Wats. in Atkinson (rosha, palmarosa, and gingergrass), *C. nardus* (L.) Rendle (Ceylon citronella), and *C. winterianus* Jowitt (Java citronella).

The Latin name *Cymbopogon* is derived from the Greek *kymbe*, a boat, and *pogon*, a beard; this is a rather technical term alluding to the form of the flowers. *Citratus*, of course, means "resembling *Citrus*."

The best atmospheric conditions for growing lemongrass are full sun and temperatures between 64 and 100°F (18 to 38°C) and 40 to 100 percent relative humidity. Lemongrass tops will be killed at 28°F (–2°C), and prolonged temperatures below freezing will eventually kill the entire plant. Lemongrass prefers well-drained, sandy soils. It rarely flowers, so propagation is by divisions.

A single pot of lemongrass will suffice for most home cooks. If your local nurseries do not sell lemongrass, check the Asian food markets for lemongrass pieces with stems. Place the unrooted pieces in pots of sterile potting soil and cover with a polyethylene bag for about two weeks, or until roots appear. Then gradually remove the bag. Lemongrass, once rooted and placed in optimum conditions, will grow rapidly and demand to be repotted in a few months or less.

For commercial production, divisions are planted in furrows 3 to 4 feet (0.9 to 1.2 m) apart in beds 4 to 5 feet (1.2 m to 1.5 m) wide. Raised furrows minimize crown rot that may be induced by irrigation. Lemongrass is shallow-rooted and cannot withstand water stress.

Fresh lemongrass leaves are harvested commercially up to four times a year where the climate permits. At harvest, the entire clump is severed at the base. Stems are separated from the crown, cleaned, and six to eight bundled together for immediate sale. Home gardeners may harvest a few stems at a time as needed.

For essential-oil production, maximum yields of 45 gallons per acre (419 l/ha) are achieved when lemongrass is cut at sixty-day intervals at a height of 7.8 inches (20 cm). Longer intervals and higher cutting heights give lower oil yields. Lemongrass also loses considerable oil if allowed to wilt after cutting. In a year, lemongrass removes nitrogen at the rate of 166 pounds per acre (186 kg/ha), phosphorus at the rate of 23 pounds per acre (26 kg/ha), and potassium at the rate of 343 pounds per acre (384 kg/ha). High-potassium fertilizers are recommended for prolonged cultivation of lemongrass.

The chief source of imported lemongrass oil is Guatemala; India also produces some. The essential oil is used primarily in soaps and perfumes but is considered GRAS at 4 to 290 ppm. Lemongrass oil displays antibacterial and antiprotozoal action and is documented to kill tropical cattle ticks. Lemongrass also is antioxidant, antiradical, anticarcinogenic.

Important chemistry: Lemongrass oil contains 10 to 62 percent geranial, 3 to 35 percent neral, 0 to 20 percent (*Z*)-pinocarveol, and 0 to 10 percent geranyl acetate.

Botanical Description

C. citratus (DC.) Stapf, Bull. Misc. Inform. 1906:322, 357. 1906.

Native country: Lemongrass is found only in cultivation but widely distributed in the tropics; the origin is unknown.

General habit: Lemongrass is a smooth grass to 200 cm high arising from a basal stem.

Leaves: Leaf blades are narrow and flat with parallel sides, tapering, up to 90 cm long, 5 mm wide, smooth on both surfaces, blue-green, tapering to a sheath at the base.

Flowers: Flowers, which are rarely produced, are brownish-red in a loose inflorescence with younger flowers at the center.

Dianthus

dī-ăn-thŭs

pinks

Family: Caryophyllaceae

Growth form: herbaceous perennials 3 to 31 inches (7.6 to 80 cm) high

Hardiness: many routinely hardy to central Pennsylvania (Zone 5)

Light: full sun

Water: moist but not constantly wet

Soil: well drained, pH 6.0 to 7.5

Propagation: divisions for named cultivars, seeds otherwise

Culinary use: edible flowers, beverages (not GRAS)

Craft use: potpourri

Landscape use: edges of borders, rock gardens, along paths

Sometimes the story behind a plant's name reveals the importance accorded it by different cultures; the plants we call "pinks" today are an example of a history of reverence and adulation. *Dios anthos*, literally "god's flower," was the name used by the Greek naturalist Theophrastus (371–287 B.C.E.) for the bloom most favored by Zeus. The Romans followed suit and placed the flowers at the pinnacle of their pantheon; they called them *Flos Jovis*, or Jove's flower.

The early Normans referred to pinks as *girofle*, which was derived from the Greek *karuophullon* and Latin *caryophyllum*, both names for cloves. At that time, cloves were an expensive and coveted commodity, and the fragrance of pinks resembled that of cloves. Cloves also resembled the hand-made nails, or *clavi*, of the period, so the Latin name for pinks, *clavus gariofili* came into use around 1250; this was later supplanted by the Latin-French hybrid *clavus de gylofre* and the French *clou de girofle*. Chaucer

called the flowers *clowe-gilofre* in *The Canterbury Tales* (1386–1400); *gillofloure* was reported by Ruellius about 1536, and *gelofer* and *clowgelofer* were reported by Turner in 1538. The modern terms "gilliflower" or "gillyflower" arose from this period. The word "carnation," the common name for *D. caryophyllus*, is probably derived from the name "incarnacyon" as first reported in print by Turner in 1538.

The word "pink" itself has enriched the English language because of these flowers. "To pink" originally meant "to pierce," which referred to the serrated edges of the flowers (think of today's pinking shears). Before the middle of the eighteenth century, when "pink" came into use to indicate a color, pale red flowers were described as flesh-, blush-, or rose-colored. The etymology of the word may even be more involved than this, as the word "pink" may be derived from the Dutch "pinkster," which refers to Whitsuntide (the first three days of Pentecost), when pinks were supposedly used as floral decorations for religious festivals.

Many species of *Dianthus* are particularly adapted to well-drained alkaline soil and rockeries in full sun to Zone 5 and sometimes even to Zone 3. Clove pinks and grass pinks have low, spiky blue foliage and make effective foreplantings or groundcovers, particularly in rock gardens. Propagation, especially of the named cultivars, is primarily from cuttings or layerings. Because the stems of pinks are hollow, these cuttings are sometimes called "pipings." Pipings may be taken any time of the year but root best during cool weather. Seed propagation is easy but will not perpetuate the identical genetic constitution of named cultivars.

Many pinks have a pronounced clove fragrance, so heavy in some that they can perfume the whole yard. Unfortunately, the more genes from *D. caryophyllus*, and the larger and more gorgeous the flower, the more pinks tend to become woody at the base, which seems to shorten their lives. Cuttings or layerings may be taken from year to year, but the wise gardener who savors at least some time to enjoy the garden should choose pinks with grass or cheddar pink genes. When derivatives of the latter two species are mowed after flowering, they come back stockier than ever.

We particularly recommend the very old hybrid 'Gloriosa' for its intense clove perfume and exceptional vigor. 'Gloriosa' is a double pink-carnation hybrid with a darker "eye."

Pinks were once employed to flavor wine. In English literature, these were called "sops-in-wine" (1573–1625), which explains the name of a later cultivar that goes by the same name. Carnation-based fragrances such as Old Spice and Cashmere Bouquet are typically compounded not from *Dianthus* but instead from clove oil and other naturals, isolates, and synthetics. Some carnations, however, are raised in Grasse, France, to produce a concrète and absolute of limited use in perfumery.

Dianthus caryophyllus
dī-ăn-thŭs kăr-ĭ-ō-fĭl-ŭs
clove pink

French: *oeillet-giroflée*
German: *Gartennelke*
Italian: *garofano*
Spanish: *clavel*

Dianthus caryophyllus was the basic genetic material for the modern florist carnation. However, almost all cultivated material is of some hybrid origin. Even the clone widely sold as "clove pink" is a hybrid (*D. caryophyllus* × *D.*

plumarius). Similar in origin to the recently rediscovered 'Gloriosa', it is of shorter stature.

Monks from Normandy, following William the Conqueror to Britain, are said to have introduced clove pinks there around 1100 C.E. Some seed may have arrived in England by clinging to stone brought from the region of Caen for use in Normandy castles.

Important chemistry: The essential oil of carnation is dominated by 12 to 40 percent benzyl benzoate, 2 to 30 percent eugenol, and 1 to 11 percent cis-3-hexenyl benzoate. The absolute of carnation is dominated by trace to 15 percent benzyl benzoate.

Clove pinks and grass pinks have low, spiky blue foliage and make effective fore-plantings or groundcovers, particularly in rock gardens.

Dianthus plumarius

dī-ăn-thŭs plū-măr-ĭ-ŭs

grass pink

Grass pink, alias the cottage pink, is usually cultivated in hybrid form; the cheddar pink, *D. gratianopolitanus* Vill., has infiltrated its genes into many selections sold as *D. plumarius*. The uses of the grass pinks are similar to that of the clove pinks because of their intense clove fragrance, the result of hybridization with other clove-scented species.

Botanical Key and Description

Key:

1. Petal limb narrowly incised or slashed to nearly halfway or more . . . . *D. plumarius*
1a. Petal limb toothed to almost smooth-edged . . . . *D. caryophyllus*

D. caryophyllus L., Sp. pl. 410. 1753.
Native country: The clove pink is perhaps native to southern Spain, Italy, Sardinia, Sicily, and the Ionian Islands.

Dianthus plumarius

General habit: The clove pink is a laxly tufted, usually bluish-waxy perennial to 80 cm; the base is often woody, long, and not very thick.
Leaves: Leaves are 2 to 4 mm wide, linear, nearly flat.
Flowers: Flowers are pink, rarely white, beset with c. 5 mm teeth on the edge.

D. plumarius L., Sp. pl. 411. 1753.
Native country: The grass pink is native to calcareous mountains of east-central Europe from the Italian Alps to northeastern Hungary and the Tatary Mountains of eastern Europe.
General habit: The grass pink is a more or less bluish-waxy perennial to 40 cm.
Leaves: Leaves are about 1 mm wide, narrowed only in the upper part, and sharp-pointed.
Flowers: Flowers are generally one (rarely more, except in the cultivars) with petals deeply divided to about the middle into narrow lobes, white or bright pink.

Dysphania ambrosioides

dĭs-făn-ĭ-å ăm-brō-sĭ-ōy-dēz
epazote, American wormseed

Family: Chenopodiaceae
Growth form: annual to 47 inches (1.2 m)
Hardiness: can withstand some slight frost
Light: full sun
Water: can withstand drought
Soil: well drained, pH 5.3 to 8.7, average 7.0
Propagation: seeds in spring
Culinary use: not recommended
Craft use: none
Landscape use: weedy

French: *ambroisie de Mexico, ansérine ambroisie,*
ambroisine, thé des Jesuits, ansérine américain,
ansérine vermifuge
German: *Wohlriechender Gänsefuss,*
Mexikanisches Traubenkraut, Jesuiten-Tee,
Amerikanisches Wurmsamenkraut
Italian: *chenopodio, ambrosia*
Spanish: *epazote, paico macho, caá ná, yerba de*
Santa Maria, té de los Jesuitas, té de España,
hierba hormiguera
Portuguese: *erra formigueira*
Chinese: *t'u-ching-chieh*

What potentially poisonous herb has captured the attention of food columnists and even appeared in the venerable *New York Times*?

The common English name of *Dysphania ambrosioides* is American wormseed, after its chief medicinal use, or chenopodium, but the Spanish *epazote*, derived from the Nahuatl *epatl* ("skunk"), has taken over as interest in Mexican-influenced southwestern cooking has grown in the United States. Traditionally the herb has been used as an anthelmintic (purgative to intestinal worms and amoebae), to prevent flatulence, and as a minor condiment in bean dishes

in Mexico, particularly for its bactericidal effects. The taste is intense and peppery.

In the popular literature and the nursery trade, this species is thoroughly confused with wormseed, *D. anthelmintica*, and it is difficult to tell where one ends and the other starts, illustrating the close similarity of the two. Information on both species is given here because of this confusion. Epazote has no GRAS status, and the wormseed oil is not recommended for skin applications by the International Fragrance Association. In fact, wormseed oil is poisonous, the therapeutic dose approaching the minimum toxic levels, and death may result from undesirable side effects. The death of a 14-month-old baby has been attributed to a dose of one teaspoon of wormseed oil; a two-year-old child died after being given 16 minims (0.947 cc) of wormseed oil over a period of three weeks.

Wormseed oil causes skin and mucous-

Dysphania ambrosioides

membrane irritation, headache, dizziness, nausea, vomiting, constipation, disruptions of hearing and sight, kidney and liver damage, and delirium. These may be followed by coma and sometimes death.

Researchers at Howard University and the University of Miami found that a water-based extract of the leaves produced tumors in 50 percent of rats who received it by injection. Argentinian researchers report that the aqueous extract is both cyto- and genotoxic. This rate of disease was comparable to that produced by sassafras root bark, which is banned by the FDA. Further, epazote is included in the classics on poisonous plants, such as Kingsbury's *Poisonous Plants of the United States and Canada* and Muenscher's *Poisonous Plants of the United States*. This herb should not be consumed until further studies determine its safety.

Epazote is an annual with a multibranched stem and sticky, fetid leaves. The genus *Dysphania* includes about 32 temperate species (10 in North America); the generic name is derived from the Greek *dysphanis* ("obscure"), apparently alluding to the inconspicuous flowers. The specific name of wormseed alludes to its similarity to the genus *Ambrosia*, the ragweeds.

Epazote can grow under a wide range of conditions; it is sometimes found as an urban weed sprouting from the cracks of sidewalks. J. Juan Jimenez-Osornio of the University of California has found that the ascaridole from epazote will inhibit germination of plants around it, such as beans, so this is not a plant for the vegetable and herb garden. On the other hand, leaves of epazote will protect grains against stored-product beetles.

Important chemistry: The essential oil of typical epazote is dominated by 17 to 90 percent ascaridole, trace to 80 percent para-cymene, 0 to 65 percent alpha-terpinene, 0 to 18 percent isoascaridole, 0 to 29 percent limonene, and/or 0 to 19 percent myrcene. Pure ascaridole is described as having a nauseating, choking herbaceous odor and a rather unpleasant taste. Combine this with the citrusy odor of para-cymene and limonene and the sweet-balsamic odor of myrcene, and you have a general idea of what wormseed oil smells like—rather peculiar for a faddish herb of the late twentieth century.

Rare strains have also been reported with 0 to 65 percent pinocarvone, 2 to 43 percent pinocarveol, 0 to 33 percent limonene, and trace to 33 percent alpha-pinene. These strains have more of a camphoraceous-minty odor like that of balm of Gilead (*Cedronella canariensis*). Other strains have been reported with trace to 56 percent alpha-terpinene, 16 to 74 percent alpha-terpinyl acetate, and 4 to 16 percent *p*-cymene with trace ascaridole. These strains low in ascaridole may be edible, but we know of no morphological traits to indicate low or high ascaridole content.

Epazote also contains ascaridole epoxide, which has an unknown toxicity, but typically many epoxides are more mutagenic and carcinogenic than the parent compounds.

Botanical Description

Epazote was recently reclassified from the genus *Chenopodium*. William A. Weber of the University of Colorado Museum proposed that the glandular chenopods, such as *D. ambrosioides*, should be renamed *Teloxys*. The genus *Dysphania* has priority over *Teloxys*, however, and so the correct name for epazote in a genus separate from *Chenopodium* is *D. ambrosioides*. While *D. ambrosioides* and some allied glandular species do form distinct groups within *Chenopodium* (sections *Ambrina* Benth. & J. D. Hook and *Botryoides* C. A. Mey. in Ledeb.), some botanists do not consider *Dysphania* sufficiently different from *Chenopodium* to even discuss the genus.

Dysphania ambrosioides is extremely similar but distinct from *D. anthelmintica* (L.) Mosyakin & Clemants, wormseed. Both species are widely cultivated, naturalized, and confused with each other in the literature (and since vouchers are rarely filed, it is impossible to tell what the researchers examined). The inflorescences of *D. anthelmintica* are leafless, while the inflorescences of *D. ambrosioides* have reduced, leaflike bracts.

D. ambrosioides (L.) Mosyakni & Clements, Ukrayins'k Bot. Zhurn., n.s. 59:382. 2002.

[*Chenopodium ambrosioides* L., *Teloxys ambrosioides* (L.) W. A. Weber].

Native country: Epazote is native to tropical America but naturalized worldwide.

General habit: Epazote is an annual, rarely short-lived perennial, to 1.2 m, hairy and glandular.

Leaves: Leaves are usually lance-shaped, smooth-edged, toothed, or rarely deeply lobed.

Flowers: Flowers are small and greenish arranged in a compound inflorescence with the younger flowers at the apex.

Fruits/seeds: The abundant seeds are 0.5 to 0.8 mm in diameter.

Elsholtzia

ĕl-shōl-tsĭ-å

mintshrub, heathermint

Family: Lamiaceae (Labiatae)

Growth form: herbs or shrubs, annual or perennial

Hardiness: most cannot withstand frost, but some are hardy to Zone 7

Light: full sun

Water: moist but not constantly wet

Soil: well-drained garden loam

Propagation: cuttings or seeds

Culinary use: limited (not GRAS)

Craft use: potpourri

Landscape use: front of herb or shrub border, container plant

The genus *Elsholtzia* is very similar to *Pogostemon* (patchouli) and *Mentha* (mint), differing in microscopic characteristics of the flowers. It includes about thirty-five to forty temperate and tropical Old World herbs and shrubs, commonly known as mintshrubs or heathermints. Most perennial species of *Elsholtzia* cannot withstand frost, although a few species are hardy to around Zone 7. *Elsholtzia* is named in honor of Johann Sigismund Elsholtz (1623–1688), a Prussian naturalist and physician.

Elsholtzia ciliata

ĕl-shōl-tsĭ-å sĭl-ĭ-å-tå
Vietnamese lemon balm

Japanese: *naginata-kōju*
Vietnamese: *rau kinh giôi*

Vietnamese lemon balm is named for the many hairs (cilia) that give the leaves a rough texture. The leaves are used in some Asian cuisines to impart a spicy lemon flavor. Vietnamese lemon balm is an annual that flowers in the spring and sometimes reseeds, but it is better to collect seeds to ensure a later crop. Another plant, a tender perennial, is also cultivated as Vietnamese lemon balm in the United States, but we have not yet identified it.

Vietnamese lemon balm is sometimes encountered at larger herb nurseries, but the easiest way to obtain this plant is to root cuttings from an Asian food market. Plants can be easily grown in friable garden loam, in the border or in pots.

Vietnamese lemon balm has no GRAS status. We recommend it for an unusual nuance in potpourri.

Important chemistry: The essential oil of Vietnamese lemon balm is usually dominated

Elsholtzia ciliata

by 2 to 86 percent elsholtzia ketone, and trace to 89 percent dehydroelsholtzia ketone, which provides a spicy lemony odor. Another form has been reported with 24 percent carvacrol and 18 percent thymol, with a scent of oregano, another form has been reported with 43 percent rosefuran with a minty odor, and another form has been reported with 43 percent 1,8-cineole and 13 percent acetophenone with a eucalyptus odor.

Elsholtzia stauntonii

ĕl-shōl-tsĭ-å stăn-tō-nē-ī
mintshrub

The narrow, lance-shaped leaves of this shrub are scented of mint, and the purple flowers appear in autumn when little else flowers in the herb garden. Mintshrub requires friable garden loam in full sun. While hardy to at least Zone 7, mintshrub often is killed to the ground but reappears in the spring. Semi-hardened softwood

cuttings taken in spring root quickly; establishing the plant in the ground before frost ensures its survival over the winter.

The mintshrub was introduced into North America from China in 1905. Its epithet honors Sir George C. Staunton (1737–1801), an Irish traveler in China. This herb has no GRAS status, but we recommend it for potpourri.

Important chemistry: The essential oil of mintshrub consists of 18 to 63 percent rosefuran, 0 to 41 percent rosefuran epoxide, and trace to 28 percent 1,8-cineole, providing a minty odor. One form has been reported with 25 per-cent beta-caryophyllene and 13 percent gamma-caryophyllene, providing an herbaceous odor.

Botanical Key and Description

Key:

1. Herbaceous annual, leaves usually scented of spicy lemon .... *E. ciliata*
1a. Perennial shrub, leaves usually scented of mint... *E. stauntonii*

E. ciliata (Thunb.) Hyl., Bot. Not. 1941:129. 1941 [*E. cristata* Willd., *E. patrinii* (Lepech.) Garcke].

Native country: Vietnamese lemon balm is native to central and eastern Asia but natu-ralized in Europe and North America.

General habit: Vietnamese lemon balm is an annual 30 to 60 cm tall.

Leaves: Leaves are broadly to narrowly egg-shaped, 6 to 10 × 2.5 to 6 cm, shortly taper-ing to the blunt tip, wedge-shaped to broadly wedge-shaped at the base, toothed, thinly hairy above and on nerves beneath.

Flowers: Flowers are purple and in a one-sided spike 5 to 10 cm × 7 to 8 mm with round to kidney-shaped bracts.

Fruits/seeds: Nutlets are about 1 mm long, slightly flattened.

E. stauntonii Benth., Labiat. gen. spec. 161. 1833.

Native country: Mintshrub is native to North China.

General habit: Mintshrub is a subshrub, 1 to 1.5 m tall.

Leaves: Leaves are broadly to narrowly egg-shaped, 13 × 3.8 cm, tapering to the tip, toothed.

Flowers: Flowers purplish and arranged in a narrow one-sided spike with small bracts.

Fruits/seeds: Nutlets are about 1 mm long, slightly flattened.

Eryngium foetidum

ě-rĭn-jĭ-ŭm fĕt-ĭ-dŭm
culantro

Family: Apiaceae (Umbelliferae)

Growth form: biennial about 16 inches (40 cm) high when flowering

Hardiness: cannot withstand frost

Light: full sun

Water: moist

Soil: friable garden loam, pH 4.3 to 6.8

Propagation: seeds in spring

Culinary use: used in manner of cilantro but not GRAS

Craft use: limited use for dried flowers

Landscape use: front of border, container plant

French: *chardon étoile fétide, penicaut fétide*
Chinese: *jia yuán*
Vietnamese: *ngò gai*
Malay: *ketumbar jawa*
Thai: *phakchi-farang, hom-pomkula, mae-lae-doe*
Cambodian: *chi barain, chi banal, chi sang-kaëch*

Leaves of *Eryngium* species are usually toothed. Flowers are borne in spiny, leafy heads and are often very decorative when dried. Only two other species, *E. campestre* L. and *E. maritimum* L., or eryngoes (also the ancient Greek name), have herbal uses; their roots were once candied and used as "kissing confits" in England. The genus *Eryngium* consists of 230 species in tropical and temperate areas. In Jamaica, culantro is known as spirit weed, while in Trinidad it goes under the name of *shado beni* or *bhandhanya*.

Culantro's spiny leaves are used in the same manner as the foliage of *Coriandrum sativum*, cilantro, and the epithet *foetidum* aptly describes the stinkbug odor of the leaves. Don't

be alarmed by the spines; they are surprisingly soft and easily eaten. Culantro retains its flavor rather well on drying, in contrast to the leaves of cilantro, which taste of tissue paper when dried.

Culantro is easily cultivated in moist garden loam if started early inside and transplanted after spring frost. After spring-planted cilantro has ceased to produce leaves because of heat, culantro will continue to reward the gardener with its spiny leaves.

Slugs and snails have a peculiar affinity for culantro and can become a major problem if preventive measures are not taken. Mealybugs may also infest the tightly packed leaves and are virtually impossible to eliminate; discard the parent plant and resow the seeds when mature. Storage at 50°F (10°C) with packaging will extend the shelf-life of culantro to two weeks, compared with four days under ambient marketing conditions. Blanching in hot water at 205°F (96°C) prior to drying preserves the green color.

Culantro has no GRAS status. It is documented to have anticonvulsant activity in rats and topical anti-inflammatory activity in mice.

Important chemistry: The essential oil of Chinese culantro leaves has 73 percent 2,4,5-trimethylbenzaldehyde + 5-dodecanone + 4-hydroxy-3,5- dimethylacetophenone. The Vietnamese plants have 46 percent (*E*)-2-dodecenal and 16 percent 2-dodecenoic acid in the essential oil, while Malaysian plants have 60 percent (*E*)-2-dodecenal and Fijian plants have 64 percent (*E*)-2-dodecenal and 14 percent (*E*)-2-tetradecenal. Plants from the islands of São Tomé and Príncipe in the Gulf of Guinea off the coast of West Africa have 6 to 24 percent 2,3,6-trimethylbenzaldehyde, 16 to 38 percent (*E*)-2-dodecenal, and 19 to 25 percent (*E*)-2-tetradecenal. Plants from Cuba have been found to have 21 percent 2,4,5-trimethylbenzaldehyde, 12 percent hexadecanoic acid, and 10 percent

Eryngium foetidum

carotol in the leaves. Cuban seed oil has 19 percent carotol and 10 percent (*E*)-beta-farnesene.

Botanical Description

E. foetidum L., Sp. pl. 232. 1753.
Native country: Culantro originated in the tropics and subtropics of the New World but is now widespread through tropical Africa and Asia.
General habit: Culantro is a biennial. Stems are 15 to 40 cm when flowering, erect.

Leaves: Leaves are parallel-sided lance-shaped with narrowed base, 4 to 12 cm long, 1 to 2.5 cm broad, blunt at apex, margins round-toothed to finely spine-toothed, base wedge-shaped, not stalked.
Flowers: The inflorescence is convex, open, dark green with egg-shaped heads (capitula), 4 to 10 mm long, 3 to 5 mm broad, subtended by five to seven bracts 1 to 3 cm long, linear-lance-shaped, with a few spiny teeth.
Fruits/seeds: The tiny fruits are egg-shaped and pimpled.

Ferula

fĕr-ū-lå
ferula

Family: Apiaceae (Umbelliferae)
Growth form: herbaceous perennials to almost 8 feet (2.4 m) high
Hardiness: many routinely hardy to southern Pennsylvania (Zone 7)
Light: full sun
Water: withstands drought
Soil: well drained
Propagation: fresh seeds
Culinary use: curries, sauces
Craft use: none
Landscape use: bold, striking accent plant for rear of borders

The genus *Ferula* includes 132 species ranging from the Mediterranean region to central Asia. Most are statuesque perennials with ferny leaves and large taproots. The leaves of some have been eaten in the past as a vegetable for their celery-like taste, but some, such as *F. communis* L., are considered poisonous because of their couma-

rin content. When the vegetative top is severed, the taproot releases a milky sap which hardens to a yellow to reddish brown oleoresin. The name *Ferula* was given by Pliny the Younger (61–113), a Roman naturalist.

Claims have appeared in herb books that asafetida is under cultivation in North America, but all the authors seem to be confused with another species. Both asafetida and galbanum are included here to clarify these claims, and because of the use and value of both products in food and the increasing interest in both species as natural birth control agents. Species of *Ferula* are usually propagated from ultra-fresh seeds, and some seeds of asafetida and galbanum will make their way soon to the shores of North America. Confirmation of correct identification, alas, is only possible with the work of E. Korovin, which was primarily written in Latin, published in Taschkent in 1947, and almost impossible to locate today.

Ferula assa-foetida

fĕr-ū-lå ă-så-fĕ-tĭ-då
asafetida

French: *assa foetida, férule perisque*
German: *Asant, Stink-Asant, Teufelsdreck*
Dutch: *duivelsdrek*
Italian: *assafetida, ferula del sagapeno*
Spanish: *asafetida*
Chinese: *a-wei, hsun-ch'u*
Arabic: *tyib*
Bengali: *hing*

Also called devil's dung or giant fennel, asafetida oleoresin or oil has a garlic-like odor and a slightly bitter, pungent taste. Pennsylvania German schoolchildren once wore this as an amulet around the neck to ward off colds. Well, nobody came near them, so it may have worked!

Asafetida is used in southern Indian curries and Indian pickles and is the secret ingredient of Worcestershire sauce, commonly used by Anglo-Saxon cooks for soups, boiled meats, steak tartare, and Wiltshire pork pies. The other ingredients of Worcestershire sauce are not at all mysterious, but asafetida, in minute quantities, supplies that *je ne sais quoi*. Asafetida is also believed to relieve flatulence.

Asafetida is reputed by some authors to be similar to the ancient silphium of the Romans. Silphium was both a necessary ingredient of many recipes and an early birth-control agent. True silphium was harvested from another *Ferula* species, perhaps now extinct, and was a major commodity of ancient Cyrenaica (modern northeast Libya). An inferior form of silphium came from Persia and Armenia, and this is probably our modern asafetida. The alternate Roman names of these oleoresins, laser or laserpitum, probably supplied the prefix for this oleoresin to create the name asafetida, or "stinking gum."

The essential oil of asafetida is considered GRAS at 1 to 15 ppm, the extract is GRAS at 4 to 50 ppm, while the oleoresin is GRAS at 5 to 160 ppm.

The commercial supplies of asafetida oleoresin arise from wild-collected materials in Iran, Afghanistan, Turkestan, and Kashmir. Asafetida is not in cultivation in the West at the present time. The plant sometimes offered in United States herb nurseries as asafetida is another *Ferula* species, probably *F. gracilis* Led. of Siberia.

To harvest asafetida oleoresin, the soil is first scraped away from around the crown of the plant, exposing the carrot-like root, which may be several inches in diameter. A portion of the root is then cut away or the stem cut off at crown level. After the milky juice exudes, it is allowed to air-dry before collection. Dried leaves or stones are sometimes placed over the root to protect it from the elements for subsequent scrapings of the oleoresin. The root may also be subsequently cut to increase the flow of sap. The oleoresin enters the market in three forms: "paste," "tear," and "mass" (block or lump), mainly the latter.

Ferula assa-foetida

Good samples have 40 to 64 percent resin, 10 to 17 percent volatile oil, and 25 percent water-soluble gum. Asafetida oleoresin may also be further modified as either "locked-in," encapsulated, or liquid. Locked-in asafetida is compounded with gum arabic, whereas encapsulated asafetida is blended with a gelatin base. Liquid asafetida is prepared in an oil base.

Important chemistry: The essential oil of asafetida owes it characteristic garlic-like odor to sulfurous constituents, particularly 19 to 38 percent 1-(methylthio)propyl cis-1-propenyl disulfide and 11 to 17 percent 2-butyl trans-1-propenyl disulfide. The roots also contain foetidin, a sesquiterpenoid coumarin.

Ferula galbaniflua
fĕr-ū-lå gǎl-bǎn-ĭ-flū-å
galbanum

> **French:** *galbanum*
> **German:** *Galbanum*
> **Italian:** *galbano*
> **Spanish:** *galbano*
> **Arabic:** *brada-kéma*

In contrast to asafetida, galbanum oleoresin and oil smell green and leafy, with an overall odor similar to that of green peppers. Today the primary application of yellow-green galbanum oleoresin and oil (*galbaniflua* means "with a yellow-green exudate") is in perfumery for the "green" perfumes, such as Aliage and Vent Vert; it blends well with chypres, fougères, pine, forest, and moss notes. However, galbanum oleoresin and oil are also used in nonalcoholic beverages, ice cream, ices, candy, baked goods, and condiments. Galbanum oleoresin is considered GRAS (Generally Recognized As Safe) by the U.S. Food and Drug Administration at 0.04 to 50 ppm, while the essential oil is GRAS at 0.2 to 1.8 ppm.

Commercial supplies of galbanum oleoresin were collected from the wilds of Iran and Libya prior to the Ayatollah Khomeini and Muammar al-Qaddafi regimes. Galbanum oleoresin is harvested in a similar manner to that of asafetida, but some of the gum is obtained from natural exudations from the stem of the plant. Galbanum oleoresin consists of 50 to 70 percent resin, 5 to 20 percent volatile oil, and 20 to 30 percent water-soluble gum.

Important chemistry: Galbanum essential oil is dominated by 60 percent beta-pinene and 14 percent alpha-pinene, along with guaiazulene and isoguaiazulene, which give the oil a greenish-blue color. The odor of galbanum essential oil, however, is primarily due to (E,Z)-1,3,5-undecatriene and pyrazines, particularly 2-methoxy-3-sec-butylpyrazine, 2-methoxy-3-isobutylpyrazine, 2-methoxy-3-isopropylpyrazine, tetramethylpyrazine, 2,6-diethyl-3-methylpyrazine, and 2,3-dimethyl-5-ethylpyrazine. While these pyrazines are present at levels around 0.05 percent or less in the essential oil, they carry high impact value for the characteristic green pepper–like odor.

The sulfur esters also carry high impact value, providing an asafetida-like odor, and include S-iso-propyl-3-methylbutanethioate, S-sec-butyl 3-methylbutanethioate, S-sec-butyl 2-methylbutanethioate, S-iso-propyl 3-methylbut-2-enethioate, and S-sec-butyl 3-methylbut-2-enethioate. The roots also contain umbelliferone ethers, derivatives of umbelliferone (7-hydroxycoumarin).

Botanical Key and Description

Key:

1. Style of flower elongated, apex of the erect stigma with a depressed globose head . . . . *F. assa-foetida*
1a. Style of flower not elongated, apex recessed . . . . *F. galbaniflua*

F. assa-foetida L., Sp. pl. 248. 1753 [*F. foetida* (Bunge) Regel].

Native country: Asafetida is native to Afghanistan, Iran, and Asia Minor.

General habit: Asafetida is a tall perennial, 1.5 to 2.4 m high.

Leaves: Leaves are numerous, large, and spreading, about 23 to 46 cm long, light green above, paler underneath, of a dry, leathery texture. The fern-like leaves are deeply divided with oblong-lance-shaped segments 15 × 5 cm.

Flowers: Flowers are small, yellowish, and in an umbel.

Fruits/seeds: Fruit is 16 to 22 × 12 to 16 mm, flat, thin, somewhat convex in the middle, with a dilated border, dark-reddish brown toward the center, lighter toward the margin,

perfectly smooth, with a somewhat glossy surface.

F. galbaniflua Boiss. & Buhse, Nov. Mem. Moskovsk. Obšč. Isp. Prir. 12:99. 1860 (*F. gummosa* Boiss.).

Native country: Galbanum is native to Iran, Turkestan, and western Afghanistan.

General habit: Galbanum is a tall perennial.

Leaves: Leaves are numerous, large, and spreading, deeply divided into tiny fern-like segments, the individual segments 1 to 2 mm long, finely hairy.

Flowers: Flowers are small, yellowish, in an umbel.

Fruits/seeds: Fruits are 16 × 8 mm, flat, thin, convex in the middle, with a dilated border.

Foeniculum vulgare

fē-nĭk-ū-lŭm vŭl-gā-rē
fennel

Family: Apiaceae (Umbelliferae)

Growth form: short-lived herbaceous perennial to almost 6 feet (1.8 m) high

Hardiness: perennial to Delaware (Zone 7), but often naturalized as an annual north to Zone 4

Water: moist but not constantly wet; can withstand drought

Soil: well-drained garden loam, pH 4.8 to 8.2, average 6.6

Propagation: seed in spring or fall, 8,000 seeds/oz (282/g)

Culinary use: garnish, meats, beverages

Craft use: none

Landscape use: rear of perennial or herb border

French: *fenouil*
German: *Gemiener Fenchel*
Dutch: *venkel*
Italian: *finocchio, finocchio selvatico*
Spanish: *hinojo*
Portuguese: *funcho*
Swedish: *fänkål*
Russian: *fyenkhel'*
Chinese: *hsiao-hui-hsiang, siao-hiu, shih-lo, tzu-mo-lo*
Japanese: *uikyō*
Arabic: *shamār, razeeaneja*

The ancient Greeks called fennel *marathron*, from *marainein*, to grow thin. Others have suggested that fennel was called *marathron* after a village about twenty-five miles from Athens, where fennel grew wild; Athenians defeated the Persians on this site in 490 B.C.E. Before the battle, Pheidippides had carried a stalk of fennel while running 120 miles in two days to recruit soldiers from Sparta. There, another long-distance runner took news of the victory to Athens and fell dead upon arrival. The modern marathon races owe their name to this bit of trivia.

Fennel has a long history in folklore as an appetite suppressant. William Coles remarked in *Nature's Paradise* (1650): "Both the seeds, leaves and root of our Garden Fennel are much used in drinks and broths for those that are grown fat, to abate their unwieldiness and cause them to grow more gaunt and lank." In contrast, researchers in Germany have found that caraway and fennel as flavor additives are appetite promoters in weaned piglets. Some have also believed fennel to be a digestive aid and antiflatulent, and many Indian restaurants in the United States offer a bowl of fennel seeds at the end of the meal, but no scientific studies have substantiated these historical uses. Fennel also has been hung over doors to ward off evil influences.

Foeniculum is derived from the Latin for hay, referring to the sweet odor, while the specific name, *vulgare*, means "common." A single, variable species comprises this genus. The fruits (commonly called seeds) of fennel are traditional in Italian sweet sausage; the aromatic blue-green foliage and stems are also used in a variety of dishes, especially those containing seafood. Bronze fennel, with its unusual dark foliage, is a great garnish, especially when the stems are grilled with meats and vegetables to add a hint of flavor. The essential oil of fennel seeds is used for flavoring foods, confectionery, and liqueurs such as anisette. It is also used in perfume, cosmetics, and pharmaceuticals.

For the gardener, fennel delights by attracting swallowtail butterflies, especially the anise swallowtails. The butterfly lays its eggs on the leaves, and the resulting vividly striped caterpillars, in shades of green, yellow, and black, feed on the leaves without doing much harm to the robust fennel plant. If you rub the heads of the caterpillars, they often stick out their bright orange "horns."

A comprehensive botanical/chemical/agronomic investigation is needed on the variation

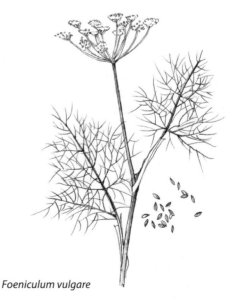

Foeniculum vulgare

of *F. vulgare*. Little is known about the differences among the German or Saxon, wild or bitter, Galician, Russian, Romanian, Indian, Persian, and Japanese fennels (to name just a few). What is the importance of Sicilian wild fennel? Is Italian mountain fennel (*finocchio di montagna*) any different? Two subspecies are known in the existing literature: subsp. *vulgare* is the cultivated fennel, while subsp. *piperitum* (Ucria) Coutinho is the wild pepper fennel.

Subspecies *vulgare* includes var. *vulgare*, perennial fennel, and var. *azoricum* (Mill.) Thell. (*F. dulce* DC., not Mill.), the Florence fennel, cultivated as an annual vegetable (the slow-bolting cultivar 'Zefa Fino' is recommended). It also includes var. *dulce* Bett. & Trab. (*F. dulce* Mill.), also called sweet or Roman fennel, which is an

---

For the gardener, fennel delights by attracting swallowtail butterflies, especially the anise swallowtails.

---

annual cultivated for its essential oil. The latter variety is confused with var. *azoricum* but lacks the thickened leaf bases. The cultivar 'Rubrum' is the perennial bronze fennel derived from var. *vulgare*.

Egypt is the chief source of fennel imported into the United States today. Seeds should be placed 11¾ to 18 inches apart in rows at the rate of 7 to 9 pounds per acre (8 to 10 kg/ha). Researchers in Australia found that low stand-density strips within standard-density commercial crops have a better yield overall and recommend 10 to 12 plants/m2. Soaking fennel seeds in water for five days prior to sowing increases germination. Additional nitrogen application at the rate of 40 to 45 pounds per acre (45 to 50 kg/ha) is recommended. Flowering starts ninety days after sowing of annual forms, and harvesting may commence 100 days later. The highest yields are obtained from two harvests, the first when the umbels reach maturity and another when the umbels are ripened. The yield of seeds may reach 1,338 to 1,784 pounds per acre (1,500 to 2,000 kg/ha), corresponding to 36 to 49 pounds per acre (40 to 55 kg/ha) of anethole. The crop must be dried under shade for four or five days to preserve the green color, then beaten to release the fruits.

Lowered yields may result from infestations by the insects *Lygus campestris*, *Orthops calmi*, and *Depressaria nervosa*. Cercospora leaf spot (*Cercosporidium punctum*), powdery mildew (*Plasmopara* spp.), and a mycoplasm also infect fennel.

In the home garden disease is rarely a problem, but preventing the spread of fennel is! Fennel can become a real weed in the garden, but this is easily remedied by cutting the heads immediately after flowering to prevent seed-set.

Fennel (50 to 6,500 ppm) and its essential oil (0.3 to 234 ppm) are considered GRAS. Some data exist to suggest that high-estragole forms of fennel may be carcinogenic in children, but this needs more study, especially since researchers in Turkey have found that both the essential and fixed oils of fennel are hepatoprotective and investigators in Italy have found that a patent medicine with fennel is useful in treating colic in breastfed infants. The high anethole content of fennel oils may exert estrogenic activity via a polymeric form, probably dianethole or photoanethole; this may support the traditional use of fennel to promote menstruation, increase milk production, alleviate the symptoms of male menopause, and increase libido. However, fennel seed tea taken to induce lactation may be toxic to the central nervous system of newborns and should be avoided. Fennel may be useful in atherosclerosis as it inhibits platelet aggregation. Besides antioxidant activity, fennel oil enhances bile secretion and is diuretic, analgesic, carminative, antipyretic, antibacterial, and antifungal.

Important chemistry: The essential oil of fennel seeds (really fruits) consists of trace to 91 percent (*E*)-anethole, 2 to 83 percent estragole (methyl chavicol), 1 to 33 percent fenchone, and 1 to 32 percent limonene. However, samples of fennel seed occur in three chemovarieties: (1) a "bitter" variety containing about 60 percent (*E*)-anethole and 34 percent fenchone, (2) a "sweet" variety containing about 80 percent (*E*)-anethole and 10 percent fenchone, and (3) an "anethole-free" variety containing up to 84 percent estragole and 26 percent fenchone. Investigation into populations in Israel found that in habitats with a high precipitation, the content of estragole was high and that of (*E*)-anethole was low; researchers found 3 to 74 percent (*E*)-anethole, 8 to 63 percent estragole, and 9 to 26 percent fenchone. Named seed lines include 'Berfena' with 55 to 72 percent (*E*)-anethole and 'Shumen' with 47 to 72 percent (*E*)-anethole/6 to 25 percent gamma-terpinene.

The essential oil of seeds of *F. vulgare* subsp. *piperitum* from Portugal consists of 7 to 31 percent fenchone, 3 to 36 percent estragole, and 44 to 74 percent (*E*)-anethole. The essential oil of the fresh aerial parts of the plants from populations of *F. vulgare* subsp. *piperitum* in Italy have 9 to 49 percent estragole and trace to 82 percent alpha-phellandrene.

In addition, other organs of fennel yield similar essential oils. The essential oils of the leaves and stems consist of 39 to 82 percent (*E*)-anethole, trace to 20 percent alpha-phellandrene, trace to 20 percent limonene, and trace to 16 percent fenchone. The essential oil of the leaves alone consists of 2 to 74 percent limonene, 11 to 60 percent (*E*)-anethole, and 1 to 30 percent alpha-phellandrene with up to 36 percent estragole and 10 percent fenchone, depending upon the variety; the essential oil of the stems alone consists of 1 to 68 percent limonene, 14 to 74 percent (*E*)-anethole, 2 to 16 percent alpha-phellandrene, and 0 to 10 percent gamma-terpinene with up to 32 percent estragole and 10 percent fenchone, depending on the variety.

The essential oil of the roots consists of 23 to 48 percent apiole, trace to 36 percent terpinolene, 1 to 29 percent myristicin, 3 to 19 percent limonene, 5 to 11 percent dill apiole, and trace to 11 percent (*E*)-anethole.

Botanical Description

F. vulgare Mill., Gard. Dict. ed. 8, No. 1. 1768.
Native country: Fennel is native to southern Europe.
General habit: Stems of this annual or perennial are erect, reaching 1 to 1.8 m high.
Leaves: Leaves are divided on opposite sides three or four times, the ultimate segments very narrow and thread-like and to 4 cm long, the leaf-stalks broad and clasping.
Flowers: Flowers are in an umbel with fifteen to twenty thread-like bracts.
Fruits/seeds: The fruit is 4 to 8 mm long, narrow with parallel sides, smooth, circular in cross-section and more or less elongated.

Galium

gā-lē-ŭm
galium

Family: Rubiaceae
Growth form: herbaceous perennials to
  about 4 inches (10 cm)
Hardiness: routinely hardy to southern
  North Dakota (Zone 4)
Light: part shade (sweet woodruff) to full sun
  (yellow bedstraw)
Water: moist but not constantly wet
Soil: friable garden loam
Propagation: division
Culinary use: May wine (sweet woodruff)
Craft use: potpourri, strewing, mattresses
Landscape use: groundcover

The 400 cosmopolitan species of the genus
Galium are all slender herbs usually with square
stem around which little circles of leaves spin.
Some species, such as sweet woodruff and yellow
bedstraw, release coumarin when dried, which
produces a newly mown hay odor similar to
sweet vernal grass, holy grass, tonka, and numerous other coumarin sources. Coumarin is normally bound to a sugar (called a glycoside) in
the living plant, but drying ruptures this bond.

The generic name, *Galium*, is derived from
the Latin for milk, because some species, such
as yellow bedstraw, were used to curdle milk
in cheesemaking. All species are easy to grow
in good, friable soil, and some are even listed
as weeds.

The leaves of sweet woodruff are considered
GRAS at 400 ppm but only in alcoholic beverages because of the coumarin content. In 1953,
approximately 200 metric tons of coumarin
were used in flavors. Since 1954, however, coumarin in foods and nonalcoholic beverages has
been banned by the U.S. Food and Drug Administration, which has classified it as a carcinogen. Coumarin is still widely used to flavor tobacco (tonka is used in pipe tobacco) and wine
(sweet woodruff flavors May wine). Coumarin
is also used as an adulterant in Mexican and
Caribbean vanilla extracts; the so-called white
vanilla extract is vanillin with coumarin added.
This use is also prohibited by the FDA

While coumarin itself is not a blood-thinner,
a derivative (3-alkyl-4-hydroxycoumarin) is
marketed as Warfarin, a rat poison, and Warfarin sodium crystalline is marketed as the pharmaceutical anticoagulant, Coumadin. Re-exam-
ination of the original carcinogenicity tests and
further in vivo and in vitro tests have shown
that coumarin does not cause mutations, cancer, or birth defects in rodents; further, coumarin has failed to produce any sensitization reactions in humans. On the other hand, coumarin
does produce liver damage in rats and dogs but
not in baboons and humans. Thus, the potential toxicity from coumarin in humans appears
to be quite low, assuming that the individual
has normal liver function and can metabolize
coumarin to 7-hydroxycoumarin, not 3-
hydroxycoumarin, as in the rat.

Galium odoratum

ga̱-lē-ŭm ō-dŏ-ra̱-tŭm
sweet woodruff

French: *aspérule odorante, petit muguet des bois*
German: *Waldmeister*
Dutch: *onze lieve vrouwenbedstro, meikruid*
Italian: *stellina odorosa, piccolo murghetto, asperula odorosa*
Spanish: *asperula, asperilla olorsa, rubilla, hepática estrellada*

Galium odoratum

Sweet woodruff has earned its German name of Waldmeister, or master-of-the-woods. In partial shade and good, friable, slightly acid, moist humus with leaf litter, it will literally take over a forest. Don't worry about trying to grow this, but rather how to control it under conditions to its liking! Sweet woodruff grows to an average of 8 inches (20 cm) from a slender, creeping rhizome. Whorls of six to eight, slightly shiny, somewhat rough, pointed leaves surround the square, glossy stem. The small starry flowers appear in May and tiny, prickly fruits may follow.

Sweet woodruff is indispensable for the traditional May wine or Mai bowle, usually prepared with white Rhine-type wine (white grape juice serves as a good nonalcoholic substitute) and strawberries and decorated with edible spring flowers such as violets and rose petals. German researchers have extensively studied the use of sweet woodruff in May wine and concluded the coumarin content is not affected by drying the herb, nor is gathering it before bloom important.

Thus, although many recipes for May wine call for dried woodruff leaves, add the fresh herb, plucked without concern for bloom time, to the white Rhine wine of your choice. The researchers recommended, however, that the wine contain no more than 0.001 ounce coumarin per gallon (5 mg/l), so 1 gallon of wine (3g/l) should contain no more than 0.4 ounce of fresh sweet woodruff. A greater concentration could result in potential toxicity and off-flavors.

Sweet woodruff has also been employed as a strewing herb, insect repellent, and potpourri ingredient. Sweet woodruff is excellent for sachets for laying among clothing, linens, and bedding; it was once used to stuff mattresses.

Important chemistry: The leaves and stems of sweet woodruff contain about 1 percent coumarin upon enzymatic breakdown of the glycoside asperuloside.

Galium verum

gā-lē-ŭm vĕr-ŭm

yellow bedstraw

French: *caille-lait jaune, gaillet jaune*
German: *Echtes Labkraut Wegekraut, Käse-Labkraut, Glebes Labkraut*
Dutch: *echt walstro, geel walstro*
Italian: *caglio, presvola, erba solfina*
Spanish: *galio, cuaja leche*
Portuguese: *erva coalheira*
Chinese: *chu-yang-yang*

Also called cheese rennet or Our-Lady's-bedstraw, yellow bedstraw was the legendary bedding of the Christ child in the manger. Yellow bedstraw is good in potpourris and sachets stuffed between clothing, linens, and bedding. As the name implies, this was the "true" milk-curdling agent used in Europe for preparing cheeses.

Yellow bedstraw produces whorls of six to eight leaves around a square stem, similar to sweet woodruff's but smaller. As the name implies, panicles of yellow flowers are produced in late summer. Yellow bedstraw produces a gradually increasing dense groundcover in full sun and friable, moist garden loam. As with sweet woodruff, don't worry too much about how to grow yellow bedstraw but rather how to contain it. Nonetheless, the herb does make a nice groundcover. While its chemistry is still relatively unknown, it does release the distinct odor of coumarin upon drying.

Botanical Key and Description

Key:

1. Fruit with hooked hairs; flowers white.. *G. odoratum*
1a. Fruit smooth; flowers yellow .... *G. verum*

G. odoratum (L.) Scop., Fl. Carn. ed. 2. 1:105. 1771 (*Asperula odorata* L.).

Native country: Sweet woodruff is native to most of Europe but rare in the Mediterranean region.

General habit: Sweet woodruff is a creeping, perennial herb with stems 15 to 25 cm high, erect, stem four-angled, smooth except for a ring of hairs at the nodes.

Leaves: Leaves are six to eight, 20 to 50 × 5 to 14 mm, three to five times as long as wide, widest at the middle or in the upper third, whorled.

Flowers: Flowers are white, terminal.

Fruits/seeds: Fruits are 2 to 3 mm with hooked hairs.

G. verum L., Sp. pl. 107. 1753.

Two subspecies are known, but subsp. *verum* is the cultivated yellow bedstraw.

Native country: Yellow bedstraw is native to most of Europe.

General habit: Yellow bedstraw is a creeping herb 50 to 120 cm long, stem with four raised lines, rarely almost smooth.

Leaves: Leaves are six to eight, 15 to 30 × 0.5 to 2 mm, sharply pointed, shining and usually hairy above, densely hairy beneath, whorled.

Flowers: Flowers are yellow, terminal.

Fruits/seeds: Fruits are smooth, rarely hairy, but infrequently produced in the cultivated material.

Geranium macrorrhizum

jĕ-rā-nē-ŭm măk-rō-rī-zŭm
musk geranium

Family: Geraniaceae
Growth form: semi-evergreen perennial to 20 inches (50 cm) when flowering
Hardiness: routinely hardy to Zone 6
Light: part shade
Water: moist preferred but can withstand drought
Soil: rich in organic matter, well drained
Propagation: divisions of rhizome
Culinary use: none
Craft use: potpourri, perfumes
Landscape use: groundcover, woodland walkways

Bulgarian: *zdravetz*

If you like spicy Oriental perfumes such as Cinnabar by Estée Lauder, then you will love musk geranium. Musk geranium is one of about 300 species of annual and perennial herbs (and sometimes shrublets) found in the genus *Geranium*; their native habitats are the mountains of the temperate zone and tropics. These are "hardy geraniums," not the florists' geraniums (see *Pelargonium* for a discussion of *Geranium* vs. *Pelargonium*). The name *geranion* was used by Dioscorides in the first century C.E.; the name is the diminutive form of *geranos*, or crane, referring to the shape of the fruit, which resembles the head of a crane.

Musk geranium, alias Bulgarian geranium or *zdravetz*, derives its specific name, *macrorrhizum*, from its long, stout rhizome. The plant is generally sticky with a peculiar warm, fresh, musk-like fragrance. This complex fragrance has been described by Steffen Arctander as "sweet-woody with a floral and faintly herba-ceous undertone, reminiscent of clary sage, tobacco, broom absolute (fruity notes), tea leaves, and *Ulex europaeus*."

Musk geranium does well in shade (even relatively dry shade) but generally requires annual splitting and replanting to best maintain it. Alternatively, use a loose leaf mulch in which the musk geranium will root itself and gradually form a good groundcover. In nature, the musk geranium grows among rocks and scrub, usually in shade, in mountains and subalpine woodlands. In gardens, several cultivars are grown: 'Album', with very pale pink petals; 'Bevan's Variety', with deep red sepals and deep magenta petals; 'Czakor', similar to 'Bevan's Variety' but with no visible veins on the petals; 'Grandiflorum', with large flowers; 'Ingwersen's Variety', with pale pink flowers; 'Pindus', with magenta-red flowers on a low plant; 'Snow Sprite', with white petals and similar to 'White-Ness'; 'Spes-

Geranium macrorrhizum

sart', with dark pink petals; 'Variegatum', with leaves irregularly splashed with cream; 'Velebit', similar to 'Pindus'; and 'White-Ness' with completely white flowers, in contrast to 'Album'. *Geranium ×cantabrigiense* Yeo is a hybrid of this species with *G. dalmaticum* (Beck) Rechinger; 'Biokovo' is the most famous cultivar selected from this cross.

The oil of musk geranium, called zdravetz oil (or incorrectly "geranium oil"), is imported from Bulgaria and sometimes used in perfumery. In Bulgarian, *zdrave* means "health," alluding to the warm-fresh aroma of musk geranium. Zdravetz oil blends well with oakmoss, labdanum, frankincense, sandalwood, clary sage, lavender, and bergamot. It could be used in fougères, chypres, crepe de Chines, Oriental bases, colognes, and fantasy fragrances; its limitation is an irregular market and price. Try the leaves in potpourri.

Important chemistry: Zdravetz oil contains about 50 percent germacrone backed by a number of sesquiterpenes.

Botanical Description

G. macrorrhizum L., Sp. pl. 680. 1753.

Native country: Musk geranium is native to the south side of the Alps, Apennines, Balkan Peninsula, and southern and eastern Carpathians but often naturalized elsewhere in Europe.

General habit: Musk geranium is a perennial 30 to 50 cm tall with fleshy, underground rhizomes and a thick, ascending aboveground stem that lasts for several years.

Leaves: Leaves are 10 to 20 cm wide, deeply divided as far as two-thirds to three-fourths into seven lobes, clothed with minute glandular hairs and usually more or less densely covered with long glandular and eglandular hairs.

Flowers: Flowers are pink, borne in a dense inflorescence, usually with umbrella-like clusters above the first few flowering nodes.

Fruits/seeds: Fruits are separated into two halves (mericarps), each 2.5 to 3 mm, with wavy horizontal ribs.

Glycyrrhiza glabra

glī-sĕ-rhī-zȧ glā-brȧ
licorice

Family: Fabaceae (Leguminosae)
Growth form: herbaceous perennial to 7 feet (2 m)
Hardiness: hardy to Zone 6
Light: full sun
Water: moist preferred but can withstand drought
Soil: deep sandy soil, pH 5.5 to 8.2, average 7.1
Propagation: crown divisions in late autumn
Culinary use: sweetener, primarily in confections

Craft use: none
Landscape use: rear of herb garden, shrub

French: *réglisse*
German: *Süssholz*
Dutch: *zoethout*
Italian: *liquirizia*
Spanish: *orozuz*
Swedish: *lakritsväxt*
Russian: *solodka*

Licorice whips, licorice shoestrings, licorice jujubes, licorice bars, and licorice jelly beans all bring back memories of childhood. The use of licorice is ancient; the earliest written reference to the use of licorice is the Codex Hammaurabi, dating from 2100 B.C.E. Licorice was known as Scythian root to the Greek naturalist Theophrastus (371–287 B.C.E.), who noted that it was sweet and grew in the neighborhood of Lake Maeotis (Sea of Azov). Legend maintained that Scythian warriors could go for twelve days without drink when supplied with licorice and mare's-milk cheese.

If you have ever sucked on a licorice (liquorice in England) root, you probably were impressed, just like Theophrastus, with the smooth, sweet taste. Licorice roots (and stolons), which are wrinkled and brown on the outside but yellow on the inside, are the source of the sweetener glycyrrhizin, which is about 50 to 150 times sweeter than cane sugar. Many people confuse the root, however, with the commercial licorice candy; they insist that anise, fennel, and French tarragon smell like licorice, which is technically incorrect. Licorice roots have no

Glycyrrhiza glabra

other significant flavor beyond sweet glycyrrhizin and a pea-like odor; licorice candy is usually flavored with anise oil, sometimes in combination with peppermint oil and laurel oil. Some "licorice-flavored" candies are not even sweetened with licorice root. Hence, anise, fennel, and French tarragon smell of licorice candy or anise, not licorice itself. Genuine licorice candy is usually composed of wheat flour, gum arabic, gum tragacanth, gelatin, and/or carbohydrate sweeteners.

Glycyrrhiza glabra is an erect herbaceous perennial to 7 feet (2 m) high. Its native range is from southern Europe to Asia Minor. The herb bears a large creeping rhizome and branched roots, alternate leaves, and pale blue to violet flowers. The genus *Glycyrrhiza* is derived from the Greek words *glykys*, "sweet," and *rhiza*, "root"; the specific name means "destitute of hairs," referring to the smooth seed pod of the typical variety.

The English word licorice is actually a corruption of the medieval *gliquiricia*, in turn derived from the Greek name. The typical variety, var. *glabra*, is called Spanish or Italian licorice, while var. *glandulifera* is called Russian licorice. The genus includes about twenty species native to Eurasia with a few species in Australia, North America, and temperate South America. Mongolian or Chinese licorice, *G. uralensis* Fisch. ex DC. (known as *gan cao* in Chinese), and Manchurian licorice, *G. pallidiflora* Maxim., are closely related and are used similarly.

Extracts of licorice stolons and roots are used in baked goods, dairy products, meat products, sauces, gelatins, chewing gum, cough mixtures, lozenges, plug and pipe tobacco, and beverages, including beer, in addition to candies. Grocer-apothecaries of the Middle Ages were probably the first to combine licorice juice with honey and sugar, and extruded licorice sweets were available in the Netherlands toward the end of the seventeenth century. Today's licorice candies date from the "Pontefract cakes" of English chemist George Dunhill of Pontefract, who prepared them from *G. glabra* var. *glabra* with molasses, sugar, and flour.

In the days of the pharaohs, licorice was used by the Egyptians to prepare a drink known as *mai sus*, and Lord Carnarvon discovered a generous supply of licorice root in the tomb of Tutankhamun. Today, licorice is still used to prepare soft drinks during the Islamic holy month of Ramadan. Extract of licorice root is considered GRAS at 16 to 1,424 ppm, the root

---

At least three to four years are required to produce marketable roots, and only roots two years and older have any commercial value.

---

is GRAS at 12 to 2,400 ppm, and the isolated glycyrrhizin is GRAS at 51 to 2,278 ppm. The principal suppliers of licorice root to the United States are Spain, Turkey, Greece, and countries of the former Soviet Union, while Australia today is one of the chief foreign suppliers of licorice candy to North America.

Licorice is so easy to cultivate that it may become weedy. It is usually planted in spring in deep, sandy soil from crown divisions set about 18 inches (46 cm) apart in rows spaced to permit cultivation. At least three to four years are required to produce marketable roots, and only roots two years and older have any commercial value. Maximum yield of glycyrrhizin is about the time of flowering. Since the roots are deep and up to 25 feet (7.6 m) long, harvest is arduous. The highest concentration of glycyrrhizin occurs in roots with a diameter greater than 2.5 inches (more than 6.3 cm).

After digging, the roots are washed and dried. Licorice "juice" consists of the dry extract prepared by extraction of the semidried roots with hot water, although fluxing for three times with 60 percent ethyl alcohol and 0.3 percent ammonia results in greater yields of glycyrrhizic acid. Licorice is sold commercially in large loaves or cylindrical sticks. Spent licorice roots make an excellent mulch.

In the human intestine, glcyrrhizin is hydrolyzed by bacteria to glucuronic acid and glycyrrhetinic acid, which is not well absorbed from the intestinal tract. Glycyrrhizin prevents dental caries. Glycyrrhizic acid inhibits the growth of many fungi and bacteria, such as *Helicobacter pylori*, which is directly implicated in the development of peptic ulcers. Glycyrrhetinic acid has been demonstrated to be an antioxidant, antiinflammatory, antiasthmatic, antithrombotic, and antiarthritic, while glabradin is also antiinflammatory and inhibits melanogenesis. This provides modern affirmation for Arad-Nana, personal physician to King Esarhaddon (seventh century B.C.E.), son of Sennacherib of Assyria, who prescribed licorice for the relief of rheumatic pain. In the test tube, glycyrrhizin and/or glycyrrhizic acid inhibit the virus that causes chickenpox as well as the viruses HIV-1, HHV-6, HHV-7, KSHV, Epstein-Barr, SARS, Hepatitis C, and other viruses. An extract of licorice has been demonstrated to be anticarcinogenic and antimutagenic. Licorice flavonoids suppress abdominal fat accumulation and increase blood glucose level in obese mice. Licorice may be helpful in canine Addison's disease.

Korean researchers have found that licorice root and glycyrrhizin activate glucuronidation and thus may influence the detoxification of foreign biological substances in the liver in rats. Glycyrrhizin and related compounds also are active against leukemia cells in vitro.

In the area of cardiovascular research, Israeli scholars found that four isoflavans and two chalcones from licorice roots are very potent antioxidants against low-density lipoprotein oxidation, and thus may prevent the formation of early atherosclerotic lesions; glabradin and isoflavan were the most abundant and potent antioxidants. Antioxidant activity of licorice root, however, is a synergistic effect of the isoflavonoid mixture, rather than isolated flavonoids, as demonstrated in test tubes by researchers in the United Kingdom. Licorice extract produces bile production in rats and may relieve symptoms of chronic fatigue syndrome.

Yet licorice consumption may produce serious side effects, including headaches, edema, weight gain, and disturbances in the body's electrolyte balance. A report from the Netherlands concerned a 15-year-old boy, who became very ill within three hours of eating 1.1 pounds (0.5 kg) of licorice candy; he exhibited vomiting, serious headache, right-sided weakness, and elevated blood pressure, but recovered in five months. Pulmonary edema was reported in a 64-year-old man who consumed four packages (35 oz or 1020 g) of licorice candy within three days. A Danish woman experienced a life-threatening incident of hypokalaemia caused by consuming 3.5 to 7 ounces (100 to 200 g) of licorice per day for five days. Hypokalaemia and hypertension were also observed in two Dutch women after chewing licorice chewing gum. If licorice is consumed in excess, the risk of apparent mineralocorticoid excess, producing sodium retention, can occur. Licorice also exhibits estrogenic or antiestrogenic effects, but the mechanism of action and the overall effect are controversial. Glycyrrhetinic acid inhibits two enzymes important in prostaglandin synthesis. Elderly individuals or individuals with high blood pressure or disease of the heart, kidneys, or liver should avoid licorice altogether.

Important chemistry: Licorice roots yield 2 to 24 percent glycyrrhizin, a calcium and potassium salt of glycyrrhizic acid. Licorice roots also contain trace levels of the aglycone of glycyrrhizin, glycyrrhetinic acid. The essential oil of licorice root contains trace to 32 percent hexanoic acid, 0 to 15 percent hexadecanoic acid, and significant levels of acetol, propionic acid, 2-acetylpyrrole, 2-acetylfuran, and furfuryl alcohol, but the pea-like odor is probably due to 4 ppm 2,6-dimethylpyrazine, 2 ppm 2-methylpyrazine, and other alkylpyrazines.

Many different flavonoid glycosides (such as glabrene, glabrol, liquiritin, isoliquiritin, liquiritoside, isoliquiritoside, rhamnoliquiritin, and rhamnoisoliquiritin) provide the yellow color of the roots. Licorice roots also contain coumarin derivatives (herniarin and umbelliferone), asparagine, 22,23-dihydrostigmasterol, 3 to 16 percent sugars (glucose, mannitol, fructose, and sucrose), and about 20 to 30 percent starch. Commercial licorice confections in Britain have trace to 1 percent glycyrrhizin; commercial British health products have trace to 5 percent glycyrrhizin with the highest values measured in throat lozenges.

Botanical Key and Description

At least three varieties are recognized.

Key:
1. Flowers blue, native to Mediterranean and Caucasian regions .... var. *glabra*
1a. Flowers violet, native from eastern Europe to Asia Minor 2
   2. Fruit smooth, native to Iraq .... var. *violacea* Boiss.
   2a. Fruit glandular-bristly, native from Hungary to southern Siberia, Turkistan, and Afghanistan ....
   .... var. *glandulifera* (Waldst. & Kit.) Regel & Herder

G. glabra L., Sp. pl. 742. 1753.

Native country: Licorice is native to southern Europe and Asia Minor but naturalized in North America.

General habit: Licorice is an herbaceous perennial 0.5 to 2 m tall.

Leaves: Leaves are alternate and divided into nine to seventeen egg-shaped leaflets, 2 to 5 cm long, arranged as in a feather.

Flowers: The pale blue to violet pea-like flowers appear from June to July in spikes shorter than the leaves.

Fruits/seeds: The bean-like fruits, 30 mm long, have two to five kidney-shaped seeds.

Hedeoma pulegioides

hē-dē-ō̱-må̍ pŭ-lē-gī-ō̱y-dēz
American pennyroyal

Family: Lamiaceae (Labiatae)

Growth form: annual to about 16 inches (40 cm)

Hardiness: can withstand slight frost

Light: part shade

Water: can withstand slight drought

Soil: well-drained garden loam

Propagation: seeds in spring

Culinary use: none

Craft use: flea pillows

Landscape use: wildflower meadow, edges of woodland, front of herb border

---

French: *menthe pouliot américain*

German: *Amerikanische Poleiminze*

Dutch: *amerikaans poleikruid*

The specific name of *Hedeoma pulegioides* was originally derived from *pulex*, or flea, which alludes to the herb's use in folklore: like pennyroyal (*Mentha pulegium*), it was used as a flea repellent. When the Europeans discovered the plants of eastern North America, the one that smelled exactly like their old pennyroyal was named American pennyroyal. The generic name was derived from *hedyosmon*, an ancient name for mint derived from the Greek *hedys*, which means "sweet," and *osma*, or "scent." In the American West, other species of *Hedeoma* grow wild, including some (*H. floribundum* and *H. patens*) that smell like European oregano. The genus includes about thirty-eight species found in North and South America.

The essential oil (1 to 24 ppm) is considered GRAS. Higher doses, however, can be poison-

Hedeoma pulegioides

ous (see discussion under the European penny-royal, *Mentha pulegium*).

Hedeoma pulegioides is an annual easily grown from seed and cultivated in well-drained garden loam. In partially shaded areas in soils rich in organic matter, it readily reseeds. These light, wispy plants must be planted in a mass to make an impression in the garden or on the senses.

Important chemistry: The essential oil of American pennyroyal consists of 61 to 82 percent pulegone.

Botanical Description

H. pulegioides (L.) Pers., Syn. pl. 2:131. 1806.
Native country: *H. pulegioides* is native to open woodlands and waste ground through-out central and eastern United States, east-ern Kansas and Oklahoma east to South Carolina and north to Nova Scotia.
General habit: This is an annual, 10 to 40 cm high, with upright, branched shoots.
Leaves: Leaves are spreading or nodding, often falling from the lower half of the plant at maturity, membranous, broad to narrow and widest at the center with the ends equal or nearly parallel-sided, 1.2 to 3.2 cm long, 4 to 11 mm wide, margins obscurely to sharply toothed with the teeth directed outward, apex narrowly blunt, gradually narrowing to the base and stalked. The petiole is 2.5 to 7 mm long, hairless or minutely coated with very short appressed hairs on the nerves.
Flowers: Calyx 3.5 to 4.5 mm long; corolla minute and barely visible, about 4 mm long.
Fruits/seeds: Fruits less than 0.9 mm wide, 1 mm long.

Helichrysum italicum

hĕl-ĭ-krī-sŭm ĭ-tăl-ĭ-kŭm
curry plant

Family: Asteraceae (Compositae)
Growth form: shrubs, from creeping to 20 inches (50 cm) high
Hardiness: marginally hardy to Zone 7a
Light: full sun
Water: withstands drought
Soil: well drained
Propagation: cuttings in spring or summer
Culinary use: none
Craft use: potpourri, wreaths
Landscape use: rock gardens, container plant

The genus *Helichrysum* used to include about 500 perennial, annual, or shrubby species of warm regions of the Old World. Until the recent breakup of the genus, the best known were the everlastings, such as the strawflower, *H. brac-teatum* (Vent.) Andrews, from South Africa, now known as *Xerochrysum bracteatum* (Vent.) Tzelev. The generic name is derived from the Greek *helios*, the sun, and *chrusos*, gold, alluding to the golden flowers of many species. Curry plant, alias white-leaved everlasting, is usually sold in the nursery trade by a name with no botanical standing, *H. angustifolium*.

At least three forms of curry plant are currently sold in the United States. The normal curry plant is *H. italicum* subsp. *italicum*. It forms a nice, compact shrub to about 12 inches (30 cm) high. Potted plants release a pleasant scent when brushed against, and some are even trained into topiaries. Giant curry plant is *H. italicum* subsp. *italicum* also; it may reach about 20 inches (50 cm). Dwarf curry plant, *H. italicum* subsp. *microphyllum*, is especially fine hanging out of window boxes and terra-cotta pots or trailing over rocks.

The foliage scent of *H. italicum* is of curry, but curry is actually a ground spice mixture which varies from region to region and even from family to family in Southeast Asia. The principal components of true curry are cumin, ginger, coriander, cinnamon, turmeric, red pepper, fenugreek, allspice, black pepper, cardamom, cloves, mustard, and nutmeg. Turmeric, in particular, provides the distinctive color and odor that are so characteristic of curries. The curry plant should not be confused with the curry-leaf tree of Southeast Asia, *Bergera koenigii* L.

Some popular herb books advocate the use of curry plant in soups and casseroles, but curry plant has no GRAS status and has an unknown

Helichrysum italicum

toxicity. It is fine in potpourri, nosegays, and wreaths, however, and makes a good accent plant in the herb garden. The so-called helichrysum or immortelle oils commercially used in the fragrance industry include *H. italicum* as well as *H. stoechas* (L.) Moench. The essential oil of *H. italicum* is bacteriostatic.

Curry plant is reliably hardy to Zone 8 (marginally to 7a) in sunny, well-drained situations. The wise gardener will take measures to provide curry plant with excellent air circulation and soil drainage; light-colored sand or gravel mulches aid the fungus-prone plants. Propagation is by cuttings during spring or summer; seeds, if available, have an uneven and unpredictable germination.

Important chemistry: The essential oil of the curry plant cultivated in North America, subsp. *italicum*, is dominated by 14 to 51 percent neryl acetate and 2 to 17 percent alpha-pinene, providing a rosy-pine odor, but the distinctive turmeric-like odor is apparently contributed by 0 to 16 percent gamma-curcumene. The oils of wild and non–North American cultivated curry plants include trace to 45 percent neryl acetate, 0 to 36 percent geraniol, 0 to 34 percent alpha-pinene, 0 to 15 percent geranyl acetate, 0 to 13 percent beta-selinene, 0 to 12 percent (E)-nerolidol, 0 to 11 percent beta-caryophyllene, and 0 to 14 percent gamma-curcumene. The distinctive odor of Italian wild specimens is due to two minor constituents, 3,5-dimethyloctane-4,6-dione and 2,4-dimethylheptane-3,5-dione. From six different islands in the Tuscan archipelago, trace to 20 percent 4,6,9-trimethyldec-8-en-3,5-dione has also been reported in oil of the curry plant. The essential oil of the dwarf curry plant cultivated in North America has 24 to 54 percent neryl acetate, 9 to 25 percent linalool, and 6 to 15 percent limonene, backed by traces of alpha- and gamma-curcumene. Wild plants of the dwarf curry plant from Sardinia and Corsica have 34 to 53 percent neryl acetate and trace to 14 percent (*E*)-beta-ocimene, backed by trace to 3 percent gamma-curcumene. Dwarf curry plants from Greece have 17 percent beta-selinene and 7 to 14 percent gamma-curcumene.

Botanical Key and Description

H. italicum (Roth) G. Don in Loudon, Hort. Brit. 342. 1830 (*H. angustifolium* DC.)

Key:
1. Fruits (achenes) without glands; bracts at the rear of the heads (involucre) 3 to 4 mm in diameter. . . . . subsp. *serotinum* (Boiss.) P. Fourn.
1a. Fruits with scattered white glands; bracts at the rear of the heads 2 to 3 mm in diameter 2
    2. Bracts at the rear of the head 2 to 3 mm in diameter; outer bracts without glands; lower leaves usually 20 to 50 mm . . . . subsp. *italicum*
    2a. Bracts at the rear of the head 2 mm in diameter; outer bracts glandular on the outside; leaves rarely more than 10 mm . . . . subsp. *microphyllum* (Willd.) Nyman

Native country: Curry plant is native to dry places in southern Europe.

General habit: Curry plant is a shrub 20 to 50 cm high.

Leaves: Leaves are 10 to 30 mm long, narrowly linear, greenish and sparsely hairy to almost smooth or white-hairy.

Flowers: Flowers are arranged in a head 1.5 to 8 cm across with the bracts at the back of the head 2 to 4 mm in diameter, oblong-cylindrical to narrowly bell-shaped; bracts are closely and regularly overlapping, all, except the outermost, glandular, the inner at least five times as long as the outer, narrowly oblong to linear, thin, dry, membranous, the outer broadly rounded, leathery, usually hairy.

Fruits/seeds: Fruits (achenes) have scattered shining white glands or are without glands.

Houttuynia cordata

hō-tī-nĭ-å kôr-dă-tå
"hot tuna"

Family: Saururaceae

Growth form: herbaceous perennial to 6 inches (15 cm)

Hardiness: hardy to Zone 5

Light: full sun to part shade, depending upon available water

Water: moist to edge of standing water

Soil: garden loam rich in organic matter, pH 5.0 to 6.8, average 6.1

Propagation: divisions in spring

Culinary use: limited (not GRAS)

Craft use: none

Landscape use: groundcover

Chinese: *ch'i, chu-ts'ai, yu xing cao*
Japanese: *doku-dami*
Vietnamese: *giấp cá*
Cambodian: *ghee*

This plant has earned the dubious American popular name of "hot tuna" because of mispronunciations of the genus name, *Houttuynia*. Other common names include fish mint and outhouse mint, referring to uses of the plant in different cultures. This genus of one species was named after Martin Houttuyn (1720–1794), a Dutch naturalist, while the specific name refers to the heart-shaped leaves. *Houttuynia cordata* exists in at least two chemical forms: one scented of oranges and the other scented of raw meat, fish, and fresh cilantro. The heart-shaped leaves a required garnish for Vietnamese fish stew and boiled, fertilized duck eggs (eaten three days before they would otherwise hatch). The Vietnamese also chop the leaves for fish sauce. The Chinese sometimes use the leaves in salads. The Japanese usually avoid the strange flavor altogether in food and instead plant it around their privies.

Houttuynia cordata

The flowers resemble white buttercups with yellow centers, but technically they are inflorescences of yellow flowers with petal-like bracts beneath them. A double-flowered form ('Plena') has many proliferated white bracts and dark purple-green leaves, while a variegated form ('Chameleon') has leaves splashed with red, green, and white and is often sold as groundcover in nurseries as the chameleon plant. 'Chameleon' deepens in color as the leaves harden during the summer; container-grown plants will be even deeper in color. Reversion to the green leaves is very common.

Houttuynia cordata, an herbaceous perennial, does best in semi-shaded, moist soil. The more water that can be provided, the less the leaves seem to burn in the sun. It is hardy to at least Zone 5, although it dies down to the ground at the first frost. Don't worry about trying to grow *H. cordata* but rather how to control it; in a situation to its liking it can form a dense groundcover, gradually taking over the garden by underground rhizomes.

Houttuynia cordata has no GRAS status. An investigation at Wonkwang University in Korea found that the leaves of *H. cordata* promote the immune response in mice. German researchers found that the *n*-hexane extract inhibits prostaglandin synthase in test tubes, so it may be useful as an anti-inflammatory and immunomodulatory agent. In Japan, researchers found that in test tubes the steam distillate inhibits the viruses herpes simplex type 1 (HSV-1), influenza, and HIV-1.

Important chemistry: Japanese plants have been shown to be rich in dodecanoic acid, 2-undecanone, and methyl decanoate, which would create a scent reminiscent of cilantro. Chinese plants have been shown to be rich in myrcene, 2-undecanone, limonene, and decanoyl acetaldehyde, which would be scented of lemon and cilantro. Another analysis of the

Chinese plants found 14 percent isogeranyl acetate, 10 percent 2-tridecanone, and 8 percent 2-undecanone, which would be scented of fruits and cilantro, while another analysis of Chinese plants found 45 percent 3-oxododecanal. The foliage is also rich in aporphine alkaloids (cepharanone B, aristolactam AII, aristolactam BII, piperolactam A, norcephalardione B, cepharadione, and 7-chloro-6-demethyl-depharadione B), flavonoids, phenols, fatty acids, and sterols.

Botanical Description

H. cordata Thunberg, Fl. jap. 234. t. 26. 1784.
Native country: *H. cordata* is native to eastern Asia from Japan south to the mountains of Nepal and Java.

General habit: *H. cordata* is a smooth herbaceous perennial 20 to 50 cm long with slender rhizomes.

Leaves: Leaves are simple, egg-heart-shaped, 3 to 8 × 3 to 6 mm, deep green, paler beneath.

Flowers: The individual yellow flowers are arranged on a short, stubby spike with four white bracts, 1.5 to 2 cm long, at the base.

Humulus lupulus

hū-mū-lŭs lū-pū-lŭs
hops

Family: Moraceae
Growth form: perennial vine to 33 feet (10 m) high
Hardiness: hardy to Zone 5
Light: full sun
Water: moist but not constantly wet
Soil: deep sandy loam, pH 4.5 to 8.2, average 6.5
Propagation: suckers in spring
Culinary use: beer
Craft use: hop pillows, fresh and dried bouquets
Landscape use: trellises, draped over bowers and porches

French: *houblon*
German: *Hopfen*
Dutch: *hop*
Italian: *luppulo, lupari, maschio, orticacci*

Spanish: *lúpulo, hombrecillo, vidarria, betiguera*
Portuguese: *lúpolo, engatadeira*
Swedish: *humle*
Russian: *khmel'*

With a change in federal law, home brewing of specialty beers has become a new craze to replace home brewing of wines. The home brewer may buy dried hops at specialty shops, but more and more home brewers who also garden are raising their own hops, especially organic hops. Beers are prepared by fermenting malt (soaked and germinated grain, typically barley) and then flavoring the brew with a plant full of bitter resins, typically hops.

German beer makers have used hops to flavor beers for hundreds of years, certainly since the ninth century. Beer may have been hopped before that time, but the earliest record of hopped beer dates from 822 C.E.; it is mentioned by Abbot Adalhard in his *Statutae Abbatiae Corbej*. During the Middle Ages, beer often accompanied every meal, and hop cultivation spread rapidly throughout Europe as a result. However, until hops arrived in England toward the close of the fifteenth century, bitter plants like ale-hoof (gill-over-the-ground, *Glechoma hederacea* L.) were used to flavor fermented malt. Henry VII and Henry VIII of England liked their beer without hops and therefore prohibited their use.

Hops were introduced to New York around 1629 and Virginia in 1648. European hops have become naturalized (along with Japanese hops), in waste places, fence-rows, old house sites, and so on from Canada to New Mexico.

In the American colonies, molasses was a common substitute for malt, and often rice, corn, wheat, and other grains were substituted for barley. The first commercial crop of hops was established in New York in 1808. Later, the plant moved west to Wisconsin. Today the Yakima Valley in Washington produces about 75 percent of the hops grown in the United States, with limited production in the Upper Midwest.

The genus *Humulus* includes two species (*H. japonicus* Sieb. & Zucc., Japanese hops, is the other species) and is closely aligned to *Cannabis sativa* L., marijuana; the two can even be grafted. The generic name, *Humulus*, was derived from the Slavic-German name *khmel'*, while *lupulus* was derived from the Latin *lupus*, or wolf, referring to the straggling habit of this vine on other plants ("willow wolf").

Hops are perennial dioecious ("two houses," or separate sexes) vines to 33 feet (10 m); male vines bear male flowers in loose axillary clusters, while female vines bear flowers that are cone-like at maturity. Leaves are dark green, heart-shaped, and with three to five deep lobes. The whole plant is rich in bitter resins and thus useful in brewing beer. Seedless hops, produced by preventing pollination, are considered more desirable by brewers; the weight is 30 percent less than seeded hops, but seedless hops are more shatter-resistant.

Hops are adapted to a wide range of climates. In areas where rainfall is lacking, irrigation may be required. Deep, sandy loam in full sun produces the best hops harvests. Levels of phosphorous and potassium are similar to those required for corn; a soil test is necessary before any recommendations can be made, and your county agricultural agent can provide interpretations of the results.

Approximately 100 pounds per acre (121 kg/ha) of nitrogen are removed by the harvested portion of hops every year; organic fertilizers of 2 to 5 percent nitrogen are preferred. Hops are propagated by the runners that arise from the crown just below the soil surface. In May the runners are cut into 6- to 8-inch-long (15 to 20 cm) pieces, each bearing at least two sets of buds. Cuttings are planted immediately in hills, two to four cuttings per hill, with the buds

Humulus lupulus

pointed up and covered by ¼ to 1 inch (0.6 to 2.5 cm) of soil, with a spacing of approximately 8 × 8 feet (2.4 × 2.4 m) at a density of 800 hills per acre (1,977 hills/ha).

Hops are grown on an overhead trellis system that may be designed to handle mechanical harvesting. When the vines are about 2 feet (60 cm) long, two to six vigorous vines per hill are selected and trained up a wire trellis. When the vines are securely attached to the wires, the lowest 4 feet (122 cm) of leaves and lateral branches are carefully removed to aid in preventing diseases such as downy mildew and insect pests such as spider mites. Suckers rising from the base early in the season are continually removed to promote the growth of selected vines, but the hardiness of the crown is fostered by allowing the suckers to persist later in the season.

Weed control is usually by early mechanical cultivation 6 to 10 inches deep (15 to 25 cm) to incorporate surface organic matter, followed by shallow cultivation 2 to 4 inches deep (5 to 10 cm) later in the season. Late-season cultivation inhibits growth and leads to early ripening. Some herbicides are registered for use on hops but are rarely necessary.

Hops are harvested mechanically or by hand from mid-August to mid-September in the Pacific Northwest; plants are prime for picking for only five to ten days, and delayed harvesting causes shattering of the cones and discoloration.

Home gardeners should gauge harvest readiness by the cones' growing slightly papery and giving off a pronounced odor; brown spots indicate overmaturity. To store the hops, reduce moisture content from 65 to 80 percent to 8 to 10 percent. At home, a food dehydrator may be used, but do not exceed 140°F (60°C). After drying, move the hops to a cooling room for a week to allow them to "even up." Any storage and transport should be below 40°F (4.4°C);

home brewers may prefer to refrigerate or freeze the cones.

The selection of the cultivar is particularly important for yield of dried hops, essential-oil content, and alpha acid content. Also, the source of barley malt is important; standard barley cultivars include 'Crystal', 'Klages', and 'Russell'. Old World–aroma hops varieties include the following.

Cultivar: 'Cascade'
Origin: 1972, Oregon Agricultural Experiment Station
Yield: 2,000 pounds per acre (2,242 kg/ha) dried hops
Flavor: distinct fragrance; 1 to 2 percent essential oil; alpha acid content of 5 to 7 percent
Maturation: later than 'Fuggle'
Diseases/insects: resistant to downy mildew but very susceptible to verticillium wilt and *Prunus* necrotic ringspot virus (PNRSV)

Cultivar: 'Columbia'
Origin: 1976, USDA
Yield: nearly sterile triploid well suited to mechanical harvest; potential of 1,900 pounds per acre (2,130 kg/ha) dried hops
Flavor: similar to 'Fuggle'
Maturation: medium to late maturing

Cultivar: 'Fuggle'
Origin: pre-1890, England
Yield: low, does not produce first full crop until third season; 1,100 to 1,400 pounds per acre (1,233 to 1,569 kg/ha) dried hops
Flavor: pronounced; 1 percent essential oil with 44 to 58 percent myrcene and 22 to 30 percent alpha-humulene; alpha acid content of 4 to 6 percent
Maturation: early
Diseases/insects: resistant to downy mildew, hop nettlehead disease, and verticillium wilt

Cultivar: 'Hallertauer'
Origin: Germany
Yield: 50 to 70 percent of U.S. cultivars; grown organically in Wisconsin to produce up to 800 pounds per acre (897 kg/ha) dried hops
Flavor: essential oil with 41 percent alpha-humulene, 27 percent myrcene, and 11 percent beta-caryophyllene
Diseases/insects: fairly tolerant of crown infection by downy mildew but susceptible to spider mite infestations

Cultivar: 'Liberty'
Origin: 1991, A. Haunold, USDA
Flavor: similar to 'Hallertauer'
Diseases/insects: resistant to diseases plaguing 'Hallertauer'

Cultivar: 'Mount Hood'
Origin: 1989, A. Haunold, USDA
Flavor: similar to 'Hallertauer'

Cultivar: 'Tettnanger'
Origin: Germany
Yield: see 'Hallertauer'
Diseases/insects: see 'Hallertauer'

Cultivar: 'Willamette'
Origin: selected from 'Fuggle' 1976, Oregon Agricultural Experiment Station
Yield: seedless hops in presence of male flowers; up to 2,000 pounds per acre (2,242 kg/ha) dried hops
Flavor: pleasant; 1 percent oil, alpha acid content of 6 to 7 percent
Maturation: later than 'Fuggle' (late August–early September in Oregon)
Diseases/insects: resistant to downy mildew but susceptible to potato strain of *Verticillium dahliae*

The American varieties include the following.

Cultivar: 'Early Cluster'
Origin: U.S.A.
Yield: vigorous, high yielding, well adapted to mechanical harvesting
Flavor: essential oil with 41 to 62 percent myrcene and 9 to 21 percent alpha-humulene; alpha acid content of 5 to 7 percent
Maturation: 10 to 14 days earlier than 'Late Cluster'
Diseases/insects: resistant to verticillium wilt but somewhat susceptible to downy mildew via crown and root infection

Cultivar: 'Late Cluster'
Origin: U.S.A.
Yield: 2,000 pounds per acre (2,242 kg/ha) dried hops
Flavor: similar to 'Early Cluster'; essential oil with 28 to 59 percent myrcene and 11 to 24 percent alpha-humulene
Diseases/insects: downy mildew may be problem late in season and more susceptible to viruses than 'Early Cluster'

Cultivar: 'Talisman'
Origin: 1965, Idaho Agricultural Experiment Station
Yield: potential in Idaho of 3,200 pounds per acre (3,587 kg/ha) dried hops
Flavor: 1.5 percent essential oil with 59 percent myrcene and 4 percent alpha-humulene; alpha acid content of 8 to 10 percent
Maturation: week later than 'Late Cluster'
Diseases/insects: resistant to crown rot phase of downy mildew but vulnerable to cone phase of disease; phytophthora root rot is a problem in waterlogged soils

The Extract or High-Alpha varieties include the following.

Cultivar: 'Brewer's Gold'
Origin: England, introduced in the United States in the 1930s
Yield: vigorous and well adapted to mechanical harvesting, potential of 2,500 pounds per acre (2,802 kg/ha) dried seeded hops
Flavor: high in essential oils (51 to 72 percent myrcene and 6 to 21 percent alpha-humulene); alpha acid content of 8 percent
Maturation: medium to late maturing
Diseases/insects: less susceptible to downy mildew than 'Cluster' cultivars

Cultivar: 'Bullion'
Origin: England, introduced in the United States in the 1930s
Yield: see 'Brewer's Gold'
Flavor: see 'Brewer's Gold'; essential oil with 51 to 72 percent myrcene and 6 to 18 percent alpha-humulene
Maturation: ten days earlier than 'Brewer's Gold'
Diseases/insects: see 'Brewer's Gold'

Cultivar: 'Chinook'
Origin: 1985, Washington Agricultural Experiment Station
Flavor: 0.5 percent essential oil, alpha acid content of 11 to 13 percent
Maturation: medium-early
Diseases: moderate resistance to downy mildew, hop-damson aphid and the two-spotted mite; free of PNRSV and apple mosaic virus

Cultivar: 'Eroica'
Origin: sibling of 'Galena', 1980
Yield: not as stable in storage as 'Galena' or the 'Cluster' cultivars
Flavor: essential oil with 42 percent myrcene

and 11 percent beta-caryophyllene but only 2 percent alpha-humulene, alpha acid content of 10 to 13 percent
Maturation: later than 'Galena'
Diseases/insects: moderately high degree of resistance to hop downy mildew and the potato strain of *Verticillium dahliae*

Cultivar: 'Galena'
Origin: selected from 'Brewer's Gold', 1978, Idaho Agricultural Experiment Station
Flavor: alpha acid content of 12 percent
Maturation: later than 'Early Cluster'
Diseases/insects: moderately resistant to crown stage of downy mildew, some tolerance to verticillium wilt; susceptible to frost damage and difficult to establish

Cultivar: 'Nugget'
Origin: 1983, Oregon Agricultural Experiment Station
Yield: good storage qualities
Flavor: 2 percent essential oil, alpha acid content similar to 'Eroica'
Maturation: matures later than 'Galena' but earlier than 'Eroica'
Diseases/insects: good resistance to downy mildew but susceptible to verticillium wilt

Cultivar: 'Olympic'
Origin: 1983, Washington Agricultural Experiment Station
Yield: tends to produce excessive amount of male flowers, reducing cone-cluster density and yield; easily trained and frost tolerant
Flavor: essential oil with 27 percent alpha-humulene, 25 percent myrcene, and 10 percent beta-caryophyllene
Diseases/insects: no resistance to hop-damson aphid or two-spotted mite; moderate resistance to downy mildew but some susceptibility to verticillium wilt

The essential oil of hops is GRAS at 1 to 35 ppm, while the extract of the female cones is GRAS at 0.7 to 720 ppm. About 8 to 13 ounces of hops are used for each barrel of beer. To enhance the aromatic value of beer, sometimes the essential oil is added to the finished product. While beer manufacture uses 98 percent of the world's production of hops, hop derivatives are also used in bitters and tobacco flavoring. Before the advent of pasteurization, brewers used to use hops for its antibiotic qualities, and, indeed, the bitter resins and other compounds have been documented to be antifungal and antibacterial. In some countries, the young shoots are eaten as a boiled vegetable. Some crafters prepare hop pillows, which are reputed to promote sleep.

Hops may offset the cancer-causing potential of the alcohol in beer; Japanese researchers found that topical application of humulon, the bitter principle, inhibits the development of skin tumors in mice. The hop bitter acids are antioxidant.

Important chemistry: Three important fractions may be partitioned from hops. The first, isolated at low densities, is the essential oil of hops and responsible for the aroma of the beer. In the essential oil, myrcene (10 to 82 percent) is an undesirable component, while alpha-humulene (trace to 54 percent) is desirable. The second fraction, the bitter acids, is responsible for the bitter taste. The bitter acids include the alpha-acids (humulons) and the beta-acids (lupulons). The third fraction represents the waxes and lipids, along with the bitter acids. The substance responsible for the sleep-inducing qualities of hops is 2-methyl-3-butene-2-ol, which induces sleep in mice for up to eight hours with no observable abnormal behavior.

Botanical Description

H. lupulus L., Sp. pl. 1028. 1753.
Native country: Hops are native to the northern temperate zone.
General habit: Hops are a perennial dioecious vine to 10 m, climbing clockwise. The crown becomes woody with age and produces an extensive root system to a depth of almost 5 m.
Leaves: Leaves are dark green, hairy, heart-shaped, with three to five deep lobes, and coarsely toothed.
Flowers: Female flowers are borne in clusters on lateral branches to form pale green cone-like structures 2.5 to 10 cm long and papery at maturity.
Fruits/seeds: The dry, one-seeded fruit (achene) is enclosed within the persistent calyces.

The Yakima Valley in Washington produces about 75 percent of the hops grown in the United States, with limited production in the Upper Midwest.

Hyssopus officinalis

hĭ-sō-pŭs ŏ-fĭs-ĭ-nā-lĭs
hyssop

Family: Lamiaceae (Labiatae)
Growth form: perennial subshrub to 2 feet (60 cm) high
Hardiness: hardy to Zone 6
Light: full sun
Water: moist; can withstand drought
Soil: well drained, gravelly or rocky loam, pH 5.0 to 7.5, average 6.7
Propagation: seeds in spring, 29,000 seeds per ounce (1,023/g)
Culinary use: sauces, condiments
Craft use: wreaths, potpourri
Landscape use: effective massed in shrub or perennial border, hedges, edging

French: *hysope*
German: *Ysop*
Dutch: *hyssop*
Italian: *issopo*
Spanish: *hisopo*
Swedish: *isop*
Arabic: *zufah-yabis*

The genus *Hyssopus* includes one very variable species of Europe. The specific name, *officinalis*, refers to the past medicinal use of hyssop. The generic name *Hyssopus* is derived from the Semitic *ezov*, a plant tied in bunches and used as a brush to sprinkle blood on doorposts and lintels when the house was cleansed against leprosy.

The plant we now know as hyssop is not the plant named in the Bible (Exodus 12:21–22, I Kings 4:33, Psalms 51:7, John 19:28–30); that honor belongs to "Syrian hyssop," *Origanum syriacum*. *Hyssopus officinalis* is not native to Israel or the Sinai.

Hyssop requires full sun and well-drained, gravelly or rocky soil. Trim hyssop back sharply in the early spring and after flowering, the first time to prevent the plants from becoming woody and leggy, and later to maintain trim, compact plants. Hyssop typically has blue flow-

We find it somewhat curious that hyssop is planted in so many herb gardens today despite the skunk-like odor that it develops on hot summer days. While hyssop provides good blue, pink, or white flowers in the herb garden, its continued cultivation is more traditional than useful. In the Middle Ages and Renaissance, hyssop was employed in cooking, but our ancestors also used musk and civet as flavorings and personal fragrances. On the other hand, we know of one gardener who created a wonderful potpourri of summer memories with sweet woodruff and hyssop to remind her of both new-mown hay and skunks!

Hyssopus officinalis

ers; 'Rosea' has pink ones, and 'Alba' has white. Massed hyssop is very effective in the garden, and it makes a very good hedge or edging, mimicking a green-leaved lavender with spikes of flowers. Under favorable conditions, this hardy perennial subshrub reseeds readily.

Hyssop is considered GRAS at 600 ppm; the essential oil is GRAS at 0.2 to 50 ppm, while the extract is GRAS at 13 to 300 ppm. Hyssop oil and extract have been employed in sauces, condiments, and canned foods as well as liqueurs. Yet, the pinocamphone and isopinocamphone in hyssop oil cause convulsions. Above 0.002 ounce per pound (0.13g/kg), ingestion of hyssop oil causes convulsions; above 0.020 ounce per pound (1.25g/kg), it can be fatal. For a human weighing 150 pounds, that comes out to be 0.31 ounce and 3 ounces, respectively. We thus are somewhat reticent to recommend hyssop for foods despite its GRAS status.

Researchers have isolated a polysaccharide (MAR-10) from the aqueous extract of hyssop that showed strong anti-HIV-1 activity in test tubes, with no toxic or inhibitory effects on lymphocyte functions or T-cell counts. The essential oil of hyssop is both antimicrobial and spasmolytic.

Important chemistry: The essential oil of hyssop is dominated by trace to 69 percent pinocamphone, 1 to 62 percent isopinocamphone, 0 to 53 percent 1,8-cineole, trace to 37 percent limonene, 6 to 23 percent beta-pinene, trace to 28 percent pinocarvone, trace to 22 percent germacrene D, 0 to 13 percent beta-phellandrene, and trace to 12 percent camphene. Leaves may have 32 to 60 percent pinocamphone, 3 to 16 percent camphor, and 12 to 14 percent beta-pinene, while flowers may have up to 34 percent pinocamphone, 21 percent camphor, and 10 percent beta-pinene.

Botanical Description

Four subspecies are known, but subsp. *officinalis* is the cultivated hyssop of herb gardens.

H. officinalis L., Sp. pl. 569. 1753.

Native country: Hyssop is native to dry hills and rocky ground in south, south-central, and eastern Europe but locally naturalized near gardens.

General habit: Hyssop is a dwarf shrub 20 to 60 cm high with numerous, erect branches, sometimes decumbent.

Leaves: Leaves are 10 to 50 × 1 to 10 mm, linear, lance-shaped, or oblong, blunt to tapered to the apex, smooth-edged, smooth to wavy-haired, stalked or almost stalkless.

Flowers: Flowers are blue, pink, or white spikes.

Fruits/seeds: Fruits (nutlets) are about 2 mm in diameter.

Inula helenium

ĭn-ū-lå hĕ-lē-nē-ŭm
elecampane

Family: Asteraceae (Compositae)

Growth form: herbaceous perennial to 8 feet (2.4 m) high when flowering

Hardiness: hardy to Zone 5

Light: full sun

Water: moist but not constantly wet

Soil: well-drained loam, pH 4.5 to 7.4, average 6.2

Propagation: divisions or seeds in spring

Culinary use: candied root

Craft use: none

Landscape use: rear of perennial border or as accent

French: *aunée*

German: *Echter Alant*

Dutch: *alant*

Italian: *enula campana, inula, elenio, antiveleno, erbella*

Spanish: *enula campana, ala, hierba del moro*

Swedish: *ålandsrot*

Russian: *devyasil*

Arabic: *rasan*

Women of high and low status in society often figure in the name of plants, and *Inula helenium* honors a woman and her sorrow in both its botanical and common names. One legend relates that Helen met Paris on the fields of Troy with a large bouquet of these yellow daisies in her arms, and thus the common name was derived from *Helena de la campagne*, or Helen of the fields. Another legend relates that this plant sprang from Helen's tears on the fields of Troy.

The generic name itself, *Inula*, is a corruption of *helenium* after Helen of Troy. The other English names are less noble: scabwort, alant, horseheal, and yellow starwort. The name scabwort is aptly derived from the use of elecampane to cure chronic skin inflammations at least since the time of Job. Elecampane oil is both bacteriostatic and fungistatic, and it displays antioxidative activity.

The genus *Inula* includes about ninety species that grow in the temperate and warm regions of the Old World. Elecampane is a statuesque perennial with large leaves and yellow daisies borne on stalks up to 8 feet (2.4 m) high—an herb-garden standout. Elecampane is easily propagated from seeds or by division in spring. Budded pieces of roots about 3 inches long can also be planted.

In Roman times, the fleshy roots of elecampane were once used as a vegetable, but today are used to prepare a decoction (2 percent), infusion (5 percent), tincture (20 percent in 65-percent ethyl alcohol), and fluid and soft ex-

Inula helenium

tracts. The flavor is bitter and aromatic and useful for flavoring bitters and vermouths; bitters have been documented to be a stimulant and tonic for the digestive system. The liqueur absinthe was once flavored with elecampane. A very aromatic confection prepared with elecampane root, cane sugar, cinnamon, cloves, and nutmeg was a favorite of nineteenth-century English schoolboys, who believed it gave agility and endurance in athletics. The root extract of elecampane is considered GRAS at 800 ppm.

Important chemistry: The dominant components of the essential oil of the roots of elecampane include 4 to 52 percent alantolactone and 13 to 33 percent isoalantolactone. The roots also include beta- and gamma-sitosterol.

Botanical Description

I. helenium L., Sp. pl. 883. 1753.
Native country: Elecampane is native to southeast Europe.
General habit: Elecampane is an erect, robust, hairy perennial, 60 to 250 cm high.
Leaves: Leaves are gray-hairy beneath, the lower 40 to 70 × 10 to 25 cm, egg-elliptic-shaped, the upper heart-shaped and clasping the stem.
Flowers: The daisies have a head 15 to 20 mm in diameter with yellow ray flowers (ligulate florets) 30 to 40 mm long.
Fruits/seeds: The dry one-seed fruits (achenes) are 3 to 5 mm long, smooth.

Iris

ī-rĭs
‾
orris

Family: Iridaceae
Growth form: rhizomatous herbaceous perennial from 16 inches to 4 feet (40 to 120 cm) when flowering
Hardiness: hardy to Zone 5
Light: full sun
Water: can withstand drought when established
Soil: well-drained garden loam, near-neutral (pH 6.5 to 7.0)
Propagation: divisions of the rhizomes around 4 July
Culinary use: none
Craft use: potpourri
Landscape use: front of border, along walkways

French: *iris*
German: *Iris*
Italian: *irios, ireos*
Spanish: *lirio*

Iris was the Greek for rainbow and aptly refers to the multiplicity of flower colors available in this genus of about 300 species with thousands of named cultivars. However, according to Clarence Mahan, the origin of the name *Iris* may actually stem from the rainbow iridescence of the rhizomes when cut in the dark.

Iris was also a goddess, one of the Oceanides, a messenger of the gods and one of the special attendants of Juno, so the early Greeks dedicated the flower to Juno to guide the souls of dead women to their final resting place. No wonder that *I.* ×*germanica* 'Albicans' and *I. mesopotamica* Dykes are still grown on Muslim graves in the eastern Mediterranean.

Violet-scented orris is commercially derived from the rhizomes of *I.* ×*germanica* 'Albicans', *I.* 'Florentina' and/or *I. pallida* 'Dalmatica' To add further confusion, 'Albicans' and 'Florentina' have been confused in the nursery trade.

Carl Linnaeus published the name *I. germanica* in his first edition of *Species Plantarum* in 1753. We now realized that this is a complex of "near-species" and possible hybrids and best designated as a hybrid, *I.* ×*germanica*. Unlike *I. pallida*, which has 24 somatic (body) chromosomes ($2n = 24$), *I.* ×*germanica* usually has $2n = 44$ (36 and 48 have also been reported). Various parents have been suggested, but the controversy will probably continue until DNA is applied to sort out the lineages.

The original publication of *I. albicans*, by Johan Martin Christian Lange in 1861, described it as very similar to 'Florentina' ("A proxima I. florentina"). This form is pure white. In 1913, William Rickatson Dykes cited the illustration and description of John Belenden Ker Gawler, published in *Curtis' Botanical Magazine* in 1803, and published *I. germanica* var. *florentina*. The flowers of 'Florentina' are a very pale blue, best described as pearly white (Ker Gawler says "grayish white, outer segments with a somewhat bluer tint"), and bearing a typical sweet iris odor. Dykes noticed that this was similar to those plants grown in Florence, Italy, except for minor morphological differences. It is among the very first bearded irises to bloom in early spring, around May. 'Florentina' sometimes sports back to various blue forms, each given different names but illustrating the relationship to the typical blue flowers of the species, *I.* ×*germanica*. Both 'Albicans' and 'Florentina' share the chromosome number of $2n = 44$ with *I.* ×*germanica*.

'Dalmatica' also differs in insignificant aspects from the very variable *I. pallida* and the name has been applied to more than one clone, and, like the species, the flowers of 'Dalmatica' are lilac-colored and scented of Concord grapes.

The word orris is derived from the Italian *orice* or *oris*, corruptions of the Middle Italian *irios*. The first use of orris in perfumery is attributed to Dominicans who operated a pharmaceutical factory at Santa Maria Novella in Florence in the 1600s. Orris became a major item for perfumery at the beginning of the nineteenth century and reached peak cultivation in Tuscany, Italy, from 1850 to 1920. Cultivation then declined to today's estimated 173 acres (70 ha). *Iris pallida* 'Dalmatica' is now raised principally in Tuscany, in the mountains of Chianti, and the slopes of Pratomagno. *Iris* 'Florentina' is raised in Morocco, China, and India. *Iris pallida* was very important in the early evolution of the tall, bearded iris, so the rhizomes of almost any early antique iris can be processed to yield orris of varying quality.

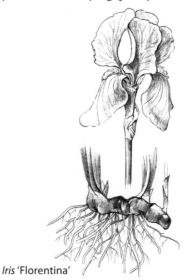

Iris 'Florentina'

Orris is cultivated like any tall bearded iris but is more resistant to leaf spot and other plagues of the modern cultivars. Provide full sun and well-drained soil; in Italy orris is cultivated on stony, hot hillsides. If fertilization is deemed necessary, use high phosphorus fertilizers, such as bonemeal. In areas with abundant rainfall, slugs may be a problem. Divide plants every two or three years, around 4 July, to prevent overcrowding. The rhizomes are branched, heavy and compact, covered with a gray or green epidermis, and usually whitish inside. Fresh orris rhizomes smell of freshly cut potatoes and develop their characteristic odor with proper aging.

In Italy, in mid-July to September, about three years after planting, the rhizomes are lifted and single shoots are removed for propagation. Then the remaining rhizomes are derooted, washed, decorticated (scraped) with a hook-shaped knife, and dried in the sun for six to ten days on cane mats or nets until shrunken and pliable. The peeled rhizomes are stored for not less than two years in a dark place with good air circulation and protected against insects and mold. Recent studies done at Nestlé and Givaudan-Roure Research have shown that a technique involving a bacterial treatment (*Rahnella aquatilis* Izard, Gavini, Trinel, and Leclerc) of fresh rhizomes shortened the maturation time from three years to a few days.

The home gardener may want to loosely stack the cleaned, scraped rhizomes on screened shelves in the garage, but maintain good air flow to prevent mold. This storage period is necessary to permit enzymatic changes that release the irones, chemicals with the scent of violets.

Orris was once widely used as hair powder but now serves only as a fixative in potpourris. Orris may also be purchased chopped or in pinhead size. Both the Greeks and Romans valued orris for cosmetics, and the unguents of Elis and Corinth were famous for their violet perfume derived from orris. Fresh rhizomes were once bleached with sulfuric acid to use for teething infants, but the bleaching process removes any odor and merely leaves a white, chewy block of starch.

Pulverized orris is steam-distilled to yield a wax-like, cream-colored mass called "orris butter" or "*beurre d'iris*" (sometimes incorrectly called "orris concrète"). From this orris butter an alcoholic extract, or absolute, is prepared.

The small yield of butter, the high starch content of the rhizomes, and the volume of the material all present problems for distillation. An orris resinoid and true concrète are sometimes commercially available. The Victorian "*extrait de civette*" was a blend of civet and orris butter. Orris butter is used in violet-type perfumes and blends well with cassis, rose, opopanax, bergamot, and lavender, but the expense limits its use in perfumery. The butter and extract also find limited use in nonalcoholic beverages, baked goods, gelatins, chewing gum, and so on.

Orris essential oil is considered GRAS at 0.5 to 8.6 ppm, while the extract is GRAS at 2 to 120 ppm.

Important chemistry: Moroccan orris butter (from *I.* 'Florentina') is rich in 58 to 66 percent *cis*-alpha-irone and 34 to 39 percent *cis*-gamma-irone. Italian orris butter (from *I. pallida* 'Dalmatica') is rich in 26 to 41 percent *cis*-alpha-irone and 55 to 69 percent *cis*-gamma-irone.

Botanical Key and Description

Key:

1. Bracts (spathes) subtending the flowers entirely thin, dry, membranous, more or less translucent at time of pollen release. . . . . *I. pallida*

1a. Spathes leafy at the time of pollen release, at least in the lower part . . . . *I. ×germanica*

I. ×germanica L., Sp. pl. 38. 1753.
Native country: The so-called German iris is a complex mix of "near-species" and may have been derived by hybridization; it is probably native to the eastern Mediterranean region. In the wild, it is found in dry, rocky, or grassy places.
General habit: The German iris is a stout, rhizomatous perennial 40 to 90 cm high upon flowering.
Leaves: Leaves are 30 to 70 cm × 20 to 35 mm, somewhat coated with a waxy bloom.
Flowers: About three to five flowers are borne upon branched stems at least 5 cm long in the upper half, the lower flowers well exserted from the bract even in bud. Flowers are typically bluish violet.

I. pallida Lam., Encycl. 3:294. 1789.
Native country: The pale iris is native to northern Italy and the western part of the former Yugoslavia.
General habit: The pale iris is a stout rhizomatous perennial 15 to 120 cm high.
Leaves: Leaves are 20 to 60 cm × 10 to 40 mm, coated or scarcely coated with a waxy bloom.
Flowers: Two to six lilac to violet flowers are borne on a branched stem.

Juniperus communis

jŏ-nĭp-ĕr-ŭs kŏ-mū-nĭs
common juniper

Family: Cupressaceae
Growth form: prostrate shrubs or trees to 49 feet (15 m)
Hardiness: hardy to southern Maine (Zone 5)
Light: full sun
Water: moist but not wet; can withstand drought
Soil: well drained
Propagation: cuttings or seeds in fall
Culinary use: meats, sauces, alcoholic beverages
Craft use: wreaths, potpourri

Landscape use: shrub border

French: *genévrier, geniévre commune*
German: *Gemeiner Wacholder, Kaddigbeere*
Dutch: *jeneverbes*
Italian: *ginepro, zinepro*
Spanish: *enebro común, junípro, baya de enebro*
Portuguese: *zimbro común, enebro real, cada, grojo, nebrina*
Swedish: *en*
Arabic: *habul hurer, shamrat-ul-arar*

Common juniper is a thickly branched, evergreen tree or shrub that may reach 49 feet (15 m) in height with many prickly, awl-like leaves. Juniper is a cone-bearing tree, not a flowering plant, and thus does not bear fruits; the fleshy cones of common juniper resemble blueberries and ripen in fall. Gin, liqueurs, and game such as venison and wild boar, poultry stuffing, beef stews, and pâtés are flavored with the cones, usually called berries. In Germany, they also flavor sauerkraut and a conserve called *Latwerge* that is eaten with cold meats. The taste is aromatic and bitter, a bit like turpentine. The flavor goes well with parsley, thyme, fennel, marjoram, bay, and other herbs as well as garlic, spices, wine, brandy, and port. Juniper berries vary in strength, and the ones from Italian hillsides are considered stronger than those that grow in Great Britain.

The extract of common juniper is GRAS at 5 to 53 ppm, the essential oil is GRAS at 0.01 to 95 ppm, and the "fruit" is GRAS at 60 to 2,000 ppm. The essential oil of juniper has been used in folk medicine as a diuretic, but it irritates the kidneys, an action that is detrimental when accompanied by existing inflammation. Thus, while juniper oil is also antimicrobial, juniper

Juniperus communis

oil is no longer recommended by competent physicians.

The genus *Juniperus* includes about fifty species of the northern hemisphere to the tropical African mountains and West Indies. The generic name is Latin of unknown derivation. Many cultivars of common juniper are available in the nursery trade, from dwarf shrubs to trees. The popular 'Hibernica', the Irish juniper, grows eventually to 10 to 16 feet (3 to 5 m) in a tight column. A miniature version for troughs and rock gardens is 'Compressa', which very slowly forms a tiny, tight column to only 47 inches (1.2 m).

The genus *Juniperus* includes both male and female plants (dioecious), and only the female plants bear fleshy cones. Many cultivars are male, and sometimes females fail to bear cones under cultivation. The only named cultivar that reliably bears cones seems to be 'Suecica'.

Common juniper requires full sun and moist but well-drained garden loam; junipers can withstand mild drought. Propagation, especially of the cultivars, is by cuttings taken in late fall and wintered over in a cold frame or cool greenhouse. The hard seeds need stratification (alternating moist freezing and thawing), and the home gardener will have most success by simply sowing cleaned seeds in fall in the garden and then waiting for spring.

The most serious disease affecting junipers is phomopsis twig blight, but *J. communis* seems to be relatively resistant. This fungus is especially active during weather in which the evaporation rate is low, especially during hot, humid summers or cold, wet springs, or when overhead irrigation is employed.

Important chemistry: The essential oil of common juniper ripe berries is dominated by 4 to 86 percent alpha-pinene, trace to 42 percent sabinene, 1 to 53 percent myrcene, 0 to 11 percent gamma-muurolene, 0 to 10 percent germacrene D, and 0 to 10 percent delta-cadinene. An alcoholic extract of common juniper berries, as would be present in gin, yields 11 to 46 percent alpha-pinene and 5 to 18 percent myrcene plus alpha-terpinene and up to 13 percent delta-cadinene.

Botanical Description

J. communis L., Sp. pl. 1038. 1753.
Native country: Common juniper is native to Europe, northern Asia, northern Africa, and North America.

General habit: Common juniper is an evergreen tree to 15 m, or a shrub, usually multistemmed, 3 to 5 m high.
Leaves: Leaves are always awl-like, 3 to 15 × 1 to 2 mm, straight, usually gray-green, shallowly grooved above and with a broad white band.
Cones: As a gymnosperm, *Juniperus* produces rather fleshy coalescing scales which become berry-like. The cones are borne on female trees and take two to three years to ripen to a waxy blue-black, 6 to 9 mm thick, from initial pollination.

Laurus nobilis

lâ-rŭs nō-bĭ-lĭs
Grecian bay

Family: Lauraceae
Growth form: tree to 66 feet (20 m)
Hardiness: routinely hardy to Zone 8
Light: full sun
Water: moist but not wet; can withstand minor drought
Soil: well-drained garden loam, pH 4.5 to 8.2, average 6.2
Propagation: cuttings or seeds
Culinary use: soups, stews, meats
Craft use: wreaths
Landscape use: container plant, specimen tree

French: *laurier franc, laurier des poétes, laurier d'Apollon*
German: *Edler Lorbeerbaum*
Dutch: *laurierboom, bakelaar*
Italian: *lauro franco, lauro poetico, lauro regio, alloro*
Spanish: *laurél común, lauro, bahia*

Portuguese: *loureiro, louro*
Swedish: *lager*
Russian: *lavr*
Chinese: *yueh-kuei*
Japanese: *gekkeiju*
Arabic: *ghār*

Grecian bay, alias laurel, Grecian laurel, or sweet bay, was called *Laurus* by the Romans, but the ultimate derivation of the name is probably from the Celtic *blaur*, or green. In Greek mythology the Grecian bay was personified by the nymph Daphne, who was transformed into a Grecian bay while being pursued by Apollo. In honor of the tree's beauty, Apollo dedicated it to the poets. As a symbol of triumph and the tree of heroes, the leaves of Grecian bay were once used to crown the victors of the Greek Olympic games (*nobilis* means "noble"); the athletes had literally won their "laurels." The genus *Laurus* includes only one other species, *L. azorica* (Seub.) Franco (*L. canariensis* Webb. & Berth, non Willd.), the Canary Island bay/laurel.

Grecian bay is an evergreen tree native to Asia Minor and cultivated extensively throughout the Mediterranean basin for both culinary and ornamental purposes. The herb is easily pruned into hedges or standards.

Grecian bay is used with meats and fish dishes and in sauces, condiments, preserves, pickles, and even pastries. Broken or powdered bay leaves may be used in cooking, but commonly the whole leaf is placed in soups and stews. Be very sure to remove all the bay leaves before serving; while some people think it lucky to find a bay leaf on their plate, individuals have choked to death on bay leaves or died from perforated intestines.

Grecian bay leaves are considered GRAS at 1,000 ppm for the leaves and 200 ppm for the essential oil. The essential oil of Grecian bay shows significant antioxidant activity. Some people are allergic to Grecian bay and break out in a rash around the mouth. The fruits have been used in nonalcoholic beverages, while the oil from the fruits has been used in soap. In case

Laurus nobilis

you're wondering how rats are able to hold their own at the local bar, Japanese researchers found that the sesquiterpenes of bay leaves "potently inhibited" the elevation of blood ethanol level in ethanol-loaded rats. Bay laurel has been found to be both antimutagenic and anticonvulsant. An old folk tale relates that Grecian bay leaves ward off cockroaches. In this case, the old folks were right, according to researchers at Kansas State University.

Grecian bay needs good, friable garden loam in full sun. It prefers warm, humid summers. Because Grecian bay is only marginally hardy to Zone 7, most North Americans find it necessary to grow the bay plants in pots and winter them over indoors on cool, sunny porches or in cool greenhouses at 40 to 50°F (4 to 10°C). Avoid temperatures below 38°F (3°C) and waterlogged soils; repot plants to a larger container every two to three years as they become pot bound. Bays will continue sporadic growth during the winter if day length is extended with supplemental artificial lighting. As new leaves form in spring, older leaves normally turn yellow and drop.

The principal commercial harvests are in autumn, but the home gardener can harvest fresh green leaves as needed. About a half fresh leaf is equal to a whole dried one. If pruning to shape, save the leaves and dry them for later use. One study in Spain found that air-drying at ambient temperature and oven drying at 45°C produced similar results and hardly any loss in volatiles, whereas freezing and freeze-drying brought about substantial losses in bay leaf aroma. Commercial Grecian bay is primarily imported from Spain, Turkey, and Morocco.

In protected spots as far north as Washington, D.C., bays can be successfully overwintered outdoors; it may take some experimentation to find the perfect spot, and in harsh winters the plant will die back like an herbaceous perennial and send up shoots from the roots in May. Nancy Howard of the Herb Society of America even found such a place for her bay tree in her Philadelphia garden. Much more selection could be done to find hardy Grecian bay trees, such as has been done with 'Arp' rosemary.

Grecian bay is easily rooted from cuttings of the suckers that are produced from the base of the plant and from the roots; tip cuttings root unevenly and often take months. In our research, we found the best success with tip cuttings of half-hardened wood (new growth that had stopped and was about ready to grow again) soaked in water for four to six weeks (be sure to change the water every day) and then placed in rooting medium. All rooted within three weeks. Commercial propagation is normally via seeds, which results in an uneven population and considerable variation, and germination is often low. Researchers in Turkey found that removal of both the pericarp (fruit wall) and seed coat significantly increased the germination, probably by removing inhibitors of seed germination.

Variations in Grecian bay have not been fully cataloged. An inventory of wild bay trees in Israel revealed twenty-one distinct varieties. This Israeli researcher found dwarfs with tiny leaves, huge bays with heavy concentrations of dark green leaves, and scents that ranged from an essential oil described as having a "good lemony" aroma to others with almost no odor at all. Below are some of the named cultivars recognized by Voloshin, author of the most recent comprehensive work on Grecian bay. Obviously much more exploration could be done to bring additional variation into cultivation into North America. While *L. nobilis* is a dioecious ("two houses," or separate sexes) species, the sex of the following cultivars is unknown, although male trees are preferred near homes to avoid the fruits, which eventually turn rancid. The cor-rect nomenclature of the cultivars is also confusing and in need of revision.

Cultivar: 'Angustifolia'
Synonyms: var. *angustifolia* Lodd., f. *angustifolia* Mouill., var. *angustifolia* (Nees) Markgr., var. *angustifolia* Batt.
Common English name: narrow-leaved bay
Comments: confused in nursery trade with 'Salicifolia'

Cultivar: 'Aurea'
Synonyms: f. *pallidus* Brizi
Common English name: golden bay
Leaves: yellow-green when grown under relatively cool conditions, particularly influenced by night temperature, otherwise green

Cultivar: 'Borziana'
Synonyms: var. *borziana* Bég.
Common English name: Borzi's bay
Leaves: thin, elongated
Fruit: spherical, large to c. ½ inch (1.5 cm)

Cultivar: 'Cylindrocarpa'
Synonyms: var. *cylindrocarpa* Bég.
Common English name: cylinder-fruited bay
Leaves: egg-shaped
Fruit: cylindrical

Cultivar: 'Eriobotryfolia'
Synonyms: f. *eriobotryfolia* Kalaida
Common English name: loquat-leaved bay

Cultivar: 'Flore Pleno'
Synonyms: var. *flore pleno* Duhamel
Common English name: double-flowered bay

Cultivar: 'Glauca'
Synonyms: f. *glauca* Kalaida
Common English name: glaucous-leaved bay

Cultivar: 'Grandiflora'
Synonyms: f. *grandiflora* Kalaida
Common English name: large-flowered bay

Cultivar: 'Holy Land'
Origin: Israel
Leaves: slightly wavy on edges

Cultivar: 'Latifolia'
Synonyms: var. *latifolia* Duhamel, var. *latifolia*
(Nees) Markgr., f. *latifolia* Mill.
Origin: native to Spain, Italy, and Asia
Common English name: broad-leaved bay
Leaves: broad and smooth
Growth: less hardy than most other varieties

Cultivar: 'Ligustrifolia'
Synonyms: f. *ligustrifolia* Kalaida
Common English name: privet-leaved bay

Cultivar: 'Macrocarpa'
Synonyms: f. *macrocarpa* Kalaida
Common English name: large-fruited bay

Cultivar: 'Macroclada'
Synonyms: var. *macroclada* Giac. & Zanib.
Common English name: large bay
Leaves: rounded apex, tapering to base, stout
Fruit: globular, large, c. ½ inch (1.5 cm)
Growth: growing to great height

Cultivar: 'Mikrocarpa'
Synonyms: f. *mikrocarpa* Kalaida
Common English name: small-fruited bay

Cultivar: 'Multiflora'
Synonyms: f. *multiflora* Kalaida
Common English name: many-flowered bay

Cultivar: 'Nancy Howard'
Origin: garden of Nancy Howard, Wayne,
Pennsylvania

Common English name: Nancy Howard bay
Comments: root hardy to Philadelphia, Pennsylvania

Cultivar: 'Olivaeformis'
Synonyms: f. *olivaeforms* Kalaida
Common English name: olive-fruited bay

Cultivar: 'Ovalifolia'
Synonyms: f. *ovalifolia* Kalaida, var. *cinnamomifolius* Brizi
Common English name: oval-leaved bay

Cultivar: 'Pallida'
Synonyms: var. *pallida* Brizi
Leaves: yellow-green
Fruit: reddish
Growth: shrubby

Cultivar: 'Parvifolia'
Synonyms: var. *parvifolia* D. J. Browne, f.
microphylla Kalaida, 'Microphylla'
Origin: French Caribbean
Common English name: small-leaved bay

Cultivar: 'Pedunculata'
Synonyms: f. *pedunculata* Kalaida
Common English name: pedunculate-flowered bay

Cultivar: 'Rotundifolia'
Origin: mentioned by Theophrastus (371–287
B.C.E.) in his *Enquiry into Plants* (3.17.3)
Synonyms: var. *rotundifolia* Emb. & Maire, f.
rotundifolia Voloshin
Common English name: round-leaved bay
Leaves: wide, mostly round

Cultivar: 'Rubrinervis'
Synonyms: f. *rubrinervis* Kalaida
Common English name: red-veined bay
Leaves: red-veined

Cultivar: 'Salicifolia'
Synonyms: var. *salicifolia* Sweet, 'Tenuifolia'
Common English name: willow-leaf bay
Leaves: narrowly lance-shaped, about 1 to 2.7 inches × ⅔ to ¾ inch (3 to 7 cm × 6 to 20 mm), not as thick as the normal variety and of a lighter green color
Growth: shrub 6 to 8 feet (1.8 to 2.4 m)
Comments: confused in nursery trade with 'Angustifolia'

Culivar name: 'Saso's Dwarf'
Origin: Louis Saso, Saso Herb Gardens, Saratoga, California
Leaves: thick, dark green
Growth: shrubby

Cultivar: 'Sphaerocarpa'
Common English name: ball-fruited bay
Leaves: small, polished
Fruit: spherical

Cultivar: 'Undulata'
Synonyms: var. *undulata* Mill., f. *undulata* Mouill., var. *crispa* (Nees) Markgr. in Hegi
Common English name: wavy-leaved bay
Leaves: margin distinctly undulate
Fruit: egg-shaped
Growth: low shrub seldom higher than 4 to 6 feet (1.2 to 1.8 m)

Cultivar: 'Variegata'
Synonyms: var. *variegata* Sweet
Common English name: gold-striped bay
Leaves: striped gold

In addition to these cultivars, the following cultivars (many originally published as botanical varieties or forms) have been listed in the literature, but relatively little is known about them: 'Baccalia', 'Communis', 'Cypria', 'Delphica', 'Elliptica', 'Ellipticifolia', 'Floribunda', 'Iterophylla', 'Lanceolata', 'Longifolia', 'Minor', 'Mustacen', 'Obscura', 'Pompeiana', 'Pyriformis', 'Regia', 'Subovata', 'Sunspot', 'Sylvatica', and 'Triumphalis'.

Important chemistry: The essential oil of Grecian bay leaves is characterized by 24 to 56 percent 1,8-cineole, 3 to 28 percent alpha-terpinyl acetate or formate, and trace to 11 percent linalool, providing a eucalyptus-like but delicate spicy fragrance. At least eight alpha-methylene gamma-butyrolactones (costunolide, costuslactone, laurenobiolide, deacetyllaurenbioloide, artemorin, verlotorin, santamarin, and reynosin) have been isolated from *L. nobilis* leaves and documented to be the chief causes of allergic contact dermatitis. Ten alkaloids, nine of them aporphines and nor-aporphines, with unknown physiological activity have also been isolated from *L. nobilis* leaves.

Botanical Description

L. nobilis L., Sp. pl. 369. 1753.
Native country: Grecian bay is native to Asia Minor.
General habit: Grecian bay is an evergreen shrub or, more commonly, an evergreen tree, 2 to 20 m high, with erect branches. Shoots are black-red, smooth.
Leaves: Leaves are alternate, narrowly parallel-sided, lance-shaped, pinched at both ends, 5 to 10 × 2 to 7.5 cm, smooth, margins undulate, glossy dark green above.
Flowers: Flowers are dioecious, greenish yellow in axillary clusters.
Fruits/seeds: Fruit is glossy black and olive-like, 10 to 15 mm round.

Lavandula

lå-văn-dū-lå
lavender

Family: Lamiaceae (Labiatae)
Growth form: perennial subshrub
Hardiness: most hardy only to southern California (Zone 9); lavender and lavandin hardy to Pennsylvania (Zone 6)
Light: full sun
Water: moist to somewhat dry, can withstand drought when established
Soil: well-drained gravelly or rocky loam, pH 6.4 to 8.2, average 7.1 (*L. angustifolia*)
Propagation: cuttings in summer, seeds in spring, 25,000 seed per ounce (882/g) (*L. angustifolia*)
Culinary use: some desserts, sugars, liqueurs
Craft use: potpourri, wreaths, dried flowers
Landscape use: effective massed in shrub or perennial border, hedges, edging

The odor of lavender is light and clean; however, its use in baths is relatively new, probably dating from prior to Tudor times. The Romans and Greeks used *L. stoechas* medicinally, but there is no evidence of the use of lavender in baths (the word *Lavandula* is probably derived from the Latin *livere*, to be livid or bluish).

The most economically important lavender has been common lavender, *L. angustifolia*. This is typically a plant of high altitudes, and the floral oil is widely used in finer perfumes. Spike or spike lavender, *L. latifolia*, is normally a plant of low altitudes, and the floral oil is usually used for what are sometimes termed by cosmetic scientists as "coarser vehicles," such as soap. Lavandin, *L.* ×*intermedia*, is a hybrid of common lavender and spike lavenders and has been increasingly substituted for both. "Lavender oil" (including that derived from lavender, lavandin, and spike) is imported primarily from France, but some also comes from Spain and Austria.

Common lavender oil is colorless or pale yellow with a sweet, floral-herbaceous odor and a pleasant, balsamic-woody undertone. The oil evaporates quickly, but it blends well with clove, oakmoss, patchouli, rosemary, clary sage, pine-needle oils, and bergamot and other citrus oils. Lavender and lavandin oils are also used in commercial moth repellents.

This genus includes about twenty species of the Atlantic Islands and the Mediterranean, but only a few have any real herbal uses. The remaining species are tender perennials and not hardy outside of southern California. This is another good genus to collect—both the species and cultivars.

Lavandula ×*allardii*

lå-văn-dū-lå å-lăr-dĭ-ī
fringed lavender, heterophylla lavender

This hybrid (*L. dentata* × *L. latifolia*), often sold as *L.* ×*heterophylla*, easily withstands the hot summers of the deep southern United States. Fringed lavender is very similar to lavandin in appearance but can be distinguished by (1) occasional toothed leaves at the base, (2) flowers which are scented of camphor and eucalyptus rather than lavender, and (3) lack of hardiness north of about Zone 8.

Goodwin Creek Gardens of Williams, Oregon, has introduced 'Goodwin Creek Grey', apparently a hybrid, *L. dentata* × *L. lanata* (*L. ×ginginsii* Upson & S. Andrews), with fuzzier foliage. In the north, both fringed lavender and 'Goodwin Creek Grey' are excellent in window boxes and large pots and often flower all summer long. Other cultivars in this hybrid series with *L. dentata* include 'African Pride', 'Antipodes', 'Anzac Pride', 'Derwent Grey', 'Devantville-Cuche', 'Jurat's Giant', 'Magella', and 'Silver Streak'.

The oil of fringed lavender may promote wound healing.

Important chemistry: The essential oil of the flowers is dominated by 34 percent 1,8-cineole and 12 percent camphor.

Lavandula angustifolia

lå-văn-dū-lå ăn-gŭs-tĭ-fō-lē-å
common lavender, true lavender

French: *lavande*
German: *Lavendel*
Dutch: *lavendel*
Italian: *lavanda vera, nardo, spigo*
Spanish: *espliego, lavandula, alhucema, alhucemilla*
Portuguese: *alfazema, rosmaninho, lavanda*
Swedish: *lavendel*
Russian: *lavanda*

Lavender is essential for many potpourris, and in the herb garden, roses and lavenders just seem to be made for each other. Lavenders make good edgings, and their blooms, draping over walkways, are a delight to brush against. Lavender attracts bees, so watch out if you are allergic to bee stings. The numerous cultivars of common lavender vary in flower color, height, vigor, and scent, and more seem to be introduced every year. Named lavender clones can be propagated only by cuttings or layers. Seed propagation introduces new variations that are not true to type; seed from 'Hidcote' lavender, for instance, will not yield 'Hidcote' lavender but only 'Hidcote'-derived lavender.

The overall flower color is derived from both the calyx and corolla. The most attractive floral colors, the whites, pinks, and dark aster violets, are, unfortunately, often borne on the weakest plants. It would be impossible, given the limited space, to fully describe all the cultivars of lavender, and so the reader is directed to *The Genus Lavandula* by Tim Upson and Susyn Andrews (2004); we have only listed some of the most popular cultivars here. In the following characterizations, "dwarf" refers to a vegetative plant after two years at around 4 to 6 inches (10 to 15

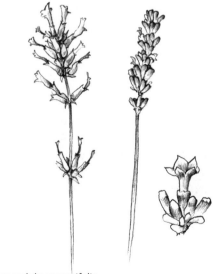

Lavandula angustifolia

cm) high, 9 to 12 inches (23 to 31 cm) high for flowering plant; "semi-dwarf" refers to a vegetative plant after two years at around 7 to 13¾ inches (18 to 35 cm) high, 15 to 20 inches (38 to 51 cm) high for a flowering plant; and "tall" refers to a vegetative plant after two years at around 8 to 24 inches (20 to 61 cm) high, 27 to 46 inches (69 to 117 cm) for a flowering plant.

Cultivar: 'Alba'
Origin: pre-1580
Hardiness: Zone 8?
Growth: semi-dwarf
Flowers: white corollas, sage-green calyces
Comments: very rare in cultivation; prone to sudden wilts in hot, humid climates

Cultivar: 'Avice Hill'
Synonyms: 'Impression'
Origin: Avice Hill, Christchurch, New Zealand, 1980, first in trade 1997
Hardiness: Zone 6?
Flowers: large violet-blue corollas, dark violet calyces
Comments: flowers all summer long

Cultivar: 'Backhouse Purple'
Synonyms: 'Backhouse', 'Backhouse Nana'
Origin: Messrs. James Backhouse & Co., York, England, 1888
Hardiness: Zone 6?
Growth: tall
Flowers: mid violet corollas, very dark purple calyces
Comments: very rare in cultivation

Cultivar: 'Blue Mountain'
Origin: Stan Hughes, Central Otago, New Zealand, mid 1950s
Hardiness: Zone 6?
Growth: compact

Flowers: vibrant violet corollas, dark violet calyces
Comments: good for hedging

Cultivar: 'Bowles Early'
Synonyms: 'Bowles Variety', 'Bowles Early Dwarf', 'Miss Donnington'/'Miss Dunnington'
Origin: given to Mr. Edward Augustus Bowles by Miss Dunnington; introduced by Mr. Amos Perry, Enfield, England, 1913
Hardiness: Zone 6?
Growth: tall
Flowers: dark violet-blue corollas, mid violet calyces
Comments: offered as 'Munstead' in the Netherlands; very rare outside England and the Netherlands

Cultivar: 'Buena Vista'
Origin: Donald Roberts, Albany, Oregon, 1981
Hardiness: Zone 6?
Flowers: bright violet-blue corollas, very dark purple calyces
Essential oil: 34 percent linalyl acetate, 31 percent linalool, 11 percent terpinen-4-ol

Cultivar: 'Carolyn Dille'
Synonyms: 'Sleeping Beauty'
Origin: Thomas DeBaggio, Arlington, Virginia, 1988
Hardiness: Zone 6?
Flowers: lavender-blue
Comments: as flower spike develops, the pointed head is bent over as if nodding but straightens up as buds begin to color

Cultivar: 'Compacta'
Synonyms: 'Nana Compacta'
Origin: U.S.A., pre-1901

Hardiness: Zone 6?
Growth: semi-dwarf
Flowers: bright violet-blue corollas, mostly dark violet calyces
Essential oil: 35 to 37 percent linalyl acetate, 20 to 22 percent linalool, 10 percent terpinen-4-ol
Comments: usually offered as 'Munstead' in the United States but is much more vigorous and bears lavender-blue rather than dark aster violet flowers

Cultivar: 'Croxton's Wild'
Origin: Europe via Pauline Croxton, 1994
Hardiness: Zone 5?
Growth: semi-dwarf
Flowers: lavender-blue
Essential oil: 36 percent linalyl acetate, 2 to 33 percent linalool, 15 to 18 percent terpinen-4-ol
Comments: very hardy with a pleasantly mounded shape

Cultivar: 'Dwarf Blue'
Synonyms: 'Blue Dwarf', 'New Dwarf Blue', 'Baby Blue', 'Hardy Dwarf', 'Nana'
Origin: Bussum, Netherlands, c. 1911
Hardiness: Zone 6?
Growth: semi-dwarf
Flowers: vibrant soft violet corollas, mid to soft violet calyces
Essential oil: 50 percent linalool, 17 percent linalyl acetate, 11 percent terpinen-4-ol
Comments: rare in cultivation

Cultivar: 'Folgate'
Synonyms: 'Colgate Blue', 'Folgate Blue', 'Folgate Variety'
Origin: Linn Chilvers, Norfolk, England, pre-1933
Hardiness: Zone 6?
Growth: tall

Flowers: vibrant violet corollas, dark violet calyces
Comments: rare in cultivation; a selection of *L. ×intermedia* has also been offered under this name

Cultivar: 'Graves'
Hardiness: Zone 5?
Growth: semi-dwarf
Flowers: lavender-blue
Essential oil: 34 percent linalool, 29 percent terpinen-4-ol plus lavandulyl acetate

Cultivar: 'Gray Lady'
Origin: J. J. Grullemans, Wayside Gardens, Mentor, Ohio, pre-1967
Hardiness: Zone 5?
Growth: semi-dwarf
Flowers: mid violet corollas, dark violet calyces
Essential oil: 46 percent linalool, 18 percent linalyl acetate, 12 percent terpinen-4-ol
Comments: rare in cultivation

Cultivar: 'Gwendolyn Anley'
Origin: Mrs. B. L. Anley, St. George's, Woking, Surrey, England; introduced by G. Jackman & Sons, Surrey, pre-1962
Hardiness: Zone 6?
Growth: tall
Flowers: lavender-blue
Comments: very rare in cultivation

Cultivar: 'Helen Batchelder'
Origin: Helen Batchelder, Rumford, Rhode Island via Well-Sweep Herb Farm, Port Murray, New Jersey
Hardiness: Zone 6?
Growth: semi-dwarf and very compact
Flowers: bright violet-blue corollas, dark violet calyces
Comments: good hedge material and produces a good mounded shape

Cultivar: 'Hidcote'
Synonyms: 'Hidcote Variety', 'Hidcote Blue', 'Hidcote Purple'
Origin: Major Lawrence Johnston, Hidcote Manor, Gloucester, England, pre-1949
Hardiness: Zone 6?
Growth: dwarf
Flowers: mid violet corollas, dark violet calyces
Essential oil: 57 percent linalyl acetate
Comments: sometimes confused with 'Nana Atropurpurea'; excellent dark color but prone to sudden wilts in hot, humid climates; often propagated from seed by careless herb growers

Cultivar: 'Hidcote Pink'
Origin: Major Lawrence Johnston, Hidcote Manor, Gloucester, England, pre-1957
Hardiness: Zone 6?
Growth: semi-dwarf
Flowers: pale pink-mauve corollas, greenish white calyces
Comments: similar to 'Rosea' except for the leaves, which are slightly more narrow and gray but otherwise not significantly different; prone to sudden wilts in hot, humid climates

Cultivar: 'Irene Doyle'
Synonyms: 'Two Seasons'
Origin: Thomas DeBaggio, Arlington, Virginia, 1981
Growth: semi-dwarf
Hardiness: Zone 6?
Flowers: vibrant violet corollas, very dark purple calyces
Essential oil: 29 to 41 percent linalyl acetate, 21 to 24 percent linalool
Comments: usually flowers twice in one season

Cultivar: 'Lady'
Origin: W. Atlee Burpee & Co., Warminster, Pennsylvania, 1993

Flowers: usually violet-blue corollas, dark violet calyces but very variable
Comments: flowers first year from seed but very variable in growth pattern and hardiness and otherwise unexceptional

Cultivar: 'Loddon Blue'
Origin: Thomas Carlile, Loddon Nurseries, Berkshire, England, pre-1963
Hardiness: Zone 6?
Growth: tall
Flowers: vibrant violet corollas, dark violet calyces
Comments: similar to 'Hidcote' but flowers are slightly less vivid and growth is taller; plants prone to sudden wilts in hot, humid climates

Cultivar: 'Maillette'
Origin: M. Maillet, Valensole, France, pre-1959
Hardiness: Zone 6?
Growth: semi-dwarf
Flowers: dark violet-blue corollas, mostly very soft purple calyces
Essential oil: 35 percent linalyl acetate, 45 percent linalool
Comments: a commercial French cultivar; may exist in five similar, closely related clones

Cultivar: 'Melissa'
Origin: Van Hevelingen Herb Nursery, Newberg, Oregon, 1994, in trade 1999
Hardiness: Zone 6?
Growth: semi-dwarf
Flowers: off-pink corollas, hints of dark pink or purple in calyces, very woolly
Essential oil: 28 to 34 percent linalyl acetate, 22 to 26 percent terpinen-4-ol, 14 to 15 percent linalool
Comments: prone to sudden wilts in hot, humid climates

Cultivar: 'Middachten'
Origin: Middachten, Rheden, Netherlands, by Moerheim, Dedemsvaart, pre-1923
Hardiness: Zone 6?
Growth: semi-dwarf
Flowers: violet-blue corollas, very dark purple calyces
Comments: plants weak and difficult to root; rare outside the Netherlands

Cultivar: 'Mitcham Grey'
Origin: selection of 'Nana Atropurpurea', pre-1978
Hardiness: Zone 6?
Growth: semi-dwarf
Flowers: dark violet corollas, very dark purple calyces
Essential oil: 55 percent linalyl acetate
Comments: prone to sudden wilts in hot, humid climates

Cultivar: 'Munstead'
Synonyms: 'Dwarf Munstead', 'Munstead Blue', 'Munstead Variety'
Origin: Gertrude Jekyll, Munstead Wood, Surrey, England; introduced by Barr, 1902
Hardiness: Zone 5?
Growth: semi-dwarf
Flowers: mid violet corollas, dark violet calyces
Essential oil: 33 to 51 percent linalool, 9 to 23 percent linalyl acetate, 10 to 17 percent terpinen-4-ol
Comments: 'Compacta' is usually offered as this cultivar, but the true 'Munstead' has dark aster violet flowers similar to those of 'Hidcote'

Cultivar: 'Nana Alba'
Synonyms: 'Baby White', 'Dwarf White'
Origin: England, 1928
Hardiness: Zone 6?
Growth: dwarf

Flowers: pure white corollas, pale green calyces
Essential oil: 32 to 36 percent linalyl acetate, 10 to 25 percent linalool, and 15 to 23 percent terpinen-4-ol
Comments: delicate and prone to sudden wilts in hot, humid climates; there are two clones in cultivation under this name

Cultivar: 'Nana Atropurpurea'
Origin: pre-1912
Hardiness: Zone 6?
Growth: dwarf
Flowers: vibrant violet corollas, violet calyces
Essential oil: 26 percent linalyl acetate, 25 percent linalool, 14 percent terpinen-4-ol
Comments: very similar to 'Hidcote' but the flowers are paler and less hairy; prone to sudden wilts in hot, humid climates

Cultivar: 'Pacific Blue'
Synonyms: '565/6'
Origin: France via New Zealand, mid 1990s
Flowers: mid violet corollas, very dark purple calyces
Comments: suitable for cutting

Cultivar: 'Pastor's Pride'
Origin: Rev. Douglas Seidel, Emmaus, Pennsylvania
Hardiness: Zone 6?
Growth: semi-dwarf
Flowers: lavender-blue
Essential oil: 35 percent linalyl acetate, 33 percent linalool, 12 percent terpinen-4-ol
Comments: often flowers twice a year

Cultivar: 'Premier'
Origin: Donald Roberts, Albany, Oregon, 1990
Hardiness: Zone 6?
Flowers: medium lavender-blue

Essential oil: 37 percent linalyl acetate, 19 percent linalool, 12 percent terpinen-4-ol

Cultivar: 'Rosea'
Synonyms: 'Jean Davis', 'Loddon Pink', 'Munstead Pink'
Origin: England, pre-1937
Hardiness: Zone 6?
Growth: semi-dwarf
Flowers: off-pink corollas, purplish green calyces
Essential oil: 34 to 47 percent linalool, 21 to 28 percent terpinen-4-ol, 10 to 11 percent linalyl acetate
Comments: good pink color but prone to sudden wilts in warm, humid climates

Cultivar: 'Royal Purple'
Origin: Linn Chilvers, Norfolk Lavender, 1944
Growth: semi-dwarf
Flowers: violet-blue corollas, dark violet calyces
Essential oil: 31 percent linalool, 27 percent linalyl acetate, 16 percent terpinen-4-ol
Comments: similar to 'Twickel Purple'

Cultivar: 'Royal Velvet'
Origin: England via Van Hevelingen Herb Nursery, Newberg, Oregon, 1980s
Hardiness: Zone 6?
Growth: semi-dwarf
Flowers: violet-blue corollas, soft violet calyces
Comments: best cultivar for dark purple dried wands that do not shatter but prone to sudden wilts in hot, humid climates

Cultivar: 'Sharon Roberts'
Origin: Donald Roberts, Albany, Oregon, 1989
Hardiness: Zone 6?
Flowers: bright violet-blue corollas, dark violet calyces

Essential oil: 41 percent linalyl acetate, 30 percent linalool
Comments: excellent recurrent blooms

Cultivar: 'Summerland Supreme'
Origin: N. May, C.D.A. Research Station, Summerland, British Columbia, Canada, 1930
Hardiness: Zone 6?
Growth: semi-dwarf
Flowers: bright violet-blue corollas, dark violet calyces
Essential oil: 48 percent linlyl acetate, 22 percent linalool, 12 percent terpinen-4-ol
Comments: delicate and very prone to sudden wilts in hot, humid climates

Cultivar: 'Tucker's Early Purple'
Origin: Thomas DeBaggio, Arlington, Virginia, 1993
Hardiness: Zone 6?
Growth: semi-dwarf
Flowers: dark violet-blue corollas, violet calyces
Essential oil: 40 percent linalyl acetate, 27 percent linalool, 11 percent terpinen-4-ol
Comments: long blooming season

Cultivar: 'Twickel Purple'
Origin: Kasteel Twickel, Delden, Netherlands, pre-1922
Hardiness: Zone 6?
Growth: semi-dwarf
Flowers: vibrant violet corollas, mid violet-mauve calyces
Essential oil: 34 percent linalyl acetate, 26 percent linalool
Comments: a selection of *L. ×intermedia* has also been offered under this name

Cultivar: 'W. K. Doyle'
Synonyms: 'Dark Supreme'

Origin: Thomas DeBaggio, Arlington, Virginia, 1987
Hardiness: Zone 6?
Growth: semi-dwarf
Flowers: electric blue-violet corollas, dark violet calyces
Essential oil: 21 percent linalyl acetate, 21 percent linalool, 14 percent terpinen-4-ol
Comments: often flowers twice in one season; prone to sudden wilts in hot, humid climates

Cultivar: 'Wyckoff'
Origin: L. J. Wyckoff, Washington, pre-1951
Hardiness: Zone 6?
Flowers: vibrant violet-blue corollas, dark violet calyces

Lavender must have full sun and excellent soil and air drainage to avoid sudden wilts (usually due to phytophthora infections of the roots) during hot, humid weather. Light colored mulches such as sand or gravel will also produce sturdier plants more resistant to sudden wilts. Lavenders grown in shade or with dark-colored mulches in the eastern United States or any climate with consistent cloud cover inevitably succumb to sudden wilts, grow spindly, and give poor fragrance. A mulch with oyster shells has been found beneficial in the climate of the Pacific Northwest. Soil pH is best near neutral; around pH 7.0 is recommended. Lavenders can also have their oil production modified and/or reduced by infection with alfalfa mosaic virus.

Lavenders that reseed unassisted signal that growing conditions are excellent. If lavender is grown from seed, moist prechilling of 37.4 to 41°F (3 to 5°C) for about one month, alone or in combination with 200 ppm gibberellic acid, results in significantly higher germination.

For forcing lavender as a flowering perennial in pots, researchers at Michigan State University have outlined the production schedule by working with seed-propagated 'Compacta' (designated 'Munstead' in their publication) and seed-propagated 'Hidcote'. 'Compacta' seedlings should be grown under natural photoperiods until they have at least forty to fifty leaves (twenty to twenty-five nodes). Plants are then subjected to at least ten weeks at 40°F (5°C) under lights; the researchers used nine hours per day with cool-white fluorescent lamps of approximately 50 footcandles.

The study showed that the flowering percentage in plants that were cooled for ten weeks increases when subsequently forced under night-interruption (NI) long days (LD), while plants cooled for fifteen weeks can be forced under natural day lengths. If plants are cooled for fewer than fifteen weeks or overwintered in a greenhouse where temperatures periodically become warm, they should be forced under LD for most rapid, uniform flowering.

LD can be provided by extending the natural day length to sixteen hours or by night-break lighting for four hours from 10 p.m. to 2 a.m. Incandescent, high-pressure sodium, cool-white fluorescent, and metal halide lamps all work if they provide a minimum light intensity of 10 footcandles. When using incandescent lamps, about 1.5 watts of lamp per square foot is required.

Lighting should be provided from the start of forcing until flower buds are visible. 'Hidcote' lavender, however, requires LD even after fifteen weeks of cold treatment; provide LD for at least three weeks from the start of flowering until flower buds are visible. Throughout, grow plants on the dry side. To keep the inflorescence more compact, apply growth retardants when shoot elongation begins (about a week before flower buds are visible).

Seed propagation, however, is recommended only to create new lavenders, as the named cultivars are asexually propagated clones. Fortunately, lavender roots easily with late spring and early summer cuttings treated with rooting hormone in flats of 1 part perlite to 1 part Turface® (clay frit) in 50 percent shade; no mist or plastic tarp is required (and either may actually result in rotting, depending upon local conditions). Layers are very easy any time of the year. Merely scrape the bark off near the base of a long stem, apply rooting hormone, bend the stem down, and cover with soil, pegging the stem down with a V bent from a wire coat hanger.

Oil yield from the flowers is maximum from mid to late bloom, or starting when about one-half of the blossoms are open. Lavender oil is considered GRAS at 20 ppm. Lavender oil is commonly used in aromatherapy, and inhalation of lavender vapors produces an anticonvulsive effect and reduces anxiety. Lavender oil is synergistic with tea tree [*Melaleuca alternifolia* (Maiden & Betche) Cheel] oil to treat tinea and onychomycosis (fungal infection of the toenails or fingernails and sometimes hair), as well as candida. While lavender oil is commonly used in massage for its sedative and relaxing effects, in addition to anti-inflammatory properties, the oil can sometimes cause allergic rashes with repeated handling (especially in conjunction with heat and light). Lavender oil may also benefit individuals with dementia. The evidence linking lavender to prepubertal gynecomastia (breast development in male children) is specious, as this condition was linked to a commercial product with lavender and tea tree, and the constituents of the commercial product were not tested individually (the reader is directed to the comments by Dr. Brian Lawrence, cited in the literature). Lavender oil also kills mites.

Important chemistry: Commercial lavender oil, distilled from the flowers, has 28 to 49 percent linalool and 12 to 45 percent linalyl acetate.

Lavandula dentata
lå-văn-dū-lå děn-tā-tå
dentate lavender

The dentate, fringed-leaf, or coarse-toothed lavender is not hardy north of Zone 9. An attractive variegated selection, 'Linda Ligon' ('Herb Companion'), was introduced by Thomas De-Baggio, Arlington, Virginia. Dentate lavender is an excellent choice for window boxes and large pots. The pale green, deeply toothed foliage blends well with the pale lavender flowers and showy bracts. See *L.* ×*allardii* for a brief discussion of hybrids of this species with *L. lanata* and *L. latifolia*.

Important chemistry: The essential oil of the flowers is dominated by 17 to 58 percent 1,8-cineole, providing a eucalyptus-like fragrance.

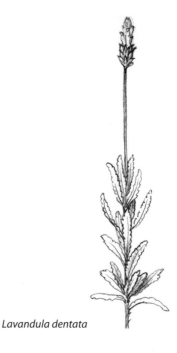

Lavandula dentata

Lavandula ×*intermedia*

lå-văn-dū-lå ĭn-tĕr-mē-dē-å
lavandin

French: *lavandin*
Italian: *lavandino*

Lavandin is an intermediate hybrid of common lavender and spike, combining characteristics of both parents in a plant that displays hybrid vigor. Both growth and flowering are, as the specific name implies, intermediate between *L. angustifolia* and *L. latifolia*. Lavandins are exceptionally resistant to sudden wilts, and their greater heights over lavender make them appropriate for hedging; their ability to hold their leaves and leaf-color through cold winters recommends them for landscaping uses. The essential oil of 'Grosso' lavandin has antiplatelet and antithrombic activities.

Many cultivars are available, all in lavender-blue except for one white-flowered cultivar. It would be impossible, given the limited space, to fully describe all the cultivars of lavandin, and so once again the reader is directed to *The Genus Lavandula* by Tim Upson and Susyn Andrews (2004); we have listed only some of the most popular cultivars here. Because the lavandins are usually seed-sterile, propagation must be by cuttings or layers.

Cultivar: 'Abrialii'
Synonyms: 'Abrialis', 'Abriali'
Origin: Claude Abrial, France, pre-1935
Hardiness: Zone 6?
Growth: tall
Flowers: mid violet corollas, dark violet calyces
Essential oil: 30 to 38 percent linalool, 19 to 33 percent linalyl acetate
Comments: once the chief commercial lavandin; many French plantings were decimated by a mycoplasm

Cultivar: 'Dutch'
Synonyms: *L. vera*, *L. hortensis*, *L. spica*, 'Early Dutch', 'Dutch Mill'
Origin: pre-1917
Hardiness: Zone 6?
Growth: tall
Flowers: bright violet-blue corollas, dark violet calyces
Essential oil: 28 to 34 percent linalool, 20 to 21 percent 1,8-cineole
Comments: probably the most common lavandin in the United States, England, and the Netherlands; the bloom is sometimes unreliable

Cultivar: 'Edelweiss'
Synonyms: 'Alba' (in part), 'Caty Blanc'
Origin: Europe, 1980s
Hardiness: Zone 6?
Growth: tall
Flowers: pure white corollas, soft mauve calyces

Cultivar: 'Grappenhall'
Synonyms: 'Giant Grappenhall', 'Grappenhall Variety'

Lavandula ×*intermedia*

Origin: Messrs. Clibran, Altricham, England, c. 1902
Hardiness: Zone 6?
Growth: the tallest
Flowers: dark violet corollas, light green calyces suffused with violet
Essential oil: 34 percent linalool, 22 percent 1,8-cineole
Comments: the clone currently cultivated in the United States fits the original descriptions of an early flowering, tall, vigorous lavender of the 'Mitcham' type

Cultivar: 'Grosso'
Synonyms: 'Fat Spike', 'Dilly Dilly'
Origin: Pierre Grosso, Vaucluse District, France, c. 1972
Hardiness: Zone 6?
Growth: tall
Flowers: mid to soft violet corollas, very dark purple and mauve-violet calyces
Essential oil: 29 to 37 percent linalyl acetate, 21 to 32 percent linalool
Comments: this commercial lavandin resists the mycoplasm that decimates many plantings

Cultivar: 'Hidcote Giant'
Origin: Major Lawrence Johnston, Hidcote Manor, Gloucester, England, pre-1957
Hardiness: Zone 6?
Growth: tall
Flowers: vibrant violet corollas, mid violet calyces
Essential oil: 31 to 34 percent linalyl acetate, 32 to 36 percent linalool
Comments: good fragrance, similar to commercial lavandins

Cultivar: 'Hidcote White'
Synonyms: 'Alba', 'White Spikes'
Origin: pre-1880

Hardiness: Zone 6?
Growth: tall
Flowers: pearly white corollas, sage-green calyces
Comments: 'Alba' is apt to be confused with *L. angustifolia* 'Alba', so the earliest synonym, 'Hidcote White', is preferred

Cultivar: 'Impress Purple'
Synonyms: 'Arabian Night', '41/70'
Origin: France via New Zealand, 1983
Flowers: vibrant violet corollas, very dark purple calyces

Cultivar: 'Old English'
Synonyms: *L. spica* (misapplied)
Origin: Herb Farm, Seal, United Kingdom, pre-1917
Hardiness: Zone 6?
Growth: very tall
Flowers: bright violet-blue corollas, very dark purple calyces
Comments: rare in cultivation

Cultivar: 'Provence'
Synonyms: 'Du Provence'
Origin: possibly Canada, mid 1950s
Hardiness: Zone 6?
Growth: tall
Flowers: lavender-violet corollas, dark purple calyces
Essential oil: 35 to 36 percent linalool, 3 to 23 percent linalyl acetate, 7 to 12 percent terpinen-4-ol
Comments: not a commercial source of lavandin oil, despite the claims in catalogs!

Cultivar: 'Seal'
Synonyms: 'Seal 7 Oaks'
Origin: Miss D. G. Hewer, Hitchin, England; introduced by The Herb Farm, Seal, Kent, England, pre-1935

Hardiness: Zone 6?
Growth: tall
Flowers: dark violet-blue corollas, very dark purple to dark purple calyces
Essential oil: 34 to 41 percent linalool, 23 to 27 percent 1,8-cineole

Cultivar: 'Super'
Synonyms: 'Arabian Night'
Origin: Chiris, Grasse, France, c. 1956
Hardiness: Zone 6?
Growth: tall
Flowers: mid violet corollas, soft dark violet calyces
Essential oil: 33 to 47 percent linalyl acetate, 27 to 34 percent linalool
Comments: a commercial French cultivar

Cultivar: 'Walvera'
Synonyms: 'Warberton's Silver Edge', 'Silver Edge'
Origin: Tim Crowther, Walberton Nursery, Arundel, West Sussex, England, c. 1987–1993 as a sport of 'Pale Pretender'; patented in 2002 (U.S. PP13,091)

Growth: tall
Flowers: violet-blue corollas, very dark purple calyces
Essential oil: 28 percent linalool, 22 percent 1,8-cineole
Comments: the first recorded variegated lavandin

Cultivar: 'Yuulong'
Origin: from seed supplied by Van Dijk & Co., Netherlands, via Yuulong Lavender Estate, Australia, 1986
Flowers: bright violet-blue corollas, very dark purple calyces
Comments: does particularly well in Queensland, Australia

Important chemistry: Commercial lavandin oil, distilled from the flowers, has 32 to 47 percent linalool, 17 to 42 percent linalyl acetate, and 6 to 12 percent 1,8-cineole. Lavandin oil is considered GRAS at 0.3 to 18 ppm.

Lavandula lanata
lå-văn-dū-lå lå-nå-tå
woolly lavender

The woolly lavender is very similar to spike except that it is less hardy and more prone to sudden wilts in hot, humid climates. In near desert conditions of Zone 9, where woolly lavender is hardy, it makes an excellent accent in the gar-den with its fuzzy, gray foliage. In the north, woolly lavender can be grown in pots, but don't expect a long life from this plant. See *L. ×allardii* for a brief discussion of hybrids of this species with *L. dentata*.

Important chemistry: The essential oil of woolly lavender is dominated by 43 to 59 percent camphor, 3 to 29 percent lavandulol, and 2 to 12 percent 1,8-cineole.

Lavandula latifolia
lå-văn-dū-lå låt-ĭ-fō-lē-å
spike, spike lavender

French: *lavande aspic, grande lavande (ordinaire)*
German: *Spik-Lavendel, Blauer Lavendel*
Dutch: *spijk-lavendel*
Italian: *lavanda spigo*
Spanish: *espliego, espigol, alhucena*
Portuguese: *alfazema brava*

Lavandula latifolia

The scientific name *latifolia* refers to the plant's broad leaves. While common lavender blooms in early summer, spike provides late summer flowers in Zone 7b—and what a mass of bloom, almost 4 feet (1.2 m) high and wide! The odor of the flowers, though, is very eucalyptus-like, not the sweet fragrance of common lavender, and the flowers are paler in color. Spike is the other parent of lavandin, along with common lavender. If some late flowers appear on 'Rosea' and other cultivars of lavender, as they do in some seasons, try creating your own lavandins.

Spike oil is considered GRAS (Generally Recognized As Safe) by the U.S. Food and Drug Administration at 10 to 50 ppm. The most common uses of spike oil are as a pigment vehicle in china painting and for scenting soaps.

Researchers in Japan and Paraguay have ascertained that topically applied crude drug "Alhucema" (*L. latifolia*) has anti-inflammatory effects due to coumarin, 7-methoxycoumarin, *trans*-phytol, and caryophyllene oxide.

Important chemistry: The essential oil of the flowers of spike is dominated by 15 to 55 percent linalool and 19 to 36 percent 1,8-cineole, providing a eucalyptus-lavender fragrance.

Lavandula multifida
lå-văn-dū-lå mŭl-tĭf-ĭ-då
fernleaf lavender

Fernleaf lavender is a tender perennial hardy only to Zone 9 but comes true from seed and is easily grown. Today, in the North American nursery trade, *L. pinnata* is usually substituted for this species, so don't trust the label! Fernleaf lavender seems to set out dark lavender blossoms almost continuously, and the fuzzy, deeply

divided leaves are excellent accents in window boxes and pots. Fernleaf lavender is rather short-lived, generally not more than one or two years in pots, but it often reseeds itself; be sure to save the occasional seedlings that appear at the base of the plant. The scent is very camphoraceous.

Important chemistry: The essential oil of the entire flowering plant is dominated by 18 to 60 percent carvacrol, 3 to 28 percent beta-bisabolene, and trace to 14 percent camphor.

Lavandula pedunculata

lå-văn-dū-lå pĕ-dŭn-cū-lå-tå
butterfly lavender

> **French:** *lavande papillon*
> **Spanish:** *cantueso*
> **Portuguese:** *rosmarinho-major*

Butterfly lavender is often listed as a subspecies of *L. stoechas*, which it resembles closely. It is very variable, with five subspecies. It would be impossible, given the limited space, to fully describe all the cultivars of butterfly lavender; for more details, see *The Genus Lavandula* by Tim Upson and Susyn Andrews (2004).

Cultivar: 'Atlas'
Origin: California, late 1980s
Hardiness: Zone 7b?
Flowers: dark purplish black with rich indigo-purple bracts

Foliage: grayish green
Comments: similar to *L. stoechas* 'Otto Quast' but taller and more upright, with narrower leaves

Cultivar: 'James Compton'
Origin: Jamie Compton, southern Spain, c. 1979
Flowers: dark purple black, large; flaring violet bracts
Foliage: greenish gray

Cultivar: 'Purple Crown'
Origin: Andy and Sonja Cameron, Cameron's Nursery, Arcadia, New South Wales, Australia, 1993
Growth: tall, to over 3 feet (1 m)
Flowers: corollas dark violet; bracts pink
Foliage: greenish gray

Lavandula stoechas

lå-văn-dū-lå stē-kăs
French lavender

> **French:** *lavande stéchas, lavande chevelure, lavande à stechade, stoechade arabique*
> **German:** *Schopflavendel*
> **Dutch:** *pruiklavendel*
> **Italian:** *steca, stigadosso*
> **Spanish:** *cantueso, azaya, estecados*
> **Portuguese:** *alfazema, rosmaninho*

French lavender derives its scientific name, *stoechas*, from the Stoechades, now the Îles d'Hyères off the southern coast of France near Toulon.

French lavender is often hardy to Zone 7b. Growth is spreading, gradually forming a

Lavandula stoechas

groundcover about 6 inches (15 cm) high. The tiny dark purple blossoms are borne in a cone-like spike and are usually capped with a purple butterfly-like "flag" of sterile bracts. The size of the bracts varies among seedlings, and some named cultivars with exceptionally large bracts are gradually appearing on the market. This is a variable species, with two subspecies. Listed below are a few French lavender cultivars, including hybrids of *L. stoechas* and *L. pedunculata* with *L. viridis*; for more, see *The Genus Lavandula* by Tim Upson and Susyn Andrews (2004).

Cultivar: 'Avonview'
Origin: Ross King, Auckland, New Zealand, 1992, as a hybrid with *L. viridis*
Hardiness: Zone 7b?
Flowers: dark blue-black corollas; fertile bracts electric-mauve with splash of green up the center; long, broad, electric-mauve sterile bracts; large, impressive spikes on long peduncles

Cultivar: 'Evelyn Cadzow'
Origin: Geoff and Adair Genge, Marshwood Gardens, Invercargill, New Zealand, c. 1992, as *L. stoechas* × *L. viridis*
Hardiness: Zone 7b?
Growth: miniature version of *L. pedunculata*
Flowers: dark purple-black corollas; fertile bracts reddish purple and green; mid reddish purple sterile bracts
Foliage: bright green

Cultivar: 'Helmsdale'
Origin: Geoff and Adair Genge, Marshwood Gardens, Invercargill, New Zealand, c. 1991, as *L. stoechas* × *L. viridis*
Hardiness: 7b?
Growth: bushy
Flowers: dark violet-blue corollas, overall appearance of burgundy; fertile bracts reddish purple, sterile bracts dark purple with centers of very dark purple
Foliage: grayish green

Cultivar: 'Kew Red'
Origin: Spain, 1991
Flowers: mid to reddish purple corollas, fertile bracts green and heavily flushed with reddish purple, sterile bracts off-white to pale pink with reddish midribs and veins
Foliage: mid green to gray-green

Cultivar: 'Marshwood'
Origin: Geoff and Adair Genge, Marshwood Gardens, Invercargill, New Zealand, late 1980s, as *L. stoechas* × *L. viridis*
Hardiness: Zone 7b?
Flowers: very dark purple corollas; fertile bracts green tinged burgundy-purple; long, mid mauve-pink sterile bracts
Foliage: grayish green

Cultivar: 'Otto Quast'
Synonyms: 'Otto Quasti', 'Otto's Quest', 'Otto Quastii', 'Quastii' (misspellings)
Origin: Otto Quast, Point Reyes Station, California, early 1980s, as *L. stoechas* × *L. viridis*
Hardiness: Zone 7b?
Flowers: dark purple-black corollas with large, butterfly-like sterile bracts that are dark purple-mauve

Cultivar: 'Pippa'
Origin: George Rainey, North Island, New Zealand, 1991, as *L. stoechas* × *L. viridis*
Hardiness: Zone 7b?
Growth: upright
Flowers: change color with age; electric dark blue corollas; fertile bracts green tinged with reddish veining; purple sterile bracts

Cultivar: 'Pippa White'
Origin: Peter Carter, South Auckland, New Zealand, 1992, as *L. stoechas* × *L. viridis*
Hardiness: 7b?
Flowers: purple corollas; fertile bracts green; peduncles long and hairy
Foliage: greenish gray

Cultivar: 'Plum'
Origin: Terry Hatch, Auckland, New Zealand, 1992, as *L. stoechas* × *L. viridis*
Hardiness: Zone 7b?
Growth: bushy
Flowers: dark purple corollas; reddish purple bracts

Cultivar: 'Pukehou'
Origin: Pukehou Nursery, Manukau, New Zealand, 1994, as *L. stoechas* × *L. viridis*
Hardiness: Zone 7b?
Growth: bushy
Flowers: dark purple corollas; fertile bracts purple; long mid mauve-violet sterile bracts
Foliage: greenish gray

Cultivar: 'St. Brelade'
Origin: David and Elizabeth Christie, 1995, as *L. pedunculata* × *L. viridis*
Flowers: dark violet corollas, pinkish green fertile bracts, subdued purple sterile bracts
Foliage: green or greenish gray

Cultivar: 'White Form'
Synonyms: 'Alba'
Hardiness: Zone 8?
Flowers: white corollas, pale green bracts
Comments: white-flowered French lavenders include 'Snowball', 'Snowman', 'Very White Form', 'White Knight', and 'Willowbridge Snow'

Cultivar: 'Willow Vale'
Synonyms: 'Willow Dale'
Origin: New South Wales, Australia, 1992, as *L. stoechas* × *L. viridis*
Hardiness: Zone 7b?
Flowers: dark purple-black corollas; wispy sterile bracts mid purple
Foliage: steely blue

Important chemistry: The essential oil of the entire flowering plant of French lavender is dominated by 31 to 88 percent fenchone, 10 to 62 percent camphor, and up to 10 percent pinocarvyl acetate. The flowers have trace to 74 percent fenchone, trace to 51 percent 1,8-cineole, and 9 to 58 percent camphor, while the leaves have 39 to 59 percent fenchone, 13 to 24 percent camphor, and trace to 21 percent 1,8-cineole. An unusual plant has been reported from Turkey with 40 percent pulegone and 18 percent menthone in the leaves, providing a minty odor.

Lavandula viridis
lå-văn-dū-lå vĭr-ĭ-dĭs
green-flowered lavender

This lavender bears white flowers with green bracts, earning it its common name. Culture is similar to French lavender. Green-flowered lavender is a good accent next to the lavandins and fringed lavender because of the light green color of the foliage and pale blossoms, but it is hardy only to southern California. In the north, green-flowered lavender is a good plant for window boxes and pots.

Botanical Key and Description

Key:
1. Leaves toothed to deeply lobed 2
    2. Leaves round-toothed (at least at base) to comblike-lobed 3
        3. Leaves distinctly comblike-lobed . . . . *L. dentata*
        3a. Leaves mixed, some margins without teeth or lobes, others (especially basal ones) with lobes . . . . .
            . . . . *L.* ×*allardii*
    2a. Leaves mostly double-lobed, fern-like . . . . *L. multifida*
1a. Leaf margins without teeth or lobes 4
        4. Upper bracts parallel-sided, lance-shaped, much larger than the flowers and without flowers
            in their axils. 5
            5. Upper bracts white or purple; leaves densely coated with a wool-like covering 6
                6. Corolla tube with a ring of hairs in the throat, fertile bracts with distinct apex . . . .
                    . . . . *L. stoechas*
                6a. Corolla tube lacking a ring of hairs in throat, fertile bracts without a distinct apex . . . .
                    . . . . *L. pedunculata*
            5a. Upper bracts green; leaves shortly hairy, fertile bracts without distinct apices or rarely
                apiculate . . . . *L. viridis*
        4a. All the bracts similar, not longer than the flowers and all with flowers in their axils. 7
            7. Bracts egg-diamond-shaped 8
                8. Bract length/width ratio 0.83 to 2.20; tiny bracts (bracteoles) absent or up to 2.5
                    mm long; flowering early (mid- to late June in Zone 7) . . . . *L. angustifolia*
                8a. Bract length/width ratio 1.33 to 3.00; tiny bracts to 1 to 4 mm long; flowering
                    midseason (early to mid-July in Zone 7) . . . . *L.* ×*intermedia*
            7a. Bracts linear to lance-shaped; bract length/width ratio 4.67 to 7.00; tiny bracts 1 to
                6 mm long; flowering late July to mid-August in Zone 7 9
                9. Leaves very shortly and densely white-woolly when young, gray-green and
                    less densely hairy when mature; calyx thirteen-veined . . . . *L. latifolia*
                9a. Leaves densely and persistently white-hairy with long tangled hairs; calyx
                    eight-veined . . . . *L. lanata*

L. ×allardii Viv., Elenchus Pl. 23 (1802) (*L. ×heterophylla* Poir., *L. ×hybrida* Balb. ex Ging.).

This seems to be the correct name for *L. dentata* × *L. latifolia*, but it is commonly sold as *L. ×heterophylla*. The complex nomenclature of this hybrid series has been published by Tim Upson and Susyn Andrews in *The Genus Lavandula* (2004).

Native country: Fringed lavender has been reported wherever dentate and spike lavender co-exist.

General habit: These hybrid lavenders combine traits of both parents.

Leaves: Typically the toothed leaves are only at the base of the stem or in young plants, the other leaves having smooth margins. Toothed leaves have one to seven teeth on each side at about the center of the leaf or toward the apex. All leaves are gray-woolly and have margins that roll backward.

Flowers: The spikes are elongated, interrupted at the base, and dark blue-violet.

L. angustifolia Mill., Gard. Dict. ed. 8, no. 2. 1768 (*L. spica* L., nom. ambig., *L. officinalis* Chaix in Villars).

Native country: Common lavender is native to the Mediterranean region.

General habit: Common lavender is a shrub which in cultivated forms does not exceed 1 m.

Leaves: Leaves are 2 to 5 cm long, lance-shaped, parallel-sided and narrow, smooth-edged, white-woolly when young, later becoming green.

Flowers: The spike is 2 to 8 cm long. Bracts subtending the flowers are egg-diamond-shaped and smaller bracts (bracteoles) are absent or minute. The flowers are lavender-violet, pink, or white.

L. dentata L., Sp. pl. 572. 1753.

Native country: The dentate lavender is native to southern and eastern Spain and the Balearic Islands.

General habit: The toothed lavender is a shrub to 1 m high.

Leaves: Leaves are 1.5 to 3.5 cm long, lance-shaped or parallel-sided and narrow, round-toothed to deeply lobed, gray-woolly below, gray-green above.

Flowers: The spike is 2.5 to 5 cm long. The bracts subtending the flowers are conspicuous and egg-diamond-shaped with pinched tips; the upper bracts commonly have no flowers and are egg-shaped and purple. The flowers are dark lavender-violet.

L. ×intermedia Emeric ex Loisel., Fl. Gal. 2:19. 1828 (*L. hybrida* Reverchon ex Briq., *L. hortensis* Hy).

Lavandin combines the characteristics of *L. angustifolia* and *L. latifolia* in a range of variation from one parent to the other.

L. lanata Boiss., Elenchus 72. 1838.

Native country: Woolly lavender is native to the mountains of southern Spain.

General habit: Woolly lavender is very similar to spike (*L. latifolia*), but the stems and leaves are persistently white-woolly with long, tangled hairs.

Leaves: Leaves are 3.5 to 5 cm long, parallel-sided, lance-shaped or narrow but broad and rounded at the apex and tapering to the base.

Flowers: The spike is 4 to 10 cm long. Bracts subtending the flowers are narrow or lance-shaped; small bracts (bracteoles) accompany the bracts. Flowers are blue-violet.

L. latifolia Medik., Bot. Beob. 1783:135. 1784
(*L. spica* auct., non L.).

Native country: Spike is native to the Mediterranean region and Portugal.

General habit: Spike is similar to lavender.

Leaves: Leaves are gray-green and densely hairy.

Flowers: Bracts subtending the flowers are narrow or narrow-lance-shaped. Small bracts (bracteoles) accompany the bracts. The flowers are blue-violet.

L. multifida L., Sp. pl. 572. 1753.

Native country: The fernleaf lavender is native to the western part of the Mediterranean and southern Portugal.

General habit: The fernleaf lavender is a shrub to 1 m, gray-hairy and sometimes also with long, straight hairs.

Leaves: Leaves are mostly deeply double-lobed, green, sparsely hairy.

Flowers: The spike is 2 to 7 cm long. The flowers are blue-violet.

L. pedunculata (Mill.) Cav., Descr. Pl. 70. 1802.

Butterfly lavender is a very variable species with five subspecies [subsp. *pedunculata*, subsp. *cariensis* (Boiss.) Upson & S. Andrews, subsp. *atlantica* (Braun-Blanq.) Romo, subsp. *lusitanica* (Chaytor) Franco, and subsp. *sampaiana* (Rozeira) Franco]. The long, naked flower stalks of butterfly lavender distinguish it from French lavender.

Native country: Butterfly lavender is native to the Mediterranean region from Spain to Turkey.

General habit: Butterfly lavender is a shrub to 1 m high, woolly-hairy.

Leaves: Leaves are 2 to 4 cm long, narrow to parallel-sided, lance-shaped, smooth-edged, usually gray-woolly.

Flowers: The spike is usually 1 to 1.5 cm long. The bracts subtending the flowers are heart-diamond-shaped, the upper ones without flowers and usually purple. The flowers are dark purple.

L. stoechas L., Sp. pl. 573. 1753.

This is a variable species with two subspecies [subsp. *stoechas*, subsp. *lusieri* (Rozeira) Rozeira], defined by the amount of hairs of the calyx and bracts.

Native country: French lavender is native to the Mediterranean region and Portugal.

General habit: French lavender is a shrub to 2 m high, woolly-hairy.

Leaves: Leaves are 1 to 3.5 cm long, narrow to parallel-sided, lance-shaped, smooth-edged, usually gray-woolly.

Flowers: The spike is usually 2 to 6 cm long. The bracts subtending the flowers are egg-shaped, the upper ones without flowers and usually purple. The flowers are dark purple.

L. viridis L'Hér., Sert. angl. 19. 1789.

Native country: The green-flowered lavender is native to southwestern Spain and southern Portugal.

General habit: Green-flowered lavender is very similar to French lavender (*L. stoechas*), but the stem and leaves bear short hairs.

Flowers: The bracts are light green, flowers white.

Levisticum officinale

lĕ-vĭs-tĭ-kŭm ō-fĭs-ĭ-nā-lē
lovage

Family: Apiaceae (Umbelliferae)
Growth form: herbaceous perennial to 6 feet (1.8 m)
Hardiness: hardy to Zone 5
Light: full sun
Water: moist but not wet
Soil: rich in organic matter, pH 5.0 to 7.6, average 6.5
Propagation: seeds or divisions in spring
Culinary use: soups, stews, salads, and so on
Craft use: none
Landscape use: tall background specimen for herb or perennial garden

---

French: *livèche*
German: *Liebstöckel, Maggikraut*
Dutch: *lavas, makkikruid*
Italian: *levistico, sedano di monte*
Spanish: *apio de montana, ligistico*
Chinese: *tang-kui, man-mu*
Arabic: *kâmûn-el-mulûki, amus*

If you find celery hard to grow, lovage is an easily cultivated plant that is a good substitute and tastes like the real thing, only more so. Use lovage wherever celery is desired: soups, stews, salads, casseroles, and stuffings, and use about half as much lovage as celery to compensate for the more concentrated flavor. The leaf stalks of lovage were once blanched like celery by piling soil around the base. The large flowering stems may be candied, while the tender young stems are good in salads. The seeds (actually fruits) have been used as an alternative to celery seeds (fruits). Both leaves, stems, and seeds may be dried for winter use. The roots are antibiotic from the content of falcarindiol. The oil and oleoresin are used in the formulation of sauces, bouillons, preserves, and condiments. Application of the root extract or oil to the skin is not recommended; they contain psorlaen and bergapten that may heighten the skin's sensitivity to light.

The genus *Levisticum* includes only one species. The generic name is the Latin equivalent of Dioscorides' name for a plant from Liguria, Italy; the specific name, *officinale*, refers to the medicinal reputation of lovage.

Given the proper nourishment and moisture, lovage is a giant plant with flowering stalks towering to over 6 feet (1.8 m) high. The dark green, shiny leaves are finely cut, and in late June or early July a large stalk with yellow flowers appears.

Lovage is easily grown from seeds planted in early spring in rich, moist garden soil with good drainage and partial shade where summers are

Levisticum officinale

hot and steamy; plants are harvested beginning the second year. Seedlings started indoors and transplanted to the garden will produce year-lings larger than giant Italian parsley that can be harvested the first year. Older plants may be cut back to a foot high in mid-season before flowers appear; they will regrow to produce more leaves before frost.

Lovage responds to rotted manure and other organic applications when deeply dug into the soil. The optimum nitrogen-level seems to be 40 to 67 pounds per acre (45 to 75 kg/ha) for fresh root yield. Mulch well to conserve moisture.

One lovage plant usually produces more leaves than a single household can use. When older leaves turn yellow, simply clip them off; there will be more to replace them later. Harvesting for leaves curtails root production. Lovage seeds remain viable for one to three years with 70 to 80 percent germination.

The essential oil of the roots is considered GRAS at 0.08 to 30 ppm; the extract is GRAS at 0.07 to 170 ppm, while the oleoresin is GRAS at 0.08 to 30 ppm.

Important chemistry: The adult roots of lovage contain many phthalides, particularly 9 to 93 percent (Z)-ligustilide and trace to 29 percent (Z)-3-butylidene phthalide, providing a celery-like note, accompanying trace to 49 percent beta-phellandrene, 0 to 26 percent alpha-terpinyl acetate, 0 to 12 percent sabinyl acetate, and 0 to 12 percent pentylcyclohexa-1,3-diene.

The seedling roots contain trace (Z)-ligustilide with 40 percent germacrene B, 22 percent beta-phellandrene, and 13 percent *trans*-beta-farne-sene, providing a sweet spicy note.

The essential oil of the lovage seeds (fruits) is dominated by 63 percent beta-phellandrene. The essential oil of lovage leaves is dominated by 29 to 56 percent terpinyl acetate with 11 to 19 percent beta-phellandrene. Commercial lovage extract is characterized by sotolon (3-hydroxy-4,5-dimethyl-2(5H)-furanone).

Botanical Description

L. officinale Koch, Nova Acta Phys. Med. Acad. Oes. Leop.-Carol. Nat. Cur. 12:101. 1824.

Native country: Lovage is native to most of Europe, particularly in mountainous regions and escaped near gardens; the exceptions are the extreme north and the south and the islands.

General habit: Lovage is a stout perennial 100 to 250 cm high. Lower branches are alternate, upper opposite, or whorled.

Leaves: Lower leaves are as large as 70 × 65 cm, triangular-diamond-shaped in outline; lobes long-wedge-shaped, irregularly and deeply toothed and lobed in upper part.

Flowers: Flowers are yellow-green and arranged in an umbel.

Fruits/seeds: Fruits (schizocarps) are 5 to 7 mm long, yellow or brown.

Limnophila chinensis subsp. *aromatica*

lĭm-nŏ-fĭ-lå chĭ-<u>něn</u>-sĭs å-rō-<u>mă</u>-tĭ-kå
rau ngô

Family: Scrophulariaceae
Growth form: annual to short-lived perennial to 20 inches (50 cm) high
Hardiness: hardy to Zone 9
Light: full sun
Water: partially submerged
Soil: garden loam
Propagation: cuttings, seeds
Culinary use: Vietnamese dishes but not GRAS
Craft use: none
Landscape use: good on edges of ponds

Vietnamese: *rau ngố, rau om, ngò om*

Rau ngô is an herb which was introduced into North America with the 1975 airlift of about 140,000 Vietnamese refugees. It is usually sold in bunches in Asian groceries (a good source of inexpensive propagating material) and is easily recognized by the whorls of three leaves, toothed and lance-shaped, and the lemony floral scent of the leaves. The lavender flowers are delicate and airy.

This is a *sina qua non* for several Vietnamese sweet-and-sour dishes, particularly a soup made with tamarinds and cantaloupe. However, rau ngô has no GRAS status.

The genus *Limnophila* includes about thirty-six species of the Old World tropics; most are aquatics or emergent aquatics, and the name *Limnophila*, not unexpectedly, comes from the Greek *limne* ("pool") and *philos* ("loving"). Rau ngô prefers mud and a film of standing water in full sun.

Important chemistry: We examined the essential oil of the leaves and stems and found 53 percent limonene and 12 percent *cis*-4-cara-none, providing an odor reminiscent of lemons, flowers, and spearmint.

Botanical Description

L. chinensis (Osb.) Merrill **subsp.** *aromatica* (Lam.) Yamazaki, J. Jap. Bot. 53:313. 1978 [*L. aromatica* (Lam.) Merr.].

Native country: Rau ngô is native to swamplands and moist habitats from China to Australia.

General habit: Rau ngô is an erect annual or perennial herb up to 50 cm high.

Leaves: Leaves are simple, egg-lance-shaped to lance-shaped with the center widest and the ends equal, opposite or more commonly in whorls of three, 10 to 60 × 3 to 22 mm, with round-toothed margins.

Limnophila chinensis subsp. *aromatica*

Flowers: The pale purple flowers with yellow centers are axillary, solitary, or sometimes in terminal or laterally leafy bunches.

Fruits/seeds: Seeds are dark brown, 0.25 to 4 mm long, borne in small pods.

Lindera benzoin

lĭn-dĕr-å bĕn-zōyn
spicebush

Family: Lauraceae
Growth form: shrub to almost 15 feet (4.5 m)
Hardiness: hardy to at least southwest Maine (Zone 5)
Light: part to full shade; full sun if adequate moisture available
Water: constantly moist
Soil: rich in organic matter, subacid
Propagation: divisions in spring
Culinary use: limited (not GRAS)
Craft use: potpourri
Landscape use: excellent background in shaded herb garden

Spicebush not only has good fragrance and a history of use as a spice but is also an admirable garden plant. Unfortunately, it is rarely cultivated and is only found at wildflower and specialty shrub nurseries, but the herb should be grown in home gardens as a handsome deciduous shrub; in the wild it prefers damp woods and stream banks. The fragrant leaves turn a brilliant gold in the fall, a wonderful contrast to the red fruits (if the birds don't get them first). Insects and diseases are few. This is a native plant that the nursery trade ought to evaluate for its beauty and fragrance.

Spicebush is also known as Benjamin bush, feverbush, or wild allspice. The genus was named after Swedish botanist Johann Linder (1676–1723), while *benzoin* was adapted from *Styrax benzoin* Dryander, or Sumatra benzoin. Three species of *Lindera* inhabit the eastern United States; the other seventy-seven species are native to Asia.

The fruits of spicebush (this species has male and female plants) have been dried and powdered and used as a substitute for allspice, while the leaves and bark produce a pleasant lemony tea. An herbal vinegar from the twigs and fruits was once used to preserve beets. Unfortunately, spicebush has no GRAS status. Dried leaves of spicebush, however, are great in potpourri.

Lindera benzoin

Important chemistry: We have examined the essential oil of two collections of spicebush. One is dominated by 11 to 16 percent 6-methyl-5-hepten-2-one and 10 to 16 percent 1,8-cineole, providing a grassy-eucalyptus odor. The other is dominated by 15 percent beta-caryophyllene and 10 percent (*E*)-nerolidol, providing a woody-floral odor. The stems contain lauroteta-nine, an alkaloid which may be toxic to cells.

Botanical Description

L. benzoin (L.) Blume, Mus. bot. 1:324. 1851.
Native country: Spicebush is native to damp woods and stream banks from Maine to the Mississippi Gulf Coastal Plain.

General habit: Spicebush is a deciduous shrub to 4.5 m.
Leaves: Leaves are emerald-green, smooth or slightly hairy, membranaceous, 6 to 15 × 3 to 6 cm, narrowed at the wedge-shaped base, pinched at the tip.
Flowers: Flowers are greenish yellow, tiny.
Fruits/seeds: Fruit is red, olive-like, 10 mm long.

Lippia

lĭp-ĭ-å
lippia

Family: Verbenaceae
Growth form: shrubs
Hardiness: cannot withstand frost; routinely hardy only to Zone 10
Light: full sun
Water: moist but not constantly wet
Soil: well drained, pH 5.8 to 6.8 (*L. micromera*)
Propagation: cuttings throughout active growing season
Culinary use: many species used as substitutes for oregano but not GRAS
Craft use: none
Landscape use: container plant, sometimes trained into topiaries

The genus *Lippia*, named after Augustus Lippi, a French traveler, includes sources of oregano and teas. Almost all the 200 species (by one estimate) are tropical shrubs, freely forming small

Lippia graveolens

cream flowers in the axils of leaves coated with rough hairs. They can be planted outside for the summer and grow rapidly to form waist-high, lax shrubs. In areas where frost is anticipated, root cuttings in the summer; carry them over the winter in the greenhouse or indoors on sunny but cool windowsills. They are fine sources of fresh oregano or leaves for teas from potted plants during the winter.

While the leaves of many *Lippia* species are commercially marketed by leading spice companies as oregano, no *Lippia* species has GRAS status. For a discussion of *L. dulcis*, the Aztec sweet herb, see *Phyla scaberrima*, its correct name.

The scent of *Lippia alba* (bushy matgrass) varies widely and includes aromas of licorice candy, lemon, and camphor, to mention a few. The licorice verbena (*L. carterae*) was originally collected from Mexico, where it is sometimes called *anis de España*. *Lippia graveolens* (Mexican oregano) is the primary commercial source of oregano from Mexico, where it is known as *orégano cimarron*, while *L. micromera* is called Jamaican oregano, false thyme, or *orégano del pais*. Both are also called simply *orégano*. Many other *Lippia* species are used locally as oregano in Latin America (*L. affinis* Schauer in DC; *L. cardiostegia* Benth.; *L. formosa* T. S. Brandeg.; *L. fragrans* Turcz.; *L. origanoides* Humb., Bonpl. & Kunth; *L. palmeri* S. Wats.; and *L. umbellata* Cav.). The plants high in carvacrol are antimicrobial, similar to that of *Origanum* species.

Important chemistry: The oil of the licorice verbena cultivated in North America (*L. carterae*) consists of 56 percent estragole (methyl chavicol) and 13 percent 1,8-cineole, providing a scent reminscent of French tarragon with undertones of eucalyptus. Otherwise, the essential oil of *L. alba* is very variable and may consist of 0 to 37 percent piperitone, 0 to 36 percent geranial, 0 to 34 percent limonene, 0 to 28 percent neral, 2 to 24 percent beta-caryophyllene, 0 to 18 percent camphor, and 0 to 35 percent 1,8-cineole. Cuban plants of *L. alba* yield 33 percent (*R*)(+)-carvone, 31 percent limonene, and 13 percent beta-guaiene, providing a spearmint-like odor. This is similar to the plants from Guadeloupe, Martinique, and French Guiana with 0 to 68 percent carvone, 0 to 51 percent limonene, 0 to 33 percent neral, 0 to 21 percent geranial, trace to 18 percent germacrene D, 0 to 15 percent alpha-guaiene, and 0 to 13 percent (*E*)-beta-ocimene. Brazilian plants yield 0 to 55 percent (*R*)(+)-carvone, 0 to 32 percent neral, and 36 to 51 percent geranial, providing a rosy spearmint odor. Brazilian and Indian plants may also be lavender-scented with 50 to 79 percent linalool. North Indian plants may have up to 26 percent myrcene. A spearmint-scented form has been reported from Brazil with 32 percent limonene, 32 percent (*R*)(+)-carvone, and 11 percent myrcene, while another spearmint-scented form has been reported from Costa Rica with 69 percent carvone and 23 percent limonene. Guatemalan plants may have 2 to 55 percent myrcenone, 0 to 25 percent 1,8-cineole, 0 to 24 percent geranial, and trace to 16 percent (*Z*)-ocimenone.

The oils of oregano-scented species of *Lippia* contain predominantly carvacrol and, to a lesser extent, the thyme-scented thymol. The essential oil of *L. graveolens* consists of trace to 81 percent thymol, trace to 48 percent carvacrol, 3 to 30 percent para-cymene, and trace to 15 percent 1,8-cineole. The essential oil of *L. micromera* consists of 27 percent carvacrol, 23 percent gamma-terpinene, and 12 percent *p*-cymene.

Botanical Key and Description

Key:

1. Flower heads four to five per node, leaves rounded or almost heart-shaped at base . . . . *L. graveolens*
1a. Flower heads two to four per node, leaves narrowed or wedge-shaped at base 2
    2. Leaves 1 to 3 cm long, flowers white, pink, light bluish purple, or yellow, flower heads borne paired in axils of leaves 3
        3. Leaves with a dense, close coating of fine, white, crinkled hairs . . . . *L. carterae*
        3a. Leaves with stiff, relatively thick-based hairs . . . . *L. alba*
    2a. Leaves 6 to 12 mm long, flowers white, flower heads borne singly in axils of leaves . . . . *L. micromera*

L. alba (Mill.) N. E. Brown ex Britton & P. Wils., Bot. Puerto Rico 6:141. 1925.

Native country: *L. alba* is native from Texas to Argentina and throughout the West Indies.

General habit: This is a much-branched shrub with long straggling slender branches, up to 5 feet (1.5 m) high.

Leaves: Leaves are opposite or in threes, essentially parallel-sided but widest at the center with the ends equal, wedge-shaped at the base, blunt to rounded at the tip, 1 to 3 cm long, 0.9 to 2 cm broad, margin finely scalloped, covered with stiff, relatively thick-based hairs, veins prominent beneath, crinkled.

Flowers: Inflorescence stalks paired, rarely as much as ½ inch (1.5 cm) long; spikes elongating to ¾ inch (2 cm) long, corolla white, pink, or light bluish purple.

L. carterae (Mold.) Nesom, Phytologia 70:187. 1991 [*L. alba* (Mill.) N. E. Brown ex Britton & P. Wils. Var. *carterae*].

Native country: The licorice verbena is native to Baja California.

General habit: The licorice verbena is a much-branched shrub with long, straggling slender branches to 5 feet (1.5 m) high.

Leaves: Leaves are opposite or in threes, essentially parallel-sided but widest at the center with the ends equal, wedge-shaped at the base, blunt to rounded at the tip, 1 to 3 cm long, 0.9 to 2 cm broad, margin finely scalloped, covered with fine, white, crinkled hairs. Leaf surfaces have an understory of fine coating with much longer, straight, stiffer, "*alba*-like" hairs intermixed on the upper surface and along the veins of the lower surface.

Flowers: Inflorescence stalks paired, rarely as much as ½ inch (1.5 cm) long; spikes elongating to ¾ inch (2 cm) long, corolla yellow.

L. graveolens Humb., Bonpl. & Kunth, Nov. gen. sp., ed. folio 2:215. 1817 (*L. berlandieri* Schauer).

Native country: *L. graveolens* is native to Texas and Mexico.

General habit: This is a shrub or small tree, 3 to 9 feet (1 to 2.7 m) high.

Leaves: Leaves are stalked, two to four times longer than wide and sides parallel, tending to be egg-shaped or lance-egg-shaped, blunt or tapering at the apex, rounded or almost heart-shaped at base, round-toothed, minutely hairy and glandular beneath.

Flowers: Heads are four to five at each node, flowers creamy white.

L. micromera Schauer in DC., Prodr. 11:587. 1847.

Native country: *L. micromera* is native to the

West Indies, Central America, and South America to Guyana.

General habit: This bushy shrub grows to 2.5 m high, but is usually smaller, with three-angled branches.

Leaves: Leaves are opposite, crowded with short stalks, narrowed at the base but widest at the center with the ends equal, 6 to 12 mm long, more or less downy on both surfaces; margins may be simply recurved, slightly toothed at the tip, or sometimes wholly toothed.

Flowers: Flowers are white, massed into hemispherical heads borne singly on short stalks in the axils of the upper leaves.

Litsea glaucescens

lĭt-sē-å glă-sĕs-ĕnz
Mexican bay

Family: Lauraceae
Growth form: tree to 20 feet (6 m)
Hardiness: probably hardy to Zone 9
Light: full sun
Water: moist but not wet; can withstand minor drought
Soil: well-drained garden loam
Propagation: cuttings or seeds
Culinary use: soups, stews, meats but not GRAS
Craft use: wreaths
Landscape use: container plant, specimen tree

Mexican bay, commonly called laurel in Mexico, has been promoted for Mexican cooking in a number of cookbooks, particularly Diana Kennedy's *Mexican Regional Cooking*. While Mexican bay has no GRAS status, the appearance and flavor are very similar to that of Grecian bay, *Laurus nobilis*, making it a good substitute.

Litsea is a genus of about 400 warm-climate and tropical species, especially abundant in Asia and Australia. The generic name was supposedly derived from a Chinese name for the genus, while *glaucescens* refers to the blue-green undersides of the leaves.

Mexican bay is gathered from the wild in Mexico. While plants of Mexican bay are not common in the United States, cultivation is similar to that for Grecian bay.

Important chemistry: The essential oil of Mexican bay is dominated by around 22 percent 1,8-cineole, 13 percent sabinene, and 10 percent terpinen-4-ol, providing a very bay-like odor.

Litsea glaucescens

Botanical Description

Four varieties of *L. glaucescens* are known, but var. *glaucescens* is the variety commonly used in cooking in Mexico.

L. glaucescens Humb., Bonpl. & Kunth., Nov. gen. sp. 2:133. 1817.

Native country: Mexican bay is native to Mexico, from Tamaulipas to Veracruz, Chiapas, and Tepic, ranging to Central America.

General habit: Mexican bay is an evergreen tree to 6 m. Branches are smooth, dark or reddish brown or olive.

Leaves: Leaves are variable, usually thinly leathery, olive-green to dark brown above when dried, blue-green to pale green below, usually lance-shaped, 7 to 9 × 2 to 3 cm, gradually narrowing to the base, pinched or tapering to the apex.

Flowers: Greenish white flowers are borne in clusters of three to five.

Fruits/seeds: Fruits are globular, 12 mm in diameter.

Matricaria

mă-trĭ-kā-rĭ-å
matricaria

Family: Asteraceae (Compositae)

Growth form: annual from 3 inches to 2 feet tall (8 to 60 cm)

Hardiness: withstands frost

Light: full sun

Water: moist but not constantly wet

Soil: well-drained garden loam, pH 4.8 to 8.0, average 6.7 (*M. recutita*)

Propagation: seeds in spring, 625,000 seeds per ounce (22,046/g) (*M. recutita*)

Culinary use: teas

Craft use: potpourri

Landscape use: edge of herb borders, along paths

The genus *Matricaria* is derived from the Latin *matrix*, or womb, because German chamomile was once used medicinally to treat feminine disorders. This genus, like many genera in the Asteraceae, is in scientific disarray, but it probably includes about five species native to Europe and Asia. Most species have fragrant, ferny leaves and are relatively low-growing, generally with daisy-like flowers bearing white rays and yellow centers.

Matricaria matricarioides

mă-trĭ-kā-rĭ-å må-trĭ-kā-rĭ-ōy-dēz
pineapple weed

Pineapple weed is normally a wayside plant found along gravelly country roads and driveways. If cultivated, it must have similar well-drained circumstances in full sun. Commercial seed is very rare, so you will have to find your own patch in the wild to transfer to your garden. As the name implies, the fragrance is a pineapple-like version of German chamomile. Pineapple weed has been used by foragers to prepare a delightful tea from the blossoms and tender foliage, but it has no GRAS status.

Important chemistry: The essential oil of pineapple weed is dominated by 4 to 47 percent (*E*)-beta-farnesene, 1 to 22 percent germacrene D, and 16 to 45 percent myrcene, providing a fruity odor. Also reported as a major constituent in pineapple weed oil is 7-methoxycoumarin.

Matricaria recutita

mă-trĭ-kā-rĭ-å rĕ-kū-tĭ-tå
German chamomile

> **French:** *camomille vulgaire, matricarie, petite camomille*
> **German:** *Echte Kamille, Gemeine Kamille*
> **Dutch:** *echte kamille, kleine kamille*
> **Italian:** *camomilla volgare, manzanilla*
> **Spanish:** *camomila, camomilda, capomilla, manzanilla de Aragón, manzanilla alemana*
> **Portuguese:** *camomila, margaça das boticas*
> **Swedish:** *kamomill, sötblomster*
> **Russian:** *aptechnaya*

German chamomile, alias Hungarian chamomile, is widely confused with Roman chamomile, *Chamaemelum nobile*, and the two have been used almost interchangeably. However, Roman chamomile is a low, ground-hugging perennial while German chamomile is an upright annual, and the essential oils are also vastly different. Ingesting Roman chamomile sometimes induces allergic responses in ragweed-sensitive individuals, but such responses are rare for German chamomile. Stinking mayweed (*Anthemis cotula* L.), a common roadside weed, is sometimes confused with German chamomile and also causes allergic responses. The actual origin of German chamomile is in the Near East and eastern Europe, but it has become naturalized throughout.

The specific name, *recutita*, refers to the similarity of the flower heads, with their reflexed rays, to a circumcised penis. Bet you didn't know *Matricaria recutita* was so sexy!

The essential oil of German chamomile is considered GRAS at 20 ppm. German chamo-

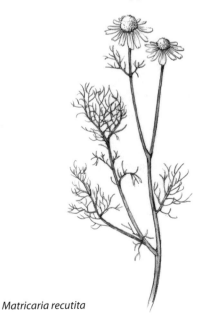

Matricaria recutita

mile oil has been used in nonalcoholic beverages, alcoholic beverages, ice cream and ices, candy, baked goods, and chewing gum. (-)-Alpha-bis-abolol and apigenin, the principal flavonoid, in particular, prevent smooth-muscle spasms and inhibit locomotor activity. Calves fed German chamomile show reduced handling stress. (-)-Alpha-bisabolol has very low toxicity and shows activity against some fungi and bacteria, inhibits ulcers, and promotes burn healing. Chamazulene has antiallergenic and anti-inflammatory properties. *Cis-* and *trans*-ene, yne-dicycloether also work against inflammation, allergies, muscle spasms, and certain fungi and bacteria. The essential oil is antimutagenic.

German chamomile grows best in a light, sandy loam with abundant moisture at pH 6. Additional fertilizers should have a nitrogen:potassium ratio of 1:2 because nitrogen delays the transition from the vegetative to the flowering stage, while potassium advances flowering. The surface of the soil should be firm to ensure good contact with the seeds in furrows 2 to 4 inches (5 to 10 cm) high at the rate of 1.3 to 1.8 pounds per acre (1.5 to 2.0 kg/ha), and plants should be established in rows 4 to 32 inches (10 to 80 cm) apart.

In the Czech Republic, plants are seeded from 15 August to 15 September, or 1 October to winter months, or 1 March to 30 April, depending upon the moisture conditions. Early autumn seeding is best in areas with regular autumn rain, late autumn seeding is best in areas with early frost and little snowfall, and spring seeding is best in areas with spring rain. Spring sowings produce a higher content of essential oils. Seeds germinate at 43 to 45°F (6 to 7°C) within seven to ten days after seeding.

Leaf rosettes form thirty to forty days after germination and flowers quickly follow. Optimal temperature for flowering is 66 to 68°F (19 to 20°C). At 82 to 90°F (28 to 32°C), the flowering time is shortened. Best yields are in areas with an average rainfall of 18 inches (45 cm).

Under optimal conditions, German chamomile flowers two to three times per year. Regeneration of flowers after cutting requires ten to twenty days, depending upon weather conditions. Flowers are mechanically harvested in commercial plantings and distilled or dried in sheds with forced hot air. Average yields of 268 to 446 pounds per acre (300 to 500 kg/ha) of dry flowers are reported in the Czech Republic, but optimization with cultivar selection and agronomic practices may result in yields of 900 to 1,000 pounds per acre (100 to 1,200 kg/ha). The highest essential oil content is found in fully developed flowers approximately one week after flowering begins.

A very large number of seed lines of German chamomile have been developed, especially by the Hungarians. If commercial cultivation is anticipated, be aware that the desirable lines have been selected for their richness in (-)-alpha-bisabolol, but many lines are rich in (-)-bisabolol oxide A. The selected lines also differ in the inheritance of matricin, which gives rise to the blue chamazulene upon distillation. The composition of the oil depends on the stage of development. Flower buds contain more alpha-bisabolol than fully developed flowers, whereas chamazulene and bisabolol oxides increase during flowering.

Important chemistry: The dominant components of the essential oil are trace to 77 percent (-)-alpha-bisabolol, 0 to 58 percent (-)-bisabolol oxide A, 0 to 44 percent (*Z*)-beta-farnesene, 0 to 35 percent chamazulene, trace to 32 percent (-)-bisabolol oxide B, 2 to 19 percent *cis/trans*-ene, yne-dicycloether, and 0 to 13 percent (*E*)-beta-farnesene. The chamazulene provides a blue color to the oil; chamazulene is not present in the raw plant but forms under distillation from matricin ("pro-chamazulene").

Botanical Key and Description

Key:

1.   White ray flowers (ligulate florets) usually present; yellow tubular flowers five-lobed . . . . *M. recutita*
1a. White ray flowers usually absent; yellow tubular flowers four-lobed. . . . . *M. matricarioides*

M. matricarioides (Less.) Porter [*Chamomilla suaveolens* (Pursh) Rydb.].

Native country: Pineapple weed is native to Europe but naturalized in North America in farmyards, roadsides, and cultivated ground.

General habit: Pineapple weed is an erect annual herb 8 to 45 cm tall, rather fleshy, branched above and often also from the base. Branches are rigid, smooth below, sometimes sparsely hairy below the flower head.

Leaves: Leaves are 2 to 6 × 1 to 2 cm, rather crowded, smooth; segments are numerous, flattened, tapering to a point.

Flowers: From five to forty yellow-green, rayless daisies are produced, 5 to 9 mm in diameter, enlarging as they mature.

Fruits/seeds: Fruits (achenes) are 1.2 to 1.5 mm long, pale brown, with three or four ribs on the ventral face.

M. recutita L. [*Chamomilla recutita* (L.) Rauschert, *M. chamomilla* L., pro parte].

Native country: German chamomile is native to the south and west of Europe in waste places and salty steppes.

General habit: German chamomile is an erect annual herb, 10 to 60 cm high, much-branched above.

Leaves: Leaves are 4 to 7 cm long; segments taper to a point and are well branched.

Flowers: From 8 to 120 white daisies are produced, 10 to 25 mm in diameter.

Fruits/seeds: Fruits (achenes) are about 1 mm long, pale grayish-brown, with four to five ribs on the ventral face.

Melissa officinalis

mĕ-lĭ-så ŏ-fĭs-ĭ-nā-lĭs
lemon balm

Family: Lamiaceae (Labiatae)

Growth form: herbaceous perennial usually reaching 3 feet (91 cm) tall

Hardiness: hardy to Zone 5

Light: full sun

Water: moist but not constantly wet

Soil: well-drained garden loam, pH 5 to 7.5, average 6.6

Propagation: divisions or seeds in spring, 43,000 seeds per ounce (1,517/g)

Culinary use: teas; where a lemon flavor is desired

Craft use: potpourri

Landscape use: mid-border or allowed to reseed in cottage-garden fashion

French: *mélisse, citronelle, citragon*
German: *Zitronen-Melisse, Garten-Melisse*
Dutch: *citroenmielisse*
Italian: *cedrina, melissa, cedronella, appiastro,*
  citraggine
Spanish: *meliza, melisa, toronjil, torongil, erba*
  cedrata
Portuguese: *erva cideira, melissa*
Swedish: *citronmeliss*
Russian: *melissa*
Arabic: *hab-ul-ban*

Lemon balm can be found growing in scrubby and sandy places in southern Europe, where it is native, and spreading across any unoccupied earth in many herb gardens in the United States and other locations throughout temperate zones. This popular lemon-scented herb has bright green, puckered, egg-shaped leaves and small, pale yellow flowers.

The genus *Melissa* includes five species native from Europe to central Asia. The generic name is derived from the Greek *melissa*, or bee, presumably because honeybees are attracted to the flowers. Indeed, the chemical composition of lemon balm oil is remarkably similar to the content of the worker honeybee's Nasonov gland, which it uses for chemical communication about food sources.

Lemon balm, or simply balm, was once medicinal. The Swiss-born alchemist and physician Paracelsus (1493–1541) selected lemon balm to prepare his elixir vitae, *primum ens melissae*, by which he professed to regenerate the strength of man and render him nearly immortal. Lemon balm has been employed in tisanes, wines, and cordials, and we still find it in liqueurs. The essential oil of lemon balm is considered GRAS at 1 to 60 ppm, while the leaf extract is GRAS at 2,000 to 5,000 ppm.

Arquebusade, Eau de Berlin, Eau des Carmes, and Hungary water have also used lemon balm in the formulations of eau de colognes. While the herb has traditionally not been used as such, some northern European forms of lemon balm high in citronellal mimic citronella oil and may thus be effective mosquito repellents. A cream formulated with 1 percent dried lemon balm significantly accelerated the healing of herpes infections. Lemon balm extract may have some value in managing mild to moderate Alzheimer's disease, modulating mood and cognitive performance. Lemon balm is also antimicrobial, antioxidant, anticarcinogenic, and antimutagenic and may have a hypolipidemic effect.

Lemon balm is easy to grow from seed— almost too easy. If allowed to reseed, it will be with you forever. Start seeds early for transplanting or sow them directly. Layerings and cuttings are also possible. Lemon balm grows in any reasonably moist garden loam at pH 5 to 7.5, and the problem is how to get rid of the copious seedlings that spread hither and yonder.

Recommendations for commercial cultivation are 12 inches (30 cm) between plants and 5 feet (1.5 m) between rows. Yields are 2,200 to 5,600 pounds per acre (1,000 to 2,700 kg/ha)

Melissa officinalis

the first year and 16,300 to 29,000 pounds per acre (7,400 to 13,000 kg/ha) for an established crop. Oil yield is less than 0.05 percent.

A virus-infected form, known as golden balm or 'Aurea', is sometimes grown but should be avoided because this is *Tulip virus* × (TVX), which heretofore has not been detected in the United States. And then there is the so-called lime balm. Every plant of it that we have purchased has proven to be nothing more than lemon balm by a new name. Does lime balm truly exist? Lime oil is characterized by limonene, backed by alpha-terpineol, terpinolene, and/or gamma-terpinene. If lime balm exists, we would expect it to have a similar constitution.

Two subspecies of *M. officinalis* are listed, but the typical subspecies, *officinalis*, is the cultivated lemon balm. The subsp. *altissima* is naturalized in New Zealand, where it is known as "bush balm." The latter subspecies has a leaf odor varying from scentless to fetid but more commonly characterized as herbal, fruity, and powdery. subsp. *altissima* is sometimes encountered as an adulterant of typical lemon balm.

Important chemistry: The essential oil of lemon balm, subsp. *officinalis*, is dominated by 1 to 40 percent geranial, trace to 39 percent citronellal, 0 to 36 percent neral, 0 to 23 percent geraniol, and trace to 20 percent beta-caryophyllene. Greek plants have 13 to 24 percent caryophyllene oxide, 6 to 18 percent beta-pinene, 7 to 17 percent sabinene, and 7 to 15 percent beta-caryophyllene and no geranial, neral, or citronellal.

The essential oil of bush balm from New Zealand, subsp. *altissima*, is dominated by 39 percent beta-cubebene and 10 percent terpinolene. Bush balm from Europe has 32 to 54 percent germacrene D and 7 to 22 percent beta-caryophyllene.

Botanical Key and Description

M. officinalis L., Sp. pl. 592. 1753.
Native country: Lemon balm is native to scrub and sandy places in southern Europe.
General habit: Lemon balm is an erect herbaceous perennial 20 to 150 cm tall.
Leaves: Leaves are 2 to 9 × 1.5 to 7 cm, broadly egg-shaped to diamond-shaped to oblong, with a blunt or sharp tip, more or less round-toothed except at the base, rugose.
Flowers: Flowers are pale yellow becoming white or pinkish in the axils of the terminal leaves.
Fruits/seeds: Nutlets are 1.5 to 2 mm round.

Key:
1. Leaves lemon-scented, smooth or sparsely hairy above . . . . subsp. *officinalis*
1a. Leaves scentless to fetid-scented, gray-hairy . . . .
. . . . subsp. *altissima* (Sibth. & Sm.) Arcang. (Comp. fl. ital. ed. 2. 427. 1984).

Mentha

měn-thå
mint

Family: Lamiaceae (Labiatae)

Growth form: herbaceous perennials from procumbent to 3 feet (90 cm) high

Hardiness: hardy to Maine (Zone 5)

Light: full sun to part shade

Water: moist

Soil: well-drained loam, pH 4.5 to 8.2, average 6.2 to 6.9

Propagation: divisions or seeds in spring, 475,000 seeds per ounce (16,755/g) (*M. spicata*)

Culinary use: teas, meats, salads

Craft use: potpourri

Landscape use: best if allowed to run rampant, cottage-garden fashion

In Greek mythology, Pluto raped the nymph Minthe; then his wife, Persephone, trampled her underfoot in a jealous rage. Minthe has had her revenge, however; nobody remembers Pluto or Persephone in a living plant genus, but almost everyone knows and loves *Mentha*.

The genus *Mentha* includes nineteen "pure" but very variable species. These species have crossed and recrossed, creating a vast confusion of plants that botanists aptly refer to as "reticulate evolution." In addition, extreme environments alter the growth forms and scents of mints; the botanists call this "phenotypic plasticity." As a result of these two evolutionary characteristics, over 3,000 names have been published for the eighteen species and their named hybrids. No wonder Walahfrid Strabo remarked in his *Hortulus* in c. 850–900 C.E.:

But if any man can name
The full list of all the kinds and all the properties
Of mint, he must be one who knows how many fish
Swim in the Indian Ocean, how many sparks Vulcan
Sees fly in the air from his vast furnace in Etna.

The most economically important mints are five basic species in section *Mentha*. These have hybridized to yield every possible combination with an additional twelve botanically named hybrids. Because of the variation and extensive hybridization, most mints are sterile or do not reproduce from seeds, but their abundant long, thin rhizomes, called stolons, offset any need for seeds. Mints are like stray cats: you take them in, give them some food, and they are yours forever.

The commercial cultivation of both peppermint and spearmint date from 1750 in England; it centered around Mitcham in County Surrey and peaked around 1850. By 1770, commercial cultivation had spread to Utrecht in the Netherlands and later into Germany and France. The industry appeared in the United States around 1790 in Cheshire, Massachusetts, and spread to nearby Ashfield, Lanesborough, Pittsfield, Lenox, and Whately, declining around 1840 in Massachusetts. From here, the industry moved west to New York, Ohio, Michigan, and finally Oregon.

Peppermint (*M. ×piperita*) is primarily grown today in the fertile sandy loam soils of the Yakima Valley of Washington, adjacent Idaho, and the Willamette Valley of Oregon.

"Native" spearmint (*M. ×villosonervata*) and Scotch spearmint (*M. ×gracilis*) are primarily grown today, along with some peppermint, in the muck soils of Michigan, Indiana, and Wisconsin.

Almost all mints relish moist, fertile soil in full to part sun. Spearmint has been found to do best at pH 6.0, while peppermint has been found to grow best at pH 7.0; damage to both may occur below pH 4.5. The total content of essential oil in peppermint is raised by nitrogenous fertilizers (178 to 268 pounds per acre or 200 to 300 kg N/ha); nitrates give better results than ammonium salts in increasing the weight of plant material, while ammonium salts enhance the production of volatile oil.

Mint is commonly planted out in dense rows ("row" or "strip" mint) and the stolons allowed to grow between the rows ("field" mint). Because mint is a shallow-rooted crop with medium to high total water requirements, irrigation is often required. Overhead watering bursts the essential oil glands, resulting in a lowered oil yield, so rill irrigation is commonly used. Weeds may be controlled by tilling, weeder geese, or a number of registered herbicides.

Distillation for oil and harvest for leaves is generally done at the time of maximum bloom, which generally coincides with the period of maximum oil yield. Mint is a long-day plant; peppermint must have a minimum of ten to fourteen hours of day length to flower, while fifteen hours of day length is normally recommended for commercial mint oil yield. Thus, mint production is generally limited in the United States to areas north of the 40th parallel. Mint that is grown in the Caribbean, Central America, and the Philippines rarely flowers; herbarium vouchers from these areas inevitably lack flowers.

Mint is very prone to verticillium wilt and leaf rust from *Puccinia menthae*. 'Todd Mitcham' and 'Murray Mitcham' peppermints were developed for resistance to wilt; otherwise, burning of stubble, crop rotation, and sometimes soil fumigation are essential for continued commercial production. Mint anthracnose, caused by *Sphaceloma menthae*, is occasionally destructive. Nematodes, particularly *Longidorus menthsolanus* and *Pratylenchus minyus*, are often a problem too and also increase infection by *Verticillium*. The mint flea beetle, *Longitarsus waterhousei*, can cause considerable leaf-fall and browning, while loopers and cutworms may defoliate the plants. The mint root borer (*Fumibotys fumalis*) is one of the most serious pests of peppermint in the Pacific Northwest.

Discussed here are the principal cultivated mints that can be assigned to species or named hybrids. Some, such as 'Hillary's Sweet Lemon' mint cannot be authoritatively assigned to any botanical name other than *Mentha*. *Mentha* 'Hillary's Sweet Lemon' was introduced by Jim Westerfield of Freeburg, Illinois; he named the herb after former First Lady Hillary Clinton. This mint may be a hybrid, *M. suaveolens* × *M. aquatica* (*M. ×maximiliana*); Jim has continued to introduce other selections. The odor is predominantly spearmint backed by nuances of lemon. Some other hybrids, such as *M. ×smithiana*, red mint, are sometimes encountered in North America but are rather rare.

Mentha aquatica
mĕn-thå å-kwă-tĭ-kå
water mint, bergamot mint

French: *menthe aquatique*
German: *Wasserminze*
Dutch: *watermunt*
Italian: *mentastro d'acqua*
Spanish: *hierba buena rizada, hierba buena morisca, azandar*
Portuguese: *hortelã da água*

Mentha aquatica

The typical form of this species is called water mint, but the form called bergamot mint is more commonly cultivated. The egg-shaped leaves of water mint are slightly hairy and often tinted red. Flowers are grouped into a head-like inflorescence at the tips of the stems.

Bergamot mint (a.k.a. eau de cologne mint, orange mint, or lemon mint, named after Italian bergamot, *Citrus bergamia* Risso & Poit., not our native bergamot, *Monarda*) usually differs from water mint by its completely smooth leaves, gene-determined pollen sterility, and lavender-like scent; it is not a hybrid and should not be designated as a variety of peppermint. While originally described as a separate species, *M. citrata* Ehrh., the correct scientific name of bergamot mint is probably var. *citrata* (Ehrh.) Fresen. 'Todd 664', developed by the mint geneticist Dr. M. J. Murray, is so like lavender that it has been dubbed "American lavender." Bergamot mint is commonly naturalized in North America, but the true water mint is rare in the United States.

"Lime mint" supposedly originated as a chance seedling from open-pollinated germplasm maintained by the U.S.D.A. at Corvallis, Oregon, but it is primarily *M. aquatica*.

Important chemistry: Water mint is high in menthofuran, 33 to 89 percent, supplemented with trace to 21 percent viridiflorol plus menthofurolactone, giving it a musty-mint odor.

The oil of bergamot mint is high in linalyl acetate (22 to 60 percent), 21 to 42 percent linalool, 1 to 20 percent limonene, and trace to 12 percent alpha-pinene, providing a lavender-like odor. Some populations of *M. aquatica* also have 28 to 49 percent isopinocamphone with up to 21 percent beta-pinene and 16 percent limonene, providing a warm-camphoraceous odor.

Mentha arvensis

měn-thå är-věn-sĭs

corn mint

The corn or field mint of Europe is only commonly cultivated in a green-leaved clone which has been previously designated as *M. gentilis* or ginger mint, and the virus-infected clone, called golden applemint. This central European form of corn mint is perfectly seed-fertile and lacks anthers because of at least one gene which regulates pollen production. Golden applemint is splashed with yellow in spring on leaves that develop in cool weather; William Sole called this form "window mint" in his monograph on mints in 1790, perhaps alluding to the yellow translucent areas on the lance-shaped leaves. Flowers are lavender and borne in the axils of the leaves. Selections of *M. arvensis* include so-called banana-, coconut-, and basil-scented forms, but don't expect these manufactured names to smell like the real thing unless you have a vivid imagination.

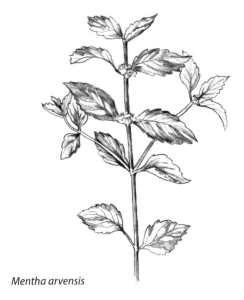

Mentha arvensis

Important chemistry: Ginger mint has 56 percent linalool. While a high linalool content would normally impart a lavender-like odor, the high gamma-terpinene/(*E*)-beta-ocimene/3-octanone content (6 percent) imparts fruity overtones.

Mentha canadensis

měn-thå kân-ă-děn-sĭs

North American cornmint, Japanese peppermint

While the North American corn- or fieldmint was previously considered an infraspecific taxon of *M. arvensis* of Europe, which it resembles closely, *M. canadensis* differs in chromosome number, distribution, and chemistry and should be considered an ancient hybrid, *M. arvensis* × *M. longifolia*. We have also accomplished resynthesis by crossing northern European forms of *M. arvensis* with a European montane form of *M. longifolia*. By chromosome number, morphology, oils, and resynthesis, this species also includes the corn- or fieldmint of eastern Asia, commonly known as Japanese peppermint in English or *hakka* in Japanese. Culture is similar to that for peppermint and spearmint.

The United States imports Japanese cornmint oil primarily from China, India, and Singapore.

Important chemistry: North American cornmint most commonly occurs in a pennyroyal/peppermint-scented form with trace to 90 percent pulegone, trace to 78 percent (*Z*)-isopulegone, trace to 76 percent isomenthone, trace to 60 percent (*E*)-isopulegone, trace to 30 percent menthone, 1 to 18 percent limonene, and trace to 12 percent 1-octen-3-ol. Another type is eucalyptus/floral/herb-scented with trace to

85 percent linalool, trace to 49 percent 1,8-cineole, 1 to 38 percent (*Z*)-beta-ocimene, and trace to 26 percent (*E*)-beta-ocimene plus gamma-terpinene. Japanese cornmint most commonly occurs in a peppermint-scented form with trace to 87 percent menthol, 3 to 84 percent menthone, trace to 22 percent menthyl acetate, trace to 21 percent piperitone, 0 to 17 percent pulegone, and 0 to 11 percent neomenthol. Pennyroyal/peppermint-scented forms, similar to North American cornmint, are also known with 14 to 83 percent pulegone, 31 to 84 percent menthone, and trace to 18 percent piperitone. Japanese cornmint contains acetoxycarvotanacetone, which has been reported to be a repellent for mosquitoes, gnats, and gadflies.

Mentha canadensis

Mentha ×gracilis

mĕn-thǎ grǎs-ĭ-lĭs
Scotch spearmint

This hybrid (*M. arvensis* × *M. spicata*) was previously called *M. ×gentilis*, but a close inspection of Linnaeus' type specimen of *M. gentilis* shows it to be a male-sterile form of *M. arvensis*.

Use Scotch spearmint in recipes calling for spearmint. Another form of this species, 'Madalene Hill', is really a "doublemint," combining the flavors of both spearmint and peppermint, and it makes an unusual substitute for spearmint. Scotch spearmint has lavender flowers in the axils of lance-shaped leaves which gradually diminish in size toward the apex of the stem.

Important chemistry: Several odors of this mint are grown or naturalized in North America. The spearmint-scented clones are high in (*R*)(+)-carvone plus dihydrocarveol, 20 to 86 percent, and up to 30 percent limonene and/or 11 percent beta-pinene. The clones scented of up to 11 percent neodihydrocarveol plus germacrene

D and/or 10 percent (*Z*)-beta-ocimene also have spearmint-like odors. The peppermint-scented clones have 38 to 91 percent menthone and 24 to 68 percent menthol and up 29 percent neomenthol, 29 percent piperitone, 24 percent menthyl acetate, and/or 23 percent pulegone. The pennyroyal-scented clones have up to 86 percent pulegone with up to 42 percent menthone, 45 percent neomenthol, 26 percent 8-hydroxy-p-menth-3-ene, 23 percent menthol, 23 percent piperitone, 22 percent menthyl acetate, 17 percent piperitenone, and/or 14 percent 1,2-epoxyneomenthyl acetate. The minty fruit-scented clones may have up to 36 percent [*E*]-piperitione oxide, 13 percent piperitone oxide, 28 percent pulegone, 28 percent menthol, 12 percent menthone, and/or 11 percent beta-pinene.

Another fruit-like odor characterizes the clones that have up to 38 percent 3-octanol, 18 percent 3-octanone, and/or 11 percent beta-pinene. The lavender-like clones have 37 to 63 percent linalool with up to 46 percent (*R*)(+)-

carvone, 17 percent 1,8-cineole, 13 percent 3-dodecanone, 12 percent (*E*)-sabinene hydrate, and/or 10 percent 3-octanol.

Some clones, such as that cultivated in North America as redstem applemint ('Madalene Hill'), are unique in that both spearmint and peppermint are in one plant, contrary to a genetic rule that says this is impossible. These "doublemints" have up to 40 percent (*R*)(+)-carvone, 22 percent menthone, 20 percent neo-dihydrocarvyl acetate, 15 percent dihydrocarveol, 14 percent menthyl acetate, and/or 13 percent limonene.

Mentha ×*piperita*
měn-thå pī-pēr-ĭ-tå
peppermint

> **French:** *mentha poivrée*
> **German:** *Pfefferminze*
> **Dutch:** *pepermunt*
> **Italian:** *menta piperita, menta inglese, menta pepe, menta piperita, menta peperina*
> **Spanish:** *menta*
> **Portuguese:** *nespereira da Europa, hortelã*
> **Swedish:** *pepparmynta*
> **Russian:** *myata*
> **Chinese:** *yang-po-ho*
> **Japanese:** *seiyo-hakka*
> **Arabic:** *na'nā, nannaul-habagul hindi*

The specific epithet refers to the genus *Piper*, which includes black pepper. Peppermint is a sterile hybrid of spearmint (*M. spicata*) and water mint (*M. aquatica*); this has been proven by resynthesis by Merritt J. Murray of A. M. Todd Co., Kalamazoo, Michigan. Since it is an interspecific hybrid of distantly related species, it rarely, if ever, sets fertile seeds; when a researcher at Michigan State University pollinated 18,000 flower spikes of 'Mitcham' peppermint containing approximately 2,888,000 ovules, the plants produced only 55 seeds, and only five of them germinated. That's 0.0002 percent seed fertility! What seed company would accept those odds?

Actually, the "peppermint" seeds now offered germinate to rank-scented forms of spearmint. Our efforts to trace this "peppermint" seed back to its source led to a single German wholesale company.

Both spearmint and water mint are very variable, so the collective hybrid *M. ×piperita* is also variable. Clones are known with leaves that are smooth or crisped, and green, purple, and/or variegated. Three clones are primarily cultivated, though: black peppermint (nothovar. *piperita*, with 'Mitcham' the most famous cultivar), white peppermint (nothovar. *officinalis* Sole), and crisped peppermint ('Crispa'). Only 'Mitcham' peppermint has achieved any economic importance.

White peppermint, so-called because it lacks the red tints on the leaves of black peppermint, was first described by John Ray from England in the second edition of his *Synopsis* (1696). After Ray died in 1705, illustrator Johann Dillenius erroneously used black peppermint in drawings for the third edition of Ray's *Synopsis* (1724), initiating a confusion of white versus black peppermint that continues today

The inflorescence of white peppermint resembles the pointed spike of spearmint, while the inflorescence of black peppermint resembles the round head of water mint. Likewise, the leaves of white peppermint resemble spearmint, while the leaves of black peppermint resemble water mint. White peppermint also lacks the dark purple to black color on the stems and leaves found in black peppermint.

Crisped peppermint, 'Crispa', has a spearmint odor inherited from the spearmint parent. It is commonly misidentified in herb books as a selection of *M. aquatica* and should not be confused with crisped spearmint. Crisped peppermint is tightly crisped with a head-like cluster of terminal flowers, while crisped spearmint has flatter leaves with a spike-like cluster of terminal flowers.

"Perfume mint," *M. ×piperita* 'Lavanduliodora', originated as a naturally occurring hybrid in the Po plain between Carmagnola and Moretta, Italy, and was discovered by Prof. Tommaso Sacco.

"Grapefruit mint" supposedly originated as a chance seedling from open-pollinated germplasm maintained by the U.S.D.A. at Corvallis, Oregon. It is hairy and crisped with a slight hint of grapefruit.

"Chocolate mint" has been applied in the U.S. trade to both black and white peppermints. The clones offered under this name differ little in morphology or odor from clones which have been cultivated for over three centuries. Apparently some vendors go by the axiom that if the plant doesn't sell, you should invent a more provocative name. "Blue balsam mint" is a slightly different variant of 'Mitcham', but not so different to warrant a separate cultivar name.

Menthol is unique in the plant kingdom, occurring in commercial quantities in only two species of *Mentha* (*M. ×piperita* and *M. canadensis*). Amazingly, this chemical produces the same effect at the level of the ion flux of membranes as that of physical cold. Menthol feels cold because it is cold! The reader is referred to the research by David McKemy on further details on the ion channels of the transient receptor potential (TRP). Knowledge that a chemical can actually produce the same effects as low temperature has led to research in "super cold" chemicals (rest assured that the obvious military applications have not gone unnoticed).

While black peppermint is grown in the United States, we also import peppermint oil, primarily from India, China, Canada, and Germany. Peppermint oil is considered GRAS at 5 to 8,300 ppm. Luteolin, a yellow pigment found in peppermint leaves, has been shown to be strongly antimutagenic. Peppermint oil is somewhat antibacterial, antiallergenic, and antispasmodic. It can be used to relieve irritable bowel syndrome and relieve intestinal cramps in humans. Maybe those after-dinner mints have some function as a digestive aid after all.

Peppermint oil is somewhat antibacterial, antiallergenic, and antispasmodic. It can be used to relieve irritable bowel syndrome and relieve intestinal cramps in humans.

On the other hand, rats exhibit encephalopathy (degeneration of the brain) in twenty-eight days when given 0.002 ounce of peppermint oil per pound of body weight (100 mg/kg); that's 0.24 ounce of oil for a 150-pound human. Menthol hypersensitivity with chronic itchy skin rash, flushing, and headaches have also been associated with peppermint in some individuals. Addiction to mentholated cigarettes has been reported to produce toxic exhaustive psychosis, while excessive peppermint consumption may lead to irregular heart rhythm. Everything in moderation! Caution on the use of peppermint oil is also indicated in patients with GI reflux, hiatal hernia, or kidney stones.

Important chemistry: 'Mitcham', *M. ×piperita* nothovar. *piperita*, or black peppermint, has an essential oil dominated by 16 to 61 percent menthol, 2 to 34 percent menthone, trace to 22 percent menthofuran, 1 to 20 percent menthyl acetate, and trace to 14 percent pulegone, depending upon slight genetic variation, the stage of harvest, and the percentage of flowers used for distillation.

As the growing season progresses, menthol and menthyl acetate levels increase while menthone decreases. Maximum oil yield results when the calyces are only barely visible or the menthol reaches about 45 to 48 percent; delaying harvest results in increased menthol but at the expense of oil yield and ratios of other significant components. *Mentha ×piperita* nothovar. *officinalis*, or white peppermint, has an oil dominated by 36 to 47 percent menthol, 9 to 15 percent menthyl acetate, 4 to 14 percent menthofuran, and 4 to 12 percent menthone. 'Lavanduliodora' has inherited 38 to 55 percent linalool and 10 to 33 percent linalyl acetate from the bergamot mint parent.

Mentha pulegium
mĕn-thå pū-lē-jē-ŭm
pennyroyal

> **French:** *pouliot, menthe pouliot, herbe aux puces, herbe de Saint-Laurent*
> **German:** *Polei*
> **Dutch:** *polei*
> **Italian:** *puleggio, pulezzo*
> **Spanish:** *poleo*
> **Portuguese:** *poejo*
> **Chinese:** *po-ho*

Pennyroyal is a creeping mint with glossy, egg-shaped leaves, ideal for carpeting paths and filling in between bricks, where mild foot traffic releases its pungent scent. The lavender blooms are tightly crowded on stems that may reach 16 inches (40 cm). This European pennyroyal should not be confused with our native American pennyroyal, *Hedeoma pulegioides*.

European pennyroyal derives its Latin name from *pulex*, or flea, alluding to its use as a strewing herb to repel fleas. The essential oil (1 to 24 ppm) is considered GRAS by the U.S. Food and Drug Administration; the GRAS maximum is approximately equivalent to 2 drops of oil in 1 quart of water. Higher doses can be poisonous, and at least one case of death has occurred from ingesting 1 ounce of pennyroyal essential oil to induce an abortion. Pennyroyal oil is not an efficient abortifacient, however, since it produces abortions by first damaging the mother's liver. The oral dose that kills 50 percent of the test rats (the LD50) of European pennyroyal is 0.006 ounce oil per pound body weight (0.4 g/kg); for a 150-pound human, that would be 0.96 ounce of oil.

Rats dosed with pulegone exhibit degeneration of the brain in twenty-eight days with 0.003 ounce pulegone per pound body weight

Mentha pulegium

(160 mg/kg); that's 0.38 oz of pulegone (or approximately 0.400 to 1.226 oz European pennyroyal oil, depending upon the relative percentage of pulegone) for a 150-pound human.

All in all, we do not recommend the consumption of pennyroyal. In addition, pennyroyal oil should not be applied to pets, as it has stimulated symptoms of poisoning in dogs. Flea pillows, yes, but please, no oil or tea!

The patented cultivars 'Snowcones Purple' (PP12,971) and 'Snowcones White' (PP12,975) are *M. cervina* L., not *M. pulegium*.

Important chemistry: European pennyroyal derives its typical scent from the content of pulegone in the essential oil, which ranges from 31 to 95 percent, sometimes with trace to 10 percent (*E*) plus (*Z*)-isopulegone. Peppermint undertones are due to a complement of 0 to 97 percent piperitone, trace to 53 percent menthone, trace to 45 percent isomenthone, 0 to 40 percent piperitenone, 0 to 24 percent isopiperitenone, trace to 16 percent menthol, trace to 15 percent neoisomenthol, and trace to 14 percent neoisomenthyl acetate. Some clones are more peppermint-like, with 70 to 88 percent piperitone and trace to 11 percent limonene but only 4 percent pulegone.

Mentha requienii
měn-thå rě-kwē-nē-ī
Corsican mint

The tiny Corsican mint is named after M. Esprit Requien (1788–1851), a botanist from Avignon and botanical explorer of Provence and Corsica. At first glance, most amateurs would not even recognize this as a *Mentha* species. It looks like a fragrant version of baby's tears [*Soleirolia soeirolii* (Req.) Dandy, a.k.a. *Helxine soleirolli* Req.], and, oddly enough, both evolved on lakeshores in Corsica. The tiny, egg-shaped leaves may reach only 4 mm.

Corsican mint will generally reseed in moist soil, although it is rarely winter-hardy above Zone 8. It is delightful if planted in front of a bench in the herb garden, causing visitors to step upon it, release its fragrance, and curiously examine the very tiny lavender flowers, borne in the axils of the leaves, while sitting down.

Mentha requienii

Important chemistry: The tiny Corsican mint is characterized by an essential oil containing 63 to 78 percent pulegone and 3 to 26 percent menthone, thus giving it a pennyroyal-peppermint odor.

Mentha spicata
mĕn-thå spī-kā-tå
spearmint

> **French:** *baume vert, menthe verte*
> **German:** *Grüne Minze*
> **Dutch:** *groene munt*
> **Italian:** *mentastro verde, menta verde, erba Santa Maria*
> **Spanish:** *hierabuena, menta verde*
> **Portuguese:** *hortelā*

The specific name refers to the spicate inflorescence. This is a very variable species, including forms with leaves that are smooth, hairy, crisped, and/or wrinkled. The hairy forms, sometimes called silver mint, are incorrectly named *M. longifolia* (L.) L. (horse mint) in American and English manuals, but *M. longifolia* is native to montane sections of Europe, Asia, and Africa and does not occur even naturalized in England or North America.

Thus the English and North American floras are wrong! The wrinkled leaf form, sometimes called *M. cordifolia* or 'Kentucky Colonel' in

Mentha spicata

some manuals, is found naturalized throughout Central America and the southwestern United States; in other words, wherever the conquistadors went. After Ferdinand Magellan claimed the Philippines for Spain in 1521, the herb was transported there. This form of spearmint deserves to be called "conquistadors footprint."

Spearmint is also variable in scent, from typical spearmint to peppermint. Regardless of the scent or hairiness of the leaves, all forms of spearmint have lavender flowers crowded into terminal, pointed spikes.

Spearmint is cultivated commercially in the United States, but we also import spearmint oil primarily from China, Hong Kong, and Canada. Spearmint oil is considered GRAS at 72 to 6,200 ppm, while ground spearmint is GRAS at 500 to 5,967 ppm and spearmint extract is GRAS at 0.2 to 2,100 ppm. Spearmint oil is somewhat antibacterial. Spearmint tea has been found to decrease total testosterone and increase luteinizing hormone, follicle-stimulating hormone, and estradiol and may thus offer help in women with hirsutism.

Important chemistry: As variable as the morphology are the scents. The commonly cultivated, or "typical" spearmint is high in $(R)(+)$-carvone at 20 to 83 percent, with up to 38 percent dihydrocarveol, 30 percent linalool, 22 percent dihydrocarvone, 20 percent limonene, 12 percent dihydrocarvyl acetate, 12 percent phellandrene, and/or 11 percent 1,8-cineole. Other spearmint-like clones may have 16 to 22 percent [Z]-dihydrocarvone and up to 21 percent [E]-dihydrocarvone, 12 percent limonene, and/or 10 percent neoisodihydrocarvyl acetate or up to 25 percent dihydrocarvyl acetate, 21 percent neoisodihydrocarvyl acetate, and/or 20 percent $(R)(+)$-carvone.

The minty fruit-scented clones have either 28 to 70 percent piperitenone oxide with up to 18 percent piperitone oxide plus germacrene D or 43 to 68 percent [*E*]-piperitone oxide with up to 15 percent 1,2-epoxyneomenthyl acetate. The pennyroyal-scented clones contain 26 to 31 percent pulegone and 17 to 44 percent menthone with up to 16 percent isomenthone and/or 10 percent neomenthol. The eucalyptus-scented forms from Zakynthos (Ionian Island, Greece) have 4 to 41 percent 1,8-cineole and 7 to 46 percent piperitenone oxide.

The peppermint-scented clones contain 9 to 43 percent isomenthone and 33 to 57 percent menthone with up to 11 percent piperitone, 11 percent neoisomenthyl acetate, and 10 percent neoisomenthol. Spearmint may also occur in a peppermint-like-scented clone with 41 to 57 percent piperitone and/or up to 16 percent piperitenone. The lavender-like clones have 85 to 94 percent linalool. The literature also reports clones that have both spearmint and peppermint odors in the same plant; these have up to 42 percent menthol, 36 percent (*R*)(+)-carvone, 21 percent menthone, 18 percent dihydrocarveol, 13 percent [*Z*]-dihydrocarvone, and/or 10 percent terpinolene.

Mentha suaveolens

měn-thå swä-vē-ō-lěnz
pineapple mint, apple mint

This sweet-scented species was originally named by J. F. Ehrhart from the variegated form known as pineapple mint. Since Ehrhart's type specimen is the clonally propagated variegated clone, the variegated pineapple mint is correctly known as *M. suaveolens* var. *suaveolens*, not *M. suaveolens* 'Variegata'. The correct name of the green form, sometimes called apple mint, is presently undetermined.

Pineapple mint has round, tightly wrinkled leaves and white flowers crowded into terminal, pointed spikes. Especially in the variegated form, it has lax stems, so plant this in the foreground of the herb garden and expect it to fall all over itself.

Important chemistry: Typical apple and pineapple mints owe their odors to an essential oil dominated by 8 to 88 percent piperitenone oxide and trace to 60 percent (*E*)-piperitone oxide, supplemented with trace to 67 percent 1,2-epoxyneomenthyl acetate. The literature also reports a spearmint-like form with 38 percent (*Z*)-dihydrocarvone and 10 percent (*Z*)-dihydrocarvone and a pennyroyal-scented from with 52 percent neo-iso-isopulegol and 13 percent isopiperitenone.

Mentha suaveolens

Mentha ×*villosa* nothovar.
alopecuroides
mĕn-thå vĭ-lō-så ăl-ō-pĕk-yĕw-rōy-dēs
woolly mint

Woolly mint has tall, upright stems with large, fuzzy, egg-shaped leaves and lavender flowers crowded into terminal, pointed spikes. Its scientific name means fox-tailed mint, probably for its long, soft hairs, and it is variously called woolly mint, apple mint, Egyptian mint, or Bowles's mint.

Woolly mint is a sterile plant, so all specimens are identical, whether found naturalized in Egypt, Italy, England, or North America. This is the mint usually designated as *M. rotundifolia* or apple mint in herb books whose authors confuse it with *M. suaveolens*. True *M. suaveolens* has a pineapple-like odor, while woolly mint is distinctly spearmint-scented.

Important chemistry: The essential oil is dominated by 60 to 75 percent $(R)(+)$-carvone and 9 to 13 percent limonene, providing a distinct odor of spearmint.

Botanical Key and Description

Key:
1. Calyx hairy in throat, with distinctly unequal teeth 2
    2. Stems thread-like, lying on the ground and mat-forming; leaves 2 to 7 mm . . . .*M. requienii*
    2a. Stems not mat-forming, though sometimes lying on the ground; leaves 8 to 30 mm . . . . . *M. pulegium*
1a. Calyx smooth in throat, with more or less equal teeth 3
        3. Bracts like the leaves; inflorescence terminated by leaves, or by very small upper groups of
           flowers 4
           4. Plant often tinged with red, usually pollen- and/or seed-sterile; calyx 2 to 4 mm, narrowly bell-
              shaped or tubular, the teeth narrowly triangular to awl-shaped . . . . *M.* ×*gracilis*
           4a. Plant green, usually pollen- and/or seed-fertile; calyx triangular. 5
              5. Leaves usually lance-shaped and gradually decreasing in size toward the apex of the
                 blooming stem, usually pennyroyal- or peppermint-odored . . . . *M. canadensis*
              5a. Leaves usually egg-shaped to egg-lance-shaped and not decreasing in size toward the
                 apex of the blooming stem, usually fruity-lavender odored . . . . *M. arvensis*
        3a. Bracts mostly small and inconspicuous, unlike the leaves; flowers in terminal spikes or heads 6
           6. Leaves stalkless (the lower rarely stalked); flowers in a spike 5 to 15 mm in diameter. . . . 7
              7. Stem and leaves smooth or hairy; star-shaped hairs rare . . . . *M. spicata*
              7a. Stem and leaves hairy; star-shaped hairs abundant. 8
                 8. Plant robust, 60 to 140 cm high, middle stem leaves 4 to 8 × 3 to 6 cm, distinct
                    odor of spearmint, seed-sterile . . . . *M.* ×*villosa* nothovar. *alopecuroides*
                 8a. Plant 40 to 100 cm high, middle stem leaves 1.5 to 4.5 × 1 to 4 cm, odor fruity,
                    seed-fertile . . . . *M. suaveolens*
           6a. Leaves distinctly stalked; flowers in a head or oblong spike 12 to 20 mm in diameter . . . 9
                 9. Flowers in a head or oblong spike; leaves egg-shaped or lance-shaped; flowers
                    sterile. . . . . *M.* ×*piperita*
                 9a. Flowers in a head, sometimes with one to three clusters of flowers below;
                    leaves usually egg-shaped; flowers pollen- and/or seed-fertile . . . . . *M. aquatica*

M. aquatica L., Sp. pl. 576. 1753 & var. *citrata* (Ehrh.) Fresen., Syll. Pl. Nov. 2:234.1828.

Native country: Water mint and bergamot mint are native to Europe.

General habit: *M. aquatica* is a perennial, smooth to hairy, often purplish, 10 to 90 cm high.

Leaves: Leaves are 1.5 to 9 × 1 to 4 cm, egg-shaped to egg-lance-shaped, usually squared at the base, stalked, toothed.

Flowers: Inflorescence is of two or three congested flower-clusters with inconspicuous bracts, forming a terminal head up to 2 cm in diameter, sometimes with one to three distinct flower-clusters below, in the axils of leaf-like bracts. Calyx is tubular, teeth awl-shaped or narrowly triangular. Corolla is lilac.

M. arvensis Sp. pl. 577. 1753.

Native country: Corn mint is native to Europe.

General habit: European corn mint is a smooth to hairy perennial or rarely annual up to 60 cm high; flowering stems ascending or erect.

Leaves: Leaves are 1.5 to 7 × 1 to 4 cm, lance-shaped but widest at the center with ends equal to broadly egg-shaped, usually narrowing to a stalk, shallowly toothed.

Flowers: Flowers are in remote flower clusters in the axils of the leaves, the leaves narrowing toward the apex of the stem. Calyx is broadly bell-shaped, teeth triangular or broadly triangular. Corolla is lilac to white.

M. canadensis L., Sp. pl. 577. 1753 [*M. arvensis* var. *villosa* (Benth.) Stewart, *M. arvensis* f. *piperascens* Malinvaud ex Holmes, *M. haplocalyx* Briq.].

North American and Japanese cornmints are similar to European corn mint except the leaves are usually more lance-shaped and decreasingly smaller toward the apex of the stem.

M. ×*gracilis* Sole, Menth. Brit. 37. t. 16. 1798 (*M. gentilis* Auct., non L.).

Native country: *M.* ×*gracilis* is native to Europe but commonly naturalized in North America.

General habit: This very variable hybrid complex is a perennial 30 to 90 cm high, often red-tinged.

Leaves: Leaves are 1.5 to 9 × 0.8 to 4.5 cm, egg-lance-shaped, lance-shaped, or parallel-sided with the ends equal, narrowing to a short stalk, usually smooth but sometimes hairy.

Flowers: Flowers are usually in remote, stalkless flower clusters in the axils of the leaves or leaf-like bracts tapering toward the apex of the stem. Calyx is bell-shaped, the teeth awl-shaped or triangular, stamens usually not exceeding the calyx.

M. ×*piperita* L., Sp. pl. 576. 1753.

Native country: Peppermint is native to Europe but commonly found naturalized in North America.

General habit: Peppermint is a perennial 30 to 90 cm high, usually almost smooth but occasionally hairy to gray-hairy, often purple-tinged.

Leaves: Leaves are 4 to 9 × 1.5 to 4 cm, egg-lance-shaped or lance-shaped, rarely egg-shaped, wedge-shaped to almost heart-shaped at the base and long-stalked, usually toothed.

Flowers: Inflorescence is of numerous congested flower clusters with inconspicuous bracts forming a terminal, oblong spike to head 3 to 8 × 1.2 to 1.8 cm, often interrupted below. Calyx is tubular, usually smooth, teeth thin; stamens usually do not exceed the calyx. Corolla is lilac-pink.

M. pulegium L., Sp. pl. 577. 1753.

Native country: Pennyroyal is primarily native

to southern Europe, but it has become naturalized in North and South America.

General habit: Pennyroyal is an almost smooth to hairy perennial 10 to 40 cm long, stems procumbent to ascending.

Leaves: Leaves are 8 to 30 × 4 to 12 mm, narrow but widest at the center with the ends equal, rarely almost rounded, shortly stalked, smooth-edged or with up to six teeth on each side, hairy at least beneath.

Flowers: Bracts are leaf-like but usually smaller. Calyx teeth are awl-shaped. Corolla is lilac.

M. requienii Benth., Labiat. gen. spec. 182. 1833.

Native country: Corsican mint is native to Corsica.

General habit: Corsican mint is a smooth or sparsely hairy perennial, 3 to 12 cm long; stems are thread-like, usually procumbent, rooting at the nodes, mat-forming.

Leaves: Leaves and bracts 2 to 4 mm, stalked, rounded egg-shaped, with a smooth or wavy edge.

Flowers: Flowers are borne in the axils of the leaves. Calyx teeth are triangular to awl-shaped. Corolla is pale lilac.

M. spicata L., Sp. pl. 576. 1753 (*M. viridis* L., *M. crispa* L., *M. longifolia* Auct., non L., *M. cordifolia* Auct., non Opiz).

Native country: Spearmint is native to Europe but naturalized around the world.

General habit: Spearmint is a perennial 30 to 100 cm high.

Leaves: Leaves are 3 to 9 × 0.7 to 3 cm, lance-shaped or lance-egg-shaped, smooth or ruffled, widest near the base, toothed with regular teeth, rarely the whole leaf strongly crisped, smooth to densely hairy, the hairs on the lower surface usually simple with some branched hairs.

Flowers: Flowers are crowded into dense spikes. Calyx is bell-shaped, smooth or hairy. Corolla is lilac, pink, or white.

M. suaveolens Ehrh., Beitr. Naturk. 7:149. 1792 [*M. rotundifolia* Auct., non (L.) Hudson].

Native country: *M. suaveolens* is native to Europe and North Africa.

General habit: Pineapple and apple mint are perennials 40 to 100 cm high. Stem is sparsely hairy to densely white-hairy.

Leaves: Leaves are 1.5 to 3 × 1 to 4 cm, stalkless or very shortly stalked, strongly ruffled, two to four times longer than wide and sides parallel, tending to be egg-shaped to almost rounded, blunt at the apex, tipped at the apex, or rarely tapering to the apex, widest near the base, toothed, with ten to twenty teeth, often apparently round-toothed due to the teeth being bent downward, hairy above, usually gray- or white-hairy beneath, the hairs on the lower surface branched.

Flowers: Flowers are crowded into dense spikes 40 to 90 × 5 to 10 mm, often interrupted below and usually branched. Calyx is bell-shaped, hairy. Corolla is whitish or pinkish.

M. ×*villosa* Hudson **nothovar.** *alopecuroides* (Hull) Briq., Bull. Herb. Boissier 4:679. 1896.

Native country: The native country of woolly mint is unknown, but it has been naturalized around the world.

General habit: Woolly mint is often confused with *M. suaveolens* but is more robust, 60 to 140 cm high, and has a spearmint scent.

Leaves: Middle leaves of the stem are 40 to 80 × 30 to 60 mm, broadly egg-shaped or round, softly hairy, the margin with spreading teeth.

Flowers: The inflorescence is a robust spike 10 to 12 mm wide. Corolla is pink.

Monarda

mō-när-då
monarda

Family: Lamiaceae (Labiatae)

Growth form: annuals and hardy perennials to 47 inches (120 cm)

Hardiness: many species hardy to Maine (Zone 4)

Light: full to part sun

Water: moist but not constantly wet

Soil: well-drained garden loam

Propagation: divisions or seeds in spring, 56,000 seeds per ounce (1,975/g) (*M.* ×*media*)

Culinary use: teas or thyme or oregano substitutes but limited (not GRAS)

Craft use: dried flowers, potpourri

Landscape use: excellent in mid-border; dried flowers in winter landscape associate well with grasses

Monarda is a native American herb named after Spanish physician and botanist N. Monardez, of Seville. Its unusual and ornamental flowers possess a distinctly architectural character with their bristly, colorful appearance. All species attract bees and are good honey plants. The twelve species of *Monarda*, all native to North America, offer a wide assortment of flavors and fragrances—from lemony to oregano—produced on annual or perennial plants. Cultivation is generally easy on moist, well-drained garden loam in full to part shade, depending upon the species. However, most selections of *Monarda* are prone to powdery mildew, turning the plant into a mass of grayish white, curled leaves that soon drop. This infection can be reduced by increasing the movement of air, by removing diseased leaves, and, most importantly, by choice of mildew-resistant selections, particularly 'Colrain Red', 'Marshall's Delight', 'Purple Mildew Resistant', 'Raspberry Wine', 'Rose Queen', 'Rosy Purple', 'Violet Queen', and *Monarda fistulolsa* f. *albescens*. None of the *Monarda* species discussed here have GRAS status.

Monarda citriodora

mō-när-då sǐ-trī-ō-dǒr-å
lemon beebalm

Monarda citriodora translates roughly to mean *Monarda* with a citrus aroma. *Monarda citriodora* subsp. *citriodora*, native to southern United States and northern Mexico, is called lemon beebalm in English; this subspecies includes var. *citriodora*, var. *parva* Scora, and var. *attenuata* Scora. *Monarda citriodora* subsp. *austromontana*, native to southwestern United States and western Mexico, is called orégano in Spanish.

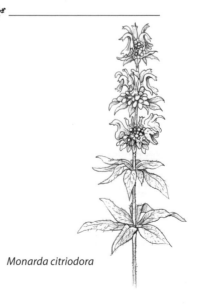

Monarda citriodora

Leaves are lance-shaped on stems 20 to 70 cm high. Flowers are white to reddish or purple on terminal heads with hairy bracts underneath; the hairs may be white, red, or purple. This annual species can be easily grown in full sun on garden loam and readily reseeds itself.

The oil of *M. citriodora* var. *citriodora* has been demonstrated to be an antioxidant.

Important chemistry: The subsp. *austro-montana* is sometimes substituted for Greek oregano, but the flavor is more similar to that of thyme, with 63 percent thymol in the essential oil. The subsp. *citriodora* has also been used as a thyme substitute and has 51 to 83 percent thymol in the essential oil.

Monarda clinopodia
mō-när-då klĭn-ō-pō-dī-å
beebalm, wild bergamot

Monarda clinopodia is named for its resemblance to the bracted leaves of *Clinopodium* (now *Pycnanthemum incanum*). No uses are recorded for *M. clinopodia*, but this perennial species is involved in the origin of many named cultivars more properly ascribed to *M. ×media*.

Lance-shaped leaves are borne on stems 12 to 49 inches (30 to 125 cm) tall. The whitish green flowers are purple-dotted or flesh-colored in a terminal head with lance-shaped, green bracts beneath. Beebalm prefers full sun and moist but well-drained garden loam.

Important chemistry: The essential oil consists of 41 percent linalyl acetate and 14 percent 1,8-cineole, providing a lavender-eucalyptus odor.

Monarda didyma
mō-när-då dĭd-ĭ-må
Oswego tea

> **French:** *monarde écarlate, thé d'Oswégo*
> **German:** *Goldmelisse, Monarde-Tee*
> **Dutch:** *scharlakenrode monarde, Pennsylvanische thee*
> **Italian:** *menta rosa*
> **Spanish:** *monarda*

This species translates roughly to mean *Monarda* with stamens in pairs. Early American settlers, particularly the Shakers in upstate New York, brought notoriety to this woodland perennial by making a tea from its leaves. From that point onward, *M. didyma* became known as Oswego tea or Oswego beebalm. The scarlet

Monarda didyma

flowers provided the other common English name, scarlet monarda.

With brilliant crimson flowers in a terminal head, Oswego tea is excellent for attracting the ruby-throated hummingbird (*Archilochus colubris*) and evening visitors, sphinx moths. Leaves are lance-shaped on stems 12 to 47 inches (30 to 120 cm) tall. This hardy perennial prefers part to full shade in a moist soil rich in organic matter. Mildew late in the season is unsightly but does not seem to damage the plant. Some of the clones identified in the plant trade as *M. didyma* may actually belong to *M.* ×*media*.

Important chemistry: The essential oil of Oswego tea consists of trace to 74 percent linalool, trace to 27 percent 1,8-cineole, trace to 13 percent limomene, 1 to 13 percent gamma-terpinene, and 12 to 19 percent para-cymene, providing a medicinal lavender-eucalyptus odor.

Monarda fistulosa

mō-när-då fĭs-tū-lō-så

wild bergamot

This species acquired its Latin name from the tubular flowers. Wild bergamot, horsemint, and beebalm are names of perennials whose native habitat covers dry, open woodlands and wood margins.

This hardy perennial consists of five varieties, but var. *fistulosa* is most commonly encountered in eastern North America, whereas var. *menthifolia* (Graham) Fern. is more commonly encountered in western North America. Controversy exists on the correct nomenclature and validity of these varieties; subsp. *fistulosa* has been proposed for the populations of eastern North America, while subsp. *menthifolia* Gill has been proposed for the populations of the prairies and Great Plains regions of North America. All variants have lance-shaped leaves on stems 12 to 47 inches (30 to 120 cm) high. Flowers are lavender to rose in a terminal head with lance-shaped, usually red-tinged bracts underneath.

Wild bergamot prefers full sun and well-drained garden soil. It tolerates drought rather well.

The high-thymol clones have been used as substitutes for thyme, and the scent of the high-geraniol clone is reminiscent of rose geranium. The high-geraniol clone is an ideal substitute for rose geranium, but it thrives only in the cool summers of its native Manitoba.

Important chemistry: The essential oil of *M. fistulosa* subsp. *fistulosa* (including var. *mollis* and var. *fistulosa*) consists of trace to 61 percent thymol, trace to 55 percent carvacrol, 20 to 43 percent para-cymene, trace to 31 percent gamma-terpinene plus 3-octanone, and 3 to 20 percent methyl carvacrol. The essential oil of *M. fistulosa* var. *brevis* consists of 67 percent thymol and 12 percent para-cymene. The essential oil of *M. fistulosa* var. *menthifolia* consists of 18 to 82 percent thymol, 0 to 29 percent para-cymene, 0 to 22 percent gamma-terpinene, 0 to 16 percent 1,8-cineole, and 0 to 10 percent alpha-terpinene. A clone ('Sweet') of *M. fistulosa* var. *menthifolia* with up to 91 to 93 percent geraniol in the essential oil has also been collected from Manitoba, Canada.

The essential oil of *M. fistulosa* var. *mollis* consists of trace to 60 percent thymol, 8 to 30 percent *p*-cymene, trace to 28 percent gamma-terpinene, 0 to 22 percent carvacrol, and 0 to 11 percent 1,8-cineole. The essential oil of an Arkansan segregate of *M. fistulosa* consists of 33 percent *p*-cymene, 22 percent gamma-terpinene, and 11 percent alpha-terpineol.

Monarda ×*media*

mō-när-då mē-dē-å
hybrid beebalm

As the Latin name implies, this is an intermediate hybrid. Hybrid beebalm represents a large portion of the monardas available in garden centers and from perennial specialists. It probably includes such cultivars as 'Adam', 'Blue Stocking', 'Croftway Pink', 'Mahogany', 'Marshall's Delight', 'Prairie Brand', 'Snow Queen', and 'Violet Queen'. 'Petite Delight' was a direct hybridization of *M. didyma* and *M. fistulosa* and is dwarf. The high-carvacrol clones have been sometimes substituted for Greek oregano; clones high in thymol can take the place of thyme.

Monarda ×*media* is a hybrid complex of *M. clinopodia*, *M. didyma*, and *M. fistulosa* usually found in rich, moist woodlands. Generally the cultivars with red flowers prefer more shade and moisture, while those with white or lavender flowers prefer full sun and less moisture.

Important chemistry: As might be expected from a hybrid complex, the essential oil of hybrid beebalm clones is quite variable. Unnamed selections have trace to 74 percent carvacrol, trace to 67 percent linalool, trace to 31 percent thymol, trace to 27 percent ocimene, trace to 22 percent 1,8-cineole, trace to 14 percent beta-pinene, and trace to 12 percent alpha-terpineol. 'Marshall's Delight' has 50 percent linalool and 18 percent carvacrol. 'Morden #3' has 93 percent geraniol.

Monarda pectinata

mō-när-då pĕk-tĭ-nā-tå
pony beebalm

The Latin epithet means "comb-like," referring to the hairs of the bracts. Because its essential oil is high in carvacrol and thymol, this herb has been occasionally substituted for Greek oregano. It is native only to Colorado, Nebraska, Arizona, and Texas. The lance-shaped leaves are borne on stems 6 to 20 inches (15 to 50 cm) tall. Flowers are white to pinkish in a terminal head with lance-shaped, green bracts underneath. This annual should be sited in well-drained soil in full sun.

Botanical Key and Description

Key:
1. Crowded clusters of flowers usually solitary, appearing terminal; dilated portion of corolla tube equaling or exceeding the unexpanded portion, the upper lip straight to only slightly moderately curved like a bow, not dotted with translucent glands, the lower lip usually unmarked; stamens exserted; leaves egg-shaped to lance-egg-shaped; perennial 2
    2. Stamen attachment 3 to 7 mm deep in expanded portion of corolla throat (except in small-flowered *M. didyma*) . . . . *M. didyma*
    2a. Stamen attachment 1 to 3 mm deep in expanded portion of corolla throat 3

3. Leaves firm, narrowly triangular-egg-shaped to lance-egg-shaped; calyx orifice densely beset with moderately coarse and stiff hairs; plants of the United States and Mexico . . . . *M. fistulosa*

3a. Leaves membranaceous or thin, broadly triangular-egg-shaped to egg-shaped; calyx orifice hairless to slightly beset with moderately coarse and stiff hairs; plants of the eastern United States 4

4. Corolla large, rose to purple, lower corolla lip mostly unmarked; bracts subtending crowded flower clusters rose to red . . . . *M. ×media*

4a. Corolla small, whitish to greenish or flesh-colored, lower corolla lip spotted with small dots at junction of lower and upper lip, or with larger dots spread over entire lower lip; bracts subtending crowded flower clusters green or whitish green . . . . *M. clinopodia*

1a. Crowded clusters of flowers, several strung along the stem; dilated portion of corolla tube shorter than unexpanded portion; the upper lip strongly curved like a bow, both lips commonly dotted with translucent glands; stamens usually included; leaves widest at the center with both ends equal to narrow and flat, rarely lance-egg-shaped; annual, biennial, or short-lived perennial 5

5. Bracts parallel-sided or lance-shaped, sparsely hairy along lower half of margin, minutely and densely hairy with white or purple hairs on adaxial surface (except *M. citriodora* var. *attenuata*); plants of southern United States and northern Mexico . . . .*M. citriodora*

5a. Bracts widest at the center with the ends equal, tending to egg-shaped, slightly hairy along entire margin, hairless on upper surface; plants of the southwestern United States . . . . *M. pectinata*

M. citriodora Cervantes ex Lag., Gen. sp. pl. 2. 1816.

Native country: *M. citriodora* is native to the southern and southwestern United States.

General habit: *M. citriodora* is an annual herb 20 to 70 cm tall, branched mainly in the inflorescence, rarely at the base or unbranched.

Leaves: Leaves are thin but firm, lance-shaped to parallel-sided, 1.5 to 8 cm long, 3 to 15 mm wide, mostly toothed, apex pinched with spinose tip, hairy to hairless on both surfaces.

Flowers: Inner bracts are parallel-sided to lance-shaped, mainly smooth-edged, 7 to 25 mm long, 3 to 9 mm wide, bract tip abruptly pinched at the tip into a spinose bristle or gradually narrowing to the tip, base tapering, hairless or densely coated with white, red, or purple short hairs above, margins with hairs. Calyx is 5 to 14 mm long; corolla is white to reddish or purple, 7 to 13 mm long.

Key:

1. Bracts lance-shaped to narrow-lance-shaped, gradually pinched at the tip to a spiny bristle, not more than 4 mm wide, strongly reflexed from the base. . . . . subsp. *austromontana* (Epling) Scora, Madroño 18(4):120. 1965 (*M. austromontana* Epling)

1a. Bracts parallel-sided, abruptly pinched at the tip to a spinelike bristle, or gradually narrowing to the apex, commonly more than 4 mm wide, spreading horizontally, or forming a cuplike whorl, but not reflexed from the base. . . . . subsp. *citriodora*

M. clinopodia L., Sp. pl. 22. 1753.

Native country: Beebalm is native from Alabama to Pennsylvania, west to Illinois.

General habit: *M. clinopodia* is a perennial herb 30 to 125 cm high, branched in the upper parts.

Leaves: Leaves are membranaceous, egg-shaped to triangular-egg-shaped, 5 to 13 cm long, 2 to 6 cm wide, mostly toothed, apex pinched (acuminate), with moderately coarse and stiff hairs above, and longer, stiff, spreading hairs below.

Flowers: Bracts are lance-shaped. Calyx is 6 to 10 mm long; corolla is whitish green with a purple-dotted lower lip or flesh colored, 8 to 12 mm long.

M. didyma L., Sp. pl. 22. 1753.

Native country: Oswego tea is native to rich, moist woodlands from Ontario to Georgia, west to Illinois.

General habit: *Monarda didyma* is a perennial herb 70 to 120 cm tall; stem axis simple or branched in the upper parts.

Leaves: Leaves are thin, egg-shaped to triangular or lance-egg-shaped, 6 to 14 cm long, 3 to 8 cm wide, toothed, apex pinched, leaf blades with occasional longer bristles, or with long hairs, especially along the veins.

Flowers: Bracts are lance-shaped. Calyx is 11 to 13 mm long; corolla is brilliant crimson, 10 to 18 mm long.

M. fistulosa L., Sp. pl. 22. 1753.

Native country: *M. fistulosa* is native from Ontario to Alberta in the north, to Hidalgo, Mexico, and Georgia in the south.

General habit: *M. fistulosa* is a perennial herb, 30 to 120 cm tall; stem axis simple or branched in the upper parts.

Leaves: Leaves are firm, lance-egg-shaped, tending to egg-shaped or lance-shaped, 2 to

12 cm long, 8 to 38 mm wide, toothed, apex pinched, leaf surface coated with fine hairs above or with longer hairs, and minutely hairy with curled hairs, with gray or white short hairs (canescent) or slightly woolly below, or both surfaces hairless. The var. *fistulosa* has thin, green leaves with moderately coarse and stiff hairs to long, soft, somewhat wavy hairs 1 to 3 mm long. The var. *menthifolia* has firm, pale green leaves with minute appressed hairs.

Flowers: Bracts are lance-shaped, frequently red-tinted. Calyx is 5 to 10 mm long; corolla is 4 to 10 mm long, lavender to rose, rarely cream to white.

M. ×media Willd., Enum. Hort. Berol. 1:32. 1809.

Native country: *M. ×media* has been encountered wherever two of the three parents occur.

General habit: *M. ×media* is a perennial herb 50 to 125 cm tall; stem axis branched in the upper parts.

Leaves: Leaves are thin, lance-egg-shaped to egg-shaped to triangular-egg-shaped, 6 to 12 cm long, 12.5 to 6 cm wide, toothed, apex pinched, upper leaf surface with a few slender, appressed hairs, lower leaf surface hairy with long and stiff spreading or curled hairs, concentrated along the midveins.

Flowers: Bracts are lance-shaped. Calyx is 8 to 12 mm long; corolla is reddish to rose-purple, 7 to 10 mm long.

M. pectinata Nutt., Acad. Phil. Ser. 2. 1:182. 1847.

Native country: Pony beebalm is native from Colorado and Nebraska to Arizona and Texas.

General habit: This is an annual herb 15 to 50 cm tall; stem axis often branched from the base.

Leaves: Leaves are thin to firm, parallel-sided, lance-shaped to parallel-sided, 1.5 to 5 cm long, 4 to 12 mm wide, mainly with very few teeth to remotely toothed, apex pinched, leaf surface somewhat beset with moderately coarse and stiff hairs with very few short bristles above and a few short bristles mainly on the veins below.

Flowers: Bracts green, lance-shaped. Calyx 6 to 8 mm long; corolla white to pinkish, 3 to 8 mm long.

Myrrhis odorata

mĭr-ĭs ō-dŏ-rā-tå
sweet cicely

Family: Apiaceae (Umbelliferae)

Growth form: herbaceous perennial to 6 feet (200 cm) when flowering

Hardiness: hardy to Zone 5

Light: part to full shade

Water: constantly moist but not wet

Soil: humusy, pH 4.5 to 7.4, average 6.6

Propagation: seeds as soon as ripe

Culinary use: limited (not GRAS)

Craft use: potpourri

Landscape use: ferny borders for shade

French: *cerfeuil d'Espagne, cerfeuil musqué, cerfuil odorant*

German: *Englischer Kerble, Spanischer Kerble, Wohlreichende Süssdolde*

Dutch: *roomse kervel*

Italian: *mirride odorosa, finocchiella, cerfolio*

Spanish: *perifolo, mirra*

Swedish: *spansk körvel*

Sweet cicely is a winter-hardy herb that is a perfect landscape specimen for that shady nook every gardener confronts with a skepticism that perennials of grace and beauty can grow in the shade. The plant's delicate, fern-like green leaves provide a soft, informal touch to any planting scheme, and it is one of the few strongly scented herbs that delights in shade and a humusy, moist soil.

Sweet cicely cannot withstand the heat of the Deep South but enjoys the cooler summers of the mountains and the upper latitudes of North America. The white flowers sparkle in umbelliferous clusters in late spring and early summer and are followed by brown fruits that stick to your socks if you brush against them.

Myrrhis odorata

The genus *Myrrhis* has only one species, and its generic name is derived from the Greek *myrrha*, "fragrant." Sweet cicely, alias garden myrrh, sweet-scented myrrh, or fern-leaved chervil, has been cultivated for its sweet, anise-scented foliage, seeds (really fruits), and roots. It flavors liqueurs such as Chartreuse, spiced wines, iced tea, baked goods, and salads, but it does not have GRAS status.

It can be frustrating to get sweet cicely seeds to germinate. You could scatter the fresh, ripe seeds where you want them to grow, and let nature take its course. Or you could try this method: About thirty to forty days after flowering, splinter-like seeds fall from the plant. Separate them from the seed head and mix them with damp peat moss in a plastic bag, then place the bag in the refrigerator (not freezer). The seeds will begin to germinate in five months and can then be transplanted into pots in the greenhouse or on the windowsill. Leave ungerminated seeds in the bag with the peat moss and return to the refrigerator for further germination. Germination will be irregular; more seed will sprout in a few weeks.

When several small ferny leaves are present and the plant becomes established in the pot, it is time to harden the young seedlings and transplant them to the garden. Light frosts should not harm properly acclimated transplants.

Important chemistry: The essential oil of sweet cicely fruits has up to 77 percent (*E*)-anethole, providing an anise-like odor. The foliage has 82 to 85 percent (*E*)-anethole.

Botanical Description

M. odorata (L.) Scop., Fl. Carn. ed. 2. 1:207. 1772.

Native country: Sweet cicely is native to the Alps, the Pyrenees, and the Apennine mountains of the western part of the Balkan Peninsula but cultivated elsewhere and widely naturalized.

General habit: Sweet cicely is a hairy perennial to 200 cm.

Leaves: Leaf lobes are oblong-lance-shaped, deeply toothed, with conspicuous sheaths on the leaf stalk.

Flowers: Flowers are white in an umbel.

Fruits/seeds: Fruit is 15 to 25 mm long, rough to the touch with bristly hairs especially near the top, dark shiny brown when mature.

Myrtus communis

mēr-tŭs kŏ-mū-nĭs
Grecian myrtle

Family: Myrtaceae

Growth form: large shrub or small tree to 16 feet (5 m)

Hardiness: hardy to Zone 9

Light: full sun

Water: moist but not wet

Soil: well-drained garden loam, pH 5.5 to 8.2, average 6.8

Propagation: cuttings or seeds

Culinary use: sometimes substituted for Grecian bay

Craft use: wreaths, potpourri

Landscape use: container plant, easily
trained into standards

French: *myrte commun*
German: *Myrte*
Dutch: *myrtus*
Italian: *mirto, mortella*
Spanish: *mirto, arryán*
Portuguese: *murta*
Swedish: *myrtem*
Japanese: *ginbaika*
Arabic: *sutre-sowa*

In his massive book, *The Food of Italy*, Waverly
Root wrote, "Sardinia's favorite flavoring is
myrtle, a preference which may well go back to
the Stone Age." On this western Italian island,
myrtle wood is used for the fires to spit-cook
whole animals; myrtle stems and leaves are used
to line holes dug in the ground for pit cooking,
a Sardinian method that imparts what Root
says is an "exquisitely delicate flavor" to meats,
especially whole pig. After the Sardinians boil a
chicken and remove it from the pot, they cover
it with myrtle leaves and put a plate over the
bird while it cools; the dish is called *Gallina col
mirto* and is eaten cold the next day. Myrtle's
flavor is close enough to that of Grecian bay
that it is often used as a substitute for it.

The genus *Myrtus* includes one very variable
species of the Mediterranean region and southwest Europe. Grecian myrtle is a large shrub
or small tree with shiny, dark green leaves and
blue-black berries. The white flowers have many
golden stamens. Grecian myrtle is now common in southern Europe; Pliny tells us that,
though it was not native to Italy, it was first
seen in Europe planted near the tomb of one
of the companions of Ulysses at Circeii. *Myrtus*
was the Latin name, derived from the Greek
murtos, which in turn was derived from *myron*,
"perfume." Other stories relate that *Myrtus* was

taken from Myrsine, an Athenian maiden and
favorite of Minerva, who allowed love to over-
power her wisdom and was changed into a myrtle by her offended mistress.

Grecian myrtle, or the common myrtle, has
a long history of uses, many entwined with mythology. Grecian myrtle is an important element in the celebration of the Jewish Feast of
the Tabernacles, or Festival of Sukkot. Beginning on the 15th day of the Hebrew month of
Tishri (September/October), this is a week-long
festival in commemoration of the time that the
Jews dwelt in small tabernacles (huts) during
the Exodus. Three Grecian myrtle shoots (*Ha-
dasim*) with leaves in groups of three are bound
onto a shoot of date palm (*Lulav*) with two
willow stems (*Aravos*) and a special citrus fruit
called *Etrog* (*Citrus medica* L. var. *ethrog* Engl.).
These four species represent Jewish unity toward God. A study by L. J. Halsall and A. M.
Dourado at Wisley found that hard pruning
will frequently produce leaves in threes upon
regrowth, but these three-leaved shoots revert
to typical branches. The cultivar 'Triloba' will
often produce three-leaved shoots.

Myrtus communis

Grecian myrtle was a symbol of love and held sacred to Venus. Venus, when she first sprang from the bosom of the sea, was supposed to have had a wreath of myrtle on her head, so the temples of Venus were always surrounded by groves of myrtle. According to Pliny, the Romans and Sabines, when they were reconciled, laid down their arms under a myrtle tree and purified themselves with its boughs. Wreaths of myrtle were the symbols of authority worn by Athenian magistrates. The weapons of war of the Greeks were also formed of this tree, and sprigs of myrtle were entwined with the laurel wreaths worn by these conquerors during their triumphs, who had gained victory without blood-shed, and so, with the Grecian bay, Grecian myrtle was worn by the victors of the Greek Olympic games, and Roman poets and playwrights were garlanded with it.

In Rome, two myrtles were placed before the temple of Romulus Quirinus to represent the plebeian and patrician orders, which were predicted to be in the ascendency according to the state of the trees. In the Middle Ages, an astringent dusting powder for babies was prepared from myrtle. The fruit was used for dyeing hair and eaten to sweeten the breath, while the Athenians used the dried berries as a spice. German brides always included a sprig of *Myrte* in their wedding bouquets, probably harking back to the association with Venus.

Grecian myrtle includes a number of cultivars, but not all have been fully characterized in the literature.

Cultivar: 'Acutifolia'
Synonyms: var. *acutifolia* L., var. *acuta* Mill., 'Mucronata'
Common English name: sharp-pointed-leaved myrtle, thyme-leaved myrtle
Common French name: *myrte pointu*
Origin: Portugal

Growth: reddish shoots
Leaves: linear-lance-shaped, gradually tapering to a point, base wedge-shaped
Flowers: sepals large, blunt
Fruit: blue-black

Cultivar: 'Belgica'
Common English name: broad-leaved Dutch myrtle
Common French name: *myrte de Belgique*
Leaves: lance-shaped, pinched at the tip, crowded together, dark green
Fruit: blue-black

Cultivar: 'Boetica'
Common English name: Andalusian myrtle, narrow-leaved Spanish myrtle, orange-leaved myrtle, upright myrtle
Common French name: *myrte d'Andalusie*
Origin: Andalucia, Spain
Leaves: lance-shaped, pinched at the tip
Fruit: blue-black
Chemistry: 24 percent myrtenyl acetate and 21 percent 1,8-cineole in leaf essential oil (spicy eucalyptus)

Cultivar: 'Flore Pleno'
Common English name: double-flowered myrtle
Origin: a double-flowered version of the broad-leaved Dutch myrtle
Flowers: double

Cultivar: 'Italica'
Synonyms: var. *italica* Mill.
Common English name: Italian myrtle, upright myrtle
Origin: central Italy
Growth: branches and shoots narrowly upright
Leaves: egg-lance-shaped, rather small, about 3 × 1 cm
Fruit: blue-black

Chemistry: 18 to 30 percent alpha-pinene, 24 to 28 percent 1,8-cineole, and trace to 24 percent myrtenyl acetate in leaf essential oil (spicy eucalyptus)

Cultivar: 'Latifolia'
Synonyms: var. *latifolia* Willk. & Lange.
Common English name: broad-leaved Jews' myrtle
Origin: Taragona, Spain
Leaves: oval-oblong to oblong-lance-shaped, tapering to the tip, 1.8 to 3 × 0.8 to 1.5 cm, frequently in multiples of three

Cultivar: 'Leucocarpa'
Synonyms: var. *leucocarpa* DC., 'Albocarpa'
Common English name: white-fruited myrtle
Origin: Greece and Balearic Islands
Fruit: white, 12 to 14 × 9 to 10 mm

Cultivar: 'Lusitanica'
Common English name: Portugal myrtle
Fruit: blue-black

Cultivar: 'Romana'
Synonyms: var. *romana* Mill.
Common English name: broad-leaved myrtle, Roman myrtle, orange-leaved myrtle, flowering myrtle
Common French name: *myrte romain*
Origin: southern Europe
Leaves: broadly egg-shaped, sharply tapering to the tip, light green, 3 to 4.5 × 11.5 cm, often in whorls of three or four
Fruit: blue-black
Flowers: free-flowering

Cultivar: 'Variegata'
Common English name: variegated myrtle
Leaves: edged in white
Chemistry: 28 percent limonene, 26 percent alpha-pinene, and 14 percent linalool (lemon-pine lavender)

Under var. *tarentina*, two cultivars are listed:

Cultivar: 'Microphylla'
Synonyms: *M. buxifolia* Raf., 'Buxifolia', var. *minima* Mill., 'Jenny Reitenbach'
Common English name: dwarf myrtle, Tarentum myrtle, box-leaved myrtle, German myrtle, Polish myrtle
Common French name: *myrte de Tarente*
Origin: southern Europe
Leaves: overlapping, linear-lance-shaped, less than 2.5 cm long
Flowers: small, opening late in autumn
Fruit: round, black

Cultivar: 'Microphylla Variegata'
Common English name: variegated dwarf myrtle
Leaves: edged in white

Additional cultivars were recorded in the past. Even Pliny tells us that eleven different sorts were cultivated by the Romans. Most of the following are now probably lost: gold-striped broad-leaved myrtle, gold-striped orange-leaved myrtle, silver-striped Italian myrtle, striped-leaved myrtle, silver-striped rosemary or thyme-leaved myrtle, nutmeg myrtle, silver-striped nutmeg myrtle, pomegranate-leaved myrtle, cock's comb or bird's nest myrtle, and spotted-leaved myrtle. Sennen and Teodoro also recorded 'Augustinii', 'Balearica', 'Baui', 'Briqueti', 'Christinae', 'Eusebii', 'Gervasii', 'Grandiflora', 'Josephi', 'Mirifolia', 'Neapolitana', 'Petri-Ludovici', 'Rodesi', 'Tarraconensis', 'Theodori', and 'Vidali', but Sennen was infamous for publishing numerous names for very slight variations (e.g., species of *Mentha*) which are no longer recognized. Regardless, research is still needed on clarification of these variations. M. Mulas and his associates at Università di Sassari, Italy, selected sixteen different Grecian myrtle cultivars grown in Tunisia and gave them names.

Grecian myrtle is not hardy above Zone 9, so it is best accommodated in a pot and carried over the winter in a cool greenhouse. A friable potting soil in full sun is preferred. Myrtle, especially the cultivar 'Microphylla', lends itself to topiaries and standards. While Grecian myrtle may be propagated by seed, it is most commonly propagated by cuttings. The named cultivars, of course, can only be propagated by cuttings.

The essential oil of Grecian myrtle is considered GRAS only in alcoholic beverages. It is also used in perfumery (the oil is sometimes known as *eau d'anges*, or angels' water) and excellent in potpourris. The essential oil of myrtle is a liver toxin at 2.2 to 3.7 ml/kg. For a 150-pound human, that's about 4.7 fluid ounces. The essential oil is active against human lice and may offer some protection against stomach ulcers.

Important chemistry: The essential oil of Grecian myrtle leaves is dominated by trace to 45 percent 1,8-cineole, 4 to 40 percent limonene, 1 to 60 percent alpha-pinene, 0 to 33 percent myrtenyl acetate, trace to 32 percent linalool, 0 to 14 percent linalyl acetate, and trace to 12 percent alpha-terpineol, providing a spicy eucalyptus/lemon/lavender scent reminiscent of Greek bay. Plants from the Mediterranean Littoral can be divided into two groups: plants from Tunisia and Corsica with 51 to 57 percent alpha-pinene, and plants from Morocco, Lebanon, and the former Yugoslavia, with 19 to 32 percent alpha-pinene. Plants from Greece have been reported with 31 percent linalyl acetate, 22 percent limonene, and 18 percent alpha-pinene. The essential oil of the mature fruits consists of 12 to 62 percent 1,8-cineole, trace to 22 percent linalool, and trace to 20 percent myrtenyl acetate.

Botanical Key and Description

M. communis L., Sp. pl. 471. 1753.

Key:
1. Tree to 5 m; leaves 2 to 5 cm, not crowded; berry broadly ellipsoid . . . . var. *communis*
1a. Shrub not more than 2 m; leaves less than 2 cm, crowded; berry subglobose . . . . var. *tarentina* (L.) Arcangeli, Comp. fl. ital. 258. 1882.

Native country: Myrtle is native to the Mediterranean region and southwest Europe.

General habit: Myrtle is an evergreen shrub or tree to 5 m.

Leaves: Leaves are up to 5 cm long, egg-lance-shaped, tapering to the tip, smooth-edged, leathery

Flowers: Flowers are white, up to 3 cm in diameter, sweet-scented.

Fruits/seeds: Fruit is a berry 7 to 10 × 6 to 8 mm, almost globular, blue-black when ripe.

Nepeta cataria

nĕ-pĕ-tå kå-tår-ĭ-å
catnip

Family: Lamiaceae (Labiatae)
Growth form: short-lived herbaceous
perennial to 39 inches (1 m) tall
Hardiness: hardy to Zone 4
Light: full sun
Water: moist but not wet
Soil: well-drained garden loam, pH 4.9 to 7.6,
average 6.6
Propagation: seeds in spring or fall, 48,000
seeds per ounce (1,693/g)
Culinary use: teas, but limited (not GRAS)
Craft use: catnip toys, insect repellents
Landscape use: allow to reseed in cottage-
garden fashion

French: *cataire, herb aux chats, chataire,
menthe de chat*
German: *Katzenminze, Katzenkraut*
Dutch: *kattenkruid*
Italian: *erba dei gatti, cataria, erba gatta, gattaja*
Spanish: *hierba gatera, mentha de gato, almaro,
nébeda*
Portuguese: *néveda dos gatos*
Chinese: *chi-hsueh-ts'ao*

If you love cats and enjoy watching their antics,
plant catnip and you'll have a free feline circus!
Strays will be attracted from all around to roll
over your catnip plants, even in winter. Unfortunately, the bacchants may also crush valuable
plants nearby; even committed cat lovers may
find this hard to overlook.

The felty, gray-green leaves of catnip are tri-
angular-shaped and held on stems to over three
feet. Flowers are white with small purple spots
in a fat terminal spike. The generic name was
probably derived from Nepete, a city of ancient

Etruria (modern Tuscany and part of Umbria
in Italy). The chief variant is lemon catnip, *N.
cataria* var. *citriodora* (Becker) Balb., but don't
let the lemony odor fool you: it still attracts cats.

While catnip has been recommended as a sedative tea in the herbal literature, it has no GRAS
status. The principal use of catnip is for exciting
cats when the leaves are wilted or crushed.

Not all cats respond to catnip, according to
Neil B. Todd who reported in his Harvard Ph.D
thesis that only about two-thirds of a sampling
of cats in Boston responded to catnip. R. C.
Hatch of the Ontario Veterinary College discovered that a cat's personality and emotions
are most important to the catnip response, but
they are also influenced by environmental
sounds, urinary infections, loss of smell, urination, defecation, and adjustment to the habitat.
Those cats that do respond, however, typically
exhibit a peculiar sequence of responses, which

Nepeta cataria

include sniffing, licking and chewing with head shaking, chin and cheek rubbing, and head-over rolling and body rubbing. Tests of other animals indicate that the catnip response is unique to the cat family, although cheetahs are notably non-responsive. Anecdotal evidence indicates that some members of the Ursidae (bear family) may respond to catnip, but this has not been tested scientifically. If you work in a zoo or game preserve that houses large cats (or bears), don't wear an insect repellent with catnip.

Why does catnip elicit this response? The most reasonable hypothesis seems to be that cats respond to catnip because they find it a supranormal stimulus, one that produces more intense reactions than those normally found. Possibly cats have some normal social odor chemically similar to the active constituents of catnip, the nepetalactones. Catnip may simply be a hallucinogen for cats. Or, maybe it's just a food cue. Examination of the stomach contents of feral cats in Germany have found a surprising amount of insects in their diet; the Felidae are suspected of having descended from insectivores, and insects use the compounds found in catnip as defensive secretions.

Do the nepetalactones occur in catnip just to attract tabbies? Not at all, according to an entomologist at Cornell, who has shown that the nepetalactones ward off insects; the catnip plant has evolved these chemical defenses to protect its leaves from insects that might eat them. What plant could have foreseen the damage a cat could do?

The insect repellency of catnip has resulted in its inclusion in a number of DEET-free sprays. U.S. Patent Application (US 2006/0121134 A1) has been submitted to separate the active nepetalactones from catnip oil. Herb growers who are interested in making their own DEET-free sprays might concentrate upon lemon catnip to utilize the additional repellency of the lemon-scented compounds, in addition to a spray that just smells better than straight catnip.

Many of the approximately 250 species of *Nepeta* also accumulate nepetalactones in their essential oils, and, as might be expected, these attract cats also. You may find such attractive garden perennials as *N. mussinii* and *N.* 'Six Hills Giant' will entice cats from all over the neighborhood to come to your garden.

This short-lived perennial herb is usually grown from seed. Field-sown seed from commercial sources is notoriously slow to germinate and may lie dormant for up to three years. Because little selection to improve plant characteristics has been done with this herb, the grower must select rapidly germinating plants that have uniform maturity and acceptable oil content.

We recommend starting seed in the greenhouse or nursery and establishing the field with transplants. Germination is best at 68 to 86°F (20 to 30°C) planted sixty to sixty-five days prior to transplanting; cuttings are also easy to root and will quickly establish a uniform field.

Well-drained soil suitable for garden vegetables is recommended for catnip. Fully acclimated transplants 6 to 8 inches tall (15 to 20 cm) are planted two weeks before the expected last frost and spaced 9 to 12 inches (23 to 30 cm) apart in rows and 30 to 38 inches (76 to 97 cm) between rows.

Plants may be harvested about two to three months later when about 25 percent of the blooms have turned brown, an indication of optimal oil levels. In early morning, just after the dew has evaporated, harvest with electric hedge clippers or with a sickle bar, cutting the stems about 3 to 5 inches (8 to 13 cm) above the crown. Regrowth will occur from basal buds, and a second harvest may be made later in fall. Yields of 3,000 to 5,000 pounds per acre (3,362 to 5,604 kg/ha) of dried catnip are normal. A good stand will last for about three years, after which weeds become a major problem.

Catnip is susceptible to septoria leaf spot, which is endemic to climates with hot, humid summers; it is identified by spotted leaves that turn yellow and die.

If you enjoy the antics of cats over catnip, then also consider growing valerian (*Valeriana officinalis*) for its roots, the leaves of various kiwi fruits (*Actinidia* spp.), and the tiny leaves of cat thyme (*Teucrium marum*); you could prepare your own special "supernip" for that special feline in your life from a combination of these ingredients and catnip. On the other hand, you may raise the shades one morning to find an orgy of spaced-out felines in your garden.

Catnip has also been found to be fungistatic, especially against *Candida*.

Important chemistry: The essential oil of catnip is dominated by 57 to 100 percent nepetalactone (*cis,trans*-nepetalactone) accompanied by trace to 30 percent epinepetalactone (*trans,cis*-nepetalactone) and 0 to 19 percent caryophyllene oxide. Lemon catnip has primarily 10 to 48 percent citronellol, 9 to 39 percent geraniol, 0 to 30 percent nerol, 10 to 21 percent geranial, and 9 to 11 percent neral, but the presence of up to 9 percent nepetalactone, 2 percent epinepetalactone, and 1 percent dihydronepetalactone means that lemon catnip still attracts cats. Catnip plants grown in Belgium (obviously lemon catnip) have 55 percent geranyl acetate and 13 percent citronellyl acetate in the essential oil.

Botanical Description

N. cataria L., Sp. pl. 570. 1753.
Native country: Catnip is native to Europe but widely naturalized in North America.
General habit: Catnip is a short-lived perennial herb, 40 to 100 cm high.
Leaves: Leaves are 2 to 8 cm long, egg-shaped, tapering to the apex, heart-shaped at the base, round-toothed or sharp-toothed, grayhairy beneath with a dense, woolly covering of matted, tangled hairs of medium length.
Flowers: Flowers are white with small purple spots.

Nigella sativa

nī-jĕl-å să-tī-vå
black cumin

Family: Ranunculaceae
Growth form: short-lived annual to 12 inches (30 cm)
Hardiness: does not withstand frost well
Light: full sun
Water: moist but not wet
Soil: light garden loam, pH 5.6 to 8.2, average 6.9

Propagation: seeds in late spring, 11,000 seeds per ounce (388/g)
Culinary use: curries, stews, breads, pastries, cheeses
Craft use: fruits can be used in dried flower arrangements
Landscape use: edges of vegetable garden, appropriate in biblical gardens

French: *cheveux de Vénus, nigelle cultivée, nigelle des jardins, cumin noire*
German: *Schwarzkümmel*
Dutch: *nigelle, zwarte komijn, zwarte kummel*
Italian: *nigella, cinnamonea, gitono, melanzio nero*
Spanish: *ajenuz commún, nigela, neguilla, pasionara*
Swedish: *jungfrun i det gröna*
Russian: *chernushka, sev kundeg, dziral*
Chinese: *ku-sheng*
Arabic: *habbah sauda, habbet el baraka, kamun-asvad, shunez*
Polish: *czarnuszka*
Bengali: *kala jeera*
Greek: *mavrokookie*
Turkish: *nigella*
Persian: *sian daneh*
Urdu: *kalonji*

Black cumin seeds have a complex flavor that is pungent, peppery, nutty, and/or acrid with an aroma reminiscent of lemony carrots or nutmeg. In India, the seeds are widely used in many spice mixtures, including *panch phoron* (Bengali five-spice) and curry blends, masalas, and kormas;

Nigella sativa

they are also added to stews, casseroles, and vegetarian recipes including lentil dishes. Nan bread baked in the clay tandoor ovens of northern India is flavored with black cumin. In Egypt and the Middle East, the seeds are sprinkled on cakes, pastries, and breads. In Syria, cheese is mixed with black cumin seeds. The wide use of the seeds underscores its long history of use; black cumin seeds are mentioned in Isaiah 28:25 (variously translated as dill, fitch, or fennel). Black cumin is considered GRAS.

Nigella is the diminutive of *niger*, which translates as "black," and refers to the very black seeds; *sativa* means cultivated. One of about fourteen Eurasian species, black cumin is also called black caraway, fennel flower, nutmeg flower, or Roman coriander.

In the garden, *N. sativa* grows 6 to 12 inches (15 to 30 cm) tall and looks like a dwarf version of its close relative *N. damascena*, love-in-a-mist or wild fennel. The flowers of black cumin are very similar to love-in-a-mist but a paler blue, almost white, carried above finely cut, fennel-like foliage.

Black cumin seeds should be broadcast or sown in rows in tilled garden loam in late spring. Plants should be sown on site as they do not transplant well. Flowering is about two months later, followed by hollow, ½-inch long, horned seed pods. When the pods turn brown, harvest and crush them to release seeds inside (about fifty per pod), winnow to remove chaff, and dry.

The essential oil of black cumin seeds is antimicrobial and effective against intestinal worms. Numerous researchers have found black cumin to be gastro- and hepatoprotective. Researchers in Jordan and the United States have found that the volatile oil is antileukemic in vitro. Others in England and Spain found that the fixed oil contains thymoquinone and thus may be useful as a treatment for rheumatism and related inflammatory diseases. Evidence also exists to support black cumin as an analgesic, antipryretic, antioxidant, anticarcinogenic, and antinociceptive, and it may also be hypoglycemic.

Important chemistry: The essential oil of Egyptian seeds is dominated by 32 percent *p*-cymene and 25 percent thymoquinone. Seed collected from the Sahara desert has 2 to 22 percent thymoquinone, 13 percent carvacrol, and 6 to 12 percent thymohydroquinone. Italian seed has 34 percent *p*-cymene, 27 percent thymol, and only 4 percent thymoquinone. Polish seed has 60 percent *p*-cymene and 13 percent gamma-terpinene and only a trace of thymoquinone. We have analyzed another commercial Polish sample, labeled *charnuska*, and found 48 percent *p*-cymene and 20 percent alpha-thujene plus alpha-pinene, but no thymoquinone; apparently the flavor varies according to the geographical source. The fixed oil consists of 49 percent oleic acid, 38 percent linoleic acid, and 2 percent linolenic acid. The total sterol content of the fixed oil is 0.51 percent and includes 63 percent beta-sitosterol, 17 percent stigmasterol, and 15 percent campesterol.

Botanical Description

N. sativa L., Sp. pl. 534. 1753.

Native country: Black cumin is native to western Asia, southeastern Europe, and the Middle East but widely cultivated.

General habit: Black cumin is an annual with erect, branched stems 15 to 30 cm tall.

Leaves: Leaves are divided into deep linear segments.

Flowers: The pale blue, almost white, flowers have egg-shaped segments, shortly clawed.

Fruits/seeds: The seed pod is united for all its length and pimpled on its back; the 3.5-mm seeds are black.

Ocimum

ŏ-sĭ-mŭm
basil

Family: Lamiaceae (Labiatae)

Growth form: shrubby annuals or perennials from 18 inches to almost 6 feet (0.45 to 2 m) tall

Hardiness: hardy only in frost-free locations

Light: full sun

Water: moist but not constantly wet

Soil: friable and porous, pH 4.3 to 9.1, average 6.6 (*O. basilicum*)

Propagation: seeds in spring, 22,000 seeds per ounce (776/g) (*O. basilicum*); cuttings also possible during summer

Culinary use: myriad

Craft use: wreaths, potpourris

Landscape use: annual border, vegetable garden

Ocimum was a Greek word for an aromatic herb, probably this genus, called basil in English. The word basil connects this genus of herbs with an ancient mythical beast, the basilisk. The Romans were confused by two Greek words, *basilicon*, or kingly herb, and *basilicus*, basilisk, the mythical king of serpents. The basilisk of the Roman Pliny was a snake with white spots on its head in the pattern of a crown, while medieval writers united parts of a rooster and snake to create their basilisk; both basilisks left death and destruction in their tracks. Pliny, in *Natural History* (79 C.E.), recorded, "Ocimum too was severely condemned by Chrysippus [280–206 B.C.E.] as injurious to stomach, urine and eyesight, adding that it causes madness, lethargus and liver troubles." This bad reputation continued into the Victorian symbolism of hatred for this herb and even into the twentieth century because of the need of a good revision of the cultivated selections of this genus, but thankfully Dr. Alan Paton at Kew has been gradually examining and publishing on the genus.

Besides many other characteristics of the mint family, such as square stem and opposite leaves, *Ocimum* is characterized by flowers in the axils of the leaves or in very loose spikes with the flowers well separated along the stem. This is similar to *Perilla*, the beefsteak plant, but in *Ocimum* each floral leaf is beneath three flowers (only one flower per floral leaf in *Perilla*). Otherwise, a general gardener's description of the genus is very difficult because of the great variety of leaf size, plant size, vegetative and floral colors, and scents.

The genus *Ocimum* includes about 64 species native to the tropics and subtropics of the Old and New World, especially Africa. Many catalogs and garden writers assume that the odors of basils are species-specific, but this is not necessarily so. Cultivars of basil may smell of anise, camphor, cinnamon, clove, eucalyptus-carnation, lemon, thyme, or other scents. In the discussion here, the high estragole forms are the ones usually consumed at the table. The spicy odors of other cultivars, though, can add novel notes to mundane recipes. This discussion leaves out the green pepper–scented basil, *O.*

selloi Benth. (*O. carnosum* Link & Otto) because of its rarity in cultivation and unknown use in cuisine.

While *O. americanum*, *O. basilicum*, *O. campechianum*, *O.* ×*citriodorum*, and *O. kilimandscharicum* are technically annuals in their native tropics, they may be treated as tender perennials and propagated by cuttings like the other species of *Ocimum* listed below. All the basils are notoriously promiscuous and will cross readily within a species; some interspecific crosses are also not that difficult. Researchers at Purdue University discovered that basils have the capacity to cross with other basil species and produce offspring up to 33 percent of the time.

If you save seeds from your plants to grow the following year, you want to maintain the genetic integrity of your basils; to do this either take cuttings in the fall or pollinate the separate lines yourself and afterward place a bag over the flowers. If you grow only a few varieties and collect your own seeds to grow the following year, you can prevent cross breeding by pruning stems to prevent flowers on one variety while another variety flowers; after seeds are produced on the plants that flowered first, allow the second variety to flower. If you permit all your different basils to flower at the same time (and you save seed to grow plant the following year) insect pollination may create a potpourri of colors and scents within a few years (of course, this may be desirable too). After many years of doing this, though, only the toughest will survive and approach homogeneity.

In the following discussion we have abstained from describing individual cultivars because of the inherent difficulty of maintaining separate seed lines and because of the rampant confusion in the herb seed and plant industry. For a further discussion of the cultivars of basil, we refer you to *Basil: An Herb Lover's Guide* by T. DeBaggio and S. Belsinger.

Ocimum americanum

ŏ-sĭ-mŭm å-mĕr-ĭ-kā-nŭm
lemon basil, spice basil, hoary basil

This species is often confused with *O. basilicum* and sometimes cited as *O. canum* or as a hybrid (*O. basilicum* × *O. canum*). In 1978 H. Keng and in 1992 Alan Paton maintained *O. americanum* as a separate species from *O. basilicum* with two varieties, var. *americanum* and var. *pilosum*, in Malaysia and Africa. Both Keng and Paton include *O. canum* as part of *O. americanum*.

The variety with hairs that are mostly short, pressed to the stem with long hairs at the nodes is the "typical" var. *americanum*. We have purchased seeds and plants of *O. americanum* var. *americanum* labeled as "sweet fine basil," 'Genoa Profumatissima' ('Genoa Perfume'), 'Green Bouquet', 'Minimum', and even "camphor basil." 'Spice' basil, occasionally designated as *O. sanctum*, the holy basil or tulsi (correctly *O. tenuiflorum*), or *O. canum* by nurseries, is part of var. *pilosum* (Willd.) Paton, the hoary basil (see *O. tenuiflorum* for further discussion). 'Spice' apparently originated in Germany (where it achieved its incorrect moniker of "holy basil") and was distributed in North America by Park's via Richard Dufresne in North Carolina and ultimately Heinz Grotzke of Meadowbrook Herb Garden.

The cultivated material is even more confused, and many selections are, in reality, hybrids of *O. basilicum* × *O. americanum*, or *O.* ×*citriodorum*, probably the result of gardeners and commercial seed firms raising both species within pollinating distance. Other selections of *O. americanum* may be scented of camphor, cinnamon, or lavender/French tarragon.

Powdered or intact *O. americanum* is effective against beetles which sometimes damage stored grains and beans. Cultivation is as for *O. basilicum*.

Important chemistry: 'Spice' is aptly named because it is rich in 30 percent eugenol and 17 percent ocimene, giving it a clove-like scent; other clove-scented forms have been reported with 37 to 66 percent eugenol, sometimes with up to 13 percent (*Z*)-beta-ocimene plus 1,8-cineole, providing a nuance of eucalyptus. A clove-scented form from India has been reported with 72 percent (*Z*)-methyl eugenol. Camphor-scented hoary basil has 15 to 99 percent camphor, sometimes with up to 15 percent camphene, 14 percent beta-bisabolene, and/or 12 percent terpinen-4-ol plus beta-caryophyllene. Camphor-eucalyptus-scented plants from Burkina Faso have 45 to 60 percent 1,8-cineole and 0 to 19 percent camphor. Cinnamon-scented hoary basil has 46 to 85 percent (*E*)-methyl cinnamate. Lavender-scented hoary basil has 21 to 88 percent linalool, sometimes with up to 35 percent terpinen-4-ol plus beta-caryophyllene, 25 percent alpha-terpineol, and/or 10 percent gamma-terpinene, and sometimes with 53 to 75 percent methyl chavicol, adding a nuance of French tarragon/sweet basil. A report from Cameroon found a rose-scented form with 38 percent geraniol and 45 percent linalool, a lemon/eucalyptus-scented form with 42 percent limonene and 10 percent 1,8-cineol, and a spicy form with 18 percent 1,8-cineole, 18 percent delta-cadinene, and 10 percent alpha-pinene. 'Genoa Profumatissima' has 57 percent linalool and 12 percent 1,8-cineole. 'Green Bouquet' has 33 percent linalool, 20 percent eugenol, 11 percent beta-caryophyllene, and 11 percent methyl eugenol. 'Sweet Fine' has 67 percent linalool.

Ocimum basilicum

ŏ-sĭ-mŭm bă-sĭl-ĭ-kŭm

sweet basil

French: *basilic, basilique, "orange de savetier"*
German: *Basilienkraut, Basilikum, Kleine Bergmünze, Königskraut, "Deutscher Pfeffer"*
Dutch: *bazielkruid, basilicum*
Italian: *basilico*
Spanish: *albahaca moruna, albahaca de limón*
Portuguese: *mangericão*
Swedish: *basilik, basilkört*
Russian: *basilik*
Chinese: *lo-le, hsiang-ts'ai*
Japanese: *bajiru*
Arabic: *raihān, firanj-mushk, faram*
Hindi: *Hindi-babui tulsi*

Ocimum basilicum is *the* basil of most kitchens; many cooks prefer the French tarragon-scented form known as sweet basil. The herb has been cultivated for thousands of years throughout the Old World tropics and is also very variable, with different growth forms, colors, and aro-

Ocimum basilicum

mas. The most stable botanical characters for identification are the flower structure and seed. Again, as mentioned under *O. americanum*, much of the cultivated material is actually *O. basilicum* × *O. americanum* or *O.* ×*citriodorum*, combining the characteristics of calyx size and stem hairiness.

Alan Paton and Eli Putievsky examined one population of dwarf basil and concluded that it should be designated as a separate species, *O. minimum*. After looking at the broad range of dwarf basils, we insist that more research is needed before reaching this conclusion. The correct designation of the dwarf basils is further complicated in that many key out to *O.* ×*citriodorum*, a hybrid complex of *O. basilicum* × *O. americanum*. Thus, for purposes of simplicity, the dwarf basils are included here as variations of *O. basilicum*, following Helen Darrah.

Many botanical varieties and forms have been described in previous literature. We recognize that these arose in cultivation and are best designated as cultivars, but some offerings seem to have no legitimate name assigned to them. Cultivars may be grouped as follows:

1. Very large green leaves (including green ruffled-leaved basils), e.g., 'Difforme' [var. *difforme* Benth., var. *crispum* (Thunb.) E. A. Camus, 'Crispum'], 'Lactucaefolium', 'Lettuce Leaf' (both a flat-leaved and a ruffled-leaved form have been sold as 'Lettuce Leaf'), 'Mammoth', 'Napoletano', 'Valentino'.
2. Large green leaves, for example 'Italian', or "large sweet basil."
3. Large purple leaves, such as 'Purpurascens' (var. *purpurascens* Benth.), 'Violaceum'.
4. Large purple, ruffled leaves, such as 'Genovese Grande Violetto' ('Italian Red'), 'Purple Ruffles'.
5. Intermediate green leaves, such as 'Genoa Green', 'Genoa Green Improved' ('Genovese

Verde Migliorato'), 'Greek', 'Thai', "sweet basil."

6. Small green leaves (green bush, fine green, compact, and ball basils), such as 'Bush Green', 'Cuban', 'Miniature Puerto Rican', 'Minimum' [*O. minimum* L., *O. basilicum* subsp. *minimum* (L.) Danert in Mansf., and *O. basilicum* var. *minimum* (L.) Alef.].

7. Small purple leaves, such as 'Minimum Purpureum', 'Miniature Purple'.

8. Compact, such as 'Blanca', 'Compactum', 'Flat Top Purple', 'Thyrsiflorum' [var. *thyrsiflorum* (L.) Benth.], 'Siam Queen' ('True Thai').

9. Purple stems, such as 'Horapha', 'New Guinea', 'Thai Purple'.

10. White flowers, such as 'Album'.

11. Purple flowers, such as 'Comosum'.

12. Aroma, such as 'Anise', 'Cinnamon', 'Licorice', 'Sweet' (including 'Piccolo'), 'Mexican Spice', 'Mrs. Burns' Lemon', and 'Sweet Fine' ('Picolo Verde Fine').

Some of these cultivar names may be synonyms, but these are the names that have been used in nursery catalogs, periodicals, and books. As regards *O. minimum* as a separate species, upon examination of three selections of 'Minimum', Robert Vieira and others concluded, "RAPD marker results strongly suggest that it should not be considered a separate species, but rather a variety of *O. basilicum*." Do not accept the catalog names of *O. basilicum* or even the cultivar names as necessarily correct. We have encountered packets labeled purple-leaved basil that produced green basils and packets labeled lettuce-leaved basil that produced regular sweet basil. This may vary from supplier to supplier and even from year to year.

The purple basils are especially fascinating and great accents in the garden. The granddaddy of purple-leaved basils may be 'Purpura-scens', which was first identified as a botanical variety of *O. basilicum* by George Bentham in 1832; while the terminal leaves of 'Purpura-scens' (which actually include a range of purple colors) are purple, these fade at the bottom from pure to light green. Olof Ryding of the Department of Systematic Botany, Uppsala, reported in 1994 that the purple basils may be a hybrid, *O. basilicum* × *O. forskolei* Benth. If true, *O. forskolei* should be sought for cultivation and further breeding. With its depth of color and subtle iridescence accompanied by deep fuchsia blossoms, 'Dark Opal' is especially notable. 'Dark Opal' was developed in the mid 1950s from seeds collected in Turkey by John Scarchuk and Joseph Lent at the University of Connecticut and later offered by Ferry-Morse Seed Co. 'Dark Opal' is distinct from *O. basilicum* 'Purpurascens' and keys out in Paton's publications to *O. basilicum* × *O. forskolei*, supporting Olof Ryding's hypothesis of hybrid origin. A descendent of 'Dark Opal' is 'Red Rubin', which was selected in Denmark and has been offered since 1992. 'Dark Opal' was probably also the parent (with *O. kilimandscharicum*?) of 'African Blue', which is scented of camphor and bologna sandwiches. 'Purple Ruffles' was bred by Ted Torrey at W. Atlee Burpee and Co. in the late 1970s and introduced in 1987; Torrey also introduced 'Green Ruffles' (seed of 'Green Ruffles' offered today seems to be *O. basilicum* × *O. americanum*). 'Genovese Grande Violette' is reputedly similar to 'Purple Ruffles'. 'Osmin' is the result of a massive selection program started in 1987 at Quedlinberg Research Station in Germany and introduced into North America in 1996; 'Osmin' is exceptional in producing almost 100 percent purple seedlings that mature into plants with even, dark purple leaves.

Fresh sweet basil leaves (usually not heated) are widely used to flavor Italian dishes, especially in the preparation of pesto and as a finishing touch to pasta sauces, but they are also found in an assortment of vegetable dishes and salads. Purple sweet basil leaves make a delightfully flavored and colored herb vinegar. In a taste test reported by Lauren Bonar Swezey in the June 1994 *Sunset*, 'Napoletano' was the hands-down favorite for fresh basil among seven judges. For pesto, judges preferred 'Sweet'.

Sweet basil oil is used to flavor nonalcoholic beverages, ice cream, candy, baked goods, gelatins, puddings, condiments, and meats. Sweet basil oil is also used in some fragrances, such as Brut.

Purple sweet basil leaves make a delightfully flavored and colored herb vinegar.

Basil is a tropical plant, and it responds with thunderous growth when nights are above 60°F and days are long and sunny with temperatures in the 80s and above; thus it is disappointing to indoor gardeners who offer their basil plants a winter windowsill. Basil may be directly seeded or transplanted; transplants provide at least a six-week head start over direct seeding (that's the equivalent of two harvests). Soil of medium fertility, about pH 6.4, is best; a heavy clay soil that bakes or crusts on the surface is not suitable because the tender seedlings are unable to penetrate if directly seeded. A soil too loose and sandy will be unable to hold sufficient water and nutrients to slake the needs of these rapidly growing plants. Sandy or clay soils should be amended with copious amounts of humus in the form of compost or sphagnum peat. Space transplanted seedlings (or thin seedlings) 12 to 18 inches apart; grown under proper conditions and with transplants provided a long growing season these plants are going to be large and

bushy. Space around the plants also allows air to circulate through the plants to dry leaves, a prophylactic effect that helps to minimize the threat of fungus diseases that can be a serious problem for some basils.

Basil is not tolerant of water stress. Water stress will decrease yield while increasing the levels of linalool and methyl chavicol; trickle irrigation is preferred to prevent stress because it keeps foliage dry. Jeanine Davis of North Carolina State University compared basil plants on raised beds watered with drip irrigation and mulched with black polyethylene, wheat straw, hardwood bark, or mixed wood chips. Bacterial soft rot (*Erwinia* spp.) was highest for basils grown on bare soil or with wheat straw or black polyethylene, while basils grown with hardwood and pine bark mulches had few soft rot symptoms. All the mulches controlled weeds. Yields were highest with black polyethylene but lowest with hardwood and pine bark mulches.

Another study by John Loughrin and Michael Kasperbauer at the U.S.D.A. in Florence, South Carolina, compared black, red, green, blue, yellow, and white plastic mulches. Leaves developing over red surfaces had greater area, moisture percentage (succulence), and fresh weight than those over black surfaces. Basil grown over yellow or green surfaces produced higher concentrations of aroma compounds than basil grown over white or blue covers. Leaves grown over yellow or green covers also contained significantly higher concentrations of phenolics than those grown over other colors. Cedric Sims and S. R. Mantreddy at Alabama A&M University also compared colored mulches and found that green cover was "significantly superior" to either red colored mulch or no mulch.

Basil leaves grow opposite each other in pairs on the plant's stems; when seedlings or transplants have six leaves (three pairs) on the main stem, it is time for the first harvest. This harvest is important for reasons gustatorial and horticultural. The gustatory reason is obvious: it's been a long winter and fresh basil is the supreme taste of summer, even when fresh tomatoes are not obtainable. Horticulturally, the pruning of the main stem starts the plant's first branches, a process essential to future large harvests and to the retardation of flower production; flower initiation ends foliage production and begins seed creation and plant death. To further retard flowering of basil plants, prune branches before they have four pairs of leaves (eight leaves); this pruning should be done just above the oldest pair of leaves and it will leave each branch with only two leaves from which two more branches will soon emerge. The summer passes in this manner and as many as 20 quarts or more of succulent, fragrant leaves may eventually be harvested from a single plant (when temperatures are high, plants may be harvest-ready every three weeks). After this harvest and each proceeding one, sidedress basil plants with liquid fertilizer to keep nitrogen levels high.

Even patio and balcony gardeners can have superb basil plants in containers; unfortunately, basil's vigorous growth means it needs to be repotted often. If you start with a basil plant in a 3-inch pot, transplant it to a container that is 6 inches wide and 6 inches deep; within a few weeks move the plant up to a 12- or 14-inch-wide container. Small basil plants started in large pots often die from too much water, which rots their roots because the growing medium in the container cannot dry fast enough, and the tender roots receive no air. Frequently transplanted basils are less likely to drown because the pots are not as large in relation to the plant's root mass.

The home gardener may start to harvest as soon as plants reach around 1 foot (30 cm) tall, although pesto-hungry gardeners often start

sooner. Storage must be above 41°F (5°C) to prevent cold-injury symptoms of blackened, wilted leaves; moderate chilling injury also occurs at 45.5 to 50°F (7.5 to 10°C). Diana Lange and Arthur Cameron of Michigan State University recommend harvesting basil later in the day, at 6 to 10 p.m., to increase shelf life, with storage at 50 to 68°F (10 to 20°C). They also found that basil can be chill-hardened preharvest at 50°F (10°C) for four hours daily (two hours at the end of the light period and two hours at the beginning of the dark period) for two days before harvesting, followed by postharvest chill-hardening of packaged basil for one day at 50°F (10°C) in darkness before transfer to 41°F (5°C). However, Shimon Meir and his associates at the Volcani Center in Israel found that cultivars vary in their sensitivity to chilling sensitivity. Steam blanching, even slight (fifteen seconds), preserves the best color upon drying; samples that are not blanched should be dried at 113 to 122°F (45 to 50°C). Marketing of basil is best in controlled-atmosphere (CA) storage; according to studies done at Michigan State University, sweet basil stored in 1.5 percent CO_2 had an average storage life of forty-five days compared with eighteen days for air control.

Farmers who intend to produce acres of basil may use different and labor-saving techniques to harvest their plants than home gardeners and will follow another cultural recipe. They may sow seeds ⅛ to ¼ inch deep (3.5 to 6.5 mm); thus the soil must be smooth and well settled before sowing. Sow about twelve seeds per foot (12 seeds/30 cm) and allow 24 to 36 inches (61 to 91 cm) between rows, or about 4 to 8 pounds of seed per acre (4.5 to 9.0 kg/ha), depending on seed viability. The germination rate should be no lower than 70 percent, with 80 to 95 percent desired. Sow after all danger of frost is past. Transplants should be about 6 inches (15 cm) apart in rows. Germination will commence about eight to fourteen days after sowing, and flowering begins within eight to ten weeks. Trim plants when about 6 inches (15 cm) tall to ensure lateral branching. The plants are ready to harvest when in full bloom and the lower leaves begin to turn yellow, about twelve to fourteen weeks after seeding. The plants should be cut at no more than 6 inches (15 cm) above the ground level with a sickle-bar gerry mower (with adjustable cutting height) in order to ensure a good second crop; closer cutting will not allow regeneration. A hay mower or hand scythe can also be adapted. If weather permits, a second crop may be harvested about eight weeks after cutting the first crop.

The home gardener may start to harvest as soon as plants reach around 1 foot (30 cm) tall, although pesto-hungry gardeners often start sooner.

In order to ensure a continuous supply of leaves, the field harvests and/or planting dates should be staggered. Leaves should be washed and extraneous materials removed. If distilled for oil, the crop should be allowed to wilt in the sun for two to three hours to facilitate packing. Cloudy or rainy weather immediately preceding the harvest will decrease the oil yield, while sunny days will have the opposite effect. Higher temperatures will increase the content of eugenol in the oil, which is preferred by some customers. Yields of 6,000 to 20,000 pounds fresh herb per acre (6,725 to 20,386 kg/ha) may be expected, with 5 to 32 pounds of oil per acre (6 to 36 kg/ha). Greater yields of 14,230 to 24,278 pounds fresh herb per acre (15,950 to 27,212 kg/ha) and 17 to 27 pounds of oil/acre (19 to 30 kg/ha) may be obtained with closer planting to 19 inches (50 cm) between rows.

Distillation with the flower spikes will increase the oil yield but will change the quality of the oil; 'Long Green' flower spikes are richer in linalool, for example. If basil is grown for seed, maximum yield and highest germination rate of seed will occur when plants are aging to produce almost dry leaves on the secondary and tertiary stems and on the lower parts of the branches, according to Eli Putievsky of Israel.

While the rate of fertilizer application will depend upon the soil type and prior history of the land, a fertilizer of 1-1-1 N-P-K ratio is recommended by broadcast and plow down at a rate of 120-120-120 pounds per acre (134-134-134 kg/ha). A sidedress application with nitrate nitrogen at a rate of 15 to 30 pounds per acre (17 to 34 kg/ha) is recommended shortly after the first harvest. Ammonium nitrogen will decrease the total oil and increase the sesquiterpene percentage.

If basil is grown hydroponically, the ionic strengths of the nutrient solutions should be monitored. Korean researchers found that lower ionic strengths will produce higher fresh weights but reduce the total oil. A comparison of three hydroponic media (rockwool slabs, perlite frames, commercial sphagnum peat/perlite/compost) with either conventional or organic fertilization by C. Elizabeth Succop and Steven E. Newman at Colorado State University found plants grown in rockwool with conventional fertilizer were 17 to 46 percent more productive than those grown with organic fertilizer. While taste panels could discern differences between the organically and conventionally fertilized basil, no preferences were shown.

For cultivation under lights, twenty-four hours of light produces the maximum yield of top growth per harvest. For photoperiods of fifteen to eighteen hours, the yield is slightly lower, but the plants reach harvest ten days earlier.

Basil is subject to fusarium (*F. oxysporum* f.

sp. *basilicum*) and rhizoctonia, both of which cause plants to wilt. Vigorous sanitation, good ventilation, crop rotation, choice of resistant strains, and good drainage are all recommended to reduce or prevent these fungal infections in the absence of fungicides registered in the United States for basil. Fusarium wilt may also be seed-borne; spores can survive in the soil and may infect other species of the mint family. Dr. Robert Wick of the University of Massachusetts at Amherst recommends that commercial growers of basil soak basil seeds in a solution of 10 percent sodium hypochlorite for twenty minutes or, alternatively, a soak for twenty minutes at 136.4°F (58°C). For soils already infected with fusarium, researchers at the University of Turin found that other strains of fusarium (particularly *F. oxysporum* and *F. moniliforme*) are antagonistic to the one that infects basil and cyclamen. Researchers at the University of Pisa found that exothermic reactions, incorporating potassium hydroxide (KOH) into the soil, were more effective than steam alone. Alternatively, the cultivar 'NUFAR' is resistant to fusarium wilt. Leaf black spots (*Marssonina rosae* and *Colletotrichum gloeosporioides*) produce dark-rayed spots. Leaf blight (*Colletotrichum capsici*), blight (*Alternaria* spp.), gray mold (*Botrytis cinerea*), stem rot (*Sclerotinia sclerotiorum*), leaf spot and blight (*Pseudomonas cichorii* and *P. syringae*), and leaf necrosis (*Pseudomonas viridiflava*) have also been reported. Researchers at Newe Ya'ar Research Center in Israel found that gray mold could be controlled by regulating the concentrations of nitrogen and calcium in the irrigation solution. Basil is also subject to alfalfa mosaic virus, cucumber mosaic virus, and tomato spotted wilt virus.

The larvae of some leaf rollers also attack basil, sticking to the undersurface of the leaves, folding them from the midrib lengthwise, and webbing them. Hector R. Valenzuela and Randal Hamasaki of the University of Hawaii at Manoa have found that compost cuts nematode populations in basil; since wilt fungi often follow nematodes when they burrow into roots, compost should thereby also cut wilt damage.

Dried sweet basil is predominantly imported from Egypt. Basil leaf is considered GRAS at 2 to 680 ppm. Basil oil is considered GRAS at 0.01 to 50 ppm. Whereas French tarragon oil with 60 percent estragole may be carcinogenic, basil oil with 8 to 17 percent methyl chavicol apparently poses no potential threat. The 1,8-cineole, linalool, methyl chavicol, and eugenol of *O. basilicum* chemotypes are fungistatic. Basil is also an effective antioxidant with radical scavenging activity.

Important chemistry: Commercial sweet basil oil from the Comoro Islands, Egypt, France, India, Italy, Madagascar, Pakistan, Reunion, Thailand, Vietnam, and the former Yugoslavia is predominantly composed of trace to 90 percent methyl chavicol (estragole) and trace to 79 percent linalool. The methyl chavicol provides a sweet taste similar to French tarragon, thus the name sweet basil, while the linalool provides a lavender-like floral odor. The basil oils from Morocco and South Africa are spicy with 2 to 3 percent methyl chavicol, 42 to 54 percent linalool, and 12 to 19 percent eugenol.

The named sweet basils include 'Anise' with 28 to 60 percent linalool and 18 to 41 percent methyl chavicol; 'Bush' with 52 percent linalool; 'Dark Opal' with 34 to 61 percent linalool and 13 to 33 percent eugenol; 'Genovese' with 42 to 61 percent linalool, trace to 25 percent eugenol, and 6 to 21 percent 1,8-cineole; 'Green Ruffles' with 47 percent methyl chavicol; 'Lettuce Leaf' (including the almost identical 'Napoletano', 'Mammoth', and 'Valentino') with 20 to 64 percent linalool, 12 to 61 percent methyl chavicol, and trace to 21 percent eugenol; 'Licorice' with trace to 50 percent methyl chavicol and 21 to 60 percent linalool; 'Little Green' (including 'Little Green Compact') with 69 to 76 percent linalool; 'Mexican Spice' with 55 percent linalool and 18 percent methyl chavicol; 'Minimum' with 18 to 53 percent linalool; 'New Guinea' with 85 percent methyl chavicol; 'Purpurascens' with 50 percent methyl chavicol and 35 percent linalool; 'Reunion' with 83 to 87 percent methyl chavicol; 'Siam Queen' ('True Thai') with 80 to 89 percent methyl chavicol; 'Sweet' with 7 to 59 percent linalool, 5 to 29 percent methyl chavicol, and 2 to 12 percent eugenol; 'Thai' with 79 percent linalool; 'Thai Purple' with 69 percent methyl chavicol; and 'Thyrsiflora' with 61 percent methyl chavicol and 26 percent linalool.

The spicy basils include 'Cinnamon' with 28 to 58 percent *trans*-methyl cinnamate and 24 to 27 percent linalool; 'Cuban' with 36 to 40 percent linalool and 24 to 27 percent 1,8-cineole; 'Dark Opal' with 57 to 71 percent linalool and 6 to 10 percent 1,8-cineole; 'Dwarf Violet' with 69 percent linalool and 12 percent 1,8-cineole; 'Genoa Green' with 48 percent linalool; 'Genovese' (including 'Giant Genovese' and 'Sanremo') with 61 to 69 percent linalool and 8 to 12 percent 1,8-cineole; 'Giant Violet Leaf' with 70 percent linalool and 13 percent 1,8-cineole; 'Miniature' with 25 percent linalool, 1 percent 1,8-cineole, and 10 percent beta-caryophyllene; 'Miniature Puerto Rican' with 58 percent *trans*-methyl cinnamate and 16 percent linalool; 'Minimum', with 35 percent linalool and 16 percent eugenol; 'Piccolo' with either 61 percent linalool and 16 percent eugenol or 31 percent beta-caryophyllene and 17 percent linalool; 'Purple Ruffles' with 26 to 47 percent linalool,

11 to 38 percent methyl chavicol, 11 to 31 percent beta-caryophyllene, and 7 to 11 percent 1,8-cineole; 'Red Rubin' with 53 percent linalool, 11 percent 1,8-cineole, and 11 percent beta-caryophyllene; 'Sweet Fine' with 57 percent linalool and 17 percent eugenol; and 'Well-Sweep Miniature Purple' with 67 percent linalool and 13 percent 1,8-cineole. 'Bush Green' has 27 percent linalool, 15 percent beta-caryophyllene, and 11 percent 1,8-cineole. 'Mrs. Burns' Lemon' seems to be *O. basilicum* with 49 percent linalool and 25 percent citral (geranial plus neral).

Other unnamed selections of *O. basilicum* may have trace to 91 percent methyl chavicol, trace to 89 percent linalool, trace to 69 percent (*E*)-methyl cinnamate, trace to 84 percent linalool, trace to 68 percent methyl eugenol, trace to 23 percent geraniol, trace to 13 percent (*Z*)-beta-ocimene plus 1,8-cineole, trace to 58 percent eugenol, and trace to 12 percent (*Z*)-methyl cinnamate. A plant from northeast India was found with 42 percent camphor. The oil of *O. basilicum* var. *hispidum* (Lam.) Chiov. from southern Somalia has 82 percent dihydrotagetone, providing it with an African marigold odor. Juvocimene I and II, potent juvenile hormone mimics affecting insects, have also been isolated from the oil of sweet basil; these compounds prevent the normal development of many insects and may have evolved as a defense mechanism.

Examination of the anthocyanins in basil by Winthrop Phippen and James Simon found 11 cyanidin-based pigments and 3 peonidin-based pigments. The highest concentration of these stable red pigments occurred just prior to flowering.

Ocimum campechianum

ŏ-sĭ-mŭm kăm-pĕsh-yă-nŭm
spice basil

Although listed as *O. micranthum* in many manuals, *O. campechianum* has priority of publication. Campeche is the name of a state and town in Mexico. This is a basil native to the New World, where it is called *albahaca, albahaca cimarrona* (Puerto Rico), *albahaca silvestre* (Guatemala), or *albahaca montés* (El Salvador). In the Lesser Antilles it goes by *balm, fon basin,* or *fonboysa*. It may be cultivated in Latin America but is often gathered from the wild for culi-nary and medicinal uses. This basil is cultivated in North America as "Peruvian basil."

This annual to 2 feet (60 cm) is very similar to sweet basil, differing in minute botanical charac-teristics. However, it can be easily distinguished from sweet basil by the brown nutlets (black in sweet basil) and the straight hairs (curved in sweet basil). Cultivation is as for *O. basilicum*.

Important chemistry: The essential oil from the leaves of *O. camphechianum* has 16 to 52 percent iso-eugenol, 4 to 23 percent 1,8-cineole, 11 to 23 percent beta-caryophyllene, and 4 to 23 percent beta-elemene, providing a eucalyptus-carnation odor.

Ocimum ×*citriodorum*

ŏ-sĭ-mŭm sĭ-trī-ō-dôr-ŭm
lemon basil

Lemon basil is a hybrid series derived from *O. basilicum* × *O. americanum* and first intro-duced into the United States from Thailand about 1940. Not all these hybrids are lemon-scented as the common and specific names would indicate. We have purchased seeds or plants of this hybrid as 'Anisatum', "ball basil," 'Bush Green', 'Citriodorum', 'Dwarf Bouquet', 'Dwarf Italian', 'Green Globe', 'Green Ruffles', 'Holly's Painted', 'Lemon', 'Minimum', 'Puerto Rican', 'Spicy Globe', 'Sweet Dani', 'Thai Lem-on', or even "sacred basil." 'Lesbos', originally from Greece and introduced into cultivation by the Rev. Douglas Seidel, is a rather unique growth form for its tight column, thus provid-ing an alternate name of 'Greek Column'. 'Aus-sie Sweetie' is very similar but supposedly origi-nated from Greece via Australia. The variegated version of 'Lesbos' has been patented (U.S. PP16,260) by Sunny Border Nurseries, Kens-ington, Connecticut, as 'Pesto Perpetuo'.

Classical *O. basilicum* has a large fruiting calyx (6 mm long) and stems are smooth or coated with tiny hairs on two opposing sides, while classical *O. americanum* has a small fruit-ing calyx (4 to 5 mm long) and stems with hairs distributed equally around the stem. A plant with a large calyx and hairy stems or a plant with a small calyx and smooth stems most likely is a hybrid of these two species.

The oil of *O.* ×*citriodorum* has been reported to be antifungal.

Important chemistry: The essential oil of lemon basil is reported in the chemical litera-ture as rich in 55 to 99 percent citral (geranial plus neral); a selected form is 'Sweet Dani' with 34 percent geranial and 22 percent neral in the leaf oil. 'Dwarf Bouquet' has 43 percent linalool and 10 percent beta-caryophyllene. 'Green Ruf-fles' has 35 to 43 percent methyl chavicol and 2 to 25 percent linalool. 'Holly's Painted' has 35 percent linalool, 29 percent methyl chavicol, and 13 percent 1,8-cineole. 'Aussie Sweetie' has 9 to 49 percent *trans*-methyl cinnamate, 9 to 16 percent linalool, and 5 to 6 percent 1,8-cineole, while the very similar 'Lesbos' ('Greek Column') has 49 percent *trans*-methyl cinnamate, 13 percent linalool, 11 percent methyl eugenol, and 10 percent 1,8-cineole. 'Puerto Rican' has

57 percent *trans*-methyl cinnamate and 22 percent linalool. 'Spicy Globe' has 36 percent linalool and 14 percent beta-caryophyllene.

Ocimum gratissimum
ŏ-sĭ-mŭm grå-tĭ-sĭ-mŭm
tree basil

French: *basilic en erbe, basilic de Ceylan, basilic Seychelles, basilic salutair, baumier*
Hindi: *vriadha tulasi, ram tulsi, Hindi-ban*
Thai: *kaphrao-chang*

This species, translated as the "very pleasing basil," is known locally as tea bush in Africa, but it is widely cultivated in India and Latin America and by serious basil buffs in North America. This shrubby perennial can grow to almost 10 feet (3 m) high and has reddish brown nutlets that produce mucilage when placed in water.

This is also known in the trade as tree basil, shrubby basil, green basil, North African basil, or East Indian basil. The seed line currently offered in North America as East Indian basil originated in Zimbabwe and was introduced by Richters in 1982. The seed line currently offered in North America as West African basil originated in Ghana and was introduced by Richters in 1995. Two subspecies are known, subsp. *gratissimum* and subsp. *iringense* Ayobangira ex Paton. The former subspecies includes what is sometimes designated as *O. viride* Willd., the fever plant or mosquito plant, also called *thé de Gambie* in French. Other species cited in the essential-oil literature, such as *O. caillei* A. Chev., *O. dalabense* A. Chev., *O. suave* Willd., *O. trichodon* Gürke, or *O. urticifolium* Roth, belong to this species.

Tree basil has distinct chemotypes: thyme-, clove-, lemon-, rose-, cinnamon-, and carnation/

herb-scented. The clove-scented form is reputed to be antimicrobial and a mosquito repellent. The oil is an effective anti-trypanosomatid. An unnamed chemical form is reputed to be effective against ticks.

Cultivation is as for *O. basilicum*.

Important chemistry: Thyme-scented tree basil (sometimes designated as *O. viride*) has 19 to 72 percent thymol, 0 to 27 percent gamma-terpinene plus (*E*)-ocimene, trace to 11 percent eugenol, and 0 to 16 percent *p*-cymene with up to 14 percent 1,8-cineole. Cinnamon-scented tree basil has up to 67 percent ethyl cinnamate. Clove-scented tree basil (sometimes reported as *O. suave* or *O. trichodon*) has trace to 98 percent eugenol, trace to 40 percent beta-caryophyllene, trace to 26 percent (*Z*)-ocimene, trace to 14 percent iso-eugenol, trace to 12 percent alpha-copaene, and trace to 10 percent beta-elemene, sometimes with up to 47 percent methyl eugenol and/or 47 percent methyl isoeugenol. Superior clove-scented cultivars, named 'Clocimum' and 'Clocimum-3c', have 60 to 95 percent eugenol and moderate oil yields. Lemon-scented tree basil has 65 percent geranial plus neral and 25 percent geraniol. The rose-scented tree basil has 85 to 88 percent geraniol in the leaves. The carnation/herb-scented tree basil has 40 percent beta-caryophyllene and 30 percent germacrene D. Ethiopian plants have a leaf oil with 23 percent (*Z*)-beta-ocimene, 17 percent delta-cadinene, 14 percent beta-caryophyllene, and 11 percent gamma-muurolene. A pine-scented form from Nigeria (as *O. suave*) has 26 percent sabinene and 24 percent beta-caryophyllene.

Ocimum kilimandscharicum

ŏ-sĭ-mŭm kĭl-ĭ-mănd-shär-ĭ-kŭm
camphor basil

Hindi: *Hindi-kapur tulsi*

The camphor basil is named after Mt. Kilimanjaro in Tanzania and has been introduced into Asia, Europe, South America, and North America. The overall appearance of this annual is similar to that of sweet basil, reaching 6 feet (2 m). 'Cattail Camphor' is probably a hybrid of this species with *O. americanum*. 'African Blue' is probably a hybrid of *O. kilimandscharicum* with *O. basilicum* 'Dark Opal' discovered in 1983 by Peter Borchard of Companion Plants.

The oil of camphor basil is reputedly antifungal.

Cultivation is as for *O. basilicum*.

Important chemistry: Typically the camphor basil produces 17 to 80 percent camphor and up to 42 percent linalool, 17 percent limonene, and 10 percent 1,8-cineole in the essential oil of the leaves. However, *O. kilimandscharicum* growing wild in Rwanda has been reported to have 62 percent 1,8-cineole, providing a eucalyptus-scented form. The oil of 'African Blue' has 55 percent linalool, with 12 percent camphor and 12 percent 1,8-cineole, providing a strong balsamy scent with a hint of turpentine.

Ocimum tenuiflorum

ŏ-sĭ-mŭm tĕn-ū-ĭ-flŭr-um
holy basil

French: *basilic sacré, basilic des moines*
Hindi: *sri tulsi (purple), Krishna tulsi (green)*
Thai: *kaprou/kaphrao, bai grapao*

The holy or sacred basil has been known as *O. sanctum* in most manuals, but *O. tenuiflorum*, meaning "slender flowers," is conspecific and has priority of publication. This species is seldom seen in the United States; *O. americanum* var. *pilosum* 'Spice' often substitutes in catalogs. We have been able to obtain *O. tenuiflorum* in North America only as plants labeled 'Purple Tulsi' and in packets of seeds from Thailand labeled "holy basil."

'Spice' is generally hairy, with long, thin hairs on the stems, leaves, calyces, and flower stalks. While often confused with holy basil in the seed trade, no morphological characteristics relate these two species. The large leaves, elongate inflorescence, stalked bracts, and mucilaginous nutlets serve as distinguishing characters to separate 'Spice' from *O. tenuiflorum*. Holy basil occurs in both green- and purple-leaved forms.

Studies on the uses of holy basil have, unfortunately, rarely designated the chemotype used.

Ocimum tenuiflorum

Medicinal uses of holy basil have shown some promise in a variety of experimental areas, but many claims should be viewed as more hype than good science until replicated and correlated with chemotype. Leaves of holy basil have an antifertility effect when ingested, according to one researcher, but more research is needed. An ethanolic extract of holy basil has been reported to reduce blood glucose in rats and is reported to prevent smooth-muscle spasms, while a crude aqueous extract has been shown to potentiate hexobarbitone-induced hypnosis in mice. The leaf extract may have radioprotective effects. In addition, some adaptogenic (antistress) activity of holy basil has been reported on experimental animals. Holy basil has also been reported to enhance the physical endurance and survival time of swimming mice, prevent stress-induced physical ulcers in rats, and protect mice and rats against the liver toxicity induced by carbon tetrachloride. Holy basil also promotes glucose utilization different from the action of insulin. The eugenol and methyl eugenol content impart an antifungal, antibacterial, and anthelmintic

activity to the oil of holy basil. The fixed oil of the seeds is anti-inflammatory, reduces fevers, and relieves pain. Leaves of *O. tenuiflorum* also repel mosquitoes.

Cultivation is as for *O. basilicum*.

Important chemistry: Lemon-scented holy basil has about 70 percent gernial plus neral. The clove-scented holy basil has 13 to 86 percent methyl eugenol and 3 to 34 percent beta-caryophyllene, sometimes with up to 23 to 62 percent eugenol, 10 to 14 percent caryophyllene oxide, and 12 percent beta-elemene. The anise-scented holy basil has trace to 19 percent 1,8-cineole plus (Z)-ocimene, 15 to 87 percent methyl chavicol, and 0 to 11 percent beta-bisabolene. The medicinal-spicy-scented holy basil has 70 percent chavibetol (betelphenol) and 20 percent eugenol. The balsamic-scented holy basil has 30 to 33 percent beta-bisabolene, 16 to 20 percent (Z)-alpha-bisabolene, and 2 to 12 percent methyl chavicol. Holy basil from India has been reported with 17 percent beta-caryophyllene as the primary constituent.

Botanical Key and Description

Key:

1. Leaves pinched at tips; mouth of calyx closed after pollen-release by up-curved lower lip; median lobes of lower lip of fruiting calyx shorter than upper lip; shrubs or undershrubs . . . . *O. gratissimum*

1a. Leaves tapering to the tip or rounded; mouth of calyx more or less open after pollen-release; median lobes of lower lip of fruit calyx as long as or longer than upper lip; herbs occasionally with stems slightly woody at base 2

   2. Leaves tapering to the tip 3

      3. Fruiting calyx 4 to 5 mm long. 4

         4. Stems hairy, hairs directed downward or spreading, distributed equally around the stem . . . .
. . . . *O. americanum*

        4a. Stems smooth or coated with tiny hairs on two opposing sides . . . . *O. ×citriodorum*

      3a. Fruiting calyx 6 to 7 mm long. 5

         5. Stems hairy, hairs directed downward or spreading, distributed equally around the stem. . . .
. . . . *O. ×citriodorum*

        5a. Stems smooth or coated with tiny hairs on two opposing faces 6

6. Pedicels divergent at right angles, decurved in fruit, not clearly separated; calyx 6 to 7 mm long in fruit, with appressed, stiff, rather short hairs outside, smooth within; nutlets brown; hairs straight. . . . . *O. campechianum*

6a. Pedicels short, erect, calyx 6 mm long in fruit, with long, straight, stiff hairs inside; nutlets black; hairs curved . . . . *O. basilicum*

2a. Leaves blunt at the tip. 7

7. Calyx tube completely smooth within; nutlets unchanged when wetted. . . . . *O. tenuiflorum*

7a. Calyx tube with a ring of hairs at the throat; nutlets mucilaginous when wet . . . . *O. kilimandscharicum*

O. americanum L., Cent. pl. I 15. 1755.

Key:

1. Stem indumentum mainly of short, retrorse, adpressed hairs with long hairs at nodes. . . . . var. *americanum*

1a. Stem indumentum with long spreading hairs only . . . . . var. *pilosum* (Willd.) Paton, Kew Bull. 47:426. 1992.

Native country: Spice and hoary basils are widely distributed in tropical and southern Africa, China, and India; naturalized in southern Europe, Australia, and tropical South America.

General habit: Spice and hoary basils are annuals or short-lived perennial herbs, 15 to 70 cm high, woody at the base.

Leaves: Leaves are narrowly egg-shaped to lance-shaped, smooth, light green, 110 to 55 × 4 to 25 cm, leaf stalk nearly half the leaf length; margin is slightly toothed.

Flowers: The inflorescence is lax, 13 to 18 cm long. Bracts, longer than the calyx, are stalked, egg-shaped, with pointed tip, glandular, hairy, with long hairs on the margins. The corolla is twice as long as the calyx, white, hairy on the outside.

Fruits/seeds: Nutlets are gray-black to black, lustrous, and show copious mucilage when moistened.

O. basilicum L., Sp. pl. 833. 1753 (including *O. minimum* L.).

Native country: Sweet basil is native to the Old World tropics.

General habit: Sweet basil is an annual herb, 0.5 to 1 m high, woody at the base. Stems and branches smooth or slightly hairy when young.

Leaves: Leaves membranaceous, egg-shaped to widest at the center with the ends equal, 3 to 5 cm long, tapering to the tip, base wedge-shaped, margin smooth-edged to few-toothed, almost smooth or hairy; leaf stalk 1 to 2 cm.

Flowers: Inflorescence is simple or branched. Bracts are lance-egg-shaped, about as long as the calyx, 2 to 3 mm. Corolla is white, pinkish, or violet, twice as long as the calyx.

Fruits/seeds: Nutlets are dark brown, pitted, swelling in water.

O. campechianum Mill., Gard. dict. ed. 8. #5. 1768 (*O. micranthum* Willd.).

Native country: *O. campechianum* is native from Florida to Brazil.

General habit: Plants are essentially annual but sometimes shrubby, up to 60 cm high.

Leaves: Leaves are parallel-sided egg-shaped to broadly egg-shaped, 2 to 9 cm long, tapering or blunt at the apex, toothed or almost smooth-edged, minutely hairy to almost smooth.

Flowers: The calyx is 6 to 7 mm long in fruit. The white corolla is spotted with purple, 4 mm long.

Fruits/seeds: Nutlets are dark brown to black, tapered to a point, producing moderate to heavy mucilage in water.

O. ×citriodorum Vis., Linnaea 15:Litteratur Bericht 102. 1841 (*O. citratum* Rumph., *O. basilicum* L. var. *anisatum* Benth., *O. dichotumum* Hochst ex Benth in DC.).

Native country: According to Alan Paton and Eli Putievsky, "*O. ×citriodorum* refers both to the products of a cross between *O. basilicum* and *O. americanum* and to the entities produced by the doubling of the F_1 chromosome number, as these forms are morphologically indistinguishable." The type of *O. ×citriodorum* is probably an allohexaploid (six times the basic chromosome number in an interspecific hybrid).

General habit, leaves, flowers, and fruits/seeds: The morphological characteristics combine a range between the two closely related parents. Classical *O. basilicum* has a large fruiting calyx (6 mm long) and a stem that is smooth or coated with tiny hairs on two opposing sides, while classical *O. americanum* has a small fruiting calyx (4 to 5 mm long) and stems with hairs distributed equally around the stem.

O. gratissimum L., Sp. pl. 1197. 1753.

Native country: Tree basil is native to tropical Africa.

General habit: Tree basil is a perennial herb, 0.6 to 3 m high, woody at the base. Stem and branches are smooth, hairy when young.

Leaves: Leaves are membranaceous, lance-shaped but widest at the center with the ends equal, 1.5 to 15 × 1 to 8.5 cm, tapering to the tip, wedge-shaped base, smooth-edged at base but elsewhere coarsely toothed, hairy.

Flowers: Inflorescences are simple or branched, 10 to 15 cm long. The calyx is 1.5 to 3 mm long at the time of pollen release, 3 to 4 mm long in fruit. The corolla is greenish white, 3 to 5 mm long.

Fruits/seeds: Nutlets are reddish brown, coarsely pitted, semilustrous, producing a small amount of mucilage in water.

O. kilimandscharicum Baker ex Gürke in Engl., Pflanzews. Ost.-Afrikas 4 (C):349. 1895.

Native country: Camphor basil is native to Tanzania, Kenya, and Uganda, introduced into Sudan.

General habit: Camphor basil is a perennial, growing to a height of about 2 m, branching repeatedly, woody at the base.

Leaves: Leaves are 15 to 55 × 10 to 30 mm, toothed, hairy, light green or gray-green, blunt-tipped. The egg-shaped leaves often fold upward, exposing the lower surfaces.

Flowers: The inflorescences are simple, up to 30 cm long. The bracts are narrow, tapering to the tip, stalked, and persistent. The calyx is similar to that of *O. canum* but with a very hairy upper lobe, kidney-shaped, abruptly turned back. The corolla is white, pink, or mauve, five or more times longer than the calyx.

Fruits/seeds: Nutlets are black, lustrous, pitted,

with a slight ridge, with moderate mucilage in water.

O. tenuiflorum L., Sp. pl. 597. 1753 (*O. sanctum* L.).

Native country: This species is native to India and Malaysia, where it is revered by the Hindus as an embodiment of Tulsi, consort to the god Vishnu, but it has become widely distributed in the Pacific Islands, Africa, and Latin America.

General habit: Holy basil is a much-branched perennial, 0.3 to 1 m tall, often woody at the base. Stems and branches are soft-hairy.

Leaves: Leaves are membranaceous, widest at the center with ends equal to parallel-sided, 15 to 33 × 11 to 20 mm, tapering to the tip or blunt, with a wedge-shaped base and smooth edges, margins elsewhere smooth or moderately toothed; hairy on both surfaces, especially on the nerves beneath; leaf stalk 7 to 15 mm long.

Flowers: Bracts egg-shaped, pinched at the tip, 2 to 3 mm long, beset with a marginal fringe of hairs. The calyx is 1 to 2.5 mm long at pollen release, about 3 to 3.5 mm long in fruit. Corolla is white or pink, 3.5 to 4 mm long.

Fruits/seeds: Nutlets are minute, brown, round-oval, more or less lustrous, finely pitted, producing small amounts of mucilage when wet.

Oenanthe javanica

ē-năn-thē jă-văn-ē-kå
water dropwort

Family: Apiaceae (Umbelliferae)
Growth form: hardy perennial to 16 inches (40 cm) tall
Hardiness: hardy to Zone 6
Light: full sun to part shade
Water: constantly moist
Soil: rich in organic matter
Propagation: easily rooted from offsets
Culinary use: celery substitute but limited (not GRAS)
Craft use: none
Landscape use: wildflower garden, cottage garden, or edge of pond

French: *fenouil d'eau, ciguë aquatica*
German: *Wasserfenchel, Ross-Fenchel, Pferde-Kümmel, Wasser-Kümmel*
Dutch: *water-venkel, watertorkruid*
Italian: *fellandrio, finocchio acquatico*
Spanish: *felandrio acuático*
Chinese: *shui qin, chin-tsai, shui-ying, chu-kuei*
Japanese: *seri*
Vietnamese: *rau cần*
Hindi: *ghora-ajowan*
Malay: *batjarongi, piopo, bamboong, pampoong*

Oenanthe includes about thirty north temperate species normally found in aquatic situations. The generic name is derived from the Greek *oinos*, "wine," and *anthos*, "flower," or flowers with a wine-like odor.

Water dropwort is favored by many Southeast Asians as a salad herb or steamed with rice.

The stalks and leaves of the plant taste and look like celery with a hint of carrot leaves, and the Japanese find this a winning combination with soups, salads, and sukiyaki.

The herb is native to pond margins, paddy fields, and wet places in China, Japan, Malaysia, India, and Australia. It is a perennial that spreads by stolons (thin, horizontal stems on the surface of the soil, just like mint). Water dropwort is far easier to grow than celery and can be potted to be maintained in the greenhouse or windowsill for winter harvests. Water dropwort prefers wet soil but will grow easily in moist garden loam and is winter hardy to at least Zone 6. Both green and red forms are known; both resemble a low celery. 'Flamingo' is a variegated cultivar in green, white, and pink. White flowers appear in early summer in an inverted umbrella-shaped inflorescence.

Water dropwort does not have GRAS status. The oil of water dropwort is antifungal and antibacterial. Hepatic detoxification is enhanced by extracts of *O. javanica*, apparently due to the content of persicarin (3-potassium sulfate ester of isorhamnetin).

Important chemistry: The essential oil of the flowering tops of water dropwort contains 68 percent dill apiole and 14 percent beta-phellandrene.

Botanical Description

O. javanica (Blume) DC., Prodr. 4:138. 1830 [*O. stolonifera* (Roxb.) Wall.].

Native country: Water dropwort is native to pond wetlands of China, Japan, Malaysia, India, and Australia.

General habit: Water dropwort is a smooth, stoloniferous perennial with erect stems to 20 to 40 cm tall.

Leaves: Leaves at 7 to 15 cm long, triangular or triangular-egg-shaped, once or twice compound, the ultimate segments egg-shaped or narrowly so, 1 to 3 cm × 7 to 15 mm, tapering to a point or almost pinched at the tip, irregularly toothed, sometimes deeply lobed.

Flowers: Flowers are white and in an umbel.

Fruits/seeds: The fruit is about 2.5 mm long with corky ribs.

Origanum

ō-rĭg-å-nŭm
marjoram

Family: Lamiaceae (Labiatae)

Growth form: herbaceous perennials 14 to 39 inches (35 to 100 cm) tall

Hardiness: many only hardy to southern California (Zone 9); wild marjoram and oregano hardy to at least Pennsylvania (Zone 6)

Light: full sun

Water: moist to somewhat dry; can withstand drought when established

Soil: well-drained gravelly or rocky loam, pH 4.9 to 8.7, average 6.9 (*O. majorana*); 4.5 to 8.7, average 6.7 (*O. vulgare* subsp. *vulgare*)

Propagation: seeds in spring, cuttings in summer; 160,000 seeds per ounce (5,644/g)

(*O. majorana*); 130,000 (4,586/g) (*O. vulgare* subsp. *vulgare*)

Culinary use: many entree dishes of the Mediterranean region

Craft use: wreaths, dried flowers

Landscape use: excellent for edgings, borders, or pots

Origanum is derived from the Greek for "beautiful mountain," a reference to the usual habitat and attractiveness of the marjorams even away from the mountains. Both the flowers and foliage are pleasing accents in the garden. The aromas of the species vary from the light, clean odor of sweet marjoram to the tarry, creosote-like scent of some oreganos native to Greece. All 43 species are perennials native to Eurasia that do well in full sun and very well-drained soil; they vary, however, in sensitivity to frost. Many species of this genus, particularly the ones designated as oregano, are particularly evocative of the Mediterranean and bring back memories of rocky hillsides covered with lovely, sweet scents and sparkling flowers, along with the regional cuisine.

Origanum majorana
ō-rĭg-å-nŭm mă-jō-rā-nå
sweet marjoram

French: *marjolaine*
German: *Majoran*
Dutch: *marjolein*
Italian: *maggiorana*
Spanish: *mejorana, amáraco*
Portuguese: *manjerona*
Swedish: *mejram*
Russian: *mayoran*
Chinese: *ma-yueh-lan-hua*
Japanese: *mayorana*
Arabic: *marzanjūsh*

The clean, sweet odor of sweet marjoram is described by perfumers as warm-spice, aromatic-camphoraceous, and woody, reminiscent of nutmeg and cardamom. The small, gray-felty leaves and terminal heads of white flowers make this a delight in pots on the patio, as this is a tender perennial probably hardy only to Zone 9b. Thus, it must be carried over in the greenhouse or treated as an annual in most North American gardens. A form known in the trade as "Greek marjoram" or "compact Greek marjoram" is grayer, hardier, and a bit more compact in habit.

The specific epithet is derived from the Greek for marjoram. Sweet marjoram is widely used in beverages, meats, baked goods, and condiments; its leaves (1.9 to 9,946 ppm), essential oil (1 to 40 ppm), and oleoresin (37 to 75 ppm) are considered GRAS. The essential oil of sweet

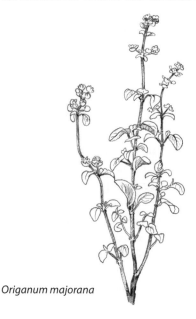

Origanum majorana

marjoram shows antimicrobial activity and is one of the few *Origanum* oils that can be used in perfumery, where it is used in fougères, colognes, and Oriental bases.

Egypt, France, and Canada are major sources of dried sweet marjoram imported into the United States. Sweet marjoram is usually grown from seeds, but in the spring greenhouse or under lights indoors, plants often succumb to root and stem diseases; cutting-grown plants are less vulnerable to these problems. A seeding density of 1 inch apart (40 plants/m) and 8 to 16 inches (20 to 40 cm) between rows is recommended for commercial production; home gardeners would probably prefer planting young plants 6 to 12 inches (15 to 30 cm) apart in rows. With harvests two to four times a year, yields of 4,015 pounds per acre (4,500 kg/ha) dried leaves and 7.8 gallons per acre (73 l/ha) essential oil can be expected. Convection drying at about 113°F (45°C) preserves the best flavor of marjoram. Blanching prior to drying preserves the green color but reduces the essential oil content.

Important chemistry: Sabinene hydrate and sabinene hydrate acetate, which supply the typical odor to marjoram, are particularly labile during distillation, and analysis of solvent extracts by researchers in Germany found that the primary components of sweet marjoram odor are 36.01±17.01 *cis*-sabinene hydrate acetate and 32.28±16.26 *cis*-sabinene hydrate. The essential oil of sweet marjoram consists of 16 to 52 percent terpinen-4-ol, 0 to 43 percent (*Z*)-sabinene hydrate, 3 to 14 percent alpha-terpineol, trace to 20 percent gamma-terpinene, trace to 12 percent sabinene, and 2 to 10 percent linalool. Selections from Turkey have been reported with 78 to 80 percent carvacrol, providing an odor of oregano. Cultivated material in Cuba has been reported with 18 percent terpinen-4-ol, 16 percent linalool, and 12 percent thymol; another report of cultivated material in Morocco showed 33 percent linalool and 22 percent terpinen-4-ol. These latter two reports may be actually *O.* ×*majoricum* from the essential-oil profile.

Origanum ×*majoricum*

ō-rĭg-å-nŭm mă-jō-rĭ-cŭm

hardy sweet marjoram

Hardy sweet marjoram is a hybrid of sweet marjoram (*O. majorana*) with wild marjoram (*O. vulgare*) and commonly confused with both. Depending upon the variability of the parents, hardy sweet marjoram may vary from tiny-leaved to large-leaved, light green to gray, and from sweetly scented to musky scented. The most commonly available form of hardy sweet marjoram in North America may be used in the same manner as sweet marjoram and has the appearance of a pale green sweet marjoram. The alternate name, "Italian oregano," does not

describe the sweet marjoram-like odor, although it may be a better name for increased sales at nurseries.

Hardy sweet marjoram requires the same culture as sweet marjoram but can be overwintered successfully with sunny, well-drained soil in Zone 7. While hardy sweet marjoram is somewhat sterile, it may occasionally set seeds that germinate in sandy soil.

Important chemistry: The most commonly available form of hardy sweet marjoram in North America has an oil with 17 percent *cis*-sabinene hydrate and 15 percent terpinen-4-ol, which supply the sweet marjoram scent; 12 percent carvacrol gives a hint of oregano. Turkish selections of hardy sweet marjoram have 26 to

27 percent *cis*-sabinene hydrate, and 7 to 18 percent carvacrol. Forms cultivated in South America under the synonym *O.* ×*applii* have

trace to 26 percent thymol, 17 to 20 percent linalyl acetate, and 10 to 13 percent terpinen-4-ol, providing a thyme/lavender-like odor.

Origanum minutiflorum

ō-rĭg-ȧ-nŭm mī-nū-tĭ-flŭr-um
Spartan oregano

Spartan oregano is commonly imported with other commercial dried oregano from Turkey. The specific epithet refers to the minute flowers. While it is commercially important and widely consumed, it has yet to enter cultivation in North America. This is probably a tender perennial requiring pot culture with the overall appearance of a fuzzy, lax pot marjoram. The oil is antimicrobial. Researchers in Turkey found that oil of Spartan oregano can be used as an antimicrobial in the leather industry.

Important chemistry: The essential oil contains 75 to 84 percent carvacrol.

Origanum onites

ō-rĭg-ȧ-nŭm ō-nī-tēz
pot marjoram

The specific epithet is derived from a kind of Greek oregano. This tasty oregano is especially esteemed in Turkey, where the common name, translated as "balls oregano," alludes to the shape of the inflorescence but also has Freudian significance because of its macho taste. This oregano has come in and out of the herb trade in the United States over the last fifty years; in past herb books, it was often confused with selections of *O. vulgare*. This finicky plant's tenderness and cultural requirements have limited its staying power.

We culled seeds of authentic pot marjoram from commercial oregano samples in the 1970s and released it to some herb nurseries. In the 1980s, the National Herb Garden, under the leadership of Holly Shimizu, released the correctly named plant again. The latter collection had been found by a member of the Herb Society of America in a meadow on a small island as the only plant that the sheep wouldn't eat.

The leaves vary from mildly hairy, providing a pale green color, to densely hairy, providing a gray color. This is a tender perennial requiring pot culture. The soil should be well-drained, and the pot should be terra-cotta. Provide cool, near freezing temperatures over winter under full sun. When spring arrives and new growth starts, trim back the dead or rambling growth. Alternatively, save the seeds each year and grow anew. Watch out, though. If you grow other species of *Origanum* nearby, you will invariably harvest hybrid seed; if you crave something new, that may be okay, but it does not preserve the original germplasm.

The oil of pot marjoram is antifungal and antibacterial, as would be expected from its high phenol (carvacrol) content.

Important chemistry: The essential oil of *O. onites* contains 2 to 90 percent carvacrol, 1 to 31 percent gamma-terpinene, 0 to 14 percent 1,8-cineole, and 1 to 12 percent *p*-cymene.

Origanum syriacum

ō-ri̱g-a̍-nŭm sĭ-rĭ-a̱-cŭm
Lebanese oregano

This is the *ezov* ("hyssop") of the Bible (Exodus 12:21–22, I Kings 4:33, Psalms 51:7, John 19:28–30). Samaritans traditionally used bunches of *O. syriacum* to sprinkle the blood of the Passover sacrifice; the hairs on the stems were reputed to prevent the coagulation of the blood. Thus, the use of branches of *ezov* to present the vinegar-soaked sponge to Christ just prior to his death would have been particularly symbolic. The oil of *O. syriacum* is antimicrobial and antioxidant, as might be expected from the high phenol (carvacrol) content.

This is similar to pot marjoram in overall appearance but more robust and with larger leaves and about as variable in leaf color, from pale green to gray. Both thyme-scented and oregano-scented forms are known. Lebanese oregano, white oregano, Syrian hyssop, and Biblical hyssop are English names attached to this species, but the Arabs call this (and a spice mixture) *za'atar*.

Origanum syriacum is harvested along with other oregano species in Turkey. It is a tender perennial that has not entered extensive cultivation, but a hybrid of this with *O. vulgare* has entered the trade simply as *O. maru*, a taxonomic synonym of *O. syriacum*, incorrectly applied. The latter hybrid has large, dark green, oregano-scented leaves and is routinely hardy to Zone 7, unlike the parental species.

Important chemistry: Rarely has the essential oil literature stated the correct botanical identification of the oregano under consideration, and investigations of *O. syriacum* are no exception. The essential oil of Turkish *O. syriacum* (i.e., var. *bevanii*) consists of 43 to 64 percent carvacrol and 6 to 12 percent *p*-cymene, sometimes with up to 25 percent thymol. The essential oil of Israeli *O. syriacum* (i.e., var. *syriacum*) consists of 12 to 44 percent thymol, 16 to 40 percent carvacrol, 11 to 15 percent gamma-terpinene, and 13 to 20 percent para-cymene. The essential oil of *O. syriacum* from the Holy Land (i.e., var. *syriacum* and *bevanii*) consists of 1 to 80 percent carvacrol and 1 to 71 percent thymol.

Origanum vulgare

ō-ri̱g-a̍-nŭm vŭl-ga̍-rē
wild marjoram, oregano

The six subspecies of *O. vulgare* are greatly confused (see the botanical keys for further diagnostic characters). The subsp. *vulgare* (called wild marjoram in English, *origan vulgaire* or *marjolaine sauvage* in French, and *Wilder Majoran* in German) is the plant that bears pretty pink flowers and purple bracts, but it is useless as a condiment, even though it is often sold as "oregano." The subspp. *virens* and *viridulum*, also called wild marjorams, are just as useless as

condiments. The subsp. *glandulosum* (Algerian oregano) is not often encountered in the United States. Some forms of subsp. *gracile* (Russian oregano) bear the typical odor of Greek oregano. The subsp. *hirtum* is *the* Greek oregano, which is now principally imported from Turkey; the harsh, creosote-like odor makes it relatively easy for any gardener with a nose to identify.

Oregano is widely used in cooking, and the leaves (320 to 2,800 ppm) are considered GRAS. Oregano essential oil is fungistatic and bacteriostatic and active against trypanosomes. The essential oil and alcoholic extract of the leaves are antioxidant. Galangin and quercetin, two flavonoids in oregano, were demonstrated to be antimutagenic in vitro against a common dietary carcinogen, Trp-P-2 (3-amino-1-methyl-5*H*-pyrido[4,3-*b*]indole). Aristolochia acid I, aristolochic acid II, and D-(+)-raffinose from *O. vulgare* were found to inhibit thrombin activity and to be anticarcinogenic. Leaves of *O. vulgare* subsp. *hirtum* were found by Greek researchers to be a natural herbal growth promoter for early maturing turkeys; they can also be useful to treat diarrhea in calves. Oregano oil may also be used as disinfectant for eggs.

All subspecies of *O. vulgare* require well-drained loam in full sun. With plants about 6 inches (16 cm) apart and rows 16 inches (40 cm) apart, yields of dried herb can achieve 2,320 to 5,424 pounds per acre (2,600 to 6,080 kg/ha) the first year and 901 to 14,944 pounds per acre (1,010 to 16,750 kg/ha) the second year. Oregano is particularly subject to sudden wilts caused by *Fusarium oxysporum* and *F. solani*.

Several cultivars of subsp. *vulgare* are grown. 'Aureum' is a very vigorous and yellow-green version. 'Dr. Ietswaart' has golden-yellow, almost translucent leaves that are wrinkled and circular. Both cultivars have been sold as 'Aure-

Origanum vulgare
subsp. *vulgare*

um', and the former has also been sold as 'Golden Creeping'. Both sometimes show irregular streaks of green and tend to become totally green late in the season or in hot weather. 'Thumble's Variety' is a more compact selection of 'Aureum'. 'Jim Best' (not 'Jim's Best') is streaked with gold and green and quite vigorous. 'White Anniversary' is edged in white but not reliably hardy and prone to leaf-fungus diseases in humid climates. 'Humile' ('Compactum') is a dwarf selection of wild marjoram. Other forms of *O. vulgare* with varying degrees of purple bracts are sold as 'Bury Hill' or *O. pulchellum*.

Important chemistry: The chemical literature rarely specifies the taxon beyond *O. vulgare* or "oregano." The essential oil of *O. vulgare* subsp. *vulgare* usually contains trace to 39 percent thymol, trace to 31 percent terpinen-4-ol, trace to 28 percent linalool, trace to 26 percent sabinene, trace to 19 percent *p*-cymene, trace to 19 percent beta-caryophyllene, 0 to 17 percent (*Z*)-beta-ocimene, 0 to 29 percent germacrene D, trace to 14 percent beta-cubenene, trace to 11 percent gamma-terpinene, trace to 11 percent 1,8-cineole, and trace to 10 percent sabinene, providing a slight musty odor; Turkish plants have been reported with 21 percent terpinen-4-ol and beta-caryophyllene and 18 percent germacrene D, providing a musty carnation-like odor. The essential oil of *O. vulgare* subsp. *glandulosum* cultivated in Italy consists of 79 to 84 percent carvacrol. The essential oil of *O. vulgare* subsp. *gracile* contains 15 to 79 percent thymol, trace to 17 percent gamma-terpinene, trace to 14 percent sabinene, and 10 percent carvacrol, providing a pine-tar odor; Turkish plants have been reported with 18 percent beta-caryophyllene and 13 percent germacrene D, providing a musty carnation-like odor. The essential oil of *O. vulgare* subsp. *hirtum* contains trace to 81 percent carvacrol, trace to 65 percent thymol,

2 to 26 percent gamma-terpinene, and 3 to 25 percent *p*-cymene; the odor of this leading source of oregano has a sharp, tarry, creosote-like odor. The essential oil of *O. vulgare* subsp. *virens* contains 10 to 70 percent linalool, trace to 19 percent beta-caryophyllene, 0 to 13 percent (*E*)-beta-ocimene, trace to 10 percent gamma-terpinene, and 0 to 10 percent (*Z*)-ocimene, providing a musty lavender-basil odor. The essential oil of *O. vulgare* subsp. *viridulum* from Iran consists of 20 percent linalyl acetate and 13 percent sabinene, providing a lavender-pine

odor. Essential oil of *O. vulgare* subsp. *viridulum* from the Liguria region of northern Italy have trace to 63 percent carvacrol, trace to 48 percent thymol, trace to 43 percent linalo, trace to 22 percent caryophyllene oxide, and trace to 16 percent germacrene-D-4-ol.

Botanical Key and Description

The calyces, which are under genetic control, are particularly important as an aid in identification.

Key:
1. Lower lip of calyces nearly absent, or the upper lip comprises ⁹⁄₁₀ or more of the length of the calyx and appears bract-like; calyx upper lip toothless to almost toothless 2
    2. Spikes arranged in flat-topped or convex open inflorescence; leaves often with small sharp teeth . . . . *O. onites*
    2a. Spikes arranged in panicles; leaves usually entire. 3
        3. Stems and leaves beset with minute hairs (hairs about 0.3 mm long); leaf apices blunt, veins not raised on lower surface. . . . . *O. majorana*
        3a. Stems and leaves with moderate coarse and stiff hairs or with dense, wool-like covering of matted, intertangled hairs (hairs about 1 mm long); leaf apices usually tapered, and veins usually raised on lower surface. . . . . *O. syriacum*
1a. Lower lip of calyx obviously present, so that calyces are one- or two-lipped for one-fifth to one-half their length and tube- or funnel-shaped; calyx upper lip often with three teeth or lobes, and lower lip consisting of two teeth or lobes. 4
        4. Calyces about 2 mm long . . . . *O. minutiflorum*
        4a. Calyces about 2.5 to 4.5 mm long 5
            5. Bracts about 4 mm long, 3 mm wide, inconspicuously dotted with glands; calyces funnel-shaped, about 3.5 mm long, teeth of lower lip much shorter to about as long as the upper lip . . . . *O. ×majoricum*
            5a. Bracts 2 to 11 mm long, 1 to 7 mm wide, conspicuously punctate; calyces tube-bell shaped, 2.5 to 4.5 mm long, with 5 (sub)equal teeth. . . . . *O. vulgare*

O. majorana L., Sp. pl. 590. 1753. (*Majorana hortensis* Moench).

Native country: *O. majorana* is native to dry, rocky (limestone) places on Cyprus and the adjacent part of southern Turkey but occurs spontaneously in the former Yugoslavia, Italy, Corsica, southern Spain, Portugal,

Morocco, and Algeria. It also is often found as a garden escape.

General habit: Stems are usually erect or ascending, sometimes branched at the bases, up to 80 cm long.

Leaves: Leaves are more or less stalked, roundish or egg-shaped or oval, apex usually blunt,

3 to 35 mm long, 2 to 30 mm wide, whitish or grayish, and coated with a dense wool-like covering of minute hairs; sessile glands inconspicuous.

Flowers: The inflorescence is a spike, usually three to five set closely together on a branch, slightly globe-shaped, egg-shaped, or a four-sided cylinder, 3 to 20 mm long, about 3 mm wide. Bracts are two to thirty pairs per spike, oval, egg-shaped attached at the narrow end, or diamond-shaped, apices usually blunt and smooth. Calyces are one-lipped, rather diamond-shaped, 2 to 3.5 mm long, outside more or less coated with dense wool-like covering of minute hairs; upper lips usually toothless, sometimes with small teeth. Corollas are two-lipped for about 3 to 7 mm long; white; outside coated with short, soft, straight hairs; upper lips divided into two lobes; lower lips divided into three subequal lobes.

O. ×majoricum Cambess., Mem. Mus. Paris 14:296. 1827 [incl. *O. ×applii* (Domin) Boros].

Native country: *O. ×majoricum* is probably a hybrid, *O. vulgare* × *O. majorana*; it has inherited the hardiness of the former and the odor of the latter. It occurs naturally in Spain and Portugal but is widely cultivated.

General habit: Stems are up to 60 cm long, coated with a dense woolly covering of minute hairs (hairs about 0.5 mm long).

Leaves: Leaves are stalked, about 9 × 5 mm.

Flowers: Spikes are usually cylindrical, up to 2 cm long, about 5 mm wide, not nodding. The green bracts are about 4 mm by 3 mm. Calyces are more or less funnel-shaped, about 3.5 mm long; upper lips with somewhat triangular teeth, less than 0.4 mm long, for one-third to one-half their length. Lower lips may be much shorter up to nearly as long as the upper lips, sometimes almost toothless but usually consisting of triangular

teeth, which are less than 0.7 mm long. The throats are coated with short, soft, straight hairs. Corollas are two-lipped for about one-third their length, 2.5 to 6 mm long and white.

O. minutiflorum Schwarz & Davis, Kew Bull. 1949:408. 1949.

Native country: *O. minutiflorum* is native to a few places in southern Turkey, where it grows on limestone at an altitude of about 1600 m.

General habit: This herb is a subshrub with erect stems up to 35 cm long, light brown, with curved and appressed hairs.

Leaves: Short-stalked green leaves occur in up to eighteen pairs per stem; they are egg-shaped or oval with tops more or less tapering to the apex or blunt at the apex and 3 to 16 mm long and 5 to 12 mm wide. They are coated with short, soft, straight hairs; sessile glands up to 150 per square cm.

Flowers: Flowering spikes are almost globe-shaped to cylindrical, sometimes rather loose at the bases, and measuring 2 to 8 mm long and about 3 mm wide. Egg-shaped to oval green bracts occur three to six pairs per spike and measure 1 to 3 mm long and 0.5 to 1.5 mm wide. The outside is coated with short, soft, straight hairs.

Calyces are two-lipped for about one-fifth their length, about 2 mm long and the outside is coated with short, soft, straight hairs. The upper lips are divided for about two-fifths their length into three almost equal and nearly triangluar teeth. The white corollas are two-lipped for about two-fifths, 2 to 4 mm long; upper lips are divided for about one-fifth into two lobes.

O. onites L., Sp. pl. 590. 1753.

Native country: *O. onites* is native from southern Greece to southern Turkey and is widely cultivated.

General habit: This herb is a subshrub with erect or ascending stems up to 1 m long, light brown, with moderately coarse and stiff hairs.

Leaves: Leaves occur in up to twenty-eight pairs per stem, the lower ones shortly stalked, heart-shaped, egg-shaped, or oval, more or less tapering to the apex or pinched at the tip, margins often with small teeth, 3 to 12 mm long and 2 to 9 mm wide, coated with moderately coarse and stiff hairs and with long, soft straight hairs with glands.

Flowers: Spikes are arranged in a flat-topped or convex open inflorescence, almost globe-shaped, ovoid, or four-sided cylindrical, 3 to 17 mm long and about 4 mm wide. Bracts are four to thirty-four pairs per spike; oval, egg-shaped, or egg-shaped and attached at the narrow end; toothless; 2 to 5 mm long, 1.5 to 4 mm wide; light green, outside hairy. Calyces are one-lipped for about nine-tenths; somewhat rhomboid, egg-shaped or egg-shaped and attached at the narrow end; 2 to 3 mm long; outside somewhat coated with short, soft, straight hairs. Corollas are two-lipped for about two-fifths; 3 to 7 mm long; white; outside somewhat coated with short, soft, straight hairs; upper lips divided for one-tenth to one-fifth their length into two lobes.

O. syriacum L., Sp. pl. 590. 1753.

Key:

1. Stems with dense wool-like covering of matted, tangled hairs of medium length; leaves whitish . . . . *O. syriacum* var. *syriacum* (*O. maru* L.).

1a. Stems with moderate coarse and stiff hairs; leaves with a slight wool-like covering of matted, intertangled hairs of medium length, leaves greenish 2

  2. Leaves about 14 by 11 mm, heart-shaped, or egg-shaped, shortly stalked (stalks about 2 mm long); corollas about 4 mm long . . . . *O. syriacum* var. *sinaicum* (Boiss.) Ietswaart, Tax. Rev. Gen. Origanum 89. 1980.

  2a. Leaves about 25 by 15 mm, egg-shaped or oval, long stalked (stalks about 5 mm long); corollas about 6 mm long . . . .*O. syriacum* var. *bevanii* (Holmes) Ietswaart, Tax. Rev. Gen. Origanum 88. 1980.

Native country: Both *O. syriacum* var. *syriacum* (native to Israel, Jordan, and Syria) and *O. syriacum* var. *bevanii* (native to Turkey, Cyprus, Syria, and Lebanon) are harvested as white oregano and are sometimes sold in the United States as Lebanese oregano. *Origanum syriacum* var. *sinaicum* is found only in the Sinai Peninsula but also has been used as oregano.

General habit: *O. syriacum* is a subshrub with ascending or erect stems, 0.4 to 13 cm long.

Leaves: Leaves are up to thirty pairs per stem; clearly stalked (petiolate) to almost stalkless; egg-shaped, oval, or heart-shaped; blunt to pinched at the tip; margins toothless or remotely with small rounded teeth; 3 to 35 mm long; 2 to 23 mm wide; green or whitish; with slightly moderately coarse, matted, stiff hairs to covered with dense wool-like covering of matted, tangled hairs of medium length.

Flowers: Spikes are four-sided cylindrical to almost globe-shaped, 3 to 25 mm long, about 4 mm wide. Bracts are four to forty pairs per spike, egg-shaped and attached at the narrow end or oval, blunt or tapering to the apex, toothless or slightly small-toothed, 2 to 5 mm long, about 2 mm wide, green or whitish, outside coated with moderately coarse, matted, stiff hairs. Calyces are one-lipped for nine-tenths or more, egg-shaped and attached at the narrow end or oval, about 2 mm long, outside coated with mod-erately coarse, matted, stiff hairs. Corollas are two-lipped for about 4 to 7.5 mm long, white, outside more or less coated with short, soft, straight hairs; upper lips divided for about one-fifth into two lobes, lower lips divided for about four-fifths into three sub-equal lobes.

O. vulgare L., Sp. pl. 590. 1753.

Key:

1. Leaves and calyces usually with conspicuous translucent dots; bracts 1.5 to 6 by 1 to 3 mm. 2
    2. Stems slightly coated with short, soft, straight hairs or becoming hairless with age; leaves with translucent dots, more or less coated with a bluish wax, almost smooth, or slightly coated with short, soft, straight hairs; branches and spikes often slender . . . . subsp. *gracile*
    2a. Stems usually with moderate coarse and stiff hairs; leaves densely coated with translucent dots, usually not glaucous, usually hirsute or pilosellous; branches and spikes not slender 3
        3. Bracts usually shorter than calyces, hairless, or slightly coated with short, straight hairs along margins; obviously coated with translucent dots; inflorescences often very wide . . . . subsp. *glandulosum*
        3a. Bracts usually as long as or somewhat longer than calyces, with moderately coarse and stiff hairs or coated with short, soft, straight hairs, more or less coated with translucent dots; inflorescence often compact . . . . subsp. *hirtum*
1a. Leaves and calyces usually conspicuously coated with translucent dots; bracts 2 to 11 by 1 to 7 mm 4
    4. Bracts usually (partly) purple; flowers pink . . . . subsp. *vulgare*
    4a. Bracts usually (yellowish) green; flowers usually white 5
        5. Bracts 3.5 to 11 by 2 to 7 mm, smooth or almost smooth, yellowish green; inflorescences often compact. . . . . subsp. *virens*
        5a. Bracts 2 to 8 by 1 to 4 mm, often (densely) coated with short, soft, straight hairs, usually green; inflorescences usually not compact . . . . subsp. *viridulum*

subsp. *vulgare*
subsp. *glandulosum* (Desf.) Ietswaart, Tax. Rev. Origanum. 110. 1980.
subsp. *gracile* (Koch) Ietswaart, Tax. Rev. Origanum. 111. 1980 (*O. tyttanthum* Gontsh-carov, *O. kopetdagnehse* Boriss.).
subsp. *hirtum* (Link) Ietswaart, Tax. Rev. Origanum. 112. 1980 (*O. hirtum* Link, *O. heracleoticum* auct., non L.)
subsp. *virens* (Hoffmanns. & Link) Ietswaart, Tax. Rev. Origanum 115:1980 (*O. virens* Hoff-manns. & Link).
subsp. *viridulum* (Martrin-Donos) Nyman, Consp. Fl. Eur. 592. 1881 [*O. vulgare* L. subsp. *viride* (Boiss.) Hayek].

Native country: *O. vulgare* is native to Europe, western Asia, and northern Africa, but it has become widely naturalized around the world.

General habit: *O. vulgare* is a woody perennial

with stems 10 to 100 cm long, usually as-cending and rooting at the bases.

Leaves: Leaves are up to forty-five pairs per stem; stalked to almost stalkless; egg-shaped, oval, or roundish; tapering to the apex to blunt; 6 to 40 mm long; 5 to 30 mm wide; with moderately coarse and stiff hairs or with long, soft, straight hairs to hairless, sometimes covered with a bluish waxy cover-ing; stalkless glands hardly visible to very conspicuous; margins smooth or remotely small-toothed.

Flowers: Spikes are 3 to 35 mm long, 2 to 8 mm wide. Bracts are two to twenty-five pairs per spike; egg-shaped and attached at the narrow end to egg-shaped or oval; more or less tapering to the apex or pinched; 2 to 11 mm long; 1 to 7 mm wide; coated with fine hairs; densely coated with short, soft, straight hairs or hairless; (partly) purple, green, or yellowish green, sometimes glau-cous. Flowers almost stalkless. Calyces are 2.5 to 4.5 mm long, outside coated with fine hairs, coated with short, soft, straight hairs, or smooth. Corollas are 3 to 11 mm long, purple, pink, or white; outside coated with short, soft, straight hairs; upper lips divided for about one-fifth into two long lobes; lower lips divided for about one-fifth into three somewhat unequal lobes.

Papaver somniferum

på-pā-vĕr sŏm-nĭ-fēr-ŭm
poppy seed

Family: Papaveraceae
Growth form: annual to 39 inches (100 cm) tall
Culinary use: primarily breads, crackers, and pastries
Craft use: pods useful in wreaths and dried flower arrangements

French: *pavot somnifère*
German: *Schlafmohn, Garten-Mohn*
Dutch: *slaapbol, papaver, maankop*
Italian: *papavero da oppio*
Spanish: *adormidera*
Portuguese: *dormideira, papoila dol ópio*
Swedish: *opiumvallmo*
Russian: *mak*
Chinese: *ying-tzu-shu*
Japanese: *keshi*
Arabic: *khas-khasa*

This poppy yields opium, yet remains the only source of edible poppy seed and poppy seed oil. The seed oil is considered GRAS. Today most poppy seed is imported from the Netherlands and Australia; the slate-blue Dutch poppy seed is standard. Because of the potential abuse of the opium-yielding sap of this plant, cultivation in the United States has been prohibited by both federal and state governments since the early twentieth century. Opium poppies were once widely cultivated for their beautiful blos-soms, and sometimes they persist at old cottage gardens. We do not advocate growing your own poppy seed, and we have omitted directions on cultivation.

The genus *Papaver* includes about fifty spe-cies native to Europe, Asia, South Africa, Aus-tralia, and western North America. All are characterized by dried fruit that resembles a small "shaker"; these are used in dried flower arrangements. *Papaver* was the Latin name for poppies, while *somniferum* means "sleep-inducing."

The opium poppy has been cultivated since ancient times. A statue of a poppy goddess was found at a sanctuary at Gazi, west of Heraklion, Crete, dating to about 1400 B.C.E. To harvest the raw material for opium, the immature seed capsules are lanced, usually with a three-pronged knife, early in the morning. The milky latex slowly exudes and congeals to a black mass. In the evening, this blackened latex is gathered and eventually pressed into bricks. The resulting raw opium contains up to twenty-five different alkaloids, especially morphine, which is a powerful analgesic and narcotic and a source of heroin. Tincture of opium, a deep ruby-red liquid called laudanum, was once widely used to alleviate pain but was also consumed as an addictive recreational drug by poets, painters, and novelists of eighteenth- and nineteenth-century Europe.

We used to be told that the black (or white) seeds (maw) do not contain measurable amounts of alkaloids unless they had been contaminated by the latex, but tests have shown commercial poppy seed to contain 0 to 1.7 ppm surface and free morphine and 0 to 0.5 ppm surface and free codeine as well as 0.6 to 2.3 ppm bound morphine and 0 to 0.5 ppm bound codeine. Perhaps those hot poppy seed milkshakes that are sometimes given to German and Eastern European children to soothe them into slumber have a real effect!

The dried poppy capsules also have trace quantities of bound morphine and codeine, and commercial seed will germinate to produce poppies that yield opium.

Poppy seeds are widely used in baking for their distinctive nutty flavor and also as birdseed. Toasting or baking the seeds will enhance the nutty flavor. The whole seeds are commonly used on dinner rolls, while the crushed seeds, mixed with sugar and other ingredients, are used in pastries. The pressed oil is used in artists' paints, salad oil, soap, and so on.

Opium poppy is a robust annual to about 3 feet (0.9 m) tall and coated with a blue wax. The flowers vary from white to mauve and from single with a distinct cross at the base ('Danebrog', or Danish flag poppies) to doubles with deeply slashed petals ("peony-flowered").

Important chemistry: The latex is rich in alkaloids, principally morphine (1 to 21 percent), and also thebaine, codeine, narceine, narcotine, and papaverine. The seeds contain about 22 percent protein and 48 percent oil, the latter rich in palmitic (31 percent), oleic (27 percent), linoleic (18 percent), and lauric (13 percent) acids.

Botanical Description

Papaver somniferum includes three subspecies, but subsp. *somniferum* is most widely cultivated.

Papaver somniferum

P. somniferum L., Sp. pl. 508. 1753.
Native country: Opium poppy was probably derived from *P. setigerum* DC. of southwest Asia.
General habit: Opium poppy is a smooth annual coated with blue wax and growing 30 to 100 cm tall.

Leaves: Leaves are 7 to 12 cm long, ovate-oblong, with lobes arranged as in a feather.
Flowers: Flowers are white to mauve with almost round petals 35 to 45 mm across.
Fruits/seeds: The dried shaker-type capsule is 5 to 9 by 3 to 6 cm, yielding white to black seeds.

Pelargonium

pĕl-är-gō-nē-ŭm
scented geranium

Family: Geraniaceae
Growth form: succulent perennial shrubs from 1 foot (30 cm) to 6 feet (1.8 m) tall
Hardiness: routinely hardy to Zone 9, although well-mulched plants snugged next to the house may be root-hardy to Zone 6
Light: full sun
Water: moist but not constantly wet; many can withstand drought
Soil: well-drained garden loam
Propagation: mostly cuttings during active growth in summer
Culinary use: limited (most not GRAS except for *P.* 'Graveolens')
Craft use: potpourri, wreaths, perfume
Landscape use: excellent for summer bedding as edgings or in borders; also excellent in pots or window boxes

---

Name a delectable fragrance—rose, lemon, orange, lime, strawberry, peppermint, camphor, nutmeg, spice, apple, apricot, coconut, filbert, ginger—and there's a scented geranium to match. *Pelargonium* is derived from the Greek *pelargos*, or stork, referring to the ripe seed head, which supposedly resembles the head and beak of the stork, hence a common name of storksbill. Most of the 280 species are native to South Africa. Many additional, complex hybrids have been created since their introduction into Europe in the early seventeenth century.

While commonly called "scented geraniums," they are often confused by the novice gardener with the hardy *Geranium* species, or cranesbills, and the hardy *Erodium* species, or heronsbills. In 1753, Linnaeus published thirty-nine species of the genus *Geranium* in his *Species Plantarum*, including storksbills, cranesbills, and heronsbills in the same genus. From 1787 to 1788 L'Héritier published forty-four plates under the title *Geraniologia*. L'Héritier's accompanying text was not published until 1802, but the unfinished manuscript was widely circulated prior to publication. From this manuscript, Aiton published the new names of *Pelargonium* and *Erodium*, separating these new genera from *Geranium*, in his *Hortus Kewensis* of 1789.

Both *Pelargonium* and *Geranium* have five petals and ten stamens, but in *Pelargonium* the two upper petals are usually larger and only five to seven anthers are fertile. The remaining are present as filaments. All three genera can also be distinguished by their fruits.

All scented geraniums do best in full sun in circumneutral garden loam with relatively cool, dry summers. The addition of 53 to 71 pounds per acre (60 to 80 kg/ha) of nitrogen is recommended for commercial production of rose geranium oil. Geranium for oil is harvested about four months after planting.

Sudden wilts and root rots from *Pythium*, *Verticillium*, *Lasiodiplodia*, and *Fusarium*, soil-borne fungi, are often encountered. Overhead watering, excessive soil moisture, and crowding will increase the incidence from wilt. Leaf spot (*Cercospora* spp.), gray mold or botrytis blight (*Botrytis cinerea*), black root rot (*Thielaviopsis basicola* and *Macrophomina phaseolina*), scab (*Sphaceloma pelargonii*), bacterial fasciation (*Corynebacterium fascians*), vascular wilts (*Xanthomonas pelargonii*), rust (*Puccinia* spp.), and several virus diseases have also been reported. Root-knot nematodes, *Meloidogyne hapla* and *M. incognita*, have been found to infect the roots of commercial stands of the rose-scented geranium. Spider mites, whiteflies, caterpillars, and aphids can be pests in the greenhouse.

Most scented geraniums flower best in late winter to early spring after a cool, but not freezing, winter. Because most species are not hardy below freezing, they are best raised as potted plants, and cuttings may be easily rooted in late summer to carry over through the winter.

Propagation by cuttings is important to preserve the unique characteristics of individual cultivars, which are often complex hybrids. While many geranium cultivars root easily and quickly in water, this is not normally recommended (see chapter 7, on propagation, for details). More traditional rooting methods use vigorous basal side-shoots ripped off in a downward tug that produces a "heel" cutting for best results. Some gardeners claim that cuttings root

most easily after "hardening" (drying) a few hours, but this is not normally required for the scenteds. Some, such as strawberry-scented geranium and 'Mabel Grey', sometimes refuse to root at all unless basal cuttings or extra watering is used.

Scented geraniums have a reputation as being more difficult to root than other geraniums; one reason for this may be because of a number of viruses that sap the plants' strength but do little else. The zonal geranium bedding-plant industry combats this by using seeds and by creating virus-free clones with special technology. These methods are expensive and are not used for scenteds because of technical difficulties and low sales when compared with bedding geraniums.

Name a delectable fragrance—rose, lemon, orange, lime, strawberry, peppermint, camphor, nutmeg, spice, apple, apricot, coconut, filbert, ginger— and there's a scented geranium to match.

An area of further research on rooting of scented geraniums is the use of Florel (ethephon). In a study, it increased rooting under supplemental lights, increased total roots per cutting, and reduced the stem length and stem diameter. Studies on basal heating are also needed.

Most of the offerings in the nursery trade, even of supposedly "pure" species, are actually complex hybrids. The herb industry, in general, has been plagued for decades with the practice of renaming plants; sometimes this is done intentionally to increase sales, but usually it is without malice by the uninformed. Scented geraniums are a case in point, and it sometimes appears that total name-anarchy exists. 'Beauty Oak' has been renamed 'Beauty', 'Cody' has been renamed 'Apple Cider', 'Logee' has become 'Old Spice', and 'Logee's Snowflake' is now sold as 'Snowflake'. The new names may have more appeal and induce more sales, but 'Beauty', for example, already designates another geranium, and the trade now has two clones called 'Citronella': one in cultivation in the United States and France and another in England. Which is correct?

In the following discussion we have omitted the mildly scented selections grown primarily for their flowers or foliage, such as *P. vitifolium* (L.) L'Hér. ex Aiton, 'Brilliant', 'Capri', 'Clorinda' ('Eucalyptus'), 'Mexican Sage', 'Mrs. Kingsley', 'Mrs. Taylor', 'Old Scarlet Unique', 'Pink Champagne', 'Red-Flowered Rose', 'Roger's Delight', 'Rollison's Unique', 'Solfrino', 'Spanish Lavender', and 'Sweet Miriam'. Some scented-leaved geraniums, such as the so-called labdanum-scented *P. cucullatum* (L.) L'Hér. ex Aiton and the apocryphal rue-scented *P. ×rutaceum* Sweet, are not in general cultivation and have also been omitted. New cultivars are introduced every year, and the correct taxonomic placement of these cultivars is often in doubt. We thus find too little published information on 'Cook's Lemon Rose', 'Copthorne', 'Dean's Delight', 'Karooense', 'Lillian Pottinger', 'Ruby Edged Oak', 'Sancho Panza', 'Sharp-Toothed Oak', 'Solferino', 'Spring Park', 'Sweet Miriam', 'Variegated Oak', or 'Variegated Shrubland Rose'.

The scented geraniums have been grouped here by species. Following the principal species and their derivatives are the complex hybrids in which no one species predominates. In all cases,

because of their rampant hybridization in years past and close similarities, only markedly distinguishing morphological characteristics are listed; detailed botanical descriptions are listed separately for the intellectually curious. These herbs were selected primarily for their odors, and thus are discussed more fully in the general introduction. Ultimately, identification of unknown scented geraniums must be done one-on-one with authentically labeled living material; not even good photographs will suffice in difficult cases.

A strong caveat must also be inserted here. Hybrid origins are only hypothetical unless artificial resynthesis has been done and compared with the type specimens (in addition to the descriptions and illustrations), and this has only been done (so far, in part) with the 'Graveolens' series. Much work remains to be done! Take any statements of hybrid origin in *Pelargonium* with a liberal dose of skepticism. They are only included here, with legitimately published names as currently accepted by taxonomists, to provide routes for future research. We have also followed the policy of the English experts in *Pelargonium* to create cultivar groups, e.g., 'Graveolens' (which see), for many of the so-called species complexes. Until nothospecies (hybrid species) are typified and the origins elucidated by resynthesis, this is probably the best temporary solution. This is obviously not the last word, and names will undoubtedly change in the future. Consider yourself warned!

Pelargonium abrotanifolium

pĕl-är-gō-nĭ-ŭm ăb-rŏ-tā-nĭ-fō-lē-ŭm
southernwood geranium

The fragrant, gray, slender leaves of this species resemble the herb southernwood (*Artemisia abrotanum*). The floating, lacy, gray leaves are a great accent with other geraniums and in window boxes.

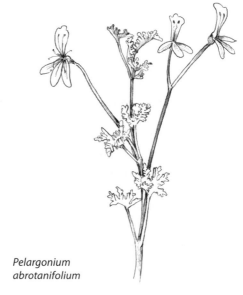

Pelargonium abrotanifolium

Pelargonium capitatum

pĕl-är-gō-nĭ-ŭm kăp-ĭ-tă-tŭm
rose-scented geranium

The specific name means "head-shaped," referring to the shape of the flower clusters. The flowers are similar to *P. vitifolium*, the grape-leaved geranium. This rose-scented geranium is one of the ancestors, along with *P. radens* and *P. graveolens*, of 'Graveolens', the leading rose-scented geranium of commercial cultivation. The hydrophilic extract of *P. capitatum* has been shown to be antimicrobial.

Important chemistry: The essential oil is very variable with trace to 48 percent alpha-pinene, 0 to 37 percent citronellyl formate, trace to 29 percent citronellol, 0 to 26 percent 10-*epi*-gamma-eudesmol, 0 to 22 percent delta-cadinene, 0 to 18 percent menthone, 0 to 18 percent germacrene D, 0 to 18 percent beta-caryophyllene, 0 to 18 percent guaia-6,9-diene, 0 to 15 percent geraniol, 0 to 4 percent linalool, 0 to 12 percent terpinen-4-ol, and 0 to 11 percent limonene.

Some cultivars derived from *P. capitatum* follow. Many of these may, in fact, be more correctly relegated to *P.* 'Graveolens' because of their lack of pollen fertility, but chromosome counts must still be done to confirm this classification.

Cultivar: 'Attar of Roses'
Synonyms: 'Otto of Roses'; more than one clone is sold in North America
Origin: England, 1817; introduced at the New York Botanical Garden in 1923
Description: differs from *P. capitatum* in that the stems are somewhat shorter, leaves are more densely lobed and harsher on the upper surfaces, small flowers on short stems are rose-pink, and the upper ones more conspicuously veined
Essential oil: 7 to 43 percent geraniol, 18 to 43 percent citronellol, and 3 to 14 percent iso-menthone (minty rose)

Cultivar: 'Both's Snowflake'
Synonyms: 'Ice Crystal Rose', a seedling introduced by Gary Scheidt of California in the 1970s, is extremely similar but not identical
Origin: bred by Edward Alfred Bernard ("Ted") Both, Flinders, South Australia, 1950s
Description: deeply divided leaves with irregular splashes of cream and white; flowers are small and lavender; fragrance is lemon-rose

Cultivar: 'Major'
Synonyms: 'Large-leaved Rose', *P. quinquevulnerum* Willd.
Origin: Veitch, England, 1879, probably of hybrid origin
Description: same habit as *P. capitatum* but grows taller; leaves are larger, margins not as sharply toothed; flowers are similar in form but rose-pink in color

Pelargonium citronellum

pĕl-är-gō-nĭ-ŭm sĭ-trō-nĕl-ŭm

This was first described in 1983. According to the discoverer, Dr. J. J. A. van der Walt, this species may be a naturally occurring, ancient hybrid involving *P. scabrum* (L.) L'Hér. ex Aiton. It flowers most abundantly in spring. 'Mabel Grey' is a selected, cultivated clone of the species with leaves slightly less deeply lobed (much as 'Mitcham' is a selected, cultivated clone of peppermint).

Important chemistry: The oil of the wild species has 36 to 48 percent geranial and 27 to 37 percent neral, providing a lemony odor. 'Mabel Grey' is bitter lemon-scented with an essential oil containing trace to 58 percent neral, 30 to 43 percent geranial, 0 to 27 per-

cent geranyl formate, 0 to 31 percent citronellol, 0 to 43 percent geraniol, and 0 to 13 percent beta-pinene.

Pelargonium citronellum 'Mabel Grey'

Pelargonium crispum

pĕl-är-gō-nĭ-ŭm krĭs-pŭm
lemon-scented geranium

The specific name refers to the crisped leaves, scented of lemons.

Important chemistry: 8 to 30 percent gera-

nial, 3 to 57 percent neral, 0 to 14 percent nerol, trace to 17 percent [*E*]-nerolidol, 0 to 14 percent germacrene D, 0 to 14 percent selina-4,11-diene, trace to 11 percent beta-bourbonene, and 0 to 10 percent guaia-6,9-diene.

Some cultivars derived from *P. crispum* follow.

Cultivar: 'Gooseberry Leaf'
Synonyms: 'Peach', 'Peach Cream', 'Variegatum', often incorrectly listed as *P. grossularioides*
Description: similar to the species but with leaves mottled green and white, growth bushy, compact

Cultivar: 'Prince Rupert'
Description: similar to the species but with larger leaves and shorter leaf stalks; flowers are the same color, the upper petals carmine-veined
Essential oil: 16 to 20 percent [*Z*]-nerolidol, 12 to 30 percent geranial, and 16 to 19 percent neral

Cultivar: 'Variegated Prince Rupert'
Synonyms: 'French Lace'
Origin: Arndt, New Jersey, 1948
Description: habit of *P. cripsum* but bushier

and of more rapid growth, pyramidal in shape, leaves green with white margins
Essential oil: 28 to 49 percent geranial and 22 to 33 percent citronellol

Pelargonium crispum

Pelargonium denticulatum
pĕl-är-gō-nĭ-ŭm dĕn-tĭk-ū-lā-tŭm
pine-scented geranium

This pungent-scented geranium has flat, sticky, leaves and rounded teeth on the leaf margins. Most of the material cultivated in the United States as this species is actually an unnamed cultivar, perhaps derived from *P. radens* × *P. denticulatum*. Plants tend to become lanky with age and should be pruned back occasionally to maintain an attractive shape.

   Important chemistry: 40 percent isomenthone, 18 percent citronellal, and 18 percent citronellol (pungent-scented).

A cultivar derived from *P. denticulatum* follows.

Cultivar: 'Filicifolium'
Synonyms: 'Fernaefolium', *P. filicifolium* Hort.
Origin: introduced by Henderson in England in 1879
Description: very similar to the wild species in South Africa with finely cut leaves, lacy in appearance
Essential oil: 24 to 32 percent n-hexyl butyrate and 14 to 17 percent *trans*-2-hexenyl butyrate in the essential oil

Pelargonium elongatum
pĕl-är-gō-nĭ-ŭm ē-lŏn-gā-tŭm

This species is called "upright coconut" in the trade, not to be confused with *P. tabulare* (Burm.f.) L'Hér. or *P. patulum* Jacq.

Pelargonium 'Fragrans' (probably not identical with *P. ×fragrans*)
pĕl-är-gō-nĭ-ŭm frā-grănz
nutmeg-scented geranium

This aromatic ("nutmeg-scented") geranium may be a hybrid, *P. exstipulatum* (Cav.) L'Hér. ex Aiton × *P. odoratissimum*; others have questioned whether this is a non-hybrid species, now extinct in South Africa.

Important chemistry: 10 to 31 percent methyl eugenol, 0 to 20 percent alpha-pinene, and 8 to 14 percent fenchone (spicy)

This species (notho- or otherwise) includes the following cultivars. Also listed are 'Aroma', 'Fringed Apple', 'Fruity', and 'Lillian Pottinger'. 'Fruit Salad' (Arndt, New Jersey) has a fruity scent.

Cultivar: 'Apple Cider'
Synonyms: 'Cody'
Origin: Dorcas Brigham, Village Hill Nursery, Williamsburg, Massachusetts, pre-1955
Description: more compact than 'Fragrans', the leaves lighter green, larger, usually kidney-shaped

Cultivar: 'Old Spice'
Synonyms: 'Logee'
Origin: Ernest Logee, Danielson, Connecticut, c. 1948

Description: erratically lobed leaves with handsomely ruffled margins, flowers like 'Fragrans'
Comments: may be a backcross to *P. odoratissimum*

Cultivar: 'Variegated Nutmeg'
Synonyms: 'Snowy Nutmeg' and 'Golden Nutmeg' were derived from this cultivar and frequently revert from one to the other
Origin: Dr. John Seeley, Cornell University, Ithaca, New York, 1957
Description: irregularly streaked with white

Pelargonium 'Fragrans'

Pelargonium glutinosum

pĕl-är-gō-nĭ-ŭm glū-tĭ-nō-sŭm
pheasant's foot geranium

Important chemistry: The odor of the gluti-
nous, clammy leaves is pungent from up to 25
percent guaia-6,9-diene, 16 to 24 percent *p*-
cymene, and trace to 12 percent citronellol in
the essential oil of the cultivated species. Hexyl
butyrate and *trans*-2-hexenyl butyrate are the
principal constituents of the oil of wild-
collected material.

A cultivar derived from this extremely variable species follows.

Cultivar: 'Viscossimum'

Origin: originally thought to be a natural species raised from seed obtained from Cape
Province, South Africa, but more probably
a variant of *P. glutinosum*

Description: habit of *P. glutinosum* but the
leaves are more deeply lobed, the lobes narrower and more strongly toothed; flowers
very small, short-spurred, five to eight in a
flat flower cluster, petals nearly equal, lilac
or white streaked with red on the upper two

Pelargonium graveolens

pĕl-är-gō-nĭ-ŭm grå-vē-ō-lĕnz

The true *P. graveolens* is similar to *P. radens*,
but it is not now in general cultivation. The
plant usually sold as *P. graveolens* in North
America is actually 'Graveolens'.

Important chemistry: This is peppermint-
or rose-scented geranium with 7 to 83 percent
isomenthone, 19 to 42 percent geraniol, 0 to 18
percent citronellol, 1 to 13 percent linalool, and
around 11 percent citronellyl formate in the
essential oil.

Pelargonium 'Graveolens'

pĕl-är-gō-nĭ-ŭm grå-vē-ō-lĕnz

The 'Graveolens' hybrids (*P. capitatum* × *P.
radens* or *P. graveolens*) include both minty and
rose-scented forms. They were once designated
by taxonomists as *P.* ×*asperum* Willd., but close
examination of Willdenow's type specimen in
Berlin reveals that the latter is a hybrid involving *P. quercifolium* or maybe *P. panduriforme*
Eckl. & Zeyh. As further proof of the hybrid
origin of this series of geraniums, we have yet
to find any fertile pollen, and all plants that we
have counted so far have a chromosome number
of $2n = 77$, supporting J. Payet and other re-

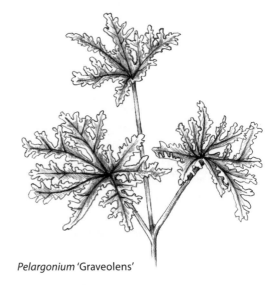

Pelargonium 'Graveolens'

searchers around the world who have not only examined the chromosome numbers of these hybrids and their parents but also created synthetic hybrids.

Pelargonium 'Graveolens' (syns. 'Old Fashioned Rose', 'Rosé', not *P. graveolens*) is the hybrid usually sold in North America as *P. graveolens*, which it closely resembles in morphology. It has narrower leaves, with more deeply cut lobes, than *P. graveolens* and the harsh hairs of *P. radens*. Because seed propagation has occurred here, introducing slight variation, we (again, following the English experts) designate 'Graveolens' as a cultivar group, or what used to be called a grex (a term taxonomists used to describe a collection of clones from the same cross) rather than one clone.

While the essential oil constituents of 'Graveolens' are not influenced by fertility, they are greatly influenced by water stress and altitude. France and China supply most of the rose geranium oil to the United States. 'Graveolens' is also raised commercially on the Island of Réunion, having been introduced in 1800, and the commercial product is called "Bourbon Geranium."

Around 1900 'Graveolens' was introduced from France to Algeria, Egypt, and Morocco, where it became known as "African geranium" in the commercial trade. A characteristic feature of the Bourbon Geranium oil is the presence of 4 to 7 percent guaia-6,9-diene, which is present in African geranium in only trace quantities. African geranium is characterized by the presence of 4 to 5 percent 10-epi-gamma-eudesmol, which is not present in Bourbon-type oils. Rose geranium oil is greenish at first, becoming yellow with age. The odor is green, leafy-rosy, with a sweet-rosy dryout. Rose geranium oil is widely used in perfumery, blends well with almost everything, and displays antimicrobial activity. The essential oil is considered GRAS at 1.6 to 200 ppm.

Important chemistry: The essential oil of *P.* 'Graveolens' is 8 to 51 percent citronellol, 1 to 28 percent citronellyl formate, trace to 23 percent geraniol, trace to 18 percent beta-caryophyllene, 0 to 16 percent linalool, and 0 to 10 percent geranyl butyrate (rose)

Selections of this hybrid complex sometimes listed in catalogs and books include 'Candy Dancer', 'Crowfoot Rose', 'Fragrantissimum', 'Giganteum' ('Giant Rose'), 'Granelous', 'Grey Lady Plymouth', 'Marginata', 'Peacock', 'Roller's Sigma Variegated Rose', 'Silver Leaf Rose', and 'Variegatum'. Other selections that seem to fall within this hybrid complex follow.

Cultivar: 'Bontrosai'
Origin: 2005 (U.S. PP15,918) by Boekestijn-Vermeer, Klazina, Naaldwiji, Netherlands, reputedly derived from 'Graveolens' by UV-radiation and hormones
Description: contorted, curled leaves

Cultivar: 'Camphor Rose'
Synonyms: 'Camphorum'
Origin: c. 1900
Description: similar to 'Graveolens' in growth habit but coarser throughout, leaves larger and bristly haired, flower cluster similar but flowers rose-pink
Essential oil: 22 percent menthone, 15 percent isomenthone, and 10 percent geranyl butyrate (minty rose)

Cultivar: 'Charity'
Origin: reputedly a sport of 'Graveolens' discovered by Dr. Durrell Nelson, Nauvoo Restoration, Illinois; distributed by Glasshouse Works, Ohio
Description: golden green leaves with deeper green veining and centers

Cultivar: 'Chicago Rose'
Origin: Chicago Botanic Garden, 1970s; distributed by Mary Peddie, Rutland, Kentucky
Description: very large leaves, up to 6 inches (15 cm) across

Cultivar: 'Cinnamon Rose'
Synonyms: 'Cinnamon'; this is often listed as *P. gratum* Willd. (a species of unknown origin) and more than one 'Cinnamon' clone exists, but the most common clone with this name is rose-scented with a hint of cinnamon
Origin: Fred Bode, California, 1950s

Cultivar: 'Citrosa'
Origin: unknown, probably Florida, but not the Netherlands
Description: similar in morphology to 'Lady Plymouth' and 'Little Gem'
Essential oil: 39 percent geraniol and 11 percent citronellol
Comments: 'Citrosa' has been touted as a somatic fusion of *Pelargonium* and *Cymbopogon nardus* (citronella grass) with the ability to repel mosquitoes. The citronellal content, the unique component of citronella grass (about 21 percent in Java citronella oil and 14 percent in Ceylon citronella oil) is only 0.09 percent. In addition, a study found no significant repellency from the whole plant, but the crushed plant had 30 to 40 percent repellency compared with Deep Woods Off; lemon thyme (*Thymus ×citriodorus*) had 60 percent repellency. In short, we have been unable to substantiate any of the claims of origin or repellency made for 'Citrosa'.

Cultivar: 'Dr. Livingston'
Synonyms: 'Dr. Livingstone', 'Skeleton Rose'
Origin: England, pre-1876
Description: morphologically similar to the *P.*
radens parent but leaves are more deeply lobed, growth is taller, and blooms less freely produced
Essential oil: 33 to 39 percent citronellol and 18 to 24 percent isomenthone (rosy mint)

Cultivar: 'Lady Plymouth'
Origin: England, c. 1852
Description: lower growing and less vigorous than 'Graveolens', leaves green, blotched cream white, flowers similar
Essential oil: 72 to 82 percent isomenthone (peppermint)

Cultivar: 'Little Gem'
Origin: England, 1860s, possibly not the same plant as originally described
Description: leaves more lobed and toothed, slightly woolly, flower clusters on short stalks and held close to the foliage, flowers rose-pink with two purple lines on the upper petals, somewhat rose/pungent-scented
Comments: sometimes cited as a derivative of *P. quercifolium* but origin unknown

Cultivar: 'Ocean Wave'
Origin: Logee's, Danielson, Connecticut
Description: wavy, almost curly leaves

Cultivar: 'Peppermint Rose'
Description: vigorous with gray-green, deeply cut leaves
Essential oil: 63 to 65 percent isomenthone and 7 to 11 percent decanoic acid (peppermint)

Cultivar: 'Rober's Lemon Rose'
Synonyms: 'Canadian Silver Seedling', 'Western Rose Seedling'
Origin: unknown, apocryphally a hybrid (*P.* 'Graveolens' × *P. tomentosum*) from Ernest Rober in California in the 1940s, but the

morphology and essential oil pattern suggests a chimera of *P.* 'Graveolens'

Description: shrubby habit of growth, stems erect to 2 feet (60 cm) or more, branching, not densely leafy, leaves intermediate in size, almost like those of tomatoes, to 2 inches (5 cm) long and as broad at the base, triangular in outline, lobed or almost-lobed to the midrib, the segments irregularly lobed and toothed, feltlike white-hairy, flower clusters dense, flowers pink, the upper petals crimson-veined

Essential oil: 1 to 26 percent beta-caryophyllene, 19 to 57 percent citronellol, 3 to 17 percent citronellyl formate, 2 to 13 percent linalool, and 4 to 10 percent geraniol (lemon-rose)

Cultivar: 'Velvet Rose'

Origin: 'Velvet Rose' was isolated from a 'Rober's Lemon Rose' tissue culture line by Robert Skirvin, Purdue University, in 1975

Description: relatively short internodes, leaves thick, gray-green, densely hairy

---

Pelargonium grossularioides
pĕl-är-gō-nĭ-ŭm grŏss-ū-lăr-ĭ-ōy-dēz
coconut-scented geranium

The coconut-scented geranium shows great variability in number of flowers per cluster and leaf shape. The specific name means "gooseberry-like," and another common name is gooseberry geranium (not to be confused with *P.* 'Gooseberry Leaf', which sometimes is sold as *P. grossularioides*). Abundant seeds are produced, and they may even overwinter and germinate in the spring.

Important chemistry: The essential oil of *P. grossularioides* is rich in 16 percent geraniol, 13 percent isomenthone, 12 percent citronellol, and 11 percent methyl eugenol, providing a complex rose-mint-lemon-clove fragrance.

Pelargonium odoratissimum
pĕl-är-gō-nĭ-ŭm ō-dŏ-rå-tĭs-ĭ-mŭm

This apple-rose-scented geranium is similar to *P.* 'Fragrans'.

Important chemistry: 32 to 80 percent methyl eugenol and 5 to 19 percent isomenthone.

Pelargonium quercifolium
pĕl-är-gō-nĭ-ŭm kwĕr-sĭ-fō-lē-ŭm
oak-leaved geranium

The plants currently cultivated under this name are mainly hybrids, probably of *P. pseudoglutinosum* R. Kunth and *P. panduriforme* Eckl. & Zeyn. The true species has pointed, not rounded leaf lobes.

Important chemistry: The odor of the typical species is pungent from 33 percent *p*-cymene and 12 percent alpha-phellandrene in the essential oil. A cultivated form has been reported with 31 percent isomenthone and 19 percent beta-pinene.

All cultivars derived from this species have pungent-scented oily leaves, including 'Harlequin Oak', a variegated oak geranium, and the following.

Cultivar: 'Fair Ellen'
Synonyms: probably originally known as 'Fair Helen'
Origin: probably of hybrid origin, originated in England in the 1840s
Description: habit of *P. quercifolium*, the stems erect, more branched and not quite as tall, leaves similar to the species, flowers somewhat larger than the species, bright magenta-pink with larger purple spot on the upper petals

Cultivar: 'Giant Oak'
Synonyms: giant oak-leaved geranium, 'Giganteum'
Origin: originated in England c. 1850
Description: leaves twice the size as those of the species, with five broader lobes, flowers slightly smaller with a smaller dark spot on the upper petals

Essential oil: 20 to 34 percent alpha-phellandrene and 11 to 19 percent *p*-cymene

Cultivar: 'Pinnatifidum'
Synonyms: sharp-toothed oak-leaved geranium
Description: smooth, stocky, deeply lobed leaves with sharply pointed teeth, flat flower clusters hold four blossoms
Essential oil: 17 to 20 percent *p*-cymene, 12 to 24 percent alpha-phellandrene, and 14 to 16 percent *trans*-2-hexenyl butyrate

Cultivar: 'Staghorn Oak'
Synonyms: 'True Oak', 'Staghorn'
Origin: introduced in England c. 1860
Description: similar to the species in habit of growth, leaves similar size and outline but differ in that each segment has an additional round lobe, suggesting incipient antlers about to emerge from a stag's horn, some leaves with the terminal lobe elongated with seven to nine smaller lobes
Essential oil: 14 to 23 percent *p*-cymene, 17 to 19 percent *trans*-2-hexenyl butyrate, 12 to 16 percent alpha-phellandrene, and 8 to 11 percent n-hexyl butyrate

Pelargonium radens
pĕl-är-gō-nĭ-ŭm rā-dĕnz

This rose-scented geranium is often called the crow's foot geranium (not to be confused with its cultivar 'Crow's Foot'); the specific epithet is adapted from *radians*, or radiating from a common center.

Important chemistry: The fragrance of the wild species is characteristically minty from 32 to 85 percent isomenthone, trace to 54 percent citronellol, and trace to 12 percent beta-caryophyllene.

Pelargonium tomentosum
pĕl-är-gō-nĭ-ŭm tō-mĕn-tō-sŭm
peppermint-scented geranium

The peppermint-scented geranium is delightful
in hanging baskets with large, fuzzy leaves on
irregular but compact growth.

Important chemistry: It owes its scent to
46 to 87 percent isomenthone and 2 to 50 percent menthone in the essential oil.

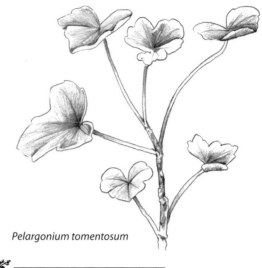

Pelargonium tomentosum

Pelargonium cultivars of uncertain parentage

Cultivar: 'Atomic Snowflake'
Also called 'Atomic Rose', this lemon-rose-
scented geranium is a variation of 'Snowflake'
originated by Merry Gardens, Camden, Maine.
It has an irregular pale yellow band on the edge
of the gray-green leaves with a slightly distorted
leaf edge. The lavender flowers are similar to
'Snowflake', and reversions to 'Round Leaf
Rose' have been reported.

Cultivar: 'Beauty'
'Beauty' ('Beauty Oak') originated at Logee's,
Danielson, Connecticut, supposedly as a
chance mint-pungent-scented hybrid, *P. quercifolium* 'Giant Oak' × *P. tomentosum*. 'Beauty'
has trailing, branching stems, leaves long-
stalked, rounded heart-shaped in outline, three-
to five-lobed, the margins of lobes and smaller
lobes sharply toothed, center of light green
leaves marked with brown-purple, flowers similar to *P. tomentosum*.

Cultivar: 'Bitter Lemon'
Often marketed simply as 'Angel' or 'Angeline',
this has a sharp harsh bitter lemon fragrance.
'Bitter Lemon' bears showy pink flowers with
leaves similar to 'Mabel Grey' but with more
teeth. This may be the same plant marketed
as 'Citronella' in England; the essential oil of
the English cultivar contains up to 31 percent
neral, 28 percent geranial, and 23 percent citronellol. Like 'Mabel Grey', which it superficially
resembles, this is probably a derivative of *P.
citronellum*.

Cultivar: 'Blandfordianum'
The rosy-scented plant currently cultivated under this name is of unknown origin but bears
some resemblance to the 'Graveolens' series.
This is probably not the same as *P. ×blandford-
ianum* (Andr.) Sweet. The leaves are five- to
seven-lobed and palmate, the lobes with
rounded teeth. Flowers are in flat clusters, the
petals white or very pale pink, the upper 1 cm
long and broader with two red spots and purplish veins below.

Cultivar: 'Chocolate Peppermint'
'Chocolate Peppermint', sometimes called 'Chocolate Mint', is of similar origin to 'Beauty' and introduced by Viva Ireland, Santa Barbara, California. This resembles 'Beauty' except that the leaves are less deeply lobed. The odor is pungent minty with no trace of chocolate (merely a chocolate splotch on the leaf). The essential oil contains trace to 39 percent menthone, trace to 22 percent isomenthone, and 3 to 18 percent alpha-phellandrene.

Cultivar: 'Citronella'
At least two different cultivars are raised under this name. The English 'Citronella' is lemon-rose-scented and probably the same cultivar as 'Angeline'/'Angel' in North America, while the French 'Citronelle', which is also cultivated in North America, is lemon-mint-scented. Leaves of the French/American 'Citronella' are heart-shaped in outline with three to five rounded lobes. The essential oil of the French/North American cultivar contains 32 to 40 percent citronellol, trace to 20 percent isomenthone, and 17 to 48 percent citronellic acid. The origin of the French/North American cultivar is unknown but has been postulated to be a hybrid of *P. vitifolium* with *P. radens* or *P.* 'Graveolens'.

Cultivar: 'Clare's Cascade'
'Clare's Cascade' is peppermint-scented. The light green leaves are similar to those of *P. odoratissimum*.

Cultivar: 'Concolor Lace'
'Concolor Lace', alias 'Filbert' or 'Shotesham Pet', originated in England in about 1820. It is probably not the same as *P.* ×*concolor* Sweet. This is a mildly filbert-scented hybrid. The leaves are light green, softly hairy, thin, egg-shaped in outline, lobed to the central axis in the manner of a feather, with five to seven more or less wedge-shaped lobes, margins of segments incised and toothed, flat flower clusters with five to seven scarlet flowers.

Cultivar: 'Endsleigh'
Pungent-scented 'Endsleigh' has been considered a hybrid, *P. quercifolium* × *P. capitatum*. It originated in the United Kingdom by Cross, 1951. It has strong, prostrate growth with five-lobed, rounded leaves with a dark blotch in the center. Flowers are pale rosy mauve with darker veins on the upper petals.

Cultivar: 'Frensham'
'Frensham', also sold under the misspelled names of 'Francais' or 'Frenchaise' was introduced by Morden in the United Kingdom in 1970 as a hybrid ('Orange' × 'Mabel Grey'). It is a short, bushy plant with moss-green palmate leaves. The mauve flowers are similar to 'Orange'. The essential oil is characterized by 51 percent citral (geranial plus neral), 26 percent citronellol, and 12 percent geranyl formate.

Cultivar: 'Godfrey's Pride'
This geranium has been postulated to be a hybrid, *P. quercifolium* × *P. capitatum*. It is a large, rangy shrub with green leaves that are yellow-streaked in some, three-lobed, the margins sharply toothed. Flowers are pink with darker veining on the upper petals. The essential oil has 25 percent beta-pinene, 15 percent geranyl butyrate, and 15 percent menthone, providing a piney-rosy-minty fragrance.

Cultivar: 'Joy Lucille'
This is a peppermint-scented hybrid of unknown origin (but listed as *P.* 'Graveolens' × *P. tomentosum*) from Logee's, Danielson, Connecticut, introduced in the 1940s; but more likely the parentage is a rose-scented geranium crossed with *P. vitifolium* (L.) L'Hér. It has a

loose and rangy habit of growth. Leaves are large, green, feltlike, white-hairy, three-lobed, all lobes scalloped and toothed. Flowers are small, pink with carmine markings in the upper petals. The essential oil is dominated by 57 percent isomenthone and 29 percent menthone. 'Variegated Joy Lucille', marbled in ivory, is also listed.

Cultivar: 'Lady Mary'
The plants in commerce do not match the original description of *P. ×limoneum* and are probably not this species. The odor is faint citrusy with rose overtones.

Cultivar: 'Lady Scarborough'
This strawberry-lemon-scented geranium is often sold in the trade as 'Countess of Scarborough'. It is of unknown origin and probably not the same as *P. ×scarboroviae* Sweet but very similar in morphology to the rose-camphor-scented *P. englerianum* Kunth. Stems are lax, densely branched. Leaves are deeply divided, glossy green, rigid, three-lobed with the central lobe usually three-parted, coarsely toothed, not crisped. The flowers have spotted upper petals, veined with red or pink-violet, the lower petals narrower, pale lilac or stained red.

Cultivar: 'Lemon Balm'
This is a rose-scented hybrid, possibly involving *P. vitifolium* and sometimes listed as *P.* 'Graveolens' × *P. quercifolium*; it is probably not the same as *P. ×melissimum* Sweet. In the United States, two different plants are sold under this invalid (because it is the simple common name of a species in another genus, *Melissa officinalis*) cultivar name, one of which is more deeply dissected and likely a derivative of *P.* 'Graveolens'; the latter is characterized by 33 to 36 percent geraniol, 30 to 35 percent decanoic acid, and 11 to 14 percent isomenthone.

Cultivar: 'Lemon Meringue'
This lemon-scented geranium is perhaps a seedling of 'Mabel Grey', introduced by Harriet Foster of The Tunnel Geranium Nursery, Santa Barbara, California.

Cultivar: 'Lime'
Again, a cultivar name representing the simple common name of a species in another genus is not valid; this geranium needs a new name. The plant now in commerce is probably not the same as *P. ×nervosum* Sweet. 'Lime' has round to oblong leaves with shallow serrate edges. Flowers vary from pale lilac to a deeper shade with purple feathering on the upper petals. 'Lime' geranium owes its fragrance to 13 to 14 percent delta-cadinene and 10 to 11 percent beta-caryophyllene.

Cultivar: 'Orange'
Another invalid name (it is the common name of a species in another genus). The lemon-scented *P. ×citrosum* Voigt ex Breiter included a clone named 'Prince of Orange', which originated in England pre-1850 and was named for the orange scent of the leaves. However, what is

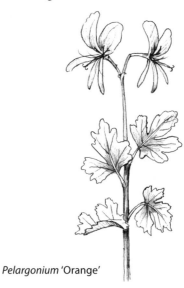

Pelargonium 'Orange'

sold in the United States is not this clone at all but one which might be called simply 'Orange'. It is of unknown parentage. Leaves are broad, the blades nearly flat.

Cultivar: 'Paton's Unique'
The so-called apricot-scented geranium, sometimes sold as 'M. Ninon', was introduced from South Africa into England in 1775. Some have postulated it is a hybrid involving *P. scabrum* (L.) L'Hér. ex Aiton, but that is doubtful. It is a bushy, much-branched, harsh-hairy, glandular plant with strong, erect stems to 4 feet (1.2 m) or more. Leaves are sticky, large, triangular in outline, deeply three-lobed with lobes again divided, margins of all lobes coarsely toothed and curled. Flower clusters in the leaf axils are many-flowered, the flowers small, white to deep pink, or even red, with a carmine spot and purple veins on the upper petals.

Cultivar: 'Pheasant's Foot'
A name applied to several different pungent-scented plants, perhaps all derivatives of *P. glutinosum*. At least some of the plants sold as 'Pheasant's Foot' are hybrids, *P. denticulatum* × *P. glutinosum*, sometimes called *P. ×jatrophaefolium* DC. The foliage is deeply cut and toothed, sticky. Flowers are small and pink.

Cultivar: 'Pretty Polly'
This mildly pungent-scented (so-called almond-scented) geranium originated in England about 1850. Some have postulated 'Pretty Polly' is a hybrid involving *P. quercifolium*, but that is doubtful. The short, thick, woody stems, branched at the top, reach a height of 1 foot (30 cm). Leaves are numerous, arising in tufts at the ends of the stems and branches, bright green with a brown or black-purple area in the center, thinner in texture than others of oak-leaved geranium heritage, triangular heart-shaped and deeply three-

lobed, the primary lobes deeply divided, the margins sharply toothed. Flowers are rarely produced but are pink with the upper petals ornamented with maroon.

Cultivar: 'Pungent Peppermint'
A suspected hybrid (*P. tomentosum* × *P. denticulatum*), 'Pungent Peppermint' ('Mopsy') is musty peppermint-scented. It has shrubby, branching, soft white-hairy stems erect to a foot (30 cm) or more. Leaves are more or less triangular in outline, five-lobed in the manner of a feather, the lobes distant, basal lobes again divided but not as deeply, segments linear and rounded at the apex, margins coarsely toothed, gray-green, velvety, white-hairy. Flowers are small, long, pale pink upper petals with carmine-feathering on the upper petals. The essential oil is characterized by 50 to 55 percent isomenthone.

Cultivar: 'Rose Bengal'
Scented of fruit, and possibly a hybrid involving *P. citronellum*. Flowers are rose-purple with the upper petals a soft pink-mauve with pale edges.

Cultivar: 'Round Leaf Rose'
Rose-scented and raised in North Street Greenhouses (now Logee's), Danielson, Connecticut, said to be a chance seedling of *P. capitatum* and *P. quercifolium*. More likely one of the parents was *P. vitifolium*. This has the habit of *P. capitatum*, the leaves somewhat similar in shape and lobing but bearing more stiff hairs, the stems more lax. Flowers are small, lavender, in dense clusters.

Cultivar: 'Shrubland Pet'
'Shrubland Pet' ('Shrubland Rose') is a hybrid involving *P. quercifolium*. It was introduced by Beaton of Shrubland Park Nursery, England, in 1849. The habit of growth is vigorous, spread-

ing, branching, the stems lax. Leaves are large, lobed somewhat like those of *P. capitatum*, glossy and sparsely hairy above with purple area in the center. Flowers are rose-pink with more purple markings in the upper petals. The essential oil is characterized by 26 percent alpha-phellandrene and 11 percent bicyclogermacrene.

Cultivar: 'Skelton's Unique'

This rosy-pungent-scented hybrid (possibly *P. capitatum* and *P. quercifolium*) originated in England about 1861. It is vigorous with lax branching stems not as densely branched as *P. capitatum*. Leaves are ruffled, light green with a dark zone, slightly woolly hairy. Flowers are dense, light pink, the upper petals purple-marked like those of *P. quercifolium*. The essential oil is characterized by 18 to 21 percent geranyl butyrate and 13 to 18 percent alpha-guaiene.

Cultivar: 'Snowflake'

This rose-scented geranium (a.k.a. 'Logee's Snowflake') is probably a sport of 'Round Leaf Rose'. It originated at Logee's, Danielson, Connecticut.

Cultivar: 'Torento'

The ginger geranium sold today is probably not the same as *P.* ×*nervosum* Sweet. Leaves are similar to 'Lime' but more sharply toothed, densely hairy beneath. Flowers are rosy lavender with darker markings on the upper petals. 'Torento' owes its fragrance to 23 to 25 percent beta-caryophyllene and 12 percent delta-cadinene.

Cultivar: 'Village Hill Oak'

This pungent hybrid (a.k.a. 'Village Hill Hybrid') of *P. quercifolium* was raised at Village Hill Nursery in Williamsburg, Massachusetts, by Dorcas Brigham as "parsley leaf hybrid." Growth is like that of *P. quercifolium*. Leaves are sometimes broader, five- to seven-lobed, lower division of the basal lobes pointed downward, all segments furnished with rounded and pointed lobes. Flowers are more densely clustered, smaller and paler with smaller dark spot on the upper petals. The essential oil has 25 percent *p*-cymene, 15 percent nerol/citronellol, and 11 percent terpinen-4-ol.

Botanical Key and Description

Only the species are included in the following key. A lifetime of work awaits someone who is willing to look at the hybrids and selections more closely.

Key:
1. Leaves divided as in a feather . . . . *P. abrotanifolium*
1a. Leaves without divisions or lobed and palmate. 2
    2. Flowers long-spurred, the spur twice as long as the sepals or more . . . . *P. elongatum*
    2a. Flowers not as above 3
        3. Leaves densely white-hairy below, especially when young . . . . *P. tomentosum*
        3a. Leaves green below 4
            4. Flowers very small, the sepals mostly 5 mm long or less, the petals seldom exceeding 10 mm in length; low, sprawling, herbaceous 5
                5. Petals deep red . . . . *P. grossularioides*
                5a. Petals white or pale pink, lined with red . . . . *P. odoratissimum*
            4a. Flowers larger, the sepals mostly 7 mm long or more, the petals 12 mm long or more; branched, shrubby. 6

6. Leaves small or very small, seldom more than 2 cm long, 1.5 cm wide, three-lobed, the margin strongly crisped, smelling of lemon or lime .... *P. crispum*

6a. Leaves larger, with lobed or toothed but not crisped blades, not lemon-scented but often fragrant or pungent-, mint-, rose-, or aromatic-scented 7

7. Leaves divided to the middle or less into three to five broad, blunt lobes; blades densely and softly hairy on both sides; flowers stalkless, numerous, in a dense, flat-topped cluster .... *P. capitatum*

7a. Leaves divided beyond the middle into rather narrow lobes; blades smooth, stocky, or roughly hairy at least on the upper surface; flowers more or less stalked in a rather loose flat-topped cluster. 8

8. Lobes of the leaves not strongly toothed, the blade often with dark markings along the veins. 9

9. Tips of lobes rounded. .... *P. quercifolium*

9a. Tips of lobes tapering to apex .... *P. glutinosum*

8a. Lobes of the leaves strongly and sharply toothed 10

10. Petals notched at the tip; upper surface of the leaf smooth, sticky. .... *P. denticulatum*

10a. Petals smooth-edged at the tip; upper surface of the leaf hairy, not sticky 11

11. Margins of the leaves rolled under, the lobes very deeply divided into narrow segments with short, stiff, rasp-like hairs on both surfaces .... *P. radens*

11a. Margins of the leaves not rolled under, the lobes rather shallowly toothed with soft, slender hairs on both surfaces. .... *P. graveolens*

P. abrotanifolium (L.f.) Jacq., Pl. hort. schoenbr. 2:6, t. 136. 1800 (*P. artemisiaefolium* Hort.).

Native country: This species is native to Cape Province to Orange Free State in South Africa and was introduced into England in 1791–1796.

General habit: The southernwood geranium grows to about 1 m, usually less. The slender, woody branches are glandular and often covered with the remains of the leaf stalk bases.

Leaves: The feathery gray-green leaves are 5 to 17 mm long and 5 to 19 mm broad and vary considerably in structure. They are usually three- or five-segmented, each segment again being subdivided into three or more lobes, which are channeled on their upper surface

along the midribs. Small, lance-shaped basal leaf appendages are found at the base of relatively long leaf stalks.

Flowers: Flower clusters are unbranched with one to five flowers per stalk. The flowers vary from white to pink or mauve, veined in red or purple. Flowering extends throughout most of the year.

P. capitatum (L.) L'Hér. in Aiton, Hort. kew ed. 1. 2:425. 1789 (*P. australe* Hort.).

Native country: This rose-scented geranium occurs from Lambert's Bay all along the coast through Transkei to Zululand in South Africa. It is abundant on sand dunes or low hillsides near the sea, commonly in disturbed areas. This was introduced into Britain by Bentick in 1690.

General habit: This rose-scented geranium is a low-growing shrub or bush with soft-wooded sprawling or erect stems, 0.25 to 1 m tall and up to 1.6 m in diameter. Individual side branches can attain a length of 60 cm. Stems are covered with long, soft hairs of variable density.

Leaves: The crinkly, velvety leaves with heart-shaped bases are shallowly to deeply three- to six-lobed and generally 4.5 cm long and about 6 cm wide. The segments themselves may also be lobed with the leaf margin toothed throughout.

Flowers: The flower clusters are head-shaped and hold eight to twenty flowers. The flowers are commonly cyclamen-purple with beet-root-purple stripes on the two upper and slightly larger petals. Pale pink and dark pink-purple flowers also occur. Plants start to flower in early spring, although scattered flowers may be found throughout the year.

P. citronellum J. J. A. van der Walt, S. African J. Bot. 2:79. t. 5. 1983.

Native country: In nature this herb is confined to a small area around Ladysmith, South Africa. It is usually found near streams in well-drained sandy soil.

General habit: This is a much-branched, evergreen shrub to 2 m and 1 m in diameter. Stems are herbaceous when young, woody at bases, with moderately stiff and coarse hairs and numerous glandular hairs.

Leaves: Leaves are simple, conspicuously veined on the bottom, sparsely coated with stiff to moderately stiff and coarse hairs, with numerous shorter glandular hairs interspersed, green; blade lobed and irregularly incised, base wedge-shaped to heart-shaped, tips of the lobes sharp, margins irregularly toothed,

3.5 to 11 cm long and 1.5 to 6 cm long; appendages at the base of the leaf stalk narrowly triangular to triangular, 6 to 10 mm long and 3 to 6 mm wide.

Flowers: Inflorescence a five- to eight-flowered, almost flat flower cluster borne on a branched system of stalks, petals pinkish purple.

P. crispum (Berg.) L'Hér. in Aiton, Hort. kew. ed. 1. 2:430. 1789 (*P. hermaniaefolium* Hort.).

Native country: This occurs in the southwestern part of the Cape Province, in the winter-rainfall region on sandy soil in the shelter of sandstone boulders. It flowers with a peak during the spring. The lemon-scented geranium was introduced into England from South Africa in 1774 by Francis Masson of Kew.

General habit: The lemon-scented geranium is an erect to decumbent, much-branched sub-shrub or shrub to 1 m high. Stems are herbaceous when young but soon become woody, densely soft- to stiff-hairy interspersed with glandular hairs, green but soon becoming brownish.

Leaves: Leaves are stiff-hairy densely interspersed with glandular hairs, green; blade kidney-shaped, three-lobed, crisped and coarsely toothed on the margin, 2 to 10 mm long and 3 to 15 mm wide; appendages at the base of the leaf stalk heart-shaped, often ending in an abrupt sharp point, 2 to 4 mm long and 2 to 5 mm wide. The inflorescence is a one- to three-flowered, almost flat flower cluster. Flowers are small, white to dark pink or almost purple.

P. denticulatum Jacq., Pl. hort. schoenbr. 2:5, t. 135. 1797.

Native country: This herb is confined to a small area in the Southern Cape of South

Africa that receives most of its rainfall during the winter months. It is found in ravines and near streams. It was introduced into England in 1789 by Masson, who was sent there to collect live plants for Kew.

General habit: The pine-scented geranium is an erect, very strongly branched shrub, 1 to 2 m high and up to 1 m in diameter. Stems are smooth, herbaceous when young, woody at base, densely coated with moderately coarse and stiff hairs and glands, dark green, and sometimes flushed with purple.

Leaves: Leaves are deeply twice-divided down to the axis with deeply divided segments, viscous, hard and rigid, densely covered with glandular hairs and covered on the bottom surface with moderately coarse and stiff hairs, green; blade triangular to heart-shaped in outline; segments narrow and grooved on the top, apices toothed, margins irregularly and finely toothed, apices of teeth sharp; blade 4 to 10 cm long and 4.5 to 11 cm wide; leaf stalk 2.5 to 9 cm long; leafy appendages at the base of the leaf stalk asymmetric-triangular, about 6 mm long and 2 to 5 mm wide.

Flowers: Flat flower clusters are three to nine-flowered. Petals are pinkish purple with dark red to purple markings. Flowers almost throughout the year with a peak in spring.

P. elongatum (Cav.) Salisb., Prodr. Stirp. Chap. Allerton 312. 1796.

Native country: The upright coconut geranium is native to South Africa.

General habit: Stems are to 20 cm, slender, erect or ascending.

Leaves: Leaves are glabrous above, zoned with purple to 5 cm across, deeply five- to seven-lobed, lobes sharply toothed, petiole hairy with narrow stipules.

Flowers: The flat flower cluster holds one to five flowers on a 15-cm peduncle, cream-colored, upper petals veined red, narrow.

P. glutinosum (Jacq.) L'Hér. in Aiton, Hort. kew. ed. 1. 2:426. 1789 [*P. viscosum* (Cav.) Harv. & Sond. ex B. D. Jacks., *P. viscosum-glutinosum* Hort.].

Native country: This occurs from South Africa's Piketberg in the southwestern Cape to the Kei River in the Eastern Cape. The distribution range is largely correlated with mountain ranges. It grows on well-drained soil in relatively moist habitats, often in close proximity to running water. It was introduced from South Africa to England about 1777.

General habit: The pheasant's foot geranium is an erect, much-branched shrub to 1.8 m or more. Stems are herbaceous when young but soon grow woody, smooth to hairy but always with numerous glandular hairs, green but becoming brownish with age.

Leaves: Leaves are smooth above, 1.5 to 12 cm long, 5 to 80 mm wide, on short stalks; blade heart-shaped in outline, three-lobed nearly to the base (palmate), lobes broad, basal lobes often irregularly incised, sharply pointed with irregularly toothed margins, often dark-colored about the main veins; appendages at the base of the leaf stalks narrowly triangular to triangular, about 7 mm long and 5 mm wide.

Flowers: The flat flower clusters hold one to eight nearly stalkless flowers, the calyx spur to 1 cm long, about as long as the sepals, petals orchid-pink to rose, the upper broader, crimson-blotched and streaked. The herb flowers sporadically throughout the year, peaking during the spring.

P. graveolens L'Hér. in Aiton, Hort. kew. ed. 1. 2:423. 1789 [*P. terebinthaceum* (Cav.) Small, non Harvey].

Native country: This was introduced from South Africa to England in 1774 by Francis Masson of Kew.

General habit: The true *P. graveolens* is erect, much-branched, to 1.3 m high and 1 m in diameter. Stems are herbaceous when young, becoming woody with age, hairy to densely hairy and densely interspersed with glandular hairs, green but becoming brown with age.

Leaves: Leaves are soft to the touch, always with numerous glandular hairs; blade heart-shaped in outline, with the segments irregularly lobed, 2 to 5 cm long and 3 to 10 cm wide; appendages at the base of the leaf stalks asymmetric-triangular, tipped with a sharp point, about 6 mm wide and 4 mm wide.

Flowers: Inflorescence is an almost flat flower cluster with three to seven flowers. Flowers are white to pinkish brown with a white margin.

P. grossularioides (L.) L'Hér. in Aiton, Hort. kew. ed. 1. 2:420. 1789 (*P. parviflorum* Hort.).

Native country: From Mozambique southward along the coast to the Southwestern Cape in South Africa. It is also recorded from Tristan da Cunha and as an alien from Kenya, India, and California. It is generally found in damp or shady places and withstands more frost than most species of *Pelargonium*. It was cultivated as early as 1731 by Philip Miller in England.

General habit: The coconut-scented geranium is a low spreading annual herb branching from the base and attaining a height of about 20 cm. Individual stems may reach a length of up to 50 cm. They are characterized by their long, angular, and furrowed reddish stems. The stems and leaves are almost smooth to fairly hairy with short hairs and glands. The leaves are round to kidney-shaped with three to five lobes in a palmate arrangement, usually 1 to 4 cm long and 1 to 6 cm wide. Upper leaves are normally much smaller and more deeply incised. Triangular leafy appendages are found at the base of the reddish leaf stalks.

Flowers: The rather small flowers are borne in a flat-topped cluster with three to fifty flowers. The flowers vary from pink to beet-root-purple, but whitish flowers are sometimes found. Plants flower throughout most of the year.

P. odoratissimum (L.) L'Hér. in Aiton, Hort. kew. ed. 1. 2:419. 1789.

Native country: This is common in the Eastern and Southern Cape of South Africa, but it is also recorded from the Lowveld of Transvaal and Natal. It occurs as undergrowth in forests or in shady places protected by bushes or rocky ledges. This was introduced into England in 1724 at the Chelsea Physic Garden.

General habit: This is a perennial and prostrate shrublet with a short, thick main stem and sprawling, herbaceous flowering branches which may attain a length of about 60 cm. The height of the plant rarely exceeds 30 cm. The main stem is rough and scaly due to the persisting leaf appendages at the base of the leaf stalks. The roots are slightly tuberous.

Leaves: The round or egg-heart-shaped leaves with blunt-tipped rounded margins are usually 3 to 4 cm in diameter. Leaves on the main stems are normally much larger, up to 12 cm in diameter, than those on the elongated flowering stems. The leaves are apple-green and are covered with fine, short hairs, making them soft to the touch. Small leaf appendages are found at the base of each very long leaf stalk.

Flowers: The flat-topped flower clusters have three to ten flowers. The flowers are relatively small, with the petals only slightly longer than the sepals. Usually the flowers are white with crimson markings on the upper two petals. Pale pink flowers are also known. Plants flower almost throughout the year except in the heat of summer.

P. quercifolium (L.f.) L'Hér. in Aiton, Hort. kew. ed. 1. 2:422. 1789 [*P. terebinthaceum* (Murr.) Harv. & Sond., non Small, *P. karrooense* Kunth].

Native country: The oak-leaved geranium was introduced from South Africa to England in 1774 by Francis Masson of Kew. This is confined to the towns of Oudtshoorn and Willowmore and environs. The annual rainfall in these Karoo regions is relatively low and spread throughout the year. The herb flowers throughout the year but most abundantly in spring.

General habit: The oak-leaved geranium is shrubby to 1.8 m. Stems are herbaceous when young but soon become woody, with long glandular hairs densely interspersed, green but becoming brownish with age.

Leaves: Leaves are sticky, hard to the touch, green, 1 to 8 cm long and about as broad at the base, deeply and wavy-lobed, often dark-marked in the center, lobes rounded, toothed, two to three on each side, the basal lobes widely separated from the upper ones.

Flowers: The flat-topped flower cluster holds two to six blossoms. Flowers are almost stalkless, calyx spur about as long as the sepals, petals rose, the upper large, smooth-edged, with large red spot and red veins.

P. radens H. E. Moore, Baileya 3:22. 1955 [*P. multifidum* Salisb., *P. radula* (Cav.) L'Hér. in Aiton].

Native country: It occurs from the Southern and Eastern Cape in South Africa, from near Barrydale eastward to Engcobo in the Transkei. It is usually found on mountainsides and often in ravines near streams. This was introduced into England in 1774 by Francis Masson of Kew.

General habit: This rose-scented geranium is an erect, densely branched shrub usually less than 1 m high, with stems becoming woody near the base. The herbaceous side branches are covered with stiff bristles.

Leaves: Leaves are deeply divided, palmate, triangular in outline, 3 to 5 cm long and 3 to 6.5 cm wide. The rough leaves have narrow segments with margins typically rolled under and blunt lobes. Leaf appendages at the base of the leaf stalk are egg-shaped with a sharp point.

Flowers: The two- to six-flowered cluster is borne on a short stem. Petals are pale purple or pink-purple with beet-root-purple streaks on the upper two. Plants usually flower in the spring.

P. tomentosum Jacq., Icon. pl. rar. 3:10. t. 537. 1794.

Native country: The peppermint-scented geranium occurs in South Africa, confined to mountains where it occurs in semi-shaded, moist habitats, usually on the margins of ravine forest near streams, in sandy soil. It was introduced to England prior to 1700, probably by Francis Masson of Kew.

General habit: The peppermint-scented geranium is a low-growing, much-branched, sprawling subshrub, up to 50 cm tall and 1.5 m in diameter. Stems are soft to the touch, herbaceous, brittle, with long, soft glands, and somewhat wavy hairs, green.

Leaves: Leaves are soft, hairy, with numerous glandular hairs, green; the blade is heart-shaped with three to five lobes, apices of lobes mostly rounded (rarely sharp), coated on the top with long, soft, somewhat wavy hairs, coated on the bottom with a dense, wool-like covering of matted, tangled hairs of medium length, margins with irregularly rounded teeth, 2.5 to 11 cm long and 3.5 to 12 cm wide; leaf stalk usually longer than blade; leaf appendages at base triangular to egg-shaped, sharp to pinched at tip, 6 to 20 mm long and 4 to 12 mm wide.

Flowers: Flat-topped cluster bears four to fifteen flowers. Petals are white with purple markings. Flowering occurs in spring.

Perilla frutescens

pĕ-rĭl-å frū-tĕs-ĕnz
beefsteak plant

Family: Lamiaceae (Labiatae)
Growth form: annual to 39 inches (1 m) tall
Hardiness: cannot withstand frost
Light: full sun
Water: moist but not constantly wet
Soil: friable garden loam, pH 5.0 to 7.5, average 6.1
Propagation: seeds in spring, 27,000 seeds per ounce (952/g)
Culinary use: limited (not GRAS)
Craft use: none
Landscape use: allow to reseed cottage-garden style; purple forms are excellent contrasts in garden

Chinese: *bai su zi*
Japanese: *shiso zoku*

Beefsteak plant looks so much like basil that some gardeners believe they have discovered a "perennial" basil, or, at the very least, a basil that self-sows so extensively that they will never have to purchase basil seeds or plants again. This claim of a reseeding basil is another example of the old adage that if it looks too good to be true, it probably is. Although it is not a perennial basil, beefsteak plant can stand on its own as an interesting, flavorful herb. An alternative name used by gardeners who must endure continual emergence of seedlings every spring is "wild coleus." And a word to the wise: 'Magilla

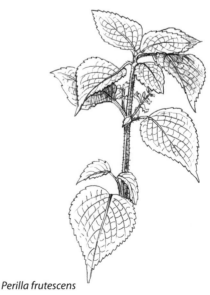

Perilla frutescens

Perilla' and 'Magilla Vanilla' are coleus [*Solenostemon scutellarioides* (L.) Codd] (tender perennial, filaments basally united), not perilla (annual, filaments not united).

Perilla is a genus of probably only one very variable species native to India and eastern Asia. The generic name is derived from a native East Indian name, while *frutescens* means "fruitful." The name beefsteak plant is probably derived from the bloody purple-red color of the leaves of many forms. Leaves may also be green, green on top and purple-red on the bottom, crisped and wrinkled or flat, but the application of the cultivar names is poorly defined in the literature. Many different scents of beefsteak plant also exist.

In Japan different forms of beefsteak plant are given different names: *e-goma*, *remon-egoma*, *tora-no-o-jiso*, *chirimen-jiso*, and *shiso*. The purple-red leaves of *shiso* are used to color apricots, gingers, and tubers of Jerusalem artichokes; when used this way the leaves are salted to remove the water-soluble cyanogenic glycosides, which reduces their harshness. The somewhat anise-scented leaves are used to flavor bean curd or as a garnish for tempura. The flower spikes are used in soups or fried, while the seedlings are used to flavor raw fish.

We cannot recommend most forms of beefsteak plant for culinary applications. *Perilla frutescens* has no GRAS status, and many forms are rich in perilla ketone, a chemical shown to be a potent lung toxin and documented to produce acute pulmonary edema in sheep, atypical interstitial pneumonia and acute pulmonary emphysema and edema in cattle, and restrictive lung disease in horses.

Most forms of beefsteak plant are documented to produce contact dermatitis on sensitive individuals after prolonged handling. Japanese researchers have reported that perilla ketone is "an active principle of intestinal pro-

pulsion in mice." We don't know if the same action follows in humans, but we shudder to think of the results of eating too much *shiso* in a Japanese restaurant! The phenolic constituents of *P. frutescens* may inhibit globular sclerosis, a kidney disease, and extracts may inhibit tumor necrosis.

Forms of *P. frutescens* high in perillaldehyde, providing a cumin-like odor, are popular in Japan as *aojiso* for suppressing the sardine odor of *niboshi* soup stock. The Vietnamese cultivar 'Tia To' has no perilla ketone but instead is rich in perillaldehyde, which has sedative and other benficial properties. Although it was recommended for GRAS status by the Flavor and Extract Manufacturers Association in 1978, its full safety remains undetermined.

Culture of beefsteak plant is almost too easy; it requires friable garden loam in full sun. The herb generously reseeds and may become a weed. 'Tia To' usually does not bloom until very late in the fall or early winter and rarely has time to produce seeds; aside from being the safest beefsteak plant to consume, it has the fewest horticultural bad habits. Other cultivars available include 'Atropurpurea' with dark purple leaves; 'Crispa' ('Nankinensis') with crinkled bright purple or bronze leaves mottled with green, rose, or pink; and 'Laciniata' with all-green, deeply incised leaves.

Important chemistry: The essential oil of beefsteak plant typically has trace to 94 percent perilla ketone, 0 to 64 percent perillaldehyde, 0 to 36 percent elemicin, 0 to 30 percent naginaketone, 0 to 26 percent beta-caryophyllene, 0 to 11 percent beta-pinene, and/or 0 to 10 percent beta-ionone, usually providing an anise-like odor. The essential oil of 'Tia To' has 48 percent perillaldehyde and 27 percent limonene, providing a wonderful lemony cumin-like odor.

An unnamed Chinese form has been reported with 55 percent piperitone and 31 percent limonene, while an unnamed Vietnamese form has 25 percent piperitone, 28 percent limonene, and 17 percent beta-caryophyllene, giving both a lemony mint odor. A chemotype from Thailand has 36 percent piperitenone and 24 percent limonene, again, with a lemony mint odor. Other types are high in elsholtziaketone, isoegomaketone, myristicin, rosefuran, and/or dill apiole. The purple-red pigment of the leaves is cyanidin-3-(6-para-coumaroyl-beta-D-glucoside) 5-beta-D-glucoside. The seeds are rich in alpha-linolenic acid (ALA), an omega-3 fatty acid.

Botanical Description

P. frutescens (L.) Britton, Mem. Torrey Bot. Club 5:277. 1894 (*P. ocymoides* L.).
Native country: Beefsteak plant is native to the Himalayan region but naturalized in Europe and North America.
General habit: Beefsteak plant is a hairy annual to 1 m.
Leaves: Leaves are 4.5 to 8 × 3 to 6 cm, broadly egg-shaped, deeply round-toothed, pinched at the tip, wedge-shaped at the base, stalked. Leaves may be purple, green, or a combination of purple and green.
Flowers: Flowers are white in a 3 to 10 cm inflorescence with floral leaves.

Persea borbonia

pĕr-sē-å bôr-bŏn-ĭ-å
red bay

Family: Lauraceae
Growth form: tree to 66 feet (20 m)
Hardiness: routinely hardy to Zone 7
Light: full sun to part shade
Water: moist but not wet
Soil: acid, well-drained, sandy soil
Propagation: cuttings or seeds
Culinary use: substitute for Grecian bay but not GRAS
Craft use: wreaths
Landscape use: evergreen specimen tree

The spicy leaves of red bay are used on the southeastern coast of North America as a substitute for Grecian bay (*Laurus nobilis*). Thus, as you might imagine, red bay looks and smells like Grecian bay. While commonly gathered from

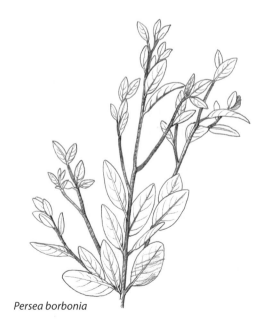

Persea borbonia

the wild, it is easily cultivated from southern Zone 7 south in sandy to rich, moist soil and full to part sun.

This attractive evergreen is nearly pest-free and deserves to be more widely known. Charles Sprague Sargent remarked in 1895: "Although it is one of the most beautiful and valuable of the evergreen trees of the North American forest, the Red Bay has been neglected as an ornament for parks and gardens, and it is now rarely seen in cultivation."

Persea was the ancient name of an Oriental tree, while *borbonia* commemorates the Gaston de Bourbon (1608–1660), a patron of botany who was Duke of Orleans and son of Henry IV of France. The genus includes about 150 tropical species, and you probably already know *P. americana* Mill., the avocado. Many species of *Persea* have fragrant leaves, from bay-like to anise-like, and a number of species are economically important for their wood.

A closely related species, swamp bay (*P. palustris* Sarg.), occurs as far north as southern Delaware and also bears spicy leaves with fuzzy, brown undersides. Neither red bay or swamp bay is considered GRAS.

Important chemistry: We examined the essential oil of the leaves of red bay from Florida and found 32 to 39 percent camphor and 12 to 22 percent 1,8-cineole, providing a camphoraceous bay-like odor.

Botanical Description

P. borbonia (L.) Sprengel, Syst. 2:268. 1825.
Native country: Red bay is native to low woodlands and coastal forests from Virginia to Florida, west to Texas along bogs, streams, and swamps.
General habit: Red bay is a tree to 20 m., often with a cylindrical shape and dense, round crown. The trunk often reaches 1 m in diameter.
Leaves: The evergreen leaves are simple, lance-shaped, broadest near the middle, or with almost uniformly wide sides, 5 to 20 × 2 to 8 cm, pointed at the tip, tapering to the base.
Flowers: The greenish flowers are produced in few-flowered, compact, branched clusters.
Fruits/seeds: The dark blue fruits are olive-like, 0.7 to 1.2 cm in diameter.

Persicaria odorata

pĕr-sĭ-kā-rĭ-å ō-dō-rā-tå
rau răm

Family: Polygonaceae
Growth form: herbaceous perennial to about 6 inches (15 cm)
Hardiness: marginally hardy to Zone 7
Light: part sun
Water: wet; standing water preferred
Soil: garden loam

Propagation: cuttings during summer
Culinary use: limited (not GRAS)
Craft use: none
Landscape use: pond margins

Vietnamese: *rau răm*

Rau răm, often pronounced "zow-zam," is widely sold in the United States as "Vietnamese coriander." The odor is that of cilantro with a hint of lemon. Rau răm is used by the Vietnamese to garnish meat dishes, especially fowl, and is also eaten with duck eggs. The herb is also an ingredient of a Vietnamese pickled dish resembling sauerkraut. Rau răm has no GRAS status.

Rau răm is a perennial that resembles the European water-pepper [*P. hydropiper* (L.) Delarbe], an annual, with smooth, pale green, lance-shaped leaves marked with red lines. From the similar reported chemistry, this may be the same plant identified as *P. minor* (Huds.) Opiz, known as *kesom* in Malaysia, but rau răm does not produce the spikes of dark pink flowers and small black seed-like fruits of *P. minor*. A further problem with its correct botanical name is that no one has comprehensively tackled the Asian species since Steward's work in 1930.

The genus *Persicaria* includes about 100 species of the north temperate region; most are aquatic scramblers. *Persicaria* is derived from Persia, similar to that of peach, *Prunus persica* (L.) Batch. Some botanists are adamant that this and similar species should be classified in the genus *Polygonum*.

Rau răm is typical for the genus and requires a rich, moist soil in semi-shade, although full sun is desired if abundant moisture is available; under less-than-desirable conditions, the leaves turn brown. Normally treated as a tender perennial, it may overwinter in Zone 7 on pond margins during mild winters.

Important chemistry: The essential oil of rau răm is dominated by 11 to 52 percent dodecanal, 3 to 37 percent beta-caryophyllene, and 5 to 28 percent decanal, providing a lemony, soapy odor that has been characterized by some as the odor of lemon dish detergent.

Botanical Description

P. odorata (Lour.) Soják, Preslia 46(2):154. 1974 (*Polygonum odoratum* Lour.).
Native country: Rau răm is native to southeastern Asia.
General habit: Rau răm bears branching, trailing stems, smooth, often reddish, reaching to about 15 cm.
Leaves: Leaves are narrowly lance-shaped to lance-egg-shaped, marked with red lines. Characteristic of the family Polygonaceae, each leaf has a tubular, sheathing, elongated appendage at the base, encircling the stem; this is called an ocrea. The ocreae of rau răm are beset with a marginal fringe of hairs but otherwise smooth.
Flowers: Flowers, when they appear, are terminal, dark pink.

Persicaria odorata

Petroselinum crispum

pĕ-trō-sĕ-lī-nŭm krĭs-pŭm
parsley

Family: Apiaceae (Umbelliferae)
Growth form: biennial to 27 inches (75 cm) when flowering
Hardiness: withstands frost
Water: moist but not constantly wet
Soil: well-drained garden loam, pH 4.9 to 8.2, average 6.2
Propagation: seeds in spring, 15,000 seeds per ounce (529/g)
Culinary use: a multitalented herb used for garnish, meats, vegetables, soups, and more
Craft use: limited
Landscape use: excellent edging

French: *persil*
German: *Petersilie*
Dutch: *peterselie*
Italian: *prezzomolo*
Spanish: *perejil*
Portuguese: *salsa*
Swedish: *persilja*
Russian: *pyetrushka*
Chinese: *yang-hu-sui*
Japanese: *paseri*
Arabic: *baqdūnis*

Parsley is the first herb that most Americans recognize on sight because it is the most-used herb in the United States, but it may be one of the most misunderstood herbs in the garden. Its most common use is as an uneaten, curly-leaved, green garnish, especially on restaurant dinner plates; it is a shame that this garnish is usually thrown away because the leaves are really quite high in vitamins: A, B_1, B_2, and C; niacin, calcium, and iron. Elsewhere in the world, parsley plays a key role in a variety of prepared foods; parsley pesto is an alternative or supplement to basil pesto, and the root of the Hamburg or turnip-rooted type is consumed. The clean, delicate flavor also provides a breath sweetener.

The leaves of parsley have GRAS status at 200 to 14,963 ppm, the oil is GRAS at 0.2 to 8.5 ppm, and the oleoresin is GRAS at 5 to 392 ppm. Because myristicin, a major component of the essential oil of parsley leaves, inhibits tumor formation and increases the detoxifying action of the enzyme system glutathione *S*-transferase, it has been nominated as a potential cancer-fighting agent. The furocoumarins from parsley leaves are antimicrobial. The essential oil of parsley is also antioxidant.

The genus *Petroselinum* includes three European species. The generic name is derived from the Greek for rock, *petros*, which alludes to its native habitat of cliffs, rocks, and old walls, and

Petroselinum crispum

selinum, celery. The specific name refers to the crisped leaves of many cultivars.

Although parsley is a biennial, it occasionally blooms the first year, which reduces yields; parsley that is subjected to thirty days of temperatures below 40°F (4.4°C) will flower. Parsley in its second year is usually useless as an herb because the leaves turn bitter after the flower stems rise from the center of the plant in early spring. Thus, when grown for its foliage, parsley is considered as an annual.

The bright green, fern-like leaves provide a delightful accent in the sunny herb garden and make an excellent edging. Three types of parsley are grown in the United States: common (curled-leaf, var. *crispum*), plain (flat-leaved or Italian, var. *neapolitanum* Danert), and Hamburg or turnip-rooted [var. *tuberosum* (Bernh.) Crov.]. The first two are used in sauces, stews, soups, prepared meat products, and condiments, while the latter's large, edible root is considered a vegetable. Essential oil varies from 0 to 0.16 percent (fresh weight) but is not correlated with flatness of the leaves; as with other herbs, genes are important to produce a flavorful parsley.

Curly-leaved cultivars include 'Afro', 'Banquet', 'Bravour', 'Curlina', 'Dark Moss Colored', 'Decorator', 'Deep Green', 'Envy', 'Evergreen', 'Ferro', 'Forest Green', 'Improved Market Gardener', 'Moss Curled', 'Paramount', 'Perfection', and 'Sherwood'. Flat-leaf types include 'Perfection', 'Plain', and 'Plain Italian Dark Green'.

In Italy, the cultivar 'Catalogno', with its long, thick stems and large, dark, flat, green leaves is considered to be the true Italian parsley, while other flat-leaved parsley selections are "comune" (common or ordinary). In the United States, few firms sell this variety, which is usually listed as 'Giant Italian', but it is superior in flavor and yield to other flat-leaved parsleys. According to research performed at Purdue University, final selection of a parsley cultivar should be based upon both yield and quality, particularly aroma, flavor, stem length, leaf color, and leaf shape. Other factors, such as insect and disease resistance, should be important quality variables regardless of the cultivar.

Seeds (technically fruits known as schizocarps containing two mesocarps) have slow and asynchronous germination, with 10 and 28 days being allowed for the first and last germination counts, respectively. Parsley's slow and erratic germination has given rise to the fanciful tale that the seed has to go to Hell nine times and back before it will germinate.

> The bright green, fern-like leaves provide a delightful accent in the sunny herb garden and make an excellent edging.

The slow germination can be attributed in part to a high concentration in the seeds of heraclenol, a coumarin, but this is easily leached out with water. Germination thus can be enhanced by soaking the seeds in aerated water for three days at 77°F (25°C), draining, rinsing, and then sowing ¼ inch deep (0.6 cm) in a fine seedbed. Seed priming also has benefitted parsley germination. Priming is the exposure of seeds to a low external water potential that is created either osmotically (by the presence of solutes) or matrically (by the presence of colloids). During this exposure, pregerminative physiological, biochemical, and anatomical activities occur, but the seed moisture concentration is sufficiently low to prevent germination. Priming benefits subsequent seed germination and seedling emergence, particularly under stressful seed bed conditions. Recent work showed that embryo volume, but most particularly that of the radicle, increased with increasing duration of osmotic priming. Dr. Wallace Pill at the University of Delaware found that seed may be primed, after leaching, with aerated polyethylene glycol (PEG) 8000 for 4.5 days at 77°F; the seed may then be dried for sowing with mechanical equipment (Pill and Killian, 2000). They also found that matric priming in fine, exfoliated vermiculite at -0.5 MPa for 4 to 7 days at 68 or 86°F (20 or 30°C) will result in greater germination (89 percent) than priming, but priming at 86°F (30°C) with 1 mM GA$_3$ (gibberellic acid) resulted in the greatest emergence percentage, hypocotyl length, and shoot dry weight . Sowing "pre-germinated seeds" (germinated for four days at 59°F [15°C] in aerated water) in a hydroxyethyl cellulose gel carrier resulted in improved seedling emergence compared to sowing primed seeds. Seed started indoors and transplanted into pots shows a more rapid and uniform germination without special treatment, probably because of constant moisture levels and warm soil temperatures. Parsley presents no problems as a transplant as long as it is properly hardened off for increased light and decreased temperature before it is planted in the garden.

In other aspects, parsley should be treated as a leafy green vegetable and grown in rich, moist soil with good drainage and a pH of 5.3 to 7.3. Depending upon the soil and environmental conditions, commercial seeding rates may be 12 to 60 pounds per acre (14 to 67 kg/ha). For the home gardener, plant seeds ⅜ to 2 inches apart in 3 to 4 rows 18 to 22 inches apart on raised beds. Sow seeds in the early spring as soon as the soil can be worked. An N-P-K fertilizer ratio of 1-1-1 or 3-1-2 should be used, depending upon soil tests. Sidedress with nitrogen fertilizer after the first cutting if a second crop is desired. In the garden parsley is allelopathic, that is, it prevents the growth of closely surrounding plants by releasing chemicals from its leaves and roots. Yet hoeing is necessary to remove weeds, even when registered herbicides are used.

Parsley may be harvested by hand continuously throughout the year as a fresh market culinary green. The outer leaves should be clipped to 1 to 3 inches (2.5 to 7.6 cm) above the crown. Up to three sowings of seeds may be possible in some states for harvests April to December, and the home gardener will find that a cold frame will provide fresh parsley all winter.

Parsley is best preserved by freezing rather than drying, because its subtle flavor dissipates with heat; yet, dried parsley has a market, and we import dried parsley from Israel and Mexico. Parsley can be stored for long periods using modified atmosphere packaging (MAP) for 77 days at 32°F (0°C) and 35 days at 41°F (5°C). Parsley may also be distilled for an oil which has some use in flavor work. If parsley is grown for seed, the most common pollinators are syrphid flies and honeybees.

Pythium damp-off of seedlings and adult plants may be a problem, but it is easily avoided by treating the seeds with a registered fungicide, avoiding overcrowding, and maximizing ventilation around the plants. Aphids, cabbage loopers, beet armyworms, carrot weevils, corn earworms, flea beetles, leafhoppers, or tarnished plant bugs may cause problems and should be controlled with registered insecticides. The black swallowtail caterpillar, *Papilio polyxenes* Fabricius, can consume a small plant in a day or two. Root-knot nematode, *Meloidogyne incognita*, must be controlled with fumigants. Septoria leaf spot and aster yellows have also been reported on parsley.

Important chemistry: The typical odor of parsley is primarily due to para-1,3,8-menthatriene. The essential oil of parsley leaves is dominated by 1 to 92 percent myristicin, 6 to 65 percent para-1,3,8-menthatriene, trace to 54 percent apiole, and 4 to 30 percent beta-phellandrene, providing a nutmeg-spearmint-celery-oily odor. The essential oil of parsley seeds is dominated by 1 to 94 percent myristicin and trace to 80 percent apiole, trace to 41 percent alpha-pinene, and 1 to 27 percent beta-pinene, providing a nutmeg-celery-pine odor. The essential oil of parsley root is dominated by 17 to 77 percent apiole and 3 to 30 percent myristicin, providing a celery-nutmeg odor.

Botanical Description

P. crispum (Mill.) Nym. ex A. W. Hill, Handlist Herb. Plt. Kew ed. 3. 122. 1925 (*P. hortense* Auct., *P. sativum* Hoffm.).

Native country: Parsley is native to southeast Europe and western Asia.

General habit: Parsley is a biennial herb to 75 cm.

Leaves: Leaves are triangular in outline, fern-like, and lobed three times, the lobes 10 to 20 mm, often crispate in cultivars.

Flowers: Flowers are greenish yellow, in an umbel.

Fruits/seeds: Fruits are 2.5 to 3 mm, broadly egg-shaped.

Phyla scaberrima

fī-lå skā-bĕr-ĭ-må
Aztec sweet herb

Family: Verbenaceae
Growth form: herbaceous shrubby perennial to 2 feet (60 cm)
Hardiness: hardy only to Zone 9
Light: full sun
Water: moist but not wet
Soil: well-drained garden loam
Propagation: cuttings or seeds
Culinary use: camphor-scented sweetener but not recommended (not GRAS)
Craft use: none
Landscape use: container plant

The Aztec sweet herb was mentioned in a monograph *Natural History of New Spain* written between 1570 and 1576 by Spanish physician Francisco Hernández. The herb was known by the Nahuatl name *Tzonpelic xihuitl*, literally translated as "sweet herb." The earliest available book on medicinal herbs used by the Aztecs is *Libellus de Medicinalibus Inodorum Herbis*, an herbal written in Nahuatl by Aztec physician Martín de la Cruz and published in Latin in 1552; in this work the Aztec sweet herb is called *Tzopelicacoc*. The *General History of the Things of New Spain* by Spanish friar Bernardino de Sahagún also mentions *Tzopelic xiuitl*. Common names in Latin America are *hierba dulce*, *hierba buena*, *neuctixihuitl* ("honey herb"), *orozuz*, *orozul*, *salvia santa*, and *corronchoco*.

In the late nineteenth century, Parke, Davis and Co. used the Aztec sweet herb under the name "Lippia Mexicana" in a concentrated tincture for the treatment of bronchitis, and in Mexico, an aqueous decoction of it is still used to treat a variety of ills.

The Aztec sweet herb has been more frequently known in the horticultural literature as *Lippia dulcis*, but following Harold Moldenke, who wrote the latest monograph of the Verbenaceae, the correct name should be *Phyla scaberrima*. The scientific name is derived from the Greek for "tribe," *phyla*, referring to the compound flower heads that characterize the genus, and the Latin for "most rough," *scaberrima*.

The Aztec sweet herb bears small, rough-surfaced, egg-shaped leaves, which often turn red-purple in bright sun, arising from a central rosette and bearing terminal elongated, football-like heads of white flowers. Since it is hardy only in tropical and semi-tropical areas, this is best grown as a potted plant. In winter the stems drop their leaves, dying back to the central rosette, and produce new green shoots in spring.

The vegetative parts of the Aztec sweet herb contain hernandulcin, which is about three times sweeter than sucrose but with a perceptible aftertaste and some bitterness. No toxicity or mutagenesis has been observed for hernandulcin. The raw leaves are also scented with camphor, so the overall effect is similar to con-

suming sweet moth balls. Camphor is toxic, particularly for small children, causing nausea, vomiting, central nervous system depression, and coma. Additionally, the long use of the *P. scaberrima* as an emmenagogue in Mexico alludes to its potential abortifacient properties, possibly from the camphor. Thus, since *P. scaberrima* does not have GRAS status, we cannot recommend its consumption.

Important chemistry: The leaves of the Aztec sweet herb contain a bisbolane sesquiterpene, hernandulcin, as 0.004 percent (w/w) of the dried herb. The essential oil of typical *P. scaberrima* is characterized by 53 percent camphor and 16 percent camphene, providing a camphoraceous odor. Plants from Cuba have 11 percent beta-caryophyllene and 9 percent 6-methyl-5-hepten-2-one and only a trace of camphor.

Botanical Description

P. scaberrima (A. L. Juss.) Moldenke, Repert. Spec. Nov. Regni Veget. 41:64. 1936 (*Lippia dulcis* Trevir.).

Native country: The Aztec sweet herb is native to Tamaulipas, Veracruz, Morelos, Oaxaca, and Yucatán in Mexico, Central America, the West Indies, and Colombia.

General habit: The Aztec sweet herb is an erect shrubby perennial to less than 60 cm high.

Leaves: The leaves are long-stalked, egg-shaped, coarsely toothed, rough-surfaced, and green to red-purple.

Flowers: The white flowers are produced in a head about 6 mm in diameter, elongating with age.

Fruits/seeds: The fruits are tiny and pale brown.

Phyla scaberrima

Pimpinella anisum

pĭm-pĭ-nĕl-å å-nĭ-sŭm
anise

Family: Apiaceae (Umbelliferae)
Growth form: annual to 2 feet (60 cm)
Hardiness: seedlings can withstand minor frost
Light: full sun
Water: moist but not constantly wet
Soil: light, pH 6.5 to 8.2, average 7.2
Propagation: seeds in spring, 6,500 seeds per ounce (230/g)
Culinary use: candies, liqueurs, chewing gum, teas, pastries
Craft use: none
Landscape use: short-lived; rear of border, best in vegetable plot

French: *anis vert*
German: *Anis*
Dutch: *anijs*
Italian: *anice verde, anisio, anacio*
Spanish: *anís, matalahuga, matalahuva*
Portuguese: *aniz, erva doce*
Swedish: *gran*
Russian: *anis*
Chinese: *huai-hsiang, huei-hsiang, pa-yueh-chu*
Japanese: *anason*
Arabic: *shâmar, razianaj, anisun*

Anise reminds us of those anonymous perfumers who create widely recognized fragrances but under the name of a couturier: anise never quite gets the recognition that it deserves. Anise seeds (really fruits) are used to flavor licorice candy; the notion that there are "licorice-scented" plants should be amended to reflect the relative lack of aroma in the sweetener licorice; "anise-scented" more accurately describes the scent.

Anise seeds are also used to flavor liqueurs (Anisette, Ouzo, Raki) and are also useful in some meat dishes (lamb shanks), ice cream, candy, chewing gum, condiments, teas, and pastries (pizzelles). Because of a similarity of flavor, anise seeds are sometimes confused with the seeds of fennel, which are used in sweet Italian sausage; the seeds themselves, however, are not identical in appearance. The seeds of anise are considered GRAS at 2 to 5,000 ppm, while the essential oil is GRAS at 7 to 3,200 ppm.

The genus *Pimpinella* includes about 150 species of Eurasia. The generic name is of uncertain medieval origin, while the specific name is Latin for anise.

Anise seed is primarily imported from Turkey, but Spain and China also supply the United States market. Anise oil (sometimes confused with essential oil from Chinese star anise, *Illicium verum* J. D. Hook.) comes primarily from China, Spain, and Guatemala. Anise essential

Pimpinella anisum

oil is anti-inflammatory. Aqueous suspensions of anise have been found to protect rats against chemically induced gastric ulcers. Anethole, the chief constituent of anise oil, has been shown to be antifungal and antibacterial; it is also an insecticide and effective against houseflies in laboratory experiments. *p*-Anisaldehyde has been found to be acaricidal. Anise seed tea should not be used to increase lactation because it may be toxic to newborns. Anise seed, in particular (*E*)-anethole, has some estrogenic activity.

Anise is an easily raised annual found wild in the Middle East but widely cultivated in Europe, the United States, China, and Chile. The seed (technically fruit) of this lacy, delicate plant, similar in appearance to dill and reaching to about 2 feet (60 cm) high, should be sown in warm soil in spring; it requires at least 120 days frost-free days in order to fruit properly. Choose a spot in well-drained, friable garden loam in full sun. Anise is very susceptible to drought, so irrigation may be necessary. Plant seed about half an inch (1.3 cm) deep in rows 18 to 30 inches (46 to 76 cm) apart, one or two seeds per inch (one or two seeds per 2.5 cm). This translates to a commercial rate of 5 to 10 pounds seed per acre (5.6 to 11 kg/ha). Germination occurs in seven to fourteen days at 70°F (21°C). Carefully thin seedlings to 6 to 12 inches (15 to 30 cm) apart; anise transplants poorly. Growth is spindly, and plants tend to flop unless soil is firmed at the base of the plant.

While the seed in the umbel is still green, pull the plants out of the ground or cut the tops by hand, tie into bundles, and stack in conical piles with the fruiting heads toward the center. Thresh after drying and separate seeds from chaff. For the home gardener, expect a harvest of about 1 to 2 tablespoons of seed from each plant. In California, average commercial yields range from 500 to 700 pounds seed per acre (560 to 785 kg/ha).

Important chemistry: The essential oil of anise seeds is dominated by 67 to 94 percent (*E*)-anethole. The essential oil of the foliage is dominated by 29 percent (*E*)-anethole, 15 percent germacrene D, and 12 percent beta-bisabolene. Anethole is very similar in structure to estragole (methyl chavicol) in tarragon and safrole in sassafras, and so these oils smell similar but not identical.

All three constituents supply a somewhat sweet flavor, and the greater the concentration of anethole in anise oil, the sweeter the flavor. The roots contain 52 percent beta-bisabolene and 13 to 16 percent pregeijerene (1,5-dimethyl-cyclodeca-1,5,7-triene), and the *trans*-anethole is only 3 percent.

Botanical Description

P. anisum L., Sp. pl. 264. 1753.
Native country: The native distribution of anise is unknown, but it probably originated in Asia.
General habit: Anise is a finely hairy annual 10 to 61 cm high.
Leaves: Young leaves are broad, up to 2.5 cm wide, and kidney-shaped, resembling flat parsley, while the older leaves are feathery like dill.
Flowers: Flowers have white petals and are arranged in an umbel.
Fruits/seeds: The fruits of anise are 3 to 5 mm long, flattened, egg-shaped to oblong, downy, and gray-brown, with lengthwise ribs.

Piper

p̲ī-pḗr
piper

Family: Piperaceae

Growth form: vines, shrubs, or small trees

Hardiness: most not hardy above Zone 9

Light: part shade

Water: moist but not constantly wet

Soil: well-drained garden loam

Propagation: cuttings during summer

Culinary use: limited beyond black pepper and cubebs (most not GRAS)

Craft use: potpourri

Landscape use: container plant, sun room or greenhouse

The genus *Piper*, derived from the ancient Latin name, includes over 1,000 species of vines, shrubs, and small trees. The best-known species are *P. nigrum* L., black pepper; *P. cubeba* L. fil., cubebs; and *P. betle* L., the betel leaf or pan. The fruits or leaves of many other species are also used for seasoning. Many have heart-shaped leaves, and all have an inflorescence of tiny white flowers on a fleshy spike. All are tropical greenhouse plants not hardy above Zone 9.

Piper auritum

p̲ī-pḗr âw-r̲ī-t̲ŭm
makulan

Spanish: *hojas, acuyo, hinojo sabalero, hoja santa* (misapplied)

Piper auritum is the only Central American *Piper* species in general cultivation in the United States, but it is often confused with *P. sanctum* (Miq.) Schlecht, ex Miq., *hoja santa*, *hierba santa*, or *acuyo*. The bases of the leaves of *P. auritum* are unequal and overlapping and create an ear-like appearance, which is the meaning of the specific name. The large, velvety, heart-shaped leaves, studded with crystal-like glands, have a wonderful sassafras odor from which derives the alternate common name, root beer plant. The stems have swollen nodes and become quite woody; they are frequently used as canes or walking sticks.

Crushed makulan leaves are used by natives

in Panama to attract fish during the dry season, and the fish taste of this sassafras-scented herb after feeding regularly on the leaf. In Veracruz the leaves are ground with garlic, chiles, and roasted tomatoes to make a sauce for fish; the leaves are sautéed with shrimp and roasted peppers. The large leaves are also used to line fish or chicken casseroles that are laced with spicy chile sauces; in the southwestern United States, the leaves are wrapped around pork tamales before cooking.

Because of the known liver toxicity and carcinogenicity of safrole, the main component of the plant's essential oil, and because the U.S. Food and Drug Administration has prohibited safrole in foods since 1960, we cannot recommend makulan in food (see sassafras for a discussion of safrole).

If you want to grow makulan for non-food applications, grow it in rich, well-drained soil in dappled afternoon shade. Ample moisture should be supplied. Since this must be moved indoors north of Zone 9, we recommend the plant be grown in large pots.

Important chemistry: The essential oil of makulan is dominated by about 65 to 93 per-

cent safrole. Makulan also has capharadione A and B, two aporphine-type alkaloids of un-known physiological activity.

Piper lolot
pī-pér lō-lŏt
lá lốt

Vietnamese: *lá lốt, cay lốt*

This is one of a number of herbs that reached U.S. shores with refugees who fled Vietnam at the end of the war in 1975. The glossy heart-shaped leaves of *P. lolot* are used by the Viet-namese to impart a delicate flavor to roast beef or to a type of shish kabob; to use the leaves for such dishes it is necessary to first dip them in boiling water to keep them from burning. They are then wrapped around small pieces of beef, secured with a toothpick, and placed on a skewer.

Lá lốt is a very tender perennial vine, sensi-tive to frost but easily overwintered in the green-house or sunny windowsill. Otherwise it can be purchased from Asian food stores that handle

Piper lolot

fresh Vietnamese herbs. Lá lốt does not have GRAS status.

Important chemistry: The essential oil of the leaf of lá lốt has 26 percent beta-caryophyl-lene. The stem oil has 31 percent beta-caryophyl-lene, while the rhizome oil has 28 percent beta-caryophyllene.

Botanical Key and Description

Key:
1. Leaves hairy underneath, 20 to 55 × 12 to 30 cm. . . . . *P. auritum*
1a. Leaves smooth underneath, 6 to 10 × 5 to 9 cm. . . . . *P. lolot*

P. auritum Humb., Bonpl. & Kunth, Nov. gen. sp. 1:54. 1815.
Native country: Makulan ranges from Mexico to Colombia and to some of the islands of the West Indies.

General habit: Makulan is a shrub or slender tree to about 6 m tall.
Leaves: Leaves are stalked on 4 to 10 cm peti-oles, 20 to 55 × 12 to 30 cm, egg-shaped to widest at the center with the ends equal but with very unequal heart-shaped bases, taper-

ing abruptly to the sharp, blunt, or pinched tip. The upper surface is smooth to the touch, while the lower surface has whitish hairs.

Flowers: Flowers are tiny and white on a fleshy spike.

P. lolot C. DC., Annuaire Conserv. Jard. Bot. Genève 2:272. 1898.

Native country: Lá lốt is native to Vietnam.

General habit: Lá lốt is a perennial vine to several meters.

Leaves: Leaves are smooth, glossy, unequally heart-shaped, tapering to a point, 6 to 10 × 5 to 9 cm.

Flowers: The tiny white flowers are carried on a fleshy spike.

Plectranthus

plĕc-trăn-thŭs
plectranthus

Family: Lamiaceae (Labiatae)
Growth form: succulent shrubs
Hardiness: very sensitive to frost
Light: full to part sun
Water: moist but not constantly wet
Soil: well-drained garden loam, pH 5.2 to 6.8 (*P. amboinicus*)
Propagation: cuttings during summer
Culinary use: limited (not GRAS)
Craft use: none
Landscape use: container plant

The botanical name means "spurflower" and is derived from two Greek words, *plectron*, a spur, and *anthos*, a flower. Controversy exists on whether Cuban oregano should be designated as *Coleus* or *Plectranthus*. *Plectranthus*, *Coleus*, and several allied genera contain similar species in which the genera are delineated on the basis of rather trivial characteristics. *Coleus* was described by João de Loureiro in his *Flora Cochinchinensis* in 1790 to separate those species in which the stamens are fused into a tube (monadelphous stamens). Other botanists have not consistently followed Loureiro and instead have

lumped these species into the genus *Plectranthus*, described by Charles-Louis L'Héritier de Brutelle in his *Stirpes Novae aut Minus Cognitae* (1788), primarily because the stamens do not form a satisfactory basis for consistently separating these genera.

Controversy also exists on the correct identity of the plants commonly called Vick's™ plant, after the aromatic chest rub traditionally used to treat colds. At least three different species of *Plectranthus* are cultivated under this name, and the correct botanical identities are still unknown. The Vick's™ plant may include *P. intraterraneus* S. T. Blake of Australia, *P. marrubioides* Benth. of Kenya, *P. ornatus* Codd of Ethiopia to Tanzania, and *P. coeruleus* (Guerke) Agnew of Kenya, but many incorrect specific epithets of *Plectranthus* are used by growers. To confuse matters even more, one of these three, small-leaved Vick's™ plants is sold as Cuban oregano. More study is needed to correctly identify these species, and it may prove monumental because the genus *Plectranthus* includes some 300 species of the tropics and warm Old World.

No *Plectranthus* species has GRAS status.

Plectranthus amboinicus
plĕc-trăn-thŭs ăm-boy-nĭ-kŭs
Cuban oregano

> **Spanish:** *orégano, orégano brujo, orégano de Cartagna, orégano de España, orégano Frances, sugánda, clavo, limon, orégano torogil de limon, bildu, latai*
>
> **Bengali:** *pathor chur, pater chur, owa, pashana bledi*
>
> **Vietnamese:** *cần dầy lá*

The botanical name is derived from *Amboina* (the Moluccas Islands) in Indonesia. Also called Puerto Rican oregano, Indian borage, or Spanish thyme, Cuban oregano may be substituted for Greek oregano (*Origanum vulgare* subsp. *hirtum*), but the large (up to 2¾ inches or 7 cm long), fleshy, fuzzy leaves are not easily manipulated by cooks accustomed to using crushed, dried oregano. In parts of India, the leaves are dipped in batter and fried. Like the other members of the genus *Plectranthus* (including Swedish ivy, *P. australis*), this is a low perennial shrub that requires full sun and good, fertile garden loam with constant moisture. Under optimum conditions in the garden, Cuban oregano may reach 39 inches (1 m) tall, but plants in pots rarely reach half that height. Winter temperatures should not be below 40°F (4.4°C).

Two cultivars are known: 'Variegata' (of unknown origin and a name which is technically incorrect because it is in Latin and published after 1 January 1959) with edges in white, and 'Well Sweep Wedgewood' with a creamy center. 'Well Sweep Wedgewood' tends to grow laterally and is best displayed in a hanging basket.

The essential oil of Cuban oregano has been found to be insecticidal.

Important chemistry: The essential oil of Cuban oregano, depending upon the geographical source, consists of 0 to 88 percent thymol, 0 to 80 percent carvacrol, and 0 to 21 percent beta-phellandrene, trace to 21 percent beta-caryophyllene, 0 to 20 percent gamma-terpinene, 0 to 17 percent alpha-terpinene, and 0 to 17 percent *p*-cymene.

Botanical Description

P. amboinicus (Lour.) Spreng., Syst. veg. 2. 690. 1825 (*Coleus amboinicus* Lour., *C. aromaticus* Benth.).

Native country: Cuban oregano is probably native to India (or possibly Africa) but is widely distributed throughout the tropics, from Africa, India, Malaysia, and the Philippines to the Virgin Islands, Cuba, and Mexico.

General habit: This is a more or less succulent herb, 0.3 to 1 m high. Stems and branches are almost circular in cross-section, densely hairy when young, becoming smooth in age.

Leaves: Leaves are thick, fleshy, broadly egg-shaped, almost round, or kidney-shaped, 5 to 7 cm long, 4 to 6 cm wide, blunt or rounded at apex, rounded or squared at the

Plectranthus amboinicus

base, often tapering to the base, sparsely hairy above and with moderately coarse and stiff hairs on the nerves beneath; margin coarsely round-toothed.

Flowers: Flowers are in dense, ten- to more than twenty-flowered clusters, the corolla lavender-blue.

Pogostemon

pō-gō-stĕ-mŏn
patchouli

Family: Lamiaceae (Labiatae)
Growth form: herbaceous perennials about 1.5 to 3 feet (0.5 to 1 m) tall
Hardiness: very sensitive to frost
Water: moist but not constantly wet
Soil: well-drained garden loam, pH 4.3 to 6.3, average 5.3
Propagation: cuttings when in active growth in spring or summer; seeds possible but not routine
Culinary use: none
Craft use: scenting, moth repellent
Landscape use: large pots, front of border

French: *patchouli*
German: *Patschouli*
Dutch: *patchouli*
Italian: *patchouli*
Spanish: *pacholí*

It is thanks to Napoleon Bonaparte (1769–1821), the Corsican-born military leader and Emperor of France, that patchouli found its way to Europe and now enriches our herb gardens with its sweet, spicy, balsamic aroma. It all happened in a roundabout way.

After exploring the Egyptian marketplaces during his North African campaign (1798–1799), Napoleon brought back to Paris several cashmere shawls. The fabric of these shawls, woven from the under-fleece of the Kashmir or down goat, was so supple and fine that the Moguls called them "ring shawls" because they could be drawn through a finger-ring. The dark-colored shawls were also marked by an intricate pattern of tiny floral components arranged in a large comma shape culminating in a tilted finial. In addition, the shawls were scented of patchouli to protect them from moths, both during the lengthy time of weaving (up to eighteen months) and during transport. The source of the mysterious and luscious scent was a closely held secret.

Soon European manufacturers at Paisley, Scotland, and Reims, France, began to duplicate the shawl patterns with coarser wools, but the perfumed shawls from India always demanded a higher price. When patchouli oil was imported into France for scenting the shawls—as early as 1826—sales soared.

In 1837, Blanco first described true patchouli as *Mentha cablin* in his *Flora de Filipinas*, finally revealing the source of the mysterious aroma. Patchouli may be one of the first aromas used as a marketing tool; some hundred years later, American marketing consultants "discovered" the value of scent for selling everything from toilet paper to cars. So what else is new?

Mystery continues to surround patchouli because the fragrance is not the property of a single species or cultivar. Many of the seventy-one *Pogostemon* species of the Indomalaysian region have leaves scented with a rich, sweet-herbaceous, aromatic-spicy, and woody-balsamic aroma. Two species, *P. cablin* and *P. heyneanus*, are harvested and often mixed to produce an oil that contains 14 to 46 percent patchoulol (patchouli alcohol), but the chief aromatic component appears to be norpatchoulenol, which is only about 0.3 to 6 percent of the oil. In addition, at least three unnamed cultivars of *P. cablin* are raised commercially. Thus far, research has usually centered upon the commercial product rather than individual species.

While both *P. cablin* and *P. heyneanus* are available in cultivation, an inferior species is sometimes pawned off as their scented sibling in the United States. This large-leaved, slightly hairy and essentially scentless species is *P. benghalensis* (N. L. Burm.) Kuntze (*P. plectranthoides* Desf.). Some gardeners are familiar only with this species and thus have a very poor impression of patchouli.

In addition, gardeners who come to patchouli, the plant, after becoming familiar with patchouli, the oil, are sometimes baffled because the essential oil is so overpowering and the leaf scent so subtle. The strength of patchouli oil's odor is so strong that, when mixed volume for volume with any other oil, patchouli always predominates. The intensity of commercial patchouli oil is developed after controlled fermentation of the dried leaves, thereby releasing more odor. Chemists note that many scented components are actively metabolized while bound to a sugar, but in this form they are not volatile and are hence scentless; fermentation breaks the sugar bond and releases the "free" chemicals to eventually evaporate and be detected as scent.

Patchouli is also unique in the mint family because the essential oil is synthesized in both internal and external glands; most other members of the Lamiaceae secrete most of their essential oil beneath a layer of cutin (plant wax) from either three-celled or ten-celled epidermal glands. Along with its dominance, the rich, distinctive scent of patchouli has staying power; it will remain perceptible for weeks or months on unwashed clothing and is thus described as having good "tenacity." Thus patchouli is sometimes described as having "fixative" qualities.

Patchouli is a loose-growing, somewhat weedy, upright tender perennial. The generic name for patchouli, *Pogostemon*, refers to the bearded filaments of the four erect stamens, a distinguishing characteristic of the genus. The common name is derived from *paccilai*, meaning "green leaf" in the Tamil language of southern India.

Patchouli oil blends well with labdanum, vetiver, sandalwood, cedarwood, oakmoss, rose geranium, clove, lavender, rose, bergamot, clary sage, and pine needle. Patchouli forms an integral part of Oriental perfumes, woody bases, fougères, chypres, and powdery perfumes. Combined with geranium, the violet-scented ionones and orris extracts, anise, clove, and so on, it formed the basis of the tiny, black, paper-like squares of Sen-Sen, a breath sweetener that was particularly popular during Prohibition. In India, ink was once scented of camphor and patchouli, a custom that deserves resurrection. Patchouli oil has also been used in baked goods, beverages, candies, gelatins, puddings, chewing gum, and low-tar cigarettes; it is reputed to have insecticidal and antimicrobial activities. The essential oil is considered GRAS at 2 to 220 ppm.

All *Pogostemon* species are extremely sensitive to temperature and grow rapidly in warm weather. At temperatures much below 70°F (21°C) growth slows and, as temperatures drop further, the plants go dormant and lose some leaves; severe, permanent damage may be caused if temperatures dip to 35°F (2°C), and they will certainly not withstand hard freezes. This temperature sensitivity demands that home gardeners grow patchouli as a warm-weather annual or cultivate it in containers that can be brought into a house or greenhouse during winter. Because of its rapid growth rate, a plant in a 2.5-inch pot purchased in spring will step up to a 6-to 12-inch pot easily within a single season. A soilless growing medium provides good stability and should be fertilized every two weeks during rapid growth periods. Frequent pinching or small harvests produce more compact growth and increase branching.

Patchouli is a plant for a shady or partly shady location; it will show heat stress in direct, hot sun. Indonesia provides most of the patchouli oil imported into the United States.

Pogostemon cablin

pō-gō-stĕ-mŏn kăb-lĭn
true patchouli

True patchouli is cultivated in Indonesia, Malaysia, China, and Brazil for its oil, but Indonesia accounts for over 80 percent of the total annual oil production. Patchouli oil derived primarily from *P. cablin* is commercially marketed as "Singapore patchouli oil." The specific name is derived from the native Tagalog (Philippine) name *kablin*. The herb is called *dilem wangi*, the "cultivated patchouli," in Indonesia because it rarely flowers there or in Malaya and is propagated from cuttings.

At least three unnamed cultivars of true patchouli are commercially raised. The apocryphal story has circulated, sometimes reprinted in rather reputable manuals, that this species *never* flowers. Yet it flowers prolifically, particularly in the fall, in our greenhouses. This is not an unusual phenomenon in the Lamiaceae because many high-latitude mints, when taken to areas near the equator, do not flower under the almost equal lengths of day and night.

For commercial production, cuttings are raised in a nursery. From there they are placed in well-tilled and well-drained soil 2 feet (60 cm) apart in rows 3 feet (1 m) apart. Because patchouli does best in part shade, it is commonly interplanted with coconut palms in Indomalaysia. Moisture must be constant, and irrigation is necessary in dry climates.

The first cutting takes place after five to nine months of growth, with further harvests every three to six months for two to three years. Only the top 10 to 24 inches (25 to 60 cm) are harvested, so that four to six juvenile sprouting buds remain at the basal region to provide rapid regeneration. Next, the leaves are dried in the shade and turned frequently to prevent fungal growth, for three to six days. Fresh yields vary

Pogostemon cablin

from 3,569 to 7,138 pounds per acre (4,000 to 8,000 kg/ha); up to 80 to 85 percent of that weight is lost on drying. Distillation may vary from six to twenty-four hours, depending upon the lot, with oil yields of about 2 percent of the weight of the dried leaves.

In order to get the highest yield of the essential oil by steam distillation, the leaves are either given a controlled, light fermentation, scalded with superheated steam, or stacked or baled, thus "curing" them by modest and interrupted fermentation. The latter method produces the best oil. Patchouli oil is a dark orange or brownish orange, viscous liquid; this native oil is often redistilled.

Patchouli is said to deplete the soil rapidly and is thus commonly grown for a single season without additional nitrogen fertilizer; the plots are later rotated with coffee or rubber crops, or nitrogen fertilizers are applied at the rate of 45 pounds per acre (50 kg/ha) after each harvest.

For home gardeners, this equals a rate of about 2 pounds 5-10-5 fertilizer per 100 square feet.

Patchouli is very susceptible to root-knot nematode, *Meloidogyne incognita*, and care must be taken to prevent its infestation. Leaf blight, caused by a *Cercospora* species, is evidenced by brown spots near the margins and can be controlled by fungicides.

Important chemistry: In one of the few projects to analyze the essential oil of authentic *P. cablin* from Vietnam rather than a commercial oil, Dung et al. found 38 percent patchouli alcohol and 15 percent alpha-bulnesene. Sugimura et al. also defined variations of essential oils from three unnamed cultivars of *P. cablin* and found 19 to 29 percent patchouli alcohol, 7 to 12 percent alpha-patchoulene plus delta-guaiene, and 5 to 17 percent alpha-guaiene plus beta-caryophyllene. Indonesian patchouli oil has 32 percent patchouli alcohol, 17 percent delta-guaiene, and 16 percent alpha-guaiene.

Pogostemon heyneanus
pō-gō-stĕ-mŏn hā-nē-ă-nŭs
false patchouli

This herb is called "false" because it is a substitute for the more desirable true patchouli, *P. cablin*. The specific name is derived from Benjamin Heyne (1770–1819), the superintendent of the Bangalore Gardens in India. In Indonesia, the herb is called *dilem kembang*, the "flowering patchouli." Cultivation and uses are similar to true patchouli, and both are commonly mixed on the market. The commercial oil derived primarily from this species is called "Java" or "Sumatra patchouli oil."

Botanical Key and Description

Key:
1. Habit proportionally slender, segments of the inflorescences evenly spaced, with internodes always visible, less than 1 cm, short appressed-hairy, calyx 3 to 3.5 mm (in fruit 3.5 to 4 mm) long .... *P. heyneanus*
1a. Habit more robust, axis not slender, segments of inflorescences in an almost continuous thick spike 1 to 2 cm wide, densely hairy, calyx 4 to 6 mm (in fruit 5.5 to 6 mm) long .... *P. cablin*

P. cablin (Blanco) Benth in DC., Prodr. 12:146. 1848 (*P. petchouly* Pellet.).

Native country: True patchouli is native to clearings and settled areas in Sri Lanka and continental southeastern Asia but cultivated elsewhere and often escaped.

General habit: True patchouli is an erect branched herb, 0.5 to 1 m high. Stems and branches are coated with a dense, wool-like covering of matted, tangled hairs of medium length.

Leaves: Leaves are thin- or thick-membranaceous, narrowly egg-shaped or egg-shaped, 5 to 14 × 3.5 to 10 cm, with short appressed hairs, tapering to the apex, base rounded-wedge-shaped, base always smooth-edged, margin with rounded teeth or doubly toothed.

Flowers: Flowers are white, lavender-blue, or violet, 6 to 7 mm long.

P. heyneanus Benth in Wall., Pl. asiat. rar. 2:16. 1830–1831 (*P. patchouli* J. D. Hook.).

Native country: False patchouli is native to thickets, old clearings, and stream banks in Sri Lanka and continental southeastern Asia but cultivated elsewhere and often escaped.

General habit: False patchouli is an erect branched herb, 0.5 to 1.5 m high. Stems and branches are slender, sparsely hairy.

Leaves: Leaves are thin-membranaceous, egg-shaped to broadly egg-shaped, 5 to 8 × 3.5 to 5.5 cm, tapering to the apex, base broadly wedge-shaped, base smooth-edged, margin with rounded teeth or doubly toothed.

Flowers: Flowers are white, or the upper lip pale violet, 4.5 to 5 mm long.

Poliomintha bustamanta

pō-lī-ō-mĭn-thå būs-tå-mǎn-tå
Mexican oregano

Family: Lamiaceae (Labiatae)
Growth form: subshrub to 39 inches (1 m)
Hardiness: root hardy to Zone 8
Light: full sun
Water: moist but not constantly wet; withstands drought
Soil: well-drained garden loam
Propagation: cuttings in spring and summer
Culinary use: limited (not GRAS)
Craft use: none
Landscape use: container plant, middle of border

Spanish: *orégano*

Poliomintha bustamanta

The name of this genus of seven species is probably derived from the Spanish for pennyroyal plus the Greek for mint. The specific epithet refers to Bustamante in Nuevo León in Mexico. As the Spanish name, *orégano*, implies, this is used in the same manner as Greek oregano (*Origanum vulgare* subsp. *hirtum*) in Mexico. This plant was first used in Texas in the early 1970s as a landscape plant by Lynn Lowry; he acquired the plants from the Sierra Picachos, which are south of Laredo about one hour on the Monterrey Highway. He observed men coming out of the mountains with bundles of cut branches, tied on mules, to be sold at the local markets.

Mexican oregano has been identified in previous articles as *P. longiflora* A. Gray, but the publication of *P. bustamanta* in 1993 by B. L. Turner alerted Kim Kuebel of Texas that the cultivated material was incorrectly identified. However, because the cultivated plants combine the characteristics of both *P. longiflora* and *P. glabrescens* A. Gray and because they do not fit *P. bustamanta* exactly, we wonder whether a hybrid complex may be involved here; we also wonder whether other local, endemic species (such as *P. dendritica* Turner and *P. maderensis* Henrickson) may also be hybrids.

Mexican oregano is a subshrub occasionally hardy to short freezes down to -5°F (-20.6°C) in well-drained soil and full sun. The glossy, green leaves on a shrub to almost 39 inches (1 m) are attractive in themselves, but the long lavender flowers to about 1 inch (30 cm) long, produced almost all summer, really make this desirable in the herb garden or mixed herbaceous border.

While widely consumed in Mexico and Texas, Mexican oregano has no GRAS status.

Important chemistry: The essential oil of *Poliomintha bustamanta* consists of 41 to 45 percent carvacrol, 14 percent carvacryl methyl ether, and 11 percent gamma-terpinene.

Botanical Description

P. bustamanta Turner, Phytologia. 74:164. 1993.

Native country: *P. bustamanta* is native to Nuevo León, Mexico.

General habit: This is a subshrub 1 m high.

Leaves: Leaves are well spaced; spreading or nodding; oval to broadly or narrowly elliptical; 16 to 19 mm long, 4 to 5 mm wide; with smooth edges, tapering to the base and shortly stalked; the stalk 2 mm long; blunt at apex; young leaves hairy, almost smooth upon maturity.

Flowers: Flowers are solitary in the axils of the upper leaves, rarely two-flowered in the axils, corolla lavender.

Porophyllum ruderale subsp. *macrocephalum*

pôr-ō-fĭl-ŭm rū-dĕ-rā-lē măk-rō-sĕf-ă-lŭm
papaloquelite

Family: Asteraceae (Compositae)
Growth form: annual to 6 feet (1.8 m)
Hardiness: very sensitive to frost
Water: moist but not wet
Soil: well-drained garden loam
Propagation: seeds in spring
Culinary use: cilantro-like but limited (not GRAS)
Craft use: none
Landscape use: container plant (in southern Texas and Mexico), rear of the vegetable/herb garden

Papaloquelite is used in Mexico and Texas for flavoring foods. Branches are kept in glasses of water on the tables of the cafes, and the leaves are torn up fresh on beans or eaten with tortillas and garlic. The leaves impart a unique cilantro–green pepper–cucumber flavor. In South America the leaves of the normal subspecies (subsp. *ruderale*) are used in foods under the name *quinquiña* (Bolivia) or *cravo de urubu* ("black vulture's marigold," Brazil). Each marigold-like plant may grow to 6 feet (1.8 m) high and provide plenty of foliage, but ray-less flowers are rarely produced in the northern United States before frost. If you grow this outside of southern Texas and Mexico, grow it in pots so that you gather the dandelion-like fruits with their tiny, bristly parachutes.

The generic name means "pored-leaf" and refers to the translucent oil glands scattered on the margin and surface of the blue-green leaves; a ruderal plant grows in waste places. *Macrocephalum* means "large-headed." The normal subspecies has lance-shaped leaves, while subsp. *macrocephalum* has egg-shaped leaves. The genus *Porophyllum* includes about twenty-eight species of the warm Americas. Most other species of this genus are described by botanists as "smelly."

The cultivated material is not *P. coloratum* (Humb., Bonpl. & Kunth.) DC., as claimed in a 2001 article in *Herb Companion*; *P. coloratum* has linear leaves, unlike the lance-shaped leaves of *P. ruderale*. Some ethnic markets in the United States will sometimes offer another species of similar odor, *P. tagetoides* (Humb., Bonpl. & Kunth.) DC.; this species has linear leaves but has not entered general cultivation in the United States.

Despite its consumption in southern Texas and Latin America, *P. ruderale* has no GRAS status.

Important chemistry: The essential oil of the type, *P. ruderale* subsp. *ruderale*, from

Porophyllum ruderale subsp. *macrocephalum*

Brazil is characterized by 0 to 75 percent limonene, 0 to 63 percent beta-phellandrene, and 0 to 22 percent (*E*,*E*)-dodecadienal, providing a lemony cilantro-like odor. Plants from Bolivia have 64 percent sabinene and 10 percent terpinen-4-ol, providing a piney odor.

Botanical Description

P. ruderale (Jacq.) Cass. **subsp.** *macrocephalum* (DC.) R. R. Johnson, Univ. Kansas Sci. Bull. 48:233. 1969.

Native country: Papaloquelite is native from Texas to South America.

General habit: This an erect annual, smooth and somewhat covered with a bluish waxy covering. Stems are branching above, 15 cm to 1.8 m high, green to purplish, circular in cross-section, marked with fine longitudinal lines.

Leaves: Leaves are borne opposite or singly; blades are 1 to 3.5 cm long and 2.5 cm wide, thin, broadly egg-shaped to narrowed at the base; rarely lance-shaped or lance-shaped with narrow base, wavy-margined with one gland in each depression and one at each tip, surfaces of the blades with or without glands, tip rounded, base usually rounded or sometimes gradually narrowing. Leaf stalks are 0.5 to 2 cm long.

Flowers: Heads are solitary at the ends of branches; stalks erect, club-shaped, 1.5 to 6 cm long, bracts five, green, purple-tinged, lance-shaped with two rows of lance-shaped glands. Flowers are thirty or more per head, corolla purple to olive-green.

Pycnanthemum

pĭk-năn-thĕ-mŭm
mountain mint

Family: Lamiaceae (Labiatae)

Growth form: herbaceous perennials to 59 inches (150 cm)

Hardiness: many hardy to Zone 5

Light: full sun

Water: moist but not wet; many can withstand drought

Soil: well-drained garden loam

Propagation: seeds or divisions of clumps in spring

Culinary use: limited (not GRAS)

Craft use: dried flowers, wreaths, tussymussies, sachets

Landscape use: wildflower and meadow gardens, herbaceous borders (with caution)

This genus, usually called mountain mint, was derived from the Greek *pyknos*, "dense," and *anthos*, "flower," alluding to the densely packed flower clusters. All eighteen species of North America are good herbaceous perennials with scents varying from eucalyptus to mint to lemon; they are good plants for foraging bees and produce distinctively scented honey. The foliage in many species is hairy, which produces a silvery cast that often intensifies upon drying; flower stems, picked at their peak (about midflowering) are used in dried arrangements. Most species propagate easily from seeds (actually tiny nuts, or nutlets), but abundant stolons and/or rhizomes are also produced and can be divided. Some may even become weeds, and if you grow many of the species, new hybrids may result.

These native American plants are underused in the herbaceous border, potpourri, flea pillows, tussy-mussies, dried flower arrangements, and sachets. None have GRAS status, and while no poisonous constituents have been identified in the literature, you're on your own with culinary applications.

Pycnanthemum incanum

pĭk-năn-thĕ-mŭm ĭn-kă-nŭm
gray mountain mint

The gray mountain mint is scented of pennyroyal and peppermint. The fat spear-shaped leaves increase in hairiness at the apex of the 59-inch (150 cm) stems and appear almost white; they're coated with soft velvety hairs. The flowers are white to pale lilac. The herb is excellent for dried arrangements.

Important chemistry: The oil of gray mountain mint has 31 to 54 percent pulegone and 28 to 53 percent menthone.

Pycnanthemum pilosum

pĭk-năn-thĕ-mŭm pĭ-lō-sŭm
hairy mountain mint

The hairy mountain mint is intensely scented of peppermint and pennyroyal. The stems reach to 59 inches (150 cm) high with dark green, spear-shaped leaves. The heads of white to pale lilac flowers of hairy mountain mint have been touted as an excellent for bees, which then produce a mint-scented honey. The growth habit of this herb is floppy and rather weedy, and the seed heads shatter so readily that seedlings appear in every nook and cranny. We recommend this herb enthusiastically for meadow-gardening; in other situations, its spreading habit may cause problems.

Important chemistry: The oil of hairy mountain mint has 3 to 44 percent menthone, 27 to 84 percent pulegone, and trace to 16 percent neomenthol.

Pycnanthemum pilosum

Pycnanthemum virginianum
pĭk-năn-thĕ-mŭm vĕr-jĭn-ē-ă-nŭm
Virginia mountain mint

Also called wild basil, Virginia mountain mint is very variable in morphology and chemistry. Most individuals are scented of pennyroyal and peppermint, but some smell distinctly of lemon meringue pie and others smell medicinal. The narrow, spear-shaped leaves are usually pale green and smooth; heads of white to pale lilac flowers appear at the apex of 39-inch (1 m) stems. This species too is excellent in dried flower arrangements.

Important chemistry: The essential oil of Virginia mountain mint has 0 to 78 percent isomenthone, 2 to 66 percent pulegone, trace t o 51 percent limonene, and trace to 23 percent germacrene D.

Botanical Key and Description

Key:

1. Median leaf stalks (about halfway up the stem) 3 to 12 mm long; calyces bearing elongate, jointed bristles 1 to 3 mm long . . . . *P. incanum*
1a. Median leaf stalks rarely over 3 mm long; calyces never tipped with jointed bristles 2
    2. Stems hairy on the angles only; leaves smooth or rarely slightly hairy . . . . *P. virginianum*
    2a. Stems hairy on all sides; leaves hairy . . . . *P. pilosum*

P. incanum (L.) Michx., Fl. bor.-amer. 2:7. 1803.
Native country: Gray mountain mint is native to dry woods and thickets from Vermont, south to North Carolina and west to Tennessee and Kentucky.
General habit: Gray mountain mint is a perennial herb to 150 cm, commonly about 80 cm, the stems loosely branched in the upper part, densely hairy with both short curled hairs and a few longer spreading hairs.
Leaves: Leaves are egg-spear-shaped, less often spear-shaped, somewhat rounded at the base, lighter beneath, toothed, the median 4.5 to 11 × 1.5 to 5.5 cm.
Flowers: The tightly packed terminal flowers are white to pale lilac, purple-spotted.

P. pilosum Nutt., Gen. N. Amer. pl. 2:33. 1818.
Native country: Hairy mountain mint is native to dry to moist woods, thickets, and clearings from Michigan to Illinois, south to North Carolina, and west to Iowa.
General habit: Hairy mountain mint is a perennial herb to 150 cm, commonly 90 to 100 cm, the stems rather densely coated with spreading hairs, branching freely in the inflorescence.
Leaves: Leaves are spear-shaped, 3.5 to 7 × 0.8 to 2 cm, smooth-edged or shallowly toothed, the upper surface of the lower leaves essentially smooth, those of the upper sparingly hairy, the lower surfaces of all coated with long, soft, straight hairs.
Flowers: The tightly packed terminal flowers are white to pale lilac, purple-spotted.

P. virginianum (L.) Th. Durand & B. D. Jacks. ex B. L. Robinson & Fernald, Gray's manual, ed. 7, 707. 1908.
Native country: Virginia mountain mint is native to gravelly shores, meadows, dry to wet

thickets, and so on from Ontario to North Carolina, west to Oklahoma and Minnesota.

General habit: Virginia mountain mint is an herbaceous perennial herb to 1 m or more tall, commonly about 70 cm, bearing short leafy lateral branches in the upper parts.

Leaves: Leaves are spear-shaped or narrow with the sides parallel to spear-shaped, smooth, stalkless, smooth-edged or rarely shallowly toothed, the median 35 to 65 × 6 to 11 mm.

Flowers: The tightly packed terminal flowers are white to pale lilac, purple-spotted.

Rhus coriaria

rŭs kō-rĭ-ār-ĭ-å
Sicilian sumac

Family: Anacardiaceae

Growth form: shrubby tree to about 10 feet (3 m)

Hardiness: potentially hardy to Zone 8

Light: full sun

Water: moist but not wet

Soil: well-drained garden loam; can withstand drought

Propagation: seeds

Culinary use: limited (not GRAS)

Craft use: none

Landscape use: rear of shrub border; accent

French: *sumac des corroyeurs, corroyére*

German: *Färberbaum, Gerber-Sumach, Sumach, Sizilianische Sumach*

Dutch: *siliciaanse sumak*

Italian: *sommacco di Sicilia*

Spanish: *zumaque de tenerías*

Portuguese: *sumagra*

Swedish: *sumack*

Russian: *sumakh dubil'nyy*

Arabic: *sammak, timtima*

The genus *Rhus* includes about 200 temperate and subtropical species, usually trees, shrubs, or vines with clinging roots and simple or compound leaves and tiny, olive-like fruits. Many species, such as poison ivy, sometimes relegated to the genus *Toxicodendron*, produce contact dermatitis. Other species, such as *R. verniciflua* Stokes, the Chinese or Japanese lacquer tree, produce lacquers. *Rhus* was an ancient Greek name, while *coriaria* is derived from the Latin *corium*, "leather," perhaps alluding to the use of sumac leaves in tanning leather.

Sicilian sumac has bright red fruits about ⅛ inch (2 to 4 mm) in diameter, similar to the

Rhus coriaria

North American *R. glabra* L., smooth sumac. While not yet in cultivation in North America, sumac trees are grown commercially in Sicily and southern Italy for the coating around the seeds; the taste is sour but not astringent, rather a rounded fruity sourness, as in sour apples. Sumac is used in Middle Eastern cooking for such dishes as *samak el harrah*, a fish stew of Lebanon and Syria. Sumac fruits, blended with thyme and oregano, are an integral part of the Arabic spice za'tar. The Iranians and Georgians season kebobs with sumac. The Lebanese extract the juice of the fruit as an alternative to lemon juice for salads; to extract the juice, the fruits are first soaked in water for fifteen to twenty minutes and then squeezed out thoroughly. Unfortunately, the fruits of sumac are not listed as GRAS.

The leaves of sumac are used for tanning Cordoba and Morocco leather, earning this plant the alternate name of tanner's sumac. The dried leaves have been used by the Turks to adulterate their oregano, especially after shortages from the radioactive fallout from Chernobyl, but the leaves may be carcinogenic.

Important chemistry: The essential oil of fruits of Turkish *R. coraria* is characterized by 3 to 42 percent (E)-2-decenal, 2 to 13 percent nonanal, and trace to 9 percent limonene, providing a lemony-cucumber-like odor. The essential oil of the leaves is characterized by trace to 17 percent beta-caryophyllene and 3 to 24 percent patchoulane, providing a somewhat resinous odor.

Botanical Description

R. coriaria L., Sp. pl. 265. 1753.
Native country: Sicilian sumac is native to densely wooded uplands from southern Europe to western Asia.
General habit: Sicilian sumac is a shrub or small tree about 3 m high.
Leaves: Leaves are divided into seven to twenty-one leaflets arranged as a feather, each leaflet 1 to 5 cm long, egg-shaped to widest at the center, tip sharp or blunt, coarsely toothed, sometimes with one or two small lobes at the base, hairy beneath, nearly smooth above.
Flowers: Flowers are greenish and arranged in a dense compound inflorescence with the younger flowers at the apex.
Fruits/seeds: Fruits are red to brownish purple and hairy, 2 to 4 mm in diameter.

Rosa

rō-zå
rose

Family: Rosaceae
Growth form: shrubs 2 to 30 feet (61 cm to 9 m)
Hardiness: many routinely hardy to Zone 6
Light: full sun
Water: moist but not constantly wet
Soil: well-drained garden loam
Propagation: cuttings or grafts
Culinary use: salads, desserts
Craft use: potpourri, sachets, beads
Landscape use: shrubbery or rear of herb border

French: *rosier*
German: *Rose*
Dutch: *roos*
Italian: *rosa*
Spanish: *rosa, gavanzo, escaramujo*
Portuguese: *roseira*
Swedish: *ros*
Russian: *rosa*
Chinese: *ch'iang-wei, mei-kuei*
Japanese: *bara*
Arabic: *ward(a)*

Gertrude Stein's "A rose is a rose is a rose" strikes us as pitifully naive when you consider that the genus *Rosa* includes about 100 species of the temperate regions to tropical mountains and thousands of different named cultivars. The genus *Rosa* derives its name from the Latin *rosa*, in turn from the Greek *rhodon*, which, in turn, was derived the original Indo-European root-word, *ward*, still retained in the Arabic.

As implied from such an ancient Indo-European origin of the name, roses have been cultivated since ancient times; we find, for example, the depiction of what may be *R. pulverulenta* M. Bieb. in the House of Frescoes at Knossos dated to around 1450 B.C.E. Roses have enthralled humans for their beauty of form and scent down through the ages, and today we use rose petals for perfumes, cosmetics, and even salads, while the fruits, known as hips, are high in vitamin C with a tomato-like taste. Roses have long symbolized romance, and we find special pleasure and meaning in being able to grow, touch, and inhale the fragrance of the same rose that grandmother grew in West Virginia or Napoleon's Josephine grew at Malmaison.

The choice of a rose cultivar for its beauty and usefulness is an individual choice, but the nursery's methods of producing roses should be an important consideration as well. Roses sold today in North America and Europe are usually budded upon one of three different rootstocks, *R. canina*, *R. multiflora* Thunb., or 'Dr. Huey', but some companies sell plants grown on their own roots. There are advantages and disadvantages to both methods. Generally, most heritage roses perform better with their own roots, but modern hybrids such as teas and floribundas, whose own roots tend to be weak, do better grafted to a more vigorous rootstock.

Some own-root roses often produce shoots from their roots, especially if they have *R. gallica* ancestry; these suckers can be as troublesome as spreading mints and as difficult to manage. 'Dr. Huey' rootstock is fine for the sandy, alkaline soils of California and Texas, but for the acid soils of the northeastern United States, either *R. canina* or *R. multiflora* is preferred. For Florida and other subtropical areas, *R.* ×*fortuniana* Lindl. is a must as a rootstock because of the combination of heat and nematodes. The choice of the rootstock is almost as important as the grafted scion, and if the commercial company which sells the rose you desire does not give that information in their catalog, write or call them.

Also look for grading of the budded roses and buy only grade 1 to 1½; these are the top grades awarded to plants with more canes and higher quality. An indication of a really good company is authentication that their budwood and rootstock have been indexed as virus-free. Expect, even with the best of companies, some misidentification, and if the company does not admit fault or refer you to a source for authentication, you may wish to look for another source.

Most roses do best on deep, fertile, moist but well-drained soils with a pH of 5.5 to 6.5; a position that provides full sun and good air circulation helps reduce disease and insects. The choice of species or cultivar (as well as your climate) will dictate spacing. If rooting of the scion is desired, plant the bud union about 2 to 3 inches (5 to 8 cm) below the soil level; otherwise, be sure that the bud union sets above the soil level. Some gardeners prefer fall-planting to give the roots extra time to establish themselves, but we have found that in Zone 7 and north, some winters will be so cold that the fall-planted roses will not survive.

Do not fertilize newly planted roses; wait four to six weeks for the plants to become established. Authorities do not agree on the type of fertilizer or the rate, only that roses are heavy feeders. We recommend yearly feedings of about a cupful of 5-10-5 fertilizer per established rose bush sprinkled in a circle around the base, supplemented with monthly feedings of fish emulsion, manure tea, or other organic sources of nutrients for maximum growth. Robust roses, such as 'Gardenia', which puts out 40-foot canes even on poor soil, require additional fertilizer.

Do not expect typical blossoms of a species or cultivar until the second year after planting. The blooms of the first year are smaller and sparser than are typical.

Many of the heritage roses are easily propagated by cuttings. Those that don't root easily from cuttings, such as the roses with heavy *R. gallica* ancestry, produce suckers, which are easily transplanted. Many people swear on pencil-sized green cuttings taken in the fall, but we have had good success with "heel" cuttings of blooming stalks. Cuttings taken at the time of flowering also guarantee proper labeling. The cleanliness, temperature, and humidity of the rooting chamber are of primary importance; rooting media that suffers from fungi contamination, high temperatures, or low humidity guarantees failure.

To prepare a spring rose cutting, choose a healthy blooming side shoot with at least three good terminal leaves. Rip the side branch off in a quick downward movement, removing some of the tissue of the main stem. Dip the cutting

in rooting hormone and treat as advised in the propagation chapter.

We have found that a well-drained rooting medium of 1 part perlite to 1 part Turface® (clay frit) with clean mason jars and semi-shade work very well for small batches of rose cuttings; for larger volumes of roses, you may want to experiment with mist systems. For budding and other methods of propagation of roses, please see the books and articles cited in the selected references.

Roses have long symbolized romance, and we find special pleasure and meaning in being able to grow, touch, and inhale the fragrance of the same rose that grandmother grew in West Virginia or Napoleon's Josephine grew at Malmaison.

The worst rose pests are thrips, leafhoppers, rose slugs, and Japanese beetles. The first three can be controlled by spraying a dormant oil in early spring when you have twenty-four hours of above-freezing temperatures but before the buds have begun to burst. Japanese beetles can be controlled by strains of *Bacillus thuringiensis* applied to the adjacent lawns. If you use the Japanese beetle traps that have sex attractants and/or rose oil, be sure to place the trap far away from the roses and empty the traps often; placing the traps near the roses will guarantee that your roses are eaten.

Black spot and mildew are the most common diseases, and various claims of success have been made for sprays of baking soda (3 tablespoons per gallon of water) applied with an insecticidal soap (5 tablespoons per gallon water) or summer horticultural oil. Baking soda sprays must be reapplied after each heavy rain. Avoid overhead watering.

Picking rose petals is extremely labor-intensive. Pickers in New Zealand do not exceed 13.2

pounds per hour (6 kg/hr), but the average is 6.6 pounds per hour (3 kg/hr). At 0.09 to 0.18 ounce per flower (2.5 to 5.0 g/flower), this represents 91 to 181 flowers per pound (200 to 400 flowers/kg). A report from New Zealand indicates that *R. damascena* 'Trigintipetala' produced 12.3 pounds (5.6 kg) of flowers per plant during the third flowering season, for a total flower yield of 4.10 tons per acre (9.2 t/ha) at a density of 668 plants per acre (1650 plants/ha).

Either yields in New Zealand are exceptional, their plants are misidentified, or the decimal has been moved because in Delaware we only found 0.57 pounds (0.26 kg) of flowers per plant for authentic 'Trigintipetala' and 0.68 pounds (0.31 kg) of flowers per plant for 'Prof. Émile Perrot'. Typically, after picking, the rose petals are spread over cool concrete floors in the shade, where the rose petals may continue to produce rose scent, until they can be distilled.

The distillation of rose petals is unique in a number of aspects. The essential oil of most herbs can be steam-distilled by passing steam over the leaves, but rose petals "glop together" under steam to form an impenetrable mass. Hence, the best method to distill the essential oil from rose petals is water distillation; the rose petals are placed in a distillation unit, often a copper still, often with salty water, and then boiled. The heating drives off both the steam and the volatile components that are condensed by a cold-water condenser.

The resulting product in most other plants is an oil, but in the case of rose petals, many plant waxes (paraffins) are also distilled, resulting in a waxy, oily product called an "attar" or "otto" (derived from the Arabic 'itr, meaning "perfume" or "essence"). The water contains many water-soluble components, particularly beta-phenylethanol, and this rose water is marketed for use in cosmetics or food. Rose petals may also be extracted with petroleum ether, produc-ing a yellow-colored, waxy concrète. Extraction of the odoriferous principles into ethyl alcohol, leaving behind the yellow pigments and waxes, produces an absolute from concrète.

The typical rose scent is due to a simple water-soluble alcohol, beta-phenylethanol, and three monoterpenic oil-soluble alcohols, geraniol, nerol, and citronellol. The acetate esters of these alcohols are also rose-scented but of a slightly different fragrance. The clove-scented eugenol and methyl eugenol provide spiciness, while ionones give hints of violets. The relative concentrations of these chemicals determine the final odor. The attar may also be characterized by various waxes, such as nonadecane, eicosane, and heneicosane, but these are essentially odorless.

All the following old roses, unfortunately, flower only once, in spring. The fruit of some species, such as *R. canina* and *R. rugosa*, are large and red. These hips, as the fruit is called, softened by the first heavy frost, have a tomato-like taste and are rich in vitamin C (ascorbic acid) and especially good prepared as conserves and jams with cream cheese for tea cakes. Under ideal conditions, rose hips may have 0.5 percent vitamin C. However, vitamin workers have reported asthma-like symptoms induced by inhalation of powdered rose hips.

In our discussion we have included seven basic rose species and ancient hybrids which have utility in the herb garden. Many cultivars, particularly those designated as "heritage" roses, could also be recommended, but remain beyond the scope of this book.

The literature on roses is voluminous: for a survey of this literature, we recommend Keith L. Stock's *Rose Books*. Gerd Krüssmann's encyclopedic *The Complete Book of Roses* provides a general history and guide through the complex evolution of roses. For descriptions and dates of cultivars, Thomas Cairn's *Modern Roses XI* is a good introduction. For color pictures of the species and heritage roses, we recommend, in particular, Peter Beales's *Classic Roses*, Trevor Griffiths's *The Book of Old Roses* and *The Book of Classic Old Roses*, and Roger Phillips and Martyn Rix's *Roses*. Look for books on rose culture in your region, such as Liz Druitt and G. Michael Shoup's *Landscaping with Antique Roses*, which is great for the Deep South.

Rosa alba

rō-zǎ ǎl-bǎ

white rose

The white rose is unknown outside of cultivation and has an unknown pedigree. The white rose has clean, white petals with bluish green foliage and a wonderful old-rose scent; it is typified by a Linnaean specimen with nine petals. This is var. *alba*, sometimes incorrectly designated as 'Semi-Plena'; it may bear up to twelve petals. *Rosa alba* var. *alba* has been called the "York" rose because it was chosen by Edward IV (reigned 1461–1470) as a symbol of the House of York. Another cultivar is 'Suaveolens', the white rose of perfumers since before 1899, with twelve to sixteen petals. 'Suaveolens' is typically used as a windbreak for the damask rose fields in Bulgaria, and the petals are also harvested for the commercial attar. 'Maxima', with forty-four to fifty-one petals, was the rose of the Jacobites, chosen by the supporters of the House of Stuart after James II lost his throne in 1688. 'Maxima' predates 1400 and was often pictured in fifteenth-century paintings.

Important chemistry: The attars of 'Suaveolens' and 'Maxima' are very similar, with 32 to 34 percent geraniol and 18 percent nerol.

Rosa canina

rō-zǎ kǎ-nī-nǎ

dog rose

The dog rose or dog hip is typically used as a rootstock for grafting hybrids, particularly by nurseries in England, and it is frequently naturalized in North America. This is a large shrub to 8 feet (2.4 m). The flowers are single and pink; the hips (fruits) are orange-red, large, tasty, and high in vitamin C. The seeds yield an oil rich in *trans*-retanoic acid and are potentially useful for cosmetics.

Rosa centifolia

rō-zǎ sěn-tǐ-fō-lē-ǎ

cabbage rose

> **French:** *rose de Mai, rose pâle, rose centfeuilles, rose de Provins*

German: *Zentifolien-Rose, Centifolien-Rose, Provence Rose*
Dutch: *centifolia roos, Provence roos*
Italian: *rosa centofoglie*
Spanish: *rosa centifolia, rosa de cien hojas, rosa común*

Rosa centifolia 'Crested Moss'

Cabbage rose may date from ancient times, but it definitely appeared in the form 'Maxima' from Dutch nurseries in the sixteenth century. 'Maxima' is now difficult to locate, and some modern nurseries pawn off other cultivars that do not match the 'Maxima' pictured in early Dutch paintings. The true 'Maxima' looks like a small, pink cabbage, as the name implies. While desirable for form, color, and texture, true cabbage roses tend to be rather weak plants.

Rosa centifolia, translated as the hundred-leaved (petaled) rose, gave rise to many cultivars in Dutch and French nurseries. Some nurseries still offer 'Bullata' (c. 1801), the cabbage-leaved cabbage rose, with red-tinged leaves that are crinkled like those of a cabbage.

The cabbage rose was particularly noted for sporting in the past to the moss roses; these roses have a distinctive pine-scented mossiness on the flower stem, hypanthium, and sepals. The most distinctive early moss is 'Crested Moss' ('Chapeau de Napoléon', 1827). These cultivars also have that full, cabbagey form and old-rose scent typical of the true cabbage rose in addition to the moss.

The rose water of *R. centifolia* is listed as GRAS at 100 ppm. Rose oil from Morocco, reputedly *R. centifolia*, was found to have anti-conflict effects from the content of beta-phenylethanol and citronellol.

Important chemistry: The attar of 'Crested Moss' petals is dominated by 34 percent geraniol and 18 percent nerol. Oil from Morocco, supposedly *R. centifolia*, has 34 percent citronellol, 15 percent nonadecane, and 14 percent geraniol.

Rosa damascena

rō-zå dăm-å-sē-nå

summer damask rose

French: *rose de Damas*
German: *Damaszener Rose*
Dutch: *damast roos*
Spanish: *rosa damascena*

The scientific name of *R. damascena*, the summer damask rose, was first published by Jean Herrmann in his *Dissertatio Inauguralis Botanico-Medica de Rosa* in 1762. However, Herrmann's rose is not the damask rose we know, but an unidentified hybrid. Six years after Herrmann's description was published, Philip Miller published *R. damascena* for the rose that we grow today. Because Herrmann's prior use of this name takes precedence under the International Code of Botanical Nomenclature, the correct name of today's damask rose is actually unknown, but this is only one of many instances of confusion concerning the correct identity of roses. We use *R. damascena* here simply because no other name is currently available and generally understood. The damask rose may be derived from hybridization of *R. moschata* Herrm., *R. gallica*, and *R. fedtschenkoana* Regel, but futher studies are need to confirm this.

The rose commercially cultivated in the Kazanlik Valley of Bulgaria is usually listed in rose books as 'Trigintipetala', a name first published by G. Dieck in 1889. This cultivar has become thoroughly confused in the nursery trade with 'Prof. Émile Perrot', which was gathered from commercial fields in Iran and introduced by the rosarian Turbat in 1931. 'Prof. Émile Perrot' is the cultivar offered as 'Trigintipetala' by American, Canadian, and British nurseries; one leading American heritage-rose nursery even has the audacity to offer 'Alika' of 1906 as 'Trigintipetala'. A rose similar to 'Trigintipetala' is 'Gloire de Guilan', which was gathered from commercial fields in the Caspian provinces of Iran by Nancy Lindsay and introduced by Hilling, a British rose nursery, in 1949. All these damask roses bear double flowers, usually pink, with typical damask scent.

'York and Lancaster' ('Versicolor', 'Variegata') is called the Tudor rose and supposedly originated about the time Henry VII ascended the throne in 1485; this story may be apocryphal because the rose can be dated with certainty only to the description of Clusius in 1601.

Rosa damascena

The petals are usually white but sometimes streaked light pink, thereby uniting in a floral emblem the Houses of York and Lancaster (see *R. alba* var. *alba*, earlier, and *R. gallica* 'Officinalis', to come; also Shakespeare's *King Henry VI*, part 1, act 2, scene 4, which explains the connection of the red and the white roses with the dispute: in this scene, English noblemen gathered in London discuss whose claim to the throne they will support).

The attar of *R. damascena* is listed as GRAS at 0.01 to 15 ppm. The essential oil is antibacterial. The tea made from the petals is rich in antioxidants.

Important chemistry: The commercial Bulgarian attar is dominated by 33 to 36 percent citronellol, 16 to 26 percent geraniol, and 5 to 14 percent nonadecane. Iranian oil is rich in 15 to 47 percent citronellol, 0 to 40 percent nonadecane, 0 to 19 percent docosane, 0 to 19 percent disiloxane, 0 to 18 percent geraniol, 0 to 18 percent heneicosane. Indian oil is rich in 15 to 36 percent geraniol, 12 to 36 percent citronellol, and trace to 25 percent nonadecane. Chinese oil is rich in 31 to 44 percent citronellol, 16 to 22 percent geraniol, and 2 to 17 percent nonadecane. Gülbirlik rose oil from Turkey has 31 to 44 percent citronellol, 8 to 15 percent nonadecane, and 9 to 14 percent geraniol. Turkish absolute is rich in 50 to 86 percent beta-phenylethanol. The attar of 'York and Lancaster' is dominated by 25 percent geranyl acetate plus citronellol, 17 percent geraniol, and 11 percent heneicosane. The attar of 'Trigintipetala' is dominated by 19 percent nonadecane, 15 percent geranyl acetate plus citronellol, 14 percent geraniol, and 11 percent heneicosane. The attar of 'Prof. Émile Perrot' is dominated by 21 percent geraniol, 19 percent geranyl acetate plus citronellol, and 13 percent nonadecane. The attar of 'Gloire de Guilan' is dominated by 33 percent geraniol and 12 percent nonadecane.

Rosa gallica
rō-zå gă-lĭ-kå
French rose

French: *rose rouge*
German: *Gallische Rose*
Dutch: *rode franse roos*
Spanish: *rosa frances*

Rosa gallica 'Officinalis'

The French or Provins rose is usually cultivated as the semidouble, cherry-pink cultivar 'Officinalis', the apothecary's rose. 'Officinalis' dates to about 1240 and was the red rose of the House of Lancaster, chosen by Edmund, Earl of Lancaster, in 1277. 'Officinalis' was the source of rose water as prepared in Provins, France. 'Versicolor' ('Rosamundi'), a striped version of 'Officinalis', has been sometimes ascribed to the "Fayre Rosamonde," the mistress of King Henry II of England, who died about 1176, but this rose can be dated with authority only to the description by L'Obel in 1581.

Rosa gallica 'Officinalis', sometimes called the "red damask," was often pictured in paintings of the Virgin Mary, along with *R. alba* 'Maxima'. The apothecary's rose is a vigorous shrub to about 2.5 feet (0.8 m), but it sets out suckers like crazy from its own roots. The petals of 'Officinalis' retain their color nicely on drying and are thus good for potpourri. The petals are also reputed to retain their fragrance when dried, but we have not found any scientific proof for this tale.

Important chemistry: The attar of 'Officinalis' is dominated by 17 percent nonadecane, 17 percent geraniol, and 12 percent nerol.

Rosa rubiginosa
rō-zå rŭ-bĭg-ĭ-nō-så
eglantine

The eglantine or sweet briar, known in French as *églantier*, has apple-scented young leaves, a unique characteristic among roses (the incense rose, *R. primula* Boulenger, has sandalwood-scented leaves). It is full of prickles with single, pink roses and grows to about 8 feet (2.4 m) in height. The eglantine was important in the Penzance hybrids, such as 'Lord Penzance' of 1894, with apple-scented young leaves and single, coppery pink flowers.

Rosa rugosa
rō-zå rū-gōs-å
rugosa rose

The rugosa or ramanas rose is worth growing, not only for its large, red hips rich in vitamin C, but also because the curly, green foliage of this rose is rarely troubled by mildew or blackspot. The stems are coated with many fine green to brown prickles. Some hybrids of this rose, such as 'Hansa' (1905), have fine, damask rose–like odors besides good form and color. If you are interested in this species and its progeny, we recommend Suzanne Verrier's book *Rosa Rugosa*. Aqueous and ethanol extracts of dried ramanas rose flowers have been shown to have HIV-1 reverse transcriptase inhibitory activity.

Important chemistry: The attar of rugosa rose petals is dominated by 31 to 38 percent beta-phenylethanol, trace to 29 percent citronellol, 0 to 19 percent geranyl formate, trace to 14 percent nerol, and 6 to 14 percent geraniol.

Botanical Description

Note: A key has been omitted for two reasons. First, a key would not be useful unless the thousands of cultivars could be included. Secondly, while rose books continue to designate cultivars, such as 'Mme. Hardy', as pure species, most roses are hybrids ('Mme. Hardy' is probably a damask × cabbage hybrid, not a pure damask rose).

R. alba L., Sp. pl. 492. 1753.
Native country: The white rose is not known outside cultivation.
General habit: The white rose is a deciduous shrub to 2 m.
Leaves: Leaves are divided into five leaflets, 2 to 6 cm long, broad-elliptic or egg-shaped, toothed, hairy beneath.

Flowers: Flowers are semidouble to double, white.
Fruits/seeds: Fruit is oblong-egg-shaped, red.

R. canina L., Sp. pl. 491. 1753.
Native country: The dog rose is native to Europe.
General habit: The dog rose is a deciduous shrub with green stems to 2.4 m.
Leaves: Leaves are divided into five to seven leaflets, 15 to 40 × 12 to 20 mm, egg-shaped or ellipse-shaped, toothed or doubly toothed, smooth and lacking in glands, dark to blue-green, shining or dull above.
Flowers: Flowers have 15 to 25 mm petals, pink to white.
Fruits/seeds: Fruit is globose, ovoid, or ellipse-shaped, smooth, red.

R. centifolia L., Sp. pl. 491. 1753.
Native country: The cabbage rose is not known outside cultivation.
General habit: The cabbage rose is a deciduous shrub to 2 m.
Leaves: Leaves are divided into five leaflets, hairy on both sides or only beneath, toothed.
Flowers: Flowers are very double, pink.
Fruits/seeds: Fruit is ellipsoid to almost globose.

R. damascena Mill., Gard. Dict. ed. 8. 1768.
Native country: The damask rose is not known outside cultivation.
General habit: The damask rose is a deciduous shrub to 2 m with numerous stout prickles.
Leaves: Leaves are divided into five to seven leaflets, egg-shaped to oblong-egg-shaped, toothed, smooth above, more or less hairy beneath.
Flowers: Flowers are double, pink.
Fruits/seeds: Fruit is almost egg-shaped, hairy, red.

R. gallica L., Sp. pl. 492. 1753.

Native country: The French rose is native to southern and central Europe.

General habit: The French rose is a deciduous shrub, 0.4 to 0.8 m high, forming large patches.

Leaves: Leaves are divided into three to seven leaflets, 20 to 60 × 18 to 30 mm, leathery, almost globe-shaped to egg-shaped, rounded at the apex, usually doubly toothed, dull bluish green and smooth above, paler, hairy, and glandular below.

Flowers: Solitary flowers, rarely two to four per stalk, are 6 to 9 cm in diameter, deep pink.

Fruits/seeds: Fruit is globose to spindle-shaped, densely glandular hairy, bright red.

R. rubiginosa L., Mant. pl. 2:564. 1771 (*R. eglanteria* L.).

Native country: The eglantine is native to most of Europe.

General habit: The eglantine is a deciduous shrub to 3 m.

Leaves: Leaves are divided into five to seven leaflets, 10 to 25 × 8 to 15 mm, almost orbicular to egg-shaped, doubly toothed, smooth or hairy above, usually hairy and more or less glandular beneath.

Flowers: Flower has 8 to 15 mm petals, deep pink.

Fruits/seeds: Fruit is almost globe-shaped, ovoid, or ellipse-shaped, smooth or glandular hairy, bright red.

R. rugosa Thunb., Fl. jap. 213. 1784.

Native country: The rugosa rose is native to China and Japan.

General habit: The rugosa rose is a deciduous shrub to 2 m, densely bristly and prickly.

Leaves: Leaves are divided into five to nine leaflets, 2 to 5 cm long, slightly waxy, wrinkled, lustrous, dark green, smooth above, hairy beneath.

Flowers: Flowers are single, cherry-pink to purple to white.

Fruits/seeds: Fruit is depressed globe-shaped, smooth, brick-red.

Rosmarinus officinalis

rŏs-må-rī-nŭs ŏ-fĭs-ĭ-nā-lĭs
rosemary

Family: Lamiaceae (Labiatae)

Growth form: shrub to 6 feet (2 m)

Hardiness: routinely hardy to North Carolina (Zone 8), but some cultivars hardy to New Jersey, Delaware, and Maryland (Zone 7)

Light: full sun

Water: moist but not wet; can withstand mild drought

Soil: well drained, sandy or gravelly, pH 4.5 to 8.7, average 6.8

Propagation: cuttings easiest and necessary for named cultivars, otherwise seeds in spring, 25,000 seeds per ounce (882/g)

Culinary use: lamb, venison, poultry, and other dishes

Craft use: wreaths, potpourri, scents

Landscape use: groundcover to tall shrubs

French: *romarin*
German: *Rosmarin*
Dutch: *rozemarijn*
Italian: *ramerino*
Spanish: *romero, rosmarino*
Portuguese: *alecrim*
Swedish: *rosmarin*
Russian: *rozmarin*
Chinese: *mi-tieh-hsiang*
Japanese: *mannenrō*
Arabic: *iklil al-ajbal*

Rosemary symbolizes remembrance, and for good reason. After working with rosemary plants for any length of time or even brushing against them, its piney fragrance clings with special fondness to wool, hair, and human skin. Its fragrance invokes images of fresh-roasted lamb on skewers of rosemary branches prepared over a campfire on a gravelly beach with the Mediterranean Sea breaking in the background.

Rosmarinus species are often found clinging to sea-cliffs; the generic name is aptly derived from the Latin *ros*, "dew" ("spray"), and *marinus*, "sea." The specific epithet, *officinalis*, means "of the shops," or medicinal. The narrow leaves are tightly arranged along branches, giving it, along with the piney scent, the general appearance of a conifer. The brilliant blue flowers, which can appear almost any time of the year, depending upon the cultivar, supposedly assumed their color when the Virgin Mary draped her cloak to dry upon the plant on her flight into Egypt.

Rosmarinus officinalis is the chief species cultivated, but this genus also includes two other species, *R. eriocalyx* Jord. & Fourr. and *R. tomentosus* Huber-Morat & Maire. Both are restricted to southeastern Spain and northwestern Africa. The upright rosemarys are hardy to Zone 8, but 'Arp' and 'Madalene Hill' have withstood winters in Zone 6. The prostrate rosemarys are mar-ginally hardy to Zone 8 but more reliably survive Zone 9 winters.

Rosemary is difficult to grow from seed because of low viability and slow growth, and of course named cultivars do not remain true to type when seed-grown. Cuttings root readily in water, a variety of aggregates, or a combination of sphagnum peat and perlite; a rooting hormone such as 0.8 percent indole butyric acid (IBA) or 5,000 ppm naphthalene acetic acid (NAA) in talc may encourage a more vigorous root structure but does not speed the rooting process. For maximum growth, rosemary does well in a perlite or soilless mix composed of about 50 percent perlite and 50 percent coarse sphagnum peat moss with some lime and trace elements. For greenhouse production of rosemary, Paul Westervelt and Holly Scoggins at Virginia Tech found that a peat medium (Fafard 3B) produced the largest plants.

Rosemary in pots is especially sensitive to overwatering; the soil must dry slightly between waterings, but not to the point that the plant wilts. Overwatered rosemary develops browned leaf tips, an indication that some roots

Rosmarinus officinalis

may have begun to rot. Clay pots will allow the soil to dry faster, a property that lessens root-rot problems during periods of low light in winter. Pot-grown plants may become root-bound quickly (yellowing of lower leaves at the base of the plant is an early warning of the stress from this condition) and should be repotted during periods of rapid growth—spring and summer in most parts of North America.

The ratios of the nitrogen and potassium, in particular, can influence the oil, depending upon the cultivar. In pots of soilless mix, fertilize weekly with a water-soluble 20-5-20 formula in combination with a 10-5-10 controlled-release fertilizer. Plants in the garden may be fertilized once in the season with a granular 5-10-5 or 10-10-10 during active growth.

Rosemary grows rapidly in the heat of summer and may be pruned severely to shape the plants or to keep them from interfering with nearby herbs. Pruning is also a good method of maintaining air flow around and through rosemary plants, an important cultural feature that helps prevent foliar diseases that cause wilts.

Rosemary is subject to attacks from spider mites, mealybugs, whiteflies, and thrips. Web (aerial) blight from *Rhizoctonia solani* produces twig and branch blight on the interior of the plant, so be sure to maintain good air circulation. A stem rot, caused by *Sclerotinia sclerotiorum*, has been reported. A "stem knot" is quite common; the cause is unknown but it resembles bacterial infections caused by *Pseudomonas*, *Agrobacterium*, and *Xanthomonas* species, bacterial stem galls that are difficult to control because they are essentially systemic, growing from the inside out. This infection spreads through dirty pruning clippers and nearby plants, and newly propagated cuttings may carry it. Overhead watering and exceedingly damp and rainy summers are often associated with the arrival of rosemary stem gall. Organic

mulches near the base of the plant often hold water and moisture near low-lying foliage, which provides a home and pathways for water-borne fungi and bacteria. Mulches of pea gravel or sand, which dry rapidly and radiate drying heat into the interior of dense rosemary plants, help to lessen diseases.

France, Spain, Portugal, the former Yugoslavia, and California supply most of the rosemary consumed in the United States, while Spain and France supply most of the rosemary oil.

Rosemary has many varieties of growth pattern, floral color, and scent. Both upright and prostrate growth patterns are available. Floral color varies from intense blue-violet to lavender to pink to white. Scent varies from robust and piney to those with subtle, flowery, spicy undertones. While some cultivars are grown merely for their landscape value, all can be used in cooking and each imparts its own individual flavor. The distinguishing characteristics of some of the cultivars are listed here (infraspecific taxonomy is still uncertain because of a good, recent revision of the genus and is omitted).

Cultivar: 'Albus'
Synonyms: 'Albiflorus', 'White Flower'
Origin: This general name has been applied to a variety of different cultivars, ranging from pure white to pale blue and does not denote a specific clone (see, for example, 'Huntington Blue', 'Logee White', and 'Nancy Howard').

Cultivar: 'Alderley'
Origin: France, by Alvilde Lees-Milne in 1960s; selected at Alderley Grange, Gloucestershire, England
Foliage/growth: small sprawling shrub with some pendant stems reaching to the ground and arching upward
Flowers: pale sky-blue

Cultivar: 'Alida Hyde'
Synonyms: 'Prostrate #4'
Origin: Cyrus Hyde, Port Murray, New Jersey
Foliage/growth: green, prostrate
Flowers: medium blue-violet
Essential oil: 29 percent alpha-pinene, 16 percent 1,8-cineole (eucalyptus-pine)

Cultivar: 'Argenteus'
Foliage/growth: edged with white, upright
Flowers: blue-violet
Comments: noted as early as 1654, the silver-striped rosemary has apparently been lost to cultivation, but Silver Spires™ is another, recent mutation

Cultivar: 'Arp'
Origin: Arp, Texas; selected by Madalene Hill, Cleveland, Texas, in 1972
Hardiness: Zone 7
Foliage/growth: upright
Flowers: pale blue-violet
Essential oil: 42 percent 1,8-cineole, 19 percent camphor, 10 percent alpha-pinene (pine-camphor-eucalyptus)
Comments: very hardy

Rosmarinus officinalis 'Arp'

Cultivar: 'Athens Blue Spires'
Origin: University of Georgia, Athens, introduced by Allan Armitage, James Garner, and Jimmy Greer
Foliage/growth: upright
Flowers: light blue

Cultivar: 'Aureus'
Synonyms: 'Gilded', var. *foliis aureis*
Foliage/growth: splashed with yellow, upright
Flowers: pale blue-violet
Comments: variegation of the gilded rosemary, probably of viral origin, shows up only in certain climates and weather

Cultivar: 'Benenden Blue'
Synonyms: var. *angustifolius*, var. *angustissimus*, 'Collingwood Ingram', 'Ingrami'
Origin: 1930 Bonifacio, Corsica; selected by Collingwood Ingram, Benenden, Kent, England, and introduced into California by Elizabeth de Forest
Foliage/growth: narrow green, upright
Flowers: medium blue-violet
Essential oil: 51 percent alpha-pinene (pine)
Comments: initially erect branches soon arch and flow sideways

Cultivar: 'Blue Boy'
Origin: Huntington Botanical Gardens, San Marino, California
Foliage/growth: narrow green, sprawling
Flowers: pale blue-violet
Comments: unique small leaves make it a beautiful plant for pots and bonsai

Cultivar: 'Blue Lady'
Origin: 'Prostratus' × 'Majorca' by Sandy Mush Herb Nursery, Leicester, North Carolina
Foliage/growth: narrow green, flowing
Flowers: blue-violet

Cultivar: 'Blue Spire'
Origin: England
Foliage/growth: green, columnar
Flowers: medium blue-violet
Essential oil: 44 percent alpha-pinene, 30 percent 1,8-cineole (eucalyptus-pine)

Cultivar: 'Bolham Blue'
Origin: found and selected by Mrs. Lena Hickson, Bolham, Devon
Foliage: glossy, yellow-green, lower surface pale gray-green
Flowers: calyx dark purple tinged green, corollas blue-purple, blotched with dark purple and a paler center

Cultivar: 'Calabriensis'
Origin: England

Cultivar: 'Capercaillie'
Origin: Scotland
Foliage/growth: pale, vibrant green, bushy
Flowers: bright blue

Cultivar: 'Capri'
Foliage/growth: prostrate

Cultivar: 'Cascade'
Foliage/growth: prostrate

Cultivar: 'Corsican Blue'
Synonyms: *R. corsicus*
Origin: originally from Corsica and introduced by Jackmans, Woking, Surrey, England
Foliage/growth: narrow, glossy dark green, upright
Flowers: lobelia blue

Cultivar: 'Dancing Waters'
Origin: 'Majorca' × 'Prostratus' by Sandy Mush Herb Nursery, Leicester, North Carolina

Foliage/growth: dark green, sprawling
Flowers: medium blue-violet

Cultivar: 'Dark Logee Blue'
Origin: Country Greenhouses, Danielson, Connecticut
Foliage/growth: green, upright
Flowers: medium blue-violet

Cultivar: 'Duplici'
Flowers: double blue
Comments: the double-flowered rosemary, listed by Parkinson in 1629, has been lost to cultivation

Cultivar: 'Dutch Mill'
Origin: Barbara Remington, Forest Grove, Oregon
Hardiness: Zone 7?
Foliage/growth: green, upright
Flowers: pale blue-violet
Essential oil: 32 percent alpha-pinene, 30 percent 1,8-cineole (eucalyptus-pine)

Cultivar: 'Fota Blue'
Origin: Fota Island, Ireland
Foliage/growth: short, rather wide leaves, predominantly prostrate
Flowers: dark blue

Cultivar: 'Gorizia'
Origin: Italy; introduced by Thomas DeBaggio, Arlington, Virginia
Foliage/growth: gray-green, upright
Flowers: lobelia blue
Essential oil: 21 percent bornyl acetate, 19 percent camphor, 15 percent borneol (camphor-rosemary)
Comments: good sturdy growth

Cultivar: 'Hawaii'
Foliage/growth: upright
Flowers: blue

Cultivar: 'Herbal Gem'
Foliage/growth: upright

Cultivar: 'Herb Cottage'
Synonyms: 'Foresteri'
Origin: Cathedral Herb Garden, Washington, D.C.
Foliage/growth: green, upright
Flowers: pale blue-violet
Essential oil: 53 percent alpha-pinene, 21 percent 1,8-cineole (eucalyptus-pine)

Cultivar: 'Holly Hyde'
Synonyms: 'Yellow Green Leaf'
Origin: Cyrus Hyde, Port Murray, New Jersey
Foliage/growth: yellow-green, prostrate
Flowers: medium blue-violet
Essential oil: 28 percent 1,8-cineole, 17 percent camphor, 14 percent alpha-pinene (pine-camphor-eucalyptus)

Cultivar: 'Howe'
Origin: Keith Howe, Country Gardens, Seattle, Washington
Hardiness: Zone 7?
Foliage/growth: green, upright
Flowers: blue-violet

Cultivar: 'Huntington Blue'
Synonyms: 'Alba'
Origin: Huntington Botanical Garden, San Marino, California
Foliage/growth: green, upright
Flowers: very pale blue-violet

Cultivar: 'Israeli Commercial'
Origin: Israel
Hardiness: Zone 8

Foliage/growth: large leaves
Flowers: very pale blue, infrequent
Comments: withstands shipping and storage better than most cultivars; stems produce aerial roots readily

Cultivar: 'Joyce DeBaggio'
Synonyms: 'Golden Rain'
Origin: Thomas DeBaggio, Arlington, Virginia
Foliage/growth: edged in gold, upright
Flowers: pale blue-violet
Essential oil: 19 percent camphor
Comments: good stable variegation; unique camphoraceous odor; similar to 'Genges Gold' from New Zealand

Rosmarinus officinalis 'Joyce DeBaggio'

Cultivar: 'Kent Taylor'
Origin: sport of 'Majorca', named after Kent Taylor of Taylor's Herb Farm in Pasadena, California
Foliage/growth: green, prostrate
Flowers: dark blue
Comments: rare in cultivation

Cultivar: 'Lady in White'
Foliage/growth: delicate, dark green, yellow-tinged young shoots
Flowers: pure white

Cultivar: 'Light Logee Blue'
Synonyms: 'Pale Blue'
Origin: Country Greenhouses, Danielson, Connecticut
Foliage/growth: green, upright
Flowers: medium blue-violet in center, light blue violet on lower lips
Essential oil: 58 percent alpha-pinene, 19 percent 1,8-cineole (eucalyptus-pine)

Cultivar: 'Lockwood de Forest'
Synonyms: sold under various aliases, such as 'Prostratus' or 'Prostrate #5'
Origin: probably selfed selection of 'Prostratus' mid 1930s by Mrs. Lockwood de Forest, Santa Barbara, California
Foliage/growth: green, sprawling
Flowers: light blue-violet
Essential oil: 27 percent 1,8-cineole, 20 percent alpha-pinene, 15 percent camphor (camphor-pine-eucalyptus)
Comments: the plant usually sold as 'Lockwood de Forest' is 'Prostratus'

Cultivar: 'Logee White'
Synonyms: 'Alba'
Origin: Logee's, Danielson, Connecticut
Foliage/growth: green, upright
Flowers: white
Essential oil: 52 percent alpha-pinene, 19 percent 1,8-cineole (eucalyptus-pine)

Cultivar: 'Lottie DeBaggio'
Origin: Thomas DeBaggio, Arlington, Virginia
Hardiness: Zone 8, marginal in Zone 7
Foliage/growth: green, upright
Flowers: very pale blue-violet

Cultivar: 'Madalene Hill'
Synonyms: 'Hill Hardy'
Origin: introduced by Thomas DeBaggio, Arlington, Virginia
Hardiness: Zone 7
Foliage/growth: green, upright
Flowers: pale blue-violet
Comments: very hardy

Cultivar: 'Majorca'
Synonyms: 'Collingwood Ingram', 'Rex #4', 'Wood'
Origin: Majorca
Foliage/growth: green, sprawling-upright
Flowers: medium blue-violet
Essential oil: 32 percent alpha-pinene, 11 percent camphor, 11 percent bornyl acetate, 10 percent 1,8-cineole (eucalyptus-rosemary-camphor-pine)
Comments: flowers of intense bluebird blue, the lower perianth segments with a deeper blotch

Cultivar: 'Majorca Pink'
Synonyms: *R. prostrata rosea*, 'Roseus'
Foliage/growth: pale green, sprawling
Flowers: amethyst-violet
Essential oil: 57 percent camphor
Comments: unique growth form and camphoraceous odor, but floral color more lavender than pink

Cultivar: 'McConnell's Blue'
Synonyms: 'Mrs. McConnell'
Origin: Ireland
Hardiness: Zone 8
Foliage/growth: leaves short and rather wide; low growing, rather sprawling habit with erect laterals
Flowers: medium blue

Cultivar: 'Mercer Hubbard'
Origin: Mercer Hubbard, Pittsboro, North Carolina
Hardiness: Zone 7?
Foliage/growth: green, sprawling
Flowers: blue-violet

Cultivar: 'Miss Jessopp's Upright'
Synonyms: 'Miss Jessup's Upright' (typographical error), 'Miss Jessopp's Variety'
Origin: Euphemia Jessopp via E. A. Bowles, England
Foliage/growth: green, columnar
Flowers: medium blue-violet
Essential oil: 53 percent alpha-pinene, 14 percent 1,8-cineole (eucalyptus-pine)
Comments: 'Corsicus', 'Fastigiatus', and 'Trusty' are probably not sufficiently different to warrant separate names; 'Miss Jessopp's Upright' has been applied to many different upright selections

Cultivar: 'Mrs. Reed's Dark Blue'
Origin: Joanna Reed, Malvern, Pennsylvania
Foliage/growth: green, upright
Flowers: medium blue-violet
Comments: good intense floral color

Cultivar: 'Mt. Vernon'
Origin: Mt. Vernon, Virginia
Foliage/growth: green, upright
Flowers: medium blue-violet
Comments: no special reason to grow this other than its origin

Cultivar: 'Nancy Howard'
Synonyms: 'Alba Heavy Leaf'
Origin: Cyrus Hyde, Port Murray, New Jersey
Hardiness: marginal in Zone 7
Foliage/growth: green, upright
Flowers: white

Essential oil: 46 percent alpha-pinene, 23 percent 1,8-cineole (eucalyptus-pine)
Comments: good semi-hardy white rosemary

Cultivar: 'Pinkie'
Origin: Huntington Botanical Garden, San Marino, California
Foliage/growth: yellow-green, sprawling
Flowers: pink-lavender
Comments: probably closest to pink flowers in rosemary

Cultivar: 'Portuguese Pink'
Origin: Portugal via Judy Kehs, Cricket Hill Herb Farm, Rowley, Massachusetts
Flowers: pink

Cultivar: 'Portuguese Red'
Origin: Portugal via Judy Kehs, Cricket Hill Herb Farm, Rowley, Massachusetts
Flowers: dark pink

Cultivar: 'Primley Blue'
Synonyms: 'Frimley Blue' (typographical error)
Origin: Paignton Zoo, Devon, England
Foliage/growth: narrow olive-green, upright
Flowers: China blue

Cultivar: 'Prostratus'
Synonyms: 'Dwarf Prostrate', 'Golden Prostrate', 'Huntington Carpet', 'Kenneth Prostrate', 'Prostrate #3', 'Santa Barbara' (offered as separate clones, all these are seemingly identical)
Foliage/growth: green, prostrate
Flowers: medium blue-violet
Essential oil: 25 percent 1,8-cineole, 23 percent alpha-pinene, 13 percent camphor (camphor-pine-eucalyptus)
Comments: plant sometimes offered under this name is actually 'Lockwood de Forest', and 'Prostratus' is sometimes sold as 'Lock-

wood de Forest'; 'Prostratus' has, unfortunately, been applied by nurserymen to any prostrate rosemary

Cultivar: 'Pyramidalis'
Synonyms: 'Robinson's Variety'
Origin: W. Robinson, Gravetye Manor, England
Foliage/growth: narrow green, columnar
Comments: very similar to 'Miss Jessopp's Upright' and possibly not sufficiently different to warrant a separate cultivar name

Cultivar: 'Rampant Boule'
Origin: France
Foliage/growth: dense, ground-hugging

Cultivar: 'Renzels'
Synonyms: Irene™
Origin: spontaneous seedling discovered in a California garden by Philip Johnson; named for Princess Irene (a.k.a. Renzels), Johnson's black labrador
Foliage/growth: prostrate
Flowers: pale blue
Comments: U.S. PP124

Cultivar: 'Rexford'
Origin: Rexford Talbot, Williamsburg, Virginia
Foliage/growth: upright
Flowers: blue

Cultivar: 'Roman Vivace'
Synonyms: 'Roman Vicace' (typographical error)
Foliage/growth: green, upright
Flowers: wisteria blue
Essential oil: 27 percent camphor, 21 percent alpha-pinene, 14 percent camphene, 13 percent 1,8-cineole (eucalyptus-pine-camphor)

Cultivar: 'Russian River'
Origin: Janis Teas, Teas Herbs and Orchids, Magnolia, Texas
Foliage/growth: upright

Cultivar: 'Salem'
Origin: originally from Old Salem, North Carolina; introduced by Sandy Mush Herb Nursery, Leicester, North Carolina
Hardiness: marginal in Zone 7
Foliage/growth: green, upright
Flowers: blue-violet

Cultivar: 'Sarah's White'
Origin: Bernard Sparkes, Wye College, Kent, England
Flowers: white

Cultivar: 'Severn Sea'
Synonyms: 'Seven Seas' (typographical error)
Origin: raised by Norman Hadden from a seedling, selected and obtained from Herbert Whitley, growing at Paignton Zoo, Devon, England, in the 1950s
Hardiness: marginal in Zone 8
Foliage/growth: green, upright
Flowers: medium blue-violet
Essential oil: 36 percent 1,8-cineole, 26 percent alpha-pinene (pine-eucalyptus)
Comments: branches arch and dip when they reach 2 to 3 feet (61 to 91 cm)

Cultivar: 'Shady Acres'
Origin: Theresa Mieseler, Shady Acres Herb Farm, Chaska, Minnesota
Foliage/growth: dark green, upright
Flowers: deep blue
Essential oil: 27 percent alpha-pinene, 23 percent 1,8-cineole, 7 percent verbenone (pine-eucalyptus)

Cultivar: 'Sheila Dore'
Origin: South Wight Council, Ventnor Botanic Garden, England
Foliage/growth: green, prostrate
Flowers: blue
Comments: may not remain in cultivation

Cultivar: 'Shimmering Stars'
Origin: 'Prostratus' × 'Majorca Pink' by Sandy Mush Herb Nursery, Leicester, North Carolina
Foliage/growth: broad green, sprawling
Flowers: pink buds opening to pale blue-violet

Cultivar: 'Sissinghurst Blue'
Synonyms: 'Brevifolia'
Origin: chance seedling found in 1958 at Sissinghurst Castle, Cranbrook, Kent, England
Foliage/growth: green, upright
Flowers: blue-violet

Cultivar: 'Sudbury Blue'
Foliage/growth: dense blue-green, upright
Flowers: speckled blue

Cultivar: 'Talbot Blue'
Origin: Talbot Manor, Suffolk, England
Foliage/growth: upright
Flowers: blue

Cultivar: 'Taylor's Blue'
Synonyms: 'False Tuscan Blue'
Origin: Taylor's Herb Gardens, Vista, California
Foliage/growth: green, prostrate
Flowers: medium blue-violet
Essential oil: 31 percent 1,8-cineole, 28 percent alpha-pinene, 14 percent beta-thujone plus 1-octen-3-ol (sage-pine-eucalyptus)
Comments: unique sage-like odor

Cultivar: 'Topsy'
Origin: Betty Rollins, Berkeley, California
Foliage/growth: green, sprawling
Flowers: medium blue-violet

Cultivar: 'Tuscan Blue'
Synonyms: 'Erectus'
Origin: prior to 1948 from Tuscany, Italy, by W. Arnold-Forster, Cornwall, England
Foliage/growth: broad green, columnar
Flowers: dark blue-violet
Essential oil: 45 percent alpha-pinene, 15 percent 1,8-cineole (eucalyptus-pine)

Cultivar: 'Very Oily'
Origin: Huntington Botanical Gardens, San Marino, California
Hardiness: Zone 7?
Foliage/growth: green, upright
Flowers: medium blue-violet
Essential oil: 39 percent alpha-pinene, 31 percent 1,8-cineole (eucalyptus-pine)

Cultivar: 'Well Sweep'
Synonyms: 'Alba Thin Leaf'
Origin: Cyrus Hyde, Port Murray, New Jersey
Foliage/growth: narrow green, upright
Flowers: pale blue-violet

Cultivar: 'Well Sweep Golden'
Synonyms: 'Golden'
Origin: Cyrus Hyde, Port Murray, New Jersey
Foliage/growth: yellow-green, maturing to green, upright
Flowers: pale blue-violet
Essential oil: 46 percent alpha-pinene, 12 percent myrcene, 11 percent 1,8-cineole (eucalyptus-pine)

Cultivar: 'Wolros'
Synonyms: Silver Spires™

Origin: discovered in 1986 by Christine Wolters, United Kingdom
Foliage/growth: pale green margined with white
Flowers: blue
Comments: Silver Spires™ is the trademark name at the U.K. Patent Office

Other cultivars merely mentioned in the literature with little qualifying characteristics are 'Blue Gem', 'Blue Spears', 'Corsicus Prostratus', 'Heavenly Blue', 'Maggie's Choice', 'Marshall Street', 'Robustifolius', 'Sawyer's Selection', 'Tough Stuff', and 'Wonderful'. The cultivars of rosemary have been selected from several botanical varieties and forms. Please remember that a cultivar is a category unto itself and is not subordinate to the botanical taxa. Many cultivars are also hybrids of botanical taxa and thus difficult to fit within any classification scheme. Thus, we may speak of 'Nancy Howard' as being selected from var. *officinalis* f. *albiflorus* but don't bother to cite it as *R. officinalis* var. *officinalis* f. *albiflorus* 'Nancy Howard'.

An evaluation of rosemary cultivars by Daniel Warnock and Charles Voigt at the University of Illinios found that five were especially good for use as Christmas topiaries: 'Athens Blue Spires', 'Herb Cottage', 'Joyce DeBaggio', 'Shady Acres', and 'Taylor's Blue' (a sixth cultivar, listed as 'Rex', is a name that has been applied to more than one cultivar).

Rosemary leaves are GRAS at 380 to 4,098 ppm, while the oil is GRAS at 0.5 to 40 ppm. Rosemary leaves have antioxidant and antimutagenic properties from the content of phenolic diterpenes, particularly carnosic acid, carnosol, epirosmanol, and isorosmanol. These compounds show higher antioxidative activity than the commonly used BHA (butylated hydroxyanisole) and BHT (butylated hydroxytoluene) and have been commercially produced as natural food preservatives for fatty foods, such as potato chips. Luteolin is an antioxidant flavonoid in rosemary leaves.

Rosemary oil has also been demonstrated to be antifungal, antibacterial, and antiviral. It stimulates the production of bile, prevents liver damage, and possesses anti-inflammatory and antimutagenic effects. Researchers have found that the volatile oil of rosemary leaves may be useful in treating diabetes and dementia; the extract has shown an anti-implantation effect in rats. Rosemary oil may also repel aphids and mites.

Aromatherapists who use rosemary oil should be aware that rosemary oil increases locomotor activity, apparently from the content of 1,8-cineole. Aromatherapists should also be aware that rosemary oils vary considerably and there is not a standard rosemary oil, so the physiologic effects from one rosemary oil to another may vary. Rosemary oil has also been reported to induce contact dermatitis.

Important chemistry: The oil of commercial rosemary is predominantly composed of trace to 47 percent alpha-pinene, trace to 60 percent camphene, 4 to 60 percent 1,8-cineole, trace to 47 percent camphor, trace to 23 percent bornyl acetate, and trace to 18 percent borneol. Dried rosemary leaves have 2 to 4 percent carnosic acid and 0.2 to 0.4 percent carnosol. Cultivars vary in content of rosmarinic acid, but one of the highest is 'Benenden Blue'.

Botanical Description

R. officinalis L., Sp. pl. 23. 1753.
Native country: Rosemary is native to the Mediterranean region.
General habit: Rosemary is an erect or procumbent shrub to 2 m.
Leaves: Leaves are 15 to 40 × 1.2 to 3.5 mm, linear, leather-textured, with margins rolled

back upon the lower side, bright green and wrinkled above, with a dense wool-like covering of white, matted, tangled hairs of medium length beneath, stalkless.

Flowers: Inflorescence and flower stalk have star-shaped, tangled hairs. Calyx is 3 to 4 mm, green or purplish and sparsely coated with matted, tangled hairs when young, later 5 to 7 mm, almost smooth, and distinctly veined. Flower is pale blue, pink, or white.

Ruta graveolens

rū-tå grå-vē-ō-lĕnz
garden rue

Family: Rutaceae

Growth form: shrubby semi-evergreen perennial to 20 inches (50 cm)

Hardiness: Zone 6

Light: full sun

Water: moist but not wet; can withstand minor drought

Soil: well-drained garden loam, pH 5.5 to 8.2, average 6.7

Propagation: seeds in spring, 16,300 seeds per ounce (575/g)

Culinary use: limited; may be toxic to sensitive individuals

Craft use: none

Landscape use: avoid paths where bare legs can brush against it

---

French: *rue odorante, péganion, rue fétide*

German: *Gartenraute, Raute, Weinkraut, Weinraute, Edelraute*

Dutch: *wijnruit*

Italian: *ruta*

Spanish: *ruda, armaga, arruda*

Chinese: *yün-hsiang-ts'ao*

Arabic: *sadab*

Garden rue is appreciated for its wonderful blue-green leaves with an acrid, orange-like, poppyseed-like scent, but don't touch those leaves on a hot, summer day or you'll "rue the day." Large, watery blisters will develop within the hour and, depending upon your sensitivity and the sunlight, will leave nasty scars. Scientifically, garden rue is called a "photosensitizer" because it requires sunlight to produce skin sensitization.

Garden rue is a semi-evergreen perennial shrublet widespread in sunny, arid areas of southern Europe and North Africa but perhaps

Ruta graveolens

native to the Balkans and the Crimea. This 20-inch (50 cm) high herb has slightly greenish yellow flowers in May to June and unusual sparse leaves coated with a blue wax.

Ruta was the ancient Latin name for rue. The genus *Ruta* includes about seven species of Macronesia and the Mediterranean. Some authors have divided *R. graveolens* into *R. hortensis* Mill. and *R. divaricata* Tenore, but these species are not widely recognized. A variegated form ('Variegata') and a compact blue form ('Blue Mound') are sometimes available.

Southern Europeans, especially country folk, have a decided taste for rue leaves chopped in cheese and in salads. One of the lesser-known decorative and gustatory uses of rue is as a flavoring agent in *grappa*, once a home-brew moonshine of Italian peasants distilled from fermented grape skins left over after the wine pressing; *grappa* has taken on a more sophisticated image as a grape brandy in recent years. After the *grappa* is distilled, a rue stem is placed in a bottle and the grape brandy is poured over it; soon the blue-green rue stem is white. The bleached rue branches dances suggestively in the clear liquid with each movement of the bottle. This *aqua vitae* burns a path down your throat and leaves a slight, lingering, earthy taste of rue.

Solvent extracts of garden rue have been documented to have antifertility activity in rats when added to the diet up to ten days after coitus. The oil is documented to produce hemorrhage effects when taken internally, as well as stomach pain, nausea, vomiting, confusion, convulsions, and death; abortion may also result. The International Fragrance Association recommends that rue oil not be used for applications on areas of skin exposed to sunshine and to limit rue oil to 3.9 percent in a compounded fragrance. Steffen Arctander has advised, in his *Perfume and Flavor Materials of Natural Origin*, to avoid rue oil completely in fragrance and flavor work. Paradoxically, the essential oil of rue is considered GRAS at 1 to 10 ppm, and the Council of Europe has included garden rue oil in the list of flavoring substances temporarily admitted for use. On top of that, Japanese rsearchers have found that an extract of rue stimulates the growth of hair.

Rue is easily grown in well-drained garden loam in full sun. Its fertilizer and cultural requirements are minimal. In the spring, after the first year of growth, prune the stems of rue 6 to 8 inches above the ground. Follow this procedure each spring, and a well-shaped, handsome plant will result. Beware, though: rue can inhibit the growth of nearby plants, and Italian researchers have even isolated potential allelochemicals that could be used as pre-emergent herbicides.

Rue is a magnet for black swallowtail butterflies, which lay their eggs on the plant's leaves; these hatch a colorful yellow, chartreuse, and black caterpillar that may defoliate the plant if the gardener is unaware. Garden rue has an unusual horticultural use as a breeding area for the tiny parasitic wasp *Encarsia formosa*, which serves as a natural control of whiteflies in the greenhouse; Doug Walker at the University of California-Davis noticed that garden rue plants were always infested with whiteflies in his greenhouse. He now uses the plants in his Integrated Pest Management program to propagate *Encarsia* and serve as an early warning monitor of whitefly invasion. Rue oil is toxic to some insects, such as *Rhizopertha dominica* and *Tribolium castaneum*, two pests of stored grain.

Important chemistry: The essential oil of garden rue is dominated by 2 to 84 percent 2-undecanone (methyl nonylketone), 5 to 39 percent 2-nonanone, 0 to 15 percent 2-undecyl acetate, and trace to 10 percent 2-nonyl acetate. The photosensitization is primarily produced by psoralen (0.126g/kg dry herb), bergapten (0.514 g/kg dry herb), and xanthotoxin (1.274 g/kg dry herb). Garden rue also contains a large number of quinoline and acridone alkaloids, such as rutaverine, arborinine, dictamnine, kokusaginine, skimmianine, fagarine, platydesminium, ribaliniu, and rutalinium.

Botanical Description

R. graveolens L., Sp. pl. 383. 1753.

Native country: Rue is native to the Balkan Peninsula and the Crimea but widely naturalized from gardens throughout Europe and North America.

General habit: Rue is a smooth, blue-green semi-evergreen perennial 14 to 50 cm high.

Leaves: Lower leaves are more or less long-stalked, the uppermost almost stalkless; the ultimate segments 2 to 9 mm wide, lance-shaped to narrowly oblong to almost egg-shaped.

Flowers: Flowers are greenish yellow in a rather lax inflorescence.

Fruits/seeds: Fruits are smooth pockets with black seeds.

Salvia

săl-vĭ-å
sage

Family: Lamiaceae (Labiatae)

Growth form: from tufted herbaceous perennials to shrubs many feet high

Hardiness: some hardy to Zone 6 but most cannot withstand frost

Light: full sun

Water: moist but not constantly wet; many can withstand minor drought

Soil: well-drained garden loam, pH 4.9 to 8.2, average 6.4 (*S. officinalis*)

Propagation: seeds or cuttings in spring, 3,400 seeds per ounce (119/g) (*S. officinalis*)

Culinary use: varied

Craft use: wreaths, potpourri

Landscape use: excellent in mixed borders

Salvia was a name used by the Romans for *S. officinalis* and was probably derived from *salvus*, a Latin word that denoted good health (sage was believed to have many healing properties). Fragrant foliage and brilliant flowers are typical of many of the 900 species of *Salvia*, so many of them make handsome additions to the herb garden and/or perennial border. Most species grow best when sited in full sun and well-drained soil, particularly those with gray foliage. *Salvia* is a genus with worldwide distribution but the greatest diversity is in the subtropics, especially the Americas, Sino-Himalayas, and southwestern Asia. Growth patterns range from herbaceous tufted alpines to woody shrubs.

Salvia clevelandii
săl-vē-å clēv-lăn-dĭ-ī
Cleveland sage

Cleveland or blue sage was named by Harvard's Asa Gray after the collector of the type specimen, Daniel Cleveland (1838–1929), but the commercial offerings of this species are actually hybrids, *S. clevelandii* × *S. leucophylla* Greene. In 1938 Carl Epling reported only one hybrid in existence, at the Rancho Santa Ana Botanic Garden in California, and we suspect that this hybrid was later distributed in the trade simply as *S. clevelandii*. All the hybrids have pebbly gray foliage on stems to about 3 feet (1 m) high, and the foliage is scented of rose potpourri, a characteristic in common with *S. leucophylla*. While the flowers of the typical species are a good blue, backed by reddish calyces, they are lavender-blue in the hybrids. In both the species and hybrids, flowers are irregularly produced and do not present a dramatic show.

At least five selections of *S. clevelandii* × *S. leucophylla* are known, differing only slightly in scent, growth pattern, and/or floral color: 'Allen Chickering', 'Aromas', 'Compact Form', 'Santa Cruz Dark', and 'Whirley Blue'. Even the unnamed clone passed around in the herb trade as simply *S. clevelandii* is from this cross. As might be expected of their southern California origins, Cleveland sage and its hybrids want well-drained, gravelly soil in full sun, probably hardy only to Zone 9. While some books have advocated that Cleveland sage be used in cooking, it does not have GRAS status.

'Winifred Gilman' seems to be the only cultivar in the trade that may be pure *S. clevelandii*. 'Winifred Gilman' is more difficult to grow than the hybrids and is characterized by pebbly green foliage scented of eucalyptus. Flowers should be dark violet-blue, but it has never flowered for us.

Important chemistry: The foliage of the hybrids is scented of rose potpourri with about 44 percent camphor and 19 percent 1,8-cineole in the essential oil; a multivariate analysis of the essential oil components confirmed no statistical differences among the named cultivars. The essential oil of 'Winifred Gilman' is characterized by around 20 percent 1,8-cineole with a eucalyptus-like scent.

Salvia dorisiana
săl-vē-å dō-rĭs-ĭ-å-nå
peach sage

Peach sage, also known as fruit sage, was named by Paul Standley, who documented the trees and shrubs of Mexico and Central America in the early twentieth century. The name honors Doris Zemurray Stone (1909–1994), a friend of the Escuela Agricola Panamericana, not some ancient goddess named Doris (as apocryphally repeated in most horticultural books on sage). Doris Zemurray Stone was the daughter of Sam

Salvia dorisiana

Zemurray (Schmuel Zmurri), founder of the United Fruit Company; she was an archaeologist and ethnographer and served as director of the National Museum of Costa Rica.

The leaves of peach sage can be dried and used in potpourri but have also been used to complement peach dishes, such as cobbler, despite its lack of GRAS status.

Peach sage is a robust, open plant with large leaves, 21 to 50 inches (7 to 14 cm) long by 2 to 4 inches (5 to 10 cm) wide, pale green, fleshy, and bristly-pebbly. Peach sage prefers part shade and constantly moist soil. This sage is extremely sensitive to frost, and since the rose-red flowers start forming very late in fall, it is often cut down before peak flowering. Under good conditions, peach sage may reach 47 inches (1.2 m) high.

Important chemistry: The essential oil is dominated by 27 to 28 percent perillyl acetate, 17 to 21 percent methyl perillate, and around 10 percent beta-caryophyllene, providing a peach-like odor reminiscent of perilla.

Salvia elegans
săl-vē-å ĕl-ĕ-gănz
pineapple sage

Salvia elegans ("elegant sage") is a vigorous, strong-stemmed plant with red-tinged green leaves that are scented of pineapples, giving it its common name. *Salvia rutilans*, a name sometimes applied to pineapple sage, is known only from cultivation, differing only in the smaller calyces and downier stems and probably not specifically different from *S. elegans*. Contrary to some popular horticultural books, pineapple sage is not a variety of *S. splendens* F. Sellow ex Roem. & Schult., the scarlet sage. 'Honeydew Melon' is a selection with a melon-like scent; 'Golden Delicious' has golden leaves, and 'Frida Dixon' is somewhat dwarf.

The young shoots of pineapple sage have been used to flavor cold drinks, and its fresh leaves and flowers have been used as garnishes for desserts despite its lack of GRAS status. Leaves are egg-shaped, tapering to a tip, 1 to 4 inches (2.5 to 10 cm) long arising from dark red, downy stems. The pineapple sage, like the peach sage, produces brilliant scarlet flowers just about the time it is cut down by frosts. Pineapple sage may reach 47 inches (1.2 m) high under optimum conditions.

Important chemistry: The essential oil of pineapple sage leaves contains 27 percent beta-caryophyllene, 22 percent 2-propanol, and 10 percent (*E*)-beta-ocimene.

Salvia elegans

Salvia fruticosa

săl-vē-å frö-tĭ-kō-så
Greek sage

Greek sage often comprises up to 95 percent of the dried, imported sage sold in the United States. Its eucalyptus-like aroma lacks the understated sweetness of garden sage, and the heavy presence of Greek sage may account for the musty odor of the commercial dried product. Often referred to as *S. triloba* in older literature, Greek sage has historical uses similar to garden sage. Greek sage is illustrated with what may be *Rosa pulverulenta* on the "blue bird fresco" in the House of Frescoes at Knossos (c. 1450 B. C.E.). The elongated egg-shaped leaves have two smaller lobes near the base. All vegetative parts are covered with a dense wool-like covering of matted, tangled hairs of medium length. Bright blue flowers appear in early winter.

Greek sage is extremely variable in both morphology and oil. Greek sage usually has a higher oil yield than garden sage. The oil is antimicrobial, cytotoxic, and antiviral.

While Greek sage is only reliably hardy in Zone 8b, hybridization with *S. officinalis* offers potential for new morphological and chemical types hardy further north. 'Newe 'Ya'ar', a hybrid (primarily *S. officinalis* × *S. fruticosa*) cultivated in Israel, withstands heat very well, occasionally appears on the U.S. market, and is easily rooted; unfortunately, it is not routinely hardy above Zone 8.

Important chemistry: The oil of *S. fruticosa* consists of 19 to 68 percent 1,8-cineole, trace to 45 percent camphor, trace to 38 percent viridiflorol, 3 to 27 percent alpha-pinene, 2 to 11 percent beta-pinene, and trace to 10 percent beta-caryophyllene.

Salvia lavandulifolia

săl-vē-å lå-văn-dū-lĭ-fō-lē-å
Spanish sage

The nine subspecies of *Salvia lavandulifolia*, the lavender-leaved sage, vary greatly in morphology and essential oils. In the cultivated plants in North America, the simple, stalked leaves are narrowly parallel-sided and covered with a dense wool-like covering of matted, tangled hairs. The blue flowers are rarely produced.

The essential oil is considered GRAS at 2 to 50 ppm but finds very little use in flavor work; it is primarily used to scent soaps. Ingestion of Spanish sage oil brings on convulsions from the toxicity of the camphor content. The dose at which rats show symptoms of toxicity is 0.005 ounce oil per pound of body weight (0.3 g/kg), while above 0.008 ounce per pound (0.5 g/kg)

convulsions occur; above 0.05 ounces per pound (3.2 g/kg), the dose is lethal. Translating this to a 150-pound human, these numbers would be 0.72 ounce, 1.2 ounces, and 7.7 ounces, respectively.

The sabinyl acetate in the essential oil induces birth defects in mice, a cautionary indication that this oil should not be used in aromatherapy by pregnant women. Research has shown that an extract of *S. lavandulifolia* significantly decreases the blood-sugar levels of diabetic rats; it also displays anticholinesterase activity. Spanish sage oil has been found to enhance the memory in healthy young volunteers and may have usefulness in dementia therapy, particularly Alzheimer's disease.

Important chemistry: The essential oil has 6 to 59 percent 1,8-cineole, 1 to 39 percent camphor, 2 to 28 percent beta-pinene, 3 to 28 percent alpha-pinene plus tricyclene, trace to 16 percent myrcene, trace to 14 percent camphene, 2 to 12 percent limonene, trace to 23 percent borneol, and trace to 12 percent viridiflorol, plus alpha-terpineol plus alpha-terpinyl acetate.

Salvia officinalis
săl-vē-å ŏ-fĭs-ĭ-nā-lĭs
garden sage

French: *sauge*
German: *Salbei*
Dutch: *salie*
Italian: *salvia*
Spanish: *salvia*
Portuguese: *salva*
Swedish: *salvia*
Russian: *shalfey*
Chinese: *chjing-chieh*
Japanese: *sēji*
Arabic: *mariyamiya*

The specific epithet, *officinalis*, refers to the medicinal value of the sage in years past. Imported sage is chiefly gathered from the wild along the Dalmatian coast of the former Yugoslavia and Albania, hence an alternative name is Dalmatian sage. As a wild-gathered herb, it actually consists of not only *S. officinalis* but also *S. fruticosa* and hybrids of the two species. In fact, only 5 to 50 percent of imported sage may be *S. officinalis*.

Garden sage is widely used in flavoring condiments, cured meats (particularly sausage and poultry stuffing), liqueurs, and bitters. Garden sage oil is used to impart herbaceous notes to fragrances. The leaf is GRAS at 300 to 4,777 ppm; the oleoresin is GRAS at 10 to 139 ppm, while the essential oil is GRAS at 2 to 126 ppm. Sage yields an effective antioxidant that is relatively odorless and tasteless; this has been proposed as a preservative for fatty foods such as potato chips. The essential oil of sage is antimutagenic. Sage extract has also been found to be effective in the management of mild to moderate Alzheimer's disease. Sage kills both bacteria and fungi. Sage extract may be useful in the control of *Varroa* mites in bee colonies.

Depending upon the source, garden sage seed may germinate unevenly and produce very variable plants, few of which have heavy, thick leaves with robust growth and the desired odor. Named cultivars are easily propagated from hormone-treated cuttings about 1½ to 2 inches (4 to 5 cm) long. If taken in late fall to early winter, the cuttings will establish ample roots in the greenhouse for transplanting by spring. Cuttings should be taken from new growth of nonflowering stems, preferably from the base of the plant if available.

Transplants should be set 15 to 24 inches (39

Salvia officinalis

to 61 cm) apart in rows set about 3½ feet (about 1 m) apart. Approximately 7,000 plants per acre (17,297 plants/ha) would be required with these spacings.

The home gardener will usually be satisfied with one or two large plants of sage. Home gardeners should pinch the growing tips regularly throughout the first summer to create many branches; also cut the plant back about a third before new growth starts in the second year. Before planting, a high grade commercial fertilizer (depending on the results of the soil test), with 89 to 134 pounds per acre (100 to 150 kg/ha) of nitrogen, should be drilled into the rows. A side-dressing of fertilizer should be given six to eight weeks later. After plants are established, fertilize about the time that growth starts in spring and repeat about the first week in June. Cultivate lightly through the spring and summer to control weeds. The first year should have one harvest of the terminal 3 to 5 inches (8 to 13 cm) during the fall; afterward, harvesting can be two to three times per summer.

Leaves and small tops will bring the best prices; keep the percentage of stems below 12 percent. In the first year, the yield is usually small, ranging from 200 to 600 pounds dried leaves per acre (224 to 672 kg/ha). In the second and subsequent years 1,500 to 2,000 pounds per acre (1,681 to 2,241 kg/ha) may be obtained. A regimen of three successive harvests produces the highest biomass yield. Experimental plantings in New Zealand have produced the phenomenal yield of 1,106 to 2,432 pounds per acre (1,240 to 5,080 kg/ha) the first year.

Sage loses its color and flavor rapidly with age, so bale and market the product as soon as possible. Blooming significantly reduces the harvest, so choose a cultivar with low flowering potential.

Sudden phytophthora, verticillium, and fusarium wilts are the most obnoxious diseases to confront sage. These can usually be remedied by increasing the drainage of the soil. Powdery mildew (*Oidium* spp.) occurs sometimes in hot, humid weather. Nematodes will also attack sage, and their presence accelerates sudden wilts.

Garden sage has a few cultivars, selected mainly for foliar or floral colors. All may be used for cooking, imparting their own particular flavors, but some taste better than others.

Cultivar: 'Albiflora'
Foliage/growth: broad leaves, low height
Flowers: white
Essential oil: 37 percent beta-thuone and 23 percent camphor
Comments: tends to be weak and prone to wilts in hot climates

Cultivar: 'Aurea'
Foliage/growth: gold-flushed leaves, low height
Flowers: lavender-blue
Comments: vastly confused in the horticultural literature with 'Icterina' (which see); 'Aurea' is a uniform golden green and very weak plant, not worth growing except as a curiosity

Cultivar: 'Berggarten' ("mountain garden")
Synonyms: 'Herrenhausen'
Origin: Herrenhausen Grosser Garten, Hanover, Germany
Foliage/growth: broad leaves, low height
Flowers: lavender-blue, infrequent
Essential oil: 25 percent camphor and 10 percent camphene
Comments: the best agronomic plant of the available cultivars, with very large leaves, few flowers, and an oil that matches much of the imported Dalmatian sage

Cultivar: 'Compacta'
Foliage/growth: narrow, upright, medium height
Flowers: lavender-blue
Essential oil: 21 percent 1,8-cineole and 19 percent camphor

Cultivar: 'Crispa'
Foliage/growth: variegated with wavy margins

Cultivar: 'Grandiflora'
Foliage/growth: leaves larger and wider with a heart-shaped base
Flowers: larger than typical

Cultivar: 'Grete Stolze'
Foliage/growth: pointed, pale gray
Flowers: mauve-blue

Cultivar: 'Icterina'
Synonyms: 'Aurea' (incorrect name, see earlier)
Foliage/growth: edged in gold, low height
Flowers: lavender-blue
Essential oil: 22 percent camphor, 11 percent alpha-thujone, and 10 percent alpha-humulene
Comments: generally not hardy above Zone 8

Cultivar: 'Kew Gold'
Origin: a sport of 'Icterina', to which it sometimes reverts, selected by Brian Halliwell, Royal Botanic Gardens, Kew, England
Foliage/growth: gold on green
Comments: seems to be a more vigorous version of 'Aurea'

Cultivar: 'Milleri'
Foliage/growth: red, blotched (maculae)

Cultivar: 'Purpurascens'
Synonyms: 'Purpurea'

Foliage/growth: broad, purple leaves, low height
Flowers: lavender-blue
Essential oil: 17 percent alpha-thujone, 17 percent alpha-humulene, 15 percent camphor, and 13 percent beta-pinene
Comments: oil matches much of the imported Dalmatian sage; good garden accent; a selection of this is 'Robin Hill'

Cultivar: 'Purpurascens Variegata'
Foliage/growth: cream markings on some leaves
Comments: a sport of 'Purpurascens'

Cultivar: 'Rubriflora'
Foliage/growth: narrow, upright, somewhat sparse
Flowers: pink
Essential oil: 27 percent alpha-thujone and 19 percent camphor
Comments: oil matches much of the imported Dalmatian sage

Cultivar: 'Salicifolia'
Foliage/growth: leaves very long and narrow

Cultivar: 'Sturnina'
Foliage/growth: white-green

Cultivar: 'Tricolor'
Synonyms: Parkinson's "party-colored sage"
Origin: probably a variegated 'Purpurascens'
Foliage/growth: purple edged in white, low height
Flowers: lavender-blue
Essential oil: 20 percent camphor, 19 percent alpha-humulene, 14 percent alpha-thujone, and 12 percent beta-pinene
Comments: not hardy above Zone 8 and rather weak in growth but a good garden accent

Cultivar: 'Woodcote Farm'
Synonyms: 'Woodcote'
Foliage/growth: broad leaves, low height
Flowers: lavender-blue, infrequent
Essential oil: 17 percent camphor and 11 percent alpha-thujone
Comments: good culinary sage and garden plant; occasionally offered in a variegated form

'Holt's Mammoth' is another cultivar that needs clarification. What is the real 'Holt's Mammoth'? The original clone reputedly had larger leaves than the type; the cultivar usually offered in the United States is often propagated from seeds and no different from the type or any other seed-propagated sage. Is the sage now known as 'Woodcote Farm' the real 'Holt's Mammoth'? No original good description exists of 'Holt's Mammoth', so we are at a loss to clarify this problem. 'Woodcote Farm' is the most frequently offered sage cultivar for fresh leaves at vegetable counters in the United States. In Great Britain, besides 'Woodcote Farm', some other commercial cultivars include 'Archers Long Leaf', 'Archers Broad Leaf', 'Andrews', 'Extracta', 'Preen 38', and 'Wisley'.

Additional cultivars with few published descriptions include 'Emanuel', 'Jefferson', and 'Wurzburg'.

Important chemistry: The essential oil and dried sage from the Dalmatian coast of the former Yugoslavia and Albania show tremendous variability in the principal components: trace to 47 percent alpha-thujone, 1 to 36 percent beta-thujone, 3 to 38 percent camphor, 4 to 25 percent 1,8-cineole, and trace to 16 percent borneol. Populations from Serbia and Montenegro have 8 to 25 percent alpha-thujone, trace to 25 percent camphor, and 6 to 13 percent 1,8-cineole. An examination of the essential oil of *S. officinalis* from nine European countries showed 3 to 45 percent 1,8-cineole, 11 to 29 percent camphor, 3 to 24 percent alpha-thujone, and five to 13 percent beta-thujone. A collection identified as var. *angustifolia* Ten. from Italy showed 39 percent alpha-thujone and 12 percent alpha-humulene. As in rosemary, the antioxidative activity is due to the content of phenolic diterpenes, particularly carnosic acid, carnosol, epirosmanol, isorosmanol, rosmadial, and methyl carnosate. Also, like rosemary, luteolin, a flavonoid, exhibits antioxidative activity.

Salvia pomifera
săl-vē-å pō-mĭf-ēr-å
apple sage

The specific epithet, which means "bearing apples," refers to the curious fruitlike, semitransparent insect galls that form on the branches. These agreeably flavored but astringent growths are sometimes candied as sage apples. Apple sage was used for cooking and medicine, along with *S. officinalis* and *S. fruticosa*, by the ancient Greeks and Romans, but apple sage does not currently have GRAS status.

The leaves of apple sage are egg-shaped with rounded- to heart-shaped bases, 2 to 3 inches (5 to 8 cm) long, wrinkled and densely hairy when young. The violet-blue flowers often have a reddish calyx.

Important chemistry: The essential oil contains 15 to 72 percent alpha-thujone, 7 to 51 percent beta-thujone, and trace to 10 percent 1,8-cineole.

Salvia sclarea
săl-vē-å sklă-rē-å
clary sage

French: *toute-bonne, sauge sclarée*
German: *Scharlei, Muskatsalbei*
Italian: *sclarea, erba moscatella, scanderona, trippa di dama, scarleggia*
Spanish: *hierba de los ojos, amaro, almaro, salvia romana*

The herb's traditional use for clearing the eyes give it the specific epithet—meaning "clear"—as well as its common name. The seeds are mucilaginous in water and were once used to pick up small particles of dirt from the eyes.

Clary sage imparts a muscatel flavor to alcoholic beverages and is used to flavor wines, vermouths, and liqueurs, so an alternative common name is muscatel sage. The essential oil is widely used in perfumery. Sclareol, an amber-scented compound present as trace to 3 percent of the oil, is isolated from clary sage by hydrocarbon extraction and is useful for tobacco flavoring. The oil of clary sage is GRAS at 1 to 155 ppm. The oil has both anti-inflammatory and pain-relieving action.

Clary sage is a biennial that readily reseeds in the garden. The winter rosette is relatively lacking in fragrance, but the entire inflorescence, rising to 39 inches (1 m) high and bearing white or pink flowers with leafy bracts, has a pronounced cloying, amber/lavender note. Leaves are broadly egg-shaped, heart-shaped at the base, about 3 to 5 inches (8 to 14 cm) long.

The var. *turkestanica* Mottet has been used to designate forms with long bracts, but the offerings of this variety in the seed trade differ little from normal seed lots of clary sage; seed lots of 'Vatican' also differ very little.

Important chemistry: The essential oil of typical clary inflorescences has 14 to 74 percent linalyl acetate, 8 to 32 percent linalool, and 2 to 12 percent alpha-terpineol. The diffusive, onion-like odor of perspiration is from trace amounts of 1-methoxyhexant-3-thiol. A lemon/rose-scented form of clary has also been isolated in Israel; this has 36 to 37 percent geranyl acetate, 16 to 25 percent geraniol, 11 to 19 percent geranial, 8 to 11 percent neral, and 1 to 0 percent germacrene D. Leaves are typically less odorous, being scented with about 68 percent germacrene D.

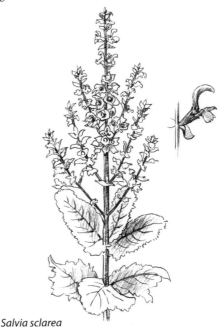

Salvia sclarea

Salvia viridis
săl-vē-å vĭr-ĭ-dĭs
bluebeard sage

The specific epithet means green, but this is known as bluebeard sage, Joseph sage, red-topped sage, or horminum clary. The sterile bracts, often colored violet, green, pink, or white, are very decorative in the garden. The leaves of bluebeard sage are egg-shaped or parallel-sided, rounded or heart-shaped at the base, blunt at the apex, and 2 inches (5 cm) long. While bluebeard sage is grown today only as an ornamental, it was once used by the Greeks and Romans to flavor wine.

Important chemistry: The essential oil of bluebeard sage contains 29 percent beta-pinene and 15 percent alpha-humulene.

Botanical Key and Description

Key:
1.   Annual bearing brilliantly colored sterile bracts at the terminus of the branches . . . . *S. viridis*
1a. Perennial without sterile bracts 2
   2.   Leaves usually tri-lobed and velvety . . . . *S. fruticosa*
   2a. Leaves usually simple and not velvety 3
      3.   Corolla brilliant red. . . . . *S. elegans*
      3a. Corolla blue, pink, or white, not red. 4
         4.   Leaves rounded or heart-shaped at the base. 5
            5.   Leaves 5 to 8 cm long . . . . *S. pomifera*
            5a. Leaves 8 to 18 cm long 6
               6.   Hardy biennial from winter rosette. . . . . *S. sclarea*
               6a. Tender shrub . . . . *S. dorisiana*
         4a. Leaves narrowed to the base 7
            7.   Corolla dark blue-violet; flowers many in compact, crowded clusters . . . . *S. clevelandii*
            7a. Corolla blue, blue-violet, pink, or white; flowers in five- to ten-flowered clusters 8
               8.   Leaves to 5 cm long, parallel-sided . . . . *S. lavandulifolia*
               8a. Leaves 4 to 7.7 cm long, broadly parallel-sided . . . . *S. officinalis*

S. clevelandii (A. Gray) Greene, Pittonia 2:236. 1892.

As mentioned earlier, we do not usually cultivate "pure" *S. clevelandii*, but rather hybrids with *S. leucophylla*. The hybrid differs from *S. clevelandii* in having lavender-blue flowers and branched hairs.

Native country: Cleveland sage is a component of the chaparral of western San Diego County, California, extending down to Baja California.

General habit: Cleveland sage grows about 1 m tall. Branchlets are hairy with backward-directed hairs, ashy.

Leaves: Leaves are 1.5 to 2 cm long, usually widest at the center with the ends equal, blunt at the apex, narrowed to the base with stalks 3 to 6 mm long, margins with rounded small teeth, the upper surfaces puckered, coated with fine hairs, the lower ashy or, especially when young, whitened with minute appressed hairs, with prominent veins.

Flowers: Flowers are many in one to three compact, crowded clusters in remotely interrupted spikes, these evenly branched, subtended by firm egg-shaped bracts shorter than the calyces. Corolla is dark violet-blue.

S. dorisiana Standley, Ceiba 1:43. 1950.
Native country: Peach sage is a native of Honduras.
General habit: Peach sage is a shrub to about 1 to 1.2 m, with long, soft, somewhat wavy hairs, leafy and freely branched.
Leaves: Leaves are egg-shaped, pinched at the tip, heart-shaped at the base with lobes often overlapping, toothed, thinly papery, hairy, gland-dotted below, 7 to 14 × 5 to 10 cm.
Flowers: Inflorescence is showy, glandular; flower cluster two- to ten-flowered; corolla is magenta, with long, soft, somewhat wavy hairs.

S. elegans Vahl, Enum. pl. 1:238. 1804 (*S. rutilans* Carrière).
Native country: Pineapple sage is native to Mexico.
General habit: Pineapple sage is a shrubby herb, 61 to 120 cm.
Leaves: Leaves are egg-shaped, tapering to the tip, rounded at the base, finely toothed, hairy, 2.5 to 10 cm long.
Flowers: The inflorescence is branched, flower clusters distinct, about six-flowered; corolla is deep crimson to blood red, densely coated with long, soft, straight hairs.

S. fruticosa Mill., Gard. Dict. ed. 8. 1768 (*S. triloba* L.f.).
Native country: Greek sage is native to the central and eastern Mediterranean region.
General habit: Greek sage is a shrub to about 1 m, white-hairy.
Leaves: Leaves are usually three-lobed, the laterals much smaller than the terminal. Terminal lobe is two to four times longer than

wide with the sides parallel tending to egg-shaped, 2 to 5 × 0.75 to 2 cm, wrinkled, lower surface white to velvety with dense, wool-like covering of matted, tangled hairs of medium length.
Flowers: Inflorescence is branched, flower clusters two- to eight-flowered; corolla is bright blue.

S. lavandulifolia Vahl, Enum. pl. 1:222. 1804.
In 1983, De Bolòs and Vigo reclassified the subspecies of *S. lavandulifolia* into five forms of *S. officinalis* subsp. *lavandulifolia* (Vahl) Gams, later publishing subsp. *lavandulifolia* as a variety [*S. officinalis* L. var. *lavandulifolia* (Vahl) O. de Bolòs & J. Vigo, Fl. Països Catalans 3:342. 1995], but *S. lavandulifolia* is maintained as a species here, following popular custom.
Native country: Spanish sage is native to central, southern, and eastern Spain, extending slightly into southern France.
General habit: Spanish sage is a small shrub or herb, woody at the base, up to 50 cm high, stems erect or ascending, hairy.
Leaves: Simple leaves are stalked, narrow, narrowly parallel-sided, edged with small rounded teeth, up to 5 cm long, with a dense, wool-like covering of matted, tangled hairs of medium length.
Flowers: Flower clusters six- to eight-flowered; calyx is often reddish purple, hairy, corolla is blue or blue-violet.

S. officinalis L. Sp. pl. 23. 1753.
Native country: Garden or Dalmatian sage is native to northern and central Spain, southern France, and the western part of the Balkan Peninsula but is widely cultivated and naturalized in southern and south-central Europe.
General habit: Garden sage is a shrub to 61 cm high, stems erect, covered with dense, woolly

covering of matted, tangled hairs of medium length.

Leaves: Leaves are simple, stalked, parallel-sided, more or less narrowed at the base, ruffled, white-hairy beneath, greenish above, densely hairy when young, 4.1 to 7.7 × 0.9 to 5.0 cm.

Flowers: Flower clusters are five- to ten-flowered; corolla is violet-blue, pink, or white.

S. pomifera L., Sp. pl. 24. 1753 (*S. calycina* Sibth. & Sm.).

Native country: Apple sage is native to southern Greece and the southern Aegean region.

General habit: Apple sage is a shrub to 1 m, much-branched, short-hoary.

Leaves: Leaves are simple, stalked, egg-shaped, rounded or heart-shaped at the base, 5 to 8 cm long to about 3 cm wide, wrinkled, densely short-hoary when young.

Flowers: Flower clusters two- to four-flowered; calyx is often reddish purple with non-glandular hairs and sessile glands, corolla is violet-blue, the lower lip paler.

S. sclarea L., Sp. pl. 27. 1753.

Native country: Clary sage is native to southern Europe.

General habit: Clary sage is a biennial or short-lived perennial up to 1 m high. Stems are erect, much branched, glandular above.

Leaves: Leaves are simple, stalked, broadly egg-shaped, heart-shaped at base, hairy, about 8 to 14 × 5 to 10 cm.

Flowers: Flower clusters are four- to six-flowered. Bracts exceed the lilac or white corollas. Calyx has spiny teeth, hairy and dotted with glands.

S. viridis L., Sp. pl. 24. 1753 (*S. horminum* L.).

Native country: Bluebeard sage is native to southern Europe.

General habit: Bluebeard sage is an annual with stems to 50 cm, erect, simple or branched, non-glandular or glandular-hairy.

Leaves: Leaves are simple, stalked, egg-shaped or parallel-sided, rounded or heart-shaped at the base, blunt at the apex, regularly edged with round teeth, hairy, about 5 × 2.5 cm.

Flowers: Flower clusters are four- to eight-flowered. Terminal sterile bracts are usually prominent and violet, green, pink, or white. Corolla is pink or violet.

Sanguisorba minor

săn-gwĭ-sôr-bå mī-nôr
burnet

Family: Rosaceae
Growth form: herbaceous perennial to about 18 inches (46 cm)
Hardiness: hardy to Zone 5
Light: part to full sun

Water: constantly moist but not wet
Soil: well-drained garden loam rich in organic matter, pH 4.8 to 8.2, average 6.8
Propagation: seeds in fall or spring, 5,000 seeds per ounce (176/g)

Culinary use: salads but not GRAS
Craft use: none
Landscape use: front of herb or vegetable garden

French: *grande pimprenelle, pimprenelle commune des prés*
German: *Pimpinelle, Kölbel, Blutsauge, Kleiner Wiesenknopf, Bibernelle*
Dutch: *klien sorbenkruid, bloedkruid*
Italian: *pimpinella, bilbernella, salvastrella, meloncello*
Spanish: *pimpinela menor*
Portuguese: *pimpinela*

Salad burnet is one of those herbs that can shine in the garden and in the kitchen. As a landscape plant, it possesses unusual accordion-like, dark green leaves. Its lacy, ferny appearance provides texture and contrast in the herb garden. In the kitchen, burnet's light cucumber-flavored leaves are useful in several ways. In France, the leaves are used for dressings, salads, soups, and sauces, wherever a light cucumber

Sanguisorba minor

flavor is needed. Burnet's decorative leaves make it especially useful as a garnish for pâtés and aspics. Burnet makes a good alternative to decorative sprigs of parsley in other dishes, too.

Burnet is easily grown from seeds planted in fall or spring and will easily reseed (the reseeded plants are often healthier than the original plants). Provide a light, well-drained organic soil in full sun with good moisture retention.

Start cutting one-year-old plants early in spring through early summer. The plant grows to 12 to 18 inches (30 to 46 cm) when flowering but normally exists as a tight rosette of leaves. Flowers are minute and green in small, tight heads; the red stigmas are often visible. To keep the plants vigorous and limit self-seeding, cut the flowers as they appear; they are good to eat but can become fibrous if cut too late.

The genus *Sanguisorba* includes about 18 species. Some were once believed to have styptic qualities, so the generic name translates to "blood-stauncher." The specific name translates to "small."

In spite of centuries of consumption by Europeans, burnet has no GRAS status.

Botanical Description

Six subspecies are known, but subsp. *minor* (*Poterium sanguisorba* L.) is the burnet of gardens.

S. minor Scop., Fl. Carn. ed. 2. 1:110. 1772.
Native country: Burnet is native to dry grassland and rocky ground, southern, western, and central Europe, extending to southern Sweden and central Russia.
General habit: Burnet is a smooth herb with a well-developed basal rosette of leaves, reaching 30 to 46 cm when flowering.
Leaves: Leaves have three to twelve pairs of globe-shaped to elliptical leaflets; each leaflet

is 0.5 to 2 cm, more or less stalked, round-toothed to incised, mostly of equal size.

Flowers: The green flowers are arranged in globose to egg-shaped heads.

Fruits/seeds: The fruits are ridged or winged with pimpled and sculptured faces.

Santolina

săn-tō-lī-nå
lavender cotton

Family: Asteraceae (Compositae)

Growth form: perennial subshrub to 2 feet (60 cm)

Hardiness: most hardy to Zone 6

Light: full sun

Water: moist to somewhat dry; can withstand drought when established

Soil: well-drained gravelly or rocky loam

Propagation: layerings or cuttings in summer

Culinary use: none

Craft use: tussy-mussies, potpourri

Landscape use: small, tight hedges, knot gardens

French: *petit cyprès, santoline, aurone femelle, garde-robe*

German: *Heiligenkraut, Cypressenkraut*

Dutch: *heiligenbloem*

Italian: *santolina, crespolina*

Spanish: *abròtano hembra, hierba lombriguera hembra, hierba piojera, santolina, bolina, manzanilla cabezudo*

Portuguese: *abrotano fêmea, guarda roupa*

In the landscape, the compact, short gray lances of *Santolina* resemble cotton balls, hence the common name "lavender cotton" or "cotton lavender" in England. The lavender cottons were used in culinary and medicinal applications at one time (particularly to rid the body of worms), but none have GRAS status. The fragrance of the plants is penetrating and unusual, and the branches are attractive for Christmas decorations, tussy-mussies, and as additions to potpourris. An old tale suggests that lavender cotton acts as a moth preventive, and the French name, *garde-robe*, indicates its value in closets (this French name is also applied to southernwood), but we cannot find any research to validate the efficacy of this use. The greatest value

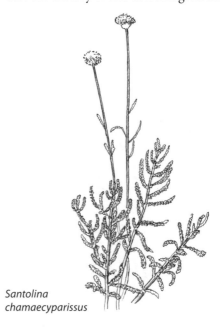

Santolina chamaecyparissus

of the lavender cottons, however, is in the herb garden as hedges, especially for decorative, intricate hedges that form "knots."

Santolina is an example of botanists and horticulturists going about their own merry ways without communication. Names that have proliferated in catalogs and herb books either have been misapplied or have no botanical meaning. Our interpretation is the best that can be done with the existing literature.

Santolina is a genus of about twelve species of subshrubs native to the western Mediterranean region. The generic name was derived from *sanctum linum*, "holy flax," an old name for green lavender cotton.

The plant cultivated as gray lavender cotton is actually one self-sterile clone that keys out to *S. chamaecyparissus* subsp. *insularis* in E. Guinea and T. G. Tutin's account in *Flora Europaea*. The specific name is derived from the Greek word *chamai*, which means "on the ground," and a second word, *kuparissos*, which translates as cypress; *insularis* refers to Corsica and Sardinia, where this subspecies is common. In the wild, the cultivated clone of gray lavender cotton is very rare, and our clone seems to have originated in the former Yugoslavia, according to Hugh McAllister of the University of Liverpool Botanic Garden, who has introduced other clones of this gray lavender cotton into England and has been able to effect seeds. He now proposes that since Linnaeus' type specimen (*S. chamaecyparissus* subsp. *chamaecyparissus*) is similar to the Sardinian populations, the cultivated Yugoslavian plants should be designated as *S. chamaecyparissus* subsp. *dalmaticum*.

The plant cultivated as dwarf lavender cotton ('Nana' or 'Compacta') occurs in the wild in Majorca and Minorca in the Balearic Islands. This dwarf entity with crisped-branched hairs keys out to *S. chamaecyparissus* subsp. *squarrosa* in *Flora Europaea*. McAllister has proposed

that this is actually a separate species, *S. magonica*. Another, taller-growing lax shrub with long, feathery leaves, bearing numerous lobes, originated in central Italy, and McAllister notes this should be designated as *S. neapolitana*, the Naples lavender cotton.

The green lavender cotton has usually been designated as *S. virens* but designated as synonymous with *S. viridis*, or *S. rosmarinifolia* in the horticultural literature. Yet *S. rosmarinifolia* (alias *S. viridis*) has remote leaf lobes on the juvenile foliage, thus the designation of rosemary-leaved. This species is not hardy north of Zone 8 and is not our green lavender cotton.

What, then, is our green lavender cotton? The green-leaved, almost herbaceous, creamy-white flowered, smooth plants from the Alpi Apuane northeast of Genoa key out to *S. chamaecyparissus* subsp. *tomentosa* in *Flora Europaea*. McAllister has designated these as a separate species, *S. pinnata*.

A few named cultivars are grown. Here we have tried to describe these and their taxonomic placement.

Cultivar: 'Edward Bowles'
Origin: Hillier and Sons, England; *S. neapolitana*
Leaves: gray-green
Flowers: cream-yellow

Cultivar: 'Lemon Queen'
Origin: *S. pinnata*
Leaves: green
Flowers: pale yellow

Cultivar: 'Morning Mist'
Origin: *S. rosmarinifolia*
Growth: 15 inches (38 cm) tall; tolerant of compacted, wet soils
Leaves: grayish-waxy green
Flowers: yellow

Cultivar: 'Nana'
Origin: perhaps *S. magonica*?
Growth: dwarf
Leaves: gray
Flowers: yellow

Cultivar: 'Pretty Carroll'
Origin: Carroll Gardens, Westminster, Maryland; *S. chamaecyparissus*
Leaves: gray
Flowers: yellow

Cultivar: 'Primrose Gem'
Origin: *S. pinnata*; probably the same as 'Lemon Queen'
Leaves: green
Flowers: pale yellow

Cultivar: 'Sulphurea'
Origin: *S. neapolitana*
Leaves: similar to 'Edward Bowles' but more gray
Flowers: pale primrose yellow

Both the gray and green lavender cottons, no matter what their names, are easily grown in full sun in sandy, well-drained soil. Pythium wilt of the foliage and sudden root wilts are problems that can be avoided with excellent drainage, good air circulation, and neutral to slightly alkaline soil. These subshrubs do best with a hard annual pruning in spring, which allows increased air circulation and permits more sunlight to penetrate the plant. In late summer the white to yellow heads ("rayless daisies") appear; these can be removed later, but do not prune heavily at this time or the plant may die.

Most of the cultivated material produces few seeds, and the cultivars cannot be seed propagated reliably. Layering stems is the easiest route to increasing your collection of lavender cottons, but rooting summer stem-tip cuttings, although difficult, is reliable if you need many new plants. The grayer the foliage, however, the less the humidity required for rooting, and rooting of gray lavender cotton can be easily accomplished during summer under a 50-percent shade cloth if the humidity is 80 percent or above.

The oil of *S. chamaecyparissus* has been shown to be anticandidal.

Important chemistry: The essential oil of a plant identified as *S. chamaecyparissus* subsp. *squarrosa* from eastern Spain is dominated by 25 percent camphor and 19 percent *allo*-aromadendrene, providing a spicy-camphoraceous odor. French oils of *S. chamaecyparissus* are dominated by 31 to 34 percent artemisia ketone and 9 to 18 percent beta-phellandrene, providing an odor of annual wormwood (sweet Annie). German and Hungarian oils of *S. chamaecyparissus* are dominated by 17 percent longiverbenone (vulgarone B), providing a dusty miller–like odor similar to some forms of *Artemisia douglasiana*. The essential oil of plants identified as *S. chamaecyparissus* from Turkey has 38 percent artemisia ketone, 12 percent camphor, and 9 percent beta-phellandrene with an artemisia-like odor. Cultivated plants of *S. chamaecyparissus* in India have 32 percent artemisia ketone, 16 percent 1,8-cineole, and 15 percent myrcene. Plants identified as *S. rosmarinifolia* from Bulgaria have 14 percent beta-eudesmol and 13 percent 1,8-cineole in the essential oil of the flower heads, providing a eucalyptus-like odor.

Botanical Key and Description

Key:

1. Leaves green to grayish-waxy green, not hairy 2
    2. Leaves green; flowers whitish. . . . . *S. pinnata*
    2a. Leaves grayish-waxy green; flowers yellow. . . . . *S. rosmarinifolia*
1a. Leaves gray, finely hairy 3
    3. Leaves feathery in appearance with numerous, long lobes . . . . *S. neapolitana*
    3a. Leaves knobby in appearance with short lobes 4
        4. Peg-like lobes of leaves not more than 2 mm, eight to nine per longitudinal row . . . .
        . . . . *S. magonica*
        4a. Peg-like lobes of leaves at least 2.5 mm, nine to fourteen per longitudinal row . . . .
        . . . . *S. chamaecyparissus*

S. chamaecyparissus L., Sp. pl. 842. 1753 [*S. chamaecyparissus* L. subsp. *insularis* (Genn. ex Fiori) Yeo, *S. incana* Lam.].

The clone in cultivation is *S. chamaecyparissus* subsp. *dalmaticum*.

Native country: Gray lavender cotton is native to Sardinia and the former Yugoslavia.

General habit: Gray lavender cotton is an erect to ascending subshrub.

Leaves: Leaves are densely toothed and coated with a dense wool-like covering of matted, tangled hairs of medium length; lobes are more than 2.5 mm long.

Flowers: Head is usually coated with hairs like the leaves. Flowers are yellow.

S. magonica (Bolòs, Molin. & P. Monts.) Romo, Flores Silvestres Baleares 303. 1994.

Native country: Dwarf lavender cotton is native to the Balearic Islands and perhaps North Africa.

General habit: Dwarf lavender cotton is an erect to ascending subshrub.

Leaves: Leaves are smooth to coated with a dense wool-like covering of matted, crisped-branched hairs of medium length; lobes are no more than 2 mm long.

Flowers: Head is usually smooth. Flowers are pale yellow.

S. neapolitana Jord. & Four., Icon. fl. eur. 2:10. 1869.

Native country: Naples lavender cotton is native to central Italy.

General habit: Naples lavender cotton is an erect to ascending subshrub 30 to 61 cm tall and 61 to 91 cm wide.

Leaves: Leaves appear feathery with long numerous lobes and are coated with a dense wool-like covering of matted hairs of medium length.

Flowers: Head is coated with hairs like the leaves. Flowers are yellow.

S. pinnata Viviani, Elench. pl. hort. Dinegro 31. 1802 [*S. chamaecyparissus* L. subsp. *tomentosa* (Pers.) Arcangeli, *S. ericoides*].

Native country: Green lavender cotton is native from the Pyrenees to central Italy.

General habit: Green lavender cotton is an erect or ascending subshrub.

Leaves: Leaves are green and smooth with lobes 2.5 to 7 mm long.

Flowers: Head is usually smooth. Flowers are whitish to pale yellow.

S. rosmarinifolia L., Sp. pl. 842. 1753.
Native country: Rosemary-leaved lavender cotton is native to the Iberian Peninsula and southern France.
General habit: Rosemary-leaved lavender cotton is an erect or ascending subshrub, 35 to 45 cm high.

Leaves: Leaves are grayish-waxy green. Juvenile leaves are erect to erect-deflexed, narrowly linear, tapering to the tip, very shortly and remotely pimpled-toothed to lobed. Adult leaves have closely pressed teeth, the uppermost smooth.
Flowers: Flowers are bright yellow.

Sassafras albidum

săs-å-frăs ăl-bĭd-ŭm
sassafras

Family: Lauraceae
Growth form: tree to 66 feet (20 m)
Hardiness: hardy to Maine (Zone 5)
Light: full sun
Water: moist but not constantly wet
Soil: well-drained and rich in organic matter
Propagation: seeds in fall
Culinary use: root bark toxic; leaves as flavoring and thickener in soups
Craft use: potpourri
Landscape use: vigorous tree for fall color

French: *sassafras*
German: *Sassafras, Fenchelholz*
Dutch: *sassafras, venkelhout, zweethout*
Italian: *sassafraso*
Spanish: *sasafras*

Sassafras is a rapidly growing but short-lived tree found in young forests from the U.S. Midwest to New England to the Deep South. When mature, the tree may reach more than 66 feet (20 m) high. Its fall plumage radiates brilliant orange and crimson. The root bark has the unmistakable aroma of root beer, the leaves have a fatty lemon odor, and the birds are drawn to the small, black, olive-like fruits, which they avidly consume.

Sassafras was apparently a vernacular name used by early European settlers in Florida. The specific name, *albidum* ("white"), refers to the blue-green smooth-to-hairy undersides of the leaves. Two other species of *Sassafras* grow in China, *S. tzumu* (Hemsley) Hemsley and *S. randaiense* (Hayata) Rehder.

Sassafras roots and leaves are usually gath-

Sassafras albidum

ered from the wild. If you cultivate sassafras in your garden, start it from seed or transplant seedlings very early before the taproot develops; transplanting later is difficult. Soil should be well drained but rich in organic matter and in full sun.

Sassafras has been a tree of many uses. The tea from the root bark, mixed with milk and sugar, was once consumed as a beverage called *saloop*, and the root bark was used to brew root beer. The chief constituent of the roots, safrole, has been prohibited by the U.S. Food and Drug Administration (FDA) since 1960 in foods because it is metabolized to a liver toxin and carcinogen. Yet, sassafras root tea is still sold (the FDA does not have enough time and money to police every farmers' market) and has many adherents as a "blood-purifier."

Other health conditions have been tied to sassafras tea; overindulgence (about ten cups a day for an adult) has been linked to a medical condition called diaphoresis that is characterized by profuse sweating with an elevated body temperature. Consumption of as little as 0.17 ounces (5 ml) of sassafras oil may kill an individual or induce vomiting, tachycardia (irregular heartbeat), and tremors. While you may or may not personally accept the toxicity and carcinogenicity of sassafras roots and safrole, you may be sued by someone who becomes ill or develops liver cancer if you sold them or advised the consumption of safrole-rich beverages or foods. Lawyers from the FDA could also be petitioned as a witness for the litigant.

The controversy over the safety of sassafras arises from the long consumption of sassafras root tea by the Appalachian community and because safrole itself is not carcinogenic. However, safrole is metabolized to very active carcinogens in the body on ingestion. Complicating matters in the ban on sassafras tea is that safrole is also present in trace quantities in some spices,

such as nutmeg (0.12 to 0.43 percent safrole) and mace (0.43 to 1.99 percent). However, these levels are considered relatively minor, and so the FDA does not prohibit nutmeg and mace; both spices are also consumed daily in beverages and foods at levels below that of routine sassafras root tea drinkers.

The FDA does approve safrole-free extracts of sassafras at 10 to 290 ppm, while the leaves, known as filé, are GRAS at 30,000 ppm. Artificial sassafras oil is safrole-free and relatively safe, based upon wintergreen. Filé, or gumbo filé (from the Choctaw *kombo ashish*), is used in Cajun cooking, sometimes mixed with other herbs and spices, as a thickener and flavoring in soups and stews. Add the filé at the last few minutes of cooking or else a stringy mass will result (the French *filé* means thread). The egg-shaped or two- to three-lobed ("mitten-shaped") leaves may be ground fresh or dried and powdered for later use. Fortunately safrole is either absent or present in only trace levels in sassafras leaves.

Important chemistry: The essential oil of the roots of sassafras contains 74 to 80 percent safrole, providing a warm-spice, woody-floral odor. The essential oil of the leaves has around 30 percent (*Z*)-nerolidol, 22 percent beta-caryophyllene, and 20 percent linalool, providing a woody-floral, green odor, sometimes with various fatty acids that provide a sour-fatty note. The young twigs of sassafras have an essential oil with around 27 percent limonene, 24 percent linalool, and 16 percent alpha-terpineol, providing a sweet lemony odor.

Botanical Description

S. albidum (Nutt.) Nees, Syst. laur. 490. 1836.
Native country: Sassafras is native from southwestern Maine, west to northern Illinois, and south to eastern and central Florida.

General habit: Sassafras is a tree to 20 m.
Leaves: Leaves are egg-shaped to widest at the center with the ends equal, 8 to 18 by 2 to 8 cm, wedge-shaped at the base, unlobed or usually one- to three-lobed (rarely four- to five-lobed), characteristically mitten-shaped, the lobes almost tapering to the apex or blunt. Upper surfaces are bright green, smooth, and blue-green below, sometimes hairy below in southern trees.
Flowers: Flowers are greenish yellow.
Fruits/seeds: Fruits are olive-like, about 1 cm long, borne on bright red, fleshy stalks.

Satureja

săt-ū-rē-yå
savory

Family: Lamiaceae (Labiatae)
Growth form: annuals and perennials, from trailing groundcovers to tiny shrubs
Hardiness: mostly subtropical but some hardy to Zone 6
Light: most full sun
Water: moist but not constantly wet; many can withstand drought
Soil: well-drained garden loam, pH 5.6 to 8.2, average 6.8 (*S. hortensis*); pH 6.5 to 7.0, average 6.7 (*S. montana*)
Propagation: seeds in spring, 52,000 seeds per ounce (1,834/g) (*S. hortensis*)
Culinary use: teas; many oregano-scented
Craft use: none
Landscape use: groundcover, front of border, container plant

Satureja was most probably adapted from *za'atar*, an Arabic name used for all oregano-scented herbs. A mythological yarn claims that *Satureja* was the herb eaten by satyrs to give them their extraordinary sexual stamina; we cannot promise that effect for humans.

The genus *Satureja* includes approximately thirty species, but many are moved back and forth among the genera *Acinos*, *Micromeria*, *Calamintha*, and *Clinopodium*. Most savories are dwarf shrubs adapted to rather sunny, dry sites; the major exception is yerba buena, which is trailing and prefers part shade and somewhat moister soil.

Satureja douglasii

săt-ū-rē-yå dŭg-lăs-ĭ-ī
yerba buena, Oregon tea

Spanish: *yerba buena*

Yerba buena, which translates as "good herb," is a link to the padres of Spanish California. It conjures visions, as related by Mary Elizabeth Parsons in *The Wild Flowers of California*, of "long, low, rambling mission buildings of adobe, with their picturesque red-tiled roofs; the flocks and herds tended by gentle shepherds in cowls; and the angelus sounding from those quaint belfries, and vibrating in ever-widening circles over hill and vale."

The Spanish padres used this herb for medicinal purposes. Further north, in Oregon, yerba buena was used to make a tea; however, it has no GRAS status by the U.S. Food and Drug Administration. Yerba buena has at least five forms with different aromas: a spearmint-scented form, a pennyroyal-scented form, two peppermint-scented forms, and a camphor-scented form.

The round, pale green, aromatic, evergreen leaves on trailing stems grow in dry, open woods throughout California, Oregon, Washington, and British Columbia; it does not seem to be hardy north of Zone 8b. With solitary small, white flowers in the axils of the leaves, yerba buena is similar to many species of *Micromeria*, in which genus it is often classified.

Important chemistry: The essential oil of yerba buena contains 23 to 46 percent camphor, 13 to 22 percent camphene, trace to 52 percent pulegone, trace to 18 percent carvone, trace to 16 percent isomenthone, trace to 15 percent menthone, and trace to 15 percent piperitenone. The composition is greatly influenced by moisture stress, light intensity, day temperature, and herbivory by slugs.

Satureja hortensis

săt-ū-rē-yå hôr-těn-sĭs
summer savory

French: *sarriette des jardins*
German: *Bohnenkraut*
Dutch: *ibonenkruid*
Italian: *satureia, peverella, santoreggia*
Spanish: *ajedrea de jardin*
Portuguese: *seguerelha*
Swedish: *kyndel*
Russian: *chabyor*
Chinese: *hsiang po ho*
Japanese: *saborí*
Arabic: *nadgh*

Savory bespeaks flavor by its name alone, and its oregano-like taste goes well with vegetable dishes, especially beans, as well as stuffings, sausages, and other meats. As noted by the epithet *hortensis*, or "of the garden," this is the preferred savory for culinary purposes. Summer savory is used commercially in the formulation of vermouths and bitters, sauces, soups, and prepared meats. The essential oil and oleoresin of summer savory are considered GRAS at 4 to 373 ppm; the leaf is GRAS at 200 to 5,190 ppm. Summer savory has been demonstrated to be antibacterial and antifungal, probably from the high concentrations of carvacrol and thymol, two phenols. Summer savory is also antioxidant.

Satureja hortensis

One seed line, 'Saturn', with 41 percent gamma-terpinene and 39 percent carvacrol, has been registered in Poland. H. J. Hannig, K. P. Svoboda, and R. I. Greenaway discuss ten native seed lines ('Aromata', 'Budakalászi', 'Classic', 'Compacta', 'Einjähriges Blatt', 'Lozenka', 'Mestina', 'Pikanta', 'Saturn', and 'SAT 10/97') with 38 to 48 percent carvacrol.

The seeds of this annual may be sown in April and will germinate in two to three weeks. Seeds older than one year quickly lose their viability. Light is necessary for germination, so sow the seeds shallowly. For best growth and development, thin plants to about 6 inches apart. This 18-inch herb has narrow, dark green leaves with light pink flowers. Summer savory grows rapidly and young, tender shoot tips may be har-vested when the plant reaches 6 inches in height; this serves two purposes: to slow flower production and to encourage branching. As the season progresses, the plant may be harvested regularly to retard flowering. Before the first autumn freeze, the entire plant may be cut for drying. Freezing may also preserve the fresh leaves.

The commercial summer savory is commonly adulterated with *S. montana* (winter savory) and *Thymbra spicata*.

Important chemistry: The essential oil of summer savory contains 24 to 63 percent carvacrol and trace to 53 percent gamma-terpinene, providing an oregano-like odor. Wild *S. hortensis* is often scented of thyme from 29 to 43 percent thymol.

Satureja montana
săt-ū-rē-yå mŏn-tā-nå
winter savory

French: *sarriette des montagnes*
German: *Winterbohnenkraut, Guisopillo*
Italian: *santoreggia invernale*
Spanish: *hisopillo*

Winter savory is a perennial plant of the high country (hence, its epithet) of southern Europe, hardy to at least Zone 6. Its perennial nature along with smaller, paler green leaves, white flowers, and lower stature set it apart from its annual relative, summer savory.

Winter savory is used in similar fashion to summer savory. The essential oil of winter savory is considered GRAS at 4 to 50 ppm; the oleoresin is GRAS at 4 to 127 ppm. Winter savory has been demonstrated to be antibacterial and antifungal, primarily from the content of carvacrol and thymol, two phenols. The essen-tial oil of winter savory may also be useful in treating ascosphaerosis of honeybees.

A low-growing dwarf winter savory is often listed as *S. repanda* or *S. spicigera* in popular herb books, but in all botanical revisions and

Satureja montana

floras this appears to be a dwarf variant of *S. montana* subsp. *montana*. It is probably *S. montana* subsp. *montana* var. *prostrata* Boiss. (Voy. bot. Espagne 495. 1841), which is native to the mountains of Spain. Dwarf winter savory is appropriate for the rock garden.

Important chemistry: The essential oil of *S. montana* subsp. *montana*, typical winter savory, has trace to 68 percent carvacrol, trace to 61 percent thymol, trace to 47 percent para-cymene, trace to 23 percent gamma-terpinene, and trace to 20 percent 1,8-cineole, providing an oregano/thyme-like odor. Local populations in the Balkans include a *p*-cymene-type (15 to 48 percent *p*-cymene, 5 to 21 percent borneol, trace to 21 percent *trans*-sabinene hydrate, trace to 14 percent gamma-terpinene), a *trans*-sabinene hydrate-type (14 to 27 percent *trans*-sabinene hydrate, trace to 19 percent *p*-cymene, 4 to 14 percent terpinen-4-ol), a linalool-type (8 to 74 percent linalool, 2 to 18 percent borneol, trace to 12 percent terpinen-4-ol), a borneol-type (22 to 30 percent borneol, 3 to 29 percent *p*-cymene), a p-cymen-8-ol-type (11 to 27 percent p-cymen-8-ol, 2 to 19 percent *p*-cymene, trace to 16 percent linalool, 2 to 14 percent limonene, trace to 11 percent thymol), and a carvacrol/thymol type (5 to 52 percent carvacrol, 3 to 45 percent thymol, and 4 to 26 percent *p*-cymene).

Satureja thymbra

săt-ū-rē-yå tĭm-brå

za'atar rumi

Arabic: *za'atar rumi, za'atar franji*
Greek: *throumbi, thymbri, thymbros, thrymbi, thryvi, throumba, thryba*

Thymbra was the Greek name for this plant. The Arabic name *za'atar rumi* means "Roman hyssop," while *za'atar franji* means "European hyssop." This species exists in both thyme- and oregano-scented forms and has been used as a substitute for both herbs.

This savory is a small, woody perennial with small whorls of tiny, egg-shaped leaves and clusters of pink flowers at narrow intervals. Za'atar rumi does not seem to be hardy north of Zone 9, so it is best cultivated in pots.

Za'atar rumi is antibacterial and antifungal from the high content of thymol and carvacrol, two phenols. It is also antinociceptive and anti-inflammatory.

Important chemistry: The essential oil of za'atar rumi has trace to 66 percent thymol, 3 to 49 percent carvacrol, 10 to 46 percent gamma-terpinene, and 8 to 35 percent para-cymene, providing an oregano/thyme-like odor.

Botanical Key and Description

Key:

1. Plant trailing; leaves egg-shaped. . . . . *S. douglasii*
1a. Plant upright; leaves linear to inversely egg-shaped 2
    2. Annual; at least the lower calyx-teeth much longer than the tube . . . . *S. hortensis*
    2a. Dwarf shrub or perennial woody herb; calyx-teeth shorter than to slightly longer than tube 3
        3. Small bracts numerous, oblong or lance-shaped, about as long as the calyx . . . . *S. thymbra*
        3a. Small bracts absent or short, rarely a few almost as long as calyx . . . . *S. montana*

S. douglasii (Benth.) Briq. in Engl. & Prantl, Nat. Pflanzenfam. 4(3A):300. 1896 [*Micromeria chamissonis* (Benth.) Greene, *M. douglasii* (Benth.) Benth.].

Native country: Yerba buena is found in dry brushy tracts and open woods from Vancouver Island to Los Angeles County, California.

General habit: Yerba buena is a trailing perennial herb with stems 30 to 122 cm long.

Leaves: Leaves are opposite, short-stalked, egg-shaped, round-toothed, green above, purple beneath.

Flowers: Flowers, which appear in the axils of the leaves, are solitary, small, and white.

S. hortensis L., Sp. pl. 568. 1753.

Native country: Summer savory is native to the Mediterranean region.

General habit: Summer savory is an annual herb, slightly hairy, 10 to 25 cm high.

Leaves: Leaves are 10 to 40 by 1 to 5 mm, linear or linear-lance-shaped, blunt at the apex.

Flowers: Flowers are pink or lavender in two- to five-flowered clusters.

S. montana L., Sp. pl. 568. 1753.

Winter savory, according to P. W. Ball and F. M. Getliffe, includes five subspecies in Europe, but only subsp. *montana* is economically important:

subsp. *montana*

subsp. *variegata* (Host) P. W. Ball, Bot. J. Linn. Soc. 65:352. 1972.

subsp. *illyrica* Nyman, Consp. fl. eur. 591. 1881.

subsp. *kitaibelii* (Wierzb.) P. W. Ball, Bot. J. L. Soc. 65:332. 1972.

subsp. *taurica* (Velen.) P. W. Ball, Bot. J. Linn. Soc. 65:352. 1972.

Native country: Winter savory is native to southern Europe.

General habit: Winter savory is a perennial woody herb 10 to 70 cm high, smooth or slightly hairy.

Leaves: Leaves are 5 to 30 by 1 to 7 mm, linear to lance-shaped with narrowed bases, usually tapering to the apex.

Flowers: Flowers are white to pale pink in clusters of up to fourteen.

S. thymbra L., Sp. pl. 567. 1753.

Native country: Za'atar rumi is native to the southern Aegean region to the eastern Mediterranean.

General habit: Za'atar rumi is a much-branched, usually gray-hairy dwarf shrub 20 to 35 cm tall.

Leaves: Leaves are 5 to 20 by 1 to 9 mm, two to four times longer than wide and the sides parallel or nearly so to inversely egg-shaped, tapering to the apex.

Flowers: Flowers are bright pink or reddish purple.

Sesamum orientale

sĕs-å-mŭm ôr-ĭ-ĕn-tā-lē
sesame

Family: Pedaliaceae
Growth form: annual to 4 feet (1.2 m)
Hardiness: cannot withstand frost
Light: full sun
Water: moist but not constantly wet
Soil: well-drained garden loam with near-neutral pH
Propagation: seeds in spring, 10,200 seeds per ounce (360/g)
Culinary use: oil, seeds for breads
Craft use: none
Landscape use: vegetable garden

French: *sésame*
German: *Sesamstrauch*
Dutch: *sesamstruik*
Italian: *sesamo, ginggiolena*
Spanish: *sésamo, ajonjolí, alegría*
Portuguese: *gergelim*
Swedish: *sesam*
Russian: *kunzhut*
Chinese: *hu-ma, ch'ing-jang*
Japanese: *goma*
Arabic: *simsim*

Sesame, alias gingelly, jingili, or benné, is cultivated for its oil or for its edible seeds. The seeds have about 45 to 63 percent oil and 25 percent protein. Records of sesame cultivation go back to the Tigris and Euphrates valleys of 1600 B.C.E. and even further to Harappa (c. 3500–3050 B.C.E.). Biochemical evidence further supports an origin in India, possibly *S. latifolium* J. B. Gillett × *S. radiatum* Schumach. & Thonn. We also know that sesame seed was pressed for its oil in the empire of Urartu (now Armenia) about 900 to 700 B.C.E. Today India and China are the world's largest producers of sesame. The United States also produces sesame; its cultivation is centered around Paris, Texas.

Sesame is a rough, hairy, gummy annual plant to 2.6 feet (80 cm) high with linear, lance-shaped leaves to 4 inches (10 cm) long. The pale or rose-colored flowers are followed by black or white seeds, which are tiny but sweet and oily. The seeds are commonly used to flavor breads, and the oil is used in baking. Sesame seeds may be eaten raw or roasted; the temperature for roasting to achieve the best flavor is around 392°F (200°C) for a few minutes until lightly browned on the edges. Sesame seeds are considered GRAS, although some people have demonstrated a life-threatening allergy to sesame seeds. Sesamin, a lignan from sesame oil, is antihypertensive. Sesame oil may also be protective against hepatotoxicity. Sesame oil also has a synergistic effect with some insecticides,

Sesamum orientale

particularly pyrethrins, due to the content of sesamolin.

The genus *Sesamum* includes about fifteen species of the Old World and South Africa. The generic name is derived from a Semitic word similar to the Egyptian *sesemt*; this is mentioned in the Ebers Papyrus of about 1500 B.C.E.

Commercial varieties of sesame require 90 to 120 frost-free days; the home gardener on the margins of cultivation can start transplants earlier to speed the process. Sesame should not be planted before the soil reaches a temperature of 70°F (21°C). Sesame can be directly seeded at 250,000 to 300,000 plants per acre in 18- to 30-inch (46 to 76 cm) rows for highest yields. Because of slow early growth, sesame is a poor competitor against weeds. Select fields with low weeds and cultivate very shallowly in order to avoid injury to the surface roots. Daytime temperatures of 77 to 80°F (25 to 27°C) are optimal for cultivation.

Sesame has an extensive root system and is very drought tolerant, but it requires adequate moisture for germination and early growth. A minimum rainfall of 20 to 26 inches (51 to 66 cm) during the growing season is required for reasonable yields. Rainfall late in the season prolongs growth and increases loss due to shattering.

The best soils for sesame growth are well-drained, fertile soils of medium texture and neutral pH. Increased levels of nitrogen result in increased protein and decreased oil content, while potassium demonstrates a similar, but smaller response; phosphorous alone has no effect on protein or oil content.

Sesame is ready for harvesting 90 to 150 days after planting. As the seed pods ripen, the long pockets split and release the seeds ("open sesame"). Because of shattering problems, the dis-covery of non-shattering sesame in 1943 was an innovation toward the development of high yielding, shatter-resistant varieties that can be mechanically harvested. Yields of 1,000 to 2,300 pounds per acre (1,207 to 2,577 kg/ha) are generally expected.

Important chemistry: Sesame oil, which contains about 47 percent oleic acid and 39 percent linoleic acid, stores well because of a natural antioxidant, sesamol. The flavor components of the seed oil are primarily 9 to 17 percent 2-methylpyrazine, 0 to 6 percent furfuryl alcohol, 5 to 15 percent 2,5-dimethylpyrazine, and 0 to 3 percent pyrrole. The most important odorants in roasted black and white sesame seeds are (*E*,*E*)-2,4-decadienal, 2-methoxyphenol, 2-pentylpyridine, 2-furfurylthiol, 2-ethyl-3,5-dimethylpyrazine, 4-hydroxy-2,5-dimethyl-3(2H)-furanone, and 2-phenylethylthiol. These flavor chemicals provide a green pepper–baked bread-like odor.

Botanical Description

S. orientale L., Sp. pl. 634. 1753 (*S. indicum* L.).
Native country: Sesame is probably native to Southeast Asia but naturalized in southeastern Europe.
General habit: Sesame is an erect, hairy annual 30 to 80 cm high, simple or with branches.
Leaves: Leaves are about 10 cm long, stalked, the lower usually lobed or divided into threes, opposite, the upper oblong to linear-lance-shaped, smooth-edged, alternate.
Flowers: Flowers are white, often with purplish or yellow markings, about 3 cm long, in the axils of the leaves.
Fruits/seeds: Fruits are 25 by 5 mm pockets, oblong, erect, rough. Seeds may be whitish or black.

Sinapis

sī-nāp-ĭs
sinapis

Family: Brassicaceae (Cruciferae)

Growth form: annuals to about 32 inches (80 cm)

Hardiness: withstands frost

Light: full sun

Water: moist but not constantly wet

Soil: good garden loam, pH 4.5 to 8.2, average 6.6 (*S. alba*)

Propagation: seeds in spring, 15,000 seeds per ounce (535/g) (*S. alba*)

Culinary use: mustards

Craft use: none

Landscape use: wildflower garden

Yellow mustard and charlock resemble brown mustard and black mustard, species of the genus *Brassica* (which see), but yet are sufficiently different to warrant a separate genus. This is reflected in the Greek name, *sinapi* ("cabbage"), which is said to be derived from *nap*, Celtic for plants resembling cabbage or turnip. The genus *Sinapis* includes about ten species of Europe.

While these plants are raised commercially for their seeds, they are not often cultivated by the home gardener because of the work involved. With the advent of novel homemade mustards, however, we may see more small-scale cultivation.

Sinapis alba

sī-nāp-ĭs ăl-bâ
yellow mustard

French: *moutarde blanche (jaune, anglaise)*

German: *Weisser (Gelber) Senf*

Dutch: *witte (gele) mosterd*

Italian: *sanape bianca, rucherttone*

Spanish: *mostaza blanca, jenabe, jenable*

Portuguese: *mostarda branca*

Swedish: *vit senap*

Russian: *gorchitsa byepaya*

Chinese: *pai-chieh*

Japanese: *karashi*

Arabic: *khardal*

In English this is also known as white mustard (and the specific epithet means white). Yellow mustard provides a sharp taste distinct from that of brown or Oriental mustard (see *Brassica*).

Seeds of *Sinapis alba* are listed as GRAS at 20 to 124,274 ppm, while the essential oil is GRAS at 201 ppm.

For culture, see *Brassica juncea* var. *juncea*. Yield of yellow mustard is about 800 pounds per acre (897 kg/ha). Under relatively cold conditions with a day/night rhythm rising from 64.4/48.2°F at seed planting to 75.2/57.2°F at seed formation (18/9°C to 24/14°C), the yield of seeds per plant may be up to 78 percent higher. Commercial sources are the same as for *B. juncea* var. *juncea*.

Important chemistry: In the presence of water, sinalbin (sinapine *p*-hydroxybenzyl glucosinolate) is acted upon by myrosinase to liberate 2 to 4 percent *p*-hydroxybenzyl isothiocyanate, a non-volatile isothiocyanate. The essential oil of the leafy tops is dominated by 53 percent thymol and 27 percent linalool, providing a thyme/lavender odor.

Sinapis arvensis
sī-nāp-ĭs är-vĕn-sĭs
charlock

Sinapis arvensis

French: *moutarde sauvage, moutarde des champs, sénève*
German: *Acker-Senf*
Dutch: *herik*
Italian: *senapa salvatica, senape arvense, serafini*
Spanish: *mostaza negra, jenable, jenabe*
Portuguese: *mostarda dos campos*

In English, charlock is also known as wild mustard or corn mustard. Seeds of charlock have been used to prepare poor quality mustard, and the active constituents are similar to *S. alba*. Charlock is sometimes cultivated as an oil crop or vegetable but may become a serious weed (aptly illustrated by the specific epithet, which means "of cultivated land"). For culture, see *Brassica juncea* var. *juncea*. Limited production of charlock occurs in the former Soviet Union, France, Hungary, and Romania, but not at levels of commercial significance.

Botanical Key and Description

Key:
1. Surface of long capsules smooth or at most only finely hairy or with a very few falling prematurely fine erect points; eight to seventeen small seeds, not much exceeding 1 mm thick . . . . *S. arvensis*
1a. Surface of long capsules bristly-hairy; four to eight large seeds, often exceeding 2 mm thick . . . . . . *S. alba*

S. alba L., Sp. pl. 668. 1753.
Native country: Yellow mustard is an annual herb native to the Mediterranean region.
General habit: Stems are up to 80 cm tall, usually with stiff, deflexed hairs, sometimes smooth.
Leaves: Leaves are usually with stiff and rigid bristles (hispid) but not rough to the touch, all stalked.
Flowers: Flowers are yellow, stalked, on many short stems.

Fruit/seeds: Long capsules are 20 to 40 by 3 to 6.5 mm. Seeds are about 3 mm in diameter, flattened laterally, usually a pale straw color but sometimes with a slight pinkish cast.

S. arvensis L., Sp. pl. 668. 1753 [*S. orientalis* L., *S. kaber* DC., *B. kaber* (DC.) Wheeler, *B. arvensis* (L.), Rabenh.].
Native country: Charlock is an annual herb native to the Mediterranean region but naturalized throughout Europe.

General habit: Stems grow to 80 cm high, with stiff and rigid bristles at least below, sometimes smooth.
Leaves: Leaves are up to 20 cm long, usually with stiff and rigid bristles; lower stalked, lobed, with a large, coarsely toothed termi-nal lobe, usually with several smaller lateral lobes; upper leaves are not stalked, usually simple, lance-shaped.
Flowers: Flowers are yellow, small.
Fruit/seeds: Long capsules are 25 to 55 by 1.5 to 4 mm. Seeds are reddish brown or black.

Solidago odora

sŏl-ĭ-dā-gō ō-dŏ-rå
sweet goldenrod

Family: Asteraceae (Compositae)
Growth form: perennial to 5 feet (160 cm)
Hardiness: hardy to New Hampshire (Zone 5)
Light: full sun
Water: moist but not constantly wet
Soil: sandy, acid soil preferred
Propagation: seeds or divisions of clumps in spring
Culinary use: limited (not GRAS)
Craft use: potpourri, dye
Landscape use: rear of perennial border, meadow gardens

On 24 June 1996, Governor Thomas Carper signed Senate Bill No. 364 proclaiming sweet goldenrod as the State Herb of Delaware. Delaware thus became the first state in the Union to designate an herb in this manner.

Sweet goldenrod, alias Texas goldenrod, licorice goldenrod, Blue Mountain tea, or fragrant goldenrod, smells and looks like French tarragon (*Artemisia dracunculus* 'Sativa') but without that characteristic full, warm, herbaceous odor. After the Boston Tea Party in 1773, the colonists substituted a Liberty tea composed of equal parts of sweet goldenrod, betony, red clover, and New Jersey tea (*Ceanothus americanus*

L.). By 1816, according to nineteenth-century botanist Frederick Pursh, sweet goldenrod became an article of export to China, fetching a high price. The oil extracted from sweet goldenrod was listed as official in the *U.S. Pharmacopoeia* from 1820 to 1882 and it was once raised commercially in Texas for its oil, but today sweet goldenrod is not considered GRAS. If it were more commercially available, its primary use would now be in perfumes of the fougère

Solidago odora

type, chypres, moss, and so on, or in trace amounts in lilac, muguet, and similar scents. Try it in potpourri! Sweet goldenrod, like other goldenrods, can also be used as a dye herb.

The genus *Solidago* includes about 100 species primarily in North America with a few in South America and Eurasia. The generic name is derived from the Latin *solido*, "to make whole," an allusion to its reputed healing qualities.

Sweet goldenrod is a short-lived herbaceous perennial easily raised in full sun and very sandy, slightly acid soil. Under favorable conditions, it readily reseeds but never to the extent of becoming weedy. It would be excellent in wildflower mixtures, and the golden yellow flowers from July to September blend well in the border with plants like the beebalms (*Monarda* spp.). The erect, often sprawling stems of sweet goldenrod, up to 5 feet (160 cm) tall, bear long linear leaves up to 4 inches (11 cm) long and dotted with glandular dots that are visible when held to the light.

Cases of livestock deaths from consuming sweet goldenrod have been reported, but the culprit seems to be a rust fungus (*Colesporium asterum*) that sometimes grows on the foliage, not the herb itself. This rust is widespread in the northern hemisphere and also infects other members of the aster family; it requires two hosts to complete its life cycle and uses pine trees as the alternate host. Hence, cultivation should be as separate as possible from other composite flowers and pine trees.

Goldenrods have come into vogue for the fall perennial border with their many forms, from short to tall, most with golden yellow flowers. Most other species have no herbal uses.

No discussion of goldenrods would be complete without tackling the great myth that they cause hay fever. Goldenrod pollen does not cause allergic reactions, but the belief that goldenrods cause hay fever is tenacious. This mistaken belief probably started because goldenrod's bright flowers stand out in the late summer weedscape, but the real culprits are the greenish brown ragweeds (*Ambrosia* spp.) that bloom at the same time. The ragweeds have light, airborne pollen that is easily inhaled by the hapless allergic individual, while goldenrods have heavy, insect-borne pollen. Well, you might be able to induce an allergic response by stuffing the flowers up your nose, but you could do the same thing with many other flowers.

Important chemistry: The essential oil of sweet goldenrod is dominated by about 71 to 75 percent estragole (methyl chavicol) and about 12 percent myrcene, providing a characteristic tarragon-like odor. A "scentless" form, f. *inodora* Gray, has also been described with about 31 percent myrcene, 27 percent limonene, and 13 percent (*E*)-methyl isoeugenol

Botanical Description

S. odora Aiton, Hort. kew. 3:214. 1789.
Native country: Sweet goldenrod is native to dry, open woods, especially in sandy soil, from Massachusetts and New Hampshire and Vermont to southern Ohio and southern Missouri, south to Florida and Texas.
General habit: Sweet goldenrod is an herbaceous perennial with 60 to 160 cm stems arising from a stout, persistent, woody base.
Leaves: Leaves are 4 to 11 cm long by 0.5 to 2 cm wide, stalkless, smooth, smooth-edged, finely dotted with glandular dots, not prominently veined.
Flowers: Flowers are golden yellow in a branched inflorescence with the younger flowers at the center.

Stevia rebaudiana

stē-vǐ-å rě-bâw-dǐ-ǎn-å
Paraguayan sweet herb, stevia

Family: Asteraceae (Compositae)
Growth form: shrubby perennial to 18 inches (45 cm)
Hardiness: hardy only to Zone 9
Light: full sun
Water: moist but not constantly wet
Soil: well-drained garden loam
Propagation: cuttings in summer
Culinary use: sweetener but limited (not GRAS)
Craft use: none
Landscape use: container plant

The leaves of *S. rebaudiana* have been known to the Guarani Indians of Paraguay as *kaá hâ-é, caá-êhé, caá-hê-hê, caá-enhem, azucá-caá, eira-caa,* or *ca-a-yupe,* all loosely translated as "sweet herb," and used for centuries as a sweetener for bitter drinks such as maté (*Ilex paraguariensis* St.-Hil.); it is also called sugar grass or *yerbe dulce.* In 1931 M. Bridel and R. Lavieille of France discovered a sweet diterpenic glycoside that they termed stevioside (a.k.a. stevin or eupatorin). While some species of *Stevia* have sweet leaves, no other species of *Stevia* seems to possess such intensely sweet leaves (but stevioside also occurs in the leaves of a raspberry, *Rubus suavissimus* S. Lee).

Stevioside is 100 to 300 times more sweet than sucrose, non-caloric, anticariogenic (inhibits tooth decay), non-fermentable, does not darken upon cooking, and is highly stable when exposed to both acids and heat. Stevioside has a detectable taste at a threshold of 0.002 percent, but large amounts of the leaves taste bitter. Stevioside is used as a sweetener in Japan, China, Korea, Israel, Brazil, and Paraguay. In Japan,

stevia extracts and stevioside are used to sweeten Japanese-style pickles, dried sea foods, fish, meat pastes, soy sauce, and bean paste products, fruit-flavored drinks, and other beverages, and dessert items, such as ice cream and chewing gum. In the United States, leaves of *S. rebaudiana* have been used to flavor herbal teas.

The discovery of the Paraguayan sweet herb was revealed to the world by Moisés Santiago Bertoni, a scientist in Paraguay. He first published it in 1899 as a species of *Eupatorium,* to which it is very similar, later changing it to a species of *Stevia* in 1905. Overall, the flowering plant has the appearance of a small white-flowering boneset with papery leaves that may reach 2 inches (5 cm) long. The genus *Stevia* includes about 120 to 300 tropical and subtropical species of the New World and was named after P. J. Esteve, a botanist of Valencia, Spain; *rebaudi-*

Stevia rebaudiana

ana was coined to honor the Paraguayan chemist Ovidio Rebaudi.

Stevioside is passed through the human digestive system apparently unaltered and does not appear to be toxic to guinea pigs, rabbits, or chickens. Stevioside is not mutagenic or teratogenic, and no indications exist that stevioside causes cancer in humans. In experiments with rats, stevioside produced no significant changes in blood glucose or liver glycogen levels and did not change the relative sizes of the liver, thyroid gland, or adrenal gland with a normal diet; stevioside with a high carbohydrate diet in rats produced a significant decrease in liver glycogen. Chronic administration of an aqueous extract, though, induced systemic and renal widening of the blood vessels, causing abnormally low blood pressure, diuresis (increased urination), and natriuresis (excretion of greater than normal amounts of sodium in the urine). Prenatal exposure to stevioside is not toxic for the chicken embryo. No allergic reactions have been reported. A study done on tolerability of oral stevioside in hyperlipidemic patients found that stevia was safe.

Stevia may actually be beneficial for your health. A number of studies have focused on its antidiabetic activity in both rats and humans. A study done in China found that stevia should be considered as a supplemental therapy for patients with hypertension. Stevia may also be anti-carcinogenic and antibacterial.

Blood pressure, respiration, cardiogram, and body temperature of rabbits are unaffected by stevioside. One report showed a slight contraceptive effect of leaf extracts in female rats, but this has not been confirmed, and tests for anti-androgenic activity were negative. Despite such scientific documentation, in May 1991 the U.S. Food and Drug Administration (FDA) issued an import alert on *S. rebaudiana*, and the herb has mysteriously failed to achieve GRAS status despite repeated attempts from American Herbal Products Association (AHPA). In September 1995, the FDA lifted the import alert on *S. rebaudiana*; the herb can be imported only as a "dietary supplement," not as a sweetener! However, now the big companies have discovered stevia; Cargill and Coca-Cola are poised to produce the stevia derivative Truvia, and Corn Products International is readying its Enliten.

Why does *S. rebaudiana* produce stevioside? Experiments with herbivorous insects have concluded that stevioside is an antifeedent: many insects would rather face starvation than eat the leaves. Stevioside also has growth-regulating properties similar to gibberellin in some plants.

Paraguayan sweet herb is easily cultivated in pots or good garden loam in full sun. Since this species is normally found in moist to wet areas, it does not stand drought well. Seeds may be set after flowering in late fall to early winter, but these inevitably fail to germinate. Propagation is best from cuttings during active growth in summer. Harvesting of leaves should be on a sunny, dry day and then the leaves rapidly dried to a moisture content of 15 to 20 percent in an oven at 158°F (70°C) or by sun drying; leaves should be subsequently kept dry. Most of the commercial culture today is done in South Korea, Japan, and Taiwan, where several products from *S. rebaudiana* are sold: crude extract (about 20 percent stevioside), crude product (about 50 percent stevioside), stevioside (about 95 percent stevioside), Stevix (50 to 90 percent steviosides, rebaudiosides, etc.), and Steviosin (greater than 95 percent stevioside).

The content of sweet compounds in leaf tissue can vary by method of propagation, day length, and agronomic practices. Canadian researchers found that plants spaced 12 inches (30 cm) apart in rows 12 inches (30 cm) apart yielded 2,677 pounds per acre (3,000 kg/ha) of leaves with a stevioside content of 10.5 percent or 281 pounds per acre (315 kg/ha). If stevioside is estimated to be 210 times sweeter than sucrose, this yield of stevioside is equivalent to 29 tons of sugar per acre (66.2 tons/ha)!

Important chemistry: The leaves of *S. rebaudiana* are characterized by eight different *ent*-kaurene glycosides with sweetening properties. The four major ones are stevioside, rebaudioside A, rebaudioside C, and dulcoside A with sweetness relative to sucrose 100 to 300, 242 to 450, 30 to 120, and 40 to 120, respectively. Stevioside comprises 6 to 20 percent of the dried leaves and about 4 percent of the dried flowers of *S. rebaudiana*, and upon hydrolysis yields three moles of D-glucose to one mole of steviol. Other sweet diterpene glycosides include rebaudioside B, rebaudioside D, rebaudioside E, and steviolbioside with sweetness relative to sucrose 300 to 350, 200 to 300, 250 to 300, and 100 to 125, respectively.

The essential oil is characterized by 0 to 23 percent spathulenol I, 6 to 20 percent caryophyllene oxide, 1 to 12 percent beta-caryophyllene, 0 to 12 percent beta-cubebene, 0 to 12 percent gamma-elemene, and trace to 11 percent *trans*-beta-farnesene, providing a light green-flowery fragrance.

Botanical Description

S. rebaudiana (Bertoni) Bertoni, Anales Ci. Parag. Ser. I, 5:1. 1905 [*Eupatorium rebaudianum* Bertoni, *S. rebaudiana* (Bertoni) Hemsl.].

Native country: The Paraguayan sweet herb is native to edges of marshes and grassland communities on soils with shallow water tables in northeastern Paraguay and bordering Mato Grosso do Sul in Brazil.

General habit: The Paraguayan sweet herb is a shrubby perennial herb to 45 cm.

Leaves: Leaves are opposite, sessile, lance-oblong to spoon-shaped, blunt-tipped, lightly toothed above the middle, toothless on the narrowed base, with a papery texture, three-nerved, 3 to 5 cm long.

Flowers: White flowers have a purple throat.

Fruit/seeds: The brown fruit is a bristly achene.

Tagetes lucida

tå-jē-tēz lū-sĭ-då
Mexican tarragon

Family: Asteraceae (Compositae)

Growth form: herbaceous perennial to 310 inches (80 cm)

Hardiness: marginally hardy to Zone 7b

Light: full sun

Water: constant moisture but not wet

Soil: well-drained garden loam

Propagation: cuttings throughout summer

Culinary use: has been substituted for French tarragon but not GRAS

Craft use: none

Landscape use: mid-border or container plant

Spanish: *pericon, Santa Maria, anisillo*

Annual marigolds have been popular for so long with the general public that they have become a landscape cliché in America. These familiar, bright flowers in yellows and oranges are mostly the product of selection from the African marigold (*T. erecta* L.) and the French marigold (*T. patula* L.), and their pungent foliage ("stink flowers" is a common name) does not endear them to many gardeners. Mexican tarragon (also called sweet marigold or sweet mace) has an entirely different aroma, superficially similar to French tarragon (*Artemisia dracunculus* 'Sativa') but without the full, warm herbaceous odor of that classic herb of haute cuisine. The flowers of Mexican tarragon, unlike its flamboyant bedding plant cousins, are small enough to be overlooked and appear in late fall. However, in warm climates with high rainfall or high summer humidity (such as southern U.S. Gulf Coastal states), where French tarragon is difficult to impossible to grow because of its susceptibility to diseases, Mexican tarragon is often grown as a substitute. Unfortunately, while the essential oils of African and French marigolds (and *T. minuta* L.) have GRAS status, Mexican tarragon lacks this critical legal classification. Yet, this has not halted its entry into supermarkets, where it is sometimes sold as "winter tarragon" or "Texas tarragon."

Tagetes lucida

The genus *Tagetes* includes about forty-two species of tropical America from southwestern United States to Argentina with the greatest diversity in south and central Mexico. The generic name is derived from the name of an Etruscan deity, Tages, said to have sprung from the earth as it was being plowed.

Mexican tarragon, sometimes called Mexican mint marigold in the herb trade, is a perennial with smooth, toothed, egg-lance-shaped leaves to 4 inches (10 cm) long. Plants raised under optimum conditions can reach 310 inches (80 cm) high, but pot-grown plants or plants grown in the ground in temperate areas normally do not reach more than 18 to 24 inches (46 to 61 cm). The small, golden orange-yellow marigold flowers appear in very late fall just before frost in the northeastern United States.

Mexican tarragon, under the Nahuantl names *yahutli* or *tumutsáli*, is one of the ingredients in a mixture smoked by Huichal Indians in Mexico. In many parts of Latin America today, sweet marigold is used to brew a tea. Crude and semipurified extracts of *T. lucida* have been demonstrated to have an anticholinergic activity and may thus have usefulness as a remedy for several muscular problems. An aqueous leaf sample was also demonstrated to block spontaneous uterus contractability in rats in the laboratory, supporting its postpartum folk use in Mexico. Mexican tarragon is antifungal and antibacterial.

Propagation of Mexican tarragon is easy from cuttings, and branches near the base often have adventitious roots already formed and can be broken off and planted. Seed is difficult to find and often slow to germinate, perhaps because of poor storage practices. Plants may be grown in pots, where a soilless growing medium works well, or in the garden with good, friable, well-drained soil in full sun. This herb is marginally hardy in Zone 7, where, in an average winter, about 25 percent of the plants will be lost; it should be fully hardy in Zone 8. While French tarragon droops under summer heat, Mexican tarragon luxuriates under high temperatures; keep the moisture constant, however, to prevent wilting from water stress.

Several other species of *Tagetes*, such as *T. lemmonii* Gray, are sometimes used by Tex-Mex cooks. Irish lace, *T. filifolia* Lag., primarily grown as an ornamental, has an odor of anise and French tarragon, with small, white, marigold blossoms. *Tagetes minuta* L. (sometimes called Mexican marigold) is a tall marigold (up to 12 feet, 3.7 m, in a season) with tiny flowers in clusters in the fall. It is used in South America for tea or a pesto-like sauce prepared from its aromatic leaves with peanut oil and hot peppers to serve on vegetables, especially potatoes.

Important chemistry: The essential oil of *T. lucida* is dominated by 34 to 90 percent estragole (methyl chavicol) with 0 to 24 percent (*E*)-anethole and trace to 24 percent methyl eugenol.

Botanical Description

Two subspecies are recorded, but the plant under cultivation is usually *T. lucida* subsp. *lucida*.

T. lucida Cav., Icon. 3. 1794.
Native country: Mexican tarragon is native to rocky, wooded slopes, disturbed roadsides, and agricultural areas in Mexico, from Sonora south into Chiapas, and infrequently in Guatemala, from 1,100 to 4,100 m.
General habit: Mexican tarragon is an erect and nearly smooth perennial 30 to 80 cm high with a short, thick base.
Leaves: Leaves are egg-lance-shaped, extremely variable in size, 2 to 10 by 0.5 to 2 cm, finely toothed, often with elongate bristle tips on the lower teeth.
Flowers: Blooms with heads of golden orange-yellow flowers.

Tanacetum

tăn-å-sē-tŭm
tanacetum

Family: Asteraceae (Compositae)
Growth form: herbaceous perennials to 4 to 5 feet (1.2 to 1.5 m)
Hardiness: hardy to Nova Scotia and Quebec (at least Zone 4)
Light: full sun
Water: not constantly moist; can withstand some mild drought
Soil: average garden soil, pH 4.8 to 7.5, average 6.3 (*T. vulgare*); 4.9 to 7.2, average 6.2 (*T. balsamita*)
Propagation: divisions in spring or fall easiest, seeds and cuttings also possible; 240,000 seeds per ounce (8,466/g) (*T. vulgare*)
Culinary use: very limited; may be poisonous in excess
Craft use: dried flowers, potpourri, natural insecticides
Landscape use: front to middle of herb or perennial border

Tansy and costmary were once listed as species of *Chrysanthemum*, but in the realignment of that genus of 200 species with mixed origins, tansy and costmary were moved to *Tanacetum*, a genus with about 150 species mostly native to the Old World. This genus, defined by microscopic characteristics, chemistry, and so on, also includes two familiar medicinal herbs beyond the scope of this book, *T. cinerariifolium* (Trevir.) Schultz-Bip., pyrethrum, and *T. parthenium* (L.) Schultz-Bip., feverfew.

The immediate source of the generic name is from the medieval Latin name for tansy, *tanazeta*, but the root is believed to be derived from the Greek word *athanatos* ("immortal"). This is perhaps an allusion to the long-lasting flowers or perhaps an allusion to the ancient practice of using tansy for embalming and meat preservation.

Tanacetum balsamita
tăn-ȧ-sē-tŭm bâl-sȧ-mĭ-tȧ
costmary

> **French:** *balsamite, tanaise balsamite, menthe-coq*
> **German:** *Balsamkrautes, Marien Balsam, Marienblatt, Frauen Münze, Frauenblatt, Minzenartiger Rainfarn, Garten-Rainfarn*
> **Dutch:** *tuinbalsem*
> **Italian:** *balsamite, erba costa, tanaceto balsamino, erba di San Pietro, erba di Santa Maria, erba amara*
> **Spanish:** *balsamite, tanaceto*
> **Portuguese:** *tanaceto*

Costmary is usually represented in the herb garden by large, upright, yellow-green leaves, sometimes coated with a blue-green wax. Then, at the time of flowering, straggly stems ascend with daisy-like flowers, yellow centers with or without white rays. The large leaves of costmary have been used as an herb and pot herb, but its principal use today is in liqueurs, the only use for which it has GRAS status. Costmary has a relatively minor use in perfumery today, but it was once used with lavender for "sweet washing water." For the home gardener, it's excellent in potpourri and blends well with rosemary, cloves, bay, cinnamon, and sage.

Costmary was once used for strewing, and appropriately enough it is insecticidal because it contains pyrethrin I. Thus, flaked or powdered dry costmary leaves may be effective against fleas and other insect pests of the home and garden; experimentation is needed. Costmary has some curative effects on liver damage.

If botanists are a bit uncertain exactly where costmary fits in the scheme of evolution (*Tanacetum* or *Chrysanthemum*), they are not the only ones in the garden who are confused. Some people have found that confusion and mystery abound even in the meanings of common names that have been applied to *T. balsamita*. To look at a list of past common names for this plant leaves one mystified and full of questions. Why was costmary originally called *Costus Marie*, or Mary Magdalene's balsam? It has also been called maudeline or maudelinewort, again after Mary Magdalene, but the texts are curiously silent on the dedication of this particular herb to Mary Magdalene. Why are the alternate German names *Marien Balsam* and *Frauen Münze*, which signify dedication to the Virgin Mary? Was the Latin name originally *Costus amarus* (bitter balsam) rather than *Costus Marie*? The meaning of alecost, another common name, is obvious: the herb was once used to flavor beer and beverages containing wine. The aptness of another, Bible leaf, is also clear: the large, thin leaves were once used as bookmarks.

Mint geranium is another confusing name. The reference to mint is clear, since spearmint is a predominant odor in many forms of costmary. But where does geranium come from? The English have also called this plant garden mace or garden allspice. One thing is certain, though, in this welter of confusion: *T. balsamita* translates into English as "balsam tansy."

Another confusion is the distinction between costmary and camphor plant. Costmary (known to herbalists as *Balsamita Mas* or *Balsamita major*) is the form with yellow, rayless daisies and yellow-green leaves scented of tansy and spearmint. Camphor plant, or lesser costmary (known to herbalists as *Balsamita Foemina* or *Balsamita minor*), is the form with white-rayed, yellow-centered daisies and blue-green leaves scented of camphor. The former is sometimes designated in texts as var. *tanacetoides* Boiss., so the latter would then be var. *balsamita*, but no one has looked at Linnaeus' type specimen (probably in his *Hortus Cliffortianus*), so the correct nomenclature of the varieties is, as yet, unknown.

Costmary is normally propagated by divisions planted in well-drained soil in full sun. Normally the herb serves as a groundcover, but at the time of flowering it rises to a sprawling 3 to 4 feet (0.9 to 1.2 m) high. These two uneven heights make it difficult to place in many gardens.

Important chemistry: At least three chemotypes of costmary exist:

1. a camphor-scented form with 51 to 92 percent camphor, 0 to 4 percent alpha-thujone, and 0 to 1 percent carvone;
2. a camphor/tansy-scented form with 35 to 47 percent camphor, 28 to 41 percent alpha-thujone, and trace to 1 percent carvone;
3. a spearmint-scented form with 20 to 68 percent carvone, trace to 15 percent alpha-thujone, and no camphor in the essential oil.

Tanacetum vulgare
tăn-å-sē-tŭm vŭl-gă-rē
tansy

French: *tanaise, tanaise commune, barbotine*
German: *Rainfarn, Wurmkraut*
Dutch: *boerenwormkruid, reinvaren*
Italian: *tanaceto, atanasia, aniceto*
Spanish: *tanaceto, balsamita menor, hierba lombriguera*
Portuguese: *tanaceto, atanásia da boticas*
Swedish: *renfana*

Tansy, or golden buttons, is a pleasure to have in the garden just for its dark green, ferny leaves on stems to 5 feet (1.5 m) tall. The bright yellow buttons, or rayless daisies, add extra interest.

Tanacetum vulgare

The scent is variable. The typical form, scented with beta-thujone, is very toxic; 4 cc of essential oil represents a lethal adult dose. Yet, tansy is considered GRAS in liqueurs. Tansy was once used in an Easter dish—a peculiar green custard served in a pie shell—and cakes flavored with tansy acquired the name "tansies."

The oil of tansy prevents the growth of fungi and gram-positive bacteria in the laboratory, supporting the folk use of tansy in both embalming (branches were often interred with corpses) and meat preservation (tansy was once rubbed on meat, and this also helped to repel flies).

Tansy is extremely easy to grow in well-drained soil in full sun: so easy, in fact, that it should be called weedy.

Tansy is recommended as a companion plant for potatoes because it repels Colorado potato beetle, and aqueous extracts of tansy will repel cabbageworms and diamondback moths. Experiment by soaking tansy leaves in water overnight, filtering, and spraying the remaining liquid on potato and cabbage plants well in advance of harvest. Tansy can also effectively repel mosquitoes if crushed and rubbed on clothing—if you don't mind green stains.

Tansy is extremely easy to grow in well-drained soil in full sun: so easy, in fact, that it should be called weedy. Thus, tansy would be best situated in a cottage or meadow garden. The chief named variation is var. *crispum* L., curly tansy. 'Isla Gold' is a golden form of tansy.

Important chemistry: Tansy is characterized by the following seven chemotypes based upon foliar essential oil.

1. A form scented of arborvitae (typical tansy) has 22 to 98 percent beta-thujone, trace to 37 percent sabinene, trace to 26 percent camphor, and 0 to 14 percent umbellulone.
2. A form scented of camphor/eucalyptus has 12 to 80 percent camphor and 4 to 31 percent 1,8-cineole.
3. A form scented of sweet Annie has 60 to 79 percent artemisia ketone.
4. A form scented of California bay has up to 61 percent umbellulone.
5. A form scented of chrysanthemums has either 32 to 82 percent *trans*-chrysanthenyl acetate and 2 to 18 percent *trans*-chrysanthenol or 22 to 49 percent chrysanthemum epoxide or 26 to 30 percent lyratol, 7 to 28 percent lyratyl acetate, and 0 to 24 percent camphor.
6. A form scented of rosemary/eucalyptus has 8 to 52 percent 1,8-cineole and 9 to 21 percent borneol.
7. A form scented of eucalyptus/arborvitae/myrtle has 0 to 78 percent alpha-thujone, trace to 46 percent 1,8-cineole, 0 to 44 percent beta-thujone, 0 to 25 percent myrtenol, and 0 to 16 percent vulgarone B.

A study at the University of Helsinki and Purdue University grouped the volatile compounds from the flower heads of tansy from 20 genotypes collected in Finland into six groups based upon a complete linkage cluster analysis. Another study grouped 40 collections of tansy from Norway into seven groups and correlated these with leaf morphology.

Other compounds present in amounts greater than 10 percent in tansy oil include tricyclene, davadone D, bornyl acetate, terpinen-4-ol, thymol, myrtenol, gamma-terpinene, alpha-pinene, and/or isopinocamphone. High parthenolides have also been reported in thujone-free forms from the Netherlands. A shame that these other scented types are not commonly cultivated!

Botanical Key and Description

Key:

1. Leaves deeply divided into segments . . . . *T. vulgare*
1a. Leaves simple, not divided. . . . . *T. balsamita*

T. balsamita L., Sp. pl. 845. 1753 [*Chrysanthe-mum balsamita* (L.) Baillon, non L.; *Balsamita major* Desf.; *Pyrethrum majus* (Desf.) Tzelev.].

Two subspecies are known [subsp. *balsamita* and subsp. *balsamitoides* (Sch. Bip.) Grierson], but subsp. *balsamita* is our costmary.

Native country: Costmary is native to southwest Asia but widely cultivated and naturalized throughout Europe and North America.

General habit: The flowering stems of costmary rise to 30 to 120 cm. Stems may be simple or branched and densely leafy.

Leaves: Basal and stem-leaves are oblong or elliptic, wedge-shaped at the base, round-toothed, stalked, silvery-hairy, 15 to 31 cm; the upper leaves are reduced in size, 3.8 to 12.7 cm.

Flowers: Individual yellow flower heads are 6 to 10 mm in diameter in the form without rays, or 10 to 16 mm in the form with 4 to 6 mm white rays.

T. vulgare L., Sp. pl. 844. 1753 [*Chrysanthe-mum vulgare* (L.) Bernh., non (Lam.) Gaterau; *C. tanacetum* Karsch, non Vis.].

Native country: Tansy is native to Europe but naturalized in North America.

General habit: Stems are 30 to 150 cm high, branched above.

Leaves: Leaves are deeply divided, smooth to sparsely hairy, glandular, to 12 cm long; lower stem leaves are more than 5 cm long, stalked, oblong to oblong-egg-shaped, while the upper stem leaves are similar but stalkless.

Flowers: Five to 100 individual flower heads, each to 8 mm across, are arranged in a dense inflorescence.

Thymbra

tǐm-brå
thymbra

Family: Lamiaceae (Labiatae)

Growth form: woody subshrubs to 22 inches (55 cm)

Hardiness: probably Zone 9a

Light: full sun

Water: moist to somewhat dry; can withstand drought when established

Soil: well-drained gravelly or rocky loam

Propagation: seeds in spring or cuttings during spring and summer

Culinary use: oregano and thyme substitutes

Craft use: wreaths

Landscape use: container plant

This genus is very similar to *Thymus* in appearance and horticultural requirements, but it is not reliably hardy above Zone 9a. The name is derived from the Greek name, which actually refers to *Satureja thymbra* L. The genus includes four species, but the following two species provide another source of an oregano or thyme-like odor.

Thymbra capitata
tĭm-brȧ kăp-ĭ-tă-tȧ
conehead thyme

The dense head-like inflorescences provided the name for this species. In English it is known as conehead thyme, "corido thyme," Cretan thyme, thyme of the ancients, Spanish origanum, or headed savory. This was the thyme of the ancient Greeks and is still the source of "thyme honey" of the Greek Islands. This is a woody subshrub with bright lilac flowers on stems up to almost 20 inches (50 cm) tall. Linear leaves are up to about ½ inch (15 mm) long and up to 2.5 mm wide.

The Arabic name is *za'atar farsi* (Persian hyssop). Conehead thyme exists in both high carvacrol (oregano-scented) and high thymol (thyme-scented) forms. The leaves of oregano-scented conehead thyme may be used in the same fashion as Greek oregano and are commonly used in za'atar, a Middle Eastern spice mixture. It is probably hardy to Zone 9b. See *Thymus vulgaris* for details of culture.

Spain provides the oil of conehead thyme as Spanish "origanum oil." The essential oil of *T. capitatus* is considered GRAS at 0.5 to 99 ppm. The oil of conehead thyme has been demonstrated in the laboratory to be antibacterial, antifungal, and antioxidant, and has application as a fumigant for stored grain and citrus.

Important chemistry: The essential oil of conehead thyme contains 5 to 86 percent carvacrol, trace to 72 percent thymol, 0 to 21 percent *p*-cymene, and 0 to 19 percent gamma-terpinene.

Thymbra spicata
tĭm-brȧ spī-kā-tȧ
za'atar hommar

The spike-like inflorescence provided the name for this species. In Arabic this is known as *za'atar hommar* (donkey hyssop) or *za'atar sahwari* (desert hyssop). This is a woody subshrub with pink flowers on stems to 22 inches (55 cm) tall. Linear leaves are up to almost 1 inch (23 mm) long and up to ⅛ inch (3 mm) wide.

The essential oil of *T. spicata* exists in either high carvacrol (oregano-scented) or high thymol (thyme-scented) chemotypes. The essential oil of *T. spicata* is antifungal, antibacterial, and

Thymbra spicata

antioxidant. The leaves of the high carvacrol chemotype of *T. spicata* may be used in the same fashion as Greek oregano, and they too are a common ingredient in za'atar. This herb is probably reliably hardy to Zone 9a. See *Thymus vulgaris* for details of culture.

Important chemistry: The essential oil consists of 7 to 71 percent carvacrol, trace to 62 percent thymol, 5 to 30 percent gamma-terpinene, and 9 to 26 percent *p*-cymene. Examination of 115 individuals in southern Puglia, Italy, found three principal chemotypes: carvacrol, carvacrol/thymol, and thymol. This is similar to other studies, as those from Israel and Sinai.

Botanical Key and Description

Key:
1. Larger leaves up to ³/₈ by ¹/₆ inch (10 by 1.5 mm), inflorescences generally head-shaped . . . . *T. capitata*
1a. Larger leaves up to ¹¹/₁₆ by ¹/₈ inch (18 by 3 mm), inflorescences generally spike-shaped . . . . *T. spicata*

T. capitata (L.) Cav., Elench. pl. horti matr. 37. 1803 [*Satureja capitata* L., *Thymus capitatus* (L.) Hoffmanns. & Link, *Coridothymus capitatus* (L.) Rchb. fil.].

Native country: Conehead thyme is native to arid plains and dry, rocky hills throughout the Mediterranean region of Europe, eastern Asia, and northern Africa.

General habit: This is a woody subshrub 15 to 50 cm tall, stems erect.

Leaves: Leaves are in pairs alternately at right angles, almost three-angled, stalkless, linear to parallel-sided, 5 to 12 mm long, 1.0 to 2.5 mm wide, tapering to the apex, stiff and leathery, minutely hairy, margin flat. Inflorescence a terminal globose or oblong-conical head, 1 to 2 cm in diameter.

Flowers: Calyx is 4 to 5 mm long, dorsally flattened. Corolla is bright lilac, pale lilac, or white.

T. spicata L., Sp. pl. 569. 1753.

Native country: Za'atar hommar is native to dry calcareous (high calcium) sites from Anatolia to Israel.

General habit: This is a woody subshrub to 55 cm tall, stems erect. Leaves are 15 to 23 × 2 to 3 mm, linear to linear-lance-shaped, toothless, hairless or beset with a marginal fringe of hairs, stalkless.

Flowers: Calyx is 5 to 8.5 mm. Corolla is pink.

Thymus

tī-mŭs
thyme

Family: Lamiaceae (Labiatae)

Growth form: trailing or erect woody sub-shrubs to 14 inches (35 cm)

Hardiness: many hardy to Zone 6

Light: full sun

Water: moist to somewhat dry; can withstand drought when established

Soil: pH 4.5 to 8.0, average 6.3 (*T. vulgaris*)

Propagation: 125,000 seeds per ounce (4,409/g) (*T. vulgaris*)

Culinary use: meats, vegetables, tea

Craft use: wreaths, potpourri

Landscape use: from groundcover to borders of beds

The thymes provide a variety of scents, from sweet to coarse, and growth patterns, from dainty to shrubby, but variety does not stop there. The genus *Thymus* includes about 350 species native to mostly Eurasia with many variations in appearance and scent within a single species, and hybridization is common. Thyme fanciers who set out to possess every thyme may have a lifetime of collecting ahead of them. All thymes are trailing to erect perennial subshrubs with terminal white to magenta flowers, often in a head-like inflorescence, and tiny, linear leaves. Most of the cultural parameters have been established based upon the requirements of common thyme (*T. vulgaris*), and the reader is directed to that species for further detail.

The generic name was derived from one of three ancient Greek root words: *thumus* ("soul," or "spirit"), *thymon* ("fumigate"), and/or *thumon* ("mind"). The latter is related to the semantic notions of breath, perception, or wits. Of similar etymology is the thymus gland, which was once believed to be the residence of the human soul. Today we also use *thym* and *thymis* as a prefix and suffix in words describing psychic disorders. Supporting this etymology was the ancient Greek use of thyme as a gravesite planting or an adornment for the dead.

Thymus ×*citriodorus*

tī-mŭs sĭ-trī-ŏ-dŏr-ŭs
lemon thyme

As the name implies, lemon thyme may be used in cooking and tea to impart a lemony flavor. This spreading subshrub, perhaps *T. pulegioides* × *T. vulgaris*, forms a mound reaching about 12 inches (30 cm) tall with tiny, egg-shaped leaves. 'Aureus' (a.k.a. 'Gold Edge'), perhaps better assigned to *T. pulegioides*, is the golden lemon thyme with variegation generally along the mar-

Thymus ×*citriodorus*

gins but sometimes with a pattern that is more irregular and mottled. 'Archer's Gold', which might also be better assigned to *T. pulegioides*, is golden yellow, becoming green in summer. 'Golden King' is reputed to be more gold than green and to hold its variegation better through the summer. 'Silver Queen' has a cream or light yellow edge that superficially appears to be silver and may not be different from 'Aureus'. 'Silver King' is mottled and margined cream to silver, more widely than 'Silver Queen'. These cultivars are also listed under this species but only occasionally encountered in cultivation and need further clarification (some may be better assigned to *T. pulegioides*): 'Bertram Anderson', 'Boothman', 'Golden Lemon', 'Golden Queen', 'Golden Upright', 'Lemon Frost', 'Lime', 'Nyewoods', 'Pink Ripple', 'Pygmy Lemon', 'Silver Lemon', and 'Villa Nova'. See *T. vulgaris* for general cultural directions.

The oil of lemon thyme repels mosquitoes and is antibacterial.

Important chemistry: The essential oil of lemon thyme consists of 39 to 71 percent geraniol with 3 to 8 percent geranial and 2 to 6 percent neral. The latter two chemicals provide the distinctive lemony odor, in spite of their low concentrations, to complement the rosy odor of geraniol. 'Archer's Gold' has 44 percent carvacrol and 21 percent *p*-cymene.

Thymus herba-barona

tī-mŭs hēr-bă-bă-rōn-å
caraway thyme

Caraway thyme was once used to flavor a "baron" of beef (two sirloins of beef not cut entirely apart), but today caraway thyme is commonly used as a leafy substitute for caraway seeds. Besides the typical caraway-scented form, caraway thyme also occurs in an unnamed oregano-scented form.

Hailing from Corsica and Sardinia, the ecological and evolutionary origin of this thyme is different from other species of thyme. Corsica is mostly of ancient crystalline rock, different from the mainland, and has many endemic species as, for example, Corsican mint (*Mentha requienii*). While the cultural directions of *T. vulgaris* apply to this thyme, caraway thyme can take more moisture and humidity than many other species of thyme. It is probably the only species that can be successfully used for creating a thyme lawn in the hot, humid areas of the eastern United States. Most other creeping species of thyme gradually die out, but caraway thyme just keeps mounding up, creating a springy mat with heads of pink flowers and tiny linear leaves. The so-called nutmeg thyme is identical to the normal caraway thyme. These cultivars are also listed under this species but only occasionally encountered in cultivation and need further clarification: 'Bob Flowerdew', 'Lemon Scented', and Lemon Carpet™. See *T. vulgaris* for details of culture.

Important chemistry: The essential oil of caraway thyme may contain 0 to 85 percent carvone, 3 to 79 percent carvacrol, 0 to 20 percent *trans*-dihydrocarvone, and 0 to 13 percent *p*-cymene.

Thymus mastichina
tī-mŭs măs-tĭ-chī-nå
mastic thyme

Spanish: *mejorana*

Mastic thyme is distinctive for its unusual complement of eucalyptus and lavender scents in the same plant. This forms a woody shrub to 50 cm tall with tiny, egg-shaped leaves and white fowers in a terminal head. Mastic thyme finds some use in soaps and shampoo as well as meat sauces, processed meats, and mixed spices for soup. Spain is the major producer of mastic thyme oil, but it is also native to Portugal. More tender than most thymes, it is probably only reliably hardy to Zone 8. These cultivars are also listed under this species but only occasionally encountered in cultivation and need further clarification: 'Didi', 'Eucalyptus-scented', and 'Lavender-scented'. See *T. vulgaris* for details of culture.

Important chemistry: Mastic thyme has two unnamed major chemotypes: a eucalyptus-scented form with 1,8-cineole (3 to 75 percent) or a lavender-scented form with linalool (6 to 83 percent).

Thymus praecox subsp. *britannicus*
tī-mŭs prē-kŏks brĭ-tă-nĭ-cŭs
creeping thyme

The epithet is derived from the Latin meaning "very early" and "British." Previously this was referred to subsp. *arcticus*, but rules of priority dictate subsp. *britannicus* as the correct name. This sometimes nearly scentless, low-growing thyme spreads by self-layering its stems as it creeps across the soil. Creeping thyme or mother-of-thyme are two English names applied to this European thyme in its confusion with *T. serpyllum*.

'Albus' and 'White Moss' have white flowers. 'Emerald Cushion' has white flowers combined with somewhat smooth, bright green leaves. 'Mayfair' has leaves variegated with yellow during cool weather. 'Minor' is very tiny and excellent for growing between paving stones. 'Coccineus' has deep red-purple or magenta flowers. 'Lanuginosus' has densely woolly foliage. 'Pink Chintz' has pale pink flowers. 'Hall's Woolly' has scattered hairs on the leaves. 'Wild Garden Lavender' has clear lavender flowers. 'Annie Hall' has bright green, essentially smooth leaves and rose flowers. These cultivars are also listed under this species but only occasionally encountered in cultivation and need further clarification: 'Atropurpureus', 'Carol Ann', 'Coccineus Major', 'Doretta Klaber', 'East Lodge', 'Elfin', 'Flossy', 'Fulney Red', 'Goldstream', 'Hans Stam', 'Hardstoft Red', 'Hazel Camplin', 'Iden', 'Lemon Curd', 'Magic Carpet', 'Minimus', 'Minor Albus', 'Mint', 'Mudcross Hill', 'Petite',

Thymus praecox subsp. *britannicus*

'Purple Beauty', 'Purple Kiss', 'Purpurteppich" ('Purple Carpet'), 'Rainbow Falls', 'Reiter's Red', 'Roseum', 'Russetings', 'September', 'Snowdrift', 'Splendens', 'Thomas's White', and 'Vey'.

While beautiful in the herb garden landscape, its use seems to be limited to potpourri. See *T. vulgaris* for details of culture.

Important chemistry: At least two chemotypes of *Thymus praecox* subsp. *britannicus* exist: a musty lavender-scented form with high linalool/linalyl acetate (19 to 88 percent), sometimes with hedycarol (0 to 51 percent); and a musty form with high hedycarol (30 to 55 percent), beta-caryophyllene (4 to 28 percent), germacrene D (trace to 13 percent), and beta-bisabolene (trace to 26 percent).

Thymus pulegioides

tī-mŭs pŭ-lē-gī-ōy-dēz

wild thyme

Called mother-of-thyme or Pennsylvania Dutch tea thyme, this European thyme is named after its superficial resemblance to pennyroyal (*Mentha pulegium*). Wild thyme is variable in height, leaf shape, and flower color. 'Fosterflower' has white flowers and an acrid, spicy scent. 'White Magic' has white flowers and lemon-scented foliage. 'Gold Dust' has bright yellow-green leaves. 'Kermesinus', crimson thyme or creeping red thyme, bears especially intense magenta flowers. 'Oregano-scented' (sometimes sold as *T. nummularius*) has a spicy, somewhat antiseptic scent. These cultivars are also listed under this species but only occasionally encountered in cultivation and need further clarification: 'Doone Valley', 'Dot Wells Creeping', 'Dot Wells Upright', 'Elliott's Gold', 'Fosley', 'Golden Dwarf', 'Goldentime', 'Lemon', 'Lemon King', 'Sir John Lawes', and 'Tabor'. Some of the lemon-scented forms previously assigned to *T. ×citriodorus* (which see) may actually belong to this species. See *T. vulgaris* for details of culture.

The oil of *T. pulegioides* is antibacterial and antifungal.

Important chemistry: At least five different chemotypes can be distinguished: a sweet camphoraceous odor from fenchone (average 34 percent), a lavender odor from linalool (average 55 percent), a lemon-rose odor from citral (geranial plus neral, average 29 percent) and geraniol (average 22 percent), a thyme odor from thymol (average 21 percent), and an oregano odor from carvacrol (average 33 percent). The oil of *T. pulegioides* contains 0 to 88 percent alpha-terpinyl acetate, 1 to 55 percent linalool, trace to 55 percent carvacrol, 0 to 39 percent thymol, trace to 34 percent fenchone, 6 to 29 percent citral, trace to 25 percent gamma-terpinene, trace to 22 percent geraniol, trace to 25 percent thymol, 0 to 20 percent alpha-terpineol, and 2 to 12 percent germacrene D. In Lithuania, six chemo-

Thymus pulegioides

types have been reported: (1) thyme-scented with 26 to 31 percent thymol, 5 to 12 percent thymyl methyl ether, 10 to 11 percent *p*-cymene, and 10 percent beta-caryophyllene; (2) oregano-scented with 6 to 33 percent carvacrol, 11 to 31 percent gamma-terpinene, and 8 to 27 percent *p*-cymene; (3) oregano/thyme-scented with 12 to 23 percent carvacrol, 8 to 21 percent gamma-terpinene, 13 to 16 percent *p*-cymene, and 12 to 14 percent thymol; (4) rose/lemon-scented with 3 to 44 percent geraniol, 11 to 29 percent geranial, trace to 19 percent nerol, and 0 to 17 percent neral; (5) lavender-scented with 80 percent linalool, and (6) spicy with 18 to 19 percent beta-caryophyllene, 15 to 16 percent beta-bisabolene, 13 to 15 percent germacrene D, and 8 to 13 percent (*E*)-nerolidol. A sweet marjoram-scented form has been reported from Denmark with 62 to 63 percent *cis*-sabinene hydrate.

Thymus quinquecostatus
tī-mŭs kwĭn-kwē-kŏ-stă-tŭs
Japanese or Chinese thyme

> **Chinese:** *bao xiang*
> **Japanese:** *ibuki-jakō-sō*

Japanese or Chinese thyme may be substituted for common thyme, but the flavor is slightly different. The overall appearance of this very hardy thyme is similar to *T. serpyllum*. Japanese/Chinese thyme occurs in high and low carvacrol forms, and f. *albiflorus* has white flowers. The specific epithet refers to the five-ribbed leaf. See *T. vulgaris* for details of culture.

Important chemistry: The oil may consist of 1 to 73 percent linalool, 0 to 56 percent thymol, 0 to 21 percent carvacrol, 0 to 18 percent geranyl acetate, trace to 29 percent *p*-cymene, and 7 to 4 percent borneol.

Thymus serpyllum
tī-mŭs sēr-pĭl-ŭm
mother-of-thyme

> **French:** *serpolet, thym sauvage (bâtard)*
> **German:** *Quendel, Feld-Thymian, Wilder Thymian*
> **Dutch:** *wilde tijm, veld-tijm*
> **Italian:** *timo serpillo, timo selvatico, serpillo, pepolino, sermollino selvatico, pepolino*
> **Spanish:** *tomillo, serpol*
> **Portuguese:** *serpil, serpol, serpao*
> **Swedish:** *backtimjan*

This species is called mother-of-thyme, wild thyme, or brotherwort in English. The "mother" here refers to the use of high thymol forms for treating the soft muscles in the uterus after childbirth. The specific epithet is derived from an old Greek name for wild thyme.

This creeping thyme, native to northern Europe, has linear leaves and heads of purple flowers. While this species is often listed in catalogs or believed to be naturalized in the United States, the plant is inevitably *T. pulegioides* or *T. praecox* subsp. *britannicus*; the primary distinguishing characteristics are tiny. Thyme-scented (high thymol) mother-of-thyme is sometimes substituted for common thyme. See *T. vulgaris* for details of culture.

The oil of *T. serpyllum* may be highly antifungal, antibacterial, and antioxidant in the high phenolic (thymol and/or carvacrol) forms.

Important chemistry: The essential oil of cultivated *T. serpyllum* contains trace to 43 percent thymol, trace to 37 percent carvacrol, trace to 21 percent limonene, trace to 21 percent para-cymene, trace to 23 percent gamma-terpinene, and 2 to 12 percent beta-caryophyllene. In Lithuania, *T. serpyllum* has six chemotypes: (1) eucalyptus-scented with 30 percent 1,8-cineole and 4 to 16 percent beta-caryophyllene; (2) eucalyptus/spearmint-scented with 22 percent

(*E*)-caryl acetate and 14 percent 1,8-cineole, (3) basil-scented with 35 percent (*E*)-beta-ocimene; (4) camphor-scented with 24 to 27 percent caryophyllene oxide and 9 to 12 percent camphor; (5) spicy with 23 to 27 percent beta-caryophyllene and 9 to 16 percent myrcene; and (6) mint/spicy with 24 percent *cis-p*-menth-2-en-1-ol and 14 percent caryophyllene oxide. In Finland, chemotypes of *T. serpyllum* may be characterized by the content of hedycarol, germacra-1(10),4-dien-6-ol, germacra-1(10),5-dien-4-ol, linalool, and linalyl acetate.

Thymus vulgaris

tī-mŭs vŭl-gā-rĭs
common thyme

French: *thym vrai*
German: *Thymian, Römisher Quendel*
Dutch: *echte tijm*
Italian: *timo, erbuccia, pepolino, sermillino*
Spanish: *tomillo común, salsero, tomillo vulgar*
Portuguese: *tomilho*
Swedish: *timjan*
Russian: *tim'yan*
Chinese: *pai-li-hsiang*
Japanese: *taimu*

Common ("vulgar") thyme or garden thyme, native from the western Mediterranean to southeastern Italy, is normally used in cooking, while the oil is also antibacterial and antifungal. *Thymus vulgaris* has wide variation, often not characterized by cultivar names, in its native range. Individual plants exhibit a wide range of growth habits, leaf sizes, leaf colors, and scents.

'Narrow-leaf French' is the name appended to the seed strain high in thymol and often offered as 'German Winter', 'French Summer', or 'Greek Gray'. In common parlance, this is *the*

garden thyme or common thyme. Many forms of 'Narrow-leaf French' have female flowers and hence will not come completely true from seed (since they must outcross to set seed). If you find a particularly favorable clone, propagate it by cuttings or layerings.

'Miniature' forms tiny tufts and is perfect for troughs. 'Orange Balsam' has a strong, bitter orange, turpentine-like odor; place this where it can be casually stepped upon. 'Bittersweet' has

Thymus vulgaris

an acrid, tar-like odor. 'Fragrantissimus' has a fragrance of rose geranium. 'Well-Sweep Variegated' has leaves edged in creamy white. These cultivars are also listed under this species but only occasionally encountered in cultivation and need further clarification: 'Albus', 'Chamay', 'Compactus', 'Dorcas White', 'English Wild', 'Erectus', 'Forcalquer', 'Golden Pins', 'Gray Hill', 'Haute Vallée de l'Lude', 'Les Baux', 'Lucy', 'Miniature', 'Pinewood', 'Provençal', 'Silver Posie', 'Snow White', and 'Victoria Becker'.

Spain is the leading supplier of thyme leaf, while Spain and France are the leading suppliers of thyme oil (while *T. vulgaris* is commercially cultivated in France, both *T. vulgaris*. and *T. zygis* L. are harvested from the wild in Spain). The leaf and essential oil are considered GRAS. Thyme has antioxidant, antifungal, and antibacterial activity. Luteolin, a flavonoid in thyme, has been characterized as a strong antimutagen; one report attributes complete remission of cutaneous melanoma metastases to thyme oil. Thyme oil is also antitrypanosomal. The oil of thyme may also help to control *Varroa* mites in bees.

All thymes demand well-drained, near-neutral soil and a position in full sun. Up to 50 percent or more of sand, gravel, or similar aggregate is beneficial because water is not retained for long periods of time and the roots are less likely to rot. While common thyme may be directly seeded, the process is slow and mined with environmental risks, as is true with most small-seeded perennial herbs, and much time is gained the first year from transplants; the propagation of favored chemotypes demands vegetative propagation by cuttings, layers, or divisions. In France, plants are placed 12 to 18 inches (30 to 45 cm) between plants and 16 to 32 inches (40 to 80 cm) between rows. The terminal 6-inch (15 cm) shoots of common thyme are typically harvested at full bloom, but another har-

vest can be made at the end of summer (end of August, beginning of September). At a maximum density of 16,188 plants per acre (40,000 plants/ha) in France, a harvest of 867 pounds per acre (972 kg/ha) dried leaves may be expected for the first harvest. Recommendations from Quebec are 40,469 plants per acre (100,000 plants/ha). New Zealand has reported the phenomenal yields of dried herb at 1,410 to 5,585 pounds per acre (1,580 to 6,260 kg/ha) for first year plantings and 6,744 to 11,955 pounds per acre (7,560 to 13,400 kg/ha) for established crops with about 2.44 gallons per acre (22.8 l/ha) of oil.

Early spring pruning that removes one-half to one-third of the stem length is beneficial if plants are not completely harvested at one time in the late summer. Regular pruning will increase the number of stems and reduce the amount of old wood on the plant. The more old wood on the plant, the shorter its life is likely to be, and woody thyme plants are more susceptible to winter damage.

Important chemistry: Many different fragrances are recorded: high linalool (trace to 98 percent), alpha-terpineol (trace to 96 percent), geraniol (0 to 93 percent), *p*-cymene (1 to 80 percent), carvacrol (trace to 80 percent), thymol (trace to 65 percent), or *trans*-4-thujanol (trace to 42 percent). The essential oil may also contain 0 to 67 percent geranyl acetate, trace to 62 percent terpinyl acetate, trace to 70 percent 1,8-cineole, 1 to 32 percent terpinen-4-ol, trace to 28 percent gamma-terpinene, trace to 18 percent linalyl acetate, trace to 25 percent 8-myrcenol, trace to 15 percent camphor, trace to 13 percent alpha-pinene, trace to 13 percent beta-pinene, trace to 11 percent camphene, 2 to 11 percent beta-caryophyllene, and trace to 10 percent 8-myrcenyl acetate. 'Bittersweet' is a clone high in carvacrol, while 'Orange Balsam' is a clone high in alpha-terpineol.

Thymus cultivars

Cultivar: 'Argenteus'
Silver thyme, as this hybrid is commonly known, has an essential oil with 55 percent thymol and can be substituted for common thyme. This often masquerades as silver lemon thyme, but smells like *T. vulgaris* 'Narrow-leaf French'; "lemon" here refers to the slight yellow color that this thyme often assumes.

Cultivar: 'Broad-leaf English'
English thyme has 55 percent thymol and 13 percent para-cymene and may be substituted for common thyme, from which it differs by its flat leaf margins.

Thymus 'Clear Gold' (creeping golden thyme, yellow transparent thyme), 'Doone Valley', 'Long-leaf Gray', 'Longwood', 'Variegated English' (a mutation of 'Broad-leaf English' with irregular blotches on the leaves and some albino shoots), 'Wedgewood English' (a mutation of 'Variegated English' with the central portion of most leaves a distinct yellow), and 'Woolly-stemmed Sharp' (in reference to its scent) seem to be limited to landscaping and potpourri. For all these hybrids, see *T. vulgaris* for cultural directions.

Botanical Key and Description

Key:
1. Upper calyx teeth similar in size and shape to lower, calyx nearly radially symmetrical. . . . . . . *T. mastichina*
1a. Upper calyx teeth different in size and/or shape from lower, calyx two-lipped. 2
   2. Leaf margin rolled backward from each margin upon the lower side (or distinctly thickened). . . . .
    . . . . *T. vulgaris*
  2a. Leaf margin flat or only slightly revolute, not thickened 3
     3. Stems with hairs on the angles of the stems only. . . . . *T. pulegioides*
    3a. Stems hairy all around or with hairs on two opposite faces of the stem, the other faces smooth . . . .
    4
       4. Venation clearly with lateral nerves curving toward the margin, the upper pair anastomosing
        with the midvein at the apex. . . . . *T. praecox*
      4a Venation with lateral veins curving toward the leaf apex, but becoming faint and disappearing
        before reaching the margin 5
         5. Stems hairy all around with hairs clearly more prominent on the angles than the faces 6
           6. Plant to 15 cm tall, broad-spreading, stems decumbent or weakly ascending, leaves
             bright yellow-green . . . . *T.* 'Clear Gold'
          6a. Plant 20 to 30 cm tall, suberect, stems erect or ascending, leaves dark green or with a
             distinct yellow marginal band . . . . *T.* ×*citriodorus*
        5a. Stems with hairs on two opposite faces of the stem, the other two faces smooth or hairy all
         around but hairs not clearly more prominent on the angles than faces 7

T. ×*citriodorus* (Pers.) Schreb. ex Schweigg.
and Körte, Fl. Erlang. 2:17. 1811 (*T. lanuginosus*
Mill. var. *citriodorum* Pers.; *T. serpyllum* L. var.
vulgaris Benth.; *T. comptus* Hort., non Friv.; *T.
jankae* Hort., in part, non Čelak; *T. serpyllum*
auct., non L., var. *citriodorus* Hort.; *T.*
'Lemoneum')

Native country: Lemon thyme is suspected to
be a hybrid of *T. pulegioides* and *T. vulgaris*.

General habit: This is a spreading subshrub
forming a rather broad mound 20 to 30 cm
tall. The stems are erect or ascending but
often woody and decumbent at the base;
stems are hairy all around with short hairs
directed downward, more dense on the angles than faces; flowering stems are usually
10 to 25 cm long.

Leaves: Leaves are stalked, narrowly to broadly
widest at the center with ends equal or egg-
shaped, 8 to 14 mm long, 3 to 6 mm wide,
tapering to the apex or blunt at the apex,
usually wedge-shaped at the base.

Flowers: Inflorescence is terminal, oblong, interrupted, 1 cm in diameter. Calyx is 2.5 to
4 mm long. Corolla is 4 to 5 mm long, pale
rose-lavender.

T. herba-barona Loisel., Fl. gall. 360. 1807
(*T.* 'Nutmeg', in part).

Native country: Caraway thyme is native only
to Corsica and Sardinia on dry, barren
slopes.

General habit: Caraway thyme, sometimes
offered as "nutmeg" thyme, is a broad, low
mound 15 to 20 cm tall, stems woody and
hairy all around, or with hairs denser on two
opposite faces; flowering stems erect or ascending, sterile shoots arching or decumbent.

Leaves: Leaves are shortly stalked, lance-

shaped, narrow and widest at center with
ends equal, 5 to 9 mm long, 1.5 to 3 mm
wide, gradually narrowing to the apex, or
wedge-shaped, almost hairless.

Flowers: Inflorescence is almost globular, lax,
occasionally the lowermost flowers remote,
1.5 cm in diameter. Calyx is 3 to 5 mm long.
Corolla is rose-purple, 4.5 to 7 mm long.

T. mastichina L., Sp. pl. ed. 2. 827. 1763.

Native country: Mastic thyme is native to
Spain and Portugal.

General habit: Mastic thyme is a woody shrub
25 to 50 cm tall, stems erect or spreading,
hairy all around, creeping shoots absent.

Leaves: Leaves are shortly stalked, green or
grayish, narrow and widest at the center with
ends equal to egg-shaped, 7 to 12 mm long,
1.5 to 4 mm wide, gradually narrowing to
the apex, with short dense wool-like covering
of matted, tangled hairs to almost hairless.

Flowers: Inflorescence is a globose to oblong
head, lowermost flowers remote, 1 to 2 cm
in diameter. Calyx is 5 to 8 mm long, nearly
radially symmetrical, very long-hairy, giving
the inflorescence a feathery appearance.
Corolla is white, 3 to 6 mm long.

T. praecox Opiz, Naturalientausch 6:40. 1824.
Five subspecies are recognized, but the most
pertinent for cultivation is as follows:

subsp. *britannicus* (Ronniger) Holub, Preslia
45:359. 1973 [*T. praecox* Opiz subsp. *arcticus*
(E. Durand), Jalas, *T. drucei* Ronn.; *T. serpyllum* auct., in part, non L.; *T. serpyllum* L. 'Car-
neus'; *T. serpyllym* L. 'Roseus'; *T. jankae* Hort.
in part, non Čelak; *T. minus* Hort.; *T. minus*
Hort.; *T.* 'Nutmeg', in part].

Key:

1. Flowers white 2
    2. Corolla 5 to 7 mm long, greatly exceeding the calyx; flowers hermaphroditic, profuse. 3
        3. Leaf margin ciliate all around; leaves often with scattered long hairs above; stem hairs prominent
        . . . . 'Albus'
        3a. Leaf margin ciliate only at base; leaves smooth and shiny above; stems hairs minute and indistinct
        . . . . 'Emerald Cushion'
    2a. Corolla 2.5 to 3.5 mm long, scarcely exceeding the calyx; flowers female, sparse . . . . 'White Moss'
1a. Flowers pink, rose, purple, or magenta. 4
    4. Leaves variegated with yellow in spring, winter, and fall. . . . . 'Mayfair'
    4a. Leaves green or gray, not variegated 5
        5. Plant dwarf, compact, cushion-like, rarely more than 11 to 30 cm in diameter; largest leaves
        3.5 mm long, but most smaller, long-hairy above. . . . . 'Minor'
        5a. Plant broad-spreading, prostrate, often to 1 m in diameter; largest leaves 5 mm or more
        long. 6
            6. Flowers deep red-purple or magenta . . . . 'Coccineus'
            6a. Flowers pink, rose, lavender, or rose-purple 7
                7. Plant densely woolly in all parts, distinctly gray in color; flowers sparse . . . .
                . . . . 'Lanuginosus'
                7a. Plant of variable pubescence, but not woolly; greenish; flowers usually profuse 8
                    8. Flowers pale pink . . . . 'Pink Chintz'
                    8a. Flowers lavender, rose, or rose-purple 9
                        9. Leaves broadly egg-shaped to nearly rounded, the largest 3.5 to 4.5 mm wide
                        with scattered long hairs on upper surface, margin hairy all around . . . .
                        . . . . 'Hall's Woolly'
                        9a. Leaves egg-shaped or narrowed at the base, the largest usually less than 3 mm
                        wide, margin and upper leaf surface of variable hairiness 10
                            10. Flowers clear lavender . . . . 'Wild Garden Lavender'
                            10a. Flowers rose or rose-purple 11
                                11. Leaves bright green; flowers rose, leaf margins hairy below the middle,
                                essentially smooth otherwise . . . . 'Annie Hall'
                                11a. Leaves medium to dark green; flowers rose-purple; margin and leaf
                                surface of variable hairiness. . . . . subsp. *britannicus*

Native country: This subspecies is found in western Europe.

General habit: This subspecies has been confused with *T. serpyllum*. Plants are prostrate, flowering stems erect, hairs on two opposite faces, the other two faces smooth, at least in the lower part of the flowering stem.

Leaves: Leaves are stalked, 3 to 8 mm long, mostly narrowed at the base. Inflorescence head-shaped to somewhat elongated, with the lowermost flowers remote.

Flowers: Calyx is 3 to 4 mm long. Corolla is various shades of rose-purple, to 8 mm long.

T. pulegioides L., Sp. pl. 592. 1753. (*T. alpestris* auct., not Tausch ex A. Kern; *T. chamaedrys* Fries; *T. serpyllum* auct., in part, non L.; *T. serpyllum* L. subsp. *montanus* Arcang.; *T. enervius* Klok.; *T. serpyllum* L. subsp. *carniolicus* (Borb.) Lyka in Hegi; *T. serpyllum* L. subsp. *effusus* (Host) Lyka in Hegi; *T. serpyllum* L. subsp. *parviflorus* (Opiz ex H. Braun) Lyka in Hegi)

Key:

1. Flowers white 2
   2. Foliage with a somewhat acrid, spice scent . . . . 'Fosterflower'
   2a. Foliage lemon-scented . . . . 'White Magic'
1a. Flowers of various shades of purple 3
   3. Leaves bright yellow-green . . . . 'Gold Dust'
   3a. Leaves medium to dark green 4
      4. Flowers very deep red-purple . . . . 'Kermesinus'
      4a. Flowers pale lavender to purple 5
         5. Leaves very broadly egg-shaped to nearly rounded, 10 to 12 mm long, 6 to 8 mm wide; with a penetrating spice, somewhat antiseptic, scent . . . . 'Oregano-scented'
         5a. Leaves egg-shaped, widest at the center with the ends equal or narrowed at the base, variously scented . . . . *T. pulegioides*

Native country: Mother-of-thyme is native to Europe but naturalized in North America.

General habit: This species has been confused by herb growers with *T. serpyllum*, but hairs occur *only* on the angles of the stems. Plants are procumbent to suberect, 10 to 35 cm tall, usually quite broadly spreading. Stems had hairs on the angles of the stems only (goniotrichous).

Leaves: Leaves are stalked, egg-shaped, widest at the center with the ends equal, more rarely lance-shaped, 3 to 5 mm long, 2.5 to 20 mm wide, usually blunt at the apex, sometimes almost tapering to the apex, wedge-shaped to gradually narrowing at the base, hairless or nearly so.

Flowers: Inflorescence elongated or almost head-shaped, usually interrupted, at least below. Calyx is 3 to 4 mm long, green or purple. Corolla is various shades of rose-lavender and purple, 3.5 to 6.5 mm long.

T. quinquecostatus Čelak, Oesterr. Bot. Z. 39:263. 1899.

Key:

1. Flowers rosy-purple . . . . var. *quinquecostatus*
1a. Flowers white . . . . f. *albiflorus* H. Hara, Bot. Mag. (Tokyo) 51:145. 1937.

Native country: As the name implies, Japanese or Chinese thyme makes its home in Japan, Korea, Manchuria, Mongolia, and Siberia.

General habit: This species has been confused with *T. serpyllum*, especially in Japan. Plants are suberect with an ascending flowering stems to 15 cm long, hairy all around (holotrichous), but sometimes with hairs sparser on two opposite sides.

Leaves: Leaves are widest at the center with the ends equal to egg-shaped, 6 to 11 mm long, 2 to 5 mm wide, blunt or tapering to the apex, wedge-shaped at base into a short stalk, smooth.

Flowers: Inflorescence is a terminal, lax, egg-shaped head, 1 to 3 cm long. Calyx is 3 to 5 mm long, tinged red-purple toward the apex. Corolla is rosy-purple, 6 to 8 mm long.

T. serpyllum L., Sp. pl. 590. 1753.

Key:

1. Calyx 3 to 4 mm, upper teeth usually 0.5 to 0.8 mm; leaves usually 2 to 3 mm wide . . . . var. *serpyllum* [*T. serpyllum* L. subsp. *angustifolius* (Pers.) Archang., *T. serpyllum* L. subsp. *rigidus* (Wimm. & Grab.) Lyka]

1a. Calyx 4 to 5 mm, upper teeth to 1.2 mm; leaves usually 3 to 5 mm wide . . . . var. *tanaensis* (Hyl.) Jalas, Acta Bot. Fenn. 39:20. 1947 (*T. subarcticus* Klok. & Shost.)

Native country: While *T. serpyllum* is rarely cultivated, this name is repeatedly used for forms of *T. pulegioides* and *T. praecox* subsp. *britannicus*. The species itself is primarily native to northern Europe.

General habit: Plants are prostrate; stems long, creeping, hairy all around.

Leaves: Leaves are almost stalkless or shortly stalked, linear, widest at the center with the ends equal, or narrowed at base, 5 to 13 mm long, 1 to 5 mm wide, hairless or hairy.

Flowers: Inflorescences are head-like or some-what elongated, about 1 cm in diameter. Calyx is 3 to 5 mm long. Corolla is purple, 6 to 8 mm long.

T. vulgaris L., Sp. pl. 591. 1753 (*T. aestivus* Reut. ex Willk., *T. ilerdensis* F. Gonzalez ex Costa, *T. webbianus* Rouy, *T. valentianus* Rouy).

This species includes a host of cultivars: 'Bittersweet', 'Fragrantissimus', 'Miniature', 'Narrow-leaf French', 'Orange Balsam', and 'Well-Sweep Variegated'.

Key:

1. Leaves uniformly green or grayish 2
   2. Plant 10 to 15 cm tall; leaves 0.5 to 1.5 mm wide . . . . 'Miniature'
   2a. Plant 20 to 35 cm tall; leaves 1 to 3.5 mm wide 3
      3. Foliage with a sweet, somewhat spicy, warm herbaceous scent . . . . 'Narrow-leaf French'
      3a. Foliage without typical fragrance of the culinary herb. 4
         4. Foliage with strong, bitter orange, turpentine-like odor. . . . . 'Orange Balsam'
         4a. Foliage not scented as above. 5
            5. Foliage with a somewhat acrid, tar-like odor. . . . . 'Bittersweet'
            5a. Foliage with the odor of rose geranium . . . . 'Fragrantissimus'
1a. Leaves variegated with yellow-white. . . . . 'Well-Sweep Variegated'

Native country: Common thyme is native from the western Mediterranean to south-eastern Italy.

General habit: Plants are erect subshrubs, 10 to 35 cm tall, stems hairy all around.

Leaves: Leaves are shortly stalked, linear to narrowly egg-shaped, 4 to 10 mm long, 0.5 to 3.5 mm wide, tapering to the apex, wedge-shaped to gradually narrowing to the base, hairy to coated with dense wool-like covering of matted, tangled hairs of short length.

Flowers: Inflorescence is lax, head-like or elongated and interrupted, 1 to 1.5 cm in diameter. Calyx is 3 to 4 mm long. Corolla is nearly white to pale purple, 3.5 to 7.5 mm long.

T. **'Argenteus'** (*T.* ×*citriodorus* Hort. 'Argenteus', *T. vulgaris* Hort. 'Argenteus')

Native country: Silver thyme is a hybrid involving *T. vulgaris*.

General habit: This is a low, spreading subshrub, 15 to 25 cm tall, hairy all around the stem.

Leaves: Leaves are stalked, egg-shaped, narrowly egg-shaped, parallel-sided, or narrowed at the base, 5 to 8 mm long, 2 to 3 mm wide, blunt or tapering to the apex, gradually narrowing to the base; grayish or olive-green with a narrow, irregular, marginal band of yellowish white.

Flowers: Inflorescence is loosely head-shaped, the lowermost flowers remote, about 1 cm in diameter. Calyx is 2 to 3 mm long, hairy (pubescent), streaked green and yellowish white, often tinged red-purple on the teeth and dorsal side of the tube. Corolla is pale rose-violet, 3 to 3.5 mm long. Only female plants are known.

T. **'Broad-leaf English'**

Native country: A hybrid involving *T. vulgaris*.

General habit: English thyme is a dense, much-branched subshrub to 25 cm high, stems hairy all around.

Leaves: Leaves are stalked, 6 to 8 mm long, 2.5 to 4 mm wide, tapering to the apex, gradually narrowing to the base or wedge-shaped.

Flowers: Inflorescence is terminal and frequently branched. Calyx is 2.5 to 3 mm long, hairy. Corolla is pale lavender, 3 to 4 mm long. Only female plants are known.

T. **'Clear Gold'** (*T. serpyllum* auct. 'Aureus', in part)

Native country: Probably a hybrid involving *T. pulegioides*.

General habit: Creeping golden thyme forms a low, spreading mound to 15 cm; stems are hairy all around, but hairs are more prominent on the angles and sparser on the faces.

Leaves: Leaves are stalked, egg-shaped, widest at the center with the ends equal, or narrowed at the base, 7 to 13 mm long, 2 to 4 mm wide, blunt at the apex, wedge-shaped at the base, bright yellow-green but often greener toward the center.

Flowers: Inflorescence is elongate, lax, interrupted, about 1 cm in diameter. Calyx is 2.5 to 3.5 mm long, often purplish. Corolla is lavender, 3 to 4 mm long. Only female plants known.

T. **'Long-leaf Gray'** (*T. glabrescens loevyanus* Hort.; *T. lanicaulis* Hort., in part, non Ronn.; *T. tracicus* Hort., non Velen.)

Native country: Flannery proposed this cultivar name because of the lack of definitive information on the placement of this taxon of cultivation.

General habit: 'Long-leaf Gray' is broad-spreading to 25 cm tall, stems decumbent, hairy all around.

Leaves: Leaves are shortly stalked, gray-green, narrow and widest at the center with the ends equal or tending to be broad and rounded at the apex, 8 to 20 mm long, 2 to 3 mm wide, tapering to the apex or rather blunt. Inflorescence is loosely head-shaped or slightly elongated, about 1.5 cm in diameter.

Flowers: Calyx is 3.5 to 4.5 mm long, hairy, often purplish on dorsal side. Corolla is pale purple, 5 to 6.5 mm long.

T. **'Woolly-stemmed Sharp'** (*T. lanuginosus* auct., in part, non Mill.; *T. lanicaulis* Hort. in part, non Ronn.)

Native country: Another taxon found only in cultivation.

General habit: Stems to 30 cm tall, decumbent or ascending, terminating in an inflorescence, hairy all around.

Leaves: Leaves are almost stalkless, pale greenish gray, with a sharp, biting, somewhat antiseptic scent, narrow but widest at the center with ends equal to narrowed at the base, 8 to 13 mm long, 2 to 2.5 mm wide, tapering to the apex or blunt at the apex, with scattered long hairs above and below.

Flowers: Inflorescence is elongate, weakly branched. Calyx is 2.5 to 3 mm long, hairy. Corolla lavender, scarcely exceeding the calyx. Only female plants are known.

Trachyspermum ammi

trā-kē-spēr-mŭm ā-mĭ
ajowan

Family: Apiaceae (Umbelliferae)
Growth form: annual to 3 feet (90 cm)
Hardiness: cannot withstand frost
Light: full sun
Water: moist but not constantly wet
Soil: light garden loam, pH 7.4 to 7.8, average 7.6
Propagation: seeds in spring, 11,000 seeds per ounce (388/g)
Culinary use: Indian and Ethiopian cuisine but not GRAS
Craft use: none
Landscape use: vegetable garden

French: *carvi oriental*
German: *Ostindischer Kümmel, Ajowan*
Dutch: *oost-indische kummel*
Italian: *ajowan*
Sanskrit: *yamani*
Indian: *ajuan, omum*

The genus *Trachyspermum* is similar to *Carum*, caraway, and includes about 20 species ranging from tropical and northeast Africa to central Asia and western China. The generic name means "rough-seeded," while the specific epithet was adapted from the Sanskrit name. Alternate English names include white cumin, bishop's weed (mistakenly, for its resemblance to *Ammi majus*), and Ethiopian caraway.

Trachyspermum ammi

The seeds (actually fruits) of this annual are used to impart a flavor of thyme in Indian savories, particularly *ompadi*, *namkin boodi*, and *sev*. In Ethiopia the fruits are used to flavor *berbere* (a spice rub)and *injera* (wet bread) and are also used in the preparation of *katikala*, an alcoholic drink. The essential oil of the fruits is antifungal from the content of thymol, a simple phenol. Ajowan fruits also yield an antioxidant. K. C. Sristava of Odense University in Denmark found that the fruits of ajowan show antiaggregatory effects and alter arachidonic acid metabolism in human platelets in vitro. K. Aftab and his associates at the University of Karachi in Pakistan found that the fruits of ajowan contain a calcium channel blocker-like constituent (thymol) which exerts hypotensive and bradycardiac effects in rats. However, in spite of its wide use in Indian and Ethiopian foods, ajowan has never achieved GRAS status (probably because no one ever lobbied for it).

In India, the commercial sowing rate is 2.2 to 3.1 pounds per acre (2.5 to 3.5 kg/ha). For the home gardener, this translates to about 12 to 16 inches between plants, but because of the lax growth and uneven germination of culinary ajowan, which is easily obtained from food stores specializing in Indian foods, seeds may be planted about 3 to 6 inches apart or even closer. Seedlings appear within seven to fifteen days. Application of nitrogen at the rate of 71 pounds per acre (80 kg/ha) is recommended. Additional potassium and sulfur may be needed depending upon soil tests. Flowering takes place in about two months, and harvesting commences when flower heads turn brown. The plants are then dried in sheds and the fruits separated from the chaff. Collar- and root-rot (*Sclerotium rolfsii*) affect ajowan, and the spice beetle (*Stegobium paniceum*) attacks the stored seeds.

Important chemistry: The essential oil of Indian ajowan fruit is dominated by 45 to 61 percent thymol, 16 to 24 percent *p*-cymene, and 12 to 23 percent gamma-terpinene, providing a thyme-like odor. A new chemotype of ajowan was isolated from northeast India with 46 percent carvone and 38 percent limonene. Ethiopian plants have fruits with 69 percent carvacrol, 11 percent alpha-phellandrene, and 10 percent alpha-terpinene.

Botanical Description

T. ammi (L.) Sprague, Kew Bull. 1929:228. 1929 [*T. copticum* (L.) Link, *Carum copticum* (L.) Hiern. in Oliver].

Native country: Ajowan is native to Asia, North Africa, and Europe.

General habit: Ajowan is a smooth annual herb 15 to 90 cm high.

Leaves: Leaves are feather-like and divided two to three times.

Flowers: Flowers have white or pinkish petals and are arranged in an umbel.

Fruits/seeds: The fruit is egg-shaped with parallel sides.

Trigonella foenum-graecum

trī-gō-nĕl-å fē-nŭm-grē-kŭm
fenugreek

Family: Fabaceae (Leguminosae)
Growth form: annual to about 1 foot (30 cm)
Hardiness: does not withstand frost
Light: full sun
Water: evenly moist
Soil: average garden loam, pH 5.5 to 8.2, average 7.3
Propagation: seeds in spring, 1588 seeds per ounce (56/g)
Culinary use: maple flavoring, curries
Craft use: none
Landscape use: short-lived in the border, best grown in vegetable garden

---

French: *fenugrec*
German: *Bockshornklee, Schabzieberklee, Griechische Hausamen*
Dutch: *fenegriek, hoornklaver*
Italian: *fieno greco*
Spanish: *alholva, fenugreco, heno griego*
Portuguese: *alforva feno greco, fenacho*
Swedish: *bockhornsklöver*
Russian: *pazhitnik*
Chinese: *hu-lu-pa, k'u-tou*
Japanese: *koroha*
Arabic: *hulabaha, hulba*

Fenugreek lends a subtle but distinctive flavor of celery and maple to food and is an important ingredient today in the cuisines of India and Pakistan, but it has been used since the times of the ancient Egyptians, Greeks, and Romans. The herb produces golden, quadrangular seeds that are crushed or powdered and used in breads and with meats, poultry, and vegetables; the powdered seed is also a staple ingredient in curries.

As the less-well known food of South Asia becomes more accessible in the United States, this visually humble but fast-growing member of the pea family is likely to be a more familiar sight in herb gardens. A maple-syrup flavored extract from fenugreek seed has already found its way into candy, baked goods, pickles, gelatins, puddings, beverages, ice cream, and syrups manufactured in America. Its sprouted seeds are also used in salads, while the leaves are infrequently consumed as a potherb.

Recent medical research suggests the fenugreek seeds may reduce blood sugar in Type II (non-insulin dependent or maturity-obesity onset) diabetics and lower blood cholesterol. Zecharia Madar and associates in Israel found that consumption of 0.5 ounces (15 g) of powdered fenugreek soaked in water significantly lowers postprandial blood glucose levels in Type II diabetes. A study done in India by R. D. Sharma and associates found that consumption of 1.75 ounces (50 g) daily of powdered fenu-

Trigonella foenum-graecum

greek seed in soup significantly decreases LDL cholesterol while significantly increasing HDL cholesterol. In Type I diabetes, R. D. Sharma and associates in India found that 3.5 ounces (100 g) of fenugreek flour in bread consumed daily by human volunteers significantly reduces fasting blood sugar and improves the glucose tolerance test. This hypoglycemic (blood glucose lowering) effect seems to be primarily from an alkaloid, trigonelline. Fenugreek also promotes significant wound healing as discovered by A. D. Taranalli and I. J. Kuppast in India. A leaf extract has been found to be antinociceptive in rats.

Fenugreek also has historical interest in the United States because it was an ingredient of Lydia Pinkham's Vegetable Compound, according to the original formula in her own handwriting:

> 12 ounces fenugreek seeds
> 8 ounces unicorn root (*Aletris farinosa* L.)
> 6 ounces life root (*Senecio aureus* L.)
> 6 ounces black cohosh [*Cimicifuga racemosa* (L.) Nutt.]
> 6 ounces pleurisy root (*Asclepias tuberosa* L.) enough alcohol to make 100 pints

No doubt the alcohol was the principal active ingredient, since none of these ingredients is sufficiently active to account for the properties attributed to Lydia Pinkham's Vegetable Compound.

Fenugreek is an easy-to-grow, but short-lived, annual. The English common name is derived from the Latin *faenum-graecum*, which means "Greek hay." This Latin name refers to its early use as a food for livestock, and fenugreek is still used today as a self-improving, winter cover crop.

The genus *Trigonella* includes about 80 species found in the Mediterranean, Macaronesia, South Africa, and Australia. Fenugreek is a wiry, pea-like plant that possesses green, clover-like leaves and a distinctive triangular white flower, ½ inch long, that is almost stalkless. *Trigonella* (Greek for "three-angled") refers to this flower. The plant has a stem with subtle but sparse hairs and grows 1 to 2 feet high. Bean-like, curved pods 3 to 7 inches long are produced and hold ten to twenty seeds.

India, France, Egypt, and Argentina raise fenugreek commercially in open, sunny fields, much like American farmers produce wheat and rye. The cultivation research we have located originates in India and Hungary and is somewhat incomplete and often lacks specifics. We have tempered this research with our own garden experience to reach our recommendations.

Soil for growing fenugreek should drain well and have moderate to high fertility; a sidedressing of about half a pound of 10-10-10 fertilizer per 100 square feet at first flowering increases yields. In dry, hot areas, irrigation may be necessary to keep plants from becoming stunted. Early planting is recommended so that the plant may mature before the heat of August.

Fenugreek seed is sometimes slow to germinate; seed soaked in lukewarm water overnight will germinate faster. Once soil warms to 50 to 55°F (about the time tomatoes are planted), fenugreek seed is broadcast at a rate of about 18 seeds per square foot. Alternatively, sow 2 to 3 inches apart in rows 12 to 18 inches apart (the commercial rate is 31 pounds per acre or 35 kg/ha in India); cover seed with about ⅛ to ½ inch of soil. A single plant should yield thirty to forty pods. Seeds ripen about four to five weeks after flowering and are harvested when the drying pods become a lighter green and the seeds are mature; pods should be harvested before they become brittle and open on their own to scatter seeds on the ground. Plants are often yanked from the ground and taken to another location to separate the pods from the plant and the seeds from the pods. The home gardener may use a screen in a warm room to make drying easier. The seeds may be separated from the dried pods by placing them in a strong paper bag and pressing it several times with a heavy rolling pin. The seeds can then be winnowed free with a vacuum cleaner; lay the seeds out on newspaper and lower the nozzle slowly until the chaff is picked up, leaving the heavier seeds behind.

Common diseases that may attack fenugreek plants are root rot, powdery mildew, downy mildew, and cercospora leaf spot (*Cercospora traversiana*). Sulfur dust is often recommended by researchers in India to control powdery mildew. Aphids, thrips, and leaf-eating caterpillars may also cause damage.

Fenugreek has GRAS status in the following amounts: as an extract (7 to 500 parts per million), seed (15 to 800 ppm), and oleoresin (7 to 500 ppm).

Important chemistry: The characteristic aroma of fenugreek seeds is due to sotolone (3-hydroxy-4,5-dimethyl-2(5H)-furanone). One analysis of the aerial parts of fenugreek found 28 percent delta-cadinene, 12 percent alpha-cadinol, 11 percent gamma-eudesmol, and 11 percent alpha-bisabolol. Seeds and leaves of fenugreek are rich in diosgenins, widely used materials for steroid manufacture.

Botanical Description

T. foenum-graecum L., Sp. pl. 777. 1753.
Native country: Fenugreek is native to southern Europe and Asia but widely naturalized.
General habit: Main stems are 10 to 50 cm long, sparsely hairy.
Leaves: Three leaflets/leaf are 20 to 50 × 10 to 15 mm, parallel-sided with narrowed base, and edged with small teeth.
Flowers: Flowers are solitary or paired, almost stalkless. Calyx is 6 to 8 mm long, the teeth about as long as the tube. Corolla is 12 to 18 mm long, yellowish white tinged with violet at the base.
Fruits/seeds: The fruit is a long, dry bean-like fruit opening along two lines, 60 to 110 × 4 to 6 mm, erect or spreading, linear, somewhat curved, smooth or becoming smooth with age, with longitudinal veins. Seeds are about 5 × 3 mm, quadrangular, somewhat compressed, yellow or pale brown, finely pimpled.

Umbellularia californica

ŭm-bĕl-ū-lār-ĭ-å kăl-ĭ-fôr-nĭ-cå
California bay

Family: Lauraceae
Growth form: tree to 147 feet (45 m)
Hardiness: marginally hardy to Zone 8
Light: full sun
Water: moist but not wet; can withstand minor drought

Soil: well-drained garden loam
Propagation: seeds or cuttings
Culinary use: not recommended (not GRAS and toxic)
Craft use: wreaths
Landscape use: specimen tree, container plant

*Umbellularia
californica*

This genus of only one species derives its name from the Latin *umbella*, an umbel, from the shape of the inflorescence on the tree. California bay or California laurel is very similar to Grecian bay (*Laurus nobilis*), and some forms of both are superficially identical but readily separable by chemical and microscopic botanical characters. California bay would be a great bay substitute for cooking were it not for the fact that it has no GRAS status and the principal constituent, umbellulone, is toxic to the central nervous system when eaten and causes convulsive sneezing, headaches, and sinus irritation when inhaled deeply. Despite this, one major U.S. spice company markets California bay, and Californians insist *this* is the *only* bay. Other than that, California bay is a great orna-

mental troubled by few insects and other pests (deer usually avoid it unless starving).

If you grow California bay as an ornamental, it is easily pruned and used in the same fashion as *Laurus nobilis*. It is only marginally hardy to Zone 8. It normally grows in the wild in various soils under both cool-humid and hot-dry atmospheric conditions in full sun. It responds to the same pot culture as Grecian bay.

Important chemistry: The essential oil of California bay is characterized by 5 to 39 percent umbellulone and 19 to 28 percent 1,8-cineole, providing a spicy bay-like note.

Botanical Description

U. californica (Hook. & Arnott) Nutt., N. Amer. Sylv. 1:87. 1842.

Native country: California bay is native from southwestern Oregon (Coos County) south to San Diego County, California.

General habit: California bay is an evergreen tree to 45 m.

Leaves: Leaves are parallel-sided to lance-shaped, 3 to 10 × 1.5 to 3 cm, obtusely pinched tips and wedge-shaped to subrounded bases. Surfaces of the blades are finely netted, shining dark green above, paler green and dull beneath.

Flowers: Flowers are greenish yellow in clusters of four to nine.

Fruits/seeds: Fruits are olive-like, 2 to 2.5 cm long, greenish, becoming brownish purple when mature.

Valeriana officinalis

vå-lē-rĭ-ā-nå ŏ-fĭs-ĭ-nā-lĭs
garden valerian

Family: Valerianaceae

Growth form: herbaceous perennial to 5 feet (1.5 m)

Hardiness: hardy to Zone 4

Light: part shade preferred

Water: moist; standing moisture tolerated

Soil: well-drained garden loam rich in organic matter

Propagation: seeds in spring

Culinary use: limited

Craft use: cat toys

Landscape use: rear of herbaceous border or herb garden

French: *valériane*

German: *Baldrian*

Dutch: *valeriaan*

Italian: *valeriana*

Spanish: *valeriana*

Portuguese: *valeriana*

Swedish: *vändelrot*

Russian: *valer'yana*

Garden valerian is known by a number of other garden names: garden heliotrope, cat's valerian, setwell, or St. George's herb. It is an herbaceous perennial with dark green, deeply cut leaves and terminal pinkish white flower heads on stems up to 5 feet (1.5 m) high and smelly rhizomes and roots. The odor of the rhizomes and roots has been described as balsamic-root-like, warm-woody, and somewhat sour with distinct animal undertones of musk. This is an aroma that many cats find irresistible and as with catnip, if you don't like cats, this is not the plant to grow, as it also induces the "catnip response" (see *Nepeta cataria*). We have even observed cats locat-

ing and pawing at the fragrant rhizomes and roots of garden valerian in the middle of winter when a foot of snow lay upon the ground! The rhizomes and roots of garden valerian are also reputed to be equally attractive to rats, and the success of the Pied Piper of Hamelin has been attributed to the use of garden valerian.

The genus *Valeriana* includes about 250 species of the northern temperate region, South Africa, and the Andes. The generic name may be derived from the Latin *valere*, to be strong or vigorous, alluding to its medieval medicinal use. The specific name, *officinalis*, of course, refers to its medicinal qualities. The Swedish name, *vändelrot*, refers to the use of this herb by the invading Teutonic tribes, collectively called the Vandals.

The extract of garden valerian is considered GRAS at 24 to 100 ppm, while the essential oil is GRAS at 0.02 to 17 ppm. Garden valerian

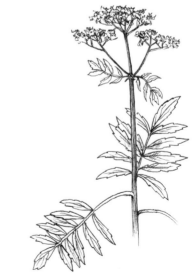

Valeriana officinalis

extract and oil are employed in flavoring tobaccos, beer, and other products. In the Middle Ages, when musk and animalic notes were more widely appreciated, garden valerian was used for seasoning meats and stews.

The primary use of garden valerian today, though, is as a mild, nonaddictive sedative to combat insomnia, excitability, and exhaustion. This is marketed widely in Europe, particularly Germany. An advantage of valerian tincture as a sedative is that it does not interact with alcohol, and overdosage is highly unlikely. The sedative action has been attributed to a group of unstable compounds called valepotriates, as well as GABA (gamma-aminobutyric acid), glutamine, valerenic acid, valerenone, eugenyl esters, and isoeugenyl esters. The reader is referred to the two excellent reviews by Hobbs and Foster for further considerations of the medicinal application of garden valerian.

While garden valerian is extremely variable in its botanical characteristics, only the species is available. Two listed cultivars are 'Anthos', advertised as yielding up to 1 ton per acre (2.5 tonnes/ha), and 'Select', which has a more uniform habit best suited for mechanical harvesting. Red valerian is not *V. officinalis*; it is actually *Centranthus ruber* (L.) DC. (which also exists in a white-flowered form, giving rise to the oxymoron "white red valerian").

Garden valerian is easily grown in moist but well-drained garden loam in part to full sun. Allowed to reseed, it will proliferate in moist forest margins and edges of fields. Seed germinates readily in about five weeks with constant moisture but lose their viability after two years. Division of old clumps is easy in early spring. Space plants about 16 inches (40 cm) between plants in rows about 16 inches (40 cm) apart. Fertilizers high in nitrogen are required.

Valepotriate content, the active constituent, decreases in autumn, while essential oil content is not correlated with the season. The best time to harvest the rhizomes and roots is at the end of September of the first year, in the morning during a cool period. This is the time the roots reach 85 percent of the maximum root weight and contain about 0.8 percent valepotriates and 0.5 percent essential oil. For maximum essential oil, spring harvest is best. Drying is best accomplished, after washing the roots free of soil, at 104°F (40°C) with an air flow of 0.25 kg/m2. For home or commercial use, fresh-dried rhizomes are ground to a coarse powder. One part (by weight) is macerated for up to two weeks in 5 parts (by volume) of a menstruum consisting of 1 part distilled water to 3 parts 95 percent grain alcohol; press and filter for use. The most effective extraction method involves premoistening the dried drug in water; shaking or vibrating the drug and menstruum decreases extraction time from four days under normal conditions to only 30 minutes, but then repeat three successive extractions at 1.6 hours, 1 hour, and 1 hour, respectively.

Important chemistry: The characteristic sour odor of the rhizomes and roots of garden valerian is primarily due to small quantities of isovaleric acid. The dominant components of the essential oil of garden valerian rhizomes and roots are 2 to 51 percent bornyl acetate, 0 to 18 percent valeranone, trace to 16 percent valerenal, trace to 14 percent camphene, and 0 to 12 percent elemol. The attractant for cats is probably due to low levels of actinidine, a volatile alkaloid that is released from *N*-(2-*para*-hydroxy-phenyl)ethyl-actinidine upon drying and heating. The valepotriates, a series of poorly characterized iridoid epoxides, vary from 0.2 to 6 percent in the roots of garden valerian (see Houghton for a more thorough discussion of the rhizome/root chemistry of garden valerian). The rhizomes and roots also have a heavy concentration of unusual sesquiterpenoids.

Analysis of the atmosphere around garden valerian flowers reveals primarily 15 to 24 percent lavandulyl isovalerate and 4 to 21 percent *para*-methyl anisole, providing a flowery anise-like note.

Botanical Description

Valeriana officinalis is extremely variable with three subspecies, but subsp. *officinalis* is the one commonly cultivated.

V. officinalis L., Sp. pl. 31. 1753.
Native country: Garden valerian is native to most of Europe but has been naturalized in North America.

General habit: Garden valerian is a smooth herbaceous perennial arising from a simple rhizome. The stem is 30 to 150 cm, usually solitary, robust, grooved, hairy or smooth.

Leaves: Leaves are lobed like a feather with three to five pairs of leaflets; opposite leaflets are linear, lance-shaped, or elliptical, smooth-edged or toothed.

Flowers: Flowers are arranged in a compound inflorescence, pink or white.

Fruits/seeds: Fruit is 2 to 5 mm, hairy or smooth, with a feathery crown.

Wasabia japonica

wå-să-bĭ-å jå-pŏn-ĭ-kå
Japanese horseradish

Family: Brassicaceae (Cruciferae)
Growth form: herbaceous perennial to 16 inches (40 cm)
Hardiness: hardy to Zone 8
Light: 50 to 80 percent shade
Water: cool running water essential
Soil: organic, slightly alkaline
Propagation: offsets from rhizomes in spring
Culinary use: limited (not GRAS)
Craft use: none
Landscape use: stream edges

Japanese: *wasabi*

Japanese horseradish is sold in Asian food stores as a can of dried green powder. Add water, and presto, instant horseradish to add extra bite to such dishes as *sashimi* (raw fish), *soba* (cold buckwheat noodles), *nigiri sushi* (small kneaded ball of sour rice and fish slices), and *norimaki sushi* (Japanese sour rice wrapped in sheets of *nori*, or red seaweed, with cucumber and/or shiitake mushrooms). Japanese horseradish may also be used to decorate cucumber and carrots and, mixed with soy sauce, as a dip. Besides the green color, the Japanese insist that their *wasabi* has a flavor unmatched by European horseradish.

Wasabia japonica is a smooth, evergreen perennial superficially resembling a giant nasturtium. It demands the cool, running water of streams and springs in open woodlands for best cultivation. Large clumps are formed with large, long-stemmed, heart-shaped leaves to about 16 inches (40 cm). Ultimately, clusters of white mustard-like flowers are produced. The genus, whose name is derived from the native Japanese name, includes two species.

Superior taste is claimed when the water is

slightly alkaline and where the temperature is maintained at 50 to 56°F (10 to 13°C); a spring-fed stream in a limestone area would be ideal. At higher temperatures the leaf and rhizome growth fall off substantially and more diseases are observed. In Japan, stream beds are artificially widened with rock walls and terraces.

Japanese growers recognize at least three cultivars based principally on the color of the rhizome (rootstock) and the leaf stalks: (1) a form with green leaf stalks and large, knobby greenish rhizomes having a strong pungency; (2) a form with reddish petioles with rhizomes of acceptable size and color but less vigorous and less resistant to cold; and (3) a form, called "white wasabi," of less vigor, pungency, and green color. Japanese horseradish is propagated vegetatively by offsets separated from the rhizomes of two-year-old plants after the latter are dug for harvest, usually in June. The offsets are planted 10 inches (25 cm) apart in rows about 18 inches (45 cm) apart. Organic fertilizers rich in nitrogen are applied in November and March in Japan. Over two tons of Japanese horseradish rhizomes may be produced per acre (4,483 kg/ha) from two-year-old plants in Japan.

At the time of harvest the crop is initially prepared by digging, washing, and removing the leaves. In its simplest form, Japanese horseradish is obtained by grating the fresh rhizomes. While usually sold as a dried powder, the best storage of Japanese horseradish is by freezing. When the dried powder is rehydrated, it must be used immediately and does not store well.

While Japanese horseradish has been used for centuries in Japan, it has no GRAS status. As with European horseradish, too much Japanese horseradish may induce excessive sweating, confusion, and collapse. Hitomi Kumagai and his associates at Nihon University in Japan found that the isothiocyanates in Japanese horseradish inhibited platelet aggregation in vitro. One of the principal compounds responsible for the distinctive flavor of wasabi, 6-methylsulfinylhexyl isothiocyanate, has been demonstrated to be anticarcinogenic.

Important chemistry: In a solvent extract of Japanese horseradish, the dominant components are 81 to 90 percent allyl isothiocyanate and 3 to 13 percent 4-pentenyl isothiocyanate. As in conventional horseradish, these compounds normally exist in the plant as glucosinolates, or sugar-bound compounds, and are enzymatically acted upon by myrosinase with the cellular disruption produced by grating. Heating changes the chemical profile, so in an essential oil the dominant components are 39 percent 6-methylthiohexanonitrile and 15 percent 7-methylthioheptanonitrile.

Botanical Description

W. japonica (Miq.) Matsumura, Index pl. jap. 2(2):161. 1912 [*Eutrema wasabi* (Sieb.) Maxim.].

Native country: Japanese horseradish is native to wet places along streams in mountains of Japan.

Wasabia japonica

General habit: Japanese horseradish is an herbaceous perennial with creeping, stout rhizomes; stems are ascending, 20 to 40 cm long, several-leaved.

Leaves: Leaves of the basal rosette have a long stalk and are heart-kidney-shaped, 8 to 15 cm long and as wide, rounded at the apex, undulate-toothed, the stalks dilated at the base. Leaves along the stem are stalked, broadly egg-shaped, 2 to 4 cm long, shallowly heart-shaped at the base.

Flowers: White mustard-like flowers are arranged in a simple inflorescence with bracts similar to the stem-leaves.

Fruits/seeds: Fruits are long pockets on 3 to 5 mm stalks.

Zingiber mioga

zĭn-jĭ-bĕr mī-ō-gå
mioga ginger

Family: Zingiberaceae

Growth form: herbaceous perennial to 10 feet (3 m)

Hardiness: hardy to Zone 7b

Light: part shade to full sun

Water: moist but not constantly wet

Soil: well-drained organic soil

Propagation: division of offsets in spring

Culinary use: limited (not GRAS)

Craft use: none

Landscape use: bold tropical look for herbaceous border or herb garden

Japanese: *myōga*

The genus *Zingiber* includes about 85 species of herbs with aromatic rhizomes; their native habitat stretches from Indomalaysia to eastern Asia and tropical Australia. The leading economically important species is ginger, *Z. officinale* Roscoe. The generic name is derived from ancient Sanskrit.

Mioga ginger grows to about 2 to 3 feet (0.6 to 0.9 m) in the average garden, but up to 10 feet (3 m) under optimum conditions, with fragrant rhizomes and bamboo-like leaves. For all its aerial abundance, however, the choice culinary portions are the young buds and the fleshy inflorescences that appear at the base of the leaves in the fall. The pale yellow flower clusters are usually pickled in salted rice vinegar and sake and then sliced for soups, stir-fry dishes,

Zingiber mioga

and sour dishes. A 4- to 6-inch (10 to 15 cm) layer of sawdust provides a substrate to locate and pick the buds. The young leaves and sheaths are minutely chopped and used as a garnish for soup, and raw fish. The young shoots are also blanched and used in soups, tempura, and as a spice for bean curd.

Most species of the Zingiberaceae are not hardy except in tropical climates. However, mioga ginger is fully hardy to at least Zone 7. Provide the plant with good, humusy soil and part shade to full sun. Propagation is via the abundant rhizomes, which will quickly form a dense colony (but not to the point of being weedy). Plant about 10-inch (25 cm) long pieces in spring, about 4 inches (10 cm) deep and 16 inches (40 cm) apart, in rows. Harvest the flower buds in the second year. Yields in New Zealand have been 3.6 to 5.8 tons per acre (8 to 13 t/ha). One ornamental cultivar, 'Dancing Crane', has white stripes on the leaves and yellow flowers.

Mioga ginger is not considered GRAS.

Important chemistry: The principal components of the essential oil of the young buds of mioga ginger are 25 percent beta-phellandrene, 20 percent beta-elemene, and 10 percent beta-pinene. The red pigment on the floral bracts is malvidin 3-rutinoside.

Botanical Description

Z. mioga (Thunb.) Roscoe, Trans. Linn. Soc. London 8:348. 1807.

Native country: Mioga ginger is native to Japan.

General habit: Mioga ginger is a smooth, rhizomatous perennial to 3 m.

Leaves: Leaves appear in a sheathed arrangement forming a false stem with lance-shaped to narrowly oblong blades 20 to 35 × 3 to 6 cm, pointed at the tip, narrowed to a short stalk-like base.

Flowers: Pale yellow flowers appear in August through October in fleshy, basal spikes.

Selected References

Chapter 1

Bailey, L. H. 1949. *Manual of Cultivated Plants*. New York: Macmillan.

Balashev, L. L. 1970. *Dictionary of Useful Plants in Twenty European Languages*. Moscow: Publ. House Nauka.

Bedevian, A. K. 1936. *Illustrated Polyglottic Dictionary of Plant Names*. Cairo: Argus & Papazian Presses.

Burdock, G. A., ed. 1995. *Fenaroli's Handbook of Flavor Ingredients*. 3rd ed. Boca Raton, Florida: CRC Press.

Cathey, H. M. 1990. *USDA Plant Hardiness Zone Map*. USDA Misc. Publ. 1475.

Duke, J. A. 1982. Ecosystematic data on medicinal plants. In *Cultivation and Utilization of Medicinal Plants*. Ed. C. K. Atal and B. M. Kapur. Jammu Tawi, India: Regional Res. Lab. 13–23.

Farr, D. F., et al. 1989. *Fungi on Plants and Plant Products in the United States*. St. Paul, Minnesota: Amer. Phytopath. Soc. Press.

Glanze, W. D., et al., eds. 1990. *Mosby's Medical, Nursing, and Allied Health Dictionary*. 3rd ed. St. Louis, Missouri: C. V. Mosby Co.

Harris, J. G., and M. W. Harris. 1994. *Plant Identification Terminology: An Illustrated Glossary*. Spring Lake, Utah: Spring Lake Publ.

International Fragrance Association. 1989. *Code of Practice*. Geneva: IFRA.

Johnson, A. T., and H. A. Smith. 1972. *Plant Names Simplified*. Bromyard, England: Landsmans Bookshop.

Kays, S. J., and J. C. Silva Dias. 1995. Common names of commercially cultivated vegetables of the world in 15 languages. *Econ. Bot.* 49: 115–152.

Leung, A. Y., and S. Foster. 1996. *Encyclopedia of Common Natural Ingredients Used in Food, Drugs, and Cosmetics*. 2nd ed. New York: John Wiley & Sons.

McGuffin, M., et al., eds. 1997. *American Herbal Products Association's Botanical Safety Handbook*. Boca Raton, Florida: CRC Press.

Nikolov, H. 1996. *Dictionary of Plants Names in Latin, German, English and French*. Berlin: J. Cramer.

Quattrocchi, U. 2000. *CRC World Dictionary of Plant Names*. Boca Raton, Florida: CRC Press.

Rehder, A. 1949. *Manual of Cultivated Trees and Shrubs Hardy in North America*. New York: Macmillan.

Stafleu, F. A., and R. S. Cowan. 1976–88. *Taxonomic Literature*. 2nd ed. 7 vols. Utrecht: Bohn, Scheltema & Holkema.

Steinmetz, E. F. 1957. *Codex Vegetabilis*. Amsterdam: E. F. Steinmetz.

Tisserand, R., and T. Balacs. 1995. *Essential Oil Safety*. Edinburgh: Churchill Livingstone.

Torkelson, A. R. 1996–99. *The Cross Name Index to Medicinal Plants*. Boca Raton, Florida: CRC Press.

Walters, S. M., et al., eds. 1984–2000. *The European Garden Flora*. 6 vols. Cambridge Univ. Press.

Zebovitz, T. C. 1989. *Compendium of Safety Data Sheets for Research and Industrial Chemicals. Part 7. Flavor and Fragrance Substances*. New York: VCH Publ.

Chapter 2

American Association of Nurserymen. c. 1989. *How to Use, Select, and Register Cultivar Names*. Washington, D.C.: Amer. Assoc. Nurserymen.

Bailey, L. H. 1933. *How Plants Get Their Names*. New York: Macmillan Co.

Bailey, R. 1948. *The Home Garden Self-pronouncing Dictionary of Plant Names*. New York: *Amer. Gard.* Guild.

Brickell, C. D., chairman. 2004. International Code of Nomenclature for Cultivated Plants. *Acta Hort.* 647.

Coombes, A. J. 1987. *Dictionary of Plant Names*. Beaverton, Oregon: Timber Press.

Cronquist, A. 1988. *The Evolution and Classification of Flowering Plants*. 2nd ed. Bronx, N.Y.: New York Bot. Gard.

DeWolf, G. P. 1968. Notes on making an herbarium. *Arnoldia* 28: 69–111.

Florists' Publishing Company. 1980. *New Pronouncing Dictionary of Plant Names*. Chicago: Florists' Publ. Co.

Gledhill, D. 1990. *The Names of Plants*. 2nd ed. New York: Cambridge Univ. Press.

Hicks, A. J., and P. M. Hicks. 1978. A selected bibliography of plant collection and herbarium curation. *Taxon* 27: 63–99.

Hottes, A. C. 1937. *The Home Gardener's Pronouncing Dictionary*. Des Moines, Iowa: Meredith Publ. Co.

Hyams, R., and R. Pankhurst. 1995. *Plants and Their Names: A Concise Dictionary*. Oxford Univ. Press.

McNeill, J., chairman. 2006. *International Code of Botanical Nomenclature (Vienna Code)*. Koenigstein: Koeltz Sci. Books.

Savile, D. B. O. 1973. *Collection and Care of Botanical Specimens*. Ottawa: Res. Branch, Canad. Dept. Agric.

Smith, A. W. 1963. *A Gardener's Book of Plant Names*. New York: Harper and Row.

Smith, C. E. 1971. *Preparing Herbarium Specimens of Vascular Plants*. USDA Inform. Bull. 348.

Stearn, W. T. 1992. *Botanical Latin: History, Grammar, Syntax, Terminology and Vocabulary*. 4th ed. London: David & Charles.

———. 1992. *Stearn's Dictionary of Plant Names for Gardeners*. London: Cassell Publ. Ltd.

Zycherman, L. A., and J. R. Schrock. 1988. *A Guide to Museum Pest Control*. Washington, D.C.: Assoc. Systematic Collections.

Chapter 3

Arctander, S. 1969. *Perfume and Flavor Chemicals (Aroma Chemicals)*. 2 vols. Montclair, New Jersey: Steffen Arctander.

Arnason, J. T., et al., eds. 1989. *Insecticides of Plant Origin*. Washington, D.C.: Amer. Chem. Soc.

Benezet, L., and G. Igolen. 1951. Note sur le basiliquage de la menthe poivrée et la teneur élevée de son essence en menthofurane. *Bull. Soc. Chim. France* 18: 912–914.

Birch, G. G. 1987. Sweeteners and sweetness. *Endeavour* 11: 21–24.

Brieskorn, C. H. 1978. "... und gibt ihm bittre Arznei." *Pharmazie Unserer Zeit* 7(5): 143–150.

Fenwick, G. R., et al. 1990. Bitter principles

in food plants. *Bitterness in Food and Beverages.* Ed. R. L. Rouseff. Amsterdam: Elsevier. 205–250.

Firth, G. 1983. *Secrets of the Still.* McLean, Virginia: PM Publ.

Furia, T. E., and N. Bellanca. 1975. *Fenaroli's Handbook of Flavor Ingredients.* 2nd ed. Cleveland, Ohio: CRC Press.

Grainge, M., and A. Ahmed. 1988. *Handbook of Plants with Pest-control Properties.* New York: John Wiley & Sons.

Guenther, E. 1948–52. *The Essential Oils.* 6 vols. New York: Van Nostrand Co.

Heath, H. B. 1978. *Flavor Technology: Profiles, Products, Applications.* Westport, Connecticut: AVI Publ.

Inglett, G. E. 1984. Sweeteners: an overall perspective. In *Aspartame: Physiology and Biochemistry.* Ed. L. D. Stegink and L. J. Filer. New York: Marcell Dekker. 11–25

International Fragrance Association. 1989. *Code of Practice.* Geneva: IFRA.

———. 1996. Amendments to the IFRA guidelines. *Perfumer Flavor.* 21(2): 51–54.

Jacobson, M. 1990. *Glossary of Plant-derived Insect Deterrents.* Boca Raton, Florida: CRC Press.

Leung, A. Y. 1980. *Encyclopedia of Common Natural Ingredients Used in Food, Drugs, and Cosmetics.* New York: John Wiley & Sons.

Muller, W. H., et al. 1969. Volatile growth inhibitors produced by *Salvia leucophylla*: effect on oxygen uptake by mitochondrial suspensions. *Bull. Torrey Bot. Club* 96: 89–96.

Ney, K. H. 1990. Aromagrams: a new approach to flavour classification and description. In *Flavor and Off-flavor '89.* Ed. G. Charalambous. Amsterdam: Elsevier. 561–576.

Richmond, C. 1985. Effectiveness of two pine oils for protecting lodgepole pine from attack by mountain pine beetle (Coleoptera: Scolytidae). *Canad. Entomol.* 117: 1445–1446.

Rothe, M. 1988. *Introduction to Aroma Research.* Dordrecht: Kluwer Acad. Publ.

Theimer, E. T., ed. 1982. *Fragrance Chemistry: The Science of the Sense of Smell.* New York: Academic Press.

Tucker, A. O., and J. E. Simon. 1990. Techniques to distill essential oils: an overview and demonstration. In *Herbs '90 Proceedings, The Fifth Annual Conference of the International Herb Growers and Marketers Association, June 30–July 3, 1990, Baltimore, Maryland.* Ed. J. E. Simon et al. 209–211.

Williams, N. H., and W. M. Whitten. 1983. Orchid floral fragrances and male euglossine bees: methods and advances in the last sesquidecade. *Biol. Bull.* 164: 355–395.

Winter, R. 1989. *A Consumer's Dictionary of Food Additives.* New York: Crown Publ.

Chapter 4

Adler, P. R., et al. 1989. Nitrogen form alters sweet basil growth and essential oil content and composition. *HortScience* 24: 789–790.

Bassuk, N. 1986. Year-round production of greenhouse-grown French tarragon. *HortScience* 21: 258.

Boyle, T. H., et al. 1991. Growing medium and fertilization regime influence growth and essential oil content of rosemary. *HortScience* 26: 33–34.

Charles, D. J., et al. 1990. Effects of osmotic stress on the essential oil content and composition of peppermint. *Phytochemistry* 29: 2837–2840.

Clery, R. A. 1992. *An Investigation of the Variability of Essential Oil Production in Plants.* Ph.D. thesis, Univ. Reading.

Franz, C. 1983. Nutrient and water management for medicinal and aromatic plants. *Acta Hort.* 132: 203–215

Lawrence, B. M. 1986. Essential oil production: a discussion of influencing factors. In *Biogeneration of Aromas.* Ed. T. H. Parliament and R. Croteau. Washington, D.C.: American Chemical Society. 363–369.

Liberty Hyde Bailey Hortorium, staff. 1978. *Hortus Third.* New York: Macmillan Publishing Co.

Phillips, H. F. 1982. *A Study of the Taxa of* Thymus *L. (Labiatae) Cultivated in the United States.* Ph.D. thesis, Cornell Univ., Ithaca, New York. (University Microfilms International, Ann Arbor, Michigan, order number DA 8228439)

Piccaglia, R., et al. 1989. Effect of mineral fertilizers on the composition of *Salvia officinalis* oil. *J. Essential Oil Res.* 2: 73–83.

Putievsky, E. 1988. Selection and breeding of aromatic plants. In *Proceedings of the Third National Herb Growing and Marketing Conference, July 24–27, 1988, Louisville, Kentucky.* Ed. J. E. Simon and L. Z. Clavio. 34–45.

———. 1990. Fertilization of aromatic plants. In *Herbs '90 Proceedings, The Fifth Annual Conference of the International Herb Growers and Marketers Association, June 30–July 3, 1990, Baltimore, Maryland.* Ed. J. E. Simon et al. 22–29.

Simon, J. E., and D. Charles. 1989. Environmental and cultural effects of essential oils. In *Proceedings of the Fourth National Herb Growing and Marketing Conference: International Herb Growers and Marketers Association. July 22–25, 1989, San Jose, California.* Ed. J. E. Simon et al. 66.

Simon, J. E., et al., 1989. Cultivar evaluation of culinary herbs. In *Proceedings of the Fourth National Herb Growing and Marketing Conference: International Herb Growers and Marketers Association, July 22–25, 1989, San Jose, California.* Ed. J. E. Simon et al. 12–21.

Torrey, T. C. 1989. Breeding herbs for culinary and ornamental use. In *Proceedings of the Fourth National Herb Growing and Marketing Conference: International Herb Growers and Marketers Association, July 22–25, 1989, San Jose, California.* Ed. J. E. Simon et al. 38–40.

Treadwell, D. D., et al. 2007. Nutrient management in organic greenhouse herb production: where are we now? *HortTechnology* 17: 461–466.

Tucker, A. O., and M. J. Maciarello. 1987. Plant identification. In *Proceedings of the First National Herb Growing and Marketing Conference, July 19–22, 1986, West Lafayette, Indiana.* Ed. J. E. Simon and L. Grant. 126–172.

Tucker, A. O., and E. Rollins. 1989. The species, hybrids, and cultivars of *Origanum* (Lamiaceae) cultivated in the United States. *Baileya* 23: 14–27.

Tucker, A. O., et al. 1984. The effect of sand topdressing and fertilizer on inflorescence and essential oil yield in 'Dutch' lavandin. *HortScience* 19: 526–527.

———. 1990. Essential oils of cultivars of Dalmatian sage (*Salvia officinalis* L.). *J. Essential Oil Res.* 2: 139–144.

Chapter 5

Barker, A. V. 1986. Organic fertilizers for herbs. *Herb, Spice, Med. Pl. Dig.* 4(3): 1–2,4–7.

———. 1989. Liming of soils for production of herbs. *Herb, Spice, Med. Pl. Dig.* 4 (4): 1–5.

Bennett, J. 1990. The undercover plot. *Harrowsmith Country Life* Sept.-Oct.: 80–92.

Dinda, K. M., and L. E. Craker. 1997. *Breaking Ground: A Resource Guide for Specialty Crop Growers.* Amherst, Massachusetts: HSMP Press.

Duke, J. A. 1977. Ecosystematic data on economic plants. *Quart. J. Crude Drug Res.* 17 (3–4): 91–110.

———. 1982. Ecosystematic data on medicinal plants. In *Cultivation and Utilization of Medicinal Plants.* Ed. C. K. Atal and B. M. Kapur. Jammu Tawi, India: Regional Res. Lab. 13–23.

———. 1983. The USDA economic botany laboratory's data base on minor economic plant species. In *Plants: The Potentials for Extracting Protein, Medicines, and Other Useful Chemicals: Workshop Proceedings.* Washington, D.C.: U.S. Congress, Office of Technology Assessment. 196–214.

Green, R. J. 1987. Peppermint and spearmint production in the Midwestern states. In *Proceedings of the Second National Herb Growing and Marketing Conference, Purdue Univ., West Lafayette, Indiana.* Ed. J. E. Simon and L. Grant. 40–42.

Hälvä, S., and L. E. Craker. 1996. *Manual for Northern Herb Growers*. Amherst, Massachusetts: HSMP Press.

Hay, R. K. M., and P. G. Waterman, eds. 1993. *Volatile Oil Crops: Their Biology, Biochemistry and Production*. Essex, England: Longman Sci. Techn.

Kammel, D. W., and J. H. Pedersen. 1989. *Preservative Treated Wood for Farm and Home*. Midwest Plant Serv., Iowa State Univ. AED-30.

Kumar, N., et al. 1993. *Introduction of Spices, Plantation Crops, Medicinal and Aromatic Plants*. Nagercoil, India: Rajalakshmi Publ.

Lamb, F. M. 1986. Wood for use in gardens and outdoor applications. *Green Scene* 15(2): 30.

Landing, J. E. 1969. *American Essence: A History of the Peppermint and Spearmint Industry in the United States*. Kalamazoo, Michigan: Kalamazoo Publ. Mus.

Long, C., and M. McGrath. 1994. Treated wood: yes, it's still toxic! *Organic Gard.* 41(1): 71–74.

Lorenz, O. A., and D. N. Maynard. 1980. *Knott's Handbook for Vegetable Growers*. 2nd ed. New York: John Wiley & Sons.

Marczewski, A. E., et al. 1989. *Guidelines for Use of Chemically Treated Wood on the Farm and in the Home*. Michigan State Univ. Ext. Bull. E-1813.

Norman, C. 1986. Wood preservatives. *Green Scene* 15(2): 31–33.

Peter, K. V., ed. 2001 *Handbook of Herbs and Spices*. Boca Raton, Florida: CRC Press.

———, ed. 2004. *Handbook of Herbs and Spices Vol. 2*. Boca Raton, Florida: CRC Press.

———, ed. 2006. *Handbook of Herbs and Spices Vol. 3*. Boca Raton, Florida: CRC Press.

Putievsky, E. 1990. Irrigation of aromatic plants. In *Herbs '90 Proceedings, The Fifth Annual Conference of the International Herb Growers and Marketers Association, June 30–July 3, 1990, Baltimore, Maryland*. Ed. J. E. Simon et al. 15–21.

Raloff, J. 2004. Danger on deck? *Sci. News* 165: 74–75.

Ricotta, J. A., and J. B. Masiunas. 1991. The effects of black plastic mulch and weed control strategies on herb yield. *HortScience* 26: 539–541.

Rist, C. 1998. Arsenic and old wood. *Herb Growing Marketing Network* 6(4): 28–31.

Weiss, E. A. 2002. *Spice Crops*. New York: CABI Publ.

Chapter 6

Aung, L. H., and G. J. Flick Jr. 1980. The influence of fish solubles on growth and fruiting of tomatoes. *HortScience* 15: 32–33.

Baker, K., et al. 1957. *The U.C. System for Pro-ducing Healthy Container-grown Plants*. California Agricultural Experiment Station Extension Service. Manual 23.

Bell, S. M., and G. D. Coorts. 1979. The effects of growth mediums on three selected herb species. *Florists' Rev.* Jan. 11: 48–49.

Boyle, T. H., et al. 1991. Growing medium and fertilization regime influence growth and essential oil content of rosemary. *HortScience* 26: 33–34.

Buchanan, R. 1990. Evaluating potting soil. *Fine Gard.* 12: 23–26.

Bunt, A. C. 1976. *Modern Potting Composts*. Pennsylvania State Univ. Press, University Park.

Emino, E. R. 1981. Effectiveness of fish soluble nutrients as fertilizers on container-grown plants. *HortScience* 16: 338.

Fosler, G. M. n.d. *Soil Sterilization Methods for the Indoor Gardener*. Univ. of Illinois Coll. of Agric. Extens. Bull. 793.

Grace Horticultural Products. 1988. *Water Quality: Effects on Nutritional Management*. Bull. PTB-133.

Heins, R., and J. Erwin. 1990. Control plant growth with temperature. *Greenhouse Grower.* May, page 72.

Kuack, David L. 1989. Beneficials bag media diseases. *Greenhouse Grower.* May 84–89.

Logan, W. B. 1991. Rot is hot. *New York Times Mag.* Sept. 8: 46.

Martin, C. A., and D. L. Ingram. 1991. Evaluation of thermal properties and effect of irrigation on temperature dynamics in container media. *J. Environm. Hort.* 9: 1.

Mastalerz, J. W., ed. 1976. *Bedding Plants: A Manual on the Culture of Bedding Plants as a Greenhouse Crop*. 2nd ed. University Park, Pennsylvania: Pennsylvania Flower Growers.

Peck, K. 1990. Measuring pH with meters and colorimetric methods. *Hummert's Quart.* 14: 1–2.

Purohit, A., and R. P. Athanas. n.d. *Fish Hydrolysate as an Alternate Fertilizer for Growing Chrysanthemums*. Hawthorne, Massachusetts: Essex Ag. & Tech. Inst.

Purohit, A., et al. n.d. *Effects of Fish Hydrolysate on Greenhouse Grown Capsicum frutescens*. Hawthorne, Massachusetts: Essex Ag. & Tech. Inst.

Wright, R. D. 1987. *The Virginia Tech Liquid Fertilizer System for Container Grown Plants*. Dept. of Hort., Virginia Tech. Information Ser. 86–5.

Chapter 7

Cowen, R., et al. 1990. The effect of media on the percentage germination of thyme, oregano, and marjoram. *Herb Proceedings 1990 Illinois Specialty Growers Convention, Jan 15–18*. University of Illinois at Urbana-Champaign Cooperative Extension Service, College of Agriculture, Horticulture Series 84.

Craker, L. E. 1987. Agronomic practices for dill production. In *Proceedings of the Second National Herb Growing and Marketing Conference, Purdue Univ., West Lafayette, Indiana*. Ed. J. E. Simon and L. Grant. 58–61.

DeBaggio, T. 1987. Growing rosemary as a holiday pot plant at Christmas. In *Proceedings of the Second National Herb Growing and Marketing Conference, Purdue Univ., West Lafayette, Indiana*. Ed. J. E. Simon and L. Grant. 91–95.

———. 1988. Scheduling production of potted herb plants. In *Proceedings of Third National Herb Growers and Marketers Conference, Purdue Univ., West Lafayette, Indiana*. Ed. J. E. Simon and L. Z. Clavio. 103–109.

DeBaggio, T., and T. Boyle. 1988. Rosemary. *GrowerTalks* 52(4): 16,18.

Hartmann, H. T., and D. E. Kester. 1983. *Plant Propagation: Principles and Practices*. New York: Prentice Hall.

Hershfeld, S. 1990. Raising herbs as bedding plants. In *Herbs '90 Proceedings, The Fifth Annual Conference of the International Herb Growers and Marketers Association, June 30–July 3, 1990, Baltimore, Maryland*. Ed. J. E. Simon et al. 66–70.

Powell, C. C. 1991. Managing seedling root diseases. *Greenhouse Manager* December: 48–54.

———. 1992. Managing foliar diseases of plugs. *Greenhouse Manager* December: 93–95.

Powell, C. C., and R. K. Lindquist. 1992. *Ball Pest & Disease Manual*. Geneva, Illinois: Ball Publ.

Putievsky, E. 1990. Fertilization of aromatic plants. In *Herbs '90 Proceedings, The Fifth Annual Conference of the International Herb Growers and Marketers Association, June 30–July 3, 1990, Baltimore, Maryland*. Ed. J. E. Simon et al. 22–29.

Chapter 8

Adekunle, O. K., et al. 2007. Toxicity of pure compounds isolated from *Tagetes minuta* oil to *Meloidogyne incognita*. *Australasian Pl. Dis. Notes* 2: 101–104.

Barker, A. V. 1990. Mulches for herbs. *Herb Spice Med. Pl. Dig.* 8(3): 1–5.

Barrons, K. C. 1984. How effective are pest-repellent companion plantings? *Herbarist* 50: 39–43.

Batish, D. R., et al. 2007. Potential utilization of dried powder of *Tagetes minuta* as a natural herbicide for managing rice weeds. *Crop. Prot.* 26: 566–571.

Chitwood, D. J. 1993. Naturally occurring nematicides. In *Pest Control with Enhanced Environmental Safety*. Ed. S. O. Duke et al. Washington, D.C.: Amer. Chem. Soc. 300–315.

Festing, S. 1989. *The Story of Lavender*. 2nd

rev. ed. Surrey, England: Heritage in Sutton Leisure.

Hutton, M. G., and D. T. Handley. 2007. Effects of silver reflective mulch, white inter-row mulch, and plant density on yields of pepper in Maine. *HortTechnology* 17: 214–219.

Kourik, R. 1986. *Designing and Maintaining Your Edible Landscape Naturally.* Santa Rosa, California: Metamorphic Press.

Gessell, S. G., et al. 1975. Companionate plantings: do they work? *Pl. Gard.* 31(1): 24–28.

Gill, S., and J. Sanderson. 1998. *Greenhouse Pests and Beneficials.* Batavia, Illinois: Ball Publ.

Hough-Goldstein, J. A. 1990. Antifeedant effects of common herbs on the Colorado potato beetle (Coleoptera: Chrysomelidae). *Environ. Entomol.* 19: 234–238.

Hough-Goldstein, J., and S. P. Hahn. 1992. Antifeedant and oviposition deterrent activity of an aqueous extract of *Tanacetum vulgare* L. on two cabbage pests. *Environ. Entomol.* 21: 837–844.

López-Escudero, F. J., et al. 2007. Reduction of *Verticillium dahliae* microsclerotia viability in soil by dried plant residues. *Crop. Prot.* 26: 127–133.

Manukyan, A. E., and W. H. Schnitzler. 2006. Influence of air temperature on productivity and quality of some medicinal plants under controlled environmental conditions. *Eur. J. Hort. Sci.* 71: 36–44.

Natarajan, N., et al. 2006. Cold aqueous extracts of African marigold, *Tagetes erecta,* for control of tomato root knot nematode, *Meloidogyne incognita. Crop. Prot.* 25: 1210–1213.

Palevitch, D., and L. E. Craker. 1994. Volatile oils as potential insecticides. *Herb Spice Med. Pl. Dig.* 12(2): 1–5.

Philbrick, H. 1969. Herb symbiosis: companion plants. *Herbarist* 35: 58–66.

Powell, C. C., and R. K. Lindquist. 1992. *Ball Pest & Disease Manual.* Geneva, Illinois: Ball Publ.

Regnault-Roger, C., et al. 1993. Insecticidal effect of essential oils from Mediterranean plants upon *Achantoscelides obtectus* Say (Coleoptera, Bruchidae), a pest of kidney bean (*Phaseolus vulgaris* L.). *J. Chem. Ecol.* 19: 1233–1244.

Smith, Judith G. 1975. Influence of crop background on aphids and other phytophagous insects on Brussels sprouts. *Ann. Appl. Biol.* 83: 1–13.

Tucker, A. O., and M. J. Maciarello. 1990. Control of sudden dieback in herbs. In *Herbs '90 Proceedings, The Fifth Annual Conference of the International Herb Growers and Marketers Association, June 30–July 3, 1990, Baltimore, Maryland.* Ed. J. E. Simon et al. 43–47.

Tunç, I., and S. Sahinkaya. 1998. Sensitivity of two greenhouse pests to vapours of essential oils. *Entomol. Exp. Appl.* 86: 183–187.

Van Tol, R. W. H. M., et al. 2007. Plant odours with potential for a push-pull strategy to control onion thrips, *Thrips tabaci. Ent. Exp. Appl.* 122: 69–76.

Walker, J. T. 1995. Garden herbs as hosts for southern root knot nematode [*Meloidogyne incognita* (Kofold & White) Chitwood race 3]. *HortScience* 30: 292–293.

Weller, S. C. 1987. Weed control considerations in herb production. In *Proceedings of the First National Herb Growing and Marketing Conference, July 19–22, 1986, West Lafayette, Indiana.* Ed. J. E. Simon and L. Grant. 92–96.

Chapter 9

Bell, K. Y., et al. 1997. Reduction of food borne microorganisms on beef carcass tissue using acetic acid, sodium bicarbonate, and hydrogen peroxide spray washes. *Food Microbiol.* 14: 439–448.

Basker, D., and E. Putievsky. 1978. Seasonal variation in the yields of herb and essential oil in some Labiatae species. *J. Hort. Sci.* 53: 179–183.

Fonseca, J. M., and S. Ravishankar. 2007. Safer salads. *Amer. Sci.* 95: 494–499.

Grella, G. E., and V. Picci. 1988. Variazioni stagionali dell-olio essenziale di *Salvia officinalis. Fitoterapia* 59: 97–102.

Kapadia, G. J. Rao, et al. 1983. Herbal tea consumption and esophageal cancer In *Carcinogens and Mutagens in the Environment. Vol. 3. Naturally Occurring Compounds: Epidemiology and Distribution.* Ed. H. F. Stich. Boca Raton, Florida: CRC Press. 3–12.

Nykänen, L., and I. Nykänen. 1987. The effect of drying on the composition of the essential oil of some Labiatae herbs cultivated in Finland. In *Flavor Science and Technology.* Ed. M. Martens et al. New York: John Wiley & Sons. 83–88.

Richards, K., et al. 2000. Survival and growth of *E. coli* O157:H7 on broccoli, cucumbers and green peppers. *Dairy, Food, and Environ. Sanitation* 20: 24–28.

Tucker, A. O., and M. J. Maciarello. 1989. Drying herbs with a low capital investment: two prototypes. In *Proceedings of the Third National Herb Growing and Marketing Conference, Louisville, Kentucky, July 17–20, 1988.* Ed. J. E. Simon and L. Grant. 95–102.

———. 1993. Shelf life of culinary herbs and spices. In *Shelf Life Studies of Foods and Beverages.* Ed. G. Charalambous. Amsterdam: Elsevier. 469–485.

Wright, J. R., et al. 2000. Reduction of *Escherichia coli* O157:H7 on apples using wash and chemical sanitizers. *Dairy, Food, and Environ. Sanitation* 20: 120–126.

Acorus

Alankararao, G. S. J. G., and Y. Rajendra Prasad. 1981. Antimicrobial property of *Acorus calamus* Linn: in vitro studies. *Indian Perfumer* 25: 4–6.

Anonymous. 1996. Calamus. In *Lawrence Review of Natural Products.* St. Louis: Facts and Comparisons.

Bogner, J., and D. H. Nicolson. 1991. A revised classification of Araceae with dichotomous keys. *Willdenowia* 21: 35–50.

Chamorro, G., et al. 1998. Dominant study of alpha-asarone in male mice. *Toxicology Lett.* 99: 71–77.

Deng, C., et al. 2004. Rapid determination of essential oil in *Acorus tatarinowii* Schott. By pressurized hot water extraction followed by solid-phase microextraction and gas chromatography-mass spectrometry. *J. Chromatogr.* 1059: 149–155.

Duvall, M. R., et al. 1993. Phylogenetic analysis of the *rbcL* sequences identifies *Acorus calamus* as the primal extant monocotyledon. *Proc. Natl. Acad. Sci.* 90: 4641–4644.

Garneau, F.-X., et al. Aromas from Quebec. I. Composition of the essential oil of the rhizome of *Acorus calamus. J. Essential Oil Res.* 20: 250–254.

Grayum, M. H. 1987. A summary of evidence and arguments supporting the removal of *Acorus* from the Araceae. *Taxon* 36: 723–729.

Héthelyi, B. E., et al. 2002. Orvosi kálmos: *Acorus calamus* L. termesztése rekultivációs területen és hatóanyagának fitokémiai vizsgálata. *Olaj Szappan Kosmetika* 51: 185–191.

Keller, K., et al. 1985. Spasmolytische Wirkung des Isoasaronfreien Kalmus. *Pl. Med.* 1985: 6–9.

Lander, V., and P. Schreier. 1990. Acorenone and gamma-asarone: Indicators of the origin of calamus oils (*Acorus calamus,* L.). *Flavour Fragrance J.* 5: 75–79.

Liao, J.-Fet al. 1998. Central inhibitory effects of water extract of Acori graminei rhizoma in mice. *J. Ethnopharmacol.* 61: 185–193.

Locock, R. A. 1987. *Acorus calamus. Canad. Pharm. J.* 120: 340–342, 344.

Marongiu, B., et al. 2005. Chemical composition of the essential oil and supercritical CO_2 extract of *Commiphora myrrha* (Nees) Engl. and of *Acorus calamus* L. *J. Agric. Food Chem.* 53: 7939–7943.

Mazza, G. 1985. Gas chromatographic and mass spectrometric studies of the constituents of the rhizome of calamus. I. The volatile constituents of the essential oil. *J. Chromatogr.* 328: 179–194.

———. 1985. Gas chromatographic and mass spectrometric studies of the constituents of the rhizome of calamus. II. The volatile constituents of alcoholic extracts. *J. Chromatogr.* 328: 195–206.

Morgan, G. R. 1980. The ethnobotany of sweet flag among North American Indians. *Bot. Mus. Leafl.* 28: 235–246.

Motley, T. J. 1994. The ethnobotany of sweet flag, *Acorus calamus* (Araceae). *Econ. Bot.* 48: 397–412.

Raina, V. K., et al. 2003. Essential oil composition of *Acorus calamus* L. from the lower region of the Himalayas. *Flavour Fragrance J.* 18: 18–20.

Röst, L. C. M. 1979. Biosystematic investigations with *Acorus*. 4. Communication. A synthetic approach to the classification of the genus. *Pl. Med.* 37: 289–307.

Röst, L. C. M., and R. Bos. 1979. Biosystematic investigations with *Acorus*. 3. Communication. Constituents of essential oils. *Pl. Med.* 36: 350–361.

Saxena, B. P., and J. B. Srivastava. 1972. Effect of *Acorus calamus* L. oil vapours on *Dysdercus koenigii* F. *Indian J. Exp. Biol.* 10: 391–393.

Sugimoto, N., et al. 1997. Pharmacognostical investigations of acori rhizomes (1). Histological and chemical studies of rhizomes of *A. calamus* and *A. gramineus* distributed in Japan. *Nat. Med.* 51: 259–264.

———. 1999. DNA profiling of *Acorus calamus* chemotypes differing in essential oil composition. *Biol. Pharm. Bull.* 22: 481–485.

Tanker, M., et al. 1993. Results of certain investigations on the volatile oil-containing plants of Turkey. In *Essential Oils for Perfumery and Flavour. Proceedings of an International Conference 26–30 May 1990 Antalya, Turkey.* Ed. K. H. C. Baser and N. Güler. Istanbul. 16–29.

Taylor, J. M., et al. 1967. Toxicity of oil of calamus (Jammu variety). *Toxicol. Appl. Pharmacol.* 10: 405.

Thompson, S. A. 2000. *Acorus*. In *Flora of North America North of Mexico.* New York: Oxford Univ. Press. Ed. Flora of North America Editorial Committee. 22: 125–127

Todorova, M. N., et al. 1995. Chemical composition of essential oil from Mongolian *Acorus calamus* L. rhizomes. *J. Essential Oil Res.* 7: 191–193.

van Lier, F. P., et al. 1986. Isolation and synthesis of (*Z,Z*)-4,7-decadienal, the character impact compound in the oil of *Acorus calamus* L. In *Progress in Essential Oil Research.* Ed. E.-J. Brunke. Berlin: Walter de Gruyter. 215–225.

Zanoli, P., et al. 1998. Sedative and hypothermic effects induced by β-asarone, a main component of *Acorus calamus. Phytotherapy Res.* 12:S114–S116.

Agastache

Ayers, G. S., and M. P. Wirdlechner. 1994. The genus *Agastache* as bee forage: an analysis of reader returns. *Amer. Bee J.* 134: 621–627.

Charles, D. J., et al. 1991. Characterization of essential oil of *Agastache* species. *J. Agric. Food Chem.* 39: 1946–1949.

Bruni, R., et al. 2007. Essential oil composition of *Agastache anethiodora* Britton (Lamiaceae) infected by cucumber mosaic virus (CMV). *Flavour Fragrance J.* 22: 66–70.

Dũng, N. X., et al. Constituents of the leaf and flower oils of *Agastache rugosa* (Fisch. et Mey) O. Kuntze from Vietnam. *J. Essential Oil Res.* 8: 135–138.

Fuentes-granados, R. G., et al. 1998. An overview of *Agastache* research. *J. Herbs Spices Med. Pl.* 6(1): 69–97.

———. 2000. Inheritance studies of aromatic compounds in *Agastache foeniculum* (Pursh) Kuntze. *J. Essential Oil Res.* 12: 581–594.

Fujita, Y., and S.-i. Fujita. 1965. Miscellaneous contributions to the essential oils of the plants from various territories (18). Essential oil of *Agastache rugosa* O. Kuntze (4). *Nippon Kagaku Zasshi* 86: 635–637.

Fujita, S.-i., and Y. Fujita. 1973. Miscellaneous contributions to the essential oils of the plants from various territories (33). Essential oil of *Agastache rugosa* O. Kuntze (6). *J. Pharm. Soc. Japan* 93: 1679–1681.

Galambosi, B., and Z. Galambosi-Szebeni. 1992. Studies on the cultivation methods of *Agastache foeniculum* (Pursh) Kuntze in Finland. *Acta Agron. Hung.* 41: 107–115.

Henning, J. 1994. After July: agastache. *Amer. Hort.* 73(8): 32–35.

Kim, M. H., et al. 2001. The effect of the oil of *Agastache rugosa* O. Kuntze and three of its components on human cancer cell lines. *J. Essential Oil Res.* 13: 214–218.

Lawrence, B. M. 1981. *Essential Oils 1979–1980.* Wheaton, Illinois: Allured.

———. 1993. *Essential Oils 1988–1991.* Wheaton, Illinois: Allured.

Lint, H., and C. Epling. 1945. A revision of *Agastache. Amer. Midl. Naturalist* 33: 207–230.

Mallavarapu, G. R., et al. 2004. The essential oil composition of anise hyssop grown in India. *Flavour Fragrance J.* 19: 351–353.

Manjarrez, A., and V. Mendoza. 1966. The volatile oils of *Agastache mexicana* (Benth) Epling and *Cunila lythrifolia* Benth. *Perfumery Essential Oil Rec.* 57: 561–562.

Mazza, G., and F. A. Kiehn. 1992. Essential oil of *Agastache foeniculum*, a potential source of methyl chavicol. *J. Essential Oil Res.* 4: 295–299.

Nykänen, I., et al. 1989. Composition of the essential oil of *Agastache foeniculum. Pl. Med.* 55: 314–315.

Sanders, R. W. 1987. Taxonomy of *Agastache* section Brittonastrum (Lamiaceae-Nepeteae). *Syst. Bot. Monogr.* Vol. 15.

Shin, S. 2004. Essential oil compounds from *Agastache rugosa* as antifungal agents against *Trichophyton* species. *Arch. Pharm. Res.* 27: 295–299.

Svoboda, K. P., et al. 1995. Analysis of the essential oils of some *Agastache* species grown in Scotland from various seed sources. *Flavour Fragrance J.* 10: 139–145.

Tirillini, B. R., et al. 1997. Constituents of the leaf secretory hairs of *Agastache foeniculum* Kuntze. *J. Essential Oil Res.* 9: 19–21.

Van Hevelingen, A. 1994. Agastaches. *Herb Companion* 6(5): 48–55.

Venskutonis, P. R. 1995. Essential oil composition of some herbs cultivated in Lithuania. In *Flavour, Fragrances and Essential Oils.* Ed. K. H. C. Baser. Istanbul: AREP Publ. 108–123.

Vogelman, J. E. 1985. Crossing relationships among North American and eastern Asian populations of *Agastache* sect. *Agastache* (Labiatae). *Syst. Bot.* 10: 445–452.

Weyerstahl, P., et al. 1992. Volatile constituents of *Agastache rugosa. J. Essential Oil Res.* 4: 585–587.

Zhu, L., et al. 1995. *Aromatic Plants and Essential Constituents (Supplement 1).* Hong Kong: Hai Feng Publ. Co.

Allium

Abul-Nasr, S. M., and K. F. Mahrous. 2000. *Allium sativum* (garlic) and its significance for the protection against lead-induced toxicity in albino rats: a chromosomal study. *Mansoura J. Forensic Med. Clin. Toxicol.* 8: 95–111.

Abul-Nasr, S. M., et al. 1999. *Allium sativum* (garlic) and its significance for the protection against lead-induced toxicity in albino rats: a male fertility study. *Mansoura J. Forensic Med. Clin. Toxicol.* 7: 163–188.

———. 1999. *Allium sativum* (garlic) and its significance for the protection against lead-induced toxicity in albino rats: a biochemical and histological study on the liver, kidney and brain. *Mansoura J. Forensic Med. Clin. Toxicol.* 7: 103–142.

———. 1999. *Allium sativum* (garlic) and its significance for the protection against lead-induced toxicity in albino rats: physical growth and mortality rate. *Mansoura J. Forensic Med. Clin. Toxicol.* 7: 75–101.

———. 1999. *Allium sativum* (garlic) and its significance for the protection against lead-induced toxicity in albino rats: a haematological study. *Mansoura J. Forensic Med. Clin. Toxicol.* 7: 143–162.

Adamu, I., et al. 1982. Hypolipidemic action of onion and garlic unsaturated oils in sucrose fed rats over a two-month period. *Experientia* 38: 899–901.

Afzal, M., et al. 1985. *Allium sativum* in the control of atherosclerosis. *Agric. Biol. Chem.* 49: 1187–1188.

Ali, M. 1995. Mechanism by which garlic (*Allium sativum*) inhibits cyclooxygenase activity. Effect of raw versus boiled garlic extract on the synthesis of prostanoids. *Prostaglandins Leukotrienes Essential Fatty Acids* 53: 397–400.

Anonymous. 2008. Garlic. *Rev. Nat. Prod. (Wolters Kluwer Health).*

Ariga, T., et al. 1981. Platelet aggregation inhibitor in garlic. *Lancet* 1981(1): 151.

Ariga, T., and T. Seki. 2006. Antithrombic and anticancer effects of garlic-derived sulfur compounds: a review. *BioFactors* 26: 93–103.

Augusti, K. T., et al. 2001. Beneficial effects of garlic (*Allium sativum* Linn.) on rats fed with diets containing cholesterol and either of the oil seeds, coconuts or ground nuts. *Indian J. Exp. Biol.* 39: 660–667.

———. 2001. A comparative study on the beneficial effects of garlic (*Allium sativum* Linn.), amla (*Emblica officinalis* Gaertn) and onion (*Allium cepa* Linn.) on the hyperlipidemia induced by butter fat and beef fat in rats. *Indian J. Exp. Biol.* 39: 760–766.

Awe, S. O., et al. 1998. Effects of *Allium sativum* and *Vernonia amygdalina* on thrombosis in mice. *Phytotherapy Res.* 12: 57–58.

Bachman, J. 2001. *Organic Garlic Production.* ATTRA (Appropriate Technology Transfer for Rural Areas).

Bailey, C. J., and C. Day. 1989. Traditional plant medicines as treatments for diabetes. *Diabetes Care* 12: 553–564.

Banerjee, M., and P. K. Sarkar. 2003. Inhibitory effect of garlic on bacterial pathogens from spices. *World J. Microbiol. Biotechnol.* 19: 565–569.

Basoglue, N., and M. Pala. 1993. Investigation on the production parameters of garlic essential oil. In *Essential Oils for Perfumery and Flavour. Proceedings of an International Conference 26–30 May 1990 Antalya, Turkey.* Ed. K. H. C. Baser and N. Güler. Istanbul. 165–177.

Bernhard, R. A. 1969. The sulfur components of *Allium* species as flavour matter. *Qual. Pl. Mater. Veg.* 18: 72–84.

Berthold, H. K., et al. 1998. Effect of a garlic oil preparation on serum lipoproteins and cholesterol metabolism: a randomized controlled trial. *JAMA* 279: 1900–1902.

———. 1998. Garlic preparations for prevention of atherosclerosis. *Current Opinion Lipidology* 9: 565–569.

Block, E. 1985. The chemistry of garlic and onions. *Sci. Amer.* 252(3): 114–119.

———. 1986. Antithrombotic agent of garlic: a lesson from 5,000 years of folk medicine. In *Folk Medicine.* Ed. R. P. Steiner.

Washington, D.C.: Amer. Chem. Soc. 125–137.

———. 1992. *Allium* chemistry: HPLC analysis of thiosulfinates from onion, garlic, wild garlic (ramsoms), leek, scallion, shallot, elephant (great-headed) garlic, chive, and Chinese chive. Uniquely high allyl-to-methyl rations in some garlic samples. *J. Agric. Food Chem.* 40: 2418–2430.

———. 1993. Flavour artifacts. *J. Agric. Chem. Soc.* 41: 992.

———. 1994. Flavour from garlic, onion, and other alliums and their cancer-preventive properties. In *Food Phytochemicals for Cancer Prevention I. Fruits and Vegetables.* Ed. H.-T. Huang et al. Washington, D.C.: Amer. Chem. Soc. 84–96.

———. 1998. Garlic as a functional food: a status report. In *Functional Foods for Disease Prevention II. Medicinal Plants and Other Foods.* Ed. T. Shibamoto et al. Washington, D.C.: Amer. Chem. Soc. 125–143.

Block, E., and E. M. Calvey. 1994. Facts and artifacts in *Allium* chemistry. In *Sulfur Compounds in Foods.* Ed. C. J. Mussinan and M. E. Keelan. Washington, D.C.: Amer. Chem. Soc. 63–79.

Block, E., et al. 1984. (E,Z)-Ajoene: a potent antithrombotic agent from garlic. *J. Amer. Chem. Soc.* 106: 8295–8296.

———. 1992. *Allium* chemistry: GC-MS analysis of thiosulfinates and related compounds from onion, leek, scallion, shallot, chive, and Chinese chive. *J. Agric. Food Chem.* 40: 2431–2438.

———. 1993. Organosulfur chemistry of garlic and onion: Recent results. *Pure Appl. Chem.* 65: 625–632.

Blumenthal, M., et al. 2003. *The ABC Clinical Guide to Garlic.* Austin, Texas: Amer. Bot. Council.

Boullin, D. J. 1981. Garlic as a platelet inhibitor. *Lancet* 1981(1): 776–777.

Breithaupt-Grogler, K., et al. 1997. Protective effect of chronic garlic intake on elastic properties of aorta in the elderly. *Circulation* 96: 2649–2655.

Brueckner, B., and H. Perner. Distribution of nutritive compounds and sensory quality in the leaves of chives (*Allium schoenoprasum* L.). *J. Appl. Bot. Food Qual.* 80: 155–159.

Calvey, E. M., et al. 1997. *Allium* chemistry: Supercritical fluid extraction and LC-APCI-MS of thiosulfinates and related compounds from homogenates of garlic, onion, and ramp. Identification in garlic and ramp and synthesis of 1-propanesulfinothioic acid S-allyl ester. *J. Agric. Food Chem.* 45: 4406–4413.

———. 1998. *Allium* chemistry: Identification of organosulfur compounds in ramp (*Allium tricoccum*) homogenates. *Phytochemistry* 49: 359–364.

Camergo, A., et al. 2007. QSAR study for the soybean 15-lipoxygenase inhibitory activity of organosulfur compounds derived from the essential oil of garlic. *J. Agric. Food Chem.* 55: 3096–3103.

Campbell, J. H., et al. 2001. Molecular basis by which garlic suppresses atherosclerosis. *J. Nutr.* 131: 1006S–1009S.

Caruso, P., et al. 1994. Comportamento di cultivar-popolazioni di aglio in Sicilia. *Colture Protette* 12: 79–85.

Chang, K. W., et al. 1988. A study of sulfur nutrition on the flavour components of garlic (*Allium sativum* L.). *J. Korean Soc. Soil Sci. Fertilizer* 21: 183–193.

Chung, H.-D. 1996. The effects of temperature and daylength on growth and bolting of the Korean native Chinese chive. *J. Korean Soc. Hort. Sci.* 37: 505–510.

Chung, J. G., et al. 1998. Effects of garlic compounds diallyl sulfide and diallyl disulfide on arylamide N-acetyltransferase activity in strains of *Helicobacter pylori* from peptic ulcer patients. *Amer. J. Chin. Med.* 26: 353–364.

Das, I., et al. 1995. Potent activation of nitric oxide synthase by garlic: a basis for its therapeutic applications. *Curr. Med. Res. Opinion* 13: 257–263.

Davies, D. 1992. *Alliums: The Ornamental Onions.* Portland, Oregon: Timber Press.

Davis, J. 1997. Chives. North Carolina Hort. Inform. Leafl. 124.

———. 1998. Influence of planting stock clove size, nitrogen rate, and planting method on elephant garlic production. *HortScience* 33: 517.

Davis, L. E., et al. 1994. In vitro synergism of concentrated *Allium* extract and amphotericin B against *Cryptococcus neoformans.* *Pl. Med.* 60: 546–549.

Deb-Kirtaniya, S., et al. 1980. Extracts of garlic as possible source of insecticides. *Indian J. Agric. Sci.* 50: 507–509.

Dehghani, F., et al. 2004. Healing effect of garlic extract on warts and corns. *Intern. J. Dermatology* 44: 612–615.

Del Tredici, P. 1987. Never enough garlic. *Horticulture* 65(10): 14–16, 18, 21.

Deruaz, D., et al. 1994. Analytical strategy by coupling headspace gas chromagraphy, atomic emission spectrometric detection and mass spectrometry: application to sulfur compounds from garlic. *J. Chromatogr.* 677: 345–354.

Dobrzanski, W., and M. Kuzminska. 1994. The influence of freeze drying parameters and storage time on the antibacterial property of garlic (*Allium sativum* L.). *Biul. Warzywniczy* 41: 127–133.

Durak, I., et al. 2004. Effects of garlic extract consumption on blood lipid oxidant/antioxidant parameters in humans with high blood cholesterol. *J. Nutr. Biochem.* 15: 373–377.

Edris, A. E., and H. M. Fadel. 2002. Investigation of the volatile aroma components of garlic leaves essential oil. Possibility of utilization to enrich garlic bulb oil. *Eur. Food Res. Technol.* 214: 105–107.

Edris, A. E., et al. 2003. Effect of organic agricultural practices on the volatile flavour components of some essential oil plants growing in Egypt: I. Garlic essential oil. *Bull. NRC Egypt* 28: 369–376.

Engeland, R. L. 1991. *Growing Great Garlic.* Okanogan, Washington: Filaree Prod.

Ernst, E. 1997. Can *Allium* vegetables provent cancer? *Phytomedicine* 4: 79–83.

———. 1999. Is garlic an effective treatment for *Helicobacter pylori* infection? *Arch. Intern. Med.* 159: 2484–2485.

Fenwick, G. R., and A. B. Hanley. 1985. The Genus *Allium.* Part 1. *CRC Crit. Rev. Food Sci. Nutr.* 22: 199–271.

———. 1985. The genus *Allium.* Part 2. *CRC Crit. Rev. Food Sci. Nutr.* 22: 273–377.

———. 1986. The genus *Allium.* Part 3. *CRC Crit. Rev. Food Sci. Nutr.* 23: 1–73.

Fleischauer, A. T., and L. Arab. 2001. Garlic and cancer: a critical review of the epidemiologic literature. *J. Nutr.* 2001: 1032A–1040A.

Fleischauer, A. T., et al. 2000. Garlic consumption and cancer prevention: meta-analysis of colorectal and stomach cancers. *Amer. J. Clin. Nutr.* 72: 1047–1052.

Foster, S. 1991. Garlic. *Allium sativum.* Amer. Bot. Council Bot. Ser. 311.

Friesen, N. 1996. A taxonomic and chronological revision of the genus *Allium* L. sect. *Schoenoprasum* Dumort. *Candollea* 51: 461–473.

Friesen, N., et al. 1999. RAPDs and noncoding chloroplast DNA reveal a single origin of the cultivated *Allium fistulosum* from *A. altaicum* (Alliaceae). *Amer. J. Bot.* 86: 554–562.

Fritsch, R. M. 2005. Arznei- und Gewürzpflanzen in der Gattung *Allium* L. Ihre systematische Einodnung von Linné bis zur Gegenwart. *Z. Arzn. Gew. Pfl.* 10: 123–132.

———. 2005. Herkunft, Taxonomie und Geschichte von *Allium.* In *Zwiebelanbau: Handbuch für Praxis und Wissenschaft.* Ed. G. F. Backhaus et al. Bergen/Dumme: AgriMedia. 15–37.

Fulder, S., and J. Blackwood. 1991. *Garlic: Nature's Original Remedy.* Rochester, Vermont: Healing Arts Press.

Galeone, C., et al. 2007. Onion and garlic intake and the odds of benign prostatic hyperplasia. *Urology* 70: 672–676.

Gardner, C. D., et al. 2007. Effect of raw garlic vs commercial garlic supplements on plasma lipid concentrations in adults with moderate hypercholesterolemia. *Arch. Intern. Med.* 167: 346–353.

Gebhardt, R. 1993. Multiple inhibitory effects of garlic extracts on cholesterol biosynthesis in hepatocytes. *Lipids* 28: 613–619.

———. 1995. Amplification of palmitate-induced inhibition of cholesterol biosynthesis in cultured rat hepatocytes by garlic-derived organosulfur compounds. *Phytomedicine* 2: 29–34.

Ghannoum, M. A. 1988. Studies on the anticandidal mode of action of *Allium sativum* (garlic). *J. Gen. Microbiol.* 134: 2917–2924.

Graham, D. Y., et al. 1999. Garlic or halapeno peppers for treatment of *Helicobacter pylori* infection. *Amer. J. Gastroent.* 94: 1200–1202.

Greenfield, J., and J. Davis. 2001. *Cultivation of Ramps* (Allium tricoccum *and* A. burdickii). North Carolina Hort. Inform. Leafl. 133.

Griffith, L., and F. Griffith. 1998. *Garlic, Garlic, Garlic.* Boston: Houghton Mifflin.

Grudzinski, I. P., et al. 2001. Diallyl sulfide: a flavour component from garlic (*Allium sativum*) attenuates lipid peroxidation in mice infected with *Trichinella spiralis*. *Phytomedicine* 8: 174–177.

Guerard, J. 1988. Fertilizer requirements of garlic. *Amer. Veg. Grower* 36(5): 38–39.

Gupta, R., and N. K. Sharma. 1994. Screening garlic cultivars for their toxicity against *Meloidogyne incognita* (Kofoid and White) Chitwood. *J. Appl. Zool. Res.* 5: 41–42.

———. 1995. Action of garlic (*Allium sativum* L.) extract on the juveniles of *Meloidogyne incognita* (Kofoid & White) Chitwood. *Curr. Res.* 24: 91–92.

Gupta, R., et al. 1992. Effect of garlic aqueous extract on soil micro-organisms. *Narendra Deva J. Agric. Res.* 7: 62–66.

Hankins, A. 1992. Elephant garlic production. *Business Herbs* 10(3): 34–35.

Hanson, B., et al. 2002. Garlic in clay loam soil thrives on little irrigation. *California Agric.* 56: 128–132.

Hara, Y., et al. 1998. Suppression of garlic odor by milk or milk components. *Res. Bull. Faculty Agric. Gifu Univ.* 63: 145–151.

Harris, L. J. 1986. *The Official Garlic Lovers Handbook.* Berkeley, California: Aris Books.

Hashimoto, S., et al. 1983. Volatile flavour components of chive (*Allium schoenoprasum* L.). *J. Food Sci.* 48: 1858–1859.

Helm, J. 1956. Die zu Würz- und Spiesewecken kultivierten Arten der Gattung *Allium* L. *Kulturpflanze* 4: 130–180.

Hile, A., et al. 2004. Aversion of European starlings (*Sturnus vulgaris*) to garlic oil treated granules: garlic oil as an avian repellent. Garlic oil analysis by nuclear magnetic resonance spectroscopy. *J. Agric. Food Chem.* 52: 2192–2196.

Holder, K., and G. Duff. 1996. *A Clove of Garlic.* Edison, New Jersey: Chartwell Books.

Hughes, J., et al. 2006. Effect of low storage temperature on some of the flavour precursors in garlic (*Allium sativum*). *Pl. Foods Human Nutr.* 61: 81–85.

Iberl, B., et al. 1990. Quantitative determination of allicin and aliin from garlic by HPLC. *Pl. Med.* 56: 320–326.

Ide, N., and B. H. S. Lau. 1997. Garlic compounds protect vascular endothelial cells from oxidized low density lipoprotein-induced injury. *J. Pharm. Pharmacol.* 49: 908–911.

Ide, N., et al. 1996. Scavenging effect of aged garlic extract and its constituents on active oxygen species. *Phytotherapy Res.* 10: 340–341.

———. 1997. Aged garlic extract and its constituents inhibit Cu2+-induced oxidative modification of low density lipoprotein. *Pl. Med.* 63: 263–264.

Iida, H., et al. 1983. Volatile flavour components of nira (*Allium tuberosum* Rottl.) *J. Food Sci.* 48: 660–661.

Ikram, M. 1972. A review on chemical and medicinal aspects of *Allium sativum*. *Pakistan J. Sci. Industr. Res.* 15: 81–86.

Imai, J., et al. 1994. Antioxidant and radical scavenging effects of aged garlic extract and its constituents. *Pl. Med.* 60: 417–420.

Isaacsohn, J. L., et al. 1998. Garlic powder and plasma lipids and lipoproteins. *Arch. Intern. Med.* 158: 1189–1194.

Ishikawa, K., et al. 1996. Antimutagenic effects of ajoene, an organosulfur compound derived from garlic. *Biosci. Biotech. Biochem.* 60: 2086–2088.

Jain, A. K., et al. 1993. Can garlic reduce levels of serum lipids? A controlled clinical study. *Amer. J. Med.* 94: 632–635.

Jain, M. K., and R. Apitz-Castro. 1994. Garlic: a matter of taste. In *Spices, Herbs and Edible Fungi.* Ed. G. Charalambous. Amsterdam: Elsevier. 309–327.

Jang, H.-W., et al. 2008. Antioxidant activity and characterization of volatile extracts of *Capsicum annuum* L. and *Allium* spp. *Flavour Fragrance J.* 23: 178–184.

Jenderek, M. M., and Y. Zewdie. 2005. Within- and between-family variability for important bulb and plant traits among sexually derived progenies of garlic. *HortScience* 40: 1234–1236.

Jones, A. G. 1979. A study of wild leek, and the recognition of *Allium burdickii* (Liliaceae). *Syst. Bot.* 4: 29–43.

Jones, H. A., and L. K. Mann. 1963. *Onions and Their Allies.* London: Leonard Hill.

Jonkers, D., et al. 1999. Antibacterial effect of garlic and omeprazole on *Helicobacter pylori. J. Antimicrobial Chemotherapy* 43: 837–839.

Joshi, D. J., et al. 1987. Gastrointestinal actions of garlic oil. *Phytotherapy Res.* 1: 140–141.

Josling, P., et al., eds. 1992. The action of garlic in the pathogenesis of atherosclerosis. *Eur. J. Clin. Res.* 3A: 1–12.

Kamenetsky, R., et al. 2004. Environmental control of garlic growth and florigenesis. *J. Amer. Soc. Hort. Sci.* 129: 144–151.

Kameoka, H., and A. Miyake. 1974. The constituents of the steam volatile oil from *Allium tuberosum* Rottler. *Nipon Nogei Kagaku Zasshi* 48: 385–388.

Kameoka, H., et al. 1984. Sulphides and furanones from steam volatile oils of *Allium fistulosum* and *Allium chinense*. *Phytochemistry* 23: 155–158.

———. 1988. Study of the flavour components of storage vegetables. Nira (*Allium tuberosum* Rottl.). *Kinki Daigaku Rikogakubu Kenkyu Hokoku* 1988: 99–103.

Kaye, A. D., et al. 1995. Analysis of responses of allicin, a compound from garlic, in the pulmonary vascular bed of the cat and in the rat. *Eur. J. Pharmacol.* 276: 21–26.

Kim, S. G., et al. 1995. Enhanced effectiveness of dimethyl-4,4'-dimethoxy-5,6,5',6'-dimethylene diosybiphenyl-2,2'-dicarboxylate in combination with garlic oil against experimental hepatic injury in rats and mice. *J. Pharm. Pharmacol.* 47: 678–682.

Kline, R. A. 1990. *Garlic.* Cornell Univ. VC Rep. 387.

Kocabatmaz, M., et al. 1997. Effect of garlic oil on plasma, erythrocyte and erythrocyte membrane total lipids, cholesterol and phospholipid levels of hypercholesterolaemic dogs. *Med. Sci. Res.* 25: 265–267.

Koch, H. P., and W. Jäger. 1990. Knoblauch-Ölmazerate. Analytische Bewertung von Knoblauchzubereitungen in öliger Lösung. *Deutsche Apotheker Zeit.* 130: 2469–2474.

Koch, H. P., and L. D. Lawson. 1996. *Garlic: The Science and Therapeutic Application of Allium sativum L. and Related Species.* 2nd ed. Baltimore: Williams & Wilkins.

Koike, S. T., et al. 2001. Rust disease continues to threaten California garlic crop. *California Agric.* 55: 35–39.

Koscielny, J., et al. 1999. The antiatherosclerotic effect of *Allium sativum*. *Atherosclerosis* 144: 237–249.

Kumar, G. R., and K. P. Reddy. 1999. Reduced nociceptive responses in mice with alloxan induced hyperglycemia after garlic (*Allium sativum* Linn.) treatment. *Indian J. Exp. Biol.* 37: 662–666.

Kuo, M.-C., and C.-T. Ho. 1992. Volatile constituents of the distilled oils of Welsh onions (*Allium fistulosum* L. variety 'Maichuon') and scallions (*Allium fistulosum* L. variety 'Caespitosum'). *J. Agric. Food Chem.* 40: 111–117.

Kyo, E., et al. 1997. Anti-allergic effects of aged garlic extract. *Phytomedicine* 4: 335–340.

Laakso, I., et al. 1989. Volatile garlic odor components: gas phases and adsorbed exhaled air analysed by headspace gas chromatography-mass spectrometry. *Pl. Med.* 55: 257–261.

Lamm, D. L., and D. R. Riggs. 2001. Enhanced immunocompetence by garlic: role in bladder cancer and other malignancies. *J. Nutr.* 131: 1067S–1070S.

Larkeom, J. 1987. Chinese chives. *Garden* (London) 112: 432–437.

Lash, L., and E. J. Staba. 1999. Garlic dietary supplements: an assessment of product information provided by garlic manufacturers. *Minnesota Pharm.* 53: 13–18, 24–26.

Lau, B. H. S., et al. 1983. *Allium sativum* (garlic) and atherosclerosis: a review. *Nutrition Res.* 3: 119–128.

Lawson, L. D. 1998. Effect of garlic on serum lipids. *JAMA* 280: 1568.

———. 1998. Garlic powder for hyperlipidemia: analysis of recent negative results. *Quart. Rev. Nat. Med.* 1998: 187–189.

Lee, J.-H., et al. 1999. Protective effects of garlic juice against emtryotoxicity of methylmercuric chloride administered to pregnant Fischer 344 rats. *Yonsei Med. J.* 40: 483–489.

Lee, J.-W., et al. 1997. Comparison of the chemical components between fresh and odorless garlic. *Agric. Chem. Biotechnol.* 40: 400–403.

Lees, P. D. 1980. *Culinary and Medicinal Herbs.* 4th ed. Minist. Agric. Fish. Food Ref. Book 325.

Leino, M. E. 1992. Effect of freezing, freeze-drying, and air-drying on odor of chive characterized by headspace gas chromatography and sensory analysis. *J. Agric. Food Chem.* 40: 1379–1384.

Liu, C.-T., et al. 1998. Effect of garlic oil on hepatic arachidonic acid content and immune response in rats. *J. Agric. Food Chem.* 46: 4642–4647.

Longbrake, T. 1989. *Garlic Production in Texas.* Texas Agric. Exp. Sta. Serv. I-2239.

Lopes, D., et al. 1997. Sulphur constituents of the essential oil of nira (*Allium tuberosum* Rottl.) cultivated in Brazil. *Flavour Fragrance J.* 12: 237–239.

Lucier, G., and B.-H. Lin. 2000. Garlic: flavour of the ages. *Agric. Outlook* June/July 2000: 7–10.

Maczka, T. 1989. Successful garlic growing. *Herb Grower & Marketer* October/November: 26–27.

Maidment, D. C. J., et al. 1999. A study into the antibiotic effect of garlic *Allium sativum* on *Escherichia coli* and *Staphylococcus albus*. *Nutr. Food Sci.* 1999: 170–172.

———. 2001. The anti-bacterial activity of 12 alliums against *Escherichia coli*. *Nutr. Food Sci.* 31: 238–241.

Makheja, A., et al. Inhibition of platelet aggregation and thromboxane synthesis by onion and garlic. *Lancet* 1979(1): 781.

Martin, N., et al. 1994. Anti-arrhythmic profile of a garlic dialysate assayed in dogs and isolated atrial preparations. *J. Ethnopharmacol.* 43: 1–8.

Mathew, B. 1996. *A review of* Allium *sect.* Allium. Richmond, England: RBG Kew.

Matus, I., et al. 1999. Evaluation of phenotypic variation in a Chilean collection of garlic (*Allium sativum* L.) clones using multivariate analysis. *Pl. Gen. Res. Newsl.* 117: 31–36.

Mayeux, P. R., et al. 1988. The pharmacological effects of allicin, a constituent of garlic oil. *Agents & Actions* 25: 182–190.

McCollum, G. D. 1984. Onion and allies. In *Evolution of Crop Plants.* Ed. N. W. Simmonds. London: Longman. 186–190.

McCrindle, B. W., et al. 1998. Garlic extract therapy in children with hypercholesterolema. *Arch. Pediatr. Adolesc. Med.* 152: 1089–1094.

Milner, J. A. 2001. A historical perspective on garlic and cancer. *J. Nutr.* 2001: 1927S–1031S.

Milner, J. A., and E. M. Schaffer. 1998. Garlic and associated allyl sulfur constituents depress chemical carcinogenesis. In *Functional Foods for Disease Prevention II. Medicinal Plants and Other Foods.* Ed. T. Shibamoto et al. Washington, D.C.: Amer. Chem. Soc. 144–152.

Minami, T., et al. 1989. Odor components of human breath after the ingestion of grated raw garlic. *J. Food Sci.* 54: 763–765.

Nagae, S., et al. 1994. Pharmacokinetics of the garlic compounds S-allylcysteine. *Pl. Med.* 60: 214–217.

Naganawa, R., et al. 1996. Inhibition of microbial growth by ajoene, a sulfur-containing compound derived from garlic. *Appl. Environm. Microbiol.* 62: 4238–4242.

Nagourney, R. A. 1998. Garlic: medicinal food or nutritious medicine? *J. Med. Food* 1: 13–28.

Neil, H. A. W., et al. 1996. Garlic powder in the treatment of moderate hyperlipidaemia: a controlled trial and meta-analysis. *J. Roy. Coll. Physicians London* 30: 329–334.

Nguansangiam, S., et al. 2003. Effects of elephant garlic volatile oil (*Allium ampeloprasum*) and T-2 toxin on murine skin. *Southeast Asian J. Trop. Med. Public Health* 34: 899–905.

Nichols, E. 1989. Growing elephant garlic. *Fine Gard.* 8: 28–31.

Nikolić, V. D., et al. 2004. Antimicrobial effect of raw garlic (*Allium sativum* L.) extracts, garlic powder and oil and commercial antibiotics on pathogen microorganisms. *Chem. Ind.* 58: 109–113.

O'Gara, E. A., et al. 2000. Activities of garlic oil, garlic powder, and their diallyl constituents against *Helicobacter pylori*. *Appl. Environm. Microbiol.* 66: 2269–2273.

Ohta, R., et al. 1999. In vitro inhibition of the growth of *Helicobacter pylori* by oil-macerated garlic constituents. *Antimicrobial Agents Chemotherapy* 43: 1811–1812.

Orekhov, A. N., et al. 1995. Direct anti-atherosclerosis-related effects of garlic. *Ann. Med.* 27: 63–65.

Öztürk, Y., et al. 1994. Endothelium-dependent and independent effects of garlic on rat aorta. *J. Ethnopharmacol.* 44: 109–116.

Palada, M. C., et al. 2000. Organic mulch improves yield and economic returns from chive production. *HortScience* 35: 464.

Park, I.-K., and S.-C. Shin. 2005. Fumigant activity of plant essential oils and components from garlic (*Allium sativum*) and clove bud (*Eugenia caryophyllata*) oils against the Japanese termite (*Reticulitermes speratus* Kolbe). *J. Agric. Food Chem.* 53: 4388–4392.

Park, I.-K., et al. 2005. Nematicidal activity of plant essential oils from garlic (*Allium sativum*) and cinnamon (*Cinnamomum verum*) oils against the pine wood nematode (*Bursaphelenchus xylophilus*). *Nematology* 7: 767–774.

Phelps, S., and W. S. Harris. 1993. Garlic supplementation and lipoprotein oxidation susceptibility. *Lipids* 28: 475–477.

Pino, J. A., et al. 2001. Volatile constituents of Chinese chive (*Allium tuberosum* Rottl. ex Sprengel) and rakkyo (*Allium chinense* G. Don). *J. Agric. Food Chem.* 49: 1328–1330.

Poncavage, J. 1993. Grow garlic like a pro. *Org. Gard.* 40(7): 52–57.

Rabinowitch, H. D., and J. L. Brewster, eds. 1990. *Onions and Allied Crops.* 3 vols. Boca Raton, Florida: CRC Press.

Rahman, K. 2001. Historical perspective on garlic and cardiovascular disease. *J. Nutr.* 2001: 977S–979S.

Raleigh Gardens. n.d. *Elephant Garlic Growing Guide.* Shedd, Oregon: Weavers Garlic Shedd.

Rasmussen, P. 1998. Garlic: a review. *Austral. J. Med. Herbalism* 10: 94–99.

Rekka, E. A., and P. N. Kourounakis. 1994. Investigation of the molecular mechanism of the antioxidant activity of some *Allium sativum* ingredients. *Pharmzie* 49: 539–540.

Reuter, H. D., and A. Sendl. 1994. *Allium sativum* and *Allium ursinum*: chemistry, pharmacology and medicinal applications. In *Economic and Medicinal Plant Research Vol. 6.* Ed. H. Wagner and N. R. Farnsworth. New York: Academic Press. 56–113.

———. 1995. *Allium sativum* and *Allium ursinum*. Part 2: pharmacology and medicinal application. *Phytomedicine* 2: 73–91.

Riaz, M., et al. 1998. Volatile flavour components of *Allium sativum* essential oil from Pakistan. *Pak. J. Sci. Ind. Res.* 41: 240–241.

Riggs, D., et al. 1997. *Allium sativum* (garlic) treatment for murine transitional cell carcinoma. *Cancer* 79: 1987–1994.

Rivlin, R. S. 2001. Historical perspectives on garlic. *J. Nutr.* 131: 951S–954S.

Rosin, S., et al. 1992. Garlic: a sensory pleasure or a social nuisance? *Appetite* 19: 133–143.

Ross, Z. M., et al. 2001. Antimicrobial properties of garlic oil against human enteric bacteria: evaluation of methodologies and comparisons with garlic oil sulfides and garlic powder. *Appl. Environm. Microbiol.* 67: 475–480.

Sánchez-Mirt, A., et al. 1993. Efecto inhibitorio y alteraciones ultraestracturales producidas por ajoeno sobre el crecimiento in vitro de los hondos dermatiáceos: *Cladosporium carrionii* y Fonsecaea pedrosoi. *Revista Iberoamer. Micol.* 10: 74–78.

———. 1994. Actividad in vitro e in vivo del ajoeno sobre *Coccidioides immitis*. *Revista Iberoamer. Micol.* 11: 99–104.

Sanchez, J. H. 1992. Step-by-step growing and harvesting garlic. *Horticulture* 70(8): 52–53.

Saradeth, T., et al. Does garlic alter the lipid pattern in normal volunteers? *Phytomedicine* 1: 183–185.

Sendl, A. 1995. *Allium sativum* and *Allium ursinum*. Part 1: chemistry, analysis, history, botany. *Phytomedicine* 4: 323–339.

Seo, H. M., and K. J. Jeo. 2007. Volatile flavour components of freeze dried garlic and garlic roasted with oils. *J. Korean Soc. Food Sci. Nutr.* 36: 332–341.

Shuford, J. A., et al. 2005. Effects of fresh garlic extract on *Candida albicans* biofilms. *Antimicrobial Agents Chemotherapy* 49: 473.

Siegel, G., et al. 1998. Molecular evidence for phytopharmacological K+ channel opening by garlic in human vascular smooth muscle cell membranes. *Phytotherapy Res.* 12: S149–S151.

Siegers, C.-P. 1992. *Allium sativum*. In *Adverse Effects of Herbal Drugs 1.* Ed. P. A. G. M. De Smet et al. Berlin: Springer-Verlag. 73–77.

Siegers, C.-P., et al. 1999. The effects of garlic preparations against human tumor cell proliferation. *Phytomedicine* 6: 7–11.

———. 1999. Effects of garlic preparations on superoxide production by phorbol ester activated granulocytes. *Phytomedicine* 6: 13–16.

Sigouras, G., et al. 1997. *S*-Allylmercaptocysteine, a stable thioallyl compound, induces apoptosis in erythroleukemia cell lines. *Nutrition Cancer* 28: 153–159.

———. 1997. *S*-Allylmercaptocysteine inhibits cell proliferation and reduces the viability of erythroleukemia, breast, and prostate cancer cell lines. *Nutrition Cancer* 27: 186–191.

Skala, D., et al. 2000. Etheric oil from garlic (*Allium sativum* L.) obtained by CO_2-SFE comparison with steam distillation. *Chem. Ind.* 54: 539–545.

Snow, K., and R. Cutler. 2006. A preliminary note on the evaluation of garlic as a mosquito repellent. *Eur. Mosquito Bull.* 21: 23.

Song, K., and J. A. Milner. 2001. The influence of heating on the anticancer properties of garlic. *J. Nutr.* 2001: 1054S–1057S.

Srivastava, K. C. 1984. Aqueous extracts of onion, garlic and ginger inhibit platelet aggregation and alter arachidonic acid metabolism. *Biomed. Biochim. Acta* 43: S335–S346.

———. 1989. Effect of onion and garlic consumption on platelet thrombaxane production in humans. *Prostaglandins Leukotrienes Essential Fatty Acids* 35: 183–185.

Srivastava, K. C., and U. Justesen. 1989. Isolation and effects of some garlic components on platelet aggregation and metabolism of arachidonic acid in human blood platelets. *Wien. Klin. Wochenschr.* 101: 293–299.

Srivastava, K. C., and T. Mustafa. 1989. Spices: antiplatelet activity and prostanoid metabolism. *Prostaglandins Leukotrienes Essential Fatty Acids* 38: 255–266.

Srivastava, K. C., and O. D. Tyagi. 1992. Effects of a garlic-derived principle (ajoene) on aggregation and arachidonic acid metabolism in human blood platelets. *Prostaglandins Leukotrienes Essential Fatty Acids* 49: 587–595.

Srivastava, K. C., et al. 1995. Garlic (*Allium sativum*) for disease prevention. *South African J. Sci.* 91: 68–77.

Štajner, et al. 1998. Antioxidant abilities of cultivated and wild species of garlic. *Phytotherapy Res.* 12: S13–S14.

———. 1998. Study on antioxidant enzymes in *Allium cepa* L. and *Allium fistulosum* L. *Phytotherapy Res.* 12: S15–S17.

Stearn, W. T. 1980. *Allium*. In *Flora Europaea Vol. 5.* Ed. T. G. Tutin et al. Cambridge Univ. Press. 49–70.

Stearn, W. T., and E. Campbell. 1986. *Allium*. In *The European Garden Flora Vol. 1.* Ed. S. M. Walters et al. Cambridge Univ. Press. 233–246.

Steiner, M., and R. S. Lin. 1998. Changes in platelet function and susceptibility of lipoproteins to oxidation associated with administration of aged garlic extract. *J. Cardiovascular Pharmacol.* 31: 904–908.

Steiner, M., and G. Sigounas. 1998. Garlic and related *Allium* derived compounds: their health benefits in cardiovascular disease and cancer. In *Functional Foods for Disease Prevention II. Medicinal Plants and Other Foods*. Ed. T. Shibamoto et al. Washington, D.C.: Amer. Chem. Soc. 112–124.

Steiner, M., et al. 1996. A double-blind crossover study in moderately hypercholesterolemic men that compared the effect of aged garlic extract and placebo administration on blood lipids. *Amer. J. Clin. Nutr.* 64: 866–870.

Stevinson, C., et al. 2000. Garlic for treating hypercholesterolemia. *Ann. Inter. Med.* 133: 420–429.

Tamaki, T., and S. Sonoki. 1999. Volatile sulfur compounds in human expiration after eating raw or heat-treated garlic. *J. Nutr. Sci. Vitaminol.* 45: 213–222.

Tanaka, S., et al. 2007. Aged garlic extract has potential suppressive effect on colorectal adenomas in humans. *J. Nutr.* 136: S821–S826.

Tardif, B., and P. Morisset. 1990. Clinical morphological variation of *Allium schoenoprasum* in eastern North America. *Taxon* 39: 417–429.

Thomas, H. F., et al. 1998. What sort of men take garlic preparations. *Compl. Therapies Med.* 6: 195–197.

Tatlioglu, T., and G. Wricke. 1980. Genetisch-züchterische Untersuchungen am Schnittlauch (*Allium schoenoprasum* L.). *Gartenbauwissenschaft* 45: 278–282.

Valerio, L., and M. Maroli. 2005. Valutazione dell'effetto repellente ed *anti-feeding* dell'olio d'aglio (*Allium sativum*) nei confronti di flebotomi (Diptera: Psychodidae). *Ann. Ist. Super Sanità* 41: 253–256.

Vernin, G., et al. 1986. GC-MS (EI, PCI, NCI) computer analysis of volatile sulfur compounds in garlic essential oils. Application of the mass fragmentometry SIM technique. *Pl. Med.* 1986: 96–101.

Volk, G. M., et al. 2004. Genetic diversity among U.S. garlic clones as detected using AFLP methods. *J. Amer. Soc. Hort. Sci.* 129: 559–569.

Voss, R., and C. Myers. 1991. Chinese chives, garlic chives, gow choy, Japanese bunching onion, Welsh onion, multiplier onion. In *Specialty and Minor Crops Handbook*. Ed. C. Meyers. Oakland: Small Farm Center, Univ. California. SMC-0018-019

Walkey, D. G. A., and D. N. Antill. 1989. Agronomic evaluation of virus-free and virus-infected garlic (*Allium sativum* L.) *J. Hort. Sci.* 64: 53–60.

Walters, S. A. 2008. Production method and cultivar effects on garlic over-wintering survival, bulb quality, and yield. *HortTechnology* 18: 286–289.

Wargovich, M. J., et al. 1988. Chemoprevention of N-nitrosomethylbenzylamine-induced esophageal cancer in rats by the naturally occurring thioether, diallyl sulfide. *Cancer Res.* 48: 6872–6875.

Weber, N. D., et al. 1992. In vitro virucidal effects of *Allium sativum* (garlic) extract and compounds. *Pl. Med.* 58: 417–423.

Whitfield, F. B., and J. H. Last. 1991. Vegetables. In *Volatile Compounds in Foods and Beverages*. Ed. H. Maarse. New York: Marcel Dekker. 203–281.

Wilson, H. 1995. Yield responses and nutrient uptake of chive as affected by nitrogen, phosphorous and potassium fertilization. *Commun. Soil Sci. Pl. Anal.* 26: 2079–2096.

Wolkomir, R. 1995. Without garlic, life would be just plain tasteless. *Smithsonian* 26(9): 71–78.

Woltz, S. S., and W. E. Waters. 1976. Chives production as affected by fertilizer practices, soil mixes and methyl bromide soil residues. *Proc. Florida State Hort. Soc.* 88: 133–137.

Woodward, P. 1996. *Garlic and Friends*. South Melbourne, Victoria: Hyland House.

Wu, C.-C., et al. 2002. Differential effects of garlic oil and its three major organosulfur components on the hepatic detoxification system in rats. *J. Agric. Food Chem.* 50: 378–383.

———. 2004. Differential effects of allyl sulfides from garlic essential oil on cell cycle regulation in human liver tumor cells. *Food Chem. Toxicol.* 42: 1937–1947.

Yeh, H. C., and L. Liu. 2001. Cholesterol-lowering effect of garlic extracts and organisulfur compounds: human and animal studies. *J. Nutr.* 2001: 989S–993S.

Yoshida, H., et al. 1998. Antimicrobial activity of a compound isolated from an oil-macerated garlic extract. *Biosci. Biotechnol. Biochem.* 62: 1014–1017.

———. 1999. Antimicrobial activity of the thiosulfinates isolated from oil-macerated garlic extract. *Ciosci. Biotechnol. Biochem.* 63: 591–594.

Yüncü, M., et al. 2006. Effect of aged garlic extract against methotrexate-induced damage to the small intestine in rats. *Phytotherapy Res.* 20: 504–510.

Zhao, C., and H. Shichi. 1998. Prevention of acetaminophen-induced cataract by a combination of diallyl disulfide and N-acetylcysteine. *J. Ocular Pharmacol. Therap.* 14: 345–355.

Aloysia

Armada, J., and A. Barra. 1992. On *Aloysia* Palau (Verbenaceae). *Taxon* 41: 88–90.

Bellakhdar, J., et al. 1994. Composition of lemon verbena [*Aloysia triphylla* (L'Herit.) Britton] oil of Moroccan origin. *J. Essential Oil Res.* 6: 523–526.

Botta, S. M. 1979. Las especies argentinas del género *Aloysia* (Verbenaceae). *Darwiniana* 22: 67–108.

Carnat, A., et al. 1995. Luteolin 2-diglucuronide, the major flavonoid compound from *Verbena triphylla* and *Verbena officinalis*. *Pl. Med.* 61: 490.

———. 1999. The aromatic and polyphenolic composition of lemon verbena tea. *Fitoterapia* 70: 44–49.

Di Leo Lira, P., et al. 2008. Characterization of lemon verbena (*Aloysia citriodora* Palau) from Argentina by the essential oil. *J. Essential Oil Res.* 20: 350–353.

Frazao, S., and M. M. Carmo. 1982. L'huile essentielle de verveine protugaise. Première études. (*Lippia citriodora* Kunth). In *VIII International Congress of Essential Oils, October 12–17, 1980, Cannes-Grasse, France*. Paper no. 84.

Garnero, J. 1977. L'huile essentielle de verveine de Provence. *Parfums, Cosmétiques, Arômes* 1977: 29–37.

Guarrera, P. M., et al. 1995. Antimycotic activity of essential oil of *Lippia citriodora* Kunt (*Aloysia triphylla* Britton). *Rivista Ital. EPPOS* 6: 23–25.

Kaiser, R., and D. Lamparsky. 1976. Inhaltsstoffe des Verbenaöls. 1. Mitteilung. Natürliches Vorkommen der Photocitrale und einiger ihrer Derivate. *Helv. Chim. Acta* 59: 1797–1802.

Lamparsky, D. 1985. Headspace technique as a versatile complementary tool to increase knowledge about constituents of domestic or exotic flowers and fruits. In *Essential Oils and Aromatic Plants*. Ed. A. Baerheim Svendsen and J. J. C. Scheffer. Dordrecht: Martinus Nijhoff. 79–92.

Nakamura, T., et al. 1997. Acetoside as the analgesic principle of cedron (*Lippia triphylla*), a Peruvian medicinal plant. *Chem. Pharm. Bull.* 45: 499–504.

Özek, T., et al. 1996. Composition of the essential oil of *Aloysia triphylla* (L'Hérit.) Britton grown in Turkey. *J. Essential Oil Res.* 8: 581–583.

Pérez, G. S., et al. 1995. Composition of the flowers oils of some *Lippia* and *Aloysia* species from Argentina. *J. Essential Oil Res.* 7: 593–595.

———. 1998. Antidiarrhoeal activity of C-9 aldehyde isolated from *Aloysia triphylla*. *Phytotherapy Res.* 12: S45–S46.

Santos-Gomes, P. C., et al. 2005. Composition of the essential oil from flowers and leaves of vervain [*Aloysia triphylla* (L'Hér.) Britton] grown in Portugal. *J. Essential Oil Res.* 17: 73–78.

Valentão, P., et al. 2002. Studies on the antioxidant activity of *Lippia citriodora* infusion: Scavenging effect on superoxide radical, hydroxyl radical and hypochlorous acid. *Biol. Pharm. Bull.* 25: 1324–1327.

Vogel, H., et al. 1999. Seasonal fluctuation of essential oil content in lemon verbena (*Aloysia triphylla*). *Acta Hort.* 500: 75–77.

Zygadlo, J. A., et al. Volatile constituents of *Aloysia triphylla* (L'Herit.) Britton. *J. Essential Oil Res.* 6: 407–409.

Anethum

Ahmad, A., et al. 1990. A dihydrobenzofuran from Indian dill seed oil. *Phytochemistry* 29: 2035–2037.

Ashraf, M., et al. 1977. Studies on the essential oils of the Pakistani species of the family Umbelliferae. Part 6. *Anethum graveolens* (dill, sowa) seed oil. *Pakistan J. Sci. Industr. Res.* 20: 53–54.

Badoc, A., and A. Lamarti. 1991. A chemotaxonomic evaluation of *Anethum graveolens* L. (dill) of various origins. *J. Essential Oil Res.* 3: 269–278.

Bandele, O., et al. 1990. Effects of N fertility, plant density and cultivar on yield of dill. *HortScience* 25: 1165.

Bélafi-Réthy, K., and K. Kerényi. 1977. Untersuchung der Zusammensetzung von eiheimischen und ausländischen ätherischen Ölen, VI. Kumaranderivate im ätherischen öl der Dillpflanze. *Acta Chim. Acad. Sci. Hung.* 94: 1–9.

Blank, I., et al. 1992. Sensory study on the character-impact flavour compounds of dill herb (*Anethum graveolens* L.). *Food Chem.* 43: 337–343.

Brunke, E.-J., et al. 1991. Constituents of dill (*Anethum graveolens* L.) with sensory importance. *J. Essential Oil Res.* 3: 257–267.

Charles, D. J., et al. 1995. Characterization of essential oil of dill (*Anethum graveolens* L.). *J. Essential Oil Res.* 7: 11–20.

Chou, J. S.-T., and J.-I. Iwamura. 1978. Studies on an unknown terpenoid contained in dill weed oil and extract of *Anethum graveolens* Linn. from USA; and on the analysis of some other dill oils. *Formosa Sci.* 32: 131–148.

Craker, L. E. 1987. Agronomic practices for dill production. In *Proceedings of the Second National Herb Growing and Marketing Conference, Purdue Univ., West Lafayette, Indiana.* Ed. J. E. Simon and L. Grant. 58–60.

Dille, C. 1993. A cook's notes on dill. *Herb Companion* 5(6): 623–629.

Embong, M. B., et al. 1977. Essential oils from spices grown in Alberta. Dill seed oil, *Anethum graveolens* L. (Umbelliferae). *Canad. Inst. Food Sci. Technol. J.* 10: 208–214.

Garrabants, N. L., and L. E. Craker. 1987. Optimizing field production of dill. *Acta Hort.* 208: 69–72.

Gupta, R. 1982. Studies in cultivation and improvement of dill (*Anethum graveolens*) in India. In *Cultivation and Utilization of*

Aromatic Plants. Ed. C. K. Atal and B. M. Kapur. Jammu Tawi, India: Regional Res. Lab. 545–558.

Hälvä, S. 1987. Yield and aroma of dill varieties (*Anethum graveolens* L.) in Finland. *Acta Agric. Scand.* 37: 329–334.

———. 1987. Studies on production techniques of some herb plants. Part 2. Row spacing and cutting height of dill herb (*Anethum graveolens* L.). *J. Agric. Sci. Finland* 59: 37–40.

Hälvä, S., et al. 1991. Light levels, growth and essential oil in dill (*Anethum graveolens* L.). *Herbs Spices Med. Pl.* 1: 47–58.

———. 1992. Light quality, growth, and essential oil in dill (*Anethum graveolens* L.). *Herbs Spices Med. Pl.* 1: 59–69.

Henry, B. S. 1982. Composition and characteristics of dill: a review. *Perfumer Flavor.* 7(1): 39–44.

Hornok, L. 1980. Effect of nutrition supply on yield of dill (*Anethum graveolens* L.) and the essential oil content. *Acta Hort.* 96: 337–342.

Huopalahti, R. 1983. Effect of latitude on the composition and content of aroma compounds in dill, *Anethum graveolens* L. In *Instrumental Analysis of Foods: Recent Progress Vol. 1.* Ed. Charalambous and G. Inglett. New York: Academic Press. 57–64.

———. 1984. Effect of latitude on the composition and content of aroma compounds in dill, *Anethum graveolens*, L. *Lebensm. Wiss. Technol.* 17: 16–19.

———. 1985. The content and composition of aroma compounds in three different cultivars of dill, *Anethum graveolens* L. *Z. Lebensm. Unters. Forsch.* 181: 92–99.

———. 1985. Dill aroma and its changes during the storage in two kinds of frozen bags. In *Progress in Flavor Research.* Ed. J. Adda. Amsterdam: Elsevier. 309–315.

———. 1986. Gas chromatographic and sensory analyses in the evaluation of the aroma of dill herb, *Anethum graveolens* L. *Lebensm. Wiss. Technol.* 19: 27–30.

Huopalahti, R., and E. Kesalahti. 1985. Effect of drying and freeze-drying on the aroma of dill (*Anethum graveolens* cv. 'Mammut'). In *Essential Oils and Aromatic Plants.* Ed. A. Baerheim Svendsen and J. J. C. Scheffer. Dordrecht: Martinus Nijhoff. 179–184.

Huopalahti, R., and R. R. Linko. 1983. Composition and content of aroma compounds in dill, *Anethum graveolens* L., at three different growth stages. *J. Agric. Food Chem.* 31: 331–333.

Huopalahti, R., et al. 1985. Effect of hot-air and freeze-drying on the volatile compounds of dill (*Anethum graveolens* L.) herb. *J. Agric. Sci. Finland* 57: 133–138.

———. 1988. Studies on the essential oils of dill herb, *Anethum graveolens* L. *Flavour Fragrance J.* 3: 121–125.

Jirovetz, L., et al. 1994. Vergleichende Inhaltsstoffeanalyse verschiedener Dillkraut-und Dillsamenöle mittels GC/FID and GC/MS. *Ernährung/Nutrition* 18: 534–536.

———. 2003. Composition, quality control, and antimicrobial activity of the essential oil of long-time stored dill (*Anethum graveolens* L.) seeds from Bulgaria. *J. Agric. Food Chem.* 51: 3854–3857.

———. 2004. Antimicrobial testings and chiral phase gas chromatographic analysis of dill oils and related key components. *Ernährung/Nutrition* 28: 257–260.

Koedam, A., et al. 1979. Comparison of isolation procedures for essential oils. Part 1. Dill (*Anethum graveolens* L.). *Chem. Mikrobiol. Technol. Lebensm.* 6: 1–7.

Kmiecik, W., and J. Słupski. 2004. Effects of freezing and storing of frozen products on the content of nitrates, nitrites, and oxalates in dill (*Anethum graveolens* L.). *Food Chem.* 86: 105–111.

Kmiecik, W., et al. 2001. Effect of the cultivar, usable part, and growing period on the content of selected antioxidative components in dill (*Anethum graveolens* L.). *Acta Agraria Silvestria* 39: 35–48.

———. 2001. Effect of storage conditions on the technological value of dill (*Anethum graveolens* L.) *Folia Hort.* 13: 33–43.

Krüger, H., and K. Hammer. 1996. A new chemotype of *Anethum graveolens* L. *J. Essential Oil Res.* 8: 205–206.

Lisiewska, Z., et al. 2004. Contents of chlorophylls and carotenoids in frozen dill: effect of usable part and pre-treatment on the content of chlorophylls and carotenoids in frozen dill (*Anethum graveolens* L.), depending on the time and temperature of storage. *Food Chem.* 84: 511–518.

Miyazawa, M., and H. Kameoka. 1974. The constitution of the volatile oil from dill seed. *Yukagaku* 23: 746–749.

Morkūnas, V. 2002. Investigation of the genetic toxicology of dill essential oil and benzo(a)pyrene in mouse bone marrow by micronucleus test. *Biologija* 2002: 14–16.

Mukherjee, P. K., and I. Constance. 1993. *Umbelliferae (Apiaceae) of India.* New Delhi: Oxford & IBH Publ. Co.

Nitz, S., et al. 1991. Gas chromatographic and sensory analysis of dill blossoms (*Anethum graveolens* L.). *Chem. Mikrobiol. Technol. Lebensm.* 13: 183–186.

Orav, A., et al. 2003. Composition of the essential oil of dill, celery, and parsley from Estonia. *Proc. Estonia Acad. Sci. Chem.* 52: 147–154.

Pino, J. A., et al. 1995. Herb oil of dill (*Anethum graveolens* L.) grown in Cuba. *J. Essential Oil Res.* 7: 219–220.

———. 1995. Evaluation of flavour characteristic compounds in dill herb essential oil by sensory analysis and gas chromatography. *J. Agric. Food Chem.* 43: 1307–1309.

Porter, N. G., et al. 1983. Content and composition of dill herb oil in the whole plant and the different plant parts during crop development. *New Zealand J. Agric. Res.* 26: 119–127.

Prechur, R. J., and N. L. Garrabants. 1983. Weed control in dill. *Herb Spice Med. Pl. Dig.* 1(2): 3.

———. 1984. Weed control in dill. *Herb Spice Med. Pl. Dig.* 2(1): 5–6.

Pundarikakshudu, K., and G. C. Bhavsar. 1990. The effect of seed and foliar treatment of ascorbic acid on the yield and composition of Indian dill (*Anethum sowa* Roxb.). *J. Essential Oil Res.* 2: 133–135.

Randhawa, G. S., and A. Singh. 1991. Effect of sowing time and harvesting state on oil content, herbage and oil yield of dill (*Anethum graveolens* L.). *Indian Perfumer* 35: 204–208.

Randhawa, G. S., et al. 1987. Optimising agronomic requirements for seed yield and quality of dill (*Anethum graveolens* L.) oil. *Acta Hort.* 208: 61–68.

Robinson, C., and C. Myers. 1991. Dill. SMC-016. In *Specialty and Minor Crops Handbook.* Ed. C. Meyers. Oakland: Small Farm Center, Univ. California.

Saxena, A. K., and S. B. Saxena. 1981. Powdery mildew of *Anethum sowa*. *Indian Phytopathol.* 34: 266.

Scheffer, J. J. C., et al. 1977. Analysis of essential oils by combined liquid-solid and gas-liquid chromatography. Part 2. Monoterpenes in the essential seed oil of *Anethum graveolens* L. *Meddel. Norsk. Farm. Selskap* 39: 161–188.

Schreier, P., et al. 1981. The quantitative composition of natural and technologically changed aromas of plants. Part 8. Volatile constituents of fresh dill herb, *Anethum graveolens* L. (Umbelliferae). *Lebensm. Wiss. Technol.* 14: 150–152.

Shah, C. S. 1977. Varieties of Indian dill and their importance. In *Cultivation and Utilisation of Medicinal and Aromatic Plants.* Ed. C. K. Atal and B. M. Kapur. Jammu Tawi, India: Regional Res. Lab. 335–337.

Shah, C. S., et al. 1971. Constituents of two varieties of Indian dill. *J. Pharm. Pharmacol.* 23: 448–450.

———. 1971. Intraspecific variability in Indian dill. *Curr. Sci.* 40: 328–329.

———. 1972. Indian dill as substitute for European dill. *Indian J. Pharm.* 34: 69–70.

Singh, A., et al. 1987. Oil content and oil yield of dill (*Anethum graveolens* L.) herb under some agronomic practices. *Acta Hort.* 208: 51–60.

Singh, G., et al. 2005. Chemical constituents, antimicrobial investigations, and antioxidative potentials of *Anethum graveolens* L.

essential oil and acetone extract: part 52. *J. Food Sci.* 70: 208–215.

Thomann, R. J., et al. 1993. Distillation and use of essential oils from dill, celery, lovage, and parsley, made in Germany. *Acta Hort.* 333: 101–111.

Tutin, T. G. 1968. *Anethum.* In *Flora Europaea Vol. 2.* Ed. T. G. Tutin et al. Cambridge Univ. Press. 342–342.

Wall, D. A., and G. H. Friesen. 1986. The effect of herbicides and weeds on the yield and composition of dill (*Anethum graveolens* L.) oil. *Crop. Protect.* 5: 137–142.

Zawirska-Wojtasiak, R., and E. Wąsowicz. 2000. Enantiomeric composition of limonene and carvone in seeds of dill and caraway grown in Poland. *Polish J. Food Nutr. Sci.* 9/50(3): 9–13.

———. 2002. Estimation of the main dill seeds odorant carvone by solid-phase microextraction and gas chromatography. *Nahrung/Food* 46: 357–359.

Angelica

Anonymous. 2004. Angelica. *Rev. Nat. Prod. (Wolters Kluwer Health).*

Bernard, D., and G. Clair. 1997. Essential oils of three *Angelica* L. species growing in France. Part 1: root oils. *J. Essential Oil Res.* 9: 289–294.

———. 2001. Essential oils of three *Angelica* L. species growing in France. Part 2: fruit oils. *J. Essential Oil Res.* 13: 260–263.

Bomme, U., et al. 2000. Evaluierung von Engelwurz (*Angelica archangelica*): Herkünften unter besonderer Berücksichtigung von Gehalt und Zusammensetzung des ätherischen Öls. *Z. Arzn. Gew. Pfl.* 2000: 28–35.

Cannon, J. F. M. 1968. *Angelica*. In *Flora Europaea Vol. 2.* Ed. T. G. Tutin et al. Cambridge Univ. Press. 357–358.

Carbonnier, J., and J. Molho. 1982. Contribution à l'étude des furocoumarines du genre *Angelica*. Distribution du β-cyclo-lavandulyloxy-5 psoralène. *Pl. Med.* 44: 162–165.

Chalchat, J. C., and R. Garry. 1993. Pentane extracts of the roots of *Angelica archangelica* L. from France. *J. Essential Oil Res.* 5: 447–449.

———. 1997. Essential oil of angelica roots (*Angelica archangelica* L.): optimization and distillation, location in plant and chemical composition. *J. Essential Oil Res.* 9: 311–319.

Doneanu, C., and G. Anitescu. 1998. Supercritical carbon dioxide extraction of *Angelica archangelica* L. root oil. *J. Supercritical Fluids* 12: 59–67.

Formanowiczowa, H., and J. Kozlowski. 1971. The germination biology and laboratory valuation of medicinal plant seeds used for seeding purposes. Part 6c. The seeds of two Umbelliferae species: *Archan-*

gelica officinalis Hoffm. and *Levisticum officinalis* Koch. cultivated in Poland. *Herba Pol.* 17: 355–366.

Fornasiero, U., et al. 1969. Identificazione della sostanze attrattiva per i maschi della *Ceratitis capitata*, contenuta nell'olio essenziale dei semi de *Angelica archangelica*. *Gazz. Chim. Ital.* 99: 700–710.

Forsén, K. 1979. Aroma constituents of *Angelica archangelica*. Variations in the composition of the essential root oil of strains of var. *norvegica* and var. *sativa*. *Rep. Kevo Subarctic Res. Sta.* 15: 1–7.

Hälvä, S. 1990. Angelica: plant from the North. *Herb Spice Med. Pl. Dig.* 8(1): 1–3.

Härmälä, P., et al. 1992. Strategy for the isolation and identification of coumarins with calcium antagonistic properties from the roots of *Angelica archangelica*. *Phytochem. Anal.* 3: 42–48.

Héthelyi, I., et al. 1985. Mass-spectrometric examination of the oil components of *Angelica archangelica* [in Hungarian]. *Herba Hung.* 24: 141–163.

Kallio, H., et al. 1987. Extraction of angelica root with liquid carbon dioxide. In *Flavor Science and Technology.* Ed. M. Martens et al. New York: John Wiley & Sons. 111–114.

Kerrola, K., and H. P. Kallio. 1994. Extraction of volatile compounds of angelica (*Angelica archangelica* L.) root by liquid carbon dioxide. *J. Agric. Food Chem.* 42: 2235–2245.

Kerrola, K., et al. 1988. Characterization of volatile composition and odor of angelica (*Angelica archangelica* subsp. *archangelica* L.) root extracts. *J. Agric. Food Chem.* 42: 1979–1988.

Kiss, I., et al. 1981. Monoterpenes of *Angelica archangelica* L. fruit. *Revista Med.* 27: 182–185.

Laufer, G. A. 1984. The effect of stratification on *Angelica archangelica* L. seed germination after storage. *Pl. Propag.* 32(2): 13–15.

Letchamo, W., et al. 1995. Growth and essential oil content of *Angelica archangelica* as influenced by light intensity and growing media. *J. Essential Oil Res.* 7: 497–504.

Matsukura, T. 1981. On *Angelica archangelica* oil and *Amyris balsamifera* oil. *Koryo* 134: 11–12.

Nivinskienė, R., et al. 2003. Changes in the chemical composition of essential oil of *Angelica archangelica* L. roots during storage. *Chemija* 14: 52–56.

———. 2005. Chemical composition of seed (fruit) essential oils of *Angelica archangelica* L. growing wild in Lithuania. *Chemija* 16: 51–54.

———. 2007. The seed (fruit) essential oils of *Angelica archangelica* L. growing wild in Lithuania. *J. Essential Oil Res.* 19: 477–481.

Ojala, A. 1984. Variation of *Angelica arch-angelica* subsp. *archangelica* (Apiaceae) in northern Fennoscandia. 1. Variation in fruit morphology. *Ann. Bot. Fenn.* 21: 103–115.

———. 1985. Variation of *Angelica archangelica* subsp. *archangelica* (Apiaceae) in northern Fennoscandia. 2. Phenological life strategy and reproductive output. *Ann. Bot. Fenn.* 22: 183–194.

———. 1985. Seed dormancy and germination in *Angelica archangelica* subsp. *archangelica* (Apiaceae). *Ann. Bot. Fenn.* 22: 53–62.

———. 1986. Variation of *Angelica archangelica* subsp. *archangelica* (Apiaceae) in northern Fennoscandia. 3. Interpopulational variation in reproductive and life-history characters. *Ann. Bot. Fenn.* 23: 11–21.

———. 1986. Variation of *Angelica archangelica* subsp. *archangelica* (Apiaceae) in northern Fennoscandia. 4. Pattern of geographic variation. *Ann. Bot. Fenn.* 23: 23–31.

———. 1986. Variation of *Angelica archangelica* subsp. *archangelica* (Apiaceae) in northern Fennoscandia. 5. Variation in composition of essential oil. *Ann. Bot. Fenn.* 23: 325–332.

Paroul, N., et al. 2002. Chemical composition of the volatiles of angelica root obtained by hydrodistillation and supercritical CO_2 extraction. *J. Essential Oil Res.* 14: 282–285.

Pasqua, G., et al. 2003. Accumulation of essential oils in relation to root differentiation in *Angelica archangelica* L. *Eur. J. Histochem.* 47: 87–90.

Rácz, G., et al. 1978. Composition of the essential oil *Angelica archangelica* L. *Revista Med.* 24: 10–12.

Sigurdsson, S., et al. 2005. The cytotoxic effect of two chemotypes of essential oils from the fruits of *Angelica archangelica* L. *Anticancer Res.* 25: 1877–1880.

Taskinen, J., and L. Nykänen. 1975. Chemical composition of *Angelica* root oil. *Acta Chem. Scand.* 29B: 757–764.

Anthoxanthum

Anonymous. 2004. Sweet vernal grass. *Rev. Nat. Prod. (Wolters Kluwer Health)*.

Arctander, S. 1960. *Perfume and Flavor Materials of Natural Origin*. Elizabeth, New Jersey: Steffen Arctander.

Bernreuther, A., et al. 1990. Enantioselective analysis of dec-2-en-5-olide (massoia lactone) from natural sources by multidimensional capillary gas chromatography. *Flavour Fragrance J.* 5: 71–73.

English, M. 1982. Sweet grass: a sacred herb. *Herbarist* 48: 5–9.

Jones, V. H. 1936. Some Chippewa and Ottawa uses of sweet grass. *Pap. Mich. Acad. Sci., Arts Lett. Pap.* 21: 21–31.

Nykänen, I. 1984. The volatile compounds of *Hierochloë odorata*. In *Flavour Research of Alcoholic Beverages*. Ed. L. Nykänen and P. Lehtonen. Helsinki: Found. Biotechn. & Industr. Ferment. Res. 131–139.

Pereira, M. P., et al. 2007. European sweet vernal grasses (*Anthoxanthum*: Poaceae, Pooideae, Aveneae): a morphometric taxonomical approach. *Syst. Bot.* 32: 43–59.

Shebitz, D. J., and R. M. Kimmerer. 2004. Population trends and habitat characteristics of sweetgrass, *Anthoxanthum nitens*: integration of traditional and scientific ecological knowledge. *J. Ethnobiol.* 24: 93–111.

Tava, A. 2001. Coumarin-containing grass: volatiles from sweet vernalgrass (*Anthoxanthum odoratum* L.). *J. Essential Oil Res.* 13: 367–370.

Tutin, T. G. 1980. *Anthoxanthum*. In *Flora Europaea Vol. 5*. Ed. T. G. Tutin et al. Cambridge Univ. Press. 229–230.

Ueyama, Y., et al. 1991. Volatile constituents of ethanol extracts of *Hierochloe odorata* L. var. *pubescens* Kryl. *Flavour Fragrance J.* 6: 63–68.

Weimarck, G. 1971. Variation and taxonomy of *Hierochloë* (Gramineae) in the northern hemisphere. *Bot. Not.* 124: 129–175.

Anthriscus

Baser, H. H. C., et al. 1998. The essential oil of *Anthriscus cerefolium* (L.) Hoffm. (chervil) growing wild in Turkey. *J. Essential Oil Res.* 10: 463–464.

Dille, C., and S. Belsinger. 1992. *Herbs in the Kitchen*. Interweave Press, Loveland, Colorado.

Edwards, J. 1984. *The Roman Cookery of Apicius*. Pint Roberts, Washington: Hartly & Marks Publ.

Feres, S., et al. 2003. Antioxidant activity of different compounds from *Anthriscus cerefolium* L. (Hoffm.). *Acta Hort.* 597: 191–198.

Lemberkovics, E., et al. 1994. Essential oil composition of chervil growing wild in Hungary. Part 1. *J. Essential Oil Res.* 6: 421–422.

Reduron, J.-P., and K. Spalik. 1995. Le genre *Anthriscus* (Apiaceae) dans la flore française. *Acta Bot. Gallica* 142: 55–96.

Rigaud, J., and J. Sarris. 1982. Les constituants volatils de l'arôme du cerfeuil. *Sci. Aliments* 2: 163–172.

Rosengarten, F. 1981. *The Book of Spices*. Rev. ed. New York: Jove Publ.

Simándi, B., et al. 1996. Comparison of the volatile composition of chervil oil obtained by hydrodistillation and supercritical fluid extraction. *J. Essential Oil Res.* 8: 305–306.

Spalik, K., and C. E. Jarvis. 1989. Typification of Linnaean names now in *Anthriscus* (Apiaceae). *Taxon* 38: 288–293.

Zwaving, J. H., et al. 1971. The essential oil of chervil, *Anthriscus cerefolium* (L.) Hoffm. Isolation of 1-allyl-2,4-dimethoxy-benzene. *Pharm. Weekbl.* 106: 182–189.

Armoracia

Anonymous. 2004. Horseradish. *Rev. Nat. Prod. (Wolters Kluwer Health)*.

Ball, P. W. 1964. *Armoracia*. In *Flora Europaea Vol. 1*. Ed. T. G. Tutin et al. Cambridge Univ. Press. 284.

Courter, J. W., and A. M. Rhodes. 1969. Historical notes on horseradish. *Econ. Bot.* 23: 156–164.

Courter, J. W., et al. 1970. Illinois leads the nation in horseradish. *Living Mus.* 32: 244–245.

Delaquis, P. J., et al. 1999. Microbiological, chemical, and sensory properties of precooked roast beef preserved with horseradish essential oil. *J. Food Sci.* 64: 519–524.

Doll, C. C., et al. 1973. *Illinois Horseradish: A Natural Condiment*. Univ. Illinois Coop. Extens. Serv. Circ. 1084.

Etoh, H., et al. 1990. Stabilization of flavour in wasabi and horseradish (application of freeze-concentration method on flavour of wasabi, part 1). *Nippon Shokuhin Kogyo Gakkaishi* 37: 953–958.

Fosberg, F. R. 1965. Nomenclature of the horseradish (Cruciferae). *Baileya* 13: 1–3.

———. 1966. The correct name of the horseradish [Cruciferae]. *Baileya* 14: 60.

Foster, R. E., et al. 1979. Treatment of propagative stocks for control of the imported crucifer weevil. *J. Econ. Entomol.* 72: 555–556.

Grob, K., and P. Matile. 1979. Vacuolar location of glucosinolates in horseradish root cells. *Pl. Sci. Lett.* 14: 327–335.

———. 1980. Capillary GC of glucosinolate-derived horseradish constituents. *Phytochemistry* 19: 1789–1793.

Ina, K., et al. 1981. Volatile components of wasabi (*Wasabi japonica*) and horseradish (*Cochlearia armoracia*). (Studies on the volatile components of wasabi and horseradish, part 1). *Nippon Shokuhin Kogyo Gakkaishi* 28: 365–370.

Kraxner, U., et al. 1982. Bitterer Meerrettich. *Industr. Obst.- Gemüsewerwertung* 67: 148–150.

———. 1986. Einfluss der Wasserversorgung auf den Wachstumsverlauf auf die ontogenetische Veränderung wertgebender Inhaltsstoffe und auf die Bitterkeit von Meerrettich (*Armoracia rusticana* Ph. Gaertn., B. Mey. et Scherb.) *Landwirtsch. Forsch.* 39: 274–286.

Lüthy, B., and P. Matile. 1984. The mustard oil bomb: rectified analysis of the subcellular organisation of the myrosinase system. *Biochem. Physiol. Pflanzen* 179: 5–12.

Masuda, H., et al. 1996. Characteristic odorants of wasabi (*Wasabia japonica* Matsum.), Japanese horseradish, in comparison with those of horseradish (*Armoracia rusticana*). In *Biotechnology for Improved Foods and Flavor*. Ed. G. R. Takeoka et al. Washington, D.C.: Amer. Chem. Soc. 67–78.

———. 1999. Wasabi, Japanese horseradish, and horseradish: Relationship between stability and antimicrobial properties of their isothiocyanates. In *Flavor Chemistry of Ethnic Foods*. Ed. F. Shahidi and C.-T. Ho. New York: Kluwer Academic. 85–96.

Mazza, G. 1984. Volatiles in distillates of fresh, dehydrated and fresh dried horseradish. *Canad. Inst. Food Sci. Technol.* 17: 18–23.

McClung, C. A., and F. D. Schales. 1982. *Commercial Production of Horseradish*. Univ. Maryland Coop. Ext. Serv. HE 127–82.

Rhodes, A. M. 1977. Horseradish: problems and research in Illinois. In *Crop Resources*. Ed. D. S. Seigler. New York: Academic Press. 137–148.

Rhodes, A. M., et al. 1965. Identification of horseradish types. *Trans. Illinois State Acad. Sci.* 58: 115–122.

———. 1965. Improving horseradish through breeding. *Illinois Res.* 1965(3): 17.

———. 1969. Measurement and classification of genetic variability in horseradish. *J. Amer. Soc. Hort. Sci.* 94: 98–102.

Schaffer, A. 1981. The history of horseradish as the bitter herb of Passover. *Gesher* 8: 217–237.

Artemisia

Adams, J. 2004. *Hideous Absinthe: A History of the Devil in a Bottle*. Madison: Univ. Wisconsin Press.

Albasini, A., et al. 1983. Indagini su piante di *Artemisia dracunculus* L. s.l. (estragone). *Fitoterapia* 54: 229–235.

Albert-Puleo, M. 1978. Mythobotany, pharmacology, and chemistry of thujone-containing plants and derivatives. *Econ. Bot.* 32: 65–74.

Anonymous. 2006. Sweet wormwood. *Rev. Nat. Prod. (Wolters Kluwer Health)*.

———. 2008. Wormwood. *Rev. Nat. Prod. (Wolters Kluwer Health)*.

Arabhosseini, A., et al. 2005. Modeling of the equilibrium moisture content (EMC) of tarragon (*Artemisia dracunculus* L.). *Intern. J. Food Eng.* 1(5): 1–15.

———. 2006. Loss of essential oil of tarragon (*Artemisia dracunculus* L.) due to drying. *J. Sci. Food Agric.* 86: 2543–2550.

———. 2007. Long-term effects of drying conditions on the essential oil and color of tarragon leaves during storage. *J. Food Eng.* 79: 561–566.

Bassuk, N. 1986. Year-round production of greenhouse-grown French tarragon. *HortScience* 21: 258–259.

Basta, A., et al. 2007. Chemical composition of *Artemisia absinthium* from Greece. *J. Essential Oil Res.* 19: 316–318.

Bianchi-Santamaria, et al. 1993. Antimutagenic action of beta carotene, canthaxanthin and extracts of *Rosmarinus officinalis* and *Melissa officinalis*. Genotoxicity of basil and tarragon oil. In *Food and Cancer Prevention: Chemical and Biological Aspects*. Ed. K. W. Waldron et al. Cambridge: Roy. Soc. Chem. 75–81.

Bicchi, C., et al. 1982. On the composition of the essential oils of *Artemisia genipi* Weber and *Artemisia umbelliformis* Lam. *Z. Lebensm. Unters. Forsch.* 175: 182–185.

Blagojević, P., et al. 2006. Chemical composition of the essential oils of Serbian wild-growing *Artemisia absinthium* and *Artemisia vulgaris*. *J. Agric. Food Chem.* 54: 4780–4789.

Borland, J. 1993. The essence of the west. *Amer. Nurseryman* 178(3): 30–43.

Brass, M., et al. 1983. Neue Substanzen aus etherischen Ölen verschiedener Artemisia-Species. 5. Mitt.: Elemicin sowie weitere Phenylpropan-Derivate. *GIT Fachz. Lab.* 3 (Suppl.): 35–36, 38–42.

Briggs, C. J. 1991. Wormwood, herbal tea or poison? *Prairie Gard.* 37: 119–120.

Carnat, A. P., et al. 1985. L'armoise: *Artemisia vulgaris* L. et *Artemisia verlotiorum* Lamotte. *Ann. Pharm. Franç.* 43: 397–405.

Chalchat, J. C., et al. 1991. A contribution to chemotaxonomy of *Artemisia annua* L., Asteraceae. *Acta Pharm. Jugosl.* 41: 233–236.

———. 1994. Influence of harvest time on yield and composition of *Artemisia annua* oil produced in France. *J. Essential Oil Res.* 6: 261–268.

Chan, K. L., et al. 1995. Selection of high artemisinin-yielding *Artemisia annua*. *Pl. Med.* 61: 285–287.

Charchari, S., et al. 1996. Activite antimicrobienne in vitro des huiles essentielles d'*Artemisia herba-alba* Asso. et d'*Artemisia judaïca* L. d'Algerie. *Revista Ital. EPPOS* 1996(18): 3–6.

Charles, D. J., et al. 1991. Characterization of the essential oil of *Artemisia annua* L. *J. Essential Oil Res.* 3: 33–39.

Charles, D. J., et al. 1993. Effect of water stress and post-harvest handling on artemisinin content in the leaves of *Artemisia annua* L. In *New Crops*. Ed. J. Janick and J. E. Simon. New York: John Wiley & Sons. 640–643.

Chialva, F., and P. A. P. Liddle. 1981. Sur la composition de l'huile essentielle de *Artemisia pontica* Linnaeus cultivée en Piémont. *Revista Ital. EPPOS* 62: 350–352.

Chialva, F., et al. 1983. Chemotaxonomy of wormwood (*Artemisia absinthium* L.). I. Composition of the essential oil of several chemotypes. *Z. Lebensm. Unters. Forsch.* 176: 363–366.

Chiasson, H., et al. 2001. Acaricidal properties of *Artemisia absinthium* and *Tanacetum vulgare* (Asteraceae) essential oils obtained by three methods of extraction. *J. Econ. Entomol.* 94: 167–171.

Conrad, B. 1998. *Absinthe: History in a Bottle*. San Francisco: Chronicle Books.

Curini, M., et al. 2006. Composition and antimicrobial activity of the essential oil of *Artemisia dracunculus* "Piemontese" from Italy. *Chem. Nat. Comp.* 42: 738–739.

Deans, S. G., and K. P. Svoboda. 1988. Antibacterial activity of French tarragon (*Artemisia dracunculus* Linn.) essential oil and its constituents during ontogeny. *J. Hort. Sci.* 63: 503–508.

Debrunner, N., et al. 1996. Selection of genotypes of *Artemisia annua* L. for the agricultural production of artemisinin. In *Proceedings: International Symposium Breeding Research on Medicinal and Aromatic Plants, June 30–July 4, 1996, Quedlinburg, Germany*. Ed. F. Pank. 222–225.

De Gaviña Mugica, M., and J. T. Ochoa. 1974. *Contribucion al Estudio de los Aceites Esenciales Españoles. II. Aceites Esenciales de la Provincia de Guadalajara*. Madrid: Inst. Nac. Invest. Agr.

Delahaye, M.-C. 1990. *L'Absinthe: Art et Histoire*. Paris: Editions Trame Way.

del Castillo, J., et al. 1975. Marijuana, absinthe, and the central nervous system. *Nature* 253: 365–366.

Dob, T., and T. Benabdelkader. 2006. Chemical composition of the essential oil of *Artemisia herba-alba* Asso grown in Algeria. *J. Essential Oil Res.* 18: 685–690.

Ferreira, J. F. S., and J. Janick. 1995. Production and detection of artemisinin from *Artemisia annua*. *Acta Hort.* 390: 41–49.

———. 1996. Immunoquantitative analysis of artemisinin from *Artemisia annua* using polyclonal antibodies. *Phytochemistry* 41: 97–104.

———. 1996. Distribution of artemisinin in *Artemisia annua*. In *Progress in New Crops*. Ed. J. Janick. Alexandria, Virginia: ASHS Press. 578–584.

Ferreira, J. F. S., et al. 1995. Developmental studies of *Artemisia annua*: flowering and artemisinin production under greenhouse and field conditions. *Pl. Med.* 61: 167–170.

———. 1997. *Artemisia annua*: botany, horticulture, pharmacology. *Hort. Rev.* 19: 319–371.

Feuerstein, I., et al. 1986. The constitution of essential oils from *Artemisia herba-alba* populations of Israel and Sinai. *Phytochemistry* 25: 2343–2347.

Gimpel, M., et al. 2006. Absinth: Abschätzun des Thujongehaltes von Absinthgetränken nach historischen Rezepten. *Deutsche Lebensmittel-Rundschau* 102: 457–463.

Goel, D., et al. 2008. Volatile metabolite compositions of the essential oil from aerial parts of ornamental and artemisinin rich cultivars of *Artemisia annua*. *J. Essential Oil Res.* 20: 147–152.

Haider, F., et al. 2004. Influence of transplanting time on essential oil yield and composition in *Artemisia annua* plants grown under the climatic conditions of sub-tropical north India. *Flavour Fragrance J.* 19: 51–53.

Haseeb, A., and R. Pandey. 1990. Root-knot nematodes: a constraint to cultivation of davana, *Artemisia pallens*. *Trop. Pest Managem.* 36: 317–319.

Héthelyi, E., and G. Bertalan. 2005. *Artemisia abrotanum* L. (istenfa – istenfü, ürömcserje) species botanikai és fitokémiai vizsgálata. *Olajk Szappan Kozmetika* 54: 118–126.

Héthelyi, E., et al. 1995. *Artemisia maritima* illóolajok kapillár gázkormatográfiás vizsgálata. *Olaj Szappan Kozmetika* 44: 117–120.

———. 1995. Chemical composition of the *Artemisia annua* essential oils from Hungary. *J. Essential Oil Res.* 7: 45–48.

Hien, T. T., and N. J. White. 1993. Qinghaosu. *Lancet* 341: 603–608.

Hien, T. T., et al. 1996. A controlled trial of artemether or quinine in Vietnamese adults with severe falciparum malaria. *New England J. Med.* 335: 76–83.

Höld, K. M., et al. 2000. α-Thujone (the active component of absinthe): γ-aminobutyric acid type A receptor modulation and metabolic detoxification. *Proc. Natl. Acad. Sci.* 97: 3826–3831.

———. 2001. Detoxification of α- and β-thujones (the active ingredients of absinthe): site specificity and species differences in cytochrome P450 oxidation in vitro and in vivo. *Chem. Res. Toxicol.* 14: 589–595.

Holm, Y., et al. 1997. Variation in the essential oil composition of *Artemisia annua* L. of different origin cultivated in Finland. *Flavour Fragrance J.* 12: 241–246.

Hudaib, M. H., and T. A. Aburjai. 2006. Composition of the essential oil from *Artemisia herba-alba* grown in Jordan. *J. Essential Oil Res.* 18: 301–304.

Huisman, M., et al. 2007. Absinthe: is its history relevant for current public health? *Int. J. Epidemiol.* 36: 739–744.

Hurabielle, M., et al. 1982. Presence de davanone et de deux autres sesquiterpenes a noyau furane dans l'huile essentielle d'*Artemisia abrotanum* L. *Pl. Med.* 45: 55–63.

Hwang, Y.-s., et al. 1985. Isolation and identification of mosquito repellents in *Artemisia vulgaris*. *J. Chem. Ecol.* 11: 1297–1306.

Jain, D. C., et al. 1996. Isolation of high artemisinin-yielding clones of *Artemisia annua*. *Phytochemistry* 43: 993–1001.

Judzentiene, A., and D. Mockutė. 2004. Chemical composition of essential oils of *Artemisia absinthium* L. (wormwood) growing wild in Vilnius. *Chemija* 15(4): 64–68.

Juteau, F., et al. 2002. Antibacterial and antioxidant activities of *Artemisia annua* essential oil. *Fitoterapia* 73: 532–535.

———. 2003. Composition and antibacterial activity of the essential oil of *Artemisia absinthium* from Croatia and France. *Pl. Med.* 69: 158–161.

Kaul, V. K., et al. 1978. Insecticidal activity of some essential oils. *Indian J. Pharm.* 40: 22.

Klayman, D. L. 1985. Qinghaosu (artemisinin): an antimalarial drug from China. *Science* 228: 1049–1055.

Kordall, S., et al. 2005. Determination of the chemical composition and antioxidant activity of the essential oil of *Artemisia dracunculus* and of the antifungal and antibacterial activities of Turkish *Artemisia absinthium*, *A. dracunculus*, *Artemisia santonicum*, and *Artemisia spicigera* essential oils. *J. Agric. Food Chem.* 53: 9452–9458.

Kroes, B. H., et al. 1995. Modulatory effects of *Artemisia annua* extracts on human complement, neutrophil oxidative burst and proliferation of T lymphocytes. *Phytotherapy Res.* 9: 551–554.

Lachenmeier, D. W. 2007. Assessing the authenticity of absinthe using sensory evaluation and HPTLC analysis of the bitter principle absinthin. *Food Res. Intern.* 40: 167–175.

Lachenmeier, D. W., and D. Nathan-Maister. 2007. Systematic misinformation about thujone in pre-ban absinthe. *Deutsche Lebensmittel-Rundschau* 103: 255–262.

Lachenmeier, D. W., et al. 2005. Authentifizierung von Absinth: Bittere Wahrheit über eine Legende. *Deutsche Lebensmittel-Rundschau* 101: 100–104.

———. 2006. Absinthe: a review. *Crit. Rev. Food Sci. Nutr.* 46: 365–377.

———. 2006. Thujone: cause of absinthism? *Forensic Sci. Intern.* 158: 1–8.

———. 2008. Chemical composition of vintage preban absinthe with special reference to thujone, fenchone, pinocamphone, methanol, copper, and antimony concentrations. *J. Agric. Food Chem.* 56: 3073–3081.

Lanier, D. 1995. *Absinthe: The Cocaine of the Nineteenth Century*. London: McFarland and Co.

Lemberg, S. 1982. Armoise: *Artemisia herba alba*. *Perfumer Flavor.* 7(2): 58–60, 62–63.

Libbey, L. M., and G. Sturtz. 1989. Unusual essential oils grown in Oregon. Part 2. *Artemisia annua* L. *J. Essential Oil Res.* 1: 201–202.

Ma, C., et al. 2007. Analysis of *Artemisia annua* L. volatile oil by comprehensive two-dimensional gas chromatography time-of-flight mass spectrometry. *J. Chrom. A* 1150: 50–53.

Maw, M. G., et al. 1985. The biology of Canadian weeds. 66. *Artemisia absinthium* L. *Canad. J. Pl. Sci.* 65: 389–400.

Meepagala, K. M., et al. 2002. Antifungal constituents of the essential oil fraction of *Artemisia dracunculus* L. var. *dracunculus*. *J. Agric. Food Chem.* 50: 6989–6992.

Michaelis, K., et al. 1982. Essential oil from blossoms of *Artemisia vulgaris*. *Z. Naturforsch.* 37c: 152–158.

Misra, L. N., et al. 1991. Fragrant components of oil from *Artemisia pallens*. *Phytochemistry* 30: 549–552.

Mitchell, I. 1978. The plant and painting that shocked Paris. *Horticulture* 56(4): 32–37.

Nagy, F. 1968. The tarragon rust disease (*Puccinia dracunculina* Fahrend.) and the method of its control. *Acta Phytopathol. Acad. Sci. Hung.* 3: 331–336.

Nano, G. M., et al. 1976. On the composition of some oils from *Artemisia vulgaris*. *Pl. Med.* 30: 211–215.

Narayana, M. R., et al. 1978. *Davana and Its Cultivation in India*. Centr. Inst. Med. Aromatic Pl. Farm Bull. No. 12.

Neetu Jain, et al. 2002. Essential oil composition of *Artemisia annua* L. 'Asha' from the plains of northern India. *J. Essential Oil Res.* 14: 305–307.

Nin, S., et al. 1995. Quantitative determination of some essential oil components of selected *Artemisia absinthium* plants. *J. Essential Oil Res.* 7: 271–277.

Ouyaha, A., et al. 1990. Essential oils from Moroccan *Artemisia negrei*, *A. mesatlantica* and *A. herba alba*. *Lebensm. Wiss. Technol.* 23: 528–530.

Padosch, S. A., et al. Absinthism: a fictitious nineteenth century syndrome with present impact. *Substance Abuse Treatment Prevention Policy* 1: 1–14.

Pappas, R. S., and G. Sturtz. 2001. Unusual alkynes found in the essential oil of *Artemisia dracunculus* L. var. *dracunculus* from the Pacific Northwest. *J. Essential Oil Res.* 13: 187–188.

Pino, J. A., et al. 1996. Chemical composition of the essential oil of *Artemisia dracunculus* L. from Cuba. *J. Essential Oil Res.* 8: 563–564.

———. 1997. Chemical composition of the essential oil of *Artemisia absinthium* L. from Cuba. *J. Essential Oil Res.* 9: 87–89.

Ram, M., et al. 1995. Effect of planting time on the yield of essential oil and artemisinin in *Artemisia annua* under subtropical conditions. *J. Essential Oil Res.* 9: 137–197.

———. 1997. *Cultivation of Quinghaosu* Artemisia annua. Lucknow, India: Cent. Inst. Med. Aromatic Pl.

———. 1997. Effect of plant density on the yields of artemisinin and essential oil in *Artemisia annua* cropped under low input cost management in North-Central India. *Pl. Med.* 63: 372–374.

Renderath, O., et al. 1997. Immunomodulation mit Herba-abrotani-Tee und Propionibacterium avidum KP-40 bei professionellen Eishockeyspielern. *Biol. Med.* 26: 105–109.

Rousi, A. 1969. Cytogenetic comparison between two kinds of cultivated tarragon (*Artemisia dracunculus*). *Hereditas* 62: 193–213.

Sacco, T., and F. Chialva. 1988. Chemical characteristics of the oil from *Artemisia absinthium* collected in Patagony (Argentina). *Pl. Med.* 54: 93.

Salido, S., et al. 2004. Composition and infraspecific variability of *Artemisia herba-alba* from southern Spain. *Biochem. Syst. Ecol.* 32: 265–277.

Simon, J. E., and E. Cebert. 1988. *Artemisia annua*: a production guide. In *Proceedings of the Third National Herb Growing and Marketing Conference, Purdue Univ., West Lafayette, Indiana*. Ed. J. E. Simon and L. Z. Clavio. 78–83.

Simon, J. E., et al. 1990. *Artemisia annua*: a promising aromatic and medicinal. In *Advances in New Crops*. Ed. J. Janick and J. E. Simon. Portland, Oregon: Timber Press. 522–526.

Sirisoma, N. S., et al. 2001. α- and β-Thujones (herbal medicines and food additives): synthesis and analysis of hydroxyl and dehydro metabolites. *J. Agric. Food Chem.* 49: 1915–1921.

Smith, R. L., et al. 2002. Safety assessment of allylalkoxybenzene derivatives used as flavour substances: methyl eugenol and estragole. *Food Chem. Toxicol.* 40: 851–870.

Soylu, E. M., et al. 2005. Chemical composition and antifungal activity of the essential oil of *Artemisia annua* L. against foliar and soil-borne fungal pathogens. *Z. Pflanzenkrankheiten Pflanzenschutz* 112: 229–239.

Subramoniam, A., et al. 1996. Effects of *Artemisia pallens* Wall. on blood glucose levels and normal and alloxan-induced diabetic rats. *J. Ethnopharmacol.* 50: 13–17.

Sutton, S., et al. 1985. Tarragon. *Garden* (London) 110: 237–240.

Talzhanov, N. A., et al. 2005. Components of *Artemisia pontica*. *Chem. Nat. Comp.* 41: 178–181.

Tateo, F., et al. 1989. Basil oil and tarragon oil: Composition and genotoxicity evaluation. *J. Essential Oil Res.* 1: 111–118.

Tellez, M. R., et al. 1999. Differential accumulation of isoprenoids in glanded and glandless *Artemisia annua* L. *Phytochemistry* 52: 1035–1040.

Thomas, A. F., and R. Dubini. 1974. Terpenoids derived from linalyl oxide. Part 3. The isolation, structure, absolute configuration and synthesis of the davanafurans, nor-sesquiterpenes isolated from *Artemisia pallens*. *Helv. Chim. Acta* 57: 2066–2075.

Thomas, A. F., and M. Ozainne. 1974. Terpenoids derived from linalyl oxide. Part 2. The isolation and synthesis of nordavanone, a C11-terpenoid from *Artemisia pallens*. *Helv. Chim. Acta* 57: 2062–2065.

Thomas, A. F., and G. Pitton. 1971. The isolation, structure, and synthesis of davana ether, an odoriferous compound of the oil of *Artemisia pallens* Wall. *Helv. Chim. Acta* 54: 1890–1891.

Thomas, A. F., et al. 1974. Terpenoids derived from linalyl oxide. Part 1. The stereochemistry of the davanones. *Helv. Chim. Acta* 57: 2055–2061.

Thomason, I. J., et al. 1960. Thermotherapy for root-knot nematodes, *Meloidogyne* spp., of sweet potato and tarragon propagating stocks. *Pl. Dis. Rep.* 44: 354–358.

Tognolini, M., et al. 2006. Comparative screening of plant essential oils: phenylpropanoid moiety as basic core for antiplatelet activity. *Life Sci.* 78: 1419–1432.

Trigg, P. I. 1989. *Qinghaosu* (artemisin) as an antimalarial drug. In *Economic and Medicinal Plants Research Vol. 3*. Ed. H. Wagner et al. New York: Academic Press. 19–55.

Tucker, A. O., and M. J. Maciarello. 1987. Plant identification. In *Proceedings of the First National Herb Growing and Marketing Conference, July 19–22, 1986, West Lafayette, Indiana*. Ed. J. E. Simon and L. Grant. 126–172.

Tucker, A. O., et al. 1993. The essential oil of *Artemisia* 'Powis Castle' and its putative parents, *A. absinthium* and *A. arborescens*. *J. Essential Oil Res.* 5: 239–242.

Tutin, T. G., et al. 1976. *Artemisia*. In *Flora Europaea Vol. 4*. Ed. T. G. Tutin et al. Cambridge Univ. Press. 178–186.

Tyler, V. E. 1981. Wormwood's green alchemy. *Garden* 5(5): 14–15, 31.

Van Hensbroek, M. B., et al. 1996. A trial of artemether or quinine in children with cerebral malaria. *New England J. Med.* 335: 69–75.

Vernin, G., and L. O. Merad. 1994. Mass spectra and Kovats indices of some new cis-chrysanthenyl esters found in the essential oil of *Artemisia herba alba* from Algeria. *J. Essential Oil Res.* 6: 437–448.

Vienne, M., et al. 1989. Chemotaxonomic study of two cultivars of *Artemisia dracunculus* L.: ("French" and "Russian" tarragon). *Biochem. Syst. Ecol.* 17: 373–374.

Vostrowsky, O., et al. 1981. Über die Komponenten des ätherischen Öls aus *Artemisia absinthium*. *Z. Naturf.* 36c: 369–377.

———. 1981. Über die Komponenten des ätherischen Öls aus Estragon (*Artemisia dracunculus* L.). *Z. Lebensm. Unters. Forsch.* 173: 365–367.

———. 1984. Das ätherische Öl von *Artemisia abrotanum* L. *Z. Lebensm. Unters. Forsch.* 179: 125–128.

White, N. J. 2008. Qinghaosu (artemisinin): the price of success. *Science* 320: 330–334.

Yashphe, J., et al. 1987. The antibacterial and antispasmodic activity of *Artemisia herba-alba* Asso. Part 2. Examination of essential oils from various chemotypes. *Int. J. Crude Drug Res.* 25: 89–96.

Zeller, A., and M. Rychlik. 2007. Impact of estragole and other odorants on the flavour of anise and tarragon. *Flavour Fragrance J.* 22: 105–113.

Zentner, J. 1996. Absinthe makes the heart grow fonder. *Herb Quarterly* Spring: 40–45.

Zolotov, M. 1971. Absinthe. *Playboy* 18(6): 169–170, 172, 174, 176, 178.

Asarum

Doskotch, R. W., and P. W. Vanevenhoven. 1967. Isolation of aristolochic acid from *Asarum canadense*. *Lloydia* 30: 141–143.

Motto, M. G., and N. J. Secord. 1985. Composition of the essential oil from *Asarum canadense*. *J. Agric. Food Chem.* 33: 789–791.

Bergera

Bhattacharyya, P., and A. Chakraborty. 1984. Mukonal, a probable biogenetic intermediate of pyranocarbazole alkaloids from *Murraya koenigii*. *Phytochemistry* 23: 471–472.

Chakrabarty, M., et al. 1998. Carbazole alkaloids from *Murraya koenigii*. *Phytochemistry* 46: 751–755.

Hohmann, B. 1971. Zur Mikroscopie von "Curry-leaves," den Blättern von *Murraya koenigii*. *Z. Lebensmittel-Untersuch. Forsch.* 145: 169–164.

Joseph, S., and K. V. Peter. 1985. Curry leaf (*Murraya koenigii*), perennial, nutritious, leafy vegetable. *Econ. Bot.* 39: 68–73.

Lal, R. K., et al. 2001. Phenotypic and genetic diversity for morphometric traits and essential oil components in diverse origin germplasm lines of curry neem (*Murraya koenigii*). *J. Med. Aromatic Pl. Sci.* 23: 392–398.

———. 2001. Genetic associations and diversity in the genetic resources of curry neem *Murraya koenigii*. *J. Med. Aromatic Pl. Sci.* 22/23: 216–221.

———. 2003. Diversity pattern in curry neem (*Murraya koenigii*). *J. Med. Aromatic Pl. Sci.* 25: 13–18.

———. 2005. Genetic diversity in the secondary metabolic traits of curry leaf (*Murraya koenigii* (Linn.) Spreng). *Indian Perfumer* 49: 519–524.

MacLeod, A. J., and N. M. Pieris. 1982. Analysis of the volatile essential oils of *Murraya koenigii* and *Pandanus latifolius*. *Phytochemistry* 21: 1653–1657.

Mallavarapu, G. R., et al. 1999. Composition of Indian curry leaf oil. *J. Essential Oil Res.* 11: 176–178.

———. 2000. Volatile constituents of the leaf and fruit oils of *Murraya koenigii* Spreng. *J. Essential Oil Res.* 12: 766–768.

Nutan, M., et al. 1998. Antibacterial and cytotoxic activities of *Murraya koenigii*. *Fitoterapia* 69: 173–175.

Onayade, O. A., and A. C. Adebajo. 2000. Composition of the leaf volatile oil of *Murraya koenigii* growing in Nigeria. *J. Herbs Spices Med. Pl.* 7(4): 59–66.

Raina, V. K., et al. 2002. Essential oil composition of genetically diverse stocks of *Murraya koenigii* from India. *Flavour Fragrance J.* 17: 144–146, 404.

Ramsewak, R. S., et al. 1999. Biologically active carbazole alkaloids from *Murraya koenigii*. *J. Agric. Food Chem.* 47: 444–447.

Rana, V. S., et al. 2004. Chemical constituents of the volatile oil of *Murraya koenigii* leaves. *Intern. J. Aromatherapy* 14: 23–25.

Ranade, S. A., et al. 2006. Molecular differentiation in *Murraya* Koenig ex L. species in India inferred through ITS, RAPD and DAMD analysis. *Curr. Sci.* 90: 1253–1257.

Ratnasooriya, W. D., et al. 1995. Protection by *Murraya koenigii* extract against ethanol-induced gastric lesions in rats. *Med. Sci. Res.* 23: 11–13.

Reisch, J., et al. 1994. Chemotypes of *Murraya koenigii* growing in Sri Lanka. *Pl. Med.* 60: 295–296.

———. 1994. Two carbazole alkaloids from *Murraya koenigii*. *Phytochemistry* 36: 1073–1076.

Walde, S. G., et al. 2006. Flavour volatiles of flowers and stalk of *Murraya koenigii* L. *Flavour Fragrance J.* 21: 581–584.

Wassmuth-Wagner, I., et al. 1993. Isolation and identification of decahydrotetramethylcyclopazulenol in the essential oil of *Murraya koenigii* (L.) Sprengor. *Fresenius J. Anal. Chem.* 347: 286–292.

Wong, K. C., and D. Y. Tie. 1993. The essential oil of *Murraya koenigii* Spreng. *J. Essential Oil Res.* 5: 371–374.

Wong, K. C., and S. G. Chee. 1996. Volatile constituents of *Murrya koenigii* Spreng. flowers. *J. Essential Oil Res.* 8: 545–547.

Borago

Awang, V. C. 1990. Borage. *Canad. Pharm. J.* 123(3): 121, 123, 125–126.

Bandonienė, D., et al. 2002. Antioxidative activity of sage (*Salvia officinalis* L.), savory (*Satureja hortensis* L.) and borage (*Borago officinalis* L.) extracts in rapeseed oil. *Eur. J. Lipid Sci. Technol.* 104: 286–292.

Beaubaire, N. A., and J. E. Simon. 1987. Production potential of *Borago officinalis* L. *Acta Hort.* 208: 101–113.

Chater, A. O. 1972. *Borago*. In *Flora Europaea Vol. 3*. Ed. T. G. Tutin et al. Cambridge Univ. Press. 109.

De Smet, P. A. G. M. 1993. *Borago officinalis*. In *Adverse Effects of Herbal Drugs 2*. Ed. P. A. G. M. De Smet et al. Berlin: Springer-Verlag. 147–152.

Dodson, C. D., and F. R. Stermitz. 1986. Pyrrolizidine alkaloids from borage (*Borago officinalis*) seeds and flowers. *J. Nat. Prod.* 49: 727–728.

Janick, J., et al. 1989. Borage: a source of gamma-linolenic acid. In *Herbs, Spices, and Medicinal Plants: Recent Advances in Botany, Horticulture, and Pharmacology Vol. 4*. Ed. L. E. Craker and J. E. Simon. Phoenix, Arizona: Oryx Press. 145–168.

Larson, K. M., et al. 1984. Unsaturated pyrrolizidines from borage (*Borago officinalis*), a common garden herb. *J. Nat. Prod.* 47: 747–748.

Lüthy, J., et al. 1984. Pyrrolizidin-Alkaloide in Arzneipflanzen der Boraginaceen: *Borago officinalis* L. und *Pulmonaria officinalis* L. *Pharm. Acta Helv.* 59: 242–246.

Mierendorff, H.-J. 1995. Bestimmung von Pyrrolizidinalkaloiden durch Dünnschichtchromatographie in Samenölen von *Borago off.* L. *Fat Sci. Technol.* 97: 33–36.

Quinn, J., et al. 1989. Recovery of beta-linolenic acid from somatic embryos of borage. *J. Amer. Soc. Hort. Sci.* 114: 511–515.

Selvi, F., et al. 2006. Karyotype variation, evolution and phylogeny in *Borago* (Boraginaceae), with emphasis on subgenus *Buglossites* in the Corso-Sardinian system. *Ann. Bot.* 98: 857–868.

Brassica

Anonymous. 2005. Mustard. *Rev. Nat. Prod. (Wolters Kluwer Health)*.

Bassett, B. 1993. The amazing mustard seed. *Herb Companion* 5(6): 33–37.

Daniel, G. H. 1972. Pest control trials in commercial crops of brown mustard. *Int. Pest Control* 14: 6–10.

Easterday, O. 1997. Safety evaluation of trans-anethole and allyl isothiocyanate (mustard oil). *Riv. Ital. EPPOS Spec. Num.*: 99–104.

Fahey, J. W., et al. 2001. The chemical diversity and distribution of glucosinolates and isothiocyanates among plants. *Phytochemistry* 56: 5–51.

———. 2003. Brassicas. In *Encyclopedia of Food Sciences and Nutrition*. Ed. B. Caballero et al. London: Academic Press. 606–615.

Hälvä, S., et al. 1986. Yield and glucosinolates in mustard seeds and volatile oils in caraway seeds and coriander fruit. Part 1. Yield and glucosinolate contents of mustard (*Sinapis* spp., *Brassica* spp.) seeds. *J. Agric. Sci. Finland* 58: 157–162.

Hazen, J. 1993. *Mustard: Making Your Own Gourmet Mustards*. San Francisco: Chronicle Books.

Heywood, V. H. 1964. *Brassica*. In *Flora Europaea Vol. 1*. Ed. T. G. Tutin et al. Cambridge Univ. Press. 335–339.

Hopley, C. 1991. *Making and Using Mustards*. Pownal, Vermont: Storey.

Jiang, A.-T., et al. 1999. Composition of essential oil of *Brassica juncea* (L.) Coss. from China. *J. Essential Oil Res.* 11: 503–506.

Kim, Y. S., et al. 2001. Volatile compounds and antimicrobial effects of mustard seeds and leaf mustard seeds according to extraction method. *Food Sci. Biotechnol.* 10: 468–474.

———. 2002. Extension of shelf life by treatment with allyl isothiocyanate in combination with acetic acid on cooked rice. *J. Food Sci.* 67: 274–279.

Prakash, S., and K. Hinata. 1980. Taxonomy, cytogenetics and origin of crop *Brassica*. *Opera. Bot.* 55: 1–57.

Shankaranarayana, M. L., et al. 1972. Mustard: varieties, chemistry and analysis. *Lebensm. Wiss. Technol.* 5: 191–197.

Sinskaia, E. N. 1927. Geno-systematical investigations of cultivated *Brassica*. *Bull. Appl. Bot. Pl. Breed.* 17: 1–166.

Sun, V. G. 1946. The evaluation of taxonomic characters of cultivated *Brassica* with a key to species and varieties. *Bull. Torrey Bot. Club* 73: 244–281, 370–377.

Tollsten, L., and G. Bergström. 1988. Headspace volatiles of whole plants and macerated plant parts of *Brassica* and *Sinapis*. *Phytochemistry* 27: 4013–4018.

Vaughan, J. G., et al. 1963. Contributions to a study of variation in *Brassica juncea* Coss. & Czern. *J. Linn. Soc. Bot.* 58: 435–447.

Yu, H. C., et al. 2003. Chemical composition of the essential oils of *Brassica juncea* (L.) Coss. grown in different regions, Hebei, Shaaxi and Shandong, of China. *J. Food Drug Anal.* 11: 22–26.

Zhao, D., et al. 2007. Analysis of volatile components during potherb mustard (*Brassica juncea* Coss.) pickle fermentation using SPME-GC-MS. *LWT-Food Sci. Technol.* 40: 439–447.

Calamintha

Adzet, T., and J. Passet. 1972. Chemotaxonomie du genre *Satureia-Calamintha*. *Rivista Ital. EPPOS* 54: 482–486.

Akgül, A., et al. 1991. The essential oil of *Calamintha nepeta* subsp. *glandulosa* and *Ziziphora clinopodioides* from Turkey. *J. Essential Oil Res.* 3: 7–10.

Ball, P. W., and T. Getliffe. 1972. *Cala-*

mintha. In *Flora Europaea Vol. 3*. Ed. T. G. Tutin et al. Cambridge Univ. Press. 166–167.

Bellomaria, B., and G. Valentini. 1987. Composizione dell'olio essenziale di *Calamintha nepeta* subsp. *glandulosa*. *Giron. Bot. Ital.* 119: 237–245.

Couladis, M., and O. Tzakou. 2001. Essential oil of *Calamintha nepeta* subsp. *glandulosa* from Greece. *J. Essential Oil Res.* 13: 11–12.

de Pooter, H. L., and N. M. Schamp. 1986. Comparison of the volatile composition of some *Calamintha/Satureja* species. In *Progress in Essential Oil Research*. Ed. E-J. Brunke. Berlin: Walter de Gruyter & Co. 139–150.

de Pooter, H. L., et al. 1986. The volatiles of *Calamintha nepeta* subsp. *glandulosa*. *Phytochemistry* 25: 691–694.

———. 1987. Variability in composition of the essential oil of *Calamintha nepeta*. *Phytochemistry* 26: 3355–3356.

Flamini, G., et al. 1999. Antimicrobial activity of the essential oil of *Calamintha nepeta* and its constituent pulegone against bacteria and fungi. *Phytotherapy Res.* 13: 349–351.

Frazao, S., et al. 1974. Characteristics of the essential oil *Calamintha ascendens* Jord. [*Satureja calamintha* (L.) Schell]. In *VI International Congress of Essential Oils, San Francisco, California, September 8–12, 1974*. Paper no. 118.

Hanlidou, E., et al. 1991. Glandular trichomes and essential oil constituents of *Calamintha menthifolia* (Lamiaceae). *Pl. Syst. Evol.* 177: 17–26.

Kirimer, N., et al. 1992. Composition of the essential oil of *Calamintha nepeta* subsp. *glandulosa*. *J. Essential Oil Research* 4: 189–190.

Kitic, D., et al. 2001. The volatile constituents of *Calamintha sylvatica* Bromf. subsp. *sylvatica*. *Flavour Fragrance J.* 16: 257–258.

———. 2002. Chemical composition and antimicrobial activity of the essential oil of *Calamintha nepeta* (L.) Savi ssp. *glandulosa* (Req.) P. W. Ball from Montenegro. *J. Essential Oil Res.* 14: 150–152.

Kokkalou, E., and E. Stafanou. 1990. The volatile oil of *Calamintha nepeta* (L.) Savi subsp. *glandulosa* (Req.) P. W. Ball, endemic to Greece. *Flavour Fragrance J.* 5: 23–26.

Lawrence, B. M. 1993. *Essential Oils 1988–1991*. Wheaton, Illinois: Allured.

McKean, D. R., and A. C. Whiteley. 2000. *Calamintha*. In *The European Garden Flora Vol. 6*. Ed. J. Cullen et al. Cambridge Univ. Press. 211.

Nickavar, B., and F. Mojab. 2005. Hydrodistilled volatile constituents of *Calamintha officinalis* Moench from Iran. *J. Essential Oil-Bearing Pl.* 8: 23–37.

Ortiz de Urbina, A. V., et al. 1988. Pharmacologic screening and antimicrobial activity of the essential oil of *Calamintha sylvatica* subsp. *ascendens*. *J. Ethnopharmacol.* 23: 323–328.

———. 1989. Sedating and antipyretic activity of the essential oil of *Calamintha sylvatica* subsp. *ascendens*. *J. Ethnopharmacol.* 25: 165–171.

Pavlovis, S., et al. 1983. Anatomic structure of organs and essential oil of the plants of a population of *Calamintha glandulosa* (Reg.) Bentham. (Lamiaceae) from the Orjen Mountains. *Bull. Mus. Hist. Nat.* (Belgrade) 38B: 27–33.

Ristorcelli, D., et al. 1996. Essential oils of *Calamintha nepeta* subsp. *nepeta* and subsp. *glandulosa* from Corsica (France). *J. Essential Oil Res.* 8: 363–366.

Sarer, E., and S. S. Pançali. 1998. Composition of the essential oil from *Calamintha nepeta* (L.) Savi ssp. *glandulosa* (Req.) P. W. Ball. *Flavour Fragrance J.* 13: 31–32.

Sevarda, A. L., et al. 1987. Comparative studies of the composition of the essential oil of species *Calamintha glandulosa* (Reg.) Bentham, *C. vardarensis* Silic and *C. sylvatica* Bromf. *Acta Pharm. Jugosl.* 37: 103–106.

Souleles, C., et al. 1987. Constituents of the essential oil of *Calamintha nepeta*. *J. Nat. Prod.* 50: 510–522.

Stanić, G., et al. 1999. The composition of essential oils of *Calamintha nepeta* (L.) Savi subsp. *glandulosa* (Req.) P. W. Ball and *C. sylvatica* Bromf. subsp. *sylvatica*. *Acta Pharm.* 49: 107–112.

Stephanou, E., and E. Kokkalou. 1990. Phytochemical study of *Chaerophyllum bulbosum* L., growing wild in Greece and *Calamintha nepeta* L., endemic to Greece. In *Flavor and Off-flavor '89*. Ed. G. Charalambous. Amsterdam: Elsevier. 839–845.

Velasco-Negueruela, A., et al. 1987. Aceites esenciales de Lamiaceas Ibericas con pulegona como componente fundamental. *Anales Bromatol.* 39: 357–372.

Calendula

Adler, G., and Z. Kasprzyk. 1976. Distribution of triterpene alcohols in subcellular fractions from *Calendula officinalis* flowers. *Phytochemistry* 15: 205–207.

Al-Badawy, A. A., et al. 1995. Response of *Calendula officinalis* L. plants to different nitrogenous fertilizers. *HortScience* 30: 858.

Anonymous. 2008. Calendula. *Rev. Nat. Prod.* (Wolters Kluwer Health).

Ansari, M. A., et al. 1997. Effect of *Calendula officinalis* ointment, Charmil and gelatin granules on wound healing in buffaloes: a histological study. *Indian Vet. J.* 74: 594–597.

Bako, E., et al. 2002. HPLC study on the carotenoid composition of *Calendula* products. *J. Biochem. Biophys. Methods* 53: 241–250.

Barajas-Farias, L. M., et al. 2006. A dual and opposite effect of *Calendula officinalis* flower extract: chemoprotector and promoter in rat carcinogenesis model. *Pl. Med.* 72: 217–221.

Bashir, S., et al. 2006. Studies on spasmogenic and spasmolytic activities of *Calendula officinalis* flowers. *Phytotherapy Res.* 20: 906–910.

Bezáková, L., et al. 1996. Inhibitory activity of isorhamnetin glycosides from *Calendula officinalis* L. on the activity of lipoxygenase. *Pharmazie* 51: 126–127.

Četković, G. S., et al. 2003. Thin-layer chromatography analysis and scavenging activity of marigold (*Calendula officinalis* L.) extracts. *Acta Periodica Technol.* 34: 93–102.

Chalchat, J. C., et al. 1991. Chemical composition of essential oil of *Calendula officinalis* L. (pot marigold). *Flavour Fragrance J.* 6: 189–192.

Crabas, N., et al. 2003. Extraction, separation and isolation of volatiles and dyes from *Calendula officinalis* L. and *Aloysia triphylla* (L'Her.) Britton by supercritical CO_2. *J. Essential Oil Res.* 15: 272–277.

Della Loggia, R., et al. 1994. The role of triterpenoids in the topical anti-inflammatory activity of *Calendula officinalis* flowers. *Pl. Med.* 60: 516–520.

El-Gengaihi, S., et al. 1982. The effect of fertilization levels on flowering, oleanolic acid and phytosterol content of *Calendula officinalis* L. *Pharmazie Beih. Ergänzungsband* 37: 511–514.

Friedrich, H. 1962. Über das Vorkommen von Isorhamnetinglykosiden in den Blüten von *Calendula officinalis* L. *Arch. Pharm. Ber. Deutsch. Pharm. Ges.* 295: 59–66.

Gazim, Z. C., et al. 2007. Identificação dos constituinetes químicos da fração volatile da *Calendula officinalis* produzida no Paraná. *Hort. Bras.* 25: 118–121.

Gopinathan, A., et al. 2006. Effect of *Calendula officinalis* in burn wounds of bovine calves and heifers. *Indian J. Animal Sci.* 76: 437–441.

Góra, J., et al. 1980. Chemical substances from inflorescences of *Arnica montana* L. and *Calendula officinalis* L. soluble in isopropyl myristate and propylene glycol. *Acta Hort.* 96(2): 165–171.

Herb Society of America. 2007. *Calendula*. Kirtland, Ohio: Herb Soc. Amer.

Herold, M., et al. 1989. Verfahrenstechnische Entwicklungen zum Anbau von *Chamomilla recutita* L. (Rauschert) und *Calendula officinalis* L. für die Gewinnung von Blütendrogen. *Drogen Rep.* 2(2): 43–62.

Heyn, C. C., and A. Joel. 1983. Reproductive relationships between annual species of *Calendula* (Compositae). *Pl. Syst. Evol.* 143: 311–329.

János, D., et al. 2000. Kosmetikaipari növényünk a körömviräg (*Calendula officinalis* L.). *Olaj Szappan Kosmetika* 49: 139–143.

Khalid, K. A., and A. H. El-Ghorab. 2006. The effect of presowing low temperature on essential oil content and chemical composition of *Calendula officinalis*. *J. Essential Oil Bearing Pl.* 9: 32–41.

Khan, N. A., et al. 1984. A preliminary physico-chemical study of azariyun (*Calendula officinalis* Linn.). *Nagarjun* 28(4–6): 3–5.

———. 1987. Pharmacological studies of azariyun (*Calendula officinalis* Linn.). *Hamdard* 30(4): 75–82.

Khanna, P., et al. 1979. Investigations into possible new sources of pyrethrins. *Pyrethrum Post* 15(1): 9–10.

Lavagna, S. M., et al. 2001. Efficacy of *Hypericum* and *Calendula* oils in the epithelial reconstruction of surgical wounds in childbirth with caesarean section. *Il. Farmaco* 56: 451–453.

Martin, R. J., and B. Deo. 2000. Effect of plant population on calendula (*Calendula officinalis* L.) flower production. *New Zealand J. Crop Hort. Sci.* 28: 37–44.

Meikle, R. D. 1976. *Calendula*. In *Flora Europaea Vol. 4*. Ed. T. G. Tutin et al. Cambridge Univ. Press. 206–207.

Meusel, H., and H. Ohle. 1966. Zur Taxonomie und Cytologie der Gattung *Calendula*. *Oesterr. Bot. Z.* 113: 191–210.

Neukrich, H., et al. 2004. Simultaneous quantitative determination of eight triterpenoid monoesters from flowers of 10 varieties of *Calendula officinalis* L. and characterization of a new triterpenoid monoester. *Phytochem. Anal.* 15: 30–35.

———. 2005. Improved anti-inflammatory activity of three new terpenoids derived, by systematic chemical modifications, from the abundant triterpenes of the flower plant *Calendula officinalis*. *Chem. Biodiversity* 2: 657–671.

Novak, J., and C. Franz. 2000. Breeding aspects of *Calendula officinalis* L. *Z. Phytotherapie* 21: 160–165.

Novak, J., et al. 1999. Genotype × environment interaction in *Calendula officinalis* L. *Acta Hort.* 502: 67–70.

Petrović, L., et al. 2007. An investigation of CO_2 extraction of marigold (*Calendula officinalis* L.). *J. Serb. Chem. Soc.* 72: 407–413.

Piccaglia, R., et al. 1997. Effects of harvesting date and climate on the flavonoid and carotenoid contents of marigold (*Calendula officinalis* L.). *Flavour Fragrance J.* 12: 85–90.

Pommier, P., et al. 2004. Phase III randomized trial of *Calendula officinalis* compared with trolamine for the prevention of acute dermatitis during irradiation for breast cancer. *J. Clin. Oncol.* 22: 1447–1453.

Stevenson, R. 1961. Some constituents of *Calendula officinalis*. *J. Org. Chem.* 26: 5228–5229.

Willuhn, G., and R.-G. Westhaus. 1987. Loliolide (calendin) from *Calendula officinalis*. *Pl. Med.* 1987: 304.

Yoshikawa, M., et al. 2001. Medicinal flowers. III. Marigold. (1): Hypoglycemic, gastric emptying inhibitory, and gastroprotective principles and new oleanane-type triterpene oligoglycosides, calendasaponins A, B, C, and D, from Egyptian *Calendula officinalis*. *Chem. Pharm. Bull.* 49: 863–870.

Zitterl-Eglseer, K., et al. 1997. Anti-oedematous activities of the main triterpendiol esters of marigold (*Calendula officinalis* L.). *J. Ethnopharmacol.* 57: 139–144.

———. 2000. Stabilität der Faradiolmonester in Ringelblumenblüten (*Calendula officinalis* L.) bei verschiedenen Trochnungstemperaturen. *Z. Arzn. Gew. Pfl.* 5: 68–70.

———. 2001. Morphogenetic variability of faradiol monoesters in marigold *Calendula officinalis* L. *Phytochem. Anal.* 12: 199–201.

Capparis

Anonymous. 2004. Capers. *Rev. Nat. Prod. (Wolters Kluwer Health).*

Barbera, G., and R. Di Lorenzo. 1984. The caper culture in Italy. *Acta Hort.* 144: 167–171.

Bond, R. E. 1990. The caper bush. *Herbarist* 56: 77–85.

Brevard, H., et al. 1992. Occurrence of elemental sulphur in capers (*Capparis spinosa* L.) and first investigation of the flavour profile. *Flavour Fragrance J.* 7: 313–321.

Cena, T. L. 1972. Action des extraits de *Capparis spinosa* L. (var. *inermis*). *Actual. Dermopharmacol.* 4: 185–193.

Cena, T. L., and R. Rovesti. 1979. Ricerche sperimentali sull'azione cosmetologica dei Capperi. *Rivista Ital. EPPOS* 61: 2–9.

Giuffrida, D., et al. 2002. Initial investigation on some chemical constituents of capers (*Capparis spinosa* L.) from the island of Salina. *Ital. J. Food Sci.* 14: 25–33.

Heywood, V. H. 1964. *Capparis*. In *Flora Europaea Vol. 1*. Ed. T. G. Tutin et al. Cambridge Univ. Press. 259.

Kontaxis, D. G. 1989. *Capers: A New Crop for California?* Davis, California: Family Farm Ser., Small Farm Center, Univ. Calif.

Rodrigo, M., et al. 1992. Composition of capers (*Capparis spinosa*): influence of cultivar, size, and harvest date. *J. Food Sci.* 57: 1152–1154.

Romeo, V., et al. 2007. Flavour profile of capers (*Capparis spinosa* L.) from the Eolian Archipelago by HS-SPME/GC-MS. *Food Chem.* 101: 1272–1278.

Shirwaikar, A., et al. 1996. Chemical investigation and antihepatotoxic activity of the root bark of *Capparis spinosa*. *Fitoterapia* 67: 200–204.

Sozzi, G. O., and A. Chiesa. 1995. Improvement of caper (*Capparis spinosa* L.) seed germination by breaking seed coat-induced dormancy. *Sci. Hort.* 62: 255–261.

Capsicum

Abdel-Salam, O. M. E., et al. 1997. Capsaicin and the stomach. A review of the experimental and clinical data. *J. Physiology* 91: 151–171.

Almela, L., et al. 1991. Carotenoid composition of new cultivars of red pepper for paprika. *J. Agric. Food Chem.* 39: 1606–1609.

Andrews, J. 1984. *Peppers: The Domesticated Capsicums*. Austin: Univ. Texas Press.

———. 1998. *The Pepper Lady's Pocket Pepper Primer*. Austin: Univ. Texas Press.

Anonymous. 2004. Capsicum peppers. *Rev. Nat. Prod. (Wolters Kluwer Health).*

Asai, A., et al. 1999. Antioxidative effects of turmeric, rosemary and capsicum extracts on membrane phospholipid peroxidation and liver lipid metabolism in mice. *Biosci. Biotechnol. Biochem.* 63: 2118–2122.

Bajaj, K. L., et al. 1980. Varietal variations in some important chemical constituents in chili (*Capsicum annuum* L.) fruits. *Veg. Sci.* 7: 48–54.

Balaban, C. D., et al. 1999. Time course of burn to repeated applications to capsaicin. *Physiol. Behav.* 66: 109–112.

Baranyai, M., et al. 1982. Determination, by HPLC, of carotenoids in paprika products. *Acta Aliment.* 11: 309–323.

Ben-Chaim, A., and I. Paran. 2000. Genetic analysis of quantitative traits in pepper (*Capsicum annuum*). *J. Amer. Soc. Hort. Sci.* 125: 66–70.

Ben-Chaim, A., et al. 2006. QTL Analysis for capsaicinoid content in *Capsicum*. *Theor. Appl. Genet.* 113: 1481–1490.

Bevacqua, R. F., and D. M. VanLeeuwen. 2003. Planting date effects on stand establishment and yield of chile pepper. *HortScience* 38: 357–360.

Black, L. L., and L. H. Rolston. 1972. Aphids repelled and virus diseases reduced in peppers planted on aluminum foil mulch. *Phytopathology* 62: 747.

Bosland, P. W. 1992. Chiles: a diverse crop. *HortTechnology* 2: 6–10.

———. 1992. *Capsicum: A Comprehensive Bibliography*. Chile Inst., Las Cruces, New Mexico.

———. 1994. Chiles: history, cultivation, and uses. In *Spices, Herbs and Edible*

Fungi. Ed. G. Charalambous. Amsterdam: Elsevier. 347–366.

Bosland, P. W., and J. B. Baral. 2007. 'Bhut Jolokia': the world's hottest known chile pepper is a putative naturally occuring interspecific hybrid. *HortScience* 42: 222–224.

Bosland, P. W., et al. 1992. *Growing Chiles in New Mexico*. New Mexico State Univ. Coop. Extens. Serv. Guide H-230.

———. 1992. *Capsicum Pepper Varieties and Classification*. New Mexico State Univ. Coop. Extens. Serv. Circ. 530.

Boswell, V. R., et al. 1964. *Pepper Production*. Agric. Inform. Bull. U.S.D.A. No. 276.

Breithaupt, D. E., and W. Schwack. 2000. Determination of free and bound carotenoids in paprika (*Capsicum annuum* L.) by LC/MS. *Eur. Food Res. Technol.* 211: 52–55.

Brzozowski, T., et al. 1992. Studies on gastroprotection induced by capsaicin and papaverine. *J. Physiol. Pharmacol.* 43: 309–322.

Buttery, R. G., et al. 1969. Characterization of some volatile constituents of bell peppers. *J. Agric. Food Chem.* 17: 1322–1327.

Carobi, C. 1996. A quantitative investigation of the effects of neonatal capsaicin treatment on vagal afferent neurons in the rat. *Cell Tissue Res.* 283: 305–311.

Carter, A. K., and C. S. Vavrina. 2001. High temperature inhibits germination of Jalapeño and cayenne pepper. *HortScience* 36: 724–725.

Cisneros-Pineda, O., et al. 2007. Capsaicinoids quantification in chili peppers cultivated in the state of Yucatan, Mexico. *Food Chem.* 104: 1755–1760.

Cordell, G. A., and O. E. Araujo. 1993. Capsaicin: identification, nomenclature, and pharmacotherapy. *Ann. Pharmacotherapy* 27: 330–336.

Cowart, B. J. 1987. Oral chemical irritation: does it reduce perceived taste intensity? *Chem. Senses* 12: 467–479.

Cremer, D. R., and K. Eichner. 2000. Formation of volatile compounds during heating of spice paprika (*Capsicum annuum*) powder. *J. Agric. Food Chem.* 48: 2454–2460.

D'Alonzo, A. J., et al. 1995. In vitro effects of capsaicin: antiarrhythmic and anti-ischemic activity. *European J. Pharmacol.* 272: 269–278.

Daood, H. G., et al. 1996. Antioxidant vitamin content of spice red pepper (paprika) as affected by technological and varietal factors. *Food Chem.* 55: 365–372.

———. 2006. Antioxidant content of bio and conventional spice red pepper (*Capsicum annuum* L.) as determined by HPLC. *Acta Agron. Hung.* 54: 133–140.

D'Arcy, W. G., and W. H. Eshbaugh. 1974. New World peppers (*Capsicum-Solana-ceae*) north of Colombia: a résumé. *Baileya* 19: 93–105.

Dasgupta, P., and C. J. Fowler. 1997. Chillies: from antiquity to urology. *Brit. J. Urology* 80: 845–852.

Davis, C. B., et al. 2007. Determinaton of capsaicinoids in Habanero peppers by chemometric analysis of UV spectral data. *J. Agric. Food Chem.* 55L: 5925–5933.

De, A. K., ed. 2003. *Capsicum: The Genus* Capsicum. New York: Taylor & Francis.

Deli, J., et al. 2001. Separation and identification of carotenoids from different coloured paprika (*Capsicum annuum*) by reversed-phase high-performance liquid chromatography. *Eur. Food Res. Technol.* 213: 301–305.

DeWitt, D., and N. Gerlach. 1990. *The Whole Chile Pepper Book*. New York: Little, Brown and Co.

———. 1990. Chile peppers: growing fire in the garden. *Fine Gard.* 11: 54–57.

DeWitt, D., and P. W. Bosland. 1993. *The Pepper Garden*. Berkeley, California: Ten Speed Press.

———. 1996. *Peppers of the World: An Identification Guide*. Berkeley, California: Ten Speed Press.

Ellis, C. N., et al. 1993. A double-blind evaluation of topical capsaicin in pruritic psoriasis. *J. Amer. Acad. Dermatol.* 29: 438–442.

Eshbaugh, W. H. 1970. A biosystematic and evolutionary study of *Capsicum baccatum* (Solanaceae). *Brittonia* 22: 31–43.

———. 1980. The taxonomy of the genus *Capsicum* (Solanaceae)–1980. *Phytologia* 47: 153–166.

———. 1993. Peppers: history and exploitation of a serendipitous new crop discovery. In *New Crops*. Ed. J. Janick and J. E. Simon. New York: John Wiley & Sons. 132–139.

Eshbaugh, W. H., et al. 1983. The origin and evolution of domesticated *Capsicum* species. *J. Ethnobiol.* 3: 49–54.

Estrada, B., et al. 1998. Effects of mineral fertilizer supplementation on fruit development and pungency in 'Padrón' peppers. *J. Hort. Sci. Biotechnol.* 73: 493–497.

Fang, J.-Y., et al. 1997. Percutaneous absorption and skin erythema: quantification of capsaicin and its synthetic derivatives from gels incorporated with benzalkonium chloride by using non-invasive bioengineering methods. *Drug Dev. Res.* 40: 56–67.

Fujimoto, K., et al. 1980. Antioxidant activity and pungency of synthetic capsaicin homologues. *Yukagaku* 29: 419–422.

Fujiwake, H., et al. 1982. Capsaicinoid formation in the protoplast from the placenta of *Capsicum* fruits. *Agric. Biol. Chem.* 46: 2591–2592.

Fung, T., et al. 1983. The identification of capsaicinoids in tear-gas spray. *J. Forensic Sci.* 27: 812–821.

Galindo, H. S. G., et al. 1995. La capsaicina, el principio pungente del chile; su naturaleza, absorción, metabolismo y efectos farmacológicos. *Ciencia* 46: 84–102.

Gardner, C. S., and G. L. Queeley. 1999. Production guidelines for the Scotch Bonnet hot pepper. *Florida A&M Res. Ext. Bull.* Vol. 1, No. 1.

Glinsukopn, T., et al. 1980. Acute toxicity of capsaicin in several animal species. *Toxicon* 18: 215–220.

Gnayfeed, M. H., et al. 2001. Supercritical CO_2 and subcritical propane extraction of pungent paprika and quantification of carotenoids, tocophernols, and capsaicinoids. *J. Agric. Food Chem.* 49: 2761–2766.

Golcz, A., and P. Kujawski. 2004. Evaluation of the biological value of the fruit of several hot pepper (*Capsicum annuum* L.) cultivars. *Rocz. Akad. Roln. Pozn.* 38: 37–42.

Gómez, R., et al. 1998. Color differences in paprika pepper varieties (*Capsicum annuum* L.) cultivated in greenhouse and in the open air. *J. Sci. Food Agric.* 77: 268–272.

Greenleaf, W. H. 1975. The Tabasco story. *HortScience* 10: 98.

Guadayol, J. M., et al. 1997. Extraction, separation, and identification of volatile organic compounds from paprika oleoresin (Spanish type). *J. Agric. Food Chem.* 45: 1868–1872.

Hanson, B., and P. W. Bosland. 1999. *Chile Peppers: Hot Tips and Tasty Picks for Gardeners and Gourmets*. Brooklyn Bot. Gard.

Harness, J. 1982. *Growing Hot Peppers*. Alcorn State Univ. Coop. Extens. Serv. Publ. 851.

Haymon, L. W., and L. W. Aurand. 1971. Volatile constituents of Tabasco peppers. *J. Agric. Food Chem.* 19: 1131–1134.

Heiser, C. B. 1976. Peppers. *Capsicum* (Solanaceae). In *Evolution of Crop Plants*. Ed. N. W. Simmonds. New York: Longman. 265–268.

Heiser, C. B., and B. Pickersgill. 1969. Names for the cultivated *Capsicum* species (Solanaceae). *Taxon* 18: 277–283.

———. 1975. Names for the bird peppers (*Capsicum*–Solanaceae). *Baileya* 19: 151–156.

Henderson, D. E., and S. K. Henderson. 1992. Thermal decomposition of capsaicin. Part 1. Interactions with oleic acid at high temperatures. *J. Agric. Food Chem.* 40: 2263–2268.

Howard, L. R. 2001. Antioxidant vitamin and phytochemical content of fresh and processed pepper fruit (*Capsicum annuum*). In *Handbook of Nutraceutical and Functional Foods*. Ed. R. E. C. Wildman. Boca Raton, Florida: CRC Press. 209–233.

Howard, L. R., et al. 2000. Changes in phytochemical and antioxidant activity of selected pepper cultivars (*Capsicum* species) as influenced by maturity. *J. Agric. Food Chem.* 48: 1713–1720.

Hudgins, S. 1993. Red dust: powdered chiles and chili powders. In *Spicing Up the Palate: Studies of Flavour: Ancient and Modern.* Ed. H. Walker. Totnes, England: Prospect Books. 107–120.

Iorizzi, M., et al. 2000. Chemical components of *Capsicum annuum* L. var. *acuminatum* and their activity on stored product insect pests. In *Flavor and Fragrance Chemistry.* Ed. V. Lanzotti and O. Taglialatela-Scafati. Boston: Kluwer Acad. Publ. 77–85.

IPGRI, AVRDC and CATIE. 1995. *Descriptors for Capsicum (*Capsicum *spp.).* Rome: Intern. Pl. Gen. Res. Inst.

Iwai, K., et al. 1979. Formation and accumulation of pungent principle of hot pepper fruits, capsaicin and its analogues, in *Capsicum annuum* var. *annuum* cv. Karayatsubusa at different growth states after flowering. *Agric. Biol. Chem.* 43: 2493–2498.

Jang, H.-W., et al. 2008. Antioxidant activity and characterization of volatile extracts of *Capsicum annuum* L. and *Allium* spp. *Flavour Fragrance J.* 23: 178–184.

Jarret, R. E. 2007. Morphologic variation for fruit variation for fruit characteristics in the USDA/ARS *Capsicum baccatum* L. germplasm collection. *HortScience* 42: 1303–1305.

Jarret, R. E., et al. 2007. Diversity of fruit quality characteristics in *Capsicum frutescens. HortScience* 42: 16–19.

Jaworski, C. A., and R. E. Webb. 1971. Pepper performance after transplant clipping. *HortScience* 6: 480–482.

Jensen-Jarolim, L. A., et al. 1998. Allergens in pepper and paprika. *Allergy* 53: 36–41.

Jun, H.-R., and Y.-S. Kim. 2002. Comparison of volatile compounds in red pepper (*Capsicum annuum* L.) powders from different origins. *Food Sci. Biotechnol.* 11: 293–302.

Jun, H.-R., et al. 2005. Comparison of volatile components in fresh and dried red peppers (*Capsicum annuum* L.). *Food Sci. Biotechnol.* 14: 392–398.

Jurentisch, J. 1981. Scharfstoffzusammensetzung in Früchten definierter *Capsicum*-Sippen-Konsequenzen für Qualitätsforderungen und taxonomische Aspekte. *Sci. Pharm.* 49: 321–328.

Jurentisch, J., and R. Leinmüller. 1980. Quantifizierung von Nonylsäurevanillylamid und anderen Capsaicinoiden in Scharfstoffgemischen von *Capsicum*-Früchten und -Zubereitungen durch Gas-Flüssig-Chromatographie an Glaskapillarsäulen. *J. Chromatogr.* 189: 389–397.

Jurentisch, J., et al. 1979. Einfache Bestimmung des Gesamt- und Einzelcapsaicinoidgehaltes in *Capsicum*-Früchten mittels HPLC. *Pl. Med.* 36: 54–60.

———. 1979. Nachweis und Identifizierung neuer Scharfstoffe in *Capsicum*-Früchten. *Pl. Med.* 36: 61–67.

———. 1979. Identifizierung kultivierter *Capsicum*-Sippen. Taxonomie, Anatomie und Scharfstoffzusammensetzung. *Pl. Med.* 35: 174–183.

Kang, J.-H., et al. 2007. Capsaicin, a spice component of hot peppers, modulates adipokine gene expression and protein release from obese-mouse adipose tissues and isolated adipocytes, and suppresses the inflammatory responses of adipose tissue macrophages. *FEBS Lett.* 581: 4389–4396.

Kang, J. Y., et al. 1995. Chili: protective factors against peptic ulcer? *Dig. Dis. Sci.* 40: 576–579.

Kawada, T., et al. 1991. Intake of sweeteners and pungent ingredients increases the thermogenin content in brown adipose tissue of rats. *J. Agric. Food Chem.* 39: 651–654.

Kirschbaum-Titze, P., et al. 2002. Pungency in paprika (*Capsicum annuum*). 1. Decrease of capsaicinoid content following cellular disruption. *J. Agric. Food Chem.* 50: 1260–1263.

———. 2002. Pungency in paprika (*Capsicum annuum*). 2. Heterogeneity of capsaicinoid content in individual fruits from one plant. *J. Agric. Food Chem.* 50: 1264–1266.

Kocsis, N., et al. 2002. GC-MS Investigation of the aroma compounds of Hungarian red paprika (*Capsicum annuum*) cultivars. *J. Food Comp. Anal.* 15: 195–203.

Kogure, K., et al. 2002. Mechanism of potent antiperoxidative effect of capsaicin. *Biochem. Biophys. Acta* 1573: 84–92.

Konisho, K., et al. 2005. Inter- and intraspecific variation of capsaicinoid concentration in chili pepper (*Capsicum* spp.). *Hort. Res. Japan* 4: 153–158.

Kurtz, O. 1972. *The Paprika Manual.* Englewood Cliffs, New Jersey: Amer. Spice Trade Assoc.

Lawless, H., et al. 1985. Effects of oral capsaicin on gustatory, olfactory, and irritant sensations and flavour identification in humans who regularly or rarely consume chili pepper. *Chem. Senses* 10: 579–589.

Lee, S.-A., et al. 2007. Capsaicin promotes the development of burst-forming uniterythroid (BFU-E) from mouse bone marrow cells. *Exp. Mol. Med.* 39: 278–283.

Locock, R. A. 1985. Capsicum. *Canad. Pharm. J.* 118: 516–519.

Long, A. C., and D. M. Medeiros. 2001. Evaluation of capsaicin's use in analgesic medicine. *J. Nutraceuticals Functional Med. Foods* 3: 39–46.

López-Carrillo, L., et al. 1994. Chili pepper consumption and gastric cancer in Mexico: a case-control study. *Amer. J. Epidemiology* 139: 264–271.

———. 2003. Capsaicin consumption, *Helicobacter pylori* positivity and gastric cancer in Mexico. *Int. J. Cancer* 106: 277–282.

Lv, C.-s., et al. 2005. Light intensity affects pungency of hot pepper (*Capsicum annuum* L.) fruits. *J. Northeast Agric. Univ.* 12: 33–36.

Maillard, M.-N., et al. 1997. Analysis of eleven capsaicinoids by reversed-phase high performance liquid chromatography. *Flavour Fragrance J.* 12: 409–413.

Maoka, T., et al. 2001. Cancer chemoprevention activity of carotenoids in the fruits of red paprika *Capsicum annuum.* L. *Cancer Lett.* 172: 103–109.

———. 2001. Antioxidative activity of capsorubin and related compounds from paprika (*Capsicum annuum*). *J. Oleo Sci.* 50: 663–665.

———. 2004. Biological function and cancer prevention by paprika carotenoids. *Foods Food Ingred. J. Jap.* 209: 203–210.

Mateo, J., et al. 1997. Volatile compounds in Spanish paprika. *J. Food Comp. Anal.* 10: 225–232.

Matsufuji, H., et al. 1998. Antioxidant activity of capsanthin and the fatty acid esters in paprika (*Capsicum annuum*). *J. Agric. Food Chem.* 46: 3468–3472.

Mazida, M. M., et al. 2005. Analysis of volatile compounds of fresh chili (*Capsicum annuum*) during stages of maturity using solid phase microextraction (SPME). *J. Food Comp. Anal.* 18: 427–437.

Meek, A. J., and J. Gulledge. 1986. *Red-pepper Paradise.* New Orleans: Audubon Park Press.

Miller, M. 1991. *The Great Chile Book.* Berkeley, California: Ten Speed Press.

Minami, M., et al. 1998. Quantitative analysis of capsaicinoid in chili pepper (*Capsicum* sp.) by high performance liquid chromatography-operating condition, sampling and sample preparation. *J. Fac. Agric. Shinshu Univ.* 34: 97–102.

Mínguez-Mosquera, M. I., and D. Hornero-Méndez. 1997. Changes in provitamin A during paprika processing. *J. Food Practice* 60: 853–857.

Mínguez-Mosquera, M. I., and A. P. Gàlvez. 1998. Color quality in paprika oleoresins. *J. Agric. Food Chem.* 46: 5124–5127.

Mínguez-Mosquera, M. I., et al. 1994. Influence of the industrial drying processes of pepper fruits (*Capsicum annuum* Cv. *Bola*) for paprika on the carotenoid content. *J. Agric. Food Chem.* 42: 1190–1193.

Molina-Torres, J., et al. 1999. Antimicrobial properties of alkamides present in flavour plants traditionally used in Mesoamerica:

affinin and capsaicin. *J. Ethnopharmacol.* 64: 241–248.

Mósik, Gy., et al. 1997. *Capsaicin-sensitive Afferent Nerves in Gastric Mucosal Damage and Protection.* Budapest: Akad. Kiadó.

———. 2004. Capsaicin-sensitive afferent nerves and gastric mucosal protection in the human healthy subjects: a critical overview. In *Mediators in Gastrointestinal Protection and Repair.* Ed. K. Takeushi and Gy. Mósik. Kerala, India: Res. Signpost. 43–62.

———. 2005. Gastroprotection induced by capsaicin in healthy human subjects. *World J. Gastroenterol.* 11: 5180–5184.

———. 2005. Participation of vanilloid/capsaicin receptors, calcitonin-gene-related peptide and substance P in gastric protection of omeprazole and omeprazole-like compounds. *Inflammopharmacology* 13: 139–159.

Naj, A. 1992. *Peppers: A Story of Hot Pursuits.* New York: Alfred A. Knopf.

Noble, D. 1992. Cultivating peppers. *Green Scene* 21(1): 11–14.

Odoemena, C. S., et al. 1998. Antibacterial activity of the essential oils from four selected varieties of *Capsicum annuum. Nig. J. Nat. Prod. Med.* 2: 49–50.

Pabst, M. A., et al. 1993. Ablation of capsaicin sensitive afferent nerves impairs defense but not rapid repair of rat gastric mucosa. *Gut* 34: 897–903.

Palevitch, D., and L. E. Craker. 1993. Nutritional and medical importance of red peppers. *Herb Spice Med. Pl. Dig.* 11(3): 1–4.

Park, H., and K-P. Park. 1993. Capsaicin induces acute spinal analgesia and changes in the spinal norepinephrine level. *Kor. J. Pharmacol.* 29: 3–41.

Park, K.-K., et al. 1998. Lack of tumor promoting activity of capsaicin, a principal pungent ingredient of red pepper, in mouse skin carcinogenesis. *Anticancer Res.* 18: 4201–4206.

Parrish, M. 1996. Liquid chromatographic method for determining capsaicinoids in capsicums and their extractives: collaborative study. *J. AOAC Intern.* 79: 738–745.

Pérez-Grajales, M., et al. 2004. Physiolgoical characterization of manzano hot pepper (*Capsicum pubescens* R & P) landraces. *J. Amer. Soc. Hort. Sci.* 129: 88–92.

Perfumi, M., and M. Massi. 1996. Effect of capsaicin pretreatment in neonatal or adult rats on glucose load-induced hyperglycaemia. *Phytotherapy Res.* 10: S22–S24.

Perucka, I., and M. Materska. 2003. Antioxidant activity and content of capsaicinoids isolated from paprika fruits. *Pol. J. Food Nutr. Sci.* 12: 15–18.

Peusch, M., et al. 1997. Extraction of capsaicinoids from chillies (*Capsicum frutescens* L.) and paprika (*Capsicum annuum* L.) using supercritical fluids and organic solvents. *Z. Lebensm. Unters. Forsch.* A 204: 351–355.

Pino, J., et al. 2007. Characterization of total capsaicinoids, colour and volatile compounds of Habanero chilli pepper (*Capsicum chinense* Jack.) cultivars grown in Yucatan. *Food Chem.* 104: 1682–1686.

Porter, W. C., and W. W. Etzel. 1982. Effects of aluminum-painted and black polyethylene mulches on bell pepper, *Capsicum annuum* L. *HortScience* 17: 942–943.

Poyrazoğlu, E. S., et al. 2005. Determination of capsaicinoid profile of different chilli peppers grown in Turkey. *J. Sci. Food Agric.* 85: 1435–1438.

Proulx, E. A. 1985. Some like them hot. *Horticulture* 63(1): 46–54.

Purseglove, J. W., et al. 1981. *Spices.* 2 vols. London: Longman.

Quinones-Seglic, C. R., et al. 1989. Capsaicinoids and pungency in various capsicums. *Lebensm. Wiss. Technol.* 22: 196–198.

Reilly, C. A., et al. 2001. Quantitative analysis of capsaicinoids in fresh peppers, oleoresin capsicum and pepper spray products. *J. Forensic Sci.* 46: 502–509.

Rowland, B. J., et al. 1983. Capsaicin production in sweet bell and pungent jalapeno peppers. *J. Agric. Food Chem.* 31: 484–487.

Russo, V. M. 2003. Planting date and plant density affect yield of pungent and nonpungent jalapeño peppers. *HortScience* 38: 520–523.

Saga, K., and G. Sato. 2003. Varietal differences in phenolic, flavonoid and capsaicinoid contents in pepper fruits (*Capsicum annuum* L.). *J. Jap. Soc. Hort. Sci.* 72: 335–341.

Saimbhi, M. S., et al. 1977. Chemical constituents in mature green and red fruits of some varieties of chili (*Capsicum annuum* L.). *Qual. Pl.* 27: 171–175.

Saito, A., and M. Yamamoto. 1996. Acute oral toxicity of capsaicin in mice and rats. *J. Toxicol. Sci.* 21: 195–200.

Seller, H., et al. 1997. Activation of chemosensitive neurons in the ventrolateral medulla by capsaicin in rats. *NeuroSci. Lett.* 226: 195–198.

Serra, C. I., et al. 1996. Cáncer vesicular: estudio de casos y controles en Chile. *Rev. Chilena Cirugía* 48: 139–147.

Shannon, E. 1989. *Chile Disease Control.* New Mexico State Univ. Coop. Extens. Serv. Guide H-219.

Smith, P. G., and C. B. Heiser. 1951. Taxonomic and genetic studies on the cultivated peppers, *Capsicum annuum* L. and *C. frutescens* L. *Amer. J. Bot.* 38: 362–368.

———. 1957. Taxonomy of *Capsicum sinense* Jacq. and the geographic distribution of the cultivated *Capsicum* species. *Bull. Torrey Bot. Club* 84: 413–420.

———. 1957. Breeding behavior of cultivated pepper. *Proc. Amer. Soc. Hort. Sci.* 70: 286–290.

Smith, P. G., et al. 1987. Horticultural classification of peppers grown in the United States. *HortScience* 22: 11–13.

Sundstrom, F. J., et al. 1987. Effect of seed treatment and planting method on Tabasco pepper. *J. Amer. Soc. Hort. Sci.* 112: 641–644.

Surh, Y.-J. 1997. Effects of capsaicin, a major pungent principle in hot red pepper, on chemically induced carcinogensis and mutagenesis. In *Food Factors in Cancer Protection.* Ed. H. Ohigashi et al. Tokyo: Springer-Verlag. 257–261.

———. 1998. Cancer chemoprevention by dietary phytochemicals: a mechanistic viewpoint. *Cancer J.* 11: 6–10.

Surh, Y.-J., and S. S. Lee. 1995. Capsaicin, a double-edged sword: toxicity, metabolism, and chemopreventive potential. *Life Sci.* 56: 1845–1855.

———. 1996. Capsaicin in hot chili pepper: carcinogen, co-carcinogen or anticarcinogen? *Food Chem. Toxic.* 34: 313–316.

Surh, Y.-J., and K.-K. Park. 1997. Carcinogenic vs. anticarcinogenic properties of capsaicin in hot red pepper: an overview. *J. Korean Assoc. Cancer Prot.* 1: 55–61.

Surh, Y.-J., et al. 1995. Chemoprotective effects of capsaicin and diallyl sulfide against mutagenesis or tumorigenesis by vinyl carbamate and N-nitrosodimethylamine. *Carcinogenesis* 16: 2467–2471.

———. 1998. Chemoprotective properties of some pungent ingredients present in red pepper and ginger. *Mutation Res.* 402: 259–267.

Suzuki, T., and K. Iwai. 1984. Constituents of red pepper species: chemistry, biochemistry, pharmacology, and food science of the pungent principle of *Capsicum* species. *Alkaloids* 23: 227–299.

Swezey, L. B. 1998. Homegrown paprika beats the bottled spice. *Sunset* March: 74.

Tandan, R., et al. 1992. Topical capsaicin in painful diabetic neuropathy. *Diabetes Care* 15: 8–14.

Tanksley, S. D. 1984. High rates of cross-pollination in chile pepper. *HortScience* 19: 580–582.

Terpó, A. 1966. Kritische Revision der wildwachsenden Arten und der kultivierten Sorten der Gattung *Capsicum* L. *Feddes Repert.* 72: 155–191.

Todd, P. H., et al. 1977. Determination of pungency due to capsicum by gas-liquid chromatography. *J. Food Sci.* 42: 660–665, 680.

Van Rijswijk, J. B., and R. G. van Wijk. 2006. Capsaicin treatment of idiopathic rhinitis: the new panacea? *Curr. Allergy Asthma Rep.* 6: 132–137.

Vesper, H., and S. Nitz. 1997. Isolation and characterization of carotenoids in paprika (*Capsicum annuum* L.). *Adv. Food Sci.* 19: 124–130.

———. 1997. Composition of extracts from paprika (*Capsicum annuum* L.) obtained by conventional and supercritical fluid extraction. *Adv. Food Sci.* 19: 172–177.

Viñas, P., et al. 1992. Liquid chromatographic determination of fat-soluble vitamins in paprika and paprika oleoresin. *Food Chem.* 45: 349–355.

Wall, M. M., et al. 2001. Variation in β-carotene and total carotenoid content in fruits of *Capsicum*. *HortScience* 36: 746–749.

Watanabe, T., et al. 1987. Capsaicin, a pungent principle of hot red pepper, evokes catecholamine secretion from the adrenal medulla of anesthetized rats. *Biochem. Biophys. Res. Commun.* 142: 259–264.

———. 1988. Effect of capsaicin pretreatment on capsaicin-induced catecholamine secretion from the adrenal medulla in rats. *Proc. Soc. Exp. Biol.* 187: 370–374.

———. 1989. Effects of capsaicin pretreatment on 2-deoxy-D-glucose- and acetylcholine-induced catecholamine secretion from the adrenal medulla. *Agric. Biol. Chem.* 53: 3397–3309.

Wood, A. B. 1987. Determination of the pungent principles of chilies and ginger by reversed-phase high-performance liquid chromatography with use of a single standard substance. *Flavour Fragrance J.* 2: 1–12.

Woodbury, J. E. 1980. Determination of capsicum pungency by high-pressure liquid chromatography and spectrofluorometric detection. *J. Assoc. Off. Anal. Chem.* 63: 556–558.

Wu, C. M., and S.-E. Liou. 1986. Effect of tissue disruption on volatile constituents of bell peppers. *J. Agric. Food Chem.* 34: 770–772.

Yajima, M., et al. 2000. Isolation and structure of antimicrobial substances from paprika seeds. *Food Sci. Technol.* 6: 99–101.

Yao, J., et al. 1994. Supercritical carbon dioxide extraction of Scotch bonnet (*Capsicum annuum*) and quantification of capsaicin and dihydrocapsaicin. *J. Agric. Food Chem.* 42: 1303–1305.

Yeoh, K. G., et al. 1995. Chili protects against aspirin-induced gastroduodenal mucosal injury in humans. *Dig. Dis. Sci.* 40: 580–583.

Zewdie, Y., and P. W. Bosland. 2000. Pungency of chile (*Capsicum annuum* L.) fruit is affected by node position. *HortScience* 35: 1174.

———. 2001. Capsaicinoid profiles are not good chemotaxonomic indicators for *Capsicum* species. *Biochem. Syst. Ecol.* 29: 161–169.

Zhang, Z., et al. 1997. Effects of orally administered capsaicin, the principal component of capsicum fruits, on the in vitro metabolism of the tobacco-specific nitrosamine NNK in hamster lung and liver microsomes. *Anticancer Res.* 17: 1093–1098.

Carthamus

Anonymous. 2004. Safflower. *Rev. Nat. Prod. (Wolters Kluwer Health).*

Claassen, C. E. 1949. Safflower, a potential oilseed crop in the western states. *Econ. Bot.* 3: 143–149.

Dajue, L., and H.-H. Mündel. 1996. *Safflower:* Carthamus tinctorius *L.* Rome: Intern. Pl. Gen. Res. Inst.

Gacsó, L., and D. Földesi. 1979. Chemical weed control experiments in false saffron (*Carthamus tinctorius* L.). *Herba Hung.* 18: 75–80.

Hanelt, P. 1963. Monographische Übersicht der Gattung *Carthamus* L. (Compositae). *Feddes Repert.* 67: 41–180.

———. 1976. *Carthamus.* In *Flora Europaea Vol. 4.* Ed. T. G. Tutin et al. Cambridge Univ. Press. 302–303.

Hang, A. N., et al. 1982. *Safflower in Central Washington.* Wash. State Univ. Coop. Ext. Bull. 1065.

Kasahara, Y., et al. 1994. Carthami flos extract and its component, stigmasterol, inhibit tumour promotion in mouse skin two-stage carcinogenesis. *Phytotherapy Res.* 8: 327–331.

Knowles, P. F. 1955. Safflower: production, processing and utilization. *Econ. Bot.* 9: 273–299.

———. 1969. Centers of plant diversity and conservation of crop germplasm: safflower. *Econ. Bot.* 23: 324–329.

———. 1977. Safflower germplasm: domesticated and wild. *Calif. Agric.* 31 (P9): 12–13.

McCorriston, J. 1998. Syrian origins of safflower production: new discoveries in the agrarian prehistory of the Habur Basin. In *The Origins of Agriculture and Crop Domestication.* Ed. A. B. Damania et al. Rome: ICARDA, IPGRI, FAO, UC and GRCP. 39–48.

Okuno, T., and K. Kazuma. 2000. Flavonoid constituents in the petals of *Carthamus tinctorius*: structures of quinochalcones and flavonols, and their biosynthetic pathway. *FFI J.* 189: 5–13.

Patra, G. J. 1976. Adaptability of strains of safflower from different sources. *Indian J. Genet. Pl. Breed.* 36: 332–336.

Smith, H. A. 1989. *Safflower: A Montana Specialty Crop.* Montana State Univ. Extens. Serv. MT 8916.

United States Department of Agriculture. 1966. *Growing Safflower: An Oilseed Crop.* U.S.D.A. Farmers Bull. No. 2133.

Carum

Aghro, M., et al. 2001. Low-resolution gasphase FT-IR method for the determination of the limonene/carvone ratio in supercritical CO_2-extracted caraway fruits. *J. Agric. Food Chem.* 49: 3140–3144.

Alhaider, A. A., et al. 2006. Effect of *Carum carvi* on experimentally induced gastric mucosal damage in Wistar albino rats. *Intern. J. Pharmacol.* 2: 309–315.

Analytical Methods Committee. 1988. Application of gas-liquid chromatography to the analysis of essential oils. Part 14. Monographs for five essential oils. *Analyst* 113: 1125–1136.

Anonymous. 1970. Caraway. *Flavor Industr.* 1: 524–526.

Argañosa, G. C., et al. 1998. Seed yields and essential oils of annual and bienniel caraway (*Carum carvi* L.) grown in western Canada. *J. Herbs Spices Med. Pl.* 6(1): 9–17.

Bouwmeester, H. J., and A.-M. Kuijpers. 1993. Relationship between assimilate supply and essential oil accumulation in annual and biennial caraway (*Carum carvi* L.). *J. Essential Oil Res.* 5: 143–152.

Bouwmeester, H. J., and H. G. Smid. 1995. Seed yield in caraway (*Carum carvi*). 1. Role of pollination. *J. Agric. Sci.* 124: 235–244.

Bouwmeester, H. J., et al. 1995. Seed yield in caraway (*Carum carvi*). 2. Role of assimilate availability. *J. Agric. Sci.* 124: 245–251.

———. 1995. Physiological limitations to carvone yield in caraway (*Carum carvi* L.). *Industr. Crops Prod.* 4: 39–51.

Chemat, S., et al. 2004. Comparison of conventional and ultrasound-assisted extraction of carvone and limonene from caraway seeds. *Flavour Fragrance J.* 19: 188–195.

Chou, J. S.-T. 1974. Analytical results on the volatile components of cardamom oil, caraway oil, and coriander oil by gas chromatography, IR-spectroscopy and etc. *Koryo* 106: 55–60.

Chowdhury, A. R. 2002. GC-MS studies on essential oil from *Carum carvi* L. raised in Kumaon. *J. Essential Oil-Baring Pl.* 5: 158–161.

Davis, J. M. 1997. *Caraway.* North Carolina State Univ. Leafl. No. 128.

Duke, J. A., and C. F. Reed. 1978. Caraway: an economic plant. *Quart. J. Crude Drug Res.* 16: 116–118.

Embong, M. B., et al. 1977. Essential oils from spices grown in Alberta. Caraway oil (*Carum carvi*). *Canad. J. Pl. Sci.* 57: 543–549.

Fehr, D. 1980. Untersuchungen zur Lagerstabilität von Anis, Fenchel und Kümmel. *Pharm. Zeitung* 125: 1300–1303.

Fleisher, A., and Z. Fleisher. 1988. The essential oil of annual *Carum carvi* L. grown in Israel. In *Flavor and Fragrances: A World*

Perspective. Ed. B. M. Lawrence et al. Amsterdam: Elsevier. 33–40.

Forster, H. B., et al. 1980. Antispasmodic effects of some medicinal plants. *Pl. Med.* 40: 309–319.

Gabler, J., and F. Ehrig. 2000. *Phomopsis diachenii* Sac., ein aggressiver Krankheitserreger an Kümmel (*Carum cavi* L.) – Erstnachweis für Deutschland. *Z. Arzn. Gew. Pfl.* 2000: 36–39.

Galambosi, B., and P. Peura. 1996. Agrobotanical features and oil content of wild and cultivated forms of caraway (*Carum carvi* L.). *J. Essential Oil Res.* 8: 389–397.

Hälvä, S., et al. 1986. Yield and glucosinolate of mustard seeds and volatile oils of caraway seeds and coriander fruit. II. Yield and volatile oils of caraway seeds (*Carum carvi* L.). *J. Agric. Sci. Finland* 58: 163–167.

Hirvi, T., et al. 1987. Yield and volatile oils of caraway seeds (*Carum carvi* L.). In *Flavor Science and Technology.* Ed. M. Martens et al. New York: John Wiley & Sons. 73–78.

Ibrahim, S. M., et al. 2006. Effect of organic manures and chemical fertilizers on *Foeniculum vulgare* Mill and *Carum carvi*, L. *Bull. Pharm. Sci. Assiut Univ.* 29: 187–201.

Karim, A., et al. 1977. Studies on the essential oils of the Pakistani species of the family Umbelliferae. Part 8. *Carum carvi* Linn. (caraway, kala zira) oil of the mature and the immature seeds and the whole immature plant. *Pakistan J. Sci. Industr. Res.* 20: 100–102.

Maghami, P. 1984. Carvi blond (*Carum carvi* L.). *Acta Hort.* 144: 21–24.

McVicar, R., et al. 2000. *Caraway in Saskatchewan.* Saskatchewan Agric. Food.

Németh, É. 1998. *Caraway: The Genus* Carum. Amsterdam: Harwood Acad. Publ.

Németh, É., et al. 1997. Factors influencing flower initiation in caraway (*Carum carvi* L.). *J. Herbs Spices Med. Pl.* 5(3): 41–50.

Pank, F. 2000. Heil- und Gewürzpflanzen aus der Sicht des Pflanzenzüchters. 3. Mitteilung: Kümmel (*Carum carvi* L.). *Beitr. Züchtungsforsch.* 6 (2): 31–45

Putievsky, E. 1978. Yield components of annual *Carum carvi* L. growing in Israel. *Acta Hort.* 73: 283–287.

———. 1980. Germination studies with seed of caraway, coriander and dill. *Seed Sci. Technol.* 8: 245–254.

Ravid, U., et al. 1992. Chiral GC analysis of (*S*)(+)- and (*R*)(-)-carvone with high enantiomeric purity in caraway, dill, and spearmint oils. *Flavour Fragrance J.* 7: 289–292.

Sanchez, J. H. 1992. Seeds for the kitchen. *Horticulture* 70(8): 54–60.

Sedláková, J., et al. 2001. Determination of essential oils content and composition in caraway (*Carum carvi* L.). *Czech. J. Food Sci.* 19: 31–36.

Shwaireb, M. H. 1993. Caraway oil inhibits skin tumors in female BALB/c mice. *Nutr. Cancer* 19: 321–325.

Sijtsma, R., et al. 1975. Chemische onkruidbestrijding in karwij. *Meded. Fak. Landbouwwetensch. Gent.* 40: 961–973.

Syed, M., et al. 1987. Antimicrobial activity of the essential oils of the Umbelliferae family. Part 5. *Carum carvi, Petroselinum cripsum*, and *Dorema ammoniacum* oils. *Pakistan J. Sci. Industr. Res.* 30: 106–110.

Tutin, T. G. 1968. *Carum.* In *Flora Europaea Vol. 2.* Ed. T. G. Tutin et al. Cambridge Univ. Press. 354.

Wichtmann, E.-M., and E. Stahl-Biskup. 1987. Composition of the essential oils from caraway herb and root. *Flavour Fragrance J.* 2: 83–89.

Cedronella

Bramwell, D. 1972. *Cedronella.* In *Flora Europaea Vol. 3.* Ed. T. G. Tutin et al. Cambridge Univ. Press. 157.

Carreiras, M. C., et al. 1987. A dimer of *d*-pinocarvone from *Cedronella canariensis. Phytochemistry* 26: 3351–3353.

Engel, R., et al. 1995. Composition of the essential oils of *Cedronella canariensis* (L.) Webb et Berth. ssp. *canariensis* and ssp. *anisata* f. *glabra* and f. *pubescens. J. Essential Oil Res.* 7: 473–487.

López-García, R. E., et al. 1992. Essential oils and antimicrobial activity of two varieties of *Cedronella canariensis* (L.) W. et B. *J. Ethnopharmacol.* 36: 207–211.

Pérez de Paz, P. L., et al. 1996. Variación morfológica y aceites esenciales de *Cedronella canariensis* (L.) Webb & Berthel. (Labiatae). *Anales Jard. Bot. Madrid* 54: 303–307.

Chamaemelum

Antonelli, A., and C. Fabbri. 1998. Study on Roman chamomile (*Chamaemelum nobile* L. All.) oil. *J. Essential Oil Res.* 10: 571–574.

Berry, M. 1995. The chamomiles. *Pharm. J.* 254: 191–193.

Bouverat-Bernier, J. P., and P. Gicquiaud. 1989. Incidence des densites de plantation de la camomile romaine sur la teneur en essence des somites fleuries recoltées pour la distillation. *Herb Gallica* 1: 67–71.

———. 1989. Incidence de camomile romaine, destines a l'herboristerie, sur la teneur en essence des sommites fleuries, recoltées ulterieurement pour la production d'huile essentielle. *Herba Gallica* 1: 73–81.

Brunke, E.-J., et al. 1993. Flower scent of some traditional medicinal plants. In *Bioactive Compounds from Plants.* Ed. R. Teranishi et al. Washington, D.C.: Amer. Chem. Soc. 282–296.

Carnat, A., et al. 2004. The aromatic and polyphenolic composition of Roman chamomile tea. *Fitoterapia* 75: 32–38.

Chialva, F., et al. 1982. Qualitative evaluation of aromatic herbs by direct head space (GC)2 analysis. Applications of the method and comparison with the traditional analysis of essential oils. In *Aromatic Plants: Basic and Applied Aspects.* Ed. N. Margaris et al. The Hague: Martinus Nijhoff. 183–195.

Farkas, P., et al. 2003. Composition of the essential oil from the flowerheads of *Chamaemelum nobile* (L.) All. (Asteraceae) cultivated in Slovak Republic. *J. Essential Oil Res.* 15: 83–85.

Fauconnier, M.-L., et al. 1996. II *Anthemis nobilis* L. (Roman chamomile): in vitro culture, micropropagation, and the production of essential oils. *Biotechnol. Agric. For.* 37: 16–37.

Foster, S. 1990. *Chamomile:* Matricaria recutita & Chamaemelum nobile. Austin, Texas: Amer. Bot. Council.

Franke, R., and H. Schilcher, eds. 2005. *Chamomile Industrial Profiles.* Boca Raton, Florida: Taylor & Francis.

Héthelyi, É., et al. 1999. Római kamilla (*Anthemis nobilis* L.) illóolajának GC-, GC/MS vizsgálata. *Olaj Szappan Kosmetika* 48: 116–123.

Jolivet, J. 1977. Importance de la nutrition minérale sur le rendement de la production de chamomille romain (*Anthemis nobilis* L.) en capitules et en huile essentielle. *Pl. Med. Phytotherap.* 11: 119–123.

Kirsch, K. 1990. Chamomile cultivation in Argentina. *Dragoco Rep.* 1990(2): 67–75.

Lewis, W. H. 1992. Allergenic potential of commercial chamomile, *Chamaemelum nobile* (Asteraceae). *Econ. Bot.* 46: 426–430.

Mann, C., and E. J. Staba. 1986. The chemistry, pharmacology, and commercial formulations of chamomile. In *Herbs, Spices, and Medicinal Plants: Recent Advances in Botany, Horticulture, and Pharmacology Vol. 1.* Ed. L. E. Craker and J. E. Simon. Phoenix, Arizona: Oryx Press. 235–280.

Oberprieler, C. 2002. A phylogenetic analysis of *Chamaemelum* Mill. (Compositae: Anthemideae) and related genera based upon nrDNA ITS and cpDNA *trn*L/*trn*F IGS sequence variation. *Bot. J. Linn. Soc.* 138: 255–273.

Omidbaigi, R., et al. 2004. Influence of drying methods on the essential oil content and composition of Roman chamomile. *Flavour Fragrance J.* 19: 196–198.

Povilaityte, V., et al. 2002. Aroma and antioxidant properties of Roman chamomile (*Anthemis nobilis* L.). In *Food Flavor and Chemistry: Advances of the New Millennium.* Ed. A. Spanier et al. London: Roy. Soc. Chem. 567–577.

Shaath, N. A., et al. 1990. The analysis of chamomile Roman. In *Proceedings of the 11th International Congress of Essential Oils, Fragrances and Flavour, New Delhi, India, 12–16 November 1989 Vol. 4*. Ed. S. C. Bhattacharyya et al. London: Aspect Publ. 207–213.

Tutin, T. G. 1976. *Chamaemelum*. In *Flora Europaea Vol. 4*. Ed. T. G. Tutin et al. Cambridge Univ. Press. 165.

Chrysopogon

Adams, R. P., and M. R. Dafforn. 1997. *DNA Fingerprints (RAPDs) of the Pantropical Grass Vetiver, Vetiveria zizanioides (L.) Nash (Gramineae), Reveal a Single Clone 'Sunshine' Is Widely Utilized in Erosion Control*. Leesburg, Virginia: Vetiver Network.

———. 1997–98. Lesson diversity: DNA sampling of the pantropical vetiver grass uncovers genetic uniformity in erosion-control germplasm. *Diversity* 13: 27–28.

———. 1999. DNA fingerprints of the pantropical grass vetiver, *Vetiveria zizanioides*. *AU J. Technol*. 2: 173–180.

Adams, R. P., and M. Zhong. 1998. DNA genetic diversity of *Vetiveria zizanioides* (Poaceae). *Phytologia* 85: 85–95.

Adams, R. P., et al. 1998. DNA fingerprinting reveals clonal nature of *Vetiveria zizanioides* (L.) Nash, Gramineae and sources of potential germplasm. *Mol. Ecol*. 7: 813–818.

———. 2003. Vetiver DNA-fingerprinted cultivars: effects of environment on growth, oil yields and composition. *J. Essential Oil Res*. 15: 363–371.

———. 2004. Preliminary comparison of vetiver root essential oils from cleansed (bacteria- and fungus-free) versus non-cleansed (normal) vetiver plants. *Biochem. Syst. Ecol*. 32: 1137–1144.

Akhila, A., et al. 1981. Vetiver oil: a review of chemistry. *Curr. Res. Med. Aromatic Pl.* 3: 195–211.

Anonis, D. P. 2005. Woody notes in perfumery. Vetiver, derivatives and aroma chemicals. Part 2. *Perfumer Flavor*. 30(6): 46–51.

Bhatwadekar, S. V., et al. 1982. A survey of sesquiterpenoids of vetiver oil. In *Cultivation and Utilization of Aromatic Plants*. Ed. C. K. Atal and B. Kapur. Jammu Tawi, India: Regional Res. Lab. 412–426.

Champagnat, P., et al. 2006. A study on the composition of commercial *Vetiveria zizanioides* oils from different geographical origins. *J. Essential Oil Res*. 18: 416–422.

Chauhan, K. R., and A. K. Raina. 2005. Modified vetiver oil: economic biopesticide. In *Natural Products for Pest Management*. Ed. A. M. Rinando and S. O. Duke. Washington, D.C.: Amer. Chem. Soc. 210–219.

Clary, R. A., et al. 2005. Nitrogen compounds from Haitian vetiver oil. *J. Essential Oil Res*. 17: 591–592.

Garnero, J. 1972. Mise au point sur la composition des essences de Vétyver. *Rivista Ital. EPPOS* 54: 315–336.

Gupta, R. S., et al. 1983. Vetiver hybrid clones. *Perfumer Flavor*. 8(3): 41–43.

Jain, S. C., et al. 1982. Insect repellents from vetiver oil: I. Zizanal and epizizanal. *Tetrahedron Lett*. 23: 4639–4642.

Karkhanis, D. W., et al. 1978. Minor sesquiterpene alcohols of North Indian vetiver oil: isolation and structure of isoalencenol, vetiselinol and isovetiselinenol. *Indian J. Chem*. 16B: 260–263.

Kim, H.-J., et al. 2005. Evaluation of antioxidant activity of vetiver (*Vetiveria zizanioides* L.) oil and identification of its antioxidant constituents. *J. Agric. Food Chem*. 53: 7691–7695.

Klemme, D. 1986. Vetiver. *H&R Contact* 40: 16–17.

Konrad, V. 1986. How Indian vetiver oil is produced. *H&R Contact* 40: 18–19.

Kresovich, S., et al. 1994. Application of molecular methods and statistical analyses for discrimination of accessions and clones of vetiver grass. *Crop Sci*. 34: 805–809.

Lal, R. K., et al. 1997. Genetic diversity in germplasm of vetiver grass, *Vetiveria zizanioides* (L.) Nash ex Small. *J. Herbs Spices Med. Pl*. 5(1): 7–84.

Lemberg, S., and R. B. Hale. 1979. Vetiver oils of different geographical origins. In *VII International Congress of Essential Oils, October 7–11, 1977, Kyoto, Japan*. 402–413.

Maffei, M., ed. 2002. *Vetiveria: The Genus Vetiveria*. London: Taylor & Francis.

Martinez, J., et al. 2004. Valorization of Brazilian vetiver (*Vetiveria zizanioides* (L.) Nash ex Small) oil. *J. Agric. Food Chem*. 52: 6578–6584.

Morris, E. T. 1983. Vetiver: gift of India. *Dragoco Rep*. 1983: 130–137.

National Research Council. 1993. *Vetiver Grass: A Thin Green Line Against Erosion*. Washington, D.C.: Natl. Acad. Press.

Peyron, L. 1995. Le vétyver et sa culture dans le monde. *Rivista Ital. EPPOS* 1995(17): 3–17.

Smadja, J., et al. 1988. Essais d'identification des constituants de l'huile essentielle de vétyver bourbon. *Parfums, Cosmétiques, Arômes* 84: 61–66.

Sobti, S. N., and B. L. Rao. 1977. Cultivation and scope of improvement in vetiver. In *Cultivation and Utilization of Medicinal and Aromatic Plants*. Ed. C. K. Atal and B. M. Kapur. Jammu Tawi, India: Regional Res. Lab. 319–323.

Veldkamp, J. F. 1999. A revision of *Chrysopogon* Trin. including *Vetiveria* Bory (Poaceae) in Thailand and Malesia with notes

on some other species from Africa and Australia. *Austrobaileya* 5: 503–530.

Weyerstahl, P., et al. 1996. New sesquiterpene ethers from vetiver oil. *Liebigs Ann.* 1996: 1195–1199.

———. 2000. Analysis of the polar fraction of Haitian vetiver oil. *Flavour Fragrance J.* 15: 153–173.

———. 2000. Constituents of Haitian vetiver oil. *Flavour Fragrance J.* 15: 395–412.

Zhu, B. C. R., et al. 2001. Evaluation of vetiver oil and seven insect-active essential oils against the Formosan subterranean termite. *J. Chem. Ecol.* 27: 1617–1625.

Citrus

Davidson, A. 1998. Kaffir lime. *Petis Propos Culinaires* 60: 62–63.

Hongratanworakit, T., and G. Buchbauer. 2007. Chemical composition and stimulating effect of *Citrus hystrix* oil on humans. *Flavour Fragrance J.* 22: 443–449.

Karp, D. 2004. Caffre-lime. *Petis Propos Culinaires* 77: 144–145.

Karp, D., and C. de Silva. 1998. Infidel lime. *Petis Propos Culinaires* 58: 59–60.

Khuwijitjaru, P., et al. 2008. Phenolic content and radical scavenging capacity of kaffir-lime fruit peel extracts obtained by pressurized hot water extraction. *Food Sci. Technol. Res.* 14: 1–4.

Lawrence, B. M., et al. 1971. Constituents of the leaf and peel oils of *Citrus hystrix* DC. *Phytochemistry* 10: 1404–1405.

Murakami, A., et al. 1995. Glyceroglycolipids from *Citrus hystrix*, a traditional herb in Thailand, potently inhibit the tumor-promoting activity of 12-O-tetradecanoylphorbol 13-acetate in mouse skin. *J. Agric. Food Chem.* 43: 2779–2783.

———. 1999. Identification of coumarins from the fruit of *Citrus hystrix* DC. as inhibitors of nitric oxide generation in mouse macrophage RAW 264.7 cells. *J. Agric. Food Chem.* 47: 333–339.

Owen, S. 1998. On 'infidel lime.' *Petis Propos Culinaires* 59: 62–63.

Piyachaturawat, P., et al. 1985. Antifertility effect of *Citrus hystrix* DC. *J. Ethno-Pharmacol.* 13: 105–110.

Sato, A., et al. 1990. The chemical composition of *Citrus hystrix* DC. (Swangi). *J. Essential Oil Res.* 2: 179–183.

Wijaya, C. H. 1995. Oriental natural flavour: liquid or spray-dried flavour of "jeruk purut" (*Citrus hystrix* DC.) leaves. In *Food Flavor, Generation, Analysis and Process Influence*. Ed. G. Charalambous. Amsterdam: Elsevier. 235–248.

Coriandrum

Al-Mofleh, I. A., et al. 2006. Protection of gastric muscosal damage by *Coriandrum sativum* L. pretreatment in Wistar albino rats. *Environm. Toxicol. Pharmacol.* 22: 64–69.

Baratta, M. T., et al. 1998. Chemical composition, antimicrobial and antioxidative activity of laurel, sage, rosemary, oregano and coriander essential oils. *J. Essential Oil Res.* 10: 618–627.

Benyoussef, E.-H., et al. 2001. Modelisation du transfert de matiere lors de l'extraction de l'huile essentielle des fruits de coriander. *Chem. Eng. J.* 3820: 1–5.

Biertümpfel, A., et al. 2006. Höhere und sichere Kornerträge durch Hoerbstrassaat von Koriander (*Coriandrum sativum* L.). *Z. Arzn. Gew. Pfl.* 11: 30–34.

Birosik, P. J. 1994. *Cilantro.* New York: Collier Books.

Cadwallader, K. R., et al. 1999. Character-impact aroma components of coriander (*Coriandrum sativum* L.) herb. In *Flavor Chemistry of Ethnic Foods.* Ed. F. Shahidi and C.-T. Ho. New York: Kluwer Acad. 77–84.

Chialva, F., et al. 1982. Qualitative evaluation of aromatic herbs by direct headspace GC analysis. Applications of the method and comparison with the traditional analysis of essential oils. *J. High Resolution Chromatogr. Chromatogr. Commun.* 5: 182–188.

Cooksey, D. A., et al. 1991. Leaf spot of cilantro in California caused by a nonfluorescent *Pseudomonas syringae*. *Pl. Dis.* 75: 101.

Delaquis, P. J., and K. Stanich. 2004. Antilisterial properties of cilantro essential oil. *J. Essential Oil Res.* 10: 409–414.

Diedrichsen, A. 1996. *Coriander:* Coriandrum sativum *L.* Gatersleben, Germany: Intern. Pl. Genet. Res. Inst.

Eyres, G., et al. 2005. Identification of character-impact odorants in coriander and wild coriander leaves using gas chromatography-olfactometry (GCO) and comprehensive two-dimensional gas chromatography-time-of-flight mass spectrometry (GCxGC-TOFMS). *J. Sep. Sci.* 28: 1061–1074.

Fan, X., and J. K. B. Sokorai. 1002. Changes in volatile components of γ-irradiated fresh cilantro leaves during cold storage. *J. Agric. Food Chem.* 50: 7622–7628.

Formácek, V., and K.-H. Kubeczka. 1982. *Essential Oil Analysis by Capillary Gas Chromatography and Carbon-13 NMR Spectroscopy.* New York: John Wiley & Sons.

Frank, C., et al. 1995. GC-IRMS in the authenticity control of the essential oil of *Coriandrum sativum* L. *J. Agric. Food Chem.* 43: 1634–1637.

Ghannadi, A., and D. Sadeh. 1999. Volatile constituents of the fruit of *Coriandrum sativum* L. from Isfahan. *DARU* 7: 12–13.

Gil, A., et al. 2002. Coriander essential oil composition from two genotypes grown in different environmental conditions. *J. Agric. Food Chem.* 50: 2870–2877.

Hooper, P., and J. Dennis. 2002. *Coriander: Overcoming Production Limitations.* RIRDC Publ. No. 02/147.

Hornok, L. 1986. Effect of environmental factors on growth, yield, and on the active principles of some spice plants. *Acta Hort.* 188: 169–176.

Kalra, A., et al. 1995. Variable cultivar response to control of powdery mildew in coriander (*Coriandrum sativum* L.). *J. Essential Oil Res.* 7: 403–406.

———. 2003. Screening of *Coriandrum sativum* accessions for seed and essential oil yield and early maturity. *Pl. Gen. Res. Newsl.* 133: 19–21.

Kaur, P., et al. 2006. Quality of dried coriander leaves as affected by pretreatments and method of drying. *Eur. Food Res. Technol.* 223: 189–194.

Kizil, S., and T. Söğüt. 2002. An investigation on antimicrobial effects of essential oils of coriander and cumin at different concentrations. *Turkish J. Field Crops* 7: 1–5.

Kubo, I., et al. 2004. Antibacterial activity of coriander volatile compounds against *Salmonella choleraesuis*. *J. Agric. Food Chem.* 52: 3329–3332.

Lawrence, B. M. 1991. Progress in essential oils. *Perfumer Flavor.* 16(1): 49–54, 56–58.

Luayza, G., et al. 1996. Coriander under irrigation in Argentina. In *Progress in New Crops.* Ed. J. Janick. Alexandria, Virginia: ASHS Press. 590–594.

MacLeod, A. J., and R. Islam. 1976. Volatile flavour components of coriander leaf. *J. Sci. Food Agric.* 27: 721–725.

Mangan, T. X., et al. 2000. Effects of short-term postharvest treatments on cilantro (*Coriandrum sativum* L.) storage quality. *HortScience* 35: 409–410.

Mayberry, K., and C. Myers. 1991. Cilantro, Chinese parsley, coriander. SMC-012. In *Specialty and Minor Crops Handbook.* Ed. C. Meyers. Oakland: Small Farm Center, Univ. California.

Mazza, G. 2002. Minor volatile constituents of essential oil and extracts of coriander (*Coriandrum sativum* L.) fruits. *Sci. Aliments* 22: 617–627.

McVicar, R., et al. 2000. *Coriander in Saskatchewan.* Saskatchewan Agric. Food.

Melena, J. L. 1976. Coriander on the Knossos tablets. *Minos* 25: 133–163.

Mookherjee, B. D., et al. 1990. The chemistry of flowers, fruits and spices: live vs. dead, a new dimension in fragrance research. *Pure Appl. Chem.* 62: 1357–1364.

Morales-Payan, J. P. 1998. Influence of methanol and nitrogen on the yield of cilantro (*Coriandrum sativum*). *HortScience* 33: 494.

Msaada, K., et al. 2007. Variations in the essential oil composition from different parts of *Coriandrum sativum* L. cultivated in Tunisia. *Ital. J. Biochem.* 56: 47–52.

———. 2007. Changes on essential oil composition of coriander (*Coriandrum sativum* L.) fruits during three stages of maturity. *Food Chem.* 102: 1131–1134.

Nagy, F. 1971. Results of phytophylacological investigations related to the injury of coriander (*Coriandrum sativum* L.). *Herb Hung.* 10: 37–46.

Perineau, F., et al. 1991. Hydrodistillation du fruit de coriandre (*Coriandrum sativum*). *Parfums, Cosmétiques, Arômes* 98: 79–84.

Pillai, P. K. T., and M. C. Nambiar. 1982. Condiments. In *Cultivation and Utilization of Aromatic Plants.* Ed. C. K. Atal and B. M. Kapur. Jammu Tawi, India: Regional Res. Lab. 167–189.

Pino, J. A., et al. 1996. Chemical composition of the seed oil of *Coriandrum sativum* L. from Cuba. *J. Essential Oil Res.* 8: 97–98.

Potter, T. L. 1996. Essential oil composition of cilantro. *J. Agric. Food Chem.* 44: 1824–1826.

Potter, T. L., and I. S. Fagerson. 1990. Composition of coriander leaf volatiles. *J. Agric. Food Chem.* 38: 2054–2056.

Purseglove, J. W., et al. 1981. Coriander. In *Spices Vol. 2.* Ed. J. W. Purseglove. London: Longman. 736–788.

Putievsky, E. 1980. Germination studies with seed of caraway, coriander, and dill. *Seed Sci. Technol.* 8: 245–254.

Ramadan, M. F., and J.-T. Mörsel. 2002. Oil composition of coriander (*Coriandrum sativum* L.). *Eur. Food Res. Technol.* 215: 204–209.

Rangappa, M., et al. 1997. Cilantro response to nitrogen fertilizer rates. *J. Herbs Spices Med. Pl.* 5: 63–68.

Rao, V. K., et al. 2004. A comparative study of whole herb and leaf essential oils of coriander. *J. Essential Oil-Bearing Pl.* 7: 49–55.

Ravi, R., et al. 2007. Aroma characterization of coriander (*Coriandrum sativum* L.) oil samples. *Eur. Food Res. Technol.* 225: 367–374.

Singh, D., et al. 2006. Genetic variation for seed yield and its components and their association in coriander (*Coriandrum sativum* L.) germplasm. *J. Spices Aromatic Crops* 15: 25–29.

Singh, G., et al. 2006. Studies on essential oils. Part 41: chemical composition, antifungal, antioxidant and sprout suppressant activities of coriander (*Coriandrum sativum*) essential oil and its oleoresin. *Flavour Fragrance J.* 21: 472–479.

Smallfield, B. 1993. *Coriander*: Coriandrum sativum. New Zealand Inst. Crop Food Res. Broadsheet No. 30.

Stoyanova, A., et al. 2002. Investigation on the essential oil of coriander from Bulgaria. *Herba Pol.* 48: 67–70.

Taylor, J. D., and C. L. Dudley. 1980. Bacterial disease of coriander. *Pl. Pathol.* 29: 117–121.

Tucker, A. O., and T. DeBaggio. 1991. Cilantro around the world. *Herb Companion* 4(4): 36–41.

Wangensteen, H., et al. 2004. Antioxidant activity in extracts from coriander. *Food Chem.* 88: 293–297.

Worku, T., and Ch. Franz. 1997. Essential oil yield from different plant organs and various coriander-accessions. In *Essential Oils: Basic and Applied Research.* Ed. Ch. Franz et al. Carol Stream, Illinois: Allured. 333–335.

Zheljazkov, V., and I. Zhalnov. 1995. Effects of herbicides on yield and quality of *Coriandrum sativum* L. *J. Essential Oil Res.* 7: 633–639.

Crocus

Al-Mofleh, I. A., et al. 2006. Antigastric ulcer studies on saffron *Crocus sativus* L. in rats. *Pakistan J. Biol. Sci.* 9: 1009–1013.

Alonso, G. L., and R. Salinas Fernandez. 1993. *Color, Sabor y Aroma del Azafran de Determinadas Comarcas de Castilla-La Mancha.* Albacete, Spain: Escuela Superior de Ingenieros Agrónomos.

Alonso, G. L., et al. 1993. Auto-oxidation of crocin and picrocrocin in saffron under different storage conditions. *Bol. Chim. Farm.* 132: 116–120.

———. 1996. Determination of safranal from saffron (*Crocus sativus* L.) by thermal desorption-gas chromatography. *J. Agric. Food Chem.* 44: 185–18.

———. 1998. Method to determine the authenticity of aroma of saffron (*Crocus sativus* L.). *J. Food Protection* 61: 1525–1528.

Anonymous. 2004. Saffron. *Rev. Nat. Prod.* (Wolters Kluwer Health).

Basker, D. 1993. Saffron, the costliest spice: drying and quality, supply and price. *Acta Hort.* 344: 86–97.

Basker, D., and M. Negbi. 1983. Uses of saffron. *Econ. Bot.* 37: 228–236.

Bowles, E. A. 1952. *A Handbook of* Crocus *and* Colchicum *for Gardeners.* London: Bodley Head.

Brighton, C. A. 1977. Cytology of *Crocus sativus* and its allies (Iridaceae). *Pl. Syst. Evol.* 128: 137–157.

Buchecker, R., and C. H. Eugster. 1973. Absolute Konfiguration von Picrocrocin. *Helv. Chim. Acta* 56: 1121–1124.

Camps, A. B. 2008. Saffron in perfumery and flavors. *Perfumer Flavor.* 33(1): 26–36.

Cappelli, C., and G. DiDonato. 1994. Attachi di *Fusarium oxysporum* Schlecht. in coltivazioni di safferano in Abruzzo. *L'Informatore Agrario* 25: 75–76.

Carmona, M., et al. 2007. A new approach to saffron aroma. *Crit. Rev. Food Sci. Nutr.* 47: 145–159.

———. 2007. Identification of the flavonoid fraction in saffron spice by LC/DAD/MS/MS: comparative study of samples from different geographical origins. *Food Chem.* 100: 445–450.

Chichiriccò, G. 1989. Fertilization of *Crocus sativus* ovules and development of seeds after stigmatic pollination with *C. thomasii* (Iridaceae). *Giornale Bot. Ital.* 123: 31–37.

———. 1990. Sterility and improvement of saffron crocus. In *Lo Zafferano: Proceedings of the International Conference on Saffron* (Crocus sativus L.) *L'Aquila (Italy) 27–29 October 1989.* Ed. Tammaro and L. Marra. L'Aquila, Italy: Univ. Degli Studi L'Aquila Accad. Ital. dell Cucina. 99–107.

D'Auria, M., et al. 2004. Volatile organic compounds from saffron. *Flavour Fragrance J.* 19: 17–23.

Delgado, M. C., et al. 2006. *The Chemical Composition of Saffron: Color, Taste and Aroma.* Albacete, Italy: Editorial Bomarzo.

De Mastro, G., and C. Ruta. 1993. Relation between corm size and saffron (*Crocus sativus* L.) flowering. *Acta Hort.* 344: 512–517.

———. 1993. Effect of corm size at planting time on corm enlargement and flower production in saffron (*Crocus sativus* L.). *Rivista Ital. EPPOS* Spec. Num.: 299–307.

Escribano, J., et al. 1996. Crocin, safranal and picrocrocin from saffron (*Crocus sativus* L.) inhibit the growth of human cancer cells in vitro. *Cancer Lett.* 100: 23–30.

———. 1999. In vitro activation of macrophages by a novel proteoglycan isolated from corms of *Crocus sativus* L. *Cancer Lett.* 144: 107–144.

———. 1999. Isolation and cytotoxic properties of a novel blycoconjugate from corms of saffron plant (*Crocus sativus* L.). *Biochim. Biophys. Acta* 1426: 217–222.

———. 2000. The cytolytic effect of a glycoconjugate extracted from corms of saffron plant (*Crocus sativus*) on human cell lines in culture. *Pl. Med.* 66: 157–162.

Estilai, A. 1978. Variability in saffron (*Crocus sativus* L.). *Experientia* 34: 725.

Fakhrai, F., and P. K. Evans. 1990. Morphogenic potential of cultured floral explants of *Crocus sativus* L. for the in vitro production of saffron. *J. Exp. Bot.* 41: 47–52.

Fernández, J.-A., and F. Abdullaev, eds. 2003. Proceedings of the First International Symposium on saffron biology and biotechnology. *Acta Hort.* 650: 1–499.

Ferrence, S. C., and G. Bendersky. 2004. Therapy with saffron and the goddess at Thera. *Perspectives Biol. Med.* 47: 199–226.

Freiburghaus, F., et al. 1998. Geheimnisse des Safrans. *Naturw. Rdsch.* 51: 91–95.

Giaccio, M. 2004. Crocetin from saffron: an active component of an ancient spice. *Crit. Rev. Food Sci. Nutr.* 44: 155–172.

Hozzeinzadeh, H., and J. Ghenaati. 2006. Evaluation of the antitussive effect of stigma and petals of saffron (*Crocus sativus*) and its components, safranal and crocin in guinea pigs. *Fitoterapia* 77: 446–448.

Hozzeinzadeh, H., and F. Talebzadeh. 2005. Anticonvulsant evaluation of safranal and crocin from *Crocus sativus* in mice. *Fitoterapia* 76: 722–724.

Hozzeinzadeh, H., and H. M. Younesi. 2002. Antinociceptive and anti-inflammatory effects of *Crocus sativus* L. stigma and petal extracts in mice. *BMC Pharmacol.* 2: 7–14.

Hozzeinzadeh, H., et al. 2004. Antidepressant effect of *Crocus sativus* L. stigma extracts and their constituents, crocin and safranal, in mice. *Acta Hort.* 650: 435–445.

Humphries, J. 1996. *The Essential Saffron Companion.* Berkeley, California: Ten Speed Press.

Ingram, J. S. 1969. Saffron (*Crocus sativus* L.). *Trop. Sci.* 11: 176–184.

Interreg IIIC. n.d. *Saffron in Europe.* Athens: Editions Alexandros.

Jacobsen, N., and M. Øgaard. 2004. *Crocus cartwrightianus* on the Attica Peninsula. *Acta Hort.* 650: 65–69.

Johnson, R. 1992. Saffron and the good life. *Petits Propos Culinaires* 41: 30–51.

Kirk, E. B. 1958. Saffron crocus. *Natl. Hort. Mag.* 37: 140–146.

Konoshima, T., and M. Takasaki. 2003. Anti-carcinogenic activities of natural pigments from beet root and saffron. *Foods Food Ingred. J. Jap.* 208: 615–622.

Konoshima, T., et al. 1998. Crocin and crocetin derivatives inhibit skin tumour production in mice. *Phytotherapy Res.* 12: 400–404.

Koocheki, A., et al., eds. 2007. II International Symposium on saffron biology and technology. *Acta Hort.* 739: 1–461.

Koyama, A., et al. 1987. Formation of stigma-like structures and pigments in cultured tissues of *Crocus sativus. Shoyakugaku Zasshi* 41: 226–229.

———. 1988. Formation of stigma-like structures and pigment in cultured tissues of *Crocus sativus. Pl. Med.* 1988: 375–376.

Loskutov, A. V., et al. 2000. Development of an improved procedure for extraction and quantification of safranal in stigmas of *Crocus sativus* L. using high performance liquid chromatography. *Food Chem.* 69: 87–95.

Lozano, P., et al. 1999. Quantitative high-performance liquid chromatographic method to analyse commercial saffron (*Crocus sativus* L.) products. *J. Chromatogr. A* 830: 477–483.

Madan, C. L., et al. 1966. Saffron. *Econ. Bot.* 20: 377–385.

Mannino, S., and G. Amelotti. 1977. Determinazione dell'umidità ottimale di conservazione dello zafferano. Nota 2. *Rivista Ital. Sci. Alimentazione* 6(2): 95–98.

Mathew, B. 1977. *Crocus sativus* and its allies (Iridaceae). *Pl. Syst. Evol.* 128: 89–103.

———. 1982. *The Crocus: A Revision of the Genus* Crocus *(Iridaceae)*. Portland, Oregon: Timber Press.

McGimpsey, J. A. 1993. *Saffron*: Crocus sativus. New Zealand Inst. Crop Food Res. Broadsheet No. 20.

McGimpsey, J. A., et al. 1997. Evaluation of saffron (*Crocus sativus* L.) production in New Zealand. *New Zealand J. Crop Hort. Sci.* 25: 159–168.

Miller, P. 1768. *The Gardeners Dictionary*. 8th ed. London: Philip Miller.

Mishra, R. S., et al. 1977. Economics of saffron cultivation in Kashmir Valley. *JNKVV Res. J.* 11: 59–66.

Moshiri, E., et al. 2006. *Crocus sativus* L. (petal) in the treatment of mild-to-moderate depression: a double-blind, randomized and placebo-controlled trial. *Phytomed.* 13: 607–611.

Négbi, M., ed. 1999. *Saffron*: Crocus sativus *L.* Amsterdam: Harwood Acad. Publ.

Nétien, G., and L. Méry. 1962. Recherches sur les falsifications du safran par technique chromatographique. *Bull. Trav. Soc. Pharm. Lyon* 6: 35–39.

Petersen, G., et al. 2008. A phylogeny of the genus Crocus (Iridaceae) based on sequence data from five plastic regions. *Taxon* 57: 487–499.

Pfander, H., and F. Wittwer. 1975. Carotenoid-Glykoside. 2. Mitteilung. Untersuchungen zur Carotinoid-Zusammensetzung im Safran. *Helv. Chim. Acta* 58: 1608–1620.

———. 1979. Carotenoid-Glycosylester. 3. Mitteilung. Die Synthese von Crocetin-di-(β-D-glucosyl)-ester. Eine neue Methode zur selektiven Veresterung von ungeschutzter β-D-glucose. *Helv. Chim. Acta* 62: 1944–1951.

Pfander, H., and H. Schurtenberger. 1982. Biosynthesis of C20-carotenoids in *Crocus sativus*. *Phytochemistry* 21: 1039–1042.

Radjabian, T., et al. 2001. Comparative analysis of crocetin and its glycosyl esters from Crocus sativus L. and *Crocus haussknechtii* Boiss. As an alternative source of saffron. *J. Food Sci. Technol.* 38: 324–328.

Raina, B. L., et al. 1996. Changes in pigments and volatiles of saffron (*Crocus sativus* L.) during processing and storage. *J. Sci. Food Agric.* 71: 27–32.

Rees, A. R. 1988. Saffron: an expensive plant product. *Plantsman* 9: 210–217.

Reppert, B. 1983. Saffron: grow gold! *Green Scene* 12(1): 12–15.

Ríos, J. L., et al. 1996. An update review of saffron and its active constituents. *Phytotherapy Res.* 10: 189–193.

Rödel, W., and M. Petrzika. 1991. Analysis of the volatile components of saffron. *J. High Resolution Chromatogr.* 14: 771–774.

Rukšāns, J. 1981. *Krokusi* [in Latvian]. Avots, Riga.

Sampathu, S. R., et al. 1984. Saffron (*Crocus sativus* Linn.): cultivation, processing, chemistry and standardization. *CRC Crit. Rev. Food Sci. Nutr.* 20(2): 123–157.

Solinas, M., and A. Cichelli. 1988. Analisi HPLC dei composti responsabili del colore e dell'aroma dello zafferano. *Ind. Aliment.* 27: 634–639.

Sonnino, R. 2007. Embeddedness in action: saffron and the making of the local in southern Tuscany. *Agric. Human Values* 24: 61–74.

Srivastava, R. P. 1968. Some practical hints on growing saffron in Uttar Pradesh. *Indian Hort.* 13(1): 15–16, 27, 29.

Straubinger, M., et al. 1997. Novel glycosidic constituents from saffron. *J. Agric. Food Chem.* 45: 1678–1681.

———. 1998. Identification of novel glycosidic aroma precursors in saffron (*Crocus sativus* L.). *J. Agric. Food Chem.* 46: 3238–3243.

Sugiura, M., et al. 1994. Crocin (crocetin digentiobiose ester) prevents the inhibitory effect of ethanol on long-term potentiation in the dentate gyrus in vivo. *J. Pharmacol. Exp. Therap.* 271: 703–707.

———. 1995. Crocin improves the ethanol-induced impairment of learning behaviors of mice in passive avoidance tasks. *Proc. Jap. Acad. B.* 71: 319–324.

Suvatabandhu, K. 1964. Buddhist rules prescribe dyes for monks' robes. *Pl. Gard.* 20(3): 45–45.

Szita, E. 1987. *Wild About Saffron: A Contemporary Guide to an Ancient Spice*. Daly City, California: Saffron Rose.

———. 1990. Saffron. *Herb Companion* 2(3): 18–27.

———. 2001. The saffron mystique. *Herb Companion* 13(3): 51–55.

Tarantilis, P. A., and M. G. Plissiou. 1997. Isolation and identification of the aroma components from saffron (*Crocus sativus*). *J. Agric. Food Chem.* 45: 459–462.

Tarantilis, P. A., et al. 1994. Inhibition of growth and induction of differentiation of promyelocytic leukemia (HL-60) by carotenoids from *Crocus sativus* L. *Anticancer Res.* 14: 1913–1918.

Winterhalter, P., and M. Straubinger. 2000. Saffron: renewed interest in an ancient spice. *Food Rev. Int.* 16: 39–59.

Zarghami, N. S., and D. E. Heinz. 1971. Monoterpene aldehydes and isophorene-related compounds of saffron. *Phytochemistry* 10: 2755–1761.

———. 1971. The volatile constituents of saffron. *Lebensm. Wiss. Technol.* 4: 43–45.

Zhang, Y., et al. 1994. Effects of *Crocus sativus* L. on the ethanol-induced impairment of passive avoidance performances in mice. *Biol. Pharm. Bull.* 17: 217–221.

Zougagh, M., et al. 2006. Determination of total safranal by *in situ* acid hydrolysis in supercritical fluid media: application to the quality control of commercial saffron. *Anal. Chim. Acta* 578: 117–121.

Zubor, A. A., et al. 2004. Molecular biological approach of the systematics of *Crocus sativus* L. and its allies. *Acta Hort.* 650: 85–93.

Cryptotaenia

Abe, K., et al. 1994. Effects of cultivation methods and cultivar variations on characteristic aroma of Japanese honewort (*Cryptotaenia japonica* Hassk.). *J. Jap. Soc. Hort. Sci.* 62: 903–908.

Hara, H. 1962. Racial differences in widespread species, with special reference to those common to Japan and North America. *Amer. J. Bot.* 49: 647–652.

Hiroe, M., and L. Constance. 1958. Umbelliferae of Japan. *Univ. California Publ. Bot.* 30: 1–144.

Kami, T., et al. 1969. A study on low-boiling chemical constituents of *Cryptotaenia japonica* Hassk. *Agric. Biol. Chem.* 33: 1717–1722.

Miyazawa, M., et al. 1999. Components of the essential oil of *Cryptotaenia japonica* Hassk. 'Itomitsuba' for Japanese food. *Flavour Fragrance J.* 14: 273–275.

Cuminum

Anonymous. 2005. Cumin. *Rev. Nat. Prod. (Wolters Kluwer Health)*.

Bandoni, A. L., et al. 1991. Contribucion al estudio de las esencias de comino (*Cuminum cyminum* L.). *Essenze Derivati Agrumari* 61: 32–49.

Baser, K., et al. 1992. Composition of Turkish cumin seed oil. *J. Essential Oil Res.* 4: 133–138.

El-Sawi, S. A., and M. A. Mohamed. 2002. Cumin herb as a new source of essential oils and its response to foliar spray with some micro-elements. *Food Chem.* 77: 75–80.

Janahmadi, M., et al. 2006. Effects of the fruit essential oil of *Cuminum cyminum* Linnj. (Apiaceae) on pentylenetetrazol-induced epileptiform activity in F1 neurons of *Helix aspersa*. *J. Ethnopharmacol.* 104: 278–282.

Jangir, R. P., and R. Singh. 1996. Effect of irrigation and nitrogen on seed yield of cumin (*Cuminum cyminum*). *Indian J. Agron.* 41: 140–143.

Karim, A., et al. 1976. Studies on the essential oils of the Pakistan species of the family Umbelliferae. Part 3. *Cuminum cyminum* Linn. (cumin, safred zira) seed oil. *Pakistan J. Sci. Industr. Res.* 19: 239–242.

Li, R., and Z.-T. Jiang. 2004. Chemical composition of the essential oil of *Cuminum cyminum* L. from China. *Flavour Fragrance J.* 19: 311–313.

Maiti, R. G. 1978. Grow cumin, it pays. *Intensive Agric.* 16(8): 22–23.

Mann, J. S. 1980. More profit from zeera. *Indian Farming* 30(9): 13–14.

Parveen, S., and Z. Ullah. 1979. Diseases of cumin: a review. *Pakistan J. Forest.* 29: 195–198.

Patel, R. M., and M. V. Desai. 1971. Alternaria blight of *Cuminum cyminum* and its control. *Indian Phytopathol.* 24: 16–22.

Pillai, P. K. T., and M. C. Nambiar. 1982. Condiments. In *Cultivation and Utilization of Aromatic Plants*. Ed. C. K. Atal and B. M. Kapur. Jammu Tawi, India: Regional Res. Lab. 167–189.

Sayyah, M., et al. 2002. Anti-nociceptive effect of the fruit essential oil of *Cuminum cyminum* L. in rat. *Iranian Biomed. J.* 6: 141–145.

———. 2002. Anticonvulsant effect of the fruit essential oil of *Cuminum cyminum* in mice. *Pharm. Biol.* 40: 478–480.

Srivastava, K. C., and T. Mustafa. 1989. Spices: Antiplatelet activity and prostanoid metabolism. *Prostaglandins Leukiotrienes Fatty Acids* 38: 255–266.

Syed, M., et al. 1986. Antimicrobial activity of the essential oils of the Umbelliferae family. Part 1. *Cuminum cyminum*, *Coriandrum sativum*, *Foeniculum vulgare*, and *Bunium persicum* oils. *Pakistan J. Sci. Ind. Res.* 29: 183–188.

Thippeswamy, N. B., and K. A. Naidu. 2005. Antioxidant potency of cumin varieties—cumin, black cumin and bitter cumin—on antioxidant systems. *Eur. Food Res. Technol.* 220: 472–476.

Tutin, T. G. 1968. *Cuminum*. In *Flora Europaea Vol. 2*. Ed. T. G. Tutin et al. Cambridge Univ. Press. 352.

Wang, Z., et al. 2006. Improved solvent-free microwave extraction of essential oil from dried *Cuminum cyminum* L. and *Zanthoxylum bungeanum* Maxim. *J. Chromatogr. A* 1102: 11–17.

Cunila

Iffland, D. 1969. The frost mint. *Morris Arbor. Bull.* 20: 70.

Lawrence, B. M. 1980. Aromatic flora of North America. Part 1. Labiatae. In *Essential Oils 1979–1980*. Wheaton, Illinois: Allured. 53–102

———. 1991. Labiatae oils: Mother Nature's chemical factory. In *Essential Oils 1988–1991*. Carol Stream, Illinois: Allured. 188–206.

Cymbopogon

Ali, M., et al. 2004. Volatile constituents of *Cymbopogon citratus* (DC.) Stapf leaves. *J. Essential Oil-Bearing Pl.* 7: 56–59.

Anonymous. 2004. Lemongrass. *Rev. Nat. Prod. (Wolters Kluwer Health)*.

Baratta, M. T., et al. 1998. Antimicrobial and antioxidant properties of some commercial essential oils. *Flavour Fragrance J.* 13: 235–244.

Beech, D. F. 1977. Growth and oil production of lemongrass (*Cymbopogon citratus*) in the Ord irrigation area, Western Australia. *Austral. J. Exp. Agric. Anim. Husb.* 17: 301–307.

Blake, S. T. 1974. Revision of the genera *Cymbopogon* and *Schizachyrium* (Gramineae) in Australia. *Contrib. Queensland Herb.* 17: 1–70.

Boelens, M. H. 1994. Sensory and chemical evaluation of tropical grass oils. *Perfumer Flavor.* 19(2): 29–45.

Chisowa, E. H., et al. 1998. Volatile constituents of the essential oil of *Cymbopogon citratus* Stapf grown in Zambia. *Flavour Fragrance J.* 13: 29–30.

Chungsamarnyart, N., and S. Jiwajinda. 1992. Acaricidal activity of volatile oil from lemon and citronella grasses on tropical cattle ticks. *Kasetsart J. (Nat. Sci. Suppl.)* 26: 46–51.

Corrigan, D. 1992. *Cymbopogon* species. In *Adverse Effects of Herbal Drugs 1*. Ed. P. A. G. M. De Smet et al. Berlin: Springer-Verlag. 115–123.

Ekundayo, O. 1985. Composition of the leaf volatile oil of *Cymbopogon citratus*. *Fitoterapia* 56: 339–342.

El-Kamali, H. H., et al. 1998. Antibacterial properties of essential oils from *Nigella sativa* seeds, *Cymbopogon citratus* leaves and *Pulicaria undulata* aerial parts. *Fitoterapia* 69: 77–78.

Hood, S. C. 1917. *Possibility of the Commercial Production of Lemon-grass Oil in the United States*. U.S.D.A. Bull. No. 442. 12 pp.

Igbokwe, P. E., and S. Asumeng. 2007. Lemongrass *Cymbopogon citratus* production in southwest Mississippi. *J. Herbs Spices Med. Pl.* 13(2): 69–77.

Kulkarni, R. N. 2000. Lemongrass breeding: past progress and future prospects. *J. Med. Aromatic Pl. Sci.* 22: 278–284.

Kumar, S., et al., eds. 2000. Cymbopogon: *The Aromatic Grass Monograph*. Lucknow, India: Cent. Inst. Med. Aromatic Pl

Menut, C., et al. 2000. Aromatic plants of Tropical West Africa. XI. Chemical composition, antioxidant and antiradical properties of the essential oils of three *Cymbo-*

pogon species from Burkina Faso. *J. Essential Oil Res.* 12: 207–212.

Negrelle, R. R. B., and E. C. Gomes. 2007. *Cymbopogon citratus* (DC.) Stapf: chemical composition and biological activities. *Rev. Bras. Pl. Med. Botucafu* 9: 80–92.

Onawumi, G. O., et al. 1984. Antibacterial constituents in the essential oil of *Cymbopogon citratus* (DC.) Stapf. *J. Ethnopharmacol.* 12: 279–286.

Pedroso, R. B., etr al. 2006. Biological activities of essential oil obtained from *Cymbopogon citratus* on *Crithidia deanei*. *Acta ProtoZoologica* 45: 231–240.

Santoro, G. F., et al. 2007. Anti-proliferative effect of the essential oil of *Cymbopogon citratus* (DC.) Stapf (lemongrass) on intracellular amistigotes, bloodstream trypomastigotes and culture apimastigotes of *Trypanosoma cruzi* (Protozoa: Kinetoplastida). *Parasitology* 134: 1649–1656.

Sarer, E., et al. 1983. Composition of the essential oil of *Cymbopogon citratus* (DC.) Stapf cultivated in Turkey. *Sci. Pharm.* 51: 58–63.

Schaneberg, B. T., and I. A. Khan. 2002. Comparison of extraction methods for marker compounds in the essential oil of lemon grass by GC. *J. Agric. Food Chem.* 50: 1345–1349.

Soenarko, S. 1977. The genus *Cymbopogon* Sprengel (Gramineae). *Reinwardtia* 9: 225–375.

Suaeyun, R., et al. 1997. Inhibitory effects of lemon grass (*Cymbopogon citratus* Stapf) on formation of azoxymethane-induced DNA adducts and aberrant crypt foci in the rat colon. *Carcinogenesis* 18: 949–955.

Thappa, R. K., et al. 1981. Citral-containing *Cymbopogon* species. *Indian Perfumer* 25: 15–18.

Tzortzakis, N. G., and C. D. Economakis. 2007. Antifungal activity of lemongrass *Cymbopogon citratus* L.) essential oil against key postharvest pathogens. *Innovative Food Sci. Emerging Technol.* 8: 253–258.

Valencia, J., and C. Meyers. 1991. Lemongrass. SMC-037. In *Specialty and Minor Crops Handbook*. Ed. C. Meyers. Oakland: Small Farm Center, Univ. California.

Viturro, C. I., and C. W. Bucu. 1998. Composicion del aceite esencial de lemongrass de Jujuy. *Anales Asoc. Quim. Argentina* 86: 45–48.

Dianthus

Allwood, M. C. 1954. *Carnations, Pinks, and All Dianthus*. Hayward's Heath, England: Allwood Bros.

———. 1962. *Carnations for Everyman*. New York: St. Martin's Press.

Anonis, D. P. 1985. The application of carnation in perfumery. *Flavour Fragrance J.* 1: 9–15.

Anonymous. 1928. The pink, carnation, and clove in the perfumer's art. *Perfumery Essential Oil Rev.* 19: 213–216.

Bailey, L. H. 1938. *The Garden of Pinks, with Decorations.* New York: Macmillan.

Bailey, S. 1962. *Growing Perpetual-flowering Carnations.* London: Garden Book Club.

Buil, P., et al. 1983. Newly discovered constituents in concrète from carnation flowers. *Parfums, Cosmétiques, Arômes* 52: 45–49.

Cook, J. H. 1911. *Carnations and Pinks.* New York: Frederick A. Stokes.

Derbesy, M., et al. 1982. Comparaison d'absolues oeillets de différentes origines géographiques. In *VIII International Congress of Essential Oils, October 12–17, 1980, Cannes-Grasse, France.* Paper no. 130.

Dowdall, R. K. 1962. *Growing Carnations and Pinks.* London: British Natl. Carnation Soc.

Genders, R. 1962. *Garden Pinks.* London: John Gifford Ltd.

Harvey, J. H. 1978. Gilliflower and carnation. *Gard. Hist.* 6(1): 46–47.

Hensen, K. J. W. 1981. Het onderzoek van het sortiment grasanjers (*Dianthus gratianopolitanus* en *plumarius*). *Groen* 37: 265–277.

Ingwersen, W. 1949. *The Dianthus: A Flower Monograph.* London: Collins.

Jarratt, J. 1988. *Growing Carnations.* Kenthurst: Kangaroo Press.

Köhlein, F. 1991. Pfingstnelken neu bewertet. *Gartenpraxis* 1991(2): 16–21.

Mansfield, T. C. 1951. *Carnations in Color and Cultivation.* London: Collins.

McCully, K. F. 1949. *Commercial Carnation Growing.* Saugus, Massachusetts: Sim Carnation Co.

Moreton, C. O. 1955. *Old Carnations and Pinks.* London: George Rainbird.

Sedanko, J. 1989. Pinks: the divine flowers. *Pacific Hort.* 50(3): 35–42.

Tutin, T. G. 1964. *Dianthus.* In *Flora Europaea Vol. 1.* Ed. T. G. Tutin et al. Cambridge Univ. Press. 188–204.

Vernin, E., et al. 1989. Le girofle. *Parfums, Cosmétiques, Arômes* 89: 81–94.

Weston, T. A. 1931. *Practical Carnation Culture.* New York: A. T. De La Mare Co.

Whitehead, S. B. 1956. *Carnations Today.* London: John Gifford.

Dysphania

Bauer, A., and G. A. de Assiss Brasil e Silva. 1973. Os óleos essenciais de *Chenopodium ambrosioides* e *Schinus terebinthifolius* no Rio Grande do Sul. *Rev. Bras. Farm.* 54: 240–242.

Brenan, J. P. M. 1964. *Chenopodium.* In *Flora Europaea Vol. 1.* Ed. T. G. Tutin et al. Cambridge Univ. Press. 92–95.

Cavalli, J.-F., et al. 2004. Combined analysis of the essential oil of *Chenpodium ambrosioides* by GC, GC-MS and 13D-NMR spectroscopy: quantitative determination of ascaridole, a heat-sensitive compound. *Phytochem. Anal.* 15: 275–279.

Clemants, S. E., and S. L. Mosyakin. 2004. *Dysphania.* In *Flora of North America North of Mexico Vol. 4.* Ed. Flora of North America Editorial Committee. New York: Oxford Univ. Press. 267–275.

De Amorin, A., et al. 1998. Ação anti-helmíntica de plantas, XIII. Ação de extratos aquosos de *Chenopodium ambrosioides* L. "in vitro" sobre larvas de primeiro e terceiro estádios de estrongiliüno. *R. Brax. Med. Vet.* 20: 14–16.

Gadano, A. B., et al. 2006. Argentine folk medicine: genotoxic effects of Chenopodiaceae family. *J. Ethnopharmacol.* 103: 246–251.

Gupta, D., et al. 2002. Chemical examination of the essential oil of *Chenopodium ambrosioides* L. from the southern hills of India. *J. Essential Oil Res.* 14: 93–94.

Hutson, L. 1992. Mexican culinary herbs. *Fine Gard.* 23: 52–55.

Jimenez-Osornio, J. J. 1991. Ethnoecology of *Chenopodium ambrosioides. Amer. J. Bot.* 78(6, Suppl.): 139.

Jirovetz, L., et al. 2000. Analysis of the essential oil of the leaves of the medicinal plant *Chenopodium ambrosioides* var. *anthelminticum* (L.) A. Gray from India. *Sci. Pharm.* 68: 123–128.

Kapadia, G. J., et al. 1978. Carcinogenicity of some folk medicinal herbs in rats. *J. Natl. Cancer Inst.* 60: 683–686.

Kasali, A. A., et al. 2006. 1,2,3,4-Diepoxy-p-menthane and 1,4-epoxy-p-menth-2-ene: rare monoterpenoids from the essential oil of *Chenopodium ambrosioides* L. var. *ambrosioides* leaves. *J. Essential Oil Res.* 18: 13–15.

Kennedy, D. 1989. *The Art of Mexican Cooking.* New York: Bantam Books.

Kingsbury, J. M. 1964. *Poisonous Plants of the United States and Canada.* Englewood Cliffs, New Jersey: Prentice-Hall.

Kowal, T. 1953. A key for determination of the genera *Chenopodium* L. and *Atriplex* L. *Monogr. Bot.* 1: 87–163.

Lewis, W. H., and M. P. F. Elvin-Lewis. 1977. *Medical Botany: Plants Affecting Man's Health.* New York: John Wiley & Sons.

Logan, M. H., et al. 2004. An empirical assessment of epazote (*Chenopodium ambrosioides* L.) as a flavour agent in cooked beans. *J. Ethnobiol.* 24: 1–12.

Monzote, L., et al. 2006. Activity of the essential oil from *Chenopodium ambrosioides* grown in Cuba against *Leismania amazonensis. Chemotherapy* 52: 130–136.

———. 2006. Activity, toxicity and analysis of resistance of essential oil from *Chenopodium ambrosioides* after intraperitoneal, oral and intralesional administration in BALB/c mice infected with *Leismania amazonensis*: a preliminary study. *Biomed. Pharmacotherapy* 61: 148–153.

Muenscher, W. C. 1951. *Poisonous Plants of the United States.* Rev. ed. New York: Macmillan.

Muhayimana, A., et al. 1998. Chemical composition of essential oils of *Chenopodium ambrosioides* L. from Rwanda. *J. Essential Oil Res.* 10: 690–692.

Muniz, L. P. 1990. On the trail of the accent herb of Mexico. *New York Times* January 10: C1, C4.

Narva, S. M. 1996. A most surprising worm-killer: a history of the use and cultivation of wormseed (*Chenopodium ambrosioides* var. *anthelminticum*) in early America. In *Plants and People.* Ed. P. Benes et al. Boston Univ. Press. 78–91.

Olajide, O. A., et al. 1997. Pharmacological screening of the methanolic extract of *Chenopodium ambrosioides. Fitoterapia* 68: 529–532.

Onocha, P. A., et al. 1999. Essential oil constituents of *Chenopodium ambrosioides* L. leaves from Nigeria. *J. Essential Oil Res.* 11: 220–222.

Opdyke, D. L. J. 1976. Monographs on fragrance raw materials. *Food Cosmet. Toxicol.* 14: 659–893.

Palomino H., et al. 1990. Cytogenetic distinction between *Teloxys* and *Chenopodium* (Chenopodiaceae). *SouthW. Naturalist* 35: 351–353.

Pamo, E. T., et al. 2004. Chemical composition and acaricide effect of the essential oils of leaves of *Chenopodium ambrosioides* and *Eucalyptus saligna* on ticks (*Rhipicephalus lunulatus*) of West African dwarf goat in West Cameroon. *Bull. Anim. Health Prod. Afr.* 52: 221–228.

Pino, J. A. 2003. Essential oil of *Chenopodium ambrosioides* L. from Cuba. *J. Essential Oil Res.* 15: 213–214.

Quintana, P. 1986. *The Taste of Mexico.* New York: Stewart, Tabori & Chang.

Sagrero-Nieves, L., and J. P. Bartley. 1995. Volatile constituents from the leaves of *Chenopodium ambrosioides* L. *J. Essential Oil Res.* 7: 221–223.

Scott, A. J. 1978. A review of the classification of *Chenopodium* L. and related genera (Chenopodiaceae). *Bot. Jahrb. Syst.* 100: 205–220.

Tapondjou, L. A., et al. 2002. Efficacy of powder and essential oil from *Chenopodium ambrosioides* leaves as post-harvest grain protectants against six-stored product beetles. *J. Stored Prod. Res.* 38: 395–402.

Tucker, A. O., and M. J. Maciarello. 1998. Some toxic culinary herbs in North America. In *Food Flavor: Formation, Analysis and Packaging Influences.* Ed. E. T. Contis et al. Amsterdam: Elsevier. 401–414.

Umemoto, K. 1978. Essential oil of *Cheno-podium ambrosioides* L. containing (-)-pinocarveol as a major component. *J. Agric. Chem. Soc. Japan* 52: 149–150.

Wahl, H. A. 1954. A preliminary study of the genus *Chenopodium* in North America. *Bartonia* 27: 1–46.

Weber, W. A. 1988. The genus *Teloxys* (Chenopodiaceae). *Phytologia* 58: 477–478.

Weiland, G. S., et al. 1935. *Wormseed Oil Production*. Maryland Agric. Exp. Sta. Bull. No. 384.

Elsholtzia

Bakova, N. I., et al. 1988. Characterization of essential oils of different *Elsholtzia ciliata* Thunb. biotypes [in Russian]. *Izv. Timiryazevsk. S-kh. Akad.* 1988(2): 162–166.

Dmitriev, L. B., et al. 1987. Composition of *Elsholtzia stauntoni* Benth. essential oil [in Russian]. *Izv. Timiryazevsk. S-kh. Akad.* 1987(5): 167–170.

Du, H-q., et al. 1989. Components of essential oils of *Elsholtzia stauntonii* Benth. [in Chinese]. *Yaowu Fenxi Zazhi* 9: 18–21.

Kobold, U., et al. 1987. Terpenoids from *Elsholtzia* species; II. Constituents of essential oil from a new chemotype of *Elsholtzia cristata*. *Pl. Med.* 1987: 268–270.

Korolyuk, E., et al. 2002. Composition of essential oil of *Elsholtzia ciliata* (Thunb.) Hyl. from the Novosibirisk region, Russia. *Khimiya Rastitel'nogo Syr'ya* 202(1): 31–36.

Liu, A.-L., et al. 2007. *Elsholtzia*: review of traditional uses, chemistry and pharmacology. *J. Chin. Pharm. Sci.* 2007(16): 73–78.

Liu, G., et al. 2006. GC-MS analysis of essential oils from the *Elsholtzia ciliata* Hyland. *Zhongguo Shiyan Fangjixue Zazhi* 12: 18–21.

Sohn, K., et al. 1998. Morphological observation of glandular trichomes of *Elsholtzia ciliata* (Thunb.) Hylander by scanning electron microscope. *J. Kor. Soc. Hort. Sci.* 39: 814–818.

———. 1998. The growth and essential oil of *Elsholtzia ciliata* (Thunb.) Hylander. *J. Kor. Soc. Hort. Sci.* 39: 809–813.

Tucker, A. O., and M. J. Maciarello. 1995. Volatile oil of *Elsholtzia stauntonii* Benth. *J. Essential Oil Res.* 7: 653–655.

Walker. 1825. *Elsholtzia cristata*: crested elsholtzia. *Bot. Mag.* 52: t. 2560.

Zheng, S.-z., et al. 2001. Composition of *Elsholtzia stauntonii* essential oil prepared by steam distillation and supercritical CO_2 fluid extraction. *J. Northwest Normal Univ. (Nat. Sci.)* 37: 37–40.

Zheng, X.-d., and H.-b. Hu. 2005. A study of chemical compositions of Qinyang *Elsholtzia ciliata* (Thunb.) Hyland. *Guangpu Shiyanshi* 22: 179–182.

Zhu, L., et al. 1995. *Aromatic Plants and Essential Constituents. Supplement 1*. Hong Kong: South China Inst. Bot.

Eryngium

Bohlmann, F., and C. Zdero. 1971. Über weitere Terpenaldehydester aus *Eryngium*-Arten. *Chem. Ber.* 104: 1957–1961.

Calpouzos, L. 1954. Botanical aspects of oregano. *Econ. Bot.* 8: 222–233.

Chater, A. O. 1968. *Eryngium*. In *Flora Europaea Vol. 2*. Ed. T. G. Tutin et al. Cambridge Univ. Press. 320–324.

Eyres, G., et al. 2005. Identification of character-impact odorants in coriander and wild coriander leaves using gas chromatography-olfactometry (GCO) and comprehensive two-dimensional gas chromatography-time-of-flight mass spectrometry (GCxGC-TOFMS). *J. Sep. Sci.* 28: 1061–1074.

García, M. D., et al. 1999. Topical anti-inflammatory activity of phytosterols isolated from *Eryngium foetidum* on chronic and acute inflammation models. *Phytotherapy Res.* 13: 78–80.

Krahulik, J. L., and W. L. Theobald. 1981. Umbelliferae. In *A Revised Handbook to the Flora of Ceylon Vol. 3*. Ed. M. D. Dassanayake. Washington, D.C.: Smithsonian Institution. 479–499.

Leclercq, P. A., et al. 1992. Composition of the essential oil of *Eryngium foetidum* L. from Vietnam. *J. Essential Oil Res.* 4: 423–424.

Martins, A. P., et al. 2003. Essential oil composition of *Eryngium foetidum* from S. Tomé e Príncipe. *J. Essential Oil Res.* 15: 93–95.

Pino, J. A., et al. 1997. Chemical composition of the seed oil of *Eryngium foetidum* L. from Cuba. *J. Essential Oil Res.* 9: 123–124.

———. 1997. Composition of the leaf oil of *Eryngium foetidum* L. from Cuba. *J. Essential Oil Res.* 9: 467–468.

Sankat, C. K., and V. Maharaj. 1994. Drying the green herb shado beni (*Eryngium foetidum* L.) in a natural convection cabinet and solar driers. *ASEAN Food J.* 9: 17–23.

———. 1995. Shelf life of the green herb "shado beni" (*Eryngium foetidum* L.) stored under refrigerated conditions. *Postharvest Biol. Technol.* 7: 109–118.

Simon, O. R., and N. Singh. 1986. Demonstration of anticonvulsant properties of an aqueous extract of spirit weed (*Eryngium foetidum* L.). *West Indian Med. J.* 35: 121–125.

Wong, K. C., et al. 1994. Composition of the leaf and root oils of *Eryngium foetidum* L. *J. Essential Oil Res.* 6: 369–374.

Yeh, P.-H. 1974. Essential oils XVI. Oil of *Eryngium foetidum* Linn. *J. Chinese Chem. Soc.* 21: 139–147.

Ferula

Abraham, K. O., et al. 1979. Studies on asafetida oil. In *VII International Congress of Essential Oils, October 7–11, 1977, Kyoto, Japan*. 373–375.

———. 1982. Odorous compounds of asafetida VII: isolation and identification. *Indian Food Packer* 36(5): 65–76.

Aishima, T. 1986. Application of multivariate analysis to silica capillary GC profiles to differentiate the aroma characteristics of Worcestershire sauces. In *The Shelf Life of Foods and Beverages*. Ed. G. Charalambous. Amsterdam: Elsevier. 755–774.

Aitchison, I. E. T. 1887. Some plants of Afghanistan, and their medicinal products. *Amer. J. Pharm. Bot. Med. Monogr.* Sundry Vol. 59, no. 1.

Anonymous. 2004. Asafoetida. *Rev. Nat. Prod.* (Wolters Kluwer Health).

Arctander, S. 1960. *Perfume and Flavor Materials of Natural Origin*. Elizabeth, New Jersey: Steffen Arctander.

Balasubrahmanyam, N., et al. 1979. Asafetida VI. Packaging and storage studies on asafetida products. *Indian Food Packer* 33(3): 15–22.

Bramwell, A. F., et al. 1969. Characterisation of pyrazines in galbanum oil. *Tetrahedron Lett.* 1969: 3215–3216.

Breckle, S.-W., and W. Unger. 1977. Afghanische Drogen und ihre Stammpflanzen (1). Gummiharze von Umbelliferen. *Afghanistan J.* 4: 88–93.

Buddrus, J., et al. 1985. Foetidin, a sesquiterpenoid coumarin from *Ferula assa-foetida*. *Phytochemistry* 24: 869–870.

Burrell, J., et al. 1970. Characterisation of pyrazines in galbanum oil. *Chem. Industr.* 1970: 1409–1410.

———. 1971. Characterisation of thiol esters in galbanum oil. *Tetrahedron Lett.* 1971: 2837–2838.

Dalby, A. 1992. Silphium and asafetida: Evidence from Greek and Roman writers. In *Spicing Up the Palate: Studies of Flavour: Ancient and Modern*. Ed. H. Walker. Totnes, England: Prospect Books. 67–72.

Falconer, H. 1851. Description of the asafoetida plant of central Asia. *Trans. Linn. Soc. London* 20: 285–291.

Graf, E., and M. Alexa. 1985. Über 5 neue Umbelliferonether aus Galbanumharz. *Pl. Med.* 1985: 428–431.

Hiscox, G. D. 1927. *Henley's Twentieth Century Formulas, Recipes and Processes*. New York: Norman W. Henley Publ. Co.

Howes, F. N. 1949. *Vegetable Gums and Resins*. Waltham, Massachusetts: Chron. Bot. Co.

Ikeda, R. M., et al. 1962. The monoterpene hydrocarbon composition of some essential oils. *J. Food Sci.* 27: 455–458.

Khajeh, M., et al. 2005. Comparison of essential oils compositions of *Ferula assa-*

foetida obtained by supercritical carbon dioxide extraction and hydrodistillation methods. *Food Chem.* 91: 639–644.

Kjaer, A., et al. 1976. 2-Butyl propenyl disulfides from asafetida: separation, characterization, and absolute configuration. *Acta Chem. Scand.* 30B: 137–140.

Korovin, E. 1947. *Generis* Ferula *(Tourn.) L.: Monographia Illustrata.* Taschkent: Acad. Sci. UzRss.

Martinez, D. 1991. Galbanum. *H&R Contact* 50: 9–13.

Martinez, D., and K. Lohs. 1987. Der Asant: ein vergessenes Heilmittel und Gewürz. *Naturwiss. Rundschau* (Stuttgart) 40(3): 85–91.

———. 1988. Asa foetida: Heilmittel der asiatischen Volksmedizin. *Pharmazie Beih. Ergänzungsband* 43: 720–722.

McAndrew, F. A., and D. M. Michalkiewicz. 1988. In *Flavor and Fragrances: A World Perspective.* Ed. B. Lawrence et al. Amsterdam: Elsevier. 573–585.

Naimie, H., et al. 1972. Über die flüchtigen Inhaltstoffe von Asa Foetida: zwei neuen natürlichen Schwefelverbindungen mit pestizider Wirkung. *Collect. Chem. Commun.* 37: 1166–1177.

Nassar, M. I., et al. 1995. Sesquiterpene coumarins from *Ferula assafoetida* L. *Pharmazie* 50: 766–767.

Naves, Y.-R. 1967. Études sur les matières végétales volatiles CCIII. Présence de n-undécatriènes-1,3,5 dans l'huile essentielle de la gomme-résine de galanum. *Bull. Soc. Chim. France* 9: 3152–3154.

———. 1969. Sur quelques constituants inédits de la gomme-résine de galbanum. *Parfum. Cosmet. Savon* 12: 586–589.

Noleau, I., et al. 1991. Volatile compounds in leek and asafoetida. *J. Essential Oil Res.* 3: 241–246.

Raghavan, B., et al. 1979. Asafetida v. asafetida products and flavour losses during cooking and frying. *Indian Food Packer* 33(3): 11–14.

Riddle, J. M. 1992. *Contraception and Abortion from the Ancient World to the Renaissance.* Cambridge, Massachusetts: Harvard Univ. Press.

Samimi, M. N., and W. Unger. 1979. Die Gummiharze afghanischer "Asa foetida"-liefernder *Ferula*-Arten. Beobachtungen zur Herkunft und Qualitat afghanischer "Asa Foetida." *Pl. Med.* 36: 128–133.

Siddiqui, R. R., et al. 1995. Antimicrobial activity of essential oils from *Schinus terebinthifolia, Cypress sempervirens, Citrus limon, Ferula assafoetida.* Part 1. *Pak. J. Sci. Ind. Res.* 38: 358–361.

Takeoka, G. 2001. Volatile constituents of asafetida. In *Aroma Active Compounds in Foods: Chemistry and Sensory Properties.* Ed. G. Takeoka et al. Washington, D.C.: Amer. Chem. Soc. 33–44.

Teisseire, P. 1964. A contribution to the knowledge of essential oil of galbanum. *Recherches* 14: 81–88.

Thomas, A. F., and M. Ozainne. 1978. New sesquiterpene alcohols from galbanum resin: the occurrence of C(10)-epi-sesquiterpenoids. *Helv. Chim. Acta* 61: 2874–2880.

Foeniculum

Akgül, A. 1986. Studies on the essential oils from Turkish fennel seeds (*Foeniculum vulgare* M. var. *dulce*). In *Progress in Essential Oils.* Ed. E.-J. Brunke. Berlin: Walter de Gruyter. 487–489.

Akgül, A., and A. Bayrak. 1988. Comparative volatile oil composition of various parts from Turkish bitter fennel (*Foeniculum vulgare* var. *vulgare*). *Food Chem.* 30: 319–323.

Albert-Puleo, M. 1980. Fennel and anise as estrogenic agents. *J. Ethnopharmacol.* 2: 337–344.

Anonymous. 2007. Fennel. *Rev. Nat. Prod. (Wolters Kluwer Health).*

Arslan, N., et al. 1989. The yield and components of essential oil in fennels of different origin (*Foeniculum vulgare* Mill.) grown in Ankara conditions. *Herba Hung.* 29: 27–31.

Ashraf, M., and M. K. Bhatty. 1975. Studies on the essential oils of the Pakistani species of the family Umbelliferae. Part 2. *Foeniculum vulgare* Miller (fennel) seed oil. *Pakistan J. Sci. Industr. Res.* 18: 236–240.

Badoc, A., et al. 1995. Hybridation intraspécifique chez le fenouil, *Foeniculum vulgare* Mill. *Bull. Soc. Pharm. Bordeaux* 134: 107–126.

Baqrazani, O., et al. 1999. Chemical variation among indigenous populations of *Foeniculum vulgare* var. *vulgare* in Israel. *Pl. Med.* 65: 486–489.

Bellomaria, B., et al. 1999. L'olio essenziale di *Foeniculum vulgare* Mill. ssp. *vulgare. Rivista Ital. EPPOS* Spec. Num.: 43–48.

Bernáth, J., and É. Németh. 2007. Chemical systematization of the genus *Foeniculum* Mill. based on the accumulation and qualitative differentiation of the essential oil. *Nat. Prod. Commun.* 2: 309–314.

Bernáth, J., et al. 1996. Morphological and chemical evaluation of fennel (*Foeniculum vulgare* Mill.) populations of different origin. *J. Essential Oil Res.* 8: 247–253.

Betts, T. J. 1976. Possible new western Australian fennel chemovar. *Australian J. Pharm.* 5: 78.

———. 1992. Possible value for the gas chromatographic analysis of essential oils for some unusual phase commercial capillaries. *J. Chromatogr.* 626: 294–300.

Bowes, K. M., and V. D. Zheljazkov. 2005. Essential oil yields and quality of fennel grown in Nova Scotia. *HortScience* 39: 1640–1643.

Braun, M., and G. Franz. 1999. Quality criteria of bitter fennel oil in the German pharmacopoeia. *Pharm. Pharmacol. Lett.* 9: 48–51.

Cavaleiro, C. M. F., et al. 1993. Contribution for the characterization of Portuguese fennel chemotypes. *J. Essential Oil Res.* 5: 223–225.

Creasy, R. 1995. Fennel: a handsome plant with fine flavour and stature in the garden. *Herb Companion* 7(4): 26–33.

Dadalioğlu, I., and G. A. Evrendilek. 2004. Chemical compositions and antibacterial effects of essential oils of Turkish oregano (*Origanum minutiflorum*), bay laurel (*Laurus nobilis*), Spanish lavender (*Lavandula stoechas* L.), and fennel (*Foeniculum vulgare*) on common foodborne pathogens. *J. Agric. Food Chem.* 52: 8255–8260.

Desmarest, P. 1978. New aspects of fennel cultivation in France. *Acta Hort.* 73: 289–295.

Díaz-Maroto, M. C., et al. 2005. Volatile components and key odorants of fennel (*Foeniculum vulgare* Mill.) and thyme (*Thymus vulgaris* L.) oil extracts obtained by simultaneous distillation-extraction and supercritical fluid extraction. *J. Agric. Food Chem.* 53: 5385–5389.

El-Gengaihi, S., and N. Abdallah. 1978. The effect of date of sowing and plant spacing on yield of seed and volatile oil of fennel (*Foeniculum vulgare* Mill.). *Pharmazie Beih. Ergänzungsband* 33: 605–606.

Embong, M. B., et al. 1977. Essential oils from spices grown in Alberta. Fennel oil (*Foeniculum vulgare* var. *dulce*). *Canad. J. Pl. Sci.* 57: 829–837.

Falzari, L. M., et al. 2005. Reducing fennel stand density increases pollen production, improving potential for pollination and subsequent oil yield. *HortScience* 40: 629–634.

———. 2006. Optimum stand density for maximum essential oil yield in commercial fennel crops. *HortScience* 41: 646–650.

Fehr, D. 1980. Untersuchungen zur Lagerstabilität von Anis, Fenchel und Kümmel. *Pharm. Zeitung* 125: 1300–1303.

Fujita, S.-i., et al. 1980. Miscellaneous contributions to the essential oil of the plants from various territories (46). The constituents of the essential oils from *Foeniculum vulgare* Miller. *J. Agric. Food Chem. Soc. Japan* 54: 765–767.

García-Jiménez, N., et al. 2000. Chemical composition of fennel oil, *Foeniculum vulgare* Miller, from Spain. *J. Essential Oil Res.* 12: 159–162.

Gross, M., et al. 2002. Biosynthesis of estragole and *t*-anethole in bitter fennel (*Foeniculum vulgare* Mill. var. *vulgare*) chemotypes. Changes in SAM:phenylpropene *O*-methyltransferase activities during development. *Pl. Sci.* 163: 1047–1053.

Guillén, M. D., and M. J. Manzanos. 1994. A contribution to the study of Spanish wild-growing fennel (*Foeniculum vulgare* Mill.) as a source of flavour compounds. *Chem. Mikrobiol. Technol. Lebensm.* 16: 141–145.

———. 1996. A study of several parts of the plant *Foeniculum vulgare* as a source of compounds with industrial interest. *Food Res. Intern.* 29: 85–88.

Harvey, I. C., et al. 1988. Essential oil yields from blighted fennel. In *Proc. 41st New Zealand Weed & Pest Control Conference.* 96–98.

Holt, S., et al. 1996. Essential oils smooth gastric functioning. *Altern. Compl. Therap.* 2(1): 46–50.

Hussain, R. A., et al. 1990. Sweetening agents of plant origin: Phenylpropanoid constituents of seven sweet-tasting plants. *Econ. Bot.* 44: 174–182.

Ibrahim, S. M., et al. 2006. Effect of organic manures and chemical fertilizers on *Foeniculum vulgare* Mill and *Carum carvi* L. *Bull. Pharm. Sci. Assiut Univ.* 29: 187–201.

Jahromi, B. N., et al. 2003. Comparison of fennel and mefenamic acid for the treatment of primary dysmenorrhea. *Intern. J. Gynecol. Obst.* 80: 153–157.

Keller, K. 1992. *Foeniculum vulgare*. In *Adverse Effects of Herbal Drugs 1*. Ed. P. A. G. M. De Smet et al. New York: Springer-Verlag. 135–142.

Koşar, M., et al. 2007. Comparison of microwave-assisted hydrodistillation and hydrodistillation methods for the fruit essential oils of *Foeniculum vulgare*. *J. Essential Oil Res.* 19: 426–429.

Kraus, A., and F. J. Hammerschmidt. 1980. An investigation of fennel oils. *Dragoco Rep.* 27: 31–40.

Krüger, H., and K. Hammer. 1999. Chemotypes of fennel (*Foeniculum vulgare* Mill.). *J. Essential Oil Res.* 11: 79–82.

Lamarti, A., et al. 1993. Étude chromatographique de l'huile essentielle de la plantule de fenouil amer (*Foeniculum vulgare* Mill.); caractéristiques spectrales (UV, IR, SM) de ses constituants. *Bull. Soc. Pharm. Bordeaux* 132: 73–89.

Locock, R. A. 1994. Fennel. *Canad. Pharm. J.* 126: 503–504.

Marotti, M., and R. Piccaglia. 1992. The influence of distillation conditions on the essential oil composition of three varieties of *Foeniculum vulgare* Mill. *J. Essential Oil Res.* 4: 569–576.

Marotti, M., et al. 1993. Agronomic and chemical evaluation of three "varieties" of *Foeniculum vulgare* Mill. *Acta Hort.* 331: 63–69.

Miraldi, E. 1999. Comparison of the essential oils from ten *Foeniculum vulgare* Miller samples of fruits of different origin. *Flavour Fragrance J.* 14: 379–382.

Mojab, F., et al. 2007. GC-MS Analysis of the essential oils of roots and leaves of *Foeniculum vulgare*. *J. Essential Oil-Bearing Pl.* 10: 36–40.

Morales, M., et al. 1991. Cultivation of finnochio fennel. *Herb, Spice, Med. Pl. Dig.* 9(1): 1–4.

Ostad, S. N., et al. 2001. The effect of fennel essential oil on uterine contraction as a model for dysmenorrheal, pharmacology and toxicology study. *J. Ethnopharmacol.* 76: 299–304.

Özbek, H., et al. 2003. Hypoglycemic and hepatoprotective effects of *Foeniculum vulgare* Miller seed fixed oil extract in mice and rats. *Eastern J. Med.* 8: 35–40.

———. 2003. Hepatoprotective effect of *Foeniculum vulgare* essential oil. *Fitoterapia* 74: 317–319.

———. 2004. Hepatoprotective effect of *Foeniculum vulgare* essential oil: a carbontetrachloride induced liver fibrosis model in rats. *Scand. J. Lab. Anim. Sci.* 31: 9–17.

———. 2006. Investigation of hepatoprotective effect of *Foeniculum vulgare* fixed oil in rats. *Res. J. Med. Med. Sci.* 1: 72–76.

Pank, F., et al. 2000. Ergebnisse der Auslese von kleinfrüchtigem Arzneifenchel (*Foeniculum vulgare* Mill. ssp. *vulgare* var. *vulgare*) aus Kreuzungsnachkommen verschiedener Genotypen. *Z. Arzn. Gew. Pfl.* 1: 40–48.

Park, J. S., et al. 2004. Antibacterial activity of fennel (*Foeniculum vulgare* Mill.) seed essential oil against the growth of *Streptococcus mutans*. *Food Sci. Biotechnol.* 13: 581–585.

Patra, M., et al. 2002. Utilization of essential oil as natural antifungal against nail-infective fungi. *Flavour Fragrance J.* 17: 91–94.

Pereira, C. G., and M. A. A. Meirales. 2007. Economic analysis of rosemary, fennel and anise essential oils obtained by supercritical fluid extraction. *Flavour Fragrance J.* 22: 407–413.

Piccaglia, R., and M. Marotti. 2001. Characterization of some Italian types of wild fennel (*Foeniculum vulgare* Mill.). *J. Agric. Food Chem.* 49: 239–244.

Pillai, P. K. T., and M. C. Nambiar. 1982. Condiments. In *Cultivation and Utilization of Aromatic Plants*. Ed. C. K. Atal and B. M. Kapur. Jammu Tawi, India: Regional Res. Lab. 167–189.

Randhawa, G. S., and B. S. Gill. 1985. Effect of row spacing and nitrogen level on growth and yield of fennel (*Foeniculum vulgare*). *J. Res. Punjab Agric. Univ.* 22: 39–42.

Ravid, U., et al. 1983. The volatile components of oleoresins and the essential oils of *Foeniculum vulgare* in Israel. *J. Nat. Prod.* 46: 848–851.

Robinson, C., and C. Myers. 1991. Fennel, sweet anise. SMC-017. In *Specialty and Minor Crops Handbook*. Ed. C. Meyers. Oakland: Small Farm Center, Univ. California.

Rosti, L. A., et al. 1994. Toxic effects of a herbal tea mixture in two newborns. *Acta Pediatrica* 83: 683.

Savino, F., et al. 2005. A randomized double-blind placebo-controlled trial of a standardized extract of *Matricariae recutita*, *Foeniculum vulgare* and *Melissa officinalis* (ColiMil®) in the treatment of breastfed colicky infants. *Phytotherapy Res.* 19: 335–340.

Schöne, F., et al. 2006. Effects of essential oils from fennel (*Foeniculum aetheroleum*) and caraway (*Carvi aetheroleum*) in pigs. *J. Anim. Physiol. Anim. Nutr.* 90: 500–510.

Stahl-Biskup, E., and E.-M. Wichtmann. 1991. Composition of the essential oils from roots of some Apiaceae in relation to the development of their oil duct sytems. *Flavour Fragrance J.* 6: 249–255.

Sváb, J. 1978. Problems and results of *Foeniculum vulgare* cultivation in large scale production in Hungary. *Acta Hort.* 73: 297–302.

Syed, M., et al. 1986. Antimicrobial activity of the essential oils of the Umbelliferae family. Part 1. *Cuminum cyminum*, *Coriandrum sativum*, *Foeniculum vulgare* and *Bunium persicum* oils. *Pakistan J. Sci. Industr. Res.* 29: 183–188.

Tanira, M., et al. 1996. Pharmacological and toxicological investigations on *Foeniculum vulgare* dried fruit extract in experimental animals. *Phytotherapy Res.* 10: 33–36.

Tawfik, A. A., and M. F. Mohamed. 1997. Selection for seed yield and earliness in fennel (*Foeniculum vulgare* Mill.) and correlated response in seed-yield. In *Essential Oils: Basic and Applied Research*. Ed. Ch. Franz et al. Carol Stream, Illinois: Allured. 81–86.

Tsalboukov, P. 1979. Studies on the diseases and the pests in the common fennel (*Foeniculum vulgare* Mill.) in Bulgaria and possibilities of control. In *VII International Congress of Essential Oils, October 7–11, 1977, Kyoto, Japan*. 100–104.

Tutin, T. G. 1968. *Foeniculum*. In *Flora Europaea Vol. 2*. Ed. T. G. Tutin et al. Cambridge Univ. Press. 341.

Venskutonis, P. R. 1995. Essential oil composition of some herbs cultivated in Lithuania. In *Flavor, Fragrances and Essential Oils*. Ed. K. H. C. Baser. Istanbul: AREP Publ. 108–123.

Venskutonis, P. R., et al. 1996. Essential oils of fennel (*Foeniculum vulgare* Mill.) from Lithuania. *J. Essential Oil Res.* 8: 211–213.

Yoshioka, M., and T. Tamada. 2005. Aromatic factors of anti-platelet aggregation in fennel oil. *Biogenic Amines* 19: 89–96.

Zygadlo, J. A., et al. 1995. Empleo de aceites esenciales como antioxidantes naturales. *Grasas Aceites* 46: 285–288.

Galium

Anonymous. 2004. Woodruff, sweet. *Rev. Nat. Prod. (Wolters Kluwer Health).*

Ehrendorfer, F., et al. 1976. *Galium.* In *Flora Europaea Vol. 4.* Ed. T. G. Tutin et al. Cambridge Univ. Press. 14–36.

Floreno, A. 1996. Tobacco industry battle puts coumarin in spotlight. *Chem. Market. Rep.* February 12: 22.

Laub, E., et al. 1985. Waldmeister und Maibowle. *Deutsche Apotheker Zeitung* 125: 848–850.

Marles, R. J., et al. 1987. Coumarin in vanilla extracts: its detection and significance. *Econ. Bot.* 41: 41–47.

Máthé, I., et al. 1981. Comparative study of asperuloside production of *Galium verum* L. populations from the surroundings of Budapest. *Bot. Közlem.* 68: 77–84.

———. 1984. Variation in the asperuloside production of *Galium verum* L. during the vegetation period. *Acta Hort.* 144: 49–56.

Geranium

Abbott, P. 1994. *A Guide to Scented Geraniaceae.* West Sussex, England: Hill Publicity Services.

Arctander, S. 1960. *Perfume and Flavor Materials of Natural Origin.* Elizabeth, New Jersey: Steffen Arctander.

Bendtsen, B. H. 2005. *Gardening with Hardy Geraniums.* Portland, Oregon: Timber Press.

Forty, J. 1980. A survey of hardy geraniums in cultivation and their availability in commerce. *Plantsman* 2: 67–78.

Ivanov, V., and A. Shvetz. 1974. Technology of industrial growing of *Geranium* planting material. In *VI International Congress of Essential Oils, San Francisco, California, September 8–12, 1974.* Paper no. 168.

Lis-Balchin, M., ed. 2002. Geranium *and* Pelargonium*: The Genera* Geranium *and* Pelargonium. London: Taylor & Francis.

Ognyanov, I. 1985. Bulgarian zdravetz oil. *Perfumer Flavor.* 10(5): 39–44.

Tsankova, E. T., and I. V. Ognyanov. 1972. Sesquiterpene hydrocarbons in the Bulgarian zdravetz (*Geranium macrorrhizum* L.) oil. *Compt. Rend. Acad. Bulg. Sci.* 25: 1229–1231.

———. 1977. New data on the composition of Bulgarian zdravets oil. *Izv. Khim.* 10: 593–597.

Yeo, P. F. 1985. *Hardy Geraniums.* London: Croom Helm.

Glycyrrhiza

Abe, M., et al. 2003. Glycyrrhizin enhances interleukin-10 production by liver dendritic cells in mice with hepatitis. *J. Gastroenterol.* 38: 962–967.

Akao, T., et al. 1994. Intestinal bacterial hydrolysis is indispensable to absorption of 18 beta-glycyrrhetic acid after oral administration of glycyrrhizin in rats. *J. Pharm. Pharmacol.* 46: 135–137.

Anonymous. 2004. Licorice. *Rev. Nat. Prod. (Wolters Kluwer Health).*

Arase, Y., et al. 1997. The long-term efficacy of glycyrrhizin in chronic hepatitis C patients. *Cancer* 79: 1494–1500.

Baba, M., and S. Shigeta. 1987. Antiviral activity of glycyrrhizin against *Varicella zoster* virus in vitro. *Antiviral Res.* 7: 99–107.

Baba, M., et al. 2002. Studies on cancer chemoprevention by traditional folk medicine XXV. Inhibitory effect of isoliquiritigenin on azoxymethane-induced murine colon aberrant crypt focus formation and carcinogenesis. *Biol. Pharm. Bull.* 25: 247–250.

Baschetti, R. 1995. Chronic fatigue syndrome and licorice. *New Zealand Med. J.* April 26: 156–157.

Benetti, Gl., and R. Ranzetti. 1994. Le alchilpirazine, componenti importanti dell'aroma degli estratti di liquirizia. *Industr. Alimentari* 33: 639–642.

Bielenberg, J. 1992. Lakritzerzeugnisse ó gesundheitlich unbedenklich? *Pharm. Unserer Zeit* 21: 157–158.

Cantelli-Forti, G., et al. 1994. Interaction of licorice on glycyrrhizin pharmacokinetics. *Environmental Health Perspectives* 102 (Suppl. 9): 65–68.

———. 1997. Toxicological assessment of liquorice: biliary excretion in rats. *Pharmacol. Res.* 35: 463–470.

Cermelli, C., et al. 1996. Activity of glycyrrhizin and its diastereoisomers against two new human herpesviruses: HHV-6 and HHV-7. *Phytotherapy Res.* 10: S27–S28.

Chamberlain, J., and I. Abolnik. 1997. Pulmonary edema following a licorice binge. *Western J. Med.* 167: 184–185.

Cherng, J.-M., et al. 2004. A quantitative bioassay for HIV-1 gene expression based on UV activation: effect of glycyrrhizic acid. *Antiviral Res.* 62: 27–36.

Chin, Y.-W., et al. 2007. Anti-oxidant constituents of the roots and stolons of licorice (*Glycyrrhiza glabra*). *J. Agric. Food Agric.* 55: 4691–4697.

Choi, E.-M. 2005. The licorice root derived isoflavan glabridin increases the function of osteoblastic MC3T3-E1 cells. *Biochem. Pharmacol.* 70: 363–368.

Chung, J. G. 1998. Inhibitory actions of glycyrrhizic acid on arylamine N-acetyltransferase activity in strains of *Helicobacter pylori* from peptic ulcer patients. *Drug Chem. Toxicol.* 21: 355–370.

Cinatl, J., et al. 2003. Glycyrrhizin, an active component of liquorice roots, and replication of SARS-associated coronavirus. *Lancet* 361: 2045–2046.

Curreli, G., et al. 2005. Glycyrrhizic acid alters Kaposi sarcoma: associated herpesvirus latency, triggering p53-mediated apoptosis in transformed B lymphocytes. *J. Clin. Invest.* 115: 642–652.

DeKlerk, G., et al. 1997. Hyopkalaemia and hypertension associated with the use of liquorice flavour chewing gum. *Brit. Med. J.* 314: 731–732.

Fanali, S., et al. 2005. Use of nano-liquid chromatography for the analysis of glycyrrhizin and glycyrrhetic acid in licorice roots and candles. *J. Sep. Sci.* 28: 982–986.

Feldman, E. C., et al. 2005. Liquorice and canine Addison's disease. *New Zealand Vet. J.* 53: 214.

Fenwick, G. R., et al. 1990. Liquorice, *Glycyrrhiza glabra* L.: composition, uses and analysis. *Food Chem.* 38: 119–143.

Frattini, C., et al. 1977. Volatile flavour components of licorice. *J. Agric. Food Chem.* 25: 1238–1241.

Fuhrman, B., et al. 1997. Licorice extract and its major polyphenol glabradin protect low-density lipoprotein against lipid peroxidation: in vitro and ex vivo studies in humans and in atherosclerotic apolipoprotein E-deficient mice. *Amer. J. Clin. Nutr.* 66: 267–275.

Fukai, T., et al. 2002. Anti-*Helicobacter pylori* flavonoids from licorice extract. *Life Sci.* 71: 1449–1463.

———. 2002. Antimicrobial activity of licorice flavonoids against methicillin-resistant *Staphylococcus aureus.* *Fitoterapia* 73: 536–539.

Ghosh, D., et al. 1994. Mechanism of inhibition of 3α,20β-hydroxysteroid dehydrogenase by a licorice-derived steroidal inhibitor. *Structure* 2: 973–980.

Gibson, M. R. 1978. Glycyrrhiza in old and new perspectives. *Lloydia* 41: 348–354.

Gordon, M. H., and J. An. 1995. Antioxidant activity of flavonoids isolated from licorice. *J. Agric. Food Chem.* 43: 1784–1788.

Gunnarsdóttir, S., and T. Jóhannesson. 1997. Glycyrrhetic acid in human blood after ingestion of glycyrrhizic acid in licorice. *Pharmacol. Toxicol.* 81: 300–302.

Hartley, M. J. 1996. Weed control in licorice. *Proc. New Zealand Plant Protection Conf.* 1996: 169–172.

Hatano, T., et al. 1991. Phenolic constituents of licorice. IV. Correlation of phenolic constituents and licorice specimens from various sources, and inhibitory effects of licorice extracts on xanthine oxidase and monoamine oxidase. *J. Pharm. Soc. Japan* 111: 311–321.

———. 1998. Bioactive phenolics from licorice: their radical-scavenging effects, inhibitory effects on oxidative enzymes and antiviral effects. In *Towards Natural Medicine Research in the 21st Century.* Ed. G. Aegata et al. Amsterdam: Elsevier. 261–272.

Hayashi, H. 2007. Field surveys and comparative analysis of *Glycyrrhiza* plants. *Foods Food Ingred. J. Jap.* 212: 357–364.

Hayashi, H., et al. 1998. Seasonal variation of glycyrrhizin and isoliquiritigen glycosides in the root of *Glycyrrhiza glabra* L. *Biol. Pharm. Bull.* 21: 987–989.

———. 2000. Molecular cloning and characterization of a cDNA for *Glycyrrhiza glabra* cycloartenol synthase. *Biol. Pharm. Bull.* 23: 231–234.

———. 2000. Phylogenetic relationship of six *Glycyrrhiza* species based on *rbc*L sequences and chemical constituents. *Biol. Pharm. Bull.* 23: 602–606.

———. 2003. Field survey of *Glycyrrhiza* plants in Central Asia (1). Characterization of *G. uralensis*, *G. glabra* and the putative intermediate collected in Kazakhstan. *Biol. Pharm. Bull.* 26: 867–871.

———. 2003. Field survey of *Glycyrrhiza* plants in Central Asia (2). Characterization of phenolics and their variation in the leaves of *Glycyrrhiza* plants collected in Kazakhstan. *Chem. Pharm. Bull.* 51: 1147–1152.

———. 2003. Field survey of *Glycyrrhiza* plants in Central Asia (3). Chemical characterization of *G. glabra* collected in Uzbekistan. *Chem. Pharm. Bull.* 51: 1338–1340.

Hibashi, H., et al. 2005. Glycyrrhizin induces apoptosis in human stomach cancer KATO III and human promyelotic leukemia HL-60 cells. *Intern. J. Mol. Med.* 16: 233–236.

Hiraga, Y., and K. Kajiyama. 1997. Chemical and original guide to licorice root products. *Bull. Meiji Coll. Pharm.* 27: 9–57.

Hojo, H., and J. Sato. 2002. Antifungal activity of licorice (*Glycyrrhiza glabra*) and potential applications in beverage. *Foods Food Ingred. J. Jap.* 203: 27–33.

Hrelia, P., et al. 1996. Potential antimutagenic activity of *Glycyrrhiza glabra* extract. *Phytotherapy Res.* 10: S101–S103.

Huang, W., et al. 1994. An orthogonal method for comparing extracting techniques of licorice root extract. *Zhongguo Zhongyao Sazhi* 19: 283–284.

İbanoğlu, E., and Ş. İbanoğlu. 2000. Foaming behaviour of liquorice (*Glycyrrhiza glabra*) extract. *Food Chem.* 70: 333–336.

Jang, S. I., et al. 1998. Effect of glycyrrhizin on rainbow trout *Oncorhynchus mykiss* leukocyte responses. *J. Kor. Soc. Microbiol.* 33: 263–271.

Kamei, J., et al. 2005. Pharmacokinetic and pharmacodynamic profiles of the antitussive principles of *Glycyrrhiza radix* (licorice), a main component of the Kampo preparation Bakumondo-to (Mai-mendong-tang). *Eur. J. Pharmacol.* 507: 163–168.

Kameoka, H., and K. Nakai. 1987. Components of essential oil from the root of *Glycyrrhiza glabra. J. Agric. Chem. Soc. Japan* 61: 1119–1121.

Kent, C. 1994. Licorice: more than just candy. *Atoms* Autumn: 9–14.

Kim, S. C., et al. 2004. Cytoprotective effects of *Glycyrrhiza radix* extract and its active component liquiritigenin against cadmium-induced toxicity (effects on bas translocation and cytochroma c-mediate PARP cleavage). *Toxicology* 197: 239–251.

Kimura, M., et al. 2001. Glycyrrhizin and some analogues induce growth of primary cultured adult rat hepatocytes via epidermal growth factor receptors. *Eur. J. Pharmacol.* 431: 151–161.

Kumano, M., et al. 1985. Glycyrrhizin contents of licorice roots. *Nagasaki-ken Eisei Kogai Kenkyushoho* 27: 77–83.

Lee, C.-H., et al. 2007. Protective mechanism of glycyrrhizin on acute liver injury induced by carbon tetrachloride in mice. *Biol. Pharm. Bull.* 30: 1898–1904.

Lee, C. S., et al. 2007. Glycyrrhizin protection against 3-morpholinosydnonimine-induced mitochondrial dysfunction and cell death in lung epithelial cells. *Life Sci.* 80: 1759–1767.

Li, K-l., et al. 2001. Protective role of glycyrrhizin on experimental obstructive nephropathy in rats. *Acta Acad. Med. Militaris Tertiae* 23: 573–575.

Lin, J.-C. 2003. Mechanism of action of glycyrrhizic acid in inhibition of Epstein-Barr virus replication in vitro. *Antiviral Res.* 59: 41–47.

Lloyd, J. U. 1929. Licorice. *Eclectic Med. J.* 1929: 1–11.

Malagoli, M., et al. 1998. Effect of glycyrrhizin and its diastereoisomers on the growth of human tumour cells: preliminary findings. *Phytotherapy Res.* 12: S95–S97.

Martinez, A., et al. 1998. Protective effect of broccoli, onion, carrot, and licorice extracts against cytotoxicity of *N*-nitrosamines evaluated by 3-(4,5-dimethylthiazol-2-yl)-2,5-diphenyltetrazolium bromide assay. *J. Agric. Food Chem.* 46: 585–589.

Mauricio, I., et al. 1997. Identification of glycyrrhizin as a thrombin inhibitor. *Biochem. Biphys. Commun.* 235: 259–263.

Mendes-Silva, W., et al. 2003. Antithrombotic effect of glycyrrhizin, a plant-derived thrombin inhibitor. *Thrombosis Res.* 112: 93–98.

Mitscher, L. A., et al. 1980. Antimicrobial agents from higher plants. Antimicrobial isoflavonoids and related substances from *Glycyrrhiza glabra* L. var. *typica. J. Nat. Prod.* 43: 259–269.

Moon, A., and S. H. Kim. 1996. Effect of *Glycyrrhiza glabra* roots and glycyrrhizin on the glucuronidation in rats. *Pl. Med.* 62: 115–119.

Näf, R., and A. Jaquier. 2006. New lactones in liquorice (*Glycyrrhiza glabra* L.). *Flavour Fragrance J.* 21: 193–197.

Nakagawa, K., and M. Asami. 1981. Effect of glycyrrhizin on hepatic lysosomal systems. *Jap. J. Pharm.* 31: 849–851.

Nakagawa, K., et al. 2004. Licorice flavonoids suppress abdominal fat accumulation and increase in blood glucose level in obese diabetic KK-Ay mice. *Biol. Pharm. Bull.* 27: 1775–1778.

Nakashima, H., et al. 1987. A new anti-human-immunodeficiency-virus substance, glycyrrhizin sulfate; endowment of glycyrrhizin with reverse transcriptase-inhibitory activity by chemical modification. *Jap. J. Cancer Res.* 78: 767–771.

Nerya, O., et al. 2003. Glabrene and isoliquiritigenin as tyrosinase inhibitors from licorice roots. *J. Agric. Food Chem.* 51: 1201–1207.

Nielsen, I., and R. S. Pedersen. 1984. Life-threatening hypokalaemia caused by liquorice ingestion. *Lancet* 1984(1): 1305.

Niwa, K., et al. 2007. Preventive effects of glycyrrhizin on estrogen-related endometrial carcinogenesis in mice. *Oncology Rep.* 17: 617–622.

Nomiyama, K., and H. Nomiyama. 1993. Cadmium-induced renal dysfunction was improved by treating hepatic injury with glycyrrhizin. *J. Trace Elements Exp. Med.* 6: 171–178.

Nose, M., et al. 1994. A comparison of the antihepatotoxic activity between glycyrrhizin and glycyrrhetinic acid. *Pl. Med.* 60: 136–139.

Ofir, R., et al. 2003. Inhibition of serotonin re-uptake by licorice constituents. *J. Mol. Neurosci.* 20: 135–140.

Okada, K., et al. 1989. Identification of antimicrobial and antioxidant constituents from licorice of Russian and Xinjiang origin. *Chem. Pharm. Bull.* 37: 2528–2530.

Okamoto, T. 2000. The protective effect of glycyrrhizin on anti-Fas antibody-induced hepatitis in mice. *Eur. J. Pharmacol.* 387: 229–232.

Okamoto, T., and T. Kanda. 1999. Glycyrrhizin protects mice from concanavalin A-induced hepatitis without affecting cytokine expression. *Intern. J. Mol. Med.* 4: 149–152.

Pan, X., et al. 2000. Microwave-assisted extraction of glycyrrhizic acid from licorice root. *Biochem. Eng. J.* 5: 173–177.

Paolini, M., et al. 1999. Effect of liquorice and glycyrrhizin on rat liver carcinogen metabolizing enzymes. *Cancer Lett.* 145: 35–42.

Polyakov, N. E., et al. 2005. Complexation of lappaconitine with clycyrrhizic acid: stability and reactivity studies. *J. Phys. Chem. B* 109: 24526–24530.

———. 2006. Host-guest complexes of carotenoids with β-glycyrrhizic acid. *J. Phys. Chem. B* 110: 6991–6998.

———. 2006. Antioxidant and redox properties of supramolecular complexes of carotenoids with β-glycyrrhizic acid. *Free Rad. Biol. Med.* 40: 1804–1809.

Pompei, R. 1979. Activity of *Glycyrrhiza glabra* extracts and glycyrrhizic acid on virus growth and infectivity. *Rivista Farm. Terapia* 10: 281–284.

Pompei, R., et al. 1979. Glycyrrhizic acid inhibits virus growth and inactivates virus particles. *Nature* 281: 689–690.

———. 1979. On the antiviral action of glycyrrhizic acid. II.–Noninvolvement of cell membrane transport of ions and metabolites on the antiviral effect. *Rivista Farm. Terapia* 10: 355–359.

———. 1980. Antiviral activity of glycyrrhizic acid. *Experientia* 36: 304.

———. 1983. Glycyrrhizic acid inhibits influenza virus growth in embryonated eggs. *Microbiologica* 6: 247–250.

Raggi, M. A., et al. 1994. Bioavailability of glycyrrhizin and licorice extract in rat and human plasma as detected by a HPLC method. *Pharmazie* 49: 269–272.

———. 1995. Studio dell'effetto coleretico della liquirizia: identificazione e determinazione di componenti dell *Glycyrrhiza glabra* farmacologicamente attivi. *Boll. Chim. Farmaceutico* 134: 634–638.

Ram, A., et al. 2006. Glycyrrhizin alleviates experimental allergic asthma in mice. *Intern. Immunopharmacol.* 6: 1468–1477.

Rossi, T., et al. 1995. Influence of glycyrrhizin on the evolution and respiration of Ehrlich ascites tumour cells. *In Vivo* 9: 183–186.

———. 1999. Correlation between high intake of glycyrrhizin and myolysis of the papillary muscles: an experimental *in vivo* study. *Pharmacol. Toxicol.* 85: 221–229.

Sakagami, H., et al. 1992. Volatile components of licorice roots produced in different countries. *Nippon Shokuhin Kogyo Gakkaishi* 39: 257–263.

Sasaki, H., et al. 2002. Effect of glycyrrhizin, an active component of licorice roots, on HIV replication in cultures of peripheral blood mononuclear cells from HIV-seropositive patients. *Pathobiology* 70: 229–236.

Sato, J., et al. 2001. Identification of an antifungal substance derived from the oil-based extract of licorice. *Biocontrol Sci.* 6: 113–118.

Sato, S., et al. 2004. The effects of nutrient solution concentration on inorganic and glycyrrhizin contents of *Glycyrrhiza glabra*. *Pharm. Soc. Jap.* 124: 705–709.

Sato, Y., et al. 2006. Glycocoumarin from glycyrrhizae radix acts as a potent antispasmodic through inhibition of phophodiesterase 3. *J. Ethnopharmacol.* 105: 409–414.

Segal, R., et al. 1985. Anticariogenic activity of licorice and glycyrrhizine I: inhibition of in vitro plaque formation by *Steptococcus mutans*. *J. Pharm. Sci.* 74: 79–81.

Sekizawa, T., et al. 2001. Glycyrrhizin increases survival of mice with herpes simplex encephalitis. *Acta Virol.* 45: 51–54.

Shibata, N., et al. 2000. Characteristics of intestinal absorption and disposition of glycyrrhizin in mice. *Biopharm. Drug Disposition* 21: 95–101.

———. 2000. Application of pressure-controlled colon delivery capsule to oral administration of glycyrrhizin in dogs. *J. Pharm. Pharmacol.* 53: 441–447.

Snow, J. M. 1996. *Glycyrrhiza glabra* L. (Leguminosae). *Protocol J. Bot. Med.* Winter: 9–14.

Spinks, E. A., and G. R. Fenwick. 1990. The determination of glycyrrhizin in selected UK liquorice products. *Food Addit. Contaminants* 7: 769–778.

Stormer, F. C., et al. 1993. Glycyrrhizic acid in liquorice: evaluation of health hazard. *Food Chem. Toxic.* 31: 303–312.

Strandbert, T. E., et al. 2001. Birth outcome in relation to licorice consumption during pregnancy. *Amer. J. Epidemiology* 153: 1085–1088.

Takeda, S., et al. 1996. Bioavailability study of glycyrrhetic acid after oral administration of glycyrrhizin in rats; relevance to the intestinal bacterial hydrolysis. *J. Pharm. Pharmacol.* 48: 902–905.

Tamir, S., et al. 2001. Estrogen-like activity of glabrene and other constituents isolated from licorice root. *J. Steroid Biochem. Mol. Biol.* 78: 291–298.

Tanahashi, T., et al. 2002. Glycyrrhizic acid suppresses type 2 11β-hydroxysteroid dehydrogenase expression in vivo. *J. Steroid Biochem. Mol. Biol.* 80: 441–447.

Torshiz, N. B., and H. Ghadiri. 1997. Growth of licorice (*Glycyrrhiza glabra* L.) as affected by propagation materials. *Iran Agric. Res.* 16: 97–110.

Usai, M., et al. 1995. Glycyrrhizin variability in subterranean organs of Sardinian *Glycyrrhiza glabra* subspecies *glabra* var. *glabra*. *J. Nat. Prod.* 58: 1727–1729.

Utsunomiya, T., et al. 1997. Glycyrrhizin, an active component of licorice roots, reduces morbidity and mortality of mice infected with lethal doses of influenza virus. *Antimicrobial Agents Chemotherapy* 41: 551–556.

———. 2000. Glcyrrhizin improves the resistance of AIDS mice to opportunistic infection of *Candida albicans* through the modulation of MAIDS-assocaited Type 2 T cell responses. *Clin. Immunol.* 95: 145–155.

van der Zwan, A. 1993. Hypertension encephalopathy after liquorice ingestion. *Clin. Neurol. Neurosurgery* 95: 35–37.

Van Gelderen, C. E. M., et al. 2000. Glycyrrhizic acid: the assessment of a no effect level. *Human Exp. Toxicol.* 19: 434–439.

Van Rossum, T. G. J., et al. 1998. Glycyrrhizin as a potential treatment for chronic hepatitis C. *Aliment. Pharmacol. Ther.* 12: 199–205.

———. 1999. Pharmacokinetics of intravenous glycyrrhizin after single and multiple doses in patients with chronic hepatitis C infection. *Clin. Therapeutics* 21: 2080–2090.

Vaya, J., et al. 1997. Antioxidant constituents from licorice roots: isolation, structure elucidation, and antioxidative capacity toward LDL oxidation. *Free Radical Biol. Med.* 23: 302–313.

Walker, W. W. 1953. Licorice: dark mystery of industry. *Atlantic* 190(5): 23–26.

Wang, Y.-C., and Y.-S. Yang. 2007. Simultaneous quantification of flavonoids and triterpenoids in licorice using UPLC. *J. Chromatogr. B* 850: 392–399.

Wang, Z., et al. 1994. Mechanism of gastrointestinal absorption of glycyrrhizin in rats. *Biol. Pharm. Bull.* 17: 1399–1403.

———. 1995. Gastrointestinal absorption characteristics of glycyrrhizin from *Glycyrrhiza* extract. *Biol. Pharm. Bull.* 18: 1238–1241.

———. 1996. Pharmacokinetics of glycyrrhizin in rats with D-galactosamine-induced hepatic disease. *Biol. Pharm. Bull.* 19: 901–904.

Yamazaki, M., et al. 1994. Genetic relationships among *Glycyrrhiza* plants determined by RAPD and RFLP analyses. *Biol. Pharm. Bull.* 17: 1529–1531.

———. 1995. Extraction of DNA and RAPD analysis from dried licorice root. *Nat. Med.* 49: 488–490.

Yanagawa, Y., et al. 2004. Effects of cost of glycyrrhizin in the treatment of upper respiratory tract infections in members of the Japanese maritime self-defense force: preliminary report of a prospective, randomized, double-blind, controlled, parallel-group, alternate-day treatment assignment clinical trial. *Curr. Therapeutic Res.* 65: 26–33.

Yano, S. 1992. Recent studies on licorice. *IRYO* 46: 241–245.

Yeo, P. F. 1968. *Glycyrrhiza*. In *Flora Europaea Vol. 2*. Ed. T. G. Tutin et al. Cambridge Univ. Press. 127.

Yokotoa, T., et al. 1998. The inhibitory effect of glabridin from licorice extracts on melanogenesis and inflammation. *Pigment Cell Res.* 11: 355–361.

Zhongping, J. L., et al. 2005. Simultaneous determination of glycyrrhizin, a marker component in radix glycyrrhizae, and its major metabolite glycyrrhetic acid in human plasma by LC-MS/MS. *J. Chromatogr. B* 814: 201–207.

Hedeoma

Anonymous. 1992. Pennyroyal. In *Lawrence Review of Natural Products.* St. Louis: Facts and Comparisons.

Boyd, E. L. 1992. *Hedeoma pulegioides* and *Mentha pulegium.* In *Adverse Effects of Herbal Drugs 1.* Ed. P. A. G. M. De Smet et al. New York: Springer-Verlag. 151–156.

Calpouzos, L. 1954. Botanical aspects of oregano. *Econ. Bot.* 8: 222–233.

Handa, K. L., et al. 1964. Essential oils and their constituents XXIII. Chemotaxonomy of the genus *Mentha. J. Pharm. Sci.* 53: 1407–1409.

Irving, R. 1980. The systematics of *Hedeoma* (Labiatae). *Sida* 8: 218–295.

Lawrence, B. M. 1981. *Essential Oils 1979–1980.* Wheaton, Illinois: Allured.

Helichrysum

Bianchini, A., et al. 2003. A comparative study of volatile constituents of two *Helichrysum italicum* (Roth) Guss. Don Fil subspecies growing in Corsica (France), Tuscany and Sardinia (Italy). *Flavour Fragrance J.* 19: 487–491.

Charles, D. J., and J. E. Simon. 1991. Volatile compounds of the curry plant. *HortScience* 26: 69–70.

Chinou, I. B., et al. 1996. Chemical and biological studies on two *Helichrysum* species of Greek origin. *Pl. Med.* 62: 377–378.

Clapham, A. R. 1976. *Helichrysum.* In *Flora Europaea Vol. 4.* Cambridge Univ. Press. 128–131.

Ferrares, L., et al. 2005. Le proprietá antimicrobiche e fitocosmetiche dell'elicriso. *Cosmetic News* 28: 228–231.

Krüssmann, G. 1985. *Manual of Cultivated Broad-leaved Trees and Shrubs.* 3 vols. Trans. M. E. Epp. Portland, Oregon: Timber Press.

Manitto, P., et al. 1972. Two new beta-diketones from *Helichrysum italicum. Phytochemistry* 11: 2112–2114.

Marongiu, B., et al. 2003. Analysis of the volatile concentrate of the leaves and flowers of *Helichrysum italicum* (Roth) Don ssp. microphyllum (Willd.) Nyman (Asteraceae) by supercritical fluid extraction and their essential oils. *J. Essential Oil Res.* 15: 120–126.

Mastelic, J., et al. 2005. Composition and antimicrobial activity of *Helichrysum ital-*icum essential oil and its terpene and terpenoid fractions. *Chem. Nat. Comp.* 41: 35–40.

Paolini, J., et al. 2006. Composition of essential oils of *Helichrysum italicum* (Roth) G. Don fil subsp. *italicum* from Tuscan archipelago islands. *Flavour Fragrance J.* 21: 805–808.

Peyron, L., et al. 1978. Composition of *Helichrysum* essential oils. *Perfumer Flavor.* 3(5): 25–27.

———. 1978. Composition des essences d'*Helichrysum. Rivista Ital. EPPOS* 60: 79–82.

Roussis, V., et al. 2000. Volatile constituents of four *Helichrysum* species growing in Greece. *Biochem. Syst. Ecol.* 28: 163–175.

Tucker, A. O., et al. 1997. Volatile leaf oil of the curry plant [*Helichrysum italicum* (Roth) G. Don subsp. *italicum*] and dwarf curry plant [subsp. *microphyllum* (Willd.) Nyman] in the North American herb trade. *J. Essential Oil Res.* 9: 583–585.

Usai, M., et al. 1997. Preliminary analysis of essential oil from Sardinian *Helichrysum italicum* (Roth) G. Don ssp. *microphyllum* (Willd.) Nyman. In *Essential Oils: Basic and Applied Research.* Ed. Ch. Franz et al. Carol Stream, Illinois: Allured. 207–208.

Weyerstahl, P. 1988. Investigation of helichrysum oil. *H&R Contact* 43: 19–21.

Weyerstahl, P., et al. 1986. Isolation and synthesis of compounds from the essential oil of *Helichrysum italicum.* In *Progress in Essential Oil Research.* Ed. E.-J. Brunke. Berlin: Walter de Gruyter. 177–195.

Zola, A., and J.-P. Levanda. 1976. Quelques huiles essentielles en provenance de la Corse. *Rivista Ital. EPPOS* 57: 467–472.

Houttuynia

Bauer, R., et al. 1996. Cyclooxygenase inhibitory constituents from *Houttuynia cordata. Phytomedicine* 2: 305–308.

Bloom, A. 1988. *Houttuynia cordata* 'Chameleon'. *Garden* (London) 113: 476–479.

Hayashi, K., et al. 1995. Virucidal effects of the steam distillate from *Houttuynia cordata* and its components on HSV-1, influenza virus, and HIV. *Pl. Med.* 61: 237–241.

Kaiser, R. 2006. *Meaningful Scents Around the World.* Zurich: Verlag Helv. Chim. Acta.

Kindscher, K. 1986. *Gardening with Southeast Asian Refugees.* Lawrence, Kansas: Kelly Kindschar.

Kuebel, K. R., and A. O. Tucker. 1988. Vietnamese culinary herbs in the United States. *Econ. Bot.* 42: 413–419.

Song, H.-H., and M. K. Shin. 1987. Effects of Houttuyniae Herba on immune responses and histological findings in mice bearing pneumonitis. *Kor. J. Pharmacogn.* 18: 216–232.

Tutupalli, L. V., and M. G. Chaubal. 1975.

Saururaceae. V. Composition of the essential oil from foliage of *Houttuynia cordata* and chemosystematics of Saururaceae. *Lloydia* 38: 92–96.

Wagner, H., et al. 1997. Herba houttuyniae cordatae (xuxingcao). *Chin. Drug Monogr. Anal.* 1(6): 1–12.

Yinger, B. 1989. *Houttuynia cordata. Garden* (London) 114: 298.

Yinger, B., and C. R. Hahn. 1985. Cultivars of Japanese plants at Brookside: 2. *Arnoldia* 45(2): 7–18.

Zhu, L.-f., et al. 1993. *Aromatic Plants and Essential Constituents.* Hong Kong: South China Inst. Bot., Peace Book Co.

Humulus

Anonymous. 2004. Hops. *Rev. Nat. Prod. (Wolters Kluwer Health).*

Araki, S., et al. 1998. Identification of hop cultivars by DNA marker analysis. *J. Amer. Soc. Brew. Chem.* 56: 93–98.

Arimoto, S. 2002. Antimutagens in beer and other alcoholic beverages active against several carcinogens. *Foods Food Ingred. J. Jap.* 200: 5–11.

Bennett, J. M. 1996. *Ale, Beer, and Brewsters in England: Women's Work in a Changing World 1300–1600.* New York: Oxford Univ. Press.

Bernotienè, G., et al. 2004. Chemical composition of essential oils of hops (*Humulus lupulus* L.) growing wild in Aukštaitija. *Chemija* 15: 31–36.

Bhattacharya, S., et al. 2003. Inhibition of *Streptococcus mutans* and other oral streptococci by hop (*Humulus lupulus* L.) constituents. *Econ. Bot.* 57: 118–125.

Buhner, S. H. 1998. *Sacred and Herbal Healing Beers: The Secret of Ancient Fermentation.* Boulder, Colorado: Brewers Publ.

Burkhardt, R. J. 1986. Determination of essential oil in hops and hop products. *J. Amer. Soc. Brew. Chem.* 44: 38–40.

Buttery, R. G. 1967. Hop flavour. In *Symposium on Foods: Chemistry and Physiology of Flavor.* Ed. H. W. Schultz et al. Westport, Connecticut: AVI Publ. Co. 406–418.

Buttery, R. G., and L. C. Ling. 1967. Identification of hop varieties by gas chromatographic analysis of their essential oils. Capillary gas chromatography patterns and analyses of hop oils from American-grown varieties. *J. Agric. Food Chem.* 15: 531–535.

Carter, P. R., et al. 1990. *Hop.* Univ. Wisconsin-Madison Alternative Field Crops Manual.

Corliss, J. 1991. Hoppiness is brewing better beer. *Agric. Res.* 39(9): 18–19.

Davies, N. W. 1982. Essential oils of Tasmanian grown hops. *J. Inst. Brew.* 88: 80–83.

DeLyser, D. Y., and W. J. Kasper. 1994. Hopped beer: the case for cultivation. *Econ. Bot.* 48: 166–170.

de Mets, M., and M. Verzele. 1968. The aroma of hops. I. Origin and identification of hop aroma substances. *J. Inst. Brew.* 74: 74–81.

Edwardson, J. R. 1952. Hops: their botany, history, production and utilization. *Econ. Bot.* 6: 160–175.

Evans, R. G., et al. 1985. *Hop Production in the Yakima Valley.* Washington State Univ. Coop. Extens. EB 1328.

Eyres, G. T., et al. 2007. Comparison of odor-active compounds in the spicy fraction of hop (*Humulus lupulus* L.) essential oil from four different varieties. *J. Agric. Food Chem.* 55: 6252–6261.

Foster, R. T. 1985. Changes in hop oil content and hoppiness potential (Sigma) during hop aging. *J. Amer. Soc. Brew. Chem.* 43: 127–135.

Gardner, D. S. J. 1994. Hop flavour and aroma products (Monograph). *Eur. Brew. Conv.* 22: 114–126.

Hansel, R., et al. 1982. The sedative-hypnotic principle of hops. 3. Communication: contents of 2-methyl-3-butene-2-ol in hops and hop preparations. *Pl. Med.* 45: 224–228.

Haunold, A., and G. B. Nickerson. 1987. Development of a hop with European aroma characteristics. *J. Amer. Soc. Brew. Chem.* 45: 146–151.

———. 1990. 'Mt. Hood', a new American noble aroma hop. *J. Amer. Soc. Brew. Chem.* 48: 115–118.

Heyrick, A., et al. 2002. Modulation of the phytoestrogenicity of beer by monoterpene alcohols present in various hop oil fractions. *J. Inst. Brew.* 108: 94–101.

Hinman, H. R., and J. H. Griffin. 1986. *Cost of Establishing and Producing Hops in the Yakima Valley, Washington.* Washington State Univ. Extens. Bull. 1134.

Hums, N. 1973. Zur Chemie der Hopfenbitterstoffe. *Brauwelt* 113: 38–41.

Irwin, A. J. 1989. Varietal dependence of hop flavour volatiles in lager. *J. Inst. Brew.* 95: 185–194.

Kač, M., and M. Kovačevič. 2000. Presentation and determination of hop (*Humulus lupulus* L.) cultivars by a min-max model on composition of hop essential oil. *Monatsschrift Bruwissenschaft* 9/10: 180–184.

Kač, M., and D. Kralj. 1998. Studying biodiversity of hop (*Humulus lupulus* L.) accessions from the composition of their essential oils. *Acta Hort.* 476: 313–319.

Kaltner, D., et al. 2001. Hops: investigations into technological and flavour effects in beer. *Brauwelt Intern.* 2001: 40–45.

———. 2001. Untersuchungen zum Hopfenaroma in Pilsner Bieren bei Variation technologischer Parameter. *Monatsschrift Brauwissenschaft* 9/10: 199–205.

Kammhuber, K. 2000. Untersuchungen zur Biogenese der ätherischen Öle des Hopfens. *Monatsschrift Brauwissenschaft* 7/8: 138–142.

Kammhuber, K., and S. Hagl. 2001. Statistische Untersuchungen zur Korrelation von Hopfenölkomponenten. *Monatsschrift Brauwissenschaft* 5/6: 100–103.

Katsiotis, S. T., et al. 1989. Comparative study of the essential oils from hops of various *Humulus lupulus* L. cultivars. *Flavour Fragrance J.* 4: 187–191.

Kenny, S. T. 1990. Identification of U.S.-grown hop cultivars by hop acid and essential oil analysis. *J. Amer. Soc. Brew. Chem.* 48: 3–8.

Kovačevič, M., and M. Kač. 2001. Solid-phase microextraction of hop volatiles. Potential use for determination and verification of hop varieties. *J. Chromatogr. A* 981: 159–167.

———. 2002. Determination and verification of hop varieties by analysis of essential oils. *Food Chem.* 77: 489–494.

Krofta, K. 2003. Comparison of quality parameters of Czech and foreign hop varieties. *Pl. Soil. Environ.* 49: 261–268.

Lam, K. C., et al. 1986. Aging of hops and their contribution to beer flavour. *J. Agric. Food Chem.* 34: 763–770.

Lermusieau, G., et al. 2001. Use of GC-olfactometry to identify the hop aromatic compounds in beer. *J. Agric. Food Chem.* 49: 3867–3874.

Likens, S. T., and G. B. Nikerson. 1967. Identification of hop varieties by gas chromatographic analysis of their essential oils. Constancy of oil composition under various environmental influences. *J. Agric. Food Chem.* 15: 525–530.

Lim, U.-K., and W.-C. Cho. 1976. The study on the effects of various N.P.K. fertilization levels on hop yield. *Korean J. Bot.* 19: 37–40.

Mizobuchi, S., and Y. Sato. 1984. A new flavonone with antifungal activity isolated from hops. *Agric. Biol. Chem.* 48: 2771–2775.

———. 1985. Antifungal activity of 2,4-dihydroxyacylophenones and related compounds. *Agric. Biol. Chem.* 49: 1327–1333.

———. 1985. Antifungal activities of hop bitter resins and related compounds. *Agric. Biol. Chem.* 49: 399–403.

Moir, M. 1994. Hop aromatic compounds. (Monograph). *Eur. Brew. Conv.* 22: 165–180.

Narziss, L., et al. 1999. Das Verhalten flüchtiger Aromastoffe bei der Alterung des Bieres. *Monatsschrift Brauwissenschaft* 9/10: 164–175

———. 1999. Untersuchungen zur Beeinlussung der Geschmacksstabilität durch Variation technologischer Parameter bei der Bierherstellung. *Monatsschrift Brauwissenschaft* 11/12: 192–206

Peacock, V. E., and M. L. Deinzer. 1980. Hop aroma in American beer. *J. Agric. Food Chem.* 28: 774–777.

———. 1981. Chemistry of hop aroma in beer. *J. Amer. Soc. Brew. Chem.* 39: 136–141.

Perpète, P., et al. 1998. Varietal discrimination of hop pellets by essential oil analysis. I. Comparison of fresh samples. *J. Amer. Soc. Brew. Chem.* 56: 104–108

Pilling, R. 1980. Brewing colonial beer. *Early Amer. Life* 11(5): 23–24, 26–27, 76.

Renfrow, C. 1997. *A Sip Through Time: A Collection of Old Brewing Recipes.* Cindy Renfrow.

Roberts, D. D., et al. 1980. Genetic variability and association of maturity, yield, and quality characteristics of female hops. *Crop Sci.* 20: 523–527.

Roberts, M. T., and A. C. Lewis. 2002. Rapid characterization of hop essential oils using gas chromatography-time of flight mass spectrometry. *J. Amer. Soc. Brew. Chem.* 60: 116–121.

Schieberle, P., and M. Steinhaus. 2001. Characterization of the odor-active constituents in fresh and processed hops (variety *Spalter Select*). In *Gas Chromatography-olfactometry: The State of the Art.* Ed. J. V. Leland et al. Washington, D.C.: Amer. Chem. Soc. 23–32.

Singh, T. A., et al. 1979. *Hop and Its Cultivation in India.* Centr. Inst. Med. Aromatic Pl. Farm Bull. No. 13.

Small, E. 1978. A numerical analysis of morpho-geographic groups of *Humulus lupulus* based on samples of cones. *Canad. J. Bot.* 59: 311–324.

Srinivasan, V., et al. 2004. Contributions to the antimicrobial spectrum of hop constituents. *Econ. Bot.* 58: S230–S238.

Tagashira, M., et al. 1995. Antioxidative activity of hop bitter acids and their analogues. *Biosci. Biotech. Biochem.* 59: 740–742.

———. 1997. Inhibition by hop bract polyphenols of cellular adherence and water-insoluble glucan synthesis of *Mutans streptococci.* *Biosci. Biotech. Biochem.* 61: 332–335.

Thomas, G. G. 1980. Weather factors controlling the alpha-acid content of hops (*Humulus lupulus* L.). *J. Hort. Sci.* 55: 71–77.

Tressl, R., et al. 1982. Changes of aroma components during storage and processing of hops and their contribution to beer flavour. In *Chemistry of Foods and Beverages: Recent Developments.* Ed. G. Charalambous and G. Inglett. New York: Academic Press. 1–24.

Wohlfart, R., et al. 1983. Sedative-hypnotic principle of hops. 4. Communication: pharmacology of 2-methyl-3-buten-2-ol. *Pl. Med.* 48: 120–123.

Yasukawa, K., et al. 1995. Humulon, a bitter in the hop, inhibits tumor production by 12-O-tetradecanoylphorbol-13-acetate in two-stage carcinogenesis in mouse skin. *Oncology* 52: 156–158.

Hyssopus
Anonymous. 2004. Hyssop. *Rev. Nat. Prod. (Wolters Kluwer Health)*.

Chalchat, J.-C., et al. 2001. Composition of oils of three cultivated forms of *Hyssopus officinalis* endemic in Yugoslavia: f. *albus* Alef., f. *cyaneus* Alef. and f. *ruber* Mill. *J. Essential Oil Res.* 13: 419–421.

DeFillipps, R. A. 1972. *Hyssopus*. In *Flora Europaea Vol. 3*. Ed. T. G. Tutin et al. Cambridge Univ. Press. 170.

Fraternale, D., et al. 2004. Composition and antifungal activity of two essential oils of hyssop (*Hyssopus officinalis* L.) *J. Essential Oil Res.* 16: 617–622.

Galambosi, B., et al. 1993. Agronomical and phytochemical investigation of *Hyssopus officinalis*. *Agric. Sci. Finland* 2: 293–302.

Glamočlija, J. M., et al. 2005. Antifungal activity of essential oil *Hyssopus officinalis* L. against mycopathogen *Mycogone perniciosa* (Mang). *Proc. Nat. Sci. Matica Srpska Novi Sad* 109: 123–128.

Gollapudi, S., et al. 1995. Isolation of a previously unidentified polysaccharide (MAR-10) from *Hyssopus officinalis* that exhibits strong activity against human immunodeficiency virus type 1. *Biochem. Biophys. Res. Commun.* 210: 145–151.

Gorunovic, M. S., et al. 1995. Essential oil of *Hyssopus officinalis* L., Lamiaceae of Montenegro origin. *J. Essential Oil Res.* 7: 39–43.

Joulain, D. 1976. Contribution a l'etude de la composition chimique de l'huile essentielle d'hysope (*Hyssopus officinalis* Linnaeus). *Rivista Ital. EPPOS* 58: 479–485.

Kazazi, H., et al. 2007. Supercritical fluid extraction of flavour and fragrances from *Hyssopus officinalis* L. cultivated in Iran. *Food Chem.* 105: 805–811.

Kerrola, K., et al. 1994. Volatile components and odor intensity of four phenotypes of hyssop (*Hyssopus officinalis* L.). *J. Agric. Food Chem.* 42: 776–781.

Kreis, W., et al. 1990. Inhibition of HIV replication by *Hyssopus officinalis* extracts. *Antiviral Res.* 14: 323–337.

Lawrence, B. M. 1992. Chemical components of Labiatae oils and their exploitation. In *Advances in Labiate Science*. Ed. R. M. Harley and T. Reynolds. Richmond, England: RBG Kew. 399–436.

Letessier, M. P., et al. 2001. Antifungal activity of the essential oil of hyssop (*Hyssopus officinalis*). *J. Phytopath.* 149: 673–678.

Lu, M., et al. 2002. Muscle relaxing activity of *Hyssopus officinalis* essential oil on isolated intestinal preparations. *Pl. Med.* 68: 213–216.

Maheshwari, M. L., et al. 1988. The composition of essential oils from *Hyssopus officinalis* L. and *Cymbopogon jwarancusa* (Jones) Schult. collected in the cold desert of Himalaya. In *Flavor and Fragrances: A World Perspective*. Ed. B. M. Lawrence et al. Amsterdam: Elsevier. 171–176.

Manitto, P., et al. 2004. Gas chromatography-mass spectral analysis of Bulgarian and Italian essential oils from *Hyssopus officinalis* L. *Bulg. Chem. Industr.* 75: 89–95.

Mazzanti, G., et al. 1998. Spasmolytic action of the essential oil from *Hyssopus officinalis* L. var. *decumbens* and its major components. *Phytotherapy Res.* 12: S92–S94.

Millet, J., et al. 1979. Étude expérimentale des propriétés toxiques convulsivantes des essences de sauge et d'hysope du commerce. *Rev. E. E. G. Neurophysiol.* 9: 12–18.

———. 1980. Étude de la toxicité d'huiles essentielles végétales du commerce: essence d'hysope et de sauge. *Med. Legale Toxicol.* 23: 9–21.

Özer, H., et al. 2005. Essential oil composition of *Hyssopus officinalis* L. subsp. *angustifolius* (Bieb.) Arcangeli from Turkey. *Flavour Fragrance J.* 20: 42–44.

Schultz, G., and E. Stahl-Biskup. 1991. Essential oils and glycosidic bound volatiles from leaves, stems, flowers and roots of *Hyssopus officinalis* L. (Lamiaceae). *Flavour Fragrance J.* 6: 69–73.

Shah, N. C. 1991. Chemical constituents of *Hyssopus officinalis* L.: "Zufe Yabis," a Unani drug from U. P. Himalaya, India. *Indian Perfumer* 35: 49–52.

Shah, N. C., et al. 1986. Gas chromatographic examination of oil of *Hyssopus officinalis*. *Parfümerie Kosmetik* 67: 116, 118.

Steinmetz, M. D., et al. 1980. Sur la toxicité de certaines huiles essentielles du commerce: essence d'hysope et essence de sauge. *Pl. Med. Phytotherap.* 14: 34–45.

———. 1985. Action d'huiles essentielles de sauge, thuya, hysope et de certains constituants, sur la respiration de coupes de cortex cérébral in vitro. *Pl. Med. Phytotherap.* 29: 35–47.

Svoboda, K. P., et al. 1993. Agronomical and biochemical investigation of *Hyssopus officinalis* L. from various geographic sources. *Acta Hort.* 344: 434–443.

Tsankova, E. T., et al. 1993. Chemical composition of the essential oils of two *Hyssopus officinalis* taxa. *J. Essential Oil Res.* 5: 609–611.

Veres, K., et al. 1997. Investigation of the composition of essential oils of *Hyssopus officinalis* L. populations. In *Essential Oils: Basic and Applied Research*. Ed. Ch. Franz et al. Carol Stream, Illinois: Allured. 217–220.

Zohary, M. 1982. *Plants of the Bible*. Cambridge Univ. Press.

Inula
Ball, P. W., and T. G. Tutin. 1976. *Inula*. In *Flora Europaea Vol. 4*. Ed. T. G. Tutin et al. Cambridge Univ. Press. 133–136.

Boatto, G., et al. 1994. Composition and antibacterial activity of *Inula helenium* and *Rosmarinus officinalis* essential oils. *Fitoterapia* 65: 279–280.

Bourrel, C., et al. 1993. Chemical analysis, bacteriostatic, and fungistatic properties of the essential oil of elecampane (*Inula helenium* L.). *J. Essential Oil Res.* 5: 411–417.

El-Gammal, S. Y. 1985. Elecampane and Job's disease. *Hamdard* 28(3): 95–98.

Olechnoqicz-Stępień, W. 1963. The isolation of helenine and main components of the crystalline fraction of the essential oil of the roots of *Inula helenium* L. Compositae. *Diss. Pharm.* 15: 301–311.

Olechnoqicz-Stępień, W., and H. Rzadkowska-Bodalska. 1969. Investigations of the neutral fraction ethereal extract of the root of elecampane (*Inula helenium* L.). *Diss. Pharm. Pharmacol.* 21: 337–340.

Olechnoqicz-Stępień, W., et al. 1975. Investigations of the ethereal extract of elecampane root (*Inula helenium* L.). Part 2. *Rocz. Chem. Ann. Soc. Chem. Pol.* 49: 849–851.

Stelling, K. 1994. *Inula helenium* (elecampane). *Canad. J. Herbalism* January: 8–14.

Iris
Alessandro, B., et al. 1993. Productivity and quality of rhizomes of some different types of *Iris* spp. *Acta Hort.* 344: 98–109.

Anonymous. 1929. The iris in the perfumer's art. *Perfumery Essential Oil Rec.* 20: 447–449.

Dafni, A., et al. 2006. Ritual plants of Muslim graveyards in northern Israel. *J. Ethnobiol. Ethnomed.* 2: 38–49.

Dykes, W. R. 1913. *The Genus Iris*. Cambridge Univ. Press.

Firmin, L., et al. 1998. Evaluation of the natural variability in irone content and selection of *Iris* for perfume production. *HortScience* 33: 1046–1047.

Galfré, A., et al. 1993. Direct enantioselective separation and olfactory evaluation of all irone isomers. *J. Essential Oil Res.* 5: 265–277.

Henderson, N. C. 1992. What is *Iris germanica*? *Bull. Amer. Iris Soc.* 70(3): 6–11.

Ker Gawler, J. B. 1803. *Iris florentina*. Florentine iris. *Bot. Mag.* 1803: t. 671.

Köhlein, F. 1987. *Iris*. Portland, Oregon: Timber Press.

Landi, R. 1996. Effetti della popolazione coltivata, della concimazione e dei fattori ambientali sulla produzione del giaggiolo

(*Iris pallida* Lam.). In *Atti convegno internazionale: coltivazione e miglioramento di piante officinali, Trento, Italy, 2–3 June 1994*. 47–71.

Landi, R., et al. 1996. Differentiation of *Iris pallida* Lam. biotypes in Italy. In *Atti convegno internazionale: coltivazione e miglioramento di piante officinali, Trento, Italy, 2–3 June 1994*. 355–368.

Lange, J. M. C. 1860–65. Pugillus plantarum imprimis hispanicarum. *Vidensk. Meddel. Dansk Naturhist. Foren. Kjøbenhaven*. 4 vols.

Mahan, C. E. 2007. *Classic Irises and the Men and Women Who Created Them*. Malabar, Florida: Krieger Publ. Co.

Mathew, B. 1981. *The Iris*. London: B. T. Batsford.

Maurer, B., and A. Hauser. 1991. Identification de nouveaux constituants du beurre d'iris marocain. *Rivista Ital. EPPOS* Spec. Num.: 115–124.

Maurer, B., et al. 1989. New irone-related constituents from the essential oil of *Iris germanica* L. *Helv. Chim. Acta* 72: 1400–1415.

Naves, Y. R. 1946. Orris root: its oil and its resinoid. *Drug Cosmetic Industr*. 59: 478–479, 586–587.

Rodionenko, G. I. 1987. *The Genus* Iris *L*. London: British Iris Soc.

Species Group of the British Iris Society, ed. 1997. *A Guide to Species Irises: Their Identification and Cultivation*. Cambridge Univ. Press.

Täckholm, V., and M. Drar. 1954. *Iris*. In *Flora of Egypt Vol. 3*. Cairo: V. Täckholm and M. Drar. 459–497.

Thompson, C. J. 1927. The lore of the iris. *Perfumery Essential Oil Rec*. 18: 223–224.

Webb, D. A., and A. O. Chater. 1980. *Iris*. In *Flora Europaea Vol. 5*. Ed. T. G. Tutin et al. Cambridge Univ. Press. 87–92.

Juniperus

Adams, R. P. 1987. Yields and seasonal variation of phytochemicals from *Juniperus* species of the United States. *Biomass* 12: 129–139.

Adams, R. P., et al. 2003. Pan-Arctic variation of *Juniperus communis*: historical biogeography based on DNA fingerprinting. *Biochem. Syst. Ecol*. 31: 181–192.

Anonymous. 1987. Juniper. In *Lawrence Review of Natural Products*. St. Louis: Facts and Comparisons.

Bonanga, G., and G. C. Galletti. 1985. Analysis of volatile compounds in juniper oil by high resolution gas chromatography and combined gas chromatography/mass spectrometry. *Ann. Chim*. 75: 131–136.

Butkiene, R., et al. 2006. Differences in the essential oils of the leaves (needles), unripe and ripe berries of *Juniperus communis* L.

growing wild in Vilnius District (Lithuania). *J. Essential Oil Res*. 18: 489–494.

———. 2006. Leaf (needle) essential oils of *Juniperus communis* L. growing wild in Eastern Lithuania. *J. Essential Oil-Bearing Pl*. 9: 144–151.

Cavaleiro, C., et al. 2006. Antifungal activity of *Juniperus* essential oils against dermatophyte, *Aspergillus* and *Candida* strains. *J. Appl. Microbiol*. 100: 1333–1338.

Chatzopoulou, P. S., and S. T. Katsiotis. 1993. Study of the essential oil from *Juniperus communis* "berries" (cones) growing wild in Greece. *Pl. Med*. 59: 554–556.

———. 1993. Chemical investigation of the leaf oil of *Juniperus communis* L. *J. Essential Oil Res*. 5: 603–607.

Chatzopoulou, P. S., et al. 2002. Investigation on the supercritical CO_2 extraction of the volatile constituents from *Juniperus communis* obtained under different treatments of the "berries" (cones). *Pl. Med*. 68: 827–831.

Davidson, R. M., and R. S. Byther. 1984. *Phomopsis Twig Blight of Juniper*. Washington State Univ. Coop. Extens. Bull. 1275.

den Ouden, P., and B. K. Boom. 1978. *Manual of Cultivated Conifers Hardy in the Cold- and Warm-temperate Zone*. The Hague: Martinus Nijhoff.

Gelsomini, N., et al. 1988. Capillary gas chromatography of the terpenic fraction of *Juniperus communis* L. black, green, berry, and leaf extracts. *J. High Resolution Chromatogr. Chromatogr. Commun*. 11: 10720–10722.

Glišic, S. B., et al. 2007. Antimicrobial activity of the essential oil and different fractions of *Juniperus communis* L. and a comparison with some commercial antibiotics. *J. Serb. Chem. Soc*. 72: 311–320.

Harrison, C. R. 1975. *Ornamental Conifers*. New York: Hafner Press.

Hörster, H. 1974. Variabilität der Öle von *Juniperus communis*. II. Die Zusammensetzung der Öle reifer und unreifer Früchte. *Pl. Med*. 25: 73–79.

Koukos, P. K., and K. I. Papadopoulou. 1997. Essential oil of *Juniperus communis* L. grown in northern Greece: variation of fruit oil yield and composition. *J. Essential Oil Res*. 9: 35–39.

Krüssmann, G. 1985. *Manual of Cultivated Conifers*. Trans. M. E. Epp. Portland, Oregon: Timber Press.

Lamparsky, D., and I. Klimes. 1985. Neue Ergebnisse der Wacholderbeeröl-Analyse im Hinblick auf terpenoid Inhaltsstoffe. *Parfumerie Kosmetik* 66: 553–556, 558–560.

Melegari, M., et al. 1987. Ricerche su piante officinali nell'Appennino Modenese– piante spontanee–IV -Indagine sull'olio essenziale di *Juniperus communis* L.

(ginepro). *Att Soc. Nat. Mat. Modena* 118: 75–91.

Pepeljnjak, S., et al. 2005. Antimicrobial activity of juniper berry essential oil (*Juniperus communis* L., Cupressaceae). *Acta Pharm*. 55: 417–422.

Pourmortazavi, S. M., et al. 2004. Extraction of volatile compounds from *Juniperus communis* L. leaves with supercritical fluid carbon dioxide: comparison with hydrodistillation. *Flavour Fragrance J*. 19: 417–420.

Proença da Cunha, A., and O. L. R. Roque. 1989. Composição química do óleo essencial de bagas de *Juniperus communis*, variedade *nana*. *Revista Port. Farm*. 39: 18–20.

———. 1989. The chemical composition of the essential oil of *Juniperus communis* L. ssp. *nana* Syme. *J. Essential Oil Res*. 1: 15–17.

Stobart, T. 1977. *Herbs, Spices and Flavour*. Middlesex, England: Penguin Books.

Taskinen, J., and L. Nykänen. 1976. Volatile constituents of an alcoholic extract of juniper berry. *Intern. Flavor Food Additives* 7: 228, 233.

van Gelderen, D. M. 1986. *Conifers*. Portland, Oregon: Timber Press.

Vernin, G., et al. 1988. GC-MS-SPECMA bank analysis of *Juniperus communis* needles and berries. *Phytochemistry* 27: 1061–1064.

Vichi, S., et al. 2007. HS-SPME coupled with GC/MS for quality control of *Juniperus communis* L. berries used for gin aromatization. *Food Chem*. 105: 1748–1754.

Welch, H. J. 1979. *Manual of Dwarf Conifers*. New York: Theophrastus Publ.

Laurus

Browne, D. J. 1846. *The Trees of America*. New York: Harper & Brothers.

Caredda, A., et al. 2002. Supercritical carbon dioxide extraction and characterization of *Laurus nobilis* essential oil. *J. Agric. Food Chem*. 50: 1492–1496.

Cheminat, A., et al. 1984. Allergic contact dermatitis to laurel (*Laurus nobilis* L.): isolation and identification of haptens. *Arch. Dermatol. Res*. 276: 178–181.

Díaz-Maroto, C., et al. 2002. Effect of drying method on the volatiles in bay leaf (*Laurus nobilis* L.) *J. Agric. Food Chem*. 50: 4520–4524.

El-Feraly, F. S., and D. S. Benigni. 1980. Sesquiterpene lactones of *Laurus nobilis* leaves. *J. Nat. Prod*. 43: 527–531.

Farkas, J. 1987. Perioral dermatitis from marjoram, bay leaf and cinnamon. *Contact Dermatitis* 7: 121.

Ferguson, D. K. 1974. On the taxonomy of recent and fossil species of *Laurus* (Lauraceae). *J. Linn. Soc. Bot*. 68: 51–72.

Hausen, B. M. 1992. Sesquiterpene lactones: *Laurus nobilis*. In *Adverse Effects of Herbal Drugs 1*. Ed. P. A. G. M. De Smet et al. Berlin: Springer-Verlag. 249–253.

Kilic, A., et al. 2004. Volatile constituents and key odorants in leaves, buds, flowers, and fruits of *Laurus nobilis* L. *J. Agric. Food Chem.* 52: 1601–1606.

Kostermans, A. J. G. H. 1964. *Bibliographia Lauracearum*. Bogor: Min. Natl. Res.

Krüssmann, G. 1985. *Manual of Cultivated Broad-leaved Trees and Shrubs*. 3 vols. Trans. M. E. Epp. Portland, Oregon: Timber Press.

Matsuda, H., et al. 1999. Preventive effect of sesquiterpenes from bay leaf on blood ethanol elevation in ethanol-loaded rat: structure requirement and suppression of gastric emptying. *Bioorg. Med. Chem. Lett.* 9: 2647–2652.

McClintock, E. 1993. Trees of Golden Gate Park, San Francisco: 48. California bay and Mediterranean laurel. *Pacific Hort.* 54(1): 10–12.

Pech, B., and J. Bruneton. 1982. Alcaloïdes du laurier noble, *Laurus nobilis*. *J. Nat. Prod.* 45: 560–563.

Politeo, O., et al. 2007. Chemical composition and antioxidant activity of free volatile aglycones from laurel (*Laurus nobilis* L.) compared to its essential oil. *Croatica Chem. Acta* 80: 121–126.

Rhizopoulou, S. 2004. Symbolic plant(s) of the Olympic Games. *J. Exp. Bot.* 55: 1601–1606.

Samejima, K., et al. 1998. Bay laurel contains antimutagenic kaempferyl coumarate acting against the dietary carcinogen 3-amino-1-5*H*-pyrido[4,3-*b*]indole (Trp-P-2). *J. Agric. Food Chem.* 46: 4864–4868.

Sari, A. O., et al. 2006. Breaking seed dormancy of laurel (*Laurus nobilis* L.). *New For.* 31: 403–408.

Sayyah, M., et al. 2002. Anticonvulsant activity of the leaf essential oil of *Laurus nobilis* against pentylenetetrazole- and maximal electroshock-induced seizures. *Phytomedicine* 9: 212–216.

Strack, D., et al. 1980. Analysis of sesquiterpene lactones by high performance liquid chromatography. *Z. Naturforsch.* 35c: 915–918.

Tada, H., and K. Takeda. 1976. Sesquiterpenes of Lauraceae plants. IV. Germacranolides from *Laurus nobilis* L. *Chem. Pharm. Bull.* 24: 667–671.

Tomita, M., et al. 1963. On the alkaloids of *Laurus nobilis* Linn. *J. Pharm. Soc. Japan* 83: 763–766.

Tucker, A. O., et al. 1992. *Litsea glaucescens* Humb., Bonpl. & Kunth var. *glaucescens* (Lauraceae): a Mexican bay. *Econ. Bot.* 46: 21–24.

Tutin, T. G. 1964. *Laurus*. In *Flora Europaea Vol. 1*. Ed. T. G. Tutin et al. Cambridge Univ. Press. 246.

Verma, M., and C. E. Meloan. 1981. A natural cockroach repellent in bay leaves. *Amer. Lab.* 13(10): 64, 66–69.

Voloshin, M. P. 1959. Review of laurel forms in Crimea. *Trudy Gosud. Nikitsk. Bot. Sada* 29: 85–94.

Yoshikawa, M., et al. 2000. Alcohol absorption inhibitors from bay leaf (*Laurus nobilis*): structure-requirements of sesquiterpenes for the activity. *Bioorg. Med. Chem.* 8: 2071–2077.

Zygadlo, J. A., et al. 1995. Empleo de aceites esenciales como antioxidantes naturales. *Grasa Aceites* 46: 285–288.

Lavandula

Adams, K. L. 2001. *Lavender as an Alternative Farming Enterprise*. Fayetteville, Arkansas: Natl. Center Appropriate Technol.

———. 2004. *Lavender Production, Products, Markets, and Entertainment Farms*. Fayetteville, Arkansas: Natl. Center Appropriate Technol.

Adasoglu, N., et al. 1994. Supercritical-fluid extraction of essential oil from Turkish lavender flowers. *J. Supercrit. Fluids* 7: 93–99.

Ahmed, A., et al. 1980. Analyse quantitative d'huiles essentielles de lavandes cultivées en Algérie. *Rivista Ital. EPPOS* 62: 293–296.

Allardice, P. 1990. *Lavender*. Melbourne: Hill of Content.

An, M., et al. 2001. On-site field sampling and analysis of fragrance from living lavender (*Lavandula angustifolia* L.) flowers by solid-phase microextraction coupled to gas chromatography and ion-trap mass spectrometry. *J. Chromatogr.* 917: 245–250.

Angioni, A., et al. 2006. Chemical composition, seasonal variability, and antifungal activity of *Lavandula stoechas* L. ssp. *stoechas* essential oils from stem/leaves and flowers. *J. Agric. Food Chem.* 54: 4364–4370.

Anonymous. 2004. Lavender. *Rev. Nat. Prod.* (*Wolters Kluwer Health*).

Arabaci, O., and E. Bayram. 2006. Evaluation of chemical composition, essential oil and morphological traits in wild populations of *Lavandula stoechas* L. in the Mediterranean environment. *Asian J. Chem.* 18: 371–380.

Ballabeni, V., et al. 2004. Novel antiplatelet and antithrombotic activities of essential oil from *Lavandula hybrida* Reverchon "grosso." *Phytomedicine* 11: 596–601.

Bélafi-Réthy, K., et al. 1975. Untersuchung der Zusammensetzung von eiheimischen und ausländischen ätherischen Ölen, IV. Beiträge zur Zusammensetzung des ungarischen Lavendelöles. *Acta Chim. Acad. Sci. Hung.* 87: 91–103.

———. 1975. Untersuchung der Zusammensetzung von eiheimischen und ausländischen ätherischen Ölen, V. Beiträge zur Zusammensetzung des Lavandulöles und des Musktateller Salbeiöles. *Acta Chim. Acad. Sci. Hung.* 87: 105–119.

Bellakhdar, J., et al. 1985. Étude chimique comparative des huiles essentielles de dix populations de *Lavandula multifida* L. du Maroc. *Biruniya* 1: 95–106.

Beus, C. 2006. *Growing and Marketing Lavender*. Washington State Univ. Ext. EB2005.

Bilke, S., and A. Mosandl. 2002. Authenticity assessment of lavender oils using GC-P-IRMS 2H/1H isotope ratios of linalool and linalyl acetate. *Eur. Food Res. Technol.* 214: 532–535.

Bonari, E., et al. 1985. Effet de la densité de plantation sur une culture du lavandin (variété <<Grosso>>). Influence sur la qualité et la quantité d'essence. *Pl. Med. Phytotherap.* 19: 98–108.

Bousmaha, L., et al. 2006. Infraspecific chemical variability of the essential oil of *Lavandula dentata* L. from Algeria. *Flavour Fragrance J.* 21: 368–372.

Bradley, B. F., et al. 2007. Anxiolytic effects of *Lavandula angustifolia* odour on the Mongolian gerbil elevated plus maze. *J. Ethnopharmacol.* 111: 517–525.

Brandao, F. M. 1986. Occupational allergy to lavender oil. *Contact Dermatitis* 15: 249–252.

Bruni, R., et al. 2006. Impact of alfalfa mosaic virus subgroup I and II isolates on terpene secondary metabolism of *Lavandula vera* DC., *Lavandula ×allardii* and eight cultivars of *L. hybrida* Rev. *Physiol. Mol. Pl. Pathol.* 68: 189–197.

Bruns, K. 1979. Analytische Bewertung von Lavandinöl. *Seifen Öle Fette Wachse* 10: 291–294.

Cassella, S., et al. 2002. Synergistic antifungal activity of tea tree (*Melaleuca alternifolia*) and lavender (*Lavandula angustifolia*) essential oils against dermatophyte infection. *Intern. J. Aromather.* 12: 2–15.

Cavanagh, H. M. A., and J. M. Wilkinson. 2002. Biological activities of lavender essential oil. *Phytother. Res.* 16: 301–308.

Ceroni, A. R. 1978. *La lavanda e il Lavandino*. Bologna: Edizioni Agricole.

Chavagnat, A. 1978. Lavender seed dormancy and germination. *Acta Hort.* 83: 147–154.

———. 1978. Étude de la germination des semences de *Lavandula augustifolia* au laboratoire. *Seed Sci. Technol.* 6: 775–784.

Chaytor, D. A. 1937. A taxonomic study of the genus *Lavandula*. *J. Linn. Soc. Bot.* 51: 153–204.

Cook, S. M., et al. 2007. Responses of *Phradis* parasitoids to volatiles of lavender, *Lavandula angustifolia*: a possible repellent for their host, *Meligethes aeneus. BioControl* 52: 591–598.

Cousin, M.-T., et al. 1970. Le <<Dépérissement Jaune>> du lavandin: nouvelle maladie à mycoplasmes. *Ann. Phytopathol.* 2: 227–237.

Dadalioğlu, I., and G. A. Evrendilek. 2004. Chemical compositions and antibacterial effects of essential oils of Turkish oregano (*Origanum minutiflorum*), bay laurel (*Laurus nobilis*), Spanish lavender (*Lavandula stoechas* L.), and fennel (*Foeniculum vulgare*) on common foodborne pathogens. *J. Agric. Food Chem.* 52: 8255–8260.

D'Auria, F. D., et al. 2005. Antifungal activity of *Lavandula angustifolia* essential oil against *Candida albicans* yeast and mycelial form. *Med. Mycol.* 43: 391–396.

———. 2005. Composition of volatile fractions from *Thymus, Origanum, Lavandula* and *Acinos* species. *J. Essential Oil-Bearing Pl.* 8: 36–51.

Delaveau, P., et al. 1989. Sur les propriétés neuro-dépressives de l'huile essentielle de lavande. *Compt.-Rend. Hebd. Seances Mem. Soc. Biol.* 183: 342–348.

De Pascual-Teresa, J., et al. 1989. Chemical composition of the Spanish spike oil. *Pl. Med.* 55: 398–399.

Dob, T., et al. 2005. Chemical composition of the essential oil of *Lavandula dentata* L. from Algeria. *Intern. J. Aromather.* 15: 110–114.

Evandri, M. G., et al. 2005. The antimutagenic activity of *Lavandula angustifolia* (lavender) essential oil in the bacterial reverse mutation assay. *Food Chem. Toxicol.* 43: 1381–1387.

Evelegh, T. 1996. *Lavender.* New York: Lorenz Books.

Fausey, B. A., et al. 2005. Daily light integral affects flowering and quality of greenhouse-grown *Achillea, Gaura,* and *Lavandula. HortScience* 40: 114–118.

Festing, S. 1982. *The Story of Lavender.* London: London Borough Sutton Libr. & Arts Serv.

Gamez, M. J., et al. 1990. Study of the essential oil of *Lavandula dentata. Pharmazie* 45: 69–70.

González-Coloma, A., et al. 2006. Antifeedant effects and chemical composition of essential oils from different populations of *Lavandula luisieri* L. *Biochem. Syst. Ecol.* 34: 609–616.

Gören, A. C., et al. 2002. The chemical constituents and biological activity of essential oil of *Lavandula stoechas* ssp. *stoechas. Z. Naturforsch.* 57c: 797–800.

Granger, R., et al. 1973. A propos d'une labiée cosmopolite: *Lavandula stoechas* L. *Trav. Soc. Pharm. Montpellier* 33: 355–360.

Guinea, E. 1972. *Lavandula.* In *Flora Europaea Vol. 3.* Ed. T. G. Tutin et al. Cambridge Univ. Press. 187–188.

Guyot-Declerck, C., et al. 2002. Floral quality and discrimination of *Lavandula stoechas, Lavandula angustifolia,* and *Lavandula angustifolia × latifolia* honeys. *Food Chem.* 79: 453–459.

Hajhashemi, V., et al. 2003. Anti-inflammatory and analgesic properties of the leaf extracts and essential oil of *Lavandula angustifolia* Mill. *J. Ethnopharmacol.* 89: 67–71.

Henley, D. V., et al. 2007. Prepubertal gynecomastia linked to lavender and tea tree oils. *New England J. Med.* 3456: 479–485.

Hoeberechts, J., et al. 2004. Growth of lavender (*Lavandula officinalis*) and rosemary (*Rosmarinus officinalis*) in response to different mulches. *Acta Hort.* 629: 245–251.

Irti, M., et al. 2006. Histo-cytochemistry and scanning electron microscopy of lavender glandular trichomes following conventional and microwave-assisted hydrodistillation of essential oils: a comparative study. *Flavour Fragrance J.* 21: 704–712.

Jäger, W., et al. 1992. Percutaneous absorption of lavender oil from a massage oil. *J. Soc. Cosmet. Chem.* 43: 49–54.

Jung, J., et al. 2005. Comprehensive authenticity assessment of lavender oils using multielement/multicomponent isotope ratio mass spectrometry analysis and enantioselective multidimensional gas charomatography-mass spectrometry. *Eur. Food Res. Technol.* 220: 232–237.

Kim, H.-M., and S.-H. Cho. 1998. Lavender oil inhibits immediate-type allergic reaction in mice and rats. *J. Pharm. Pharmacol.* 51: 221–226.

Kim, N.-S., and D.-S. Lee. 2002. Comparison of different extraction methods for the analysis of fragrances from *Lavandula* species by gas chromatography-mass spectrometry. *J. Chromatogr. A* 982: 31–47.

Kokkalou, E. 1988. The constituents of the essential oil of *Lavandula stoechas* growing wild in Greece. *Pl. Med.* 54: 58–59.

Kourik, R. 1998. *The Lavender Garden.* San Francisco: Chronicle Books.

Kreis, P., et al. 1993. Methodenvergleich zur Stereodifferenzieurng von Linalool und Linalylacetat in ätherischen Ölen von *Lavandula angustifolia* Miller. *Pharm. Z. Wissen* 138: 149–155.

Lammerink, J., et al. 1989. Effects of harvest time and postharvest drying on oil from lavandin (*Lavandula ×intermedia*). *New Zealand J. Crop Hort. Sci.* 17: 315–326.

Lawrence, B. M. 1992. Chemical components of Labiatae oils and their exploitation. In *Advances in Labiate Science.* Ed. R. M. Harley and T. Reynolds. Richmond, England: RBG Kew. 399–436.

———. 2007. Estrogenic activity in lavender and tea tree oils, part 1. *Perfumer Flavor.* 32(5): 20–25.

———. 2007. Estrogenic activity in lavender and tea tree oils, part 2. *Perfumer Flavor.* 32(6): 14–20.

Lehrner, J., et al. 2005. Ambient odors of orange and lavender reduce anxiety and improve mood in a dental office. *Physiol. Behav.* 86: 92–95.

Lin, P. W.-K., et al. 2007. Efficacy of aromatherapy (*Lavandula angustifolia*) as an intervention for agitated behaviours in Chinese older persons with dementia: a cross-over randomized trial. *Int. J. Geratr. Psychiatr.* 22: 405–410.

Lis-Balchin, M., ed. 2002. *Lavender: The Genus* Lavandula. London: Taylor & Francis.

Lis-Balchin, M., and S. Hart. 1999. Studies on the mode of action of the essential oil of lavender (*Lavandula angustifolia* P. Miller). *Phytotherap. Res.* 13: 540–542.

Lusby, P. E., et al. 2006. A comparison of wound healing following treatment with *Lavandula ×allardii* honey or essential oil. *Phytotherap. Res.* 20: 755–757.

Lyman-Dixon, A. 2000. Did the Tudors invent lavender? or was it the Romans? *Lavender Bag* 14: 14–17.

———. 2001. Did the Tudors invent lavender? or was it the Romans? Part 2. *Lavender Bag* 15: 34–39.

———. 2001. Did the Tudors invent lavender? or was it the Romans? Part 3. *Lavender Bag* 16: 20–24.

———. 2003. Did the Tudors invent lavender? Epilogue. *Lavender Bag* 20: 15–18.

Marchoux, G., et al. 2003. Un virus de la Luzerne attaque des legumes et aromates en France et Italie. *Phytoma* 559: 41–45.

McGimpsey, J. A., and N. J. Rosanowski. 1993. *Lavender: A Growers' Guide for Commercial Production.* New Zealand Inst. Crop & Food Res. Crop Seed Bull. No. 2.

McLeod, J. A. 1989. *Lavender, Sweet Lavender.* Kenthurst, Australia: Kangaroo Press.

McNaughton, V. 1994. *The Essential Lavender: Growing Lavender in New Zealand.* New York: Viking Penguin.

Meunier, C. 1985. *Lavandes & Lavandins.* Aix-en-Provence: Édisud.

———. 1995. *Lavender: Fragrance of Provence.* New York: Harry N. Abrams.

Milchard, M. J., et al. 2004. Application of gas-liquid chromatography to the analysis of essential oils. *Perfumer Flavor.* 29(5): 28–36.

Miller, A. G. 1985. The genus *Lavandula* in Arabia and tropical NE Africa. *Notes Roy. Bot. Gard. Edinburgh* 42: 503–528.

Minuto, A., et al. 2001. Influence of cultural practices on incidence of *Phytophthora nicotianae* var. *parasitica* causing rot of lavender (*Lavandula officinalis* L.). *Phytopathol. Mediterr.* 40: 45–54.

———. 2001. Prime ozzervazioni sulla suscettibilità a *Phytophthora nicotianae* var. *parasitica* di selezioni di lavanda. *Inform. Fitopatol.* 5: 69–72.

Moon, T., et al. 2006. Antiparasitic activity of two *Lavandula* essential oils against *Giardia duodenalis, Trichomonas vaginalis* and *Hexamita inflata. Parasit. Res.* 99: 722–728.

Moore, C. 2004. *Growing Lavender: A Guide for Cooler Climates.* Belleville, Ontario: Epic Press.

Motomura, N., et al. 1999. A psychophysiological study of lavender odorant. *Mem. Osaka Kyoku Univ.* 47: 281–287.

———. 2001. Reduction of mental stress with lavender odorant. *Perceptual Motor Skills* 93: 713–718.

Muñoz-Bertomeu, J., et al. 2007. Essential oil variation within and among natural populations of *Lavandula latifolia* and its relation to their ecological areas. *Biochem. Syst. Ecol.* 35: 479–488.

Peracino, V., et al. 1994. Essential oils from some *Lavandula* hybrids growing spontaneously in north west Italy. *Flavour Fragrance J.* 9: 11–17.

Perrucci, S., et al. 1996. The activity of volatile compounds from *Lavandula angustifolia* against *Psoroptes cuniculi. Phytotherap. Res.* 10: 5–8.

Prager, M. J., and M. A. Miskiewicz. 1979. Gas chromatographic-mass spectrometric analysis, identification, and detection of adulteration of lavender, lavandin, and spike lavender oils. *J. Assoc. Off. Anal. Chem.* 62: 1231–1238.

———. 1981. Characterization of lavandin 'Abrialis', 'Super', and 'Grosso' by GC-MS. *Perfumer Flavor.* 6(2): 53–58.

Prashar, A., et al. 2004. Cytotoxicity of lavender oil and its major components to human skin cells. *Cell Prolif.* 37: 221–229.

Proença da Cunha, A., et al. 1985. Estudio cariológico e determinação da composição química do óleo essencial de *Lavandula latifolia* Medicus da regiao de Coimbra. *Bol. Fac. Farm. Coimbra* 6–8: 27–34.

———. 1985. Estudio cariológico e determinação da composição química do óleo essencial de *Lavandula latifolia* Medicus da regiao de Leiria. *Bol. Fac. Farm. Coimbra* 9(1): 25–35.

———. 1987. *Lavandula latifolia* Medicus: caryological study and determination of chemical composition of its essential oil. In *International Symposium on Conservation of Genetic Resources of Aromatic and Medicinal Plants.* Ed. M. Mota and J. Baeta. OEIRAS. 129–134.

Puchalska, H., and Z. Janeczko. 2003. Content and composition of the volatile oil obtained from lavender (*Lavandula angustifolia* L.) flowers cultivated in Gołcza

region, in Małopolska province. *Herba Pol.* 49: 12–16.

Putnam, M. 1991. Root rot of lavender caused by *Phytophthora nicotianae. Pl. Pathol.* 40: 480–482.

Reichner, M., and J. Reichner. 2003. *Application of Oyster Shell Mulch for Lavender Production.* SARE Proj. Rep. FW01-052.

Renaud, E. N. C., et al. 2001. Essential oil quantity and composition from 10 cultivars of organically grown lavender and lavandin. *J. Essential Oil Res.* 13: 269–273.

Salido, S., et al. 2004. Chemical composition and seasonal variations of spike lavender oil from southern Spain. *J. Essential Oil Res.* 16: 206–210.

Sgoutas,-Emch, S., et al. 2001. Stress management: aromatherapy as an alternative. *Sci. Rev. Altern. Med.* 5: 90–95.

Shaw, D., et al. 2007. Anxiolytic effects of lavender oil inhalation on open-field behaviour in rats. *Phytomedicine* 14: 613–620.

Shellie, R., et al. 2000. Characterisation of lavender essential oils by using gas chromatography-mass spectrometry with correlation of linear retention indices and comparison with comprehensive two-dimensional gas chromatography. *J. Chromatogr. A* 970: 225–230.

Shen, J., et al. 2005. Olfactory stimulation with scent of lavender oil affects autonomic nerves, lipolysis and appetite in rats. *NeuroSci. Lett.* 383: 188–193.

———. 2007. Mechanism of changes induced in plasma glycerol by scent stimulation with grapefruit and lavender essential oils. *NeuroSci. Lett.* 416: 241–246.

Shiina, Y., et al. 2007. Relaxation effects of lavender aromatherapy improve coronary flow velocity reserve in healthy men evaluated by transthroacic Doppler echocardiography. *Intern. J. Cardiology* 129: 193–197.

Shimizu, M., et al. 1990. Anti-inflammatory constituents of topically applied crude drugs. IV. Constituents and anti-inflammatory effect of Paraguayan crude drug "Alhucema" (*Lavandula latifolia* Vill.). *Chem. Pharm. Bull.* 38: 2283–2284.

Singh, A. K., et al. 1989. Multivariate analysis in relation to genetic improvement in lavender, *Lavandula officinalis* Chaix. *Pl. Breeding* 102: 302–305.

Skoula, M., et al. 1996. Essential oil variation of *Lavandula stoechas* L. ssp. *stoechas* growing wild in Crete (Greece). *Biochem. Syst. Ecol.* 24: 255–260.

Slavova, Y., et al. 2004. Vegetative propagation of lavender (*Lavandula vera* V.) by using green cuttings. *Bulg. J. Agric. Sci.* 10: 518–520.

Steltenkamp, R. J., and W. Casazza. 1967. Composition of the essential oil of lavandin. *J. Agric. Food Chem.* 15: 1063–1069.

Tanida, M., et al. 2006. Olfactory stimulation with scent of lavender oil affects auto-

nomic neurotransmission and blood pressure in rats. *NeuroSci. Lett.* 398: 155–160.

———. 2008. Effects of olfactory stimulations with scents of grapefruit and lavender oils on renal sympathetic nerve and blood pressure in Clock mutant mice. *Autonomic Neurosci. Basic Clin.* 139: 1–8.

Tanker, M., et al. 1993. Results of certain investigations on the volatile-oil-containing plants of Turkey. In *Essential Oils for Perfumery and Flavour. Proceedings of an International Conference 26–30 May 1990 Antalya, Turkey.* Ed. K. H. C. Baser and N. Güler. Istanbul. 16–29.

Tomei, P. E., et al. 1995. Evaluation of the chemical composition of the essential oils of some Lamiacae from Serania de Ronda (Andaluçia, Spain). *J. Essential Oil Res.* 7: 279–282.

Tucker, A. O., and K. J. W. Hensen. 1985. The cultivars of lavender and lavandin [Labiatae]. *Baileya* 22: 168–177.

Tucker, A. O., et al. 1984. A preliminary analysis of some lavender and lavandin clones. *Perfumer Flavor.* 9(4): 49–52.

———. 1993. The essential oil of *Lavandula* ×*hybrida* Balb. ex Ging., a distinct hybrid from *L.* ×*heterophylla* Poir. (Labiatae). *J. Essential Oil Res.* 5: 443–445.

Umezu, T., et al. 2006. Anticonflict effects of lavender oils and identification of its active constituents. *Pharmacol. Biochem. Behav.* 85: 713–721.

Upson, T., and S. Andrews. 2004. *The Genus Lavandula.* Richmond, England: RBG Kew.

Upson, T., and S. Jury. 1996. *Lavandula*: the need for new research. *Herbs* 21(2): 9–10.

Valenti, G., et al. 1993. Étude chimique comparative des huiles essentielles de quatre populations de *Lavandula stoechas* L. subsp. *stoechas* spontanées de Chypre. *Pl. Med. Phytotherap.* 26: 289–299.

Venskutonis, P. R. 1995. Essential oil composition of some herbs cultivated in Lithuania. In *Flavour, Fragrances and Essential Oils.* Ed. K. H. C. Baser. Istanbul: AREP Publ. 108–123.

Vickers, L. 1991. *The Scented Lavender Book.* Boston: Little, Brown & Co.

Vinot, M., and A. Bouscary. 1971. Studies on lavender (VI). The hybrids. *Recherches* 18: 29–44.

———. 1974. Studies on lavender (VII). Ecology and dieback. *Recherches* 19: 173–204.

Whitman, C., et al. 1996. Forcing perennials crop by crop: species, *Lavandula angustifolia*, common name, lavender. *Greenhouse Grower* May: 37–40.

Wyckoff, L. J. 1951. Producing lavender oil in the Puget Sound District. *Herb Grower* 5: 67–82.

Wyckoff, L. J., and A. F. Sievers. 1935. Lavender growing in America. *Amer. Perfumer Essential Oil Rec.* 31(1): 67–71, (2): 79–83.

Yamada, K., et al. 1994. Anticonvulsive effects of inhaling lavender oil vapors. *Biol. Pharm. Bull.* 17: 359–360.

Yasui, H., et al. 2004. Dermatological suppressive effect of lavender oil against UVA-induced reactive oxygen species (ROS) in the skin of live animals: possibility of lavender oil for both protection of ultraviolet-induced dermal injury and suppression of skin-aging. *Aroma Res.* 18: 31–37.

Levisticum

Anonymous. 2004. Lovage. *Rev. Nat. Prod. (Wolters Kluwer Health).*

Blank, I., and P. Schieberle. 1993. Analysis of the seasoning-like flavour substances of a commercial lovage extract (*Levisticum officinale* Koch.). *Flavour Fragrance J.* 8: 191–195.

Bötcher, H., et al. 2002. Physiologisches Nachernteverhalten von Liebstöckel-Kraut (*Levisticum officinale* W. D. J. Koch). *Gartenbauwissenschaft* 67: 234–242.

Bylaitë, E., et al. 1996. Dynamic headspace gas chromatography of different botanical parts of lovage (*Levisticum officinale* Koch.). *Spec. Publ. Roy. Soc. Chem.* 197: 66–69.

Cichy, M., et al. 1984. Neue Inhaltsstoffe von *Levisticum officinale* Koch (Liebsöckel). *Liebigs Ann. Chem.* 1984: 397–400.

Cu, J.-Q., et al. 1990. The chemical composition of lovage headspace and essential oils produced by solvent extraction with various solvents. *J. Essential Oil Res.* 2: 53–59.

Daukšas, E., et al. 1999. Supercritical CO_2 extraction of the main constituents of lovage (*Levisticum officinale* Koch.) essential oil in model systems and overground botanical parts of the plant. *J. Supercritical Fluids* 15: 51–62.

Formanowiczowa, H., and J. Kozowski. 1971. The germination biology and laboratory valuation of medicinal plant seeds used for seeding purposes. Part 6c. The seeds of two Umbelliferae species: *Archangelica officinalis* Hoffm. and *Levisticum officinale* Koch. cultivated in Poland. *Herba Polon.* 17: 355–366.

Galambosi, B., and Z. Szebeni-Galambosi. 1992. The effect of nitrogen fertilization and leaf-harvest on the root and leaf yield of lovage. *J. Herbs Spices Med. Pl.* 1: 3–13.

Gijbels, M. J. M., et al. 1982. Phthalides in the essential oil from roots of *Levisticum officinale*. *Pl. Med.* 44: 207–211.

Karlsen, J., et al. 1968. The furanocoumarins of *Levisticum officinale*: isolation of psoralen and bergapten. *Medd. Norsk. Farm. Selskap* 30: 169–172.

Majchrzak, M., and E. Kamiński. 2004. Flavour compounds of lovage (*Levisticum officinale* Koch.) cultivated in Poland. *Herba Pol.* 50: 9–14.

Perineau, F., et al. 1992. Studying production of lovage essential oils in a hydrodistillation pilot unit equipped with a cohobation system. *J. Chem. Tech. Biotechnol.* 53: 165–171.

Raal, A., et al. 2008. Composition of the essential oil of *Levisticum officinale* W. D. J. Koch from some European countries. *J. Essential Oil Res.* 20: 318—322.

Stahl-Biskup, E., and E.-M. Wichtmann. 1991. Composition of the essential oils from roots of some Apiaceae in relation to the development of their oil duct systems. *Flavour Fragrance J.* 6: 249–255.

Szebeni-Galambosi, Z., et al. 1992. Growth, yield and essential oil of lovage grown in Finland. *J. Essential Oil Res.* 4: 375–380.

Thomann, R. J., et al. 1993. Distillation and use of essential oils from dill, celery, lovage, and parsley, made in Germany. *Acta Hort.* 333: 101–111.

Toulemonde, B., and I. Noleau. 1988. Volatile constituents of lovage (*Levisticum officinale* Koch.). In *Flavor and Fragrances: A World Perspective*. Ed. B. M. Lawrence et al. Amsterdam: Elsevier. 641–657.

Toulemonde, B., et al. 1987. Phthalides from lovage (*Levisticum officinale* Koch.). In *Flavor Science and Technology*. Ed. M. Martens et al. New York: John Wiley & Sons. 89–94.

Tutin, T. G. 1968. *Levisticum*. In *Flora Europaea Vol. 2*. Ed. T. G. Tutin et al. Cambridge Univ. Press. 358–359.

Venskutonis, P. R. 1995. Essential oil composition of some herbs cultivated in Lithuania. In *Flavour, Fragrances and Essential Oils*. Ed. K. H. C. Baser. Istanbul: AREP Publ. 108–123.

Limnophila

Kuebel, K. R., and A. O. Tucker. 1988. Vietnamese culinary herbs in the United States. *Econ. Bot.* 42: 413–419.

Philcox, D. 1970. A taxonomic revision of the genus *Limnophila* R. Br. (Scrophulariaceae). *Kew Bull.* 24: 101–170.

Tucker, A. O., et al. 2002. Volatile leaf and stem oil of commercial *Limnophila chinensis* (Osb.) Merrill ssp. *aromatica* (Lam.) Yamazaki (Scrophulariaceae). *J. Essential Oil Res.* 14: 228–229; 15: 215.

Wannan, B. S., and J. T. Waterhouse. 1985. A taxonomic revision of the Australian species of *Limnophila* R. Br. (Scrophulariaceae). *Austral. J. Bot.* 33: 367–380.

Yamazaki, T. 1985. A revision of the genera *Limnophila* and *Torenia* from Indochina. *J. Faculty Sci. Univ. Tokyo Sec. III.* 13: 575–625.

Lindera

Babcock, P. A., and A. B. Segelman. 1974. Alkaloids of *Lindera benzoin* (L.) Blume (Lauraceae) I: isolation and identification of laurotetanine. *J. Pharm. Sci.* 63: 1495.

Tucker, A., et al. 1994. Spicebush [*Lindera benzoin* (L.) Blume var. *benzoin*, Lauraceae]: a tea, spice, and medicine. *Econ. Bot.* 48: 333–336.

Wofford, B. E. 1983. A new *Lindera* (Lauraceae) from North America. *J. Arnold Arbor.* 64: 325–331.

Lippia

Atti-Serafini, L., et al. 2002. Variation in essential oil yield and composition of *Lippia alba* (Mill.) N. E. Br. grown in southern Brazil. *Rev. Bras. Pl. Med., Boptucatu* 4(2): 72–74.

Bahl, J. R., et al. 2000. Composition of linalool rich essential oil from *Lippia alba* grown in Indian plains. *Flavour Fragrance J.* 15: 199–200.

———. 2002. Linalool-rich essential oil quality variants obtained from irradiated stem nodes in *Lippia alba*. *Flavour Fragrance J.* 17: 127–132.

Bassols, G. B., and A. A. Gurni. 1996. *Lippia* species employed in Latin America folk medicine. *Dominguezia* 13: 7–25.

Calpouzos, L. 1954. Botanical aspects of oregano. *Econ. Bot.* 8: 222–233.

Catalan, C. A. N., et al. 1977. Aceite esencial de *Lippia alba* (Miller) N. E. Brown de la provincia de Tucuman. *Rivista Ital. EPPOS* 59: 513–518.

Ciccio, J. F., and R. A. Ocampo. 2004. Aceite esencial de *Lippia alba* (Verbenaceae) cultivada en el trópico húmedo en el Caribe de Costa Rica. *Ing. Cienc. Quim.* 21: 13–16.

Craveiro, A. A., et al. 1981. Essential oils from Brazilian Verbenaceae. Genus *Lippia*. *J. Nat. Prod.* 44: 598–601.

da F. Barbosa, F., et al. 2006. Influência da temperatura do ar de secagem sobre o teor e a composição química do oleo essencial de *Lippia alba* (Mill) N. E. Brown. *Quim. Nova* 29: 1221–1225.

de Abreu Matos, F. J., et al. 1996. Essential oil composition of two chemotypes of *Lippia alba* grown in northeast Brazil. *J. Essential Oil Res.* 8: 695–698.

Dellacassa, E., et al. 1990. Essential oils from *Lippia alba* (Mill.) N. E. Brown and *Aloysia chamaedrifolia* Cham. (Verbenaceae) from Uruguay. *Flavour Fragrance J.* 5: 107–108.

Fischer, U., et al. 1997. Variability of the essential oils of *Lippia graveolens* HBK from Guatemala. In *Essential Oils: Basic and Applied Research*. Ed. Ch. Franz et al. Carol Stream, Illinois: Allured. 266–269.

———. 2004. Two chemotypes within *Lippia alba* populations in Guatemala. *Flavour Fragrance J.* 19: 333–335.

Fun, C. E., and A. B. Svendsen. 1990. The essential oil of *Lippia alba* (Mill.) N. E. Br. *J. Essential Oil Res.* 2: 265–267.

Gomes, E. C., et al. 1993. Constituintes do óleo essencial de *Lippia alba* (Mill.) N. E. Br. (Verbenaceae). *Rev. Bras. Farm.* 74: 29–32.

Hennebell, T., et al. 2006. The essential oil of *Lippia alba*: analysis of samples from French overseas departments and review of previous works. *Chem. Biodiversity* 3: 1116–1125.

———. 2006. Phenolics and iridoids of *Lippia alba*. *Nat. Prod. Commun.* 9: 727–730.

———. 2007. Antioxidant and neurosedative properties of polyphenolis and iridoids from *Lippia alba*. *Phytotherapy Res.* 22: 256–258.

Kintzios, S. E., ed. 2002. *Oregano: The Genera Origanum and Lippia*. New York: Taylor & Francis.

Mallavarapu, G. R., et al. 2000. Essential oil of *Lippia alba*, a rich source of linalool. *J. Med. Arom. Pl. Sci.* 22: 765–767.

Moldenke, H. N. 1965. Materials toward a monograph of the genus *Lippia*. I. *Phytologia* 12: 6–71.

———. 1965. Materials toward a monograph of the genus *Lippia*. III. *Phytologia* 12: 130–181.

———. 1965. Materials toward a monograph of the genus *Lippia*. IV. *Phytologia* 12: 187–242.

———. 1965. Materials toward a monograph of the genus *Lippia*. V. *Phytologia* 12: 252–312.

———. 1965. Materials toward a monograph of the genus *Lippia*. VI. *Phytologia* 12: 331–367.

———. 1978. Additional notes on the genus *Lippia*. I. *Phytologia* 13: 343–368.

———. 1978. Additional notes on the genus *Lippia*. II. *Phytologia* 14: 400–419.

———. 1978. Additional notes on the genus *Lippia*. III. *Phytologia* 38: 230–266.

———. 1978. Additional notes on the genus *Lippia*. IV. *Phytologia* 38: 385–406.

———. 1978. Additional notes on the genus *Lippia*. VI. *Phytologia* 39: 24–46.

———. 1978. Additional notes on the genus *Lippia*. VII. *Phytologia* 39: 78–106.

———. 1978. Additional notes on the genus *Lippia*. VIII *Phytologia* 39: 162–182.

———. 1978. Additional notes on the genus *Lippia*. IX. *Phytologia* 39: 252–267.

———. 1978. Additional notes on the genus *Lippia*. X. *Phytologia* 39: 390–395.

———. 1978. Additional notes on the genus *Lippia*. XI. *Phytologia* 39: 434–456.

———. 1978. Additional notes on the genus *Lippia*. XII. *Phytologia* 40: 58–85.

———. 1979. Additional notes on the genus *Lippia*. XV. *Phytologia* 41: 145–151.

Morton, J. F. 1981. *Atlas of Medicinal Plants of Middle America: Bahamas to Yucatan*. Springfield, Illinois: Charles C. Thomas.

Nesom, G. L. 1991. Taxonomic adjustments in *Bouchea* and *Lippia* (Verbenaceae) of México. *Phytologia* 70: 185–187.

Obledo, E. N., et al. 2002. Antimicrobial activity of the essential oil of Mexican oregano (*Lippia graveolens* H. B. K.) against pathogens of *Agave tequilana* Weber var. *azul*. *Phyton* 51: 249–254.

Pascual, M. E., et al. 2001. *Lippia*: traditional uses, chemistry and pharmacology: a review. *J. Ethnopharmacol.* 76: 201–214.

Pino, J. A., et al. 1989. Analysis of the essential oil of Mexican oregano (*Lippia graveolens* HBK). *Nahrung* 33: 289–295.

———. 1995. Solvent extraction and supercritical carbon dioxide extraction of *Lippia alba* (Mill.) N. E. Brown leaf. *J. Essential Oil Res.* 9: 341–343.

———. 1996. Producción de orégano en Cuba: una alternativa a la importación. *Alimentaria* 1996: 69–71.

Rao, G. P., et al. 2000. Studies on chemical constituents and antifungal activity of leaf essential oil of *Lippia alba* (Mill). *Indian J. Chem. Technol.* 7(6): 332–335.

Retamar, J. A. 1994. Variaciones fitoquimicas de la especie *Lippia alba* (Salvia morada) y sus aplicaciones en quimica fina. *Essenze Derivati Agrumari* 64: 55–60.

Silva, N. A., et al. 2006. Caracterização quimica do oleo essencial da erva cidreira (*Lippia alba* (Mill.) N. E. Br.) cultivada em Ilhéus na Bahia. *Rev. Bras. Pl. Med. Botucato* 8: 52–55.

Singh, G., et al. 1999. Studies on essential oils. Part 15. GC/MS analysis of chemical constituents of leaf oil of *Lippia alba* (Mill.) from North India. *J. Essential Oil Res.* 11: 206–208.

Standley, P. C. 1924. Trees and shrubs of Mexico. *Contr. U.S. Natl. Herb.* 23: 1–1721.

Tucker, A. O., and M. J. Maciarello. 1994. Oregano: botany, chemistry, and cultivation. In *Spices, Herbs and Edible Fungi*. Ed. G. Charalambous. Amsterdam: Elsevier. 439–456.

———. 1999. Volatile leaf oil of the "licorice verbena" [*Lippia alba* (Mill.) N. E. Brown ex Britton and P. Wils. var. *carterae* Moldenke] from the North American herb trade. *J. Essential Oil Res.* 11: 314–316.

Tucker, A. O., et al. 1993. The essential oil of *Lippia micromera* Schauer in DC. (Verbenaceae). *J. Essential Oil Res.* 5: 683–685.

Uribe-Hernádez, C. J., et al. 1992. The essential oil of *Lippia graveolens* H. B. K. from Jalisco, Mexico. *J. Essential Oil Res.* 4: 647–649.

Vazquez, R. S., and N. T. Dunford. 2005. Bioactive components of Mexican oregano oil as affected by moisture and plant maturity. *J. Essential Oil Res.* 17: 668–671.

Zogbhi, M. das G. B., et al. 1998. Essential oils of *Lippia alba* (Mill.) N. E. Br. growing wild in the Brazilian Amazon. *Flavour Fragrance J.* 13: 47–48.

Litsea

Kennedy, D. 1990. *Mexican Regional Cooking*. Rev. ed. New York: Harper Collins Publ.

Tucker, A. O., et al. 1992. *Litsea glaucescens* Humb., Bonpl. & Kunth var. *glaucescens* (Lauraceae): a Mexican bay. *Econ. Bot.* 46: 21–24.

Matricaria

Achterrath-Tuckermann, U., et al. 1980. Pharmakologische Untersuchungen von Kamillen-Inhaltsstoffen. V. Untersuchungen über die spasmolytische Wirkung von Kamillen-Inhaltstoffen und von KAMILLOSAN am isolierten Meerschweinschen-ileum. *Pl. Med.* 39: 38–50.

Anonymous. 2007 Chamomile. *Rev. Nat. Prod. (Wolters Kluwer Health)*.

Avallone, R., et al. 1996. Benzodiazepine-like compounds and GABA in flower heads of *Matricaria chamomilla*. *Phytotherapy Res.* 10: S177–S179.

———. 2000. Pharmacological profile of apigenin, a flavonoid isolated from *Matricaria chamomilla*. *Biochem. Pharmacol.* 59: 1387–1394.

Bötcher, H., et al. 2001. Physiological postharvest responses of matricaria (*Matricaria recutita* L.) flowers. *Postharvest Biol. Technol.* 22: 39–51.

Breinlich, J., and K. Scharnagel. 1968. Pharmakologische Eigenschaften des EN-IN-Dicycloäthers aus *Matricaria chamomilla*. *Arzneimittel-Forsch.* 18: 429–431.

Brunke, E.-J., et al. 1992. The headspace analysis of flower fragrances. *Dragoco Rep.* 1992(1): 3–31.

———. 1993. Flower scent of some traditional medicinal plants. In *Bioactive Volatile Compounds from Plants*. Ed. R. Teranishi et al. Amer. Chem. Soc. 282–296.

Cekan, Z., et al. 1954. A chamazulene precursor from chamomile (*Matricaria chamomilla* L.). *Chem. Industr.* 1954: 604–605.

Das, M., et al. 1998. Chamomile (*Chamomilla recutita*): economic botany, biology, chemistry, domestication and cultivation. *J. Med. Aromatic Pl.* 20: 1074–1109.

———. 1999. Composition of the essential oils of the flowers of three accessions of *Chamomilla recutita* (L.) Rausch. *J. Essential Oil Res.* 11: 615–618.

Der Marderosian, A., and L. Liberti. 1988. *Natural Product Medicine*. Philadelphia: George F. Stickley Co.

ESCOP. 1991. Proposal for a European monograph on the medicinal use of matricariae flos, *Matricaria* (chamomile) flower. *HerbalGram* 24: 44–45.

Falzari, L. M., and R. C. Menary. 2003.

Chamomile for Oil and Dried Flowers. RIRDC Publ. No. 02/156.

Farnsworth, N. R., and B. M. Morgan. 1972. Herb drinks: chamomile tea. *JAMA* 221: 410.

Flaskamp, E., et al. 1982. Untersuchungen zur Charakterisierung des Prochamazulens Matrizin aus *Matricaria chamomilla* L. *Z. Naturforsch.* 87b: 508–511.

Forster, H. B., et al. 1980. Antispasmodic effects of some medicinal plants. *Pl. Med.* 40: 309–319.

Foster, S. 1990. *Chamomile:* Matricaria recutita & Chamaemelum nobile. Austin, Texas: Amer. Bot. Council.

Franke, R., and H. Schilcher, eds. 2005. *Chamomile Industrial Profiles.* New York: Taylor & Francis.

Franz, C. 1980. Content and composition of the essential oil in flower heads of *Matricaria chamomilla* L. during its ontogenetical development. *Acta Hort.* 96: 317–321.

———. 1992. Genetica biochimica e coltivazione della camomilla (*Chamomilla recutita* (L.) Rausch.) *Agric. Ricerca* 131: 87–96.

Franz, C., and J. Hölzl. 1978. Variation in the essential oil of *Matricaria chamomilla* L. depending on plant age and stage of development. *Acta Hort.* 73: 229–238.

Franz, C., and C. Kirsch. 1974. Wachsum und Blütenbildung von *Matricaria chamomilla* L. in Abhängigkeit variierter Stickstoff- und Kalidüngung. *Gartenbauwissenschaft* 39: 9–19.

Franz, C., and H. Massoud. 1989. Genotype-environment interactions and breeding of *Chamomilla recutita. Pl. Med.* 55: 528.

Franz, C., et al. 1978. Preliminary morphological and chemical characterization of some populations and varieties of *Matricaria chamomilla* L. *Acta Hort.* 73: 109–114.

———. 1986. Influence of ecological factors on yield and essential oil of camomile (*Chamomilla recutita* (L.) Rauschert (syn. *Matricaria chamomilla* L.). *Acta Hort.* 188: 157–161.

Galambosi, B., et al. 1988. Comparative examination of chamomile varieties grown in Finland and Hungary. *Herba Hung.* 27: 45–55.

———. 1991. Variation in the yield and essential oil of four chamomile varieties grown in Finland in 1985–1988. *J. Agric. Sci. Finland* 63: 403–410.

Gasic, O., et al. 1983. Chemical study of *Matricaria chamomilla* L.–II. *Fitoterpaia* 54: 51–55.

———. 1986. Variation in the content and the composition of the essential oils in flower heads of *Matricaria chamomilla* L. during its ontogenetical development. *Acta Pharm. Hung.* 56: 283–288.

———. 1989. Variability of content and composition of essential oil in various camomile cultivars (*Matricaria chamomilla* L.). *Herba Hung.* 28: 21–28.

———. 1991. The influence of sowing and harvest time on the essential oils of *Chamomilla* (L.) Rausch. *J. Essential Oil Res.* 3: 295–302.

Habersang, S., et al. 1979. Pharmakologische Untersuchungen von Kamillen-Inhaltsstoffen. IV. Untersuchungen zur Toxizität des (-)-alpha-Bisabolols. *Pl. Med.* 37: 115–123.

Hausen, B. M. 1992. Sesquiterpene lactones: *Chamomilla recutita.* In *Adverse Effects of Herbal Drugs 1.* Ed. P. A. G. M. De Smet et al. Berlin: Springer-Verlag. 243–264.

Hausen, B. M., et al. 1984. Über das Sensibilisierungsvermögen von Compositenarten. VII. Experimentelle Unbersuchungen mit Auszügen und Inhaltsstoffen von *Chamomilla recutita* (L.) Rauschert und *Anthemis cotula* L. *Pl. Med.* 1984: 229–234.

Hempel, B., and R. Hirschelmann. 1998. Kamille. *Deutsche Apotheker Z.* 138(44): 43–48.

Heneka, N. 1993. *Chamomilla recutita. Austral. J. Med. Herbalism* 5: 33–39.

Hernández-Ceruelos, A., et al. 2002. Inhibitory effect of chamomile essential oil on the sister chromatid exchanges induced by daunorubicin and methyl methansulfonate in mouse bone marrow. *Toxicol. Lett.* 135: 103–110.

Herold, M., et al. 1989. Verfahrenstechnische Entwicklungen zum Anbau von *Chamomilla recutita* L. (Rauschert) und *Calendula officinalis* L. für die Gewinnung von Blütendrogen. *Drogen Rep.* 2(2): 43–62.

Hölzl, J., and G. Demuth. 1975. Einfluss ökologischer Faktoren auf de Bildung des ätherischen Öls und der Flavone verschiedene Kamillenherkunfte. 1. Kritischer Vergleidh der quantitativen Bestimmungsmethoden. *Pl. Med.* 27: 37–45.

Hölzl, J., et al. 1975. Untersuchungen Über die Bildung des ätherischen Öls von *Matricaria chamomilla* L. *Z. Naturforsch.* 30c: 853–854.

Honcariv, R., and M. Repcak. 1979. Chemotypes of *Matricaria chamomilla* L. *Herba Polon.* 25: 261–267.

Isaac, O. 1979. Pharmakologische Untersuchungen von Kamillen-Inhaltsstoffen. I. Zur Pharmakologie des (-)-alpha-Bisabolols und der Bisabololoxide (Übersicht). *Pl. Med.* 35: 118–124.

———. 1980. Die Kamillentherapie–Erfahrung und Bestätigung. *Deutsche Apotheker Z.* 120: 567–570.

Jain, T. C., and J. J. Karchesy. 1971. Concerning the chemical constituents of *Matricaria matricarioides. Phytochemistry* 10: 2825–2826.

Jakolev, V., et al. 1979. Pharmakologische Untersuchungen von Kamillen-Inhaltsstoffen. II. Neue Untersuchungen zur antiphlogistischen Wirkung des (-)-alpha-Bisabolols und der Bisabololoxide. *Pl. Med.* 35: 125–140.

———. 1983. Pharmakologische Untersuchungen von Kamillen-Inhaltsstoffen. VI. Untersuchungen zur antiphlogistischen Wirkung von Chamazulen und Matricin. *Pl. Med.* 49: 67–73.

Jeffrey, C. 1979. Note on the lectotypification of the names *Cacalia* L., *Matricaria* L. and *Gnaphalium* L. *Taxon* 28: 349–351.

Karawya, M. S., et al. 1972. Study of effect of pH of soil on yield of flower heads and oil content of chamomile. *Bull. Fac. Pharm. Cairo Univ.* 11: 329–338.

Kay, Q. O. N. 1976. *Chamomilla.* In *Flora Europaea Vol. 4.* Ed. T. G. Tutin et al. Cambridge Univ. Press. 167.

Kirsch, K. 1990. Chamomile cultivation in Argentina. *Dragoco Rep.* 1990(2): 67–75.

Lawrence, B. M., et al. 1971. Volatile constituents of *Matricaria matricarioides. Phytochemistry* 10: 2827.

Letchamo, W. 1993. Nitrogen application affects yield and content of active substances in chamomile genotypes. In *New Crops.* Ed. J. Janick and J. E. Simon. New York: John Wiley & Sons. 636–639.

———. 1995. Organic cultivation of camomile in North America. *Hort Science* 30: 906.

Lima de Souza Reis, L., et al. 2006. *Matricaria chamomilla* CH12 decreases handling stress in Nelore calves. *J. Vet. Sci.* 7: 189–192.

Mann, C., and E. J. Staba. 1986. The chemistry, pharmacology, and commercial formulations of chamomile. In *Herbs, Spices, and Medicinal Plants: Recent Advances in Botany, Horticulture, and Pharmacology Vol. 1.* Ed. L. E. Craker and J. E. Simon. Phoenix, Arizona: Oryx Press. 235–280.

Marczal, G., and G. Verzár-Petri. 1980. Essential oil production and composition during the ontogeny in *Matricaria chamomilla* L. *Acta Hort.* 96: 325–329.

Massoud, H. Y., and C. M. Franz. 1990. Quantitative genetical aspects of *Chamomilla recutita* (L.) Rauschert. II. Genotype-environmental interactions and proposed breeding methods. *J. Essential Oil Res.* 2: 299–305.

Matos, F. J. A., et al. 1993. Constituents of Brazilian chamomile oil. *J. Essential Oil Res.* 5: 337–339.

Medić-Šarić, M., et al. 2001. The use of information theory and numerical taxonomy methods for evaluating the quality of thin-layer chromatographic separations of flavonoid constituents of matricariae flos. *Pharmazie* 56: 156–159.

Miller, T., et al. 1996. Effects of some components of the essential oil of chamomile, *Chamomilla recutita*, on histamine release from rat mast cells. *Pl. Med.* 61: 60–61.

Mishra, D. K., et al. 1999. Effect of drying *Matricaria chamomilla* flowers on chemical composition of essential oil. *J. Med. Aromatic Pl. Sci.* 21: 1020–1025.

Motl, O., et al. 1977. Zur GC Analyse und zu chemischen Typen von Kamillenöl. *Arch. Pharm. Ber. Deutsch. Pharm. Ges.* 310: 210–215.

Ohe, C., et al. 1995. Seasonal variation in production of the head and accumulation of glycosides in the head of *Matricaria chamomilla. Acta Hort.* 390: 75–82.

———. 1995. Studies on the cultivation and evaluation of chamomilae flos. Seasonal variation in the production of the head (capitula) and accumulation of glycosides in the capitula of *Matricaria chamomilla* L. *Yakugaku Zasshi* 115: 130–135.

Orav, A., et al. 1999. Volatile constituents of *Matricaria matricarioides* (Less.) Port. *J. Essential Oil Res.* 11: 243–245.

Orav, A., and K. Ivask. 2001. Volatile constituents of *Matricaria recutita* L. from Estonia. *Proc. Estonian Acad. Sci. Chem.* 50: 39–45.

Pekic, B., et al. 1999. Essential oil of chamomile ligulate and tubular flowers. *J. Essential Oil Res.* 11: 16–18.

Povh, N. P., et al. 2001. Supercritical CO_2 extraction of essential oil and oleoresin from chamomile (*Chamomilla recutita* [L.] Rauschert). *J. Supercrit. Fluids* 21: 245–256.

Presibella, M. M., et al. 2006. Comparison of chemical constituents of *Chamomilla recutita* (L.) Rauschert essential oil and its anti-chemotactic activity. *Braz. Arch. Biol. Technol.* 49: 717–724.

———. 2007. *In vitro* antichemotactic activity of *Chamomilla recutita* hydroethanol extract. *Pharm. Biol.* 45: 1–7.

Raal, A., et al. 2003. Comparación de aceites esenciales de *Matricaria recutita* L. de origen diverso. *Ars Pharm.* 44: 159–165.

Ram, M., et al. 1997. *Chamomile and Its Cultivation in India.* Lucknow, India: Central Inst. Med. Aromatic Pl.

Rauschert, S. 1974. Nomenklatorische Probleme in der Gattung *Matricaria* L. *Folia Geobot. Phytotax.* 9: 249–260.

Repcak, M., et al. 1993. The essential oil content and composition in diploid and tetraploid *Chamomilla recutita* during the ontogenesis of anthodia. *J. Essential Oil Res.* 5: 297–300.

Rubiolo, P., et al. 2006. Headspace-solid-phase microextraction fast GC in combination with principle component analysis as a tool to classify different chemotypes of chamomile flower-heads (*Matricaria recutita* L.). *Phytochem. Anal.* 17: 217–225.

Salamon, I. 1992. Chamomile: a medicinal plant. *Herb Spice Med. Pl. Dig.* 10(1): 1–4.

———. 2004. The Slovak gene pool of German chamomile (*Matricaria recutita* L.) and comparison in its parameters. *Hort. Sci.* (Prague) 31: 70–75.

———, ed. 2006. *Program and Abstract Book of the I. International Symposium on Chamomile Research, Development and Production.* Presov, Slovak Republic: Presov Univ.

Savino, F., et al. 2005. A randomized double-blind placebo-controlled trial of a standardized extract of *Matricariae recutita, Foeniculum vulgare* and *Melissa officinalis* (ColiMil®) in the treatment of breast-fed colicky infants. *Phytotherapy Res.* 19: 335–350.

Schilcher, H. 1973. Neuere Erkenntnisse bei der Qualitätsbeurteilung von Kalmillenblüten bzw. Kamillenöl. Teil 2. Qualitative Beurteilung des ätherischen Öles in Flores Chamomillae. *Pl. Med.* 23: 132–144.

Singh, A. 1982. Cultivation of *Matricaria chamomilla*. In *Cultivation and Utilization of Aromatic Plants.* Ed. C. K. Atal and B. M. Kapur. Jammu Tawi, India: Regional Res. Lab. 653–658.

Smokinski, A. T., and J. J. Pestka. 2003. Modulation of lipopolysaccharide-induced proinflammatory cytokine production in vitro and in vivo by the herbal constituents apigenin (chamomile), ginsenoside Rb1 (ginseng) and parthenolide (feverfew). *Food Chem. Toxicol.* 41: 1381–1390.

Stanić, G., et al. 2000. Essential oil of chamomile cultivated in Slavonija. *Farm. Glas.* 56: 139–147.

Surburg, H., et al. 1993. In *Bioactive Volatile Compounds from Plants.* Ed. R. Teranishi et al. Amer. Chem. Soc. 103–119.

Szalontai, M., et al. 1977. Beitrag zur Untersuchung der antimykotischen Wirkung biologisch aktiver Komponenten der *Matricaria chamomilla* L. *Parfumerie Kosmetik* 58: 121–127.

Szelenyi, I., et al. 1979. Pharmakologische Untersuchungen von Kamillen-Inhaltsstofen. III. Tierexperimentelle Untersuchungen über die ulkusprotektive Wirkung der Kamille. *Pl. Med.* 35: 218–227.

Szöke, É., et al. 2003. Analysis of biological active essential oil components of chamomiles in Hungary (in vivo-in vitro). *Acta Hort.* 597: 275–284.

———. 2004. New terpenoids in cultivated and wild chamomile (in vivo and in vitro). *J. Chromatogr. B* 800: 231–238.

Tanker, M., et al. 1993. Results of certain investigations on the volatile-oil-containing plants of Turkey. In *Essential Oils for Perfumery and Flavour. Proceedings of an International Conference 26–30 May 1990 Antalya, Turkey.* Ed. K. H. C. Baser and N. Güler. Istanbul. 16–29.

Tirillini, B., et al. 2006. Essential oil composition of ligulate and tubular flowers and receptacle from wild *Chamomilla recutita* (L.) Rausch. grown in Italy. *J. Essential Oil Res.* 18: 42–45.

Tyler, V. E. 1987. *The New Honest Herbal.* Philadelphia: George F. Stickley Co.

van Ketel, W. G. 1987. Allergy to *Matricaria chamomilla. Contact Dermatitis* 16: 50–51.

Yamada, K., et al. 1996. Effect of inhalation of chamomile oil vapour on plasma ACTH level in ovariectomized rat under restriction stress. *Biol. Pharm. Bull.* 19: 1244–1246.

Melissa

Adzet, T., et al. 1992. Genetic variability of the essential oil content of *Melissa officinalis. Pl. Med.* 58: 558–561.

———. 1992. Content and composition of *M. officinalis* oil in relation to leaf position and harvest time. *Pl. Med.* 58: 562–564.

Akhondzadeh, S., et al. 2003. *Melissa officinalis* extract in the treatment of patients with mild to moderate Alzheimer's disease: a double blind, randomized, placebo controlled trial. *J. Neurol. Neurosurg. Psychiatry* 74: 863–866.

Anonymous. 1930. The sweet balm in the perfumer's art. *Perfumery Essential Oil Rec.* 21: 451–452.

———. 2004. Lemon balm. *Rev. Nat. Prod. (Wolters Kluwer Health).*

Basta, A., et al. 2005. Composition of the leaves essential oil of *Melissa officinalis* s.l. from Greece. *Flavour Fragrance J.* 20: 642–644.

Bianchi-Santamaria, A., et al. 1993. Antimutagenic action of beta carotene, canthanxantin and extracts of *Rosmarinus officinalis* and *Melissa officinalis.* Genotoxicity of basil and tarragon oil. In *Food and Cancer Prevention: Chemical and Biological Aspects.* Ed. K. W. Waldron et al. Cambridge: Roy. Soc. Chem. 75–81.

Blank, A. F., et al. 2005. Influência do horário de colheita e secagem de folhas no oleo essencial de melissa (*Melissa officinalis* L.) cultivada em dols ambientes. *Rev. Bras. Pl. Med. Botucatu* 8: 73–78.

———. 2006. Efeitos da adubação química e da calagen na nutrição de melissa e hortelã-pimenta. *Hort. Bras.* 24: 195–198.

Bolkent, S., et al. 2005. Protective role of *Melissa officinalis* L. extract on liver of hyperlipidemic rats: a morphological and biochemical study. *J. Ethnopharmacol.* 99: 391–398.

Brendler, T., et al. 2005. Lemon balm (*Melissa officinalis* L.): an evidence-based systematic review by the natural standard research collaboration. *J. Herbal Phamacotherapy* 5: 71–107.

Burgett, M. 1980. The use of lemon balm (*Melissa officinalis*) for attracting honeybee swarms. *Bee World* 61(2): 44–46.

Carnat, A. P., et al. 1998. The aromatic and polyphenolic composition of lemon balm (*Melissa officinalis* L. subsp. *officinalis*) tea. *Pharm. Acta Helv.* 72: 301–305.

Carvalho de Sousa, A., et al. 2004. *Melissa officinalis* L. essential oil: antitumoral and antioxidant activities. *J. Pharm. Pharmacol.* 56: 677–681.

Cerny, A., and K. Schmid. 1999. Tolerability and efficacy of valerian/lemon balm in healthy volunteers (a double-blind, placebo-controlled, multi-centre study). *Fitoterapia* 70: 221–228.

Davis, J. M. 1991. *Lemon Balm*. North Carolina State Univ. Leafl. No. 126.

Dawson, B. S. W., et al. 1988. Essential oil of *Melissa officinalis* L. subsp. *altissima* (Sibthr. et Smith) Arcang. *Flavour Fragrance J.* 3: 167–170.

de Vries, J. 1996. *Melissa Extract: The Natural Herbal Remedy for Herpes*. New Canaan, Connecticut: Keats Publ.

Duke, J. A. 2007. The evidence for lemon balm. *Altern. Complementary Therapies* 2007: 173–177.

Enjalbert, F., et al. 1983. Analyse des essences de melisse. *Fitoterapia* 54: 59–65.

Fernandes, R. 1972. *Melissa*. In *Flora Europaea Vol. 3*. Ed. T. G. Tutin et al. Cambridge Univ. Press. 162–163.

Harshavardhan, P. G., et al. 2005. Effect of spacing and integrated nutrient management on biomass and oil yield in *Melissa officinalis* L. *Indian Perfumer* 49: 349–354.

Hefendehl, F. W. 1970. Zusammensetzung des ätherischen Öls von *Melissa officinalis* L. und sekundäre Veränderungen der Ölkomposition. *Arch. Pharm.* 303: 345–357.

Hener, U., et al. 1995. On the authenticity evaluation of balm oil (*Melissa officinalis* L.). *Pharmazie* 50: 60–62.

Holla, M., et al. 1997. Composition of the essential oil from *Melissa officinalis* L. cultivated in Slovak Republic. *J. Essential Oil Res.* 9: 481–484.

Hose, S., et al. 1997. Ontogenetic variation of the essential leaf oil of *Melissa officinalis* L. *Pharmazie* 52: 247–253.

Kato-Noguchi, H. 2003. Assessment of allelopathic potential of shoot powder of lemon balm. *Sci. Hort.* 97: 419–423.

Kennedy, D. O., et al. 2002. Modulation of mood and cognitive performance following acute administration of *Melissa officinalis* (lemon balm). *Pharmacol. Biochem. Behav.* 72: 953–964.

———. 2003. Modulation of mood and cognitive performance following acute administration of single doses of *Melissa officinalis* (lemon balm) with human CNS nicotinic and muscarinic receptor-binding properties. *Neuropsychopharmacology* 28: 1871–1881.

———. 2004. Attenuation of laboratory-induced stress in humans after acute administration of *Melissa officinalis* (lemon balm). *Psychosomatic Ed.* 66: 607–613.

———. 2006. Anxiolytic effects of a combination of *Melissa officinalis* and *Valeriana officinalis* during laboratory induced stress. *Phytotherapy Res.* 20: 96–102.

Koytchev, R., et al. 1999. Balm mint extract (Lo-701) for topical treatment of recurring Herpes labialis. *Phytomedicine* 6: 225–230.

Lukic, V., et al. 1989. The contents of essential oil and its components in some *Melissa officinalis* L. genotypes. *Zborn. Matice Srpske Prir. Nauke* 77: 77–82.

Marongiu, B., et al. 2004. Antioxidant activity of supercritical extract of *Melissa officinalis* subsp. *officinalis* and *Melissa officinalis* subsp. *inodora*. *Phytotherapy Res.* 18: 789–792.

McGimpsey, J. A. 1993. *Lemon Balm*: Melissa officinalis. New Zealand Inst. Crop Food Res. Broadsheet No. 17.

Mimica-Dukic, N., et al. 2004. Antimicrobial and antioxidant activities of *Melissa officinalis* (Lamiaceae) essential oil. *J. Agric. Food Chem.* 52: 2485–2489.

Mrlianova, M., et al. 2002. The influence of the harvest cut height on the quality of the herbal drugs melissae folium and melissae herba. *Pl. Med.* 68: 178–180.

Mulkens, A. 1987. *Étude phytochimique des feuilles de* Melissa officinalis *L. (Lamiaceae)*. Thèse, Univ. Genève.

Mulkens, A., and I. Kapetanidis. 1988. Étude de l'huile essentielle de *Melissa officinalis* L. (Lamiaceae). *Pharm. Acta Helv.* 63: 266–270.

Nykänen, I. 1985. Composition of the essential oil of *Melissa officinalis* L. In *Progress in Flavor Research 1984*. Ed. J. Adda. Amsterdam: Elsevier. 329–338.

Nykänen, I., et al. 1986. Flavour composition of lemon balm (*Melissa officinalis* L.) cultivated in Finland. *Lebensm. Wiss. Technol.* 19: 482–485.

Pellecuer, J., et al. 1981. Contribution a l'étude de l'huile essentielle de mélisse: *Melissa officinalis* L. (Lamiacées). *Pl. Med. Phytotherap.* 15: 149–153.

Putievsky, E. M., et al. 1983. Development and regeneration ability of lemon balm (*Melissa officinalis* L.) and marjoram (*Majorana hortensis* L.) on various media. *Biol. Agric. Hort.* 1: 327–333.

Savino, F., et al. 2005. A randomized double-blind placebo-controlled trial of a standardized extract of *Matricariae recutita*, *Foeniculum vulgare* and *Melissa officinalis* (ColiMil®) in the treatment of breastfed colicky infants. *Phytotherapy Res.* 19: 335–340.

Schultze, W., et al. 1989. Die Melisse. Dünnschichtchromatographische Untersuchung des ätherischen Öles. *Deutsche Apotheker Z.* 129: 155–163.

———. 1995. Melissenöle. *Deutsche Apotheker Z.* 135: 557–577.

Shalaby, A. S., et al. 1995. Oil of *Melissa officinalis* L., as affected by storage and herb drying. *J. Essential Oil Res.* 7: 667–669.

Tagashira, M., and Y. Ohtake. 1998. A new antioxidative 1,3-benzodioxole from *Melissa officinalis*. *Pl. Med.* 64: 555–558.

Tittel, G., et al. 1982. Über die chemische Zusammensetzung von Melissenölen. *Pl. Med.* 46: 91–98.

Tzanetakis, I. E., et al. 2005. *Tulip virus* × (TVX) associated with lemon balm (*Melissa officinalis*) variegation: first report of TVX in the USA. *Pl. Path.* 54: 562.

Van den Berg, T., et al. 1997. *Melissa officinalis* subsp. *altissima*: characteristics of a possible adulteration of lemon balm. *Pharmazie* 52: 802–808.

Venskutonis, P. R., et al. 1995. Flavour composition of some lemon-like aroma herbs from Lithuania. In *Food Flavor: Generation, Analysis and Process Influence*. Ed. G. Charalambous. Amsterdam: Elsevier. 833–847.

Werker, E., et al. 1985. Structure of glandular hairs and identification of the main components of their secreted material in some species of the Labiatae. *Israel J. Bot.* 34: 31–45.

Wölbing, R. H., and K. Leonhardt. 1994. Local therapy of herpes simplex with dried extract from *Melissa officinalis*. *Phytomedicine* 1: 25–31.

Wolf, H.-T., et al. 1999. Identification of *Melissa officinalis* subspecies by DNA fingerprinting. *Pl. Med.* 65: 83–85.

Mentha

Akdoğan, M., et al. 2007. Effect of spearmint (*Mentha spicata* Labiatae) teas on androgen levels in women with hirsutism. *Phytotherapy Res.* 21: 444–447.

Allard, H. A. 1941. Further studies of the photoperiodic behavior of some mints (Labiatae). *J. Agric. Res.* 63: 55–64.

Al-Marzouqi, A. H., et al. 2007. Comparative evaluation of SFE and steam distillation methods on the yield and composition of essential oil extracted from spearmint (*Mentha spicata*). *J. Liquid Chromatogr. Rel. Technol.* 30: 463–475.

Al-Mofleh, I., et al. 2006. Antisecretagogue, antiulcer and cytoprotective effects of 'peppermint' *Mentha piperita* L. in laboratory animals. *J. Med. Sci.* (Pakistan) 6: 930–936.

Alpman, G. 1975. Gas chromatographic studies on *Mentha pulegium* L. collected from several parts of Istanbul. *Istanbul Ecz. Fak. Mec.* 11: 95–102.

Anderson, I. B., et al. 1996. Pennyroyal toxicity: measurement of toxic metabolite levels in two cases and review of the literature. *Ann. Internal Med.* 124: 726–734.

Anonymous. 1998. Pennyroyal. In *Lawrence Review of Natural Products*. St. Louis: Facts and Comparisons.

Arakawa, T., et al. 1992. Antiallergic effects of peppermint oil, chicle, and jelutong. *J. Food Hygienic Soc. Japan* 33: 569–575.

Bachthaler, G., et al. 1976. Vergleichende Untersuchungen verschiedener Herkünfte und Sorten von *Mentha piperita* L. 2. Teil: Anbaueignung (Wachstum, Ertrag, Inhaltsstoffe) an verschiedenen Standorten in der Bundesrepublik Deutschland. *Bayer. Landwirtsch. Jahrb.* 53: 35–47.

Baird, J. V. 1957. The influence of fertilizers on the production and quality of peppermint in central Washington. *Agron. J.* 49: 225–230.

Baquar, S. R., and G. Reese. 1965. Cytotaxonomische und gaschromatographische Untersuchungen an norddeutschen Mentha-Formen. 2. Teil. Gaschromatographische Untersuchungen. *Pharmazie Beih. Ergänzungsband* 20: 214–220.

Baslas, R. K. 1970. Chemistry of Indian essential oils. Part 9. *Flavor Industr.* 1: 475–478.

Baslas, R. K., and K. K. Baslas. 1970. Chemistry of Indian essential oils. Part 8. *Flavor Industr.* 1: 473–474.

Bayraktar-Alpmen, G. 1975. Gas chromatographic studies on some samples of *Mentha aquatica* L. and *M. longifolia* (L.) Huds. *Istanbul Ecz. Fak. Mec.* 13: 178–183.

Bélafi-Réthy, K., et al. 1973. Untersuchung der Zusammensetzung von einheimischen und ausländischen ätherischen Ölen, I. Kombinierte Methode zur Analyse von ätherischen Ölen mittels wirksamer Trennung der Gemische und instrumenteller identifizierung der Komponenten. *Acta Chim. Acad. Sci. Hung.* 76: 1–11.

Ben Fadhel, N., et al. 2006. Allozyme and essential oil variation within and among natural Tunisian *Mentha pulegium* L. (Lamiaceae) populations. *Acta Hort.* 723: 117–125.

Berry, R. E., et al. 1977. *Insects on Mint*. Pacific Northwest Coop. Ext. Publ. 182.

Bhagat, S. D., et al. 1975. Oil of bergamot mint (*Mentha citrata* Ehrh.). *Indian Perfumer* 19: 31–33.

Bowen, I. H., and I. J. Cubbin. 1992. *Mentha piperita* and *Mentha spicata*. In *Adverse Effects of Herbal Drugs 1*. Ed. P. A. G. M. De Smet et al. New York: Springer-Verlag. 171–178.

Boyd, E. L. 1992. *Hedeoma pulegioides* and *Mentha pulegium*. In *Adverse Effects of Herbal Drugs 1*. Ed. P. A. G. M. De Smet et al. New York: Springer-Verlag. 151–156.

Bozin, B., et al. 2006. Variability of content and composition of *Mentha aquatica* L. (Lamiaceae) essential oil in different phenophases. *J. Essential Oil-Bearing Pl.* 9: 223–229.

Briggs, C. J. 1973. Effects of polybutene emulsion sprays on the composition of peppermint oils. *Pl. Med.* 24: 120–126.

———. 1989. Pennyroyal: a traditional herb with toxic potential. *Canad. Pharm. J.* 122: 369, 371–372.

———. 1993. Peppermint: medicinal herb and flavour agent. *Canad. Pharm. J.* 126: 89–92.

Bullis, D. E., et al. 1948. *Relationship of Maturing and Weathering to Yield and Quality of Peppermint*. Oregon Agric. Exp. Sta. Bull. 458.

Carnat, A. P., and J. L. Lamaison. 1987. La menthe (Auvergne Tradition), *Mentha ×piperita* L., f. *rubescens* Camus, source potentielle d'huile essentielle officinale. *Pl. Med. Therap.* 21: 242–251.

Cash, D. B., et al. 1971. Effect of individual components on peppermint oil flavour. *Food Technol.* 25: 53–54, 58.

Chamura, S. 1953. Chemical changes of reserved matters in rhizome cuttings of peppermint in special relation to its sprouting. *Proc. Crop. Sci. Soc. Japan* 21: 313–314.

Chialva, F., et al. 1982. Qualitative evaluation of aromatic herbs by direct headspace GC analysis. Applications of the method and comparison with the traditional analysis of essential oils. *J. High Resolution Chromatogr. Chromatogr. Commun.* 5: 182–188.

Chopra, M. M., et al. 1964. The essential oils of the species of genus Mentha. *Perfumery Essential Oil Rec.* 55: 323–329.

Clark, G. S. 2007. Aroma chemical profile: menthol. *Perfumer Flavor.* 32(12): 38–47.

Clark, R. J., and R. C. Menary. 1979. The importance of harvest date and plant density on the yield and quality of Tasmanian peppermint oil. *J. Amer. Soc. Hort. Sci.* 104: 702–706.

———. 1980. The effect of irrigation and nitrogen on the yield and composition of peppermint oil (*Mentha piperita* L.). *Austral. J. Agric. Res.* 31: 489–498.

———. 1980. Environmental effects on peppermint (*Mentha piperita* L.). I. Effect of daylength, photon flux density, night temperature and day temperature on the yield and composition of peppermint oil. *Austral. J. Pl. Physiol.* 7: 685–692.

———. 1980. Environmental effects of peppermint (*Mentha piperita* L.). II. Effects of temperature on photosynthesis, photorespiration and dark respiration in peppermint with reference to oil composition. *Austral. J. Pl. Physiol.* 7: 693–697.

———. 1981. Variations in composition of peppermint oil in relation to production areas. *Econ. Bot.* 35: 59–69.

———. 1982. Environmental and cultural factors affecting the yield and composition of peppermint oil (*Mentha piperita* L.). In *VIII International Congress of Essential*

Oils, October 12–17, 1980, Cannes-Grasse, France. Paper no. 14.

Cook, C. M., et al. 2007. *Mentha spicata* essential oils rich in 1,8-cineole and 1,2-epoxy-*p*-menthane derivatives from Zakynthos (Ionian Island, W Greece). *J. Essential Oil Res.* 19: 225–230.

———. 2007. Differences between the inflorescence, leaf and stem essential oils of wild *Mentha pulegium* plants from Zakynthos, Greece. *J. Essential Oil Res.* 19: 239–243.

Crane, F. A., and F. C. Steward. 1962. Growth, nutrition, and metabolism of *Mentha piperita* L. Part 5. Effects of acute deficiency of specified nutrients on *Mentha piperita* L. *Cornell Univ. Agric. Exp. Sta. Mem.* 379: 91–129.

Croteau, R. 1977. Effect of irrigation method on essential oil yield and rate of oil evaporation in mint grown under controlled conditions. *HortScience* 12: 563–565.

da Cunha, A. P., et al. 1976. Estudio cromatográfico e químico do óleo essencial de *Mentha pulegium* L. de Angola. *Bol. Fac. Farm. Coimbra* 1: 23–36.

de Pooter, H. L., and N. M. Schamp. 1987. The essential oil of *Mentha ×villosa* nv. *alopecuroides*. *Flavour Fragrance J.* 2: 163–165.

Dimitrova-Rousseva, E., and H. Chouldjiyan. 1971. Mineral composition of *Mentha piperita* L. grown without N, P, K, Ca, Mg, S or Fe. *Ses. Inst. Genet. Sel. Rast., Sofia* 1971: 261–267.

Ding, D., and H. Sun. 1983. Structural determination of a repellent principle in the essential oil of *Mentha haplocalyx* Briq. *Zhiwu Xuebao* 25: 62–66.

Duriyaprapan, S., et al. 1986. The effect of temperature on growth, oil yield, and oil quality of Japanese mint. *Ann. Bot.* (London) 58: 729–736.

Dutta, P. K. 1971. Cultivation of *Mentha arvensis* in India. *Flavor Industr.* 2: 233–240, 245.

Faulkner, L. R., et al. 1970. Interaction of *Verticillium dahliae* and *Pratylenchus minyus* in *Verticillium* wilt of peppermint: influence of the nematode as determined by a double root technique. *Phytopathology* 60: 100–103.

Fenwick, A. L., and S. M. Ward. 2001. Use of random amplified polymorphic DNA markers for cultivar identification in mint. *HortScience* 36: 761–764.

Forster, H. B., et al. 1980. Antispasmodic effects of some medicinal plants. *Pl. Med.* 40: 309–319.

Franz, C. 1972. Einfluss der Nährstoffe Kalium und Stickstoff auf die Bildung des ätherischen Öls von *Mentha piperita*. *Pl. Med.* 22: 160–183.

Franz, C., and Y. Fujita. 1970. Studies on the essential oils of the genus *Mentha*. Part

5. A biochemical study of the essential oils of *Mentha pulegium* Linn. *J. Agric. Chem. Soc. Japan* 44: 293–298.

———. 1972. On the high boiling components of the essential oil of *Mentha pulegium* Linn. (Studies on the essential oils of the genus *Mentha* VII). *J. Agric. Chem. Soc. Japan* 46: 303–307.

Franz, C., et al. 1977. On the components of the essential oils of *Mentha rotundifolia* (Linn.) Huds. (Studies on the essential oils of the genus *Mentha*, part 10). *J. Agric. Chem. Soc. Japan* 51: 699–702.

Fujita, Y., and S.-i. Fujita. 1967. Essential oil of *Mentha pulegium* Linn. and *M. gattefossei* Maire viewed from the stand-point of comparative biochemistry. *Nippon Kagaku Zasshi* 88: 767–769.

Gasic, O., et al. 1992. Variability of content and composition of essential oil of different *Mentha arvensis* L. var. *piperascens* cultivars. *J. Essential Oil Res.* 4: 49–56.

Gilly, G. 1984. La menthe poivrée blanche de Grasse. *Acta Hort.* 144: 15–19.

Gordon, W. P., et al. 1982. Hepatotoxicity and pulmonary toxicity of pennyroyal oil and its constituent terpenes in the mouse. *Toxicol. Appl. Pharmacol.* 65: 413–424.

———. 1987. The metabolism of the abortifacient terpene, (*R*)-(+)-pulegone, to a proximate toxin, menthofuran. *Drug Metabolism Disposition* 15: 589–594.

Green, R. J. 1963. *Mint Farming*. Rev. ed. U.S.D.A. Inform. Bull. No. 212.

Grundschober, F. 1979. Literature review of pulegone. *Perfumer Flavor.* 4(1): 15–17.

Guéedon, D. J., and B. P. Pasquier. 1994. Analysis and distribution of flavonoid glycosides and rosmarinic acid in 40 *Mentha* ×*piperita* clones. *J. Agric. Food Chem.* 42: 679–684.

Guenther, E. 1929. Spanish essential oils. *Amer. Perfumer Essential Oil Rev.* 24: 291–294, 297.

Hadley, S. K., and S. M. Gaarder. 2005. Treatment of irritable bowel syndrome. *Amer. Family Physician* 72: 2501–2506.

Haginiwa, J., et al. 1963. Pharmacological studies on crude drugs. VII. Properties of essential oil components of aromatics and their pharmacological effects on mouse intestine. *J. Pharm. Soc. Japan* 83: 624–628.

Handa, K. L., et al. 1964. Essential oils and their constituents XXIII. Chemotaxonomy of the genus *Mentha*. *J. Pharm. Sci.* 53: 1407–1409.

Harley, R. M. 1972. *Mentha*. In *Flora Europaea Vol. 3*. Ed. T. G. Tutin et al. Cambridge Univ. Press. 183–186.

Hefendehl, F. W. 1967. Zusammensetzung des ätherischen Öls von *Mentha aquatica* L. Beiträge zur Terpenbiogenese. *Arch. Pharm.* (Berlin) 300: 438–448.

———. 1970. Beiträge zur Biogenese ätherischer Öle Zusammensetzung zweier ätherischer Öle von *Mentha pulegium* L. *Phytochemistry* 9: 1985–1995.

Hefendehl, F. W., and M. J. Murray. 1972. Changes in monoterpene composition in *Mentha aquatica* produced by gene substitution. *Phytochemistry* 11: 189–195.

Hefendehl, F. W., and E. Ziegler. 1975. Analytik von Pfefferminzölen. *Deutsche Lebensmittel-Rundschau* 8: 287–290.

Hendriks, H. 1973. Beschreibung eines Gerätes für die Gewinnung grösser Mengen ätherischen Öle für die Analyse. *Pl. Med.* 24: 158–164.

Horner, C. E. 1955. *Control of Peppermint Diseases*. Oregon Agric. Exp. Sta. Bull. 547.

Ikeda, N., et al. 1968. *Mentha arvensis* L. var. *piperascens* Mal. which grows wild in the north-eastern part of Japan. I. Wild mint in Nasu and Aizuwakamatu-city. *Jap. J. Breed.* 18: 272–276.

———. 1971. *Mentha arvensis* L. var. *piperascens* Mal. which grows wild in the northeastern part of Japan. III. Studies on the essential oils. *Sci. Rep. Fac. Agric. Okayama Univ.* 37: 1–8.

Inamori, M., et al. 2007. Early effects of peppermint oil on gastric emptying: a crossover study using continuous real-time 13C breath test (BreathID system). *J. Gastroenterol.* 42: 539–542.

Karasawa, D., et al. 1991. The essential oil of *Mentha spicata* L. var. *crispa* Benth. from Nepal. *J. Essential Oil Res.* 3: 447–448.

Karousou, R., et al. 2007. "Mints," smells and traditional uses in Thessaloniki (Greece) and other Mediterranean countries. *J. Ethnopharmacol.* 109: 248–257.

Kartnig, Th., and F. Still. 1975. Die Zusammensetzung des ätherischen Öles verschiedener *Mentha*-Sorten aus der Landesversuchsanlange für Spezialkulturen in Burgstall/Wies (Stmk.). *Sci. Pharm.* 43: 236–242.

Kizil, S., and Ö. Tonçer. 2006. Influence of different harvest times on the yield and oil composition of spearmint (*Mentha spicata* L. var. *spicata*). *J. Food Agric. Environm.* 4: 135–137.

Kofidis, G., et al. 2004. Seasonal variation of essential oils in a linalool-rich chemotype of *Mentha spicata* grown wild in Greece. *J. Essential Oil Res.* 16: 469–472.

Kokkini, S., and V. P. Papageorgiou. 1982. Morphological, cytological and chemical investigations of *Mentha spicata* L. in Greece. In *Aromatic Plants: Basic and Applied Aspects*. Ed. N. Margaris et al. The Hague: Martinus Nijhoff. 131–140.

Kokkini, S., and D. Vokou. 1989. *Mentha spicata* (Lamiaceae) chemotypes growing wild in Greece. *Econ. Bot.* 43: 192–202.

Kokkini, S., et al. 2004. Clinal variation of *Mentha pulegium* essential oils along the climatic gradient of Greece. *J. Essential Oil Res.* 16: 588–593.

Kokkini-Gouzkouni, S. 1983. *Taxonomic Studies in the Genus* Mentha *in Greece*. D. thesis., Univ. Thessaloniki, Greece.

Kostecka-Madalska, O. 1970. Investigations on the nourishment of different *Mentha* species in pot cultures. Part 1. The influence of nitrates or ammonium salts upon the growth of *Mentha piperita* L. forma *nigra* and on the content of volatile oil. *Herba Polon.* 16: 379–388.

Kostecka-Madalska, O., et al. 1968. Trials on *Mentha sachalinensis* (Briq.) Kudo cultivation and analysis of its essential oil. *Herba Polon.* 14: 72–78.

Lamaison, J. L., et al. 1987. Différenciation des menthes poivrées, *Mentha* ×*piperita* L. type Mitcham et type Hongrie, cultivées en Auvergne. *Pl. Med. Phytotherap.* 21: 252–261.

Lammerink, J., and T. D. R. Manning. 1971. Yields and composition of oil from peppermint grown at Lincoln, New Zealand. *New Zealand J. Agric. Res.* 14: 745–751.

———. 1973. Peppermint oil composition and yield, flowering time, and morphological characters of four naturalized South Island clones and the Mitcham strain of *Mentha piperita*. *New Zealand J. Agric. Res.* 16: 181–184.

Landing, J. E. 1969. *American Essence: A History of the Peppermint and Spearmint Industry in the United States*. Kalamazoo, Michigan: Kalamazoo Publ. Mus.

Lawrence, B. M. 1978. *A Study of the Monoterpene Interrelationships in the Genus* Mentha *with Special Reference to the Origin of Pulegone and Menthofuran*. D. thesis, Univ. Groningen.

———. 1979. A fresh look at the biosynthetic pathways for most compounds found in *Mentha* oils. In *VII International Congress of Essential Oils, October 7–11, 1977, Kyoto, Japan*. 121–126.

———. 1981. *Essential Oils 1979–1980*. Wheaton, Illinois: Allured.

———. 1981. Monoterpene interrelationships in the *Mentha* genus: a biosynthetic discussion. In *Essential Oils*. Ed. B. D. Mookherjee and C. J. Mussinan. Wheaton, Illinois: Allured. 1–81.

———. 1982. The chemical composition of uncommon members of the *Mentha* genus. In *VIII International Congress of Essential Oils, October 12–17, 1980, Cannes-Grasse, France*. Paper no. 91.

———, ed. 2007. *Mint: The Genus* Mentha. Boca Raton, Florida: CRC Press.

———. 2008. *Peppermint Oil*. Carol Stream, Illinois: Allured.

Lawrence, B. M., and J. K. Morton. 1974. Infraspecific differentiation in the *Mentha* genus. In *VI International Congress of Essential Oils, San Francisco, California, September 8–12, 1974*. Paper no. 16.

Lawrence, B. M., et al. 1972. Essential oils and their constituents. X. Some new trace constituents in the oil of *Mentha piperita* L. *Flavor Industr.* 3: 467–472.

———. 1972. Terpenoids of some *Mentha* hybrids from Canada. *Phytochemistry* 11: 2638–2639.

———. 1989. Peppermint oil differentiation. *Perfumer Flavor.* 14(6): 21–24, 26, 28–30.

Leicester, R. J., and R. H. Hunt. 1982. Peppermint oil to reduce colonic spasm during endoscopy. *Lancet* 1982(2): 989.

Lemli, J. A. J. M. 1955. Opbrengst en samenstelling der vluchtige olie van in Nederland gekweekte pepermunt. *Pharm. Weekbl.* 90: 906–914.

Ley, T. W., and R. G. Stevens. 1992. *Mint Irrigation Management.* Wash. State Univ. Coop. Extens. EM4827.

Lincoln, D. E., et al. 1971. Genetic basis for high limonene-cineole content of exceptional *Mentha citrata* hybrids. *Theor. Appl. Genet.* 41: 365–370.

Luke, E. 1962. Addiction to mentholated cigarettes. *Lancet* 1962(1): 110–111.

Maffei, M., et al. 1986. Glandular trichomes and essential oils of developing leaves in *Mentha viridis lavanduliodora. Pl. Med.* 1986: 187–193.

Malingré, Th. M. 1968. Het gaschromatografische onderzoek van vluchtige oliën. I. *Pharm. Weekbl.* 103: 985–986.

———. 1969. Het gaschromatografische onderzoek van vluchtige oliïn. II. De vluchtige van *Mentha piperita* L. gedurende de ontwikkeling van de plant. *Pharm. Weekbl.* 104: 381–406.

McGimpsey, J. A. 1993. *Mints:* Mentha *Species.* New Zealand Inst. Crop Food Res. Broadsheet No. 18.

McKay, D. L., and J. B. Blumberg. 2006. A review of the bioactivity and potential health benefits of peppermint tea (*Mentha piperita* L.). *Phytotherapy Res.* 20: 619–633.

Mehra, B. K. 1982. *Mentha* oil and menthol production in India: past, present and future. In *Cultivation and Utilization of Aromatic Plants.* Ed. C. K. Atal and B. M. Kapur. Jammu Tawi, India: Regional Res. Lab. 241–272.

Mkaddem, M., et al. 2007. Variability of volatiles in Tunisian *Mentha piperita* L. (Lamiaceae). *J. Essential Oil Res.* 19: 211–214.

Morteza-Semnani, K., et al. 2006. The essential oil composition of *Mentha aquatica* L. *J. Essential Oil-Bearing Pl.* 9: 283–286.

Murray, M. J., and F. W. Hefendehl. 1973. Changes in monoterpene composition of *Mentha aquatica* produced by gene substitution from a high limonene strain of *M. citrata. Phytochemistry* 12: 1875–1880.

Murray, M. J., and D. E. Lincoln. 1970. The genetic basis of acyclic oil constituents in

Mentha citrata Ehrh. *Genetics* 65: 457–471.

———. 1972. Oil composition of *Mentha aquatica–M. longifolia* F1 hybrids and *M. dumetorum. Euphytica* 21: 337–343.

Murray, M. J., et al. 1971. Inter-subgeneric hybrids in the genus *Mentha. J. Hered.* 62: 363–366.

———. 1972. Chemical composition of *Mentha arvensis* var. *piperascens* and four hybrids with *Mentha crispa* harvested at different times in Indiana and Michigan. *Crop Sci.* (Madison) 12: 742–745.

———. 1972. Oil composition of *Mentha aquatica* × *M. spicata* F1 hybrids in relation to the origin of ×*M. piperita. Canad. J. Genet. Cytol.* 14: 13–29.

Nagell, A., and F. W. Hefendehl. 1974. Zusammensetzung des ätherischen Öles von *Mentha rotundifolia. Pl. Med.* 26: 1–8.

Naves, Y. R. 1942. Etude sur les matières végétales volatiles. XVI. Sur la présence de la p-menthadiene-1,4(8)-one-(3) (pipéritéone) et de la p-menthadien-1,8(9)-one-(3) (isopipériténone) dans l'essence de menthe pouliot marocaine. *Helv. Chim. Acta* 25: 732–745.

Ogg, A. G. 1975. *Evaluation of Herbicides for Weed Control in Mint.* Wash. State Agric. Exp. Stat. Bull. 810.

Olsen, P., and I. Thorup. 1984. Neurotoxicity in rats dosed with peppermint oil and pulegone. *Arch. Toxicol.* Suppl. 7: 408–409.

Opdyke, D. L. J. 1974. Monographs on fragrance raw materials. *Food Cosmet. Toxicol.* 12: 807–1016.

Papa, C. M., and W. B. Shelley. 1964. Menthol hypersensitivity. *JAMA* 189: 546–548.

Parker, R., and A. G. Ogg. 1985. *Chemical Weed Control in Mint.* Wash. State Univ. Cooperative Extens. EB 1341.

Pereira, C., et al. 2007. Short-term toxicity study of dl-menthol in rats. *Toxicol. Int.* 14: 41–46.

Perrin, A., and M. Colson. 1991. Timing of the harvest date for *Mentha ×piperita* based on observations of the floral development. *J. Essential Oil Res.* 3: 17–25.

Pichitakul, N., and K. Sthapitanonda. 1977. The constituents of oil from different mint varieties. *J. Natl. Res. Council Thailand* 9(2): 1–12.

Pike, K. S., et al. 1988. *Mint Root Borer in the Pacific Northwest.* Pacific Northwest Extens. Publ. PNW 322.

Piper, T. J., and M. J. Price. 1975. Atypical oils from *Mentha arvensis* var. *piperascens* (Japanese mint) grown from seed. *Intern. Flavor* 6: 196–198.

Póvoa, O., et al. 2006. Pennyroyal (*Mentha pulegium*) and Hart's pennyroyal (*Mentha cervina*) biodiversity in Alentejo, Portugal. *Acta Hort.* 723: 91–97.

Powers, W. L. 1927. Effect of hydrogen-ion

concentration on the growth of certain plants. *Soil Sci.* 24: 1–7.

Rasooli, I., et al. 2007. Antibacterial and antioxidative characterization of essential oils from *Mentha piperita* and *Mentha spicata* grown in Iran. *Acta Alimentaria* 37: 41–52.

Rees, W. D. W., et al. 1979. Treating irritable bowel syndrome with peppermint oil. *Brit. Med. J.* 1979: 835–836.

Retamar, J. A., and E. D. De Riscala. 1980. Aceite esencial de *Mentha arvensis* Linnaeus, variedad *piperascens. Rivista Ital. EPPOS* 62: 127–129.

Sacco, T. 1959. Una nuova forma di menta. *Mentha viridis* (L.) L. cultivar × *lavanduliodora* Sacco, n. cult. Secondo contributo. *Allionia* 5: 185–194.

———. 1966. Comparative considerations on the *Mentha viridis* (L.) L. cultivar × *Lavanduliodora* Sacco n. cult. sown in Italy and Brazil. *Perfumery Essential Oil Rec.* 57: 489–491.

Sacco, T., and M. Calvarano. 1964. Sulla composizione dell'essenza ottenuta da una nuova forma selezionata di menta (*Mentha viridis* (L.) L. cultivar × *lavanduliodora* Sacco n. cult.). *Essenze Deriv. Agrumari* 34: 121–136.

Sacco, T., and G. M. Nano. 1970. Contributo allo studio botanico e chimico del genere *Mentha* gruppo *arvensis. Allionia* 16: 59–64.

Samejima, K., et al. 1995. Luteolin: a strong antimutagen against dietary carcinogen, Trp-P-2, in peppermint, sage, and thyme. *J. Agric. Food Chem.* 43: 410–414.

Schnell, F. J., and H. Hörster. 1968. GLC-Analyse des ätherischen Öles von *Mentha requienii. Pl. Med.* 16: 48–53.

Shasany, A. K., et al. 2007. Chemotypic comparison of AFLP analyzed Indian peppermint germplasm to selected peppermint oils of other countries. *J. Essential Oil Res.* 19: 138–145.

Shimizu, S., et al. 1967. Contributo allo studio citotassonomico e chimico della *Mentha viridis* (L.) L. cultivar × *lavanduliodora* Sacco n. cult. *Allionia* 13: 215–219.

———. 1969. Studies on the essential oils of *Mentha aquatica* L. I–III. *J. Fac. Agric. Shinshu Univ.* 6: 67–82.

Sigmund, C. J., and E. F. McNally. 1969. The action of a carminative on the lower esophageal sphincter. *Gastroenterology* 56: 13–18.

Sivropoulou, A., et al. 1995. Antimicrobial activity of mint essential oils. *J. Agric. Food Chem.* 43: 2384–2388.

Smith, D. M., and L. Levi. 1961. Treatment of compositional data for the characterization of essential oils. Determination of geographical origins of peppermint oils by gas chromatographic analysis. *J. Agric. Food Chem.* 9: 230–244.

Spindler, P. and C. Madsen. 1992. Sub-chronic toxicity study of peppermint oil in rats. *Toxicology Lett.* 62: 215–220.

Sticher, O., and H. Flück. 1968. Die Zusammensetzung von genuinen, extrahierten und destillierten ätherischen Ölen einiger Mentha-Arten. *Pharm. Acta Helv.* 43: 411–446.

Sudekum, M., et al. 1992. Pennyroyal oil toxicosis in a dog. *J. Amer. Veterin. Med. Assoc.* 200: 817–818.

Sullivan, J. B., et al. 1979. Pennyroyal oil poisoning and hepatotoxicity. *JAMA* 242: 2873–2874.

Szentmihályi, K., et al. 2001. In vitro study on the transfer of volatile oil components. *J. Pharm. Biomed. Anal.* 24: 1073–1080.

Tassou, C. C., et al. 1995. Effects of essential oil from mint (*Mentha piperita*) on *Salmonella enteritidis* and *Listeria monocytogenes* in model food systems at 4° and 10°C. *J. Appl. Bacteriol.* 78: 593–600.

Taylor, B. A., et al. 1983. Inhibitory effect of peppermint oil on gastrointestinal muscle. *Gut* 24: 992.

Thomas, J. G. 1962. Peppermint fibrillation. *Lancet* 1962(1): 222.

Thomassen, D., et al. 1991. Partial characterization of biliary metabolites of pulegone by tandem mass spectrometry. Detection of glucuronide, glutathione, and glutathionyl glucuronide conjugates. *Drug Metabolism Disposition* 19: 997–1003.

Tucker, A. O. 1992. The truth about mints. *Herb Companion* 4(6): 51–52.

Tucker, A. O., and D. E. Fairbrothers. 1972. *Mentha* ×*gentilis* L. 'Variegata': nomenclature and viral origin. *Taxon* 21: 209–210, 733.

———. 1990. The origin of *Mentha* ×*gracilis* (Lamiaceae). I. Chromosome numbers, fertility, and three morphological characters. *Econ. Bot.* 44: 183–213.

Tucker, A. O., et al. 1980. The Linnaean types of *Mentha* (Lamiaceae). *Taxon* 29: 233–255.

———. 1991. The origin of *Mentha* ×*gracilis* (Lamiaceae). II. Essential oils. *Econ. Bot.* 45: 200–215.

Tzanetakis, I. E., et al. 2006. Mint virus S: a novel potexvirus associated with symptoms in 'Variegata' mint. *Arch. Virol.* 151: 143–153.

Vejdani, R., et al. 2006. The efficacy of an herbal medicine, Carmint, on the relief of abdominal pain and bloating in patients with irritable bowel syndrome: a pilot study. *Dig. Dis. Sci.* 51: 1501–1507.

Younis, Y. M. H., and S. M. Beshir. 2004. Carvone-rich essential oils from *Mentha longifolia* (L.) Huds. ssp. *schimperi* Briq. and *Mentha spicata* L. grown in Sudan. *J. Essential Oil Res.* 16: 539–541.

Zwaving, J. H., and D. Smith. 1971. Composition of the essential oil of Austrian *Mentha pulegium*. *Phytochemistry* 10: 1951–1953.

Monarda

Burt, J. B. 1936. *Monarda pectinata* Nutt., a phytochemical study. The volatile oil. *J. Amer. Pharm. Assoc.* 25: 682–687.

Calpouzos, L. 1954. Botanical aspects of oregano. *Econ. Bot.* 8: 222–233.

Carnat, A. P., et al. 1991. Composition of leaf and flower essential oil from *Monarda didyma* L. cultivated in France. *Flavour Fragrance J.* 6: 79–80.

Chubey, B. B. 1982. Geraniol-rich essential oil from *Monarda fistulosa* L. *Perfumer Flavor.* 7(3): 32–34.

Collicutt, L. M., and C. G. Davidson. 1999. 'Petite Delight' *Monarda*. *HortScience* 34: 149–150.

Collins, J. E., et al. 1994. Composition of the essential oil from the leaves and flowers of *Monarda citriodora* var. *citriodora* grown in the United Kingdom. *J. Essential Oil Res.* 6: 27–29.

Davidson, C. G. 2002. 'Petite Wonder' monarda. *HortScience* 37: 235–236.

———. 2006. *Monarda*, bee-balm. In *Flower Breeding and Genetics: Issues, Challenges and Opportunities for the 21st Century*. Ed. N. O. Anderson. Netherlands: Springer. 735–777.

Dorman, H. J., and S. G. Deans. 2004. Chemical composition, antimicrobial and *in vitro* antioxidant properties of *Monarda citriodora* var. *citriodora*, *Myristica fragrans*, *Origanum vulgare* ssp. *hirtum*, *Pelargonium* sp. and *Thymus zygis* oils. *J. Essential Oil Res.* 16: 145–150.

Dorman, H. J. D., et al. 1995. Evaluation in vitro of plant essential oils as natural antioxidants. *J. Essential Oil Res.* 7: 645–651.

Gill, L. S. 1977. A cytosystematics study of the genus *Monarda* L. (Labiatae) in Canada. *Caryologia* 30: 381–394.

Hawke, R. 1999. Evaluations of *Monarda*-powdery mildew. *Herbal Connection* 7(1): 28–31.

Henning, J. 1995. Mildew-resistant monardas. *Hardy Pl. Soc. Mid-Atlantic Group* 9(3): 3–4.

———. 1998. Monarda and powdery mildew resistance. *Pl. Evaluation Notes* No. 12.

Keefover-Ring, K. 2006. *Monarda fistulosa*: making good scents in Colorado. *Aquilegia* 30(2): 3–4.

Keith, J. 2005. Must-have monardas. *Amer. Gard.* 84(4): 18–22.

Lawrence, B. M. 1981. *Essential Oils 1979–1980*. Wheaton, Illinois: Allured.

———. 1982. The existence of infraspecific differences in specific genera in the Labiatae family. In *VIII International Congress of Essential Oils, October 12–17, 1980, Cannes-Grasse, France*. Paper no. 35.

Marshall, H. H., and R. W. Scora. 1972. A new chemical race of *Monarda fistulosa* (Labiatae). *Canad. J. Bot.* 50: 1845–1849.

Mattern, A. 1993. Neue *Monarda*-Sorten aus Holland. *Gartenpraxis* 1993(2): 8–15.

———. 1994. Monardas of merit. *Garden* (London) 119: 516–519.

Mazza, G., et al. 1993. *Monarda*: a source of geraniol, linalool, thymol and carvacrol-rich essential oils. In *New Crops*. Ed. J. Janick and J. E. Simon. New York: John Wiley & Sons. 628–631.

Oudolf, P. 1993. Neue *Monarda*-Sorten aus Holland. *Gartenpraxis* 1993(2): 8–16.

Scora, R. W. 1967. Interspecific relationships in the genus *Monarda* (Labiatae). *Univ. Calif. Publ. Bot.* 41: 1–71.

———. 1967. Study of the essential leaf oils of the genus *Monarda* (Labiatae). *Amer. J. Bot.* 54: 446–452.

———. 1969. El genero *Monarda* en México. *Bol. Soc. Bot. México* 30: 31–71.

Myrrhis

Cannon, J. F. M. 1968. *Myrrhis*. In *Flora Europaea Vol. 2*. Ed. T. G. Tutin et al. Cambridge Univ. Press. 327.

DeBaggio, T. 1988. Sweet cicely: Seed germination tricks. *Herb Spice Med. Pl. Dig.* 6(1): 6.

Hussain, R. A., et al. 1990. Sweetening agents of plant origin: phenylpropanoid constituents of seven sweet-tasting plants. *Econ. Bot.* 44: 174–182.

Kubeczka, K.-H. 1982. Chemical investigations of essential oils of umbelifers. In *Aromatic Plants: Basic and Applied Aspects*. Ed. N. Margaris et al. The Hague: Martinus Nijhoff. 165–173.

Tkachenko, K. G., and I. G. Zenkevich. 1993. Chemical composition of the leaf of *Myrrhis odorata* (L.) Scop. *J. Essential Oil Res.* 5: 329–331.

Uusitalo, J. S., et al. 1999. Essential oil composition of *Myrrhis odorata* (L.) Scop. grown in Finland. *J. Essential Oil Res.* 11: 423–425.

Myrtus

Agrimonti, C., et al. 2007. Understanding biological conservation strategies: a molecular-genetic approach to the case of myrtle (*Myrtus communis* L.) in two Italian regions: Sardinia and Calabria. *Conserv. Genet.* 8: 385–396.

Akgül, A., and A. Bayrak. 1989. Essential oil content and composition of myrtle (*Myrtus communis* L.) leaves. *Doga: Turk Tarim Ormancilik Derg.* 13: 143–147.

Anonymous. 1928. The myrtle in the perfumer's art. *Perfumery Essential Oil Rec.* 19: 384–386.

Asllani, U. 2000. Chemical composition of Albanian myrtle oil (*Myrtus communis* L.). *J. Essential Oil Res.* 12: 140–142.

Boelens, M. H. 1989. A royal story about myrtle. *Perfumer Flavor.* 14(4): 33–34, 36–38.

Boelens, M. H., and R. Jimenez. 1991. The chemical composition of Spanish myrtle leaf oils. Part 1. *J. Essential Oil Res.* 3: 173–177.

———. 1992. The chemical composition of Spanish myrtle oils. Part 2. *J. Essential Oil Res.* 4: 349–353.

Bouzouita, N., et al. 2003. Antimicrobial activity of essential oils from Tunisian aromatic plants. *Flavour Fragrance J.* 18: 380–383.

Brandesi, P., et al. 1997. Chemical composition of myrtle leaf essential oil from Corsica (France). *J. Essential Oil Res.* 9: 283–288.

Browne, D. J. 1846. *The Trees of America.* New York: Harper & Brothers.

Bullitta, P., et al. 1996. Prime indagini sulla risposta del *Myrtus communis* L. ad interventi agronomici. *Rivista Ital. EPPOS* 1994(19): 111–116.

Cakir, A. 2004. Essential oil and fatty acid composition of the fruits of *Hippophae rhamnoides* L. (sea buckthorn) and *Myrtus communis* L. from Turkey. *Biochem. Syst. Ecol.* 32: 809–816.

Chalchat, J.-C., et al. 1998. Essential oils of myrtle (*Myrtus communis* L.) of the Mediterranean littoral. *J. Essential Oil Res.* 10: 613–617.

Curini, M., et al. 2003. Composition and *in vitro* antifungal activity of essential oils of *Erigeron canadensis* and *Myrtus communis* from France. *Chem. Nat. Comp.* 39: 191–194.

Deriu, A., et al. 2007. In vitro activity of essential oil of *Myrtus communis* L. against *Helicobacter pylori*. *Intern. J. Antimicrobial Agents* 30: 562–563.

Farah, A., et al. 2006. Fractional distillation effect on the chemical composition of Moroccan myrtle (*Myrtus communis* L.) essential oils. *Flavour Fragrance J.* 21: 351–354.

Frazao, S., et al. 1974. Characteristics and composition of essential oil of *Myrtus communis* L. In *VI International Congress of Essential Oils, San Francisco, California, September 8–12, 1974*. Paper no. 112.

Fujita, S.-i., et al. 1992. Miscellaneous contributions to the essential oils of plants from various territories (53). On the components of the essential oils of myrtle (*Myrtus communis* Linn.). *Bull. Mukogawa Women's Univ. Nat. Sci.* 40: 33–37.

Gauthier, R., et al. 1988. A propos de l'huile essentielle de *Myrtus communis* L. var. *italica* recolte au Maroc. I. Rendements et compositions durant un cycle végétif annuel. *Biruniya* 4: 97–116.

———. 1988. A propos de l'huile essentielle de *Myrtus communis* L. var. *italica* et var. *baetica* recolte au Maroc. II. Rendement et composition selon le mode d'extraction; comparison avec diverses sources. *Biruniya* 4: 117–132.

———. 1989. Activité d'extraits de *Myrtus communis* contre *Pediculus humanus capitis*. *Pl. Med. Phytotherap.* 23: 95–108.

Grigoriadou, K., and N. Leventakis. 2000. Preliminary study on large scale *in vitro* propagation of *Myrtus communis* L. *Acta Hort.* 541: 299–302.

Halsall, L. J., and A. M. Dourado. 2001. Myrtle in a whorl. *New Plantsman* 8: 224–226.

Jamoussi, B., et al. 2005. Effect of harvest time on the yield and composition of Tunisian myrtle oils. *Flavour Fragrance J.* 20: 274–277.

Koukos, P. K., et al. 2001. Chemicals from Greek forestry biomass: constituents of the leaf oil of *Myrtus communis* L. grown in Greece. *J. Essential Oil Res.* 13: 245–246.

Krüssmann, G. 1985. *Manual of Cultivated Broad-leaved Trees and Shrubs.* 3 vols. Trans. M. E. Epp. Portland, Oregon: Timber Press.

Lawrence, B. M., et al. 1970. Essential oils and their constituents. V. Oil of *Myrtus communis* L. *Amer. Perfumer Cosmetics* 85: 53–55.

Maurizio, M., and M. R. Cani. 1996. Variability of rooting ability of softwood cuttings in myrtle germplasm. In *Proceedings: International Symposium Breeding Research on Medicinal and Aromatic Plants, June 30–July 4, 1996, Quedlinburg, Germany*. Ed. F. Pank. 191–194.

Maurizio, M., et al. 1996. First observation of myrtle (*Myrtus communis* L.) germplasm for characters related to intensive plant cultivation. In *Proceedings: International Symposium Breeding Research on Medicinal and Aromatic Plants, June 30–July 4, 1996, Quedlinburg, Germany*. Ed. F. Pank. 29–32.

Messaoud, C., et al. 2005. *Myrtus communis* in Tunisia: variability of the essential oil composition in natural populations. *Flavour Fragrance J.* 20: 577–582.

Milia, M., et al. 1996. Propagazione del mirto (*Myrtus communis* L.) mediante l'uso di tecniche diverse. *Rivista Ital. EPPOS* 1994(19): 117–123.

Miller, P. 1754. *The Gardeners Dictionary.* London: Philip Miller.

Mulas, M., et al. 2002. Myrtle (*Myrtus communis* L.) as a new aromatic crop: cultivar selection. *J. Herbs Spices Med. Pl.* 9(2/3): 127–131.

Özek, T., et al. 2000. Chemical composition of Turkish myrtle oil. *J. Essential Oil Res.* 12: 541–544.

Pirisino, G., et al. 1996. Studio della resa e della composizione chimica dell'olio essenziale di *Myrtus communis* L. sponaneo di cuglieri (Sardegna). *Rivista Ital. EPPOS* 1994(19): 159–169.

Queirós, M., and J. Ormonde. 1987. Conservation of the medicinal and aromatic myrtle (*Myrtus communis* L.) in the Açores. In *International Symposium on Conservation of Genetic Resources of Aromatic and Medicinal Plants*. Ed. M. Mota and J. Baeta. OEIRAS. 139–143.

Scora, R. W. 1973. Essential leaf oil variability in green, variegated and albino foliage of *Myrtus communis*. *Phytochemistry* 12: 153–155.

Sennen and Teodoro. 1929. Les formes du *Myrtus communis* L. sur le territoire de Tarragone (Espagne). *Bull. Soc. Dendrol. France* 69: 5–19.

Tateo, F., and V. Picci. 1982. Prime indagini sulla caratterizzazione GLC-MS dell'olio essenziale di mirto di Sardegna (*Myrtus communis* L.). *Rivista Soc. Ital. Sci. Aliment.* 11: 53–58.

Trochain, J.-L., and M. Delpoux. 1970. Le myrte à fruits blanc: *Myrtus communis* L. var. *leucocarpa* DC. Nouvelle localité française. *Bull. Soc. Hist. Nat. Toulouse* 106: 303–305.

Uehleke, H., and M. Brinkschulte-Freitas. 1979. Oral toxicity of an essential oil from myrtle and adaptive liver stimulation. *Toxicology* 12: 335–342.

Vanhaelen, M., and R. Vanhaelen-Fastré. 1980. Constituents of essential oil of *Myrtus communis*. *Pl. Med.* 39: 164–167.

Walters, S. M. 1968. *Myrtus.* In *Flora Europaea Vol. 2*. Ed. T. G. Tutin et al. Cambridge Univ. Press. 303–304.

Weyerstahl, P., et al. 1994. Constituents of the essential oil of *Myrtus communis* L. from Iran. *Flavour Fragrance J.* 9: 333–337.

Nepeta

Anonymous. 2004. Catnip. *Rev. Nat. Prod.* (*Wolters Kluwer Health*).

Baranauskiene, R., et al. 2003. Sensory and instrumental evaluation of catnip (*Nepeta cataria* L.) aroma. *J. Agric. Food Chem.* 51: 3840–3848.

Bourrel, C., et al. 1993. Catnip (*Nepeta cataria* L.) essential oil: analysis of chemical constituents, bacteriostatic and fungistatic properties. *J. Essential Oil Res.* 5: 159–167.

Das, S., et al. 2001. *Catnip*. Virginia Tech Fact Sheet No. 4.

de Pooter, H. L., et al. 1988. The essential oils of five *Nepeta* species: a preliminary evaluation of their use in chemotaxonomy by cluster analysis. *Flavour Fragrance J.* 3: 155–159.

Ferguson, J. M., et al. 1988. Catnip production in North Carolina. *Herb, Spice, Med. Pl. Dig.* 6(4): 1–4.

———. 1990. Production of catnip in North Carolina. In *Advances in New Crops*. Ed. J.

Janick and J. E. Simon. Portland, Oregon: Timber Press. 527–528.

Héthelyi, É., et al. 2002. Volatile constituents of *Nepeta cataria* L., *N. glechoma* Benth. and *N. parviflora* M. Bieb. from Hungary. *Intern. J. Hort. Sci.* 7: 47–50.

Hoffman, M. H. A. 2001. *Nepeta*: sortimentsonderzoek en keuringsrapport. *Dendroflora* 38: 88–113

Huffman, M., and E. Huffman. 1980. Catnip as a cash crop. *Mother Earth News* 62: 31.

Ibrahim, M. E., and A. A. E. El-Din. 1999. Cultivation of *Nepeta cataria* L. in Egypt: its growth, yield and essential oil content as influenced by some agronomic practices. *Egypt. J. Hort.* 26: 281–302.

Jamzad, Z., et al. 2003. Phylogenetic relationships in *Nepeta* L. (Lamiaceae) and related genera based on ITS sequence data. *Taxon* 52: 21–32.

Malizia, R. A., et al. 1996. Volatile constituents of the essential oil of *Nepeta cataria* L. grown in Cordoba Province (Argentina). *J. Essential Oil Res.* 8: 565–567.

Oliver, P. C. 1998. Catnip: not just for kitty anymore. *Business Herbs* 16(1): 1–2, 6–7, 16.

Peterson, C. J., et al. 2002. Behavioral activity of catnip (Lamiaceae) essential oil components to the German cockroach (Blattodea: Blattellidae). *J. Econ. Entomol.* 95: 377–380.

Regnier, F. E., et al. 1967. Studies on the composition of the essential oils of three *Nepeta* species. *Phytochemistry* 6: 1281–1289.

Sakurai, K., et al. 1988. Both (4a*S*,7*S*,7a*R*)-(+)-nepetalactone and its antipode are powerful attractants for cats. *Agric. Biol. Chem.* 52: 2369–2371.

Schultz, G., et al. 2004. Catnip, *Nepeta cataria* (Lamiales: Lamiaceae)—a closer look: seasonal occurrence of nepetalactone isomers and comparative repellency of three terpenoids to insects. *Environ. Entomol.* 33: 1562–1569.

Svoboda, K., et al. 1996. Cultivation and volatile oil analysis of *Nepeta cataria* ssp. *citriodora* grown in Finland and Scotland. *Beitr. Zuechtungsforsch* 2: 377–380.

Tittel, G., et al. 1982. Über die chemische Zusammensetzung von Melissenölen. *Pl. Med.* 46: 91–98.

Tucker, A. O., and S. S. Tucker. 1988. Catnip and the catnip response. *Econ. Bot.* 42: 214–231.

van Hevelingen, A. 1995. Catnip and cousins: nepetas cater to a collector's fancy. *Herb Companion* 7(5): 30–36.

Venskutonis, P. R., et al. 1995. Flavour composition of some lemon-like aroma herbs from Lithuania. In *Food Flavor: Generation, Analysis and Process Influence*. Ed. G. Charalambous. Amsterdam: Elsevier. 833–847.

Nigella

Abdel-Fattah, A. M., et al. 2000. Antinociceptive effects of *Nigella sativa* oil and its major component, thymoquinone, in mice. *Eur. J. Pharmacol.* 400: 89–97.

Aboutabl, E. A., et al. 1986. Aroma volatiles of *Nigella sativa* L. seeds. In *Progress in Essential Oil Research*. Ed. E.-J. Brunke. New York: Walter de Gruyter & Co. 49–55.

Agarwal, R., et al. 1979. Antimicrobial and antihelmintic activities of the essential oil of *Nigella sativa* Linn. *Indian J. Exp. Biol.* 17: 1264–1265.

Al-Ghamdi, M. S. 2001. The anti-inflammatory, analgesic and antipyretic activity of *Nigella sativa*. *J. Ethnopharmacol.* 76: 45–48.

Anonymous. 2008. Kalanji. *Rev. Nat. Prod.* (*Wolters Kluwer Health*).

Ashraf, M., et al. 2006. Effect of nitrogen application on the content and composition of oil, essential oil and minerals in black cumin (*Nigella sativa* L.) seeds. *J. Sci. Food Agric.* 86: 871–876.

Atia, F., et al. 2002. Stimulatory effects of Na+ transport in renal epithelia induced by extracts of *Nigella arvensis* are caused by adenosine. *J. Exp. Biol.* 205: 3729–3737.

Bankaci-Ali, F., et al. 2006. Etude comparative de la composition chimique de la *Nigella sativa* Linn. de quelques regions du monde, extraites par micro-ondes. *Rivista Ital. EPPOS* 41: 23–32.

———. 2007. Chemical composition of seed essential oils from Algerian *Nigella sativa* extracted by microwave and hydrodistillation. *Flavour Fragrance J.* 22: 148–153.

Bourrel, C., et al. 1993. Etude des composes aromatiques des graines de nigelle (*Nigella sativa* L.): evaluation des proprietes antibacteriennes et antifongiques. *Rivista Ital. EPPOS* 1993(10): 21–27.

Burits, M., and F. Bucar. 2000. Antioxidant activity of *Nigella sativa* essential oil. *Phytotherapy Res.* 14: 323–328.

Daba, M. H., and M. S. Abdel-Rahman. 1998. Hepatoprotective activity of thymoquinone in isolated rat hepatocytes. *Toxicol. Lett.* 95: 23–29.

D'Antuono, L. F., et al. 2002. Seed yield, yield components, oil content and essential oil content and composition of *Nigella sativa* L. and *Nigella damascena* L. *Industr. Crops. Prod.* 15: 59–69.

Daukšas, E., et al. 2002. Comparison of oil from *Nigella damascena* seed recovered by pressing, convention solvent extraction and carbon dioxide extraction. *J. Food Sci.* 67: 1021–1024.

El-Abhar, H. S., et al. 203. Gastroprotective activity of *Nigella sativa* oil and its constituent, thymoquinone, against gastric mucosal injury induced by ischaemia/reperfu-sion in rats. *J. Ethnopharmacol.* 84: 251–258.

El-Dakhakhny, M. 1963. Studies on the chemical constitution of Egyptian *Nigella sativa* L. seeds. II. The essential oil. *Pl. Med.* 11: 465–470.

El-Dakhakhny, M., et al. 2002. The hypoglycemic effect of *Nigella sativa* oil is mediated by extrapancreatic actions. *Pl. Med.* 68: 465–466.

El-Hadiyah, T. M., et al. 2003. Evaluation of *Nigella sativa* seed constituents for their in vivo toxicity in mice. *Nat. Prod. Sci.* 9: 22–27.

Fico, G., et al. 2004. Biological screening of *Nigella damascena* for antimicrobial and molluscicidal activities. *Phytotherapy Res.* 18: 468–470.

Gad, A. M., et al. 1963. Studies on the chemical constitution of Egyptian *Nigella sativa* L. oil. *Pl. Med.* 11: 134–138.

Gilani, A. H., et al. 2001. Bronchodilator, spasmolytic and calcium antagonist activities of *Nigella sativa* seeds (kalonji): a traditional herbal product with multiple medicinal uses. *J. Pakistan Med. Assoc.* 51: 115–120.

Hailat, N., et al. 1995. Effect of *Nigella sativa* volatile oil on Jurkat T cell leukemia polypeptides. *Intern. J. Pharmacogn.* 33: 16–20.

Havlik, J., et al. 2006. Chemical composition of essential oil from the seeds of *Nigella arvensis* L. and assessment of its antimicrobial activity. *Flavour Fragrance J.* 21: 713–717.

Herrmann, W. 1998. *Nigella* macht wieder von sich reden: Neues im Busch. *Gartenpraxis* 1998(2): 47.

Hitchings, C., and J. Bird. 1993. *Nigella sativa*. *Herbarist* 59: 20–32.

Houghton, P. J., et al. 1995. Fixed oil of *Nigella sativa* and derived thymoquinone inhibit eicosanoid generation in leukocytes and membrane lipid peroxidation. *Pl. Med.* 61: 33–36.

Ibraheim, Z. Z. 2002. Effect of *Nigella sativa* seeds and total oil on some blood parameters in female volunteers. *Saudi Pharm. J.* 10: 54–59.

Kacem, R., and Z. Meraihi. 2006. Effects of essential oil extracted from *Nigella sativa* (L.) seeds and its main components on human neutrophil activity. *Iakugaku Zasshi* 126: 301–305.

Kanter, M., et al. 2003. Effects of *Nigella sativa* L. and *Urtica dioica* L. on lipid peroxidation, antioxidant enzyme systems and some liver enzymes in CCl4-treated rats. *J. Vet. Med. A* 50: 264–268.

Khan, M. A. U., et al. 2003. The *in vivo* antifungal activity of the aqueous extract from *Nigella sativa* seeds. *Phytotherapy Res.* 17: 183–186.

Mahmood, M. S., et al. 2003. The *in vitro* effect of aqueous extract of *Nigella sativa* seeds on nitric oxide production. *Phytotherapy Res.* 17: 921–924.

Mahmoud, M. R., et al. 2002. The effect of *Nigella sativa* oil against the liver damage induced by *Shistosoma mansoni* infection in mice. *J. Ethnopharmacol.* 79: 1–11.

Mansour, M. A. 2000. Protective effects of thymoquinone and desferrioxamine against hepatotoxicity of carbon tetrachloride in mice. *Life Sci.* 26: 2583–2591.

Michelitsch, A., and A. Rittmannsberger. 2003. A simple differential pulse polarographic method for the determination of thymoquinone in black seed oil. *Phytochem. Anal.* 14: 224–227.

Meral, I., et al. 2004. Effect of *Nigella sativa* L. on heart rate and some haematological values of alloxan-induced diabetic rats. *Scand. J. Lab. Animal Sci.* 31: 49–53.

Özgüven, M., et al. 2001. Ertrags- und Qualitäts-eigenschaften von Schwarzkümmel (*Nigella sativa* L.) aus dem Cukurova-Gebiet der Süd-Türkei. *Z. Arzn. Gew. Pfl.* 6: 20–24.

Parker, T. D., et al. 2003. Fatty acid composition and oxidative stability of cold-pressed edible seed oils. *J. Food Sci.* 68: 1240–1243.

Parry, J. W., et al. 2005. Radical scavenging properties of cold-pressed edible seed oils. In *Phenolic Compounds in Foods and Natural Health Products.* Ed. F. Shahidi and C.-T. Ho. Washington, D.C.: Amer. Chem. Soc. 107–117.

Ramadan, M. F., and J.-T. Mörsel. 2003. Analysis of glycolipids from black cumin (*Nigella sativa* L.), coriander (*Coriandrum sativum* L.), and niger (*Guizotia abyssinica* Cass.) oilseeds. *Food Chem.* 80: 197–204.

Ramadan, M. F., et al. 2003. Radical scavenging activity of black cumin (*Nigella sativa* L.), coriander (*Coriandrum sativum* L.), and niger (*Guizotia abyssinica* Cass.) crude seed oils and oil fractions. *J. Agric. Food Chem.* 51: 6961–6969.

Rao, M. V., et al. 2007. Comparative evaluation of SFE and solvent extraction methods on the yield and composition of black seeds (*Nigella sativa*). *J. Liquid Chromatogr. Rel. Technol.* 30: 2545–2555.

Salama, R. B. 1973. Sterols in the seed oil of *Nigella sativa. Pl. Med.* 24: 375–377.

Salim, E. I., and S. Fukushima. 2003. Chemopreventive potential of volatile oil from black cumin (*Nigella sativa* L.) seeds against rat colon carcinogenesis. *Nutr. Cancer* 45: 195–202.

Sanchez, J. H. 1992. Seeds for the kitchen. *Horticulture* 70(8): 54–60.

Sorvig, K. 1983. The genus *Nigella. Plantsman* 4: 229–235.

Stoyanova, A., et al. 2003. A comparative investigation on the composition of the vola-

tiles of *Nigella sativa* L. from Bulgaria. *J. Essential Oil-Bearing Pl.* 6: 207–209.

Tennekoon, K. H., et al. 1991. Possible hepatotoxicity of *Nigella sativa* seeds and *Dregea volubilis* leaves. *J. Ethnopharmacol.* 31: 283–289.

Thippeswamy, N. B., and K. A. Naidu. 2005. Antioxidant potency of cumin varieties—cumin, black cumin and bitter cumin—on antioxidant systems. *Eur. Food Res. Technol.* 220: 472–476.

Türkdoğan, M. K., et al. 2003. The role of *Utica dioica* and *Nigella sativa* in the prevention of carbon tetrachloride-induced hepatotoxicity in rats. *Phytotherapy Res.* 17: 942–946.

Tutin, T. G. 1964. *Nigella*. In *Flora Europaea Vol. 1*. Ed. T. G. Tutin et al. Cambridge Univ. Press. 209–210.

Wajs, A., et al. 2008. Composition of essential oil from seeds of *Nigella sativa* L. cultivated in Poland. *Flavour Fragrance J.* 23: 126–132.

Whiteley, A. C. 1989. *Nigella*. In *The European Garden Flora Vol. 3*. Ed. S. M. Walters et al. Cambridge Univ. Press. 338.

Yu, L. L., et al. 2005. Antioxidant properties of cold-pressed black caraway, carrot, cranberry, and hemp seed oils. *Food Chem.* 91: 723–729.

Zohary, M. 1983. The genus *Nigella* (Ranunculaceae): a taxonomic revision. *Pl. Syst. Evol.* 142: 1–107.

Ocimum

Adler, P. R., et al. 1989. Nitrogen form alters sweet basil growth and essential oil content and composition. *HortScience* 24: 789–790.

Albuquerque, U. P. de, and L. de Holanda C. Andrade. 1998. El género *Ocimum* L. (*Lamiaceae*) en el nordeste del Brasil. *Anales Jard. Bot. Madrid* 56: 43–64.

———. 1998. Etnobotánica del género *Ocimum* L. (*Lamiaceae*) en las comunidades afrobrasileñas. *Anales Jard. Bot. Madrid* 56: 107–118.

Ali, M. E., and L. A. M. Shamsuzzaman. 1968. Investigations on *Ocimum gratissimum* Linn. Part 3. Constituents of the essential oil. *Sci. Res.* (Dacca) 5(2/3): 91–94.

Amvam Zollo, P. H., et al. 1998. Aromatic plants of Tropical Central Africa. Part 32. Chemical composition and antifungal activity of thirteen essential oils from aromatic plants of Cameroon. *Flavour Fragrance J.* 13: 107–114.

Anonymous. 1997. Fusarium wilt of basil: it may be in your seed, so take action to prevent it. *Growing Market* 6(4): 1, 4.

———. 2006. Amazonian basil. *Rev. Nat. Prod.* (Wolters Kluwer Health).

———. 2008. African mint. *Rev. Nat. Prod.* (Wolters Kluwer Health).

Aquino Lemos, J. de, et al. 2005. Antifungal

activity from *Ocimum gratissimum* L. towards *Cryptococcus neoformans. Mem. Inst. Oswaldo Cruz* 100: 55–58.

Asha, M. K., et al. 2001. Anthelmintic activity of essential oil of *Ocimum sanctum* and eugenol. *Fitoterapia* 72: 669–670.

Ayobangira, F. X., and L. Ntezurubanza. 1987. Variations morphologiques et chimiques chez *Ocimum urticifolium* Roth (= *O. suave* Willd.) au Rwanda: significations taxonomiques de ces observations. *Pl. Med. Phytotherap.* 21: 236–241.

Badshah, K., and C. Zakaullah. 1979. Diseases of sweet basil: a review. *Pakistan J. Forest.* 29: 188–294.

Baratta, M. T., et al. 1998. Antimicrobial and antioxidant properties of some commercial essential oils. *Flavour Fragrance J.* 13: 235–244.

Basker, D., and E. Putievsky. 1978. Seasonal variation in the yields of herb and essential oil in some Labiatae species. *J. Hort. Sci.* 53: 179–183.

Batta, S. K., and G. Santhakumari. 1970. The antifertility effect of *Ocimum sanctum* and *Hibiscus rosa sinensis. Indian J. Med. Res.* 59: 777–781.

Bekers, A. G. M., and M. Kroh. 1978. Carbohydrate composition of the mucilage on *Ocimum basilicum* L. seeds. *Acta Bot. Neerl.* 27: 121–123.

Bianchi-Santamaria, A., et al. 1993. Antimutagenic action of beta carotene, canthaxanthin and extracts of *Rosmarinus officinalis* and *Melissa officinalis.* Genotoxicity of basil and tarragon oil. In *Food and Cancer Prevention: Chemical and Biological Aspects.* Ed. K. W. Waldron et al. Cambridge: Roy. Soc. Chem. 75–81.

Boniface, C., et al. 1987. Les diverses techniques d'analyse de données. II.–Application aux arômes huiles essentielles de basilic. *Parfums, Cosmétiques, Arômes* 74: 75–77.

Bonnardeaux, J. 1992. The effect of different harvesting methods on the yield and quality of basil oil in the Ord River irrigation area. *J. Essential Oil Res.* 4: 65–69.

Boonklinkajorn, P., and N. Chomchalow. 1968. Preliminary study on the effect of plant variety on the yield of *Ocimum* spp. *Appl. Sci. Res. Corp. Thailand Rep.* No. 3.

Borchard, P., and S. Borchard. 1993. Better basils. *Fine Gard.* 32: 56–57.

Bouzouita, N., et al. 2003. Antimicrobial activity of essential oils from Tunisian aromatic plants. *Flavour Fragrance J.* 18: 380–383.

Bowers, W. S., and R. Nishida. 1980. Juvocimenes: potent juvenile hormone mimics from sweet basil. *Science* 209: 1030–1032.

Bowes, K. M., and V. D. Zheljazkov. 2004. Factors affecting yields and essential oil quality of *Ocimum sanctum* L. and *Oci-*

mum basilicum L. cultivars. *J. Amer. Soc. Hort. Sci.* 129: 789–794.

Bradu, B. L., et al. 1990. Development of superior alternate source of clove oil from 'Clocimum' (*Ocimum gratissimum* Linn.). In *Proceedings of the 11th International Congress of Essential Oils, Fragrances and Flavour, New Delhi, India, 12–16 November 1989 Vol. 3.* Ed. S. C. Bhattacharyya et al. London: Aspect Publ. 97–103.

Brophy, J., and M. K. Jogia. 1984. Essential oils from two varieties of Fijian *Ocimum sanctum* (Tulsi). *Fiji Agric. J.* 46: 21–26.

———. 1986. Essential oils from Fijian *Ocimum basilicum* L. *Flavour Fragrance J.* 1: 53–55.

Brophy, J., et al. 1993. The essential oil of *Ocimum tenuiflorum* L. (Lamiaceae) growing in northern Australia. *J. Essential Oil Res.* 5: 459–461.

Bucar, F., et al. 2001. Investigations of basil cultivars on estragole content. In *Biologically-active Phytochemicals in Food Analysis, Metabolism, Bioavailability and Functions.* Ed. W. Pfannhauser et al. London: Roy. Chem. Soc. 277–279.

Carmo, M. M., et al. 1990. The essential oil of *Ocimum basilicum* L. from Portugal. *J. Essential Oil Res.* 2: 263–264.

Chalchat, J. C., et al. 1996. Plantes aromatiques du Mali: etude de deux espèces d'*Ocimum*: *O. basilicum* L. et *O. canum* Sims. *Rivista Ital. EPPOS* 1996(7): 619–626.

Chang, X., et al. 2007. Flavour and aroma of fresh basil are affected by temperature. *J. Sci. Food Agric.* 87: 1381–1385.

Charles, D. J., and J. E. Simon. 1992. Essential oil constituents of *Ocimum kilimandscharicum* Guerke. *J. Essential Oil Res.* 4: 125–128.

———. 1992. A new geraniol chemotype of *Ocimum gratissimum* L. *J. Essential Oil Res.* 4: 231–234.

Charles, D. J., et al. 1990. Essential oil components of *Ocimum micranthum* Willd. *J. Agric. Food Chem.* 38: 120–122.

Chien, M.-J. 1988. A computer database of essential oils. In *Flavor and Fragrances: A World Perspective.* Ed. B. M. Lawrence et al. Amsterdam: Elsevier. 923–929.

Chiocchetti, A., et al. 1999. Identification of *Fusarium oxysporum* f.sp. *basilica* isolated from soil, basil seed, and plants by RAPD analysis. *Pl. Dis.* 83: 576–581.

Chogo, J. B., and G. Crank. 1981. Chemical composition and biological activity of the Tanzanian plant *Ocimum suave. J. Nat. Prod.* 44: 308–311.

Choudhary, R., et al. 1989. Role of phytohormones on the cultivar and essential oil of *Ocimum canum* Sims: a potential source of citral. *Indian Perfumer* 33: 224–227.

Choudhary, S. N., and D. N. Bordoloi. 1984. Yield and eugenol content of *Oci-*

mum gratissimum Linn. under different plant densities. *PAFAI J.* 6(4): 24–28.

———. 1986. Effect of sowing on the growth, yield, and oil quality of *Ocimum gratissimum* Linn. *Indian Perfumer* 30: 254–260.

Choudhary, S. N., et al. 1985. *Ocimum gratissimum* L.: a potential source of eugenol for commercial exploitation in Assam. In *5th ISHS Symposium, Medicinal and Aromatic Spice Plants, Darjeeling, India, 1985.* 47–50.

———. 1986. Studies on the growth, yield and oil quality of *Ocimum gratissimum* Linn. under different NPK and harvesting time. *PAFAI J.* 8(2): 23–27.

Codignola, A. 1984. Un basilico canforato di interesse farmaceutico: *Ocimum kilimandscharicum* Gürke. *Essenze Derivati, Agrumari* 54: 91–101.

Copetta, A., et al. 2006. Effects of three AM fungi on growth, distribution of glandular hairs, and essential oil production in *Ocimum basilicum* L. var. *genovese. Mycorrhiza* 16: 485–494.

———. 2006. Three arbuscular mycorrhizal fungi differently affect growth, distribution of glandular trichomes and essential oil composition in *Ocimum basilicum* var. *genovese. Acta Hort.* 723: 151–156.

Cortez, D. A. G., et al. 1998. Análise do óleo essencial da alfavaca *Ocimum gratissimum* L. (Labiatae). *Arq. Ciênc. Saúde Unipar.* 2(2): 125–127.

Cramer, L. H. 1981. Lamiaceae (Labiatae). In *A Revised Handbook to the Flora of Ceylon Vol. 3.* Ed. M. D. Dassanayake. Washington, D.C.: Smithsonian Institution. 108–194.

Crespo, S., et al. 1988. Estudio del mechanismo de accion hipoglicemiante de la albahaca morada (*Ocimum sanctum* L.). II. Efecto sobre la incorporacion de glucosa en adipocitos aislados de rata. *Rev. Cubana Farm.* 22: 86–91.

Darrah, H. 1980. *The Cultivated Basils.* Independence, Missouri: Buckeye Printing Co.

Davis, J. M. 1993. In-row plant spacing and yields of fresh-market basil. *J. Herbs Spices Med. Pl.* 2(1): 35–43.

———. 1994. Comparison of mulches for fresh-market basil production. *HortScience* 29: 267–268, 835.

———. 1997. *Basil.* North Carolina Hort. Inform. Leafl. 125.

DeBaggio, T. 1994. Purple basils: a journal of discovery. *Herb Companion* 6(4): 62–71.

DeBaggio, T., and S. Belsinger. 1996. *Basil: An Herb Lover's Guide.* Loveland, Colorado: Interweave Press.

De Masi, L., et al. 2006. Assessment of agronomic, chemical and genetic variability in common basil (*Ocimum basilicum* L.). *Eur. Food Res. Technol.* 223: 273–281.

Demissew, S. 1993. A description of some essential oil bearing plants in Ethiopia and their indigenous uses. *J. Essential Oil Res.* 5: 465–479.

Deschamps, C., et al. 2006. Developmental regulation of phenylpropanoid biosynthesis in leaves and glandular trichomes of basil (*Ocimum basilicum* L.). *Int. J. Pl. Sci.* 167: 447–454.

Devagiri, U., et al. 2006. Chemical profiling and evaluation of cytotoxic properties of *Ocimum* species. *HortScience* 41: 964.

Devi, P. U., and A. Ganasoundari. 1995. Radioprotective effects of leaf extract of Indian medicinal plant *Ocimum sanctum. Indian J. Exp. Biol.* 33: 205–208.

Dey, B. B., and M. A. Choudhari. 1984. Essential oil of *Ocimum sanctum* L. and its antimicrobial activity. *Indian Perfumer* 28: 82–87.

Dharmagadda, V. S. S., et al. 2005. Biocidal activity of the essential oils of *Lantana camara, Ocimum sanctum* and *Tagetes patula. J. Sci. Industr. Res.* 64: 53–56.

Diaz-Maroto, M. C., et al. 2004. Changes produced in the aroma compounds and structural integrity of basil (*Ocimum basilicum* L.) during drying. *J. Sci. Food Agric.* 84: 2070–2076.

Djibo, A. K., et al. 2004. Composition chimique de l'huile essentielle de *Ocimum americanum* Linn., syn. *O. canum* Sims du Burkina Faso. *Comptes Rendu Chimie* 7: 1033–1037.

Dro, A. S., and F. W. Hefendehl. 1974. Analyse des ätherischen Öls von *Ocimum gratissimum* L. *Arch. Pharm. Ber. Deutsch. Pharm. Ges.* 307: 168–176.

Dubey, N. K., et al. 2000. Antifungal properties of *Ocimum gratissimum* essential oil (ethyl cinnamate chemotype). *Fitoterapia* 72: 567–569.

Dzidzaria, O. M. 1979. The principal diseases of essential oil-bearing crops in Georgia and the measures that control them. In *VII International Congress of Essential Oils, October 7–11, 1977, Kyoto, Japan.* 106–107.

Edemeka, D. B. U., and A. S. Ogwu. 2000. Blood coagulation activities of the leaf extracts of *Ocimum gratissimum* plant in man. *J. Herbs Spices Med. Pl.* 7(4): 9–14.

Ekundayo, O., et al. 1989. Constituents of the volatile oil from leaves of *Ocimum canum* Sims. *Flavour Fragrance J.* 4: 17–18.

Elementi, S., et al. 2006. Biodiversity and selection of "European" basil (*Ocimum basilicum* L.) types. *Acta Hort.* 723: 99–104.

Elmer, W. H., et al. 1994. Vegetative compatibility among *Fusarium oxysporum* f. sp. *basilicum* isolates recovered from basil seed and infected plants. *Pl. Dis.* 78: 789–791.

El-Sadek, S. A. M., et al. 1991. Occurrence of leaf blight of basil caused by *Pseudomonas syringae* in Egypt. *Assiut J. Agric. Sci.* 22(2): 91–109.

Farrag, N. M. 1995. Further analysis of the volatile oil of *Ocimum basilicum* and *Ocimum rubrum* grown in Egypt. *Bull. Fac. Pharm. Cairo* 33: 39–42.

Filho, J. L. S. C., et al. 2006. Influence of the harvesting time, temperature and drying period on basil (*Ocimum basilicum* L.) essential oil. *Rev. Bras. Farmacog.* 16: 24–30.

Fleisher, A. 1981. Essential oils from two varieties of *Ocimum basilicum* L. grown in Israel. *J. Sci. Food Agric.* 32: 119–1122.

Fleisher, Z., and A. Fleisher. 1992. Volatiles of *Ocimum basilicum* traditionally grown in Israel: aromatic plants of the Holy Land and the Sinai. *J. Essential Oil Res.* 4: 97–99.

Fun, C. E., and A. B. Svendsen. 1990. Composition of the essential oils of *Ocimum basilicum* var. *canum* Sims and *O. gratissimum* L. grown on Aruba. *Flavour Fragrance J.* 5: 173–177.

Gamliel, A., et al. 1996. Fusarium wilt and crown rot of sweet basil: involvement of soilborne and airborne inoculum. *Phytopathology* 86: 56–62.

Gangrade, S. K., et al. 1989. Evaluation of antifungal properties of essential oils of *Ocimum* species. *Indian Perfumer* 33: 97–101.

Garibaldi, A., et al. 1995. *Colletotrichum gloeosporioides* Penz. nuovo parassita del basilico in Italia. *Inform. Fitopat.* 45(2): 34–35.

———. 1997. Diseases of basil and their management. *Pl. Dis.* 81: 124–132.

González, R. M., et al. 1988. Estudio del mechanismo de accion hipoglicemiante de la albahaca morada (*Ocimum sanctum* L.). III. Efecto sobre la lipolisis y la adenilciclasa en tejido adiposo de rata. *Rev. Cubana Farm.* 22: 92–100.

Grayer, R. J., et al. 1996. Infraspecific taxonomy and essential oil chemotypes in sweet basil, *Ocimum basilicum*. *Phytochemistry* 43: 1033–1039.

———. 1996. External flavones in sweet basil, *Ocimum basilicum*, and related taxa. *Phytochemistry* 43: 1041–1047.

———. 2000. The application of atmospheric pressure chemical ionization liquid chromatography-mass spectrometry in the chemotaxonomic study of flavonoids: characterisation of flavonoids from *Ocimum gratissimum* var. *gratissimum*. *Phytochem. Anal.* 11: 257–267.

———. 2001. Distribution of 8-oxygenated leaf-surface flavones in the genus *Ocimum*. *Phytochemistry* 56: 559–567.

———. 2002. Leaf flavonoid glycosides as chemosystematic characters in *Ocimum*. *Biochem. Syst. Ecol.* 30: 327–342.

Guillaumin, A. 1930. Les <<Ocimum>> à essence. *Bull. Sci. Pharmacol.* 37: 431–449.

Gulati, B. C., et al. 1977. Essential oil of *Ocimum canum* Sims (linalool type). *Indian Perfumer* 21: 21–25.

Gulati, B. C., and G. K. Sinha. 1990. Studies on some important species of *Ocimum*. In *Proceedings of the 11th International Congress of Essential Oils, Fragrances and Flavour, New Delhi, India, 12–16 November 1989 Vol. 4*. Ed. S. C. Bhattacharyya et al. London: Aspect Publ. 197–206.

Gülçin, I., et al. 2007. Determination of antioxidant and radical scavenging activity of basil (*Ocimum basilicum* L. family Lamiaceae) assayed by different methodologies. *Phytotherapy Res.* 21: 354–361.

Gupta, S. C., and S. N. Sobti. 1990. Inheritance pattern of methyl chavicol and citral in *Ocimum americanum*. *Indian Perfumer* 34: 253–259.

Hamasaki, R. T., et al. 1994. *Fresh Basil Production Guidelines for Hawai'i*. Univ. Hawai'i Res. Ext. Ser. 154.

Hempstead, M. 1984. *The Basil Book*. New York: Long Shadow Books.

Hiltunen, R., and Y. Holm, eds. 1999. *Basil: The Genus Ocimum*. Amsterdam: Harwood Acad. Publ.

Holcomb, G. E., and M. J. Reed. 1994. Stem rot of basil caused by *Sclerotinia sclerotiorum*. *Pl. Dis.* 78: 924.

Holtz, F. B., et al. 2003. Effect of essential oil of *Ocimum gratissimum* on the trypanosomatid *Herpetomonas samuelpessaoai*. *Acta Protozool.* 42: 269–276.

Hussain, R. A., et al. 1990. Sweetening agents of plant origin: phenylpropanoid constituents of seven sweet-tasting plants. *Econ. Bot.* 44: 174–182.

Hymete, A., and J. Rohloff. 2003. GC and GC-MS analysis of essential oil from leaves and flowers of *Ocimum urticifolium*. *J. Med. Aromatic Pl. Sci.* 25: 971–973.

Interaminense, L. F. L., et al. 2005. Enhanced hypotensive effects of the essential oil of *Ocimum gratissimum* leaves and its main constituents, eugenol, in DOCA-salt hypertensive conscious rats. *Pl. Med.* 71: 376–378.

Javanmardi, J., et al. 2002. Chemical characterization of basil (*Ocimum basilicum* L.) found in local accessions and used in traditional medicines in Iran. *J. Agric. Food Chem.* 50: 5878–5883.

Jirovetz, L., et al. 1998. Aroma compounds of leaf and flower essential oils of the spice plant *Ocimum gratissimum* L. from Cameroon. *Öster. Spirit. Z.* 97: 395–397.

———. 2001. Analysis, chemotype and quality control of the essential oil of a new cultivated basil (*Ocimum basilicum* L.) plant from Bulgaria. *Sci. Pharm.* 69: 85–89.

———. 2003. Chemotaxonomical analysis of the essential oil aroma compounds of four different *Ocimum* species from southern India. *Eur. Food Res. Technol.* 217: 120–124.

———. 2005. Combined investigation of the chemical composition of essential oils of *Ocimum gratissimum* and *Xylopia aethiopica* from Cameroon and their insecticidal activities against stored maize pest *Sitophilus zeamis*. *Ernährung* 29: 55–60.

Johnson, C. B., et al. 1999. Substantial UV-B-mediated induction of essential oils in sweet basil (*Ocimum basilicum* L.). *Phytochemistry* 51: 507–510.

Karawya, M. S., et al. 1974. Oils of *Ocimum basilicum* L. and *Ocimum rubrum* L. grown in Egypt. *J. Agric. Food Chem.* 322: 520–522.

Kasali, A. A., et al. 2005. Volatile oil composition of new chemotype of *Ocimum basilicum* L. from Nigeria. *Flavour Fragrance J.* 20: 45–47.

Katan, T., et al. 1996. Vegetative compatibility of *Fusarium oxysporum* from sweet basil in Israel. *Pl. Pathol.* 45: 656–661.

Kegler, H., et al. 1995. Beiträge zur Virusresistenz des Basilienkrautes (*Ocimum basilicum* L.). I. Virusresistenzprüfung. *Gartenbauwissenschaft* 60(2): 85–90.

Keinath, A. P. 1994. Pathogenicity and host range of *Fusarium oxysporum* from sweet basil and evaluation of disease control methods. *Pl. Dis.* 8: 1211–1215.

Keng, H. 1978. Labiatae. In *Flora Malesiana Vol. 8, Part 3*. Ed. C. van Steenis. Alphen aan den Rijn, Netherlands: Sijthoff & Noordhoff. 301–394.

Khanna, R. K., et al. 1988. Essential oil of *Ocimum*: a strain of *Ocimum gratissimum* L. raised on alkaline soils. *Parfümerie Kosmetik* 69: 564–568.

Khosla, M. K. 1992. Study on genetic variability in *Ocimum*, development of *O. canum* as a potent source of methyl cinnamate. *PAFAI J.* 14: 34–36.

———. 1995. Study of inter-relationship, phylogeny and evolutionary tendencies in genus *Ocimum*. *Indian J. Genet.* 55: 71–83.

Khosla, M. K., et al. 1985. Genetic studies on the inheritance pattern of different essential oil constituents of *Ocimum* species. *Indian Perfumer* 29: 151–160.

Kopsell, D. A., et al. 2005. Carotenoid and chlorophyll pigments in sweet basil grown in the field and greenhouse. *HortScience* 40: 1230–1233.

Kothari, S. K., et al. 2004. Essential oil yield and quality of methyl eugenol in *Ocimum tenuiflorum* L.f. (syn. *O. sanctum* L.) grown in south India as influenced by method of harvest. *J. Chromatogr. A* 1054: 67–72.

———. 2005. Volatile constituents in oil from different plant parts of methyl eugenol-rich *Ocimum tenuiflorum* L.f. (syn. *O. sanctum* L.) grown in South India. *J. Essential Oil Res.* 17: 656–658.

Krüger, H., et al. 2002. The chemical variability of *Ocimum* species. *J. Herbs Spices Med. Pl.* 9: 335–344.

Lacowicz, K. J., et al. 1997. Characteristics of plants and plant extracts from five varieties of basil (*Ocimum basilicum* L.) grown in Australia. *J. Agric. Food Chem.* 45: 2660–2665.

Lange, D. L., and A. C. Cameron. 1994. Postharvest shelf life of sweet basil (*Ocimum basilicum*). *HortScience* 29: 102–103.

———. 1997. Pre- and postharvest temperature conditioning of greenhouse-grown sweet basil. *HortScience* 32: 114–116.

———. 1998. Controlled-atmosphere storage of sweet basil. *HortScience* 33: 741–743.

Lawrence, B. M. 1988. A further examination of the variation of *Ocimum basilicum* L. In *Flavor and Fragrances: A World Perspective.* Ed. B. M. Lawrence et al. Amsterdam: Elsevier. 161–170.

———. 1992. Chemical components of Labiatae oils and their exploitation. In *Advances in Labiate Science.* Ed. R. M. Harley and T. Reynolds. Richmond, England: RBG Kew. 399–436.

Lawrence, B. M., et al. 1972. Essential oils and their constituents. IX. The oils of *Ocimum sanctum* and *Ocimum basilicum* from Thailand. *Flavor Industr.* 3: 47–49.

———. 1982. Variation in the genus *Ocimum.* In *VIII International Congress of Essential Oils, October 12–17, 1980, Cannes-Grasse, France.* Paper no. 34.

Lee, B. S., et al. 1993. Changes in growth and essential oil content as affected by the different ionic strength of nutrient solution in sweet basil (*Ocimum basilicum* L.). *J. Korean Soc. Hort. Sci.* 34: 330–338.

Little, E. L., et al. 1994. First report of *Pseudomonas viridiflava* causing a leaf necrosis in basil. *Pl. Dis.* 78: 831.

Loughrin, J. H., and M. J. Kasperbauer. 2001. Light reflected from colored mulches affects aroma and phenol content of sweet basil (*Ocimum basilicum* L.) leaves. *J. Agric. Food Chem.* 49: 1331–1335.

Lowman, M. S. 1935. Growing sweet basil in Virginia. *Amer. Perfumer* 30(2): 76–79.

Lowman, M. S., and J. W. Kelly. 1945. Camphor from camphor basil (*Ocimum kilimandscharicum* Güerke). *J. Amer. Pharm. Assoc., Sci. Ed.* 34: 153–162.

Lu, R.-M., and Y.-h. Li. 2006. Analysis of the chemical constituents of essential oil in *Ocimum basilicum* from Guangxi. *Guihala* 26: 456–458.

Luvisi, A., et al. 2006. Steam and exothermic reactions as alternative techniques to control soil-borne diseases in basil. *Agron. Sustain. Dev.* 26: 201–207.

Maheshwari, N., et al. 1988. Composition of *Jamrosa* and *Clocimum* oils. *Indian Perfumer* 32: 7–17.

Maia, J. G. S., et al. 1988. Uncommon Brasilian essential oils of the Labiatae and Compositae. In *Flavor and Fragrances: A World Perspective.* Ed. B. M. Lawrence et al. Amsterdam: Elsevier. 177–188.

Makri, O., and S. Kintzios. 2007. *Ocimum* sp. (basil): botany, cultivation, pharmaceutical properties, and biotechnology. *J. Herbs Spices Med. Pl.* 13: 123–150.

Marotti, M., et al. 1996. Differences in essential oil composition of basil (*Ocimum basilicum* L.) Italian cultivars related to morphological characteristics. *J. Agric. Food Chem.* 44: 3926–3929.

Martins, A. P., et al. 1999. Composition of the essential oils of *Ocimum canum, O. gratissimum* and *O. minimum. Pl. Med.* 65: 187–189.

Marzell, H. 1970. Zur Geschichte des Basilienkrautes (*Ocimum basilicum*). *Regnum Veg.* 71: 135–143.

Masiunas, J., et al. 2001. A foam mulch system provides weed control in tomatoes and basil. *HortScience* 36: 588.

Meir, S., et al. 1995. Correlation studies between chilling sensitivity of stored basil leaves and their composition of membrane lipids. In *Plant Lipid Metabolism.* Ed. J.-C. Kader and P. Masliak. Amsterdam: Kluwer Acad. Publ. 381–388.

———. 1997. Assessment of chilling injury during storage: chlorophyll fluorescence characteristics of chilling-susceptible and triazole-induced chilling tolerant basil leaves. *Portharvest Biol. Technol.* 10: 213–220.

Miele, M., et al. 2001. Methyleugenol in *Ocimum basilicum* L. Cv. Genovese Gigante. *J. Agric. Food Chem.* 49: 517–521.

Miller, J. W., and S. M. Burgess. 1987. *Leaf-spot and Blight of Basil Caused by* Pseudomonas cichorii. Florida Dept. Agric. & Consumer Serv. Pl. Pathol. Circ. No. 293.

Minuto, A., et al. 1995. Preliminary trials on biological control of fusarium wilt of basil. *Acta Hort.* 382: 173–177.

———. 1995. Evaluation of antagonistic strains of *Fusarium* spp. in the biological and integrated control of fusarium wilt of cyclamen. *Crop Prot.* 14: 221–226.

———. 1997. Effect of antagonistic *Fusarium* spp. and of different commercial biofungicide formulations on fusarium wilt of basil (*Ocimum basilicum* L.). *Crop Prot.* 16: 765–769.

Morales, M. R., and J. E. Simon. 1997. 'Sweet Dani': a new culinary and ornamental lemon basil. *HortScience* 32: 148–149.

———. 2000. 'African Beauty': a new ornamental camphor basil. *HortScience* 35: 396.

Morales, M. R., et al. 1993. New aromatic lemon basil germplasm. In *New Crops.* Ed. J. Janick and J. E. Simon. New York: John Wiley & Sons. 632–634.

———. 1993. Comparison of essential oil content and composition between field and greenhouse grown genotypes of methyl cinnamate basil (*Ocimum basilicum* L.). *J. Herbs Spices Med. Pl.* 1(4): 25–30.

Morhy, L. 1973. Metil-chavicol, cis e trans-anetol no oleo essencial de *Ocimum selloi* Benth. *Anais Acad. Brasil. Ciênc.* 45: 401–412

Morton, J. K. 1962. Cytotaxonomic studies on the West African Labiatae. *J. Linn. Soc. Bot.* 58: 231–283.

Moudachirou, M., et al. 1999. Chemical features of some essential oils of *Ocimum basilicum* L. from Benin. *J. Essential Oil Res.* 11: 779–782.

Mwangi, E. N., et al. 1995. Repellent and acaricidal properties of *Ocimum suave* against *Rhipicephalus appendiculatus* ticks. *Exp. Appl. Acarology* 19: 11–18.

Nacar, S., and S. Tansi. 2000. Chemical components of different basil (*Ocimum basilicum* L.) cultivars grown in Mediterranean regions in Turkey. *Israel J. Pl. Sci.* 48: 109–112.

Nakamura, C. V., et al. 1999. Antibacterial activity of *Ocimum gratissimum* L. essential oil. *Mem. Inst. Oswaldo Cruz* 94: 675–678.

———. 2004. In vitro activity of essential oil from *Ocimum gratissimum* L. against four *Candida* species. *Res. Microbiol.* 155: 579–586.

Nation, R. G., et al. 1992. Estimation of outcrossing in basil. *HortScience* 27: 1221–1222.

Nébié, R. H. Ch., et al. 2002. Contribution a l'etude des plantes aromatiques du Burkina Faso: composition chimique des huiles essentielles d'*Ocimum basilicum* L. *J. Soc. Ouest-Afr. Chim.* 13: 89–98.

Ngassoum, M. B., et al. 2004. Aroma compounds of essential oils of two varieties of the spice plant *Ocimum canum* Sims from northern Cameroon. *I. Food Comp. Anal.* 17: 197–204.

Nianga, M., et al. 1995. Huiles essentielles d'*Ocimum basilicum* L.: composition chimique et influence des zones climatiques sur les chimiotypes. In *Valorisation de la Biomasse Végétale par les Produits Naturels.* Ed. F.-X. Garneau and G. J. Collin. Ottawa: Cent. Recherches Dév. Intern. 197–204.

Nishida, R., et al. 1984. Synthesis of highly active juvenile hormone analogs, juvocimene I and II, from the oil of sweet basil, *Ocimum basilicum* L. *J. Chem. Ecol.* 10: 1435–1451.

Ntezurubanza, L., et al. 1984. Composition of essential oil of *Ocimum kilimandscharicum* grown in Rwanda. *Pl. Med.* 50: 385–388.

———. 1985. Composition of the essential oil of *Ocimum canum* grown in Rwanda. *Pharm. Weekbl., Sci. Ed.* 7: 273–276.

———. 1986. Composition of the essential oil of *Ocimum trichodon* grown in Rwanda. *J. Nat. Prod.* 49: 945–947.

———. 1987. Composition of the essential oil of *Ocimum gratissimum* grown in Rwanda. *Pl. Med.* 53: 421–423.

———. 1995. Composition chimique de l'huile essentielle de *Pelargonium graveolens*, *Mentha sachalinensis*, *Cymbopogon citratus* et de *Ocimum canum* cultivés au Rwanda. In *Valorisation de la Biomasse Végétale par les Produits Naturels*. Ed. F.-X. Garneau and G. J. Collin. Ottawa: Cent. Recherches Dév. Intern., Ottawa. 317–320.

Ogden, E. 1990. *Growing and Using Basil*. Pownal, Vermont: Storey.

Olonisakin, A., et al. 2005. Volatile constituents and antibacterial activity of *Ocimum suave* (wild) found in Middle Belt of Nigeria. *Bull. Pure Appl. Sci.* 24C: 93–97.

Orafidiya, L. O., et al. 2004. A study of the effect of the leaf essential oil of *Ocimum gratissimum* Linn. on cyclophosphamide-induced hair loss. *Intern. J. Aromatherapy* 14: 119–128.

Oxenham, S. K., et al. 2005. Antifungal activity of the essential oil of basil (*Ocimum basilicum*). *J. Phytopath.* 153: 174–180.

Özek, T., et al. 1995. Comparison of the essential oil of *Ocimum basilicum* L. cultivated in Turkey. *J. Essential Oil Res.* 7: 203–205.

Pandey, A. K., and A. R. Chowdhury. 2000. Composition of the essential oil of *Ocimum gratissimum* grown in Madhya Pradesh. *J. Med. Aromatic Pl. Sci.* 22: 26–28.

Pascuel-Villalobos, M. J., and M. C. Ballesta-Acosta. 2003. Chemical variation in an *Ocimum basilicum* germplasm collection and activity of the essential oils on *Callosobruchus maculates*. *Biochem. Syst. Ecol.* 31: 673–679.

Paton, A. 1992. A synopsis of *Ocimum* L. (Labiatae) in Africa. *Kew Bull.* 47: 403–435.

Paton, A., and E. Putievsky. 1996. Taxonomic problems and cytotaxonomic relationships between and within varieties of *Ocimum basilicum* and related species (Labiatae). *Kew Bull.* 51: 509–524.

Paton, A., et al. 1999. *Ocimum*: an overview of classification and relationships. In *Basil: The Genus Ocimum*. Ed. R. Hiltunen and Y. Holm. Amsterdam: Harwood Acad. Publ. 1–38.

———. 2004. Phylogeny and evolution of basils and allies (Ocimeae, Labiatae) based on three plastic DNA regions. *Mol. Phylogenetics Evol.* 31: 277–299.

Pérez-Alonso, M. J., et al. 1995. Composition of the essential oils of *Ocimum basilicum* var. *glabratum* and *Rosmarinus officinalis* from Turkey. *J. Essential Oil Res.* 7: 73–75.

Phippen, W. B., and J. E. Simon. 1998. Anthocyanins in basil (*Ocimum basilicum* L.). *J. Agric. Food Chem.* 46: 1734–1738.

Pino, J. A., et al. 1996. Composition of the essential oil from the leaves and flowers of *Ocimum gratissimum* L. grown in Cuba. *J. Essential Oil Res.* 8: 139–141.

Politeo, O., et al. 2007. Chemical composition and antioxidant capacity of free volatile aglycones from basil (*Ocimum basilicum* L.) compared with its essential oil. *Food Chem.* 101: 379–385.

Purkayastha, J., and S. C. Nath. 2006. Composition of the camphor-rich essential oil of *Ocimum basilicum* L. native to northeast India. *J. Essential Oil Res.* 18: 332–334.

Pushpangadan, P., and S. N. Sobti. 1977. Medicinal properties of *Ocimum* (Tulsi) species and some recent investigations of their efficacy. *Indian Drugs* 14: 207–208.

———. 1982. Cytogenetical studies in the genus *Ocimum*. I. Origin of *O. americanum*, cytotaxonomical and experimental proof. *Cytologia* 47: 575–583.

Putievsky, E. 1993. Seed quality and quantity in sweet basil as affected by position and maturity. *J. Herbs Spices Med. Pl.* 2(1): 15–20.

Radovich, T. J., et al. 2000. Effect of compost and mineral fertilizer applications on the sensory quality of basil (*Ocimum basilicum* L.). *HortScience* 35: 464.

Randhawa, G. S., and B. S. Gill. 1995. Transplanting dates, harvesting stage, and yields of French basil (*Ocimum basilicum* L.). *J. Herbs Spices Med. Pl.* 3(1): 45–56.

Randriamihairsoa, R., et al. 1986. Étude de la variation de la composition chimique et classification des huiles essentielles de basilic de Madagascar. *Sci. Aliments* 6: 221–231.

Rathore, H. S. 1978. Preliminary observations on the mosquito repellent efficacy of the leaf extract of *Ocimum sanctum*. *Pakistan J. Zool.* 10: 303.

Retamar, I. A., et al. 1995. Estudio del rendimiento y composición de diferentes variedades de albahaca (*Ocimum basilicum* L.) cultivadas en Sante Fe. *Essenze Derivati Agrumari* 65: 503–510.

Reuveni, R., et al. 1984. Fungistatic activity of essential oils from *Ocimum basilicum* chemotypes. *Phytopathol. Z.* 110: 20–22.

———. 1998. NUFAR: a sweet basil cultivar resistant to fusarium wilt. *HortScience* 33: 159.

Rocha, T., et al. 1992. Effect of drying conditions and of blanching on drying kinetics and color of mint (*Mentha spicata* Huds.) and basil (*Ocimum basilicum*). In *Drying '92*. Ed. A. S. Majumdar. Amsterdam: Elsevier. 1360–1369.

Rodríguez, M. D., et al. 1988. Estudio del mechanismo de accion hipoglicemiante de la albahaca morada (*Ocimum sanctum* L.). IV. Efecto sobre la resistencia a la insulina inducida por Dexametasona en modelos animales. *Rev. Cubana Farm.* 22: 101–108.

Rodriguez Roque, O. L. 1991. Composiçao do oleo esencial de *Ocimum basilicum* L. cultivars. *Bol. Fac. Farm. Coimbra* 15(1): 47–51.

Ruberto, G., et al. 1991. Volatile flavour components of *Ocimum basilicum* var. *hispidum* (Lam.) Chiov. *Flavour Fragrance J.* 6: 225–227.

Ryding, O. 1994. Notes on the sweet basil and its wild relatives (Lamiaceae). *Econ. Bot.* 48: 65–67.

Sacchetti, G., et al. 2004. Composition and functional properties of the essential oil of Amazonian basil, *Ocimum micranthum* Willd., Labiatae in comparison with commercial essential oils. *J. Agric. Food Chem.* 52: 3486–3491.

Sainsbury, M., and E. A. Sofowora. 1971. Essential oil from the leaves and inflorescences of *Ocimum gratissimum*. *Phytochemistry* 10: 3309–3310.

Sakina, M. R., et al. 1990. Preliminary psychopharmacological evaluation of *Ocimum sanctum* leaf extract. *J. Ethnopharmacol.* 28: 143–150.

Sanda, K., et al. 1998. Chemical investigation of *Ocimum* species growing in Togo. *Flavour Fragrance J.* 13: 226–232.

———. 2001. Teneur et composition chimique de l'huile essentielle de *Ocimum basilicum* L. et *Ocimum gratissimum* L. a différentes periodes de recolte après semis. *Rivista Ital. EPPOS* 31: 3–7.

Santoro, G. F., et al. 2007. *Trypanosoma cruzei*: activity of essential oils from *Achillea millefolium* L., *Syzygium aromaticum* L. and *Ocimum basilicum* L. on epimastigotes and trypomastigotes. *Exp. Parasitol.* 116: 283–290.

Sebald, O. 1987. Studien an afrikanischen und arabischen Sippen von *Becium* und *Ocimum* (Lamiaceae). Teil I. *Stuttgarter Beitr. Naturk. A* 405: 1–15.

Segall, B. 1997. A taste of the Mediterranean. *Garden* (London) 122: 264–267.

Shaath, N. A., and N. A. Azzo. 1994. Egyptian basil. In *Spices, Herbs and Edible Fungi*. Ed. G. Charalambous. Amsterdam: Elsevier. 427–438.

Sheen, L.-Y., et al. 1991. Flavour characteristic compounds found in the essential oil of *Ocimum basilicum* L. with sensory evaluation and statistical analysis. *J. Agric. Food Chem.* 39: 939–943.

Sifola, M. I., and G. Barbieri. 2006. Growth, yield and essential oil content of three cultivars of basil grown under different levels of nitrogen in the field. *Sci. Hort.* 108: 408–413.

Silva, F. da, et al. 2003. Teor e composição do oleo essencial de manjericão (*Ocimum basilicum* L.) em dois horários e duas épocas de colheita. *Rev. Bras. Pl. Med. Botucatu* 6: 33–38.

Simon, J. E. 1985. *Sweet Basil: A Production Guide.* Purdue Univ. HO-189.

Simon, J. E., and D. Reiss-Bubenheim. 1988. Field performance of American basil varieties. *Herb, Spice Med. Pl. Digest* 6(1): 1–4.

Simon, J. E., et al. 1990. Basil: a source of essential oils. In *Advances in New Crops.* Ed. J. Janick and J. E. Simon. Portland, Oregon: Timber Press. 484–489.

———. 1992. Water stress-induced alterations in essential oil content and composition of sweet basil. *J. Essential Oil Res.* 4: 71–75.

Sims, C., and S. R. Mantreddy. 2007. Response of basil accessions to different mulch treatments. *HortScience* 42: 937–938.

Singh, C., et al. 1980. Effect of X-radiation on growth and oil composition in *Ocimum canum* Sims. *Indian Perfumer* 24: 142–147.

Singh, R. S., and D. N. Bordoloi. 1987. Biological yield manipulation by nitrogen on *Ocimum* crop. *PAFAI J.* 9: 18–19.

———. 1991. Changes in the linalool and methyl cinnamate amounts in a methyl cinnamate-rich clone of *Ocimum basilicum* at different growth stages. *J. Essential Oil Res.* 3: 475–476.

———. 1992. Evaluation of a methyl cinnamate-rich clone of basil to organic matter in relation to bio-mass production and essential oil. *J. Assam Sci. Soc.* 34: 49–51.

Singh, R. S., et al. 1986. Dynamics of prime constituents in oil of *Ocimum basilicum* L. *PAFAI J.* 8: 16–17.

Singh, S., and D. K. Majundar. 1995. Analgesic activity of *Ocimum sanctum* and its possible mechanism of action. *Intern. J. Pharmacogn.* 33: 188–192.

———. 1995. Anti-inflammatory and antipyretic activities of *Ocimum sanctum* fixed oil. *Intern. J. Pharmacogn.* 33: 288–292.

Singh, S., et al. 1996. Evaluation of anti-inflammatory potential of fixed oil of *Ocimum sanctum* (holy basil) and its possible mechanism of action. *J. Ethnopharmacol.* 54: 19–26.

Skaltsa-Diamantidis, H., et al. 1990. Analyse de l'huile essentielle d'*Ocimum sanctum* L. Nouveaux résultats. *Pl. Med. Phytotherap.* 24: 79–81.

Skrubis, B., and P. Markakis. 1976. The effect of photoperiodism on the growth and the essential oil of *Ocimum basilicum* (sweet basil). *Econ. Bot.* 30: 389–393.

Sobti, S. N., and P. Pushpangadan. 1977. Studies in the genus *Ocimum*: cytogenetics, breeding and production of new strains of economic importance. In *Cultivation and Utilisation of Medicinal and Aromatic Plants.* Ed. C. K. Atal and B. M. Kapur. Jammu Tawi: Regional Res. Lab. 273–286.

Sothy, N. 1989. *Contribution a l'Étude des*

Plantes Medicinales du Kampuchea. Résumé de la Thèse de Doctorat en Pharmacie, Fac. Pharm., Hanoi.

Sousa Maia, M. B. de, et al. 2005. Evaluation of the gastric antiulcer, antimicrobial and antioxidant activities of the essential oil from *Ocimum minimum* Linn. *Acta Farm. Bonaerense* 24: 331–336.

Srivastava, A. K. 1980. *French Basil and Its Cultivation in India.* Centr. Inst. Med. Aromatic Pl. Farm. Bull. No. 16.

Standley, P. C. 1924. Trees and shrubs of Mexico. *U.S. Natl. Herb.* Vol. 23.

Succop, D. E., and S. E. Newman. 2004. Organic fertilization of fresh market sweet basil in a greenhouse. *HortTechnology* 14: 235–239.

Suh, E. J., and K. W. Park. 1999. Composition and content of essential oil in hydroponically-grown basils at different seasons. *J. Korean Soc. Hort. Sci.* 40: 331–335.

———. 1999. Effect of magnesium on the content and composition of essential oil of basil cultivars grown in hydroponics. *J. Korean Soc. Hort. Sci.* 40: 336–340.

———. 1999. Composition and content of essential oil in hydroponically-grown basils at different seasons. *J. Korean Soc. Hort. Sci.* 40: 331–335.

Suppakul, P., et al. 2003. Animicrobial properties of basil and its possible application in food packaging. *J. Agric. Food Chem.* 51: 3197–3207.

Szabó, K., et al. 1996. Morpholgical and chemical variability of basil genotypes. In *Proceedings: International Symposium Breeding Research on Medicinal and Aromatic Plants, June 30–July 4, 1996, Quedlinburg, Germany.* Ed. F. Pank. 76–79.

Tamietti, G., and A. Matta. 1989. La tracheomicosi del basilico causata da *Fusarium oxysporum* f. sp. *basilicum*, in Liguria. *Difesa Piante* 12(1–2): 213–220.

Tassou, Ch., and G. J. E. Nychas. 1995. The inhibitory effect of the essential oils from basil (*Ocimum basilicum*) and sage (*Salvia officinalis*) in broth and in model food system. In *Food Flavor, Generation, Analysis and Process Influence.* Ed. G. Charalambous. Amsterdam: Elsevier. 1925–1935.

Tateo, F. 1989. The composition of various oils of *Ocimum basilicum* L. *J. Essential Oil Res.* 1: 137–138.

Tateo, F., et al. 1989. Basil oil and tarragon oil: composition and genotoxicity evaluation. *J. Essential Oil Res.* 1: 111–118.

Tchoumbougnang, F., et al. 2006. Variability in the chemical compositions of the essential oils of five *Ocimum* species from tropical Africa area. *J. Essential Oil Res.* 18: 194–199.

Telci, I., et al. 2006. Variability in essential oil composition of Turkish basils (*Ocimum basilicum* L.). *Biochem. Syst. Ecol.* 34: 489–497.

Tétényi, P., et al. 1986. Essential oil variations of *Ocimum suave* in Rwanda. *Herba Hung.* 25: 27–42.

Thind, T. S., and R. K. Suri. 1979. In vitro antifungal efficacy of four essential oils. *Indian Perfumer* 23: 138–140.

Thoppil, J. E., et al 1998. Antibacterial and antifungal activity of four varieties of *Ocimum basilicum. Fitoterapia* 69: 191–192.

Tonzibo, Z. F., et al. 2000. Composition chimique des huiles essentielles d'*Ocimum basilicum* L. de Côte d'Ioire. *J. Soc. Ouest Afr. Chim.* 9: 19–26.

Trevisan, M. T. S., et al. 2006. Characterization of the volatile pattern and antioxidant capacity of essential oils from different species of the genus *Ocimum. J. Agric. Food Chem.* 54: 4378–4382.

Ueda-Nakamura, T., et al. 2006. Antileishmanial activity of eugenol-rich essential oil from *Ocimum gratissimum. Parasitology Intern.* 55: 99–105.

Valenzuela, H. R., and R. Hamasaki. 1995. Effect of composts and synthetic nitrogen fertilizer on growth and nematode infestation in lettuce and basil. *HortScience* 30: 864.

Vannacci, G., et al. 1999. Seed transmission of *Fusarium oxysporum* f.sp. *basilici* in sweet basil. *J. Pl. Pathol.* 81: 47–53.

Vasconcelos Silva, M. G. de, et al. 1999. Chemical variation during daytime of constituents of the essential oil of *Ocimum gratissimum* leaves. *Fitoterapia* 70: 32–34.

———. 2004. Composition of essential oils from three *Ocimum* species obtained by steam and microwave distillation and supercritical CO_2 extraction. *Arkivoc* 2004: 66–71.

Vernin, G., et al. 1984. Analysis of basil oils by GC-MS data bank. *Perfumer Flavor.* 9(5): 71–86.

Vieira, R. F., and J. E. Simon. 2000. Chemical characterization of basil (*Ocimum* spp.) found in the markets and used in traditional medicine in Brazil. *Econ. Bot.* 54: 207–216.

———. 2006. Chemical characterization of basil (*Ocimum* spp.) based on volatile oils. *Flavour Fragrance J.* 21: 214–221.

Vieira, R. F., et al. 2001. Genetic diversity of *Ocimum gratissimum* L. based on volatile oil constituents, flavonoids and RAPD markers. *Biochem. Syst. Ecol.* 29: 287–304.

———. 2003. Genetic diversity of basil (*Ocimum* spp.) based on RAPD markers. *J. Amer. Soc. Hort. Sci.* 128: 94–99.

———. 2003. Chemical profiling of *Ocimum americanum* using external flavonoids. *Phytochemistry* 63: 555–567.

Viña, A., and E. Murillo. 2003. Essential oil composition from twelve varieties of basil (*Ocimum* spp) grown in Colombia. *J. Braz. Chem. Soc.* 14: 744–749.

Vostrowsky, O., et al. 1990. Essential oil of alfavaca, *Ocimum gratissimum*, from Brazilian Amazon. *Z. Naturforsch.* 45C: 1073–1076.

Wahab, A. S. A., and L. Hornok. 1981. Effect of NPK fertilisation on yield and essential oil content of sweet basil (*Ocimum basilicum* L.). *Kert. Egypt. Közlem. Univ. Hort. Sep. Publ.* 45: 67–73.

Wan, J., et al. 1998. The effect of essential oils of basil on the growth of *Aeromonas hydrophila* and *Pseudomonas fluorescens. J. Appl. Microbiol.* 84: 152–158.

Warner, J., and A. H. Markhart. 1998. The effect of mild water deficit on basil yield and quality. *HortScience* 33: 517.

Weaver, D. K., et al. 1991. The efficacy of linalool, a major component of freshly-milled *Ocimum canum* Sims (Lamiaceae), for protection against postharvest damage by certain stored product Coleoptera. *J. Stored Prod. Res.* 27: 213–220.

———. 1994. Contact and fumigant efficacy of powdered and intact *Ocimum canum* Sims (Lamiales: Lamiaceae) against *Zabrotes subfasciatus* (Boheman) adults (Coleoptera: Bruchidae). *J. Stored Prod. Res.* 30: 243–252.

Werker, E., et al. 1993. Glandular hairs and essential oil in developing leaves of *Ocimum basilicum* L. (Lamiaceae). *Ann. Bot.* 71: 43–50.

Wick, R. L., et al. 1993. *Fusarium* wilt of basil. *Business Herbs* 11(5): 36.

Wolf, J. 1980. Basil. *Garden* (New York) 4(5): 30.

Wu, Y., et al. 1990. Study on chemical components of the essential oil from an escape: *Ocimum gratissimum* L. var. *suave* Willd. in Miyi County, Sichuan. *Tianran Chanwu Yanjiu Yu Kaifa* 2(2): 58–60.

Yamaguchi, N., and T. Akai. 1994. Species, flavour and uses of basil. *Foods Food Ingred. J. Jap.* 161: 27–35.

Yermiyahu, U., et al. 2006. Reduction of *Botrytis cinerea* sporulation in sweet basil by altering the concentrations of nitrogen and calcium in the irrigation solution. *Pl. Pathol.* 55: 544–552.

Yousif, A. N., et al. 1990. Flavour volatiles and physical properties of vacuum-microwave- and air-dried sweet basil (*Ocimum basilicum* L.). *J. Agric. Food Chem.* 47: 4777–4781.

Yu, L., et al. 1996. Essential oil of leaves and flowers of 'Sweet Dani': a lemon basil (*Ocimum basilicum*). *HortScience* 31: 689.

Yu, X., and B. Cheng. 1986. Analysis of the chemical constituents of *Ocimum gratissimum* var. *suave* oil. *Yunnan Zhiwu Yanjiu* 8: 171–174.

Yusuf, M., et al. 1998. Studies on the essential oil bearing plants of Bangladesh. Part 6. Composition of the oil of *Ocimum gra-*

tissimum L. *Flavour Fragrance J.* 13: 163–166.

Zamureenko, V., et al. 1984. Gas-liquid chromatography-mass spectrometry in the analysis of essential oils. *J. Chromatogr.* 303: 109–115.

Zheljazkov, V. D., et al. 2008. Yield and composition of *Ocimum basilicum* L. and *Ocimum sanctum* L. grown at four locations. *HortScience* 43: 737–741.

———. 2008. Content, composition, and bioactivity of the essential oils of three basil genotypes as a function of harvesting. *J. Agric. Food Chem.* 56: 380–385.

Zola, A., and J. Garnero. 1973. Contribution à l'étude de quelques essences de basilic de type européen. *Parfums Cosmétiques Savons France* 3: 15–19.

Oenanthe

Geda, A., et al. 1979. Chemical investigations of *Oenanthe stolonifera* Wall. *Indian Perfumer* 23: 63–64.

Kuebel, K. R., and A. O. Tucker. 1988. Vietnamese culinary herbs in the United States. *Econ. Bot.* 42: 413–419.

Park, J. C., and J. W. Choi. 1997. Effects of methanol extract of *Oenanthe javanica* on the hepatic alcohol-metabolizing enzyme system and its bioactive component. *Phytotherapy Res.* 11: 260–262.

Park, J. C., et al. 1996. Protective effect of *Oenanthe javanica* on the hepatic lipid peroxidation of bromobenzene-treated rats and its bioactive component. *Pl. Med.* 62: 488–490.

Sharma, S. K., and V. P. Singh. 1979. Antifungal study of the essential oil of *Oenanthe javanica* Blume DC. *Indian Drugs* 16: 289–291.

———. 1980. Biochemical study of a medicinal plant *Oenanthe javanica* Blume DC.: volatile oil and fixed oil. *Indian Drugs Pharm. Industr.* 15: 25–26.

Sharma, S. K., et al. 1980. In vitro antibacterial effect of the essential oil of *Oenanthe javanica* (Blume) DC. *Indian J. Med. Res.* 71: 149–151.

Watanabe, I., et al. 1979. Volatile components of seri (*Oenanthe stolonifera* DC.). In *VII International Congress of Essential Oils, October 7–11, 1977, Kyoto, Japan.* 442–445.

Origanum

Afsharypuor, S., et al. 1997. Volatile constituents of *Origanum vulgare* ssp. *viride* (syn. *O. heracleoticum*) from Iran. *Pl. Med.* 63: 179–180.

Akgül, A., and A. Bayrak. 1987. Constituents of essential oils from *Origanum* species growing wild in Turkey. *Pl. Med.* 53: 114.

Alma, M. H., et al. 2003. Screening chemical composition and *in vitro* antioxidant and antimicrobial activities of the essential

oils from *Origanum syriacum* L. growing in Turkey. *Biol. Pharm. Bull.* 26: 1725–1729.

Anonymous. 2007. Oregano. *Rev. Nat. Prod. (Wolters Kluwer Health).*

Arciba-Lozano, C. C., et al. 2004. El oregano: propiedades, composicióon y actividad biológica de sus components. *Arch. Latinoamer. Nutr.* 54: 100–111.

Arnold, N., et al. 1993. Comparative study of the essential oils from three species of *Origanum* growing wild in the eastern Mediterranean region. *J. Essential Oil Res.* 5: 71–77.

Azcan, N., et al. 2000. Lipids and essential oil of *Origanum onites. Chem. Nat. Compd.* 36: 132–136.

Bampidis, V. A., et al. 2005. Effect of dietary dried oregano leaves supplementation on performance and carcass characteristics of growing lambs. *Animal Food Sci. Technol.* 121: 285–295.

———. 2005. Effect of dried oregano leaves on growth performance, carcass characteristics and serum cholesterol of female early maturing turkeys. *Brit. Poultry Sci.* 46: 595–601.

———. 2006. Effect of dried oregano leaves versus neomycin in treating newborn calves with colibacillosis. *J. Vet. Med. A* 53: 154–156.

Baranska, M., et al. 2005. Chemotaxonomy of aromatic plants of the genus *Origanum* via viabrational spectroscopy. *Anal. Bioanal. Chem.* 381: 1241–1247.

Baratta, M. T., et al. 1998. Chemical composition, antimicrobial and antioxidative activity of laurel, sage, rosemary, oregano and coriander essential oils. *J. Essential Oil Res.* 10: 618–627.

Barreyo, R., et al. 2005. Fertilización nitrogenada y rendimiento en oregano (*Origanum* ×*applii*). *Cien. Inv. Agr.* 32: 39–43.

Baser, K. H. C., et al. 1991. The essential oil of *Origanum minutiflorum* O. Schwarz and P. H. Davis. *J. Essential Oil Res.* 3: 445–446.

———. 1993. Composition of the essential oil of *Origanum majorana* L. from Turkey. *J. Essential Oil Res.* 5: 577–579.

———. 1993. Composition of the essential oils of Turkish *Origanum* species with commercial importance. *J. Essential Oil Res.* 5: 619–623.

———. 1994. The essential oil of *Origanum vulgare* subsp. *hirtum* of Turkish origin. *J. Essential Oil Res.* 6: 31–36.

Bayramoglu, E. E. 2005. Natural and environmentally-friendly new bactericide for leather industry: essential oil of *Origanum minutiflorum. J. Biol. Sci.* 5: 455–457.

Bayramoglu, E. E., et al. 2006. Ecological and innovative fungicide for the leather industry: essential oil of *Origanum minutiflorum. JALCA* 101: 96–103.

Bendahou, M., et al. 2007. Influence of the processes extraction on essential oil of *Origanum glandulosum* Desf. *J. Appl. Sci.* 7: 1152–1157.

Bertelli, D., et al. 2003. Effect of microwaves on volatile compounds in origanum. *Lebensm. Wiss. Technol.* 36: 555–560.

Biondi, D., et al. 1993. Antimicrobial activity and chemical composition of essential oils from Sicilian aromatic plants. *Flavour Fragrance J.* 8: 331–337.

Bosabalidis, A. M., and S. Kokkini. 1997. Infraspecific variation of leaf anatomy in *Origanum vulgare* grown wild in Greece. *Bot. J. Linn. Soc.* 123: 353–362.

Botsoblou, N. A., et al. 2002. The effect of dietary oregano essential oil on lipid oxidation in raw and cooked chicken during refrigerated storage. *Meat Sci.* 62: 259–265.

———. 2003. The effects of dietary oregano essential oil and α-tocopheryl acetate on lipid oxidation in raw and cooked turkey during refrigerated storage. *Meat Sci.* 65: 1193–1200.

———. 2003. Antioxidant activity of dietary oregano essential oil and α-tocopheryl acetate supplementation in long-term frozen stored turkey meat. *J. Agric. Food Chem.* 51: 2930–2936.

Bouclier, N., and W. D. Koller. 1986. Influence of temperature on odor and volatile ingredients of comminuted marjoram and its CO_2 extract. In *The Shelf Life of Foods and Beverages.* Ed. G. Charalambous. Amsterdam: Elsevier. 439–450.

Brosche, T., et al. 1981. Über die Komponenten des ätherischen Öls aus *Majorana hortensis* Moench. *Z. Naturforsch.* 36c: 23–29.

Buil, P., et al. 1977. Sur quelques huiles essentielles en provenance de Turquie. *Rivista Ital. Essenze EPPOS* 59: 379–384.

Caillet, S., et al. 2005. Effect of gamma radiation and oregano essential oil on murein and ATP concentration of *Escherichia coli* O157:H7. *J. Food Prot.* 68: 2571–2579.

Calpouzos, L. 1954. Botanical aspects of oregano. *Econ. Bot.* 8: 222–233.

Calzolari, C., et al. 1966. Sulla caratterizzazione della spezie olio essenziale di origano. *Univ. Studi Trieste, Fac. Econ. Commercio Ist. Merceologia Pubbl.* 28: 1–19.

Carmo, M. M., et al. 1989. The chemical composition of Portuguese *Origanum vulgare* oils. *J. Essential Oil Res.* 1: 69–71.

Cetin, H., et al. 2006. Toxicity of essential oils extracted from *Origanum onites* L., and *Citrus aurantium* L. against the pine processionary moth, *Thaumetopoea wilkinsoni* Tams. *Folia Biol.* (Krakow) 54: 3–4.

———. 2007. A comparative evaluation of *Origanum onites* essential oil and its four major components as larvicides against the pine processionary moth, *Thaumetopoea*

wilkinsoni Tams. *Pest Managm.* 63: 830–833.

Cetin, H., and A. Yanikoglu. 2006. A study of the larvicidal activity of *Origanum* (Labiatae) species from southwest Turkey. *J. Vector Ecol.* 31: 118–122.

Ceylan, A., et al. 1996. Selective breeding with *Origanum onites* based on collections from the wild flora in West-Turkey. In *Proceedings: International Symposium Breeding Research on Medicinal and Aromatic Plants, June 30–July 4, 1996, Quedlinburg, Germany.* Ed. F. Pank. 167–170.

———. 2003. Yield performance and essential oil composition of individual plants and improved clones of *Origanum onites* L. grown in the Aegean region of Turkey. *Israel J. Pl. Sci.* 51: 285–290.

Chalchat, J. C., and B. Pasquier. 1998. Morphological and chemical studies of *Origanum* clones: *Origanum vulgare* L. ssp. *vulgare*. *J. Essential Oil Res.* 10: 119–125.

Charai, M., et al. 1996. Chemical composition and antimicrobial activities of two aromatic plants: *Origanum majorana* L. and *O. compactum* Benth. *J. Essential Oil Res.* 8: 657–664.

Chorianopoulos, N., et al. 2004. Essential oils of *Satureja, Origanum,* and *Thymus* species: chemical composition and antibacterial activities against foodborne pathogens. *J. Agric. Food Chem.* 52: 8261–8267.

Chouliara, E., et al. 2007. Combined effect of oregano essential oil and modified atmosphere packaging on shelf-life extension of fresh chicken breast meat, stored at 4°C. *Food Microbiol.* 24: 607–617.

Circella, G., et al. 1995. Influence of day length and leaf insertion on the composition of marjoram essential oil. *Flavour Fragrance J.* 10: 371–374.

Dadalioğlu, I., and G. A. Evrendilek. 2004. Chemical compositions and antibacterial effects of essential oils of Turkish oregano (*Origanum minutiflorum*), bay leaf (*Laurus nobilis*), Spanish lavender (*Lavandula stoechas* L.), and fennel (*Foeniculum vulgare*) on common foodborne pathogens. *J. Agric. Food Chem.* 52: 8255–8260.

D'Antuono, L. F., et al. 200. Variability of essential oil content and composition of *Origanum vulgare* L. populations from a North Mediterranean area (Liguria Region, northern Italy). *Ann. Bot.* 86: 471–478.

Daouk, R. K., et al. 1995. Antifungal activity of the essential oil of *Origanum syriacum* L. *J. Food Prot.* 58: 1147–1149.

D'Auria, M., et al. 2005. Composition of volatile fractions from *Thymus, Origanum, Lavandula* and *Acinos* species. *J. Essential Oil Bearing Pl.* 8: 36–51.

Deans, S. G., and K. P. Svoboda. 1990. The antimicrobial properties of marjoram

(*Origanum majorana* L.) volatile oil. *Flavour Fragrance J.* 5: 187–190.

Dellacassa, E., et al. 1994. New chemotypes of *Origanum* ×*applii* (Domin) Boros from Uruguay. *J. Essential Oil Res.* 6: 389–393.

Dimitrijević, S. I., et al. 2007. A study of the synergistic antilisterial effects of a sublethal dose of lactic acid and essential oils of *Thymus vulgaris* L., *Rosmarinus officinalis* L. and *Origanum vulgare* L. *Food Chem.* 104: 774–782.

Dorman, H. J., and S. G. Deans. 2004. Chemical composition, antimicrobial and *in vitro* antioxidant properties of *Monarda citriodora* var. *citriodora, Myristica fragrans, Origanum vulgare* ssp. *hirtum, Pelargonium* sp. and *Thymus zygis* oils. *J. Essential Oil Res.* 16: 145–150.

Dorman, H. J. D., et al. 1995. Evaluation in vitro of plant essential oils as natural antioxidants. *J. Essential Oil Res.* 7: 645–651.

Dudai, N., et al. 1988. Glandular hairs and essential oils in the leaves and flowers of *Majorana syriaca. Israel J. Bot.* 37: 11–18.

Edris, A. E., et al. 2003. Effect of organic agriculture practices on the volatile aroma components of some essential oil plants growing in Egypt II: sweet marjoram (*Origanum majorana* L.) essential oil. *Flavour Fragrance J.* 18: 345–351.

El-Gengaihi, S., et al. 2006. *In vivo* and *in vitro* comparative studies of *Origanum* species. *J. Food Agric. Environm.* 4: 127–134.

El-Ghorab, A. H., et al. 2004. Effect of extraction methods on the chemical composition and antioxidant activity of Egyptian marjoram (*Majorana hortensis* Moench). *Flavour Fragrance J.* 19: 54–61.

Esen, G., et al. 2007. Essential oil and antimicrobial activity of wild and cultivated *Origanum vulgare* L. subsp. *hirtum* (Link) Ietswaart from the Marmara region, Turkey. *Flavour Fragrance J.* 22: 371–376.

Ezzeddine, N. B. H.-B., et al. 2001. Antibacterial screening of *Origanum majorana* L. oil from India. *J. Essential Oil Res.* 13: 295–297.

Faleiro, L., et al. 2005. Antibacterial and antioxidant activities of essential oils isolated from *Thymbra capitata* L. (Cav.) and *Origanum vulgare* L. *J. Agric. Food Chem.* 53: 8162–8168.

Figuérédo, G., et al. 2006. Studies of Mediterranean oregano populations. VIII: Chemical composition of essential oils of oreganos of various origins. *Flavour Fragrance J.* 21: 134–139.

———. 2006. Studies of Mediterranean oregano populations. IX: Chemical composition of essential oils of oreganos of various origins. *J. Essential Oil Res.* 18: 411–415.

Fischer, N., et al. 1987. Original flavour compounds and the essential oil composition of marjoram (*Majorana hortensis* Moench). *Flavour Fragrance J.* 2: 55–61.

Fleisher, A., and Z. Fleisher. 1988. Identification of Biblical hyssop and origin of the traditional oregano-group herbs in the Mediterranean region. *Econ. Bot.* 42: 232–240.

———. 1991. Chemical composition of *Origanum syriacum* L. essential oil. Aromatic plants of the Holy Land and the Sinai, part 5. *J. Essential Oil Res.* 3: 121–123.

Fleisher, A., and N. Sneer. 1982. Oregano spices and *Origanum* chemotypes. *J. Sci. Food Agric.* 33: 441–446.

Fleisher, A., et al. 1982. Chemical and botanical aspects of the Biblical hyssop. In *VIII International Congress of Essential Oils, October 12–17, 1980, Cannes-Grasse, France.* Paper no. 212.

Garbagnoli, C., and S. A. Gaetán. 1994. Marchitamiento del orégano (*Origanum vulgare* L.) causado por especies del género *Fusarium* en la República Argentina. *Fitopatologia* 29: 150–155.

Gaspar, F., and G. Leeke. 2004. Essential oil from *Origanum vulgare* L. ssp. *virens* (Hoffm. et Link) Ietswaart: content, composition and distribution within the bracts. *J. Essential Oil Res.* 16: 82–84.

Gomes, A., et al. 1980. Oleos de <<mangerona>>—tipos e caracterizaçao. *Rev. Port. Quim.* 22: 21–28.

Gönüz, A., and B. Özörgücü. 1999. An investigation on the morphology, anatomy and ecology of *Origanum onites* L. *Turk. J. Bot.* 23: 19–32.

Goun, et al. 2002. Antithrombin activity of some constituents from *Origanum vulgare*. *Fitoterapia* 73: 692–694.

Ietswaart, J. H. 1980. *A Taxonomic Revision of the Genus* Origanum *(Labiatae).* The Hague: Leiden Univ. Press.

Jerković, I., et al. 2001. The impact of both the season of collection and drying on the volatile constituents of *Origanum vulgare* L. ssp. *hirtum* grown wild in Croatia. *Intern. J. Food Sci. Technol.* 36: 649–654.

Johnson, C. B., et al. 2004. Seasonal, populational and ontogenetic variation in the volatile oil content and composition of individuals of *Origanum vulgare* subsp. *hirtum*, assessed by GC headspace analysis and by SPME sampling of individual oil glands. *Phytochem. Anal.* 15: 286–292.

Kanazawa, K., et al. 1995. Specific desmutagens (antimutagens) in oregano against a dietary carcinogen, Trp-P-2, are galangin and quercetin. *J. Agric. Food Chem.* 43: 404–409.

Karpouhtsis, I., et al. 1998. Insecticidal and genotoxic activities of oregano essential oils. *J. Agric. Food Chem.* 46: 1111–1115.

Khaosaad, T., et al. 2006. Arbuscular mycorrhiza alter the concentration of essential oils in oregano (*Origanum* sp., Lamiaceae). *Mycorrhiza* 16: 443–446.

Kintzios, S. E., ed. 2002. *Oregano: The Gen-era* Origanum *and* Lippia. New York: Taylor & Francis.

Kofidis, G., et al. 2003. Contemporary seasonal and altitudinal variations of leaf structural features in oregano (*Origanum vulgare* L.). *Ann. Bot.* 92: 635–645.

Kokkini, S., and D. Vokou. 1989. Carvacrol-rich plants in Greece. *Flavour Fragrance J.* 4: 1–7.

Kokkini, S., et al. 1991. Morphological and chemical variation of *Origanum vulgare* L. in Greece. *Bot. Chron.* 10: 337–346.

———. 1994. Pattern of geographic variation of *Origanum vulgare* trichomes and essential oil content in Greece. *Biochem. Syst. Ecol.* 22: 517–528.

———. 1997. Autumn essential oils of Greek oregano. *Phytochemistry* 44: 883–886.

———. 2004. Essential oil composition of Greek (*Origanum vulgare* ssp. *hirtum*) and Turkish (*O. onites*) oregano: a tool for their distinction. *J. Essential Oil Res.* 16: 334–338.

Kulišić, T., et al. 2007. The effects of essential oils and aqueous tea infusions of oregano (*Origanum vulgare* L. spp. *hirtum*), thyme (*Thymus vulgaris* L.) and wild thyme (*Thymus serpyllum* L.) on the copper-induced oxidation of human low-density lilpoproteins. *Intern. J. Food Sci. Nutr.* 58: 87–93.

Lagouri, V., and D. Boskou. 1996. Nutrient antioxidants in oregano. *Intern. J. Food Sci. Nutr.* 47: 493–497.

Lagouri, V., et al. 1993. Composition and antioxidant activity of essential oils from oregano plants grown wild in Greece. *Z. Lebensm. Unters. Forsch.* 197: 20–23.

Lambert, R. J. W., et al. 2001. A study of the minimum inhibitory concentration and mode of action of oregano essential oil, thymol and carvacrol. *J. Appl. Microbiol.* 91: 453–462.

Lawrence, B. M. 1981. *Essential Oils 1979–1980.* Wheaton, Illinois: Allured.

———. 1984. The botanical and chemical aspects of oregano. *Perfumer Flavor.* 9(5): 41–51.

Lin, Q., et al. 1997. Effects of volatile oil of *Origanum vulgare* L. on specific immunological functions in mice. *Chin. J. Appl. Environm. Biol.* 3: 389–391.

Lindberg, H., et al. 1996. Screening of antioxidative activity of spices: a comparison between assays based on ESR spin trapping and electrochemical measurement of oxygen consumption. *Food Chem.* 57: 331–337.

Maarse, H., and F. H. L. van Os. 1973. Volatile oil of *Origanum vulgare* L. ssp. *vulgare*. I. Qualitative composition of the oil. *Flavor Industr.* 4: 477–481.

McGimpsey, J. A. 1993. *Oregano:* Origanum vulgare. New Zealand Inst. Crop Food Res. Broadsheet No. 19.

Melegari, M., et al. 1995. Chemical characterization of essential oils of some *Origanum vulgare* L. sub-species of various origin. *Rivista Ital. EPPOS* 1995(16): 21–28.

Mockute, D., et al. 2001. The essential oil of *Origanum vulgare* L. ssp. *vulgare* growing wild in Vilnius district (Lithuania). *Phytochemistry* 57: 65–69.

———. 2003. The essential oil of the aerial parts of cultivated *Origanum vulgare* L. in Lithuania. *J. Essential Oil Bearing Pl.* 6: 109–115.

———. 2004. Volatile constituents of cultivated *Origanum vulgare* L. inflorescences and leaves. *Chemia* 15: 33–37.

Müller-Riebau, F., et al. 1995. Chemical composition and fungitoxic properties to phytopathogenic fungi of essential oils of selected aromatic plants growing wild in Turkey. *J. Agric. Food Chem.* 43: 2262–2266.

———. 1997. Seasonal variations in the chemical compositions of essential oils of selected aromatic plants growing wild in Turkey. *J. Agric. Food Chem.* 45: 4821–4825.

Nakatani, N., and H. Kikuzaki. 1987. A new antioxidative glucoside isolated from oregano (*Origanum vulgare* L.). *Agric. Biol. Chem.* 51: 2727–2732.

Novák, I., et al. 2001. Sensory analysis as a supporting method for marjoram breeding. *Intern. J. Hort. Sci.* 7: 73–77.

———. 2003. Study of essential oil components in different *Origanum* species by GC and sensory analysis. *Acta Alimentaria* 32: 141–150.

Novak, J., et al. 2000. Ratios of *cis*- and *trans*-sabinene hydrate in *Origanum majorana* L. and *Origanum microphyllum* (Bentham) Vogel. *Biochem. Syst. Ecol.* 28: 697–704.

———. 2002. Inheritance of calyx shape in the genus *Origanum* (Lamiaceae). *Pl. Breeding* 121: 462–463.

———. 2002. Distribution of the *cis*-sabinene hydrate acetate chemotype in accessions of marjoram (*Origanum majorana* L.). *Euphytica* 127: 69–74.

———. 2004. Determination of growing location of marjoram (*Origanum majorana* L.) samples by comparison of essential oil profiles. *Flavour Fragrance J.* 19: 263–267.

———. 2008. The essential oil composition of wild growing sweet marjoram (*Origanum majorana* L., Lamiaceae) from Cyprus: three chemotypes. *J. Essential Oil Res.* 20: 339–341.

Nurmi, A., et al. 2006. Consumption of juice fortified with oregano extract markedly increases excretion of phenolic acids but lacks short- and long-term effects on lipid peroxidation in healthy nonsmoking men. *J. Agric. Food Chem.* 54: 5790–5796.

———. 2006. Ingestion of oregano extract increases excretion of urinary phenolic metabolites in humans. *J. Agric. Food Chem.* 54: 6916–6923.

Nykänen, I. 1986. High resolution gas chromatographic-mass spectrometric determination of the flavour composition of marjoram (*Origanum majorana* L.) cultivated in Finland. *Z. Lebensm. Unters. Forsch.* 183: 172–176.

———. 1987. The effect of drying on the composition of the essential oil of some Labiatae herbs cultivated in Finland. In *Flavor Science and Technology*. Ed. M. Martens et al. New York: John Wiley & Sons. 83–88.

Oberdieck, R. 1981. Ein Beitrag zur Kenntnis und Analytik von Majoran (*Majorana hortensis* Moench.). *Deutsch. Lebensm.-Tundsch.* 77: 63–74.

Omer, E. A. 1999. Response of wild Egyptian oregano to nitrogen fertilization in a sandy soil. *J. Pl. Nutr.* 22: 103–114.

Ösgüven, M., et al. 1996. Yield and quality aspects of *Origanum* wild species collected in the Çukorova region of Turkey. In *Proceedings: International Symposium Breeding Research on Medicinal and Aromatic Plants, June 30–July 4, 1996, Quedlinburg, Germany*. Ed. F. Pank. 1–24.

Oussalah, M., et al. 2004. Antimicrobial and antioxidant effects of milk protein-based film containing essential oils for the preservation of whole beef muscle. *J. Agric. Food Chem.* 52: 5598–5605.

Paludosi, S., ed. 1997. *Oregano*. Rome: Intern. Pl. Gen. Res. Inst.

Pande, C., and C. S. Mathela. 2000. Essential oil composition of *Origanum vulgare* L. ssp. *vulgare* from the Kumaon Himalayas. *J. Essential Oil Res.* 12: 441–442.

Pank, F., et al. 1999. Eignung verschiedener Merkmale des Majorans (*Origanum majorana* L.) zur Differenzierung von Populationen und für die indirekte Selektion. *Z. Arzn. Gew. Pfl.* 4: 8–10.

Paster, N., et al. 1990. Inhibitory effect of oregano and thyme essential oils on moulds and food-borne bacteria. *Lett. Appl. Microbiol.* 11: 33–37.

———. 1995. Antifungal activity of oregano and thyme essential oils applied as fumigants against fungi attacking stored grain. *J. Food Prot.* 58: 81–85.

Pino, J. A., et al. 1997. Essential oil of marjoram (*Origanum majorana* L.) grown in Cuba. *J. Essential Oil Res.* 9: 479–480.

Prieto, J. M., et al. 2007. *In vitro* activity of the essential oils of *Origanum vulgare*, *Satureja montana* and their main constituents in peroxynitrile-induced oxidative processes. *Food Chem.* 104: 889–895.

Puertas-Mejia, M., et al. 2002. *In vitro* radical scavenging activity of essential oils from Colombian plants and fractions from oregano (*Origanum vulgare* L.) essential oil. *Flavour Fragrance J.* 17: 380–384.

Putievsky, E., and D. Basker. 1977. Experimental cultivation of marjoram, oregano and basil. *J. Hort. Sci.* 52: 181–188.

Radušienė, J., et al. 2005. Chemical composition of essential oil and antimicrobial activity of *Origanum vulgare*. *Biologija* 2005(4): 53–58.

———. 2006. Variability and antimicrobial activity of *Origanum vulgare* subsp. *vulgare* essential oils. *Acta Hort.* 723: 393–398.

Raghavan, B., et al. 1997. Effect of drying methods on the flavour quality of marjoram (*Origanum majorana* L.). *Nahrung* 41: 159–161.

Ravid, U., and E. Putievsky. 1983. Constituents of essential oils from *Majorana syriaca*, *Coridothymus capitatus* and *Satureja thymbra*. *Pl. Med.* 49: 248–249.

———. 1985. Essential oils of Israeli wild species of Labiatae. *Essential Oils and Aromatic Plants*. Ed. A. Baerheim Svendsen and J. J. Scheffer. Dordrecht: Martinus Nijhoff. 155–161.

———. 1986. Carvacrol and thymol derivatives of East Mediterranean wild Labiatae herbs. In *Progress in Essential Oil Research*. Ed. E.-J. Brunke. Berlin: Walter de Gruyter & Co. 163–167.

Rhayour, K., et al. 2003. The mechanism of bactericidal action of oregano and clove essential oils and their phenolic major components of *Escherichia coli* and *Bacillus subtilis*. *J. Essential Oil Res.* 15: 286–292.

Rhyu, H. Y. 1979. Gas chromatographic characterization of oregano and other selected spices of the Labiatae family. *J. Food Sci.* 44: 1373–1378.

Ruberto, G., et al. 1993. Volatile flavour components of Sicilian *Origanum onites* L. *Flavour Fragrance J.* 8: 197–200.

———. 2002. Chemical composition and antioxidative activity of essential oils from Algerian *Origanum glandulosum* Desf. *Flavour Fragrance J.* 17: 251–254.

Şahin, F., et al. 2004. Biological activities of the essential oils and methanol extract of *Origanum vulgare* ssp. *vulgare* in the Eastern Anatolia region of Turkey. *Food Control* 15: 549–557.

Salgueiro, L. R., et al. 2003. Chemical composition and antifungal activity of the essential oil of *Origanum virens* on *Candida* species. *Pl. Med.* 69: 871–874.

Sarer, E., et al. 1985. Composition of the essential oil of *Origanum majorana* grown in different localities in Turkey. In *Essential Oils and Aromatic Plants*. Ed. A. Baerheim Svendsen and J. J. about Scheffer. Dordrecht: Martinus Nijhoff. 209–212.

Sari, M., et al. 2006. Chemical composition, antimicrobial and antioxidant activities of the essential oil of several populations of Algerian *Origanum glandulosum* Desf. *Flavour Fragrance J.* 21: 890–898.

Scheffer, J. J. C., et al. 1986. The essential oils of three *Origanum* species grown in Turkey. In *Progress in Essential Oil Research*. Ed. E.-J. Brunke. Berlin: Walter de Gruyter. 151–156.

Sezik, E., et al. 1993. Essential oil composition of four *Origanum vulgare* subspecies of Anatolian origin. *J. Essential Oil Res.* 5: 425–431.

Shimoni, M., et al. 1993. Antifungal activity of volatile fractions of essential oils from four aromatic wild plants in Israel. *J. Chem. Ecol.* 19: 1129–1133.

Singh, M., et al. 1996. Processing of marjoram (*Majorana hortensis* Moench.) and rosemary (*Rosmarinus officinalis* L.). Effect of blanching methods on quality. *Nahrung* 40: 264–266.

Šipailienė, A., et al. 2006. Antimicrobial activity of commercial samples of thyme and marjoram oils. *J. Essential Oil Res.* 18: 698–703.

Sivropoulou, A., et al. 1996. Antimicrobial and cytotoxic activities of *Origanum* essential oils. *J. Agric. Food Chem.* 44: 1202–1205.

Skandamis, P., and G.-J. E. E. Nychas. 2000. Development and evaluation of a model predicting the survival of *Escherichia coli* O157:H7 NCTC 12900 in homemade eggplant salad at various temperatures, pHs, and oregano essential oil concentrations. *Appl. Environm. Microbiol.* 66: 1646–1653.

———. 2001. Effect of oregano essential oil on microbiological and physico-chemical attributes of minced meat stored in air and modified atmospheres. *J. Appl. Microbiol.* 91: 1011–1022.

———. 2002. Preservation of fresh meat with active and modified atmosphere packaging conditions. *Intern. J. Food Microbiol.* 79: 35–45.

Skandamis, P., et al. 2000. Ecophysiological attributes of *Salmonella typhimurium* in liquid culture and within a gelatin gel with or without the addition of oregano essential oil. *World J. Microbiol. Biotechnol.* 16: 31–35.

———. 2001. Inhibition of oregano essential oil and EDTA on *Escherichia coli* O157: H7. *Ital. J. Food Sci.* 13: 65–75.

———. 2002. The effect of oregano essential oil on survival/death of *Salmonella typhimurium* in meat stored at 5°C under aerobic, VP/MAP conditions. *Food Microbiol.* 19: 97–103.

———. 2002. A vitalistic approach for nonthermal inactivation of pathogens in traditional Greek salads. *Food Microbiol.* 19: 405–421.

Skoula, M., et al. 1999. A chemosystematic investigation on the mono- and sesquiterpenoids in the genus *Origanum* (Labiatae). *Phytochemistry* 52: 649–657.

Skrubis, B. G. 1972. Seven wild aromatic plants growing in Greece and their essential oils. *Flavor Industr.* 3: 566–568, 571.

Su, L., et al. 2007. Total phenolic contents, chelating capacities, and radical-scavenging properties of black peppercorn, nutmeg, rosehip, cinnamon and oregano leaf. *Food Chem.* 100: 990–997.

Tabanca, N., et al. 2004. Comparison of the essential oils of *Origanum majorana* L. and *Origanum ×majoricum* Cambess. *J. Essential Oil Res.* 16: 248–252.

Takácsová, M., et al. 1995. Study of the antioxidative effects of thyme, sage, juniper and oregano. *Nahrung* 39: 241–243.

Tarján, G., et al. 2002. Data for the gasliquid chromatographic analysis of essential oils: determination of the composition of the essential oil of marjoram. *Chromatographia* 56: S155–S163.

Taskinen, J. 1974. Composition of the essential oil of sweet marjoram obtained by distillation with steam and by extraction and distillation with alcohol-water mixture. *Acta Chem. Scand.* 28B: 1121–1128.

Tepe, B., et al. 2004. The *in vitro* antioxidant and antimicrobial activities of the essential oil and various extracts of *Origanum syriacum* L. var. *bevanii. J. Sci. Food Agric.* 84: 1389–1396.

Tsigarida, E., et al. 2000. Behaviour of *Listeria monocytogenes* and autochthonous flora on meat stored under aerobic, vacuum and modified atmosphere packaging conditions with or without the presence of oregano essential oil at 5°C. *J. Appl. Microbiol.* 89: 901–909.

Tucker, A. O. 1981. Which is the true oregano? *Horticulture* 59(7): 57–59.

Tucker, A. O., and M. J. Maciarello. 1994. Oregano: botany, chemistry, and cultivation. In *Spices, Herbs and Edible Fungi.* Ed. G. Charalambous. Amsterdam: Elsevier. 439–456.

Tucker, A. O., and E. D. Rollins. 1989. The species, hybrids, and cultivars of *Origanum* (Lamiaceae) cultivated in the United States. *Baileya* 23: 14–27.

Tümen, G., and K. H. Baser. 1993. The essential oil of *Origanum syriacum* L. var. *bevanii* (Holmes) Ietswaart. *J. Essential Oil Res.* 5: 315–316.

Vági, E., et al. 2005. Essential oil composition and antimicrobial activity of *Origanum majorana* L. extracts obtained with ethyl alcohol and supercritical carbon dioxide. *Food Res. Intern.* 38: 51–57.

van der Mheen, H. 2006. Selection and production of oregano rich in essential oil and carvacrol. *Acta Hort.* 709: 95–99.

Varkar-Üniü, G., et al. 2007. Chemical composition and *in vitro* antimicrobial activity of the essential oil of *Origanum minutiflorum* O. Schwarz and P. H. Davis. *J. Sci. Food Agric.* 87: 255–259.

Vekiari, S. A., et al. 1993. Oregano flavonoids as lipid antioxidants. *J. Amer. Oil Chem. Soc.* 70: 483–487.

Vender, C., ed. 2000. *Maggiorana.* Trento: ISAFA Commun. Ricerca.

Veres, K., et al. 2007. Chemical composition and antimicrobial activities of essential oils of four lines of *Origanum vulgare* subsp. *hirtum* (Link) Ietswaart grown in Hungary. *Nat. Prod. Commun.* 2: 1155–1158.

Vernon, F., et al. 1978. Huile essentielle de marjolaine (*Majorana hortensis* Moench) en provenance d'Egypte. *Parfums, Cosmétiques, Arômes* 21: 85–88.

Vokou, D., et al. 1988. *Origanum onites* (Lamiaceae) in Greece: distribution, volatile oil yield, and composition. *Econ. Bot.* 42: 407–412.

Werker, E., et al. 1985. The essential oils and glandular hairs in different chemotypes of *Origanum vulgare* L. *Ann. Bot.* (London) 55: 793–801.

Xu, H., et al. 2006. Oregano, thyme and clove-derived flavour and skin sensitizers activate specific TRP channels. *Nature Neurosci.* 9: 628–635.

Yaldiz, G., et al. 2005. Seasonal and diurnal variability of essential oil and its components in *Origanum onites* L. grown in the ecological conditions of Çukurova. *Grasas Aceitas* 56: 254–258.

Yildrin, I., et al. 2003. The use of oregano (*Origanum vulgare* L.) essential oil as alternative hatching egg disinfectant versus formaldehyde fumigation in quails (*Copturnix coturnix japonica*) eggs. *Rev. Méd. Vét.* 154: 367–370.

Zohary, M. 1982. *Plants of the Bible.* Cambridge Univ. Press.

Papaver

Anonymous. 2003. Poppy. *Rev. Nat. Prod.* (*Wolters Kluwer Health*).

Baldwin, B. J. 1977. Chemical weed control in oil-seed poppy (*Papaver somniferum*). *Austral. J. Exp. Agric. Animal Husbandry* 17: 837–841.

Bare, C. E., et al. 1978. Temperature and light effects on germination of *Papaver bracteatum* Lindl., *P. orientale* L., and *P. somniferum* L. *Pl. Med.* 34: 135–143.

Bernáth, J., 1980. Alteration in compositional character of poppy chemotaxa affected by different light and temperature conditions. *Acta Hort.* 96: 91–99.

———. 1981. The effect of environmental factors on growth, development and alkaloid production of poppy (*Papaver somniferum* L.). II. Interaction of light and temperature. *Biochem. Physiol. Pflanzen* 176: 599–605.

———. 1982. Production characteristics of *Papaver somniferum* L. cultivars of different origin and vegetation cycles. *Bull. Narcotics* 34: 113–127.

———, ed. 1998. *Poppy: the Genus* Papaver. Amsterdam: Harwood Acad. Publ.

Bernáth, J., and P. Tétényi. 1979. The effect of environmental factors on growth, development and alkaloid production of poppy (*Papaver somniferum* L.). I. Responses to day-length and light intensity. *Biochem. Physiol. Pflanzen* 174: 408–478.

Choudhary, D. K., et al. 1977. Cultivation and utilisation of opium poppy in India: a review. *Indian Drugs* 15(2): 1–8.

Cullen, J. 1968. The genus *Papaver* in cultivation. 1. The wild species. *Baileya* 16: 73–91.

Duke, J. A. 1973. Utilization of *Papaver. Econ. Bot.* 27: 390–400.

Finetto, G. 2008. Opium poppy: societal blessing and cure. *Chron. Hort.* 48(3): 18–23.

Griffith, W. 1993. *Opium Poppy Garden: The Way of a Chinese Grower.* Berkeley, California: Ronin Publ.

Grove, M. D., et al. 1976. Morphine and codeine in poppy seed. *J. Agric. Food Chem.* 24: 896–897.

Hatakeyama, Y., et al. 1974. Studies on cultivation of *Papaver somniferum* L. and extraction of the alkaloids. I. Effect of planting density on the growth and yield. *Eisei Shikenjo Hokoku* 92: 32–39.

Husain, A., and J. R. Sharma. 1983. The opium poppy. *Centr. Inst. Med. Aromatic Pl. Med. Aromatic Pl. Ser.* I: 1–167.

Kapoor, L. D. 1995. *Opium Poppy: Botany, Chemistry, and Pharmacology.* New York: Haworth Press.

Laughlin, J. C. 1978. The effect of time of harvest on the yield components of poppies (*Papaver somniferum* L.). *J. Agric. Sci.* 95: 667–676.

Mowat, A. B., and S. M. Walters. 1964. *Papaver.* In *Flora Europaea Vol. 1.* Ed. T. G. Tutin et al. Cambridge Univ. Press. 247–251.

Nyman, U., and O. Hall. 1974. Breeding oil poppy (*Papaver somniferum*) for low content of morphine. *Hereditas* 78: 49–54.

———. 1978. Selection for high thebaine/low morphine content in *Papaver somniferum* L. *Hereditas* 89: 43–50.

Stermitz, F. R. 1968. Alkaloid chemistry and the systematics of *Papaver* and *Argemone. Rec. Adv. Phytochem.* 1: 161–183.

Tin-Wa, M., et al. 1975. Germination and morphine content of *Papaver somniferum* plants produced from commercially available seed. *J. Pharm. Sci.* 64: 2024–2025.

Ulubelen, A., et al. 1977. Analysis of poppy seed oil by gas-liquid chromatography. *Pl. Med.* 32: 76–80.

Wold, J. K. 1978. Bound morphine and codeine in the capsule of *Papaver somniferum. Phytochemistry* 17: 832–833.

Pelargonium

Abbott, P. 1994. *A Guide to Scented Geraniaceae*. West Sussex, England: Hill Publicity Services.

Albers, F., and J. J. A. van der Walt. 1984. Untersuchungen zur Karyologie und Microsporogenese von *Pelargonium* sect. *Pelargonium* (Geraniaceae). *Pl. Syst. Evol.* 147: 177–188.

Babu, K. G. C., and V. K. Kaul. 2005. Variation in essential oil composition of rosescented geranium (*Pelargonium* sp.) distilled by different distillation techniques. *Flavour Fragrance J.* 20: 222–231.

Bakker, F. T., et al. 2004. Phylogeny of *Pelargonium* (Geraniaceae) based on DNA sequences from three genomes. *Taxon* 53: 17–28.

Becker, J., and F. Brawner. 1996. *Scented Geraniums: Knowing, Growing, and Enjoying Scented Pelargoniums*. Loveland, Colorado: Interweave Press.

Brawner, F. 2003. *Geraniums: The Complete Encyclopedia*. Atglen, Pennsylvania: Schiffer Publ. Co.

Charlwood, B. V., et al. 1988. Pelargoniums: flavour, fragrances and the new technology. *Plants Today* 1(2): 42–46.

Chatterjee, A., and A. K. Sharma. 1970. Chromosome studies in Geraniales. *Nucleus* 13: 179–200.

Cilek, J. E., and E. T. Schreiber. 1994. Failure of the "mosquito plant," *Pelargonium* ×*citrosum* 'Van Leenii', to repel adult *Aedes albopictus* and *Culex quinquefasciatus* in Florida. *J. Amer. Mosquito Control Assoc.* 10: 473–476.

Conagin, C. H. T. M., and D. D'Andréa Pinto. 1970. Caracteres morfologicos e número de cromosomos em *Pelargonium*. *Bragantia* 29: 249–262.

Cu, J.-Q. 1988. Yunnan: the kingdom of essential oil plants. In *Flavor and Fragrances: A World Perspective*. Ed. B. M. Lawrence et al. Amsterdam: Elsevier. 231–241.

Daker, M. G. 1969. Chromosome numbers of *Pelargonium* species and cultivars. *J. Roy. Hort. Soc.* 94: 346–353.

Demarne, F. 1985. Sélection des pelargonium à parfum. *Parfums, Cosmétiques, Arômes* 62: 77–79.

———. 1989. *L'amelioration Varietale du "Geranium Rosat"*(Pelargonium *sp.): Contribution Systematique, Caryologique, et Biochimique*. D. Sci. thesis, Univ. Paris.

———. 1990. Essential oils in *Pelargonium*, sect. *Pelargonium*. In *Proceedings of the International Geraniaceae Symposium held at the University of Stellenbosch, Republic of South Africa, 24–26 September, 1990*. Ed. P. Vorster. 245–308.

———. 1990. *Pelargonium tomentosum*: a potential source of peppermint-scented essential oil. *S.-Afr. Tydskr. Pl. Grond* 7: 36–39.

———. 1993. Composition of the essential oil of *Pelargonium citronellum* (Geraniaceae). *J. Essential Oil Res.* 5: 233–238.

Demarne, F., and J. J. A. Van der Walt. 1989. Origin of the rose-scented *Pelargonium* cultivar grown on Réunion Island. *S. African Tydskr. Plank.* 55: 184–191.

Demarne, F., et al. 1984. Intérêt de la chromatographie en phase gazeuse des extraits hexaniques pour la sélection des *Pelargonium* à parfum. *Agron. Trop.* 39: 346–349.

———. 1986. L'Huile essentielle de *Pelargonium tomentosum* Jacquin (Geraniaceae). *Parfums, Cosmétiques, Arômes* 70: 57–60.

———. 1993. A study of the variation in the essential oil and morphology of *Pelargonium capitatum* (L.) L'Hérit. (Geraniaceae.) Part 1. The composition of the oil. *J. Essential Oil Res.* 5: 493–499.

———. 1995. La variabilite des populations naturelles de *Pelargonium capitatum* (L.) L'Herit. (Geraniaceae). *Riv. Ital. EPPOS* Spec. Num.: 597–607.

Doraswamy, K., and M. Sundarm. 1982. Geranium cultivation in South India. In *Cultivation of Aromatic Plants*. Ed. C. K. Atal and B. M. Kapur. Jammu Tawi, India: Regional Res. Lab. 573–577.

Dorman, H. J. D., and S. G. Deans. 2004. Chemical composition, antimicrobial and *in vitro* antioxidant properties of *Monarda citriodora* var. *citriodora*, *Myristica fragrans*, *Origanum vulgare* subsp. *hitum*, *Pelargonium* sp. and *Thymus zygis* oils. *J. Essential Oil Res.* 16: 145–150.

Dzidzaria, O. M. 1979. The principal diseases of essential oil-bearing crops in Georgia and the measures of controlling them. In *VII International Congress of Essential Oils, October 7–11, 1977, Kyoto, Japan.* 106–107.

Fleisher, A., and Z. Fleisher. 1985. Yield and quality of essential oil from *Pelargonium graveolens* cultivated in Israel. *J. Sci. Food Agric.* 36: 1047–1050.

Fritz, J. 1976. Effet de la fertilisation azotée sur la production du geranium rosat. *Agron. Trop.* (Paris) 31: 369–374.

Gauger, W. 1937. Ergebnisse einer zytologischen Untersuchung der Familie der Geraniaceae. I. *Planta* 26: 529–531.

Gauvin, A., et al. 2004. Comparative investigations of the essential oils of two scented geranium (*Pelargonium* spp.) cultivars grown on Reunion Island. *Flavour Fragrance J.* 19: 455–460.

Gomes, P. B., et al. 2004. Characterization of Portuguese-grown geranium oil (*Pelargonium* sp.). *J. Essential Oil Res.* 16: 490–495.

Guerere, M., et al. 1985. Etude d'huiles essentielles de géranium Bourbon obtenues de trois façons différentes. *Ann. Falsif. Expert. Chim. Toxicol.* 78: 131–136.

Hefendehl, F. W. 1972. Beiträge zur Biogen-

ese ätherischen Öle. Zusammensetzung des ätherischen Öls von *Pelargonium tomentosum*. *Pl. Med.* 22: 378–385.

Hill, M. 1978. But we did too! *Herbarist* 44: 64–67.

James, C. M., et al. 2001. A rapid PCR based method to establish the potential for paternal inheritance of chloroplasts in *Pelargonium*. *Pl. Mol. Biol. Rep.* 19: 163–167.

Jeyabalan, D., et al. 2003. Studies on effects of *Pelargonium citrosa* leaf extracts on malarial vector, *Anopheles stephansi* Liston. *Bioresource Technol.* 89: 185–189.

Kang, J. 1989. *Analysis of Essential Oils from Geranium Plants by Gas Chromatography/Fourier Transform Infrared Spectroscopy*. Ph.D. thesis, Univ. Connecticut, Storrs.

Karawya, M. S., et al. 1979. Study of essential oil of *Pelargonium fragrans* L. growing in Egypt. *Egypt. J. Pharm. Sci.* 20: 139–145.

Kaul, P. N., and B. R. R. Rao. 1999. Quality variations in the essential oils of young and old leaves of three varieties of rosescented geranium (*Pelargonium* species). *Fafai J.* 1: 35–37.

Kothari, S. K., et al. 2002. Weed control in rose-scented geranium (*Pelargonium* spp.). *Pest Managm. Sci.* 58: 1254–1258.

Krauss, H. K. 1955. *Geraniums for Home and Garden*. New York: Macmillan Co.

Lawrence, B. M., et al. 1975. Essential oils and their constituents. XIII. The chemical composition of some *Pelargonium* species. *Int. Flavor Food Addit.* 6: 42–44.

Lis-Balchin, M. 1991. Essential oil profiles and their possible use in hybridization of some common scented geraniums. *J. Essential Oil Res.* 3: 99–105.

———. 1993. The essential oils of *Pelargonium grossularioides* and *Erodium cicutarium* (Geraniaceae). *J. Essential Oil Res.* 5: 317–318.

———. 1996. Geranium oil. *Intern. J. Aromather.* 7(3): 18–19.

———, ed. 2002. Geranium *and* Pelargonium: *The Genera* Geranium *and* Pelargonium. London: Taylor & Francis.

Lis-Balchin, M., and S. G. Deans. 1996. Antimicrobial effects of hydrophilic extracts of *Pelargonium* species (Geraniaceae). *Lett. Appl. Microbiol.* 23: 205–207.

Lis-Balchin, M., et al. 1995. Potential agrochemical and medicinal usage of essential oils of *Pelargonium* species. *J. Herbs Spices Med. Pl.* 3(2): 11–22.

———. 1998. Comparative antibacterial effects of novel *Pelargonium* essential oils and solvent extracts. *Lett. Appl. Microbiol.* 27: 135–141.

Llewellyn, J. D., ed. 1978. *A Check List and Register of* Pelargonium *cultivar names*. Part 1, A to B. Part 2, C to F. Sydney: Austral. Geranium So.

Luthra, R., et al. 1995. Yield and quality of essential oil in the growing and aging leaves of geranium (*Pelargonium graveolens*). *Curr. Res. Med. Aromatic Pl.* 17: 21–23.

Maholay, M. N., and V. R. Naragund. 1981. Wilt of scented geranium caused by *Botrydoipiodia theobromae* Pat. *Indian Perfumer* 25: 71–73.

Margarida Carmo, M., and S. Frazao. 1982. L'huile essentielle de geranium. Etude sur l'huile portugaise. In *VIII International Congress of Essential Oils, October 12–17, 1980, Cannes-Grasse, France*. Paper no. 111.

Mastalerz, J. W., ed. 1971. *Geraniums*. University Park, Pennsylvania: Pennsylvania Flower Growers.

Matsuda, B. M., et al. 1996. Essential-oil analysis and field evaluation of the citrosa plant *Pelargonium citrosum* as a repellent against populations of *Aedes* mosquitoes. *J. Amer. Mosquito Control Assoc.* 12: 69–74.

McNenny, B. R. 1978. It can't be done. *Herbarist* 44: 62–65.

Milchard, M. J., et al. 2004. Application of gas-liquid chromatography to the analysis of essential oils. *Perfumer Flavor.* 29(5): 28–36.

Miller, D. M. 1996. *Pelargoniums: A Gardener's Guide to the Species and Their Hybrids and Cultivars*. Portland, Oregon: Timber Press.

———. 1997. *Pelargonium*. In *The European Garden Flora*. Ed. J. Cullen et al. Cambridge Univ. Press. 57–67.

Moore, H. E. 1955. Pelargoniums in cultivation. I. *Baileya* 3: 5–25, 41–46.

———. 1955. Pelargoniums in cultivation. II. *Baileya* 3: 70–97.

Narayana, M. R., et al. 1979. *Geranium and Its Cultivation in India*. Centr. Inst. Med. Aromatic Pl. Farm. Bull. No. 15.

Payet, J. 1982. *Etude des Caracteres Morphologiques, Anatomiques, et Cytologiques de Pelargoniums a Feuilles Odorantes et Essai d'une Classification Numerique*. D. Sci. thesis, Univ. Paris-Sud, Centre D'Orsay, France.

Peddie, M., et al. 1991. *Growing and Using Scented Geraniums*. Storey/Garden Way Publ. Bull. A-131.

Pesnelle, P., et al. 1971. Comparison between Bourbon and African geranium oils at the level of their sesquiterpenic components. *Recherches* 18: 45–52.

Putievsky, E., et al. 1990. The effect of water stress on yield components and essential oil of *Pelargonium graveolens* L. *J. Essential Oil Res.* 2: 111–114.

Ram, P., et al. 2004. Productivity and quality assessment of different chemotypes of geranium under tarai of Uttaranchal. *J. Med. Arom. Pl. Sci.* 26: 482–485.

———. 2005. Post-harvest storage effect on quantity and quality of rose-scented geranium (*Pelargonium* sp. cv. 'Bourbon') oil in Uttaranchal. *Flavour Fragrance J.* 20: 666–668.

Raman, K. R., et al. 1982. Effect of certain growth regulators on the rooting of geranium (*Pelargonium* L'Hérit.). In *Cultivaton and Utilization of Aromatic Plants*. Ed. C. K. Atal and B. M. Kapur. Jammu Tawi, India: Regional Res. Lab. 566–569.

Ranade, G. S. 1988. Chemistry of geranium oil. *Indian Perfumer* 32: 61–68.

Rao, B. R. R. 1997. Yield and chemical composition of the essential oil of rose-scented geranium (*Pelargonium* species) grown in the presence and absence of weeds. *Flavour Fragrance J.* 12: 201–204.

———. 2000. Rose-scented geranium (*Pelargonium* species): Indian and international perspective. *J. Med. Aromatic Pl. Sci.* 22: 302–312.

———. 2002. Biomass yield, essential oil yield and essential oil composition of rose-scented geranium (*Pelargonium* species) as influenced by rose spacings and intercropping with cornmint (*Mentha arvensis* L. f. *piperascens* Malinv. ex Holmes). *Industr. Crops Prod.* 16: 133–144.

Rao, B. R. R., and A. K. Bhattacharya. 1992. History and botanical nomenclature of rose-scented geranium cultivars grown in India. *Indian Perfumer* 36: 155–160.

Rao, B. R. R., and K. P. Sastry. 1990. Variation in yields and quality of geranium (*Pelargonium graveolens* L'Hér. ex Aiton) under varied climatic and fertility conditions. *J. Essential Oil Res.* 2: 73–79.

Rath, C. C., et al. 2005. Antifungal activity of rose-scented geranium (*Pelargonium* species) essential oil and its six constituents. *J. Essential Oil-Bearing Pl.* 8: 218–222.

Ross, M. E. 1956. Scented leaved geraniums. *Natl. Hort. Mag.* 35: 225–234.

Salomon, B., and I. Kapetanidis. 1982. Influence du facteur édaphique sur la production de terpènes par *Pelargonium ×apserum* Ehrh. ex Willd. (Geranium rosat). In *VIII International Congress of Essential Oils, October 12–17, 1980, Cannes-Grasse, France*. Paper no. 30.

Sarwar, M., et al. 1982. Chemical and cultural management of wilt of geranium. *Indian Perfumer* 26: 122–124.

Sashidhara, K. V., et al. 2004. Evaluation of geranium cultivars (*Pelargonium graveolens*) in Tarai region of Uttaranchal. *Indian Perfumer* 48: 273–276.

Saxena, G., et al. 2004. Composition of the essential oil of a new isomenthone-rich variant of geranium obtained from geraniol-rich cultivar of *Pelargonium* species. *J. Essential Oil Res.* 16: 85–88.

Shellie, R. A., and P. J. Marriott. 2003. Comprehensive two-dimensional gas chromatography-mass spectrometry analysis of *Pelargonium graveolens* essential oil using rapid scanning quadrupole mass spectrometry. *Analyst* 128: 879–883.

Skirvin, R. M., and J. Janick. 1976. 'Velvet Rose' *Pelargonium*, a scented geranium. *HortScience* 11: 61–62.

Southwell, I. A., and I. A. Stiff. 1995. Chemical composition of an Australian geranium oil. *J. Essential Oil Res.* 7: 545–547.

Southwell, I. A., et al. 1995. An Australian geranium oil. *Perfumer Flavor.* 20(4): 11–14.

Spalding, G. C. 1975. *Complete Copy of the Spalding* Pelargonium *Check List*. Ed. F. Hartsook. Intern. Geranium Soc.

Swain, R. 1974. Aromatic pelargoniums. *Arnoldia* 34: 97–124.

Takagi, F. 1928. On the chromosome numbers of *Pelargonium*. *Sci. Rep. Tohoku Imperial Univ.* 3(4): 665–671.

Teisseire, P. 1987. Industrial quality control of essential oils by capillary GC. In *Capillary Gas Chromatography in Essential Oil Analysis*. Ed. P. Sandra and C. Bicchi. Heidelberg: Alfred Huethig. 215–248.

Thornton-Wood, S. 1996. A clearer view. *Garden* (London) 121: 644–645.

Tokumasu, S., and M. Kato. 1979. Variation of chromosome numbers and essential oil components of plants derived from anther culture of the diploid and the tetraploid in *Pelargonium roseum*. *Euphytica* 28: 329–338.

Tsujita, M. J., and P. M. Harney. 1978. The effects of Florel and supplemental lighting on the production and rooting of geranium cuttings. *J. Hort. Sci.* 53: 349–350.

Tyagi, B. R. 2003. 2n Pollen formation in rose-scented geranium (*Pelargonium* sp.). *Nucleus* 46: 13–19.

Tyagi, B. R., et al. 2004. Composition of the essential oil of *Pelargonium tomentosum* Jacq. grown in the plains of northern India. *Indian Perfumer* 48: 51–53.

Van der Walt, J. J. A. 1977. *Pelargoniums of Southern Africa Vol. 1*. Cape Town: Purnell.

———. 1985. A taxonomic revision of the type section of *Pelargonium* L'Hérit. (Geraniaceae). *Bothalia* 15: 345–385.

Van der Walt, J. J. A., and F. Demarne. 1988. *Pelargonium graveolens* and *P. radens*: a comparison of their morphology and essential oils. *S. African J. Bot.* 54: 617–622.

Van der Walt, J. J. A., and P. J. Vorster. 1981. *Pelargoniums of Southern Africa Vol. 2*. Cape Town: Juta.

———. 1988. *Pelargoniums of Southern Africa Vol. 3*. Kirstenbosch, South Africa: Natl. Bot. Gard.

Vernin, G., et al. 1983. Étude des huiles essentielles par CG-SM-banque SPECMA:

Essences de géranium. *Parfums, Cosmétiques, Arômes* 52: 51–61.
———. 2002. Classification of *Geranium* essential oils by chemometrics. *Rivista Ital. EPPOS* 12: 3–19.
Viljoen, A. M., et al. 1995. A study of the variation in the essential oil of *Pelargonium capitatum* (L.) L'hérit. (Geraniaceae). Part 2. The chemotypes of *P. capitatum. J. Essential Oil Res.* 7: 605–611.
Widmer, W. W., and R. P. Collins. 1991. Analysis of essential oils from selected cultivars of *Pelargonium quercifolium* by GC/MS. *J. Essential Oil Res.* 3: 331–340.
Yu, S.-N., and W. A. H. Horn. 1988. Additional chromosome numbers in *Pelargonium* (Geraniaceae). *Pl. Syst. Evol.* 159: 165–171.

Perilla

Anonymous. 2005. Perilla. *Rev. Nat. Prod.* (Wolters Kluwer Health).
Aritomi, M., et al. 1985. Cyanogenic glycosides in leaves of *Perilla frutescens* var. *acuta. Phytochemistry* 24: 2438–2439.
Bittman, M. 1995. What's that mysterious taste? Shiso captivates chefs. *New York Times* May 17: C3.
Breeze, R. G., et al. 1978. A reappraisal of atypical interstitial pneumonia in cattle. *Bovine Practitioner* 1978: 75–81.
———. 1984. Perilla ketone toxicity: a chemical model for the study of equine restrictive lung disease. *Equine Veterin. J.* 16: 180–184.
Brenner, D. M. 1993. Perilla: botany, uses and genetic resources. In *New Crops.* Ed. J. Janick and J. E. Simon. New York: John Wiley & Sons. 322–328.
Chen, G., et al. 2004. Analysis of volatile components of fresh *Perilla frutescens* (L.) Britt. var. *acuta* (Thunb.) Kudo by headspace GC/MS. *J. Essential Oil Res.* 16: 435–436.
Coggeshall, J. W., et al. 1987. Perilla ketone: a model of increased pulmonary microvascular permeability pulmonary edema in sheep. *Amer. Rev. Respir. Dis.* 136: 1453–1458.
Dung, N. X., et al. 1995. Essential oil constituents from the aerial parts of *Perilla frutescens* (L.) Britton. *J. Essential Oil Res.* 7: 429–432.
Follett, J. 1996. *Perilla: An Asian Culinary Herb.* New Zealand Inst. Crop Food Res. Broadsheet No. 75.
Fujita, T., et al. 1995. Inhibitory effect of perillosides A and C, and related monoterpene glucosides on aldose reductase and their structure-activity relationships. *Chem. Pharm. Bull.* 43: 920–926.
Habegger, R., and W. H. Schnitzler. 2004. Aroma compounds in the essential oil of perilla red (*Perilla frutescens* L. Britt.). *J. Appl. Bot. Food Qual.* 78: 141–143.

Harada, J. 1987. Identification of plant growth inhibiting substances contained in *Perilla frutescens* (L.) Britt. and *P. crispa* Tanaka by gas chromatography-mass spectrometry. In *Proceedings of the 11th Asian-Pacific Weed Science Society Conference, Taipei, Republic of China, November 29–December 5.* Weed Society of the Republic of China. 601–605.
Honda, G., et al. 1984. Antidermatophytic compounds of *Perilla frutescens* Britton var. *crispa* Decne. *Shoyakugaku Zasshi* 38: 127–130.
———. 1986. Isolation of sedative principles from *Perilla frutescens. Chem. Pharm. Bull.* 34: 1672–1677.
Ito, M., and G. Honda. 2007. Geraniol synthases from perilla and their taxonomical significance. *Phytochemistry* 68: 446–453.
Ito, M., et al. 1999. Chemical composition of the essential oil of *Perilla frutescens. Nat. Med.* 53: 32–36.
———. 1999. Essential oil composition of hybrids and amphiploids of Japanese wild *Perilla. Nat. Med.* 53: 118–122.
———. 1999. Genetic analysis of nothoapiol formation in *Perilla frutescens. Biol. Pharm. Bull.* 22: 598–601.
———. 2002. A new type of essential oil from *Perilla frutescens* from Thailand. *J. Essential Oil Res.* 14: 416–419.
Jadot, J., and P. Niebes. 1968. Identification et caractérisation de l'anthocyane acylée présente dans les feuilles de *Perilla nankinensis* (Lour.) Decne. *Bull. Soc. Roy. Sci. Liège* 37: 593–604.
Jung, Y.-Y., et al. 2008. Variations in nutraceutical compound contents in seeds of Korean and Japanese beefsteak plant (*Perilla frutescens* var. *crispa*) varieties. *HortScience* 43: 1178.
Kameoka, H., and K. Nishikawa. 1976. The composition of the essential oil from *Perilla frutescens* L. Brit. var. *acuta* Thunb. Kudo and *Perilla frutescens* L. Brit. var. *acuta* Thunb. Kudo f. *discolor* Makino. *J. Agric. Chem. Soc. Japan* 50: 345–349.
Kang, R., et al. 1992. Antimicrobial activity of the volatile constituents of *Perilla frutescens* and its synergistic effects with polygodial. *J. Agric. Food Chem.* 40: 2328–2330.
Kasahara, K., et al. 1996. The suppressing effect of perilla on the odor of *niboshi* soup stock. *Fish. Sci.* 62: 838–839.
Kerr, L. A., et al. 1986. Intoxication of cattle by *Perilla frutescens* (purple mint). *Veterin. Human Toxicol.* 28: 412–416.
Koezuka, Y., et al. 1984. Essential oil types of the local varieties and their F1 hybrids of *Perilla frutescens. Shoyakugaku Zasshi* 38: 238–242.
———. 1985. An intestinal propulsion promoting substance from *Perilla frutescens*

and its mechanism of action. *Pl. Med.* 1985: 480–482.
———. 1986. Genetic control of the chemical composition of volatile oils in *Perilla frutescens. Phytochemistry* 25: 859–863.
Kuebel, K. R., and A. O. Tucker. 1988. Vietnamese culinary herbs in the United States. *Econ. Bot.* 42: 413–419.
Kurowska, E. M., et al. 2003. Bioavailability of omega-3 essential fatty acids from perilla seed oil. *Prostaglandins Leukotrienes Essential Fatty Acids* 68: 207–212.
Lawrence, B. M. 1991. Labiatae oils: Mother Nature's chemical factory. In *Essential Oils 1988–1991.* Ed. B. M. Lawrence. Carol Stream, Illinois: Allured. 188–206.
———. 1992. Chemical components of Labiatae oils and their exploitation. In *Advances in Labiate Science.* Ed. R. M. Harley and T. Reynolds. Richmond, England: RBG Kew. 399–436.
Lee, Y.-J., and C.-M. Yang. 2006. Growth behavior and perillaldehyde concentration of primary leaves of *Perilla frutescens* (L.) Britton grown in different seasons. *Crop. Environm. Bioinform.* 3: 135–146.
Makino, T., et al. 1998. Inhibitory effect of *Perilla frutescens* and its phenolic constituents on cultured murine mesangial cell proliferation. *Pl. Med.* 64: 541–545.
Morton, J. F. 1991. Food, medicinal and industrial uses of *Perilla,* and ornamental and toxic aspects. In *Progress on Terrestrial and Marine Natural Products of Medicinal and Biological Interest.* Ed. J. M. Pezzuto et al. Austin: Amer. Bot. Council. 34–38.
Nabeta, K., and H. Sugisawa. 1983. Volatile components produced by callus tissues from three *Perilla* plants. In *Instrumental Analysis of Foods Vol. 1.* Ed. G. Charalambous and G. Inglett. New York: Academic Press. 65–84.
Nakazawa, T., and K. Ohsawa. 2000. Metabolites of orally administered *Perilla frutescens* extract in rats and humans. *Biol. Pharm. Bull.* 23: 122–127.
Nitta, M., et al. 2003. Asian *Perilla* crops and their weedy forms: their cultivation, utilization and genetic relationships. *Econ. Bot.* 57: 245–253.
Okazaki, N., et al. 1982. Contact dermatitis due to beefsteak plant (*Perilla frutescens* Britton var. *acuta* Kudo). *Skin Res.* 24: 250–256.
Omer, E. A., et al. 1998. First cultivation trial of *Perilla frutescens* L. in Egypt. *Flavour Fragrance J.* 13: 221–225.
Opdyke, D. L. J., and C. Letizia. 1982. Monographs on fragrance raw materials. *Food Chem. Toxicol.* 20: 633–852.
Opdyke, D. L. J., et al. 1988. Monographs on fragrance raw materials. *Food Chem. Toxicol.* 26: 273–416.

Phillips, W. A., and D. Von Tungein. 1986. Acute pulmonary edema and emphysema in steers fed Old-World bluestem hay. *Modern Veterin.* Practice 67: 252–253.

Richardson, I. B. K. 1972. *Perilla.* In *Flora Europaea Vol. 3.* Ed. T. G. Tutin et al. Cambridge Univ. Press. 186–187.

Schnitzler, W. H., and R. Habegger. 2004. *Perilla frutescens:* perilla red and its secondary plant metabolism. *Acta Hort.* 659: 371–374.

Sugaya, A., et al. 1981. Pharmacological studies of perillae herba. I. Neuropharmacological action of water extract and perillaldehyde. *J. Pharm. Soc. Japan* 101: 642–648.

Tucker, A. O., and M. J. Maciarello. 1998. Some toxic culinary herbs in North America. In *Food Flavor: Formation, Analysis and Packaging Influences.* Ed. E. T. Contis et al. Amsterdam: Elsevier. 401–414.

Ueda, H., and M. Yamazaki. 1887. Inhibition of tumor necrosis factor-α oproduction by orally administering a perilla leaf extract. *Biosci. Biotech. Biochem.* 61: 1292–1295.

Wilson, B. J., et al. 1977. Perilla ketone: a potent lung toxin from the mint plant, *Perilla frutescens* Britton. *Science* 197: 573–574.

Yeh, P.-H. 1960. A new perilla oil containing mainly (-)-piperitone and the stereospecific reduction of the alpha, beta-unsaturated ketone. *Perfumery Essential Oil Rec.* 51: 293–296.

Yu, H.-C., et al., eds. 1997. *Perilla: The Genus* Perilla. Amsterdam: Harwood Acad. Publ.

Zhao, S., et al. 1992. Essential oils isolated from *Perilla frutescens* and MS determination of the structures of three furan-type compounds [in Chinese]. *Yaowu Fenxi Zazhi* 12: 206–210.

———. 1993. Chemical components of essential oil of different chemical type from *Perilla frutescens* (L.) Britt. var. *arguta* and *P. frutescens* [in Chinese]. *Tianran Chanwu Yanjiu Yu Kaifa* 5(3): 8–20.

Persea

Kopp, L. E. 1966. A taxonomic revision of the genus *Persea* in the western hemisphere. (Perseae-Lauraceae). *Mem. New York Bot. Gard.* 14: 1–117.

Sargent, C. S. 1895. *The Silva of North America Vol. 7.* Boston: Houghton Mifflin and Co.

Tucker, A. O., et al. 1997. Volatile leaf oils of *Persea borbonia* (L.) Spreng., *P. humilis* Nash, and *P. palustris* (Raf.) Sarg. (Lauraceae) of North America. *J. Essential Oil Res.* 9: 209–211.

Wofford, B. E. 1973. *A Biosystematic Study of the Genus* Persea *(Lauraceae) in the Southeastern United States.* Ph.D. thesis, Univ. Tennessee, Knoxville.

Persicaria

Dung, N. Z., et al. 1995. Volatile constituents of the aerial parts of Vietnamese *Polygonum odoratum* L. *J. Essential Oil Res.* 7: 339–340.

Hunter, M. V., et al. Composition of *Polygonum odoratum* Lour. from southern Australia. *J. Essential Oil Res.* 9: 603–604.

Kuebel, K. R., and A. O. Tucker. 1988. Vietnamese culinary herbs in the United States. *Econ. Bot.* 42: 413–419.

Oyen, L. P. A., and D. D. Huyen. 1999. *Persicaria odorata* (Lour.) Soják. In *Plant Resources of South-east Asia. No. 13. Spices.* Ed. C. C. de Guzman and J. S. Siemonsma. Leiden: Backhuys Publ. 170–172.

Potter, T. L., et al. 1993. Composition of Vietnamese coriander leaf oil. *Acta Hort.* 344: 305–311.

Steward, A. N. 1930. The Polygoneae of eastern Asia. *Contr. Gray Herb.* 88.

Wilson, K. L. 1988. *Polygonum sensu lato* (Polygonaceae) in Australia. *Telopea* 3: 177–182.

Yaacob, K. B. 1990. Essential oil of *Polygonum minus* Huds. *J. Essential Oil Res.* 2: 167–172.

Petroselinum

Akers, S., et al. 1987. Germination of parsley seed primed in aerated solutions of polyethylene glycol. *HortScience* 22: 250–252.

Andrews, A. C. 1949. Celery and parsley as foods in the Greco-Roman period. *Classical Philology* 44: 91–99.

Anonymous. 2004. Parsley. *Rev. Nat. Prod. (Wolters Kluwer Health).*

Berenbaum, M. 1980. That devilish herb. *Horticulture* 58(7): 22–24.

Broda, S., et al. 2001. Characterization of parsley by chemosensory and other analytical methods. *J. Appl. Bot.* 75: 201–206.

Burgett, M. 1980. Pollination of parsley (*Petroselinum crispum*) grown for seed. *J. Apic. Res.* 19: 79–82.

Calabrese, N., and G. Cirella. 1997. Cutting time, yield and essential oil composition in three cultivars of parsley. In *Essential Oils: Basic and Applied Research.* Ed. Ch. Franz et al. Carol Stream, Illinois: Allured. 308–311.

Díaz-Maroto, M. C., et al. 2002. Effect of different drying methods on the volatile compounds of parsley (*Petroselinum crispum* L.). *Eur. Food Res. Technol.* 215: 227–230.

———. 2003. Evaluation of the effect of drying on aroma of parsley by free choice profiling. *Eur. Food Res. Technol.* 216: 227–232.

Franke, W. 1978. On the contents of vitamin C and thiamin during the vegetation period in leaves of three spice plants [*Allium schoenoprasum* L., *Melissa officinalis*

L. and *Petroselinum crispum* (Mill.) Nym. ssp. *crispum*]. *Acta Hort.* 73: 205–212.

Franz, C., and H. Glasl. 1974. Zur Kenntnis der ätherischen Öle von Petersilie. I. Dünnschichtchromatographische und gaschromatographische Untersuchung des Blattöls einiger Petersiliensorten. *Qual. Pl.* 24: 175–182.

———. 1976. Zur Kenntnis der ätherischen Öle von Petersilie II. Vergleichende Untersuchung des Frucht-, Blatt- und Wurzelöles einiger Petersiliensorten. *Qual. Pl.* 25: 253–262.

Guenther, E. 1943. Oil of parsley. *Chemurgic Dig.* 2: 57, 59–60.

Harada, J. 1989. Plant growth-inhibiting substance contained in parsley plants. *Twelfth Asian-Pacific Weed Sci. Soc. Conf., Seoul, Korea.*

Hassell, R. L., and D. W. Kretchman. 1997. The effects of umbel order, soaking, and scarification on germination inhibiting substances in *Petroselinum crispum* L. and other Apiaceae seeds. *HortScience* 32: 1227–1230.

International Seed Testing Association. 1985. International rules for seed testing. *Seed Sci. Technol.* 13: 299–355.

Kasting, R., et al. 1972. Volatile constituents in leaves of parsley. *Phytochemistry* 11: 2277–2282.

Kato, T., et al. 1978. The coumarin heraclenol as a growth inhibitor in parsley seeds. *Phytochemistry* 17: 158–159.

Kim, Y.-H., et al. 1990. Volatile components of parsley leaf and seed (*Petroselinum crispum*). *J. Korean Agric. Chem. Soc.* 33: 62–67.

Kuroska, A., and I. Gałązka. 2006. Essential oil composition of the parsley seed of cultivars marketed in Poland. *Flavour Fragrance J.* 21: 143–147.

Kurt, S., and F. M. Tok. 2006. Influence of inoculum concentration, leaf age, temperature and duration of leaf wetness on septoria blight of parsley. *Crop Prot.* 25: 556–561.

Lamarti, A., and A. Badoc. 1997. Étude chimiotaxonomique de l'huile essentielle des fruits de persil (*Petroselinum crispum* (Mill.) A. W. Hill). In *Plantes Aromatiques et Médicinales et Leurs Huiles Essentielles.* Ed. B. Genjilali et al. Rabat: Actes Éditions. 9020.

Lamarti, A., et al. 1991. A chemotaxonomic evaluation of *Petroselinum crispum* (Mill.) A. W. Hill (parsley) marketed in France. *J. Essential Oil Res.* 3: 425–433.

———. 1993. Étude des arylpropènes extraits de l'huile essentielle des fruits de persil [*Petroselinum crispum* (Mill.) A. W. Hill]. *Bull. Soc. Pharm. Bordeaux* 132: 90–98.

MacLeod, A. J., et al. 1985. Volatile aroma constituents of parsley leaves. *Phytochemistry* 24: 2623–2627.

Manderfeld, M. M., et al. 1997. Isolation and identification of antimicrobial furocoumarins from parsley. *J. Food Prot.* 60: 72–77.

Masanetz, C., and W. Gerosch. 1998. Key odorants of parsley leaves (*Petroselinum crispum* [Mill.] Nym. ssp. *crispum*) by odour-activity values. *Flavour Fragrance J.* 13: 115–124.

———. 1998. Hay-like off-flavour of dry parsley. *Z. Lebensm. Unters Forsch.* 206: 114–120.

McCracker, A. R. 1984. A root-rotting disease of parsley associated with *Pythium paroecandrum. Rec. Agric. Res.* 32: 47–53.

Molli, J. S., et al. 1993. Comparación de los aceites esenciales obtenidos de semillas de diversas variedades horticolas de perejil (*Petroselinum crispus* Mill. Nyman). *Essenze Derivati Agrumari* 63: 414–422.

Olszewski, M., et al. 2005. Priming duration influences anatomy and germination responses of parsley mericarps. *J. Amer. Soc. Hort. Sci.* 130: 754–758.

Orav, A., et al. 2003. Composition of the essential oil of dill, celery, and parsely from Estonia. *Proc. Estonian Acad. Sci. Chem.* 52: 147–154.

Parera, C. A., and D. J. Cantliffe. 1994. Presowing seed priming. *Hort. Rev.* 16: 109–141.

Park, K.-W., et al. 1999. Effects of film package and storage temperature on the quality of parsley in modified atmosphere storage. *Acta Hort.* 483: 291–298.

Partridge, B. 1986. Parsley trial 1984/5. *Garden* (London) 111: 194–196.

Petropoulos, S. A., et al. 2004. The effect of sowin date and growth stage on the essential oil composition of three types of parsley (*Petroselinum crispum*). *J. Sci. Food Agric.* 84: 1606–1610.

Pill, W. G. 1986. Parsley emergence and seedling growth from raw, osmoconditioned, and pregerminated seeds. *HortScience* 21: 1134–1136.

———. 1991. Advances in fluid drilling. *HortTechnology* 1: 59–65.

———. 1994. Low water potential and presowing germination treatments to improve seed quality. In *Seed Quality: Basic Mechanisms and Agricultural Implications.* Ed. A. S. Basra. Binghampton, New York: Haworth Press. 319–359.

Pill, W. G., and E. A. Kilian. 2000. Germination and emergence of parsley in response to osmotic or matric seed priming and treatment with gibberellin. *HortScience* 35: 907–909.

Pino, J. A., et al. 1997. Herb oil of parsley (*Petroselinum crispum* Mill.) from Cuba. *J. Essential Oil Res.* 9: 241–242.

Porter, N. G. 1989. Composition and yield of commercial essential oils from parsley.

1: Herb oil and crop development. *Flavour Fragrance J.* 4: 207–219.

Porter, N. G., and N. D. Hood. 1986. The recovery of parsley seed oil. *Perfumer Flavour* 10(6): 49–54.

Rabin, J., and G. A. Berkowitz. 1986. Successful parsley production programs in New Jersey. *Herb Spice Med. Pl. Dig.* 4(1): 1–2, 5–6.

Rabin, J., et al. 1988. Field performance of osmotically primed parsley seed. *HortScience* 23: 554–555.

Radewald, J. D., et al. 1972. The influence of the root-knot nematode, *Meloidogyne incognita,* on parsley yields under controlled greenhouse conditions. *Calif. Agric.* 26(8): 6–8.

Shaath, N. A., et al. 1988. The chemical composition of Egyptian parsley seed, absolute, and herb oil. In *Flavor and Fragrances: A World Perspective.* Ed. B. M. Lawrence et al. Amsterdam: Elsevier. 715–729.

Simon, J. E., and M. L. Overley. 1986. A comparative evaluation of parsley cultivars. *Herb Spice Med. Pl. Dig.* 4(1): 3–4, 7.

Simon, J. E., and J. Quinn. 1988. Characterization of essential oil of parsley. *J. Agric. Food Chem.* 36: 467–472.

Simon, J. E., et al. n.d. *Parsley: A Production Guide.* Purdue Univ. Dept. Hort. HO-202.

———. 1985. Response of parsley to varying plant populations and rates of nitrogen. *HortScience* 20: 558.

Spraul, M. H., et al. 1991. About the chemical composition of parsley root and seed extractives. *Chem. Mikrobiol. Technol. Lebensm.* 13: 179–182.

Stanković, M. Z., et al. 2005. The effect of parsley (*Petroselinum crispum* (Mill.) Nym. ex A. W. Hill) seeds milling and fermentation conditions on essential oil yield and composition. *CI&CEQ* 11: 177–182.

Syed, M., et al. 1987. Antimicrobial activity of the essential oils of the Umbelliferae family. Part 5. *Carum carvi, Petroselinum crispum* and *Dorema ammoniacum* oils. *Pakistan J. Sci. Industr. Res.* 30: 106–110.

Thomann, R. J., et al. 1993. Distillation and use of essential oils from dill, celery, lovage, and parsley, made in Germany. *Acta Hort.* 333: 101–111.

Thomas, T. H. 1996. Relationships between position on the parent plant and germination characteristics of parsley (*Petroselinum crispum* Nym.) *Pl. Growth Reg.* 18: 175–181.

Tutin, T. G. 1968. *Petroselinum.* In *Flora Europaea Vol. 2.* Ed. T. G. Tutin et al. Cambridge Univ. Press. 352.

United States Department of Agriculture. 1970. *Production of Parsley.* Leafl. Dept. Agric. No. 136.

Vernin, G., et al. 1994. Studies of plants in the Umbelliferae family. GC/MS analysis

of parsley leaf essential oils from Hungary and France: closely related diterpenes from *Petroselinum crispum* (Mill.) Nym. In *Spices, Herbs and Edible Fungi.* Ed. G. Charalambous. Amsterdam: Elsevier. 457–467.

Vernon, F., and H. M. J. Richard. 1983. Etude des constituants volatils de l'huile essentielle de feuille de persil frisé (*Petroselinum hortense* Hoff.). *Lebensm. Wiss. Technol.* 16: 32–35.

Welbaum, G. E., et al. 1997. The evolution and effects of priming vegetable seeds. *Seed Technol.* 19: 209–235.

Zhang, H., et al. 2006. Evaluation of antioxidant activity of parsley (*Petroselinum crispum*) essential oil and identification of its antioxidant constituents. *Food Res. Intern.* 39: 833–839.

Zheng, G.-q., et al. 1992. Myristicin: a potential cancer chemopreventative agent from parsley leaf oil. *J. Agric. Food Chem.* 40: 107–110.

———. 1992. Inhibition of benzo[*a*]pyrene-induced tumorigenesis by myristicin, a volatile aroma constituent of parsley leaf oil. *Carcinogenesis* 13: 1921–1923.

Phyla

Compadre, C. M., et al. 1985. Hernandulcin: an intensely sweet compound discovered by review of ancient literature. *Science* 227: 417–419.

———. 1986. The intensely sweet herb, *Lippia dulcis* Trev.: historical uses, field inquiries, and constituents. *J. Ethnopharmacol.* 15: 89–106.

———. 1987. The intensely sweet sesquiterpene hernandulcin: isolation, synthesis, characterization, and preliminary safety evaluation. *J. Agric. Food Chem.* 35: 273–279.

———. 1988. Analysis of structural features responsible for the sweetness of the sesquiterpene hernandulcin. *Experientia* 44: 447–449.

Moldenke, H. N. 1971. *A Fifth Summary of the* Verbenaceae, Avicenniaceae, Stilbaceae, Dicrastylidaceae, Symphoremaceae, Nyctanthaceae, *and* Eriocaulaceae *of the World as to Valid Taxa, Geographic Distribution, and Synonymy.* Wayne, New Jersey: Harold N. Moldenke.

Pino, J. A., et al. 1998. Leaf oil of *Phyla scaberrima* (L.) Small from Cuba. *J. Essential Oil Res.* 10: 211–212.

Souto-Bachiller, F. A., et al. 1997. Terpenoid composition of *Lippia dulcis.* *Phytochemistry* 44: 1077–1086.

Standley, P. C. 1924. Trees and shrubs of Mexico. *Contr. U.S. Natl. Herb.* 23: 1–1721.

Pimpinella

Al Mofleh, I. A., et al. 2007. Aqueous suspension of anise "*Pimpinella anisum*" protects rats against chemically induced gastric ulcers. *World J. Gastroenterol.* 13: 1112–1118.

Anonymous. 2005. Anise. *Rev. Nat. Prod.* (*Wolters Kluwer Health*).

Burkhardt, G., et al. 1986. Terpene hydrocarbons in *Pimpinella anisum* L. *Pharm. Weekbl.* 8: 190–193.

Embong, M. B., et al. 1977. Essential oils from spices grown in Alberta. Anise oil (*Pimpinella anisum*). *Canad. J. Pl. Sci.* 57: 681–688.

Fehr, D. 1980. Untersuchungen zur Lagerstabilität von Anis, Fenchel und Kümmel. *Pharm. Zeitung* 125: 1300–1303.

Hérisset, A., et al. 1972. Différenciation de quelques huiles essentielles présentant une constitutio voisine (en particulier par l'examen de leurs spectres UV, IR, Raman). V. Essences de badiane de chine (*Illicium verum* Hook. F.), d'anise vert (*Pimpinella anisum* L.) et de fenouil doux (*Foeniculum dulce* D. C.). *Pl. Med. Phytotherap.* 6: 137–148.

Karaali, A., and N. Basoglu. 1995. Essential oils of Turkish anise seeds and their use in the aromatization of raki. *Z. Lebensmittel-Untersuch. Forsch.* 200: 440–442.

Kosalec, I., et al. 2005. Antifungal activity of fluid extract and essential oil from anise fruits (*Pimpinella anisum* L., Apiaceae). *Acta Pharm.* 55: 377–385.

Kubeczka, K.-H., and I. Ullmann. 1980. Occurrence of 1,5-dimethylcyclodeca-1,5,7-triene (pregeijerene) in *Pimpinella* species and chemosystematic implications. *Biochem. Syst. Ecol.* 8: 39–41.

Kubeczka, K.-H., et al. 1986. New constituents from the essential oils of *Pimpinella* species. In *Progress in Essential Oil Research.* Ed. E.-J. Brunke. Berlin: Walter de Gruyter & Co. 279–286.

Kubo, I., and M. Himejima. 1991. Anethole, a synergist of polygodial against filamentous microorganisms. *J. Agric. Food Chem.* 39: 2290–2292.

Lee, H.-S. 2004. *p*-Anisaldehyde: acaricidal component of *Pimpinella anisum* seed oil against the house dust mites *Dermatophagoides farinae* and *Dermatophagoides pteronyssinus*. *Pl. Med.* 70: 279–281.

Maheshwari, S. K., et al. 1984. Differential responses of methods for sowing and seed rates on seed yield and quality of anise oil. *Indian Perfumer* 28: 133–137.

Marcus, C., and E. P. Lichtenstein. 1979. Biologically active components of anise: toxicity and interactions with insecticides in insects. *J. Agric. Food Chem.* 27: 1217–1223.

Pareek, S. K., et al. 1980. Studies on cultivation of anise in India. *Indian Perfumer* 24: 88–92.

Pereira, C. G., and M. A. A. Meireles. 2007. Economic analysis of rosemary, fennel and anise essential oils obtained by supercritical fluid extraction. *Flavour Fragrance J.* 22: 407–413.

Reichling, J., et al. 1985. Vergleichende Untersuchungen zur Bildung und Akkumulation von ätherischen Öl in der intakten Pflanze und in Zellkulturen von *Pimpinella anisum* L. *Z. Naturforsch.* 40c: 465–468.

Romdhane, M., and C. Tizaoui. 2005. The kinetic modeling of a steam distillation unit for the extraction of aniseed (*Pimpinella anisum*) essential oil. *J. Chem. Technol. Biotechnol.* 80: 759–766.

Rosti, L. A., et al. 1994. Toxic effects of a herbal tea mixture in two newborns. *Acta Pediatrica* 83: 683.

Sanchez, J. H. 1992. Seeds for the kitchen. *Horticulture* 70(8): 54–60.

Savio, Y., and C. Myers. 1991. Anise, sweet Alice. SMC-001. In *Specialty and Minor Crops Handbook.* Ed. C. Meyers. Oakland: Small Farm Center, Univ. California.

Shukla, H. S., and S. C. Tripathi. 1987. Antifungal substance in the essential oil of anise (*Pimpinella anisum* L.). *Agric. Biol. Chem.* 51: 1991–1993.

Syed, M., et al. 1986. Antimicrobial activity of the essential oils of the Umbelliferae family. Part 3. *Pimpinella anisum, Pimpinella acuminata* and *Pimpinella stewartii*. *Pakistan J. Sci. Industr. Res.* 29: 352–356.

Tabacchi, R., et al. 1974. Contribution à l'étude de la composition de l'huile essentielle de fruits d'anis de Turquie. *Rivista Ital. Essenze, Profumi, Piante Off., Aromi, Saponi, Cosmetici, Aerosol.* 56: 683–398.

Tabanca, N., et al. 2004. Estrogenic activity of isolated compounds and essential oils of *Pimpinella* species from Turkey, evaluated using a recombinant yeast screen. *Pl. Med.* 70: 728–735.

———. 2007. Effect of essential oils and isolated compounds from *Pimpinella* species on NF-κB: a target for anti-inflammatory therapy. *Phytotherapy Res.* 21: 741–745.

Tort, N., and B. Honermeier. 2005. Investigations on the ratio of methylchavicol and *trans*-anethol components in essential oil of anis (*Pimpinella anisum* L.) from different regions of Turkey. *Asian J. Chem.* 17: 2365–2370.

Tutin, T. G. 1968. *Pimpinella*. In *Flora Europaea Vol. 2*. Ed. T. G. Tutin et al. Cambridge Univ. Press. 331–333.

Zeller, A., and M. Rychlik. 2007. Impact of estragole and other odorants on the flavour of anise and tarragon. *Flavour Fragrance J.* 22: 105–113.

Piper

Burger, W. 1971. Flora Costaricensis. Family #41 Piperaceae. *Fieldiana* 35: 5–227.

Castro, C. O., and L. J. Povenda. 1983. *Piper auritum* (H. B. K.) familia Piperaceae. Estudio preliminar del aceite esencial de sus hojas. *Ing. Ci. Quim.* 7(1–2): 24–25.

Cicció, J. F. 1995. Aceite esencial de los hojas de *Piper auritum* (Piperaceae) de Costa Rica. *Ing. Ci. Quim.* 15: 39–41.

Dung, N. X., et al. 1996. Compositional analysis of the leaf, stem, and rhizome oils of *Piper lolot* C. DC. from Vietnam. *J. Essential Oil Res.* 8: 649–652.

Gupta, M. P., et al. 1985. Safrole, the main component of the essential oil from *Piper auritum* of Panama. *J. Nat. Prod.* 48: 330–343.

Hänsel, R., et al. 1975. Aporphine-type alkaloids from *Piper auritum*. *Lloydia* 38: 529–530.

Hutson, L. 1992. Mexican culinary herbs. *Fine Gard.* 23: 52–55.

Joly, C. G. 1981. Feeding and trapping fish with *Piper auritum*. *Econ. Bot.* 35: 383–390.

Kuebel, K. R., and A. O. Tucker. 1988. Vietnamese culinary herbs in the United States. *Econ. Bot.* 42: 413–419.

Pino, J. A., et al. 1998. Composition of leaf oil of *Piper auritum* H. B. K. grown in Cuba. *J. Essential Oil Res.* 10: 333–334.

Setzer, W. N., et al. 2008. Chemical compositions and biological activities of leaf essential oils of twelve species of *Piper* from Monteverde, Costa Rica. *Nat. Prod. Commun.* 3: 1–8.

Tucker, A. O., and M. J. Maciarello. 1998. Some toxic culinary herbs in North America. In *Food Flavor: Formation, Analysis and Packaging Influences.* Ed. E. T. Contis et al. Amsterdam: Elsevier. 401–414.

Vogler, B., et al. 2006. Chemical constituents of the essential oils of three *Piper* species from Monteverde, Costa Rica. *J. Essential Oil-Bearing Pl.* 9: 230–238.

Plectranthus

Agnew, A. D. Q. 1974. *Upland Kenya Wild Flowers: A Flora of the Ferns and Herbaceous Flowering Plants of Upland Kenya.* London: Oxford Univ. Press.

Baslas, R. K., and P. Kumar. 1981. Chemical examination of essential oil of *Coleus aromaticus* Benth. *J. Indian Chem. Soc.* 58: 103–104.

Blake, S. T. 1971. A revision of *Plectranthus* (Labiatae) in Australasia. *Contr. Queensland Herb.* 9: 1–120.

———. 1980. *Plectranthus. Austral. Pl.* 10: 313–327.

Codd, L. E. 1975. *Plectranthus* (Labiatae) and allied genera in Southern Africa. *Bothalia* 11: 371–442.

Dung, N. X., et al. 1990. Chemical composition of the essential oil of *Coleus amboinicus* Lour. from Vietnam and Kampuchea. *Natl. Cent. Sci. Res. Vietnam* 2: 123–127.

Gurib-Fakim, A., et al. 1995. Aromatic plants of Mauritius: volatile constituents of the essential oils of *Coleus aromaticus* Benth., *Triphasia trifolia* (Burm. f.) and *Eucalyptus kirtoniana* F. Muell. *J. Essential Oil Res.* 7: 215–218.

Hafiz, S. S. 1994. Essential oil of *Coleus aromaticus* Benth. *Zagazig J. Pharm. Sci.* 3(3): 93–96.

Haque, I. U. 1988. Analysis of volatile constituents of Pakistani *Coleus aromaticus* plant oil by capillary gas chromatography/mass spectrometry. *J. Chem. Soc. Pakistan* 10: 369–371.

Keng, H. 1978. Labiatae. In *Flora Malesiana Vol. 8, Part 3*. Ed. C. van Steenis. Alphen aan den Rijn, Netherlands: Sijthoff & Noordhoff. 301–394.

Kuebel, K. R., and A. O. Tucker. 1988. Vietnamese culinary herbs in the United States. *Econ. Bot.* 42: 413–419.

Malik, M. S., et al. 1985. Studies on the essential oil of the *Coleus aromaticus* plant. *Pakistan J. Sci. Industr. Res.* 28: 10–12.

Mallavarapu, G. R., et al. 1999. Essential oil of *Coleus aromaticus* Benth. From India. *J. Essential Oil Res.* 11: 742–744.

Mangathayaru, K., et al. 2005. Essential oil composition of *Coleus amboinicus* Lour. *Indian J. Pharm. Sci.* 67: 122–123.

Morton, J. K. 1962. Cytotaxonomic studies on the West African Labiatae. *J. Linn. Soc. Bot.* 58: 231–283.

Pino, J. A., et al. 1996. Comparative chemical composition of the volatiles of *Coleus aromaticus* produced by steam distillation, solvent extraction and supercritical carbon dioxide extraction. *J. Essential Oil Res.* 8: 373–375.

Prudent, D., et al. 1995. Analysis of the essential oil of wild oregano from Martinique (*Coleus aromaticus* Benth.): evaluation of its bacteriostatic and fungistatic properties. *J. Essential Oil Res.* 7: 165–173.

Singh, G., et al. 2002. Studies on essential oils. Part 33: chemical and insecticidal investigations on leaf oil of *Coleus amboinicus* Lour. *Flavour Fragrance J.* 17: 440–442.

Sothy, N. 1989. *Contribution a l'Étude des Plantes Medicinales du Kampuchea. Résumé de la Thèse de Doctorat en Pharmacie*. Hanoi: Fac. Pharm.

Tucker, A. O., and M. J. Maciarello. 1987. Plant identification. In *Proceedings of the First National Herb Growing and Marketing Conference, July 19–22, 1986, West Lafayette, Indiana*. Ed. J. E. Simon and L. Grant. 126–172.

Valera, D., et al. 2003. The essential oil of *Coleus amboinicus* Loureiro: chemical composition and evaluation of insect antifeedant effects. *Ciencia* 11: 113–118.

van Jaarsveld, E. n.d. *The Plectranthus Handbook*. Kirstenbosch, South Africa: Natl. Bot. Gard.

Pogostemon

Akhila, A., and R. Tewari. 1984. Chemistry of patchouli oil: a review. *Curr. Res. Med. Aromatic Pl.* 6: 38–54.

Analytical Methods Committee. 1987. Application of gas-liquid chromatography to the analysis of essential oils. Part 12. Determination of patchouli alcohol in oil of patchouli. *Analyst* 112: 1315–1318.

Backer, C. A., and R. C. Bakhuizen den Brink. 1965. *Pogostemon*. In *Flora of Java*. Ed. C. A. Backer and R. C. Bakhuizen van den Brink. Groningen: N. V. P. Noordhoff. 632–633.

Benveniste, B. 1980. Indonesian oil of patchouli. *Perfumer Flavor.* 5(3): 43–45.

Bertrand, M., et al. 1980. Sur une nouvelle synthese du (±) norpatchoulenol. *Tetrahedron Lett.* 21: 2051–2054.

Bruns, K. 1978. Ein Beitrag zur Untersuchung un Qualitätsbewertung von Patchouliöl. *Pärfumerie Kosmetik* 59: 109–115.

Buré, C. M., and N. M. Sellier. 2004. Analysis of the essential oil of Indonesian patchouli (*Pogostemon cablin* Benth.) using GC/MS (EI/CI). *J. Essential Oil Res.* 16: 18–19.

Cramer, L. H. 1981. Lamiaceae (Labiatae). In *A Revised Handbook to the Flora of Ceylon Vol. 3*. Ed. M. D. Dassanayake. Washington, D.C.: Smithsonian Institution. 108–194.

Dung, N. X., et al. 1989. Chemical composition of patchouli oil from Vietnam. *J. Essential Oil Res.* 1: 99–100.

Henderson, W., et al. 1970. Chemical and morphological studies on sites of sesquiterpene accumulation in *Pogostemon cablin* (patchouli). *Phytochemistry* 9: 1219–1228.

Keng, H. 1978. Labiatae. In *Flora Malesiana Vol. 8, Part 3*. Ed. C. van Steenis. Alphen aan den Rijn, Netherlands: Sijthoff & Noordhoff. 301–394.

Mookherjee, B. D., et al. 1981. A study on the odor-structure relationship of patchouli compound. In *Essential Oils*. Ed. B. D. Mookherjee and C. J. Mussinan. Wheaton, Illinois: Allured. 247–272.

Morris, E. T. 1983. Patchouli: the scent that intrigues. *Dragoco Rep.* 1983: 128–133.

Nikiforov, A., et al. 1986. (+)-Patchoulol, der dominante Geruchsträger des Patchouliöls (singapur.). *Monatsh. Chem.* 117: 1095–1098.

Sarwar, M., et al. 1982. Appraisal of patchouli in Indian root knot problem and control. *Indian Perfumer* 26: 117–121.

———. 1983. *Patchouli and Its Cultivation in India*. Centr. Inst. Med. Aromatic Pl. Farm Bull. No. 17.

Sugimura, Y., et al. 1990. Cultivarietal comparison of patchouli plants in relation to essential oil production and quality. *Flavour Fragrance J.* 5: 109–114.

Teisseire, P., et al. 1974. Contribution to the knowledge of patchouli oil. *Recherches* 19: 8–35.

Poliomintha

Irving, R. S. 1972. A revision of the genus *Poliomintha* (Labiatae). *Sida* 5: 8–22.

Tucker, A. O., and M. J. Maciarello. 1987. Plant identification. In *Proceedings of the First National Herb Growing and Marketing Conference, July 19–22, 1986, West Lafayette, Indiana*. Ed. J. E. Simon and L. Grant. 126–172.

———. 1994. Oregano: botany, chemistry, and cultivation. In *Spices, Herbs and Edible Fungi*. Ed. G. Charalambous. Amsterdam: Elsevier. 439–456.

Turner, B. L. 1993. Two new species of *Poliomintha* (Lamiaceae) from northeastern Mexico. *Phytologia* 74: 164–167.

Porophyllum

Andrade Neto, M., et al. 1994. Volatile constituents of *Porophyllum ruderale* Cass. *J. Essential Oil Res.* 6: 415–417.

Beserra, M. Z. B., et al. 2002. The essential oil of *Porophyllum ruderale* Cass (Asteraceae). *J. Essential Oil Res.* 14: 14–15.

Bohlmann, F., et al. 1980. A dithienylacetylene from *Porophyllum ruderale*. *Phytochemistry* 19: 2760.

Correll, D. S., and M. C. Johnston. 1970. *Manual of the Vascular Plants of Texas*. Renner, Texas: Texas Res. Found.

Fonseca, M. C. M., et al. 2006. Essential oil from leaves and flowers of *Porophyllum ruderale* (Jacq.) Cassini (Asteraceae). *J. Essential Oil Res.* 18: 345–347.

Gruenberg, L. 2001. A south of the border cilantro cousin. *Herb Companion* 13(2): 43–45.

Johnson, R. R. 1969. Monograph of the plant genus *Porophyllum* (Compositae: Helenieae). *Univ. Kansas Sci. Bull.* 48: 225–267.

Loayza, I., et al. 1999. Composition of the essential oil of *Porophyllum ruderale* (Jacq.) Cass. from Bolivia. *Flavour Fragrance J.* 14: 393–398.

von Reis Altschul, S. 1973. *Drugs and Foods from Little-known Plants: Notes in Harvard University Herbaria*. Cambridge: Harvard Univ. Press.

Pycnanthemum

Chambers, H. L. 1961. Chromosome numbers and breeding systems in *Pycnanthemum* (Labiatae). *Brittonia* 13: 116–128.

Chambers, H. L., and K. L. Chambers. 1971. Artificial and natural hybrids in *Pycnanthemum* (Labiatae). *Brittonia* 23: 71–88.

Chambers, H. L., and J. Hamer. 1992. More about picky pycnanthemums. *Tipularia* 7(1): 19–24.

Chambers, K. L., and H. L. Chambers. 2008. Infrageneric classification and nomenclatural notes for *Pycnanthemum* (Lamiaceae). *J. Bot. Res. Inst. Texas* 2: 193–199.

Djao, E. H., and A. E. Schwarting. 1951. Chemical investigation of the volatile oil of *Pycnanthemum pilosum* Nutt. *J. Amer. Pharm. Assoc.* 40: 101–103.

Galambosi, B., et al. 1999. Agronomical and phytochemical investigation of *Pycnanthemum* sp. in Finland. *Z. Arzn. Gew. Pfl.* 1999(4): 19023.

Grant, E., and C. Epling. 1943. A study of *Pycnanthemum* (Labiatae). *Univ. Calif. Publ. Bot.* 20: 195–240.

Lawrence, B. M. 1982. Addition to the chemical composition of pycnanthemum essential oils. In *Cultivation and Utilization of Aromatic Plants*. Ed. C. K. Atal and B. M. Kapur. Jammu Tawi, India: Regional Res. Lab. 677–680.

———. 1982. The existence of infraspecific differences in specific genera in the Labiatae family. In *VIII International Congress of Essential Oils, October 12–17, 1980, Cannes-Grasse, France*. Paper no. 35.

———. 1999. The composition of essential oils of *Pycnanthemum*, a North American endemic genus. In *Essential Oils*. Ed. N. Kirimer and A. Mat. Eskisehir, Turkey: Anadolu Univ. Basimevi. 164–195.

Lawrence, B. M., et al. 1972. Terpenoid composition of some Canadian Labiatae. *Phytochemistry* 11: 2636–2638.

———. 1974. An introduction to the cytology and chemistry of the *Pycnanthemum* genus (Labiatae). In *VI International Congress of Essential Oils, San Francisco, California, September 8–12, 1974*. Paper no. 42.

Pellett, F. C. 1947. Mountain mint. *Amer. Bee J.* 87(4): 172–173.

———. 1950. Mountain mint. *Amer. Bee J.* 90(2): 66–67.

Ranger, L. S. 1990. Those picky pycnanthemums. *Tipularia* 5(2): 11–14.

Sorensen, P. D., and P. A. Matekaitis. 1981. A lemon-scented *Pycnanthemum* (Lamiaceae). *Rhodora* 83: 145–146.

Rhus

Brunke, E.-J., et al. 1993. The essential oil of *Rhus coriaria* L. fruits. *Flavour Fragrance J.* 8: 209–214.

Kurucu, S., et al. 1993. The essential oils of *Rhus coriaria* L. (sumac). *J. Essential Oil Res.* 5: 481–486.

Schmaus, G., et al. 1993. Volatile constitu-

ents of *Rhus coriaria* and *Achillea wilhelmsii* from Turkey. In *Essential Oil for Perfumery and Flavour*. Ed. K. H. C. Başer and N. Güler. Istanbul. 178–197.

Seino, Y., et al. 1978. Identification of a mutagenic substance in a spice, sumac, as quercetin. *Mutat. Res.* 58: 225–229.

Stobart, T. 1977. *Herbs, Spices and Flavour*. New York: Penguin Books.

Tutin, T. G. 1968. *Rhus*. In *Flora Europaea* Vol. 2. Ed. T. G. Tutin et al. Cambridge Univ. Press. 236–237.

Rosa

Antonelli, A., et al. 1997. Characterization of 24 old garden roses from their volatile compositions. *J. Agric. Food Chem.* 45: 4435–4439.

Aydinli, M., and M. Tuta. 2003. Production of rose absolute from rose concrète. *Flavour Fragrance J.* 28: 26–31.

Azimi, M., and R. J. Bisgrove. 1975. Rooting of hardwood cuttings of rose rootstocks and cultivars. *Exp. Hort.* 27: 22–27.

Babu, K. G. D., et al. 2002. Essential oil composition of damask rose (*Rosa damascena* Mill.) distilled under different pressures and temperatures. *Flavour Fragrance J.* 17: 136–140.

Balinova-Tsvetkova, A. 1997. On the extraction of *Rosa damascena* Miller. In *Essential Oils: Basic and Applied Research*. Ed. Ch. Franz et al. Carol Stream, Illinois: Allured. 300–303.

Baser, K. H. C., et al. 2003. Turkish rose research: recent results. *Perfumer Flavor.* 28(2): 34–42.

Basim, E., and H. Basim. 2003. Antibacterial activity of *Rosa damascena* essential oil. *Fitoterapia* 74: 394–396.

Baydar, H., and N. G. Baydar. 2005. The effects of harvest date, fermentation, duration and Tween 20 treatment on essential oil content and composition of industrial oil rose (*Rosa damascena* Mill.). *Industr. Crops Prod.* 21: 251–255.

Beales, P. 1985. *Classic Roses*. New York: Holt, Rinehart and Winston.

Bruneau, A., et al. 2007. Phylogenetic relationships in the genus *Rosa*: new evidence from chloroplast DNA sequences and an appraisal of current knowledge. *Syst. Bot.* 32: 366–378.

Cairns, R., ed. 2000. *Modern Roses XI*. San Diego: Acad. Press.

Caissard, J.-C., et al. 2006. Chemical and histochemical analysis of 'Quatre Saisons Blanc Mousseaux', a moss rose of the *Rosa* ×*damascena* group. *Ann. Bot.* 97: 231–238.

Cao, Y.-l., et al. 1996. Vitamin contents in the hips of 38 species of *Rosa* and their relation to division of sections. *Acta Bot. Sin.* 38: 822–827.

Concha, J., et al. 2006. Effect of rosehip extraction process on oil and defatted meal

physicochemical properties. *J. Amer. Oil Chem. Soc.* 83: 771–775.

Dobson, H. E. M., et al. 1990. Differences in fragrance chemistry between flower parts of *Rosa rugosa* Thunb. (Rosaceae). *Israel J. Bot.* 39: 143–156.

Druitt, L., and G. M. Shoup. 1992. *Landscaping with Antique Roses*. Newtown, Connecticut: Taunton Press.

Eikani, M. H., et al. 2005. Recovery of water-soluble constituents of rose oil using simultaneous distillation-extraction. *Flavour Fragrance J.* 20: 555–558.

Ercisli, S. 2005. Rose (*Rosa* spp.) germplasm resources of Turkey. *Gen. Resources Crop. Evol.* 52: 787–795.

Fu, M., et al. 2006. Compounds from rose (*Rosa rugosa*) flowers with human immunodeficiency virus type 1 reverse transcriptase inhibitory activity. *J. Pharm. Pharmacol.* 58: 1275–1280.

Griffiths, T. 1984. *The Book of Old Roses*. London: Mermaid Books.

———. 1987. *The Book of Classic Old Roses*. London: Michael Jackson.

Gudin, S. 2000. Rose: genetics and breeding. *Pl. Breeding Rev.* 17: 159–189.

Gupta, R., et al. 2000. Composition of flower essential oil of *Rosa damascena* and *Rosa indica* grown in Lucknow. *J. Med. Aromatic Pl. Sci.* 22–23: 9–12.

Hayward, M. R. 1997. The roses of Taif. *Saudi Aramco World* 48(6): 2–9.

Illés, V., et al. 1997. Extraction of hiprose fruit by supercritical CO_2 and propane. *J. Supercritical Fluids* 10: 209–218.

Iwata, H., et al. 2000. Triparental origin of damask roses. *Gene* 259: 53–59.

Jan, C. H., et al. 1999. Rose germplasm analysis with RAPD markers. *HortScience* 34: 341–345.

Jeremias, C. G. 1979. Rooting rose cuttings. *Amer. Rose Annual* 64: 91–108.

Jirovetz, L., et al. 2002. Comparative investigations of essential oils and their SPME headspace volatiles of *Rosa damascena* from Bulgaria and *Rosa centifolia* from Morocco using GC-FID, GC-MS and olfactometry. *J. Essential Oil-Bearing Pl.* 5: 111–121.

———. 2005. Solid phase microextraction/gas chromatographic and olfactory analysis of the scent and fixative properties of the essential oil of *Rosa damascena* L. from China. *Flavour Fragrance J.* 20: 7–12.

Klástersky, I. 1968. *Rosa*. In *Flora Europaea* Vol. 2. Ed. T. G. Tutin et al. Cambridge Univ. Press. 25–32.

Knapp, H., et al. 1998. (*S*)-3,7-Dimethyl-5-octene-1,7-diol and related oxygenated monoterpenoids form petals of *Rosa damascena* Mill. *J. Agric. Food Chem.* 46: 1966–1970.

Koopman, W. J. M., et al. 2008. AFLP markers as a tool to reconstruct complex relationships: a case study in *Rosa* (Rosaceae). *Amer. J. Bot.* 95: 353–366.

Kovacheva, N, et al. 2006. Study on the morphological characteristics and essential oil constituents of Bulgarian oil-bearing rose. *HortScience* 41: 1013.

Kováts, E. 1987. Composition of essential oils. Part 7. Bulgarian oil of rose (*Rosa damascena* Mill.). *J. Chromatogr.* 406: 185–222.

Krüssmann, G. 1981. *The Complete Book of Roses*. Portland, Oregon: Timber Press.

Kurkcuoglu, M., and K. H. C. Baser. 2003. Studies on Turkish rose concrète, absolute, and hydrosol. *Chem. Nat. Compd.* 39: 457–464.

Kwaselow, A., et al. 1990. Rose hips: a new occupational allergen. *J. Allergy Clin. Immunol.* 85: 704–708.

Lawrence, B. M. 1991. Progress in essential oils. *Perfumer Flavor.* 16(3): 43–44, 46, 51–52, 54–56, 58–64, 66–70, 72–74, 76–77.

Loghmani-Khouzani, H., et al. 2007. Essential oil composition of *Rosa damascena* Mill cultivated in central Iran. *Sci. Iran.* 14: 316–319.

MacGregor, J. C. 1980. *A Portfolio of Rose Hips*. Palo Alto, California: Sweetbriar Press.

McGimpsey, J. A. 1993. *Rose*: Rosa damascena *'Trigintipetala'*. New Zealand Inst. Crop Food Res. Broadsheet No. 29.

Moore, R. S. 1963. Mist propagation of miniature roses. *Proc. Int. Pl. Propag. Soc.* 13: 208–210.

Naqvi, A. A., and S. Mandel. 1997. Investigation of rose oils from different places in India by capillary gas chromatography. *J. Med. Aromatic Pl. Sci.* 19: 1000–1002.

Nowak, R. 2004. Chemical composition of hips essential oil of some *Rosa* L. species. *Z. Naturforsch.* 60c: 369–378.

Oka, N., et al. 1999. Aroma evolution during flower opening in *Rosa damascena* Mill. *Z. Naturforsch.* 54c: 889–895.

Palairet, M. 1999. Primary production in a market for luxury: the rose-oil trade of Bulgaria, 1771–1941. *J. Eur. Econ. Hist.* 28: 551–597.

Phillips, R., and M. Rix. 1988. *Roses*. New York: Random House.

Rusanov, K., et al. 2005. Microsatellite analysis of *Rosa damascena* Mill. accessions reveals genetic similarity between genotypes used for rose oil production and old damask rose varieties. *Theor. Appl. Genet.* 111: 804–809.

Scalliet, G., et al. 2002. Biosynthesis of the major scent components 3,5-dimethyloxytoluene and 1,3,5-trimethoxybenzene by novel rose *O*-methyltransferases. *FEBS Lett.* 523: 113–118.

———. 2006. Role of petal-specific orcinal

O-methyltransferases in the evolution of rose scent. *Pl. Physiol.* 140: 18–29.

Schieber, A., et al. 2005. Flavonol glycosides from distilled petals of *Rosa damascena* Mill. *Z. Naturforsch.* 60c: 379–384.

Singh, S. P., et al. 2000. Correlated response for increased flower yield in 'damask rose' (*Rosa damascena* Mill). *Sci. Lett.* 23(7/8): 95–97.

Stock, K. L. 1984. *Rose Books*. Milton Keynes, England: K. Stock.

Thomas, G. S. 1979. *The Old Shrub Roses*. Rev. ed. London: J. M. Dent & Sons.

Tucker, A. O. 2004. Identification of the rose, sage, iris, and lily in the "Blue Bird Fresco" from Knossos, Crete (ca. 1450 B.C.E.). *Econ. Bot.* 58: 733–736.

Tucker, A. O., and M. J. Maciarello. 1986. Nomenclature and chemistry of the Kazanlik damask rose and some potential alternatives from the horticultural trade of North America and Europe. In *Flavor and Fragrances: A World Perspective*. Ed. B. M. Lawrence et al. Amsterdam: Elsevier. 99–114.

Umezu, T., et al. 2002. Anticonflict effects of rose oil and identification of its active constituents. *Life Sci.* 72: 91–102.

Verrier, S. 1991. Rosa rugosa. Deer Park, Wisconsin: Capability's Books.

Vinokur, Y., et al. 2006. Rose petal tea as an antioxidant-rich beverage: cultivar effects. *J. Food Sci.* 71: S42–S47.

Wissemann, V., and C. M. Ritz. 2005. The genus *Rosa* (Rosoideae, Rosaceae) revisited: molecular analysis of nrITS-1 and *atp*B-*rbc*L intergeneric spacer (IGS) versus conventional taxonomy. *Bot. J. Linn. Soc.* 147: 275–290.

Rosmarinus

Al-Hader, A. A., et al. 1994. Hyperglycemic and insulin release inhibitory effects of *Rosmarinus officinalis*. *J. Ethnopharmacol.* 43: 217–221.

Amaral Franco, J., et al. 1972. *Rosmarinus*. In *Flora Europaea Vol. 3*. Ed. T. G. Tutin et al. Cambridge Univ. Press. 187.

Angioni, A., et al. 2004. Chemical composition, plant genetic differences, antimicrobial and antifungal activity investigation of the essential oil of *Rosmarinus officinalis* L. *J. Agric. Food Chem.* 52: 3530–3535.

Anonymous. 2004. Rosemary. *Rev. Nat. Prod. (Wolters Kluwer Health)*.

Armitage, A. M., et al. 2004. *Rosmarinus officinalis* 'Athens Blue Spires'. *HortScience* 39: 1789.

Arnold, N., et al. 1997. Comparative study of the essential oils from *Rosminarus eriocalyx* Jordan & Fourr. from Algeria and *R. officinalis* L. from other countries. *J. Essential Oil Res.* 9: 167–175.

Aruoma, O. I., et al. 1992. Antioxidant and pro-oxidant properties of active rosemary

constituents: carnosol and carnosic acid. *Xenobiotica* 22: 257–268.

———. 1996. An evaluation of the antioxidant and antiviral action of extracts of rosemary and Provençal herbs. *Food Chem. Toxicol.* 34: 449–456.

Asai, A., et al. 1999. Antioxidative effects of turmeric, rosemary and capsicum extracts on membrane phospholipid peroxidation and liver lipid metabolism in mice. *Biosci. Biotechnol. Biochem.* 63: 2118–2122.

Atti-Santos, A. C., et al. 2004. Estudio da qualidade de amostras comerciais de óleos essenciais de alecrim (*Rosmarinus officinalis* L.). *Rev. Bras. Pl. Med. Botucatu* 6: 44–47.

———. 2005. Physico-chemical evaluation of *Rosmarinus officinalis* L. essential oils. *Braz. Arch. Biol. Technol.* 48: 1035–1039.

Barranco, R., et al. 1982. Étude comparative entre les huiles essentielles de romarin sylvestre et cultivée. In *VIII International Congress of Essential Oils, October 12–17, 1980, Cannes-Grasse, France*. Paper no. 110.

Benhabiles, N. E. H., and H. Aït-Amar. 2001. Comparative study of Algeria's *Rosmarinus eriocalyx* and *Rosmarinus officinalis* L. *Perfumer Flavor.* 26(5): 40–48.

Bianchi-Santamaria, A., et al. 1993. Antimutagenic action of beta carotene, canthanxanthin and extracts of *Rosmarinus officinalis* and *Melissa officinalis*. Genotoxicity of basil and tarragon oil. In *Food and Cancer Prevention: Chemical and Biological Aspects*. Ed. K. W. Waldron et al. Cambridge: Roy. Soc. Chem. 75–81.

Boelens, M. H. 1985. The essential oil from *Rosmarinus officinalis* L. *Perfumer Flavor.* 10(5): 21–24, 26, 28–37.

Boutekedjiret, C., et al. 1998. The essential oil from *Rosmarinus officinalis* L. in Algeria. *J. Essential Oil Res.* 10: 680–682.

———. 1999. Study of *Rosmarinus officinalis* L. essential oil yield and composition as a function of the plant life cycle. *J. Essential Oil Res.* 11: 238–240.

———. 2003. Extraction of rosemary essential oil by steam distillation and hydrodistillation. *Flavour Fragrance J.* 18: 481–484.

———. 2005. Characterisation of rosemary essential oil of different areas of Algeria. *J. Essential Oil-Bearing Pl.* 8: 65–70.

———. 2006. Isolation of rosemary oils by different processes. *J. Essential Oil Res.* 16: 195–199.

Boyle, T. H., et al. 1991. Growing medium and fertilization regime influence growth and essential oil content of rosemary. *HortScience* 26: 33–34.

Catalano, S., et al. 1993. Studio della resa e della composizione chimica di oli essenziali ottenuti da pianta intera, rami e foglie con fiori di *Rosmarinus officinalis* L. *Rivista Ital. EPPOS* 1993(10): 17–19.

Celiktas, O. Y., et al. 2007. In vitro antioxidant activities of *Rosmarinus officinalis* extracts treated with supercritical carbon dioxide. *Food Chem.* 101: 1457–1464.

———. 2007. Screening of free radical scavenging capacity and antioxidant activities of *Rosmarinus officinalis* extracts with focus on location and harvesting times. *Eur. Food Res. Technol.* 224: 443–451.

———. 2007. Antimicrobial activities of methanol extracts and essential oils of *Rosmarinus officinalis*, depending on location and seasonal variations. *Food Chem.* 100: 553–559.

Centeno, L. M. M. 2002. Plantas medicinales Españolas. *Rosmarinus officinalis* L. (Lamiaceae) (romero). *Stud. Bot.* 21: 105–118.

Chalchat, J.-C., et al. 1933. Essential oils of rosemary (*Rosmarinus officinalis* L.). The chemical composition of oils of various origins (Morocco, Spain, France). *J. Essential Oil Res.* 5: 613–618.

Chan, M. M.-Y., et al. 1995. Effects of three dietary phytochemicals from tea, rosemary, and turmeric on inflammation-induced nitrite production. *Cancer Lett.* 96: 23–29.

Chang, S. S., et al. 1977. Natural antioxidants from rosemary and sage. *J. Food Sci.* 42: 1102–1106.

Charlesworth, S. 2001. Dew of the sea. *Garden* (London) 126(4): 266–269.

Cioni, P. L., et al. 1991. Indagine preliminare su una coltivazione di *Rosmarinus officinalis* L. in provincia de Pisa: caratterizzazione dell'olio essenziale. *Rivista Ital. EPPOS* 1991(3): 3–6.

———. 1993. Indagine su una coltivazione di *Rosmarinus officinalis* L. in provincia di Pisa: studio della variabilità della resa e della composizione chimica dell'olio essenziale. *Rivista Ital. EPPOS* 1993(9): 31–33.

Cuvelier, M.-E., et al. 1996. Antioxidative activity and phenolic composition of pilot-plant and commercial extracts of sage and rosemary. *J. Amer. Oil Chem. Soc.* 73: 645–652.

DeBaggio, T. 1988. Growing rosemary: an herb to plant for many reasons. *Fine Gard.* 2: 51–55.

Dellacassa, E., et al. 1999. *Rosmarinus officinalis* L. (Labiatae) essential oils from the south of Brazil and Uruguay. *J. Essential Oil Res.* 11: 27–30.

De Mastro, G., et al. 2004. Bio-morphological and chemical characterization of rosemary (*Rosmarinus officinalis* L.) biotypes. *Acta Hort.* 629: 471–482.

Diab, Ya., et al. 2002. Chemical composition of Lebanese rosemary (*Rosmarinus officinalis* L.) essential oil as a function of the geographical region and the harvest time. *J. Essential Oil Res.* 14: 449–452.

Domokos, J., et al. 1997. Essential oil of rosemary (*Rosmarinus officinalis* L.) of Hungarian origin. *J. Essential Oil Res.* 9: 41–45.

Elamrani, A., et al. 2000. A study of Moroccan rosemary oils. *J. Essential Oil Res.* 12: 487–495.

El Naggar, H. M., et al. 2005. Rosmarinic acid (RA) content in leaves and callus of five different rosemary genotypes. *HortScience* 40: 1062.

El-Shattory, Y., et al. 2005. Effect of rosemary leaves on autoxidation of purified corn and soybean triacylglycerols. *Egypt. J. Chem.* 48: 155–167.

Estévez, M., and R. Cava. 2006. Effectiveness of rosemary essential oil as an inhibitor of lipid and protein oxidation: contradictory effects in different types of frankfurters. *Meat Sci.* 72: 348–355.

Fahin, F. A., et al. 1999. Allied studies on the effect of *Rosmarinus officinalis* L. on experimental hepatotoxicity and mutagenesis. *Intern. J. Food Sci. Nutr.* 50: 413–427.

———. 2005. Influence of the addition of rosemary essential oil on the volatiles pattern of porcine frankfurters. *J. Agric. Food Chem.* 53: 8317–8324.

———. 2005. Protein oxidation in frankfurters with increasing levels of added rosemary essential oil: effect on color and texture deterioration. *J. Food Sci.* 70: C427-C432.

Falchi Delitala, L., and F. Soccolini. 1980. Ricerche sul *Rosmarinus officinalis* Linnaeus di Sardegna. *Rivista Ital. EPPOS* 62: 195–201.

Fehr, D., and G. Stenxhorn. 1979. Untersuchungen zur Lagerstabilität von Pfefferminzblättern, Rosmarinblättern und Thymian. *Pharm. Zeitung* 124: 2342–2349.

Flamini, G., et al. 2002. Main agronomic-productive characteristics of two ecotypes of *Rosmarinus officinalis* L. and chemical composition of their essential oils. *J. Agric. Food Chem.* 50: 3512–3517.

Formácek, V., and K.-H. Kubeczka. 1982. *Essential Oil Analysis by Capillary Gas Chromatography and Carbon-13 NMR Spectroscopy.* New York: John Wiley & Sons.

Fournier, G., et al. 1989. Étude de divers échatillons d'huile essentielle de romarin de Tunisie. *Pl. Med. Phytotherap.* 23: 180–185.

Frutos, M. J., and J. A. Hernández-Herrero. 2005. Effects of rosemary extract (*Rosmarinus officinalis*) on the stability of bread with an oil, garlic and parsley dressing. *LWT* 38: 651–655.

Gaviña Mugica, M. de, and J. T. Ochoa. 1974. *Contribucion al Estudio de los Aceites Esenciales Españoles. II. Aceites Esenciales de la Provincia de Guadalajara.* Madrid: Inst. Nac. Invest. Agrarias.

Granger, R., et al. 1973. L'essence de *Rosmarinus officinalis*. Influence du mode de traitement de material vegetal. *Parfums Cosmétiques Savons France* 3(3): 133–138.

———. 1973. L'essence de *Rosmarinus officinalis* L. II. Influence des facteurs écologiques et individuels. *Parfums Cosmétiques Savons France* 3(6): 307–312.

Grayer, S. 2006. New cultivar descriptions. *Hanburyana* 1: 17.

Gjuazzi, E., et al. 2001. *Rosmarinus officinalis* L. in the Gravine of Palagianello (Taranto, South Italy). *J. Essential Oil Res.* 13: 231–233.

Hernández, C. M. L., et al. 2001. Multiplicación vegetativa de *Rosmarinus officinalis* L. (romero). *Rev. Cubana Pl. Med.* 2001(3): 79–82.

Herrera, J. 2005. Flower size variation in *Rosmarinus officinalis*: individuals, populations and habitats. *Ann. Bot.* 95: 431–437.

Héthelyi, É., et al. 1987. GC/MS investigations of the essential oils *Rosmarinus officinalis* L. *Acta Pharm. Hung.* 57: 159–169.

Ho, C.-T., et al. 1998. Antioxidative and antitumorigenic properties of rosemary. In *Functional Foods for Disease Prevention II. Medicinal Plants and Other Foods.* Ed. T. Shibamoto et al. Washington, D.C.: Amer. Chem. Soc. 153–161.

Hoefler, C., et al. 1987. Comparative choleretic and hepatoprotective properties of young sprouts and total plant extracts of *Rosmarinus officinalis* in rats. *J. Ethnopharmacol.* 19: 133–143.

Holcomb, G. E. 1992. Web blight of rosemary caused by *Rhizoctonia solani* AG-1. *Pl. Dis.* 76: 859–860.

Hori, M. 1998. Repellency of rosemary oil against *Myzus persicae* in a laboratory and in a screenhouse. *J. Chem. Ecol.* 24: 1425–1432.

Ikeda, R. M., et al. 1962. The monoterpene hydrocarbon composition of some essential oils. *J. Food Sci.* 27: 455–458.

Jirovetz, L., et al. 2005. Antimicrobial testings and gas chromatographic analysis of pure oxygenated monoterpenes 1,8-cineole, α-terpineol, terpinen-4-ol and camphor as well as target compounds in essential oils of pine (*Pinus pinaster*), rosemary (*Rosmarinus officinalis*), tea tree (*Melaleuca alternifolia*). *Sci. Pharm.* 73: 27–39.

Karawya, M. S., et al. 1970. Essential oils of certain labiaceous plants of Egypt. *Amer. Perfumer Cosmetics* 85(8): 23–28.

Katerinopoulos, H., et al. 2005. Composition and insect attracting activity of the essential oil of *Rosmarinus officinalis. J. Chem. Ecol.* 31: 111–122.

Koedam, A. 1982. Composition of the volatile oils from Dalmatian rosemary and sage: influence of the method of isolation on terpene patterns. *Fitoterapia* 53: 125–141.

Koedam, A., et al. 1980. Comparison of isolation procedures for essential oils. Part 6.

Rosemary and sage. *Riechstoffe Aromen Kosmetik* 1980: 271–276.

Koga, K., et al. 2006. Effects of 50% ethanol extract from rosemary (*Rosmarinus officinalis*) on α-glucosidase inhibitory activity and the elevation of plasma glucose level in rats, and its active compound. *J. Food Sci.* 71: S507–S512.

Kovar, K. A., et al. 1987. Blood levels of 1,8-cineole and locomotor activity of mice after inhalation and oral administration of rosemary oil. *Pl. Med.* 1987: 315–318.

Kreis, P., et al. 1994. Chiral compounds of essential oils. Part 18: on the authenticity assessment of the essential oil of *Rosmarinus officinalis* L. *Pharmazie* 49: 761–765.

Kumar, N., and R. Arumugan. 1980. Effect of growth regulators on rooting of rosemary (*Rosmarinus officinalis* L.). *Indian Perfumer* 24: 210–213.

Kumar, N., et al. 2004. Composition of oil from rosemary (*Rosmarinus officinalis* L.) grown in Kumaon hills of Uttaranchal. *Indian Perfumer* 48: 411–414.

Lacroix, M., et al. 1997. Prevention of lipid radiolysis by natural antioxidants from rosemary (*Rosmarinus officinalis* L.) and thyme (*Thymus vulgaris* L.). *Food Res. Intern.* 30: 457–462.

Lamparsky, D., and H. P. Schenk. 1982. Analyse des Rosmarinols. In *Ätherische Ole: Analytik, Physiologie, Zusammensetzung, etc.* Ed. K.-H. Kubeczka. Stuttgart: Georg Thieme Verlag. 136–148.

Lemberkovics, E., et al. 1988. Gas chromatographic determination of mono- and sesquiterpenes in some commercial Hungarian essential oils. In *Flavor and Fragrances: A World Perspective.* Ed. B. M. Lawrence et al. Amsterdam: Elsevier. 243–245.

Lemonica, I. P., et al. 1996. Study of the embryotoxic effects of an extract of rosemary (*Rosmarinus officinalis* L.). *Braz. J. Med. Biol. Res.* 29: 223–227.

Liu, X.-sh., et al. 2004. Progress on research of natural rosemary antioxidant. *Chem. Industr. Forest Prod.* 24S: 132–138.

Maness, N. E., and J. E. Motes. 1991. Propagating rosemary (*Rosmarinus officinalis*) by cuttings. *HortScience* 26: 487.

Mangena, T., and N. Y. O. Muyima. 1999. Comparative evaluation of the antimicrobial activities of essential oils of *Artemisia afra*, *Pteronia incana* and *Rosmarinus officinalis* on selected bacteria and yeast strains. *Lett. Appl. Microbiol.* 28: 291–296.

Martinetti, L., et al. 2006. Effect of the mineral fertilization on the yield and the oil content of two cultivars of rosemary. *Acta Hort.* 723: 399–405.

Martinez-González, M. C., et al. 2007. Concomitant allergic contact dermatitis due to *Rosmarinus officinalis* (rosemary) and *Thymus vulgaris* (thyme). *Contact Dermatitis* 56: 49–50.

Marzouk, Z., et al. 2006. Chemical composition, antibacterial and antimutagenic activities of four populations of *Rosmarinus officinalis* L. oils from Tunisia. *J. Food Agric. Environm.* 4: 89–94.

———. 2006. Chemical composition and antibacterial and antimutagenic activity of Tunisian *Rosmarinus officinalis* L. oil from Kasrine. *J. Food Agric. Environm.* 4: 61–65.

Masuda, T. 2004. Antioxidant mechanism of the potent diterpenoid antioxidants found in sage and rosemary. *Food Food Ingred.* 10: 858–865.

McCormick, K. A., et al. 2006. Effect of sample preparation on the amounts of α-pinene and verbenone extracted from rosemary. *J. Essential Oil Res.* 18: 478–480.

McCue, P. P., and K. Shetty. 2004. Inhibitory effects of rosmarinic acid extracts on porcine pancreatic amylase *in vitro*. *Asia Pasific J. Clin. Nutr.* 13: 101–106.

Miguel, G., et al. 1999. Study of the substrate and fertilization effects on the production of essential oils of *Rosmarinus officinalis* L. cultivated in pots. In *Improved Crop Quality by Nutrient Management.* Ed. D. Anaç and P. Martin-Prével. Dordrecht: Kluwer Acad. Publ. 185–188.

Miresmailli, S., et al. 2006. Comparative toxicity of *Rosmarinus officinalis* L. essential oil and blends of its major constituents against *Tetranychus urticae* Koch (Acari: Tetranychidae) on two different host plants. *Pest Managm.* 62: 366–371.

Mizrahi, I., et al. 1991. The essential oil of *Rosmarinus officinalis* growing in Argentina. *J. Essential Oil Res.* 3: 11–15.

Momen, F. M., and S. A. Amer. 1999. Effect of rosemary and sweet marjoram on three predacious mites of the family Phytoseiidae (Acari: Phytoseiidae). *Acta Phytopathol. Entomol. Hung.* 34: 355–361.

Mookherjee, B. D., et al. 1989. New dimensions in flavour research: herbs and spices. In *Flavor Chemistry: Trends and Developments.* Ed. R. Teranishi et al. Washington, D.C.: Amer. Chem. Soc. 176–187.

Mulas, G., and L. E. Craker. 2005. Effect of light quality on growth and essential oil composition of rosemary. *HortScience* 40: 1062.

Mulè, A., et al. 1996. Studio della resa e della composizione chimica dell'olio essenziale di *Rosmarinus officinalis* L. spontaneo di Cala Gonone (Sardegna). *Rivista Ital. EPPOS* 1996(19): 147–157.

Munné-Bosch, S., et al. 2000. The formation of phenolic diterpenes in *Rosmarinus officinalis* L. under Mediterranean climate. *Eur. Food Res. Technol.* 210: 263–267.

Murphy, A., et al. 1998. The antioxidative properties of rosemary oleoresin and inhibition of off-flavour in precooked roast beef slices. *J. Sci. Food Agric.* 77: 235–243.

Nakasuti, T., and K. Koma. 1996. Antimutagens in the leaves of *Rosmarinus officinalis* L. *Nat. Med.* 50: 354–357.

Nakatani, N., and R. Inatani. 1984. Antioxidative compounds of spices: diterpenes from rosemary and their activities. *Koryo* 143: 11–20.

———. 1984. Two antioxidative diterpenes from rosemary (*Rosmarinus officinalis* L.) and a revised structure of rosmanol. *Agric. Biol. Chem.* 48: 2081–2085.

Navarro, M. C., et al. 1993. Free radical scavenger and antihepatotoxic activity of *Rosmarinus tomentosus*. *Pl. Med.* 59: 312–314.

Okamura, N., et al. 1994. High-performance liquid chromatographic determination of carnosic acid and carnosol in *Rosmarinus officinalis* and *Salvia officinalis*. *J. Chromatogr. A* 679: 381–386.

———. 1994. Flavonoids in *Rosmarinus officinalis* leaves. *Phytochemistry* 37: 1463–1466.

Özcan, M. 1999. Antioxidant activity of rosemary (*Rosmarinus officinalis* L.) extracts on natural olive and sesame oil. *Grasas Aceites* 50: 355–358.

Palic, A., and Z. Dikanovin-Lucan. 1995. Antioxidative effect of "Herbalox" on edible oils. *Fat Sci. Technol.* 10: 379–381.

Panizzi, L., et al. 1993. Composition and antimicrobial properties of essential oils of four Mediterranean Lamiaceae. *J. Ethnopharmacol.* 39: 167–170.

Papageorgiou, V., et al. Variation of the chemical profile and antioxidant behavior of *Rosmarinus officinalis* L. and *Salvia fruticosa* Miller grown in Greece. *J. Agric. Food Chem.* 56: 7254–7264.

Pereira, C. G., and M. A. A. Meireles. 2007. Economic analysis of rosemary, fennel and anise essential oils obtained by supercritical fluid extraction. *Flavour Fragrance J.* 22: 407–413.

Pérez-Alonso, M., et al. 1995. Composition of the essential oils of *Ocimum basilicum* var. *glabratum* and *Rosmarinus officinalis* from Turkey. *J. Essential Oil Res.* 7: 73–75.

Perry, N., et al. 1996. European herbs with cholinergic activities: potential in dementia therapy. *Intern. J. Geriatric Psychiatry* 11: 1063–1069.

Pino, J. A., et al. 1998. Essential oil of rosemary (*Rosmarinus officinalis* L.) from Cuba. *J. Essential Oil Res.* 10: 111–112.

Pintore, G., et al. 2002. Chemical composition and antimicrobial activity of *Rosmarinus officinalis* L. oils from Sardinia and Corsica. *Flavour Fragrance J.* 17: 15–19.

Proença da Cunha, A., and O. R. Roque. 1986. Contribuição a o estudio do óleo essencial de alecrim nacional. II. Variações quantitativas dos principais constituintes durante a floracao da primavera. *Bol. Fac. Farm. Coimbra* 10: 5–13.

Putnam, M. L. 2004. First report of stem rot of rosemary caused by *Sclerotinia sclerotiorum* in the United States. *Pl. Pathol.* 53: 252.

Réblová, Z., et al. 1999. Effect of rosemary extract on the stabilization of frying oil during deep fat frying. *J. Food Lipids* 6: 13–23.

Rhyu, H. Y. 1979. Gas chromatographic characterization of oregano and other selected spices of the Labiatae family. *J. Food Sci.* 44: 1373–1378.

Richheimer, S. L., et al. 1996. Antioxidant activity of lipid-soluble phenolic diterpenes from rosemary. *J. Amer. Oil Chem. Soc.* 73: 507–514.

Rosúa, J. L. 1981. El complejo *Rosmarinus eriocalyx-tomentosus* en la Península Ibérica. *Anales Jard. Bot. Madrid* 37: 587–595.

———. 1985. Notas cariosistemáticazs del género *Rosmarinus* L. (Lamiaceae) en la Península Ibérica. *Anales Jard. Bot. Madrid* 42: 93–100.

———. 1986. Contribucion al estudio del genero *Rosmarinus* L. en el Mediterraneo Occidental. *Lagascalia* 14: 179–187.

Rosúa, J. L., and A. Garcia-Granados. 1987. Analyse des huiles essentielles d'espèces du genre *Rosmarinus* L. et leur intérêt en tant que caractère taxonomique. *Pl. Med. Phytotherap.* 21: 138–143.

Roussel, J.-L., et al. 1973. Propriétés antifongiques comparées des essences de trois Labiées méditerranéennes: romarin, sarriette et thym. *Trav. Soc. Pharm. Montpellier* 33: 587–592.

Saricoban, C., and M. Ozcan. 2004. Antioxidative activity of rosemary (*Rosmarinus officinalis* L.) and sage (*Salvia fruticosa* L.) essential oils in chicken fat. *J. Essential Oil-Bearing Pl.* 7: 94–95.

Shelef, L. A., et al. 1980. Sensitivity of some common food-borne bacteria to the spices sage, rosemary, and allspice. *J. Food Sci.* 45: 1042–1044.

Skrubis, B. G. 1972. Seven wild aromatic plants growing in Greece and their essential oils. *Flavor Industr.* 3: 566–568.

Soliman, F. M., et al. 1994. Analysis and biological activity of the essential oil of *Rosmarinus officinalis* from Egypt. *Flavour Fragrance J.* 9: 29–33.

Solinas, V., et al. 1996. Effects of water and nutritional conditions on the *Rosmarinus officinalis* L. phenolic fraction and essential oil yields. *Rivista Ital. EPPOS* 1996(19): 189–198.

Stefanovits-Bányai, É., et al. 2003. Antioxidant effect of various rosemary (*Rosmarinus officinalis* L.) clones. *Acta Biol. Szegediensis.* 47: 111–113.

Svoboda, K. P., and S. G. Deans. 1991. A study of the variability of rosemary and sage and their volatile oils on the British

market: their antioxidative properties. *Flavour Fragrance J.* 7: 81–87.

Tateo, F., et al. 1988. *Rosmarinus officinalis* L. extract production antioxidant and antimutagenic activity. *Perfumer Flavor.* 13(6): 48–54.

Tena, M. T., et al. 1997. Supercritical fluid extraction of natural antioxidants from rosemary: comparison with liquid solvent sonification. *Anal. Chem.* 69: 521–526.

Tomei, P. E., et al. 1995. Evaluation of the chemical composition of the essential oils of some Lamiaceae from Serrania de Ronda (Andaluçia, Spain). *J. Essential Oil Res.* 7: 279–282.

Trojáková, L., et al. 2001. Antioxidant activity of rosemary and sage extract in rapeseed oil. *J. Food Lipids* 8: 1–13.

Tuberoso, C. I. G., et al. 1998. Chemical composition of *Rosmarinus officinalis* oils of Sardinia. *J. Essential Oil Res.* 10: 660–664.

Tucker, A. O., and M. J. Maciarello. 1986. The essential oils of some rosemary cultivars. *Flavour Fragrance J.* 1: 137–142.

Upson, T. 2006. 551. *Rosmarinus eriocalyx*. *Curtis's Bot. Mag.* 23: 62–68.

Warnock, D., and C. Voigt. 2004. Evaluating rosemary cultivars for use as Christmas tree–shaped topiaries. *HortScience* 39: 860.

Westervelt, P. M., and H. L. Scogins. 2003. Challenges in the greenhouse production of rosemary (*Rosmarinus officinalis* L.). *HortScience* 38: 1270.

Zawirska-Wojtasiak, R., et al. 2005. Estimation of rosemary aroma by sensory analysis, gas chromatogrpahy and electronic nose. In *State-of-the-art in Flavor Chemistry and Biology.* Ed. T. Hofmann and M. Rothe. Garching, Germany: Deutsche Forsch. Lebensmittelchem. 130–136.

Ruta

Aboutabl, E. A., et al. 1988. The essential oil of *Ruta graveolens* L. growing in Egypt. *Sci. Pharm.* 56: 121–124.

Anonymous. 1992. Herb can help win whitefly battle. *Greenhouse Manager* 10(12): 59–60.

Anonymous. 2007. Rue. *Rev. Nat. Prod. (Wolters Kluwer Health).*

Arctander, S. 1960. *Perfume and Flavor Materials of Natural Origin.* Elizabeth, New Jersey: Steffen Arctander.

Bakewell, M. 1998. Toxicology of *Ruta graveolens. Austral. J. Med. Herbalism* 10: 23–25.

Classen, B., and K. Knobloch. 1985. Über die ätherischen Öle der Weinraute (*Ruta graveolens* L.). *Z. Lebensm. Unters. Forsch.* 181: 28–31.

Dall'acqua, F., et al. 1973. Ricerche sul contenuto della *Ruta graveolens* in psoralene, bergaptene e xantotossina. *Atti Ist. Veneto Sci., Lett. Arti, Cl. Sci. Mat. Nat.* 131: 17–27.

De Feo, V., et al. 2002. Potential allelochemicals from the essential oil of *Ruta graveolens. Phytochemistry* 61: 573–578.

International Fragrance Association. 1989. *Code of Practice.* Geneva: IFRA.

Kong, Y. C., et al. 1989. Antifertility principle of *Ruta graveolens. Pl. Med.* 55: 176–178.

Kubeczka, K. H. 1971. Die ätherischen Öle verschiedener *Ruta*-Arten. *Herb Hung.* 10: 109–117.

Mouna, B. H. F., et al. 2007. Analysis of Tunisian *Ruta graveolens* L. oils from Jemmel. *Intern. J. Food Agric. Environm.* 5: 52–55.

Opdyke, D. L. J. 1975. Monographs on fragrance raw materials. *Food Cosmet. Toxicol.* 13: 449–457.

Petit-Paly, G., et al. 1982. Étude de quelques rutacées a alcaloides II.-*Ruta graveolens*: Revue botanique, chimique et pharmacologique (Étude particulière des alcaloides quaternaires quinoléiques). *Pl. Med. Phytotherap.* 16: 55–72.

———. 1989. *Ruta gravolens*: in vitro production of alkaloids and medicinal compounds. In *Biotechnology in Agriculture and Forestry 7. Medicinal and Aromatic Plants II.* Ed. Y. P. S. Bajaj. Berlin: Springer-Verlag. 488–505.

Pino, J. A., et al. 1995. Leaf oil of *Ruta graveolens* L. grown in Cuba. *J. Essential Oil Res.* 9: 365–366.

San Miguel, E. 2003. Rue (*Ruta* L., Rutaceae) in traditional Spain: frequency and distribution of its medicinal and symbolic applications. *Econ. Bot.* 57: 231–244.

Stashenko, E. E., et al. 1995. Comparative study of Colombian rue oils by high resolution gas chromatography using different detection systems. *J. Microcol. Sep.* 7: 117–122.

Tabata, H., et al. 2005. Hair-growing activity in the extract of *Ruta graveolens* L. *Fragrance J.* 12: 58–62.

Tanker, M., et al. 1993. Results of certain investigations on the volatile oil-containing plants of Turkey. In *Essential Oils for Perfumery and Flavour. Proceedings of an International Conference 26–30 May 1990 Antalya, Turkey.* Ed. K. H. C. Baser and N. Güler. Istanbul. 16–29.

Townsend, C. C. 1968. *Ruta.* In *Flora Europaea Vol. 2.* Ed. T. G. Tutin et al. Cambridge Univ. Press. 227.

Xu, H., et al. 1994. Preliminary studies on insecticidal activity of the rue oil and analysis of its components. *Tainran Chanwu Yanjiu Yu Kaifa* 6(4): 56–61.

Salvia

Adams, R., and T. Yanke. 2007. Clary sage oils. *Perfumer Flavor.* 32(9): 36–39.

Aiello, N., et al. 2001. Caratterischtiche morfologiche, produttive e qualitative di una nuova varietà sintetica di *Salvia* confrontata con alter cultivar. *ISAFA Commun. Ricerca* 2001(1): 5–16.

Akhondzadeh, S., et al. 2003. *Salvia officinalis* extract in the treatment of patients with mild to moderate Alzheimer's disease: a double blind, randomized and placebo-controlled trial. *J. Clin. Pharm. Therapeutics* 28: 53–59.

Alziar, G. 1988. Rectifications nomenclature et chorologiques dans les genres *Salvia* L. (Lamiaceae) et *Kickxia* Dumort. (Scrophulariaceae). *Biocosme Mésogéen, Nice* 5(3–4): 85–86.

———. 1988. Catalogue synonymique des *Salvia* L. du monde (Lamiaceae). I. *Biocosme Mésogéen, Nice* 5(3–4): 87–136.

———. 1989. Rectifications nomenclatures dans le genre *Salvia*. Catalogue synonymique des *Salvia* du monde. II. *Biocosme Mésogéen, Nice* 6(1–2): 79–115.

———. 1989. Catalogue synonymique des *Salvia* L. (Lamiaceae). III. *Biocosme Mésogéen, Nice* 6(4): 163–204.

———. 1990. Catalogue synonymique des *Salvia* L. (Lamiaceae). IV. *Biocosme Mésogéen, Nice* 7(1–2): 59–109.

Andrews, A. C. 1956. Sage as a condiment in the Graeco-Roman era. *Econ. Bot.* 10: 263–266.

Anonymous. 2004. Sage. *Rev. Nat. Prod. (Wolters Kluwer Health)*.

Arikat, N. A., et al. 2004. Micropropagation and accumulation of essential oils in wild sage (*Salvia fruticosa* Mill.). *Sci. Hort.* 100: 193–202.

Asllani, U. 2000. Chemical composition of Albanian sage oil (*Salvia officinalis* L.). *J. Essential Oil Res.* 12: 79–84.

Bandonienė, D., et al. 2002. Antioxidative activity of sage (*Salvia officinalis* L.), savory (*Satureja hortensis* L.) and borage (*Borago officinalis* L.) extracts in rapeseed oil. *Eur. J. Lipid Sci. Technol.* 104: 286–292.

Baratta, M. T., et al. 1998. Chemical composition, antimicrobial and antioxidative activity of laurel, sage, rosemary, oregano and coriander essential oils. *J. Essential Oil Res.* 10: 618–627.

Baricevic, D., et al. 2001. Topical anti-inflammatory activity of *Salvia officinalis* L. leaves: the relevance of ursolic acid. *J. Ethnopharmacol.* 75: 125–132.

Baser, K., et al. 1993. The essential oil of *Salvia pomifera* L. *J. Essential Oil Res.* 5: 347–348.

Bayrak, A., and A. Akgül. 1987. Composition of essential oils from Turkish *Salvia* species. *Phytochemistry* 26: 846–847.

Bélafi-Réthy, et al. 1975. Untersuchung der Zusammensetzung von eiheimischen und ausländischen ätherischen Ölen, V. Beiträge zur Zusammensetzung des Lavandinöles und des Muskateller Salbeiöles. *Acta Chim. Acad. Sci. Hung.* 87: 105–119.

Bezzi, A. 1987. Prova di concimazione di *Salvia officinalis* L. (Villazzano, Trento). In *Atti convegno sulla coltivazione delle piante officinali, Trento, 9–10 October 1986.* 315–335.

———. 1988. La coltivazione della salvia (*Salvia officinalis* L.). *Ann. Ist. Sperim. Assestamento For. Alpicoltura* 9: 265–304.

———. 1996. Selezione clonale e costituzione di varietà di salvia (*Salvia officinalis* L.). In *Atti convegno internazionale: coltivazione e miglioramento di piante officinali, Trento, Italy, 2–3 June 1994.* 97–117.

Biondi, D., et al. 1993. Antimicrobial activity and chemical composition of essential oils from Sicilian aromatic plants. *Flavour Fragrance J.* 8: 331–337.

Bodor, Zs., et al. 2006. Produktionspotenzial ein- und zweijähriger Formen des Muskatellersalbeis (*Salvia sclarea* L.) und Einfluss unerschiedlicher Aussaatzeiten. *Z. Arzn. Gew. Pfl.* 11: 40–47.

Boelens, M. H., and H. Boelens. 1997. Chemical and sensory evaluation of three sage oils. *Perfumer Flavor.* 22(2): 19–40.

Böttcher, H., et al. 2002. Quantitative Veränderungen der Wirkstoffe des Salbei (*Salvia officinalis* L.) während der Nacherntezeit. *Z. Arzn. Gew. Pfl.* 7: 382–386.

Bowden, R. A. 1944. Commercial sage production in Georgia. *Market Growers J.* 73: 198, 203.

Brieskorn, C. H., and S. Dalferth. 1964. Die Mono- und Sesquiterpenoide ätherischer Salbeiöle. Ein Beitrag zur arzneilichen Bewertung von *Salvia officinalis*, *Salvia lavandulaefolia*, und *Salvia triloba*. *Deutsche Apotheker-Zeitung* 104: 1388–1392.

Čanadanović, J. M., et al. 2001. ESR spectroscopic charaterization of free radicals, peroxyl radical scavenging activity of sage during lipid oxidation. *APTEFF* 31: 3–11.

Carlen, C., et al. 2006. Sauge officinale: effets de la fréquence des récoltes, de la hauteur et de la date de la dernière coupe avant l'hiver sur la productivité et la qualité. *Rev. Suisse Vitic. Arbor. Hort.* 38: 315–320.

Carruba, A., et al. 2002. Characterization of an Italian biotype of clary sage (*Salvia sclarea* L.) grown in a semi-arid Mediterranean environment. *Flavour Fragrance J.* 17: 191–194.

———. 2003. Four years of observations on the major bio-agronomical and qualitative traits in clary sage (*Salvia sclarea* L.). *Agroindustria* 2: 87–89.

———. 2006. Modifications over years of volatile compounds and agronomic features in a Sicilian clary sage biotype. *Acta Hort.* 723: 203–206.

Catsiotis, S., and N. G. Iconomou. 1984. Qualitative and quantitative comparative gas-liquid-chromatographic analysis of the essential oil of *Salvia triloba* grown in Greece. *Pharm. Acta Helv.* 59: 29–32.

Cenci, C. A., and I. Clavarano. 1967. Caratteristiche degli olii essenziali di alcune salvie perugine. *Essenze Deriv. Agrumari* 37: 141–178.

Ceschel, G. C., et al. 1998. *In vitro* permeation through porcine buccal mucosa of *Salvia sclarea* L. essential oil from topical formulations. *S. T. P. Pharma Sci.* 8(2): 103–106.

Chalchat, J. C., al. 1998. Study of clones of *Salvia officinalis* L. yields and chemical composition of essential oil. *Flavour Fragrance J.* 13: 68–70.

Chang, S. S., et al. 1977. Natural antioxidants from rosemary and sage. *J. Food Sci.* 42: 1102–1106.

Chiumenti, R., and F. da Borso. 1996. Essiccazione artificiale di cimette di salvia: resultati di prove sperimentali. In *Atti convegno internazionale: coltivazione e miglioramento di piante officinali, Trento, Italy, 2–3 June 1994.* 381–390.

Chiumenti, R., et al. 1996. Un prototipo di attrezzatura per la selezione foglia-stelo delle piante officinali. In *Atti convegno internazionale: coltivazione e miglioramento di piante officinali, Trento, Italy, 2–3 June 1994.* 475–480.

Clebsch, B. 1997. *A Book of Salvias: Sages for Every Garden*. Portland, Oregon: Timber Press.

———. 2003. *The New Book of Salvias: Sages for Every Garden*. Portland, Oregon: Timber Press.

Colin, M. E. 1990. Essential oils of Labiatae for controlling honey bee varroosis. *J. Appl. Entomol.* 110: 19–25.

Colsson, M., et al. 1985. L'essence de sauge sclarée (*Salvia sclarea* L.). *Parfums, Cosmétiques, Arômes* 66: 53–58.

Couladis, M., et al. 2002. Essential oil of *Salvia officinalis* L. from Serbia and Montenegro. *Flavour Fragrance J.* 17: 119–126.

Crespo, M. E., et al. 1986. The essential oil of *Salvia lavandulifolia* subspecies *oxyodon*: a study of its vegetative cycle. *Pl. Med.* 5: 367–369.

Cuvelier, M.-E., et al. 1994. Separation of major antioxidants in sage by high performance liquid chromatography. *Sci. Aliments* 14: 811–815.

———. 1994. Antioxidant constituents in sage (*Salvia officinalis*). *J. Agric. Food Chem.* 42: 665–669.

———. 1996. Antioxidative activity and phenolic composition of pilot-plant and commercial extracts of sage and rosemary. *J. Amer. Oil Chem. Soc.* 73: 645–652.

D'Antuono, L. F., et al. 2002. Investigation of individual variability of sage (*Salvia officinalis* L.) based on morphological and chemical evaluation. *Acta Hort.* 576: 181–187.

de Gavina Mugica, M., et al. 1969. L'huile essentielle de sauge espagnole (*Salvia lavandulifolia*, Vahl.)—oleum salviae. *Parfumerie Cosmétique Savons* 12: 334–344.

Delamare, A. P. L., et al. 2007. Antibacterial activity of the essential oils of *Salvia officinalis* L. and *Salvia triloba* L. cultivated in South Brazil. *Food Chem.* 100: 603–608.

De Mastro, G., et al. 2006. Herbage yield and essential oil quality of three cultivars of sage (*Salvia officinalis* L.) grown in two Italian environments. *Acta Hort.* 723: 233–236.

Dobos, Á., et al. 1997. Comparative analysis of *Salvia officinalis* and *Salvia tomentosa* essential oils. In *Essential Oils: Basic and Applied Research*. Ed. Ch. Franz et al. Carol Stream, Illinois: Allured. 241–243.

Doran, W. L., and A. M. Davis. 1942. Propagation of sage by cuttings. *Amer. Nurseryman* 76(5): 12.

Drain, B. D., et al. 1949. A preliminary report on the yield and oil content of clonal strains of garden sage. *Proc. Amer. Soc. Hort. Sci.* 53: 371–374.

Dudai, N., et al. 1999. Dynamics of yield components and essential oil production in a commercial hybrid sage (*Salvia officinalis* × *Salvia fruticosa* cv. Newe Ya'ar No. 4. *J. Agric. Food Chem.* 47: 4341–4345.

Dzumayev, K., et al. 1995. Essential oils of *Salvia sclarea* L. produced from plants grown in southern Uzbekistan. *J. Essential Oil Res.* 7: 597–604.

Edris, A. E., et al. 2007. Chemical composition, antimicrobial activities and olfactive evaluation of a *Salvia officinalis* L. (sage) essential oil from Egypt. *J. Essential Oil Res.* 19: 186–189.

Elder, H. V., and J. A. Retamar. 1993. Comportamiento de la *Salvia officinalis* L. en la provincia de Santa Fe, Argentina. *Essenze Derivati Agrumari* 63: 191–195.

Elementi, S., et al. 2006. *Salvia officinalis* L. essential oil and carnosic acid analysis by means of NIR spectroscopy. *Acta Hort.* 723: 243–247.

Elnir, O., et al. 1991. The chemical composition of two clary sage chemotypes and their hybrids. *Flavour Fragrance J.* 6: 153–155.

Embong, M. B., et al. 1977. Essential oils from herb and spices grown in Alberta. Sage oil, *Salvia officinalis*, L. (Labiatae). *J. Inst. Canad. Sci. Technol. Aliment.* 10: 201–207.

Epling, C. 1938. The Californian salvias: a review of *Salvia*, section Audibertia. *Ann. Missouri Bot. Gard.* 25: 95–188.

———. 1938–39. A revision of *Salvia*, subgenus Calosphace. *Repert. Spec. Nov. Regni Veg. Beih.* 110: 1–383.

Fellah, S., et al. 2006. Chemical composition and antioxidant properties of *Salvia*

officinalis L. oil from two culture sites in Tunisia. *J. Essential Oil Res.* 18: 553–556.

Fournier, G., et al. 1993. Contribution to the study of *Salvia lavandulifolia* essential oil: potential toxicity attributable to sabinyl acetate. *Pl. Med.* 59: 96–97.

Gali-Muhtasib, H. U., and N. I. Affara. 2000. Chemoprotective effects of sage oil on skin papillomas in mice. *Phytomedicine* 7: 129–136.

Grassi, P., et al. 2004. A direct liquid, non-equilibrium solid-phase micro-extraction application for analyzing chemical variation of single peltate trichomes on leaves of *Salvia officinalis*. *Phytochem. Anal.* 15: 198–203.

Guillén, M. D., and M. L. Ibargoitia. 1995. Wild growing Spanish sage as a raw material in the food industry. Study of gas chromatography/mass spectrometry of its essential oil and extracts in several organic solvents. *Chem. Mikrobiol. Technol. Lebensm.* 17: 129–134.

Guillén, M. D., and M. J. Manzanos. 1999. Extractable components of the aerial parts of *Salvia lavandulifolia* and compositions of the liquid smoke flavour obtained from them. *J. Agric. Food Chem.* 47: 3016–3027.

Halim, A. F., and R. P. Collins. 1975. Essential oil of *Salvia dorisiana* (Standley). *J. Agric. Food Chem.* 23: 506–510.

Hanson, W. I., and G. M. Hocking. 1957. Garden sage. *Econ. Bot.* 11: 64–74.

Hedge, I. C. 1957. Studies in east Mediterranean species of *Salvia*. *Notes Roy. Bot. Gard. Edinburgh* 22: 173–188.

———. 1959. Studies in east Mediterranean species of *Salvia*: II. *Notes Roy. Bot. Gard. Edinburgh* 23: 47–69.

———. 1960. Notes on some cultivated species of *Salvia*. *J. Roy. Hort. Soc.* 85: 451–454.

———. 1965. Studies in the flora of Afghanistan III. An account of *Salvia*. *Notes Roy. Bot. Gard. Edinburgh* 26: 407–425.

———. 1969. *Salvia*. In *The Royal Horticultural Society Supplement to the Dictionary of Gardening: A Practical and Scientific Encyclopaedia of Horticulture*. 2nd ed. Ed. P. M. Synge. Oxford: Clarendon Press. 497–504.

———. 1972. *Salvia*. In *Flora Europaea Vol. 3*. Ed. T. G. Tutin et al. Cambridge Univ. Press. 188–192.

———. 1974. A revision of *Salvia* in Africa including Madagascar and the Canary Islands. *Notes Roy. Bot. Gard. Edinburgh* 33: 1–121.

———. 1982. *Salvia*. In *Flora of Turkey and the East Aegean Islands*. Ed. P. H. Davis. Edinburgh: Univ. Press. 400–461.

Héthelyi, É., et al. 1996. Muskotálysálya (*Salvia sclarea* L.) illóolajok kapillár

gázkromatográfiás vizsgálata. *Olaj Szappan Kosmetika* 45: 156–160.

Jalsenjak, V., et al. 1987. Microcapsules of sage oil: essential oils content and antimicrobial activity. *Pharmazie Beih. Ergänzungsband* 42: 419–420.

Jiménez, I., et al. 1995. Effects of *Salvia lavandulifolia* Vahl. ssp. *oxyodon* extract on pancreatic endocrine tissue in streptozotocin-diabetic rats. *Phytotherapy Res.* 9: 536–537.

Jirovets, L., et al. 2006. Chemical composition, antimicrobial activities and odor descriptions of various *Salvia* sp. and *Thuja* sp. essential oils. *Ernährung/Nutrition* 30: 152–159.

Kanias, G. D., et al. 1998. Statistical study of essential oil composition in three cultivated sage species. *J. Essential Oil Res.* 10: 395–403.

Karioti, A., et al. 2003. Effect of nitrogen concentration of the nutrient solution on the volatile constituents of leaves of *Salvia fruticosa* Mill. in solution culture. *J. Agric. Food Chem.* 51: 6506–6508.

Karousou, R., and S. Kokkini. 1997. Distribution and clinal variation of *Salvia fruticosa* Mill. (Labiatae) on the island of Crete (Greece). *Willdenowia* 27: 113–120.

Karousou, R., et al. 1998. Distribution and essential oils of *Salvia pomifera* subsp. *pomifera* (Labiatae) on the island of Crete (S Greece). *Biochem. Syst. Ecol.* 26: 889–897.

———. 1998. Variation of *Salvia fruticosa* essential oils on the island of Crete (Greece). *Bot. Acta* 111: 250–254.

Kedzia, B., et al. 1990. Chemical content and antimicroorganism activity of sage essential oil (*Ol. Salviae*). *Herba Pol.* 36(4): 155–164.

Kintzios, S. E., ed. 2000. *Sage: The Genus Salvia*. Netherlands: Harwood Acad. Publ.

Köhlein, F. 1998. Gartensalbei, universelle Nutz- und Zierpflanze. *Gartenpraxis* 1998: 20–23.

Koike, S. T., and D. M. Henderson. 1997. Phytophthora root and crown rot of sage caused by *Phytophthora cryptogea* in California. *Pl. Dis.* 81: 959.

Kokkalou, E., et al. 1982. Composition de l'huile essentielle de *Salvia horminum* L. (Labiatae). *Pharm. Acta Helv.* 57: 317–320.

Kovatcheva, N., and V. D. Zheljazkov. 1997. Essential oil content and components of *Salvia officinalis* L. from Bulgaria. In *Essential Oils: Basic and Applied Research*. Ed. Ch. Franz et al. Carol Stream, Illinois: Allured. 237–239.

Landi, R., and G. Bertone. 1996. Tecniche seguite nella costituzione di una varietà sintetica di *Salvia officinalis* L. In *Atti convegno internazionale: coltivazione e miglioramento di piante officinali, Trento, Italy, 2–3 June 1994*. 667–672.

Länger, R. 1997. Blattanatomie europäischer und kleinasiatischer *Salvia*-Arten. *Pharmazie* 52: 64–70.

Länger, R., et al. 1991. Mikroskopische Identifizierung von Arzneidrogen pharmazeutisch wichtiger Salbei-Arten. *Sci. Pharm.* 59: 321–331.

———. 1992. Quality control of folium salviae by GC analysis of the essential oil. *Pl. Med.* 58: A677.

———. 1993. Differences of the composition of the essential oil within an individuum of *Salvia officinalis*. *Pl. Med.* 59: A635-A636.

———. 1996. Composition of the essential oils of commercial samples of *Salvia officinalis* L. and *S. fruticosa* Miller: a comparison of oils obtained by extraction and steam distillation. *Phytochem. Anal.* 7: 289–293.

Lawrence, B. M. 1992. Chemical components of Labiatae oils and their exploitation. In *Advances in Labiate Science*. Ed. R. M. Harley and T. Reynolds. Richmond, England: RBG Kew. 399–436.

Lawrence, B. M., et al. 1970. Essential oils and their constituents. III. Some new trace constituents in the essential oil of *Salvia lavandulaefolia* Vahl. *J. Chromatogr.* 50: 59–65.

Lazreg, H., et al. 2007. Chemical composition of Tunisian *Salvia officinalis* essential oil. *J. Soc. Alger. Chem.* 17: 43–50.

Lees, P. D. 1980. *Culinary and Medicinal Herbs*. 4th ed. Minist. Agric. Fish. Food Ref. Book 325.

Leffingwell, J. C., et al. 1974. Clary sage production in the southeastern United States. In *VI International Congress of Essential Oils, San Francisco, California, September 8–12, 1974*. Paper no. 3.

Li, Y.-I., et al. 1996. Effect of light level on essential oil production of sage (*Salvia officinalis*) and thyme (*Thymus vulgaris*). *Acta Hort.* 426: 419–426.

Lokar, L. C., and M. Moneghini. 1990. Terpenes of *Salvia* species leaf oils: chemosystematic implications. *Studia Geobotanica* 10: 105–117.

Lovejoy, A. 2001. *The Sage Garden*. San Francisco: Chronicle Books.

Makino, T., et al. 1996. Aroma components of pineapple-scented sage (*Salvia elegans* Vahl). *Foods Food Ingredients J.* 169: 121–124

Maness, N. E., et al. 1995. Effects of nitrogen rates and final fall harvest timing on sage (*Salvia officinalis*). *HortScience* 30: 426–427.

Marcos Sanz, M. E., et al. 1988. Essential oils of *Salvia lavandulaefolia* Vahl. In *Flavor and Fragrances: A World Perspective*. Ed. B. M. Lawrence et al. Amsterdam: Elsevier. 147–180.

Maric, S., et al. 2006. The impact of the locality altitudes and stages of development on the volatile constituents of *Salvia officinalis* L. from Bosnia and Herzegovina. *J. Essential Oil Res.* 18: 178–180.

Masaki, H., et al. 1995. Active-oxygen scavenging activity of plant extracts. *Biol. Pharm. Bull.* 18: 162–166.

Masuda, T. 2004. Antioxidant mechanism of the potent diterpenoid antioxidants found in sage and rosemary. *Food Food Ingred.* 10: 858–865.

Máthé, I., et al. 1997. Comparative studies of the essential oils of some species of sect. *Salvia*. In *Essential Oils: Basic and Applied Research*. Ed. Ch. Franz et al. Carol Stream, Illinois: Allured. 244–247.

McGimpsey, J. A. 1993. *Sage*: Salvia officinalis. New Zealand Inst. Crop Food Res. Broadsheet No. 21.

Mihalik, E., et al. 2005. Photosynthetic and morphological characters of leaves of the annual and biennial *Salvia sclarea* biotypes. *Acta Biol. Szegediensis* 49: 161–163.

Millet, Y., et al. 1979. Étude expérimentale des propriétés toxiques convulsiviantes des essences de sauge et d'hysope du commerce. *Rev. E. E. G. Neurophysiol.* 9: 12–18.

———. 1980. Étude de la toxicité d'huiles essentielles végétales du commerce: essence d'hysope et de sauge. *Med. Legale Toxicol.* 23: 9–21.

Mincione, A., et al. 2002. Osservazioni sull'olio essenziale di ecotipi di *Salvia officinalis* L. presenti in Calabria. Influenze dell'epoca di raccolta sulla composizione. *Essenze Derivati Agrumari* 72: 123–126.

Mirjalili, M. H., et al. 2006. Essential oil variation of *Salvia officinalis* aerial parts during its phonological cycle. *Chem. Nat. Compd.* 42: 19–23.

Mockuté, D., et al. 2003. The cis-thujone chemotype of *Salvia officinalis* L. essential oils. *Chemija* 14: 216–220.

Moretti, M., et al. 1997. A study on antiinflammatory and peripheral analgesic action of *Salvia sclarea* oil and its main components. *J. Essential Oil Res.* 9: 199–204.

Müller-Riebau, F., et al. 1995. Chemical composition and fungitoxic properties to phytopathogenic fungi of essential oils of selected aromatic plants growing wild in Turkey. *J. Agric. Food Chem.* 43: 2262–2266.

———. 1997. Seasonal variations in the chemical compositions of essential aromatic plants growing wild in Turkey. *J. Agric. Food Chem.* 45: 4821–4825.

Novak, J., et al. 2006. An α-pinene chemotype in *Salvia officinalis* (Lamiaceae). *J. Essential Oil Res.* 18: 239–241.

Olszesaka, I., and K. Milkowska. 1997. Chemical analysis of essential oil and solvents extracts of sage (*Salvia officinalis* L.) plant from Poland. In *Essential Oils: Basic and Applied Research*. Ed. Ch. Franz et al. Carol Stream, Illinois: Allured. 233–236.

Overcash, J. P. 1945. Propagation and culture of garden sage in Tennessee. *Proc. Amer. Soc. Hort. Sci.* 46: 345–349.

Ozdemir, C., and G. Şenel. 1999. The morphological, anatomical and karyological properties of *Salvia sclarea* L. *Turk. J. Bot.* 23: 7–18.

Pace, L., and R. Piccaglia. 1995. Characterization of the essential oil of a wild Italian endemic sage: *Salvia officinalis* L. var. *angustifolia* Ten. (Labiatae). *J. Essential Oil Res.* 7: 443–446.

Pages, N., et al. 1992. Potential teratogenicity in mice of the essential oil of *Salvia lavandulifolia* Vahl: study of a fraction rich in sabinyl acetate. *Phytotherapy Res.* 6: 80–83.

Papageorgiou, V., et al. 2008. Variation of the chemical profile and antioxidant behavior of *Rosmarinus officinalis* L. and *Salvia fruticosa* Miller grown in Greece. *J. Agric. Food Chem.* 56: 7254–7264.

Pazłoa, Z., et al. 1990. Studies on the antioxidative properties of spices from the Labiatae family. II. Attempt at identification of antioxidative components of rosemary and sage. *Roczn. Akad. Roln. Poznan.* 218: 93–107.

Peana, A. T., et al. 1999. Chemical composition and antimicrobial action of the essential oils of *Salvia desoleana* and *S. sclarea*. *Pl. Med.* 65: 752–754.

Perry, N. B., et al. 1996. Dalmatian sage. Part 1. Differing oil yields and compositions from flowering and non-flowering accessions. *Flavour Fragrance J.* 11: 231–238.

———. 1996. European herbs with cholinergic activities: potential in dementia therapy. *Intern. J. Geriatric Psychiatry* 11: 1063–1069.

———. 1999. Essential oils from Dalmatian sage (*Salvia officinalis* L.): variations among individuals, plant parts, seasons, and sites. *J. Agric. Food Chem.* 47: 2048–2054.

Perry, N. S. L., et al. 2001. In-vitro activity of *S. lavandulaefolia* (Spanish sage) relevant to treatment of Alzheimer's disease. *J. Pharm. Pharmacol.* 53: 1347–1356.

———. 2003. *Salvia* for dementia therapy: review of pharmacological activity and pilot tolerability clinical trial. *Pharmacol. Biochem. Behav.* 75: 651–659.

Piccaglia, R., et al. 1989. Effect of mineral fertilizers on the composition of *Salvia officinalis* oils. *J. Essential Oil Res.* 2: 73–83.

———. 1993. Antibacterial and antioxidant properties of Mediterranean aromatic plants. *Industr. Crops Prod.* 2: 47–50.

———. 1997. Effect of planting density and harvest date on yield and chemical composition of sage oil. *J. Essential Oil Res.* 9: 187–191.

Pino, J. A., et al. 1997. Essential oil of sage (*Salvia officinalis* L.) grown in Cuba. *J. Essential Oil Res.* 9: 221–222.

Pitarokili, D., et al. 2003. Volatile metabolites from *Salvia fruticosa* as antifungal agents in soilborne pathogens. *J. Agric. Food Chem.* 51: 3294–3301.

Povh, J. A., and E. O. Ono. 2006. Rendimento de oleo essencial de *Salvia officinalis* L. sob ação de eguladores vegetais. *Acta Sci. Biol. Sci.* 28: 189–193.

Putievsky, E., and U. Ravid. 1984. Selection and cultivation of *Salvia fruticosa* Mill. (syn. *S. triloba*) from wild populations in Israel. In *EUCARPIA International Symposium on Conservation of Genetic Resources of Aromatic and Medicinal Plants, Ociras, Portugal.* 87–94.

Putievsky, E., et al. 1986. The essential oil and yield components from various plant parts of *Salvia fruticosa*. *J. Nat. Prod.* 49: 1015–1017.

———. 1992. Morphological observations and essential oils of sage (*Salvia officinalis* L.) under cultivation. *J. Essential Oil Res.* 4: 291–293.

Raal, A., et al. 2007. Composition of the essential oil of *Salvia officinalis* L. from various European countries. *Nat. Prod. Res.* 21: 406–411.

Radulescu, V., et al. 2004. Capillary gas chromatography-mass spectrometry of volatile and semi-volatile compounds of *Salvia officinalis*. *J. Chromatogr. A* 1027: 121–126.

Ravid, U., and E. Putievsky. 1985. Essential oils of Israeli wild species of Labiatae. In *Essential Oils and Aromatic Plants.* Ed. A. Baerheim Svendsen and J. J. C. Scheffer. Dordrecht: Martinus Nijhoff/W. Junk Publ. 155–164.

Ravid, U., et al. 1984. Rooting stem cuttings of sage (*Salvia officinalis* L.). *Pl. Propag.* 30(3): 8–9.

Reales, A., et al. 2004. Numerical taxonomy study of *Salvia* sect. *Salvia* (Labiatae). *Bot. J. Linn. Soc.* 145: 353–371.

Reverchonm E., et al. 1995. Extraction of sage oil by supercritical CO_2: influence of some process parameters. *J. Supercrit. Fluids* 8: 302–309.

Rey, Ch. 1991. Incidence de la date et de la hauteur de coupe en première année de culture sur la productivité de la sauge officinale et du thym vulgaire. *Rev. Suisse Vitic. Arbor. Hort.* 23: 137–143.

———. 1995. Comparaison du semis direct et du plant motté pour la mise en place de la sauge officinale (*Salvia officinalis* L.). *Rev. Suisse Vitic. Arbor. Hort.* 27: 375–381.

Rey, Ch., et al. 2000. Des hybrides de sauge prometteurs. *Rev. Suisse Vitic. Arbor. Hort.* 32: I–VIII.

Rosúa, J. L., and G. Blanca. 1986. Revisión del género *Salvia* L. (Lamiaceae) en el Mediterráneo Occidental: La Sección *Salvia. Acta Bot. Malacitana* 11: 227–272.

Rónyai, E., et al. 1997. Supercritical fluid extraction of clary sage and study of sclareol and element content in parts of plant. In *Essential Oils: Basic and Applied Research.* Ed. Ch. Franz et al. Carol Stream, Illinois: Allured. 152–156.

Samejima, K., et al. 1995. Luteolin: a strong antimutagen against dietary carcinogen, Trp-P-2, in peppermint, sage, and thyme. *J. Agric. Food Chem.* 43: 410–414.

Santos-Gomes, P. C., and M. Fernandes-Ferreira. 2001. Organ- and season-dependent variation in the essential oil composition of *Salvia officinalis* L. cultivated at two different sites. *J. Agric. Food Chem.* 49: 2908–2916.

Saricoban, C., and M. Ozcan. 2004. Antioxidative activity of rosemary (*Rosmarinus officinalis* L.) and sage (*Salvia fruticosa* L.) essential oils in chicken fat. *J. Essential Oil-Bearing Pl.* 7: 94–95.

Savelev, S. U., et al. 2003. Synergistic and antagonistic interactions of anticholinesterase terpenoids in *Salvia lavandulaefolia* essential oil. *Pharmacol. Biochem. Beh.* 75: 661–668.

———. 2004. Butyryl- and acetyl-cholinesterase inhibitory activities in essential oils of *Salvia* species and their constituents. *Phytotherapy Res.* 18: 315–324.

Scartezzini, F., et al. 2006. Influence of two plant materials on oil content and composition of three garden sage varieties. *Acta Hort.* 723: 227–231.

Shapiro, S., et al. 1994. The antimicrobial activity of essential oils and essential oil components towards oral bacteria. *Oral Microbiol. Immunol.* 9: 202–208.

Shelef, L. A., et al. 1980. Sensitivity of some common food-borne bacteria to the spices sage, rosemary, and allspice. *J. Food Sci.* 45: 1042–1044.

———. 1984. Growth of enteropathogenic and spoilage bacteria in sage-containing broth and foods. *J. Food Sci.* 49: 737–740, 809.

Shimoni, M., et al. 1993. Antifungal activity of volatile fractions of essential oils from four aromatic wild plants in Israel. *J. Chem. Ecol.* 19: 1129–1133.

Sievers, A. F. 1948. *Production of Drug and Condiment Plants.* U.S.D.A. Farmers Bull. No. 1999.

Singh, A. K., and Taj-ud-din. 1984. *Clary Sage and Its Cultivation in India.* Central Inst. Med. Aromatic Pl., Lucknow.

Sivropoulou, A., et al. 1997. Antimicrobial, cytotoxic, and antiviral activities of *Salvia fruticosa* essential oil. *J. Agric. Food Chem.* 45: 3197–3201.

Skoula, M., et al. 1999. Evaluation of the genetic diversity of *Salvia fruticosa* Mill. clones using RAPD markers and comparison with the essential oil profiles. *Biochem. Syst. Ecol.* 27: 559–568.

———. 2000. Genetic variation of volatiles and rosmarinic acid in populations of *Salvia fruticosa* Mill. growing in Crete. *Biochem. Syst. Ecol.* 28: 551–561.

Snyder, K. M. 1944. Domestic sage cultivation. *Chemurgic Dig.* 3(24): 360–361.

Soules, Chr., and N. Argyriadou. 1997. Constituents of the essential oil of *Salvia sclarea* growing wild in Greece. *Intern. J. Pharmacogn.* 35: 218–220.

Srinivas, S. R. 1986. *Atlas of Essential Oils.* New York: S. R. Srinivas.

Standley, P. C. 1924. Trees and shrubs of Mexico. *U.S. Natl. Herb.* 23: 1–1721.

———. 1950. New plants from Honduras. *Ceiba* 1: 38–49.

Steinmetz, M. D., et al. 1980. Sur la toxicité de certaines huiles essentielles du commerce: essence d'hysope et essence de sauge. *Pl. Med. Phytotherap.* 14: 34–45.

Sutton, J. 1999. *The Gardener's Guide to Growing Salvias.* Portland, Oregon: Timber Press.

Svoboda, K. P., and S. G. Deans. 1992. A study of the variability of rosemary and sage and their volatile oils on the British market: their antioxidative properties. *Flavour Fragrance J.* 7: 81–87.

Szenmihályi, K., et al. 2004. Comparative study on tannins, flavonoids, terpenes and mineral elements of some *Salvia* species. *Acta Hort.* 629: 463–470.

Takácsová, M., et al. 1995. Study of the antioxidative effects of thyme, sage, juniper and oregano. *Nahrung* 39: 241–243.

Tassou, C., and G. Nychas. 1995. The inhibitory effect of the essential oils from basil (*Ocimum basilicum*) and sage (*Salvia officinalis*) in broth and in model food system. In *Food Flavor: Generation, Analysis and Process Influence.* Ed. G. Charalambous. Amsterdam: Elsevier. 1925–1935.

Then, M., et al. 2003. Study of plant anatomical characteristics and essential oil composition of Hungarian *Salvia* species. *Acta Hort.* 597: 143–148.

———. 2004. Polyphenol-, mineral element content and total antioxidant power of sage (*Salvia officinalis* L.) extracts. *Acta Hort.* 629: 123–129.

Tildsley, N. T. J., et al. 2003. *Salvia lavandulaefolia* (Spanish sage) enhances memory in healthy young volunteers. *Pharmacol. Biochem. Behav.* 75: 669–674.

Torres, M., et al. 1997. Volatile constituents of two *Salvia* species grown wild in Spain. *J. Essential Oil Res.* 9: 27–33.

Trojáková, L., et al. 2001. Antioxidant activity of rosemary and sage extract in rapeseed oil. *J. Food Lipids* 8: 1–13.

Tsankova, E. T., et al. 1994. Constituents of essential oils from three *Salvia* species. *J. Essential Oil Res.* 6: 375–378.

Tucker, A. O., and M. J. Maciarello. 1990. Essential oils of cultivars of Dalmatian sage (*Salvia officinalis* L.). *J. Essential Oil Res.* 2: 139–144.

———. 1994. The essential oil of *Salvia dorisiana* Standley. *J. Essential Oil Res.* 6: 79–80.

Tucker, A. O., et al. 1980. Botanical aspects of commercial sage. *Econ. Bot.* 34: 16–19.

———. 1995. Volatile leaf oils of cultivars of *Salvia clevelandii* (Gray) Greene × *S. leucophylla* Greene. *J. Essential Oil Res.* 7: 101–104.

Ululeben, A., et al. 1994. Terpenoids from *Salvia sclarea*. *Phytochemistry* 36: 971–974.

van der Waal, M., et al. 2002. 1-Methoxyhexane-3-thiol, a powerful odorant of clary sage (*Salvia sclarea* L.). *Helv. Chim. Acta* 85: 1246–1260.

Vaverkova, S., et al. 1995. The effect of herbicides on the qualitative properties of healing plants. Part 2: content and composition of the essential oil from *Salvia officinalis* L. after application of Afalon® 50WP. *Pharmazie* 50: 143–144.

Velickovic, D. T., et al. 2002. Chemical composition and antimicrobial characteristic of the essential oils obtained from the flower, leaf and stem of *Salvia officinalis* originating from Southeast Serbia. *J. Essential Oil Res.* 14: 453–458.

Venskutonis, P. R. 1995. Essential oil composition of some herbs cultivated in Lithuania. In *Flavour, Fragrances and Essential Oils*. Ed. K. H. C. Baser. Istanbul: AREP Publ. 108–123.

Vera, R. R., et al. 1999. Chemical composition of the essential oil of sage (*Salvia officinalis* L.) from Reunion Island. *J. Essential Oil Res.* 11: 399–402.

Vernin, G., and J. Metzger. 1986. Analysis of sage oils by GC-MS data bank: *Salvia officinalis* L. and *Salvia lavandulaefolia* Vahl. *Perfumer Flavor.* 11(5): 79–84.

Vuković-Gačić, B., et al. 2006. Antimutagenic effect of essential oil of sage (*Salvia officinalis* L.) and its monoterpenes against UV-induced mutations in *Escherichia coli* and *Saccharomyces cerevisiae*. *Food Chem. Toxicol.* 44: 1730–1738.

Walker, J. B., et al. 2004. *Salvia* (Lamiaceae) is not monophyletic: implications for the systematics, radiation, and ecological specialization of *Salvia* and tribe *Mentheae*. *Amer. J. Bot.* 91: 1115–1125.

Yeo, C. 1995. *Salvias*. Newton Abbot, Devon, England: Pleasant View.

———. 1997. *Salvias II*. Newton Abbot, Devon, England: Pleasant View.

Zrira, S., et al. 2004. A study of the essential oil of *Salvia lavandulifolia* Vahl from Morocco. *J. Essential Oil-Bearing Pl.* 7: 232–238.

Sanguisorba

Proctor, M. C. F., and G. Nordborg. 1968. *Sanguisorba*. In *Flora Europaea Vol. 2*. Ed. T. G. Tutin et al. Cambridge Univ. Press. 33–34.

Santolina

Barrero, A. F., et al. 1999. Bioactive sesquiterpenes from *Santolina rosmarinifolia* subsp. *canescens*: a conformational analysis of the germacrane ring. *Phytochemistry* 51: 529–541.

Brunke, E.-J., et al. 1992. The essential oil of *Santolina chamaecyparissus* L. *Dragoco Rep.* 4: 151–167.

Demirci, B., et al. 2000. Chemical composition of *Santolina chamaecyparissus* L. essential oil. *J. Essential Oil Res.* 12: 625–627.

Garg, S. N., et al. 2001. Volatile constituents of the essential oil of *Santolina chamaecyparissus* Linn. from the southern hills of India. *J. Essential Oil Res.* 13: 234–235.

Guinea, E. 1970. *Santolina* europaeae. *Anales Inst. Bot. Cavanilles* 27: 29–44.

Guinea, E., and T. G. Tutin. 1976. *Santolina*. In *Flora Europaea Vol. 4*. Ed. T. G. Tutin et al. Cambridge Univ. Press. 144–145.

Ioannou, E., et al. 2007. Chemical composition and *in vitro* antimicrobial activity of the essential oils of flower heads and leaves of *Santolina rosmarinifolia* L. from Romania. *Nat. Prod. Res.* 21: 18–23.

Lancaster, R. 1971. Santolinas. *Gard. Chron.* 169(9): 37, 39.

McAllister, H. 1987. Conservation and taxonomy of *Santolina chamaecyparissus*. agg. *Natl. Council Conserv. Pl. Gard. Newsl.* 10: 7–10.

McAllister, H., et al. 2000. *Santolina*. In *The European Garden Flora Vol. 6*. Ed. J. Cullen et al. Cambridge Univ. Press. 606–607.

Suresh, B., et al. 1997. Anticandidal activity of *Santolina chamaecyparissus* volatile oil. *J. Ethnopharmacol.* 55: 151–159.

Villar, A., et al. 1986. Chemical composition of *Santolina chamaecyparissus* ssp. *squarrosa* essential oil. *J. Nat. Prod.* 49: 1143–1144.

Sassafras

Anonymous. 1997. Sassafras. In *Lawrence Review of Natural Products*. St. Louis: Facts and Comparisons.

Boberg, E. W., et al. 1983. Strong evidence from studies with brachymorphic mice and pentachlorphenol that 1'-sulfo-öxysafrole is the major ultimate electrophilic and carcinogenic metabolite of 1'-hydroxysafrole in mouse liver. *Cancer Res.* 43: 5163–5173.

Carlson, M., and R. D. Thompson. 1997. Liquid chromatographic determination of safrole in sassafras-derived herbal products. *J. Amer. Oil Chem. Intern.* 80: 1023–1028.

Clepper, H. 1989. The singular sassafras. *Amer. Forests* 95 (3/4): 33–34, 57.

Dathe, M. 1984. Sassafras in spite of itself. *Horticulture* 63(9): 19–24.

Sargent, C. S. 1895. *The Silva of North America Vol. 7*. Boston: Houghton Mifflin and Co.

Tucker, A. O., et al. 1993. Filé and the essential oils of the leaves, twigs, and commercial root teas of *Sassafras albidum* (Nutt.) Nees (Lauraceae). In *Spices, Herbs and Edible Fungi*. Ed. G. Charalambous. Amsterdam: Elsevier. 595–604.

Weaver, R. E. 1976. Sassafras: a neglected native ornamental. *Arnoldia* 36: 22–27.

Wilson, J. B. 1959. Determination of safrole and methyl salicylate in soft drinks. *J. Amer. Oil Chem. Soc.* 42: 696–698.

Wiseman, R. W., et al. 1985. Further characterization of the DNA adducts formed by electrophilic esters of the hepatocarcinogens 1'-hydroxysafrole and 1'-hydroestragole in vitro and in mouse liver in vivo, including new adducts at C-8 and N-7 of guanine residues. *Cancer Res.* 45: 3096–3105.

Satureja

Anonymous. 2005. Savory. *Rev. Nat. Prod. (Wolters Kluwer Health)*.

Azaz, A. D., et al. 2005. *In vitro* antimicrobial activity and chemical composition of some *Satureja* essential oils. *Flavour Fragrance J.* 20: 587–591.

Ball, P. W., and F. M. Getliffe. 1972. *Satureja*. In *Flora Europaea Vol. 3*. Ed. T. G. Tutin et al. Cambridge Univ. Press. 163–165.

Bandonienė, D., et al. 2002. Antioxidative activity of sage (*Salvia officinalis* L.), savory (*Satureja hortensis* L.) and borage (*Borago officinalis* L.) extracts in rapeseed oil. *Eur. J. Lipid Sci. Technol.* 104: 286–292.

Baser, K. H. C., et al. 2004. A comparative study of the essential oil of wild and cultivated *Satureja hortensis* L. *J. Essential Oil Res.* 16: 422–424.

Bellomaria, B., and G. Valentini. 1985. Composizione dell'olio essenziale di *Satureja montana* subsp. *montana* dell'Appennino marchigiano. *Giorn. Bot. Ital.* 119: 81–87.

Bezić, N., et al. 2005. Phytochemical composition and antimicrobial activity of *Satureja montana* L. and *Satureja cuenifolia* Ten. essential oils. *Acta Bot. Croat.* 64: 313–322.

Bianchi, A., et al. 1986. Indagini su plante del genere *Satureja*. *Atti Soc. Naturalisti Mat. Modena* 117: 49–64.

Bilia, A. R., et al. 1992. Essential oil of *Satureja montana* L. ssp. *montana*. Composition and yields of plants grown under different environmental conditions. *J. Essential Oil Res.* 4: 563–568.

Böttcher, H., et al. 2000. Physiologisches Nachernteverhalten von Bohnenkraut (*Satureja hortensis* L.). *Gartenbauwissenschaft* 65: 22–29.

Boyraz, N., and M. Özcan. 2006. Inhibition of phytopathogenic fungi by essential oil, hydrosol, ground material and extract of summer savory (*Satureja hortensis* L.) growing wild in Turkey. *Intern. J. Food Microbiol.* 107: 238–242.

Briquet, J. 1891–95. *Les Labiées des Alpes Maritimes.* Genève: George & Co.

Capone, W. C., et al. 1989. Chemical composition and antibacterial activity of the essential oil from Sardinian *Satureja thymbra*. *Fitoterapia* 60: 90–92.

Chialva, F., and G. Gabri. 1987. Headspace versus classical analysis. In *Capillary Gas Chromatography in Essential Oil Analysis.* Ed. P. Sandra and C. Bicchi. Heidelberg: Alfred Huethig. 123–145.

Chialva, F., et al. 1980. Indagine sulla composizione dell'oleo essenziale di *Satureja hortensis* Linnaeus coltivata in piemonte e confronto con altre di diversa origine. *Revista Ital. EPPOS* 62: 297–300.

———. 1982. Qualitative evaluation of aromatic herbs by direct headspace (GC) analysis. Applications of the method and comparison with the traditional analysis of essential oils. *J. High Resolution Chromatogr. Chromatogr. Commun.* 5: 182–188.

———. 1982. Qualitative evaluation of aromatic herbs by direct headspace (GC) analysis. In *Aromatic Plants: Basic and Applied Aspects.* Ed. N. Margaris et al. The Hague: Martinus Nijhoff. 183–195.

Chorianopoulos, N., et al. 2004. Essential oils of *Satureja*, *Origanum*, and *Thymus* species: chemical composition and antibacterial activities against foodborne pathogens. *J. Agric. Food Chem.* 52: 8261–8267.

———. 2006. Characterization of the essential oil volatiles of *Satureja thymbra* and *Satureja parnassica*: influence of harvesting time and antimicrobial activity. *J. Agric. Food Chem.* 54: 3139–3145.

Ciani, M., et al. 2000. Antimicrobial properties of essential oil of *Satureja montana* L. on pathogenic and spoilage yeasts. *Biotechnol. Lett.* 22: 1007–1010.

Deans, S. G., and K. P. Svoboda. 1989. Antibacterial activity of summer savory (*Satureja hortensis* L.) essential oil and its constituents. *J. Hort. Sci.* 64: 205–210.

Esquivel, M. M., et al. 1999. Supercritical extraction of savory oil: study on antioxidant activity and extract characterization. *J. Supercritical Fluids* 14: 129–138.

Fleisher, A., et al. 1982. Chemical and botanical aspects of the Biblical hyssop. In *VIII International Congress of Essential Oils, October 12–17, 1980, Cannes-Grasse, France.* Paper no. 212.

Fleisher, Z., and A. Fleisher. 2005. Extract analyses of *Satureja thymbra* L. and *Thymbra spicata* L. Aromatic plants of the Holy Land and the Sinai, part 17. *J. Essential Oil Res.* 17: 32–35.

Fououmadi, A., et al. 2005. Chemical composition of the essential oil of *Satureja hortensis* L. var. *laxiflora*. *Chem. Indian J.* 1: 701–702.

Garnero, J., and J. Pellecuer. 1982. Étude de la composition chimique de l'huile essentielle de *Satureia montana* L. (Labiées). In *VIII International Congress of Essential Oils, October 12–17, 1980, Cannes-Grasse, France.* Paper no. 14.

Garnero, J., et al. 1981. Étude de la composition chimique de l'huile essentielle de *Satureia montana* Linnaeus (Labiées). *Revista Ital. EPPOS* 62: 344–349.

Gershenzon, J., et al. 1978. The effect of moisture stress on monoterpenoid yield and composition of *Satureja douglasii*. *Biochem. Syst. Ecol.* 6: 33–43.

Glamočlija, J., et al. 2006. Chemical composition and antifungal activities of essential oils of *Satureja thymbra* L. and *Salvia pomifera* ssp. *calycina* (Sm.) Hayek. *J. Essential Oil Res.* 18: 115–117.

Góra, J., et al. 1996. Chemical composition of the essential oil of cultivated summer savory (*Satureja hortensis* L. cv. 'Saturn'). *J. Essential Oil Res.* 8: 427–428.

Gören, A. C., et al. 2004. Analysis of essential oil of *Satureja thymbra* by hydrodistillation, thermal desorber, and headspace GC/MS techniques and its antimicrobial activity. *Nat. Prod. Res.* 18: 189–195.

Güllce, M., et al. 2003. In vitro antibacterial, antifungal, and antioxidant activities of the essential oil and methanol extracts of herbal parts and callus cultures of *Satureja hortensis* L. *J. Agric. Food Chem.* 51: 3958–3965.

Hannig, H. J. 1997. Inhaltsstoffgehalte von Bohnenkrautsorten. *Gemüse* 11: 627–628.

Hérisset, A., et al. 1973. A propos des falsifications de la sarriette des jardins (*Satureja hortensis* L.) *Pl. Med. Phytotherap.* 7: 121–134.

———. 1974. Nouvelles observations concernant les falsifications de la sarriette des jardins (*Satureja hortensis* L.). *Pl. Med. Phytotherap.* 8: 287–294.

Kanias, G. D., and A. Loukis. 1992. Statistical analysis of essential oil percentage composition of *Coridothymus capitatus* Reichb. f. and *Satureja thymbra* L. *J. Essential Oil Res.* 4: 577–584.

Karabay-Yavasoglu, N. U., et al. 2006. Evaluation of the antinociceptive and anti-inflammatory activities of *Satureja thymbra* L. essential oil. *Pharm. Biol.* 44: 585–591.

Karousou, R., et al. 2005. Essential oil composition is related to the natural habitats: *Coridothymus capitatus* and *Satureja thymbra* in NATURA 2000 sites of Crete. *Phytochemistry* 66: 2668–2673.

Kokkini, S., and D. Vokou. 1989. Carvacrol-rich plants in Greece. *Flavour Fragrance J.* 4: 1–7.

Krüger, H., et al. 2006. Eine einfache Schnellmethode zur Bestimmung von Carvacrol in ätherischen Bohnenkrautölen (*Satureja hortensis* L.). *Z. Arzn. Gew. Pfl.* 11: 55–56.

Kustrak, D., et al. 1996. Comparison of the essential oil composition of two subspecies of *Satureja montana*. *J. Essential Oil Res.* 8: 7–13.

Lincoln, D. E., and J. H. Langenheim. 1976. Geographic patterns of monoterpenoid composition in *Satureja douglasii*. *Biochem. Syst. Ecol.* 4: 237–248.

———. 1978. Effect of light and temperature on monoterpenoid yield and composition in *Satureja douglasii*. *Biochem. Syst. Ecol.* 6: 21–32.

———. 1979. Variation of *Satureja douglasii* monoterpenoids in relation to light intensity and herbivory. *Biochem. Syst. Ecol.* 7: 289–298.

Lokar, L. C., et al. 1983. Considerazioni chemotassonomiche sulle relazione fra *Satureja montana* L. subsp. *variegata* (Host) P. W. Ball e *Satureja subspicata* Bartl. ex Vis. subsp. *liburnica* Silic (Labiatae). *Webbia* 37: 197–206.

Mastelić, J., and I. Jerković. 2003. Gas chromatography-mass spectrometry analysis of free and glycoconjugated aroma compounds of seasonally collected *Satureja montana* L. *Food Chem.* 80: 135–140.

Melegari, M., et al. 1985. Ricerche su caratteristiche chimiche e proprietà antibatteriche di olii essenzialii di *Satureja montana*. *Fitoterapia* 56: 85–91.

Menghini, A., et al. 1992. Activité antifongique in vitro de l'huile essentielle de *Satureja montana* L. et de ses composants. *Rivista Ital. EPPOS* 1993(4): 566–571.

Novak, J., et al. 2006. Composition of individual essential oil glands of savory (*Satureja hortensis* L., Lamiaceae) from Syria. *Flavour Fragrance J.* 21: 731–734.

Oussalah, M., et al. 2006. Mechanism of action of Spanish oregano, Chinese cinnamon, and savory essential oils against cell membranes and walls of *Escherichia coli* O157:H7 and *Listeria monocytogenes*. *J. Food Prot.* 69: 1046–1055.

Palić, R., et al. 1998. Composition of essential oil of selected *Satureja* species and chemotaxonomic implications. *J. Essential Oil-Bearing Pl.* 1: 66–82.

Panizzi, L., et al. 1993. Composition and antimicrobial properties of essential oils of four Mediterranean Lamiaceae. *J. Ethnopharmacol.* 39: 167–170.

Parsons, M. E. 1907. *The Wild Flowers of California.* San Francisco: Cunningham, Curtiss & Welch.

Pascual, M. H., et al. 1998. Eficacia del aceite esencial de ajedrea (*Satureja montana*) en el control de la ascosferosis de la abeja (*Apis mellifera*) en condiciones de campo. *Rev. Iberamer. Micol.* 15: 151–154.

Pellecuer, J. 1974. L'Huile essentielle de *Satureja montana* L. et l'aromathérapie. *Bull. Tech. Gattefosse SFPA* 68: 77–86.

Pellecuer, J., et al. 1975. Place de l'essence de *Satureja montana* L. (Labiées) dans l'arsenal thérapeutique. *Pl. Med. Phytotherap.* 9: 99–106.

———. 1980. Therapeutic value of the cultivated mountain savory, *Satureja montana* L. (Labiatae). *Acta Hort.* 96: 35–39.

———. 1982. Etude de l'huile essentielle de *Satureia montana* L. (Labiées) en fonction de l'écologie et de la physiologie de la plante. In *VIII International Congress of Essential Oils, October 12–17, 1980, Cannes-Grasse, France.* Paper no. 37.

Pfefferkorn, A., et al. 2006. Einfluss von Entwicklungsstadium und Jahreszeit aur Ertrag und Zusammensetzung des ätherischen Öls von Bohnenkraut (*Satureja hortensis* L.). *Z. Arzn. Gew. Pfl.* 11: 92–100.

———. 2008. Chemical composition of *Satureja hortensis* L. essential oils depending on ontogenetic stage and season. *J. Essential Oil Res.* 20: 303–305.

Philianos, S. M., et al. 1984. Constituents of the essential oil of *Satureia thymbra* L., from different regions of Greece. *Int. J. Crude Drug Res.* 22: 145–149.

Piccaglia, R., et al. 1991. Characterization of essential oil from a *Satureja montana* L. chemotype grown in northern Italy. *J. Essential Oil Res.* 3: 147–152.

———. 1993. Antibacterial and antioxidant properties of Mediterranean aromatic plants. *Industrial Crops Prod.* 2: 47–50.

Radonic, A., and M. Milos. 2003. Chemical composition and *in vitro* evaluation of antioxidant effect of free volatile compounds from *Satureja montana* L. *Free Radical Res.* 37: 673–679.

———. 2003. Chemical composition and antioxidant test of free and glycosidically bound volatile compounds of savory (*Satureja montana* L. subsp. *montana*) from Croatia. *Nahrung/Food* 47: 236–237.

Ravid, U., and E. Putievsky. 1983. Constituents of essential oils from *Majorana syriaca*, *Coridothymus capitatus* and *Satureja thymbra*. *Pl. Med.* 49: 248–249.

———. 1985. Essential oils of Israeli wild species of Labiatae. In *Essential Oils and Aromatic Plants.* Ed. A. Baerheim Svendsen and J. J. C. Scheffer. Dordrecht: Martinus Nijhoff/ W. Junk Publ. 155–161.

———. 1985. Composition of essential oils of *Thymbra spicata* and *Satureja thymbra* chemotypes. *Pl. Med.* 1985: 337–338.

Rhoades, D. G., et al. 1976. Preliminary studies of monoterpenoid variability in *Satureja douglasii*. *Biochem. Syst. Ecol.* 4: 5–12.

Rhyu, H. Y. 1979. Gas chromatographic characterization of oregano and other selected spices of the Labiatae family. *J. Food Sci.* 44: 1373–1378.

Rice, R. L., et al. 1978. Palatability of monoterpenoid compositional types of *Satureja douglasii* to a generalist moluscan herbivore, *Ariolimax dolichophallus*. *Biochem. Syst. Ecol.* 6: 45–53.

Roussel, J.-L., et al. 1973. Propriétés antifongiques comparées des essences de trois Labiées méditerranéennes: romarin, sarriette et thym. *Trav. Soc. Pharm. Montpellier* 33: 587–592.

Şahin, F., et al. 2003. Evaluation of antimicrobial activities of *Satureja hortensis* L. *J. Ethnopharmacol.* 87: 61–65.

San Martin, R., et al. 1973. Le polymorphisme chimique chez deux Labiées Mediterranéennes: *Satureja montana* L. et *Satureja obovata* Lag. *Pl. Med. Phytotherap.* 7: 95–103.

Sefidkon, F., et al. 2006. Influence of drying and extraction methods on yield and chemical composition of the essential oil of *Satureja hortensis*. *Food Chem.* 99: 19–23.

Skočibuašić, M., and N. Bezić. 2004. Chemical composition and antimicrobial variability of *Satureja montana* L. essential oils produced during ontogenesis. *J. Essential Oil Res.* 16: 387–391.

Skoula, M., and R. J. Grayer. 2005. Volatile oils of *Coridothymus capitatus*, *Satureja thymbra*, *Satureja spinosa* and *Thymbra calostachya* (Lamiaceae) from Crete. *Flavour Fragrance J.* 20: 573–576.

Slavkovska, V., et al. 1997. Variability of the essential oil composition of the species *Satureja montana* L. (Lamiaceae). *J. Essential Oil Res.* 9: 629–634.

———. 2001. Variability of essential oils of *Satureja montana* L. and *Satureja kitaibelii* Wierzb. ex Heuff. from the central part of the Balkan peninsula. *Phytochemistry* 57: 71–76.

Šrepel, B., et al. 1974. Herba *Satureiae montanae* L.: Untersuchung der Droge und des ätherischen Öles. *Acta Pharm. Jugosl.* 4: 167–171.

Stancher, B., and L. Poldini. 1969. Gli olii essenziali di *Satureja variegata* Host (=*S. montana* auct. plur., non L.) nel Carso di Trieste. *Giorn. Bot. Ital.* 103: 65–77.

Stanic, G., et al. 1991. Gas chromatographic investigations of essential oils of *Satureja montana* and *Satureja subspicata* from Yugoslavia. *J. Essential Oil Res.* 3: 153–158.

Svoboda, K. P., and R. I. Greenaway. 2003. Investigation of volatile oil glands of *Satureja hortensis* L. (summer savory) and phytochemical comparison of different varieties. *Intern. J. Aromatherapy* 13: 196–202.

Svoboda, K. P., et al. 1990. Growing summer savory (*Satureja hortensis*) in Scotland: quantitative and qualitative analysis of the volatile oil and factors influencing oil production. *J. Sci. Food Agric.* 53: 193–202.

Velasco Negueruela, A., and J. P. Alonso. 1983. Estudio químico del aceite esencial de diversas *Satureiae* ibéricas. *Anales Jard. Bot. Madrid* 40: 107–118.

Venskutonis, P. R. 1995. Essential oil composition of some herbs cultivated in Lithuania. In *Flavour, Fragrances and Essential Oils.* Ed. K. H. C. Baser. Istanbul: AREP Publ. 108–123.

Whallon, D., and R. Whallon. 1977. The herbal teas of Crete: thryba (*Satureja thymbra* L.). *Herbarist* 43: 43–45.

Yanishlieva, N. V., et al. 1997. Effect of an ethanol extract from summer savory (*Saturejae hortensis* L.) on the stability of sunflower oil at frying temperature. *J. Sci. Food Agric.* 74: 524–530.

Sesamum

Bedigian, D. 2004. History and lore of sesame in Southwest Asia. *Econ. Bot.* 58: 329–353.

Bedigian, D., and J. R. Harlan. 1986. Evidence for cultivation of sesame in the ancient world. *Econ. Bot.* 40: 137–154.

Bedigian, D., et al. 1985. Sesamin, sesamolin and the origin of sesame. *Biochem. Syst. Ecol.* 13: 133–139.

———. 1986. Patterns of morphological variation in *Sesamum indicum*. *Econ. Bot.* 40: 353–365.

Delgado, M., and D. M. Yermanos. 1975. Yield components of sesame (*Sesamum indicum* L.) under different population densities. *Econ. Bot.* 29: 69–78.

James, C., et al. 1991. Sesame seed anaphylaxis. *New York State J. Med.* 91: 457–458.

Keskinen, H. P., et al. 1991. A case of occupational asthma, rhinitis and urticaria due to sesame seed. *Clin. Exp. Allergy* 21: 623–624.

Liu, P.-n. 2005. Study on volatile flavour components of sesame seed oil. *J. Chin. Cereals Oils Assoc.* 20(6): 87–90.

Lyon, C. K. 1972. Sesame: current knowledge of composition and use. *J. Amer. Oil Chem. Soc.* 49: 245–249.

Matsumura, Y., et al. 1998. Antihypertensive effect of sesamin. III. Protection against development and maintenance of hypertension in stroke-prone spontaneously hypertensive rats. *Biol. Pharm. Bull.* 21: 469–473.

Mitchell, G. A., et al. 1974. Growth, mineral composition and seed characteristics of sesame as affected by nitrogen, phosphorus, and potassium nutrition. *Soil Sci. Soc. Amer. Proc.* 38: 925–931.

Nakamura, S., et al. 1989. Identification of volatile flavour components of the oil from roasted sesame seeds. *Agric. Biol. Chem.* 53: 1891–1899.

———. 1990. Identification of volatile flavour components of roasted sesame oil. In *Proceedings of the 11th International Congress of Essential Oils, Fragrance and Flavour, New Delhi, India, 12–16 November 1989 Vol. 5.* Ed. S. C. Bhattacharyya et al. London: Aspect Publ. 73–87.

Nayar, N. M., and K. L. Mehra. 1970. Sesame: its uses, botany, cytogenetics, and origin. *Econ. Bot.* 24: 20–31.

Özbek, H., et al. 2004. Are fixed oils of *Sesamum indicum* L. and *Apium graveolens* L. protective against hepatotoxicity? *Genel. Tip. Derg.* 14: 49–55.

Ryu, S. N., et al. 1999. Influence of seed roasting process on the changes in volatile compounds of the sesame (*Sesamum indicum* L.) oil. In *Flavor Chemistry of Ethnic Foods.* Ed. F. Shahidi and C.-T. Ho. New York: Kluwer Acad. 229–237.

Schieberle, P. 1993. Important odorants in roasted white and black sesame seeds. In *Olfaction and Taste XI.* Ed. K. Kurihara et al. New York: Springer-Verlag. 263–267.

Seegeler, C. J. P. 1989. *Sesamum orientale* L. (Pedaliaceae): sesame's correct name. *Taxon* 38: 656–659.

Soliman, M. M., et al. 1975. Aroma of roasted sesame seeds. *Agric. Biol. Chem.* 39: 973–977.

Sun, B.-Y., et al. 1999. Taxonomy and seed morphology of *Sesamum* (Pedaliaceae). In *XVI International Botanical Congress, St. Louis, August 1–7, 1999.* Abstract 766.

Tutin, T. G. 1972. *Sesamum.* In *Flora Europaea Vol. 3.* Ed. T. G. Tutin et al. Cambridge Univ. Press. 284.

Yen, G.-C. 1990. Influence of seed roasting process on the changes in composition and quality of sesame (*Sesamum indicum*) oil. *J. Sci. Food Agric.* 50: 563–570.

Sinapis

Anonymous. 2006. Mustard. *Rev. Nat. Prod. (Wolters Kluwer Health).*

Bassett, B. 1993. The amazing mustard seed. *Herb Companion* 5(6): 33–37.

Bernth, J., et al. 1986. Effect of temperature on the dry-matter and fatty-oil production of mustard (*Sinapis alba* L.). *Herba Hung.* 25: 7385.

Chater, A. O. 1964. *Sinapis.* In *Flora Europaea Vol. 1.* Ed. T. G. Tutin et al. Cambridge Univ. Press. 339.

Hälvä, S., et al. 1986. Yield and glucosinolates in mustard seeds and volatile oils in

caraway seeds and coriander fruit. I. Yield and glucosinolate contents of mustard (*Sinapis* sp., *Brassica* sp.) seeds. *J. Agric. Sci. Finland* 58: 157–162.

Hazen, J. 1993. *Mustard: Making Your Own Gourmet Mustards.* San Francisco: Chronicle Books.

Hopley, C. 1991. *Making and Using Mustards.* Pownal, Vermont: Storey.

Mulligan, G. A., and L. G. Bailey. 1975. The biology of Canadian weeds. 8. *Sinapis arvensis* L. *Canad. J. Pl. Sci.* 55: 171–183.

Prakash, S., and K. Hinata. 1980. Taxonomy, cytogenetics and origin of crop brassicas. *Opera Bot.* 55: 1–57.

Sefidkon, F., et al. 2002. Essential oil composition of the aerial parts of *Sinapis alba* L. *J. Essential Oil-Bearing Pl.* 5: 90–92.

Shankaranarayana, M. L., et al. 1972. Mustard: varieties, chemistry and analysis. *Lebensm. Wiss. Technol.* 5: 191–197.

Solidago

Arctander, S. 1960. *Perfume and Flavor Materials of Natural Origin.* Elizabeth, New Jersey: Steffen Arctander.

Helmer, J. 1893. Acute toxic anaemia. *J. Comp. Med. Veterin. Arch.* 14: 150–156.

Holland, B. R. 1948. The terpenes of oil of sweet goldenrod. *J. Amer. Chem. Soc.* 70: 2597–2598.

Holland, B. R., et al. 1948. *Essential Oil Production in Texas. II. Sweet Goldenrod.* Texas Eng. Exp. Sta. Bull. No. 107.

Jepson, J. 1993. Goldenrod: a paradoxical native weed with a colorful story. *Herb Companion* 5(6): 44–48.

Kingsbury, J. M. 1964. *Poisonous Plants of the United States and Canada.* Englewood Cliffs, New Jersey: Prentice-Hall.

Miller, E. R., and J. M. Moseley. 1915. The volatile oils of the genus *Solidago. J. Amer. Chem. Soc.* 37: 1285–1294.

Muenscher, W. C. 1966. *Poisonous Plants of the United States.* New York: Macmillan Co.

Pursh, F. 1816. *Flora Americae Septentrionalis; etc.* London: James Black and Son.

Tucker, A. O. 1997. The official goldenrod. *Herb Companion* 9(3): 24–25.

Tucker, A. O., et al. 1999. Sweet goldenrod (*Solidago odora,* Asteraceae): a medicine, tea, and state herb. *Econ. Bot.* 53: 281–284.

Stevia

Anonymous. 2004. Stevia. *Rev. Nat. Prod. (Wolters Kluwer Health).*

Badawi, A. M., et al. 2002. Stevioside as a low caloric sweetener to milk drink and its protective role against oxidative stress in diabetic rats. *Egypt. J. Hosp. Med.* 20: 163–167.

Blumenthal, M. 1995. FDA lifts import alert on stevia. *HerbalGram* 35: 17–18.

Brandle, J. E., and N. Rosa. 1992. Heritabil-

ity for yield, leaf:stem ratio and stevioside content estimated from a landrace cultivar of *Stevia rebaudiana. Canad. J. Pl. Sci.* 72: 1263–1266.

Brandle, J. E., et al. 1998. *Stevia rebaudiana*: its agricultural, biological, and chemical properties. *Canad. J. Pl. Sci.* 78: 527–536.

Cavalcante da Silva, G. E., et al. 2006. Investigation of the tolerability of oral stevioside in Brazilian hyperlipidemic patients. *Braz. Arch. Biol. Technol.* 49: 583–587.

Chan, P., et al. 2000. A double-blind placebo-controlled study of the effectiveness and tolerability of oral stevioside in human hypertension. *Brit. J. Clin. Pharmacol.* 50: 215–220.

Cheng, T.-F., et al. 1981. A study of the post-harvest changes in steviosides contents of *Stevia* leaves and stems. *Natl. Sci. Council Monthly, ROC* 9: 775–782.

Crammer, B., and R. Ikan. 1986. Sweet glycosides from the stevia plant. *Chem. Britain* 22: 915–917.

Crosby, G. A., and T. E. Furia. 1980. New sweeteners. In *CRC Handbook of Food Additives Vol. 2.* 2nd ed. Ed. T. E. Furia. Boca Raton, Florida: CRC Press. 187–227.

Dyrskog, S. E. U., et al. 2005. Preventive effects of a soy-based diet supplement with stevioside on the development of the metabolic syndrome and type 2 diabetes in Zucker diabetic rats. *Met. Clin. Exp.* 54: 1181–1188.

Ferrigno, B. 1997. The politics of stevia. *Herbs Health* 2(2): 55.

Fujita, S., et al. 1977. Miscellaneous contributions to the essential oils of the plants from various territories (41). On the components of the essential oil of *Stevia rebaudiana* Bertoni. *Yakugaku Zasshi* 97: 692–694.

Gardana, C., et al. 2003. Metabolism of stevioside and rebaudioside A from *Stevia rebaudiana* extracts by human microflora. *J. Agric. Food Chem.* 51: 6618–6622.

Geuns, J. M. 2000. Safety of *Stevia* and stevioside. *Recent Res. Dev. Phytochem.* 4: 75–88.

———. 2002. Safety evaluation of *Stevia* and stevioside. In *Studies in Natural Products Chemistry.* Ed. Atta-ur-Rahman. Netherlands: Elsevier Sci. 299–319.

———. 2003. Stevioside. *Phytochemistry* 64: 913–921.

Geuns, J. M., et al. 2003. Effect of stevioside and steviol on the developing broiler embryos. *J. Agric. Food Chem.* 51: 5162–5167.

———. 2003. Metabolism of stevioside in pigs and intestinal absorption characteristics of stevioside, rebaudioside A and steviol. *Food Chem. Toxicol.* 41: 1599–1607.

Goto, A., and E. Clemente. 1998. Influência do rebaudiosídeo na solubilidade e no sabor do esteviosídeo. *Ci. Tecnol. Alimment.* 18: 3–6.

Gregerson, S., et al. 2004. Antihyperglycemic effects of stevioside in Type 2 diabetic subjects. *Metabolism* 53: 73–76.

Handro, W., and C. M. Ferreira. 1989. *Stevia rebaudiana* (Bert.) Bertoni: production of natural sweeteners. In *Biotechnology in Agriculture and Forestry 7. Medicinal and Aromatic Plants II.* Ed. Y. P. S. Bajaj. Berlin: Springer-Verlag. 468–487.

Huttapea, A., et al. 1997. Digestion of stevioside, a natural sweetener, by various digestive enzymes. *J. Clin. Biochem. Nutr.* 23: 177–186.

Inglett, G. E. 1978. Potential intense sweeteners of natural origin. In *Sweeteners and Dental Caries.* Ed. G. G. Roussos. Washington, D.C.: Inform. Retrieval. 327–337.

———. 1981. Sweeteners: a review. *Food Technol.* 35(3): 37, 38, 40, 41.

Kasai, R., et al. 1981. Sweet diterpeneglycosides of leaves of *Stevia rebaudiana* Bertoni. Synthesis and structure-sweetness relationship of rebaudiosides-A, -D, -E and their related glycosides. *Nipon Kagaku Kaishi* 1981: 726–735.

Kim, H.-S., et al. 1979. Acceptability of the sweetness of stevioside as a natural sweetener. *Korean J. Food Sci. Technol.* 11: 56–62.

Kinghorn, A. D. 1982. Potential sweetening agents of plant origin. I. Purification of *Stevia rebaudiana* sweet constituents by droplet counter-current chromatography. *J. Chromatogr.* 237: 478–483.

———. 1988. The search for noncariogenic sweetening agents from plants. *Acta Pharm. Indonesia* 13: 175–199.

Kinghorn, A. D., and D. D. Soejarto. 1985. Current status of stevioside as a sweetening agent for human use. In *Economic and Medicinal Plant Research Vol. 1.* Ed. H. Wagner et al. London: Academic Press. 2–52.

Konoshima, T., and M. Takasaki. 2003. Anti-carcinogenic activities of natural sweeteners. *Food Food Ingred.* 208: 184–190.

Kurahashi, H., et al. 1982. Pharmacological studies of stevioside. *Matsumoto Shigaku* 8: 56–62.

Lee, C.-N, et al. 2001. Inhibitory effect of stevioside on calcium influx to produce antihypertension. *Pl. Med.* 67: 796–799.

Lee, J. I., et al. 1979. High-yielding stevia variety 'Suweon 2'. *Nongsa Sihom Yongu Pogo* 21: 167–169.

———. 1979. Studies on new sweetening resources plant stevia (*Stevia rebaudiana* Bertoni) in Korea. I. Effects of transplanting-date shifting by cutting and seeding dates on agronomic characteristics and dry leaf yields of stevia. *Nongsa Sihom Yongu Pogo* 21: 171–179.

———. 1980. Studies on the new sweetening resource plant stevia (*Stevia rebaudiana*

Bertoni M.) in Korea. II. Effect of fertilizer application level and planting density on the dry leaf yields and some agronomic characteristics of stevia. *Nongsa Sihom Yongu Pogo* 22: 138–144.

Lewis, W. H. 1992. Early uses of *Stevia rebaudiana* (Asteraceae) leaves as a sweetener in Paraguay. *Econ. Bot.* 46: 336–337.

Lin, L.-H., et al. 2004. Study on the stevioside analogues of steviolbioside, steviol, and isosteviol 19-alkyl amide dimmers: synthesis and cytotoxic and antibacterial activity. *Chem. Pharm. Bull.* 52: 1117–1122.

Liu, H.-C., et al. 2003. Mechanism of the antihypertensive effect of stevioside in anesthetized dogs. *Pharmacology* 67: 14–20.

Martelli, A., et al. 1985. Unusual essential oils with aromatic properties, I. Volatile components of *Stevia rebaudiana* Bertoni. *Flavour Fragrance J.* 1: 3–7.

Melis, M. S. 1995. Chronic administration of aqueous extract of *Stevia rebaudiana* in rats: renal effects. *J. Ethnopharmacol.* 47: 129–134.

Midmore, D. J. 2002. *A New Rural Industry—Stevia—to Replace Imported Chemical Sweeteners.* RIRDC Project No. UCQ-16A.

Miyazaki, Y., and H. Watanabe. 1974. Studies on the cultivation of *Stevia rebaudiana* Bertoni. I. On the propagation of the plant. *Jap. J. Trop. Agric.* 49: 154–157.

Miyazaki, Y., et al. 1974. Studies on the cultivation of *Stevia rebaudiana* Bertoni. II. On the growth and stevioside content of the plant. *Jap. J. Trop. Agric.* 49: 158–163.

———. 1978. Studies on the cultivation of *Stevia rebaudiana* Bertoni. III. Yield and stevioside content of 2-year-old plants. *Eisei Shikensho Hokoku* 96: 86–96.

Mizukami, H., et al. 1983. Effect of temperature on growth and stevioside formation of *Stevia rebaudiana* Bertoni. *Shoyakugaku Zasshi* 37: 175–179.

Nishiyama, P., et al. 1991. Determinação dos teores de steviosideo e carboidratos solúveis nas folhas de *Stevia rebaudiana* por "espectroscopia de reflectância no infravermelho próximo" (ERIP). *Arg. Biol. Tecnol.* 34: 361–374.

———. 1992. Quantitative analysis of stevioside in the leaves of *Stevia rebaudiana* by near infrared reflectance spectroscopy. *J. Sci. Food Agric.* 59: 277–281.

———. 1992. Water soluble carbohydrates in leaves of *Stevia rebaudiana* and its relationship to the stevioside content. *Ci. Tecnol. Aliment.* 12: 128–133.

Okumura, M., et al. 1978. Studies on the safety of stevioside with rec-assay and reversion test. *Shokuhin Eiseigaku Zasshi* 19: 486–490.

Park, C. H., et al. 1980. Influences of cut-

ting parts of stevia on seedling characters and yield in late season cultivation. In *The Memorial Papers for the Sixtieth Birthday of Dr. Ki Chang Hong.* Korea. 163–166.

Pól, J., et al. 2007. Characterisation of *Stevia rebaudiana* by comprehensive two-dimensional liquid chromatography time-of-flight mass spectrometry. *J. Chrom. A* 1150: 85–92.

Robinson, B. L. 1930. Part 4. The stevias of Paraguay. *Contr. Gray Herb.* 90: 79–90

Sakagushi, M., and T. Kan. 1982. As pesquisas japonesas com *Stevia rebaudiana* (Bert.) Bertoni e o esteviosídeo. *Ci. Cult.* 34: 235–248.

Sakamaki, N., et al. 2004. Simultaneous determination of stevioside, rebaudioside A and glycyrrhizic acid in foods by HPLC. *J. Food Hyg. Soc. Jap.* 45: 81–86.

Salvatore, G., et al. 1983. Stevioside: occurrence, uses, chemical and biological properties. *Chimicaoggi* 1983(8): 31–37.

Soejarto, D. D., et al. 1982. Potential sweetening agents of plant origin. III. Organoleptic evaluation of *Stevia* leaf herbarium samples for sweetness. *Lloydia* 45: 590–599.

———. 1983. Ethnobotanical notes on *Stevia. Bot. Mus. Leafl.* 29: 1–25.

———. 1983. Potential sweetening agents of plant origin. II. Field search of sweet-tasting *Stevia* species. *Econ. Bot.* 37: 71–79.

Suttajit, M., et al. 1993. Mutagenicity and human chromosomal effect of stevioside, a sweetener from *Stevia rebaudiana* Bertoni. *Environmental Health Perspectives Suppl.* 101(3): 53–56.

Tanaka, O. 1980. Chemistry of *Stevia rebaudiana* Bertoni: a new source of natural sweeteners. *Recent Adv. Nat. Prod. Res.* 1979: 111–119.

Tateo, F., et al. 1999. Stevioside content of *Stevia rebaudiana* (Bertoni) Bertoni grown in East Paraguay. *Ital. J. Food Sci.* 11: 265–269.

Tucker, A. O. 1997. Sweet alternatives. *Herbs Health* 2(2): 50–54.

Unterhalt, B. 1978. Süsstoffe in Vergangenheit und Gegenwart. *Pharm. Heute* 2: 111–114.

Usami, M., et al. 1995. Teratogenicity study of stevioside in rats. *Shikensho Hokoku* 113: 31–35.

Van Calsteren, M.-R., et al. 1993. Spectroscopic characterization of two sweet glycosides from *Stevia rebaudiana. Spectroscopy* 11: 143–156.

Vaněk, T., et al. 2004. Determination of stevioside in plant material and fruit teas. *J. Food Comp. Anal.* 14: 383–388.

Wasuntarawat, C., et al. 1998. Development of toxicity of steviol, a metabolite of stevioside, in the hamster. *Drug Chem. Toxicol.* 21: 207–222.

Yoda, S. K., et al. 2003. Supercritical fluid extraction from *Stevia rebaudiana* Bertoni using CO_2 and CO_2 + water: extraction kinetics and identification of extracted components. *J. Food Eng.* 57: 125–134.

Tagetes
Bicchi, C., et al. 1997. Constituents of *Tagetes lucida* Cav. ssp. *lucida* essential oil. *Flavour Fragrance J.* 12: 47–52.

Céspedes, C. L., et al. 2006. Antifungal and antibacterial activities of Mexican tarragon (*Tagetes lucida*). *J. Agric. Food Chem.* 54: 3521–3527.

Cotrés, A. R., et al. 1990. *Tagetes lucida* Cav. II: Anticholinergic effect on skeletal muscle and heart of rat. *Phyton* 51: 77–82.

Jayme, V., et al. 1998. Effect on rat uterus contractility of *Tagetes lucida* Cav. leaf extracts. *Phyton* 62: 161–165.

Lawrence, B. M. 1985. Essential oils of the *Tagetes* genus. *Perfumer Flavor.* 10(5): 73–82.

López, F. J., et al. 1990. *Tagetes lucida* Cav. I: Inhibitory effect on smooth muscle contractility. *Phyton* 51: 71–76.

Neher, R. T. 1966. *Monograph of the Genus Tagetes (Compositae).* Ph.D. thesis, Indiana Univ., Bloomington.

———. 1968. The ethnobotany of *Tagetes.* *Econ. Bot.* 22: 317–325.

Rivera, B., et al. 1992. Efecto de compuestos cumarínicos sobre la contractilidad de músculo liso. *Phyton* 53: 5–10.

Siegel, R. K., et al. 1977. On the use of *Tagetes lucida* and *Nicotiana rustica* as a Huichol smoking mixture: the Aztec "Yahutli" with suggestive hallucinogenic effects. *Econ. Bot.* 31: 16–23.

Soule, J. A. 1993. *Tagetes minuta*: a potential new herb from South America. In *New Crops.* Ed. J. Janick and J. E. Simon. New York: John Wiley & Sons. 649–654.

Tucker, A. O., and M. J. Maciarello. 1987. Plant identification. In *Proceedings of the First National Herb Growing and Marketing Conference, July 19–22, 1986, West Lafayette, Indiana.* Ed. J. E. Simon and L. Grant. 126–172.

Tanacetum
Abad, M. J., et al. 1995. An approach to the genus *Tanacetum* L. (Compositae): phytochemical and pharmacological review. *Phytotherapy Res.* 9: 79–92.

Anonymous. 2004. Tansy. *Rev. Nat. Prod. (Wolters Kluwer Health).*

Bestmann, H. J., et al. 1984. Pflanzliche Insektizide. II: Das ätherische Öle aus Blättern des Balsamkrautes, *Chrysanthemum balsamita* L. Insektizide Wirkung und Zusammensetzung. *Z. Naturforsch.* 39c: 543–547.

———. 1986. Pflanzliche Insektizide. III: Pyrethrin I im etherischen Öl von Chry-

santhemum balsamita L. *Z. Naturforsch.* 41c: 725–728.

———. 1988. Pflanzliche Insektizide. VIII: Die synergistische Wirkung von (-)-Carvon und Pyrethrin I im etherischen Öl von *Chrysanthemum balsamita* L. *J. Appl. Entomol.* 106: 144–149.

Bos, R., et al. 1990. Analysis of *Tanacetum vulgare* L. oils by GC-MS and GC-FTIR. *Pharm. Weekbl. (Sci.)* 12: A13.

Bylaité, E., et al. 2000. Composition of essential oil of costmary [*Balsamita major* (L.) Desf.] at different growth phases. *J. Agric. Biol. Chem.* 48: 2409–2414.

Clarkson, R. E. 1938. Costmary vs. camphor plant. *Herb J.* 2(11): 3–5.

de Pooter, H. L., et al. 1989. The essential oils of *Tanacetum vulgare* L. and *Tanacetum parthenium* (L.) Schultz-Bip. *J. Essential Oil Res.* 1: 9–13.

Forsén, K. n.d. Über die infraspezifische chemische Variation bei *Chrysanthemum vulgare.* *Ann. Acad. Sci. Fenn. Ser. A. IV. Biol.* 207: 1–54.

Forsén, K., and M. von Schantz. 1971. Neue Hauptbestandteile im ätherischen Öl des Rainfarns in Finnland. *Arch. Pharm.* (Berlin) 304: 944–952.

———. 1973. Chemotypen von *Chrysanthemum vulgare* (L.) Benth. In *Chemistry in Botanical Classification.* Ed. G. Bendz and J. Santesson. New York: Academic Press. 145–152.

Gallino, M. 1988. Essential oil from *Tanacetum vulgare* growing spontaneously in "Tierra del Fuego" (Argentina). *Pl. Med.* 54: 182–183.

Gallori, S., et al. 2001. Chemical composition of some traditional herbal drug preparations: essential oil and aromatic water of costmary (*Balsamita suaveolens* Pers.). *J. Agric. Food Chem.* 49: 5907–5910.

Hanganu, D., et al. 1995. Identification of some compounds of the essential oil from *Chrysanthemum balsamita* L. (Asteraceae). *Clujul. Med.* 68: 244–247.

Hendriks, H., et al. 1990. The essential oil of Dutch tansy (*Tanacetum vulgare* L.). *J. Essential Oil Res.* 2: 155–162.

Héthelyi, É., et al. 1991. Phytochemical and antimicrobial studies on the essential oils of *Tanacetum vulgare* clones by gas chromatography/mass spectrometry. *Herba Hung.* 30: 82–90.

Heywood, V. H. 1976. *Tanacetum, Balsamita.* In *Flora Europaea Vol. 4.* Ed. T. G. Tutin et al. Cambridge Univ. Press. 169–172.

Hough-Goldstein, J. A. 1990. Antifeedant effects of common herbs on the Colorado potato beetle (Coleoptera: Chrysomelidae). *Environ. Entomol.* 19: 234–238.

Hough-Goldstein, J. A., and S. P. Hahn. 1992. Antifeedant and oviposition deterrent activity of an aqueous extract of *Tana-*

cetum vulgare L. on two cabbage pests. *Environ. Entomol.* 21: 837–844.

Judzentiene, A., and D. Mokute. 2005. The inflorescence and leaf essential oils of *Tanacetum vulgare* L., var. *vulgare* growing wild in Lithuania. *Biochem. Syst. Ecol.* 33: 487–498.

Keskitalo, M., et al. 2001. Variation in volatile compounds from tansy (*Tanacetum vulgare* L.) related to genetic and morphological differences of genotypes. *Biochem. Syst. Ecol.* 29: 267–285.

Matthews, D., and W. Schearer. 1984. *Tansy: A Potential Repellent for the Colorado Potato Beetle.* Rodale Res. Cent. EN-84.

Nano, G. M., et al. 1982. Chemical and botanical researches on wild growing Piedmontese plants: *Chrysanthemum vulgare* L.: components, distribution and variation. In *VIII International Congress of Essential Oils, October 12–17, 1980, Cannes-Grasse, France.* Paper no. 126.

Neszmélyi, A., et al. 1992. Composition of the essential oil of clone 409 of *Tanacetum vulgare* and 2D NMR investigation of trans-chrysanthenyl acetate. *J. Essential Oil Res.* 4: 243–250.

Panasiuk, O. 1984. Response of Colorado potato beetles, *Leptinotarsa decemlineata* (Say), to volatile components of tansy, *Tanacetum vulgare.* *J. Chem. Ecol.* 10: 1325–1333.

Rohloff, J., et al. 2004. Chemotypical variation of tansy (*Tanacetum vulgare* L.) from 40 different locations in Norway. *J. Agric. Food Chem.* 52: 1742–1748.

Rusu, M. A., et al. 1994. Effects of the *Chrysanthemum balsamita* hydroalcoholic extract upon the intoxicated liver. *Fitoterapia* 65: 211–213.

Schearer, W. R. 1984. Components of oil of tansy (*Tanacetum vulgare*) that repel Colorado potato beetles (*Leptinotarsa decemlineata*). *J. Nat. Prod.* 47: 964–969.

Soreng, R. J., and E. A. Cope. 1991. On the taxonomy of cultivated species of *Chrysanthemum* genus-complex (Anthemideae; Compositae). *Baileya* 23: 145–165.

Sorsa, M., et al. 1968. Variability of essential oil components in *Chrysanthemum vulgare* L. in Finland. *Ann. Acad. Sci. Fenn., Ser. A, IV. Biol.* 135: 1–13.

Strobel, H., and K. Knobloch. 1987. Über die ätherischen Öle von *Chrysanthemum balsamita* L. *Z. Naturforsch.* 42c: 502–506.

Vaverková, Š., et al. 2006. A study of qualitative properties of the essential oil of *Tanacetum vulgare* L. *Ceska Slov. Farm.* 60: 181–184.

von Schantz, M., et al. 1966. Die Veranderungen des ätherischen Öles während der Entwicklung der Blütenkörbchen von *Chrysanthemum vulgare* L. *Pl. Med.* 14: 421–435.

Wolbis, M. 1979. Investigation of *Chrysanthemum balsamita* L. I. Studies of the volatile oil with consideration of botanical characteristics of the taxon. *Acta Polon. Pharm.* 36: 707–714.

Zielinska-Sowicka, R., and M. Wolbis. 1970. Examination of *Chrysanthemum balsamita* leaves. *Herba Polon.* 16: 286–295.

Thymbra

Akgül, A., et al. 1999. Essential oil of four Turkish wild-growing Labiatae herbs: *Salvia cryptantha* Ten., *Thymbra spicata* L. and *Thymus cilicicus* Boiss. et Bal. *J. Essential Oil Res.* 11: 209–214.

Andrews, A. 1958. Thyme as a condiment in the Graeco-Roman era. *Osiris* 13: 150–156.

Arras, G., et al. 1995. Fungicide effect of volatile compounds of *Thymus capitatus* essential oil. *Acta Hort.* 379: 593–600.

Arras, G., and G. E. Grella. 1992. Wild thyme, *Thymus capitatus*, essential oil seasonal changes and antimycotic activity. *J. Hort. Sci.* 67: 197–202.

Arras, G., and A. Piga. 1995. *Thymus capitatus* essential oil reducing citrus fruit decay. In *Postharvest Physiology, Pathology and Technologies for Horticultural Commodities: Recent Advances.* Ed. A. Ait-Oubahou and M. El-Otmani. Agardir, Morocco: Inst. Agron. Vet. Hassa II. 426–428.

Arras, G., et al. 1993. The use of *Thymus capitatus* essential oil under vacuum conditions to control *Penicillium digitatum* development on citrus fruit. *Acta Hort.* 344: 147–153.

Basim, H., et al. 2000. Antibacterial effect of essential oil of *Thymbra spicata* L. var. *spicata* on some plant pathogenic bacteria. *Z. Pflanzenkrankheiten Pflanzenschutz* 279: 279–284.

Biondi, D., et al. 1993. Antimicrobial activity and chemical composition of essential oils from Sicilian aromatic plants. *Flavour Fragrance J.* 8: 331–337.

Bouzouita, N., et al. 2003. Antimicrobial activity of essential oils from Turkish aromatic plants. *Flavour Fragrance J.* 18: 380–383.

Bozkurt, H. 2006. Utilization of natural antioxidants: green tea extract and *Thymbra spicata* oil in Turkish dry-fermented sausage. *Meat Sci.* 73: 442–450.

D'Auria, M., et al. 2005. Composition of volatile fractions from *Thymus, Origanum, Lavandula* and *Acinos* species. *J. Essential Oil-Bearing Pl.* 8: 36–51.

Falchi-Delitala, L., et al. 1981. Ricerche sulle variazioni dei componenti fenolici dell'olio essenziale di *Thymus capitatus* Hoffm. e Lk. durante il ciclo vegetativo mediante HPLC. *Rivista Ital. EPPOS* 63: 62–67.

Faleiro, L., et al. 2005. Antibacterial and antioxidant activities of essential oils isolated from *Thymbra capitata* L. (Cav.) and *Origanum vulgare* L. *J. Agric. Food Chem.* 53: 8162–8168.

Flannery, H. B. 1982. *A Study of the Taxa of* Thymus *L. (Labiatae) Cultivated in the United States.* Ph.D. thesis, Cornell Univ., Ithaca, New York.

Fleisher, A., et al. 1984. Chemovarieties of *Coridothymus capitatus* L. Rchb. growing in Israel. *J. Sci. Food Agric.* 35: 495–499.

———. 1988. Identification of biblical hyssop and the origin of the traditional use of oregano-group herbs in the Mediterranean region. *Econ. Bot.* 42: 232–241.

Fleisher, Z., and A. Fleisher. 2002. Volatiles of *Coridothymus capitatus* chemotypes growing in Israel. Aromatic plants of the Holy Land and the Sinai, part 15. *J. Essential Oil Res.* 14: 105–106.

———. 2005. Extract analyses of *Satureja thymbra* L. and *Thymbra spicata* L. Aromatic plants of the Holy Land and the Sinai, part 17. *J. Essential Oil Res.* 17: 32–35.

Goren, A. C., et al. 2003. Analysis of essential oil of *Coridothymus capitatus* (L.) and its antibacterial and antifungal activity. *Z. Naturforsch.* 58c: 687–690.

Hedhili, L., et al. 2002. Variability in essential oil composition of Tunisian *Thymus capitatus* (L.) Hoffmanns. et Link. *Flavour Fragrance J.* 17: 26–28.

Kanias, G. D., and A. Loukis. 1992. Statistical analysis of essential oil percentage composition of *Coridothymus capitatus* Reichb. f. and *Satureja thymbra* L. *J. Essential Oil Res.* 4: 57–584.

Karousou, R., et al. 2005. Essential oil composition is related to the natural habitats: *Coridothymus capitatus* and *Satureja thymbra* in NATURA 2000 sites of Crete. *Phytochemistry* 66: 2668–2673.

Kiliç, T. 2006. Analysis of essential oil composition of *Thymbra spicata* var. *spicata*: antifungal, antibacterial and antimycobacterial activities. *Z. Naturforsch.* 61c: 324–328.

Kizil, S., and Ö. Tonçer. 2005. Effect of different planting densities on yield and yield components of wild thyme (*Thymbra spicata* var. *spicata*). *Acta Agron. Hung.* 53: 417–422.

Kizil, S., and F. Uyar. 2006. Antimicrobial activities of some thyme (*Thymus, Satureja, Origanum* and *Thymbra*) species against important plant pathogens. *Asian J. Chem.* 18: 1455–1461.

Kubtrak, D., et al. 1990. Composition of the essential oils of some *Thymus* and *Thymbra* species. *Flavour Fragrance J.* 5: 227–231.

Miceli, A., et al. 2006. Essential oil variability in *Thymbra capitata* (L.) Cav. growing wild in southern Apulia (Italy). *Biochem. Syst. Ecol.* 34: 528–535.

Miguel, M. G., et al. 2003. Effect of the volatile constituents isolated from *Thymus albicans, Th. mastichina, Th. carnosus* and *Thymbra capitata* in sunflower oil. *Nahrung/Food* 6: 397–402.

———. 2003. Effect of the essential volatile oils isolated from *Thymbra capitata* (L.) Cav. on olive and sunflower oils. *Grasas Aceites* 54: 219–225.

———. 2005. Evaluation of the antioxidant activity of *Thymbra capitata, Thymus mastichina* and *Thymus camphoratus* essential oils. *J. Food Lipids* 12: 181–197.

Morales Valverde, R. 1986. Taxonomía de los géneros *Thymus* (excluida la sección *Serpyllum*) y *Thymbra* en la Península Ibérica. *Ruizia.* 3: 1–324.

———. 1987. El género *Thymbra* L. (Labiatae). *Anales Jard. Bot. Madrid* 44: 349–380.

Oussalah, M., et al. 2006. Mechanism of action of Spanish oregano, Chinese cinnamon, and savory essential oils against cell membranes and walls of *Escherichia coli* O157:H7 and *Listeria monocytogenes. J. Food Prot.* 69: 1046–1055.

Özek, T., et al. 1995. Composition of the essential oil of *Coridothymus capitatus* (L.) Reichb. fil. from Turkey. *J. Essential Oil Res.* 7: 309–312.

Ozel, M. Z., et al. 2003. Subcritical water extraction of essential oils from *Thymbra spicata. Food Chem.* 82: 381–386.

Paster, N., et al. 1995. Antifungal activity of oregano and thyme essential oils applied as fumigants against fungi attacking stored grain. *J. Food Prot.* 58: 81–85.

Ravid, U., and E. Putievsky. 1985. Composition of essential oils of *Thymbra spicata* and *Satureja thymbra* chemotypes. *Pl. Med.* 1985: 337–338.

Ravid, U., et al. 1986. Carvacrol and thymol chemotypes of East Mediterranean wild Labiatae herbs. In *Progress in Essential Oil Research.* Ed. E.-J. Brunke. Berlin: Walter de Gruyter & Co. 163–167.

Salgueiro, L. R., et al. 2003. Chemical composition and antifungal activity of the essential oil of *Thymbra capitata. Pl. Med.* 70: 572–575.

Silme, R. S., and O. Yeğen. 2006. *Thymbra spicata* L. var. *spicata* essential oil assimilation by a selected bacterium and its affect to control of soil-borne pathogens. *Acta Hort.* 725: 471–476.

Skoula, M., and R. J. Grayer. 2005. Volatile oils of *Coridothymus capitatus, Satureja thymbra, Satureja spinosa* and *Thymbra calostachya* (Lamiaceae) from Crete. *Flavour Fragrance J.* 20: 573–576.

Sonsuzer, S., et al. 2004. Optimization of supercritical CO_2 extraction of *Thymbra spicata* oil. *J. Supercrit. Fluids* 30: 189–199.

Tanker, M., et al. 1993. Results of certain investigations on the volatile oil containing plants of Turkey. In *Essential Oils for Perfumery and Flavour. Proceedings of an International Conference 26–30 May 1990 Antalya, Turkey.* Ed. K. H. C. Baser and N. Güler. Istanbul. 16–29.

Tateo, F., et al. 1996. Essential oil composition and enantiomeric distribution of some monoterpenoid components of *Coridothymus capitatus* (L.) Reichenb. Fil. grown in island of Kos (Greece). *Rivista Sci. Alimentazione* 25: 103–107.

Terrab, A., et al. 2004. A preliminary palynological characterization of Spanish thyme honeys. *Bot. J. Linn. Soc.* 146: 323–330.

Tommasi, L., et al. 2007. Influence of environmental factors on essential oil variability in *Thymbra capitata* (L.) Cav. Growing wild in southern Puglia (Italy). *J. Essential Oil Res.* 19: 572–580.

Tümen, G., et al. 1994. Composition of essential oils from two varieties of *Thymbra spicata* L. *J. Essential Oil Res.* 6: 463–468.

———. 1998. Essential oil composition and enantiomeric distribution of some monoterpenoid components of *Coridothymus capitatus* (L.) Rchb. grown on the island of Kos (Greece). *J. Essential Oil Res.* 10: 241–244.

Vampa, G., et al. 1988. Études chimiques et microbiologiques sur les huiles essentielles de *Thymus. Pl. Med. Phytotherap.* 22: 195–202.

Thymus

Adzet, R., et al. 1977. Chimiotypes de *Thymus mastichina* L. *Pl. Med. Phytotherap.* 11: 275–280.

Agarwal, I., and C. S. Mathela. 1979. Study of antifungal activity of some terpenoids. *Indian Drugs Pharm. Industr.* 14(5): 19–21.

Alissandrakis, E., et al. 2007. Comparison of the volatile composition in thyme honeys from several origins in Greece. *J. Agric. Food Chem.* 55: 8152–8157.

Almeida, V., et al. 2006. Volatile constituents of leaves and flowers of *Thymus mastichina* by headspace solid-phase microextraction. *Acta Hort.* 723: 239–242.

Assoud, W. 1974. Recherches sur la génétique écologique de *Thymus vulgaris* L. Étude expérimentale du polymorphisme sexuel. *Compt. Rend. Seances Acad. Agric.* 60: 57–62.

Assoud, W., and G. Valdeyron. 1973. Remarques sur la biologie du thym *Thymus vulgaris* L. *Bull. Soc. Bot. Fr.* 122: 21–34.

Atti-Santos, A. C., et al. 2004. Seasonal variation of essential oil yield and composition of *Thymus vulgaris* L. (Lamiaceae) from South Brazil. *J. Essential Oil Res.* 16: 294–295.

Bolòs, O. de, and J. Vigo. 1983. Notes sobre

taxonomic i nomenclatura de les plantes, II. *Colect. Bot.* 14: 89–103.

Böttcher, H., et al. 2001. Physiologisches Nachernteverhalten von Thymien (*Thymus vulgaris* L.). *Gartenbauwissenschaft* 66: 172–181.

Bruni, A., and P. Modenesi. 1983. Development, oil storage and dehiscence of peltate trichomes in *Thymus vulgaris* (Lamiaceae). *Nord. J. Bot.* 3: 245–251.

Carrera, C., et al. 2005. Long-term complete remission of cutaneous melanoma metastases in association with a folk remedy. *J. Amer. Acad. Dermatol.* 52: 713–715.

Chizzola, R., et al. 2005. Variabilität im ätherischen Öl von südfranzösischgen und spanischen Wildpopulationen des Thymians (*Thymus vulgaris* L.) und daraus erstellten Feldkulturen. *Z. Arzn. Gew. Pfl.* 10: 82–90.

Cioni, P. L., et al. 1990. Studio sulla variabilità delle essenze individuali di una micropopolazione di piante di *Thymus vulgaris* L. *Rivista Ital. EPPOS* 1(1): 3–6.

Colin, M. E. 1990. Essential oils of Labiatae for controlling honey bee varroosis. *J. Appl. Entomol.* 110: 19–25.

D'Auria, M., et al. 2005. Composition of volatile fractions from *Thymus, Origanum, Lavandula* and *Acinos* species. *J. Essential Oil-Bearing Pl.* 8: 36–51.

De Gaviña Mugica, M., and J. Torner Ochoa. 1974. *Contribucion al Estudio de los Aceites Españoles. II. Aceites Esenciales de la Provincia de Guadalajara.* Madrid: Inst. Nac. Invest. Agrarias.

Díaz-Maroto, M. C., et al. 2005. Volatile components and key odorants of fennel (*Foeniculum vulgare* Mill.) and thyme (*Thymus vulgaris* L.) oil extracts obtained by simultaneous distillation-extraction and supercritical fluid extraction. *J. Agric. Food Chem.* 53: 5385–5389.

Dimitrijević, S. I., et al. 2007. A study of the synergistic antilisterial effects of a sublethal dose of lactic acid and essential oils of *Thymus vulgaris* L., *Rosmarinus officinalis* L. and *Origanum vulgare* L. *Food Chem.* 104: 774–782.

Dorman, H. J. D., et al. 1995. Evaluation in vitro of plant essential oils as natural antioxidants. *J. Essential Oil Res.* 7: 645–651.

Easter, M. 2001. *Thymus coccineus* group. *Pl. Heritage* 8(2): 18–19.

Ehler, B. K., and J. D. Thompson. 2004. Temporal variation in sex allocation in hermaphrodites of gynodioecious *Thymus vulgaris* L. *J. Ecol.* 92: 15–23.

Fang, H.-J., et al. 1988. The chemical constituents of *Thymus mongolicus* Ronn. and *T. quinquecostatus* Celak oils of Chinese origin. *Flavour Fragrance J.* 3: 73–77.

Fehr, D., and G. Stenmzhorn. 1979. Untersuchungen zur Lagerstabilität von Pfefferminzblättern, Rosmarinblättern und

Thymian. *Pharm. Zeitung* 124: 2342–2349.

Flannery, H. B. 1982. *A Study of the Taxa of Thymus L. (Labiatae) Cultivated in the United States.* Ph.D. diss., Cornell Univ., Ithaca, New York.

Fraternale, D., et al. 2003. Chemical composition and antifungal activity of essential oil obtained from in vitro plants of *Thymus mastichina* L. *J. Essential Oil Res.* 15: 278–281.

Gips, K., ed. n.d. *Thyme: An Herbal Handbook.* Cleveland, Ohio: Western Reserve Herb Society.

Granger, R., and J. Passet. 1973. *Thymus vulgaris* spontane de France: races chimiques et chemotaxonomie. *Phytochemistry* 12: 1683–1691.

———. 1974. Types chimiques de *Thymus herba-barona* Loiseleur et Deslongchamps, de Corse. *Rivista Ital. EPPOS* 56: 622–629.

Guillén, M. D., and M. J. Manzanos. 1998. Study of the composition of the different parts of a Spanish *Thymus vulgaris* L. plant. *Food Chem.* 63: 373–383.

Haddad, M., et al. 2007. Effect of gamma and e-beam radiation on the essential oils of *Thymus vulgaris thymoliferum, Eucalyptus radiata,* and *Lavandula angustifolia. J. Agric. Food Chem.* 55: 6082–6086.

Hornok, L., et al. 1975. Experiments on updating the growing methods of common thyme (*Thymus vulgaris* L.). *Herba Hung.* 14: 47–64.

Horváth, G., et al. 2004. Characterization and TLC-bioautographic detection of essential oils from some *Thymus* taxa. Determination of the activity of the oils and their components against plant pathogenic bacteria. *J. Planar Chromatogr.* 17: 300–304.

———. 2006. Essential oil composition of three cultivated *Thymus* chemotypes from Hungary. *J. Essential Oil Res.* 18: 315–317.

Hudaib, M., et al. 2002. GC/MS evaluation of thyme (*Thymus vulgaris* L.) oil composition and variations during the vegetative cycle. *J. Pharm. Biomed. Anal.* 29: 691–700.

———. 2007. Volatile components of *Thymus vulgaris* L. from wild-growing and cultivated plants in Jordan. *Flavour Fragrance J.* 22: 322–327.

Institut Technique Interprofessionnel des Plantes Medicinales, Aromatiques et Industrielles. 1983. *Domestication de la Production Conditionnement et Définition du Thym (*Thymus vulgaris *L.).* Milley-La-Forêt, France: I.T.E.P.M.A.I.

Jukić, J., and M. Miloš. 2005. Catalytic oxidation and antioxidant properties of thyme essential oils (*Thymus vulgarae* L.). *Croatica Chem. Acta* 78: 105–110.

Juliano, C., et al. 2000. Composition and *in vitro* antimicrobial activity of the essential oil of *Thymus herba-barona* Loisel growing wild in Sardinia. *J. Essential Oil Res.* 12: 516–522.

Kaloustian, J., et al. 2005. Southern French thyme oils: chromatographic study of chemotypes. *J. Sci. Food Agric.* 85: 2437–2444.

Kim, J., et al. 2008. Fumigant antifungal activity of plant essential oils and components from West Indian bay (*Pimenta racemosa*) and thyme (*Pimenta vulgaris*) oils against two phytopathogenic fungi. *Flavour Fragrance J.* 23: 272–277.

Klarić, M. Š., et al. 2006. Antifungal activity of thyme (*Thymus vulgaris* L.) essential oil and thymol against moulds from damp dwellings. *Lett. Appl. Microbiol.* 44: 36–42.

Kowal, T., and A. Krupinska. 1979. Antibacterial activity of essential oil from *Thymus pulegioides* L. *Herba Polon.* 25: 303–310.

Kubtrak, D., et al. 1990. Composition of the essential oils of some *Thymus* and *Thymbra* species. *Flavour Fragrance J.* 5: 227–231.

Kulišić, T., et al. 2007. The effects of essential oils and aqueous tea infusions of oregano (*Origanum vulgare* L. subsp. *hirtum*), thyme (*Thymus vulgaris* L.) and wild thyme (*Thymus serpyllum* L.) on the copper-induced oxidation of human low-density lipoproteins. *Intern. J. Food Sci. Nutr.* 58: 87–93.

LaFlamme, L., et al. 1994. Establishment of thyme (*Thymus vulgaris* L.) by direct sowing or transplanting at two densities. *HortScience* 29: 248.

Lawrence, B. M. 1981. *Essential Oils 1979–1980*. Wheaton, Illinois: Allured.

———. 1982. The existence of infraspecific differences in specific genera in the Labiatae family. In *VIII International Congress of Essential Oils, October 12–17, 1980, Cannes-Grasse, France.* Paper no. 35.

Lees, P. D. 1980. *Culinary and Medicinal Herbs.* 4th ed. Minist. Agric. Fish. Food Ref. Book 325.

Lens-Lisbonne, et al. 1987. Methodes d'evaluation de l'activite antibacterienne des huiles essentielles: application aux essences de thym et de canelle. *J. Pharm. Belg.* 42: 297–302.

Letchamo, W., and A. Gosselin. 1995. Effects of HPS supplemental lighting and soil water levels on growth, essential oil content and composition of two thyme (*Thymus vulgaris* L.) clonal selections. *Canad. J. Pl. Sci.* 75: 231–238.

———. 1996. Transpiration, essential oil glands, epicuticular wax and morphology of *Thymus vulgaris* are influenced by light intensity and water supply. *J. Hort. Sci.* 71: 123–134.

Letchamo, W., et al. 1995. Volatile oil and thymol accumulation in *Thymus vulgaris*. *HortScience* 30: 888.

———. 1995. Variations in photosynthesis and essential oil in thyme. *J. Pl. Physiol.* 147: 29–37.

Li, Y.-I., et al. 1996. Effect of light level on essential oil production of sage (*Salvia officinalis*) and thyme (*Thymus vulgaris*). *Acta Hort.* 426: 419–426.

Ložiene, K. 2002. Infraspecific taxa of *Thymus serpyllum* (Lamiaceae) growing in Lithuania. *Thaiszia – J. Bot. Košice* 12: 61–74.

———. 2002. Evaluation of infraspecific diversity of the *Thymus* genus (stability of morphotypes and chemotypes, selection of valuable clones). *Bot. Lithuanica* 8: 299–300.

———. 2006. Instability of morphological features used for classification of *Thymus pulegioides* infraspecific taxa. *Acta Bot. Hung.* 48: 345–360.

Ložiene, K., and J. Vaičiūniene. 1999. Keturbriaunio čiobrelio (*Thymus pulegioides* L.) vidurūšine įvairove ire augimviečių charakteristika. *Bot. Lithuanica* 5: 27–40.

Ložiene, K., and P. R. Venskutonis. 2005. Influence of environmental and genetic factors on the stability of essential oil composition of *Thymus pulegioides*. *Biochem. Syst. Ecol.* 33: 517–525.

———. 2006. Chemical composition of the essential oil of *Thymus serpyllum* L. ssp. *serpyllum* growing wild in Lithuania. *J. Essential Oil Res.* 18: 206–211.

Ložiene, K., et al. 2002. Chemical diversity of essential oil of *Thymus pulegioides* L. and *Thymus serpyllum* L. growing in Lithuania. *Biologija* 2002: 62–64.

———. 2003. Chemical composition of the essential oil of different varieties of thyme (*Thymus pulegioides*) growing wild in Lithuania. *Biochem. Syst. Ecol.* 31: 249–259.

Martinez-González, M. C., et al. 2007. Concomitant allergic contact dermatitis due to *Rosmarinus officinalis* (rosemary) and *Thymus vulgaris* (thyme). *Contact Dermatitis* 56: 49–50.

Mártonfi, P. 1992. Polymorphism of essential oil in *Thymus pulegioides* subsp. *chamaedrys* in Slovakia. *J. Essential Oil Res.* 4: 173–179.

———. 1997. Nomenclatural survey of the genus *Thymus* sect. *Serpyllum* from Carpathians and Pannonia. *Thaiszia – J. Bot. Košice* 7: 111–181.

McGimpsey, J. A. 1993. *Thyme:* Thymus vulgaris. New Zealand Inst. Crop Food Res. Broadsheet No. 22.

McGimpsey, J. A., et al. 1994. Seasonal variation in essential oil yield and composition from naturalized *Thymus vulgaris* L. in New Zealand. *Flavour Fragrance J.* 9: 347–352.

Messerschmidt, W. 1965. Gas-und dünnschichtchromatographische Untersuchungen der ätherischen Öle einiger

thymusarten. II. Der Einfluss verschiedener Herkünfte auf die Zusammensetzung des ätherischen Öls von Herba Thymi und Herba Serpylli und Vorschläge für ihre chromatographische Beurteilung. *Pl. Med.* 13: 56–72.

Michet, A., et al. 2008. Chemotypes in the volatiles of wild thyme (*Thymus pulegioides* L.). *J. Essential Oil Res.* 20: 101–103.

Miguel, M. G., et al. 1999. Study of the substrate and fertilization effects on the production of essential oils by *Thymus mastichina* (L.) L. ssp. *mastichina* cultivated in pots. In *Improved Crop Quality by Nutrient Management.* Ed. D. Anaç and P. Martin-Prével. Dordrecht: Kluwer Acad. Publ. 201–204.

———. 2002. Changes of the chemical composition of the essential oil of Portuguese *Thymus mastichina* in the course of two vegetation cycles. *Acta Hort.* 576: 83–86.

———. 2002. Chemical composition of the essential oils from *Thymus mastichina* over a day period. *Acta Hort.* 576: 87–90.

———. 2002. Effect of substrate on the essential oils composition of *Thymus mastichina* (L.) L. subsp. *mastichina* collected in Sesimbra Region (Portugal). In *Natural Products in the New Millennium: Prospects and Industrial Application.* Ed. A. P. Rauer et al. Dordrecht: Kluwer Acad. Publ. 143–148.

———. 2003. Essential oils of Portuguese *Thymus mastichina* (L.) L. subsp. *mastichina* grown on different substrates and harvested on different dates. *J. Hort. Sci. Biotechnol.* 78: 355–358.

———. 2003. Effect of the volatile constituents isolated from *Thymus albicans, Th. mastichina, Th. carnosus* and *Thymbra capitata* in sunflower oil. *Nahrung/Food* 6: 397–402.

———. 2004. Composition and antioxidant activities of the essential oils of *Thymus caespititius, Thymus camphoratus* and *Thymus mastichina. Food Chem.* 86: 183–188.

———. 2004. Main components of the essential oils from wild Portuguese *Thymus mastichina* (L.) L. ssp. *mastichina* in different developmental stages or under culture conditions. *J. Essential Oil Res.* 16: 111–114.

———. 2005. Evaluation of the antioxidant activity of *Thymbra capitata, Thymus mastichina* and *Thymus camphoratus* essential oils. *J. Food Lipids* 12: 181–197.

Milchard, M. J., et al. 2004. Application of gas-liquid chromatography to the analysis of essential oils. *Perfumer Flavor.* 29(5): 28–36.

Mockute, D., and D. Bernotiene. 1999. The main citral-geranial and carvacrol chemotypes of the essential oil of *Thymus pulegioides* L. growing wild in Vilnius District (Lithuania). *J. Agric. Food Chem.* 47: 3787–3790.

———. 2004. 1,8-Cineole-caryophyllene oxide chemotype of essential oil of *Thymus serpyllum* L. growing wild in Vilnius (Lithuania). *J. Essential Oil Res.* 16: 236–238.

———. 2005. Chemical composition of the essential oils and the odor of *Thymus pulegioides* L. growing wild in Vilnius. *J. Essential Oil Res.* 17: 415–418.

Morales Valverde, R. 1986. Taxonomía de los géneros *Thymus* (excluida la sección *Serpyllum*) y *Thymbra* en la Península Ibérica. *Ruizia.* 3: 1–324.

Ozbey, A., and U. Uygun. 2007. Behaviour of some organophosphorus pesticides residues in thyme and stinging nettle tea during infusion process. *Intern. J. Food Sci. Technol.* 42: 380–383.

Özgüven, M., and S. Tansi. 1998. Drug yield and essential oil of *Thymus vulgaris* L. as influenced by ecological and ontogenetical variation. *Turk. J. Agric. For.* 22: 537–542.

Panizzi, L., et al. 1993. Composition and antimicrobial properties of essential oils of four Mediterranean Lamiaceae. *J. Ethnopharmacol.* 39: 167–170.

Passet, J. 1979. La variabilité chimique chez le thym, ses manifestations, sa signification. *Parfums, Cosmétiques, Arômes* 28: 39–42.

Paster, N., et al. 1990. Inhibitory effect of oregano and thyme essential oils on moulds and food-borne bacteria. *Lett. Appl. Microbiol.* 11: 33–37.

Patáková, D., and M. Chládek. 1974. Über die antibakterielle Aktivität von Thymian- und Quendelölen. *Pharmazie Beih. Ergänzungsband* 29: 140, 142.

Phillips, H. F. 1991. The best of thymes. *Herb Companion* 3(4): 22–29.

Piccaglia, R., et al. 1993. Antibacterial and antioxidant properties of Mediterranean aromatic plants. *Industrial Crops Prod.* 2: 47–50.

Pina-Vaz, C., et al. 2004. Antifungal activity of *Thymus* oils and their major compounds. *DEADV* 18: 73–78.

Pinto, E., et al. 2006. Antifungal activity of the essential oil of *Thymus pulegioides* on *Candida*, *Aspergillus* and dermatophyte species. *J. Med. Microbiol.* 55: 1367–1373.

Prasad, B. L. S., et al. 2001. Rooting of cuttings in thyme (*Thymus vulgaris* L.) as influenced by growth-regulators and methods of application. *Indian Perfumer* 45: 23–29.

Raal, A., et al. 2005. Comparative chemical composition of the essential oil of *Thymus vulgaris* L. from different geographical sources. *Herba Pol.* 51: 10–16.

Rasooli, I., and S. E. Mirmostafa. 2002. Antibacterial properties of *Thymus pubescens* and *Thymus serpyllum* essential oils. *Fitoterapia* 73: 244–250.

Rasooli, I., and P. Owlia. 2005. Chemoprevention by thyme oils of *Aspergillus para-*

siticus growth and aflatoxin production. *Phytochemistry* 66: 2851–2856.

Rasooli, I., et al. 2005. Ultrastructural studies on antimicrobial efficacy of thyme essential oils on *Listeria monocytogenes*. *Intern. J. Infectious Dis.* 10: 236–241.

Reddy, M. V. B., et al. 1998. Characterization and use of essential oil from *Thymus vulgaris* against *Botrytis cinerea* and *Rhizopus stolonifera* in strawberry fruits. *Phytochemistry* 47: 1515–1520.

Rey, Ch. 1991. Incidence de la date et de la hauteur de coupe en première année de culture sur la productivité de la sauge officinale et du thym vulgaire. *Rev. Suisse Vitic. Arbor. Hort.* 23: 137–143.

Rhyu, H. Y. 1979. Gas chromatographic characterization of oregano and other selected spices of the Labiatae family. *J. Food Sci.* 44: 1373–1378.

Roussel, J.-L., et al. 1973. Propriétés antifongiques comparées des essences de trois Labiées méditerranéennes: romarin, sarriette et thym. *Trav. Soc. Pharm. Montpellier* 33: 587–592.

Salgueiro, L. R., et al. 1991. Composition de l'huile essentielle de *Thymus mastichina* du Portugal. *Rivista Ital. EPPOS* 1991: 491–495.

Samejima, K., et al. 1995. Luteolin: a strong antimutagen against dietary carcinogen, Trp-P-2, in peppermint, sage, and thyme. *J. Agric. Food Chem.* 43: 410–414.

Santoro, G. F., et al. 2007. Effect of oregano (*Origanum vulgare* L.) and thyme (*Thymus vulgaris* L.) essential oils on *Trypanosoma cruzi* (Protozoa: Kinetoplastida) growth and ultrastructure. *Parasitol. Res.* 100: 783–790.

Sattar, A., et al. 1991. Essential oils of the species of Labiatae. Part 4. Composition of the essential oil of *Thymus serpyllum*. *Pakistan J. Sci. Industr. Res.* 34: 119–120.

Sefidkon, F., et al. 2004. The composition of *Thymus serpyllum* L. oil. *J. Essential Oil Res.* 16: 184–185.

Simeon de Bouchberg, M., et al. 1976. Propriétés microbiologiques des huiles essentielles de chimiotypes de *Thymus vulgaris* Linnaeus. *Rivista Ital. EPPOS* 58: 527–536.

Singh, A., et al. 2003. Efficacy of plant essential oils as antimicrobial agents against *Listeria monocytogenes* in hotdogs. *Lebensm. Eiss. Technol.* 36: 787–794.

Singh, N., et al. 2003. Sequential disinfection of *Escherichia coli* O157:H7 inoculated alfalfa seeds before and during sprouting using aqueous chlorine dioxide, ozonated water, and thyme essential oil. *Lebensm. Wiss. Technol.* 36: 235–243.

Šipailienė, A., et al. 2006. Antimicrobial activity of commercial samples of thyme and marjoram oils. *J. Essential Oil Res.* 18: 698–703.

Stahl, E. 1982. The essential oil from *Thymus praecox* ssp. *arcticus*. In *Aromatic Plants: Basic and Applied Aspects.* Ed. N. Margaris et al. The Hague: Martinus Nijhoff. 203–206.

———. 1984. Chemical polymorphism of essential oil in *Thymus praecox* ssp. *arcticus* (Lamiaceae) from Greenland. *Nord. J. Bot.* 4: 597–600.

———. 1984. Das ätherische Öl aus *Thymus praecox* ssp. *arcticus* isländischer Herkunft. *Pl. Med.* 50: 157–160.

Stahl-Biskup, E. 1986. Das ätherische Öl norwegischer Thymian-Arten; II. *Thymus pulegioides*. *Pl. Med.* 1986: 233–235.

———. 1990. Essential oil polymorphism in Finnish *Thymus* species. *Pl. Med.* 56: 464–468.

———. 1991. The chemical composition of *Thymus* oils: a review of the literature 1960–1989. *J. Essential Oil Res.* 3: 61–82.

Stahl-Biskup, E., and J. Holthuijzen. 1995. Essential oil and glycosidically bound volatiles of lemon-scented thyme, *Thymus* ×*citriodorus* (Pers.) Schreb. *Flavour Fragrance J.* 10: 225–229.

Stahl-Biskup, E., and F. Sáez, eds. 2002. *Thyme: The Genus* Thymus. London: Taylor & Francis.

Takácsová, M., et al. 1995. Study of the antioxidative effects of thyme, sage, juniper and oregano. *Nahrung* 39: 241–243.

Tanker, M., et al. 1993. Results of certain investigations on the volatile oil containing plants of Turkey. In *Essential Oils for Perfumery and Flavour. Proceedings of an International Conference 26–30 May 1990 Antalya, Turkey.* Ed. K. H. C. Baser and N. Güler. Istanbul: 16–29.

Thompson, J. D., et al. 2000. Exploring the genetic basis and proximate causes of female fertility advantage in gynodioecious *Thymus vulgaris*. *Evolution* 54: 1510–1520.

———. 2003. Qualitative and quantitative variation in monoterpene co-occurrence and composition in the essential oil of *Thymus vulgaris* chemotypes. *J. Chem. Ecol.* 29: 859–880.

———. 2004. Multiple genetic contributions to plant performance in *Thymus vulgaris*. *J. Ecol.* 92: 45–46.

Tomei, P. E., et al. 1995. Evaluation of the chemical composition of the essential oils of some Lamiaceae from Serrania de Ronda (Andaluçia, Spain). *J. Essential Oil Res.* 7: 279–282.

Usai, M., et al. 2003. Composition and variability of the essential oil of Sardinian *Thymus herba-barona* Loisel. *Flavour Fragrance J.* 18: 21–25.

Vampa, G., et al. 1988. Études chimiques et microbiologiques sur les huiles essentielles de *Thymus*. *Pl. Med. Phytotherap.* 22: 195–202.

Van Den Broucke, C. O. 1983. The therapeutic value of *Thymus* species. *Fitoterapia* 54(4): 171–174.

Vernet, P., and P.-H. Gouyon. 1979. Le polymorphisme chimique de *Thymus vulgaris*. *Parfums, Cosmétiques, Arômes* 30: 31–45.

Vernin, G., et al. 1994. GC-MS-SPECMA analysis of *Thymus serpyllum praecox* (Opiz) Wollm (wild thyme) from Hautes Alpes (France). In *Spices, Herbs and Edible Fungi*. Ed. G. Charalambous. Amsterdam: Elsevier. 501–515.

White, K., and S. White. 1994. *Thyme in the Garden*. Woking, England: Natl. Council Conserv. *Pl. Gard.*

Xu, H., et al. 2006. Oregano, thyme and clove-derived flavour and skin sensitizers activate specific TRP channels. *Nat. Neurosci.* 9: 628–635.

Youdim, K. A., and S. G. Deans. 1999. Beneficial effects of thyme oil on age-related changes in the phospholipid C20 and C22 polyunsaturated fatty acid composition of various rat tissues. *Biochem. Biophys. Acta* 1438: 140–146.

———. 1999. Dietary supplementation of thyme (*Thymus vulgaris* L.) essential oil during the lifetime of the rat: its effects on the antioxidant status in liver, kidney and heart tissues. *Mechanism Ageing Dev.* 109: 163–175.

———. 2000. Effect of thyme oil and thymol dietary supplementation on the antioxidant status and fatty acid composition of the ageing rat brain. *Brit. J. Nutr.* 83: 87–93.

Zambonelli, A., et al. 2004. Chemical composition and fungicidal activity of commercial essential oils of *Thymus vulgaris* L. *J. Essential Oil Res.* 16: 69–74.

Zeković, Z. P. 2000. Analysis of thyme (*Thymus vulgaris* L.) extracts. *APTEFF* 31: 617–622.

Zygadlo, J. A., et al. 1995. Empleo de aceites esenciales como antioxidantes naturales. *Grasas Aceites* 46: 285–288.

Trachyspermum

Aftab, K., et al. 1995. Blood pressure lowering action of active principle from *Trachyspermum ammi* (L.) sprague. *Phytomedicine* 2: 35–40.

Anonymous. 2005. Bishop's weed. *Rev. Nat. Prod. (Wolters Kluwer Health).*

Ashraf, M., and M. K. Bhatty. 1975. Studies on the essential oils of the Pakistani species of the family Umbelliferae. Part 1. *Trachyspermum ammi* (L.) Sprague (ajowan) seed oil. *Pakistan J. Sci. Industr. Res.* 18: 232–235.

Balbaaq, S. I., et al. 1975. A study of the fixed oils of the fruits of *Carum copticum* Benth. and Hook., *Apium graveolens* L. and *Petroselinum sativum* Hoffm. growing in Egypt. *Egypt. J. Pharm. Sci.* 16: 383–390.

Chialva, F., et al. 1993. Essential oil constituents of *Trachyspermum copticum* (L.) link fruits. *J. Essential Oil Res.* 5: 105–106.

Choudhary, S., et al. 1998. Composition of the seed oil of *Trachyspermum ammi* (L.) Sprague from northeast India. *J. Essential Oil Res.* 10: 588–590.

Dale, P. W. 1973. The mysterious herb. *Horticulture* 51(1): 58–52.

Demissew, S. 1993. A description of some essential oil bearing plants in Ethiopia and their indigenous uses. *J. Essential Oil Res.* 5: 465–479.

Husain, A., et al. 1988. *Major Essential Oil-bearing Plants of India*. Lucknow, India: Central Inst. Med. Aromatic Pl.

Jirovets, L., et al. 2003. Composition and antimicrobial activity of an essential oil of long-term stored fruits of "ajowan" (*Trachyspermum ammi*) from Bulgaria. *Ernährung/Nutrition* 27: 463–466.

Klhajeh, M., et al. 2004. Comparison of essential oil composition of *Carum copticum* obtained by supercritical carbon dioxide extraction and hydrodistillation methods. *Food Chem.* 86: 587–591.

Mehta, R. L., et al. 1994. Ajowan as a source of natural lipid antioxidant. *J. Agric. Food Chem.* 42: 1420–1422.

Mohagheghzadeh, A., et al. 2007. *Carum copticum* Benth. & Hook., essential oil chemotypes. *Food Chem.* 100: 1217–1219.

Mukherjee, P. K., and L. Constance. 1993. *Umbelliferae (Apiaceae) of India*. New Delhi: Oxford & IBH Publ. Co.

Singh, A. K., et al. 1980. Fungitoxic activity of some essential oils. *Econ. Bot.* 34: 186–190.

Singh, G., et al. 2004. Chemical constituents, antifungal and antioxidative effects of ajwain essential oil and its acetone extract. *J. Agric. Food Chem.* 52: 3292–3296.

Srivastava, K. C. 1988. Extract of a spice omum-omum (*Trachyspermum ammi*) shows antiaggregatory effects and alters arachidonic acid metabolism in human platelets. *Prostaglandins Leukotrienes Essential Fatty Acids* 33: 1–6.

Srivastava, K. C., and T. Mustafa. 1989. Spices: antiplatelet activity and prostanoid metabolism. *Prostaglandins Leukotrienes Essential Fatty Acids* 38: 255–266.

Syed, M., et al. 1986. Antimicrobial activity of the essential oils of Umbelliferae. Part 2. *Trachyspermum ammi*, *Daucus carota*, *Anethum graveolens*, and *Apium graveolens* oils. *Pakistan J. Sci. Indian Res.* 29: 189–192.

Tripathi, S. C., et al. 1986. Studies on antifungal properties of essential oil of *Trachyspermum ammi* (L.) Sprague. *J. Phytopathol.* 116: 113–120.

Trigonella

Abdel-Barry, J. A., et al. 2000. Hypoglycaemic effect of aqueous extract of the leaves of *Trigonella foenum-graecum* in healthy volunteers. *Eastern Med. Health J.* 6: 83–88.

———. 2000. Acute intraperitoneal and oral toxicity of the leaf glycosidic extract of *Trigonella foenum-graecum* in mice. *J. Ethnopharmacol.* 70: 65–68.

Acharya, S. N., et al. 2006. Fenugreek: an "old world" crop for the "new world." *Biodiversity* 7(3/4): 27–30.

Adnam Salih, A. W., and L. Hornok. 1982. Influence of nutrient supply on yield and chemical composition of fenugreek (*Trigonella foenum-graecum* L.). *Herba Hung.* 21: 127–131.

Ahmadiani, A., et al. 2004. Volatile constituents from the oil of *Trigonella foenumgraecum* L. *J. Essential Oil Res.* 16: 356–357.

Ajabnoor, M. A., and A. K. Tilmisany. 1988. Effect of *Trigonella foenum graecum* on blood glucose levels in normal and alloxandiabetic mice. *J. Ethnopharmacol.* 22: 45–49.

Ali, L., et al. 1995. Characterization of the hypoglycemic effects of *Trigonella foenumgraecum* seed. *Pl. Med.* 61: 358–360.

Anonymous. 2005. Fenugreek. *Rev. Nat. Prod. (Wolters Kluwer Health).*

Billaud, C., and J. Adrian. 2001. La place du fenugrec en alimentation. *Méd. Nutr.* 37(2): 59–69.

Blank, I., et al. 1997. The principal flavour components of fenugreek (*Trigonella foenum-graecum* L.). In *Spices*. Ed. S. J. Risch and C.-T. Ho. Washington, D.C.: Amer. Chem. Soc. 12–28.

Bordia, A., et al. 1997. Effect of ginger (*Zingiber officinale* Rosc.) and fenugreek (*Trigonella foenumgraecum* L.) on blood lipids, blood sugar and platelet aggregation in patients with coronary artery disease. *Prostaglandins Leukotrienes Essential Fatty Acids* 56: 379–384.

Broca, C., et al. 1999. 4-Hydroxyisoleucine: experimental evidence of its insulinotropic and antidiabetic properties. *Amer. J. Physiol. Endocrin. Met.* 40: E617-E623.

Escot, N. 1994/95. Fenugreek. *ATOMS* Summer: 7–12.

Girardon, P., et al. 1985. Volatile constituents of fenugreek seeds. *Pl. Med.* 51: 533–534.

———. 1986. Identification de la 3-hydroxy-4,5-diméthyl-2(5H)-furanone dans l'arôme des graines de fenugrec (*Trigonella foenum graecum* L.). *Lebensm. Wiss. Technol.* 19: 44–46.

Golcz, L., and S. Kordana. 1979. Effect of nitrogen, phosphorus and potassium doses as well as magnesium and calcium fertilization on crude drug crop and uptake of mineral nutrients for *Trigonella foenumgraecum* L. *Herba Polon.* 25: 121–131.

Hannan, J. M. A., et al. 2003. Effect of soluble dietary fibre fraction of *Trigonella foenum graecum* on glycemic, insulinemic, lipidemic and platelet aggregation status of Type 2 diabetic model rats. *J. Ethnopharmacol.* 88: 73–77.

Ivimey-Cook, R. B. 1968. *Trigonella*. In *Flora Europaea Vol. 2*. Ed. T. G. Tutin et al. Cambridge Univ. Press. 150–152.

Javan, M., et al. 1997. Antinociceptive effects of *Trigonella foenum-graecum* leaves extract. *J. Ethnopharmacol.* 58: 125–129.

Knight, J. C. 1977. Analysis of fenugreek sapogenins by gas-liquid chromatography. *J. Chromatogr.* 133: 222–225.

Madar, Z., et al. 1988. Glucose-lowering effect of fenugreek in non-insulin dependent diabetics. *Eur. J. Clin. Nutr.* 42: 51–54.

Mishkinsky, J., et al. 1967. Hypoglycaemic effect of trigonelline. *Lancet* 1967(2): 1311–1312.

Petropoulos, G. A., ed. 2002. *Fenugreek: The Genus* Trigonella. London: Taylor & Francis.

Pillai, P. K. T., and M. C. Nambiar. 1982. Condiments. In *Cultivation and Utilization of Aromatic Plants*. Ed. C. K. Atal and B. M. Kapur. Jammu Tawi, India: Regional Res. Lab. 167–189.

Puri, H. S., and R. Hardman. 1977. Treatments for breaking the dormancy of seed in fenugreek. *J. Res. Indian Med. Yoga Homoeo.* 12: 109–117.

Randhawa, G. S., et al. 1996. Agronomic technology for production of fenugreek (*Trigonella foenum graecum* L.) seeds. *Herbs Spices Med. Pl.* 4(3): 43–49.

Ribes, G., et al. 1984. Effects of fenugreek seeds on endocrine pancreatic secretions in dogs. *Ann. Nutr. Metab.* 28: 37–43.

Sauvair, Y., et al. 1991. Implication of steroid saponins and sapogenins in the hypocholesterolemic effect of fenugreek. *Lipids* 26: 191–197.

———. 2000. Chemistry and pharmacology of fenugreek. In *Herbs, Botanicals and Teas*. Ed. G. Mazza and B. D. Oomah. Basel: Technomic Publ. Co. 1–7–129.

Sharma, R. D., et al. 1990. Effect of fenugreek seeds on blood glucose and serum lipids in Type I diabetes. *Eur. J. Clin. Nutr.* 44: 301–306.

———. 1996. Hypolipidaemic effect of fenugreek seeds: a chronic study in non-insulin dependent diabetic patients. *Phytotherapy Res.* 10: 332–334.

Singhal, P. C., et al. 1982. Hypocholesterolemic effect of *Trigonella foenum-graecum* (Methi). *Curr. Sci.* 51: 136–137.

Širjaev, G. 1928. *Generis* Trigonella *L. Revisio Critica*. Masaryk, Brno: Publ. Fac. Sci. Univ.

Stage, S. 1979. *Female Complaints*. New York: W. W. Norton.

Taranalli, A. D., and I. J. Kuppast. 1995. Study of wound healing activity of seeds of *Trigonella foenum-graecum* in rats. *Indian J. Pharm. Sci.* 58: 117–119.

Varshney, I. P., et al. 1984. Saponins from *Trigonella foenum-graecum* leaves. *J. Nat. Prod.* 47: 44–46.

Vörös, J., and F. Nagy. 1972. *Cercospora traversiana* Sacc., a new destructive pathogen of fenugreek in Hungary. *Acta Phytopathol. Acad. Sci. Hung.* 7: 71–76.

Umbellularia

Buttery, R. G., et al. 1974. California bay oil. I. Constituents, odor properties. *J. Agric. Food Chem.* 22: 773–777.

Lawrence, B. M., and A. C. Bromstein. 1974. Terpenoids in *Umbellularia californica*. *Phytochemistry* 13: 2009.

MacGregor, J. T., et al. 1974. California bay oil. II. Biological effects of constituents. *J. Agric. Food Chem.* 22: 777–780.

McClintock, E. 1993. Trees of Golden Gate Park, San Francisco: 48. California bay and Mediterranean laurel. *Pacific Hort.* 54(1): 10–12.

Sargent, C. S. 1895. *The Silva of North America Vol. 7*. Boston: Houghton Mifflin and Co.

Spongberg, S. A. 1975. Lauraceae hardy in temperate North America. *J. Arnold Arbor.* 56: 1–19.

Stein, W. I. 1958. *Silvical Characteristics of California-laurel*. U.S.D.A. For. Serv. Silvical Ser. No. 2.

———. 1974. *Umbellularia* (Nees) Nutt., California-laurel. In *Seeds of Woody Plants in the United States*. Techn. Coord. C. S. Schopmeyer. U.S.D.A. Agric. Handb. No. 450. 835–839.

Tucker, A. O., and M. J. Maciarello. 1998. Some toxic culinary herbs in North America. In *Food Flavor: Formation, Analysis and Packaging Influences*. Ed. E. T. Contis et al. Amsterdam: Elsevier. 401–414.

Valeriana

Anonymous. 1995. Halcion vs. valerian in treatment of insomnia. *Amer. J. Nat. Med.* 2(4): 7–9.

———. 2005. Valerian. *Rev. Nat. Prod. (Wolters Kluwer Health)*.

Backlund, A., and T. Moritz. 1998. Phylogenetic implications of an expanded valepotriate distribution in the Valerianaceae. *Biochem. Syst. Ecol.* 26: 309–335.

Béliveau, J. 1986. Herbal medicine: *Valeriana officinalis*. *Rev. Pharm. Canad.* 119(1): 24–27.

Bellardi, M. G., et al. 1999. *Valeriana officinalis*, nuovo ospite di tomato spotted wilt tospovirus. *Inform. Firopat.* 3: 47–49.

Bos, R. 1997. *Analytical and Phytochemical Studies on Valerian and Valerian Based Preparations*. Doctoral diss., Univ. Groningen.

Bos, R., et al. 1983. A structure of faurinone, a sesquiterpene ketone isolated from *Valeriana officinalis*. *Phytochemistry* 22: 1505–1506.

———. 1986. Isolation and identification of valerenane sesquiterpenoids from *Valeriana officinalis*. *Phytochemistry* 25: 133–135.

———. 1996. Analytical aspects of phytotherapeutic valerian preparations. *Phytochem. Anal.* 7: 143–151.

———. 1997. Composition of the essential oils from underground parts of *Valeriana officinalis* L. s.l. and several closely related taxa. *Flavour Fragrance J.* 12: 339–370.

———. 1997. Occurrence of valerenic acid and valepotriates in taxa related to *Valeriana officinalis* L. s.l. *Sci. Pharm.* 65: 165–168.

———. 1997. *Valeriana* species. In *Adverse Effects of Herbal Drugs 3*. Ed. P. A. G. M. De Smet et al. New York: Springer-Verlag. 165–180.

———. 1998. Seasonal variation of the essential oil, valerenic acid and derivatives, and valeprotriates in *Valeriana officinalis* roots and rhizomes, and the selection of plants suitable for phytomedicines. *Pl. Med.* 64: 143–147.

———. 1998. Cytotoxic potential of valerian constituents and valerian tinctures. *Phytomedicine* 5: 219–225.

Böttcher, H., et al 2006. Quantitative Veränderungen der Inhaltsstoffe von Baldrian-Wurzeln (*Valeriana officinalis* L.) während der Nacherntezeit. *Z. Arzn. Gew. Pfl.* 3: 149–153.

Brunke, E.-J., et al. 1992. The headspace analysis of flower fragrances. *Dragoco Rep.* 1992: 3–31.

———. 1992. Flower scent of some traditional medicinal plants. In *Bioactive Volatile Compounds from Plants*. Ed. R. Teranishi et al. Washington, D.C.: Amer. Chem. Soc. 282–296.

Cerny, A., and K. Schmid. 1999. Tolerability and efficacy of valerian/lemon balm in health volunteers (a double-blind, placebo-controlled, multicentre study). *Fitoterapia* 70: 221–228.

Douglas, J. A., et al. 1993. *Valerian*: Valeriana officinalis. New Zealand Inst. Crop Food Res. Broadsheet No. 34.

———. 1996. The effect of plant density on the production of valerian root. *Acta Hort.* 426: 375–379.

Foster, S. 1990. *Valerian*: Valeriana officinalis. Austin, Texas: Amer. Bot. Council.

Furuya, T., and H. Kojima. 1967. Gas-liquid chromatography of valerian sesquiterpenoids. *J. Chromatogr.* 29: 341–348.

Fussel, A., et al. 2000. Effect of a fixed valerian-hop extract combination

(Ze92019) on sleep polygraphy in patients with non-organic insomia: a pilot study. *Eur. J. Med. Res.* 5: 385–390.

Garges, H. P., et al. 1998. Cardiac complications and delirium associated with valerian root withdrawal. *JAMA* 280: 1566–1567.

Georgiev, E. V., et al. 1999. On the Bulgarian valerian essential oil. *J. Essential Oil Res.* 11: 352–354.

Hazelhoff, B., et al. 1979. The essential oil of *Valeriana officinalis* L. s.l. *Pharm. Weekbl.* 114: 443–449.

Hendriks, H., and R. Bos. 1984. Essential oils of some Valerianaceae. *Dragoco Rep.* 1984: 3–17.

Hendriks, H., et al. 1985. Central nervous depressant activity of valerenic acid in the mouse. *Pl. Med.* 1985: 28–31.

Hiller, K.-O., and G. Zetler. 1996. Neuropharmacological studies on ethanol extracts of *Valeriana officinalis* L.: behavioural and anticonvulsant properties. *Phytotherapy Res.* 10: 145–151.

Hobbs, C. 1994. *Valerian: The Relaxing and Sleep Herb.* Capitola, California: Botanica Press.

Houghton, P. J. 1988. The biological activity of valerian and related plants. *J. Ethnopharmacol.* 22: 121–142.

———. 1994. Herbal products. 1. Valerian. *Pharm. J.* 253: 95–96.

———, ed. 1997. *Valerian: The Genus Valeriana.* Amsterdam: Harwood Acad. Publ.

———. 1999. The scientific basis for the reputed activity of valerian. *J. Pharm. Pharmacol.* 51: 505–512.

Lawalrée, A. 1952. Le groupe de *Valeriana officinalis* L. en Belgique. *Bull. Jard. Bot. Etat* 22: 193–200.

Marder, M., et al. 2003. 6-Methylapigenin and hesperidin: new valerian flavonoids with activity on the CNS. *Pharmacol. Biochem. Behav.* 75: 37–545.1

Meyer, F. G. 1951. *Valeriana* in North America and the West Indies (Valerianaceae). *Ann. Missouri Bot. Gard.* 38: 377–503.

Morazzoni, P., and E. Bombardelli. 1995. *Valeriana officinalis*: traditional use and recent evaluation of safety. *Fitoterapia* 66: 99–112.

Nikivorov, A., et al. 1994. Headspace-analysis of valerian roots (radix valerianae). *Sci. Pharm.* 62: 331–335.

Ockendon, D. J. 1976. *Valeriana.* In *Flora Europaea Vol. 4.* Ed. T. G. Tutin et al. Cambridge Univ. Press. 52–55.

Pande, A., and Y. N. Shukla. 1993. Chemistry and pharmacology of genus *Valeriana*: a review. *Curr. Res. Med. Aromatic Pl.* 15: 39–72.

Pank, F., et al. 1980. Chemische Unkrautbekämpfung in Arzneipflanzenkulturen. 1. Mitteilung: Baldrian (*Valeriana officinalis* L.). *Pharmazie Beih. Ergänzungsband* 35: 115–119.

Pavlovic, M., et al. 2004. The essential oil of *Valeriana officinalis* L. s.l. growing wild in western Serbia. *J. Essential Oil Res.* 16: 397–399.

———. 2007. Composition of the essential oils from the aerial parts of five wild growing *Valeriana* species. *J. Essential Oil Res.* 19: 433–438.

Plushner, S. L. 2000. Valerian: *Valeriana officinalis. Amer. J. Health-Syst. Pharm.* 57: 328–335.

Santos, M. S., et al. 1994. An aqueous extract of valerian influences the transport of GABA in synaptosomes. *Pl. Med.* 60: 278–279.

———. 1994. Synaptosomal GABA release as influenced by valerian root extract: involvement of the GABA carrier. *Arch. Intern. Pharmacodynamie Thérapie* 327: 220–231.

———. 1994. The amount of GABA present in aqueous extracts of valerian is sufficient to account for [3H]GABA release in synaptosomes. *Pl. Med.* 60: 475–476.

Stahn, Th., and U. Bomme. 1998. Qualitative Beurteilung eines grossen Sortimentes von *Valeriana-officinalis*-Herkünften. *Gartenbauwissenschaft* 63: 110–116.

Stevinson, C., and E. Ernst. 2000. Valerian for insomnia: a systematic review of randomized clinical trials. *Sleep Med.* 1: 91–99.

Titz, W., et al. 1983. Valepotriate und ätherishes Öl morphologisch und chromosomal definierter Typen von *Valeriana officinalis* s.l. II. Variation charakteristischer Komponenten des ätherischen Öls. *Sci. Pharm.* 51: 63–86.

Tucker, A. O., and S. S. Tucker. 1988. Catnip and the catnip response. *Econ. Bot.* 42: 214–231.

Upton, R., ed. 1999. *Valerian Root,* Valeriana officinalis: *Analytical, Quality Control and Therapeutic Monograph.* Santa Cruz, California: Amer. Herbal Pharmacopoeia.

Valpani, C. 1995. *Valeriana officinalis.* ATOMS 1(1): 57–62.

Vonderheid-Guth, B., et al. 2000. Pharmacodynamic effects of valerian and hops extract combination (Ze 91019) on the quantitative-topographic EEG in healthy volunteers. *Eur. J. Med. Res.* 5: 139–144.

Wagner, H., et al. 1980. Vergleichende Untersuchungen über die sedierende Wirkung von Baldrianextrakten, Valepotriaten und ihren Abbauprodukten. *Pl. Med.* 38: 358–365.

Willey, L. B. 1995. Valerian overdose: a case report. *Vet. Human Toxicol.* 37: 364–365.

Wills, R. B. H. 2003. *Production of High Quality Australian Valerian Products.* RIDC Project No. UNC-11A.

Yao, M., et al. 2007. A developmental toxicity-screening test of valerian. *J. Ethnopharmacol.* 113: 204–209.

Zhu, L., et al. 1995. *Aromatic Plants and Essential Constituents. Supplement 1.* Hong Kong: South China Inst. Bot.

Wasabia

Chadwick, C. I., et al. 1993. The botany, uses and production of *Wasabia japonica* (Miq.) (Cruciferae) Matsum. *Econ. Bot.* 47: 113–135.

Douglas, J. A. 1993. *Wasabi or Japanese Horse Radish: Wasabia japonica.* New Zealand Inst. Crop Food Res. Broadsheet No. 26.

Etoh, H., et al. 1990. Stabilization of flavour in wasabi and horse radish (Application of freeze concentration method on flavour of wasabi, part 1). *Nippon Shokuhin Kogyo Gakkaishi* 37: 953–958.

Fuke, Y., et al. 1997. Anti-carcinogenic activity of 6-methylsulfinylhexyl isothiocyanate, an active anti-proliferative principle of wasabi (*Eutrema wasabi* Maxim.). *Cytotechnology* 25: 197–203.

———. 2000. Suppressive effect of tumor metastasis by 6-(methylsulfinyl)hexyl isothiocyanates from wasabi. *Nippon Shokuhin Kagaku Kogaku Kaishi* 47: 760–766.

Hara, M., et al. 2003. Changes in pungent components of two *Wasabia japonica* MATSUM. cultivars during the cultivation period. *Food Sci. Technol. Res.* 9: 288–291.

Hodge, W. H. 1974. Wasabi: native condiment plant of Japan. *Econ. Bot.* 28: 118–129.

Hou, D.-X., et al. 2000. Induction of NADPH:quinone oxidoreductase in murine hepatoma cells by methylsulfinyl isothiocyanates: methyl chain length-activity study. *Intern. J. Mol. Med.* 6: 441–44.

———. 2000. Transcriptional regulation of nicotinamide adenine dinucleotide phosphate: quinone oxidoreductase in murine hepatoma cells by 6-(methylsulfinyl)hexyl isothiocyanate, an active principle of wasabi (*Eutrema wasabi* Maxim). *Cancer Lett.* 161: 195–200.

Ina, K., et al. 1981. Volatile components of wasabi (*Wasabia japonica*) and horse radish (*Cochlearia armoracia*). (Studies on the volatile components of wasabi and horse radish, part 1). *Nippon Shokuhin Kogyo Gakkaishi* 28: 365–370.

Kameoka, H., and S. Hashimoto. 1982. Volatile flavour components from wild *Wasabia japonica* Matsum. (wasabi) and *Nasturtium officinale* R.Br. (orandagarashi). *J. Agric. Chem. Soc. Japan* 56: 441–443.

Kojima, M., and Y. Nakano. 1978. Studies on the changes of volatile components, particularly allyl isothiocyanate, during the storage of *Wasabia japonica*. *Hakkokogaku* 56: 298–303.

Kumagai, H., et al. Ariga. 1994. Analysis of volatile components in essential oil of upland *Wasabia* and their inhibitory effects on platelet aggregation. *Biosci. Biotech. Biochem.* 58: 2131–2135.

Masuda, H., et al. 1996. Characteristic odorants of wasabi (*Wasabia japonica* Matsum.), Japanese horseradish, in comparison with those of horseradish (*Armoracia rusticana*). In *Biotechnology for Improved Foods and Flavor*. Ed. G. R. Takeoka et al. Washington, D.C.: Amer. Chem. Soc. 67–78.

———. 1999. Wasabi, Japanese horseradish, and horseradish: relationship between stability and antimicrobial properties of their isothiocyanates. In *Flavor Chemistry of Ethnic Foods*. Ed. F. Shahidi and C.-T. Ho. New York: Kluwer Academic. 85–96.

Ohtsuru, M., and H. Kawatani. 1979. Studies on the myrosinase from *Wasabia japonica*: purification and some properties of wasabi myrosinase. *Agric. Biol. Chem.* 43: 2249–2255.

Sultana, T., et al. 2000. Flavour components in the rhizome of soil-grown wasabi. *Proc. Nutr. Soc. New Zealand* 25: 95–106.

———. 2002. Effects of fertilization on the allyl isothiocyanate profile of aboveground tissues of New Zealand grown wasabi. *J. Sci. Food Agric.* 82: 1477–1482.

Zingiber

Douglas, J. A. 1993. *Myoga Ginger:* Zingiber mioga. New Zealand Inst. Crop Food Res. Broadsheet No. 27.

Kato, Y., et al. 2002. Chemical structure of an anthocyanin pigment isolated from myoga (*Zingiber mioga* Rosc.). *Foods Food Ingred. J. Jap.* 197: 28–33.

Kurobayashi, Y., et al. 1991. Volatile flavour compounds of myoga (*Zingiber mioga*). *Agric. Biol. Chem.* 55: 1655–1657.

Ohwi, J. 1965. *Flora of Japan*. Washington, D.C.: Smithsonian Institution.

Ravindran, P. N., and K. N. Babu, eds. 2004. *Ginger: The Genus* Zingiber. Boca Raton, Florida: CRC Press.

Yashiroda, K., and C. H. Woodward, eds. 1968. Japanese herbs and their uses. *Pl. Gard.* 24(2): 1–72.

Index

JERICHO PUBLIC LIBRARY

31125 00 36 3658

DISCARD

5-19-10

Jericho Public Library
1 Merry Lane
Jericho, New York 11753
Phone: 935-6790

GAYLORD